To Tony,
July 1996. With love and pleasure
in seeing you again — after 40 years

Aunt Helen

ECONOMICS
second canadian edition

ECONOMICS
second canadian edition

Åke Blomqvist
University of Western Ontario

Paul Wonnacott
University of Maryland

Ronald Wonnacott
University of Western Ontario

McGRAW-HILL RYERSON LIMITED

Toronto   Montreal   New York   Auckland   Bogotá
Cairo   Hamburg   Lisbon   London
Madrid   Mexico   Milan   New Delhi   Panama
Paris   San Juan   São Paulo   Singapore
Sydney   Tokyo

ECONOMICS, Second Canadian Edition

ISBN 0-07-549159-1

4 5 6 7 8 9 0   JD   6 5 4 3 2 1 0 9 8

Printed and bound in Canada

Cover Design: Marc Mireault
Art Direction: Daniel Kewley
Cover Photo: Steve Smith/Masterfile

Care has been taken to trace ownership of copyright material contained in this text. The publishers will gladly take any information that will enable them to rectify any reference or credit in subsequent editions.

Canadian Cataloguing in Publication Data

Blomqvist, Åke G., date—
  Economics

Includes index.
ISBN 0-07-549159-1

1. Economics.   I. Wonnacott, Paul, date—
II. Wonnacott, Ronald J., date—   .   III. Title.

HB171.5.B58 1987   330   C86-094843-9

To Karen, Jennifer, Jeffrey, and Gregory

Also available from McGraw-Hill Ryerson:

AN INTRODUCTION TO MACROECONOMICS
Second Canadian Edition
by Blomqvist/Wonnacott/Wonnacott
ISBN 0-07-549160-5

AN INTRODUCTION TO MICROECONOMICS
Second Canadian Edition
by Blomqvist/Wonnacott/Wonnacott
ISBN 0-07-549161-3

STUDY GUIDE to accompany ECONOMICS
Second Canadian Edition
by Blomqvist/Wonnacott/Wonnacott
ISBN 0-07-549163-X

SUMMARY OF CONTENTS

CONTENTS

PREFACE

TO THE STUDENT

Economics is like the music of Mozart. On one level, it has great simplicity; its basic ideas can be grasped quickly by those who first encounter it. On the other hand, below the surface, there are fascinating subtleties that remain a challenge even to those who spend a lifetime in its study. We therefore hold out this promise. In this introductory study of economics, you will learn a great deal about how the economy works—the simple principles governing economic life that must be recognized by those in government and business who make policy decisions. At the same time, we also guarantee that you will not be able to master it all. You should be left with an appreciation of the difficult and challenging problems of economics that remain unsolved.

How to Use This Book

We have tried to design this book to help you grasp the basic propositions of economics as easily as possible. Definitions of important terms are highlighted by the use of colour, and key steps in the argument are emphasized with boldface type or italics. These devices are intended to draw your attention to important concepts and arguments during the initial reading of the material, and in later review. (A glossary is provided at the back of the book, containing definitions of many of the terms used in the book, as well as other common economic terms that you may encounter in class or in readings.) The basic arguments of each chapter are summarized in the Key Points section at the end of each chapter, where newly introduced concepts are also listed.

When you read a chapter for the first time, don't worry about what is in the boxes. This material is optional; it is set aside from the text to keep the main argument as simple and straightforward as possible. Several types of material are presented in the boxes. Some boxes provide levity or colour—for example,

Kurt Vonnegut's tale in Chapter 36 of the Handicapper General whose aim is to make sure that people will not only start out equal but also finish that way. Other boxes present detailed theoretical explanations that are not essential to the main argument. If you want to glance at the boxes that are fun and easy to read, fine. But when you first read a chapter, don't worry about those that contain more difficult material. On the first reading, you may also skip starred (*) sections of the text, along with the footnotes and appendices; these also tend to be more difficult. Come back to them later, after you have mastered the basic ideas. And listen to your instructor, who will tell you which of the boxes and starred sections are most important for your course.

Economics is not a spectator sport. You can't learn just from observation; you must work at it. When you have finished reading a chapter, work on the problems listed at the end; they are designed to reinforce your understanding of important concepts. (The starred (*) problems are either based on material in a box, or are more difficult questions designed to provide a challenge to students who want to do more advanced work.) Because each chapter builds on preceding ones, and because the solutions to some of the problems depend on those that come before, remember this important rule: Don't fall behind in a problem-solving course.

To help you keep up, we recommend the *Study Guide* by Åke Blomqvist, Paul Wonnacott, Ronald Wonnacott, and Peter Howitt; it is designed especially to assist you in working through each chapter. (It should be available in your bookstore.)

TO THE INSTRUCTOR

The starting point of this book is the third U.S. edition of *Economics*, by Paul Wonnacott and Ronald Wonnacott. The book has been organized in such a way as to deal with two difficult questions that have long been the concern of teachers of introductory economics.

For *macroeconomics*, the question is this: After studying an introductory text, are students able to understand public controversies over such topics as the level of government spending and deficits, the desirability of wage and price controls, and the relationship between exchange rates and monetary policy? Are we training our students to understand the front page of the newspaper? For many years, the introductory course was aimed at teaching students how policy should be run; that is, at providing a cookbook of "right" answers. While doubt about "pat" answers, and qualifications of general recommendations are more commonly expressed in books now than they were a decade ago, our course puts an even greater emphasis on balancing conflicting approaches and conclusions. We build up to six controversial questions: Is fiscal or monetary policy the key to aggregate demand? Is Canada better off with fixed or flexible exchange rates, and how does the relative effectiveness of monetary and fiscal policies depend on international transactions and the exchange rate regime? To what extent should the government and the Bank of Canada attempt to "fine-tune" the economy? How can inflation exist at the same time as a high rate of unemployment? How does the economy adjust to inflation, and what are the temporary and lasting effects of inflation? Why were productivity and growth so disappointing in the 1970s, and can we interpret the better performance in the mid-1980s as the beginning of a trend?

While there are no simple, indisputably "correct" answers to these questions, we believe that the major issues can be presented clearly to beginning students of economics, thereby providing them with an understanding of important, recurring themes in the public debate over macroeconomic policy.

For *microeconomics*, the question we asked was this. Does the introductory study of microeconomics lack coherence? For the student, does microeconomics tend to become just one thing after another—a guided tour through the economist's workshop, introducing as many polished pieces of analytical machinery as possible for later use in more advanced courses? Most students do not continue to advanced economics courses. For them, there is little point in concentrating on analytical techniques for their own sake, when time could be spent studying interesting policy issues instead.

In an attempt to make microeconomics more interesting, we have organized our discussion in parts 5 to 7 around two continuing themes: *efficiency* and *equity*. In Part 5, we provide the analytical foundations, leading up to the discussion of the efficiency of a system of competitive markets, and the problems introduced by monopoly and oligopoly. In this discussion we emphasize the interpretation of the demand curve as a marginal benefit curve and the supply curve as a marginal cost curve: For efficiency, equating marginal benefit and marginal cost is the key. In emphasizing marginal concepts, we have tried to give students an appreciation of what allocative efficiency means—why it is desirable to produce the goods that consumers demand. But we have also tried to show why it is not the last word. In particular, we have discovered that elementary students can be shown fairly easily what many, in the past, discovered only in graduate school: There is a different efficient solution for each income distribution; hence, a solution that is efficient is not necessarily best.

In Part 6, we deal with a set of microeconomic policy issues that relate primarily to efficiency: regulation; the control of pollution and the provision of public goods; the efficient exploitation of natural resources, including energy resources; and the problems and opportunities inherent in international trade policy. In Part 7, the emphasis is on equity: We discuss how the returns to factors of production and the distribution of income are determined, and how policies are designed to reduce inequality and fight poverty. But, of course, the issues of efficiency and equity are interrelated. In our discussion of efficiency in parts 5 and 6, we show how policies that are primarily aimed at improving efficiency (such as the allocation of property rights in a common property resource) may also influence income distribution and thus equity; and in Part 7 we discuss how policies that are intended primarily to improve equity (such as social assistance programs to help the poor) may also have side effects on efficiency.

Thus, the most important objective we set ourselves in our discussion of both macroeconomics and microeconomics is to provide students with an understanding of *current policy issues*. Our second objective is to meet the challenge of providing comprehensive and relatively rigorous coverage of the many topics that may be introduced in an introductory course, without making the book too difficult for the average student. To accomplish this, we have devoted the main text to a simple, step-by-step exposition of the main ideas. (To reinforce the text, key ideas are also frequently repeated in the captions that accompany the illustrations.) Thus, we believe that most students will be able to understand the fundamental concepts. At the same time, the more demanding material, which appears in the appendices, the optional boxes, and the starred (*) sections can be used by the instructor to provide a further challenge to particularly well-prepared and ambitious students.

OTHER POINTS OF INTEREST

Finally, we draw your attention to a number of ways in which this book differs from many other introductory texts, and to some changes that we have made in this edition.

- In the preparation of any Canadian economics text, one important choice that has to be made is how to treat the material on international economic relations. It could be discussed all in one section (for a more unified treatment) or the interplay between domestic and international forces could be discussed throughout the book (to reflect the fact that, in virtually all policy discussions in Canada, the repercussions of policies on our international economic relations must be taken into account). We have chosen the second alternative, because we felt that it would not be possible to provide an adequate discussion of most Canadian policy issues, especially at the macro level, without taking international transactions into account. For this reason we discuss, in parts 3 and 4, the effects of Canada's high marginal propensity to import on the value of the multiplier (Chapter 11); in Chapter 13 we look at the effects of Bank of Canada transactions in foreign currencies on chartered bank reserves and the money supply; in Chapter 16 we consider the role of foreign interest rates and exchange rates in setting targets for monetary policy; and in Chapter 17 we examine the problem of dealing with import prices when designing a program of wage and price controls in Canada.

In parts 6 and 7, the role of foreign capital in Canada is discussed in relation to the determination of the return to capital in general (Chapter 35), and in Chapter 29 the problem of foreign ownership is considered as part of the discussion of natural resource extraction in Canada. In Chapter 28, our treatment of pollution includes an examination of transboundary pollution, in the form of acid rain and water pollution in the Great Lakes basin. However, while international issues are considered throughout the book, the core material on international trade and finance is concentrated in three chapters: Chapter 15, which deals with exchange rates, the balance of payments, and stabilization policy, and chapters 31 and 32, which deal with the gains from trade and international trade policy.

- The functions of capital markets and their institutions, and the problem of financial instability, are often given very brief treatment in introductory texts. In this book, we deal with these issues in some detail in several places: in the discussion of business finance in Chapter 6; in the treatment of the functioning and regulation of the monetary system in chapters 12 and 13; and in our discussion of the breakdown of the international gold standard in the interwar period in Chapter 15. (In chapters 12 and 13 we also give an account of the failures of the Canadian Commercial Bank and the Northland Bank, and the Ontario government's takeover of Greymac Trust in 1985.)

- In this edition, the basic discussion of the theory of national income determination in Chapter 10 is preceded by two new chapters: Chapter 8, which contains a systematic discussion of Canada's recent macroeconomic performance; and Chapter 9, in which we provide a brief overview of the aggregate supply–aggregate demand framework for analysing national income determination and the price level. The descriptive material in Chapter 8 gives students a background for the subsequent discussion of macroeconomic theory and policy. The aggregate supply–aggregate demand framework in Chapter 9 serves as a background for the detailed analysis of the Keynesian model, and the discussion of the Phillips curve in Chapter 17.

- In our treatment of efficiency and the gains from specialization, we have given more than the usual attention to economies of scale. In chapters 3 and 31, economies of scale are given almost equal billing with comparative advantage. In our opinion, economies of scale are an important source of gain from specialization, and they should not be avoided because of the difficult analytical problems to which they lead. (Most of these analytical problems can be sidestepped in an elementary treatment.)

- Should indifference curves be introduced in an elementary text? We are very much of two minds on this matter. On the one hand, we do not see great value in the indifference curve demonstration that a demand curve typically slopes downward to the right. (Every analysis must start somewhere, and we find the downward sloping demand curve a more appealing starting point than indifference curves in an introductory course.) But we recognize that our view is not shared by all; consequently, we have included a discussion of indifference curves in the appendix to Chapter 21 to show the standard result. But more important—in an application not typically attempted in a book at this level—we use indifference curves (in an appendix to Chapter 24) to demonstrate the efficiency of perfect competition. (But we also illustrate this result more simply in the text itself, using supply and demand curves.)

- We also show how conflicts can exist not only between objectives (such as equity and efficiency), but also between groups of people in the economy. For example, like other authors, we develop the theory of comparative advantage to illustrate how foreign trade can increase a nation's real income. But we go one step further in emphasizing how trade affects various groups differently: Tariffs benefit domestic producers, but hurt consumers. Since it is easy for students to identify such winners and losers, they can appreciate the irony of complaints about agricultural price supports from business executives who benefit from tariffs that prop up the prices of the goods *they* produce. Moreover, this identification of different groups (and the differences in their political power) helps the student to answer one of the basic questions raised by the theory of public choice: Why is there a difference between what the government *should* do, and what it *does* do?

- The discussion of government regulation has been updated to include recent initiatives in deregulation,

and the current increase in mergers and takeovers. In our treatment of international trade policy, we pay particular attention to the possibility of negotiating a free-trade agreement with the United States, following the initiation of bilateral discussions in 1986. In Chapter 37, we discuss the issue of welfare reform, and assess the pros and cons of a negative income tax such as the one suggested by the MacDonald Royal Commission on the Economic Union and Development Prospects for Canada.

- Substantial changes have been made in the microeconomics section (chapters 20 to 38). The subject of costs and perfectly competitive supply, formerly treated in a single chapter, is now covered in two chapters; one describes the short run, and the other describes the long run. This division serves to slow the pace a little and should provide students with more time to assimilate these important elements of basic microeconomic theory.

Equally important has been the creation of a new section: Part 6, "Economic Efficiency: Issues of Our Time." In this part, we highlight a number of important policy issues in microeconomics, just as in Part 4, "Great Macroeconomic Issues of Our Time," we dealt with key macro policy questions. This new section also contains a fully reworked analysis of natural resources (Chapter 29), which is now linked to the discussion of pollution in Part 6. Just as pollution imposes an external cost on those downstream or downwind, so, too, the extraction of a nonrenewable common property resource creates an external cost—in this case, the cost to future generations, who are left with less of the resource. This reorganization has also improved the sequencing of Part 7. The chapters in Part 7 that deal with the way in which markets distribute income are followed immediately by the controversies over how income *should* be distributed, and over the policies that the government can use to alter income patterns.

WE WISH TO THANK . . .

In developing this book, and the earlier edition, we have been helped by many friends and colleagues with whom we have had discussions over the years about Canadian economic problems and policy. Though we cannot list them all, we wish to acknowledge our indebtedness to them. Several persons also helped by commenting on parts of the manuscript or by providing information on specific matters relating to Canadian institutions and policy. They are:

Ronald Bodkin, University of Ottawa
Michael Bradfield, Dalhousie University
Kevin Burley, University of Western Ontario
Thomas Courchene, University of Western Ontario
Jim Davies, University of Western Ontario
Don Gilchrist, University of Saskatchewan
Christopher Green, McGill University
Morley Gunderson, University of Toronto
Jim Hatch, University of Western Ontario
Stephen Hemphill, McLeod, Young and Weir, Ltd.
Derek Hum, University of Manitoba
Susan Johnson, University of Western Ontario
Edward Ketchum, Health and Welfare Canada

David Laidler, University of Western Ontario
John McDougall, University of Western Ontario
Gary McMahon, Laurentian University
John Palmer, University of Western Ontario
Michael Parkin, University of Western Ontario
Tom Powrie, University of Alberta
Gideon Rosenbluth, University of British Columbia
Ron Shearer, University of British Columbia
Maurice Tugwell, Acadia University
Tom Wilson, University of Toronto
Ron Wirick, University of Western Ontario

Furthermore, we would like to acknowledge the research assistance provided by Andrea Potter. We are also grateful to the editorial and production staff at McGraw-Hill Ryerson in Toronto. In particular, we would like to thank Jackie Kaiser, Carol Gurnett, and freelance editor Kathryn Dean.

Åke Blomqvist
Paul Wonnacott
Ron Wonnacott
London, Ontario, and
College Park, Maryland

Part One

BASIC ECONOMIC CONCEPTS

Chapter 1

ECONOMIC PROBLEMS AND ECONOMIC GOALS

Economy is the art of making the most out of life.

George Bernard Shaw

Some years ago, a Japanese mass-circulation newspaper, the *Mainichi*, conducted a survey of 4,000 people, asking them what they thought of first when they heard the word *takai* (high). Twelve percent responded, "Mount Fuji." The overwhelming majority—88%—said: "Prices."

In Canada, economic issues have played a crucial role in recent federal elections. In 1974, the Liberals under Trudeau narrowly defeated the Progressive Conservatives in a campaign dominated by the question of whether or not to introduce wage and price controls. In 1979, the victory of Joe Clark's Conservatives could be explained in large part by the hostility that the Liberals' energy policy had created in the Western provinces, and by public disappointment with the failure of their anti-inflation policy (the rate of inflation was 9.2% in 1979). After only nine months, Clark's government fell when its budget was defeated in Parliament, largely because of its proposed increases in the prices of gas and oil. And when the Conservatives won a landslide victory over the Liberals in 1984, the record-high unemployment rates and large federal budget deficits were important factors in explaining the massive swing in the popular vote. Issues such as inflation and unemployment are of immediate concern to almost all Canadians. With the rare exception of the individual who inherits great wealth, most of us spend a large part of our energy in the struggle to make a living.

> *Economics* is the study of how people make their living, how they acquire the food, shelter, clothing, and other material necessities and comforts of this world. It is a study of the problems they encounter, and of the ways in which these problems can be reduced.

In the words of Alfred Marshall, a great teacher and scholar of a century ago, "economics is a study of mankind in the ordinary business of life."

Under this broad definition, economics addresses many specific questions. To list but a few:

- What jobs will be available when we finish university? What will they pay?

- Why is it so difficult to get a job at some times, and so easy at others?

- Does it pay to go to university?

- How are goods produced and exchanged? How do we choose which goods to produce?

- Why has the value of the Canadian dollar fallen so low relative to the U.S. dollar?

- What are the long-term consequences of large deficits in the federal government's budget?

- Why did our economy produce so much more in 1984 than in 1948?

Economics is a study of success, and it is a study of failure.

ECONOMIC PROGRESS

From the vantage point of our comfortable homes of the late twentieth century, it is easy for us to forget how many people, throughout history, have been losers in the struggle to make a living. Unvarnished economic history is the story of deprivation, of 80-hour work weeks, of child labour—and of starvation. But it is also the story of the slow climb of civilization toward the goal of relative affluence, where the average person as well as the fortunate few can have a reasonable degree of material well-being and leisure.

One of the most notable features of the Canadian economy has been its growth. Although there have been interruptions and setbacks, economic progress has been remarkable. Figure 1-1 shows one of the standard measures of success: the increase in total production per person. (The precise measure of production in this diagram is gross national product, or GNP for short. This concept will be explained in Chapter 7.) The average Canadian now produces more than twice as much as the average Canadian of 1945, and five times as much as the average Canadian at the turn of the century. Furthermore, the higher output is produced with less effort: The average work week has declined about 35% since 1926. Thus, economic progress in Canada has been reflected both in an increase in the goods and services that we produce and enjoy, and in a greater amount of leisure time.

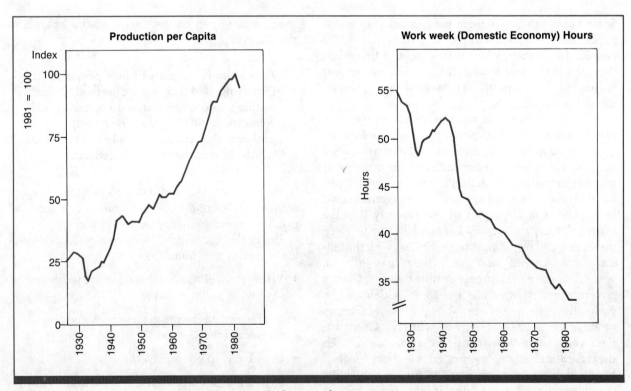

Figure 1-1 Production per person and hours worked per week.

Source: Compiled from Statistics Canada, *CANSIM Databank*, and K. Buckley and M. Urquhart, eds., *Historical Statistics of Canada*, 1st ed. (Toronto and Cambridge: Cambridge University Press and Macmillan of Canada, 1965). Reproduced by permission of the Minister of Supply and Services Canada.

A similar tale of success has occurred in many other countries, as illustrated in Figure 1-2. Between 1960 and 1983, output grew at an average annual rate of 3.4% in the United States, 4.2% in France, 3.4% in Germany, and 3.7% in Italy. Nor has growth been confined to the countries of Europe and North America. Particularly notable has been the growth of the Japanese economy. From the ashes of the Second World War, Japan has emerged as one of the leading success stories, with output per person that now exceeds that

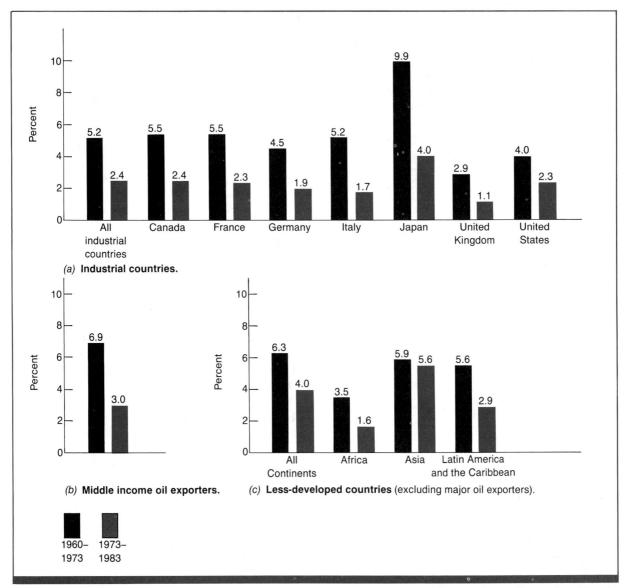

(a) **Industrial countries.**

(b) **Middle income oil exporters.**   (c) **Less-developed countries** (excluding major oil exporters).

1960– 1973–
1973   1983

Figure 1-2 Annual rates of increase in output, 1960–1983. Rapid rates of growth have occurred in many countries. Growth was particularly fast in Japan between 1960 and 1973, when output increased at an average annual rate of 9.9 percent. Note that for most countries, growth has been much slower since 1973 than during the previous decade (with the less-developed economies of Asia being an exception). This slower growth may be traced in part to the disruptions caused by the rapid increase in the price of oil.
Source: The World Bank, *Annual Report*, 1984, pp. 32–34.

of Britain.[1] Other stories of success have come from the middle-income areas of East Asia—South Korea, Hong Kong, and Singapore—where output per person has grown at a very impressive rate of 6.7% per year.

ECONOMIC PROBLEMS

Although rapid growth has occurred in many countries, it has been neither universal nor automatic. In a number of countries, the standard of living remains abysmally low. The World Bank—an international institution whose major purpose is to lend to the less developed countries (LDCs)—estimates that, between 1960 and 1982, output per person rose at an average annual rate of only 1.2% in the 25 poorest countries (excluding China). The record is even bleaker in the poorest of the poor nations, where the increase in population continuously threatens to outrun the increase in production.

In the large cities of Asia, Latin America, and Africa, millions of people are crowded together in makeshift housing, with barely enough income to feed themselves and with little access to things like basic health care and education for their children. Many have moved to the urban centres to escape even worse poverty in the countryside.

Even in a relatively prosperous country such as Canada, substantial economic problems remain. For example, we may wonder:

- Why are so many unable to find work, when so much needs to be done?

- Why do pockets of poverty remain in an affluent society?

- Why have prices spiralled upward?

- Why is the average income so much lower in the Atlantic provinces than in the rest of Canada?

- Are we really producing the right things? Should we produce more housing and fewer cars? Or more medical services and fewer sports spectaculars?

- Why is pollution such a problem? What should be done about it?

ECONOMIC POLICY

"Why?" and "What should be done?" are the two key questions in economics. The ultimate objective of economics is to develop policies to deal with our problems. However, before we can formulate policies, we must first try to understand how the economy has worked in the past, and how it works today. Otherwise, well-intentioned policies may go astray and lead to unforeseen and unfortunate consequences.

When economic policies are studied, the centre of attention is usually the policies of the government—policies such as taxation, government spending programs, international trade policy, and the regulation of particular industries, such as telephone companies, airlines, and railroads. However, the policies of private businesses are also important. How should they organize production in order to make their goods at the lowest possible cost? What prices should a business charge? When should a supermarket increase the stocks of goods in its warehouse?

The Controversial Role of Government

For more than two hundred years, economics has been dominated by controversy over the proper role of government. In what circumstances should government take an active role? When is it best for government to leave decisions to the private participants in the economy? On this topic, the giants of economics have repeatedly met to do battle.

In 1776, Scottish scholar **Adam Smith** published his pathbreaking book, *An Inquiry into the Nature and Causes of the Wealth of Nations*.[2] Modern eco-

---

[1] The success of the Japanese economy has made that country the subject of good-natured humour. In a lecture, U.S. economist Paul McCracken of the University of Michigan recalled that on his first trip to Japan in the fifties, he had gone to offer the Japanese advice on economic growth policy. Added McCracken, "I've been trying to remember ever since what we told them."

There are substantial problems in comparing output per person in various countries. However, careful work indicates that Japan passed Britain about 1970. See Irving B. Kravis et al., *A System of International Comparisons of Gross Product and Purchasing Power*, United Nations International Comparison Project: Phase One (Baltimore: Johns Hopkins University Press, 1975), p. 231.

[2] Available in Modern Library edition (New York: Random House, 1937.) Smith's book is commonly referred to as *The Wealth of Nations*.

nomics may be dated from that year. Smith's message was clear: private markets should be liberated from the tyranny of government control. In pursuit of their private interests, individual producers would make the goods that consumers want. It is not, said Smith, "from the benevolence of the butcher, the brewer, or the baker that we expect our dinner, but from their regard to their own interest." There is an "invisible hand," he wrote, that causes the producer to promote the interests of society. Indeed, "by pursuing his own interest he frequently promotes that of the society more effectually than when he really intends to promote it." In general, said Smith, the government should be cautious in interfering with the operations of the private market. According to Smith, the best policy is generally one of *laissez-faire*—leave it alone. Government intervention usually makes things worse. For example, government imposition of a tariff is generally harmful. (A tariff or duty is a tax on a foreign-produced good as it enters the country.) Even though a tariff generally helps domestic producers who are thereby given an advantage over foreign producers, the country as a whole loses. Specifically, a tariff increases the cost of goods available to consumers, and this cost to consumers outweighs the benefits to producers. Smith's work has been refined and modified during the past 200 years, but many of his laissez-faire conclusions have stood up remarkably well. For example, there is still a very strong economic argument against high tariffs on imported goods, and in recent decades, one of the principal areas of international co-operation has been the negotiation of lower tariffs.

During the Great Depression of the 1930s—a century and a half after the appearance of *The Wealth of Nations*—the laissez-faire tradition in economics came under attack. In 1936, **John Maynard Keynes** published his *General Theory of Employment, Interest and Money* (also known, more simply, as the *General Theory*). In this book, Keynes (whose name rhymes with "Danes") argued that the government has the duty to intervene in the economy, to put the unemployed back to work. Of the several ways in which this could be done, one stood out in its simplicity. Through public works, such as building roads, post offices, and dams, the government could provide jobs directly, and thus provide a cure for the Depression.

With his proposals for a more active role for government, Keynes drew the ire of many businessmen.

They feared that, as a result of his recommendations, the government would become larger and larger and private enterprise would gradually be pushed out of the picture. But Keynes did not foresee this result. He believed that by providing jobs the government could remove the explosive frustrations caused by the mass unemployment of the 1930s, and could make it possible for Western political and economic institutions to survive. His objective was to modify our economic system, and make it better. Unlike Karl Marx, he did not believe that the system would have to be destroyed and replaced by a different one in order to solve these problems.(For a brief introduction to the revolutionary ideas of Marx, see Box 1-1.)[3]

Thus, Smith and Keynes took apparently contradictory positions—Smith arguing for less government, and Keynes for more.[4] It is possible, of course, that each was right. Perhaps the government should do more in some areas, and less in others. Economic analysis does not lead inevitably to either an activist or a passive position on the part of the government. The economist's rallying cry should not be, "Do something." Rather, it should be, "Think first."

ECONOMIC GOALS

We have already noted that the ultimate goal of economics is to develop better policies to minimize our problems and to maximize the benefits from our daily toil. More specifically, there is widespread agreement that we should strive for the following goals:

1. *A high level of employment.* People willing to work should be able to find jobs reasonably quickly. Widespread unemployment is demoralizing, and it represents an economic waste, since

---

[3]Throughout this book, the boxes present illustrative and supplementary materials. They can be disregarded without losing the main thread of the discussion.

[4]Conflicting views over the proper role of government may also be found in the works of two retired professors: the University of Chicago's Milton Friedman (for laissez-faire) and Harvard's John Kenneth Galbraith (who argues for more government involvement). See John Kenneth Galbraith, *The Affluent Society* (Boston: Houghton Mifflin, 1958), and Milton Friedman and Rose Friedman, *Free to Choose* (New York: Harcourt Brace Jovanovich, 1980). (We strongly recommend that if you read one of these books, you read them both. Each of the books puts forth a convincing case, but they flatly contradict each other.)

KARL MARX

The main text refers to two towering economists—Adam Smith and John Maynard Keynes. In the formation of the intellectual heritage of most British and North American economists, Smith and Keynes have played leading roles. But, if we consider the intellectual heritage of the world as a whole, Karl Marx is probably the most influential economist of all. In the Soviet Union and the People's Republic of China, Marx is more than the source of economic "truth"; he is the Messiah of what is in effect the state religion.

Many business executives viewed Keynes as a revolutionary because he openly attacked accepted economic opinion and proposed fundamental changes in economic policy. But, by revolutionary standards, Keynes pales beside Marx. The Marxist call to revolution was shrill and direct: "Workers of the world, unite! You have nothing to lose but your chains."

Why did they have nothing to lose? Because, said Marx, workers are responsible for the production of all goods. Labour is the sole source of value. But workers get only part of the fruits of their labour. A large—and in Marx's view, unearned—share goes to the exploiting class of capitalists. (Capitalists are the owners of factories, machinery, and other equipment.) Marx believed that, by taking up arms and overthrowing capitalism, workers could end exploitation and obtain their rightful rewards.

On our main topic—the role of government—Marx was strangely ambivalent. Who would own the factories and machines once the communist revolution had eliminated the capitalist class? Ownership by the state—by all the workers as a group—was the obvious solution. And, in fact, this has been the path taken by countries such as the Soviet Union: The revolution has led to state ownership of the means of production. Yet, Marx also believed that the revolution would eventually lead to the "withering away" of the state. There has been no perceptible sign of this withering away in Marxist societies.

Courtesy Canapress Photo Service

society foregoes the goods and services that the unemployed could have produced.

2. *Price stability*. It is desirable to avoid rapid increases—or decreases—in the average level of prices.

3. *Efficiency*. When we work, we want to get as much as we reasonably can out of our productive efforts.

4. *An equitable distribution of income*. When many live in affluence, no group of citizens should suffer stark poverty.

5. *Growth*. Continuing growth, which would make possible an even higher standard of living in the future, is generally considered an important objective.

This list is far from complete. Not only do we want to produce more, but we want to do so without degrading our environment: the **reduction of pollution** is important. **Economic freedom**—the right of people to choose their own occupations, to enter contracts, and to spend their incomes as they please—is a desirable goal. So, too, is **economic security**—freedom from the fear that chronic illness or other catastrophe will place an individual or a family in a desperate financial situation. The objective of economic security has played a large and increasingly important part in Canadian policy in the last few decades.

Another long-standing (but more controversial) goal is that of more **economic independence**. Some people feel that too many decisions which affect the welfare of Canadians are made by foreign firms, and that increased control by Canadians over our own economy is an important objective.

This book will focus principally on how we try to achieve our economic goals. As a background for later chapters, let's look at the major goals in more detail.

1. A High Level of Employment

The importance of the objective of full employment was illustrated most clearly during the Great Depression of the 1930s, when Canada and many other countries conspicuously failed to achieve it. During the sharp contraction from 1929 to 1933, total output in Canada fell by 30%, and spending for new buildings, machinery, and equipment declined by more than 85%. As the economy slid downward, more and more workers lost their jobs. By 1933, almost 20% of the labour force was unemployed. (See Figure 1-3.) Long lines of

the jobless gathered at factory gates in the hope of work; disappointment was their common fate. Nor was the problem quickly solved. The downward slide into the depths of the Depression went on for a period of four years, and the road back to a high level of employment was even longer. It was not until the beginning of the 1940s, when industry began working around the clock to produce weapons that many of the unemployed were able to find jobs. During the decade from 1931 to 1940 unemployment averaged above 11% of the labour force in every year except one.

> A *depression* exists when there is a very high rate of unemployment over a long period of time.

Something had clearly gone wrong—disastrously wrong. Large-scale unemployment represents tremendous waste; time lost in involuntary idleness is gone forever. The costs of unemployment go beyond the loss of output; unemployment involves the dashing of hopes. Those unable to find work suffer frustration and a sense of worthlessness, and their skills are lost as they remain out of work.

The term **unemployed** is reserved for those who are willing and able to work, but are unable to find jobs. Thus, those of you who are full-time university students are not included among the unemployed. Your immediate task is to get an education, not a job. Similarly, the 70-year-old retiree is not included in the statistics of the unemployed. Nor are those in prisons or mental institutions, since they are not available for jobs.

> A person is *unemployed* if he or she is available and looking for work, but has not found it.

The unemployment rate is calculated as a percentage of the total labour force—the labour force being the sum of those who are actually employed, plus those who are unemployed. (Labour force and employment statistics are tied to the traditional definition of "jobs." Thus, for example, a mother who stays at home to raise her children is neither "in the labour force" nor "employed," although she certainly works.)

At the end of the Second World War, the Great Depression was still a fresh memory. The public, the

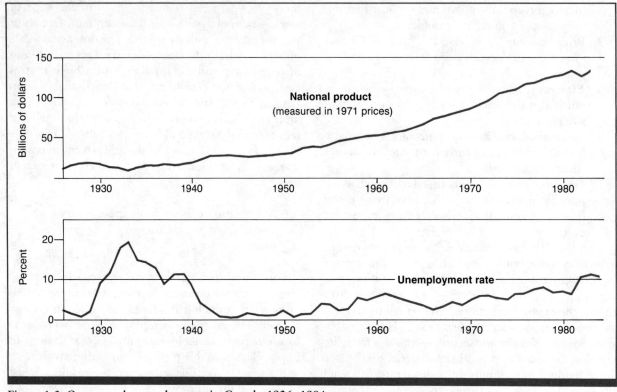

Figure 1-3 Output and unemployment in Canada 1926–1984.

Source: Compiled from Statistics Canada, *CANSIM Databank*, and K. Buckley and M. Urquhart, eds., *Historical Statistics of Canada*, 1st ed. (Toronto and Cambridge: Cambridge University Press and Macmillan of Canada, 1965). Reproduced by permission of the Minister of Supply and Services Canada.

politician, and the economist shared a common determination not to permit a repeat of the 1930s. And so far, we have been largely successful in our efforts to prevent a repetition of the prolonged period of very high unemployment of the 1930s. But the postwar years have certainly not been an unbroken story of success. From time to time, there have been downturns in the economy—much more moderate, it is true, than the slide of 1929 to 1933—but downward movements nonetheless. These more moderate declines, or **recessions**, have been accompanied by an increase in the unemployment rate. In December 1982, during the worst recession of the past four decades, the unemployment rate rose to a peak of 12.9%. While we have been successful in preventing large-scale depressions, the problem of periodic recessions has not been solved.

A *recession* is a general slowdown of economic activity, usually involving a decline in total output, income, and employment, lasting six months or more, and marked by contractions in many sectors of the economy. (The slowdown is not confined to just one or two industries, such as forest products or car manufacturing.)

2. Stability of the Average Price Level
During the Depression of the 1930s, unemployment was the overwhelming problem, and in the first half of the 1980s joblessness has once again become the dominant economic issue. During the late 1970s, *inflation* became a severe problem.

Inflation is an increase in the average level of prices. (Deflation is a fall in the average level of prices.)

We can see in Figure 1-4 how the average of prices paid by consumers has risen through most of our recent history, with the period 1920–1933 being a notable exception. Prices rose most rapidly after World War I, and for a brief period after World War II. Between 1973 and 1981, inflation was unusually severe for peacetime periods. (Details on how to draw and interpret diagrams such as Figure 1-4 may be found in the appendix to this chapter, and in the Study Guide which accompanies this text.)

While unemployment represents sheer waste—society loses the goods which might have been produced by those out of work—the problem with inflation is less obvious. When a price rises, there is both a winner and a loser. The loser is the buyer, who has to pay more. However, there is a benefit to the seller, who receives more. On balance, it is not clear whether society as a whole is better or worse off in this situation.

It is true, of course, that people resent inflation. At least some of this resentment, however, probably reflects a peculiarity of human nature. When people find the goods they sell rising in price, they see the increase as perfectly right, normal, and justified. On the other hand, when they find the goods they buy rising in price, they often view the increase as evidence of the seller's greed. When the price of wheat rises, farmers see themselves at last getting a reasonable return from their toil. When the price of oil increases, the oil companies argue that they are getting no more than the return necessary to finance the search for more oil. When the price of books rises, authors feel that they are getting no more than a "just" return for their creative efforts, and book publishers insist that they are no more than adequately compensated for their risks. However, when the farmer, the oil company, the author, and the book publisher find that the prices of the goods they buy have increased, they believe they have been cheated by inflation. We may all be the victims of an illusion—the illusion that each of us can and should have a rise in the price of what we sell, but that the

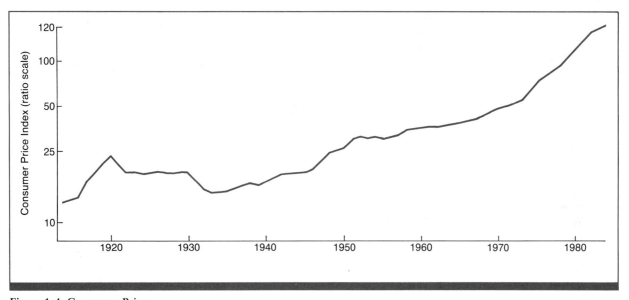

Figure 1-4 Consumer Prices.
Occasionally prices have fallen—for example, during the early 1930s. In recent decades, however, the trend of prices has been clearly upward. In 1974, and again in 1979 and 1980, Canada suffered from "double-digit" inflation—a rise in the average level of prices by more than 10 percent per year.

Source: Statistics Canada, *CANSIM Databank*. Reproduced by permission of the Minister of Supply and Services Canada.

price of what we buy should remain stable. For the economy as a whole, this is not possible.

The two-sided nature of price increases—a gain to the seller but a loss to the buyer—means that it is difficult to evaluate the dangers of inflation. Indeed, there has been considerable controversy as to whether a low rate of inflation (say, 2% or 3% per annum) is dangerous, or whether, on the contrary, it may actually be beneficial to society. (Some say that a low rate of inflation makes it easier for the economy to adjust to changes, and helps to maintain a high level of employment.)

However, when inflation increases beyond a moderate rate, there is widespread agreement that it becomes a menace. It becomes more than a mere transfer of money from the buyer to the seller; it interferes with the production and exchange of goods. This has most clearly been the situation during very rapid inflations, when economic activity was severely disrupted.

Hyperinflation—that is, a skyrocketing of prices at annual rates of 1000% or more—occurs most commonly during or soon after a military conflict, when government spending shoots upward; for example, in Germany during the early 1920s, in China during its Civil War in the late 1940s, and in the southern states during the American Civil War. With hyperinflation, money rapidly loses its power to buy goods, and people try to spend money as quickly as possible while they can still get something for it.

Clearly, hyperinflation of 1000% or more per year is an extreme example. However, lower rates of inflation, amounting to 10% or less per year, can also have serious consequences:

1. Inflation hurts people living on fixed incomes and people who have saved fixed amounts of money for their retirement or for "a rainy day" (future illness or accident). The couple who put aside $1,000 in 1960 for their retirement have suffered a rude shock. In 1985, $1,000 bought no more than $250 bought in 1960.

2. Inflation can lead to business mistakes. For good decisions, businesses need an accurate picture of what is going on. When prices are rising rapidly, the picture becomes obscured and out of focus. Decision makers cannot see clearly. (For example, business accounting is done in dollar terms. When there is rapid inflation, some businesses may report profits when, using

a more accurate calculation, they might actually be suffering losses. Consequently, inflation can temporarily hide problems.) Our economy is complex, and it depends on a continuous flow of accurate information. Prices are an important link in the information chain. For example, a high price should provide a signal to producers that consumers are especially eager to get more of a particular product. But in a severe inflation, producers find it difficult to know whether this is the message, or whether the price of their product is rising simply because all prices are rising. In brief, a severe inflation obscures the message carried by prices.

Here, it is important to distinguish between a rise in the *average level of prices* (inflation) and a change in *relative* prices. Even if the average level of prices was perfectly stable (that is, if no inflation existed), some individual prices would still change as conditions change in specific markets. For example, new inventions have cut the costs of producing computers, which has allowed computer companies to cut prices sharply. At the same time, energy prices (for oil, gasoline, electricity, and other energy sources) have risen substantially during the past 15 years, in response to the rise in the world price of oil. The resulting fall in the price of computers relative to the price of oil has performed a useful function. It has encouraged consumers and businesses to use more of the relatively cheap computers, and to conserve on the relatively expensive oil. (This is not, of course, to deny that the rise in the price of energy was painful, particularly to those living in the coldest areas of the country.)

3. Efficiency

This illustration—of how consumers and businesses use more computers when they become less expensive—is one example of economic efficiency.

In an economy, the unemployment and inflation rates may both be very low, but performance may still be poor. For example, fully employed workers may be engaged in a lot of wasted effort, and the goods being produced may not be those which are most needed. Obviously, this is not a satisfactory state of affairs.

Efficiency is the goal of getting the most out of our productive efforts. Inefficiency occurs when there is waste.

Under this broad definition, two types of efficiency can be distinguished: ***technological efficiency*** and ***allocative efficiency***.

To illustrate technological efficiency (also known as *technical efficiency*), let us consider two bicycle manufacturers. One uses a large number of workers and many machines to produce 1,000 bicycles. The other uses fewer workers and fewer machines to produce the same number of bicycles. The second manufacturer is not a magician; he is simply a better manager. He is technologically efficient, whereas the first manufacturer is not. (Technological inefficiency exists when the same output could be produced with fewer machines and fewer workers, working at a reasonable pace. [Technological efficiency does not require a sweatshop.] Technological inefficiency involves wasted effort and sloppy management; better management is the solution.)

Allocative efficiency, on the other hand, involves the production of the best combination of goods, using the lowest-cost combination of inputs. How much food should we produce, and how many houses? Suppose we produce only food, and do so in a technologically efficient way, with no wasted effort. We will still not have achieved the goal of allocative efficiency, because consumers want both food and housing.

Or consider another question: How much newsprint should we produce, and how much wine? If we produce just enough of each to meet the demand of Canadian wine drinkers and newspaper readers, we will probably not reach allocative efficiency. A better solution would be to produce more newsprint and less wine, and then to trade newsprint for imported wine in the world market.

Thus, allocative efficiency depends on the choice of the right combination of outputs. It also involves using the best (lowest-cost) combination of inputs. Consider our earlier illustration. The cost of computers is falling, while the cost of oil is rising. If businesses fail to adjust—that is, if they fail to conserve oil and to use computers more—then there is allocative inefficiency.

Relative prices perform a key role in encouraging allocative efficiency. As we have noted, the decrease in the price of computers encourages businesses to use more computers, and less of the other, relatively more expensive inputs. And low costs of producing newsprint in Canada encourage other countries to buy paper from us, while we are encouraged to buy wine from Italy and Spain because of the low wine prices in those countries.

4. An Equitable Distribution of Income

Ours is an affluent society. Yet many people remain so poor that they have difficulty buying the basic necessities of life, such as food, clothing, and shelter. In the midst of plenty, some live in need. The moral question must then be faced: Should some people have so much, while others have so little?

When the question is put this way, the compelling answer must surely be no. Our sense of compassion requires that assistance be given to those crushed by illness and to those born and raised in cruel deprivation. In the view of the large majority, society has a responsibility to help those at the bottom of the economic ladder.

Our sense of equity, or justice, is offended by extreme differences. Thus, most people think of "equity" as a move toward "equality." But not all the way. The two words are far from synonymous. While there is widespread agreement that the least fortunate should be helped, there is no consensus that the objective of society should be an equal income for all. Some individuals are willing to work overtime; it is generally recognized as both just and desirable for them to have a higher income as a consequence. Otherwise, why should they work longer hours? Similarly, it is generally considered "right" for the hardworking to have a larger share of the pie. After all, they have contributed more to the production of the pie in the first place. On the other side, some are loafers. If they were automatically given the same income as everyone else, our sense of equity would be offended. They don't deserve an equal share. And if everyone were guaranteed an equal income, how many would work?

There is no agreement on broad principles, such as how far we should go toward complete equality of incomes. The "best" division (or distribution) of income is ill-defined. As a result, much of the discussion of income distribution has focused on narrower questions, such as: What is happening to those at the bottom of the ladder? What is happening to the families who live in poverty?

Poverty is difficult to define in precise dollar terms. For one thing, people's needs differ greatly. The sickly have the greatest need for medical care. Large families have the most compelling need for food and clothing.

Those who live in cities, where the costs of food and shelter are high, need more money for basic necessities than do those who live on farms, where they can grow some of their own food. There is no simple, single measure of the "poverty line," below which families may be judged to be poor. Reasonable standards may, however, be established by taking into consideration such obvious variables as the number of individuals in a family. For example, Statistics Canada has defined different poverty standards for families of different sizes in large cities and in rural areas (see Table 1-1).

Table 1-1
Poverty Standards in Large Cities and Rural Areas, 1983

Number of people in the family	Large Cities	Rural Areas
1	$ 9,400	$ 7,000
2	12,400	9,100
3	16,600	12,200
4	19,200	14,100
5	22,300	16,400
6	24,400	17,900
7 +	26,900	19,700

SOURCE: Statistics Canada, *Income Distribution by Size in Canada*, 1983, p. 32 (1978 base). (Dollar figures have been rounded to the nearest $100.) Reproduced by permission of the Minister of Supply and Services Canada.

There are two ways of raising people above the poverty line. The first is to increase the size of the national "pie." As the level of income rises throughout the economy, the incomes of those at the lower end will also generally rise. In the words of former U.S. President John Kennedy, "A rising tide lifts all boats."

A second way to reduce poverty is to increase the share of the pie going to people with the lowest incomes. Thus, poverty may be combatted by a **redistribution of income**. For example, the well-to-do may be taxed in order to finance government programs aimed at helping the poor.

Since World War II, the Canadian federal government has organized or helped finance many major programs designed to raise the incomes of poor families. During the 1960s and 1970s, these programs were partly responsible for a substantial reduction in the number of people living in poverty. As Figure 1-5 shows, there was a steady decline in the percentage of Canada's population that could be classified as poor, from over 25% in the mid-1960s to a low of just under 10% in 1981. Since that time, however, the trend has been halted and even reversed. In 1983, the percentage had climbed back to 11.4%.

We are still far short of the objective of eliminating poverty. Why is this task so difficult? One major reason is unemployment. As unemployment rates have been rising, many of the people who have lost their jobs have fallen into poverty.

Other possible explanations include the tendency of workers to retire early (at which time they often drop into the low-income group), and the tendency for families to divide into more than one group: Young people move out of the parental home more readily than they used to, old people are less likely to live with their children, and more marriages are splitting up. When one family with an income above the poverty line splits up, each of the resulting families may be below the poverty line.

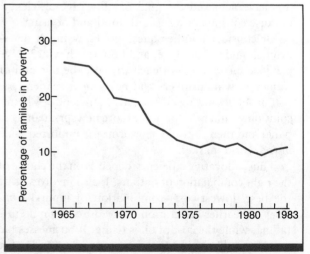

Figure 1-5 Trends in the percentage of the population below the poverty line.
By Statistics Canada's poverty standard of the mid-1970s, the proportion of the population in poverty declined substantially until about 1981, when the trend began to reverse.

Source: Statistics Canada, *Income Distribution by Size in Canada*, 1983, p. 22. Reproduced by permission of the Minister of Supply and Services Canada.

The design of policies to further reduce the extent of poverty remains a challenging problem.

5. Growth

In an economy with large-scale unemployment, output can be increased by putting the unemployed back to work. But once this is done, there is a limit to the amount that can be produced with the existing labour force and the existing factories and equipment. To increase output beyond this limit requires either an addition to the available resources (for example, an increase in the number of factories and machines) or an improvement in technology (that is, the invention of new, more productive machines or new ways of organizing production). When economists speak of growth, they typically mean an increase in output that results from technological improvement and additional factories, machines, or other resources.

The advantages of growth are obvious. If the economy grows, our incomes will be higher in the future. We and our children will have higher standards of material comfort. Moreover, some of the increase in production can be used to benefit the poor without reducing the incomes of the rich. During the early 1960s, growth became a prominent national goal in most Western countries, both because of its economic advantages, and because expansion of productive capacity was seen as an important part of Western security; the West had to "keep up with the Russians."

During the late 1960s and early 1970s, doubts began to develop about the importance of growth as an objective of economic policy. While its advantages are obvious, growth comes at a cost. If we are to grow more rapidly, more of our current efforts will have to be directed toward the production of machines, and away from the production of consumption goods. In the future, of course, as the new machines begin operating, they will turn out more consumption goods— more clothing, radios, or cars. Thus, current policies to stimulate growth will make possible higher consumption in the future. But, for the moment, consumption will be less. Thus, to evaluate a high-growth policy, the advantage of higher future consumption has to be compared with the sacrifice of lower current consumption.

Seen in this light, it is not clear that the faster the rate of growth, the better. Why, for example, should I live modestly, just so my children may at some future date live in luxury? The future generations should be considered; but so should the present one.

Even if we were concerned solely with the welfare of coming generations, it would not be so clear that the more growth, the better. Increasing levels of production use increasing quantities of raw materials, which will then be unavailable to future generations. A moderate rate of growth may be in the best interests of future generations, because it allows us to conserve raw materials.

Furthermore, very rapid rates of growth may harm the environment. If our primary objective is to produce more and more newsprint, steel, and automobiles, we may pay too little heed to the belching smoke of the pulp and paper mills, to the pollution of our lakes and rivers, or to the effect of the automobile on the quality of the air that we breathe. In the 1970s, as these side effects became apparent, less emphasis was placed on growth than in the early 1960s, and more attention was paid to other goals, such as preservation of the environment. In the 1980s, however, there has been renewed concern about finding policies to stimulate growth, in part because the economy has been growing more slowly, and in part because growth is seen as one way of creating more jobs and reducing the unemployment problem.

INTERRELATIONSHIPS AMONG THE GOALS

The achievement of one goal may help to achieve others. As we have noted, growth may make it easier to solve the poverty problem, since additional income may be provided for the poor out of the growth in total income, without reducing the income of those at the top. Social conflicts over the share of the pie may be reduced if the size of the pie is increasing.

Similarly, the poverty problem is easier to solve if the unemployment rate is kept low, so that large numbers of unemployed do not swell the ranks of the poor. When goals are **complementary** like this (that is, when achieving one helps to achieve another), economic policy making is relatively easy. One broad policy may help us attain several goals at once.

Unfortunately, however, economic goals are not always complementary. In many cases, they are in conflict. For example, when the unemployment problem is reduced, the inflation problem tends to get worse.

There is a reason for this. Heavy purchasing by the public tends to reduce unemployment, but it also tends to increase inflation. It reduces unemployment because, as the public buys more cars, unemployed workers get jobs again in the auto factories; and when families buy more homes, construction workers find it easier to get jobs. At the same time, heavy purchasing tends to increase inflation because producers are more likely to raise their prices if buyers are clamouring for their products.

Another example of conflicts among the goals of economic policy is the relationship between efficiency and economic independence. Allocative efficiency in a relatively small economy, such as we have in Canada, requires a large amount of international trade and investment. But there are many who feel that as our economic relations with foreign countries become more extensive, we will ultimately become too dependent on the policies and attitudes of those countries; the price of allocative efficiency may be a partial loss of Canada's political and economic independence. Such conflicts among goals test the wisdom of policy makers.

A PREVIEW

These, then, are the five major objectives of economic policy: high employment, price stability, efficiency, an equitable distribution of income, and growth. The first two goals are related to the stability of the economy. If the economy is unstable, moving along like a roller coaster, its performance will be very unsatisfac-tory. As it heads downhill into recession, large numbers of people will be thrown out of work. Then, as it heads upward into a runaway boom, prices will soar as the public scrambles to buy the available goods. The first two goals may therefore be looked on as two aspects of a single objective: that of achieving an *equilibrium*, with stable prices and a low unemployment rate. This will be the major topic discussed in parts 2, 3, and 4 (Chapters 7 through 19) of this book.

Equilibrium is the first of three main "E's" of economics. The second E—*efficiency*—will be studied in parts 5 and 6 (Chapters 20 through 32). Are we getting the most out of our productive efforts? When does the free market—where buyers and sellers come together without government interference—encourage efficiency? Where the free market does not encourage efficiency, what (if anything) should be done?

Part 7 (Chapters 33 through 38) deals primarily with the third E—*equity*. If the government takes a laissez-faire attitude, how much income will go to workers? to the owners of land? to others? How do labour unions affect the incomes of their members? How can the government improve the lot of the poor?

The final major objective—growth—cuts across a number of other major topics, and thus appears periodically throughout the book. However, before we get into the meat of policy issues, we must first set the stage with some of the basic concepts and tools of economics. To that task we now turn (in Chapters 2 through 6).

KEY POINTS

1. In the words of Alfred Marshall, "economics is a study of mankind in the ordinary business of life." It is the study of how people make their living, how they acquire food, shelter, clothing, and other material necessities and comforts. It is a study of the problems they encounter, and of the ways in which these problems can be reduced.

2. During the twentieth century, substantial economic progress has been made in Canada and many other countries. We are producing much more, even though we spend less time at work than did our grandparents.

3. Nevertheless, substantial economic problems remain: problems such as poverty in the less-developed countries and at home; high rates of unemployment; and inflation.

4. One of the things we study in economics is how we can deal with our problems, either through private action or through government policies.

5. In the history of economic thought, the role of government has been controversial. Adam Smith in 1776 called for the liberation of markets from the tyranny of government control. By 1936, John Maynard Keynes was appealing to the government to accept its responsibilities

and to undertake public works in order to get the economy out of the Depression.

6. Important economic goals include the following:
   (a) An equilibrium with high employment and price stability.
   (b) Efficiency. Technological efficiency occurs when goods are produced with the smallest feasible quantity of inputs (while working at a reasonable pace). Allocative efficiency involves the production of the right combination of goods, using the lowest-cost combination of inputs.
   (c) Equity in the distribution of income.
   (d) A satisfactory rate of growth.

KEY CONCEPTS

economics
laissez-faire
depression
recession
unemployment
inflation
hyperinflation

average level of prices
relative prices
technological efficiency
allocative efficiency
poverty
equitable distribution of income

equal distribution of income
redistribution of income
growth
economic freedom
economic security
complementary goals
conflicting goals

PROBLEMS

1-1 According to Smith's "invisible hand," we are able to obtain meat, not because of the butcher's benevolence, but because of his self-interest. Why is it in the butcher's self-interest to provide us with meat? What does the butcher get in return?

1-2 Suppose another depression occurs like the Depression of the 1930s. How would it affect you? (Thinking about this question provided a major motivation for an entire generation of economists. They were appalled at the prospect, and determined to play a role in preventing a repeat of the Great Depression.)

1-3 The section on an equitable distribution of income reflects two views regarding the proper approach to poverty:
   (a) The important thing is to meet the basic needs of the poor; that is, to provide at least a minimum income for the purchase of food, shelter, and other necessities.
   (b) The important thing is to reduce inequality; that is, to reduce the gap between the rich and the poor.
   These two views are not the same. For example, if there is rapid growth in the economy, objective (a) may be accomplished without any progress being made toward (b). Which is the more important objective? Why? Do you feel strongly about your choice? Why?

1-4 Explain how an upswing in purchases by the public will affect (a) unemployment and (b) inflation. Does this result illustrate economic goals that are complementary or in conflict?

1-5 In Figure 1-1, you saw that the length of the average work week in Canada has declined more or less continuously since World War II. In the United States, the decline has been less sharp, whereas in Sweden the length of the work week has fallen even more than in Canada.
   (a) Can you think of some reason for this difference?
   (b) How would you expect these trends to have affected the growth rates of total production and worker incomes? Is it necessarily true that people in a country where total income is growing rapidly are better off than people in another country where income is growing more slowly?

APPENDIX

DIAGRAMS USED IN ECONOMICS

Chapter 1 contains diagrams that illustrate important points, such as the increase in production per person since 1926 (Figure 1-1), and the fact that economic growth has slowed down since 1973 (Figure 1-2). In the study of economics, diagrams are frequently used—as you may see by flipping through this book. A picture is often worth a thousand words. Diagrams present information in a vivid and eye-catching way and can fix important ideas in our minds. But, unfortunately, they can also mislead. The first and lasting impression may be the wrong impression. This appendix explains some of the major types of diagram used in economics. It also explains some of the ways in which diagrams may be used to impress or mislead, rather than inform.[5]

Three major types of diagrams will be considered:

1. Diagrams that present and compare two facts.
2. Diagrams that show how something changes through time. For example, Figure 1-4 illustrates how the average level of prices has usually risen, but has sometimes fallen.
3. Diagrams that show how two variables are related to one another; for example, a diagram showing that people spend more on housing as their incomes rise.

1. A SIMPLE COMPARISON OF TWO FACTS

The simplest type of diagram brings together two facts for comparison. Often, the best method of presenting two facts—and the least likely to mislead—is to use a bar chart like the one in Figure 1-2. In the top left corner, the first bar shows that the average rate of growth of industrial countries between 1960 and 1973 was 5.2% per year, while the second bar shows that the rate was only 2.4% in the next decade. By comparing the heights of the two bars, we immediately see how growth rates have changed.

---

[5]For more detail on how readers may be misled, see the sprightly book by Darrell Huff, *How to Lie with Statistics* (New York: Norton, 1954).

Things to Watch

Even such a simple diagram may carry a misleading message. There are several "tricks" that an unscrupulous writer can use to fool the reader.

Suppose, for example, that someone wants to present the performance of a country or a corporation in the most favourable light possible. Consider an example—a country whose steel production rose from 10 million tonnes in 1975 to 20 million tonnes in 1985.

Figure 1-6 is a bar chart illustrating this comparison in the simplest, most straightforward way. Glancing at the height of the two bars in this diagram, the reader gets the correct impression—steel production has doubled.

This is a very good performance, but not a spectacular one. Suppose that someone wants to "gild the lily," and make things look even better. Two easy ways of doing so—without actually lying—are illustrated in Figure 1-7.

The left panel is designed to mislead because part of the diagram is omitted. The heights of the bars are measured from 5 million tonnes, rather than zero.

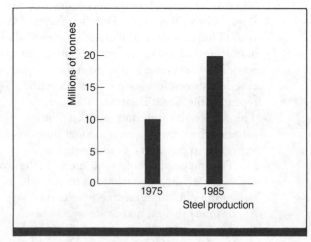

Figure 1-6 A Simple Bar Chart.
The simplest bar chart provides a comparison of two numbers, in this case the production of steel in two years. We see correctly that steel production has doubled.

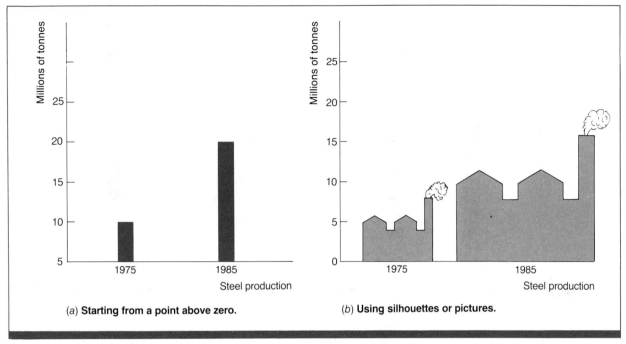

Figure 1-7 Variations on the simple bar chart.
Readers may be misled by variations on the simple bar chart. Both of the above panels present the same information as in Figure 1-6. In the left panel, the vertical axis begins with 5 million tonnes, rather than zero. In the right panel, pictures are used, rather than bars. In each case, the reader may be left with the erroneous impression that steel production has more than doubled.

Thus, the 1985 bar is three times as high as the 1975 bar, and the unwary reader may be left with the wrong impression—that steel production is three times as high in 1985, whereas in fact it is only twice as high. This, then, is the first thing to watch for: Do the numbers on the vertical axis start from zero? If not, the diagram may give the wrong impression.

The right panel shows another way in which the reader may be fooled. The bars of Figure 1-6 are replaced with something more interesting—pictures of steel mills. Because production has doubled, the steel mill on the right is twice as high as the one on the left. But notice how this picture gives the wrong impression. The mill on the right is not only twice as high. It is also twice as wide, and we can visualize it as being twice as deep, too. Therefore, it isn't just twice as large as the mill on the left; it is many times as large. Thus, the casual reader will again be left with the wrong impression—that steel output has increased manyfold, when in fact it has only doubled. This, then, is the second reason to be wary. Look carefully and skeptically at diagrams using silhouettes or pictures. Do they leave you with an exaggerated impression of the changes that have actually occurred?

A third way to mislead is illustrated in Figure 1-8. In both panels, the facts are correct regarding the average price of common stock in Canada. (Each share of common stock represents part ownership of a company.) The left panel shows that, between 1929 and 1952, the average price of stocks changed very little. The right panel shows facts which are equally true. Between 1932 and 1952—almost the same period of comparison—stock prices increased more than three-fold. How can these panels both be correct? The answer: Between 1929 and 1932, the most spectacular stock-market collapse in history occurred, with stocks losing two-thirds of their value. (The bar for 1932 is only one-third as high as the bar for 1929.)

Notice the contrast between the two panels. The left one implies that not much is to be gained by entering the stock market. The right panel gives exactly the opposite impression: The stock market is the place to

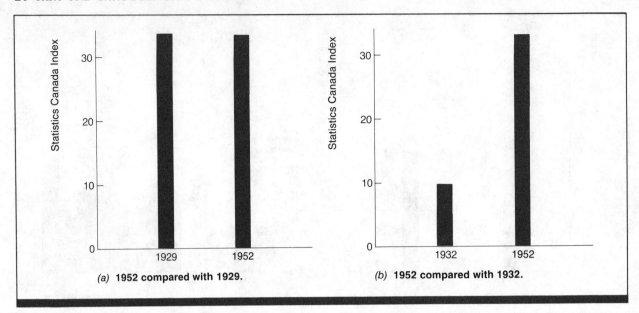

(a) **1952 compared with 1929.**

(b) **1952 compared with 1932.**

Figure 1-8 Comparisons depend on the times chosen.
Comparisons may change even when seemingly minor
changes are made in the dates. In 1952, stock prices were no
higher on average than in 1929 (left panel). However, they

were three times as high in 1952 as they had been in 1932.

Source: Statistics Canada, *CANSIM Databank*. Reproduced by permission of the Minister of Supply and Services Canada.

get rich. Thus, an author can give two completely
different messages, depending on the choice of the
initial "base" year (1929 or 1932). So beware. In any
diagram showing how something has changed over
time, ask yourself: Has the author slanted the results
by selecting a base year designed to mislead?

2. TIME SERIES: HOW SOMETHING CHANGES THROUGH TIME

That last problem can be avoided by providing the
reader with more information, using a **time series** diagram that shows stock prices in every year, not just in
a beginning and final year. Even better is to show
stock prices every month. With a more detailed figure,
the reader gets a much more complete story, including
both the collapse of 1929–1932 and the way in which
stock prices have risen since 1932.

> A *time series diagram* shows how some-
> thing (such as the price of stocks, the out-
> put of steel, or the unemployment rate)
> has changed through time.

However, even when we provide a detailed time
series, a number of issues remain. Here are some of
the most important ones.

Should We Measure from Zero?

In discussing a simple comparison between two facts,
we seem to have settled the question of how we should
measure up the vertical axis of a diagram. To start at
any figure other than zero can be misleading—as in
Figure 1-7(a), where steel production was measured
up from a starting point of 5 million tonnes.

However, once we provide the detailed information of a time series, we should reopen the question of
how to measure along the vertical axis. The problem
is that we now have two conflicting considerations.
We would like to start from zero to avoid misleading
the reader. On the other hand, starting from some
other point may make the details of a diagram much
easier to see.

This is illustrated in Figure 1-9, which shows the
rate of unemployment in each year from 1975 to 1985.
In the left panel, the unemployment rate is measured
vertically, starting from zero. This gives the best pic-

ture of how the overall unemployment rate compares in any two years we might like to choose (for example, 1981 and 1982).

Contrast this with the right panel, where the measurement of unemployment starts above zero. Like the graph in Figure 1-7(a), this panel can be misleading. For example, the bars for 1981 and 1982 might leave the impression that the unemployment rate more than doubled between those years, whereas in fact it increased by far less.

However, the right panel has a major compensating advantage. It provides a much clearer picture of how the unemployment rate changes from year to year; the year-to-year differences are much more conspicuous. (And year-to-year changes are very important, since they are one measure of fluctuations in the economy.) Consequently, the right-hand diagram can be more informative.

If panel (b) is chosen, readers must be warned that we have not started from zero. One way to do this is to leave a gap in the vertical bars, to show that something has been left out. Alternatively, a gap may be left in the vertical axis itself. (This alternative was used in Figure 1-1, where there were no bars on which to show gaps.)

How Should Growth Be Illustrated?

Some time series—such as a nation's population—have a strong tendency to grow over time. If we measure in the normal way along the vertical axis, the curve becomes steeper and steeper over time, as shown in the left panel of Figure 1-10. There is nothing necessarily wrong with this presentation—the increase in the population between 1970 and 1980 (2.7 million) was in fact much greater than the increase between 1870 and 1880 (0.6 million).

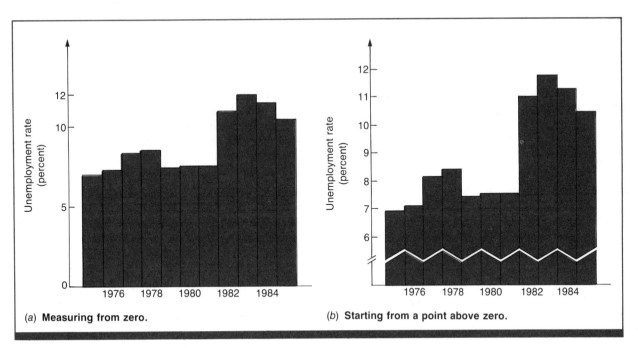

(a) **Measuring from zero.** (b) **Starting from a point above zero.**

Figure 1-9 A time series: The unemployment rate, 1975–1985.
The reader is provided with much more information in a time series that shows every year or every month, rather than every two years. In this diagram, there is an advantage in starting the vertical measurement above zero. Observe that

the detailed, year-to-year changes stand out more clearly in the right panel than in the left. To warn the reader that something has been left out, a gap has been left in the vertical bars.

Source: *Bank of Canada Review* (January 1986). Reproduced by permission of the Minister of Supply and Services Canada.

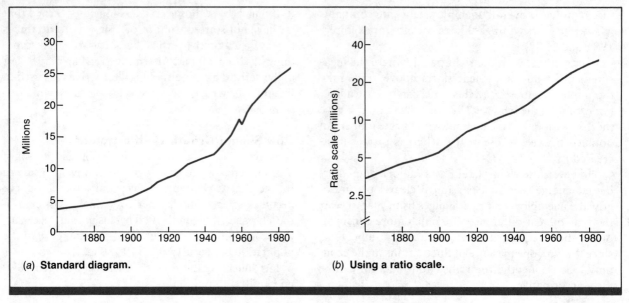

Figure 1-10 Population of Canada, 1867–1984.
By using a ratio scale, we can identify the periods when the rate of population growth was most rapid. It occurred when the slope of the curve in the right panel was steepest.

Source: Compiled from K. Buckley and M. Urquhart, eds., *Historical Statistics of Canada*, 1st ed. (Toronto and Cambridge: Cambridge University Press and Macmillan of Canada, 1965) and Statistics Canada, *Canadian Statistical Review*, various issues. Reproduced by permission of the Minister of Supply and Services Canada.

However, there are two related problems with this figure. First, the numbers in the early years—prior to 1900, say—are so small that details are hard to see. Second, we may be interested not just in the absolute numbers, but in the rate at which population is growing. Thus, the 0.6 million increase in population in the 1870s represents a much greater rate of increase (1.8% per year) than the 2.7 million increase of the 1970s (1.2% per year).

To highlight the rate of growth, a ***ratio*** or ***logarithmic*** scale is used on the vertical axis (Figure 1-10, panel (b)). On such a scale, equal percentage changes show up as equal distances. For example, the distance from 5 million to 10 million (an increase of 100%) is the same as the distance from 10 million to 20 million (also an increase of 100%). In such a diagram, if something grows at a constant rate (for example, by 2% per year), it shows up as a straight line. By looking for the steepest sections of the time series in the right panel of Figure 1-10, we can identify the periods when population has grown at the most rapid rate. Similarly,

back in Figure 1-4, the curve is steepest when the most rapid rates of inflation occurred.

A ratio scale is appropriate for a time series—like population growth—where the emphasis is on proportional rates of growth (or decline). However, it is inappropriate for a series that does not have a strong tendency to grow (or decline) at a proportional rate. For example, there is no reason to expect the unemployment rate in the economy to either grow or decline systematically over time, and there is no particular reason to use a logarithmic scale in a diagram such as the bottom half of Figure 1-3 (though we would have been justified in using one for the top half).

Finally, note that when a logarithmic scale is used, the question of whether the vertical axis is measured from zero becomes irrelevant, since zero cannot appear on such a diagram. By looking at Figure 1-10(b), we can see why. Each time we go up one centimetre (one notch on the vertical axis), the population doubles—from 5 to 10 million, and then to 20 million. We can make exactly the same statement the other way around:

Each time we go down a centimetre, the population falls by half—from 5 million to 2.5 million, then 1.25 million, and so on. No matter how far we extend the diagram downward, each additional centimetre will reduce the population by one-half. Therefore, the population can never reach zero on such a diagram.

Real or Monetary Measures?

People often complain that the federal government is getting "too big." Suppose we wanted to look at the size of the government. How would we do so?

The most obvious way is to look at the amount the government spends. Measured in dollars, the growth of government spending has been truly stupendous over the past half-century or so (Figure 1-11). But this simple measure has several shortcomings.

The first has to do with prices, which have risen substantially during the past half-century. Inflation

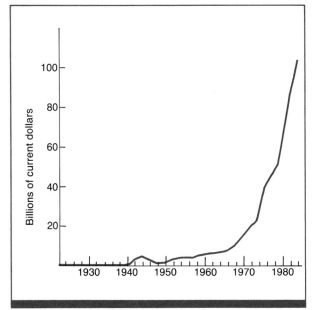

Figure 1-11 Federal government expenditures, measured in dollars.
As measured by the number of dollars spent, the size of the federal government has expanded very rapidly.

Source: Statistics Canada, *CANSIM Databank*. Reproduced by permission of the Minister of Supply and Services Canada.

means that even if the government had remained exactly the same size—building the same number of schools and roads, and keeping the same number of soldiers in the army—it would have spent many more dollars. That is, its expenditures in dollar, or **nominal**, terms would have gone up rapidly. In order to eliminate the effects of inflation, government statisticians calculate what government expenditures would have been if prices had not gone up—that is, if prices had remained at the level existing in a single year. Such a measure of government expenditures—in **constant-dollar**, or **real**, terms—is shown in panel (a) of Figure 1-12. Observe how much more slowly government expenditures appear to have grown when the effects of inflation are eliminated. (Further details on how real expenditures are calculated will be presented in a later chapter.)

Relative Measures

Even when measured in real terms, government expenditures have risen substantially. Does this, in itself, mean that the government is "too big?" The answer is, not necessarily. One reason is that, as the government has grown, so has the overall economy. Thus, we may ask the question: Has the government grown relative to the economy? (As in Figure 1-1, the size of the economy is measured by gross national product or GNP.) In Figure 1-12, panel (b), observe that government expenditures have not grown much relative to the economy (that is, as a percentage of GNP).

In passing, we should note that none of the panels of figures 1-11 and 1-12 allows us to answer the question of whether the government is too big, although each panel does provide some relevant information. If the government is spending on wasteful projects, then even a small government may be "too big." However, if it is spending wisely to meet pressing needs, then even a big government may be "too small."

Measuring things as a percentage of GNP is one way of judging their relative size. Another meaningful approach is to measure how things have changed compared to the population. For example, just because we are producing more wheat and other food now than we were a century ago, it does not necessarily follow that Canadians are better fed. The reason is that there are so many more of us than there were in 1885. To look at how well we are fed, we have to look at food consumption per capita (per person).

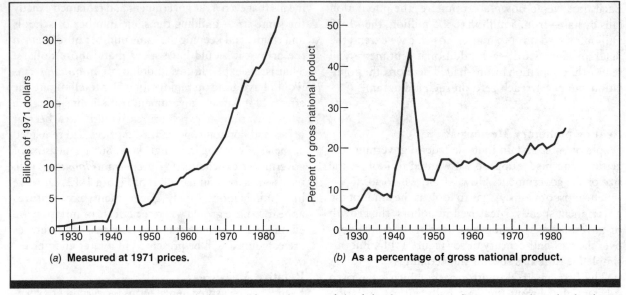

Figure 1-12 Federal government expenditures: Alternative presentations.
When the effects of inflation are removed in the left panel, the growth of government spending is much less spectacular than in Figure 1-11. As compared to the overall size of the economy (as measured by gross national product), the size

of the federal government has grown relatively slowly, as can be seen in the right panel.

Source: Compiled from Statistics Canada, *CANSIM Databank*. Reproduced by permission of the Minister of Supply and Services Canada.

3. RELATIONSHIPS BETWEEN VARIABLES

Frequently, economists want to keep track of the relationship between two variables. Table 1-2 provides an illustration—the relationship between the incomes of households and their expenditures on the basic necessities (housing, food, and clothing). The top row (Row A) indicates that a hypothetical family with an income of $10,000 spent $7,000 on the basic necessities. Similarly, Row B shows that a family with an income of $20,000 spent $11,000 on these basics.

The data in Table 1-2 may be graphed as Figure 1-13, where income is measured along the horizontal axis, and expenditures for basics up the vertical axis. (The lower left corner—labelled "0"—represents the starting point from which both income and basic expenditures are measured. This point is called the *origin*.) To plot the data in Row A of the table, we measure $10,000 in income along the horizontal axis, and $7,000 in spending for basics up the vertical axis. This gives us point A in the diagram. Similarly, points

Table 1-2
Household Income and Expenditures for Basics, 1985

	(1) Household income (after taxes)	(2) Expenditures for basics
A	$10,000	$ 7,000
B	20,000	11,000
C	30,000	14,500
D	40,000	17,500

B, C, and D represent corresponding rows B, C, and D in Table 1-2.

One question which can be addressed with such a diagram is how expenditures on the basics change as income increases. For example, as income increases from $10,000 at point A to $20,000 at point B, basic expenditures rise from $7,000 to $11,000. That is, expenditures on the basics rise by $4,000 in response to the $10,000 increase in income.

This relation can be illustrated by drawing a line

between points *A* and *B*, and looking at its *slope*—the slope being defined as the vertical change (*HB*) divided by the horizontal change (*AH*). In this example, the slope is $4,000/$10,000 = 4/10. As incomes increase from point *A* to point *B*, families spend 40% of the increase on the basics.

Observe in this diagram that the slope becomes smaller and smaller as we go further and further to the right; that is, as we move to larger and larger incomes. Whereas the slope is 4/10 between *A* and *B*, it is only $3,000/$10,000, or 3/10, between *C* and *D*. This smaller slope makes sense. Families with high incomes already have good houses, food, and clothing. When their income goes up another $10,000, they don't spend much more on the basics; they can do other things with their income.

Nevertheless, no matter how far to the right this diagram is extended, the line joining any two points will always slope upward; that is, the slope is always positive. The reason is that, as people's incomes rise, they always want somewhat better houses, food, and clothing.

However, in some relationships, there may be a downward-sloping curve. Figure 1-14 illustrates the situation facing a company producing a small business aircraft. The costs facing such a company are high—it has the expense of designing the aircraft, and it requires an expensive plant for production. If the firm produces only a few units each year (say, 10 aircraft, measured along the horizontal axis), it will operate at point *A*. It will be unable to charge a price high enough to cover its costs, and it will therefore suffer a loss. That is, its profit (measured along the vertical axis) will be negative. As it sells more, its revenues will rise, and it will begin to make profits to the right of point *B*.

However, profits do not rise indefinitely. If the company were to produce a large number of planes—say, 200—it would have to slash prices in order to sell them. This would reduce its profits. Thus, the profit curve at first slopes upward, reaches a peak at *C*, and then slopes downward.

Point *C* is very significant for the firm. At this point, the firm *maximizes its profits*. At this point, the curve

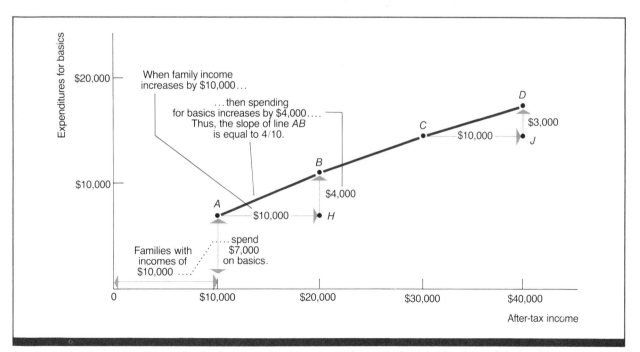

Figure 1-13 How expenditures for basics are related to income.

As family income increases (along the horizontal axis), the family's expenditures for the basics increase (as measured up the vertical axis). The *slope* of the line between any two points—such as *A* and *B*—show how strongly expenditures for basics respond (*HB*) to an increase in income (*AH*).

ceases to slope upward, and is just about to slope downward. That is, the slope is just about to switch from being positive to becoming negative. Thus, at the point of maximum profit, the slope of the curve is zero.

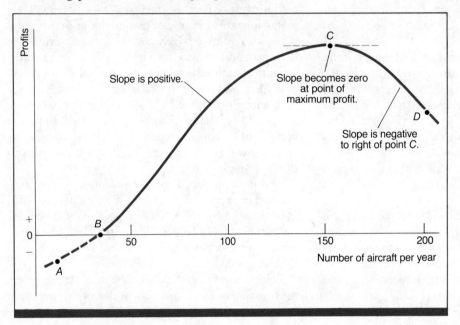

Figure 1-14 Output and profits.
If the firm produces only a few planes, it cannot cover its costs. It suffers losses. (Profits are negative.) As production increases, its losses shrink as it approaches point B. Then, to the right of B, the firm begins to make profits. So long as output is less than 150 units, the profits curve has a *positive* slope; that is, it slopes upward. Profits reach a peak at point C and thereafter begin to decline. Thus, to the right of C the curve has a *negative* slope. At the point where the curve reaches its peak, it is horizontal. The slope is zero.

Chapter 2

SCARCITY AND CHOICE

Economics studies human behaviour as a
relationship between ends and scarce means.
Lionel Robbins

In Chapter 1, we surveyed a wide range of economic issues: economic progress, economic problems such as inflation and unemployment, and economic goals such as efficiency and equity.

In this chapter, we will become more specific by exploring the most important single concept in economics: *scarcity*. Consider, for a moment, the major economic developments in Canada during the twentieth century. The average worker now produces about five times as much as the worker at the turn of the century—and does so with less effort, in a shorter work week. If the average worker can now produce so much, why don't we relax? If, with relatively little effort, we can have higher incomes than our grandparents, why do we worry about economic problems at all?

There are two fundamental reasons:

1. Our material *wants* are virtually unlimited or insatiable.

2. Economic *resources* are limited or scarce.

Because of these two basic facts, we cannot have everything we want. We therefore have to *make choices.*

UNLIMITED WANTS . . .

Consider, first, our wants. If the one-horse shay was good enough for great-grandpa, why isn't it good enough for us?

Material wants arise for two reasons. First, each of us has basic biological needs: the need for food, shelter, and clothing. But there is also a second reason. Clearly, we are prepared to work more than is required to meet our minimum needs. We want more than the basic diet of vegetables and water needed to sustain life. We want more than a shack which will provide minimal protection from the weather. We want more than the minimum clothing needed to protect us from the cold. In other words, we want the goods and services which can make life more pleasant. Of course, the two basic reasons for material wants cannot be sharply separated. When we sit down to a gourmet meal at a restaurant, we satisfy our biological need for food. But we are doing something more. When we savour exotic foods in a comfortable and stylish atmosphere, we are getting both the basics and the "frills." These frills are sufficiently pleasant that we are willing to work to obtain them.

The range of consumer wants is exceedingly broad. We want *goods*, such as houses, cars, shoes, shirts, and tennis rackets. Similarly, we want *services*, such as medical care, haircuts, and laundry services. When we get what we want, it may whet our appetites for something more. If we own a Chevrolet, perhaps we will want a Volvo next time. After we buy a house, we may wish to replace the carpets and drapes. Furthermore, as new products are introduced, we may want them too. We want video recorders, home computers, and a host of other products that earlier generations never even dreamed of. Even though it is conceivable that, some day, we will say, "Enough," that day seems far away. Our material wants show no sign of being completely satisfied.

. . . SCARCE RESOURCES

Because of the second fundamental fact of scarce resources, not all wants can be satisfied. While our productive capacity is large, it is not without limit. There are only so many workers in the labour force, and we have only a certain number of machines and factories. In other words, our resources are limited.

Resources are the basic inputs used in the production of goods and services. Therefore, they are also frequently known as *factors of production*. They can be categorized under three main headings: land, capital, and labour.

Economists use the term *land* in a broad sense, to include not only the arable land used by farmers and the city land used as building lots, but also the other gifts of nature that come with the land. The abundance of such natural resources in Canada constitutes an important explanation for the prosperity of this country's economy. Early economic development was based to a large extent on our game and fish resources, as well as on our fertile agricultural land. Other resources, such as minerals; petroleum and natural gas; forestlands; and rivers from which we can produce hydroelectric power, have become more important in the present era. All are classified as part of Canada's vast land resource.

Capital refers to buildings, equipment, and materials used in the productive process. An automobile assembly plant is "capital," and so are the machines in the plant and the steel with which automobiles will be built. In contrast to land, which has been provided by nature, capital has been produced at some time in the past. This may be the distant past: the factory may have been built 15 years ago. Or it may be the recent past: The steel may have been manufactured last month. The process of producing and accumulating capital is known as *investment*.

Unlike consumer goods (such as shoes, shirts, or food), capital goods or "investment goods" (such as tractors, factories, or machinery in the factories) are not designed to satisfy human wants directly. Rather, they are intended for use in the production of other goods. Capital produced now will satisfy wants only indirectly, and at a later time, when it will be used in the production of consumer goods. When capital is produced, therefore, it means that someone has been willing to wait. When a machine is produced rather than a car, the choice has been made to forego the car now in order to produce the machine, thus making it possible to produce more cars or other goods in the future. Thus, capital formation involves a choice between consumption *now* and more consumption *in the future.*[1]

A point of terminology should be emphasized here. Unless otherwise specified, economists use the term "capital" to mean *real capital*, not financial capital. In previous paragraphs, we've been referring to real capital: the factories and machinery used to produce other goods. *Financial capital*, on the other hand, consists of financial assets such as common stocks, bonds, or bank deposits. Such assets are important. The holder of a stock or bond, for example, has a form of wealth which is likely to produce income in the future, in the form of dividends on the stock or interest on the bond. But while an individual might consider 100 shares of Hiram Walker stock as part of his or her "capital," they are not capital in the economic sense. They are not a resource with which goods and services can be produced.

Similarly, when economists talk of investment, they generally mean *real investment*—the accumulation of machines and other real capital—and not financial investment (such as the purchase of a Canada Savings Bond).

Labour refers to the physical and mental talents of human beings, applied to the production of goods and services. The construction worker provides labour, and so does the university professor or the physician. (The professor produces educational services, and the doctor produces medical services.)[2]

---

[1]Note that the one who is willing to wait (forego present consumption in exchange for an expected future return) may be a foreign capitalist. A substantial proportion of the capital resources used in Canada is indeed owned by foreigners; the implications of this are discussed later in this chapter.

[2]The preceding paragraphs have presented the traditional division of the factors of production into the categories of land, labour, and capital. While still popular, this traditional division is not universally used by present-day economists. In particular, some economists now talk of "human capital." This is the education and training which add to the productivity of labour. Human capital has two of the important characteristics of physical capital: (1) a willingness to

One particular human resource deserves special emphasis: *entrepreneurial ability*. The entrepreneur is someone who

1. organizes production, bringing together the factors of production—land, labour, and capital—to produce goods and services.

2. makes business decisions, figuring out what goods to produce and how to produce them.

3. takes risk. (There is no guarantee that business decisions will turn out to be correct.)

4. innovates, introducing new products, new technology, and new ways of organizing business.

In order to be successful, an entrepreneur needs to be aware of changes in the economy. Is the market for adding machines declining, while that of computers is expanding? If so, the successful entrepreneur will not build a new assembly line for adding machines, but will instead consider producing computers. Some entrepreneurs are spectacularly successful: for example, Steve Jobs and Steve Wozniak, who set up Apple Computer while still in their twenties. Their mushrooming sales helped to make the microcomputer a common household appliance—and made them multimillionaires in the process (Box 2-1, p. 32). Other entrepreneurs are engaged in much more prosaic, everyday tasks. The teenager who offers to cut a neighbour's lawn for $10 is an entrepreneur. So is the university student who has a business typing other students' papers. The key questions facing an entrepreneur are these: Are people willing to pay for what I can produce? Can I sell the good or service for enough to cover costs, and have some profit left over?

Because entrepreneurs are the ones who undertake the production of new goods, they play a strategic role in determining the dynamism and growth of the economy. (The French word *entrepreneur* means, literally, "someone who undertakes" a task.)

SCARCITY AND CHOICE: THE PRODUCTION POSSIBILITIES CURVE

With unlimited wants and limited resources, we face the fundamental economic problem of *scarcity*. We can-

not have everything we want; we must make choices.

The problem of scarcity—and the need to make choices—can be illustrated with a *production possibilities curve* (PPC). This curve shows what can be produced with our existing resources (land, labour, and capital) and with our existing technology. Although our resources and our capacity to produce are limited, we have options as to what goods and services we produce. We may produce fewer cars and more aircraft, or less wheat and more corn.

In an economy with thousands of products, the choices before us are complex. In order to reduce the problem to its simplest form, consider a very basic economy, with only two goods (woollen clothing and wheat). If we decide to produce more food (wheat), then we will have to produce less clothing.

The options open to us are shown in the production possibilities table (Table 2-1) and the corresponding production possibilities curve (Figure 2-1). Consider first an extreme example, where all our resources are directed toward the production of food. In this case, illustrated by option A, we would produce 20 million tonnes of food, but no clothing. This clearly does not represent a desirable composition of output. While we would be well fed, we would be running around naked. However, no claim has been made that the points on the production possibilities curve are necessarily desirable; the only claim is that they are possible. And point A is possible.[3]

At the other extreme, if we produced nothing but clothing, we would make 5 billion metres of wool material, as illustrated by point F. Again, this is a possible outcome, but not a desirable one. We would be well dressed as we faced starvation.

The Shape of the Production Possibilities Curve: Increasing Opportunity Costs

More interesting cases, and more reasonable ones, are those where we produce some of each good. Consider how the economy might move from point A toward point F. At point A, nothing is produced but

---

wait during the training period, when the trainee does not produce goods or services; and (2) the increase it brings about in the productive capacity of the economy, since a trained worker can produce more than an untrained one.

[3]It may be advantageous for a country to specialize by devoting most of its resources to producing one good only (such as wheat) when it can sell this good (wheat) to foreign countries in exchange for all other goods (such as clothing). The possibility of specialized production and international trade is likely to be especially important for a relatively small country such as Canada.

Table 2-1
Production Possibilities

Options	Clothing (billions of metres)	Food (millions of tonnes)	Units of food that must be given up to produce one more unit of clothing (opportunity cost of clothing)
A	0	20	1
B	1	19	2
C	2	17	4
D	3	13	5
E	4	8	8
F	5	0	

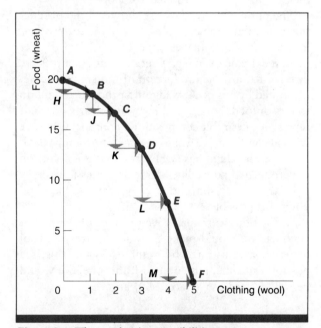

Figure 2-1 The production possibilities curve.
The curve shows the combinations of two goods that can be produced with limited resources of land, labour, and capital.

food. It is grown on all types of arable land throughout the nation. In order to begin the production of clothing, we would begin raising sheep in the areas that are comparatively best suited for wool production—on hilly meadowland in the Atlantic provinces and British Columbia, say. From these lands, we would get a lot of wool, while giving up just a small amount

of food that might have been grown there. This is illustrated as we move from point *A* to point *B* on the production possibilities curve. Only one unit of food is given up in order to produce the first unit of clothing.

As we decide to produce more wool, however, we must move to land which is somewhat less suited to wool production. As a result, we do not get the second unit of clothing quite so easily. To produce it, we must give up more than one unit of food. This is illustrated in the move from point *B* to point *C*. As clothing production is increased by one more unit (from 1 unit to 2), food production falls by two units (from 19 to 17). The **opportunity cost** of the second unit of clothing—the food we have to give up to acquire it—is thus greater than the opportunity cost of the first unit.

> The *opportunity cost* of a product is the alternative that must be given up to produce that product. (In this illustration, the opportunity cost of a unit of clothing is the food that must be given up when that unit of clothing is produced.)

Further increases in the production of clothing come at higher and higher opportunity costs. As we move to the third unit of clothing (from point *C* to point *D*), we must start grazing sheep on good cornland in Southern Ontario. A lot of food must be given up to produce that third unit of clothing. Finally, as we move from point *E* to point *F*, we are switching all our resources into the production of clothing. This comes at an extremely high opportunity cost in terms of lost output of food. Wheat production is stopped on the farms of Manitoba and Saskatchewan, which are no good at all for producing wool. The wheat lands remain idle, and prairie farmers migrate to the Atlantic region and B.C., where they can make only minor contributions to wool production. Thus, the last unit of clothing (the move from point *E* to *F*) comes at the very high cost of 8 units of food.

Thus, *the increasing opportunity cost of clothing is a reflection of the specialized characteristics of our resources*. Our resources are not completely adaptable to alternative uses. The lands of New Brunswick and Saskatchewan are not equally well suited to the production of wool and wheat. Thus, the opportunity cost of wool rises as its production is increased.

As a result of increasing opportunity cost, the production possibilities curve bows outward; that is, it is concave to the origin, as shown in Figure 2-1. The arrows in this figure illustrate why. The horizontal increases in clothing production—from point *H* to *B*, from *J* to *C*, from *K* to *D*, and so on—are each one unit. The resulting reductions in food production— measured vertically from *A* to *H*, *B* to *J*, *C* to *K*, and so on—become larger and larger, making the curve slope increasingly steeply as we move to the right.

While opportunity costs generally increase as production of a good increases, as shown in Figure 2-1, it is not logically necessary that they do so. In some cases, it is possible for opportunity costs to remain constant. For example, beef cattle and dairy cattle can graze on similar land; it is possible that the resources used to raise beef are equally suited to dairy cattle. Thus, the opportunity cost of beef in terms of milk may be constant. If we drew a production possibilities curve with milk on one axis and beef on the other, we would get a straight line.

THE PRODUCTION POSSIBILITIES CURVE IS A "FRONTIER"

The production possibilities curve in Figure 2-1 illustrates what an economy is capable of producing. It shows the maximum possible combined output of the two goods. In practice, actual production can fall short of our capabilities. Obviously, if there is large-scale unemployment, we are wasting some of our labour resources. Such a situation is shown by point *U*, inside the production possibilities curve in Figure 2-2. Beginning at such a point, we could produce more food and more clothing (and move to point *D*) by putting the unemployed back to work. (With full employment, we could also choose any other point on the production possibilities curve, such as *B*, *C*, or *E*.)

Thus, while the production possibilities curve represents options open to the society, it does not include all conceivable options. The attainable options include not only the points on the curve, but also all points in the shaded area inside the curve.

The production possibilities curve therefore traces out a frontier or boundary of the options open to us. We can pick a point on the frontier if we manage our affairs well and maintain a high level of employment.

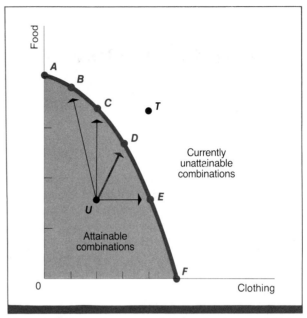

Figure 2-2 Unemployment and the production possibilities curve.
Point *U* represents a position of large-scale unemployment. If people are put back to work, the economy can be moved to point *D*, with more food and more clothing.

With its limited resources, the society can choose any point along the production possibilities curve, or any point within it. Points in the shaded area within the curve are undesirable; the society could do better by moving out to the curve. Points beyond the curve are unattainable with the resources currently at our disposal.

Or we can end up inside the curve if we mismanage the economy into a depression. But points (such as *T*) that are outside the curve are currently unattainable. We cannot reach them with our present quantities of land, labour, and capital, and with our present technology.

In summary, the production possibilities curve illustrates three important concepts: scarcity, choice, and opportunity cost.

1. Scarcity is illustrated by the fact that combinations outside the curve cannot be attained. Even though we might want such combinations, we cannot have them with the resources available to us.

2. Because we cannot have combinations outside the curve, we must settle for a choice of one of the attainable combinations outlined by the PPC.

BOX 2-1

A TALE OF TWO DREAMS

Even dreams are subject to demand curves.
John Hilton, explaining the failure of the
De Lorean automobile†

Courtesy Apple Canada Inc.

One task of the entrepreneur is to identify new opportunities and potential new products. In the business world, it is the entrepreneur who dreams dreams. But the entrepreneur must also be practical and hard-headed. Will the public share the dream? Will the new product sell? Can the entrepreneur produce it at a price low enough to attract customers?

APPLE COMPUTER

For Steve Jobs and Steve Wozniak, the answer was a resounding "yes."

In the mid-1970s, the two college dropouts were employed in the electronics industry—Wozniak at Hewlett-Packard, and Jobs as a designer of video games at Atari. In their spare time, they tinkered. In 1976, Wozniak built the first Apple, a small, easy-to-use computer. Jobs recognized its promise. They put together their available financial resources—$1,300—to start production in Jobs' garage.

For a fledgling electronics company, California's Silicon Valley was the place to be. An early task for the new entrepreneurs was to get funds for expansion by tapping into the local pool of venture capital. They were not immediately successful. One of their first prospects was put off by Jobs' cutoff jeans, sandals, and wispy beard. Then they made contact with A.C. Markkula, a former marketing manager at Intel (a maker of computer chips), who was delighted with the new machine. He put up $250,000,

†"The Decline and Fall of the De Lorean Dream," *Car and Driver* (July 1982): 70.

joined the company, and persuaded two venture capital firms to put up more money. Apple Computer was ready to go.

Wozniak quickly redesigned the original model. The trim, attractive Apple II was born. Sales surged: $800 thousand in 1977, $7.9 million in 1978, $100 million by 1980, and $500 million by 1982. The pace was frenetic. For Markkula, the problem was to "keep the race car on the track."

Apple's break-neck growth has created a major problem: how to keep the creative ferment and raw enthusiasm of a small company, while developing the structure and discipline needed in a large business. The team that developed Apple's Macintosh model—mostly young people in their twenties—wore T-shirts with their motto: "Working 90 hours a week, and loving every minute of it." The creativity of that group was remarkable, but the slightly madcap atmosphere exacted a toll. Many of Apple's young engineers burned out and left the company in their thirties. To create a more structured company, Apple in 1983 brought in as president a professional manager and marketing expert, former president John Sculley of Pepsi-Cola. Within the next two years, both Wozniak and Jobs left Apple.

DE LOREAN

The Apple dream has been generally happy, if somewhat surreal. In contrast, the dream of John Zachary De Lorean has turned into a nightmare.

During his 17 years at General Motors, De Lorean rose close to the pinnacle of the automobile industry, managing the Pontiac and Chevrolet divisions, and earning $650,000 a year. But he was restless and unhappy, chafing in the manager's role. In April, 1973, he left, to become a critic of G.M.

Courtesy Canapress Photo Service

and set up his own automobile firm to produce—in his words—an "ethical" car. His hint of social consciousness, his glittering lifestyle, and his willingness to take the big chance made him something of a folk hero.

Cars are very unlike computers. You can't start building them in your garage. An automobile assembly line takes vast amounts of capital, and most automobile companies are consequently very large. New entrants into the North American car market in the past half century have been conspicuously unsuccessful—Kaiser-Frazer, Tucker, and Bricklin. It took De Lorean seven years to design his new car, acquire a factory, and begin production. In the process, he discovered that Puerto Rico and the British government were willing to pay handsomely to attract his factory, so eager were they to provide new jobs. In spite of a consulting firm's estimate that De Lorean's project had only one chance in ten of succeeding, the British government made the high bid, offering De Lorean more than $100 million to locate his plant in Northern Ireland.

Production of De Lorean's sleek, stainless steel sports car began in 1981. The American introduction of the $26,000 vehicle was accompanied by extravagant hoopla, and sales were brisk at first. De Lorean ordered an increase in production to an annual rate of 20,000, even though his own market research estimated sales of no more than 12,000. By February of 1982, the company had an inventory of more than 4,000 unsold cars. Losses mounted. When De Lorean informed the British government that he would need $70 million more to keep his factory in operation, they coldly refused. In an angry debate in parliament, De Lorean's operation was denounced as a "rip off." It was then that his problems really began. Within a few months, he was arrested on a drug charge. The prosecutors alleged that he had offered to put up almost $2 million to buy cocaine, in the hopes of making a quick profit with which to save his company. Although he was acquitted, he faced other charges of illegal activity, and he had lost his dream. His car company had collapsed.

3. Opportunity cost is illustrated by the downward slope of the production possibilities curve.

GROWTH: THE OUTWARD SHIFT OF THE PRODUCTION POSSIBILITIES CURVE

As time passes, a point such as *T* (Figure 2-2) may come within our grasp as our productive capacity increases and the economy grows. There are three main sources of growth:

1. technological improvement, representing new and better ways of producing goods
2. an increase in the quantity of capital
3. an increase in the labour force

Consider a change in technology. Suppose a new type of fertilizer is developed that substantially increases the output of our land, whether wool or wheat is being produced. Then we will be able to produce more

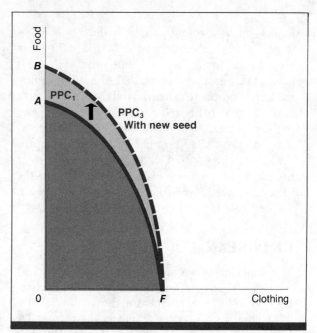

Figure 2-4 Technological improvement in a single good. When a new, improved strain of wheat is developed, the production possibilities curve moves out to PPC_3.

wheat and more wool. The production possibilities curve will shift out to the new curve (PPC_2) shown in Figure 2-3.

> *Growth* is defined as an outward movement of the production possibilities curve.

While the new fertilizer illustrated in Figure 2-3 increases our ability to produce both wheat and wool, other types of technological improvement may increase our ability to produce only one of them. For example, the development of a new disease-resistant strain of wheat will increase our ability to produce wheat, but not wool. In this case, illustrated in Figure 2-4, nothing will happen to the place where the production possibilities curve meets the axis for clothing. If we direct all our resources to the production of clothing, we can still produce no more than shown by point *F*. However, if we direct all our resources to wheat, we can produce more; the other end of the PPC therefore moves upward along the food axis, from *A* to *B*. Thus,

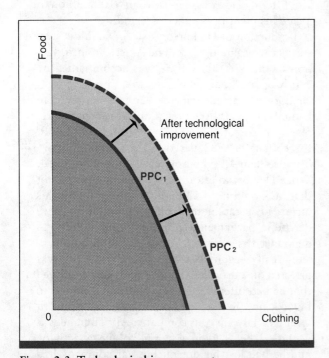

Figure 2-3 Technological improvement. As a result of the development of a new fertilizer, our productive capabilities increase. The production possibilities curve moves outward.

the development of the new wheat causes the PPC to move upward, from PPC_1 to PPC_3.

GROWTH: THE CHOICE BETWEEN CONSUMER GOODS AND CAPITAL GOODS

As an alternative to technological change, consider the second source of growth listed above: an increase in the quantity of capital. The capital which we have today is limited. However, capital itself can be produced. The quantity of capital in the year 2000 will be determined in large part by how much capital we choose to produce this year and in coming years.

In order to study this choice, we must look at a different production possibilities curve—not one showing food and clothing, but one showing the choice between the production of capital goods (such as machines and factories) and the production of consumer goods (such as food, clothing, and TV sets).

In Figure 2-5, two hypothetical economies are compared. Starting today, these two countries face the same initial production possibilities curve (PPC_{today}). The citizens of Extravagania (on the left) believe in living for the moment. They produce mostly consumption goods and very few capital goods (at point A). As a result, their capital stock will be not much greater in 2000 than it is today, so their PPC will shift out very little. In contrast, the citizens of Thriftiana (on the right) keep down the production of consumer goods in order to build more capital goods (at point B). By the year 2000, their productive capacity will be greatly increased, as shown by the large outward movement of the PPC. Because they have given up so much consumption today, their income (and ability to consume) will be much greater in the future. Thus, any society faces a choice: How much consumption should it sacrifice now in order to be able to consume more in the future?

Capital Imports and Growth

In the example illustrated by Figure 2-5, we have assumed that the increase in the capital stock of a country is made possible because its citizens are willing to forego a certain amount of current consumption.

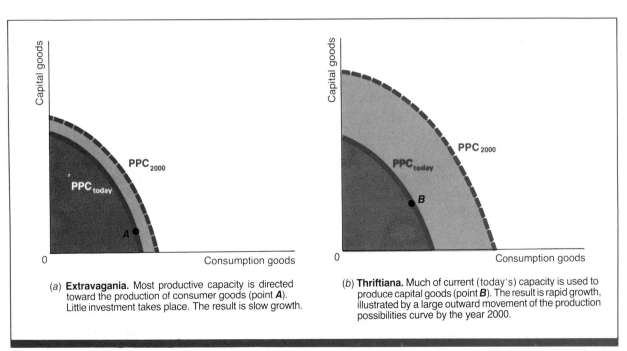

(a) **Extravagania.** Most productive capacity is directed toward the production of consumer goods (point **A**). Little investment takes place. The result is slow growth.

(b) **Thriftiana.** Much of current (today's) capacity is used to produce capital goods (point **B**). The result is rapid growth, illustrated by a large outward movement of the production possibilities curve by the year 2000.

Figure 2-5 **Capital formation now helps to determine future productive capacity.**

But a country's citizens do not necessarily have to forego consumption in order for the country to increase its capital stock. For example, an increase in Canada's capital stock may be financed by residents of foreign countries, either through their lending money to Canadians, or through foreign direct investment in Canada. (An example of foreign lending to Canadians would be if foreigners bought $10 million worth of bonds issued by B.C. Hydro, the proceeds being used to finance the building of a new generating station. Direct investment occurs when foreigners control the capital created in Canada—for example, if Ford Motor Co. spends $20 million to construct an assembly plant in St. Thomas, Ont.) When increases in Canada's capital stock are financed by foreigners in either of these ways, it is foreigners, not Canadians, who are foregoing current consumption in order to make the capital formation possible. This process is referred to as a **capital inflow** or **capital imports** into Canada.

> When foreigners finance a part of the increase in a country's capital stock, the country is said to have a *capital inflow*, or to be *importing capital.*

Although capital inflows can help to move the production possibilities curve outward at a rapid pace, all of this benefit doesn't go to Canadians. Some goes to the foreigners who have to be paid a return on their investment. To illustrate this, suppose that Canada's production possibilities curve has expanded from PPC_{today} to PPC_{2000} in panel (b) of Figure 2-5, through large-scale capital imports. While it will still be true that the large capital stock in the year 2000 will make it possible for us to produce a large amount of goods and services in that year, some of our output will have to go to the foreign capitalists as a return on their capital. (The issues faced by a country that has large capital imports will be discussed further in Chapter 35.)

Economic Development:
The Problem of Takeoff

In some countries, the question of growth may be approached in a relatively relaxed manner. For countries such as Canada or the United States, for example, the issue is not a matter of life or death. Even if we consume most of our current output and grow only slowly, we will still be comfortable in the year 2000.

The same is true for Japan and for the countries of Western Europe. (However, Japan conspicuously has not taken a relaxed approach to the growth question. Japan has been "Thriftiana" *par excellence*, investing a large share of national output in new plant and equipment, and growing rapidly.)

Some other countries, however, face a much more critical situation. They are so poor that they can scarcely take a relaxed view either of the present or of the future. Unless they can import capital, they face a cruel dilemma (illustrated in Figure 2-6). If they consume all their current output (at point A), they will not be able to move out from PPC_1. Their future will be just as bleak as the present.[4] On the other hand, if they want to grow, they will have to produce capital, and this means cutting back on their production of consumer goods. (If they choose the growth strategy and move initially to point B_1, then the production of consumer goods will decrease from A to B.) Since the already low level of consumption is depressed further, more people may starve.

In the long run, the growth strategy pays off, however. Because capital is produced at B_1, productive capacity grows. The production possibilities curve shifts out to PPC_2. Now the nation can pick point B_2, where it not only produces capital goods, but also consumes as much as it originally did at A. (B_2 is directly above point A.) The economy has achieved a *takeoff*. Because it is now producing capital goods, its PPC is continuously moving out. Consequently, the nation can produce ever-increasing amounts of both consumer and capital goods.

However, the long-run process does not solve the painful problem of the present: Should consumption be depressed, at the possible risk of starvation, in order to initiate the growth process? How can the economy take off without the danger of a crack-up halfway down the runway? (The danger may be politi-

---

[4]In this simplified example, it is assumed that only capital changes, and that technology and population remain constant. In fact, all three major determinants of growth (capital, labour, and technology) may change. If technology improves, growth may occur even in the absence of investment, and so the outlook would not be as bleak as suggested above. On the other hand, population pressures may make the outlook even worse. As population grows, output must grow if the already low standard of living is not to fall even lower. Thus, some capital formation may be required just to maintain the present standard.

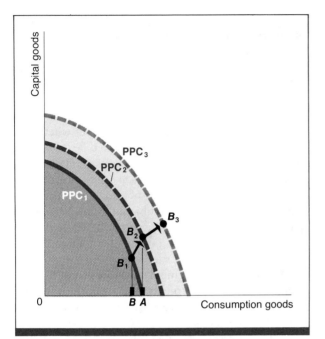

Figure 2-6 "Takeoff" into economic growth.
If point B_1 is initially chosen (on PPC_1), then growth will occur. The economy can move progressively to B_2, B_3, and beyond. However, the initial choice of B_1 instead of A means that people will have to forego some consumption goods, as measured by the distance AB. The problem therefore is: What short-term miseries will be caused by the choice of B_1 rather than A?

cal as well as economic. If a government chooses point B_1, the population may be unimpressed with "pie in the sky"—the promise of a brighter future. They may vote the government out, or rebel.)

One possible solution to this difficult dilemma lies in capital imports from other countries. Richer countries can provide the resources for the early stages of growth, either by granting aid or through private investment. (For example, a Canadian tractor manufacturer might build a plant in the developing country.) In this way, economic takeoff might occur without the sacrifices that capital formation otherwise requires.

AN INTRODUCTION TO ECONOMIC THEORY: THE NEED TO SIMPLIFY

The production possibilities curve is the first piece of theoretical equipment that the beginning economics student typically encounters. There will be many more.

At this early stage, it is appropriate to address directly a problem which often bothers both beginning and advanced students of economics. The production possibilities curve, like many other theoretical concepts that will be introduced in later chapters, represents a gross simplification of the real world. When the PPC is drawn, it is assumed that only two types of goods can be produced—food and clothing, or consumer goods and capital goods. (Diagrams are limited to two alternatives because the printed page has only two dimensions.) Yet obviously, there are thousands of goods produced in the modern economy. This raises a question: With our simple approach, can we say anything of relevance to the real world?

Since we have already used the production possibilities curve, it is not surprising that our answer to this question is yes. To see why, let us briefly consider the role of theory in economics. Economics is a study of such questions as how consumers behave; why shoes are produced in Montreal and steel in Hamilton; why prices are sometimes stable and sometimes volatile. To study economics, we must consider *cause* and *effect*.

Theory Necessarily Involves Simplification

If we wished to describe and explain the real world in detail, we could go on without end. But complete description would be useless as a guide to private behaviour or public policy; it would be too complex. In a sense, theory is like a map. A road map is necessarily incomplete. In many ways, it is not very accurate, and, indeed, downright wrong. Towns and villages are not round circles. Roads of various qualities do not really come in different colours. If a road map were more realistic, it would be less useful for its intended purpose. If it tried to show every house and every tree, it would be an incomprehensible jumble of detail. A road map is useful precisely because it is a simplification that shows in stark outline the various roads which may be travelled. Similarly, the objective of economic theory is to draw in stark outline the important relationships among producers and consumers.

When details are left out of a road map, it becomes more useful as a guide for the auto traveller. However, it becomes less useful for other purposes. A road map is a poor guide for airplane pilots. They need a map with the heights of mountains marked clearly. A road map is a poor guide for sales managers, who need a map showing regional sales targets and staff assignments. The way in which a map is constructed depends upon its intended use. Various maps are "true," but they do not represent the "whole truth." An important question for a map user thus becomes: Do I have the best map for my purpose?

The same generalization holds for economic theory. If we want to study long-run growth, we may use quite different theoretical tools from those we would use to study short-term fluctuations. If we want to study the consequences of price controls on the housing market, we may use different tools from those we would choose to investigate the economic consequences of a cut in Old-Age Security benefits. Just as in the case of the map, the "best" theory cannot be identified unless we know the purposes for which it is to be used.

The production possibilities curve is a theoretical tool whose purpose is to illustrate the concept of scarcity. If we begin on the PPC, with our resources fully employed, then we can come to a significant conclusion: to produce more of one good, we will have to cut back on the production of some other good or service. The "if" clause is important. It tells us that when we consider points along the PPC, we are making an assumption—that resources are fully utilized. When the "if" clause is violated—when the economy begins with large-scale unemployment—then we reach quite a different conclusion: The economy can produce more consumer goods and more capital goods at the same time. Thus, the "if" clause acts as a label on our theoretical road map. It tells us when the map can be used.

For the novice and old hand alike, it is essential to recognize and remember such "if" clauses. Failure to do so may lead us to use the wrong theory, and make serious policy mistakes—just as the pilot who uses the wrong map may fly a plane into the nearest mountain top.

The Distinction between Positive and Normative Economics

The uses of theory are many, but they may be divided into two main families. *Positive* or *descriptive* economics aims at understanding how the economy works. It is directed toward explaining the world as it is, and how various forces can cause it to change. In contrast, *normative* economics deals with the way the world (or some small segment of it) ought to be.

A debate over a positive statement can often be settled by an appeal to the facts. For example, the following is a positive statement: "Canadian newsprint production last year was 100 million tonnes." By looking up the statistics, we can find out whether or not this was true. A more complicated positive statement is: "There are millions of barrels of oil under the Beaufort Sea." With a geological study, we can discover whether this is likely to be so. A third positive statement is this: "If one cubic metre of tar sands is passed through steam, five litres of oil will flow out of the sand." By experimentation, we can discover whether or not this is generally true.

A normative statement is more complex: for example, "We ought to extract oil in large quantities from the Beaufort Sea." Facts are relevant here. If there is no oil under the Beaufort Sea (a positive conclusion), then the normative statement that we ought to extract oil must be rejected for the very simple reason that it can't be done. However, facts alone will seldom settle a dispute over a normative statement, since it is based on something more—on a view regarding appropriate goals or ethical values. A normative statement involves a value judgement, a judgement about what ought to be. It is possible for well-informed individuals of exemplary character to disagree over normative statements, even when they agree completely regarding the facts. For example, they may agree that there is, in fact, a large quantity of oil under the Beaufort Sea. Nevertheless, they may disagree as to whether or not it should be extracted. These differences may develop, perhaps, over the relative importance of a plentiful supply of heating oil as compared with the damage to the Arctic environment which might accompany the extraction of oil; or over a difference of opinion about whether or not the Canadian taxpayer should be required to provide the subsidy necessary for this development.

Although some positive statements may be settled easily by looking at the facts, others may be much more difficult to assess. This is particularly true of statements making claims about causation. They may be quite controversial because the facts are not easily untangled. For example: "If there is no growth in the money stock next year, then inflation will fall to zero"; or "If income tax rates are increased by 5%, government revenues will increase by $20 billion next year"; or "Rent controls have little effect on the number of apartments constructed each year."

In evaluating such statements, economists and other social scientists have two major disadvantages as compared with natural scientists. First, experiments are difficult or impossible in many instances. Society is not the plaything of economists. They do not have the power to conduct an experiment in which one large city is subjected to rent control while a similar city is not, simply to estimate the effects of rent control. Nevertheless, economists do have factual evidence to study. By looking at situations where rent controls have actually been imposed by the government, they may be able to estimate the effects of those controls. Moreover, in special situations, economic experiments are possible, particularly when the government is eager to know the results. For example, experiments have been undertaken to find out if people work less when they are provided with a minimum income by the government. (Some results from these studies will be discussed in Chapter 37.)

The second disadvantage is that the social sciences deal with the behaviour of people, and behaviour can change. Suppose that we estimate corporate profits next year to be $20 billion. We might carelessly conclude that, if the profits tax is raised by 10%, the government will receive an additional $2 billion in revenues. But this is not necessarily so. With a higher tax rate, businesses may behave differently, in order to reduce the taxes they have to pay. Furthermore, even if we have evidence as to how businesses have responded to a 10% tax increase in the past, we cannot be certain that they will respond the same way in the future. They may have become more imaginative in finding ways to avoid taxes. The possibility that people will learn and change their behaviour has been one of the most interesting areas of research in economics in recent years.

In contrast, physical scientists study a relatively stable and unchanging universe. Gravity works the same today as it did in Newton's time.

KEY POINTS

1. Scarcity is a fundamental economic problem. Because wants are virtually unlimited and resources are scarce, we are faced with the need to make choices.

2. The choices open to society are illustrated by the production possibilities curve.

3. Not all resources are uniform. For example, the land of Manitoba is different from the land of Nova Scotia. As a consequence, opportunity cost generally increases as more of a good is produced. For example, as more wool is produced, more and more wheat must be given up for each additional unit of wool. As a result, the production possibilities curve normally bows outward.

4. The production possibilities curve is a frontier, representing the choices open to society—if there is full utilization of the available resources of land, labour, and capital. If there is large-scale unemployment, then production occurs at a point within this frontier.

5. The economy can grow and the production possibilities curve can move outward if:
   (a) technology improves
   (b) the capital stock grows and/or
   (c) the labour force grows

6. By giving up consumer goods at present, we can produce more capital goods, and thus have a growing economy. The production of capital goods (investment) therefore represents a choice of more future production and less present consumption.

7. Through capital imports, a country may achieve economic growth without reducing its current consumption. However, some of the extra production which results from capital imports has to be used to pay foreign capitalists for the use of their capital.

8. For the poorest countries, a choice between present consumption and growth is particularly painful. If consumption is suppressed in order to allow for more rapid growth, people may

starve. But growth is essential to raising a low standard of living.

9. Like other theoretical concepts, the production possibilities curve represents a simplification. Because the world is so complex, theory cannot reflect the "whole truth." Nevertheless, a theory —like a road map—can be valuable if it is used correctly. In order to determine the appropriate uses of a theory, it is important to identify the assumptions on which the theory was developed.

KEY CONCEPTS

scarcity	capital	growth
goods	investment	takeoff
services	real capital	capital imports
resources	financial capital	positive economics
factors of production	entrepreneur	normative economics
land	production possibilities curve	theory
labour	increasing opportunity cost	

PROBLEMS

2-1 In Chapter 1, economics was defined broadly as the study of how people make their living, of the problems they encounter in doing so, and of the ways in which they can reduce these problems. Another common definition of economics is tied closely to the idea of scarcity. Economics is "the study of the allocation of scarce resources to satisfy alternative, competing human wants."

Clearly, the study of scarcity is an important part of economics. We cannot have all the goods and services we want. However, one of the economic problems in Chapter 1 cannot be attributed to a scarcity of resources. Which one? Why is this problem not attributable to a scarcity of resources? Is this problem covered by the broader definition in Chapter 1?

2-2 "Wants aren't insatiable. The economic wants of Peter Pocklington have been satisfied. There is no prospect that he will spend all his money before he dies. His consumption is not limited by his income." Do you agree? Does your answer raise problems for the main theme of this chapter, that wants cannot all be satisfied by the goods and services produced from our limited resources? Why or why not?

2-3 "The more capital goods we produce, the more the Canadian economy will grow, and the more we and our children will be able to consume in the future. Therefore, the government should encourage capital formation." Do you agree or disagree? Why?

2-4 Does Canada have a moral obligation to aid India with its economic development? Nigeria? Brazil? China? Jamaica?

2-5 Do your answers to questions 2-3 and 2-4 fall under the heading of "positive" or "normative" economics? Why?

Chapter 3

SPECIALIZATION, EXCHANGE, AND MONEY

Money . . . is not of the wheels of trade:
it is the oil which renders the motion of
the wheels smooth and easy.

David Hume

The past century has witnessed impressive economic progress, marked by a huge increase in the quantity of capital and a flood of new inventions. Tractors have been introduced into farming; airplanes speed the movement of people and goods; telephones and radio allow instant worldwide communication; computers help in the design of products. A long list of advances could quickly be compiled. Today, the worker has not only more tools, but also much better tools than the worker of the nineteenth century.

The new tools have led to a significant increase in the degree of *specialization*. The nineteenth-century carpenter produced a wide range of furniture and related wood products, from jewellery boxes to caskets. (Indeed, occupations were sometimes combined, with the same individual acting as both carpenter and undertaker.) On the early frontier, the settler was largely self-sufficient. Families grew their own food, built their own homes, and often made most of their own clothes. Not so today. Most farms are specialized, producing only one or a few products, such as wheat, corn, or beef. The worker in a modern factory tends a machine designed to produce a single piece of furniture, or perhaps just a single leg of a piece of furniture. The results have not been an unmixed blessing. Modern

workers are more prone to boredom, and they lack the sense of accomplishment enjoyed by the skilled workers of the past who could see their creations taking shape. However, the results have undoubtedly contributed to efficiency. By using specialized machinery, the modern worker has become very productive.

We can easily find examples where specialization contributes to efficiency. It is efficient for Canada to import coffee and to export wheat or subway cars to pay for this coffee. It might be possible to produce coffee in Canada, but only with great difficulty, and at a very high cost. Similarly, it is efficient to produce steel in Hamilton and wheat in Manitoba. Manitobans presumably could produce their own steel, but the cost would be prohibitively high. Specialization likewise takes place within towns and cities. Barbers specialize in cutting hair, doctors in treating illnesses, and factory workers in producing bicycles, cars, and home appliances.

EXCHANGE: THE BARTER ECONOMY

Specialization requires *exchange*. Farmers who specialize in raising beef (beyond their families' direct requirements) must exchange beef for furniture, cloth-

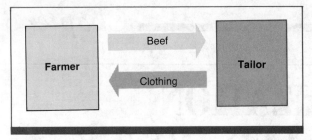

Figure 3-1 Barter.
With barter, no money is used. The farmer exchanges beef directly for clothing. Transactions involve only two parties—in this case, the farmer and the tailor.

ing, and other needs. There are two kinds of exchange: barter, and exchange for money.

In a *barter* system, no money is used: One good or service is exchanged directly for another. The farmer specializing in the production of beef may find a hungry barber and thus get a haircut, or find a hungry tailor and thus exchange meat for a suit of clothes, or find a hungry dentist and thus obtain dental treatment. A simple barter transaction is illustrated in Figure 3-1. In a barter economy, there are dozens of such bilateral (two-way) transactions: between the farmer and the tailor; between the farmer and the dentist; between the dentist and the tailor; and so on.

Clearly, barter is inefficient. Farmers in a barter system spend half their time producing beef, and the other half searching for someone willing to make the right trade. Barter requires a *coincidence of wants*: Those engaged in barter must each have a product that the other wants. The farmer not only must find

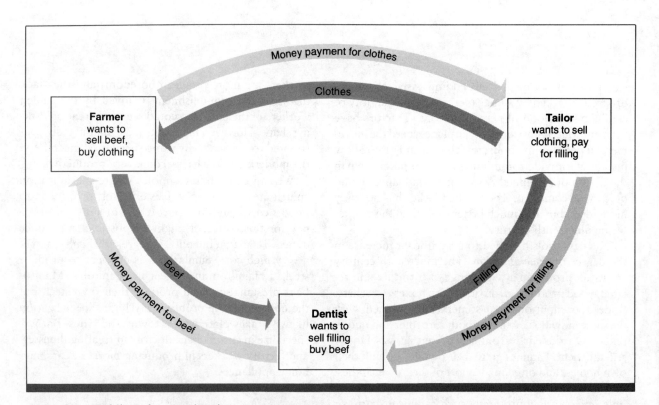

Figure 3-2 Multilateral transactions in a money economy.
In a money economy, multilateral transactions among many participants are possible. The farmer gets clothing from the tailor, even though the tailor doesn't want to buy the farmer's beef.

someone who wants beef, but that someone must also be able to provide something in exchange that the farmer wants. Furthermore, with barter, there is a problem of **indivisibility**. A suit of clothes—or an automobile or a house—should be bought all at once, and not in pieces. To illustrate, suppose that a beef farmer who wants a suit of clothes has been lucky enough to find a tailor who wants meat and is willing to make a trade. The suit of clothes may be worth 50 kg of beef, and the farmer may be quite willing to give up this amount. The problem is that the tailor may not be that hungry, perhaps wanting only 25 kg. In a barter economy, what would the farmer have to do? Get only the jacket from this tailor, and set out to find another hungry tailor in order to obtain a pair of pants? If the farmer did that, what would be the chances that the pants would match?

EXCHANGE WITH MONEY

With money, exchange is much easier. It is no longer necessary for wants to coincide. In order to get a suit of clothing, the farmer would not need to find a hungry tailor, but only someone willing to pay money for the beef. The farmer could then take the money and buy the suit of clothes. Because money represents *general purchasing power*—that is, it can be used to buy any of the goods and services offered for sale—money makes possible complex transactions among many parties. Figure 3-2 gives a simple illustration with three parties. Actual transactions in a monetary economy may be very complex, with dozens or hundreds of participants.

Money also solves the problem of indivisibility. The farmer can sell the whole carcass of beef for money, and use the proceeds to buy a complete set of clothes. It doesn't matter how much beef the tailor wants.

In the simple barter economy, there is no clear distinction between seller and buyer, or between producer and consumer. When bartering beef for clothing, the farmer is at the same time both a seller (of beef) and a buyer (of clothing). By contrast, in a monetary economy, there is a clear distinction between seller and buyer. In the beef market, the farmer is the seller; the hungry tailor is the buyer. The farmer is the producer; the tailor is the consumer.

The distinction between the producer and the con-

sumer in a money economy is illustrated in Figure 3-3. Producers—or **businesses**—are shown in the right-hand box; consumers—or **households**—in the left. Transactions between the two groups are illustrated in the loops. In the top loops, the transactions in consumer goods and services are shown. Food, clothing, and a host of other products are sold in exchange for money.

In the lower loops, transactions in economic resources are shown. In a complex exchange economy, not only are consumer goods bought and sold for money; so are resources. In order to be able to buy food and other goods, households must have money income. They acquire money by providing the labour and other resources that are the inputs of the business sector. For example, workers provide their labour in exchange for wages and salaries, and owners of land provide their property in exchange for rents.

Figure 3-3 is simplified. For example, we have excluded the government, which is a major purchaser of goods and services. (Remember the purpose of simplification discussed in Chapter 2: to show important relationships in sharp outline.) Figure 3-3 shows the circular flow of payments—that is, how businesses use the receipts from sales to pay their wages, salaries, and other costs of production, while households use their income receipts from wages, salaries, and so on, to buy consumer goods.

THE MONETARY SYSTEM

Because barter is so inefficient, people turn naturally to the use of money. In most societies, the government becomes deeply involved in the monetary system, issuing paper money and coins. But even if the government does nothing, a monetary system will evolve.

The powerful tendency for money to appear, and some of the important characteristics of a good monetary system may be illustrated by a specific example of an economy that began without money: the prisoner-of-war camp of World War II.[1] Economic relations in such a camp were primitive; the range of goods was very limited. But some things were available: rations supplied by the German captors, and the Red Cross

---

[1]This illustration is based on R. A. Radford, "The Economic Organization of a P. O. W. Camp," *Economica* (November 1945): 189–201.

parcels that arrived periodically. These parcels contained a variety of items such as canned beef, jam, margarine, and cigarettes. Nonsmokers who received cigarettes were obviously eager to trade them for other items. The basis for exchange was established.

At first, trading was rough and ready, with no clear picture of the relative values of the various items. In one instance, a prisoner started around the camp with only a can of cheese and five cigarettes, and returned with a complete Red Cross parcel. He did so by buying goods where they were cheap, and selling them where they were dear. However, as time went by, the prices of various goods tended to become stable, and all prices came to be quoted in terms of cigarettes. For example, a can of cheese was worth seven cigarettes.

Not only did cigarettes become the measuring rod for quoting prices, but they were used as the common *medium of exchange*. That is, cigarettes were the item used to buy goods. Even nonsmokers were willing to accept cigarettes in payment, although they had no desire to smoke. They knew that they would be able to use the cigarettes to buy chocolate, jam, or other items. In short, cigarettes became the money of the POW camp. This was a natural evolution; there was no government to decree that cigarettes were money, and no authority to enforce that choice. At other times and in other societies, other items have been used as money: items as diverse as beads, playing cards, empty gin bottles, porpoise teeth, rice, salt, wampum, stones, and even woodpecker scalps (Box 3-1).

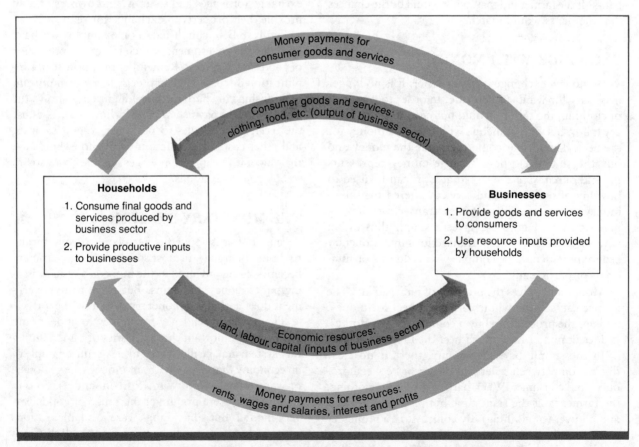

Figure 3-3   The flow of goods, services, resources, and money payments in a simple economy.
Monetary payments are shown in the outer loop. These pay for the flow of goods and services and resources shown in the inner loop.

BOX 3-1

EARLY MONEY ON THE ISLAND OF UAP†

On the south-sea island of Uap, the medium of exchange is called fei. This currency consists of large, solid, thick stone wheels ranging in diameter from one to twelve feet, and in the center a hole, so that the stones may be slung on poles and carried. They are not found on Uap itself, but are quarried in Babelthuap, some four hundred miles away. Size is the most important factor, but also the fei must be of a certain fine, white, close-grained limestone. A traveler to Uap described the fei as follows:

> A feature of this stone currency, which is also an equally noteworthy tribute to Uap honesty, is that its owner does not need to actually possess it. After concluding a bargain which involves a fei too large to be conveniently moved, its new owner is quite

†Abridged from Norman Angell, *The Story of Money* (New York: Garden City Publishing Co., 1929), pp. 88-89.

content to accept the bare acknowledgment of ownership; and without so much as a mark to indicate the exchange, the coin remains undisturbed on the former owner's premises.

There was in a village nearby a family whose wealth was unquestioned—acknowledged by everyone, and yet no one, not even the family itself, had ever laid eyes on this wealth; it consisted of an enormous fei lying at the bottom of the sea! Many years ago an ancestor of this family, on an expedition after fei, secured this remarkable stone, which was placed on a raft to be towed homeward. A violent storm arose and the party, to save their lives, were obliged to cut the raft adrift, and the stone sank out of sight. When they reached home, they all testified that the fei was of magnificent proportions and extraordinary quality, and that it was lost through no fault of the owners. Thereupon it was universally considered that the mere accident of its loss overboard was too trifling to mention. The purchasing power of the stone remained, therefore, as valid as if it were leaning visibly against the side of the owner's house.

Monetary Problems in the POW Camp

Cigarette money made the primitive economy of the prisoner-of-war camp more efficient. But problems occurred, including problems quite similar to those of more advanced monetary systems. As part of the natural trend toward simplification, distinctions among different brands of cigarettes became blurred. Although all cigarettes were not equally desirable to smokers, all were equal as money. In paying for beef or other items, a cigarette was a cigarette. What was the consequence? Smokers held back the desirable brands for their personal use and spent the others. The less desirable cigarettes therefore were the ones used as money; the "good" cigarettes were smoked. This illustrates *Gresham's law.* This law, first enunciated by Elizabethan financier Sir Thomas Gresham (1519-1579), is popularly and loosely abbreviated: "Bad money drives out good." In this case, "bad" cigarettes drove "good" cigarettes out of circulation as money. (The good cigarettes were smoked instead.)

> *Gresham's law*: If there are two types of money whose values in exchange are equal while their values in another use (like consumption) are different, the more valuable item will be retained for its other use while the less valuable item will continue to circulate as money. Thus, the "bad" (less valuable) money drives the "good" (more valuable) money out of circulation.

The tendency for every cigarette to be treated as

equal to every other cigarette caused another monetary problem. As a cigarette was a cigarette, prisoners often pulled out a few strands of tobacco before passing a cigarette along. This corresponds precisely to a problem when gold coins circulate: There is a temptation to "clip" coins by chipping off bits of gold. Furthermore, the cigarette currency became *debased*: Some enterprising prisoners rolled cigarettes from pipe tobacco or broke down cigarettes and rerolled them, reducing the amount of tobacco in each. Similarly, governments have from time to time given in to the temptation to debase gold coins by melting them down and reissuing them with a smaller gold content. (Private entrepreneurs have had a strong incentive to do the same, but they have been discouraged throughout history by severe punishments against counterfeiting.)

However, it was not clipping or debasement which led to the greatest monetary problems in the POW camp. As long as there was a balanced inflow of both cigarettes and other goods, the exchange system of the camp worked reasonably well. But from time to time the weekly Red Cross issue of 25 or 50 cigarettes per prisoner was interrupted. As the existing stock of cigarettes was consumed by smokers, cigarettes became more and more scarce. Desperate smokers had to offer more and more to get cigarettes; their value skyrocketed. To put the same point another way: Other goods now exchanged for fewer and fewer cigarettes. A can of beef which previously sold for 20 cigarettes dropped in value to 15, 10, or even fewer cigarettes. Thus, there was a *deflation*—a decline in the prices of other goods, measured in terms of money.

As cigarettes became increasingly scarce and prices continued to fall, prisoners began to revert to barter in exchanging other goods. Smokers who had the few remaining cigarettes were reluctant to give them up to make purchases. Then, from time to time, thousands of cigarettes would arrive at the camp during a brief period. Prices soared; in other words, the value of cigarettes fell. Prisoners became reluctant to accept cigarettes in payment for other goods. (Remember: Nonsmokers accepted cigarette money only when they thought they would be able to buy other goods with it.) Once again, barter became common. Thus, the monetary system worked smoothly only so long as a reasonable balance was kept between the quantity of money (cigarettes) and the quantity of other goods.

Several characteristics of a good monetary system may be drawn out of this story of the "cigarette standard." A smoothly operating monetary system should be made up of money whose value is *uniform*. Nonuniform money will set Gresham's law into operation, with "bad" money driving "good" money out of circulation. In our economy, the Bank of Canada has the responsibility of ensuring that money is uniform. It is the institution that issues paper currency. It matters not whether the one-dollar bill I have in my pocket is crisp and new, or whether it is tattered and soiled. The Bank of Canada will replace it with a new bill of equal value when it becomes excessively worn. This means that it represents one dollar in value to anyone. This uniformity in the value of each dollar bill obviously contributes to the ease of exchange—and it means that Gresham's law does not operate in our modern economy. In accepting dollar bills, we need worry only about whether they are genuine; we need not quibble over their exact physical condition.

A second important characteristic of a good monetary system is that there be the *proper quantity of money*, neither too much nor too little. The responsibility for controlling the quantity of money also lies with the Bank of Canada. The question of how the Bank discharges this responsibility will be studied in Part 3 of this book. (For other important characteristics of money, see Box 3-2.)

COMPARATIVE ADVANTAGE: A REASON TO SPECIALIZE

Money, the development of markets, and (perhaps equally important) the development of a sophisticated transportation and communications system all make possible a high degree of specialization of production. They make specialization possible and relatively smooth, but they don't provide a reason why specialization is advantageous in the first place. At the beginning of the chapter, an answer was suggested: Specialization can increase efficiency. It is now time to explain in more detail just how. A key concept in the explanation is the *principle of comparative advantage*. To understand this principle, it is useful to look first at the simpler concept of *absolute advantage*.

A good is often made in the place that is best suited for its production: wood products in British Columbia, corn in Iowa, bananas in the tropical lands of Central America, coffee in the cool highlands of Colombia, and so on. In technical terms, there is some tendency for a good to be produced in the area that has an absolute advantage in its production.

A country (or region or individual) has an *absolute advantage* in the production of a good if it can produce that good with fewer resources (less land, labour, and capital) than can other countries (or regions or individuals).

Note that this principle applies to specialization among individuals within a city or town. Consider the case of the lawyer and the professional gardener. The lawyer is better at drawing up legal documents and the gardener is generally better at gardening, so it is in the interest of each to specialize in the occupation in which he or she has an absolute advantage.

However, the truth is often more complicated than this. By looking at the complications, we will be led to

---

BOX 3-2

WHY CIGARETTES?

In the POW camp, cigarettes emerged as the commonly accepted money. Why cigarettes? Why not canned carrots or beef?

There were three reasons. First, although not everyone wanted cigarettes for his personal use, the market value of cigarettes was high. Thus, cigarettes were chosen over canned carrots because canned carrots were practically worthless. If carrots had been the "money," exchange would have been cumbersome, with prisoners lugging around many cans in order to make exchanges. A good money is one whose value is sufficiently high that the individual may conveniently carry a considerable purchasing power. Thus, in the broader society, the money that evolved was precious metals—silver, and particularly gold. Lead did not (generally) become money because its value was relatively low, and the use of lead would have been cumbersome. Of course, today our money is even more convenient than the precious metals: a $20, $50, or $100 bill may be carried easily and inconspicuously.

Thus, cigarettes were preferred to canned carrots. But why did cigarettes become money, rather than something else that had a high value—like canned beef? Here, we come to the second and third reasons why cigarettes became money. A package of cigarettes is easily divisible into subunits—20 individual cigarettes—each of which is relatively durable. A can of beef, on the other hand, cannot easily be subdivided. If it is opened and cut up, the individual chunks will be messy and will quickly spoil. Moreover, a six-ounce piece of beef is not

easily distinguished from a seven-ounce chunk. However, it is easy to tell whether you have six cigarettes or seven.

Similarly, in the broader society, monies have developed which are easily divisible and durable. Precious metals, for example, are easily divisible into units of any size. And even small units of gold or silver are durable—indeed, much more durable than the cigarettes of the POW camp. However, in another respect, gold and silver are less desirable than cigarettes. As in the case of beef, a six-ounce piece of gold is not easily distinguished from a seven-ounce piece. Therefore, governments came into the picture, minting gold coins of specific value (such as $20) that could immediately be identified.

But why did we have both gold and silver as money (for example, in the United States in the nineteenth century)? Gold is easily divisible—up to a point. Gold coins of $50, $20, or $10 could be minted without difficulty and were relatively convenient. However, suppose that the government wanted to mint a gold coin worth 25 cents. It would be so tiny that it would be easily lost. While the high value of gold made it an obvious choice for coins of high value, it was very inconvenient for coins of low value. Here, silver was the obvious choice, since it was less valuable per ounce than gold.

In summary, the evolution of the "cigarette standard" illustrated a number of the characteristics which the item chosen for money should possess: It should be sufficiently valuable that a reasonably large purchasing power can be carried conveniently by an individual; it should be easily divisible; it should be durable; and it should not be easy to lose.

the idea of comparative advantage. Suppose that a certain lawyer is better at gardening than the gardener; she's faster and more effective—in short, she has a "greener thumb." She has an absolute advantage in both the law and gardening. If absolute advantage were the key, she would practise law and do her own gardening as well. Does this necessarily happen? The answer: No. Unless this lawyer positively enjoys gardening as a recreation, she will leave the gardening to the professional gardener. Why? Even though the lawyer, being very good at it, can do as much gardening in one hour (let us say) as the gardener could in two, she will be better off to stick to law and hire the gardener to work on the flowers and shrubbery. Why? In one hour, the lawyer can draw up a will, for which she charges $50. The gardener's time, in contrast, is worth only $5 per hour. By spending the hour on the law rather than gardening, the lawyer comes out ahead. She earns $50 and can hire the gardener for $10 to put in two hours to get the gardening done. The lawyer gains $40 by sticking to law for that one hour. (This is explained in more detail in Box 3-3.)

The gardener also gains through specialization. Although he has to work 10 hours in order to earn the $50 needed to hire the lawyer to draw up his will, it would take him much more time to draw up the will himself. He would have to spend many hours—as many as 100, perhaps—poring over law books just to learn the basic traps to avoid in drawing up a will. (Even after spending the 100 hours, he could not be sure that he might not have missed something very simple that the lawyer learned in her many years of study.) Thus, by spending 10 hours on gardening and using the income to buy the lawyer's time, the gardener gains: He gets a better will than he could have had by struggling with legal books for a full 100 hours.

Thus, absolute advantage is not necessary for specialization. The lawyer has an absolute advantage in both gardening and law; the gardener has an absolute disadvantage in both. But the lawyer has a comparative advantage in law; the gardener has a comparative advantage in gardening. When the gardener and the lawyer each stick to their own comparative advantage, both gain from specialization.

British economist *David Ricardo* enunciated the principle of comparative advantage in the early nineteenth century to illustrate how countries gain from international trade. But comparative advantage pro-vides a general explanation of the advantages of specialization; it is just as relevant to domestic as to international trade. Nevertheless, it is customary to follow Ricardo and consider this principle to be part of the study of international economics. We follow the custom, and put off our more detailed analysis of comparative advantage to the chapter on international trade (Chapter 31). For the moment, we note that the concept of comparative advantage is related to opportunity cost.

> If two individuals (or cities or nations) have different opportunity costs of producing a good or service, the individual (or city or nation) with the lower opportunity cost has the *comparative advantage* in that good or service.

The opportunity cost is the alternative foregone. To prepare a will, the lawyer's opportunity cost is the 20 flowers that she could have planted instead. (Details are in Box 3-3.) In contrast, the gardener would have faced a much higher opportunity cost to prepare a will. It would take him 100 hours, in which he could have planted 1,000 flowers. Since the lawyer's opportunity cost of drawing up a will is lower than the gardener's (20 flowers vs. 1,000), the lawyer has the comparative advantage in law. She will specialize in this, leaving the flowers to the gardener. Furthermore, it follows directly that the gardener has the comparative advantage in gardening. To plant a flower, he gives up only one-thousandth of a will, compared to the one-twentieth foregone by the lawyer. Accordingly, the gardener will stick to his gardening, and leave the drafting of the will to the lawyer.

Comparative advantage, then, provides one reason to specialize. It may be considered the first great propellant driving the wheels of commerce—while money acts as the grease, making the machine run with less friction. But there is also a second fundamental reason to specialize.

ECONOMIES OF SCALE: ANOTHER REASON TO SPECIALIZE

Consider two small cities that are identical in all respects. Suppose that the citizens of these cities want both bicycles and lawnmowers, but that neither city

BOX 3-3

ILLUSTRATION OF COMPARATIVE ADVANTAGE

A. Assume the following:
  1. In one hour, the lawyer can plant 20 flowers.
  2. In one hour, the gardener can plant 10 flowers. (Therefore, the lawyer has the absolute advantage in gardening.)
  3. The lawyer's time, in the practice of law, is worth $50 per hour.
  4. The gardener's time, in gardening, is worth $5 per hour.
B. *Question:*
  How should the lawyer have 20 flowers planted?
  Option 1: Do it herself, spending one hour.
  Cost: She gives up the $50 she could have earned by practising law for that hour.

Option 2: Stick to the law, and hire the gardener to plant the 20 flowers.
  Cost: Two hours of gardener's time at $5 per hour, making a total of $10.
C. *Decision:* Choose option 2.
  Spend the available hour practising law, earning $50.
  Hire the gardener to do the planting for $10.
  Net advantage over option 1: $40.
D. *Conclusion:* The lawyer has the comparative advantage in law.

Courtesy Miller Services Limited

Devaney/Miller Services

has any advantage in the production of either good. Will each city then produce its own, without any trade existing between the two? Probably not. It is likely that one city will specialize in producing bicycles, and the other in making lawnmowers. Why?

The answer is that they will both benefit from *economies of scale*. To understand what this term means, first assume that there is no specialization. Each city directs half its productive resources into the manufacture of bicycles and half into the manufacture of lawnmowers, thus producing 1,000 bicycles and 1,000 lawnmowers. But if either city specializes by directing all its productive resources toward the manufacture of bicycles, it can acquire specialized machinery and produce 2,500 bicycles. Similarly, if the other city directs all its productive resources toward the manufacture of lawnmowers, it can produce 2,500. Note that each city, by doubling all inputs into the production of a single item, can more than double its output of that item (from 1,000 to 2,500 units). Thus, economies of scale exist.

> *Economies of scale* exist if an increase of x% in the quantity of every input causes the quantity of output to increase by more than x%. (For example, if all inputs are doubled, then output more than doubles.)

Even though neither city had any fundamental advantage in the production of either product, each can gain by specialization. Before specialization, their combined output was 2,000 bicycles and 2,000 lawnmowers. After specialization, they together make 2,500 bicycles and 2,500 lawnmowers.

While Ricardo's theory of comparative advantage dates back to the early nineteenth century, the explanation of economies of scale goes back even further, to Adam Smith's *Wealth of Nations* (1776). In Smith's first chapter, "Of the Division of Labour," there is a famous description of pin-making:

> A workman not educated to this business . . . could scarce, perhaps, . . . make one pin in a day, and certainly not twenty. But in the way in which this business is now carried on, not only the whole work

is a peculiar trade, but it is divided into a number of branches. . . . One man draws out the wire, another straightens it, a third cuts it, a fourth points it, a fifth grinds it at the top for receiving the head. . . . Ten persons, therefore, could make among them upwards of forty-eight thousand pins in a day. Each person, therefore, . . . might be considered as making four thousand and eight hundred pins in a day.[2]

What is the reason for the gain that comes from the division of pin making into a number of separate steps? Certainly it is not that some individuals are particularly suited to drawing the wire, while others have a particular gift for straightening it. On the contrary, if two individuals are employed, it matters little which activity each is assigned. Adam Smith's "production line" is efficient because of economies of scale which depend on:

1. The introduction of specialized machinery.
2. Specialization of the labour force on that machinery.

Modern corporations also derive economies of scale from a third major source:

3. Specialized research and development, which make possible the development of new equipment and technology.

In the modern world, economies of scale are especially important as an explanation of specialization. They are a major reason why the manufacturers of automobiles, aircraft, and mainframe computers are few in number and large in size. It is partly because of economies of scale that the automobile industry is concentrated in central Canada, with cars being shipped to other areas in exchange for a host of other products. And economies of scale help explain why Canada's petrochemical industry is concentrated in a small region, around Lake St. Clair in Southern Ontario.

But economies of scale explain much more than the trade among the regions and cities within a country.

---

[2] Adam Smith, *An Inquiry into the Nature and Causes of the Wealth of Nations*, Modern Library edition (New York: Random House, 1937), pp. 4–5.

They are also an important explanation of trade between countries—even in the case of large countries such as the United States. For example, economies of scale in the production of large passenger aircraft go on (and costs continue to fall) long after the U.S. market is met. Thus, there is a major advantage to Boeing—and to the United States—in producing aircraft for the world market. And there are gains to the aircraft buyers, too. For example, Swedes or Canadians can buy a Boeing 747 for a small fraction of the cost of making a comparable plane themselves. As we explain in Box 3-4, international trade is of particular importance to small countries such as Canada, since it permits us to gain from economies of scale even though our own market may be too small for large-scale production.

In this chapter, the advantages of specialization and exchange have been studied. Exchange takes place in markets; how markets operate will be the subject of the next chapter.

BOX 3-4

CARS IN CANADA: HOW DOES A COUNTRY WITH A SMALL MARKET ACHIEVE ECONOMIES OF SCALE?

Even the huge U.S. market is not large enough for some producers, such as aircraft manufacturers, to capture economies of scale fully. But it is large enough for producers of other goods, such as autos. In fact, U.S. auto manufacturers can offer a wide variety of car models and still produce most of them at the high volume necessary to achieve essentially all economies of scale. Thus, these producers can achieve low cost and at the same time provide a wide range of choice for the consumer.

But the U.S. economy is unique in this respect, because it is so large. Smaller economies (like Canada's) cannot produce a wide range of models and at the same time achieve the high-volume output necessary to lower costs. Thus, Canada has a choice among three options. It can:

1. Produce a variety of models, each on a small scale and therefore at a high cost, for the domestic Canadian market. This option would present the Canadian car purchaser with the advantage of a choice among various models, but the disadvantage of a very high cost per car.

2. Produce a small number of models, each at high volume, for the domestic market. This would provide the advantage of low cost, but the disadvantage of a severely restricted choice of models.

3. Gain both advantages (high volume, low-cost production and a wide variety of models) by engaging in international trade. Produce only a few models in Canada, at high volume and low cost. Export many of these Canadian-built cars in exchange for a variety of imported models.

Historically, up to the early 1960s, Canadian automotive policy was based on the first choice. But the twin advantages of option 3 are clear, and can come through international trade. In order to gain these advantages, Canada in 1965 entered into the so-called "auto agreement" with the United States, allowing for tariff-free passage of cars and parts for new cars both ways across the border. A similar motivation, that of gaining the advantages both of high-volume, low-cost production and of wide consumer choice, contributed to the decision of Western European countries to establish the European Economic Community, or European Common Market, in the late 1950s. (In a common market, goods are allowed to pass among the members freely, with no tariffs being collected.)

KEY POINTS

1. Specialization contributes to efficiency.
2. Specialization requires exchange. The most primitive form of exchange is barter. This has the disadvantage that it depends on a coincidence of wants.
3. Much more complex exchange, with many participants, is feasible in an economy with money. Because exchange is so much easier and more efficient with money, money will evolve even in the absence of government action—as happened in the prisoner-of-war camp.
4. In the prisoner-of-war camp, some cigarettes were more desirable than others. The desirable cigarettes were smoked, leaving the less desirable cigarettes to circulate as money. This illustrated Gresham's Law: "Bad money drives out good." In today's Canadian economy, the Bank of Canada provides a uniform currency. Every dollar bill is worth the same as every other one; there is no "bad" money to drive "good" money out of circulation.
5. The Bank of Canada also has the responsibility to control the quantity of money. (How it does so will be explained in Chapter 13.)
6. There are two major reasons why specialization and exchange lead to gains:
   (a) comparative advantage
   (b) economies of scale
7. If two individuals (or regions or countries) have different opportunity costs of producing a good or service, then the individual (or region or nation) with the lower opportunity cost has the comparative advantage in that good or service. An example of this is the lawyer who is better than the gardener at both the law and gardening. Even so, she does not do her gardening herself, because she gains by specializing in the law (her comparative advantage) and hiring the gardener to do the gardening (his comparative advantage).
8. Economies of scale exist if an increase of $x\%$ in the quantity of every input causes the quantity of output to increase by more than $x\%$.

KEY CONCEPTS

specialization	general purchasing power	deflation
exchange	medium of exchange	absolute advantage
barter	Gresham's law	comparative advantage
coincidence of wants	debasement of the currency	economies of scale
indivisibility		

PROBLEMS

3-1 Most jobs are more specialized than they were 100 years ago. Why? What are the advantages of greater specialization? What are the disadvantages?

3-2 (a) Among the goods Canada exports are newsprint and sawn timber, farm machinery, and agricultural products such as wheat. Why are these goods exported?

(b) Imports include automobiles, computers, oil, and agricultural products such as wine, coffee, and bananas. Why are these goods imported?

(c) Canada exports some agricultural products, and imports others. Why? Canada exports many cars, but it also imports some. Why is this country both an exporter and an importer of cars?

3-3 Suppose that one individual at your college is outstanding, being the best teacher and a superb administrator. If you were the college president, would you ask this individual to teach or to become the administrative vice-president? Why?

3-4 Draw a production possibilities curve (PPC) for the lawyer mentioned in Box 3-3, putting the number of wills drawn up in a week on one axis and flowers planted on the other. (Assume that the lawyer works 40 hours per week.) How does the shape of this PPC differ from that in Chapter 2?

*3-5 Draw the production possibilities curve of one of the two identical cities described in the section on economies of scale. Which way does the curve bend? Does the opportunity cost of bicycles increase or decrease as more bicycles are produced?

*Problems marked with asterisks are more difficult than the others. They are designed to provide a challenge to students who want to do more advanced work.

Chapter 4

DEMAND AND SUPPLY: THE MARKET MECHANISM

Do you know,
Considering the market, there are more
Poems produced than any other thing?
No wonder poets sometimes have to *seem*
So much more business-like than business men.
Their wares are so much harder to get rid of.

Robert Frost, "New Hampshire"

Although some countries are much richer than others, the resources of every country are limited. Choices must be made as to how those resources should be used. Moreover, every economy involves some degree of specialization. In every economy, therefore, some mechanism is needed to answer the fundamental questions raised by specialization and by the need to make choices:

1. *What* goods and services will be produced? (How do we choose among the various options represented by the production possibilities curve?)

2. *How* will these goods and services be produced? For example, will cars be produced by relatively few workers using a great deal of machinery, or by many workers using relatively little capital equipment?

3. *For whom* will the goods and services be produced? Once goods are produced, who will consume them?

THE MARKET AND THE GOVERNMENT

There are two principal mechanisms by which these questions can be answered. First, answers can be pro-

vided by Adam Smith's "invisible hand." If people are left alone to make their own transactions, then the butcher and baker will provide the beef and bread for our dinner. In other words, answers may be provided by transactions among individuals and corporations in the **market**.

> In a *market*, an item is bought and sold. Markets where transactions between buyers and sellers take place with little or no government interference are often referred to as *private* or *free* markets.

The **government** provides the second method for determining what goods and services will be produced, how they will be produced, and for whom. The government affects the economy in four principal ways: by **spending**, by **taxation**, by running **public enterprises**, and by **regulation**.

1. Spending. When the government pays Old Age Security benefits to retirees, it influences *who* gets society's output; the recipient of the benefit is able to buy more goods and services. When the government buys ships for the navy, those ships are produced; the government affects *what* is produced. When the government spends money for agricultural research, it influences *how* food will be produced.

2. Taxes. When the government collects taxes, it influences *who* gets society's output. When I pay taxes, I have less left to buy goods and services. Taxes also affect *what* is produced. For example, a tax on gasoline encourages people to buy smaller cars. More small cars are produced, and fewer large ones. Finally, the tax system may also influence *how* goods are produced. Incentives built into the tax law encourage businesses to use more machinery in producing goods. When they buy machinery, their taxes are reduced.

3. Public enterprises. The government owns and operates some businesses, including Crown corporations such as Air Canada or Canada Post. It decides *what* these enterprises will produce, and *how* they will produce it.

4. Regulation. Governmental regulations may also influence what, how, and for whom goods and services are produced. For example, the government prohibits the production of some pesticides, and requires seat belts and other safety equipment in cars, thereby affecting *what* is produced. It requires producers of steel to limit their emissions of smoke into the atmosphere, thereby influencing *how* goods are produced. The government also regulates some prices—for example, the price of telephone services. This keeps down the incomes of shareholders, as well as those of executives and workers in private phone companies. With less income, these people can buy less. Thus, the government influences *who* gets society's product.

In addition to the market and the government, there are other institutions which help to answer the three basic questions *What? How?* and *For whom?* For example, when a relief organization collects voluntary contributions of clothing or money for distribution to the poor or to the victims of a natural disaster, it is influencing who gets the output of society. Similarly, within the family, a mechanism other than the market or the government is used to determine how the budget for clothing and other items is divided among the family members. Nevertheless, economists concentrate on the market and the government when they study the way in which society answers the three basic questions.

Conceivably, a nation might depend almost exclusively on private markets to make the three fundamental decisions. The government's role might be a very limited one: providing defence, police, the courts, roads, and little else. At the other extreme, the government might try to decide almost everything, specifying what is to be produced, and using a system of rationing and allocations to decide who gets the products. But the real world is one of compromise. In every actual economy, there is a *mixture* of markets and government decision making.

In Canada, the United States, Japan, and the West European nations, most choices are made in the market. In these countries, the government plays a relatively limited role by international standards. This is especially true in the United States, where public enterprise accounts for a very small share of total economic activity, and where there has been a tendency in recent years toward *reduced* regulation of private markets. In Canada, the role of government and public enterprise is more prominent than in the United States. However, in comparison with countries at the other end of the spectrum, it still appears very limited. In the economies of the Soviet Union and Eastern Europe, decision making is carried out largely by the government.

As **Marxist** nations, they reject the idea that the market should determine *for whom* goods will be produced. They do not permit individuals to own large amounts of capital. Individuals may, of course, own small capital goods, such as hoes or hammers, but the major forms of capital—factories and heavy machinery—are owned by the state. Therefore, individuals do not own stocks and so no one receives large dividend payments with which to buy a considerable fraction of the output of the economy. In contrast, in **capitalist** or **free enterprise** countries such as Canada, the United States and Britain, most capital is privately owned.

In a Marxist nation, not only does the government own most of the capital. It is also involved in detailed decisions as to which products will be produced with this capital. For example, the Soviet Union has a **central planning agency** that issues directives to the various sectors of the economy to produce specific quantities of goods. It would, however, be a mistake to conclude that government planning is a rigid and all-pervasive method of answering the three basic questions. Markets for goods exist in all Marxist countries, and some—particularly Hungary and Yugoslavia—allow many decisions to be made through the market. China is now engaged in a major experiment in which more reliance is being placed on the market.

> A *capitalist* or *free enterprise* economy is one in which individuals are permitted to own large amounts of capital, and decisions are made primarily in markets, with relatively little government interference.
>
> A *Marxist* economy is one in which the government owns most of the capital, and makes many of the economic decisions. Political power is in the hands of a party pledging allegiance to the doctrines of Karl Marx.

Because the market is relatively important in Canada, it will be our initial concern. (Later chapters will deal in detail with the economic role of the government in Canada and with the Marxist economic system.) This chapter explains how the market answers the three basic questions: What will be produced? How? For whom?

THE MARKET MECHANISM

In most markets, the buyer and the seller come face to face. When you buy a suit of clothes, you talk directly to the salesclerk; when you buy groceries, you physically enter the seller's place of business (the supermarket). However, physical proximity of buyer and seller is not required to make a market. For example, in a typical stock-market transaction, an old-age pensioner in Medicine Hat puts in a call to her broker to buy 100 shares of Suncor common stock. At about the same time, someone in Fredericton calls his broker and asks him to sell 100 shares. The transaction takes place on the floor of the Toronto Stock Exchange, where representatives of the two brokerage houses meet. The buyer and the seller of the stock do not leave their respective homes in Alberta and New Brunswick.

Some markets are quite simple. For example, a barbershop is a "market," since haircuts are bought and sold there. The transaction is obvious and straightforward; the service of haircutting is produced on the spot. In other cases, markets are much more complex. Even the simplest everyday activity may be the culmination of a complicated series of market transactions.

As you sat at breakfast this morning drinking your cup of coffee, you were using products from distant areas. The coffee itself was probably produced in Brazil.

The brew was made with water that perhaps had been delivered in pipes manufactured in Quebec and purified with chemicals produced in Sarnia, Ontario. The sugar for the coffee may have been produced in the Caribbean. Perhaps you used artificial cream made from soybeans grown in Southern Ontario. Possibly, your coffee was poured into a cup made in Britain, and stirred with a spoon manufactured in Taiwan from Japanese stainless steel which was produced using nickel from Sudbury. All this was for one cup of coffee.

In such a complex economy, something is needed to keep things straight, to bring order out of potential chaos. *Prices* bring order by performing two important, interrelated functions:

1. Prices provide **information**.
2. Prices provide **incentives**.

To illustrate, suppose we start from the example of chaos. Most of the coffee is in Vancouver and most of the sugar, in Montreal. Coffee lovers in Montreal would clamour for coffee, even at very high prices. The high price would be a signal, providing *information* to coffee owners that there are eager buyers in Montreal. It would also provide them with an *incentive* to send coffee to Montreal. In any market, the price provides the focus for interactions between buyers and sellers.

PERFECT AND IMPERFECT COMPETITION

Some markets are dominated by a few large firms; others have thousands of sellers. The "big three" automobile manufacturers (G.M., Ford, and Chrysler) make most of the cars sold in Canada and the United States, with the rest provided by American Motors and a number of foreign firms. An industry like this, dominated by a few sellers, is an **oligopoly**. (The word *oligopoly* means "a few sellers," just as *oligarchy* means "rule by a few.") Some markets are even more concentrated. For example, there is just one supplier of local telephone services to homes in your area; so the local telephone company has a **monopoly**. On the other hand, wheat is provided by thousands of producers, so neither an oligopoly nor a monopoly exists in this case.

> A *monopoly* exists when there is only *one seller*. An *oligopoly* exists when a *few sellers* dominate a market.

The number of participants in a market has a significant effect on the way in which the price is determined. In the wheat market, where there are thousands of buyers and thousands of sellers, no individual farmer produces more than a tiny fraction of the total supply. No single farmer can affect the price of wheat. For each one, the price is given; the individual farmer's decision is limited to the number of bushels of wheat to sell. Similarly, the millers realize that they are each buying only a small fraction of the wheat supplied. They realize that they cannot, as individuals, affect the price of wheat. Each miller's decision is limited to the number of bushels to be bought at the existing market price. In such a *perfectly competitive* market, *no pricing decision* is made by the individual seller or buyer. Each buyer and seller is a *price taker*.

> *Perfect competition* exists when there are so many buyers and sellers that no single buyer or seller has any influence over the price. (Sometimes, this term is shortened simply to "competition.")

In contrast, individual producers in an oligopolistic or a monopolistic market know that they have some control over price. For example, IBM sets the prices of its computers. That does not mean, of course, that it can set *any* price it wants and still be assured of making a profit. It can offer to sell at a high price, in which case it will sell relatively few computers. Or it can charge a lower price, in which case it will sell more.

A *buyer* may also be large enough to influence price. CP Rail is a large enough purchaser of steel to be able to bargain with Canadian steel companies over the price of steel. When individual buyers or sellers can influence price, *imperfect competition* exists.

> *Imperfect competition* exists when any buyer or any seller is able to influence the price. Such a buyer or seller is said to have *market power*.

Note that the term "competition" is used differently in economics and in business. For example, a Chrysler executive would certainly not say that the automobile market was not competitive; Chrysler is very much aware of the competition from General Motors, Ford, and the Japanese. Yet, according to the economist's definition, the automobile **industry** is far *less* competitive than the wheat industry.

> An *industry* refers to all the producers of a good or service. For example, we may speak of the lumber industry, the wheat industry, or the accounting industry. Note that the term "industry" can refer to the producers of *any* good or service, not just to manufacturers.
>
> A *firm* is a business organization that produces goods and/or services. A *plant* is an establishment at a single location used in the production of a good or service; for example: a factory, mine, farm, or store. Some firms—such as General Motors—have many plants. Others have only one—for example, the local independent drug store.

Because price is determined by impersonal forces in a perfectly competitive market, the competitive market is the simplest one, and will therefore be considered first. The perfectly competitive market is also given priority because competitive markets generally operate more efficiently than imperfect markets, as we shall eventually show in Chapters 24 and 25.

THE PERFECTLY COMPETITIVE MARKET: DEMAND AND SUPPLY

> We might as reasonably dispute whether it is the upper or the under blade of a pair of scissors that cuts a piece of paper, as whether the value is governed by utility [demand] or cost of production [supply].
> Alfred Marshall, *Principles of Economics*

In a perfectly competitive market, price is determined by **demand** and **supply**.

Demand

Consider, as an example, the market for apples, in which there are many buyers and many sellers, with none having any control over the price. For the buyer, a high price acts as a deterrent. The higher the price, the fewer apples buyers purchase. Why is this so? As the price of apples rises, consumers switch to oranges or grapefruit, or they simply cut down on their total consumption of fruit. Similarly, the lower the price, the more apples are bought. A lower price brings new purchasers into the market, and each purchaser tends to buy more. The response of buyers to various possible prices is illustrated in the **demand schedule** in Table 4-1. This schedule is used to graph the **demand curve** in Figure 4-1. Points *A*, *B*, *C*, and *D* in Figure 4-1 represent the corresponding *A*, *B*, *C*, and *D* rows in Table 4-1.

> A *demand schedule*—or *demand curve*— shows the quantities of a good or service which buyers would be willing and able to purchase at various market prices.

Note carefully that the demand schedule or demand curve applies to a *specific population* and to a *specific time period*. (Clearly, the number of apples demanded during a month will exceed the number demanded during a week, and the number demanded by the people of Nova Scotia will be less than the number demanded in the whole of Canada.) In a general discussion of theoretical issues, the population and time frameworks are not always stated explicitly, but it nevertheless should be understood that a demand curve applies to a specific time and population.

Supply

While the demand curve illustrates how buyers behave, the supply curve illustrates how sellers behave; it shows how much they would be willing to sell at various prices. Needless to say, buyers and sellers look at high prices in a different light. Whereas a high price discourages buyers and causes them to switch to alternative products, a high price encourages suppliers to produce and sell more of the good. Thus, the higher the price, the higher the quantity supplied. This is shown in the **supply schedule** (Table 4-2) or, alternatively, in the **supply curve** (Figure 4-2). As in the case of the demand curve, the points on the supply curve (*F*, *G*, *H*, and *J*) are drawn from the information given in the corresponding rows of Table 4-2.

> A *supply schedule*—or *supply curve*—shows the quantities of a good or service which sellers would be willing and able to sell at various market prices.

The Equilibrium of Demand and Supply

The demand and supply curves may now be brought together (see Figure 4-3 and Table 4-3). To use Alfred Marshall's analogy, this figure shows how the two blades of the scissors jointly determine price.

The **market equilibrium** occurs at point *E*, where

Table 4-1
The Demand Schedule for Apples

	(1) Price *P* ($ per bushel)	(2) Quantity *Q* demanded (thousands of bushels per week)
A	$10	50
B	8	100
C	6	200
D	4	400

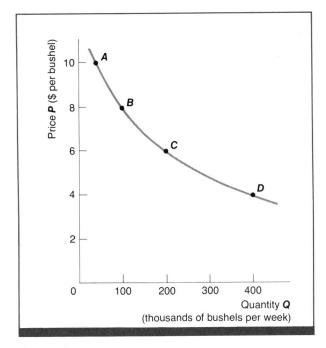

Figure 4-1 The demand curve for apples.
At each of the possible prices specified, there is a certain quantity of apples that people would be willing and able to buy. This information is provided in Table 4-1 and is reproduced in this diagram. On the vertical axis, the possible prices are shown. In each case, the quantity of apples that would be bought is measured along the horizontal axis. Since people are more willing to buy at a low price than at a high price, the demand curve slopes downward to the right.

the demand and supply curves intersect. At this equilibrium, the price is $6 per bushel, and weekly sales are 200,000 bushels.

> An *equilibrium* is a situation where there is no tendency to change.

Table 4-2
The Supply Schedule for Apples

	(1) Price P ($ per bushel)	(2) Quantity Q supplied (thousands of bushels per week)
F	$10	260
G	8	240
H	6	200
J	4	150

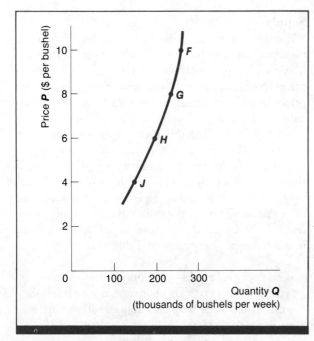

Figure 4-2   The supply curve for apples.
For each of the possible prices specified, the supply schedule (Table 4-2) indicates how many units the sellers would be willing to sell. This information is illustrated graphically in this figure, which shows how the supply curve slopes upward to the right. At a high price, suppliers will be encouraged to step up production and offer more apples for sale.

To see why E represents the equilibrium, consider what happens if the market price is initially at some other level. Suppose, for example, that the initial price is $10; that is, it is above the equilibrium price. What happens? Purchasers buy only 50,000 bushels (shown by point A in Figure 4-3), while sellers want to sell 260,000 bushels (point F). There is a large **excess supply**, or **surplus**, of 210,000 bushels. Some sellers are disappointed: They are selling much less than they want to at the price of $10. Unsold apples begin to pile up. In order to get them moving, sellers now begin to accept a lower price. The price starts to come down—to $9, and then to $8. Still, there is a surplus, or an excess of the quantity supplied over the quantity demanded. (However, the surplus is now a smaller amount, *BG*.) The price continues to fall. It does not stop falling until it reaches $6, the equilibrium. At this price, buyers purchase 200,000 bushels, which is just the amount the sellers want to sell. Both buyers and sellers are now satisfied with the quantity of their purchases or sales at the existing market price of $6. Therefore, there is no further pressure on the price to change.

> An *excess supply*, or *surplus*, exists when the quantity supplied exceeds the quantity demanded. (The price is above the equilibrium.)

Now consider what happens when the initial price is below the equilibrium—at, say, $4. Eager buyers are willing to purchase 400,000 bushels (at point D), yet producers are willing to sell only 150,000 bushels (at point J). There is an **excess demand**, or **shortage**, of 250,000 bushels. As buyers clamour for the limited supplies, the price is bid upward. The price continues to rise until it reaches $6, the equilibrium, where there is no longer any shortage because the quantity demanded is equal to the quantity supplied. At point E, and only at point E, will the price be stable.

> An *excess demand*, or *shortage*, exists when the quantity demanded exceeds the quantity supplied. (The price is below the equilibrium.)

SHIFTS IN THE DEMAND CURVE

The quantity of a product that buyers want to purchase depends on the price. As we have seen, the

Table 4-3
The Equilibrium of Demand and Supply

(1) Price *P* ($ per bushel)	(2) Quantity *Q* demanded (thousands of bushels per week)	(3) Quantity *Q* supplied (thousands of bushels per week)	(4) Surplus (+) or shortage (−) (4) = (3) − (2)	(5) Pressure on price
$10	50	260	Surplus +210	Downward
8	100	240	Surplus +140	Downward
6	200	200	0	Equilibrium
4	400	150	Shortage −250	Upward

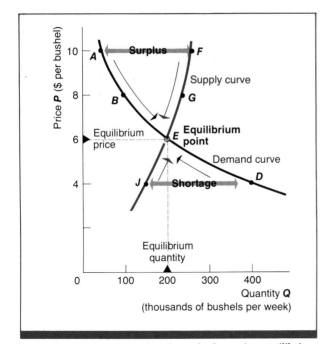

Figure 4-3   How demand and supply determine equilibrium price and quantity.
Equilibrium exists at point *E*, where the quantity demanded equals the quantity supplied. At any higher price, the quantity supplied exceeds the quantity demanded. Because of the pressure of unsold stocks, competition among sellers causes the price to be bid down to the equilibrium of $6. Similarly, at a price less than the $6 equilibrium, forces are set in motion which raise the price. Because the quantity demanded exceeds the quantity supplied, eager buyers clamour for more apples, and bid the price up to the equilibrium at $6.

demand curve illustrates this relationship between price and quantity. But the quantity that people want to purchase also depends on other influences. For example, if incomes rise, people will want to buy more apples—and more of a whole host of other products, too.

The purpose of a demand curve is to show *how the quantity demanded is affected by price, and by price alone.* When we ask how much people want to buy at various prices, it is important that our answer not be disturbed by other influences. In other words, when we draw a demand curve for a good, we must *hold constant incomes and everything else that can affect the quantity demanded*—with the sole exception of the price of the good. We make the **ceteris paribus** assumption—that other things remain unchanged. (*Ceteris* is the same Latin word that appears in *et cetera*, which literally means "and other things." *Paribus* means "equal" or "unchanged.")

Of course, as time passes, other things do not remain constant. Through time, for example, incomes generally rise. When that happens, the quantity of apples demanded at any particular price increases. The whole demand curve then shifts to the right, as illustrated in Figure 4-4. Since *economists use the term "demand" to mean the whole demand curve or demand schedule*, we may speak of this rightward shift in the curve more simply as an *increase in demand*.

Demand Shifters
A shift in the demand curve—that is, a change in demand—may be caused by a change in any one of a

number of "other things." Some of the most important are the following:

1. Income. When incomes rise, people are able to buy more. And people do in fact buy more of the typical or **normal good**. For such a good, the number of units demanded at each price increases as incomes rise. Thus, the demand curve shifts to the right with rising incomes, as illustrated in Figure 4-4.

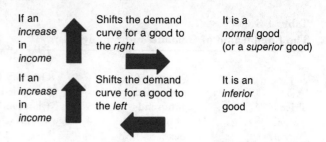

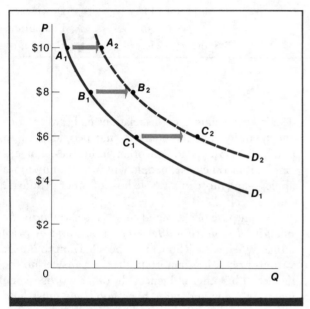

Figure 4-4   A change in the demand for apples.
When incomes rise, there is an increase in the number of apples that people want to buy at any particular price. At a price of $10, for example, the quantity of apples demanded increases from point A_1 to A_2. At other prices, the increase in incomes also causes an increase in the number of apples demanded. Thus, the whole demand curve shifts to the right, from D_1 to D_2.

Not all goods are normal, however. As incomes rise, people may buy *less* of a given good. For example, they may switch away from margarine and buy more butter, which they can afford now. When this happens—when the increase in income causes a leftward shift of the demand curve for margarine—the item is an **inferior good**.

2. Prices of related goods. A rise in the price of one good can cause a shift in the demand curve for another good.

For example, if the price of oranges were to double while the price of apples remained the same, buyers would be encouraged to buy apples instead of oranges. Thus, a rise in the price of oranges causes a rightward shift in the demand curve for apples. Goods such as apples and oranges—which satisfy similar needs or desires—are **substitutes**. Other examples are tea and coffee, butter and margarine, bus and train tickets, or heating oil and insulating materials.

For **complements**, or **complementary goods**, exactly the opposite relationship holds. In contrast to substitutes—which are used *instead* of each other—complements are used *together*, as a package. For example, gasoline and automobiles are complementary goods. If the price of gasoline spirals upward, people become less eager to own automobiles. The demand curve for cars therefore shifts to the left. So it is with other complements, such as tennis rackets and tennis balls, or formal clothes and tickets to the senior prom.

Finally, many goods are basically *unrelated*, in the sense that a rise in the price of one has no significant effect on the demand curve of the others. Thus, bus

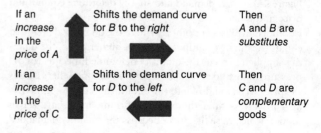

tickets and butter are unrelated, as are coffee and cameras.

3. Tastes. Tastes change over time. Because of increased interest in physical fitness, more people are jogging. This increases the demand for running shoes. Tastes, and therefore demand, are quite volatile for some products, particularly for fads like video games and Cabbage Patch dolls.

The above list covers some of the most important demand shifters, but it is far from complete. To see how it might be extended, consider the following questions:

1. How will a change in weather affect the demand for skiing equipment? for snow tires?

2. If people expect cars to be priced $2,000 higher next year, what effect will this have on the demand for cars this year?

3. As more and more families get video cassette recorders, and thereby become able to skip through the commercials with the fast-scan button, how will this affect the demand by companies buying TV ads? (A.C. Nielsen, an American firm which rates TV shows as a service for advertisers, has found that when people watch taped shows, half of them do in fact "zap" the commercials.)[1]

WHAT IS PRODUCED: THE RESPONSE TO A CHANGE IN TASTES

At the beginning of this chapter, three basic questions were listed. To see how the market mechanism can help to answer the first of these—*What* will be produced? —consider what happens when there is a change in tastes. Suppose, for example, that people develop a desire to drink more tea and less coffee. This change in tastes is illustrated by a rightward shift in the demand curve for tea and a leftward shift in the demand curve for coffee.

As the demand for tea increases, the price is bid up by eager buyers. With a higher price, growers in Sri Lanka and elsewhere are encouraged to plant more

tea. At the new equilibrium, shown as point E_2 in Figure 4-5, the price of tea is higher than it was originally (at E_1), and consumers are buying a larger quantity of tea. In the coffee market, the results are opposite. At the new equilibrium (F_2), the price is lower and a smaller quantity is bought.

Thus, competitive market forces cause producers to "dance to the consumers' tune." In response to a change in consumer tastes, prices change. Tea producers are given an incentive to step up production, and coffee production is discouraged.

SHIFTS IN SUPPLY

While the market encourages producers to "dance to the consumers' tune," the opposite is also true. As we shall now show, consumers "dance to the producers' tune," as well. The market involves a complex interaction: sellers respond to the desires of buyers, and buyers respond to the willingness of producers to sell.

Just as the demand curve reflects the desires of buyers, so the supply curve illustrates the willingness of producers to sell. In an important respect, the two curves are similar. The objective of each is to show *how the quantity is affected by the price of the good, and by this price alone.* Thus, when we draw the supply curve, once again we make the *ceteris paribus* assumption. Everything (except the price of the good) that can affect the quantity supplied is held constant.

Supply Shifters

As in the case of demand, the "other things" that affect supply can change through time, causing the supply curve to shift. Some of these "other things" are the following:

1. The cost of inputs. For example, if the price of fertilizer goes up, farmers will be less willing to produce wheat at the previously prevailing price. The supply curve will shift to the left.

2. Technology. Suppose that there is an improvement in technology that causes costs of production to fall. With lower costs, producers will be willing to supply more at any particular price. The supply curve will shift to the right.

(These first two points illustrate the dependence of the supply curve on the cost of production. The pre-

---

[1] *Answer:* It will reduce the demand. It has been estimated that this will result in a yearly loss of $200 million in advertising revenue in the United States by 1987.

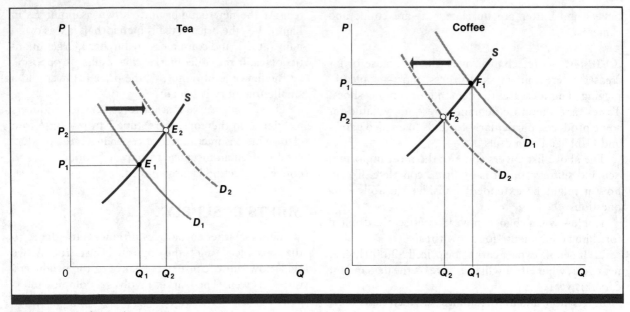

Figure 4-5 A change in tastes.
A change in tastes causes the demand for tea to increase and the demand for coffee to decrease.
As a result, more tea is bought, at a higher price. Less coffee is bought, and the price of coffee
falls.

cise relationship between production costs and supply will be considered in detail in Chapters 22 and 23.)

3. Weather. This is particularly important for agricultural products. For example, a drought will cause a decrease in the supply of wheat (that is, a leftward shift in the supply curve), and a freeze in Florida will cause a decrease in the supply of oranges.

4. The prices of related goods. Just as items can be substitutes or complements in consumption, so they can be substitutes or complements in production.

We saw earlier that substitutes in consumption are goods which can be consumed as *alternatives* to one another, satisfying the same wants (for example, apples and oranges). Similarly, **substitutes in production** are goods which can be produced as *alternatives* to one another, using the same factors of production. Thus, corn and soybeans are substitutes in production; they can be grown on similar land. If the price of corn increases, farmers are encouraged to switch their lands out of the production of soybeans and into the production of corn. The amount of soybeans they are willing to supply at any given price decreases; the supply curve for soybeans shifts to the left.

We also saw earlier that complements in consumption are used *together* (for example, gasoline and automobiles). Similarly **complements in production**, or **joint products**, are produced together, as a package. Beef and hides are one example of this. When more cattle are slaughtered for beef, more hides are produced in the process. An increase in the price of beef causes an increase in beef production, which, in turn, causes a rightward shift of the supply curve of hides.

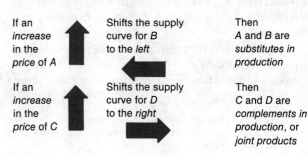

The Response to a Shift in the Supply Curve

To illustrate how "consumers dance to the producers' tune," suppose that there is a frost in Brazil, which wipes out part of the coffee crop. As a result, the quantity of coffee available on the market is reduced. That is, the supply curve shifts to the left, as illustrated in Figure 4-6. With less coffee available, the price is bid upward. At the new equilibrium (G_2), the price is higher and the quantity sold is smaller.

How do consumers respond to the change in supply? Because of the higher price of coffee, consumers are discouraged from buying. Some consumers may feel indifferent about the choice between coffee and hot chocolate, and may switch to hot chocolate because it is now less expensive than coffee. Others may simply reduce their consumption of coffee, buying it only for very special occasions. Because of the limited quantity, it is not possible for all those who might like to drink coffee to get it. Anyone who is willing and able to pay the high price will get coffee; those who are unwilling or unable to pay the price will not get it. Thus, the *high price acts as a way of allocating the limited supply among buyers*. The coffee goes only to buyers who

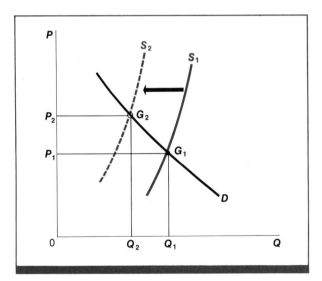

Figure 4-6   A shift in supply.
A freeze in Brazil causes a leftward shift in the supply curve of coffee. The result is a movement of the equilibrium along the demand curve from G_1 to G_2. At the new equilibrium, there is a higher price, and a smaller quantity is sold.

are sufficiently eager to be willing to pay the high price, and sufficiently affluent to be able to afford it.

SHIFTS IN A CURVE AND MOVEMENTS ALONG A CURVE

Because the term "supply" applies to a supply schedule or a supply curve, a change in supply means a *shift* in the entire curve. Such a shift took place in Figure 4-6 as a result of a freeze in Brazil.

In this figure, observe that the demand curve has not moved. However, as the supply curve shifts and the price consequently changes, there is a movement *along* the demand curve from G_1 to G_2. At the second point, less is bought than at the original point. The quantity of coffee demanded is less at G_2 than at G_1.

The distinction between a *shift in a curve* and a *movement* along a curve should be emphasized. What can we say about the move from G_1 to G_2?

1. It is correct to say that "supply has decreased." Why? Because the entire supply curve has shifted to the left.

2. It is *not* correct to say that "demand has decreased." Why? Because the demand curve has not moved.

3. It is, however, correct to say that "the quantity demanded has decreased." Why? Because a smaller quantity is demanded at G_2 than at G_1.

A similar distinction should be made when the demand curve shifts. This is shown in Figure 4-7, based on the left panel of Figure 4-5, where the demand for tea increases because of a change in tastes. The rightward movement of the demand curve causes the equilibrium to move *along* the *supply* curve, from E_1 to E_2. It is not correct to say that supply has increased, since the supply curve did not move. However, the *quantity* supplied did increase as the price rose. (Quantity Q_2 is greater than Q_1.)

The distinction between a *shift* in a curve and a movement *along* a curve is more than nitpicking. It is important in avoiding a classic error. History does not give us diagrams showing demand and supply curves, but it does give us quotations on prices and quantities. Suppose that, with a little research, we found that

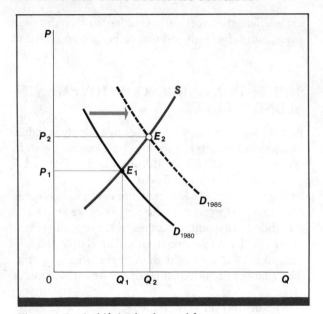

Figure 4-7   A shift in the demand for tea.
This diagram, based on the left panel of Figure 4-5, shows that there is an increase in the quantity of tea supplied as the equilibrium moves from E_1 to E_2. However, supply does not change, since the supply curve does not move.

point E_1 in Figure 4-7 was observed in 1980 and point E_2 in 1985. If we are not careful, we might jump to the following *incorrect* conclusion:

> The theory of the demand curve tells us that a rise in price should cause a decrease in the quantity demanded. Between 1980 and 1985, the price rose, but so did the quantity. Therefore, the facts contradict the theory of demand.

However, the facts do no such thing. The error in logic is this: Between 1980 and 1985, the demand curve *shifted*. As it shifted, equilibrium moved *along the supply curve*. Thus, the two points E_1 and E_2 trace out the supply curve, not the demand curve. Moreover, these two observations are exactly what we would expect as we move along a supply curve. When the price rises, so does the quantity.

(Unfortunately, the changes in equilibrium are seldom this simple. The reason is that, as time passes, both the demand and supply curves may shift. In this case, we do not know whether an increase in price will be accompanied by an increase or a decrease in the quantity sold.)

Finally, we re-emphasize:

When supply shifts while demand remains stable, the points of equilibrium trace out the demand curve (Figure 4-6). When demand shifts while supply remains stable, the points of equilibrium trace out the supply curve (Figure 4-7).

THE INTERCONNECTED QUESTIONS OF *WHAT*, *HOW*, AND *FOR WHOM*

We have explored how two tunes are played. Demand is the tune played by consumers, and supply the tune played by producers. We have also seen how each group dances to the tune played by the other.

If we now want to go beyond the question of what will be produced to the other questions—*how?* and *for whom?*—we must recognize that the world is even more complex. We don't merely have two tunes being played. We have a whole orchestra, with the tune played on any one instrument related to the tunes played on all the others.

The major segments of the economy are illustrated in Figure 4-8, which adds detail to a diagram we looked at in Chapter 3 (Figure 3-3). The **product markets** for apples, coffee, bread, housing, etc., are represented by the upper box; we have concentrated on product markets thus far. The box at the bottom indicates that there are similar **markets for factors of production**, with their own demands and supplies. For example, to produce wheat, farmers need land; they create a demand for land. At the same time, those with land are willing to sell or rent it if the price is attractive; they create a supply of land.

In answering the question, *What* will be produced? we begin by looking at the top box, where the demand and supply for products come together. If there is a large demand for bread, we may expect a lot of it to be produced. But eventually we will also have to look at the lower box, where the demand and supply for the factors of production come together. Why are the factor markets relevant? Because the demand and supply in the upper box are influenced by what happens in the factor markets in the lower box.

As an example, consider what happens when oil is

discovered in Northern Alberta. To build the pipeline needed to get the oil out, workers had to be hired. As a consequence, the demand for construction labour in Alberta increased sharply. The price of labour (that is, the wage rate) in Alberta shot up, and construction workers flocked in from the other provinces. The spiralling wage payments in Alberta (lower box) had repercussions on the demands for goods and services in Alberta (upper box). For example, the demand for housing in Alberta (in the upper box) increased as a result of the higher earnings of construction workers in the lower box.

How? and *For Whom?*

To answer the question, *What* will be produced? we began by looking at the product markets in the upper box of Figure 4-8. To answer the questions *How?* and *For whom?* we begin by looking at the lower box.

The factor prices established in the lower box help to determine *how* goods are produced. During the Black Death of 1348–1350 and subsequent plagues, an estimated quarter to a third of the Western European population died. As a consequence, labour supply was substantially reduced and wages rose sharply, by 30% to 40%. Because of the scarcity of labour and its

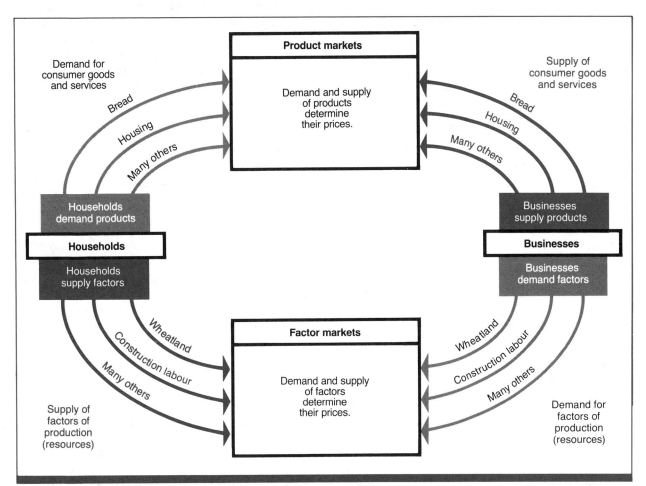

Figure 4-8 Markets answer the basic questions of *what? how?* and *for whom?*

The product markets (top box) are most important in determining *what* is produced, and the factor markets (lower box) in determining *how* goods are produced, and *for whom*.

However, there are many interrelationships between the two boxes. For example, incomes change in response to changing demand and supply conditions in the lower box, and these changing incomes in turn influence the demand for products in the upper box.

high price, wheat producers had an incentive to farm their lands with less labour. Wheat was produced in a different way, with a different combination of labour and land. In those days—as today—the market mechanism was the way in which the society conserved its scarce supply of a particular factor (in this case, labour).

The answer to the question, *For whom* is the nation's output produced? depends on incomes, which are determined by the interplay of supply and demand in factor markets (lower box in Figure 4-8). For example, the supply of accountants is small compared with the demand for accountants. The price of their "labour" is therefore high; accountants generally have high incomes. On the other hand, unskilled labour is in large supply, and is therefore cheap. Consequently, the unskilled worker receives a low income. (For further detail on the demand and supply of labour, see Appendix 4-A.)

Once again, we cannot look at only one box; we cannot look simply at the factor markets in the lower box. Influences from the product markets (upper box) must also be taken into account. For example, reconsider the Alberta pipeline workers. The increase in the demand for labour (in the lower box) drove their wage rate upward. However, that didn't mean that these workers lived like kings. Even though they had very high incomes, the Alberta economy did not provide them with luxurious accommodation. Because of the tight supply conditions in the housing market (upper box), rents for houses and hotel rooms soared. The incomes of construction workers went into paying these higher rents for housing that was not luxurious. At least in terms of living quarters, these workers did not get a much larger share of the nation's output after all.

THE MARKET MECHANISM:
A Preliminary Evaluation

There are thousands of markets in Canada, and millions of interconnections among the markets. Changes in market conditions are reflected in changes in prices. As we have seen, prices provide information to market participants; they provide them with incentives to respond to changing conditions; and they bring order out of a potentially chaotic situation—even though there is no individual or government bureaucracy in control.

Strengths of the Market

In some ways, the market works very well. Specifically:

1. *The market gives producers an incentive to produce the goods that consumers want.* If people want more tea, the price of tea is bid up, and producers are encouraged to produce more.

2. The market *provides an incentive to acquire useful skills.* For example, the high incomes that doctors earn give students an incentive to undertake the long, difficult, and expensive training necessary to become a physician.

3. The market *encourages consumers to use scarce goods carefully.* For example, when the coffee crop is partially destroyed by bad weather, the price is driven up, and people use coffee sparingly. Those who are relatively indifferent are encouraged to switch to tea. Even those who feel they must have coffee are motivated to conserve. If coffee is selling at a high price, they are careful not to brew three cups when they intend to use only two.

4. Similarly, the price system encourages producers to *conserve scarce resources.* In the pasturelands of Alberta, land is plentiful and cheap; it is used to raise cattle. In Japan, in contrast, land is relatively scarce and expensive. Because of its high price, it is used more intensively. Rice is grown rather than livestock.

5. The market involves a *high degree of economic freedom.* Nobody forces people to do business with specific individuals or firms. People are not directed into specific lines of work by government officials; they are free to choose their own occupations. Moreover, if people save, they are free to use their savings to set themselves up in their own independent businesses.

6. Markets *provide information* on local conditions. For example, if an unusual amount of hay-producing land in a specific county is ploughed up to grow corn, then the price of hay in that county will tend to rise. The higher price of hay will signal to farmers that they should put some of the land in this county back into hay. No government agency can hope to keep up-to-date and detailed information on the millions of localized markets like this one, each with its own conditions. (Note the amount of information that is relevant, even for this simple decision on whether hay or corn should be planted: the quality of the land, particularly its relative productivity in hay and corn; the number of

cattle and horses that eat hay; the cost of fertilizer for hay and for corn; the cost of seed for each; and so on and on.)

In evaluating how well a market works, we should keep in mind the most important question of all: *Compared to what?* Even a poor market may work better than the alternatives. One of the strongest arguments for the market mechanism can be made by paraphrasing Winston Churchill's case for democracy: It may not work very well, but it does work better than the alternatives that have been tried from time to time.

The alternative of price controls: Some problems. Consider, for example, some of the problems which can arise if the government interferes with the market mechanism by fixing prices. Suppose, once again, that the coffee crop is partially destroyed by bad weather. If government controls prevent the price from rising, a shortage develops. Those who get to the store first are able to buy coffee at the low price. Because they have acquired the coffee cheaply, they may use it carelessly, brewing a large pot when they will only drink a few cups, for instance. Those who get to the store later find that coffee has been sold out; they have to do without completely.

Where government price controls result in shortages, people have an incentive to get to the store first, before their neighbours. In order to get scarce goods, they waste time standing in line. To use the quip applied to Britain in the early days after World War II, the society becomes a "queuetopia." The heavily regulated economies of Eastern Europe have had chronic shortages, and queueing to buy scarce goods is common.

Moreover, as a result of price controls, goods may disappear from regular distribution channels and flow instead into illegal **black markets**. In this case, the scarce goods go to those willing to break the law.

> A *black market* is one in which sales take place at a price above the legal maximum.

Price controls can create other problems. For example, in its desire to prevent labour unrest, the Polish government kept bread fixed at a low price—so low that it was less than the price of the wheat that went into making the bread. Farmers found that it was cheaper to feed their livestock with bread than with

grain. This represented a waste of the resources that had been used to make wheat into bread. Such a problem does not occur in a market economy: Nobody will produce bread from wheat if the bread sells for a lower price. (Problems also arise when the government controls rents. See Box 4-1.)

The Market Mechanism: Limitations and Problems

While the market has impressive strengths, it is also the target of substantial criticisms:

1. While the market provides a high degree of freedom for participants in the economy, *it may give the weak and the helpless little more than the freedom to starve*. In a market, producers do not respond solely to the needs or the eagerness of consumers to have products. Rather, they respond to consumers whose needs and wants can be backed up with cash. Thus, in a *laissez-faire* system, the pets of the rich may have better meals and better health care than the children of the poor.

2. An unregulated system of private enterprise may be *quite unstable*, with periods of inflationary boom giving way to sharp recessions. Economic instability was a particularly severe problem in the early 1930s, when the economies of many countries collapsed into a deep depression.

3. In a *laissez-faire* system, *prices are not always the result of impersonal market forces*. As noted earlier, it is only in a perfectly competitive market that price is determined by the intersection of a demand and a supply curve. In many markets, one or more participants have the power to influence price. *The monopolist or oligopolist may restrict production in order to keep the price high.* (See Appendix 4-B.)

4. Activities by private consumers or producers may have *undesirable side effects*. Nobody owns the air or the rivers. Consequently, in the absence of government restraints, manufacturers use them freely as garbage dumps, harming those downwind or downstream. The market provides no incentive to limit such negative side effects.

5. Markets *simply won't work* in some areas. Where there is a military threat, individuals cannot provide their own defence. An individual who buys a rifle has no hope of standing against a foreign power. Organized military forces, financed by the government, are

BOX 4-1

RENT CONTROL

Next to bombing, rent control seems in many cases to be the most efficient technique so far known for destroying cities, as the housing situation in New York City demonstrates.

Assar Lindbeck

Because rent controls are politically popular, they have been introduced by governments in many parts of the world. In Canada, rent control programs were introduced in the 1970s in Alberta, Saskatchewan, Manitoba, and Ontario. In Europe, the markets for rental housing in the United Kingdom and the Scandinavian countries have been profoundly affected by extensive control programs that have been in place for a long time, and in Hong Kong, rent controls were introduced when rents increased in response to the inflow of refugees from mainland China after the Communist victory in 1949.

The administrative design of rent-control programs varies from place to place. In this box, we consider the effects of the simplest form of rent control: government imposition of a maximum rent that can be charged for a given type of apartment or other type of rental housing.

The early effects of such controls are illustrated in the left panel of Figure 4-9. The maximum price which can legally be charged is set at P_1, below the free-market price of P_E. Consequently, the quantity of housing demanded exceeds the quantity supplied; there is a shortage of AB units. As a result, it is difficult to find an apartment. When a renter moves out, there is a scramble to get the vacant apartment, and "knowing the right person" becomes a valuable asset. This basic effect of rent control—that it becomes hard to find an apartment—is important.

However, even greater problems arise as time passes. Rent controls result in decreased construction of new apartment buildings, because they reduce the rental income that owners can hope to receive. Furthermore, if rent ceilings are fixed at low levels,

owners may let their buildings go without proper maintenance and repair. When the buildings eventually deteriorate to the point where they cannot be rented, owners abandon them (Lindbeck's bombing effect).

This longer-run result is shown in the right panel of Figure 4-9, where the demand curve and the short-run supply (SS) are copied from the left panel. During the first year of rent control, the quantity of apartments supplied is reduced to A, on the short-run supply curve (SS). With the rent ceiling continuing at P_1, the effects become more serious as time passes. Because few new buildings are constructed and owners skimp on maintenance and abandon their older buildings, the quantity of apartments declines. After a few years, the number of apartments falls to F, and then to G. Finally it approaches point H on the long-run supply curve. (The long-run supply curve (SL) shows the ultimate effect, after apartment owners have adjusted completely to a new price.)

This illustrates the difficulties that can arise if rent controls are maintained over a long period of time. In the short term, most tenants benefit from the controls. Observe that tenants pay a lower price, and they get almost the same amount of housing at A as at the free-market equilibrium E. (Nothing much happens to the quantity of apartments supplied in the first year of rent control.) In the long run, however, it is very doubtful that renters benefit on average. While they still pay a lower price, they have less housing at H than at E. It is very hard for newcomers to find a place to live. (Desperate apartment-hunters in places like New York City have been known to watch the obituary columns, calling perfect strangers in the event of a death in the family to find out if an apartment is becoming vacant.) Furthermore, something happens that does not show up on the diagram: The housing that still can be rented at point H may be shabby and run down.

Another major effect of rent control is that owners are clearly worse off, because their rental income has fallen. Since both sides lose, a substantial case can be made against long-term rent control.

Many of the problems discussed above are, of

course, reasonably obvious, and in places where rent control programs exist, various methods have been tried to alleviate the situation. For example, in order to provide an incentive for new construction, rent control in Ontario applies only to apartments built before 1975, and not to newly constructed ones. Furthermore, in order to give owners enough income to maintain existing apartment buildings, provision is usually made to allow *some* increases in rents over time. Apartment dwellers are a politically powerful group, however, so a number of rather interesting formulae have been devised to protect current tenants. Although the details of these formulae have varied from time to time, they contain one common element. The biggest upward adjustment in rent is permitted when an apartment becomes vacant.

This provision, in turn, creates another complication. The rent for a specific apartment depends less on its quality than on how recently it has changed occupants. Consequently, it has become more and more difficult to defend rent control as being "fair." Furthermore, owners have an incentive to make life miserable for tenants, since the largest rent

increases occur when they move out. Market incentives work. When the government provides a reward for making tenants miserable, then owners will make tenants miserable. It is not clear that the provision for rent increases actually contributes to its objective of better maintenance.

In Canada, the provincial rent-control programs are of relatively recent origin, and have not led to the kind of deterioration in the housing situation that has occurred in a city like New York, for example. However, the New York experience suggests that once introduced, rent controls become more entrenched, and their consequences more severe as time passes. Writing about the Ontario rent control program, Richard Arnott of Queen's University warns:

> . . . if serious problems do start to become apparent in the rental housing market, there is a very real danger that they will be incorrectly diagnosed, and that the government will get caught in a vicious cycle in which each new policy attacks only the proximate cause of the problems and makes matters

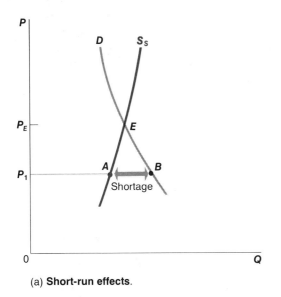

(a) **Short-run effects**.

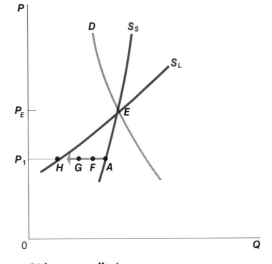

(b) **Long-run effects**.

Figure 4-9   Rent control.

worse. Thus the inefficiencies that are but a minor irritant today could become a running sore in years to come.†

While Arnott argues that there are times when temporary controls are desirable, he emphasizes that if they are introduced, they should be short-lived and should be abolished as soon as possible:

†Richard Arnott, with the assistance of Nigel Johnston, *Rent Controls and Options for Decontrol in Ontario* (Toronto: Ontario Economic Council, 1981), p. 111.

The benefits from controls fall rapidly after the temporary, unanticipated surge in demand that led to their introduction is over. The costs, meanwhile, rise exponentially. *There is, therefore, an optimal time to remove controls, and in Ontario that time is already past.*††

††Ibid., p. 113.

needed. The police and the judicial system are other services that can best be provided by the government. No matter how well the market works in general, people can't be permitted to "buy" a judge.

6. In a *laissez-faire* system, businesses may do an excellent job of satisfying consumer wants as expressed in the marketplace. But should the businesses be given high marks if they have *created the wants in the first place* by advertising? In the words of John Kenneth Galbraith, "It involves an exercise of imagination to suppose that the taste so expressed originates with the consumer."[2] In this case, the producer is sovereign, not the consumer. According to Galbraith, the consumer is a puppet, manipulated by producers with the aid of the advertising industry's bag of tricks. Many of the wants which producers create and then satisfy are trivial: for example, the demands for automobile chrome and junk food.

(Without arguing the merits of each and every product, defenders of the market system make a countercase, based in part on the question: Compared with what? If market demands are dismissed, who then is to decide which products are "meritorious" and which are not? Government officials? Should not people be permitted the freedom to make their own mistakes? And why should we assume that created wants are without merit? After all, we are not born with a taste for art or good music. Our taste for good music is created when we listen to it. Galbraith certainly

wouldn't suggest that symphony orchestras are without merit simply because they satisfy the desire for good music which they have created. But who then is to decide which "created" wants are socially desirable?)

If these criticisms of the market are taken far enough, they can be made into a case for replacing the market with an alternative system. Marxist economists lay particular emphasis on points 1 and 6 in their argument that the market should be replaced with central planning and government direction of the economy.

However, these criticisms are also often made by those who seek to reform, rather than replace, the market system. The recent economic history of Western Europe, North America, and many other parts of the globe has to a significant extent been written by such reformers. If the market does not provide a living for the weak and the helpless, then its outcome should be modified by private and public assistance programs. If monopolists have excessive market power, they should be broken up or their market power should be restrained by the government. If an unregulated market means that only American television programs would be shown in Canada, the government should regulate the television industry to protect Canadian culture. Where there are undesirable side effects, such as pollution, they should be limited by taxation or control programs. In defence, justice, the police, and other areas where the market won't work or works very poorly, the government should assume responsibility for the provision of services.

Although the market is a vital mechanism, it has many potential weaknesses. Government, therefore, has a major economic role to play. This role will be the subject of the next chapter.

[2]John Kenneth Galbraith, "Economics as a System of Belief," *American Economic Review* (May 1970): 474. See also Galbraith, *The New Industrial State* (Boston: Houghton Mifflin, 1967).

KEY POINTS

1. Every economy has limited resources, and involves specialization and exchange. In every economy, a mechanism is needed to provide answers to three fundamental questions:
   (a) *What* will be produced?
   (b) *How* will it be produced?
   (c) *For whom* will it be produced?
2. Two principal mechanisms may be used to answer these questions:
   (a) The market, where individuals are free to make their own contracts and transactions.
   (b) The government, which can use taxation, spending, regulation, and government-owned enterprises to influence the answers to the questions *What? How?* and *For whom?*

   In the real world, all countries rely on a mixture of markets and government actions. However, the mixture differs among countries. Canada and other Western countries place a relatively heavy reliance on the market. In the U.S.S.R. and the Eastern European countries, the government has a much more pervasive influence.
3. *Prices* play a key role in markets, providing information and incentives to buyers and sellers.
4. Markets vary substantially. Some are dominated by one or a few producers, while others have many producers and consumers. A market is *perfectly competitive* if there are many buyers and many sellers, with no single buyer or seller having any influence over the price.
5. In a perfectly competitive market, equilibrium price and quantity are established by the intersection of the demand and supply curves.
6. In drawing both the demand and supply curves, the *ceteris paribus* assumption is made—that "other things" do not change. Everything that can affect the quantity demanded or supplied—with the sole exception of price—is held constant when a demand or supply curve is constructed.
7. If any of these "other things"—such as consumer incomes or the prices of other goods—do change, the demand or supply curve will shift.
8. *What* the economy produces is determined primarily in the market for goods and services shown in the upper box of Figure 4-8. On the other hand, *how* and *for whom* are determined primarily in the factor markets (the lower box). However, there are numerous interactions among markets. The answer to each of the three questions depends on what happens in both the upper and lower boxes.
9. There is a substantial case to be made for the market system, because it encourages firms to produce what people demand, and because it encourages the careful use of scarce goods and resources. Nevertheless, the market also has significant weaknesses, which means that the government has an important economic role to play.

KEY CONCEPTS

market	industry	normal or superior good
central planning	firm	inferior good
capitalist economy	plant	substitutes
free enterprise	demand	complementary goods
Marxist economy	supply	supply shifter
mixed economy	equilibrium	joint products
oligopoly	surplus	product markets
monopoly	shortage	factor markets
perfect competition	*ceteris paribus*	price control
imperfect competition	demand shifter	black market
market power		

PROBLEMS

4-1 Figure 4-6 illustrates the effect of a Brazilian freeze on the coffee market. How might the resulting change in the price of coffee affect the tea market? Explain with the help of a diagram showing the demand and supply for tea.

4-2 The relatively high incomes of doctors give students an incentive to study medicine. Other than the expected income and costs of training, what are the important things that affect career decisions?

4-3 It is often said that "the market has no ethics. It is impersonal." But individual participants in the market do have ethical values, and these values may be backed up with social pressures. Suppose that in a certain society, it is considered not quite proper to be associated with a distillery. With the help of demand and supply diagrams, explain how this view will affect:

(a) The demand and/or supply of labour in the alcohol industry.

(b) The willingness of people to invest their funds in the alcohol industry, and the profitability of that industry.

4-4 Suppose that social sanctions are backed up by law, and that people caught selling marijuana are given stiff jail sentences. How will this affect the demand and supply of marijuana? the price of marijuana? the quantity sold? the incomes of those selling marijuana?

4-5 In Box 4-1, rent control is discussed. Extend the analysis by describing (a) the effects of rent control on the city's tax revenues; (b) what will happen if rent control is imposed for 20 years, and then abruptly removed.

4-6 In 1984, several New York landlords were indicted for conspiracy, coercion, and extortion. Among other things, they were charged with encouraging thieves to move into their apartment buildings, and with having garbage dumped in the hallways.

(a) What conceivable motive could the landlords have had for dumping garbage in their own buildings?

(b) What changes in law or in policy would you recommend to deal with this problem? How would your suggestion help? Are there any disadvantages to your recommendation? If you have no recommendation, describe possible policy changes, and explain the advantages and disadvantages of each.

*4-7 (Box 4-1 required as background.) "Rent control which applies only to structures in existence when the rent-control law is passed will not affect new construction." Do you agree or not? Explain.

*4-8 In distinguishing between substitutes and complements, the text listed a number of simple cases. Tea and coffee are substitutes, while cars and gasoline are complements.

However, it is worth looking more closely at one example that may not seem quite so simple: heating oil and insulation. How would you correct or rebut the following *erroneous* argument?

> Heating oil and insulation are complements, not substitutes, because they are used together. In Winnipeg, Manitoba, they use a lot of heating oil and a lot of insulation. In Miami, Florida, they don't use much of either.

Try to answer this question without looking at the following hints. But if you have difficulty, consider these hints:

(a) Think about the market for heating oil and insulation in a single place, say, Winnipeg. When the price of heating oil goes up in Winnipeg, do you think that this causes the demand curve for insulation to shift to the right or to the left? Does this make insulation a complement or substitute for heating oil, according to the definitions in the text?

---

*Problems marked with asterisks are more difficult than the others. They are designed to provide a challenge for students who want to do more advanced work.

(b) Are natural gas and oil substitutes or complements? Suppose the incorrect statement given above had mentioned heating oil and natural gas, rather than heating oil and insulation. Would it still be erroneous?

(c) If we accept the erroneous statement about heating oil and insulation shown above, can't we argue in a similar manner that there are no such things as substitutes? For example, wouldn't we also accept the following incorrect conclusion: "In the Niagara region, more apples and more cherries are sold than in the Northwest Territories.

Therefore, apples and cherries are used together. They are complements, not substitutes." Do you see that this statement is incorrect because it departs from the standard assumption that "other things remain unchanged"? In identifying complements and substitutes, we must not switch from one location and population (Northwest Territories) to another (southern Ontario); we must look at a single set of people (as in the Winnipeg example in part (a)). Do you see why economists emphasize the assumption that "other things remain unchanged" (*ceteris paribus*)?

APPENDIX 4-A

THE DEMAND AND SUPPLY FOR LABOUR: THE MALTHUSIAN PROBLEM

If we wish to explain *specific* wage rates—for example, the high wage of construction workers in Alberta—we must look at that *specific* labour market. However, we may also be interested in the average wage earned by all labour in an economy. In that case, we must look at the market for all workers.

When we do so, we follow the normal practice and assume that "other things are unchanged." Specifically, we assume that the average price of goods and services remains unchanged. Thus, a change in the wage represents a change in the *real* wage; that is, a change in the quantity of goods and services that the wage will buy. When we show an increase in the wage, the increase permits the worker to buy *more* goods and services. It is not simply used up in paying higher prices for the same goods and services.

The aggregate labour market is quite different from a specific market (such as the market for construction workers). First, consider the supply. The supply curve for construction workers in Alberta slopes upward to the right: The higher the wage, the more workers are attracted from other industries and other provinces. In contrast, the supply of labour for Canada as a whole is approximately vertical, as shown in Figure 4-10. Even if the Canada-wide wage rate were to double,

there would be little increase in the number of workers offering themselves for employment. The reason is that there are no "other industries" or "other provinces"

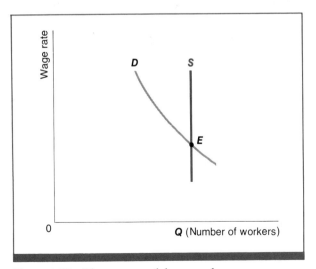

Figure 4-10   The aggregate labour market.
For the labour market as a whole, the supply curve is approximately vertical. A doubling of wage rates will not cause a large increase in the number of people who are willing to work.

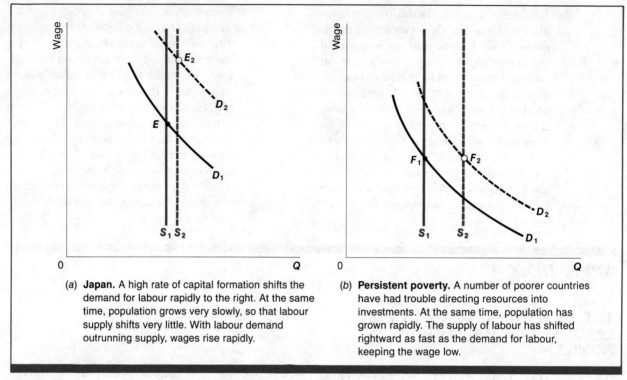

(a) **Japan.** A high rate of capital formation shifts the demand for labour rapidly to the right. At the same time, population grows very slowly, so that labour supply shifts very little. With labour demand outrunning supply, wages rise rapidly.

(b) **Persistent poverty.** A number of poorer countries have had trouble directing resources into investments. At the same time, population has grown rapidly. The supply of labour has shifted rightward as fast as the demand for labour, keeping the wage low.

Figure 4-11   Shifts in the demand and supply of labour.

from which workers can be attracted (although more workers might come in from other countries).

On the other hand, the demand curve for all Canadian labour does have the same general shape as the demand for labour in a specific industry. That is, it slopes downward to the right. The higher the wage rate, the fewer jobs are offered. At a high wage rate, businesses have an incentive to produce with less labour, and more of other inputs such as machinery. Furthermore, with the prices of goods remaining stable—in line with the *ceteris paribus* assumption—an increase in the wage rate reduces the profitability of producing goods, and therefore causes a reduction in output and in the number of jobs offered. With the demand and supply curves shown, the equilibrium is at *E*.

Now, consider what happens through time. Population increases through natural growth and immigration, and the supply curve for labour therefore shifts to the right. Forces are also at work causing the demand curve to shift. As time passes, the quantity of capital (machinery and equipment) increases, and this results in a rightward shift in the demand for labour. Why?

As the quantity of machines and other capital increases, workers have more tools to work with. As a consequence, they can produce more goods; that is, their productivity rises. Therefore, employers are more anxious to hire workers, and are able to pay them a higher wage.

With both the demand and the supply curves for labour moving to the right, the net effect on wages depends on the relative strength of the two shifts. Consider the two cases illustrated in Figure 4-11. On the left is Japan, where recent population growth has been small; the supply of labour has therefore moved only slightly to the right. At the same time, the Japanese have directed a large proportion of their productive capacity into the production of new factories and equipment. As a result of the increase in the quantity of capital, the demand curve for labour has moved rapidly to the right. The net effect has been a rapid increase in the Japanese wage rate.

In the second panel, a quite different situation is illustrated; namely, a problem which concerns a number of the poorer countries in which population growth has been very rapid. Improvements in medical services have cut mortality rates, while birth rates have remained high. As a result, the supply of labour has shifted rapidly to the right, to S_2. At the same time, a number of these countries have had trouble directing resources into the formation of capital. (Recall from Figure 2-6 that if they divert production away from satisfying their immediate consumption needs, the already low level of consumption may be depressed further.) Consequently, there has been little increase in the capital stock, and the demand curve for labour has shifted outward much less rapidly than in Japan. As a result, wage rates in a number of the poorest countries have risen very little if at all.

Thus, we come to a very important conclusion: *the key to an increase in the real wage is an increase in productivity*, which comes mainly from *improvements in technology* and from an *increase in the capital stock at the disposal of the average worker.*

THE MALTHUSIAN PROBLEM

There is a wide variation among the less-developed countries. In some, per capita output has risen rapidly in the past two decades; in others, it has remained relatively stagnant. The very poorest are haunted by the grim prospect described by the young English clergyman Thomas Malthus in his *Essay on the Principle of Population* (1798). Malthus emphasized the scarcity of natural resources—particularly land—which limits the production of food. Specifically, he argued that the output of food increases at best at an arithmetic rate (1, 2, 3, 4, 5, 6, and so on). However, the passion between the sexes means that population tends to increase at a geometric rate (1, 2, 4, 8, 16, 32, etc.):

> It may safely be pronounced that population, when unchecked, goes on doubling itself every twenty-five years, or increases in a geometrical ratio. The rate according to which the productions of the earth may be supposed to increase, will not be so easy to determine. Of this, however, we may be perfectly certain, that the ratio of their increase in a limited territory must be of a totally different nature from the ratio of the increase in population. A thousand millions are just as easily doubled every twenty-five years by the power of population as a thousand. But the food

to support the increase from the greater number will by no means be obtained with the same facility. . . .

> It may be fairly pronounced, therefore, that considering the present average state of the earth, the means of subsistence, under circumstances the most favorable to human industry, could not possibly be made to increase faster than in an arithmetic ratio. . . . The ultimate check to population appears then to be a want of food, arising necessarily from the different ratios according to which population and food increase.[3]

Because of the tendency of population to outstrip food production, the average income of those in the working class will be driven down to the subsistence

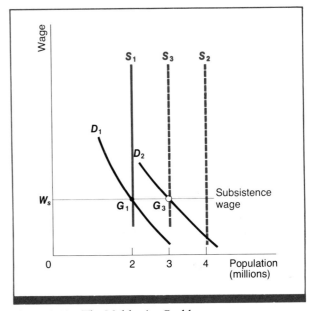

Figure 4-12 The Malthusian Problem.
The tendency for population to grow more rapidly than food production drives the wage down to the subsistence level at G_1. Thereafter, natural population growth would shift the supply of labour from S_1 to S_2, and result in a wage rate *below* the subsistence level. People starve, limiting the supply of workers to S_3, the number who can be paid the subsistence wage W_s.

[3]Thomas Malthus, *An Essay on the Principle of Population* (London: Reeves and Turner, 1888 edition), pp. 5–6.

level. During the nineteenth century, this proposition came to be known as the *iron law of wages*.

After the wage reaches the subsistence level, poor nutrition and starvation will keep the population in check. There was a cruel implication to this theory. Public relief for the poor would do nothing in the long run to improve their condition. It would simply result in an upsurge in population; there would be more people to face starvation in the future.

The Malthusian problem is illustrated in Figure 4-12. Suppose that rapid growth has already driven the wage down to the subsistence level, as shown by the intersection of S_1 and D_1; the population is 2 million. Now, in the next twenty-five-year period, population, if unchecked, would rise to 4 million (S_2). But food production can rise to no more than a level that would support 3 million. Employers cannot pay 4 million workers a high enough wage to permit them all to survive; the demand for labour increases only to D_2. Starvation, war, or pestilence take their toll, keeping the population down to the 3 million that can be supported by the available food (G_3).

As a general forecast, Malthus's theory has proved inaccurate. The standard of living in many countries has risen markedly in the past two hundred years. In these countries, birth control has been a greater restraint on population growth than Malthus anticipated. And food production has increased beyond Malthus's expectations, because of the technological revolution that has included agriculture as well as manufacturing. Nevertheless, Malthus's theory—that there can be a race between population growth and the ability to produce—is worth remembering in a world which is becoming more crowded.

KEY POINTS

10. The wage rate depends on the demand and supply of labour.
11. Increases in the productivity of labour cause the demand for labour to increase. Increases in the quantity of capital are a principal cause of increases in the productivity of labour.
12. Population growth is the main cause for an increase in the supply of labour.
13. If the demand for labour shifts out faster than the supply of labour, wages will be pulled upward. If the supply shifts out faster than demand, wages will be depressed. If the tendency for population to increase keeps wages at a very low level and under downward pressure, the country faces the *Malthusian* problem.
14. Price is determined by the intersection of the demand and supply curves only in a perfectly competitive market.

KEY CONCEPTS

supply of labour in a specific market
supply of labour in the nation as a whole

productivity of labour
Malthusian problem

iron law of wages
monopsony

PROBLEM

4-9 (a) Suppose you are the manager of a local drug store. What do you think the supply curve of clerks looks like?

    (b) What does the supply curve of labour facing a steel firm in Hamilton, Ontario, look like?

    (c) What does the supply curve for all labour in Canada look like?

    (d) Explain why the curves in parts (a), (b), and (c) have different shapes.

APPENDIX 4-B

PRICE IS DETERMINED BY DEMAND AND SUPPLY CURVES ONLY IN A PERFECTLY COMPETITIVE MARKET

It is only in a perfectly competitive market that the intersection of the demand and supply curves determines the price. To see why, consider the type of question answered by the supply schedule. If the price of apples were, say, $10 per bushel, how many apples would suppliers be willing to sell? This is a question which is relevant in a perfectly competitive market. Individual orchard owners indeed ask themselves how many apples they want to sell at the going market price. Individually, they cannot affect that price, so each owner's decision is limited to the number of bushels to be sold.

However, that is not the sort of decision a monopolist or oligopolist (such as the Ford Motor Company) has to make. Such a firm does not take the market price as given. Instead, it quotes a price for its product. For example, at the beginning of the model year, Ford announces the prices of its cars. Because Chrysler, G.M., and Ford set their own prices—rather than responding to a given market price—there is no supply curve for the auto industry.

On the other side of the market, a similar complication can arise. The demand curve is a meaningful concept only if there are many buyers, with none having any influence over price. In such a case, the demand-schedule question is relevant. If the price is, say, $10 per bushel, how many bushels will buyers be willing to purchase?

However, in a market with only one buyer (*monopsony*) or only a few buyers (*oligopsony*), the individual buyer can influence price. Therefore the question a monopsonist will ask is not, "How many units will I buy at the given market price?" but rather, "What price shall I offer?" Thus, for example, the only manufacturer in a small town will have monopsony power in the labour market, and will ask, "What wage rate shall I pay?" In such cases, where a single buyer sets market price rather than taking it as given, there is no demand curve.

The major market forms and the chapters in which they will be studied are outlined in Table 4-4.

Table 4-4
Types of Markets

Type	Characteristic	Is demand curve meaningful?	Is supply curve meaningful?	How is price determined?	Studied in Chapters
Perfect competition	Many buyers and sellers, with no single market participant affecting price	Yes	Yes	By intersection of demand and supply curves	4, 20–24
Monopoly	One seller, many buyers	Yes	No	By seller, facing market demand	25, 33
Monopsony	One buyer, many sellers	No	Yes	By buyer, facing market supply	33
More complex cases	Few buyers, few sellers	No	No	In complex manner	26, 33

Chapter 5

THE ECONOMIC ROLE OF THE GOVERNMENT

In answering that question [on the role of
the State] it would be necessary to enter
into a large consideration of what the Government
can do for the benefit of those subject to it,
and that is a very wide question, on which
people may differ.

John Stuart Mill, in evidence before
the Select Committee on the Income and
Property Tax, 1852

The defects and limitations of the market system, outlined at the end of Chapter 4, provide a reason for the government to play a significant role in the economy. In the words of Adam Smith, there are economic functions ". . . which, though they may be in the highest degree advantageous to a great society, are, however, of such a nature, that the profit could never repay the expence to any individual, or small group of individuals"; consequently, these functions must be undertaken by the government.

In Chapter 4, we described briefly how the government affects the economy in four principal ways: by **spending**, by **taxation**, by **regulation**, and by running **public enterprises**. For example, when the government *spends* for roads or for armoured personnel carriers, then production is affected: More roads and personnel carriers are built. The primary function of *taxation* is to raise revenue for the government; taxes are an unpleasant necessity. But taxes may also be used for secondary purposes. For example, if the government wants to discourage the production of some goods, it can put a tax on them. (This will raise their price and lead consumers to buy less.) The government also influences economic behaviour through *direct regulation*. Regulations regarding seat belts and other safety equipment have affected the design of automobiles; safety requirements affect the way in which coal is mined; and government regulations limit the amount of pollution that manufacturers can discharge into the air and water. Finally, the government indirectly affects many sectors of the economy through the activities of *public enterprises*. For example, because the CBC has a policy of favouring Canadian programming, more Canadians have jobs in symphony orchestras or in the television industry, and TV viewers spend less of their time watching foreign programs.

In contrast with the private market, where people have an option of buying or not, government activities generally involve compulsion. Taxes must be paid; people are not allowed to opt out of the system when it is time to pay income taxes. Similarly, government regulations involve compulsion; car manufacturers *must* install safety equipment. And compulsion sometimes exists even in a government spending program. Young people must go to school (although their parents do have the option of choosing a private school rather than one run by the government).

In later sections of this chapter, we will consider how the government can use spending, taxation, regulation, and public enterprise, to improve the outcome of activities in the private market. As a preliminary, however, we look at some facts about government: how the government's role has expanded, and what the government is currently doing.

THE GROWTH OF GOVERNMENT EXPENDITURES

During the nineteenth and early twentieth centuries, government expenditures covered little more than the expenses of the army and police, a few public works, and the salaries of judges, legislators, and a small body of government officials. Except for wartime periods when spending shot upward to pay for munitions, weapons, and personnel, government spending was low. As late as 1928, all levels of government (federal, provincial, and local) together spent less than $800 million a year. Of this total, about two-thirds was spent by the provincial and local governments. Highway maintenance and education were typical government programs. This does not mean, however, that a rigid *laissez-faire* policy was followed. Even during the nineteenth century, the Canadian government participated in some important sectors of the economy—notably railroad building.

With the Depression of the 1930s, there came a major increase in government activity. Distress and unemployment were widespread, and it was becoming increasingly hard to believe that the workings of the private market would lead to the best of all possible worlds. Public-sector spending increased rapidly as all levels of government tried to alleviate the burden on the unemployed, and to create new jobs for them in the public sector. Then, as Canada became heavily involved in the Second World War, huge federal government spending was required to pay for military

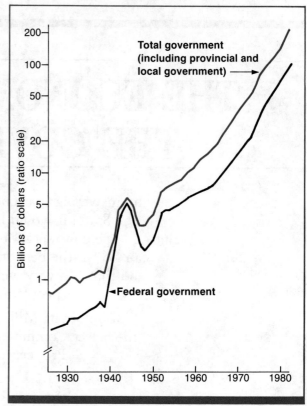

Figure 5-1   Government expenditures, 1926-1984.
The most rapid rate of increase in government spending came during 1940–1945, as the federal government had to spend enormous sums to pay for the war. In the last two decades, government spending has again increased rapidly; most of this increase has been accounted for by non-defence expenditures at all levels of government (federal, provincial, and municipal).
Source: Statistics Canada, *CANSIM Databank*. Reproduced by permission of the Minister of Supply and Services Canada.

equipment and for the salaries of military personnel.

When the war ended in 1945, the nation demobilized and government spending fell by about 30 percent. But the decline was only temporary. Over the past three decades, spending at all levels of government has increased rapidly, to total no less than $240 billion by 1984 (Figure 5-1).

Government Expenditures in Perspective
Clearly, government spending has become very large. It is hard for the average citizen, accustomed to dealing with a family budget measured in hundreds or

thousands of dollars, to comprehend government budgets measured in billions. A billion dollars may be more meaningful if it is reduced to a personal level: A billion dollars represents about $40 for every man, woman, and child in Canada. Thus, with total annual budgets amounting to $240 billion, our federal, provincial, and local governments spent more than $9,600 per Canadian in 1984. The magnitude of a billion dollars may be illustrated in another way. When the government borrows $1 billion at an interest rate of 12% per annum, its interest payments amount to $325,000 *per day.*

The rapid increase in government spending has in part been a reflection of additional responsibilities undertaken by government. In contrast to the situation that existed half a century ago, the government now has extensive programs to help people who otherwise might find themselves in difficult financial circumstances. Payments under the Old Age Security Act, the Canada Pension Plan, and the Guaranteed Income Supplement program provide financial support for retired people. The federal government pays family allowances to all families with children, and provincial governments pay most of the cost of Canadians' health care. Benefits paid out by the government's Unemployment Insurance Commission raise the incomes of people who are out of work, and social assistance helps those who are too poor to afford the basic necessities of life. All of these programs have contributed to the rapid rise in government spending.

But the expenditures shown in Figure 5-1 can give a misleading impression of the size of the government. While the government is spending more and more, so are private individuals and businesses. For both the government and the private sectors, these rising expenditures reflect two major trends: More and more goods and services are being bought, and at higher and higher prices. We can see government expenditures in better perspective by examining them, not in dollar terms (as in Figure 5-1), but rather as a percentage of national product.[1]

When we do this in Figure 5-2, the increase in government expenditures does not look quite as dramatic. Following the wartime peak of about 50% of national product, government spending fell to less than 25%

in the late forties, and the percentage then rose only slowly until the mid-1960s. However, since then it has again risen at a rapid pace, and by the mid-1980s total government spending had surpassed the wartime level of more than 50% of national product.

Government Purchases versus Transfers

A further complication in measuring the size of the government arises because of the two major categories of government expenditures: (1) **purchases of goods and services**, and (2) **transfer payments**.

Government purchases of goods include items such as typewriters, computers, and army trucks. The government purchases services when it hires schoolteachers, police officers, and employees for government departments. When the government purchases such goods and services, *it makes a direct claim on the productive capacity of the nation.* For example, when it spends $600 for a typewriter, then steel, plastic, rubber, and labour are used to manufacture the typewriter. Similarly, the purchase of services involves a claim on productive resources. The police officer hired by the government must spend time on the beat, and thus becomes unavailable for work in the private sector.

Government transfer payments, on the other hand, are payments for which the recipient does not provide any good or service in return. Family allowances and social assistance payments to low-income families are examples of transfer payments, as are Old Age Security (OAS) and Unemployment Insurance benefits.

In contrast with government purchases, transfer payments represent no direct claim by the government on the productive capacity of the nation. For example, when the government pays OAS benefits to retired people, there is no reallocation of the nation's product away from the private sector toward the government sector. Unlike the typewriter company that manufactures a typewriter and ships it to the government to get the payment of $600, the OAS benefit recipient does not use up productive resources to provide the government with a good or a service in return for the benefit. This does not mean, of course, that the Old Age Security program is unimportant. When the government collects taxes[2] to finance it and pays benefits to retirees, the pattern of consumer spending is affected. The old

---

[1] The measure of national product—gross national product (GNP)—will be explained in Chapter 7.

[2] Payments into social insurance funds such as the Canada Pension Plan or Unemployment Insurance are sometimes called *contributions,*

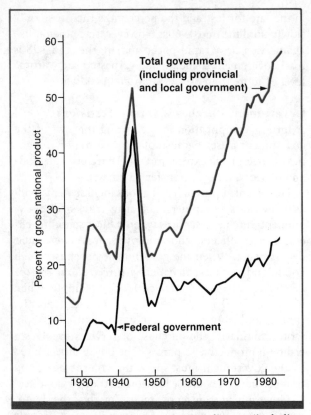

Figure 5-2 Total government expenditures (including transfers).
If we look at what the government takes for itself plus what it takes to redistribute in the form of transfers, then the government has laid claim to a larger and larger share of national product.
Source: Statistics Canada, *CANSIM Databank*. Reproduced by permission of the Minister of Supply and Services Canada.

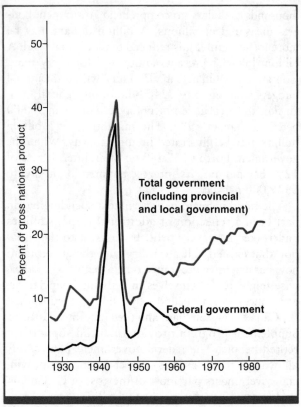

Figure 5-3 Government purchases of goods and services (excluding transfers).
However, as a percent of national product, government purchases of goods and services have changed much more slowly over the past two decades.
Source: Statistics Canada, *CANSIM Databank*. Reproduced by permission of the Minister of Supply and Services Canada.

have more to spend, and those of working age who pay taxes, have less. As a consequence, producers find they are facing greater demands for the things that old people want, and smaller demands for the products desired by the working population. Therefore, although the system of government transfer payments affects the amount of the nation's product that various indi-

on the grounds that individuals acquire a right to pensions and other benefits as a reward for their payments. But it is also correct to label the contributions as taxes, since they are involuntary payments which must be made to the government. (Furthermore, while benefits bear some relation to the "contributions" which an individual has made, they are not closely tied to those "contributions.")

viduals can purchase, it does not redirect the economy toward production for the government.

> A *transfer payment* is a payment by the government to an individual, for which the individual does not provide a good or service in return. Old Age Security benefits, Unemployment Insurance benefits, and social assistance payments are examples of transfers.

Figure 5-2 showed total government expenditures, including transfers. Another way of measuring the size of the government is to look only at government purchases of goods and services; that is, expenditures excluding transfers, as shown in Figure 5-3. These are the expenditures that make a direct claim on the productive resources of the economy. As a share of national output, government purchases of goods and services stayed relatively constant between the early 1950s and the mid-1960s. Even though the percentage has risen in the last 20 years, by the mid-1980s, it had risen just above 20%, no more than about half its wartime peak.

We can thus get two somewhat different impressions of the government's size, compared with the size of the economy. If we look only at purchases of goods and services, then the percentage of national product going to the government has been rising fairly slowly over the past two decades. If, on the other hand, we also look at transfers, the government's percentage has been increasing much more rapidly. Thus, the principal reason for the government's increasing share of the economy is not that it is directly claiming more and more of the nation's output for itself. Instead, the increasing share is mostly due to the government's claiming more revenue to be redistributed in the form of transfer payments such as Old Age Security benefits, Unemployment Insurance benefits, and social welfare assistance.

While the government is a major participant in the Canadian economy, the governments in some European countries assume an even larger role. In a country such as Sweden, taxes have to be very high to pay for the extensive welfare system and for other services provided to the public. But in other nations, the government plays a smaller role, and tax collections represent a smaller percentage of income. In spite of its rapid achievement of a standard of living similar to Western Europe's, Japan has remained a low-tax country, collecting only about half as large a share in taxes as do the Western European countries, and the U.S. government collects a significantly smaller share of total income as taxes than does the Canadian government.

THE BUDGETS OF THE CANADIAN GOVERNMENTS

Federal Government Expenditures

Details on federal government expenditures in Canada, and on the taxes that finance these expenditures, are provided in panel (a) of Table 5-1. This table includes both purchases of goods and services, and transfer payments to persons and to other levels of government. In Canada's federal system, the share of the federal government in total government spending on goods and services is comparatively small. Thus, expenditures on current goods and services in Table 5-1 are a relatively small portion of the expenditures shown (around one-fifth of the total). Included in this share is defence spending, as well as the cost of maintaining the federal civil service in Ottawa and elsewhere in Canada.

"Social services" is now the single largest expenditure item, accounting for just about a third of the federal budget. This item includes Old Age Security and Guaranteed Income Supplement payments to retired people, family allowances, and Unemployment Insurance benefits.

The federal government also transfers a large share of its revenue to provincial and local governments: In addition to item (8), "General-purpose transfers," items (4), (5) and (6) also include federal transfers to help cover provincial costs for health care, education, and social welfare.

By far the fastest-growing expenditure category in recent years has been "Debt Charges," that is, interest on the public debt. There are two reasons for this rapid growth. One is that the government has had to pay higher interest rates on its outstanding debt. In the mid-1970s, interest rates on federal government bonds were about 9%, while in 1984 they averaged well over 12%. Second, interest payments have increased because the size of the debt itself has grown rapidly. In 1975, the federal debt was less than $40 billion; at the end of 1985 it was just about $200 billion. (We will discuss the public debt in more detail in Chapter 11.)

Provincial and Local Government Expenditures

As can be seen from Figure 5-2, the share of total public expenditure accounted for by provincial and municipal governments is about as large as the federal government's share, reflecting Canada's relatively decentralized system of government. (In the United States, federal government spending is closer to two-thirds of total public sector spending.) Panel (a) in Table 5-2 gives a breakdown of provincial/local expenditure. The largest expenditure items at this level of government are the costs of education (28%) and health care (19%). These costs have been growing rapidly in the past several decades. Spending on social services other than education and health account for a

Table 5-1
Federal Government Expenditure and Revenue
Fiscal Year Ending March 31, 1983

(*a*)

Expenditure	Billions of Dollars	Percentage
1. General Services	4.4	5
2. Protection of Persons and Property	8.6	9
3. Transportation and Communication	5.3	6
4. Health	4.6	5
5. Social Services	31.2	33
6. Education	2.9	3
7. Resource Conservation & Industrial Development	9.7	10
8. General-purpose transfer to other levels of government	6.2	7
9. Debt Charges	11.9	12
10. Other Expenditure	9.1	10
Total	94.0	

(*b*)

Revenue	Billions of Dollars	Percentage
1. Personal Income Tax	27.4	37
2. Corporation Income Tax	7.1	10
3. Non-Resident Income Tax	1.0	1
4. General Sales Tax	5.9	8
5. Excise Duties and Special Taxes	2.3	3
6. Unemployment Insurance Contributions	4.9	7
7. Universal Pension Plan Levies	3.4	5
8. Other Tax Revenue	11.2	15
9. Postal Revenue	1.9	2
10. Return on Investment	5.4	7
11. Miscellaneous Non-tax Revenue	3.8	5
Total	74.3	

Source: Statistics Canada, *Federal Government Finance*, June 1984. Reproduced by permission of the Minister of Supply and Services Canada.

smaller share in the provincial/local budget than in the federal budget. While provincial and local governments pay the cost of social assistance to families or individuals with low income, the expenditures on such welfare programs are not as high as the federal government's expenditures on other kinds of social service programs such as family allowances, Old Age Security, and Unemployment Insurance.

Government Receipts
Details on the revenue derived from taxation at the federal and provincial/municipal levels are shown in panel (*b*) of tables 5-1 and 5-2.

The federal and provincial *income taxes on individuals* yield the largest share of tax revenue at both levels of government: 37% of total federal tax revenue, and 19% for provincial/local governments, come from

Table 5-2
Consolidated Provincial-Local Government Revenue and Expenditure
Fiscal Year Ended Nearest to December 31, 1981

(a)

Expenditure	Billions of Dollars	Percentage
1. General Services	6.0	6
2. Protection of Persons and Property	4.9	5
3. Transportation and Communication	8.8	8
4. Health	19.8	19
5. Social Services	11.8	11
6. Education	29.1	28
7. Resource Conservation & Industrial Development	4.8	5
8. Debt Charges	8.1	8
9. Other Expenditure	10.3	10
Total	103.6	

(b)

Revenue	Billions of Dollars	Percentage
1. Personal Income Tax	16.5	19
2. Corporation Income Tax	3.7	4
3. Non-Resident Income Tax	—	—
4. General Sales Tax	7.0	8
5. Other Consumption Taxes	4.1	5
6. Health and Social Insurance Levies	5.9	7
7. Other Tax Revenue	12.8	14
8. Natural Resource Revenue	6.7	7
9. Return on Investment	9.3	10
10. Miscellaneous Non-tax Revenue	7.8	9
11. Total transfer from the federal government and government enterprises	15.0	17
Total	88.8	

Sources: Compiled from Statistics Canada, *Local Government Finance 1981* and *Provincial Government Finance 1981*. Reproduced by permission of the Minister of Supply and Services Canada.

this source. Collection of the federal and provincial income taxes has been centralized, so that both are computed on the basis of the same income tax return prepared by the taxpayer at the end of April, and the actual taxes are paid to the federal government, which then remits the provinces' shares to the provincial treasuries. In all provinces except Quebec, a person's provincial income-tax liability is computed as a per-centage of his or her federal income tax, but the percentage varies: In 1984, it ranged from a low of 43.5% in Alberta to a high of 60% in Newfoundland.[3] For the same taxable income, the percentage paid as income

[3]In Quebec, the provincial income tax is computed directly from the individual's taxable income, and the tax is collected directly by the province.

Table 5-3
Federal and Provincial Income Tax, Ontario Residents, 1985

(1) Taxable Income	(2) Income Tax	(3) Income Tax as Percent of Income	(4) Marginal Tax Rate
$ 2,590	$ 422	16%	25%
5,180	1,073	21%	27%
7,770	1,763	23%	28%
12,950	3,220	25%	30%
18,130	4,754	26%	34%
23,310	6,516	28%	37%
36,260	11,309	31%	44%
62,160	22,808	37%	50%

Source: Revenue Canada, *Your 1985 General Tax Guide and Return for Residents of Ontario.*
Reproduced by permission of the Minister of Supply and Services Canada.

tax therefore varies from province to province.

In Table 5-3, columns 1 and 2, we have computed the 1985 federal and provincial income taxes payable for a taxpayer living in Ontario where the provincial tax was 48% of the federal tax. The **average tax rate**, shown in the third column, is simply the total tax divided by income. Observe that the income tax is *progressive*: the average percentage tax rises as taxable income increases.

Note also the concept of the **marginal tax rate** shown in the last column; this is the percentage tax payable on *additional* income. For example, in the tax bracket with income between $23,310 and $36,260 the marginal tax rate is 37%. Within this bracket, if income rises by $100 (from $27,000 to $27,100, say), an extra $37 must be paid in taxes. The marginal tax rate becomes higher and higher as taxable income rises: It is the higher and higher marginal tax rate that pulls up the average tax rate as income rises.

If a tax takes a larger percentage of income as income rises, the tax is *progressive*.

If a tax takes a smaller percentage of income as income rises, the tax is *regressive*.

If a tax takes a constant percentage of income, the tax is *proportional*.

The *corporate income tax* represents the second-largest source of tax revenue for the federal government, and is an important source of revenue for the provincial governments as well. Like the personal income tax, the total corporation income tax is collected by the federal government, which then remits the provinces' shares to the provincial treasuries.[4] The basic corporation income-tax schedule has only two rates for a given type of corporation. For example, for Canadian-controlled corporations in the manufacturing sector, the rate is 25% on the first $150,000 of business income and 46% on income above that amount. Business income (or "net income") of corporations is computed by deducting all business expenses from total revenues; in other words, the tax is levied on corporate profits.

Municipal governments raise almost nine-tenths of their tax revenue from *property taxes*; that is, taxes imposed on the ownership of land and houses. (Property taxes are included in item 7 in panel (*b*) of Table 5-2). Various kinds of *sales taxes* are levied by the federal and provincial governments. They are generally levied as a uniform percentage of the price of all goods and services, with specified exceptions. (For example, food is exempted from federal sales tax.) In addition, there are various federal and provincial excise taxes on specific commodities (such as tobacco, beer and liquor, cosmetics, gasoline, and fuel oil). The federal government also collects customs duties on goods imported into Canada. While the customs duties are imposed partly to raise revenue, they also have the function of protecting Canadian producers of various

[4]There are two exceptions to this procedure. In Quebec and Ontario, the tax is collected directly by the provincial governments.

goods and services from foreign competition, by making imported goods more expensive. (Tariffs will be discussed more fully in Chapter 32.)

With expenditures of $94.0 billion and tax revenues of $74.3 billion, the federal government ran a **deficit** of almost $20 billion in 1982/83. By historical standards, this was very large. The size of the deficit was partly attributable to the 1982 recession, which reduced the amount of revenue from various kinds of taxes and increased government expenditures under the Unemployment Insurance program. But the recession was not the only reason for large deficits in the mid-1980s. Indeed, the deficit increased in 1984, even though the economy was then pulling out of the recession. It was not until 1985 that the deficit stopped growing, and there was some hope of actually reducing it. The deficits of provincial and municipal governments have never reached anywhere near the same magnitude as those of the federal government in recent years, and in some years these governments have even registered small budget **surpluses.**

If a government's revenues exceed its expenditures, it has a budget *surplus*.

If a government's expenditures exceed its revenues, it has a budget *deficit*.

If a government's revenues are approximately equal to its expenditures, its budget is *balanced*.

INTERGOVERNMENTAL FISCAL RELATIONS IN CANADA

. . . the number of federal-provincial disputes in any one year varies in direct proportion to the number of federal-provincial meetings multiplied by the cube of the number of federal-provincial co-ordinating agencies in the respective governments.

Gordon Robertson, formerly Clerk of the Privy Council and Secretary to the Cabinet

The total expenditures of provincial and municipal governments in recent decades have been substantially larger than the amounts of *tax* revenue collected by these governments. To make up for the shortfall, they have had to rely more and more on financial support from higher levels of government.

Municipal governments, whose expenditures have

been growing rapidly, and whose only substantial source of tax revenue is the property tax, have been receiving large transfers from the provincial governments. The provincial governments, in turn, have also needed large amounts of revenue, not only to pay for the transfers to the municipal governments, but also to finance the rapidly growing cost of health care, post-secondary education, and social welfare. (Under the Constitution, and formerly under the British North America Act, programs in these areas are the responsibility of the provincial governments.) The federal government has helped meet the provinces' financial requirements in several ways:

1. It has made large transfer payments to the provincial governments.

2. By decreasing its share of the total revenue from the personal income tax, the federal government has made it easier for the provinces to increase their revenue from this source.

3. By taking responsibility for transfer payments to various groups of individuals (such as the retired, the unemployed, and families with children), the federal government has reduced the need for provincial expenditures on social welfare.

Canada's complicated system of federal-provincial transfer payments is largely governed by two Acts of Parliament: the Federal-Provincial Fiscal Arrangements Act and the Established Programs Financing Act. The system includes several types of transfers. One type is referred to as **equalization payments.** These are payments from the federal government to the "have-not" provinces; that is, provinces that have a relatively small tax base (for example, because they have low average incomes). Without such payments, "have-not" provinces wanting to raise the same per capita *revenues* as the average of Canada would be able to do so only by levying very high tax *rates*. To avoid this, the federal government makes equalization payments, so as to "ensure that all provinces are able to provide reasonably comparable levels of public services without resorting to unduly high levels of taxation."

Equalization payments represent **unconditional transfers** with no restrictions on how they are to be spent. Prior to 1977, there was also a second type of transfer—**conditional transfers**—equal to half the total provincial spending on three specific programs, namely hospital insurance, medicare, and post-secondary education. (These are the "Established Programs" referred to in the legislation.) The transfers were conditional in the sense that a province would receive the transfer only if it spent an equal amount of its own money on these programs. The transfers were designed to meet two objectives—to increase the provinces' revenues, and to encourage them to follow federal guidelines in designing their health insurance and educational systems, thus providing a certain uniformity in these systems across Canada.

There is no doubt that this conditional transfer scheme made the provincial governments more willing to spend money on the health care and higher education systems: When they spent a dollar on health care or education, they had to raise only 50 cents from taxpayers in their own province. In fact, the federal government became concerned that the system made the provinces *too* willing to spend money in these areas, especially those provinces that had comparatively large revenues to spend on their own half of the cost. To solve this problem, the federal government tried to control expenditures by limiting the grants to *some* kinds of health services only. But they then found that this "solution" distorted the system. For example, instead of building more convalescent homes (which were less expensive but were not subsidized by federal grants), the provinces enlarged the acute-care hospitals (which were more expensive but subsidized).

Because of these problems, the system was substantially modified in 1977. The existing conditional transfers were abolished. As compensation, the provinces received two things: an increase in their share of the revenue from the personal income tax, and a federal undertaking to transfer predetermined amounts to the provinces as *block grants* to help offset provincial spending on health and education. The block grants were still conditional in the sense that the provincial health insurance plans and post-secondary education systems had to conform to the existing federal guidelines. However, the amounts to be transferred were no longer determined by the amounts spent by the provinces themselves.

Federal-provincial fiscal relations are complicated, and sometimes spark considerable controversy. A recent example was the long and acrimonious debate over the 1984 Canada Health Act dealing with extra billing by physicians, and hospital user charges in some provinces. The Act authorized the federal government to withhold transfers from provinces which allowed extra billing or imposed hospital user charges. Many provincial politicians and officials saw the Act as an unwarranted federal intrusion in an area of provincial jurisdiction, and complained that it was going to make it harder for them to finance their health-care systems.

In a federal system, there will always be controversy over programs and policies for which jurisdiction and financial responsibility are divided between the federal, provincial, and local governments. As Ottawa struggles to control the federal deficit, federal-provincial friction is likely to increase: One way for the federal government to reduce spending is to try to shift more of the fiscal burden of health care, education, and social welfare assistance to the provinces.

GOVERNMENT REGULATION

The government budget, amounting to billions of dollars, has a substantial effect on the types of goods produced and on who gets those goods. But the size of the budget cannot be taken as the sole measure of the government's economic impact. Business behaviour is influenced to a great degree by various regulatory programs, even though the costs of administering these programs show up as comparatively small items in the government's budget.

For example, regulations imposed by the government of Ontario have forced the International Nickel Corporation (INCO) to install complicated antipollution equipment in order to reduce the emissions of sulphur dioxide from its plant in Sudbury, Ontario. The cost of the equipment, which will be borne by INCO, will be much higher than the cost to the government of administering the antipollution program.

Government measures to limit various abuses of private business have a long history in Canada. In 1889, a section was added to the Criminal Code which provided sanctions against attempts by business to limit competition in order to raise prices and profits in an industry. This section was the predecessor of the present Combines Investigation Act, which outlaws agreements between firms not to undercut each others' prices, and various other practices through which firms may try to create monopoly power for themselves.

Responsibility for enforcing the Act lies with the Bureau of Competition Policy in the Department of

Consumer and Corporate Affairs. While its powers have been considerably circumscribed by the courts, especially when it comes to preventing monopolies arising from mergers or takeovers, the Bureau has had some success in its efforts to prevent various forms of restrictive pricing practices. For example, Canadian General Electric, Westinghouse Canada, and Sylvania Canada were convicted in 1976 on charges of price fixing in the market for electric lightbulbs.

There are many other regulatory agencies. For example, Health and Welfare Canada tests the effectiveness and safety of drugs before they are permitted to enter the market. Government regulation is especially detailed in financial markets: Canada's chartered banks are supervised and controlled by the Bank of Canada. In those provinces with privately owned telephone companies, rates are regulated by the provincial government. Radio and television communications are regulated by the Canadian Radiotelevision and Telecommunications Commission (CRTC). The Canadian Transport Commission regulates the railroad and airline industries, while provincial Highway Transport Boards are responsible for supervising and controlling the trucking industry. The regulatory activities of the federal National Energy Board were at the forefront in the conflict between the federal government and the Western provinces over energy policy in the early 1980s. Another area of rapidly growing regulation has been agriculture, where federal and provincial agencies have been created to control and supervise the marketing of a wide variety of farm products, ranging from wheat to eggs, dairy products, and even asparagus.

Government regulation of the economy grew at a particularly rapid pace in the 1960s and 1970s. In a recent study, the Economic Council of Canada found that the number of federal regulatory statutes increased by over 200% between 1949 and 1978. Provincial regulations proliferated at an even faster rate. In the 1970s, there was particular emphasis on regulation affecting the environment, health and safety, transportation, product standards, business licensing, and land use planning.

Problems with Government Regulation

In many areas, regulation is relatively uncontroversial. For example, few people complain about a govern-ment agency that certifies the airworthiness of aircraft. Similarly, there is widespread support for government regulation aimed at keeping unsafe drugs off the market. Each of the regulatory agencies was established to deal with a problem area where the free market had been tried and found wanting.

However, by the late 1970s many observers were beginning to feel that in some areas, regulation was becoming very cumbersome and that in others it was simply becoming too restrictive. Business executives and corporations were complaining over long delays in obtaining regulatory approval for major projects; such delays, they said, could add substantially to the cost of projects. There have even been suggestions that the standards used to evaluate the safety of drugs may be too restrictive. For example, when Saccharine was temporarily banned after experiments showed that massive doses of Saccharine appeared to increase the risk of cancer in laboratory animals, critics pointed out that more lives might have been lost from problems caused by overweight (as people could no longer use Saccharine instead of sugar to keep their weight down), than from an increased incidence of cancer.

The policies of other agencies, including some of the provincial marketing boards for agricultural products have also been questioned with increasing frequency. True, unregulated markets for agricultural products may have various disadvantages; for example, they might lead to large fluctuations in the prices of such products. But regulation may also have disadvantages: It might cause waste and higher consumer prices, and be unfair to individual producers.

The criticism of excessive regulation in various sectors has gone even further in the United States than in Canada. In the United States certain sectors have already been substantially deregulated—notably the banking and airline industries—and under the Reagan administration, regulation to protect the environment has been de-emphasized. In Canada, the approach to deregulation in the first half of the 1980s was much more cautious. However, initiatives towards loosening of regulation in the transport sector were begun in 1983–84 by the Liberal government, and in 1985 the Conservative government issued a discussion paper proposing almost complete deregulation of airline fares and routes (although safety regulations would of course be maintained).

What is needed is a sense of balance. The private market mechanism has substantial defects. But government agencies also have weaknesses; they are not run by superhumans capable of solving all our problems. At some point, we should be prepared to live with the defects of the market. In some cases, the cure (regulation) may be more costly than the defects themselves.

Regulation in the public interest is made particularly difficult because of the political clout of producers. (This fact also complicates other types of economic policy, including government spending and taxation.) When regulations are being developed, the affected industry makes its views known forcefully. But the views of consumers and taxpayers are diffuse and often remain underrepresented.

The predominance of producer influence is not simply the result of a conspiracy of wealth; it is an intrinsic feature of a highly specialized economy. Each of us has a major, narrow, special interest as a producer, and each of us has a minor interest in a wide range of industries whose goods we consume. We are much more likely to react when our particular industry is affected by government policy; we are much less likely to pressure the government when our diffused interests as consumers are at stake. Narrow producer interests are expressed not only by business, but also by labour. (For example, some of the loudest early criticism of the government discussion paper on airline deregulation came from representatives of flight-attendants' unions and employees of the Canadian Transport Commission.) Unions concentrate their attention on events in their particular industry, even though the union members are also consumers, using a wide range of products. We repeat: This prevalence of producer influence is primarily a result of modern technology and a high degree of specialization; it is not primarily a result of our particular system. It exists in a wide variety of political-economic systems, including those of the United States, Britain, France, Germany, Japan, and the Soviet Union.

PUBLIC ENTERPRISE

In addition to the influence they exert over the economy through their regulatory activities, Canadian governments also participate directly in many markets through government-owned firms. Petro-Canada, the CBC, and Quebec Hydro are only a few examples of the many **Crown corporations** whose operations play an important part in the Canadian economy. Recent estimates put the number of federal Crown corporations at more than 400 and provincial ones at more than 200. Some of these Crown corporations are really just regulatory agencies or government departments. However, many others are important government enterprises that are similar to private business firms in the sense that they derive most of their revenue from selling various goods or services to the public—for example, Petro-Canada or Quebec Hydro. The economic significance of such government enterprises is much greater in Canada than in the United States. For example, it has been estimated that Crown corporations accounted for about 15% of all capital investment in Canada in the early 1980s; the corresponding figure for the United States was less than 5%.

> *Crown corporations* are government-owned firms that derive most of their revenues from selling goods or services to the public, sometimes in direct competition with privately owned firms in the same market.

Crown corporations exist in a wide variety of markets. Many of them are **natural monopolies**, where economies of scale are substantial, so that the market can support no more than one firm large enough to exploit those economies of scale. (Natural monopoly is explained in more detail in Chapter 25.) In the United States, most firms in naturally monopolistic markets are privately owned but heavily regulated by the government; in Canada they are often government-owned instead—for example, corporations producing electric power, or the telephone companies in the Prairie provinces. Crown corporations also exist in more competitive markets—for example, in transport and communication where government-owned corporations such as Air Canada, CN, and CBC operate in direct competition with privately owned firms.

Part of the function of the government-owned companies is to serve various submarkets that private companies are reluctant to serve: Air and rail service to small, remote communities, television transmissions to the Arctic, or radio programs featuring classical music, for example. In other cases, they undertake tasks which may be potentially profitable in the long run, but which require large initial investments and involve such a high degree of risk that private firms are unwilling to invest in them. Examples of such "pioneer enterprises" are Atomic Energy of Canada (AECL), and Polysar, which were both established during World War II but continued to operate and took a leading role in developing new technology in the nuclear power and synthetic rubber fields after the war. (It was the AECL that developed the CANDU nuclear reactor.) More recently, Panarctic Oils, a federally owned Crown corporation which is now a subsidiary of Petro-Canada, was a leader in creating technology for exploration of oil and gas deposits in the Arctic, and Ontario's Urban Transport Development Corporation is working on developing new rapid transit systems for large cities. Not all ventures into new technology are financial successes. For example, Canadair, a federal Crown corporation, was heavily subsidized by the Canadian taxpayer when it developed the technologically advanced Challenger executive jet. There is little prospect that much of this subsidy will ever be recovered, however—whether or not Canadair is sold to a private company.

In many provinces, government-owned development corporations provide financial support for industrial development, and in many cases governments also create Crown corporations by taking over firms which would otherwise close down. Thus, the B.C. government owns and operates a newsprint mill at Ocean Falls; Nova Scotia owns a steel mill in Sydney; and a federal Crown corporation is responsible for the operation of coal mines in Cape Breton. Often, government "bailouts" of failing private firms are undertaken to protect communities in which the firm provides a large share of total employment, and the government hopes to be able to restore the firm to profitability. Sometimes it works. For example, when the provincial government took over the wood pulp and sawmill operations of a private firm in order to stave off the closing of a large mill in Prince Rupert, B.C., it not only managed to save the mill but also made the company profitable.

Often, however, such bailouts end up being very costly to the taxpayers. The case of the Minaki Lodge in a remote area of Northern Ontario is instructive. In 1974, the Ontario government took over ownership of the lodge in order to provide about 500 local jobs, and to protect a loan of $550,000 that the govern-

ment had earlier made to the owners. At the time, the Minister of Tourism announced the government's intention to convert the lodge into "a jewel in the necklace of tourist facilities that threads throughout Ontario." By the early 1980s, the government had spent (according to newspaper estimates) about $20 million on refurbishing the lodge. However, there was little hope that it would become profitable, since mercury pollution had ruined the fishing in the local river system. (This was the reason why the lodge had become unprofitable in the first place.)

Because publicly owned enterprises use a large share of Canada's labour and other resources, and account for a large share of all goods and services produced, their operations have a substantial effect on the functioning of the Canadian economy. In recent years, there has been considerable debate over possible reforms that might improve the efficiency of government firms. The debate has focussed on two main issues: accountability and privatization.

Accountability. While the majority of Crown corporations cover most of their costs using revenue they earn from the sale of goods and services, they usually don't cover them all. As the owner, the government is often called on to pay subsidies for certain tasks the corporations undertake, to provide guarantees for repayment of money they borrow, or simply to cover operating deficits of the firms. This is not surprising: Most Crown corporations are established because governments want to use them to do things which are not privately profitable (such as providing air and rail service to distant communities), and which require a subsidy.

But once it is clear that a Crown corporation is not necessarily expected to cover *all* its costs, the question arises: Where does one draw the line? If the corporation's managers are given a "blank cheque," they are likely to spend too much. The managers must be *accountable* to someone, and since it is the government that owns the firm, their accountability must ultimately be to the politicians who make decisions about government spending. Hence, the reform proposals in this area have focused on ways of strengthening political control over Crown corporations, by providing more precise definitions of the objectives that they are expected to meet, and by providing politicians with better information about current and future spending plans. The case of the Canadair Challenger has been taken as an illustration of the need for such improvements. The argument was that if Parliament had known the extent of the development costs of the Challenger at an earlier stage, someone would have blown the whistle and the corporation would not have been allowed to incur the huge deficits it recorded in 1983.

Privatization. In some cases, the original reason for establishing a public enterprise may disappear over time. For example, an unprofitable firm which has been taken over by a provincial government in order to preserve jobs may become profitable again, or a new technology developed by a Crown corporation may become ready for commercial application. Or it may become possible for the government to accomplish the objective that the corporation was originally supposed to serve through regulation of private firms instead. In these situations, one possible strategy is to privatize the public enterprise—that is, to turn it over to private ownership.

At the federal level, a program for reducing the scope of government enterprise through privatization was an important part of the platform of the 1979-80 Conservative government under Joe Clark; its proposal to privatize Petro-Canada gave rise to considerable controversy. While Petro-Canada remained in the public sector, the privatization policy was revived when the Mulroney government came to power in 1984, and several Crown corporations were put up for sale, including the government-owned aircraft manufacturers Canadair and de Havilland. One of these firms (de Havilland) was sold to Boeing in 1986, and negotiations concerning other sales continued; there were even indications that the government might consider selling Air Canada to private interests.

At the provincial level, the most well-known instance of privatization is the case of the British Columbia Resources Investment Corporation (BCRIC). This corporation was created by the Social Credit government of Premier Bill Bennett in order to sell back to the private sector a number of resource firms which had been nationalized by the previous NDP government. Ownership of these firms was transferred to BCRIC, and the shares of BCRIC, in turn, were in part given away to residents of B.C., and in part sold to private buyers.

To some extent, the arguments for privatization are ideological. The policy is generally supported by private firms objecting to competition from Crown corporations which are supported by the government directly or indirectly. However, a second argument against privatization is based on the idea that managers of private firms have stronger incentives to perform efficiently than managers of public enterprises. The reason is that if managers of private firms perform inefficiently, this is quickly reflected in a reduction in the value of the firms' shares. To prevent this, the firms' owners (shareholders) will put pressure on the managers to perform better, or even replace the management. On the other hand, if managers of publicly owned firms perform inefficiently, the incentive to improve performance is less, for two reasons. First, the managers may be able to claim that they are losing money because the government is forcing them to continue various unprofitable activities, not because they are inefficient. Second, since shares of publicly owned firms are not traded in the market, the taxpayers (who are the ones that ultimately will carry the burden of an inefficient performance) may be only imperfectly aware of the firms' performance.

The evidence for the relative efficiency of managers in public and private firms is mixed. Some studies have shown that private firms operating in a heavily regulated market are no more efficient than public firms in the same market; furthermore, there is some evidence that public firms which have to compete with unregulated private firms also perform relatively efficiently. On the other hand, evidence from firms providing electricity and water to municipalities in the United States have shown that the privately owned companies were able to produce these services at a significantly lower cost than the government-owned ones.

THE ECONOMIC ROLE OF THE GOVERNMENT: What Should the Government Do?

With government and Crown corporation budgets reaching billions of dollars, and with an extensive list of government regulations, the Canadian economy is clearly a long way from having a pure market system of laissez-faire. What principles and objectives guide the government when it intervenes?

In part, government intervention is based on deep social attitudes that are often difficult to explain. Consider, for example, the contrasting attitudes in the

United States and Britain. Several decades ago, Americans looked askance at the government-financed, "socialized" medicine of Britain. Yet at the same time they considered British education "undemocratic" because many well-to-do Britons sent their children to privately financed elementary and secondary schools. The British, on the other hand, were proud of their educational system, and were puzzled by what they considered a quaint, emotional American objection to public financing of medical care. During the past three decades, the gap between the two societies has narrowed, with increasing governmental involvement in medicine in the United States and a decline in the importance of privately financed education in Britain.

The government intervenes in the economy for many reasons; it is hard to summarize them all. But we will look at five of the main ones.

1. The Government Provides What the Private Market Can't

Consider defence expenditures. For obvious political reasons, defence cannot be left to the private market. The prospect of private armies marching around the country is too painful to contemplate. But there is also a compelling economic reason why defence is a responsibility of the government.

The difference between defence and an average good or service is the following. If I buy food at the store, I get to eat it; if I buy a movie ticket, I get to see the film; if I buy a car, I get to drive it. In contrast, if I want a larger, better-equipped army, my offer to purchase a rifle for the army will not add in any measurable way to my own security. My neighbour and the average person in New Brunswick or Manitoba will benefit as much from the extra rifle as I do. In other words, the benefit from defence expenditures goes broadly to all citizens; it does not go specifically to the individual who pays. If defence is to be provided, it must be financed by the government, which collects taxes to ensure that everyone contributes.

Such goods—where the benefit goes to the public regardless of who pays—are sometimes known as **public goods.**

2. Externalities

An **externality** is a side effect—good or bad—of production or consumption. For example, when individuals are immunized against an infectious disease, they receive a substantial benefit; they are assured that they

won't get the disease. But there is an **external benefit** as well: others gain because they are assured that the inoculated individuals will not catch the disease and pass it along to them. Similarly, there is an external benefit when people have their houses painted; the neighbourhood becomes more attractive.

An **external cost** occurs when a factory pollutes the air. The cost is borne by those who breathe the polluted air.

> An *externality* is a side effect of production or consumption. Persons or businesses other than the producer or consumer are affected. An externality may be either positive (for example, vaccinations) or negative (for example, pollution).

Because of the effects on others, the government may wish to encourage activities that create external benefits and to discourage those with external costs. It can do so with the use of any of its four major tools: expenditures, public enterprise, regulation, or taxation. The government spends money on public health programs for the immunization of the young. It may pass regulations on the types of automobiles that can be built, in order to reduce pollution. And taxes on gasoline or on polluting factories might likewise be used to discourage pollution.

The existence of an externality does not in itself make a compelling case for government action; the government should not be concerned with insignificant externalities or other trivial matters. Thus, private incentives are generally enough to ensure that homes will be painted; the government does not usually intervene. However, there is growing concern over more serious externalities: While little was done about pollution two decades ago, major efforts are now directed toward cleaning up the air and water.

3. Merit Goods

Government intervention may also be based on the paternalistic view that people are not in all cases the best judges of what is good for them. According to this view, the government should encourage **merit goods**—those that are deemed particularly desirable—and discourage the consumption of harmful products. People's inability to pick the "right" goods may be the result of short-sightedness, ignorance, addiction, or manipulation by producers. (Recall Chapter 4's brief discussion of Galbraith's views on created wants.)

In some cases, the government attempts merely to correct ignorance in areas where the public may have difficulty determining (or facing?) the facts. The requirement of a health warning on cigarette packages is one example of this. But, in other instances, the government goes further, to outright prohibition, as in the case of heroin and other hard drugs.

The view that "the government knows best" is generally greeted with skepticism; the government intervenes relatively sparingly to tell adults what they should or should not consume. (Children are, however, another matter; they are not allowed to reject the "merit" good, education.) However, substantial government direction does occur in welfare programs, presumably on the ground that those who get themselves into financial difficulties are least likely to make wise consumption decisions. Thus, part of the assistance to the poor consists of subsidized day-care centres and housing programs, rather than outright grants of money. In this way, the government attempts to direct consumption toward housing, food, and care for the children, rather than (perhaps) toward lottery tickets for a parent.

4. Helping the Poor

The market provides the goods and services desired by those with the money to buy, but it provides little for the poor. In order to help the impoverished and to move toward a more humane society, programs have been established to provide assistance for old people, the handicapped, and the needy.

There is much resentment of the "welfare mess," and it does not all come from bigots who despise the poor. Because responsibility for the welfare of people with low incomes is dispersed among many different agencies and levels of government, it is perhaps inaccurate to speak of a welfare "system" at all. Over the years, there has been much debate about this problem, both in Canada and the United States. The difficulty lies in how to reconcile conflicting objectives. How can help be given to the needy without weakening the incentive to work? How can assistance to abandoned mothers be guaranteed without giving irresponsible fathers an incentive to desert their families? How can the poverty-stricken be given a place to live without creating ghettos of the poor? There are no easy answers to such questions.

5. The Government and Economic Stability

Finally, if we go back to the beginning of the upswing in government activity—to the Depression of the thirties—we find that the primary motivation was not to affect the kinds of products made in the economy, nor was it specifically to aid the poor. Rather, the government's main aim was to increase the quantity of production. With unemployment rates of more than 15% of the labour force year after year, the problem was to produce more—more of almost anything would help put people back to work. Since the dark days of the 1930s, a major responsibility of the government has been to promote a high level of employment and stability in the economy.

TAXATION

The art of taxation consists of plucking the goose so as to obtain the largest amount of feathers with the least possible amount of hissing.

Jean-Baptiste Colbert, Seventeenth-century French statesman

The major objective of taxation is to raise revenues—to obtain feathers, without too much hissing. But other objectives are also important in the design of a tax system.

1. Neutrality . . .

In many ways, the market system works admirably. Adam Smith's "invisible hand" provides the consuming public with a vast flow of goods and services. As a starting point, therefore, a tax system should be designed to be neutral. That is, it should disturb market forces as little as possible, unless there is a compelling reason to the contrary.

For the sake of illustration, consider a far-fetched example. Suppose that blue cars were taxed at 10% and green cars not at all. This tax would clearly not be neutral regarding blue and green cars. People would have an incentive to buy green cars; blue cars would practically disappear from the market. A tax which introduces such a distortion would make no sense.

While this illustration is silly, real taxes do introduce distortions. For example, several centuries ago, houses in parts of Europe were taxed according to the number of windows. As a result, houses were built with fewer windows. To a lesser degree, the current property tax introduces a perverse incentive. If you have your house painted and your roof repaired, the government's evaluation of your house (the assessed value) may be raised and your taxes increased as a consequence. Therefore, property taxes encourage you to let your property deteriorate.

The problem is that every tax provides an incentive to do something to avoid it. So long as taxes must be collected, complete neutrality is impossible. The objective of the tax system must therefore be more modest: to aim at neutrality. As a starting point in the design of a tax system, the disturbance to the market that comes from taxation should be minimized.

2. . . . and Nonneutrality: Meeting Social Objectives by Tax Incentives

There is, however, an important modification which must be made to the neutrality principle. In some cases, it may be desirable to disturb the private market.

For example, the government might tax polluting activities, so that firms will do less polluting. The market is disturbed, but in a desirable way. Another example is the tax on cigarettes, which, in addition to its prime objective of raising revenue for the government, also discourages cigarette consumption.

Taxation and regulation can be used to correct the failures of the private market. But the two approaches are quite different in one respect. Regulation aims at *overriding* the market mechanism, forbidding or limiting specific behaviour on the part of business. Taxation aims at *using* the market mechanism, but making it work better. When there are externalities, such as pollution, the signals of the market are incomplete; businesses or individuals who pollute the air do not have to pay the cost. Taxation of externalities can improve the outcome of the market by making the signals facing businesses and individuals more complete: Taxation makes polluters pay a penalty, and gives them an incentive to reduce pollution.

3. Simplicity

To anyone who has wasted several spring weekends sweating over an income tax form, simplicity of the tax system is devoutly desired. Of course, we live in a complex world and the tax code must to some degree reflect this complexity. Even so, it is difficult to avoid getting the impression that the Canadian code is more complicated than necessary. In part, this is due to the fact that simplification of the code would involve the abolition of various special rules which have been legislated over the years in order to provide tax relief for certain particular types of income, or for particular ways of spending or investing it. When simplifying changes are proposed, there will be vocal opposition from those taxpayers or firms who benefit from the special rules. An example of this problem occurred in the mid-sixties when a comprehensive set of revisions of Canada's tax laws were recommended by the so-called Carter Commission on Taxation.[5] If all of the Commission's proposals had been adopted, the structure of the Canadian tax system would have been greatly simplified, with a much more uniform tax treatment of different sorts of income. As it turned out, however, many of the special rules in the existing tax laws were in fact retained, and while some of the Commission's recommendations for change were accepted by the government, they were only partially implemented.

Debate on possible ways of simplifying the tax system has continued since the time of the Carter Commission. While many different proposals have been made, recent ones have emphasized two particular types of reform. First, most participants in the debate agree that the *tax base should be broadened*; that is, many existing deductions and loopholes which reduce the tax liabilities of particular groups of taxpayers should be reduced or eliminated. Not only would this simplify the tax structure, it would also make the tax system fairer; under the existing system people with the same income often end up paying very different amounts of tax depending on the deductions and exemptions they are allowed.

With a broader tax base, the amount of revenue collected at existing tax rates would rise. This has led to the other main type of recent reform proposal: a *reduction in average tax rates*. A particularly simple proposal is for a *flat tax*, which would replace the

[5] *The Royal Commission on Taxation Report* (Ottawa: Queen's Printer, 1966). The Commission derived its popular name from its chairman, K.L. Carter.

complicated structure of income tax rates with a single tax rate applied to all income over and above some basic exemption. One of the advocates of a flat tax is Peter Pocklington, the owner of the Edmonton Oilers and an unsuccessful candidate for the Conservative leadership in 1983. Under his proposal, the federal income tax would simply be 20% of all income in excess of $12,000 for a family of four ($7,500 for a single individual). Similar proposals have been made in the United States. (See Box 5-1.)

4. Equity

Taxation represents coercion; taxes are collected by force if necessary. Therefore, it is important that taxes both be fair and give the appearance of being fair. There are, however, two different principles for judging fairness.

The benefit principle. This principle recognizes that the purpose of taxation is to pay for government services. Therefore, let those who gain the most from government services pay the most. If this principle is adopted, then a question arises: Why not simply set prices for government services which people can voluntarily pay if they want the services? In other words, why not charge a price for a government service, just as Via Rail charges for railway tickets?

This approach may work in some cases—for example, for a toll road from which drivers can be excluded if they do not pay. But it will not work for public goods that benefit people even if they do not pay; for example, defence, disease-control programs, or air traffic control. Everyone will enjoy them, but no one will want to pay for them. It is the function of the government to determine whether such programs are worthwhile. Once the decision is made to go ahead, people must be required to support the program through taxes.

If the benefit principle of taxation is followed, it is up to the government to estimate how much various individuals and groups benefit, and to set taxes accordingly. (Individual citizens cannot be allowed to provide the estimates of how much they benefit personally; they have an incentive to understate their individual benefits in order to keep their taxes down.)

Ability to pay. If the government sets taxes according to the benefit principle, it does not redistribute income. People are simply taxed in proportion to their individ-

ual benefits from government programs. If the government wishes to redistribute income, it can set taxes according to the ability to pay. The usual measures of the ability to pay are income and wealth.

If the only taxes were a progressive income tax and an inheritance tax, and if at the same time the government provided assistance to those at the bottom of the economic ladder, income would be substantially redistributed from the rich to the poor. But the world is not so simple. There are different levels of government, and each one levies several different kinds of taxes. When all the taxes are taken together, it is not so clear that government is taking a significantly larger percentage of income from the rich than from the poor, as we shall see in the next section.

THE BURDEN OF TAXES:
Who Ultimately Pays?

It is difficult to determine who bears the burden of many of our taxes. For example, consider the relatively simple case of the unemployment insurance contribution. (As we noted in footnote 2, even though it is called a "contribution" it is essentially equivalent to a tax.) Part of this tax is deducted from the take-home pay of the worker. In 1985, it was deducted at the rate of 2.35% of the worker's gross income subject to a maximum contribution of $562.12. This maximum was reached at an income of $23,920. Therefore, the same $562.12 was paid by employees with an income of $24,000 as those with, say, a $48,000 income. Thus, this tax is regressive: The employee earning $24,000 per year pays twice as large a percentage of his or her gross income as the employee earning $48,000 per year. The burden in this case is simple to see. However, it is not so clear for the other portion of this tax, which was levied on the employer (3.29% of gross income). Does that tax come out of the employer's profits? Or is it passed on to the consumer in the form of higher prices? Or, possibly, this half may also fall on the worker: If there were no unemployment insurance contributions, the employer might be willing to pay a higher wage.

As another example, consider the corporation income tax. It is sometimes maintained that this tax is a relatively painless way of raising government revenue because it is levied on corporate profits and not on the incomes of individuals. However, this argument is suspect for at least two reasons. First, corporations' profits influence the individual incomes of shareholders, so that a profits tax does directly affect the income of some individuals. Second, a higher rate of corporation income tax may be "passed on" in the form of higher prices, so that the tax is in effect "paid" by the buyers of the corporations' products. When we recognize this, we cannot even tell whether the corporation income tax is ultimately progressive or regressive!

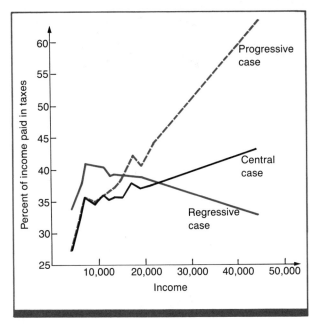

Figure 5-4 Estimates of the overall incidence of Canadian taxes.
Many estimates of the overall incidence of Canadian taxes suggest that the system is neither highly progressive (except in the lowest income brackets) nor highly regressive, as illustrated by the solid black curve.

However, with different assumptions concerning the burden of taxes on the income of those who own capital (who earn profits or interest), the estimated incidence pattern may become quite different, as shown by the solid and broken red curves.

Source: John Whalley, "Regression or Progression: The Taxing Question of Incidence Analysis," *Canadian Journal of Economics* (November 1984): tables 5 and 6.

As these examples show, the question of tax burden—of who ultimately pays—is complicated, even when we are looking at only a single particular tax. Needless to say, estimating the burden—or **incidence**—of *all* Canadian taxes (federal, provincial, and municipal) is even more difficult. Nevertheless, the problem of the incidence of the tax system as a whole *has* been studied by a number of economists, each using a somewhat different method and different assumptions. Figure 5-4 illustrates a set of recent incidence estimates by John Whalley of the University of Western Ontario; the data are from the early 1970s. The solid black curve in the middle refers to his "central case"; it implies that the system was progressive, since total taxes paid as a fraction of income rises from 27% for the lowest income group and rises to 43% as it reaches the highest income group. What is somewhat surprising, though, is that the curve is relatively flat in the intermediate range. When most of us think of taxes, we think first of the income tax with its definitely progressive rate structure. But as the estimates by Whalley and others have shown, a large part of the progressive effect of the personal income tax is offset by other taxes that are much less progressive and, in some cases, are even regressive. (Examples of taxes that are usually found to be regressive are sales and excise taxes and social insurance contributions; these taxes generally constitute a higher proportion of the income for people in the lower-income classes.)[6]

The incidence estimates of Whalley and others have to be very carefully interpreted. As Whalley notes, they all depend on both the precise definition of income, and on several somewhat arbitrary assumptions concerning the incidence of the burden of particular taxes (such as social insurance contributions or the corporation income tax). By changing these assumptions, one can produce a significantly different picture of the overall pattern of tax incidence. As an example, con-

---

[6]Earlier work by W. Irwin Gillespie indicated a much less progressive tax system than implied by Whalley's estimates. As Whalley points out, however, the difference is largely due to the fact that Gillespie measures taxes as a proportion of income *before government transfers*. Since such transfers constitute a relatively large proportion of the income of people in the lower-income classes, this substantially raises the estimate of taxes as a proportion of income in these classes.

BOX 5-1

REAGANOMICS: ANY VERDICT YET?

> Government is not the solution to our problems. Government *is* the problem.
>
> Ronald Reagan

In the 1980 presidential campaign in the United States, the basic election promise of the Republican candidate Ronald Reagan was that if elected, he would fundamentally change the economic strategy of his Democratic predecessor Jimmy Carter. He stated two goals. First, he was going to restore fiscal responsibility by eliminating, or at least sharply reducing, the federal government deficit. His second promise was a reflection of his strongly held view that government in the United States had gone far beyond its appropriate role of providing protection from external enemies and providing domestic law and order. Government, claimed Reagan, had become intrusively involved in telling business and the public what to do. One of his objectives, said Reagan, was to "get the government off the backs of the people." By loosening the heavy hand of government, the administration hoped to invigorate the private enterprise economy, and to unleash a strong economic expansion.

When he took office in January 1981, these objectives were translated into an economic program which was quickly given the label "Reaganomics."

Courtesy Canapress Photo Service

It included the following strategic components:
1. Increase defence expenditures.
2. Restrain and, where possible, reduce domestic (non-defence) spending by the federal government.
3. Restrain the growth of government regulation.
4. Cut tax rates. Specifically, the tax law enacted in 1981 provided for tax rates to be cut in stages over the period from 1981 to 1984.

Reagan and his advisors were convinced that this strategy, and especially the tax cuts and reductions in regulation, would produce an unprecedented

sider the two red curves in Figure 5-4. The solid red line implies a highly regressive distribution of the tax burden. It results from assuming that the burden of taxes on business profits and interest income is "shifted forward" to consumers in the form of higher prices (rather than resulting in lower income of the owners of capital). The broken red line, in contrast, shows a more progressive incidence pattern; it results from taking into account the burden of future taxes on the returns to savings, as well as the burden of taxes paid this year.

While this discussion illustrates that estimates of total tax incidence must be taken with more than a

grain of salt, most of those who have worked on the incidence problem agree on one thing: The degree of progressivity in the overall tax system is considerably smaller than one would be led to believe if one simply looked at the structure of tax rates in the personal income tax. This is true not only because many other types of taxes are regressive, but also because of a variety of "loopholes," some of which provide particularly attractive opportunities for rich people to reduce their tax liabilities. Loopholes not only affect the distribution of the tax burden among income classes, but may also conflict with other criteria (such as neutrality) of a well-designed tax system.

rate of economic growth. Such a strong expansion would help increase revenues, since people must pay more in taxes when their incomes rise. Cuts in domestic programs would also help to decrease government deficits. In the early budget projections made in 1981, the administration forecast a balanced budget by the end of President Reagan's first term in 1984.

Reality turned out very differently. In fiscal 1979, Jimmy Carter's last year in office, the federal deficit was estimated at less than $30 billion. During Reagan's first four years, the deficits were $74 billion, $79 billion, $128 billion, and $208 billion. What went wrong with the early predictions? Several factors can be cited.

1. Economic expansion was much less vigorous than the administration had hoped. It is true that the economy grew at a very healthy rate in 1983–84. But this came only after the severe recession of 1981–82. Because the whole economy grew less rapidly than expected for the four years as a whole, tax revenues were much less than expected.

2. Domestic spending was a great deal more difficult to cut than expected. In particular, interest on the debt was much higher than the projections made in 1981. For example, the higher interest payments in 1984 were partly the result of federal government borrowing to finance the deficits of 1981 to 1983. In short, the deficits which the government had been running had added to interest expenditures, making it even more difficult to avoid deficits in the future.

As the second Reagan administration began in 1985, the size of the deficit, and what should be done about it, dominated the debate over economic policy. The difficulty of cutting the budget was becoming increasingly clear. One fact in particular stood out. More than two-thirds of total federal spending was in three large categories: (1) interest on the debt, which the government is contractually committed to pay; (2) national defence, which the administration was firmly determined to expand further; and (3) social security, which the President had pledged not to cut. Was it realistic to expect any sizeable cuts in spending without including items (2) and (3)? Was it realistic to expect any large reduction in the deficit without an increase in tax rates?

The deficit of the U.S. federal government affects not only the American economy, but also the world economy at large. For example, many observers have argued that the trend toward higher interest rates in international capital markets in the 1980s has been due in part to the U.S. federal deficit. (The high deficit has forced the U.S. government to borrow large amounts in the U.S. capital market, and this has driven up interest rates in the United States; higher U.S. interest rates have then led to higher interest rates in other countries as well.) For this reason, many economists outside the U.S. have been concerned about the reluctance of the American public to abandon what they see as an unwarranted faith in the simple precepts of Reaganomics; they fear that this may delay the corrective action that must be taken by the U.S. government in order to actually come to grips with the deficit.

TAX LOOPHOLES

"Loopholes" are provisions of the law which permit the reduction of taxes. Thus, those who use the loopholes are acting perfectly legally to *avoid* taxes, and should be sharply distinguished from those who act illegally to *evade* taxes, perhaps by padding their deductions or understating their incomes. The term loophole clearly implies that the tax provision is unfair, and, as there can be strong disagreement over just what is fair, there is likewise some disagreement over just what constitutes a loophole. However, here are some of the items that are often put on the list.

1. Capital Gains

When an asset is sold for more than it cost, the seller has made a capital gain. For example, if you buy stock in MacMillan Bloedel Ltd. for $1,000 and the value of the stock later rises to $1,500, you have made a capital gain of $500. Until 1985, if you actually "realized" your capital gain by selling the stock, you had to pay tax on the gain, but only at half the percentage you would pay on ordinary income such as wages and salaries. In the first budget introduced by the Mulroney government, this loophole was made even bigger: A provision was introduced which completely exempted capital gains from income tax up to a lifetime maximum of $500,000 per person. This rule clearly is of great benefit to taxpayers who receive a large portion of their income as capital gains, such as those who sell large blocks of common stock.

2. Interest, Dividend, and Capital Gains Deduction

When computing taxable income, up to $1,000 of interest and dividend income from Canadian sources may be excluded. Needless to say, the amounts excluded under this provision tend to be concentrated among taxpayers with relatively high incomes.

3. Imputed Income from Owner-Occupied Housing

The Canadian tax system favours home owners by not taxing the implicit investment income of people who own their homes. Out-of-pocket housing costs (i.e., costs of maintenance, property taxes, and mortgage payments) are lower for a homeowner than for a person who *rents* housing of a comparable standard: The difference represents a *return on the homeowner's equity*. While most other income from capital is taxed, the implicit return on homeowners' equity is not. The benefits of this loophole are greater for people with high incomes—and thus, high marginal tax rates—and expensive homes. (In some countries, including the United States, homeowners are also allowed to deduct mortgage interest from taxable income. This effectively increases the tax advantage of home ownership. Mortgage interest deductibility has never been allowed in Canada, although the Conservative government of Joe Clark was planning legislation to introduce it at the time the Liberals returned to power in 1980.)

4. Preferences to Manufacturing Industry

Corporations engaged in manufacturing and processing in Canada are treated more favourably than other firms for tax purposes. The rate of federal corporate income tax applied to manufacturing firms is 40% (as opposed to 46% for others). Manufacturing firms also benefit from special rules with respect to the deductibility over time of the costs of new capital equipment (this is called *accelerated depreciation*). In addition, many of them are protected against competition from abroad by tariffs on imported foreign goods. Since 1978, corporations investing in new productive facilities have been given an *investment tax credit* equal to 7% of the cost of the investment. Higher credits are given in so-called "slow growth areas" and in the Atlantic provinces.

5. Depletion Allowances

Industries based on natural resources—such as mining, and production of oil and natural gas—are allowed to deduct costs of exploration, drilling, and prospecting from their taxable income. In addition to this, however, they are also permitted a special deduction, called a *depletion allowance*, amounting to 25% of their net taxable income. The original purpose of the depletion allowance was to compensate the owners of the mines and wells for the decline in the value of their resource as it became depleted.

CAN WE ELIMINATE THE LOOPHOLES?

The existence of these (and other) loopholes has led to a great deal of criticism of the tax system, and, as we noted above, proposals to broaden the tax base by eliminating the loopholes have been made frequently during the debate on tax reform. Yet progress in doing this has been painfully slow. Most of the far-reaching proposals by the Carter Commission to close loopholes were not implemented. In some cases, the process of loophole closing has been retarded by criticism of the way the government has gone about it. Thus the 1981 "tax reform budget" of Finance Minister Allan MacEachen was heavily criticized for imposing heavy retroactive penalties on those who had been using loopholes that were perfectly legal before the budget. As a result of the criticism, many of the reform proposals were withdrawn, and MacEachen was replaced as Finance Minister.

Although many people agree with the general principle of closing loopholes, in practice it seems that budgets that introduce new ones (such as the 1985 budget) are more popular than the ones seeking to close old ones (such as the 1981 budget). There are several reasons for this.

First, there will always be disagreement over just what is fair. For example, most economists would probably agree that fairness would require some taxation of imputed income from owner-occupied housing, but that feeling is unlikely to be shared by the majority of the population who own homes. Indeed, many Canadians believed in the fairness of Joe Clark's proposals to give more tax relief to home owners by permitting deduction of mortgage interest from taxable income: They felt that it was no more than right that the heavily burdened middle class, to which most homeowners belong, should get this sort of a break.

A second complication is the political problem. Obviously, those who benefit from loopholes have an incentive to lobby for their continuation.

Finally, reform is complicated by the fact that fairness is only one of the major objectives in a tax system. Most of the loopholes were created with the express purpose of promoting national goals that the proponents considered important. For example, the investment tax credit was introduced to stimulate capital investment in Canada, and it was made larger in the Atlantic provinces and in certain other areas with high unemployment in order to create more industrial capacity and job opportunities in these areas. The depletion allowance and the favourable tax treatment of capital gains have been considered justified as incentives for entrepreneurs to take risks. Accelerated depreciation, lower corporate tax rates, and tariff protection of manufacturing industry are defended on the grounds that they will create a more diversified economy in Canada and reduce our traditional dependence on resource-based industries. (The pros and cons of such tariff protection are discussed later, in Chapter 32.)

Many of the activities that the tax laws seek to encourage, therefore, are those which are seen as contributing to long-standing Canadian goals such as industrialization, regional equalization, and so on. But some of the arguments for special tax treatment are more convincing than others. Furthermore, the question should be asked: Is the tax system the best tool to use in promoting diverse national goals?

Unfortunately, there is no all-purpose answer to this question. Many economists favour the use of taxes for some purposes—to discourage pollution, say. But few believe in using the tax system to favour manufacturing industry through a whole host of preferential tax rules. In taxation, as in so many areas of economics, the policy maker is left with the problem of balancing conflicting national goals.

KEY POINTS

1. The defects and limitations of the market provide the government with an important role in the economy. The government affects the economy through expenditures, taxation, and regulation.

2. In dollar terms, government spending has skyrocketed since 1926. However, as a percentage of national product, the growth of government spending has been much slower.

3. Of the federal expenditures, transfer payments have risen much more rapidly than expenditures for goods and services. "Social services" is the single largest expenditure item in the federal budget. Provincial government spending has been rising especially fast in the areas of health care and education.

4. Personal income taxes, sales and excise taxes, and corporate income taxes are the main sources of revenue for the federal and provincial governments. For local governments, property taxes are the most important. Provincial governments also benefit from revenue sharing by the federal government, and local governments receive large transfers from provincial governments.

5. Government regulatory agencies are active in many areas, regulating many activities of private firms in order to protect the public against monopolies, and from business practices such as the sale of unsafe products or destruction of the environment.

6. Federal and provincial governments operate a large number of Crown corporations. There are many reasons for establishing government-owned businesses. In markets which are natural monopolies, government ownership may be a better alternative than a regulated monopoly under private ownership, or government ownership may be the best way to meet a social objective such as the provision of television programming in remote areas. Sometimes, gov-

ernment takes over private firms as a way of protecting jobs in particular communities.

7. The primary reasons for government intervention in the economy are to:

   (a) Provide public goods that cannot be supplied by the market because individuals have no incentive to buy them; individuals get the benefits regardless of who buys.

   (b) Deal with externalities, such as pollution.

   (c) Encourage the consumption of "merit" goods, and discourage or prohibit harmful products.

   (d) Help the poor.

   (e) Help stabilize the economy.

8. A number of objectives are important in the design of a tax system:

   (a) In general, neutrality is a desirable objective.

   (b) In some cases, however, the government should alter market signals by taxation. For example, a tax can be used to discourage pollution.

   (c) Taxes should be reasonably simple and easily understood.

   (d) Taxes should be fair. There are two ways of judging fairness: the benefit principle, and ability to pay.

9. The burden or "incidence" of taxes (that is, who ultimately pays the taxes) is difficult to determine. But the rich don't bear as heavy a burden as the structure of personal income-tax rates suggests.

KEY CONCEPTS

spending	proportional tax	externality
taxation	federal-provincial transfers	merit good
public enterprise	equalization payments	tax neutrality
transfer payment	unconditional transfer	tax loophole
income tax	conditional transfer	capital gain
average tax rate	regulation	return on homeowners' equity
marginal tax rate	Crown corporation	accelerated depreciation
progressive tax	privatization	investment tax credit
regressive tax	public goods	

PROBLEMS

5-1 "That government governs best which governs least." Do you agree? Why or why not? Does the government perform more functions than it should? If so, what activities would you like it to reduce or stop altogether? Are there any additional functions that the government should undertake? If so, what ones? How should they be paid for?

5-2 "Provincial and local governments are closer to the people than the federal government. Therefore, they should be given some of the functions of the federal government." Are there federal functions that might be turned over to the provinces and municipalities? Do you think they should be turned over? Why or why not? Are there federal functions that the provinces are incapable of handling? Are there functions that the federal government can do much better than the provinces or municipalities?

5-3 The government engages in research. For example, it has agricultural experimental stations, and also undertakes defence-related research. Why do you think the government engages in these two types of research, while leaving most other research to private business? Does the government have any major advantages in undertaking research? any major disadvantages?

5-4 Consider two views of the tax system:

(a) "The government promotes social goals, such as health care research and the arts, through direct payments. It also promotes health care research and the arts by encouraging private giving. This is done by allowing gifts to be deductible from taxable income. Tax deductions may be an even more effective way of supporting health research, the arts, and other desirable causes than direct government grants. Therefore, such deductions do not constitute 'loopholes.' Rather, they represent an efficient way of achieving important social goals."

(b) "The income tax is a mess. Homeowners get a tax break, but renters do not. The rich are able to escape taxes by making gifts to universities, the arts, and to charities. The only way to get equity into the system is to eliminate all deductions, and make all income subject to tax."

Which of these arguments is stronger? Why?

Chapter 6

BUSINESS ORGANIZATION AND FINANCE

Business is a game—
the greatest game in the world if
you know how to play it.

Thomas J. Watson, Sr.,

of IBM

The government is an important participant in the Canadian economy, regulating business and providing such public goods as roads, defence, and the services of the judiciary. But the primary productive role is played by private business. Businesses use the resources of society—labour, land, and capital—to produce most of the goods and services that consumers, the government, and other businesses demand.

In future chapters, we will study the behaviour of private businesses. How much do they produce? At what prices do they sell? What combination of land, labour, and capital do they use in the productive process? How do they respond to changing market conditions? Questions such as these are central subjects of any introductory study of economics. The purpose of this chapter is to provide background on the organization of businesses and the ways in which they obtain the money to finance expansion.

BUSINESS ORGANIZATIONS

There are three types of business organization: the **single proprietorship**, the **partnership**, and the **corporation**. The single proprietorship and the partnership are the most common forms of very small business, although even a one-person business may be a corporation. At the other end of the spectrum, large businesses are almost exclusively corporations, although there are some exceptions. For example, large law firms are partnerships.

Single Proprietorships and Partnerships: Their Advantages and Disadvantages

A single proprietorship is the easiest form of business to establish; there is little fuss or bother. If I decide to make pottery in my basement, or design computer software in a spare bedroom, I may do so. I can begin tomorrow, without going through legal and organizational hassles. A single proprietorship has advantages for someone who wants to experiment with a new line of work—a fact that may explain why so many single proprietorships go out of business so quickly.

The single proprietorship is flexible and uncomplicated. The proprietor buys the materials needed, hires any help that is necessary and can be afforded, and undertakes to pay the bills. The profits of the business belong to the owner, to be shared by no one—except the government, which collects its share in the form of personal income taxes paid by the owner.

However, the single proprietorship has disadvantages. Most obviously, there are limits to how much one individual can manage. Consider a typical small enterprise, the gasoline station. In this sort of business, a single owner has problems. While help can be hired to operate the pumps, there are advantages in having someone around who is "in charge." Yet one individual would find it a crushing burden to try to be present during the long hours that a gas station is open. The obvious solution is to take on a partner, who would be jointly responsible.

Some partnerships are made up of just two people; others include dozens of partners. In a typical partnership, each partner agrees to provide some fraction of the work and some of the financing. In return, each partner receives an agreed share of the profits or suffers an agreed share of the loss. Again, the partnership is easily established; a simple oral agreement will do.

Both the single proprietorship and the partnership are simple and flexible, but they share the following major limitations:

1. If a proprietorship runs into difficulty, the owner can lose more than his or her initial investment. Personal assets may be lost in order to pay the *creditors*—that is, those to whom the business owes money. In short, a proprietor has **unlimited liability** for all the debts of the business.

In the standard type of partnership, partners similarly have unlimited liability; they can lose their personal assets, as well as the money they originally put into the business. And, with a partnership, there is a particular form of risk: *Each partner is liable for the obligations undertaken by the other partner or partners*, and each partner runs the risk of being left "holding the bag" if the other partners are unable to meet their shares of the obligations of the partnership.

2. There is a problem with **continuity**. When a single proprietor dies, the business may too—although an heir may take over the shop or farm and continue to run it. Continuity is an even more awkward problem in a partnership. When a partner dies, the original partnership automatically ends, and a new partnership must be formed. A new partnership agreement is likewise necessary whenever a new partner is admitted. This is not surprising; after all, each of the partners will be liable for the acts of the new partner.

3. There is the problem of **financing growth**. A partnership or proprietorship has a number of sources of financing: the personal wealth of the owner or owners; the profits made by the business, which can be ploughed back to purchase new equipment or buildings; the mortgaging of property; and borrowing from banks, suppliers, friends, and relatives. But proprietorships and partnerships may have difficulty borrowing the money needed for expansion. Because of the risk, banks are reluctant to lend large amounts to a struggling new enterprise.

Furthermore, it may also be difficult to bring in new owners to help with the financing. It is true that a carrot, in the form of a share of the profits, can be dangled in front of potential investors. But with the carrot comes a stick. In gaining a right to a share of the profits, a new partner also undertakes unlimited liability for the debts of the business. Consequently, outside investors will be reluctant to share in the partnership unless they have carefully investigated it and have developed an exceptionally high degree of confidence in the partners. This may make it very hard for a partnership to get the financing needed for expansion.

The Corporation

Corporation, *n.* An ingenious device for obtaining individual profit without individual responsibility.

Ambrose Bierce,
The Devil's Dictionary

The major advantage of the corporate form of organization is that it **limits the liability** of its owners: All they can lose is their initial investment. When new investors buy **shares** of the **common stock** of a business, they thereby acquire partial ownership of the business without facing the danger of unlimited liability. If the business goes bankrupt and is unable to pay its debts, the owners lose the purchase price of their shares, but not their homes or other personal property. By reducing the risks of investors, the corporate form of business makes it feasible to tap a wide pool of investment funds. Thus, the corporation is the form of business most suited to rapid growth with the use of outside funds.

> Each *share of common stock* represents a fraction of the *ownership* (that is, a fraction of the *equity* of a corporation).

Because of the limited liability, a corporation's creditors cannot lay claim to the personal property of the owners if the corporation fails—although they can claim the assets of the corporation itself. Corporations must inform those with whom they do business of this limited liability; they do so by tacking to their corporate title the designation "Ltd." or "Limited." In the United States "Inc." or "Incorporated" is used. The French and Spanish use an even more colourful warning: Corporations' titles are followed by the letters S.A.—for *Société Anonyme*, or *Sociedad Anonima* (anonymous society).

When the corporate form of business was first used in Britain some centuries ago, corporation charters were awarded only rarely, by special grants of the King and Parliament. Several of these corporations played a major role in strengthening the economic connections between Britain and the colonies, operating under the protection of British military power. They included the famous East India Company, and the Hudson's Bay Company, which was originally formed in 1670 to participate in the profitable but risky fur trade between Europe and North America.

During the nineteenth century, however, a major revolution occurred in business and legal thinking, and the modern corporation emerged. General incorporation laws were passed, granting to anyone the right to form a corporation. The formation of a corporation is generally a straightforward and uncomplicated legal procedure, although there are a few important exceptions—such as banking, where government regulation is important.

In addition to limited liability, the corporation offers the advantage of continuity. In law, the corporation is a fictitious "legal person." When one of the shareholders dies, the corporation survives; the shares of the deceased are inherited by his or her heirs, without the corporation's organization being disturbed. The heirs need not be concerned about accepting the shares, since they are not liable for the corporation's debts. Furthermore, the corporation survives if some of the shareholders want to get out of the business. These shareholders can sell their shares to anyone willing to buy; there is no need to reorganize the company.

Corporation Taxes

The profits of a proprietorship or a partnership are taxed as the personal income of the proprietor or partners. When a corporation is established, taxation becomes more complicated.

Even though a corporation is owned by its shareholders, the income earned by the corporation is not considered to be part of the shareholders' taxable income until it is actually paid out to them in the form of dividends (or until the shareholder sells the stock at a profit, in which case the profit must be shown as a capital gain). Most corporations will pay out only a part of their income as dividends and will keep the rest in the business as retained earnings (which may be used to pay off the corporation's debt, finance expansion of the business, or be invested in financial assets to earn interest).

All earnings of a corporation, whether paid out as dividends or retained in the business, are of course subject to the corporation income tax. For a wealthy person who would pay a high rate of personal income tax, the tax law may nevertheless make it profitable to incorporate his or her business. While the basic rate of corporation income tax is 46%, the owner might be able to take advantage of the lower rate of roughly 25% applicable to small corporations. As long as the owner keeps dividends low and ploughs most of the earnings back into the business, the amount of tax paid will be considerably lower than they would have been if the same business had been run as a proprietorship or partnership.

Double Taxation and the Dividend Tax Credit

While there are possible tax advantages of this kind for small corporations (and wealthy shareholders with high personal tax rates), for large corporations which pay out most of their income as dividends, the situation is quite different. In fact there is *double taxation* of the owners' income from the corporation. First, it is subject to the corporation income tax (which is levied at higher rates for large corporations), and second, the dividends paid out become subject to tax as personal income of the owners. Under earlier Canadian tax law, this double taxation led to a very high effective tax rate on dividend income, and created a strong incentive for large corporations to retain most of their earnings, so that their shareholders could avoid the second round of taxation. Under present tax rules, however, the problem of double taxation has been substantially reduced, if not entirely eliminated, by means of a **dividend tax credit**. While the detailed provisions in the law are complex, the essential idea is simple. The total amount of personal income tax payable by a recipient of dividend income from a Canadian corporation is reduced by a credit which is intended to roughly represent the recipient's share of the income tax paid by the corporation. The result is that the total tax paid on corporate income paid out as dividends is similar to what it would have been if it had been treated as personal income of the shareholder in the first place—that is, before payment of corporation income tax.

Eliminating the double taxation of dividend income clearly has reduced the incentive for corporations to keep most of their profits as retained earnings. However, the change in the capital gains taxation introduced in Finance Minister Michael Wilson's budget in 1985 worked in the other direction. Shareholders in corporations that retain most of their earnings will usually experience a capital gain, as the value of the corporation's shares increases to reflect the reinvested profits. But under the new tax rules, much of such capital gains are non-taxable even if the shareholder "realizes" his or her capital gain by selling the shares.

HOW A CORPORATION FINANCES EXPANSION

The corporation can obtain funds for expansion in the same way as a proprietorship or partnership; that is, by borrowing from banks or ploughing profits back into the business. But a large corporation also has other options. It can issue common stock, bonds, or other securities.

Common Stock

When it sells additional shares of common stock, the corporation takes on new part-owners, since each share represents a fraction of the ownership of the corporation. As a part-owner, the purchaser of common stock not only receives a share of any dividends paid by the corporation, but also gets the right to vote for the corporation's directors who, in turn, choose the corporate officers and set the corporation's policies. (On the question of who actually controls a corporation, see Box 6-1.)

Bonds

Rather than take on new owners by issuing additional common stock, the corporation may raise funds by selling bonds. A **bond** represents debt of the corporation; it is an I.O.U. that the corporation is obliged to repay, whether it is making profits or not. If the corporation doesn't pay, it can be sued by the bondholder.

A bond is a long-term form of debt which does not fall due for repayment until 10, 15, or more years from the time it was initially sold (issued) by the corporation. Bonds usually come in large denominations—for example, $100,000. The original buyer normally pays the corporation a sum equal to the face value of the bond; in effect, the original buyer is lending $100,000 to the corporation. In return for the $100,000, the corporation is committed to make two sets of payments to the bondholder:

1. Interest payments that must be made periodically— normally semiannually—during the life of the bond. If the interest rate is, say, 14% per annum on a bond with a $100,000 face value, the interest payment will be $7,000 (that is, 7%) every 6 months.
2. A payment of the $100,000 **face value**, or **principal**, when the date of maturity arrives. That is, the corporation must repay the amount of the loan at maturity.

Since a bond commits the corporation to make the payments of interest and principal, it provides the purchaser with an assured, steady income—provided the corporation avoids bankruptcy. Common stock, on the other hand, involves a substantial risk. During periods of difficulty, the corporation may reduce or eliminate the dividend, and the market price of the stock may plummet. But, while bonds provide more safety than stocks, they offer less excitement. Unlike the owner of common stock, the bondholder cannot look forward to rising dividends if the company hits

---

BOX 6-1

WHO CONTROLS THE CORPORATION?

Because shareholders elect the board of directors, who in turn choose management, it would seem at first glance that the corporation is run in the interest of its shareholders.

However, things are not necessarily that simple. If a company's stock is spread among a large number of shareholders, it may, in practice, be run by a group of insiders made up of the directors and senior management. The small shareholder's problem is akin to that of the consumer. In both cases, the stakes are not sufficiently great for the individual shareholders or consumers to make their views known forcefully. If you own only a few shares of stock, it is probably not even worth your time and your travel expenses to show up at the annual meeting. Furthermore, unless the corporation is doing very badly, you are likely to grant the management's request for your proxy. That is, you give them the authorization to vote on your behalf at the annual meeting. As a result, management is likely to be in control at the annual meeting.

This does not, however, mean that the management is absolutely immune from challenge: If the corporation's performance is weak, a dissident group of shareholders can get together. They may be successful in getting enough proxies to oust the old management. But this occurs only rarely. Throwing out management is a drastic step, which dis-

rupts the everyday operation of the company. The standard advice given in the investment community is this. If you don't like the way the company is being run, don't fight management. Sell your stock. Vote with your feet.

The separation of ownership and control was pointed out in *The Modern Corporation and Private Property* by A.A. Berle and Gardner C. Means, published in 1932. They found that the stockholding of 44% of the 200 largest U.S. corporations was so diffuse that no single family, corporation, or group of business associates owned as much as 10% of the stock. More recent work indicates that, by 1963, control was even more separated from ownership than it had been when Berle and Means wrote: What was true of 44% of the 200 largest corporations in the earlier period was by then true of 84.5%.

Where control is effectively in the hands of management rather than the owners, the question arises as to what difference this makes. There is an obvious community of interest between management and shareholders: Both groups want a corporation which is profitable. Management is obviously interested in the success of the corporation, since their jobs may be lost if the corporation goes under.

But, while similar, the interests of management and shareholders are not identical. Management may be more interested in the preservation of their jobs than in profits. Furthermore, management—like a government bureaucracy—may be interested in growth for its own sake, even if growth does not contribute to profits. Why is this so? The importance of your position is in part measured by the number of people who work for you.

---

the jackpot. The bondholder will get no more than the interest and principal specified in the bond contract. Generally, bonds are safe; but they are also dull.

Bonds are not the only type of debt which a corporation can issue. It may also issue *notes*, which are similar to bonds, except that they have only a few years to maturity. *Commercial paper* is even shorter-term, normally being issued for just a few months.

Some investors desire an income-earning security

"between stocks and bonds"; that is, one that will provide more safety than common stock, while still offering a larger potential return than bonds if the company does well. These investors may choose *convertible bonds* or *preferred stock*.

Convertible Bonds
Convertible bonds are like ordinary bonds, with one additional feature. Prior to a given date, they may be

exchanged for common stock in some fixed ratio—for example, 1 bond for 10 shares of common stock. If the outlook for the corporation becomes favourable, the holder of convertible bonds may exchange them for common stock, and thus own shares of the growing corporation. If, on the other hand, the company fails to prosper, convertible bonds may be held to maturity, when the bondholder will receive repayment of the principal.

Because the holder has the option of converting, the interest rate on convertible bonds is normally less than the rate on regular bonds, often substantially less. Therefore, if you are thinking about buying convertible bonds, you have to weigh two conflicting considerations. The interest payments which you receive will be low. But you will have the option to convert into common stock, an option which may become valuable in the event that the business is successful.

Preferred Stock

Preferred stock, like common stock, represents ownership, and not debt. The corporation is legally obligated to make interest payments to bondholders, but it is not legally required to pay dividends to preferred or common shareholders.

Preferred shareholders, however, have a claim on profits which precedes—or "is preferred to"—the claim of the common shareholder. The preferred shareholder has a right to receive specific dividends (for example, $2 per share) before the common shareholder can be paid any dividend at all. But, on the other hand, the preferred shareholder does not have the possibility of large gains that is open to the common shareholder. While the common shareholder may hope for rising dividends if the corporation prospers, the preferred shareholder will at most receive the specified dividend. (A rare form of stock, the *participating preferred*, provides an exception to this rule. It gives the holder the right to participate in the growth of the company's dividends.)

As a general rule, all types of securities—common stock, preferred stock, and bonds—may be resold by the original purchasers. Securities prices tend to reflect the judgement of buyers and sellers regarding the prospects of the corporation. Thus, for example, an announcement of a new product may make purchasers eager to buy the company's stock, and make present shareholders reluctant to sell. As a result, the price of

the stock will be bid up. Purchasers also look at the position and performance of the company as indicated by a study of its financial accounts.

BUSINESS ACCOUNTING: THE BALANCE SHEET AND THE INCOME STATEMENT

Business accounts are valuable not only as a source of information for potential buyers of the company's stock or bonds. They are also an important tool for helping management keep track of how well the company is doing, and what it is worth. In addition, businesses are required to keep accounts for tax purposes.

There are two major types of business accounts:

1. The **balance sheet**, which gives a picture of the company's financial status at a point in time; for example, at the close of business on December 31 of last year.
2. The **income statement**—also called the **profit and loss statement**—which summarizes the company's transactions over a *period* of time, such as a year.

The income statement records the *flow* of payments into and out of a company *over a period* of time. It is like a record of the amount of water that has flowed into and out of Lake Huron *during* a year. The balance sheet, on the other hand, measures the situation *at a specific point* in time. It is like a measure of the *stock* of water in Lake Huron today at noon.

The Balance Sheet

The balance sheet shows (1) the **assets** that a company owns, (2) the **liabilities** that it owes, and (3) the value of the **ownership** of the shareholders. Assets must be exactly equal to the total of liabilities plus ownership. To use a simple illustration: If you have a car worth $7,000 (an asset), for which you still owe $4,000 to the bank (your debt or liability), then $3,000 is the value of your ownership in the car.

The same fundamental equation also holds for a corporation:

$$Assets = liabilities \text{ (what is owed) } + net\ worth \text{ (the value of ownership)}$$

Assets are listed on the left side of the balance sheet, while liabilities and net worth are listed on the right. Because of the fundamental equation, the two sides must add to the same total. **The balance sheet must balance**.

> The *net worth* of a corporation—the amount the shareholders own—is equal to the assets minus the liabilities of the corporation.

As an example, consider Table 6-1, which shows the balance sheet of Northern Telecom Limited, of Toronto, a producer of telephone switchboard systems and other equipment.

The left-hand, asset side. Northern Telecom has sizeable assets in the form of cash (bank accounts), marketable short-term securities issued by other corporations or the government, and accounts receivable—for example, the value of communications systems which have already been delivered to customers but not yet paid for. It has sizeable inventories of materials and parts, and of terminals and office equipment ready for sale. It also has major assets in the form of land, plant (buildings), and equipment.

The right-hand side (liabilities and net worth). Northern Telecom has a number of short-term liabilities: amounts that the company has not yet paid for the copper, plastics, and other material it has bought from suppliers (accounts payable); wages and salaries not yet paid for work already performed (accrued liabilities); and other short-term debt. In addition, at the end of 1984, Northern Telecom had an outstanding long-term debt of $416 million. (If debt matures within one year, it is short term; in more than one year, long term.)

At the end of 1984, Northern Telecom's total assets were $4.06 billion, and its liabilities were $2.24 billion. The net worth—the ownership of all shareholders—was therefore $1.82 billion. Of this, a little less than half ($798 million) had been paid in by shareholders purchasing shares from the company. The rest ($1,024 million) represented retained earnings; that is, profits made over the years that had been ploughed back into the business.[1]

At the end of 1984, there were about 115 million shares of Northern Telecom common stock outstanding. Each share represented an equity, or **book value**, of around $15.80—that is, $1,822 million in net worth ÷ 115 million shares.

> The *book value* of a stock is its net worth per share. It is calculated by dividing the total net worth of the company by the number of shares outstanding.

If you are thinking of buying common stock of a company, its book value is one of the things that should interest you. If it has a high book value, you will be buying ownership of a lot of assets. However, don't get carried away by a high book value. If the assets happen to be machinery and equipment that can be used only to produce buggy whips or other items for which there is no demand, the high book value may not be worth very much; the assets may not earn much income in the future. On the other hand, the stock of a profitable corporation like Northern Telecom may sell for substantially more than its book value. During 1984, Northern Telecom stock sold in the range between $38.75 and $55.16.

The Income Statement

While the balance sheet shows the assets, liabilities, and net worth of a corporation at a point in time, the income statement shows what has happened *during a period of time*—for example, during a calendar year. A simplified version of Northern Telecom's income statement for the year 1984 is shown in Table 6-2.

During that year, the company had $4.462 billion in revenues, mostly from the sale and servicing of telephone equipment. Costs of $3.971 billion must be subtracted from revenues to calculate before-tax profit of $491 million. Corporate income taxes were $157

---

[1]"Retained earnings" may sound like a pool of funds which the corporation has readily available. However, this is generally not the case. Most retained earnings are not held in the form of cash; most are used to buy equipment or other items.

Suppose that, in the first year of its operation, a corporation earns $1,000, and retains it all. (It pays no dividend.) The $1,000 may be used to buy a new machine. Then, as a result, the following changes occur in the balance sheet:

Change in			
Assets		Net worth	
Machinery	+$1,000	Retained earnings	+$1,000

The retained earnings have not been held in the form of idle cash; they have been put to work to buy machinery. The machinery shows up on the asset side. When the retained earnings are included in net worth, the balance sheet balances.

million, leaving an after-tax profit of $334 million, or $2.90 per share. Of this after-tax profit, $62 million was paid in dividends to shareholders, and $272 million was retained by the company. Observe that the retained earnings in Table 6-1 are substantially greater than those shown in Table 6-2. The reason is this: The income statement in Table 6-2 shows only the retained earnings during the one year, 1984. In contrast, the balance sheet in Table 6-1 shows all retained earnings accumulated over the entire lifetime of the company.

Most of Northern Telecom's costs are reasonably straightforward. The company pays wages to its work force, buys materials from outside suppliers, and spends large sums on research and development. These costs are included in items 3(a), 3(b), and 3(d) in Table 6-2. However, one cost item, **depreciation** (line 3(c)), needs to be explained. Depreciation is a way of spreading out the costs of plant and equipment used by a firm.

Depreciation

Consider the specific example of a machine acquired by Northern Telecom during 1984 for use on its production line. This machine did not wear out during 1984; it will continue to be used in coming years. Therefore, in calculating the cost of production in 1984, it would be misleading to count the full purchase price of the machine. Instead, only a fraction is counted as a cost during 1984, with other fractions being allocated to future years while the machine is still in use.

The most straightforward way to allocate the cost of a machine is to estimate its expected life, and then spread the cost evenly over the lifetime. For example, if a $10,000 machine were expected to last five years, then depreciation would be $2,000 in each of these years.

Depreciation accounting is not an exact science. Not only does the useful lifetime of a machine depend on physical wear and tear, but it also depends on obsolescence, which cannot be accurately forecast. Even if a machine could be permanently maintained in brand-new condition, it would eventually become obsolete; that is, its useful life would end as new and more efficient machines became available. (Obsolescence tends to be greatest for high-technology equipment. An early computer, built in 1946 at the University of Pennsylvania, contained 18,000 vacuum tubes, weighed 30 tons, and occupied a huge room, with other large areas needed for air conditioning. Now, a chip with greater computing capacity may be held on the tip of your finger.)

However, an even greater complication arises because of the tax laws. Note that depreciation is a cost which is subtracted before taxable income is calculated (Table 6-2). As a result, firms have an incentive to take their depreciation as soon as the law permits. The more depreciation they take, the lower is their taxable income, and therefore the lower is their tax. If the government speeds up—or *accelerates*—the rate at which firms are allowed to depreciate plant and equipment, it can encourage them to invest and expand.

> *Depreciation* is an element of cost. It is either (1) an estimate of the decline in the value of plant or equipment during the year, because of wear and obsolescence; or (2) the amount which tax laws allow business to count as a cost of using plant or equipment during the year.

FINANCIAL MARKETS

As we have seen, corporations may finance expansion by retaining their profits or by looking outside for sources of funds. They may borrow from banks, insurance companies, or other financial corporations. Or they may issue additional stocks or bonds. Financial markets and financial institutions perform a strategic role in the economy because they help to determine which businesses will receive the finances for expansion.

Financial institutions, such as banks, trust companies, and insurance companies, are **financial intermediaries**. That is, they take small amounts of funds from a large number of people, pool these funds, and lend them in larger amounts to businesses, governments, or individuals. For example, a trust company may receive 100 small deposits with an average size of $300. With the combined total of $30,000, it makes a mortgage loan to someone buying a house. In doing this, the trust company provides a useful service. The home buyer is saved the trouble of trying to locate the 100 individuals who would be willing to put up small amounts. The people who provide the funds are saved the nuisance of lending directly to the homeowner and of collecting on the loan every month. In addition to

Table 6-1
Northern Telecom Balance Sheet, December 31, 1984
(Simplified; millions of dollars)

Assets			Liabilities and Net Worth		
1. Current assets		$2,379	6. Current Liabilities		$1,238
(a) Cash & short term Investments	$ 95		(a) Notes Payable	$ 118	
(b) Accounts receivable	1,119		(b) Accounts Payable and accrued liabilities	1,120	
(c) Inventories	1,145		7. Long-term Debt		416
(d) Other current assets	20		To subsidiary companies	283	
2. Plant and equipment		1,145	To others	133	
3. Investments in subsidiary companies		478	8. Other Liabilities		584
4. Other assets		57			
5. Total assets (Items 1 + 2 + 3 + 4)		$4,060*	9. Total Liabilities		2,238
			10. Net Worth (5 − 9)		1,822
			(a) Capital stock	798	
			(b) Retained earnings	1,024	
			11. Total Liabilities and Net Worth (9 + 10)		$4,060

*Totals inexact due to rounding.
SOURCE: Adapted, with permission, from Northern Telecom Limited, *Annual Report*, 1984.

Table 6-2
Northern Telecom Income Statement
for the Year 1984
(Simplified, millions of dollars)

1. Sales revenue		$4,379
2. Investment income*		83
3. Less: Costs of operations		3,904
(a) Wages, salaries, and employee benefits	$1,770	
(b) Research and development costs	432	
(c) Depreciation	211	
(d) All other operating costs	1,491	
4. Less: Interest costs		67
5. Earnings (profit) before taxes (1 + 2 − 3 − 4)		491
6. Less: Corporation income taxes		157
7. Net earnings (net profit) (5 − 6)		334
(a) Dividends	62	
(b) Retained earnings	272	

*Includes earnings on equity in non-consolidated subsidiaries.

SOURCE: Adapted, with permission, from Northern Telecom Limited, *Annual Report*, 1984.

handling the paperwork, the trust company investigates the credit-worthiness of the potential home buyer, thus limiting the risk that the loan will not be repaid.[2] Similarly, banks and insurance companies take funds from deposits or insurance policies, pool them, and lend them to businesses, governments, or individuals who meet their standards of credit-worthiness.

Thus, a business that wants to borrow money may go to a bank or an insurance company. But what does a business do if it prefers not to borrow, and wants to raise money by selling its common stock instead? It may follow one of two courses. If it is a large corporation that already has many shareholders, it can give the current shareholders the rights or *warrants* to buy new stock at a specific price. It normally sets this price below the current market price of the stock, in order to give the shareholders an incentive to exercise the rights—that is, to use the warrants to buy stock at the bargain price. Those who already have all the stock

[2]In addition to their deposit and loan business, trust companies provide a variety of financial management services (managing the assets of estates, pension funds, and so on). Most of their incomes are in fact derived from these services.

they want can sell the warrants to someone who wants to use them to buy the bargain stock. Thus, the corporation ends up by selling the new shares of its stock either to current shareholders or to those who have bought the warrants.

Since a new company does not already have a large number of shareholders, it will use a different method of selling stock. It will approach an **investment dealer**, a firm that markets securities. The investment dealer looks for profits in the mark-up between the price she pays to the company for the stock and the price at which she sells this stock to the public. The investment dealer may simply undertake to sell as many shares as she can, up to the maximum the company is willing to issue. In this case, the company takes a risk. If buyers are unreceptive, few shares will be sold and the company will raise only a little money. However, if the dealer is confident regarding the prospects of the company, she may **underwrite** the stock issue; that is, guarantee the sale of the full issue of stock. If she is unable to find buyers for the whole issue, the investment dealer will end up buying the shares herself. In order to limit risk, she may bring in other investment dealers to form a **syndicate** which jointly underwrites the new issue.

Investment dealers may also underwrite corporation bonds. As part of their business, dealers keep close contact with pension funds and other large-scale purchasers of securities. Among the largest investment dealers are Dominion Securities Pitfield, Wood Gundy, Burns Fry, and Richardson Greenshields of Winnipeg.

The Objectives of Buyers of Securities

In some ways, the markets for stocks and bonds are similar to the markets for shirts, shoes, or automobiles. For example, just as the automobile dealer makes profits by the mark-up on cars, so the investment dealer makes profits by the mark-up on stocks and bonds. Nevertheless, in one very important way, the market for stocks and bonds is quite different from the market for shoes or cars. When you want to buy a pair of shoes or a car, you can examine the available merchandise and make a reasonably good judgment as to its quality. But when you buy common stock, you are, in effect, buying a future prospect—something which is clearly intangible and about which it may be very difficult to reach an informed and balanced judgement. Similarly, when you buy a bond, you are buying

a set of promises made by the bond issuer to pay interest and principal on schedule.

Because of the uncertainty of the future, purchasers do not simply choose the bond that has the highest interest rate; the likelihood that the company will actually repay is also important. Indeed, purchasers of securities have three objectives to balance: return, risk, and liquidity.

Return is the annual yield, measured as a percentage of the cost of the security. For example, if a bond is purchased for $10,000 and it pays interest of $1,200 per year, then it yields 12%.

Risk is the chance that something will go wrong. For example, the company may go bankrupt and the bondholder may lose both interest and principal.

Finally, **liquidity** reflects the ability of the owner to sell an asset on short notice, with little cost and bother. A passbook account in a trust company is highly liquid. Unless the trust company has run into financial difficulty, the account may be withdrawn at any time for its full dollar value. (Thus, in addition to handling paperwork and evaluating borrowers' credit-worthiness, trust companies and other financial intermediaries provide their depositors with liquidity.) At the other end of the spectrum, real estate or paintings are very illiquid. If you have to sell your home on short notice, you may have to accept a price that is much lower than you could get with a more lengthy selling effort.

While investors look for a combination of high return, low risk, and high liquidity, they do not all weigh the three objectives equally. Some—particularly those with steady incomes who are saving for the distant future—do not consider liquidity important, while others (perhaps those with children about to enter university) want to keep liquid investments on which they can draw in the near future. Different investors may have quite different attitudes toward risk.

The Objectives of Issuers of Securities

A private company raising funds also has three objectives to balance: to obtain funds in such a way as to achieve a high *return* for the corporation's shareholders; to avoid *risk*; and to ensure the *availability* of money when it is needed.

A corporation balances risk and return when it chooses whether to issue stocks or bonds. In contrast with the view from the buyer's side, the view of the corporation selling securities is that *bonds* have a *higher* risk than common stock. If the corporation sells bonds, interest payments must be made no matter how badly the company may be doing. Thus, a large outstanding debt can put a corporation in a precarious position. If business slackens, it may be unable to meet large payments for interest and principal, and may as a result be driven into bankruptcy. There is no such risk with common stock, since the company can cut dividends in the event of a downturn in business.

While it is safer for a corporation to issue stock, there is a disadvantage. Additional stock involves taking on new part-owners. If the company does well, the rising profits go partially to the new shareholders; the original stockholders must share their bonanza. In contrast, consider what happens if bonds are issued—that is, if the **leverage** of the corporation is increased. After the required payment of interest on the bonds, any large profits go only to the original shareholders. Thus, the more highly leveraged a corporation is, the greater is the uncertainty for its owners. Their potential gain is large, but so is their potential loss, including the possibility of bankruptcy.

> *Leverage* is the ratio of debt to net worth. If this ratio is large, the corporation is *highly leveraged.*

As a group, shareholders and corporate managers tend to be optimistic. They consequently may try to maximize their expected gains by a high degree of leverage. Furthermore, limited liability provides an incentive for leverage. If things go well, shareholders can earn many times their original investment. But if things go poorly, they can lose their original investment only once. Thus, a company may be highly leveraged in order to keep the potential gains in the hands of a few shareholders, while much of the risk is borne by bondholders and other creditors. Even though a company takes risk into account when it issues stocks or bonds, it has a temptation to discount the importance of risk, since someone else will suffer much of the possible loss.

If corporate managers were free to leverage to their hearts' content, the economy might be wildly unstable. When businesses go bankrupt, their employees may be thrown out of work, and other businesses to whom they owe money may also go bankrupt. Fortunately, however, there are limits to leverage. As leverage

increases, the rising risks to bondholders make them cautious. They become increasingly reluctant to buy that company's bonds unless the bonds yield a very high interest. If leverage becomes great enough, the company may find it impossible to sell bonds or to borrow from banks or others. Leverage is limited by the caution of lenders.

The final objective of corporations issuing securities is to ensure the availability of money when it is needed. As a general rule, it is not advisable to finance a new factory with short-term borrowing. It is unwise to have to keep repaying a short-term debt and borrowing money again each year to finance a factory over, say, a 20-year lifetime. In some of those years, funds may not be available to borrowers, or be available only at a very high interest rate. New factories should therefore be financed by long-term borrowing or by the issue of additional stock or by retained profits.

In order to ensure the availability of money for unpredictable requirements that can arise, a corporation may arrange a **line of credit** at a bank. A line of credit is a commitment by a bank to lend up to a specified limit at the request of the company. Similarly, builders may get commitments from trust companies to provide mortgage money in the future. Such commitments allow builders to make firm plans for construction.

The Bond Market

Because security buyers balance risk and return, risky securities generally must have higher yields, or nobody will buy them. This shows up in bond market yields: Riskier bonds will yield a **risk premium**, making their returns higher than those of safer bonds.

> A *risk premium* is the difference between the yields on two grades of bonds because of differences in their risk.

While the most important reason for differences in bond yields is difference in risk, other influences are at work as well. There are very large quantities of Canadian government bonds outstanding, and the market for these bonds is very active, with relatively small selling costs. (The gap is small between the "bid" price, at which bond dealers are ready to buy, and the "offer" price, at which they are ready to sell.) For this reason, government bonds provide a liquidity advantage; less

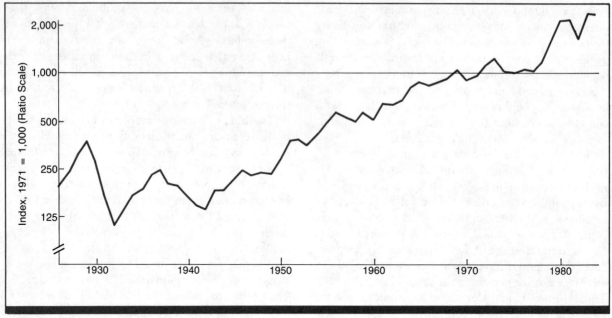

Figure 6-1 Canadian Stock Prices, 1926–1985.
The biggest swing in stock prices, in percentage terms, took place during the rising "bull" market of the 1920s and the collapsing "bear" market of 1929–32. In the 25 years following World War II, average stock prices rose about five-fold. During most of the 1970s, stock prices remained fairly stable, but they rose substantially during 1977–81. Following a steep decline in the 1982 recession, they again rose rapidly from 1982 to 1985. (Note: The vertical axis is drawn with a ratio, or logarithmic, scale. As explained in the appendix to Chapter 1, equal vertical distances represent equal percentage changes. For example, the distance from 100 to 200 is the same as the distance from 200 to 400.)
Source: Compiled from Statistics Canada, *CANSIM Databank.* Reproduced by permission of the Minister of Supply and Services Canada.

loss results if the buyer has to turn around quickly and sell them. Thus, federal government bonds have low yields for two reasons: Because they are highly liquid, and because they carry little or no risk. (In an extreme situation, the federal government has the constitutional right to print money to pay interest and principal on its bonds.)

Another notable feature in the bond market over the past few decades was the sharp upward movement of all interest rates between 1965 and 1981. An important reason for this was the acceleration of inflation during that period. When inflation is high, bondholders recognize that interest and principal will be repaid in the future when money is less valuable than at present. They therefore hesitate to purchase bonds unless interest rates are high enough to compensate for the declining value of money. Since 1981, the rate of inflation has declined, and interest rates have receded, especially in 1984 and 1985.

The Stock Market

Stocks of major corporations already held by the public are usually bought and sold on the stock exchanges, such as those in Toronto, Montreal, and Vancouver. Stockbrokers throughout the country maintain close contact with the exchanges, buying and selling stocks on behalf of their customers.

A *broker* acts as a representative of a buyer or seller, offering to buy or sell on behalf of clients.

Prices fluctuate on the stock exchanges in response to changes in demand and supply. Stock purchasers are interested in such things as the current and expected future profits of the corporation. Thus, stock prices may rise rapidly during periods of prosperity, when profit prospects appear good.

In the 1920s, the desire to "get rich quick" in the

stock market became a national mania. With stocks rising, many investors learned that individuals, too, could use leverage to increase their potential gains; they borrowed large sums to buy stocks in the expectation that their prices would rise. Then came the Great Crash of 1929.[3] As Figure 6-1 shows, by 1932 stock prices had fallen to a fraction of their 1929 values. Many investors were wiped out, especially investors who had borrowed heavily to speculate in the stock market during the 1929 boom.

Another major upswing in stock averages occurred in the 1950s and 1960s, when the Canadian economy had the longest continuous expansion on record. Common stock promised a share in the nation's prosperity. And they were widely looked on as a hedge against inflation. After all, stock represents ownership of corporations, and in a period of inflation, the dollar value of a corporation's plant and equipment should rise with the general increase in prices. This comforting viewpoint was plausible, but it was not borne out by unfolding events. From the late 1960s to 1977, stock prices rose very little, even though inflationary pressures accelerated. During most of the 1970s, stock market participants came to the view that inflation was very unhealthy for the economy, and signs of accelerating inflation were generally followed by declines in stock prices.

Between 1977 and 1981, Canadian stock prices rose rapidly. The popular Toronto Stock Exchange stock price index (the TSE 300 Composite Index) more than doubled during this period. In part, this was explained by the dramatic rise in the share values of Canada's energy resource companies in response to the increase in world oil prices in the 1979–80 period. While stock prices fell sharply during the 1981–82 recession, as Figure 6-1 shows, they rose steadily once again from 1982 to 1986. One reason for this increase was the strong expansion from the recession. Another was that inflation appeared to be under much better control than during the 1970s. Stock prices in the United States also rose substantially during this period. This was not unusual: Canadian and U.S. stock markets often move along broadly similar trends.

---

[3]For some of the drama of the collapse, see John Kenneth Galbraith, *The Great Crash, 1929* (Boston: Houghton Mifflin, 1961); or Frederick Lewis Allen, *The Lords of Creation* (New York: Harper, 1935), chap. 13.

CAPITAL MARKETS: TWO IMPORTANT PROBLEMS

The economic function of the markets for financial capital is similar to the function of markets for goods: They help to determine what will be produced in the economy. For example, if a private company develops a new product for which there is a large demand, its profits will likely rise, and it will have relatively little trouble raising funds for expansion by borrowing or by issuing stock. In this way, the company will be able to produce quickly the item in demand.

There are, however, special problems in the capital markets. First, because of difficulty in evaluating future investment prospects, money may be directed into the wrong industries or to the wrong firms. Second, private capital markets do not assure that there will be the right total quantity of investment in the economy.

The Problem of Information: Will Funds Go to the "Right" Industries?

When a company raises funds, it usually does this in order to finance expansion or new investment projects. But many investment projects (such as development and marketing of a new product, for example) are intrinsically risky. A project may go wrong for all sorts of reasons. Unexpected technical difficulties may cause cost overruns. Once a product is introduced, it may turn out that the market for it is smaller than estimated. Some projects even fail because there was no serious intention of carrying them out in the first place.

History is full of overoptimistic promoters and artful swindlers, ranging from John Law (whose Mississippi Company first provided speculative riches and then financial disaster for its shareholders in eighteenth-century Paris), to Charles Ponzi, to recent con men like Bernard Cornfeld. (Ponzi used a masterfully simple scheme to swindle more than $10 million from Bostonians in 1919–1920. His operation declared large fictitious profits, and paid dividends on outstanding stock by selling new stock which investors snapped up because of the high "profits" and dividends. Cornfeld's Investors' Overseas Service separated many Europeans and Canadians from their savings.)

When resources are invested in honest projects that fail, or in projects that are just a cover for a swindle, not only will those who have invested lose some or even all of their money; there is also a loss to society of the alternative projects that could have been financed. To protect investors from swindlers, and to help reduce the amount of resources wasted on honest but badly conceived projects, there is a strong case for regulation which requires those issuing securities to disclose full information about how the funds are going to be used. The more information that is available to investors, the better the chances that funds will flow to genuinely profitable projects.

In the Canadian financial system, regulation concerning disclosure and information is enforced by agencies such as the Ontario Securities Commission. Before offering securities to the public, companies are required to issue a **prospectus**, which is a formal statement presenting information on the current position and the future prospects of the corporation. Firms whose shares are widely traded are required to make their accounts public and to announce significant developments which may affect the price of their stock.

By and large, regulation has made financial markets function more efficiently and prevented swindles of the type that were common in the 1920s (though it did not succeed in keeping Cornfeld out of Canada). And if regulation cannot prevent the occasional spectacular financial debacle (such as the losses suffered by many of those who helped finance Dome Petroleum's takeovers of oil and gas firms shortly before world oil prices started falling in 1981–82), at least it can ensure that investors know what the odds are before they decide to risk their money.

The Capital Market and Government Enterprise
Private firms that have to rely on the capital market to raise funds for their investment projects have every incentive to come up with projects that promise a reasonable profit and yet involve relatively low risk. If they can't, they will have difficulty attracting funds. After all, investors in the capital market are putting their own money at risk. But as we saw in Chapter 5, a large share of investment in Canada is undertaken by firms that are government-owned. The incentives facing government-owned firms are likely to be different from those facing private firms, for several reasons.

First, government-owned firms such as Crown corporations are often required by the government to carry out tasks that are not commercially profitable and would not be done voluntarily if profits were the sole concern of the corporation. If they are to do this, the corporations must be funded even if they don't earn a competitive rate of return. Second, in some cases governments finance corporations to do potentially profitable projects that private firms are not willing to undertake because they are too risky. In such cases, there are bound to be failures from time to time. Third, those who decide whether or not to allocate more funds to government firms are civil servants and politicians. Since the money they put on the line is not their own, they may not be quite as concerned with the return on their investment as a private investor would be. For all these reasons, the penalty suffered by a government-owned firm which incurs losses is likely to be less severe than it would be for a privately owned firm.

The question of providing the right balance between the incentives to direct society's resources toward profitable investment opportunities and the incentives to avoid expensive "white elephant" projects is an important one for any economy. It is inevitable that large sums are sometimes channelled into honest projects that fail. As the examples of the ill-fated Ford Edsel in the 1950s and the Dome Petroleum story demonstrate, it can happen in the private sector, as well as in government-owned business. But some of the largest money losers in recent years have been projects financed by governments. In Europe, the supersonic Concorde has cost taxpayers enormous sums. In Canada, the list includes the Bricklin sports car (financed in part by the government of New Brunswick), the huge oil refinery at Come-by-Chance (government of Newfoundland), and the Canadair Challenger (federal government). Trying to prevent this list from growing longer in future years is one of the main challenges for Canada's economic policy makers.

Capital Markets and the Problem of Instability
When an economy is operating at full employment, it is producing all, or nearly all, that it can with its limited labour force and capital stock. If large additional investment is undertaken in one area, cutbacks must be made elsewhere.

However, consider the problem when the economy moves down into a recession or a depression. Then there are large amounts of unemployed labour and unused plant and equipment. The decision to proceed with one investment—such as a factory to build computers—no longer requires that we forego an alternative investment (such as an additional plant for the lumber industry). They can both be built by putting unemployed labour and unemployed equipment back to work. Indeed, if the downward slide of the economy is severe, there are available resources to produce a lot of additional capital goods of all sorts—and additional consumer goods, too. The important question ceases to be which of the competing investments is better; for example, would it be better to invest in the aircraft industry or the lumber industry? Rather, the central issue becomes: How do we get more investment in both the aircraft industry and the lumber industry—and in other industries, too?

The private financial markets do a moderately good job in determining relative risks and rewards, and thus do a moderately good job of determining which investments will be undertaken. But they suffer major shortcomings in dealing with the question that becomes important during recessions—how can the total amount of investment be increased? Consider what happened as the economy collapsed into the Depression of the 1930s. Stock market investors became panic-stricken as stock prices plummeted. At the very low prices of the Depression, the stock market was no longer an attractive place for corporations to raise funds. For a corporation to sell stock in those days meant that current shareholders were practically giving away part of their ownership to new buyers. Similarly, with the widespread difficulties of business, risk premiums on bonds rose sharply. For much of the 1930s, there was no overall shortage of funds that banks and others had available for investment. The interest rate on risk-free federal government bonds was very low. But funds were not cheap for many businesses because of extremely high risk premiums. As a result, investment was discouraged, and this deepened the Depression.

Low stock prices and high borrowing costs were not the only reasons that investment dried up during the Depression. Many business executives were so terrified that they would not have undertaken expansion even if funds had been available at very low interest rates. Their pessimism and lack of investment were not the result of a lack of information. During the 1930s, business was indeed faced with appalling prospects; an individual with perfect information would still not have invested.

Because private financial markets do not necessarily result in a stable economy, the responsibility for ensuring stability has fallen to the federal government. How the government can fulfill this responsibility is a major topic of Parts 2, 3 and 4 of this book.

KEY POINTS

1. There are three forms of business organization: (a) single proprietorships; (b) partnerships; and (c) corporations.

2. Single proprietorships and partnerships are simple and flexible. On the other hand, the advantages of the corporate form of organization are (a) limited liability; (b) automatic continuity, even if one or more of the owners should die; and (c) better access to funds for financing growth.

3. A corporation can obtain financing by issuing (selling) common or preferred stock, and bonds.

4. There are two main types of business accounts. The *balance sheet* shows assets, liabilities, and net worth at a *point* in time. The *income statement* reports sales, costs, and profits during a *period* of time.

5. A financial intermediary takes funds from individual savers and pools these funds to lend to businesses, governments, or individuals.

6. The purchaser of securities balances three important objectives: *high return, low risk,* and *high liquidity.*

7. A company that issues new securities also tries to find the best balance among three objectives: (1) to keep the *return* to the corporation's shareholders as *high* as possible, (2) to *avoid risk,* and (3) to *ensure the availability* of money when needed.

8. In general, bonds are less risky than common stock for buyers of securities, and more risky for sellers of new securities. When corporations or individuals increase their debts, they thereby increase their leverage; that is, they

increase their ratio of debt to net worth. While this raises their potential gain, it also increases their risk of bankruptcy, since they must make interest and principal payments no matter how bad business is.

9. Because stocks and bonds represent claims to future profits or interest payments, the evaluation of the issuer's prospects are extremely important for anyone buying a security. To help protect the purchaser, the provincial securities commissions require corporations to make relevant information available to the public.

10. Financial markets cannot be counted on to ensure the quantity of investment needed for full employment. The maintenance of a high level of employment is a responsibility of the federal government. This role will be studied in future chapters.

KEY CONCEPTS

single proprietorship	preferred stock	obsolescence
partnership	balance sheet	financial intermediary
limited liability	income statement	trust company
corporation	assets	return (or yield)
common stock	liabilities	risk
equity (ownership)	net worth	liquidity
double taxation of dividends	retained earnings	leverage
dividend tax credit	book value	line of credit
face value (or principal) of a bond	depreciation	risk premium
convertible bond		broker

PROBLEMS

6-1 For each of the following, state whether the sentence is true or false, and in each case explain why:
  (a) If liabilities exceed assets, net worth is negative.
  (b) If additional stock is issued at a price in excess of the book value, the book value of the corporation's stock will rise.
  (c) In general, dividends plus retained earnings are greater than corporate income taxes.

6-2 In the middle of 1984, the price of Northern Telecom common stock was approximately $40 on the Montreal and Toronto stock exchanges. There were approximately 115 million shares outstanding. What was the valuation put on Northern Telecom by the stock market? (That is, what was the total value of Northern Telecom stock outstanding?) How does this compare to the net worth of Northern Telecom, which may be found back in Table 6-1? How do you account for the fact that the stock market's valuation of Northern Telecom is different from the net worth, shown on its balance sheet?

6-3 Suppose you are an investment advisor, and a 50-year-old person comes to you for advice on how to invest $100,000 for retirement. What advice would you give? What advice would you give to a young couple who want to temporarily invest $20,000 that they expect to use for a down payment on a home two years from now?

6-4 If a corporation increases its leverage, what are the advantages and/or disadvantages for
  (a) the owner of a share of the corporation's stock;
  (b) the owner of a $100,000 bond of the corporation.

6-5 "While private enterprise does make some

mistakes and sometimes invests in losing projects, it is less likely to do so than the government. After all, businesses risk their own money, while government officials risk the public's money." Do you agree? Can you think of any investment projects that the government has undertaken which were particularly desirable? Might they have been undertaken by private businesses? Why or why not? Can you think of any government investment projects that were particularly ill-advised? Can you think of any investment projects of private corporations that were ill-advised?

6-6 In what ways do the interests of shareholders coincide with the interests of the managers of a corporation? Are there any ways in which their interests are in conflict? (See Box 6-1.)

*6-7 "High interest rates are needed to induce individuals or institutions to buy risky bonds. Similarly, high returns are required to induce corporations to invest in risky new ventures. Higher yields in response to risk are desirable, not only for the individual or corporation directly involved, but also for society. They discourage the waste of scarce resources on costly failures." Do you agree? Can you think of any exceptions, where the high risk premiums demanded by private investors discourage socially desirable expenditures? (Hint: We saw in Chapter 4 that the market mechanism does not necessarily work in a desirable way when there are side effects, or externalities. Are there ever side effects in investment decisions?)

Part Two

HIGH EMPLOYMENT AND A STABLE PRICE LEVEL

The six chapters of Part 1 have set the stage for the study of economics, providing analytical and institutional background and outlining the major objectives of high employment, price stability, growth, efficiency, and an equitable distribution of income.

The focus of Parts 2, 3, and 4 will be on the goals of **high employment**, **price stability**, and **growth**. These involve the overall aggregates of the economy. How many workers are employed in the economy as a whole? What is happening to the total quantity of output in the economy? What is happening to the average level of prices? Because they deal with economy-wide magnitudes, these questions are classified under the heading of **macroeconomics**. (*Makros* means "large" in Greek.) In contrast, the objectives of efficiency and equity, which will be the principal topics of Parts 5, 6, and 7, deal with the details of the economy. What specific goods are produced? Would we be better off if we produced more wheat and less butter? More houses and fewer speedboats? How is income divided between labour (in the form of wages and salaries) and capital (in the form of interest and profits)? Why is there so much foreign-owned capital in Canada? Since these questions deal with the detailed relation-

ships among various industries or groups in the economy, they go under the heading of **microeconomics**. (*Mikros*, the Greek word for "small," appears in such words as "microscope.")

As an introduction to Part 2 on macroeconomics, Chapter 7 describes how national output is measured. Chapter 8 provides an overview of macroeconomic problems of recent decades: how output has fluctuated, how unemployment has risen during recessions, and how prices have increased. Chapter 9 introduces the concepts of aggregate demand and aggregate supply, which are at the core of macroeconomic theory—just as the demand and supply for individual products lie at the centre of microeconomic theory. Chapter 10 addresses the question of why high unemployment can exist—and persist—in a market economy. Not surprisingly, much of the basic theory of unemployment can be traced back to the Depression of the 1930s and, in particular, to the pen of British economist John Maynard Keynes. Keynes argued that production fell and unemployment rose during the Depression because of **insufficient demand**. With the collapse in demand for raw materials in the early depression, workers in the mining and forest industries were discharged. When the demand for housing slackened, construction workers lost their jobs. When the demand for clothing declined, textile workers were laid off. Thus, the widespread increase in unemployment was due to an overall decline in the demand for the goods and services produced in the economy; that is, to a decline in aggregate demand. When people don't buy, workers don't work. The Keynesian theory of aggregate demand is explained in Chapter 10.

Chapter 7

MEASURING NATIONAL PRODUCT AND NATIONAL INCOME

Never ask of money spent
Where the spender thinks it went
Nobody was ever meant
To remember or invent
What he did with every cent.

Robert Frost,
"The Hardship of Accounting"

In our modern economy, we produce a vast array of goods and services: cars, TV sets, houses, clothing, medical care, and food, to name but a few. One way of judging the performance of the economy is to measure the production of all these goods and services. A measure of total production does not, of course, give a complete picture of the welfare of the nation. When we acquire more and more goods, we do not necessarily become happier. Other things are obviously important too; for example, the sense of accomplishment which comes from our everyday work, and the quality of our environment. Nevertheless, the total amount produced is one of the important measures of economic success.

THE MARKET AS A WAY OF MEASURING PRODUCTION

The wide range of products poses a problem: How are

we to add them all up into a single measure of national product? How do we add apples and oranges?

Market prices provide an answer. If apples sell for $10 per bushel and oranges for $20 per bushel, the market indicates that 1 bushel of oranges is worth 2 bushels of apples. Thus, when market prices are used, oranges and apples can be compared and added, as shown in the example in Table 7-1. In our complex economy, the total value of output can be found in a similar way. By taking the quantity times the market price, we find expenditures on a particular product. By adding up the expenditures for the many goods produced—clothing, food, speedboats, etc.—we can get a dollar measure of national product during the year.

National product (or equivalently, *national expenditure*) is the money value of the goods

Table 7-1
Using Market Prices to Add Apples and Oranges

	(1) Quantity (bushels)	(2) Price (per bushel)	(3) Market value (3) = (1) × (2)
Apples	3,000	$10	$30,000
Oranges	2,000	$20	$40,000
		Total	$70,000

Market prices provide a way of adding different goods to get a measure of total production.

and services produced by a nation during a specific time period, such as a year.[1]

TWO APPROACHES: EXPENDITURES AND INCOME

Before looking in detail at the national product, we should look at the overall picture. To do so, let's call once more on the circular-flow diagram introduced in Chapter 3, and repeated here as Figure 7-1. This illustrates the simplest of all possible market economies, in which the public consumes all the goods and services being produced.

The performance of this simple economy can be measured by looking at the money payments in either the upper gray loop or the lower gray loop. The upper loop shows expenditures by households buying the goods produced by business. Once business has received these payments, where do they go? The lower loop shows that they go to those who have provided the productive inputs: wages and salaries go to the labour force; rents to suppliers of land and buildings; and interest and profits to the suppliers of capital. Profits are what is left over after other payments—wages, salaries, interest, etc.—have been made. Thus, in the very simple economy shown in Figure 7-1, both gray loops give exactly the same total. We may look at the upper loop, which shows national expenditures or the expenditures for national product. Alternatively, we

may look at the lower loop, which measures *national income*.

National income is the sum of all income derived from providing the factors of production. It includes wages and salaries, rents, interest, and profits.

NATIONAL PRODUCT: THE EXPENDITURES APPROACH

To calculate national product, we look at the upper loop, examining expenditures on the goods and services that have been produced. When we calculate what has been produced, it is important to count everything once, but only once. Unless we are careful, we may make a mistake, and count some things more than once. The reason is that most products go through a number of stages in the process of production; they are sold a number of times before reaching the hands of the final user. For example, copper wiring and silicon chips are sold to electronics companies, which use them to manufacture electronic calculators. In calculating national product, government statisticians include the calculators sold to consumers. But they do not also count separately the wiring and chips that went into them. Similarly, they count the bread purchased by the consumer. But they do not also count separately the flour that was used in producing the bread. To do so would mean that the flour was counted twice.

The electronic calculators and bread bought by consumers are *final products*; the wheat that went into the bread and the chips that went into the calculators are *intermediate products*. As a first approximation, national product is found by adding up just the expenditures on final products. In this way, double counting is avoided.

> A *final product* is a good or service that is purchased by the ultimate user, and not intended for resale or further processing.
> An *intermediate product* is one that is intended for resale or further processing.

Note that it is the intended use, rather than the physical characteristics of a product that determines whether it is a final good or not. When gasoline is bought by a service station, it is an intermediate good;

---

[1] In Statistics Canada's publications, the term "national expenditure" is used, rather than "national product." However, in most of the discussion of economic policy in the newspapers and elsewhere, the term "national product" is used, and we will follow this convention here.

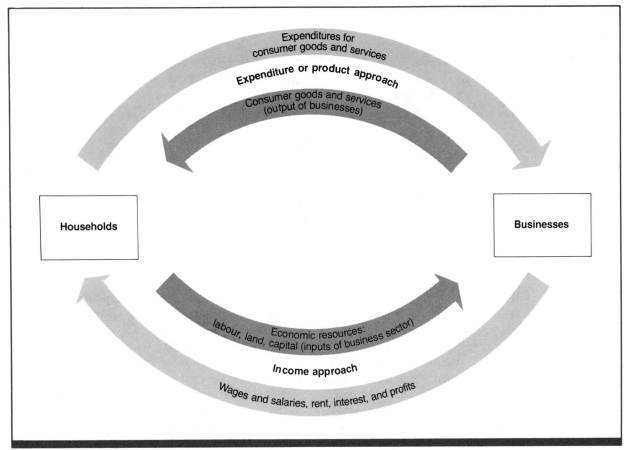

Figure 7-1   The circular flow of payments
In the upper gray loop are the payments for the goods and services produced. This loop measures national product. In the lower gray loop, we see where the receipts of businesses go: to pay wages, salaries, rents, interest, and profits. This loop measures national income.

it is intended for resale to the public. When it is bought by a farmer or trucker, it is also an intermediate product, since it will be used to harvest grain or produce trucking services. However, when it is purchased by a tourist on vacation, it is a final good. Similarly, when a family buys vegetables for its own consumption, they are final products. But when vegetables are bought by a restaurant, they are intermediate products, to be used in the production of restaurant meals.

The distinction between final products and intermediate products is illustrated in Table 7-2, which shows a simple productive process with only four stages. The first step in the production of a loaf of bread occurs when the farmer grows 20 cents' worth of wheat. The second stage is the milling of this wheat into flour, which is then worth 45 cents. In other words, 25 cents of value is added to the 20 cents' worth of wheat when it is made into flour. Similarly, the table shows how value is added at the last two stages, when the flour is baked into bread, and when the bread is delivered to the consumer. How much has been produced? The answer: The $1.25 loaf of bread. In calculating national product, we use only the $1.25 value of the bread. We must not add up the value of all the transactions in the first column, which would total $2.85.

Value added is the difference between the value of a firm's product and the cost of intermediate products bought from outside suppliers.

Table 7-2
Final and Intermediate Products

Stage of production	(1) Value of sales	(2) Cost of intermediate products	(3) Value added (1) − (2) = (3)
Intermediate goods:			
Wheat	20	0	= 20
Flour	45	20	= 25
Bread, at wholesale	95	45	= 50
Final good:			
Bread, at retail	$1.25	95	= 30
		Total	$1.25

Value is added at the various stages of production. Note that the sum of all the value-added items in the last column ($1.25) is equal to the value of the final product.

In the calculation of national product, final products are classified into four categories: (1) personal consumption expenditures, (2) domestic investment, (3) government expenditures for current goods and services, and (4) net exports—that is, exports minus imports. By including government, investment, and net exports, we are now recognizing that the world is more complicated than the simple one in Figure 7-1, where consumers were assumed to buy all the final goods produced in the economy.

1. Personal Consumption Expenditures (C)

Consumption is the ultimate objective of economic activity; we work and produce so that we will have goods and services to consume. Personal consumption expenditures (C) constitute the largest component of national product. They may be divided into three main components: durable goods, such as cars or washing machines; non-durable goods, such as food or clothing; and services, such as dental care or haircuts (Table 7-3).

Note that personal consumption expenditure includes only spending by *private individuals*. Government expenditures on various goods and services are divided between the second and third categories below, depending on whether the expenditures are classified as current spending or investment spending.

2. Domestic Investment (I)

Each year, we produce not only goods and services for immediate consumption, but also capital goods which help in production in future years. Investment may be undertaken by governments—for example, the construction of a power plant. Or it may be undertaken by private businesses—for example, the construction of new factories.

Domestic investment includes three categories: (a) investment in plant and equipment; (b) residential construction; and (c) changes in inventories.

Plant and equipment. This category includes the construction of factories, power plants, warehouses, stores, and other non-residential structures used by business and government, and the acquisition of machinery and other equipment.

Residential construction. The construction of residences is included in the investment segment of national product. The reason for including apartment buildings in investment is straightforward. An apartment building, like a factory or machine, is intended to be an income-producing asset. In future years, the apartment building will produce shelter, for which the owner will charge rent.

There is a substantial advantage in treating all residential construction similarly in the national product accounts. When housing of any kind is built, families have shelter; this is true whether they rent the new housing or own it. For consistency, construction of new owner-occupied housing is included in the investment category. More specifically, national product accountants treat owner-occupied housing as if the family had originally invested in the home, and then, in future years, rented the house to itself. Note that houses are treated differently from consumer durables such as refrigerators. Houses are included in investment; refrigerators are part of consumption expenditures.

Changes in inventories. We have seen that wheat that goes into bread is not counted separately in the national product, because its cost is included as part of the total cost of bread, and is accounted for in the price of the bread. But how about any wheat we produce above and beyond the amount consumed in bread and pastries? What happens to it? The answer is that it is either exported (a possibility that we will consider in just a moment), or it is used to build up our inventories of wheat. Any such increases in our stocks of wheat represent something we have produced this year. Therefore, they are included in this year's national product.

Similarly, increases in inventories of steel are included in national product; for example, the additional inventories of steel held by refrigerator manufacturers, or the increase in the inventory of unsold steel held by a steel company. But we do not include the steel which went into the production of refrigerators or machines, since it has already been included when we count consumer purchases of refrigerators and investment in equipment.

Earlier, we said that, as a first approximation, national product is found by adding up only expenditures on final products. That is an acceptable and commonly used generalization. It is 99% right, and that is not bad. But it is not precisely accurate. National product includes not only final products in the form of consumer goods and services, government purchases, and equipment and buildings. It also includes the intermediate products that have been added to inventories. The precisely correct statement is perhaps worth reiterating: We should measure all goods and services once, but only once.

Changes in inventories can be either positive or negative. In a bad crop year, there may be less wheat on hand at the end of the year than at the beginning. We have taken more out of our stocks than we have put back in. In this case, changes in inventories are negative, and they are subtracted in measuring national product.

Finally, note that the domestic investment category (I) includes only domestic investment in Canada, since it is Canadian national product that is being estimated. If Massey-Ferguson builds a factory in Brazil, its value is included in Brazil's national product, not in Canada's national product. On the other hand, if Honda builds an assembly plant in Ontario, that plant is included in Canadian national product.

3. Government Expenditures on Current Goods and Services (G)

The government not only engages in investment activi-

Table 7-3
The Composition of Personal Consumption Expenditures, 1983

	Billions of Dollars	Percent of Total
1. Food, Beverage, & Tobacco	45.1	20
2. Clothing & Footware	14.3	6
3. Gross Rent, Fuel, and Power	48.7	21
4. Furniture, Furnishings, Household Equipment	19.3	8
5. Medical Care and Health Services	7.9	4
6. Transport and Communication	33.3	15
7. Recreation, Entertainment, Education, and Cultural Services	23.3	10
8. Personal Goods and Services, other	37.3	16
TOTAL:	229.2	100

SOURCE: Statistics Canada, *CANSIM Databank*. Reproduced by permission of the Minister of Supply and Services Canada.

ties, such as the construction of power plants, roads, school buildings, and municipal waste treatment plants. (As we have just seen, these activities are included in the *I* category.) The government also pays for the production of goods and services for current use (*G*). The government hires workers to keep up the parks; park services are produced for the public to enjoy currently. The government hires teachers and pays the operating costs of hospitals; educational and health care services are produced. Soldiers are paid to provide national defence. Governments at all levels—federal, provincial, and municipal—undertake current expenditures for the public good.[2]

While government expenditures on goods and services (*G*) are included in the national product, transfer payments are not. When the government buys spare parts for an army truck, the parts are produced. But when the government makes transfer payments—such as Old Age Security benefits to retirees—the recipients are not required to produce anything in return. Therefore, government expenditures on truck parts are included in national product, but transfer payments are not.

4. Exports of Goods and Services (X)

Some wheat is exported. It is part of our total production of wheat, and therefore it should be included in national product. Because such wheat does not appear in the first three categories (*C, G, I*), it is included here—in exports of goods and services (*X*).

It is obvious how we export a good, such as wheat: We put it on a ship and send it abroad. But how can we export services, such as haircuts and surgical operations? The answer is this. A tourist from Tokyo visiting Vancouver has all sorts of expenditures: for hotel accommodation, for taxi rides, for haircuts, and perhaps even for medical services. Since these services have been produced by Canadians, they must be counted as part of Canada's national product. Since they are paid for by the foreigner, they are considered exports of services, even though the hotel, the taxi, the barber shop, and the hospital remain in Canada.

Interest and dividend payments by foreigners to Canadian firms or individuals, and profits of Canadian subsidiaries abroad, are also considered exports of services. They represent income to Canadians for the services provided by Canadian-owned capital. That is, they represent returns from our past investments abroad.

5. A Subtraction: Imports of Goods and Services (M)

When the Japanese buy our wheat, this export is included in our national product. What happens, on the other side, when we buy Japanese automobiles? Such purchases of imports are included in the Canadian personal consumption expenditures category. But these cars were not produced in Canada. Therefore, they should not be counted as part of our national product. Thus, a subtraction is made for cars imported from Japan (and other countries). Similarly, in calculating national product we subtract all other imports (*M*) of goods and services—including interest and dividends paid to foreigners for the use of their capital.

National Product: A Summary Statement

When we measure national product using the expenditure approach, we make use of the fact that national product is equal to national expenditure, and estimate national product as:

National product = personal consumption expenditures (*C*)
plus domestic investment (*I*)
plus government expenditures for current goods and services (*G*)
plus exports of goods and services (*X*)
minus imports of goods and services (*M*)

In symbols, this is written:

National product = $C + I + G + X - M$ (7-1)

(In this chapter, the equations are numbered—starting

[2]The inclusion of all government expenditures for goods and services in national product is a problem. While some government purchases are for "final" use, other government spending is for intermediate products. A road, for example, can carry both vacation traffic (a "final" or consumption type of use) and trucks loaded with goods (an "intermediate" stage in the productive process). Thus, it might be argued that insofar as roads are used for "intermediate" purposes, this portion of the expenditure for roads should not be included in national product. But national product accountants have ducked this problem. They simply assume that all goods and services purchased by the government are for "final" use, and they therefore include all such purchases in national product.

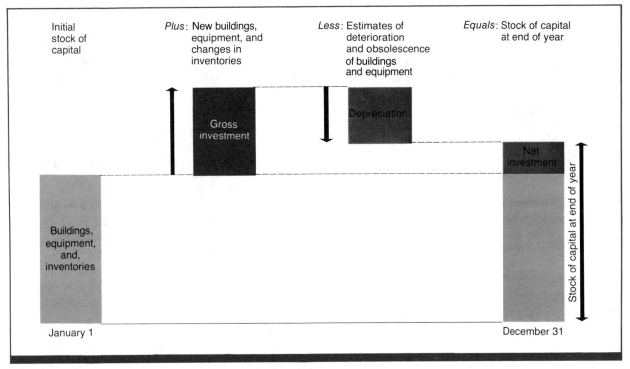

Figure 7-2   Net investment: a change in the stock of capital.
During the year the stock of capital increases by gross investment, less depreciation.

here with Equation 7-1—because we want to refer back to them at a later point.)

Finally, several details might be noted. Recall that national product includes only goods and services produced during the year. Therefore, it does not include expenditures for used goods, such as cars or houses. They were produced in a previous year, and were included in that year's national product. However, renovations of old buildings are included, as are repairs to automobiles. They represent current production. Also included in current national product are the brokerage fees for selling houses and other buildings. They represent payments for a valuable service—namely, assistance in the transfer of the building to someone who wants it.

Common stocks acquired by an individual or institution are not included in national product, since they represent a transfer of ownership rather than production. Of course, if a corporation issues stock and finances the construction of a factory with the proceeds, the factory is part of the national product. It has been produced during the current year.

THE COMPLICATION OF DEPRECIATION: GNP AND NNP

The main outline of the national product accounts has now been completed, but we still have a number of details to consider. One of the most important is the measurement of investment.

If we count the full value of capital goods such as buildings and equipment produced during this year, national product is overestimated. Why? Because existing buildings and equipment have deteriorated—or *depreciated*—during the year from wear and obsolescence. After calculating the total value of all new plant, equipment, and residential buildings produced during the year, we should deduct the amount that plant, equipment, and residences have depreciated during the year. Only if we do this will we get a true measure of how much our total stocks of buildings and equipment have increased during the year (Figure 7-2).

Thus, two concepts of investment should be distinguished:

Gross domestic investment (I_g) is equal to total expenditures for new capital goods, such as plant, equipment, and residential buildings, plus the change in inventories.

Net domestic investment (I_n) is equal to gross domestic investment (I_g), less depreciation. That is,

$$I_n = I_g - \text{depreciation}^3$$

Corresponding to these two concepts of investment, there are two concepts of national product:

Gross national product (GNP) =
$$C + I_g + G + X - M \qquad (7\text{-}2)$$
Net national product (NNP) =
$$C + I_n + G + X - M \qquad (7\text{-}3)$$

From these two equations, it follows that:

$$\textbf{GNP} - \textbf{depreciation} = \textbf{NNP} \qquad (7\text{-}4)$$

This relationship is illustrated in the second and third columns of Figure 7-3. Notice that in 1984, net exports ($X - M$) were positive: exports were larger than imports.

In theory, NNP is the measure of national product that we should use, because it takes into account the obsolescence and physical deterioration of machinery and buildings during the year. But in newspapers and statistical publications, NNP is *not* the commonly used measure; much more attention is paid to GNP (or the equivalent measure GNE, gross national expenditure). Why is this? The answer is that, while NNP is the best measure conceptually, it is difficult to estimate in practice. Gross investment—the value of new buildings and equipment, plus additions to inventories—is relatively easy to measure. But to estimate net investment, we need to measure depreciation, and this raises difficult questions. How rapidly will a machine really wear out? Will it become obsolete before it is physically worn out? If it will be scrapped in 10 years, does its value decline in a "straight line," by 10% each year? Or, does it lose most of its productive value in the first few years? Because of such questions, we cannot be confident about estimates of depreciation. In practice, therefore, GNP is used much more commonly than NNP.

NET NATIONAL PRODUCT AND NATIONAL INCOME: THE COMPLICATION OF THE SALES TAX

Earlier in this chapter, we looked at the circular flow of payments in Figure 7-1, in which upper-loop payments represented national product, and lower-loop payments represented national income. In that very simple illustration, the two loops were equal, and net national product and national income were exactly the same size. In our complex, real-world economy, they are closely related, but not precisely equal.

Net national product (NNP) is the total quantity of goods and services produced during the year, measured at market prices. National income is the sum of income earned by those who provide the factors of production. How can they possibly be different? They may be different because the factors of production do not get all the proceeds from the sale of a good. Part goes to the government in the form of sales taxes (and other similar taxes).[4]

Consider a package of razors priced, say, at $1.99. Most of the $1.99 is divided among the various participants who bring the razors to the market, in the form of wages and salaries, rents, interest, and profits. But those who contribute to the production of the blades do not get all of the $1.99: Part of it goes to the government as manufacturer's sales tax. Suppose that this tax is 10 cents. Then it is only the remaining $1.89—that is, the part which goes to wages, salaries, profits, etc.—that is part of national income. Furthermore, when you get to the cash register with your package of razor blades, you will pay more than $1.99 if there is a provincial sales tax (as there is in every

---

[3]More precisely, to go from I_g to I_n, accountants subtract Capital Consumption Allowances (CCA). These allowances include not only depreciation, but also adjustments for the effects of inflation on the measurement of capital. This is a fine point, which we henceforth ignore; we use the simpler concept of depreciation, in place of CCA.

[4]These other similar taxes include customs duties on imports, property taxes, and excise taxes on items such as cigarettes. These taxes are sometimes lumped together under the heading of indirect taxes. (This term is based on the assumption that these taxes will not be borne by the producer or importer, but will be passed along to the person who buys cigarettes, the imported good, or other item on which a tax is collected.)

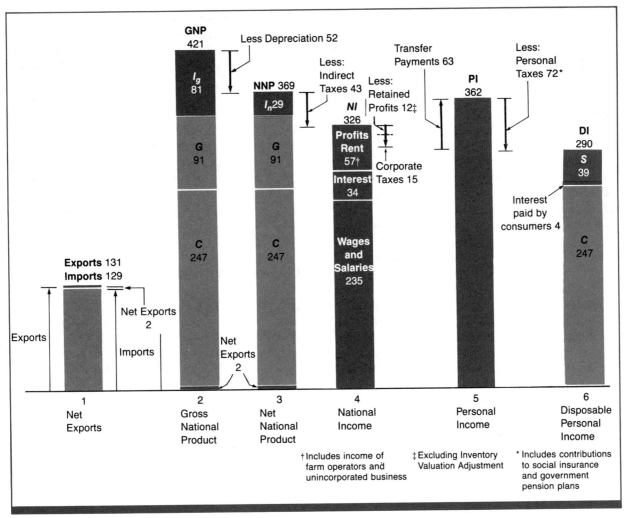

Figure 7-3 National product and income accounts, 1984 (Simplified; in billions of dollars)

GNP = Gross national product
NNP = Net national product
 NI = National income
 PI = Personal income
 DI = Disposable personal income
  C = Personal consumption expenditures
  G = Government expenditures for current goods and

services
I_g = Gross domestic investment
I_n = Net domestic investment
 S = Personal saving

Source: Compiled from Statistics Canada, *National Income and Expenditures Accounts*, First quarter, 1985. Reproduced by permission of the Minister of Supply and Services Canada.

province except Alberta). Suppose the provincial sales tax is 7%, or 14 cents, on the package of razor blades. Then the total price you pay will be $2.13. Because national product is measured at market prices, it includes the whole $2.13.

This distinction shows up in Figure 7-3, where column 3 measures NNP. We subtract sales taxes (and

other similar taxes) in order to get column 4, which shows the national income earned by the suppliers of productive resources.

The tax complication should not obscure a conclusion that is worth emphasizing. With the exception of sales taxes, the proceeds from the sale of the final product become incomes of the factors of production.

Thus:

The process of production is also the process of generating income.

In column 4 of Figure 7-3, the income generated on owner-operated farms and unincorporated business is included in the "profits, rent" category, rather than being divided into the familiar components of income—wages and salaries, profits, and so on. To understand the reason for this, note that for a large corporation, wages are sharply distinguishable from profits. Wages go to the workers, while profits are the return to the owners of the corporation. However, for some businesses—such as a family farm or a mom and pop store—it is not feasible to separate wages, profits, and other income shares. How much of a farmer's income is the result of the family's labour, and how much a return on its investment in buildings, equipment, and so on? It is not easy to say. Accordingly, no attempt is made to subdivide such income; it is treated as a single item and included in the "profits, rent" category, even though it contains some implicit labour income.

OTHER INCOME MEASURES

Thus far, we have seen that GNP includes personal consumption, government expenditures on current goods and services, gross investment, and exports less imports. The difference between GNP and NNP is depreciation, although this is difficult to measure precisely. We also saw that you have to subtract sales taxes from NNP to get national income, which is the sum of payments for providing factors of production—labour, land, and capital.

Now let's see what happens next.

Personal Income (*PI*)
Although most of *national income* is received by households as their *personal income* (*PI*), national income and personal income are not exactly the same.

One reason is that not all national income flows through the business sector to households:
- Part of corporate profit is taken by the government in the form of corporate income taxes.
- Part of profit is retained by corporations to finance expansion. Thus, dividends are the only portion

of corporate profits that do flow from corporations to households as personal income.

The other reason that personal income is not the same as national income lies in transfer payments, such as family allowances and Unemployment Insurance benefits. Such transfers are a source of personal income to households. But they are not payments to households for providing factors of production. Therefore, they are not included in national income.

Thus, to find personal income (column 5, Figure 7-3), we begin with national income (column 4), and then subtract corporation taxes and profits retained by corporations, and we add transfer payments. Personal income is the measure which corresponds most closely to the everyday meaning of "income."

Disposable Personal Income (*DI*)
Not all personal income is available to the individual or family for personal use, however. The government takes a sizeable chunk in the form of personal taxes. (These are mainly personal income taxes, but also include compulsory contributions to government pension plans and unemployment insurance, and other miscellaneous items, such as inheritance taxes.) After these taxes and contributions are paid, disposable personal income (*DI*) remains. Households can do three things with this income: spend it on consumption, use it to pay interest on consumer debt, or save it.[5] Disposable income is an important concept, because consumers look at this income when they decide how much to spend.

Relative Magnitudes
Before leaving Figure 7-3, observe the relative magnitudes of the major boxes. Consumption is by far the largest component of GNP (column 2). In 1984, it amounted to 59% of GNP. Government expenditures for goods and services constituted the next largest component, 22%. While gross investment was also substantial, most of it went to cover depreciation, leaving a relatively small proportion as net investment.

---

[5]In Canadian national accounting, interest paid by households on consumer debt is not considered part of consumption spending. Instead, it is considered as a transfer (from households which are in debt, to other households which own assets on which they earn interest). Thus the $4 billion interest payments shown in column 6 are part of the $63 billion in transfer payments in column 5.

Table 7-4
Current-dollar and Constant-dollar GNP

(1) 1971 current-dollar GNP	(2) 1986 current-dollar GNP	(3) 1986 constant-dollar GNP
100 coats @ $60 = $6,000	120 coats @ $200 = $24,000	120 coats @ $60 = $7,200
100 radios @ $40 = $4,000	120 radios @ $50 = $6,000	120 radios @ $40 = $4,800
Total $10,000	Total $30,000	Total $12,000

In the fourth column, we see that wages and salaries were by far the largest component of national income, 72%. Profits and rent was 17%. In the last column, consumption expenditures were 85% of disposable income.

While most of these items are relatively stable, a few change quite sharply from year to year. Net exports can be either positive or negative; they were usually positive in the years prior to 1978, but have been negative in recent years. Investment has been quite volatile, rising sharply during periods of business prosperity, and falling during recessions. In the quarter century from 1960 to 1984, gross investment ranged from a high of 27.2% of GNP in the second quarter of 1966 to a low of 18.7% in the third quarter of 1982. Corporate profits are even more responsive to business conditions—reaching a high of 29.2% of GNP in the first quarter of 1980, then dropping rapidly to 15.3% in the third quarter of 1982.

NOMINAL AND REAL GNP

Dollar prices provide a satisfactory basis for calculating national product in any one year; they allow us to add apples and oranges, haircuts and cars. But if we wish to evaluate the performance of the economy over a number of years, we face a major problem. The dollar is a shrinking yardstick. Because of inflation, its value is going down. On average, the dollar in 1985 buys only 46% of what it bought in 1975.

As the years pass, the dollar measure of GNP increases for two quite different reasons. First, there is an increase in the quantity of goods and services produced. This increase is desirable; we have more and more goods and services at our disposal. Second, the prices of goods and services increase. This increase is undesirable; it occurs because we have been unsuccessful in combatting inflation. To judge the performance of the economy, it is essential to separate the desirable increase in the quantity of output from the undesirable increase in prices.

To do this, economists use the concept of **constant-dollar GNP**, also known as **real GNP**. This is calculated by valuing GNP at the prices that existed in a beginning or **base year**, not at the prices which actually exist while the GNP is being produced. (Statistics Canada currently uses 1971 as the base year in GNP calculations.) A hypothetical example of an economy producing only two items is given in Table 7-4.

If we looked only at **nominal** or **current-dollar GNP** in the first two columns, we might come to the erroneous conclusion that output had trebled—up from $10,000 in 1971 to $30,000 in 1986. But this clearly misstates the increase in the quantity of goods and services produced. Observe that the quantities of coats and radios have both increased by only 20%. By measuring 1986 output at 1971 prices in the final column, we find constant-dollar GNP to be $12,000. Comparing this with 1971 GNP of $10,000, we come to the correct conclusion: Real output has increased by 20%.

Obviously, this is a very simplified example. Figure 7-4 shows the actual figures for current-dollar and constant-dollar GNP. Observe how much more rapidly the current-dollar series has risen. Most of the increase in nominal GNP between 1971 and 1984 was caused by a rise in prices (Figure 7-5).

Price Indexes

More specifically, we can use current-dollar and constant-dollar GNP to calculate how much the average level of prices has risen since the base year. Returning to the example in Table 7-4, observe that nominal (current-dollar) GNP in 1986 is 2.5 times as high as

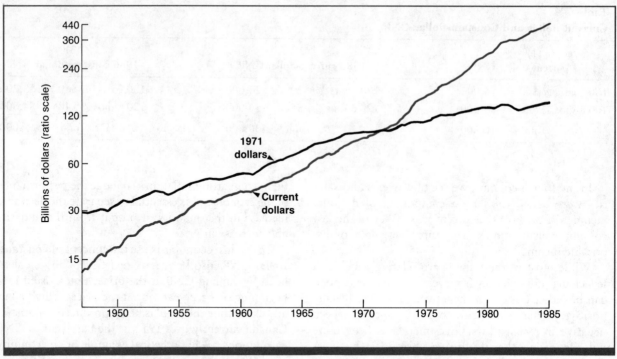

Figure 7-4 Gross national product (GNP), measured in current dollars and 1971 dollars.
Much of the increase in current-dollar national product has been the result of inflation. Observe that national product has grown much more slowly in constant (1971) dollars than in current dollars.
Source: Statistics Canada, *CANSIM Databank*. Reproduced by permission of the Minister of Supply and Services Canada.

real GNP in that year ($30,000/$12,000 = 2.5). By convention, the average price in the base year is given a value of 100 when calculating a *price index*. Thus, in the example in Table 7-4, the index of prices in 1986 is 250 (that is, 2.5 times the base of 100.)

> An *index* is a number which shows how an average (of prices, or wages, or some other economic measure) has changed over time.

The index calculated from nominal and real GNP figures is known as the *implicit GNP price deflator*, or, more simply, as the *GNP deflator*. In general, it is calculated as:

$$\text{GNP price deflator} = \frac{\text{Nominal GNP}}{\text{Real GNP}} \times 100$$

$$(7\text{-}5)$$

While the GNP deflator measures the change in the average price of the goods and services we have produced, another index—the *consumer price index (CPI)*—measures the change in the average price of the goods and services bought by the typical household. Specifically, the CPI measures changes in the cost of a basket of goods and services purchased by the typical urban family—food, automobiles, housing, furniture, repair services, etc.

When the prices of the goods and services that we produce rise, so generally do the prices of what we purchase—for the simple reason that we consume most of what we produce. Therefore, it's not surprising that the GNP price deflator and the CPI tend to move together. But the two price indexes are not identical. For example, much of Canada's production of goods such as wheat, timber, or newsprint is exported to foreign countries. Thus, these products have more

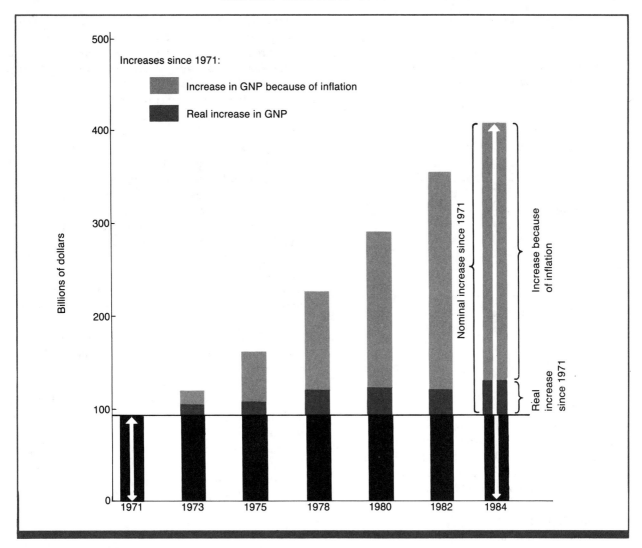

Figure 7-5   The increase in GNP, 1971–1984.
Between 1971 and 1984, nominal GNP increased more than fourfold. However, most of the
increase was attributable to inflation. Real GNP increased by only 50%.
Source: *Bank of Canada Review* (January 1986).

important weights in the GNP-deflator (which includes all wheat, timber, or newsprint produced in Canada) than in the CPI (which includes only the wheat, timber, and newsprint consumed in Canada). Partly as a result of this difference, the two indexes moved differently in the early 1970s, when there was a steep rise in the world prices of the raw materials we exported. For example, between 1973 and 1974, the GNP-deflator increased by 15.3%, while the CPI increased by a less spectacular 10.9%. (The appendix to this chapter investigates the problem of calculating real GNP when the prices of exported or imported commodities change sharply.)

Short-run movements in the two indexes may also differ because the CPI covers only the goods and services bought by the typical urban household. In contrast, the GNP deflator is calculated from the prices of every item in GNP—that is, the cost of capital goods and government services, as well as consumer goods and services.

Other Real Measures

Equation 7-5 may be rearranged this way:

$$\text{Real GNP} = \frac{\text{Nominal GNP}}{\text{GNP price deflator}} \times 100 \quad (7\text{-}6)$$

This process—of dividing by a price index—is known as **deflating**. Similar equations may be used to calculate other real measures. For example:

$$\text{Real consumption} = \frac{\text{Nominal consumption}}{\text{CPI}} \times 100 \quad (7\text{-}7)$$

$$\text{Real wage} = \frac{\text{Nominal wage}}{\text{CPI}} \times 100 \quad (7\text{-}8)$$

Suppose the nominal or money wage rises from $100 to $107 while the CPI rises by 5%. Then, using Equation 7-8, we find:

$$\text{Real wage} = \frac{\$107}{105} \times 100$$
$$= \$101.90 \quad (7\text{-}9)$$

The real wage has increased by 1.90%. That is, a worker's wage will buy almost 2% more goods and services. Observe that, in deflating the nominal wage to find the real wage, we use the CPI. This is the most appropriate price index, since it measures changes in the prices of the goods and services that the typical family buys.

While Equation 7-9 gives the precise answer, it is cumbersome. A much simpler procedure is often used to find the approximate change:

Change in real wage
$\simeq$ change in money wage $-$ change in CPI
$= 7\% - 5\% = 2\%$ $\quad (7\text{-}10)$

A MEASURE OF ECONOMIC WELFARE

Real GNP is one of the most frequently used measures of economic performance. And large changes in GNP may in fact reflect severe problems or impressive gains. When Canada's real GNP fell by 30% between 1929 and 1933, the performance of the economy was very unsatisfactory. Conversely, the large increase in real GNP in Japan in recent decades has reflected a rapid rise in the Japanese material standard of living.

Yet real GNP cannot be taken as a precise measure of the standard of living. The most obvious difficulty arises because an increase of, say, 10% in real GNP doesn't mean that the average person has 10% more goods and services. The reason is that population is growing. Rather than using total GNP figures, it is appropriate to estimate changes in the standard of living by looking at real GNP *per capita*; that is, real GNP divided by the population.

Other, more subtle problems arise because market sales are taken as the starting point in calculating GNP. When you hire a professional carpenter to build bookcases, the amount you pay appears in GNP. But if you build bookcases for your home, only the wood and materials are included in GNP; the value of your time as a carpenter is not. Similarly, a restaurant meal appears in GNP. But when you prepare an even better meal at home, only the ingredients bought from the store are included. Thus, GNP does not include some important items, simply because they do not go through the market.

However, in calculating GNP, government statisticians do not adhere blindly to the idea that GNP should include all market transactions, and nothing else. GNP includes some imputed items which do not go through the market. We have already seen that owner-occupied housing is treated as if its owners rent to themselves. Imputed rents on such housing are included in GNP, even though people do not actually pay themselves rent.

On the other hand, some items that actually do go through the market are excluded from GNP, and quite properly so. Since GNP is taken as a measure of the economy's performance, illegal products—such as heroin—are excluded from GNP on the ground that lawmakers have decided that they are "bads" rather than "goods."

Nevertheless, a number of dubious items remain in GNP. When international relations become more tense, higher expenditures for weapons are included in GNP, but our situation has scarcely improved. If there is an increase in crime, additional expenditures for police, courts, and prisons are included in GNP. Yet society is certainly no better off than it was before the increase in crime.

Furthermore, some goods are included, while the "bads" which they create or stem from are ignored. For example, GNP includes the production of automobiles and electricity, but there is no downward adjustment for the resulting pollution. Indeed, if people need medical attention as a result, GNP will go up, since payments by governments and patients for the services of doctors and hospitals are included in GNP.

Naturally enough, economists are bothered by the shortcomings of GNP as a measure of well-being. During the past two decades, a number of attempts have been made to deal with some of the inadequacies. These attempts fall under two main headings.

1. Emphasis on Additional Social Indicators

The first approach is to downplay GNP as the measure of how the economy and society are performing, and to realize that it is only one of a number of important indicators of performance. Rather than focusing on GNP, policymakers can look at a set of indicators that, taken together, provide both a way of judging performance and a set of objectives to be met in setting policy.[6] In addition to real GNP, important indicators of well-being include such things as life expectancy, infant mortality rates, the availability of health care, education and literacy, the amount of leisure, the quality of the environment, and the degree of urban crowding.

2. A Comprehensive Measure of Economic Welfare (MEW)

The second approach is more ambitious: to provide a comprehensive single measure of economic performance, including not only the standard national product, but also additions for the value of leisure and subtractions for pollution and other disadvantages of crowded urban living. Such a measure of economic welfare (MEW) has been calculated for the United States by two Yale University economists, William Nordhaus and James Tobin.[7]

The difficulties they encountered were formidable.

The most interesting implication of their study is that an entirely satisfactory index *can't* be constructed. To see why, consider the problem posed by leisure. As our ability to produce has increased, the working population has taken only part of the gain in the form of higher wages and other measured incomes; a significant part of the gain has come in the form of a shorter workweek.

For example, Nordhaus and Tobin calculated that in the United States, the average number of leisure hours had increased by 22% between 1929 and 1965, while real per capita net national product had risen by 90%. The question is, What should be made of these facts? Specifically, which of the following conclusions is correct?

1. Production per person went up by 90%, and Americans had more leisure, too. Therefore, economic welfare improved by more than 90%; it rose *more* than NNP.

2. Production per person went up by 90%. But leisure increased by less than 90%; specifically, by only 22%. Therefore, economic welfare rose by some average of the 90% and the 22%; that is, by *less* than NNP.

The choice between conclusions 1 and 2 is difficult, but it is only the beginning of the problems with evaluating economic welfare in a more comprehensive way. For example, the estimates of MEW compiled by Nordhaus-Tobin did not drop during the Great Depression; indeed, they actually rose between 1929 and 1935. The explanation for this quirk, of course, is that Nordhaus and Tobin included leisure as an element of welfare, and leisure certainly increased as people were thrown out of work. But surely there is something wrong here. Leisure after a good day's work may be bliss, but it's not so pleasant to be idle when you've lost your job.

The ultimate test of economic success is the contribution that economic activity makes to the goal of human happiness. But to seek a single, summary measure of this contribution is surely to set out on an impossible task. In the words of the late economist Arthur Okun, the calculation of "a summary measure of social welfare is a job for a philosopher king."

Because it seems impossible to develop a single comprehensive measure of welfare, we are stuck with the national product accounts. In spite of all their defects

[6]Examples of lists of such indicators may be found in Economic Council of Canada, *Eleventh Annual Review: Economic Targets and Social Indicators* (Ottawa: Supply and Services Canada, 1974).
[7]William Nordhaus and James Tobin, "Is Growth Obsolete?" in *Economic Growth, Fiftieth Anniversary Colloquium* (New York: National Bureau of Economic Research, 1972).

and shortcomings, they do provide an important measure of the health of our economy. Downturns in real GNP act as a signal that we have been unable to prevent recessions, while long-run increases in real GNP per capita are an important indicator of economic progress. GNP is a significant and useful social indicator— but we should not view it as the last word.

THE UNDERGROUND ECONOMY: THE CASE OF THE MISSING GNP

The logical question of what GNP statisticians should attempt to measure is, however, not the only controversy surrounding the GNP accounts. Another involves what they are able to measure in practice. In recent years, a number of economists and government officials have expressed concern that many transactions escape the attention of national product accountants, resulting in a substantial underestimate of GNP.

The reason is that plumbers, carpenters, and lawyers—to name but a few—have an incentive to perform services without reporting their income, in order to evade taxes. But, when such income is unreported, it not only disappears from Revenue Canada's tax records. It also disappears from the GNP accounts. Moonlighting, and the incomes of illegal aliens, are particularly unlikely to be reported.

Such "subterranean" or "irregular" activities are by no means confined to Canada and the United States. The French have their "travail au noir" (work in the dark); the Italians their "lavorno nero" (same thing); the British their "fiddle"; and the Germans their "Schattenwirtschaft" (shadow economy). The **underground economy** includes not only unreported illegal activities—which, as we have noted, national income accountants intentionally exclude from the GNP—but also such socially desirable services as the work of the moonlighting plumber, whose only illegal aspect is tax evasion. If we want an accurate measure of the goods and services produced in our economy, we should certainly include such socially desirable services.

The problem, of course, is to get information, since those in the underground economy are trying to keep their activities secret. Thus, it is difficult to measure the size of the underground economy directly. Rather, economists have looked for the traces left by irregular activities. What might these traces be?

The most obvious way to keep transactions secret is to use currency rather than cheques. Thus, if the underground economy is growing fast, one would then expect the amount of currency to increase faster than the amount of chequing deposit money. And as University of Alberta economists Rolf Mirus and Roger Smith have shown, this is exactly what has happened in Canada: The ratio of currency to chequing deposits grew from about 0.33 before World War II to 0.56 in 1980.[8] From this information, Mirus and Smith concluded that a large underground economy has developed, amounting to 14 percent of GNP. (Using a somewhat different method of calculation suggested by Edgar Feige, they arrived at an even higher estimate, 20% of GNP.)[9]

If, in fact, the underground economy is not only large but also growing relative to reported GNP (as Mirus and Smith found), a number of important conclusions follow. (1) Official statistics understate the growth of the economy. (2) Official statistics overstate the true rate of inflation, because those in the rapidly growing underground sector generally charge lower prices to gain customers. (3) Unemployment statistics overstate the true amount of unemployment. People collecting Unemployment Insurance benefits— but also working "off the record" in the underground economy—are not likely to tell interviewers from Employment and Immigration that they are employed.

In other words, things may be better than they seem from the official statistics. However, we should not take too much comfort from this conclusion. Because estimates of the underground economy are based on circumstantial evidence, they may contain large errors. Without a doubt, many transactions go unreported. But we do not know just how large the irregular economy really is, nor how much of it represents illegal activities which we do not want to count anyway.

[8]Rolf Mirus and Roger S. Smith, "Canada's Irregular Economy," *Canadian Public Policy* (Summer 1981): 444–453.

[9]Literature on the underground economy in the United States includes work by Edgar L. Feige, "How Big Is the Irregular Economy?" *Challenge* (November 1979): 5–13; Carl P. Simon and Ann D. Witte, *Beating the System: The Underground Economy* (Boston: Auburn House Publishing, 1982); and Vito Tanzi, "The Underground Economy in the United States," *International Monetary Fund Staff Papers* (June 1983): 283–305.

KEY POINTS

1. The market provides a way of adding apples, oranges, automobiles, and the many other goods and services produced during the year. Items are included in national product at their market prices.

2. In measuring national product, everything should be measured once, and only once. Intermediate products (such as wheat or steel) used in the production of other goods (such as bread or automobiles) should not be counted separately, since they are already included when we count the final product (bread or automobiles).

3. Net investment equals gross investment minus depreciation. If net investment is positive, then more buildings, equipment, and inventories are being produced than are being used up. Thus, the capital stock is rising (Figure 7-2).

4. $GNP = C + I_g + G + X - M$
   $NNP = GNP - \text{depreciation}$
   Because depreciation is difficult to measure accurately, statisticians have more confidence in the measure of GNP than NNP, and therefore GNP is used more commonly.

5. Receipts from the sale of products are distributed to those who contribute to the productive process by providing labour, capital, or land. In a simple economy, all the proceeds from the sale of goods would be distributed in the form of income payments to the factors of production. Net national product and national income would be the same. However, in a real-world economy, national income is less, because some of the proceeds from the sale of goods goes to the government in the form of sales taxes. Thus:

   National income = NNP − sales taxes.

6. Review Figure 7-3 for the relationships between NNP, national income, personal income, and disposable personal income.

7. Market prices provide a good way for adding up the many different goods and services produced in a *single* year. But they would be a misleading way of comparing the national product in *different* years. The reason is that the value of the dollar shrinks as a result of inflation. A rise in current-dollar national product reflects both an increase in prices and an increase in real production.

8. In order to estimate the increase in real output, constant-dollar figures are used. These are found by measuring GNP at the prices existing in a base year.

9. By "deflating" current data with the appropriate price index, it is possible to get a real measure of other important economic variables, such as the real wage (Equation 7-9).

10. Real GNP (or real NNP) per capita is not a good measure of economic welfare. However, attempts to calculate a more comprehensive measure of economic welfare have run into the insoluble problem of how to deal with leisure.

11. The "underground" economy is made up of two components:
    (a) Unreported income of plumbers, carpenters, lawyers, farmers, etc. The failure to report is the only illegal aspect. The services themselves are legal and socially useful, and they would be included in GNP if government statisticians knew how large they were.
    (b) Income from illegal activities such as the drug trade. Since the government has decided that these activities represent social "bads," they would not be included in GNP even if statisticians knew how large they were.
    Circumstantial evidence suggests that (a) is growing in proportion to reported GNP. This means that the official GNP statistics understate growth of real GNP.

KEY CONCEPTS

final product	net exports	constant-dollar GNP
intermediate product	gross national product (GNP)	base year
value added	net national product (NNP)	price index
consumption	gross investment	deflating with a price index
investment	net investment	GNP deflator
inventories	depreciation	consumer price index (CPI)
government expenditures for current goods and services	national income (NI)	real wage
	personal income (PI)	measure of economic welfare
exports of goods and services	disposable personal income (DI)	GNP per capita
imports of goods and services	current-dollar GNP	underground economy

PROBLEMS

7-1 Consider an economy in which the following quantities are measured (in billions of dollars):

Consumption expenditures	$1,000
Value of common shares purchased	400
Gross private domestic investment	300
Government transfer payments	100
Sales taxes	50
Government expenditures for current goods and services	200
Corporate income taxes	200
Personal income taxes	100
Exports minus imports	10
Depreciation	75
Purchases of secondhand cars	100

    (a) Calculate GNP. (Be careful. Not all the items are included.)
    (b) Calculate NNP.

7-2 The change in inventories can be negative. Can net investment also be negative? Explain.

7-3 Give an example of an import of a service.

7-4 Which of the following government expenditures are included in GNP?
    (a) the purchase of an aircraft for the Air Force
    (b) the purchase of a computer for the Department of Finance
    (c) the payment of unemployment insurance benefits to those who have lost their jobs
    (d) the salary paid to maintenance workers who mow the grass beside the highways.

7-5 Last year a family engaged in the following activities. What items are included in GNP? Explain in each case why the item is, or is not, included.
    (a) They purchased a used car from their neighbour.
    (b) They deposited $1,000 in a savings deposit at the bank.
    (c) They purchased $2,000 worth of groceries.
    (d) They flew to London, England, for a vacation.

7-6 For 1984 (shown in Figure 7-3):
    (a) Which was larger: government expenditures for current goods and services or gross investment?
    (b) Approximately what percent of NNP was net investment?
    (c) Approximately how large a percentage of national income were wages and salaries? corporate profits? rent and interest?
    (d) Approximately what fraction of disposable income was saved?

7-7 Of the two measures of economic welfare of Nordhaus and Tobin, do you think one is better than the other? If so, which one, and why? If not, would it be a satisfactory solution to avoid this problem by excluding leisure when calculating a "measure of economic welfare"?

7-8 For each of the following, state whether you

agree or disagree. If you agree, explain why. If you disagree, correct the statement.

(a) When a trucker buys gasoline, the intended use is for the production of trucking services for others, not for pleasure trips. Therefore, this gasoline is an intermediate product, while the trucking service is a final product.

(b) Bread purchased by a household is a final product, but bread purchased by a supermarket or a restaurant is an intermediate product.

(c) If new automobiles were treated like new owner-occupied housing in the national product accounts, domestic investment would be higher, and our living standards would also be higher.

(d) Defence expenditures provide no direct satisfaction to the public. They only protect our freedom to enjoy other goods and services. Therefore, defence expenditures are considered an intermediate product, and are not included separately in the calculation of GNP.

(e) A road between two manufacturing centres is an intermediate product, because it is used to transport goods in the process of production. But a road running to a summer resort is a final good, since it is used primarily for pleasure travel.

7-9 Equation 7-10 shows a simplified way of estimating the approximate change in the real wage. To see how close this approximation is, find the true change in the real wage (from Equation 7-8), and compare it to the estimate found with Equation 7-10 in each of the following cases:

(a) when the money wage increases by 10%, while the CPI increases by 2%

(b) when the money wage increases by 30%, while the CPI increases by 22%

(c) when the money wage increases by 200%, while the CPI increases by 100%.

Do your results from these examples suggest any circumstances under which it would be wise to avoid the use of Equation 7-10?

APPENDIX

EXPORTS, IMPORTS, AND REAL GNP

Nominal or current-dollar GNP is not a very useful measure. If we want to know whether the economy has performed well this year compared to last year, we should look at *real* GNP. Only if the real output of goods and services has been increasing can we say that the economy has done better than last year. Increases in nominal GNP which only reflect price increases don't make Canadians better off; but increases in the real output of goods and services do.

However, there is one component of real GNP where this argument may be misleading: net exports. Real net exports are calculated as follows. First, nominal exports are deflated by the index of export prices to get real exports, while nominal imports are deflated by the index of import prices to get real imports. Real imports are then subtracted from real exports to get real net exports; the result is then added to the esti-

mates of consumption, investment, and government spending to find real GNP.

This procedure seems reasonable enough. But sometimes it gives results that have to be interpreted carefully. Suppose, for example, that the prices of Canada's exports on average rise faster than the prices of the goods we import. (This was what happened during the commodity boom in 1978–1980, when the prices of important Canadian export goods such as wheat, metals and minerals, and natural gas, shot up rapidly.)

But consider what can happen when we calculate real GNP. Suppose we begin, in base year 1, with exports (X) of $50 billion, and imports (M) of $50 billion. Our international transactions are exactly in balance; exports are just large enough to pay for imports.

Now suppose that, by year 2, export prices double,

while the quantity of exports remains constant. The *value* of exports now amounts to $100 billion. Suppose, at the same time, that import prices remain constant, while the quantity of imports doubles. Imports now are also $100 billion. Once again, we earn enough from exports to pay for our imports. In the current-dollar GNP accounts, net exports remain zero in year 2.

But now notice what happens when real quantities are calculated. Measured in base-year prices (the prices in year 1), exports have remained constant; in constant dollars, they are still $50 billion. But in constant dollars, imports are now $100 billion. Thus our calculation shows a "real" import deficit of $50 billion. But, to say that we have a "real" import deficit is, at the very least, misleading. Remember: Our exports are still large enough to pay for our imports.

Thus, when we want to find out how well we are doing on the international side, we should not just look at constant-dollar figures: *We should look also at what has happened to the prices of our exports and imports.* In the preceding example, our real exports did not increase. But because the prices of our exports rose faster than the prices of the goods we imported, our export earnings were still sufficient to buy us a larger amount of real imports.

When the prices of a country's export goods rise faster than the prices of its imports, this is referred to as an improvement in the country's **terms of trade.** Canada's terms of trade improved substantially during the 1970s. Many other countries were less fortunate. In the United States, for example, the import price index rose substantially faster than the export price index. The main reason for this worsening of the U.S. terms of trade was the large increase in the world price of oil, which accounts for a large share of U.S. imports. Japan and most European countries also experienced worsening terms of trade because of rising oil prices.

Canada did not have this problem. While we import large amounts of oil into Eastern Canada, our total energy exports (including natural gas and electricity) are even larger, and the prices of all our energy exports rose along with the price of oil. Therefore, while rising world prices for oil and other energy resources *did* raise our import price index, they increased our export price index even more.

In the early 1980s, the recession in the world economy, and the gradual weakening of the OPEC export cartel combined to produce a rapid fall in the world oil price and falling prices for energy resources in general. As a result, Canada suffered a loss: Our terms of trade worsened once again. The worsening terms of trade, in turn, constituted one of the factors that contributed to the substantial fall in the international value of the Canadian dollar in the mid-1980s.

Chapter 8

FLUCTUATIONS IN ECONOMIC ACTIVITY: UNEMPLOYMENT AND INFLATION

A recession is when your neighbor is out of work.
A depression is when you're out of work.

Harry S. Truman

Economic conditions rarely stand still. Moderate expansions often accelerate into inflationary booms, and inflationary booms give way to recessions.

The most obvious way to measure the ups and downs of the Canadian economy is with real GNP figures, which show how aggregate output has expanded and contracted. Unfortunately, however, detailed GNP data are available for only a fraction of Canadian history; it is only since 1926 that the government has collected GNP data on a regular basis.

Of all the fluctuations in our history, the largest took place between 1929 and 1944. First came the collapse into the Great Depression, with real GNP falling by more than 30% between 1929 and 1933. This was followed by a long and painful recovery. It was not until the government began spending huge amounts of money for arms, ammunition, and military equipment during World War II that the economy recovered fully. After the war, there was a temporary drop in output as factories were converted from producing weapons to making peacetime products. Since

that time, there has been a series of recessions: in 1947, 1953–54, 1957, 1960–61, 1970, 1974–75, 1980, and 1981–82.

Fluctuations in economic activity are irregular; no two recessions are exactly alike. Nor are any two expansions. Some last for years, the 1961–69 expansion being the most notable example. Others are short-lived, such as the expansion of 1958–60 which quickly gave way to a new recession, and the expansion of 1980–81, which was interrupted by the 1981–82 recession after only about a year. The economy is not a pendulum swinging regularly at specific intervals. If it were, the analysis of business fluctuations would be simple: The movement of a pendulum is easily predicted.

THE FOUR PHASES OF THE BUSINESS CYCLE

Because business fluctuations are so irregular, it is perhaps surprising that they are called "cycles." However, they are all similar in the sense that they go through the same four phases (Figure 8-1).

The key to identifying a business cycle is to identify a **recession**—the period when economic activity is declining. This immediately raises a problem of definition. How far down does the economy have to go before we should say that it is in a recession? The answer may have considerable political significance: When the economy is in a recession, people tend to be especially critical of the government in power.

In Canada, government politicians can (and frequently do) try to reduce the extent of the political fall-out from recessions by blaming them on international economic conditions. (As we shall see later, there is a good deal of evidence that they are often justified in doing this.) In the United States, where international trade and capital flows play a less important role than in Canada, recessions are more likely to be considered as having been caused by domestic factors such as government policy. Because of this, the question of whether the economy is in a recession is a more sensitive one in the United States, and much ingenuity has been devoted to coming up with a generally acceptable way of answering it. A private research organization—the National Bureau of Economic Re-

search (NBER)—is the guardian of the keys; it decides what is, and what is not, called a recession. The NBER does not want to call every slight downward jiggle of the economy a recession; the decline should be significant. The NBER's major test is historical: Is a downswing as long and severe as declines of the past that have been labelled recessions? Prior to 1980, a simple definition was commonly used: A recession occurs when seasonally adjusted real GNP declines for two or more consecutive quarters. (For an explanation of how GNP and other data are "seasonally adjusted," see Box 8-1.) However, the NBER never actually accepted this definition, and in 1980, it declared a recession which did not meet this test. (Real GNP fell in only one quarter.)

In Canada, there is no one institution responsible for formally deciding whether or not we are in a recession, nor do we have a universally accepted definition of a recession. Canadian economic commentators sometimes use the term "recession" for periods when the *growth rate* of real GNP slows down markedly, even if there is no prolonged *decline* in real GNP. The definition offered in Chapter 1 probably comes close to the way most Canadian economists would

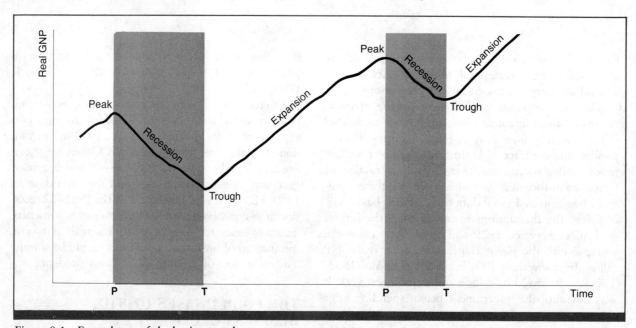

Figure 8-1   Four phases of the business cycle.
Periods of expansion and recession alternate, with peaks and troughs in between. Not every expansion reaches a high degree of prosperity with a low unemployment rate; an expansion sometimes ends prematurely and a new recession begins.

BOX 8-1

SEASONAL ADJUSTMENT OF ECONOMIC DATA

Not all ups and downs in business activity represent the misbehaviour of the economy. Crops grow by the calendar; harvests are gleaned in the summer and autumn months. The month-to-month changes in food production reflect a law of nature with which we learn to live. Retail sales boom during the holiday season in December, only to fall in January.

Such regular month-to-month swings are not our concern. The decline in retail sales in January is the aftermath of the December buying boom; it is not a symptom of an oncoming recession. In order to identify a recession, we must remove the seasonal effects from business activity. That is, we must seasonally adjust our data on production, sales, etc. The following technique is used.

Suppose the statistician discovers from past information that December sales of toys typically run at three times the average monthly rate, only to drop to one-half the average monthly rate in January. The raw data for toy sales can then be seasonally adjusted by dividing December's sales by 3, and multiplying January's sales by 2. (In fact, more complicated techniques are used, but this is the general

Courtesy Canapress Photo Service

idea.) Similarly, quarterly data for GNP or monthly indexes of industrial production can be adjusted to remove seasonal fluctuations, and help to identify fundamental movements in the economy.

---

describe a recession: a general slowdown in economic activity, usually involving a decline in total output, income, and employment, lasting six months or more, and marked by contractions in many sectors of the economy.[1]

A recession ends with the **trough**; that is, the **turning point** where economic activity is at its lowest. This is followed by the **expansion** phase. Output increases,

[1]The definition is a modified version of one suggested in Geoffrey H. Moore, *Business Cycles, Inflation, and Forecasting*, 2nd ed. (Cambridge, Mass.: Ballinger, 1983), Chapter 1.

and profits, employment, wages, prices, and interest rates generally rise. Historically, the **peak**, or upper turning point, was often associated with a financial panic, such as the panic of 1907 or "Black Tuesday"—October 29, 1929, when North American stock markets crashed. Recent peaks have been much less spectacular, with one notable exception. The economic peak in late 1973 and early 1974 coincided with war in the Middle East, an oil embargo, and skyrocketing oil prices.

Not only is it difficult to decide when a downturn

becomes strong enough to be classified as a recession. It is also difficult to decide when a serious recession should be labelled a *depression*. There is no commonly accepted definition of a depression—except, perhaps, Harry Truman's quip with which we introduced this chapter. Because the Depression of the 1930s was so deep and long-lasting, the reduction in output and employment would have to be exceptionally severe and persistent before we should talk of a depression. In Canada, seasonally adjusted unemployment rates were so high (in the range of 11% to 13% of the labour force) between early 1982 and late 1985 that some commentators wanted to classify this period as a depression. However, even though unemployment rates remained in this very high range, total output grew at healthy rates in 1983 and 1984 (real GNP surpassed its previous peak level at the end of 1983). Therefore, most economists stop short of describing 1981–82 as a depression, and refer to it instead as an exceptionally severe recession.

In any case, no matter how a depression is defined, there is no doubt that this term should be used to describe the 1930s.

THE GREAT DEPRESSION OF THE 1930s

The Great Depression of more than 50 years ago still haunts us today. Between the peak of 1929 and the depth of the Depression in 1933, real GNP declined by more than one-third. The unemployment rate shot up to almost 20% of the labour force. Prices fell, with the GNP deflator declining about 19%. The combination of falling prices and falling real output meant that current-dollar GNP decreased almost 50%. In the United States, the story was much the same.

Nor did the recovery come quickly and strongly. Business revived slowly, with the unemployment rate gradually declining to 9.1% by 1937. In 1938, there was another slowdown with increased unemployment—a recession within the Depression. It was not until 1941, after the outbreak of World War II in Europe, that the unemployment rate finally fell below 9%. By 1941, the Canadian economy was on a war footing, rushing to re-arm, with industry working around the clock to produce military equipment and supplies. Between 1938 and 1942, defence spending

shot up from less than 1% of GNP to more than 30% of GNP. The Great Depression was ended only by an even greater catastrophe—World War II.

The decade of depression was a disaster for many segments of society. Many of those thrown out of work were unable to find other jobs. Nor were the unemployed alone in their misery. Business bankruptcies came thick and fast. Between 1929 and 1932, total corporation profits fell by more than 90%. In the face of slack demand, prices of farm commodities dropped more than 50% between 1929 and 1932. In parts of the country, the plight of farmers was compounded by a natural disaster—a severe and prolonged drought, which turned much of the Prairie provinces into a dust bowl. Farmers and the unemployed struggled to get by on the small relief payments of local governments. Offering her engagement ring as collateral, an Alberta housewife wrote to Prime Minister R.B. Bennett asking for a loan:

> We are just one of many on relief and trying to keep our place without being starved out. Have a good 1/2 section not bad buildings and trying to get a start without any money and five children all small. Have been trying to send 3 to school and live on $10.00 a month relief for everything medicine meat flour butter scribblers. Haven't had any milk for 3 months . . . .
>
> My husband doesn't know I am writing this letter but I just dont know what to do for money the children come to me about everything its the women & children who suffer in these terrible times . . . .[2]

Unemployed single men (who were not eligible for relief payments) roamed the country in search of a job:

> The municipalities steer them off because if they are arrested as vagrants they become a charge on the municipality and it costs a dollar a day to keep them. So their word is "Keep them moving." The C.P.R. police advise the men that it is better travelling C.N.R. and the C.N.R. police

[2]Quoted in Michiel Horn, ed., *The Dirty Thirties: Canadians in the Great Depression* (Toronto: Copp Clark Publishing, 1972), p. 237. Reprinted by permission of Michiel Horn, *The Dirty Thirties: Canadians in the Great Depression*.

return the compliment . . . . There is no work, no hope, no place for them.[3]

The Depression was worldwide; large-scale unemployment was an international phenomenon. There were immeasurable, but perhaps even greater, political consequences. The Depression was one of the factors that brought Hitler to power, with his promises of full employment and military conquest. The world in which we live has been shaped by the events of the 1930s.

The Great Depression laid the foundation for modern macroeconomics. "Never again" was the determination of the economic scholar, the politician, and the general public. In fact, we have been successful in preventing a repeat of the 1930s. Economic problems in recent decades have been mild compared to those of the thirties.

OUTPUT, UNEMPLOYMENT, AND INFLATION IN RECENT BUSINESS CYCLES

However, in spite of successes, problems have remained. The economy has continued to fluctuate. Furthermore, and perhaps most disconcerting of all, the performance of the economy does not seem to have improved with time. Recessions have not been getting more and more mild. On the contrary, the 1981–82 recession was the most severe since the Great Depression.

Figure 8-2 shows how output, unemployment, profits, hourly wages, and inflation have changed since 1959. We have identified periods of negative or slow growth as recessions and marked them with coloured bars in the diagram.[4] Although recent recessions have caused much less economic dislocation than the collapse of 1929–33, the recent behaviour of the economy is broadly consistent with the 1930s in some important respects. Specifically:

[3]From a 1932 description by the Reverend Andrew Roddan, quoted in L. Richter, ed., *Canada's Unemployment Problem* (Toronto: Macmillan, 1939), p. 180.

[4]We have generally defined recessions as periods of slow growth with each period including at least two quarters of negative growth. The 1980 mini-recession does not quite meet this criterion. However, the fall in real GNP in early 1980 was substantial enough that GNP remained below its previous peak value for two successive quarters; therefore we include 1980 as a recession anyway.

- During recessions, when production is falling, or growing very slowly, the unemployment rate rises. Likewise, when production recovers during an expansion, more workers are needed, and the unemployment rate falls.
- During recessions, profits fall by a much larger percentage than output. They rise rapidly during expansions.
- During recessions, when output is declining, inflation generally declines, too. When the economy is expanding, the rate of inflation generally accelerates.

Observe that wages and profits behave quite differently during recessions. While profits fall sharply, money wages remain much more stable. Indeed, recessions had no readily apparent effect on the wage series shown in Figure 8-2. Recessions hit workers primarily in the form of unemployment, not lower wages.

Observe, also, that inflation responds slowly to changing business conditions. During the first half of the long expansion of the 1960s, for example, prices were quite stable. It was only in the latter part of the 1960s that inflation began to accelerate significantly. Similarly, the strong upswings in inflation occurred in the last half of the expansions of 1970–74 and 1975–79.

Furthermore, the upward momentum of inflation may continue into the early part of a recession, as it did in 1974 and 1981–82. Generally, it is toward the end of recessions that economic slack has its strongest effect in bringing down the rate of inflation. Downward pressure on the rate of inflation sometimes continues into the early recovery—as in 1971, 1976, and especially 1983–84.

The slowness of prices to respond introduces an important complication into the government's task of stabilizing the economy, as we shall see when we get to the more advanced macroeconomic topics of Part 4 (chapters 14 to 19).

Consumption, Investment, and Net Exports during Recession

During recessions, some parts of GNP decline much more than others. This is illustrated in Figure 8-3, which shows the changes in various segments of aggregate demand, between the last quarter of 1979 (which marked the end of the expansion of the 1970s) and the

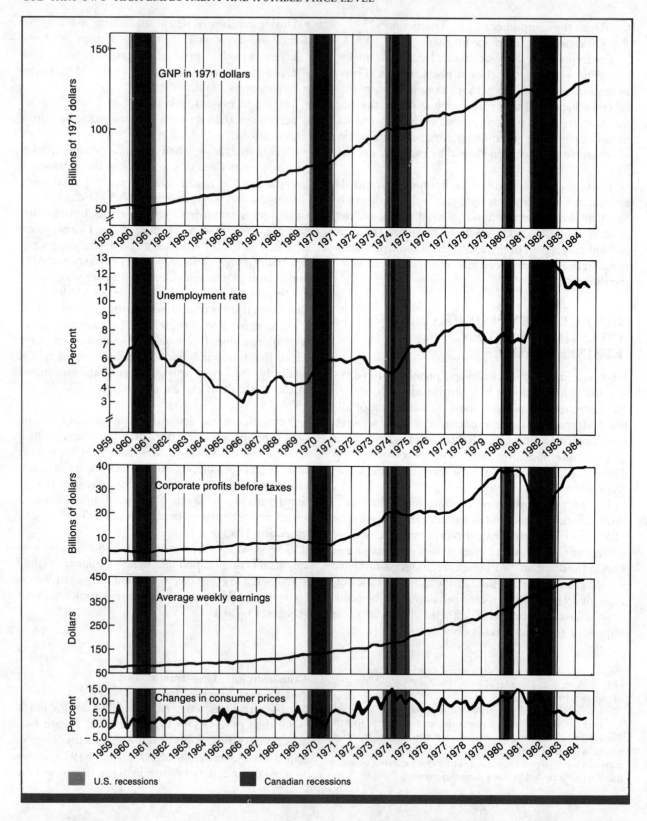

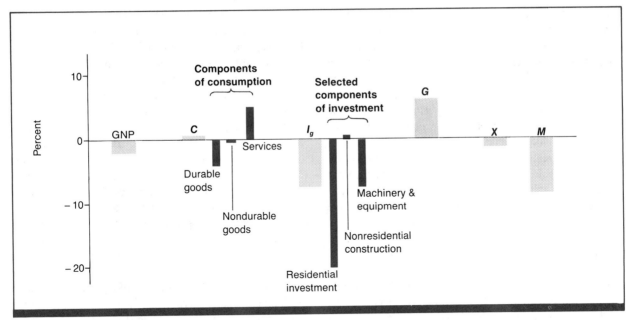

Figure 8-3   Percentage changes in real GNP and selected components between last quarter of 1979 and last quarter of 1982.

The economy reached a cyclical peak in the last quarter of 1979. There were then two quick recessions, with the trough of the second occurring in the last quarter of 1982. This figure shows how some components of GNP declined much more than others. In fact, both consumption and government purchases of goods and services increased in real terms, and real exports fell by just a small amount. The recession was concentrated in the investment sector, particularly inventory investment. Real imports fell by a substantial amount. However, because imports are a subtraction from GNP, this fall helped to moderate the severity of the recession.

Source: *Bank of Canada Review* (January 1986).

last quarter of 1982 (when the recession reached its trough).

Consumption. Over this period, real GNP declined by 2.8%, but real consumption expenditures actually rose. Expenditures for services increased by 3% and spending on semi-durables and non-durables also increased. However, consumers cut back their real spending for durable goods by almost 8%.

There is a reason for this different behaviour of durables, on the one hand, and other consumption goods, on the other. Because durables last, people have the option of postponing purchases during hard times, when they are having trouble paying their bills. For example, as incomes decline, people may decide to fix up their old cars or old refrigerators rather than splurging on new ones. They can continue to enjoy the use of durables, even if they are not currently buying them. This obviously does not apply to services such as dental care. Services are consumed as they are produced. Nor does it apply to non-durable goods. Purchases of food represent one of the last things that people will cut back on during recessions.

Investment. Much larger fluctuations occur in the investment sector. By the last quarter of 1982, total real investment had fallen by 24% from its level three years earlier. Residential investment decreased by 20%. Other private fixed investment (including machinery and equipment) declined by a less spectacular 4.6%. Inventory accumulation, which had been positive in all but two quarters during the 1976 to 1979 period, was negative for five successive quarters during 1981–82; measured in current dollars, it reached −$12.4

◀ **Figure 8-2   Recent business fluctuations.**

Areas in solid colour denote recessionary periods in the Canadian economy, while the shaded areas denote recessions in the United States.

Source: Compiled from Statistics Canada, *CANSIM Databank Historical Labour Force Statistics*, and *Review of Employment and Payrolls*. Reproduced by permission of the Minister of Supply and Services Canada.

billion (3.4% of GNP) in 1982:4. (1982:4 is an abbreviated way of writing "the fourth quarter of 1982.")

Instability of investment has been a continuing feature of business cycles; fluctuations in investment have accounted for a large fraction of overall fluctuations in the economy. Furthermore, the decline in inventories in 1982 was typical for a period of recession. Inventory investment has become negative in every recession during the last 30 years. In fact, swings in inventory investment have been as large as 70% of the declines in real GNP during the recessions of the past three decades. It is not surprising, therefore, that the business fluctuations in the postwar period have frequently been referred to as *inventory recessions*.[5]

Net exports. In the 1980–82 period, real exports declined by about 4.4%. Because exports are such a large share of GNP, this decline made a substantial contribution to the overall fall in real GNP. This is a typical pattern in Canadian recessions: Decreases in real exports have contributed to the decline in GNP in five of the six recessions during the last three decades. On average, the fall in exports has accounted for as much as 40% of the overall reductions in GNP.

Since Canadian exports are sold in foreign markets, principally the United States, one would expect that our exports would be sensitive to international economic conditions, and particularly to economic conditions in the United States. Thus, the fact that reductions in our exports usually contribute to the decline in GNP during Canadian recessions suggests that our recessions tend to happen at the same time as they do in the United States. Looking back at Figure 8-2 confirms that this is indeed what usually happens. The areas in solid colour denote periods of recession in Canada, as explained earlier, while areas marked with shaded bars mark off U.S. recessions. As the figure shows, every time there has been a recession in Canada during the past 25 years, there has also been a recession in the United States. Moreover, *every* American recession has resulted in a recessionary period of slow growth in Canada as well. This should not come as a surprise. Since about 70% of our foreign trade (on both

the export and the import sides) is with the United States, and because most of our international capital flows represent movements of funds between Canada and the United States, it is not strange that our economy is especially sensitive to business fluctuations in that country. As the saying goes: "When the United States sneezes, Canada catches a cold."

The tendency for business cycles to take place at the same time in different countries is apparent not only when one compares Canada and the United States, but also when one compares the cycles in the North American and European economies. The links between the world's economies (through trade and capital flows) are apparently strong enough to produce a powerful mechanism for *international transmission of economic fluctuations*. Because this transmission mechanism exists, the policy makers responsible for economic stabilization in the smaller countries of the world are faced with an extra difficulty. Not only will they be responsible for dealing with economic fluctuations that have their origin in domestic disturbances (such as a crop failure, or a strike in a large domestic industry); they will also be called upon to deal with fluctuations that originate with disturbances in the large foreign economies. In later chapters, we will consider this issue in more detail.

Figure 8-3 shows that there was a substantial decrease in real imports during the 1980–82 period. This is also typical of recessions. As consumption and investment fall, there is a reduction in the demand for imported consumer goods or imported goods used for investment. Since imports are a *subtraction* from GNP, the fact that imports tend to fall in recessions and rise during expansions has a *stabilizing* effect on the Canadian economy: The fluctuations in imports moderate the effects of fluctuations in consumption and investment demand on the demand for Canadian-produced goods and services. We will discuss this point further in Chapter 11.

UNEMPLOYMENT

The two principal features of a recession are a stagnation or actual decline in output, and a rise in unemployment. Changes in output are measured by the national product accounts. Changes in unemployment are measured by the unemployment rate.

---

[5]Sometimes inventory investment does not become negative until after the recession is over. But many of the cutbacks in orders, which ultimately cause the inventory reduction, occur earlier during the recession period.

Calculating the Unemployment Rate

Each month, Statistics Canada estimates the unemployment rate using an obvious, direct approach: It asks people. Because it would be prohibitively expensive and time consuming to ask everybody, a sample of about 53,000 households is surveyed.[6] Questions are asked about each member of the household who is at least 15 years old, except members of the armed forces and those who are unavailable for work, for example, those who are in prison. Each individual is classified in one of three categories: (1) employed, (2) unemployed, or (3) not in the labour force.

The first category includes all those who have worked during the week of the survey, including part-time employees who have worked as little as one hour. The second category includes people without work who (a) are on temporary layoff but expect to be recalled, (b) are waiting to report to a new job within four weeks, or (c) say they have actively looked for work during the previous four weeks, and are currently available for work. The remainder are out of the labour force. This group includes retirees, full-time students without paying jobs, and those who stay out of the labour force in order to look after young children. The unemployment rate is calculated as the number of unemployed as a percentage of the labour force (Table 8-1, line 3).

The method used in calculating the unemployment rate has caused controversy. (1) Some critics think the official unemployment rate overstates the true figure, pointing out that there is no check on those who say they are looking for work; they are simply asked. (2) On the other hand, others observe that, during hard times, workers may become discouraged and quit looking for work after they have been repeatedly rebuffed. They thereby drop out of the labour force. Thus, during recessions, the rise in the unemployment rate may not measure the full deterioration in the employment situation. This interpretation is supported by the behaviour of the labour force. During recessions, it generally grows very slowly and sometimes even declines because of the departure of discouraged workers. On the other hand, it grows rapidly during recoveries. When jobs are easier to get, people are more likely to enter the labour force, and less likely to drop out.

> *Discouraged workers* are those who want work but are no longer actively looking for it because they think no jobs are available. When they stop looking for work, they are no longer counted either as part of the labour force or as unemployed.

Finally, during recessions, there is an increase in the number of people who can't get full-time jobs, and who are therefore involuntarily limited to part-time work. The usual unemployment statistics do not take

Table 8-1
The Labour Force and Unemployment, October 1984 (thousands)

1. Total population		25,213
Less: Those under 15		5,995
Not in Labour Force		6,723
2. *Equals:* Labour Force		12,495
a) Employed	11,077	
b) Unemployed	1,418	

3. Unemployment rate as percent of labour force:
$$\frac{\text{line 2(b)}}{\text{line 2}} = \frac{1,418}{12,495} = 11.3\%$$

4. Underemployment (part-time workers who would like full-time work) 469

As percent of labour force:
$$\frac{\text{line 4}}{\text{line 2}} = \frac{469}{12,495} = 3.8\%$$

Addendum: Labour force participation rates (persons over 14 years of age; percent)

	Male	Female
1953	82.9	23.4
1961	81.1	29.3
1971	77.3	39.4
1981	78.4	51.7
1984	76.6	53.5

SOURCE: Statistics Canada, *The Labour Force*, November 1984. Reproduced by permission of the Minister of Supply and Services Canada.

[6]The survey does not include residents of the Yukon and Northwest Territories, or people living on Indian reserves.

into account such **underemployment**. However, information is collected on the number of part-time workers who wanted full-time work but were unable to find it (Table 8-1, line 4). Even though underemployment may have less serious consequences than outright unemployment, it is nevertheless a problem for a large fraction of the labour force. Not surprisingly, underemployment becomes larger during recessions when more workers are limited to part-time work.

Underemployment

We have just considered one group of the underemployed: those who can find only part-time work when they want full-time jobs. But underemployment also takes a second form, which results from the way in which businesses respond to falling sales.

During recessions, businesses do not change the number of employees quickly. As the economy begins to weaken, businesses are more likely to cancel overtime than to lay off workers. Thus, employment falls less rapidly than output. And even after overtime has been substantially eliminated, employers are reluctant to lay off workers. One reason is that a person who has been laid off may take a job somewhere else. When sales revive, the business will then have to go to the bother and expense of hiring and training a replacement. Thus, managers often conclude that it is better to keep workers on the job, even if they are not kept busy. Such workers are underemployed in the sense that they produce significantly less than they could. Thus, as the economy declines into recession, the **productivity of labour** generally declines.

> Workers are *underemployed* if (1) they can find only part-time work when they want full-time work; or (2) if they are being paid full time, but are not kept busy because of low demand for the firm's products.
>
> The *productivity of labour* is the average amount produced in an hour of work. It is measured as total output divided by the number of hours of labour input.

When the economy finally does recover, labour productivity increases very rapidly. Because many businesses have developed slack during the recession, they have underemployed labour and machinery. Thus, during the early stages of a recovery, businesses can increase their output substantially before they need to add many more workers.

As a result, output fluctuates more than unemployment during the business cycle. A study by University of Toronto economists Peter Dungan and Thomas Wilson[7] suggests that on average, every 2% cyclical change in output leads to a change in the unemployment rate of about 1% in the opposite direction. This tendency for output to fluctuate much more strongly than unemployment was originally found in studies of the U.S. economy in the 1950s and 1960s, and is known as *Okun's Law* after the late American economist Arthur Okun.

Who Are the Unemployed?

Unemployment does not fall equally on all members of society. The unemployment rate for teenagers is much higher than for adults (Figure 8-4). Unemployment rates have consistently been higher in British Columbia and the Maritimes than in the rest of Canada. The unemployment situation is particularly bleak for young people in the Maritimes. For example, teenage unemployment in Newfoundland reached a staggering 40% in the fall of 1982, and it remained in the 30–40% range well into the mid-1980s, even though the economy was expanding. Historically, the unemployment rate for women has generally been above that for men. However, there is a tendency for the difference to become smaller during recessions, when male-dominated sectors such as construction, heavy manufacturing, and resource industries, are hit hard with layoffs. The lower panel in Figure 8-4 confirms this tendency: In the recession of 1981–82, the rate for men over 25 rose much more than the rate for women in this age category, and the difference between the male and female rate remained small during the recovery in 1983–84.

Figure 8-5 illustrates two other important features about the unemployed—how they came to be unemployed, and how long they are unemployed. Not surprisingly, the duration of unemployment increases sharply during recessions, as unemployed workers experience more and more difficulty in finding jobs. At the end of the prosperous year 1979, those who had been out of work for 14 or more weeks made up

[7]D. Peter Dungan and Thomas A. Wilson, *Potential GNP: Performance and Prospects*, University of Toronto Institute for Policy Analysis, report no. 10 (Toronto, 1982).

about 30% of the total number of unemployed. As overall unemployment peaked in late 1982 and early 1983, the figure had risen to about 50%. This pattern has important implications. Short-term unemployment can be painful, but is scarcely catastrophic. It is long-term unemployment that is so demoralizing. During recessions, this type of unemployment takes up a larger share of the rising overall unemployment rate. Thus,

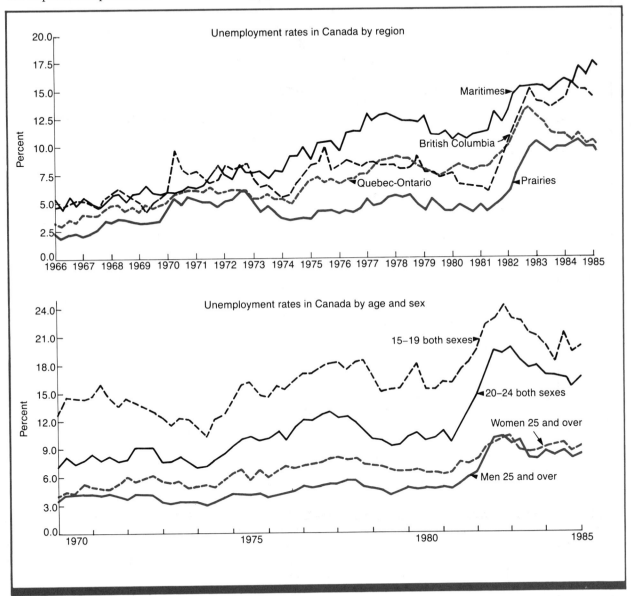

Figure 8-4 Selected unemployment rates.
Unemployment rates vary greatly among different groups in the economy. Unemployment rates in British Columbia and the Maritime provinces are consistently higher than rates in other parts of Canada. Historically, women have had higher unemployment rates than men, but the rate for men rose above the women's rate during the recession of 1982. Teen-agers have the highest unemployment rate of all. Even during the relatively prosperous years of 1973–74, the teenage unemployment rate was still above 10%. For the recession of 1982, it was more than 20%.

Source: Statistics Canada, *CANSIM Databank*. Reproduced by permission of the Minister of Supply and Services Canada.

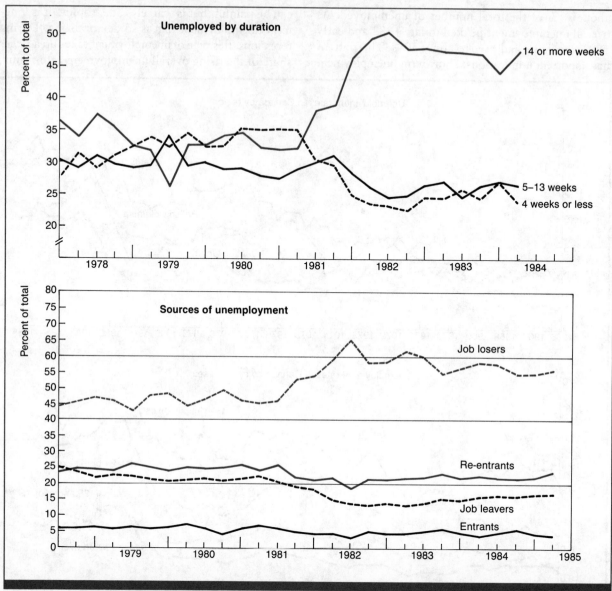

Figure 8-5 Duration of unemployment, and its sources.
The upper panel shows how the duration of unemployment increased during the 1982 recession and into the early recovery, when people were still having difficulty finding jobs. The lower panel shows the sources of unemployment. During the relatively prosperous period 1978–81, the share of the unemployed who had lost their jobs through layoff or firing was usually less than half; the rest were people who had quit their jobs and labour-force entrants who had not yet found work. However, during the recession of 1982 more than half the unemployed had lost their jobs—well over 60% in late 1982 and early 1983.

Source: Statistics Canada, *Historical Labour Force Statistics*, 1984. Data have been seasonally adjusted by authors. Reproduced by permission of the Minister of Supply and Services Canada.

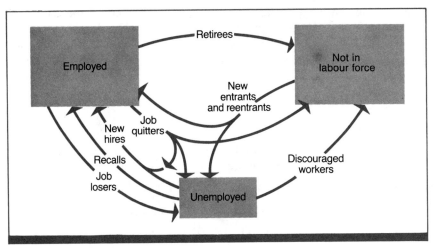

Figure 8-6   The changing labour force.
The labour force is quite fluid. Not only do many people move from job to job, but many move into and out of the labour force, and into and out of the pool of unemployed.

during recessions, the unemployment situation becomes even worse than it appears in the overall unemployment numbers. For example, while the overall number of the unemployed about doubled (from fewer than 800 thousand toward the end of 1979 to 1.6 million in early 1983), the number of long-term unemployed (14 weeks or more) nearly tripled, reaching more than 900,000 in the first quarter of 1983.

During recessions, people are much more likely to lose their jobs, either through layoff or discharge (Figure 8-5, lower panel). However, even during recessions, it is unusual if more than 60% of the unemployed have actually lost their previous jobs. The other 40% are new entrants (young people who are looking, but have not yet found work after leaving school), re-entrants (many of whom are re-entering the labour force after caring for young families), and people who have quit their last jobs to look for something better. Not surprisingly, people are more reluctant to quit during hard times, when other jobs are scarce. But even as unemployment hit its peak of about 1.6 million in early 1983, about 200,000 of the unemployed were people who had quit their previous jobs (and over 300,000 were re-entrants into the labour force).

This illustrates something important about the Canadian labour force. It is quite mobile. Many people are ready to quit their jobs to look for something better. This mobility of the labour force is illustrated in Figure 8-6. The arrows show the many ways people move into and out of employment, and into and out of the labour force. Because of this mobility, it is difficult to define precisely what is meant by "full employment." Clearly, we are not striving for an economy in which the unemployment rate is zero. To accomplish such a goal, we would have to forbid people from leaving one job until they already had another one lined up.

Types of Unemployment
Before attempting to define the elusive concept of "full employment," let us consider the various types of unemployment. The first is the one we've talked about so far: cyclical unemployment. During recessions, workers are laid off. This is the most important type of unemployment, and the one on which macroeconomic analysis is focused. But there are also other types.
Frictional unemployment.   There will always be some people who are between jobs, or looking for their first job. Others may be temporarily out of work because

of the weather—for example, those employed in construction work.

> *Frictional unemployment* is temporary unemployment associated with adjustments in a changing, dynamic economy. It arises for a number of reasons. For example, some new entrants into the labour force take time to find jobs, some workers with jobs quit to look for something better, and some are unemployed by temporary disturbances (for example, bad weather, or a temporary shutdown of an automobile factory to retool for a new model).

Such frictional unemployment is practically inevitable. It is difficult to see how it could be eliminated without a detailed government policy directing people to the first available jobs. And at least some frictional unemployment is desirable. For example, people are often willing to spend some time looking for a job. Such time can be well spent, since the first available job may be quite inappropriate. Having people search for high-paying, high-productivity jobs is not only good for them; it also contributes to the overall efficiency of the economy. Similarly, if we are to have people occupied in building houses, this will inevitably result in some unemployment: Some construction jobs can't be done in bad weather.

In our dynamic, changing economy, some industries decline; others rise. In many cases, when one firm goes bankrupt, others rise to take its place, and the labour force can move to the new jobs quite quickly and easily. Such transitional unemployment is also classified as frictional; people are temporarily between jobs as they hunt for new ones.

Structural unemployment. In other cases, the changing pattern of jobs may leave workers stranded. In the Maritimes, many jobs were lost as resource-based industries such as forestry and fishing declined. Many of the unemployed (or underemployed) forestry workers and fishermen have been unable to find local jobs; to find work, they would have had to move hundreds of miles and learn new skills. Similarly, a loss of part of the market to Japanese cars, combined with automation on the assembly line, has permanently reduced the number of jobs in the North American automobile industry. Even with the cyclical recovery of automo-

bile sales in 1983–84, employment in the Canadian automobile industry has remained well below the peak numbers reached in 1977–79; partly for this reason, unemployment in Ontario declined relatively slowly after the 1981–82 recession. These are illustrations of **structural unemployment.**

> *Structural unemployment* results when the location and/or skills of the labour force do not match the available jobs. It can occur because of declining demand for a product, because of automation or other changes in technology, because industry is moving to a different location, or because new entrants into the labour force do not have the training for available jobs.

It should be obvious that no sharp distinction can be drawn between frictional and structural unemployment. If an auto parts factory closes down, and a bicycle factory opens up a mile away, displaced auto workers may quickly and easily find jobs in the bicycle factory. The temporary unemployment is frictional. If the new jobs are 150 miles away, the workers will have to move to take them. During the extended period before they actually do move, they may be classified among the structurally unemployed. But what if the new job is 30 miles away, near the limit of the commuting range? This case is not so clear. The difference between frictional and structural unemployment is one of degree. Structural unemployment lasts longer, because to get a new job, a greater change in location or a more extensive acquisition of new skills is required.

Because it is longer-lasting and more painful than frictional unemployment, structural unemployment is a greater social problem. But, once again, it may represent a painful side effect of the desirable flexibility of the economy. After the invention of the transistor, it would have made no sense to protect glass workers' jobs by requiring radios and computers to use vacuum tubes. However, the pain associated with such structural unemployment does make a case for government assistance to ease the adjustment process; for example, by subsidized retraining for displaced workers. Thus the society that benefits from the new transistor technology can help to reduce the burden that falls on a group of glassworkers who have lost their jobs.

HOW MUCH EMPLOYMENT IS "FULL EMPLOYMENT"?

It is impossible—and undesirable—to eliminate frictional unemployment. Hence, *full employment* must be defined as something less than the employment of 100% of the labour force. Over the past quarter century, there has been a lively debate over what unemployment rate should be considered "full employment."

In the years following the 1960 recession, the Canadian unemployment rate gradually fell from a high of about 7.5% in 1960–61; by 1965 it had reached a level of 3.5–4.0%. At that time, the Economic Council of Canada suggested that it should be possible to reach a "target" rate of 3% without unleashing inflationary pressures. Based on past experience, this did not seem unrealistic: The actual unemployment rate had stayed well below 3% for many years during the 1940s and 1950s.

For a time, the 3% target seemed attainable. The unemployment rate was less than 3.5% on the average during 1966, and for a short while actually dipped below 3%. Yet there was little inflationary pressure. However, during the late 1960s, inflationary pressures gathered force. There was widespread agreement that the expansion of the 1960s had become too strong. Reluctantly, the Economic Council revised its target upward. The Council concluded that the unemployment rate could not be brought below 3.8% without causing inflation.

During the 1970s, the average unemployment rate never fell below 5% in any year; yet the government was still struggling to control inflation. Consequently, the new target of 3.8% came to be viewed as unrealistic, in the sense that it could be achieved only during temporary periods when the economy was overheating and inflation accelerating. Frictional unemployment seemed to be higher than it had been in previous decades. Several explanations were suggested:

1. Changes in the composition of the labour force. For example, teenagers had become a larger fraction of the labour force, and teenagers are more likely to drift from job to job than are adults with family responsibilities.
2. Increases in the minimum wage, which meant that it was more expensive for employers to hire workers with minimal skills.
3. Reduced pressure on unemployed workers to take the first job available. Family income was being maintained in the face of unemployment by (a) improved unemployment insurance, and (b) increases in the number of families with two or more members in the labour force.

As a result, many economists have argued that the "full-employment rate" should be revised upward again. In 1980, the Economic Council raised its estimate of a realistic target to 6%. In 1983, Ernie Stokes of the Conference Board of Canada published a careful study of the full-employment rate in Canada for the period 1966 to 1981. His results implied that even 6% may have been an underestimate, and he suggested that a realistic full-employment rate for the late 1970s and early 1980s may have been in the 7.0–7.5% range.[8]

From late 1981 through late 1985, the actual unemployment rate has been in the 8–13% range; during the worst part of the recession, it exceeded 12% for almost a year. Since these rates are higher than any reasonable estimate of the full-employment target, the issue of precisely defining the target lost some of its urgency. It was clearly desirable to bring down the unemployment rate substantially. Furthermore, changes in the composition of the labour force during the first half of the 1980s would suggest that a realistic target for the mid-1980s should involve a *lower* unemployment rate than in the late 1970s. One reason for this was the changing age structure of the Canadian population: In the late 1980s, the number of teenage entrants into the labour force will be much lower than it was in the 1970s and early 1980s.

ECONOMIC COSTS OF RECESSIONS AND UNEMPLOYMENT

Whenever the economy slips into recession, potential output is lost, never to be recovered. The weeks and months that the unemployed spend in idleness are gone forever.

The substantial economic costs of recessions—in terms of output foregone—are illustrated in Figure 8-7. The black curve represents an estimate of the path the economy would have followed in the absence of recessions and business cycles; that is, if full employment had been consistently maintained. This path is

[8]Ernie Stokes, *Canada's Output Growth: Performance and Potential, 1966–92*, Conference Board of Canada, Technical Paper, April 1983.

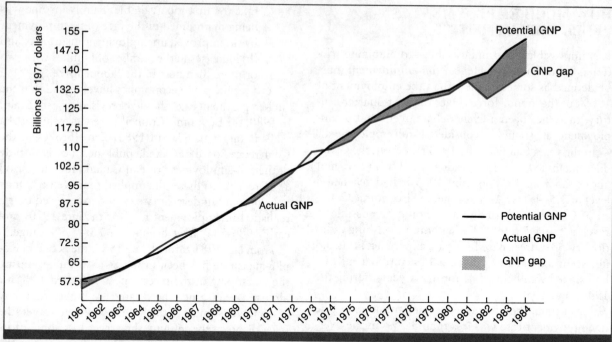

Figure 8-7   The cost of recession: The GNP gap.
During periods of slack in the economy, production is at less than the full-employment potential. The GNP gap—the amount by which actual GNP falls below potential—is a measure of output lost because of recessions.

Sources: Peter Dungan and Thomas Wilson, *Potential GNP: Performance and Prospects*, University of Toronto Institute for Policy Analysis, report no. 10 (Toronto, 1982), p. 15 (1961–78); estimates by authors (1979–84).

accordingly labelled **full-employment GNP** or **high-employment GNP** or **potential GNP**. Needless to say, it is difficult to identify this path with precision. Most obviously, there is uncertainty—described in the previous section—over just how much employment should be considered "full employment." Nevertheless, an estimate of potential output is useful in estimating the approximate amount of output lost because of recessions.

Lost output is known as the **GNP gap**. By far the greatest gap occurred during the Great Depression, prior to the period shown in Figure 8-7. In recent decades, the greatest gap has occurred during the severe recession of 1981–82 and the early recovery that followed. The estimated gaps in Figure 8-7 imply that, during 1982–84, over $35 billion in GNP was foregone, measured at 1971 prices (about 8% of potential output over those three years). In 1985 dollars, this amounts to more than $100 billion. To put this in perspective, note that $1 billion represents more than $40 for every man, woman, and child in Canada.

Thus, the economic slack of 1981–84 meant a loss of approximately $4,000 for every person in the nation. (Note: These numbers can change substantially if different estimates are made of potential output. Problems in estimating the potential GNP path will be studied in detail in Chapter 16.)

> The *GNP gap* is the amount by which actual GNP falls below potential GNP.

Observe that according to Figure 8-7, actual GNP *exceeded* the estimate of potential GNP in 1965–66 and in 1973–74. This may seem puzzling: how can the economy possibly produce more than its potential? The answer is that the economy is capable of short-term bursts of activity which are unsustainable in the long run because of their cumulative adverse effects on the economy. Most notably, the short bursts of activity can cause the overheating of the economy, and an acceleration of inflation.

The economic costs of recession and unemployment illustrated in Figure 8-7 are important; additional goods and services could be put to good use. But it is equally important to recognize the great stresses and hardships on the unemployed. Unemployment is costly not only in terms of the output foregone, but also in terms of demoralization of the population (Box 8-2).

INFLATION

The costs of inflation are much less obvious than the costs of unemployment. That may seem surprising, as people are almost unanimous in expressing dislike of inflation. But in any transaction, there is both a buyer and a seller; when a price rises, the seller gains and the buyer loses. Thus, the analysis of inflation is quite different from the study of unemployment. Unemployment represents a clear loss. When we look at inflation, we have to consider both losers and gainers.

Losers

As a result of inflation, money loses its value. Thus, the most obvious losers are those who own bonds, or have lent money in other ways. Consider the individual who purchased a $10,000 government bond in 1962 which came due in 1984. In addition to the interest of 4% per annum, the bond purchaser expected to get $10,000 back when the bond reached maturity. In a formal sense, that expectation was fulfilled: The government did pay the bondholder $10,000 in 1984. But that $10,000 represented a pale shadow of its original value. In 1984, $10,000 bought no more than $2,600 would have bought in 1962. In just 22 years, money had lost almost 75% of its value.

Some people might say that this doesn't matter much, because only wealthy people own bonds. But this is not so. Inflation does not simply steal from the rich and benefit the poor. Many elderly people of moderate means hold bonds—or savings accounts, which suffer the same disadvantages as bonds during inflation.

Because inflation reduces the real value of bonds, the elderly may also be hit by inflation in another way. They may have saved through private pension funds, which in turn hold bonds. With inflation, pensions financed by these bonds provide less and less real income for retirees. For the private pension system,

the unexpected inflation of the past two decades has been a calamity. (However, recipients of government Old Age Security have not suffered in this way, since their benefits have been increased to compensate for inflation.)

Another group of losers is made up of people whose money incomes do not keep up with inflation. Refer back to Figure 8-2, which shows that average weekly earnings fell in real terms as inflation accelerated in 1973–74 and 1978–79. Even though money wages were rising, they did not keep up with accelerating inflation during those years. In fact, there was practically no increase in real weekly earnings over the period 1976 to 1984. During these eight years, the increase in money income did little more than compensate for inflation. In contrast, real income per hour rose by more than 30% in the previous decade, from 1966 to 1976.

Winners

While almost everyone understands that there are losers from inflation, it is not so well understood that there also are winners. Businesses that employ workers at stable wages win if the prices of what they sell rise more rapidly than their costs.

Just as bondholders and other lenders lose from inflation, so bond issuers and other borrowers win. When $10,000 is repaid after a period of rapid inflation, we have seen how the lender is worse off: The lender is repaid in dollars whose value has declined. For exactly the same reason, the borrower's position has improved: The dollars that the borrower must repay have decreased in value.

The windfall to homeowners. For the average family, the mortgage on their home is by far the largest debt. Consider a typical Canadian family in a small city. In 1970, they bought their dream house for $25,000, paying $5,000 down and borrowing the rest. In 1984, when their youngest child went off to university, they decided to move into something smaller. They sold their house for $70,000. Its dollar value had soared because of the inflation of the 1970–84 period.

They found that they had a tidy gain, as illustrated in Table 8-2. The original $5,000 of their own money that they had put into the house had grown *tenfold*, to $50,000 (the $70,000 from the sale of the home, minus the $20,000 used to repay the mortgage). Even though the general price level had tripled since 1970, the

BOX 8-2

WARNING: RECESSIONS CAN BE HARMFUL TO YOUR HEALTH

Harvey Brenner of Johns Hopkins University has found that unemployment and other economic problems have adverse effects on physical and mental health, and shorten life spans. The following excerpts are from his report to the U.S. Congress:†

In addition to a high unemployment rate, three other factors— decline in labour force participation, decline in average weekly hours worked, and an increase in the rate of business failures —are strongly associated with increased mortality. . . .

Economic inequality is associated with deterioration in mental health and well-being, manifest in increased rates of homicide, crime, and mental hospital admissions.

. . . The report presents new evidence on the relationship between pathological [economic] conditions and . . . per capita alcohol consumption; cigarette consumption; illicit drug traffic and use; divorce rates; and the proportion of the population living alone.

Between 1973 and 1974, the U.S. unemployment rate rose from 4.9% to 5.6% of the civilian labour force. The chart below shows Brenner's estimate of the additional stress-related deaths and crimes associated with this increase in unemployment. The statistical relationships found by Brenner do not prove that the recession caused these results. But the evidence is strong enough to provide a warning. Recessions can be harmful to your health.

†M. Harvey Brenner, *Estimating the Effects of Economic Change on National Health and Social Well-Being*, U.S. Congress Joint Economic Committee, (Washington: June 1984), pp. 2–3.

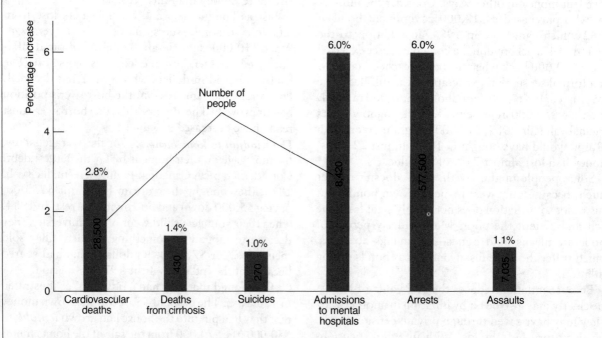

Figure 8-8   Recession, health, and crime in the 1974 U.S. recession.

Table 8-2
Inflation and Housing: A Simple Example

1970		1984	
Purchase price	$25,000	Selling price	$70,000
Borrowing (mortgage)	20,000	Repayment of mortgage	20,000
Down payment	$ 5,000	Net	$50,000
		Value in 1970 dollars =	$16,667

$50,000 represented much more buying power than their initial $5,000 down payment.

The constant-dollar or real value of the $50,000 can be calculated with an equation similar to those in Chapter 7. Specifically:

$$\text{Real value of an asset (or liability)} = \frac{\text{current dollar value}}{\text{price index}} \times 100 \qquad (8\text{-}1)$$

The price index rose from 100 in 1970 to 300 by 1984. Thus, measured in 1970 dollars, the $50,000 was worth:

$$\frac{\$50,000}{300} \times 100 = \$16,667$$

Thus, the original $5,000 investment had more than trebled in real terms. In 1984, the $50,000 would buy three times as many goods and services as the $5,000 used in 1970 to make the down payment.

This illustration has skipped over some details.[9] But it illustrates an important and valid point: *The inflation of recent decades has provided a windfall to people who borrowed to purchase homes several decades ago.* This has been particularly important for the middle class. Home ownership represents a major fraction of their assets, while home mortgages represent a major fraction of their liabilities. It is not so important for the poor, few of whom own homes, nor for the rich, who have many other assets.

Anticipated and Unanticipated Inflation

Because *inflation can lead to an arbitrary reshuffling*

[9]To simplify, we have assumed that mortgage payments cover only interest. Thus, the whole $20,000 mortgage remains to be paid off when the house is sold. In practice, each mortgage payment normally covers both interest and repayment of part of the principal. The conclusions based on Table 8-2 would not be materially changed by discarding this simplifying assumption.

of wealth and income, one of its costs is that it makes the economic system *less fair*.

This is particularly true if inflation is *unexpected*. The inflation beginning in the mid 1960s had strong effects because it came as a surprise to most people.

However, if people anticipate inflation, they can take steps to protect themselves. For example, if people anticipate inflation, then: (a) They will avoid bonds, unless interest rates rise to attractive levels; (b) workers will negotiate for higher nominal wages to compensate for the effects of inflation.

These two responses to inflation will be considered in detail in later chapters. For the moment, we note that the damage from inflation increases when it becomes *less predictable*. If people are very uncertain about what is going to happen to prices, they will have difficulty protecting themselves from its effects. Businesses that are very uncertain about inflation will have difficulty making plans. For example, should they borrow to buy machinery now, before its price rises? They cannot make good judgements if they have no clear idea regarding future prices.

One problem with high inflation is that it tends to be *variable* and *unpredictable*. Countries which suffer high rates of inflation find that the inflation rate tends to bounce around by large amounts from year to year; for example, from 100% to 75% to 150%. In contrast, when the average rate of inflation is low—say 2% or 3% per year—it is generally quite stable. Decision making can proceed in a relatively predictable environment.

Because the value of bonds is so strongly affected by inflation, high and unpredictable rates of inflation may cause people to stop buying bonds. The long-term bond market may dry up, making it difficult to raise funds for residential construction or for business expansion.

In summary, rapid inflation creates three problems:
1. An arbitrary redistribution of wealth and income.
2. An uncertain environment, in which it is difficult to make business decisions.
3. Possibly, the drying up of the long-term bond market.

KEY POINTS

1. The Canadian economy does not expand steadily. From time to time, expansion is interrupted by a recession.
2. During recessions, output declines and the unemployment rate rises. Inflation generally declines. Profits fall sharply.
3. Reductions in investment (especially residential construction and inventories) and in exports have accounted for a large part of the overall decline in GNP in Canadian recessions during the past three decades.
4. Every recession in Canada since World War II has occurred at about the same time as a U.S. recession.
5. During recessions, the increase in the unemployment rate does not reflect all the pressures on the labour force. Some workers are limited to part-time work when they want full-time employment. Some of the unemployed become discouraged. When they stop looking for work and thus drop out of the labour force, they are no longer counted among the unemployed.
6. During recessions, output declines to a greater extent than employment. Although the unemployment rate rises, the percentage decline in the number of people employed is less than the percentage decline in output.
7. The unemployment rate for young people exceeds that for the labour force as a whole. The Maritime provinces tend to have substantially higher unemployment rates than the rest of the country. Until recently, women had a higher unemployment rate than men.

8. Unemployment is classified into three categories:
   (a) frictional unemployment
   (b) structural unemployment
   (c) cyclical unemployment
   The first represents the smallest problem: people out of work temporarily as they hunt for jobs. Structural unemployment is more serious. Workers have to move or obtain additional skills in order to find jobs. Cyclical unemployment is attributable to instability in the economy.
9. There is disagreement over the amount of unemployment that should be considered "full employment." While a rate of about 4% was generally considered "full employment" during the 1960s, estimates have been substantially increased in the past 15 years, to 6%, or even 7%.
10. The GNP gap measures how much actual output falls short of the full-employment potential. The gap is an important measure of the cost of recessions; it measures how much potential output has been lost. However, it does not include all the social costs, such as the demoralization of those who are out of work.
11. Rapid inflation creates three problems:
    (a) An arbitrary redistribution of wealth and income.
    (b) An uncertain environment, in which it is difficult to make business decisions.
    (c) Possibly, the drying up of the long-term bond market.

KEY CONCEPTS

recession	underemployment	cyclical unemployment
trough	discouraged workers	potential or full-employment
expansion	labour force time lost	output
peak	Okun's Law	GNP gap
depression	frictional unemployment	anticipated and unanticipated
international transmission	structural unemployment	inflation
mechanism		

PROBLEMS

8-1 Why is it difficult to identify a recession? Why can't we simply say that there is a recession whenever real output declines?

8-2 The text notes that inflation may respond slowly to changing economic conditions. For example, the downward pressure on prices may be concentrated in the later stages of recession, and continue into the early recovery. Why might inflation be slow to respond?

8-3 During business cycles:
   (a) Why do consumer durable purchases fluctuate more than consumer purchases of non-durables and services?
   (b) Why does output fluctuate more than the unemployment rate?

8-4 Part of the reason why U.S. recessions affect the Canadian economy is that they cause a reduction in the demand for Canadian exports. Can you think of any reasons why economic conditions in the United States may also indirectly affect the amount of private investment in Canada?

8-5 Inflation is generally considered a major economic problem. How is it possible for anyone to gain from inflation?

8-6 In 1980, the National Bureau of Economic Research estimated that the downward movement of the American economy lasted six months—February to July, inclusive. Yet real GNP data show only one quarter of decline—the second quarter, from April to June. Can you explain how it is possible for a monthly GNP series to decline from February to July, while GNP measured on a quarterly basis only declines in one quarter?

Chapter 9

EXPLAINING UNEMPLOYMENT AND INFLATION: AGGREGATE SUPPLY AND AGGREGATE DEMAND

I believe myself to be writing a book on
economic theory which will largely
revolutionize—not, I suppose, at once but
in the course of the next ten years—the way
the world thinks about economic problems.

John Maynard Keynes

In studying the market for an individual product—such as apples—we illustrated the concepts of demand and supply in a diagram, with the horizontal axis showing the quantity of apples, and the vertical axis showing the price of apples. This diagram was very useful. For example, by shifting the demand and supply curves, we could see how price and quantity respond to changing conditions of demand and supply (Figures 4-5 and 4-6).

In macroeconomics, the concepts of **aggregate demand** and **aggregate supply** are useful in a similar way. Since we are now dealing with the overall magnitudes in the economy, we use the horizontal axis to show the *overall*, or *aggregate*, quantity of output—that is, real national product. On the vertical axis, we put the *average* level of prices, as measured by a price index of the type we discussed in Chapter 7.

In drawing the aggregate demand and aggregate supply curves, we must be careful. *We cannot assume that the aggregate demand curve slopes downward to the right simply because the microeconomic demand curve for an individual product slopes this way. Nor can we assume that the aggregate supply curve slopes upward to the right, simply because the supply curve for an individual product does.*

To see why, reconsider the earlier explanation in

Chapter 4 of why the demand curve for apples slopes downward to the right. This curve is drawn on the assumption that the price of apples is the *only* price that changes; when we draw the demand curve for apples, we assume that the prices of all other goods remain stable. Thus, when the price of apples falls, it declines *relative to the prices of all other goods. With apples becoming a "better buy," people are encouraged to switch* their purchases away from other goods, and buy more apples instead. Such switching—or *substitution*—is the principal reason why the demand curve for an individual product slopes downward to the right.

Now consider what happens when we turn to the macroeconomic demand curve, with total output on the horizontal axis and the average level of prices on the vertical. For the economy as a whole, a fall in the level of all prices cannot cause buyers to switch from "other goods." There are no such other goods.[1] It is not obvious how the aggregate demand curve should be drawn.

A similar problem arises on the supply side. In drawing the microeconomic supply curve for apples, we assume that the prices of all other goods remain stable. Thus, when the price of apples rises, it increases *relative to the prices* of other goods. Farmers therefore have an incentive to *switch* away from the production of other goods, and produce more apples instead. When we look at macroeconomics—studying the economy as a whole—producers can't switch away from other goods, because there aren't any. We cannot assume that the aggregate supply curve slopes upward to the right just because the supply curve for an individual product does.

How, then, are we to draw aggregate demand and aggregate supply? Historically, there have been two approaches to this problem. The first is the classical approach, which may be traced back several hundred years, to eighteenth-century British philosopher David Hume and beyond. The second is the Keynesian approach, which was introduced during the 1930s as part of an attempt to explain and combat the Great Depression.

THE CLASSICAL APPROACH

Classical theorists argued that the aggregate quantity of goods and services demanded will increase as the average price level falls, as illustrated in Figure 9-1. The reason is this. Suppose that all prices fall by, say, 50%, as illustrated by the move from P_1 to P_2. Then, each dollar buys more; the **purchasing power** of money has increased. Finding that they can buy more with their money, people will step up their purchases. Thus, the aggregate demand curve slopes downward to the right. (But remember: The additional purchases do not come about as a result of *switching* among goods. At a lower average price level, people want to buy more goods *in total*.)

Furthermore, classical economists went beyond this general statement, to be more specific. With prices

---

[1]At least, there are no other *domestic* goods. When we take account of trade with foreign countries, things become more complicated, because changes in the overall price level in a country can lead to switching between domestic and foreign goods.

To keep matters simple, the relationship between international transactions and macroeconomic activity is left out of the discussion of aggregate demand and supply in this chapter. (It is discussed in detail in Chapter 15.) However, the neoclassical economists argued that their analysis applied to an open economy (an economy with substantial international transactions), as well as to the case of a closed economy, which we focus on in this chapter. For an exposition of the classical model in an international context, see, for example, M. Parkin, *Modern Macroeconomics* (Scarborough, Ont.: Prentice-Hall Canada, 1982), Chapter 39.

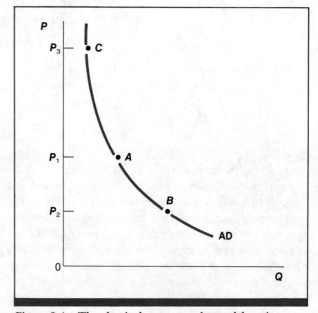

Figure 9-1 The classical aggregate demand function.
According to classical economists, the aggregate demand function slopes downward to the right. As prices fall, the money in the hands of the public will buy more. As a result, the public does buy more goods and services at *B* than at *A*.

only half as high at P_2 as at P_1, each dollar will buy twice as much. Therefore, said classical economists, the quantity of goods and services purchased at B will be about twice as great as at A. Alternatively, if prices had doubled, from P_1 to P_3, each dollar would buy only half as much as it did originally, and people would therefore buy only about half as much at C as at A. In other words, classical economists believed that we could be more specific about the shape of the aggregate demand curve than about the demand curve for an individual product. (We cannot generalize in the same way about the demand curve for an individual good. If the price of apples falls by 50%, we may expect people to buy more. But there is no reason to believe that they will buy twice as many. They may buy three or four times as many, if apples are good substitutes for other fruit. On the other hand, if the price of gasoline falls by 50%, people may not drive much more; the quantity of gasoline bought may go up only moderately—say, by 10% or 20%.)

In this theory, classical economists *put money at the centre of aggregate demand*. In their view, the willingness and ability of people to buy goods *depends on the quantity of money in their possession, and on the purchasing power of that money*.

> The *purchasing power* of money is the real quantity of goods and services that one dollar will buy. When the price level *rises*, the purchasing power of money *falls*. For example, when the price level doubles, the purchasing power of money falls to half its previous level.

Aggregate Supply: The Classical Approach

Classical economists argued that the aggregate supply function is vertical at the *potential* or *full-employment* quantity of output, as illustrated in Figure 9-2. Why?

To answer this question, consider what happens if the economy is initially at point F, with full employment. Now, suppose that all prices double, including the price of labour (that is, the wage rate). In other words, there is a **general inflation**, with *relative* prices and wages being unaffected. Workers are basically in the same position as before. While their money wages have doubled, so have prices. The real wage—the quantity of goods and services which the wage will buy—is unchanged. Therefore, workers' willingness to work

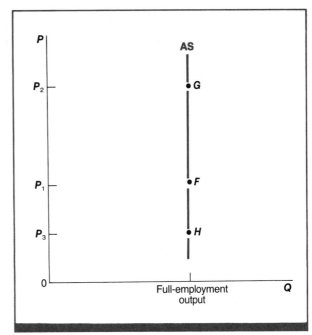

Figure 9-2   The classical aggregate supply function.
According to classical economists, the aggregate supply function is vertical at the full-employment, or potential, quantity of national product. A general rise or fall in prices and wages does not make producers any more—or any less—willing to supply goods and services.

remains the same. Businesses also are in basically the same situation as before. Their productive capacity remains unchanged, and the relationship between costs and prices also remains unchanged. As a result, businesses offer the same amount of goods and services for sale. Therefore, point G on the aggregate supply curve is directly above point F. Similarly, classical economists argued that the quantity of goods and services offered for sale would remain unchanged if all wages and prices fell by 50%, illustrated by the move from P_1 to P_3. Thus, point H is directly below point F.

Equilibrium at Full Employment

Bringing together the aggregate demand and aggregate supply curves of classical economics, we find the equilibrium at E in Figure 9-3. *Classical economists believed that the economy would be in equilibrium only at full employment*, at a point like E, *and that market forces would lead the economy to full employment*.

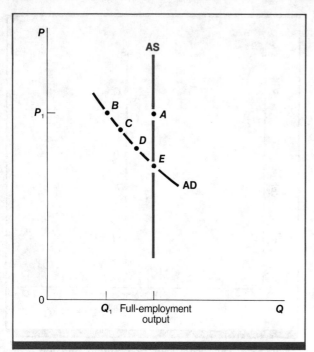

Figure 9-3 Equilibrium in classical economics.
According to classical economists, large-scale unemployment would result in an automatic movement back to full employment. Under the pressure of market forces, prices and wages would fall. The economy would gradually move down the aggregate demand curve, toward full-employment equilibrium E.

To explain this classical view, suppose that the economy is initially at a position of large-scale unemployment, such as point B in Figure 9-3. The high unemployment rate occurs because, at the initial price level P_1, the quantity of goods and services demanded (at B) is substantially less than the full-employment output (at A). What will happen, according to classical economists? At P_1, the quantity of goods and services demanded is less than producers are willing to supply. In order to sell more goods, businesses will cut their prices. At the same time, they will reduce the wage they pay, since the large number of unemployed will be so eager to get jobs that they will be willing to work for less than the prevailing wage. Thus, both prices and money wages will fall. With prices falling below P_1, the purchasing power of the money in the hands of the public will increase, and they will buy more. There will be a move along the aggregate demand curve from B to C to D. This process will continue until the economy

gets to equilibrium E, with full employment. Once this equilibrium has been reached, there will no longer be downward pressures on prices and wages.

The Classical Explanation of the Depression
Since classical economists believed that full employment always exists in equilibrium, how did they explain the Great Depression, when unemployment rates in North America rose to 20% and even higher? Their answer: Large-scale unemployment existed only when the economy was in *disequilibrium*; it was the result of temporary disturbances to the economy.

Most notably, the economy could be disturbed by a *shift* in the aggregate demand curve. As we have already seen, classical economists focused on money and its purchasing power in their analysis of aggregate demand. In drawing any single aggregate demand function (as in Figure 9-1), classical economists assumed that the nominal quantity of money was constant. That is, the number of dollars was fixed. Any changes in the quantity of money would cause a shift in the aggregate demand function. It would shift to the right if the quantity of money increased, or to the left if the quantity of money decreased.

Thus, a classical explanation of the worldwide depression goes something like this.[2] In 1929, the economy was close to a full-employment equilibrium at A in Figure 9-4, with aggregate demand AD_{1929}. Then, because of disturbances in the banking and financial system, particularly in the United States, the stock of money declined. (Between 1928–29 and 1933, money in the hands of the public fell by about 15% in Canada, and by as much as 30% in the United States.) As a result, aggregate demand shifted to the left, to AD_{1933}.

Even with this fall in demand, classical economists would say, full employment would still have been possible if prices and wages had fallen all the way to P_E. In this event, full employment would have occurred at new equilibrium E. But prices and wages were *sticky* in a downward direction; that is, they did not fall quickly in the face of slack demand and high unemployment. One reason for stickiness is that it takes some time for people searching for a job to realize that

[2]Details may be found in the very readable chapter on the Depression in Milton Friedman and Anna Schwartz, *A Monetary History of the United States, 1867–1960* (Princeton: Princeton University Press, 1963).

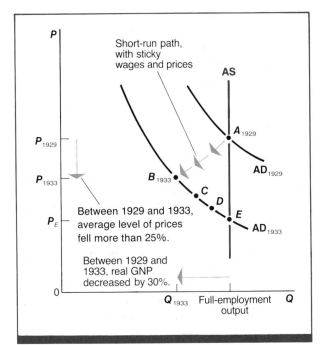

Figure 9-4   The depression in classical economics.
Classical economists believed that the principal cause of the Great Depression was a collapse in demand, caused by a sharp decline in the money stock. Because of wage and price stickiness, the economy did not move directly to its new full-employment equilibrium, *E*, but rather to *B*.

demand, price and wage adjustments could be expected to gradually restore full employment. Although it would take time, the economy would eventually move along the new aggregate demand curve from *B* to *C* to *D*, and finally to the new full-employment equilibrium *E*. So argued classical economists.

In other words, the classical aggregate supply curve illustrated where the economy would eventually go. Over the **long run**, classical economists were confident that wages and prices would in fact adjust, restoring full employment.

> In classical macroeconomics, the *long run* is the period over which prices and wages adjust completely.

This approach led classical economists to suggest two possible solutions for a depression:

1. The initial source of the disturbance might be eliminated. Steps might be taken to prevent a decline in the quantity of money in the first place, or to restore the quantity of money once it had fallen. If the money supply were increased, and aggregate demand restored to AD_{1929}, the economy might be expected to retrace its path from *B* back toward *A* in Figure 9-4.

2. Workers and businesses might be encouraged to accept lower wages and prices quickly, so the economy could move more rapidly to its new full-employment equilibrium *E*. The more willing workers and businesses were to accept lower wages and prices, the shorter would be the temporary period of unemployment. Note that the classical "long run" is not any fixed number of months or years. It is whatever period is needed for wages and prices to adjust. The faster they adjust, the sooner the economy reaches its long-run equilibrium with full employment.

However, many classical economists were quite skeptical that the government could in practice help much in promoting downward wage and price flexibility. Indeed, many believed that when the government becomes involved in markets, it is likely to keep prices up and increase their stickiness. Thus, many classical economists argued for a policy of *laissez-faire*. In macroeconomic as in microeconomic questions, they saw little role for the government, apart from providing a stable monetary system. They believed that the

they will not find the job they want, at the wage they expect. It is only after a frustrating search that they will be willing to settle for a lower wage.[3]

Because of stickiness, prices fell only to P_{1933} by 1933. With prices remaining higher than required for the new equilibrium, the amount of goods and services purchased was far less than the economy's full-employment potential. The economy was in a deep depression at point *B*.

Thus, according to the classical view, wage and price stickiness kept the economy from moving directly downward along the aggregate supply function in the face of a collapse in demand. As demand fell, the economy instead moved along the short-run path from *A* to *B*. In the absence of any further disturbance to

[3]Some classical economists argued that distortions among *relative* prices made the Depression even more severe. We skip this argument, because it was quite complex. In this section, we consider only the effects of a general, across-the-board inflation or deflation, in which all prices and wages move by the same percentage, and relative prices are accordingly left undisturbed. This allows us to grasp the central points of classical theory.

operation of market forces would work to restore full employment.

Classical Macroeconomics: A Preliminary Summary

Before proceeding, let us summarize the main points of classical macroeconomics developed thus far:

1. The aggregate demand curve slopes downward to the right. As prices fall, each dollar will buy more, and people accordingly do buy more. A single aggregate demand curve is drawn on the assumption that the nominal quantity of money is constant. If the quantity of money increases, the aggregate demand curve shifts to the right.

2. The aggregate supply curve is vertical at the full-employment output.

3. In the long run, a shift in the aggregate demand curve causes a change in prices, not in output. The reason is that, in the long run, the economy moves back to the vertical aggregate supply curve.

4. However, in the short run—when wages and prices are sticky—a collapse in aggregate demand can cause a depression. Instead of moving from A to E, the economy moves from A to B, as shown in Figure 9-4.

5. Although an economy at B will eventually move to E, a better solution is to increase the money stock, thus increasing aggregate demand back up to AD_{1929}. This will move the economy from B back toward A.

THE KEYNESIAN APPROACH

Prior to the Great Depression, most economists considered unemployment to be a relatively minor and temporary problem, associated with short-term fluctuations in the economy. The decade-long depression of the 1930s shattered this confidence, and provided the backdrop for a new theory of unemployment, put forward by British economist John Maynard Keynes. His major work—*The General Theory of Employment, Interest and Money*—attacked the prevailing classical view. Specifically, Keynes put forward three major propositions concerning unemployment in a market economy:

1. *Unemployment equilibrium.* In contrast to classical economists, Keynes argued that a market economy might have no strong tendency to move to full employment. On the contrary, a market economy might become stuck in an *equilibrium with large-scale unemployment*—often referred to, more briefly, as an **unemployment equilibrium**. Furthermore, even if the economy did temporarily reach full employment, it might be quite unstable, and fall back into depression. In other words, Keynes said that the market economy was defective in two important ways:
   (a) It might lead to a *persistent depression*, such as the Depression of the 1930s.
   (b) It might be quite *unstable*, so that even if we did achieve full employment, this happy state of affairs might be short lived.

2. *The cause of unemployment.* Keynes argued that large-scale unemployment is due to an *insufficiency of aggregate demand*—that is, too little spending for goods and services.

3. *The cure for unemployment.* To cure unemployment, aggregate demand should be increased. The best way to do that, said Keynes, is by an increase in government spending.

This third proposition was the main policy message of the *General Theory*: The government has the ability—and the *responsibility*—to *manage aggregate demand*, and thus to ensure continuing prosperity. Cast aside was the classical view that market forces would solve the unemployment problem, and that the government should strictly limit its interference in the economy. Keynes was particularly impatient with classical economists who were willing to wait for the "long run," when they expected market forces to re-establish full employment. As he put it in a now-famous phrase: "In the long run we are all dead."

Keynes held out the promise that the government could increase aggregate demand, and thus solve the appalling unemployment problem of the 1930s. His book was a spectacular success; it ranks with Adam Smith's *Wealth of Nations* and Karl Marx's *Das Kapital* as one of the most influential economics books ever written. The *General Theory* led to a sharp change in economic thinking. With its appearance in 1936, the *Keynesian Revolution* was underway.

To support his three propositions, Keynes put forward a new theoretical framework, including an approach to aggregate demand and aggregate supply which was quite different from that of classical economists.

The Simple Keynesian Aggregate Supply Function

Classical economists had recognized that prices and wages might be sticky in a downward direction, and had used this stickiness to explain *transitional* periods of large-scale unemployment when aggregate demand decreased. Keynes placed even more emphasis on stickiness. In his view, workers and businesses would *strongly* resist any cut in wages and prices. As a result, wages and prices would remain *rigid* for an *indefinitely* long period in the face of large-scale unemployment.

This idea can be represented by a horizontal section in the Keynesian aggregate supply function, as illustrated by section *BA* in Figure 9-5. Here's why. If, from an initial position of full employment at point *A*, there was a decline in aggregate demand, prices would

remain stable. The fall in demand would show up in terms of a decrease in output, not in prices. This is shown by the movement from *A* to *B*. Furthermore, there would be little tendency, even in the long run, for prices and wages to fall. If aggregate demand remained low, the economy would remain in a depression at *B*.

According to Keynes, the cure was to increase aggregate demand. In response, producers would step up production. Because of the large numbers of unemployed workers and the large quantity of unused machinery, more could be produced at existing prices, that is, without general price inflation. Output would increase, and the economy would move to the right, along the horizontal range of the aggregate supply function back toward *A*.

Once the economy got to *A*—to a point of full employment—Keynes had no major objection to the classical approach to aggregate supply. Because the economy was already operating at capacity, any further increase in aggregate demand would be reflected in

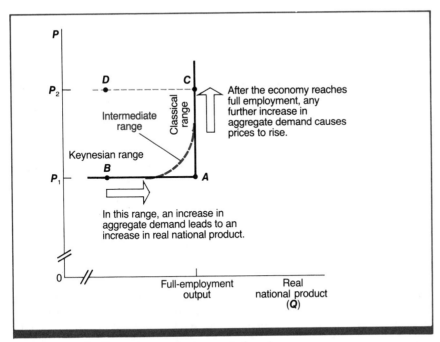

Figure 9-5 The Keynesian aggregate supply function.
There are two main segments of the Keynesian aggregate supply function. In the horizontal section, prices are stable, and a change in aggregate demand causes a change in output and employment. In the vertical section, an increase in demand causes an increase in prices.

higher prices. The economy would move vertically upward toward C. In short, the Keynesian aggregate supply function had two quite different ranges:

1. A *horizontal range*, which was relevant for analysing periods of depression and recession, when inadequate demand resulted in high rates of unemployment. This was the range which most interested Keynes. The major purpose of the *General Theory* was to explain the causes and cures of the Great Depression. Accordingly, this horizontal range of the aggregate supply function is frequently known as the *Keynesian range*.

2. A *vertical range*, which would be reached when aggregate demand was high enough to ensure full employment. Further increases in demand would simply cause inflation. Because Keynes had no quarrel with the classical approach once full employment is reached, this vertical section is sometimes known as the *classical range*.

Together, these two ranges give the aggregate supply function BAC in Figure 9-5, forming a reversed L. (In this figure, we follow the terminology of Keynesian economists, putting "real national product" on the horizontal axis. In previous diagrams, such as Figure 9-4, we used the terminology of classical economists, putting the quantity of real output Q on the axis. Q is the same as real national product, and the two terms may be used interchangeably.)

An interesting implication of the approach in Figure 9-5 is that the average level of prices will *ratchet* upward through time. As we have just seen, prices would be downwardly rigid when the economy was at point B. An increase in aggregate demand would first lead to an increase in output, to point A. But any further increase in demand would lead to higher prices. The economy would move up the vertical portion of the aggregate supply curve to point C, with prices rising to P_2. However, once C is reached, any reduction in demand would not lead the economy to retrace its path back toward A because prices and wages would not move down from the new level established at C; businesses and labour would resist such a move. Instead, the response to a fall in aggregate demand would be a decrease in output. The economy would move toward D, along the lightly dashed line. In short, the simple Keynesian aggregate supply function was a reversed L, with the horizontal part of the L shifting

upward every time a new, higher price level became established.[4]

A complication. Unfortunately, the world is more complex than indicated by the simple L-shaped function. From the early days of the Keynesian Revolution, economists recognized that there might be no sharply defined point at A where the economy suddenly reaches full employment. As the economy expands, all industries don't reach capacity at exactly the same time; some reach it before others. In the industries approaching capacity, prices begin to rise. The overall price index begins to creep up. This occurs while other industries are still operating well below capacity, and are still increasing their output as demand increases. Thus, there is a period in which both output and prices are increasing. The economy takes the curved short-cut illustrated in the dashed red curve in Figure 9-5.

While the horizontal range of aggregate supply was used by Keynesians in their explanation of the Great Depression, the sloping intermediate range is important in more normal times, when the economy is neither in an inflationary boom (the vertical section), nor in a depression (the horizontal part).

Aggregate Demand: The Keynesian Approach

As we noted above, the classical economists had a very simple view of the determination of aggregate demand: They saw it as determined by the quantity of money in the economy. Keynes instead proposed that aggregate demand be analysed by studying the demand for the various components of national product:

1. *Personal consumption expenditures*
2. *Investment demand*; that is, the demand for equipment, plant, housing, and additional inventories
3. *Government purchases of goods and services*
4. *Net exports*

Keynes was intent on explaining the Great Depression, and with finding a way to restore full employment. In his view, the Depression was caused by a collapse in aggregate demand, particularly the private investment component. Keynes stressed the instability of investment demand: Businesses are willing to invest only

[4]Both Keynesian and classical economists recognized a complication that we avoid here. As time passes, the economy grows, with the full-employment or potential output increasing. Therefore, the vertical section of the aggregate supply function shifts gradually to the right with the passage of time.

when they expect the new plant and equipment to add to profits. Expectations are fragile. Once the economy is declining sharply, business executives become pessimistic, and therefore they cut back on investment. Thus, even though a decline in private investment demand may have been the principal cause of the Depression, it was unrealistic to expect a revival of investment demand to move the economy out of the Depression. Rather, it was up to the government to provide a solution by increasing the component of aggregate demand directly under its control. That is, it was desirable for the government to increase its spending to compensate for the decline in investment demand, and thus restore full employment.

In the coming chapters, we will study the four components of aggregate demand, and the forces that cause them to increase or decrease. In these chapters, we will address two of the central questions of Keynesian theory: How large will aggregate demand be? Will it put us near full employment, or leave us in a depression?

Before passing on to these topics, we re-emphasize: The four components of aggregate demand highlighted by Keynesian theory correspond to the four components of national product studied in Chapter 7. Two major innovations in macroeconomics—the development of national product accounts and the new Keynesian theory of employment—interacted and reinforced one another during the 1930s and 1940s.

Finally, observe that in Figure 9-5, we have drawn no aggregate demand curve. Thus, something is missing from our introduction to Keynesian theory. We have not shown how the demand for goods and services responds to a change in the average level of prices. The rather complicated Keynesian approach to this issue is deferred to the appendix at the end of this chapter. All we need to note here is the principal conclusion. Except in the special case of a deep depression, Keynesian theory, like the classical theory, suggests that the aggregate demand curve slopes downward to the right.

CLASSICAL ECONOMICS AND KEYNESIAN ECONOMICS: A SUMMARY

In his *General Theory*, Keynes launched an attack on classical economists, on the ground that they had no adequate proposals for dealing with the severe unemployment problem of the 1930s. A heated debate ensued, both over policies and over the proper theoretical framework for studying macroeconomic problems.

Differences between Keynesians and the inheritors of the classical school continue to the present day. These differences attract considerable attention; debates can be interesting. But the fact that differences still exist should not obscure something even more important. On many issues, there is general agreement among macroeconomists, regardless of their intellectual heritage.

Areas of Agreement
Most notably, those in the classical and Keynesian traditions agree on these points:

1. A *sharp decline in aggregate demand* was the principal cause of the collapse into the Great Depression of the 1930s.
2. *Fluctuations in aggregate demand* have been the major cause of fluctuations in real output in recent decades.
3. Accordingly, the *stabilization of aggregate demand* should be an important macroeconomic objective.
4. When the economy is already operating at its full-employment potential, *any large increase in aggregate demand will spill over into inflation*. Both the classical and Keynesian aggregate supply functions are vertical once full employment has been reached. Thus, higher demand causes higher prices.

The second point is worth explaining in more detail. Consider Figure 9-6, with a normal, downward-sloping aggregate demand function, AD_1. The aggregate supply function slopes upward to the right; it corresponds to the intermediate range of the Keynesian supply function in Figure 9-5. Panel (*a*), in which aggregate demand shifts, is broadly consistent with the pattern already observed in Chapter 8: During expansions, output increases and inflation generally accelerates. During recession, the opposite happens: Output declines and the rate of inflation generally decreases. If shifts in aggregate supply had been the main cause of business cycles (panel (*b*)), we would expect inflation to rise during recessions (as real output contracts in the move from J to K), and fall during expansions (the move from K to J). But this is not in fact what usually happens. Therefore, we may conclude that it is not shifts in aggregate supply, but rather shifts in aggregate demand that are the major cause of business fluctuations. Not surprisingly, then, we will focus on the aggregate demand side in our early study of macroeconomics in chapters 10 to 13.

Areas of Disagreement

1. We have seen how classical economists attributed the Depression to a decline in the money stock, and believed that one solution to the Depression lay in the restoration of the money stock (a change in monetary policy). In contrast, Keynes emphasized government spending (fiscal policy) as a way of increasing aggregate demand and restoring full employment. There is a continuing difference as to whether monetary policy or fiscal policy has the stronger and more predictable effect on aggregate demand. Those in the classical tradition focus on **monetary policy**, while those in the Keynesian tradition are most likely to think first of **fiscal policy**. However, it should be emphasized that *most modern macroeconomists believe that both monetary and fiscal policies are important.*

Monetary policy involves a change in the rate of growth of the money stock. *Fiscal policy* involves a change in government expenditures or in tax rates.

2. While macroeconomists agree that it would be desirable for aggregate demand to be more stable, they differ sharply over *how* stability is best achieved. Those in the Keynesian tradition emphasize the defects and instabilities of a market economy, and believe that the government has the responsibility to *actively manage* aggregate demand in order to reduce the amplitude of business fluctuations.

   Those in the classical tradition generally

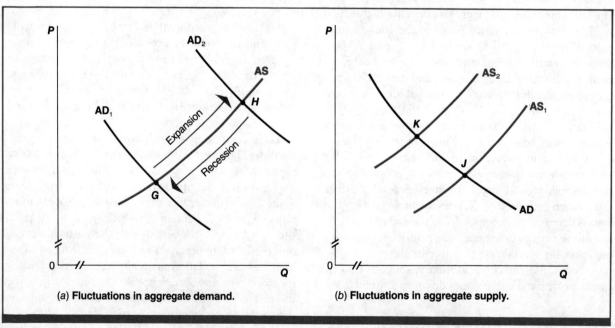

(a) **Fluctuations in aggregate demand.**

(b) **Fluctuations in aggregate supply.**

Figure 9-6   Short-run fluctuations in aggregate demand and supply.

In the left panel, aggregate demand fluctuates. During the expansion, output increases and there is upward pressure on prices (the movement from G to H). During recessions, output declines and pressure on prices subsides (H to G).

This is the pattern actually observed in most business cycles. In contrast, we do not generally observe the outcome illustrated in the right-hand panel. For example, recessions generally are not accompanied by rising inflation, as they would be if the economy were moving from J to K.

believe that the market economy will be reasonably stable, *if* monetary conditions are kept stable. As a result, many of them support a **monetary policy rule**: The authorities should aim for a *steady, moderate increase in the money stock*, at something like 3% or 4% per year. A steady growth is appropriate, since we live in a growing economy. More money is needed to buy the increasing volume of goods and services that can be produced.

Because of their emphasis on money, modern inheritors of the classical tradition are frequently known as **monetarists**. They do not argue that adherence to a monetary rule will create a perfectly stable economy, since aggregate demand will not expand in a perfectly stable way even if money does. But they are very skeptical that the government can make things better by active policy management. Like the earlier classical economists, they fear that the government attempts at stabilizing the economy might, on average, make things worse instead of better. (Some reasons for this fear will be explained in Chapter 16.)

This disagreement— between those who argue for *active management* by government and those who advocate a *policy rule*—is probably the most important single dispute among macroeconomists.

3. *The nature of equilibrium.* Those in the classical tradition associate equilibrium with full employment. High rates of unemployment represent a *temporary* problem caused by economic fluctuations and short-run *disequilibrium*. In contrast, Keynesian theory puts forward the possibility that the economy might fall into an unemployment equilibrium, involving an *extended* period of inadequate aggregate demand and high rates of unemployment.

While the possibility of an unemployment equilibrium remains a point of difference between those in the Keynesian and classical traditions, this issue has become less important with the passage of time. A major reason is that almost half a century has passed since the Great Depression. Keynesians are therefore much less worried about a lengthy depression than they used to be.

KEY POINTS

1. Just as demand and supply are useful in microeconomics, so they are also useful in macroeconomics. However, we cannot assume that the macroeconomic demand and supply curves will necessarily have slopes similar to those of microeconomic demand and supply curves.

2. There are two main approaches to aggregate demand and aggregate supply: the classical and the Keynesian approaches.

3. Classical theory stresses the importance of money as a determinant of aggregate demand. In drawing a single aggregate demand curve, we assume that the nominal quantity of money is held constant. When prices fall, the purchasing power of this fixed nominal quantity increases. Therefore, people purchase more goods and services. Accordingly, the classical aggregate demand function slopes downward to the right.

4. According to classical theory, the aggregate supply function is vertical at potential or full-employment output.

5. Consequently, full employment exists in the classical equilibrium where aggregate demand and aggregate supply intersect.

6. According to classical economists, the Depression was the result of a leftward shift in the aggregate demand curve, which in turn resulted from a fall in the money stock. In time—in the "long run"—classical economists believed that wages and prices would fall enough to restore full employment.

7. Keynes emphasized the downward rigidity of wages and prices. In its simplest form, the Keynesian aggregate supply function forms a reversed L, as illustrated in Figure 9-6.

8. According to Keynes, the principal cause of the Depression was the collapse of the investment component of aggregate demand. The solution lay in additional government expen-

ditures, whose purpose would be to increase aggregate demand to the full-employment level. Thus, Keynes rejected the laissez-faire conclusions of many classical economists.

9. Keynesian economists often stress fiscal policy as a tool for managing demand, while those in the classical tradition emphasize the importance of money. However, most modern economists believe that *both* fiscal and monetary policies can have an important effect on demand.

10. A significant debate continues over how actively the authorities should manage aggregate demand. Keynesians generally favour active management, while those in the classical tradition generally favour a monetary rule: The authorities should aim for a steady, moderate increase in the quantity of money.

KEY CONCEPTS

aggregate demand
aggregate supply
purchasing power of money
general inflation or deflation
equilibrium at full employment
wage and price stickiness
transitional periods of
   unemployment

long run (classical definition)
Keynesian unemployment
   equilibrium
reversed-L aggregate supply
   function
Keynesian and classical ranges of
   aggregate supply function

monetary policy
fiscal policy
active management of demand
monetary policy rule
monetarist

PROBLEMS

9-1 The demand curve for a specific good, such as wheat, slopes downward to the right. Why can't we simply conclude that, as a result, the aggregate demand curve will have the same general shape?

9-2 Draw a diagram showing the classical aggregate demand function. Why does it have the slope you have shown?

9-3 Why is the classical aggregate supply function vertical?

9-4 If the economy starts at a point of high unem-

ployment, explain two ways in which full employment might be restored in the classical system.

9-5 What is the reason for the horizontal section of the Keynesian aggregate supply function?

9-6 According to Keynes, what was the best way to get out of a depression?

9-7 What evidence suggests that fluctuations in aggregate demand, rather than fluctuations in aggregate supply, have been the principal reason for fluctuations in real output?

APPENDIX

THE AGGREGATE DEMAND CURVE
OF KEYNESIAN ECONOMICS

In order to complete our story about aggregate demand and aggregate supply, we need to look at what Keynes said about the slope of the aggregate demand function in his *General Theory*. Suppose that in the face of a depressed economy at *B* (Figure 9-7), a general deflation did occur, with prices and wages all falling by, say, 50%. The horizontal segment of the aggregate supply curve would then be at the new prevailing price level; aggregate supply would have shifted down from AS_1 to AS_2. What would the result be? What would

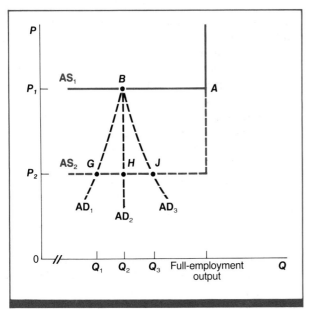

Figure 9-7   Aggregate demand in Keynesian economics.
If prices and wages fall during a depression, the result may be an increase in the quantity of goods and services demanded, as illustrated by the movement from *B* to *J*. But we cannot count on this. The quantity demanded may remain stable at *H*, or decrease to *G*. In other words, we cannot be sure which way the aggregate demand curve will slope. AD_1, AD_2, and AD_3 are all possible.

happen to the aggregate quantity of goods and services demanded? To answer this, said Keynes, we have to look at what will happen to the major components of demand, particularly consumption and investment.

1. *Consumption demand.* The amount that people consume depends primarily on their incomes. As wages and prices fall by the same proportion, people find that they are no better off: Their *real incomes* remain unchanged. Accordingly, said Keynes, we would not expect any change in the quantity of goods and services they consume. In other words, if we look only at consumption—the largest single component of aggregate demand—we would expect the aggregate demand function to be *vertical*. If it has any tendency to slope downward to the right or left, it will have to be because of the behaviour of other components of demand, most notably, investment.

2. *Investment demand.* Investment demand depends in part on what is happening to consumer purchases. For example, a rise in the sales of automobiles will encourage auto manufacturers to invest by buying more plant and machinery. However, if consumption is stable in the face of deflation—for reasons explained in point 1—then there is no reason to expect greater investment on this account.

   To identify the effects of price changes on investment, we have to look instead at two other forces:

(a) *The interest-rate effect.* As prices and wages fall, the amount of money in the system increases in real terms; that is, in terms of what it will buy. There are the same number of dollars, but each dollar is worth more. Because individuals and businesses have more real money, they are more willing to lend it; interest rates fall as a result. With lower interest rates, businesses find it cheaper to borrow the money with which to buy equipment. Investment should increase on this account.

(b) *The expectations effect.* Investment also depends on people's expectations regarding the future. If prices are expected to rise, for example, businesses have an incentive to buy buildings or equipment quickly, in order to avoid the higher prices later. In extreme cases, there can be strong speculation in real estate—there is a rush to get in while the getting is good. On the other hand, expectations of a fall in prices can cause businesses to put off investment, in the hopes of buying the plant or equipment even more cheaply in the future. This, said Keynes, is what makes deflation so dangerous. As prices fall, people may come to expect a continuing deflation. This can cause a weakening of investment demand.

There are thus two opposite forces at work as prices decline: the interest-rate effect, working toward an increase in investment, and the expectations effect, working toward a decrease.

Keynes was particularly dubious about the interest-rate effect when the economy was suffering substantial slack. During such periods, interest rates may already be very low. For example, the interest rates on long-term government bonds fell below 3% during the Great Depression. No matter what happens, interest rates can't fall much further. Clearly, interest rates can't become negative; people would simply refuse to buy bonds yielding negative rates, and hold money instead.

Thus, Keynes argued that, during a depression, a weak interest-rate effect is likely to be overpowered by a negative expectations effect. Although it's conceivable that there could be an increase in investment and aggregate demand, with aggregate demand going through point *J* in Figure 9-7, it is much more likely that investment would remain stable or decrease.

Therefore, the aggregate demand function is more likely to go through *H* or *G*.

In brief, Keynes presented two reasons for rejecting the classical argument that full employment could be restored by a general fall in prices and wages:

1. In the first place, prices and wages *won't* fall much; they are rigid in a downward direction. The downward shift of the aggregate supply curve illustrated in Figure 9-7 won't in fact occur, according to Keynes.

2. *Even if* prices and wages *did* fall, the market could not be counted on to restore full employment. A more likely outcome would be a movement toward *G* (Figure 9-7); deflation would worsen the depression.

Market forces would not lead automatically to full employment, even in the long run. Thus, Keynes came to his central policy conclusion. If the economy is at a point like *B*, the government should not stand idly by while millions remain out of work. It should accept its responsibilities, and increase its spending in order to shift aggregate demand to the right and restore full employment at *A*.

Finally, Keynesian theory suggests that the aggregate demand curve should have a normal slope during a period of prosperity; that is, it should slope downward to the right. During prosperity, interest rates are generally much higher than during a depression; they can fall substantially when the real value of the public's money holdings goes up. Thus, the interest rate effect should be relatively strong, outweighing the expectations effect and giving the aggregate demand function a normal downward slope.

As a result, Keynesian and classical theories become quite similar during prosperity. Both suggest a vertical aggregate supply function. Moreover, both foresee an aggregate demand function sloping downward to the right. The sharp differences in the two theories arise when the unemployment rate is high.

PROBLEM

*9-8 As part of Franklin Roosevelt's program to combat the Great Depression of the 1930s, the U.S. National Recovery Act contained provisions to keep prices up. Explain why someone in the classical tradition might consider such legislation a blunder. Explain why a Keynesian would be much more likely to favour such legislation.

Chapter 10

EQUILIBRIUM WITH UNEMPLOYMENT: THE KEYNESIAN APPROACH

The economic system in which we
live . . . seems capable of remaining in a
chronic condition of sub-normal activity
for a considerable period without
any marked tendency either towards recovery
or towards complete collapse.
Moreover, . . . full, or even approximately
full employment is of rare and
short-lived occurrence.

John Maynard Keynes,

The General Theory of Employment, Interest and Money

Of all our economic problems, unemployment is perhaps the most vexing. Unemployment represents an obvious waste: The society foregoes the goods and services that the unemployed might have produced. Unemployed people suffer the demoralization, frustration, and loss of self-respect that come from enforced idleness.

As we saw in Chapter 9, the deep depression of the 1930s led to a new theory of unemployment, put forward by John Maynard Keynes. This chapter will explain Keynes' major theoretical proposition, that the economy may reach an equilibrium with large-scale unemployment. (The next chapter will outline

Keynes' major policy proposals—namely, what the government can do to combat unemployment.)

Equilibrium in an economy is determined by aggregate supply and aggregate demand. To explain Keynesian theory, we begin where Keynes did, focusing on the horizontal section of the aggregate supply function (Figure 9-5), where prices are stable and changes in demand lead to changes in output. To determine how large national output will be, we need to know how big aggregate demand is. Recall from Chapter 9 that Keynes studied aggregate demand by looking at its components:

1. personal consumption expenditures

2. investment demand
3. government purchases of goods and services
4. net exports

The basic point of Keynesian theory—that the economy may reach an equilibrium with large-scale unemployment—can be illustrated most easily by considering a very simple economy, with only the first two components of aggregate demand: consumption and investment. Such a simplified economy is studied in this chapter. Government expenditures and net exports will be considered in Chapter 11.

PERSONAL CONSUMPTION EXPENDITURES

Of all the components of total spending, personal consumption is by far the largest. On what do consumption expenditures depend? An individual's consumption is influenced by many factors. Purchases of clothing depend on the weather. The purchase of an automobile depends in part on the price of gasoline and on the state of the roads. We could easily compile an extensive list of factors affecting consumption. But one stands out as the most important: *Consumption depends on the disposable income that people have left after they pay taxes.*

The behaviour of typical Canadian consumers is shown in Figure 10-1. Low-income families on the left confine their spending to little more than the necessities of life—food, clothing, and housing. Even so, they find it hard to make ends meet, and they spend more than their incomes. For example, families at G with disposable incomes of $7,500 (measured along the horizontal axis), consume, on average, about $8,125 (measured vertically). But how can low-income families possibly spend more than they have coming in? The answer: by running into debt, or by drawing on their past savings. One group of low-income people—those who are retired—are particularly likely to spend more than their current incomes. They draw on the assets, such as those in retirement savings plans, that they have accumulated during their working lives.

As the incomes of families rise, they find it easier to live within their current incomes. Thus, the family at H, with an income of $10,000, spends $10,000 for consumer goods and services. It *breaks even*, spending all its income. As incomes rise further, consumption also rises, but not as quickly as income; at incomes above $10,000, families do not consume their full incomes. For example, families at point J, with incomes of $30,000, consume considerably less than this amount and save the rest.

Figure 10-1 shows how a *family's* consumption rises as its disposable income increases. Income of the family is measured along the horizontal axis, and the family's consumption up the vertical axis. For a *nation as a whole*, consumption also rises as disposable income increases. Figure 10-2 provides an illustration, with disposable income of the whole nation on the horizontal axis, and expenditures of all consumers on the vertical axis. The numbers corresponding to Figure 10-2 are shown in Table 10-1. For example, the first line of Table 10-1 indicates that, if disposable income is $100 billion, consumption is $120 billion. This is shown at point A in Figure 10-2, measured 100 units along the horizontal income axis, and 120 units up the vertical consumption axis. Similarly, points B, C, and D in Figure 10-2 can be derived from the corresponding lines in Table 10-1. Because consumer expenditures depend primarily on real incomes, the incomes and expenditures on the axes of Figure 10-2 are measured in real, or constant-dollar, terms.

The relationship between consumption and disposable income is known as the **consumption function**. It plays a central role in Keynes' theory of unemployment.

> The *consumption function* shows how consumption expenditures depend on disposable income.

In Figure 10-2, we may find the **break-even point**—at which consumption equals disposable income—with the help of a 45° line drawn from the origin. The 45° line has an important property: Any point on it is the same distance from the two axes. Consider, for example, an economy in which disposable income is $400 billion, as shown by the horizontal distance between the origin and point G in Figure 10-2. Then the vertical distance from G to point H on the 45° line is also $400 billion. Thus, this $400 billion disposable income (DI) may be measured either along the horizontal axis from the origin to point G, or as the vertical distance from G up to the 45° line at H.

If disposable income decreases to $200 billion and we move to the left to point K, we can once again measure income as the height of the 45° line—in this

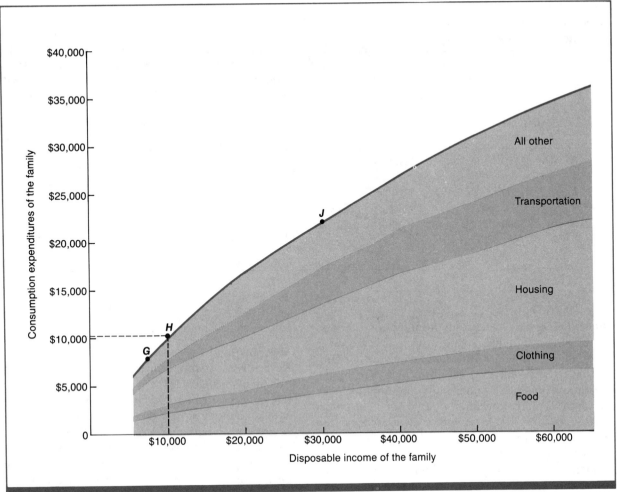

Figure 10-1 Consumption expenditures at different income levels, 1983.
Consumption depends on disposable income. Families with higher disposable incomes consume more than families with lower incomes.

Source: Statistics Canada, *Family Expenditures in Canada 1983.* Reproduced by permission of the Minister of Supply and Services Canada.

case the $200 billion vertical distance from point *K* on the horizontal axis to point *B* on the 45° line. But this vertical distance to point *B* also measures consumption; that is, *B* lies on the consumption function. Therefore, point *B*, where the consumption function and the 45° line intersect, is the break-even point.

> At the *break-even point*, consumption equals disposable income. That is, every dollar of disposable income is spent on consumer goods and services.

Saving is what is left of disposable income after consumption expenditures:

$$\text{Saving} = \text{disposable income} - \text{consumption}^{[1]} \qquad (10\text{-}1)$$

Drawing on this equation, we may derive a *saving*

[1] More precisely, saving equals disposable income less consumption less interest paid by consumers, as we saw in Chapter 7. However, when explaining the basic Keynesian theory, it is standard practice to ignore the interest complication, and use simplified equation 10-1.

Table 10-1
Consumption and Saving
(billions of dollars at constant prices)

	(1) DI Disposable income	(2) C Consumption	(3) Marginal propensity to consume $MPC = \dfrac{\Delta C}{\Delta DI}$	(4) S Saving (4) = (1) − (2)	(5) Marginal propensity to save $MPS = \dfrac{\Delta S}{\Delta DI}$
A	$100	$120		−20	
			$\dfrac{80}{100} = 0.8$		$\dfrac{20}{100} = 0.2$
B	200	200		±0	
			$\dfrac{80}{100} = 0.8$		$\dfrac{20}{100} = 0.2$
C	300	280		+20	
			$\dfrac{80}{100} = 0.8$		$\dfrac{20}{100} = 0.2$
D	400	360		+40	

function (Figure 10-3) directly from the consumption function. For example: Suppose disposable income is $400 billion, at point G measured along the horizontal axis. Disposable income is also measured by the height of H on the 45° line, while consumption is the height of D on the consumption function. The difference—distance HD—is saving. This distance is used in Figure 10-3 to measure the height of point D on the saving function. Similarly, other points on the saving function can be derived by taking the vertical distances between the consumption function and the 45° line in Figure 10-2. Thus, the consumption function (Figure 10-2) and the saving function (Figure 10-3) are two alternative ways of illustrating precisely the same information.

> The *saving function* shows the relationship between disposable income and saving.

Notice that point B in Figure 10-3 corresponds to point B on Figure 10-2's consumption function. At this break-even point, where consumption equals income, saving is zero. If we look at points even further to the left, such as point A in Figure 10-2, we see that consumption is greater than income. That is, there is negative saving, or **dissaving**, as illustrated by the

corresponding point A in Figure 10-3.

The Marginal Propensity to Consume

Keynes was interested in explaining how consumption might change. He therefore introduced an important concept: the **marginal propensity to consume**, or MPC. Economists use the term marginal to mean "extra" or "additional." (As we shall see in a later chapter, marginal revenue means additional revenue, and marginal cost means additional cost.) The marginal propensity to consume is the fraction of additional disposable income that is consumed. Formally,

Marginal propensity to consume =
$$\frac{\text{change in consumption}}{\text{change in disposable income}} \quad (10\text{-}2)$$

In abbreviated notation, this is written:

$$MPC = \frac{\Delta C}{\Delta DI} \quad (10\text{-}3)$$

where the Greek letter Δ means "change in."

If we think of a small $1 increase in disposable income, this formula reduces to:

MPC = the fraction of a $1 increase in
disposable income that is consumed

This is an obvious restatement of the idea: If your

Figure 10-2 The consumption function (billions of dollars at constant prices).

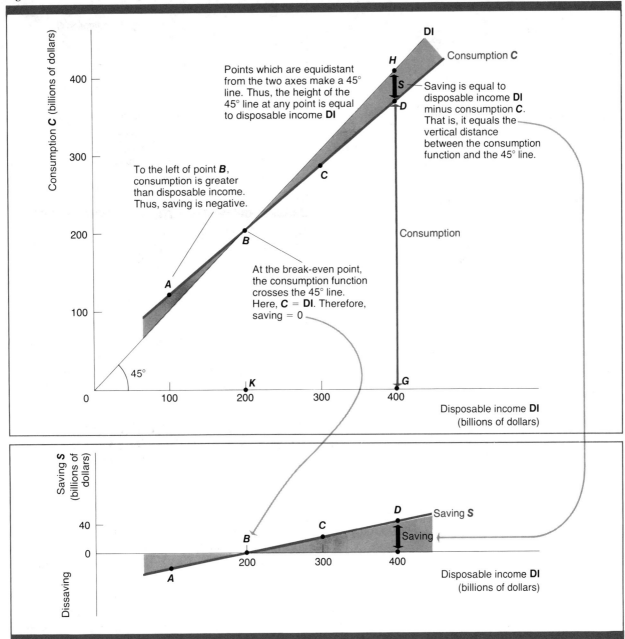

Figure 10-3 The saving function (billions of dollars at constant prices).
The saving function can be derived from the consumption function. Saving is the vertical
distance between the consumption function and the 45° line.

income increases by $1, and your consumption increases by $0.80 as a result, then your MPC is

$$\$0.80/\$1.00 = 0.80.$$

Similarly,

Marginal propensity to save (MPS) =

$$\frac{\text{change in saving}}{\text{change in disposable income}} =$$

$$\frac{\Delta S}{\Delta DI} \qquad (10\text{-}4)$$

Or:

MPS = the fraction of a $1 increase in
disposable income that is saved

In Table 10-1, the MPC and MPS are calculated in columns 3 and 5. Observe that

$$MPC + MPS = 1 \qquad (10\text{-}5)$$

This must be the case. If a person gets $1 more in income, whatever is not consumed is saved. In our example, a $1 increase in income results in an increase of consumption of $0.80. Thus, $0.20 is saved, and the MPS is

$$0.20/1.00 = 0.20.$$

In Figure 10-4, the MPC is illustrated. It is equal to the vertical change in consumption, divided by the horizontal change in income. Thus, the MPC is equal to the slope of the consumption function. Consequently, if the MPC is constant, as it is in our illustration in Table 10-1, then the consumption function has a constant slope; it is a straight line. Similarly, the MPS is the slope of the saving function. From Equation 10-5 it follows that, if the MPC is constant, so is the MPS. Thus, the saving function is also a straight line, as illustrated earlier in Figure 10-3.

The MPC plays a central role in Keynesian theory. A companion—but much less important—concept is also sometimes used; namely, the average propensity to consume (APC). This is defined:

$$APC = \frac{\text{total consumption}}{\text{total disposable income}} \qquad (10\text{-}6)$$

The difference between the marginal and average concepts may be seen by referring back to the example in Figure 10-2. Because the consumption function is a

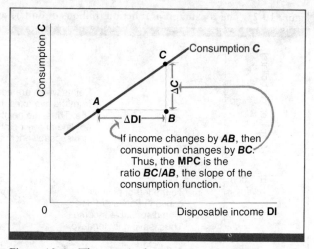

Figure 10-4 The marginal propensity to consume.
Since the slope of the consumption function gives the MPC, the consumption function is a straight line if the MPC is constant.

straight line with a slope of 0.8, the MPC is a constant 0.8. However, the APC is not constant; it changes along the consumption function. At B, for example, consumption equals disposable income, and the APC is therefore 1. At C, the APC is less than 1, specifically, 280/300 = 0.93.

THE SIMPLEST EQUILIBRIUM: AN ECONOMY WITH NO GOVERNMENT OR INTERNATIONAL TRANSACTIONS

Keynes' objective was to demonstrate that laissez-faire market economies contain a fundamental defect: They may come to rest with a very high rate of unemployment. In order to explain this central proposition as clearly and as quickly as possible, we look at a barebones economy, in which there is no international trade, no government spending, no taxes, no depreciation, and no retained corporate profits. In this very simplified economy, GNP = NNP = national income = disposable income. In other words, all the receipts from national product flow through the business sector to become the disposable income of the household sector; there are none of the subtractions explained in detail back in Chapter 7. Since GNP and NNP are the same, we can use the abbreviated term National Product, or NP.

Furthermore, the absence of government and international transactions means that there are only two components of aggregate demand in this very simple economy, namely, consumption expenditures and investment demand. (We reiterate that investment is part of national product. Specifically, investment demand means the demand for new equipment, plant, and houses, and additional inventories. When macroeconomists talk of investment demand, they do not include demand for financial assets, such as stocks or bonds, or the demand for second-hand plant, equipment, or housing.)

To make our task even simpler, we initially assume that investment demand is a constant $40 billion. We do not claim that this assumption is realistic. Indeed, as we have seen in previous chapters, investment is one of the most volatile components of GNP. However, this simple assumption will allow us to complete the main argument as quickly as possible, and then we will be in a position to consider what happens when investment demand does change.

The $40 billion of investment demand can be added to consumption demand to get aggregate demand, as shown in Table 10-2, column 5, and in Figure 10-5. In this diagram, national product NP, rather than disposable income DI, is shown on the horizontal axis and on the 45° line. We may substitute NP for DI in this diagram, because NP = DI in the simple economy we are considering here.

Equilibrium occurs where aggregate demand equals national product. Comparing columns 1 and 5 in Table 10-2, we see that this occurs at an output of $400 billion. The same equilibrium of $400 billion is shown in Figure 10-5 at point E, where the aggregate demand function cuts the 45° national product line.

To see why this is the equilibrium, consider why aggregate demand would not be sufficient to buy a larger quantity of output—say the $500 billion measured from the origin to point L on the horizontal axis, and also vertically from L to point N on the 45° line. In the right-hand part of Figure 10-5, we show a magnified view of national product LN. It is the height of the dark red bar, plus the light red bar, plus the gray bar. But aggregate demand is less than that. It's just the dark red bar (consumption demand) plus the light red bar (investment demand). Thus, at an output of $500 billion, the amount we produce (national product) exceeds the demand for it (aggregate demand).

What happens to the excess production, shown by the gray bar? It remains unsold; it piles up on retailers' shelves and in warehouses. It represents **undesired inventory accumulation**. As unwanted goods accumulate, retailers, wholesalers, and other businesses cut

Table 10-2
Equilibrium National Product
(billions of dollars)

	(1) NP National product (equals disposable income in this simple economy)	(2) C Consumption demand	(3) S Saving (3) = (1) − (2)	(4) I* Investment demand (assumed constant)	(5) AD Aggregate demand = C + I* (5) = (2) + (4)	(6) Relation of aggregate demand (5) to national product (1)	(7) Economy will:
H	$200	$200	0	$40	$240	Higher ↓	Expand
J	300	280	20	40	320	Higher ↓	Expand
K	400	360	40	40	400	Same	Stay at equilibrium
L	500	440	60	40	480	Lower ↑	Contract
M	600	520	80	40	520	Lower ↑	Contract

Figure 10-5   Equilibrium national product.
Point E represents equilibrium, with output of $400 billion. Here, aggregate demand equals national product. A higher rate of production (for example, $500 billion) is not stable, as we can see by looking at the magnified version on the right, showing what happens when national product is $500 billion. National product equals the vertical distance to the 45° line. For most of this product, there is a market. Consumption demand takes the red bar. Investment demand takes the shaded bar. But for the empty bar, there is no demand. Unsold goods pile up in the warehouses. Businesses cut back on production. Output falls to its equilibrium of $400 billion.

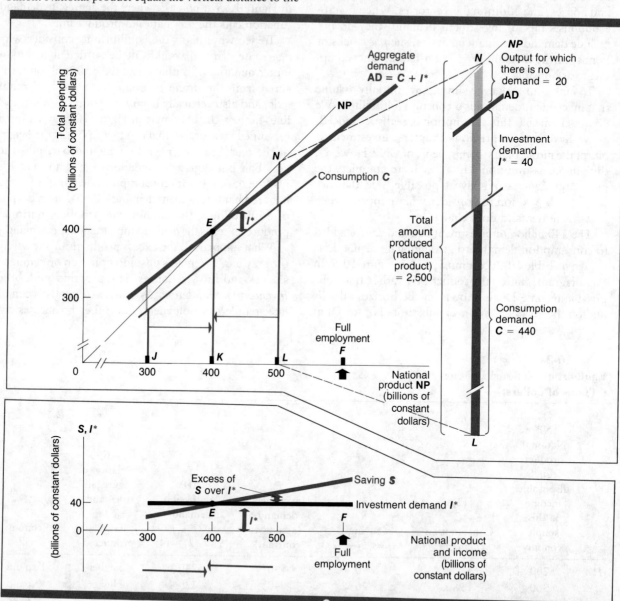

Figure 10-6   The equilibrium of saving and investment demand.
Equilibrium occurs at output of $400 billion, where saving = investment demand. At a greater national product, such as $500 billion, disequilibrium exists. Since the leakages from the spending stream (in the form of saving) are greater than the injections (in the form of investment), national product will fall toward its equilibrium at $400 billion.

back on their orders. Production falls. Moreover, it continues to contract as long as aggregate demand lies below the 45° national product line. In other words, it continues to fall until the economy reaches equilibrium E, where national product NP = aggregate demand AD and there is no further pressure of unsold goods. Therefore, $400 billion is the equilibrium quantity of output.

At a disequilibrium quantity of national product, such as $500 billion, it is important to distinguish between **actual investment** and **investment demand**. Actual investment—the quantity which shows up in the official national product accounts studied in Chapter 7—includes all investment in plant, equipment, housing, and inventories, whether that investment is desired or not. Thus, for an economy producing at $500 billion, the investment figure that appears in the national product accounts will be the light red bar plus the gray bar. ("Gray bar goods" for which there is no demand, and which therefore pile up as undesired inventory accumulation, have clearly been produced during the year, and must therefore be included in the national product statistics.) In contrast with actual investment, investment demand—also known as **desired investment** or **planned investment**—is only the investment that businesses want; that is, the light red bar. In order to keep straight the important distinction between investment demand and actual investment, we will use the symbol I^* with an asterisk to represent investment demand. As in Chapter 7, a plain I will stand for actual investment; that is, investment as it shows up in the national product accounts.

> *Actual investment* I is the amount of capital goods such as new plant, equipment, and housing acquired during the year, plus the increase in inventories. All inventory accumulation is included, *whether the inventories were desired or not.*
>
> *Investment demand* I^*—also known as *desired investment* or *planned investment*—is the amount of new capital goods acquired during the year plus *additions to inventories that businesses wanted to acquire.* It excludes undesired inventory accumulation.
>
> *Undesired inventory accumulation* is actual investment (I) less investment demand (I^*).

Just as an output initially greater than equilibrium results in contraction, so an output initially less than equilibrium generates expansion. Consider an output of $300 billion, at point J. Here, aggregate demand is higher than the 45° national product line. Buyers want to purchase more goods than are currently being produced. Retailers and wholesalers find it difficult to keep goods in stock. Inventories are run down below their desired levels; that is, there is an **undesired decrease in inventories**. Because retailers and wholesalers want to meet the large demand and rebuild their inventories, they step up their orders. To fill their larger orders, manufacturers and other producers expand their output toward the equilibrium, E.

> The *undesired decrease in inventories* is equal to investment demand (I^*) minus actual investment (I). It exists when undesired inventory accumulation is negative.

EQUILIBRIUM WITH LARGE-SCALE UNEMPLOYMENT

Now we are in a position to illustrate Keynes' key contention, that the *equilibrium national product need not be at the quantity necessary to ensure full employment.* Equilibrium national product is determined by aggregate demand, as illustrated by point E in Figure 10-5. On the other hand, the full-employment national product represents what the economy can produce with its current resources of labour, land, and capital; it is shown at national product F. The situation which Keynes feared, and which he believed would be a common outcome of a free-market economy, is the one shown in this diagram. Equilibrium national product at E is far less than the full-employment quantity at F. (See the quotation from Keynes that introduces this chapter.)

AN ALTERNATIVE APPROACH: SAVING AND INVESTMENT

Figure 10-5 showed how equilibrium national product is determined in the simple economy (with no government, etc.) by putting together consumption expenditures C and investment demand I^*. But we have already seen that the saving function (Figure 10-3) is an alternative way of presenting *exactly the same information as in the consumption function* (Figure 10-2). It is therefore not surprising that, as an alternative to *C* plus *I**, we can bring saving *S* together with investment demand *I** to determine equilibrium national product. This is done in Figure 10-6. In the simple economy, *equilibrium occurs when saving equals investment demand*; that is, at point *E* where national product is $400 billion. We may confirm in Table 10-2 that saving (Column 3) equals investment demand (Column 4) at the same $400 billion equilibrium output at which aggregate demand (Column 5) equals national product (Column 1).

The Circular Flow of Expenditure: Leakages and Injections

To explain *why* equilibrium occurs when saving equals investment demand, we call again on the circular flow of payments previously used in chapters 3 and 7, and repeated here as Figure 10-7. This figure illustrates a very rudimentary economy in which there is no investment demand, and in which consumers buy all the goods produced. Suppose that producers sell $200 billion of goods during an initial period. In turn, they pay this $200 billion to households in the form of wages, salaries, rents, and other incomes, as shown in the lower loop of the diagram. Suppose, further, that the households turn around and spend all their $200 billion of income on consumer goods (in the upper loop). Once more, the producers sell $200 billion in goods and services, and once more they pay out this amount in incomes to the households. The same $200 billion of payments keeps flowing through the system; national product is stable at this level.

Now let us introduce complications, starting with saving. Suppose that instead of consuming all their

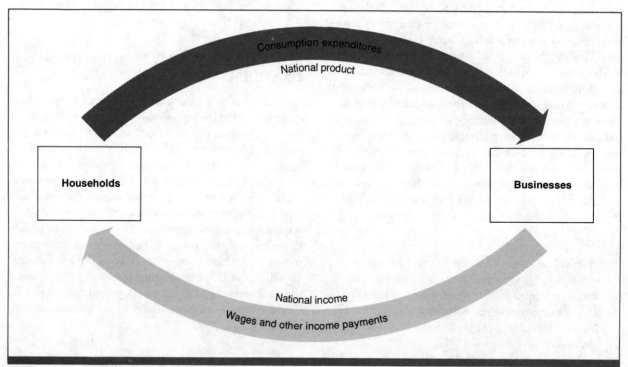

Figure 10-7   The simplest circular flow of payments. (All income is spent for consumer goods and services.)
The simplest economy is one in which people consume all their incomes. Incomes are used to buy consumer goods and services. In turn, the receipts from the sale of consumer goods and services are again paid out as incomes, in the form of wages, salaries, etc. Once more, people use all their incomes to buy consumer goods and services. Round and round the payments go.

incomes of $200 billion, people decide that they would like to save $20 billion. They spend only $180 billion on consumer goods. Producers have made $200 billion in goods, but they sell only $180 billion. Unsold goods pile up, and producers cut back on production. When they do so, they pay out less in wages and other incomes. The circular flow of national product and income is reduced. Thus, saving represents a leakage from the circular spending stream; it acts as a drag on national product and income.

Now, let us introduce investment demand. Suppose that businesses decide to increase their capital stock and that they order $20 billion worth of machinery. In response to the demand, $20 billion in machinery is produced. The machinery companies pay out the $20 billion in wages, salaries, and other incomes. Incomes rise, people consume more, and the circular flow of national product and income increases. Investment therefore acts as a stimulus to national product and income.

The Equilibrium of Saving and Investment Demand

Thus, in terms of their effect on aggregate demand and output, saving and investment have offsetting effects. Saving is a *leakage* from the circular spending stream; an increase in the desire to save leads to a decrease in national product. Investment demand represents an *injection* into the circular spending stream; an increase in investment demand leads to an increase in national product. Equilibrium exists when the forces of contraction and expansion are in balance; that is, when saving equals investment demand—as it does in Figure 10-6 at point *E*, where national product is $400 billion. At any greater national income, such as $500 billion, the leakage from the circular flow of spending—in the form of saving—exceeds the injection of investment spending, and output decreases. If, on the other hand, national product is initially at a point to the left of the $400 billion equilibrium, the injection of investment demand exceeds the saving leakage, and national product increases. This can be visualized in Figure 10-8: When more is pumped in at the investment end, the income flow becomes larger. This causes more leakages into saving at the other end. The flow stabilizes when the injections and leakages are equal.

Saving and investment decisions are made by different groups. Households save to buy a new car, to send the kids to college, or for retirement. Investment decisions are made principally by business executives; they buy additional plant and equipment when their profit prospects are good. Because of this separation of saving and investment decisions, *there is no assurance that, if an economy begins at full employment, desired investment will be as great as saving*. If it is not—as illustrated at full-employment output *F* in Figure 10-6—then national product will decrease, and unemployment will result.

The two approaches in Figures 10-5 and 10-6 are exact equivalents; either of those diagrams can be derived from the other. To summarize, we can state the condition for equilibrium in several different ways:

1. Equilibrium exists when national output is equal to aggregate demand—also sometimes referred to as aggregate expenditures. This is the **output-expenditures approach** to determining equilibrium, and is illustrated by point *E* in Figure 10-5.
2. Equilibrium exists when actual investment *I* equals investment demand *I**; that is, when inventories are at their desired level, and there is no undesired accumulation of inventories such as that shown by the gray bar in Figure 10-5.
3. Equilibrium exists when saving and investment demand are equal, as illustrated by point *E* in Figure 10-6. This is the **leakages-injections approach**.

These three statements are different ways of expressing the same basic point.

The reason for unemployment may be stated in two alternative ways. There will be an **unemployment equilibrium** if:

1. Aggregate demand is too low to buy the full-employment quantity of national product. For example, at full-employment point *F* in Figure 10-5, AD is below NP.
2. The injections of investment demand are less than the leakages into saving when national product is at the full-employment quantity. For example, at full-employment point *F* in Figure 10-6, *I** is below *S*.

(As we saw in Chapter 9, classical economists believed that equilibrium would exist only when the

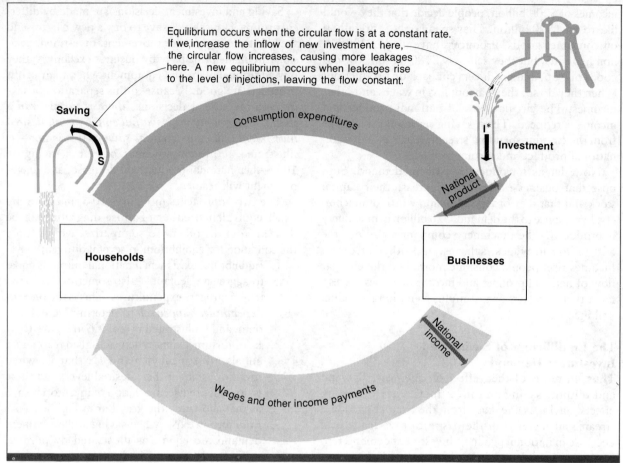

Equilibrium occurs when the circular flow is at a constant rate. If we increase the inflow of new investment here, the circular flow increases, causing more leakages here. A new equilibrium occurs when leakages rise to the level of injections, leaving the flow constant.

Saving

S

Consumption expenditures

National product

I*

Investment

Households

Businesses

National income

Wages and other income payments

Figure 10-8 The circular flow, with saving and investment.
Investment expenditures work to broaden the spending stream. Leakages into saving narrow it. Equilibrium is reached when leakages from the stream (saving) are equal to injections (investment).

economy was at full employment. Appendix 10-A provides more detail on the classical view. Specifically, it explains how classical economists fitted saving and investment into the idea of an equilibrium with full employment.)

CHANGES IN INVESTMENT DEMAND: THE MULTIPLIER

Investment is a flighty bird.

J.R. Hicks

The basic Keynesian diagrams (Figures 10-5 and 10-6) illustrate how the economy can reach an equilibrium

at less than full employment. But they can also be used to illustrate how economic activity can change, with the economy periodically moving from boom to recession and back. During the business cycle, investment demand is quite unstable.

Consider what happens if investment demand increases. Suppose that business executives become more optimistic about the future. They will plan to expand their operations, undertaking more investment in plant and equipment. Suppose, specifically, that investment demand increases by $20 billion.

The results are shown in Figure 10-9. When the increase in investment demand is added, the aggregate demand function shifts upward by $20 billion, from AD_1 to AD_2. Equilibrium once more occurs where aggregate demand and national product are equal; that is, where the new aggregate demand function AD_2 cuts the 45° line at H. Thus, the increase in investment demand moves the equilibrium from E to H. Observe that something very important has happened. The equilibrium national product has increased *by $100 billion, which is far more than the $20 billion increase in investment demand.*

How can that be? The answer is this. As businesses build more factories and order more equipment, people are put to work producing the factories and equip-ment. They earn more wages. As their incomes rise, they increase their consumption expenditures. Thus, the nation produces not only more capital goods, such as factories and equipment, but also more consumer goods. National product rises by more than investment. Specifically, as the equilibrium moves from E to H, national product increases by $100 billion. This in-cludes not only the $20 billion increase in investment spending on capital goods (shown as ΔI^* in Figure 10-9), but also an increase of $80 billion in spending on consumer goods (shown as ΔC). These are the

Figure 10-9   The multiplier.
With an MPC = 0.8, a $20 billion increase in investment demand causes a $100 billion increase in national product.

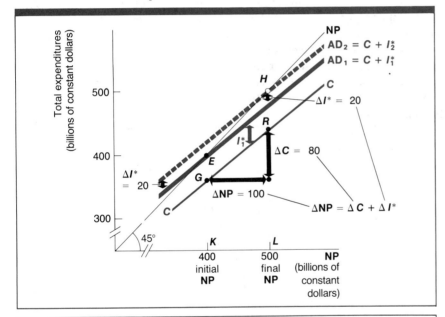

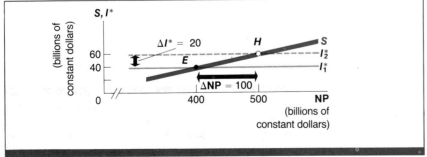

Figure 10-10   The multiplier: Saving and investment approach.
With an MPS = 0.2, an increase of $20 billion in investment demanded (from I_1^* to I_2^*) causes an increase of $100 billion in national product.

additional goods consumers buy as their incomes rise and they accordingly move up the consumption function from G to R.

Thus, the $20 billion increase in investment demand has a *multiplied* effect on national product. The relationship between the increase in national product and the increase in investment demand is known as the **investment multiplier**, or, more simply, as the **multiplier**. Formally, it is defined:

$$Investment\ Multiplier = \qquad (10\text{-}7)$$
$$\frac{change\ in\ equilibrium\ real\ national\ product}{change\ in\ investment\ demand}$$

In our illustration, equilibrium national product rises by $100 billion when investment demand increases by $20 billion. Therefore, the multiplier is 5.

The Multiplier Process: A More Detailed Look
The multiplier process may be better understood by looking in more detail at what happens when there is an additional $20 billion of investment expenditure on capital goods. The *direct impact* is a $20 billion increase in national product; more machines and other capital goods are produced. But this is not the end of the story. The $20 billion spent for plant and equipment goes in the form of wages, rents, profits, and other incomes to those who provide the resources used

to produce the capital goods. In other words, disposable incomes are $20 billion higher. (Remember, we are dealing with a highly simplified economy in which there is no government to take a tax bite.) Consumers now spend most of this increase in their disposable income, with the precise amount depending on their marginal propensity to consume (MPC). For example, if the MPC is 0.8, consumers are *induced* to spend $16 billion more, as shown in the "second-round" increase in the national product in Table 10-3 and Figure 10-11.

But again, this is not the end of the story. When consumers spend $16 billion more for clothing, food, and other consumer goods, that $16 billion in spending becomes income for producers. Thus, the incomes of textile workers, farmers, and others who produce consumer goods rise by $16 billion. With an MPC of 0.8, these people spend $16 billion × 0.8 = $12.8 billion. Once more, national product has risen, this time by $12.8 billion. The story goes on and on, with each round of consumer spending giving rise to another, smaller round.

Observe that, with an MPC = 0.8, the total spending resulting from each dollar of initial investment

Table 10-3
The Multiplier Process: Effect on National Product of an Increase in Investment Expenditure
(billions of dollars)

Round	Spending on		Resulting change in aggregate demand and national product
First	Investment	20.0	Direct initial effect
Second	Consumption	16.0	Induced increase in consumption = 80.0
Third	Consumption	12.8	
Fourth	Consumption	10.2	
Fifth	Consumption	8.2	
•		•	
•		•	
•		•	
Total increase in aggregate demand and national product		100.0	

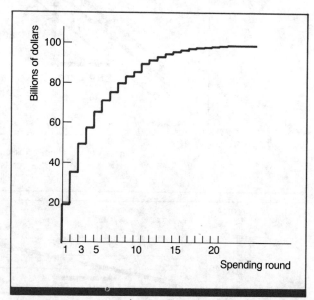

Figure 10-11   The multiplier process: The build-up of national product.
This figure portrays the various rounds of spending listed in Table 10-3, which result from an initial increase of $20 billion in investment in round 1. Notice how national product builds up toward its equilibrium increase of $100 billion.

expenditure forms the series $1 (1 + 0.8 + 0.8^2 + 0.8^3 \ldots)$. It can be shown[2] that the sum of such a series is:

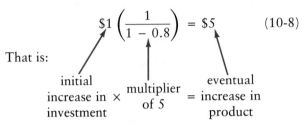

$$\$1 \left(\frac{1}{1 - 0.8} \right) = \$5 \qquad (10\text{-}8)$$

That is:

initial increase in investment × multiplier of 5 = eventual increase in product

In this case, because the MPC is 0.8, the multiplier is 5. More generally:

$$\text{Multiplier} = \frac{1}{1 - \text{MPC}} \qquad (10\text{-}9)$$

Thus, the size of the multiplier depends on the size of the MPC; that is, on the slope of the consumption function. The steeper the consumption function—that is, the higher the MPC—the larger is the multiplier.

Observe also how Table 10-3 and Figure 10-11 correspond to Figure 10-9. Each shows that a $20 billion increase in investment demand causes a $100 billion increase in national product. This $100 billion is made up of the original $20 billion increase in investment, plus $80 billion in *induced* consumption that occurs as people spend more when their disposable incomes rise.

The Multiplier Works Both Ways

We have just seen how an increase in investment demand (of $20 billion) leads to a multiplied increase in national product (of $100 billion). A similar multiplied effect occurs when investment decreases. For example, a "first-round" reduction of $20 billion in investment causes a direct reduction of $20 billion in national product and income. With smaller incomes, consumers will cut their spending by $16 billion in the "second round." They will buy fewer books, shirts, or movie tickets. This in turn will reduce the incomes of authors, textile workers, and movie producers. As a result, *their* consumption will fall. Just as in the earlier example, there will be a whole series of "rounds." The sum of all these rounds will be a $100 billion decrease in national product.

The Multiplier: The Saving-Investment Approach

Just as the saving-investment diagram may be used to show an unemployment equilibrium, so it may also be used to illustrate the multiplier. This is done in Figure 10-10, which once again provides exactly the same information as the diagram above it. When investment demand increases by $20 billion from I_1^* to I_2^*, equilibrium moves from E to H. Once again, observe that national product increases by more than the initial increase in investment. Indeed, income increases until people are willing to increase their saving by the full $20 billion injected into the spending stream by the new investment. People are not willing to increase their saving by this $20 billion until their incomes have increased by $100 billion. Remember: their marginal propensity to save (MPS) is $1/5$; they only save $1 out of every additional $5 they earn. Thus, from this other perspective, we confirm that equilibrium income rises by $100 billion. (Appendix 10-B provides a further elaboration of the saving-investment approach.)

In this saving-investment approach, it is common to define the multiplier in terms of the MPS, rather than the MPC. To do so, first note that income is either consumed or saved. Therefore:

$$\text{MPS} = 1 - \text{MPC} \qquad (10\text{-}10, \text{ from } 10\text{-}5)$$

Thus, Equation 10-9 can be rewritten:

$$\text{Multiplier} = \frac{1}{\text{MPS}} \qquad (10\text{-}11)$$

However, it should be stressed that the multiplier takes the value shown in Equation 10-11—or in similar Equation 10-9—only *if the economy is the very simplifed one we have considered so far.*

In practice, the multiplier will be smaller than indi-

---

[2]Let c stand for the MPC. As long as c is less than 1 (in our case, 0.8), then the sum of the series $1 + c + c^2 + c^3 \ldots = \dfrac{1}{1 - c}$. This can be shown by actually doing the division on the right side. In other words, divide 1 by $(1 - c)$, as follows:

$$
\begin{array}{r}
1 + c + c^2 \ldots \\
1 - c \overline{)1} \\
\underline{1 - c} \\
c \\
\underline{c - c^2} \\
c^2 \ldots
\end{array}
$$

cated by equations 10-9 and 10-11 because of several complications:

1. Part of the increase in demand may show up in terms of *higher prices*, not in terms of larger real national product.
2. *Taxes* and *imports* act as additional leakages from the spending stream. These additional leakages depress the size of the multiplier, even in a world in which prices are stable.

The second point will be explored in Chapter 11. In this chapter, we will explain the first. However, before we do so, we should bring together the analysis of this chapter—which has thus far been based on the assumption that prices are stable—and the approach of the previous chapter, in which prices were permitted to move.

BRINGING TOGETHER THE TWO APPROACHES

In Figure 10-12, panel (*a*) repeats the output-expenditures approach of this chapter. Panel (*b*), which is based on the aggregate demand and aggregate supply curves of Chapter 9, is drawn directly below it. The two diagrams may be stacked vertically in this manner, because real national product is measured on the horizontal axis of each diagram.

Observe that aggregate demand is shown in both panels. However, the aggregate demand functions in the two panels are quite different. The upper panel shows how real output and income (measured on the horizontal axis) affect the quantity of goods and services demanded (on the vertical axis). The lower panel shows how the average price level (on the vertical axis) affects the quantity of goods and services demanded (on the horizontal axis).

In the basic Keynesian theory outlined in this chapter and illustrated in panel (*a*), prices are assumed to remain constant. As investment increases and aggregate demand shifts up, equilibrium moves from *E* to *H*. In the lower panel, the increase in investment also increases aggregate demand. Specifically, it shifts rightward, and equilibrium again moves from *E* to *H*, leaving the price level unchanged. So long as the economy is moving along the horizontal range of the Keynesian aggregate supply curve in the lower panel, with prices remaining stable in the face of an increase in aggregate demand, the fixed-price assumption of the upper panel is valid. We don't need to worry about price changes. It is quite acceptable to show just the upper figure, and skip the lower one, as we have done in the previous diagrams in this chapter.

INFLATION AND THE MULTIPLIER: AN UPWARD SLOPING AGGREGATE SUPPLY CURVE

However, once we get to the range where the aggregate supply function begins to slope upward, we can no longer ignore price changes. This is illustrated in Figure 10-13. Points *E* and *H* in the upper panel repeat the multiplier analysis in a fixed-price situation. An increase of $20 billion in investment demand shifts the aggregate demand function up by $20 billion, from AD_1 to AD_2. This causes an eventual increase of $100 billion in the quantity of goods and services demanded and in equilibrium national product, as shown by the movement of the equilibrium from *E* to *H*. This increase of $100 billion in the quantity of goods and services demanded shows up as a $100 billion rightward shift in the aggregate demand function in the lower panel, from AD_1 to AD_2.

Now, suppose that there is a further increase of $20 billion in investment demand. Again, the initial investment spending will lead to various rounds of consumer spending. This multiplier process will mean that there will be another rightward shift of the aggregate demand function by $100 billion in the lower panel, from AD_2 to AD_3. Note that distance $HK = EH = \$100$ billion. If prices were to remain stable, the new equilibrium would be at *K*.

But *K* is not a possible equilibrium, because the economy cannot produce that much. As the economy approaches capacity, the aggregate supply function slopes upward. In the face of increasing demand, prices begin to rise. The new equilibrium is at *J*, where the aggregate demand and aggregate supply curves intersect in the lower panel.

Note that, in this move from *H* to *J*, real national product increases by only $60 billion, from $500 billion to $560 billion. This is less than we would have predicted from the multiplier formula (Equation 10-9); according to this formula, a $20 billion increase in investment will increase national product by $100 billion, not $60 billion.

How can this be? Why does equilibrium output

increase by only $60 billion? The answer: Part of the increase in demand goes into higher prices. In other words, even though money is being spent at each round of the multiplier, only part of the expenditure results in the production of additional goods and services. Some of it just covers the higher prices that buyers have to pay.

We conclude that, in this range where the aggregate

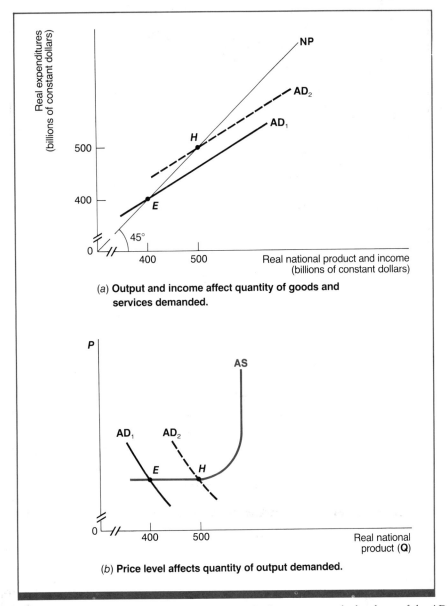

(a) **Output and income affect quantity of goods and services demanded.**

(b) **Price level affects quantity of output demanded.**

Figure 10-12   Bringing together the two approaches.
The upper panel shows the basic Keynesian approach, in which it is assumed that prices are sticky in a downward direction. Prices remain constant so long as the aggregate supply curve in the lower panel is horizontal, as shown between E and H.

In the upper panel, the slope of the AD function shows how spending increases when output and income increase. In the lower panel, the slope of the AD function shows how an increase in the price level causes a decrease in the quantity of goods and services demanded.

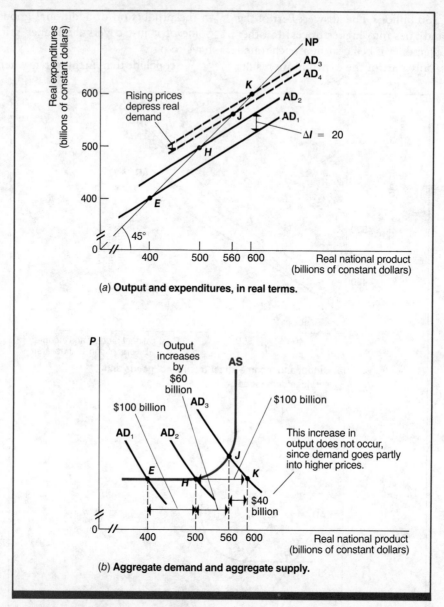

(a) **Output and expenditures, in real terms.**

(b) **Aggregate demand and aggregate supply.**

Figure 10-13 Inflation reduces the increase in real output. Consider first a situation where prices are stable, beginning from equilibrium E. A $20 billion increase in investment demand results in an eventual increase of $100 billion in the total quantity of goods and services demanded, because of the multiplier process. This is illustrated by the movement of the equilibrium from E to H in the upper panel. The increase of $100 billion in the quantity of goods and services demanded shows up as a $100 billion rightward shift in the aggregate demand function in the lower panel, from AD₁ to AD₂.

Once the economy enters the upward-sloping section of aggregate supply, a further increase of $20 billion in investment demand will not cause a full increase of $100 billion in real output. Even though the aggregate demand function shifts to the right by a full $100 billion (from AD₂ to AD₃), real national product increases by only $60 billion. Some of the increase in aggregate demand is reflected in higher prices, rather than larger output.

supply curve slopes upward to the right, a formula such as Equation 10-9 gives only the *rightward* shift of the aggregate demand function in the lower panel. The increase in real national product is less; point *J* is to the left of point *K*.

This conclusion can be carried back up to the top panel. The shift from AD$_2$ to AD$_3$ shows what would happen if prices were to remain stable. But, as part of the spending is dissipated in paying higher prices, there is a drag on the real quantities of goods and services being bought. This effect of inflation brings the aggregate demand curve in the top panel down to AD$_4$, where the equilibrium at *J* is consistent with the equilibrium in the lower panel. To understand this inflationary environment, the lower panel is essential. Without considering the effects in the lower panel, we cannot tell how much real purchases will be reduced by inflation, and we cannot find the equilibrium at *J*.

KEY POINTS

1. During the Great Depression of the 1930s, British economist John Maynard Keynes put forward a new theory of unemployment, arguing that:
   (a) A market economy can come to rest at an equilibrium with large-scale unemployment.
   (b) The cause of unemployment is insufficient aggregate demand.
   (c) The most straightforward cure for unemployment is an increase in government spending. (This point will be explained in Chapter 11.)
2. The components of aggregate demand are:
   (a) Personal consumption expenditures
   (b) Investment demand (that is, the demand for buildings, equipment, and additional inventories)
   (c) Government expenditures for current goods and services
   (d) Net exports (that is, exports minus imports)
3. In this chapter, we analysed an unrealistic but simple economy, with only two components of demand, namely, consumption and investment.
4. Consumption expenditures depend primarily on disposable personal income. As incomes rise, people consume more. The change in consumption, as a fraction of a change in disposable income, is known as the *marginal propensity to consume* (MPC).
5. Equilibrium national product occurs where the aggregate demand function cuts the 45° line.

A larger national product would be unsustainable, since demand would fall short of production and unsold goods would pile up in inventories.
6. In Keynesian theory, equilibrium national product may be less than the full-employment quantity.
7. There are several alternative ways of stating the condition for equilibrium. It exists when:
   (a) Aggregate demand and national product are equal; that is, where the aggregate demand function cuts the 45° national product line (Figure 10-5).
   (b) Inventories are at their desired level; that is, when actual investment equals desired investment and there is no undesired build-up or reduction in inventories (Figure 10-5).
   (c) Desired investment and saving are equal (Figure 10-6).
8. An increase in investment demand raises national product and income. This induces people to consume more. In the simple economy, national product increases by the rise in investment times the multiplier, where the multiplier is:

$$\text{Multiplier} = \frac{1}{1 - \text{MPC}}$$

Because saving equals income minus consumption,

Marginal propensity to save $= 1 - \text{MPC}$

Thus, the multiplier in the simple economy

may alternatively be expressed as:

$$\text{Multiplier} = \frac{1}{\text{MPS}}$$

9. In practice, the increase in real output following an increase in investment will be smaller than indicated by these two equations because of several complications:

   (a) Part of the increase in demand may show up in terms of *higher prices*, not in terms of larger real national product.

   (b) *Taxes* and *imports* act as additional leakages from the spending stream. (This point will be explained in Chapter 11.)

10. Once the economy is in a range where the aggregate supply function slopes upward to the right, only part of any increase in aggregate demand shows up in terms of larger output. Part goes to pay higher prices. In such circumstances, the formulas shown in point no. 8 represent the rightward shift of the aggregate demand function (for example, from H to K in Figure 10-13). The increase in real output is less than this rightward shift in demand.

KEY CONCEPTS

consumption function
saving function
break-even point at which
   consumption equals income
45° line
marginal propensity to
   consume (MPC)
marginal propensity to save (MPS)

investment demand—or desired
   investment or planned investment
   (I*)
actual investment (I)
undesired inventory accumulation
unemployment equilibrium
saving-investment approach

circular flow of spending
leakage
injection
output-expenditures approach
leakages-injections approach
multiplier

PROBLEMS

10-1 Draw a diagram showing the consumption function, the aggregate demand function, and the 45° line. What quantity of NP represents the equilibrium? Explain why a larger NP would be unsustainable and would lead to a contraction of production. Explain also why national product will expand, if it is initially smaller than the equilibrium quantity.

10-2 The consumption function and the saving function are two alternative ways of presenting the same information. The text explains how the saving function can be derived from the consumption function. Show how the consumption function can be derived from the saving function.

10-3 Draw a diagram showing investment demand and the saving function. What is the equilibrium national product? Explain why a higher national product would be unsustainable. Explain also why national product will expand if it is initially smaller than the equilibrium quantity.

10-4 The mathematical formula for the multiplier shows that a high MPC causes a high multiplier. By tracing the effects of $20 billion in additional investment through a number of "rounds" of spending, show that the multiplier is higher with an MPC of 0.9 than with an MPC of 0.8. (Use Table 10-3 to start.)

10-5 On a sheet of graph paper, draw a diagram similar to the one shown in Figure 10-10. (Make the diagram large, so that you will be able to see what you are doing.) Following Figure 10-10, show the multiplier effects of a

$20 billion increase in investment demand when the MPS = 0.2. Now suppose that the MPS increases to 0.5. In colour, draw in a new saving function, going through the same initial equilibrium E. When investment demand increases by $20 billion, what now is the new equilibrium national product? What is the size of the multiplier now?

10-6 What is the difference between actual investment (I) and desired investment (I^*)? What happens if desired investment is greater than actual investment? Why?

10-7 Consider an economy with the relationship between consumption and income shown in the table below.

(a) Fill in the blanks in the "Saving" column.

(b) Investment demand is originally $40 billion. Fill in the blanks in the "Initial aggregate demand" column.

(c) What is the equilibrium national product?

(d) Now assume that investment demand rises to $60 billion. What does this do to aggregate demand? (Fill in the "Later aggregate demand" column.) What is equilibrium national product now?

(e) Comparing your answers to (c) and (d), find the multiplier.

Disposable income = NP (billions)	Consumption (billions)	Saving (billions)	Initial aggregate demand (billions)	Later aggregate demand (billions)
$100	$ 90	_____	_____	_____
$110	$ 97.5	_____	_____	_____
$120	$105	_____	_____	_____
$130	$112.5	_____	_____	_____
$140	$120	_____	_____	_____
$150	$127.5	_____	_____	_____
$160	$135	_____	_____	_____
$170	$142.5	_____	_____	_____
$180	$150	_____	_____	_____

10-8 Figure 10-13 showed how the increase in real output following an increase in investment becomes smaller when the economy enters the upward-sloping section of the aggregate supply curve. Suppose that the economy was initially in the vertical, "classical" range of the aggregate supply curve. Now suppose that businesses spend $20 billion more on plant and equipment. What happens to equilibrium real national product as a result?

APPENDIX 10-A

CLASSICAL ECONOMICS: EQUILIBRIUM WITH FULL EMPLOYMENT

Chapter 9 described the main difference between the Keynesian and classical theories. Although classical economists believed that equilibrium occurs at full employment, they conceded that large-scale unemployment could occur temporarily, as a result of disturbances. However, market forces would move the economy back toward its equilibrium with full employment. This chapter has explained the revolutionary idea in Keynes' *General Theory*, that there could be an equilibrium with large-scale unemployment. The purpose of this appendix is to look in more detail at the contrasting classical argument.

The main point in the classical case was explained in Chapter 9, especially Figure 9-3. In the face of large-scale unemployment, prices fall, increasing the real quantity of money. Because households have more purchasing power at their disposal, they buy more goods and services. Prices continue to fall, and people consequently continue to buy more, until full employment is reached.

SAVING AND INVESTMENT

There was, however, also a second strand to the classical theory of full employment, related to the Keynesian theory of saving and investment which was studied in this chapter. Like Keynes, classical economists recognized that desired investment and saving would have to be equal for the economy to be in equilibrium. But, unlike Keynes (Figure 10-6), they did not believe that real national product would have to decrease if investment demand was less than saving.

Rather, classical economists argued that the price mechanism will bring desired investment and saving into equilibrium at full employment. The key price that does this is the interest rate. The interest rate is the reward received by savers, and it is also the price corporations and others pay for borrowed funds with which they construct buildings or engage in other investment projects.

Suppose that investment demand falls short of saving when the economy is at full employment. What happens? According to classical economists, savers have large quantities of funds. In their eagerness to acquire bonds and other earning assets, they are willing to settle for a lower interest rate. As the interest rate falls, businesses find it cheaper to borrow. They are encouraged to undertake more investment projects; in other words, desired investment increases. The rate of interest continues to drop until desired investment and saving are brought into equality, as illustrated in Figure 10-14. The full-employment equilibrium (E) occurs at the intersection of the investment demand curve (I^*) and the curve showing saving when the economy is at full employment (S_{FE}). An increase in the desire to save—that is, a rightward shift in S_{FE}—causes a fall in the rate of interest, which in turn causes an increase in the quantity of investment. Full employment is maintained. In other words, classical economists argued that there was something wrong with Keynes' plumbing. Savings do not simply leak from the economy, as they did back in Figure 10-8. Rather, an increase in saving causes a fall in interest rates, which in turn causes an increase in investment. Thus, the financial markets, where savers supply funds to investors, provide a pipe which connects saving and investment in Figure 10-8—that is, a pipe that brings saving leakages back into the spending stream in the form of investment demand.

THE KEYNESIAN REBUTTAL

In response, Keynes said that classical economists were in error in counting on the interest rate to fall enough to equate saving and investment at full employment. In his *General Theory*, he argued that there is "no guarantee" that the full-employment saving curve intersects investment demand "anywhere at all" when the interest rate is positive. This possibility is illustrated in Figure 10-15. Here, no full-employment equilibrium exists, since I^* and S_{FE} intersect at a negative interest rate. But it is not possible for interest rates to be negative, since people would be unwilling to lend money; they would simply lock it up in a bank vault instead. In fact, Keynes went one step further, and argued that the minimum interest rate is not zero, but at some positive rate, shown as i_{min} in Figure 10-15.

Now, if the economy were temporarily at full employment, saving would exceed desired investment by quantity BA.[3] Being at a minimum, the interest rate

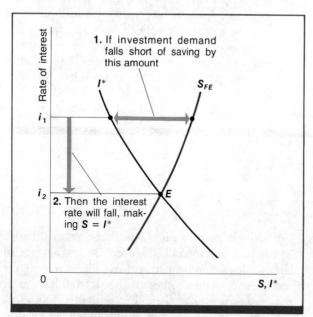

Figure 10-14   Saving and investment in classical theory. The S_{FE} curve shows how much will be saved at various interest rates in a fully employed economy. The I^* curve shows how much businesses will borrow to finance investment projects at various interest rates. Classical economists argued that if saving exceeds investment demand, the interest rate will fall until saving and investment are equalized—without large-scale unemployment.

[3]Keynes' case did not depend on i_{min} being above zero. It could be at zero and still leave a gap between full-employment saving and investment demand, although this gap would be smaller (GH, rather than BA).

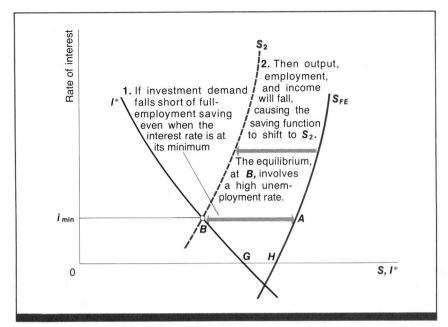

Figure 10-15   The Keynesian rebuttal.
Keynes argued that there was something wrong with the classical approach to saving and investment illustrated in Figure 10-14. Specifically, Keynes said that the full-employment saving curve (S_{FE}) might intersect the investment demand curve I^* at an interest rate below the minimum (i_{min}), which can occur in financial markets. In this case, the gap AB between saving and investment demand cannot be closed by a fall in the interest rate. It is closed by a fall in output, causing the saving function to shift to S_2.

cannot fall to bring saving and investment demand into equilibrium. Something has to give. According to Keynes, what will give will be output and employment. As leakages into saving exceed injections of investment spending, national product and employment will decrease. With smaller incomes, people will save less; the saving function in Figure 10-15 will shift to the left, all the way to S_2. Now there is an equilibrium because saving and investment demand are equal. However, there is large-scale unemployment at this equilibrium.

Incidentally, Figure 10-15 is based on the only diagram in Keynes' *General Theory*. Clearly, Keynes felt strongly about the errors of classical economists who argued that a change in the interest rate would bring saving and investment into equality at full employment.

The differences between Keynes and the classical economists may be summarized. The latter argued that an *increase in saving*, by depressing interest rates, *causes an increase in investment*, and thus stimulates growth (Figure 10-14). Saving is a benefit to society; it makes

us better off in the future. In contrast, Keynes argued that this isn't necessarily so. Saving may be antisocial. It may decrease national product and employment, a possibility we shall explore in Appendix 10-B. Furthermore, Keynes believed that it is more correct to argue that *a change in investment demand causes a change in saving* (Figure 10-10) than to argue that a change in the desire to save causes a change in investment. Thus, said Keynes, classical economists had gotten the relationship between saving and investment backwards. Because of their confusion, they had overlooked the possibility that the economy might reach an equilibrium with a high rate of unemployment.

In rebuttal, classical economists fell back on their basic argument as to why the economy would reach equilibrium at full employment—an argument already explained in Chapter 9. To recapitulate, they said that prices would fall in the event of large-scale unemployment, when aggregate demand falls far short of the productive capacity of the economy. A fall in the general level of prices would increase the purchasing power of money; the real quantity of money would rise. As a result, people would buy a greater quantity of goods and services. This process would continue until full employment was restored. Because this rebuttal was contained in an article by Cambridge professor A.C. Pigou, the idea that an increase in the real quantity of money will cause an increase in purchases is sometimes known as the *Pigou effect*. Alternatively, it is known as the *real balance effect*, because it is the proposition that people will buy more when their real money balances increase.

In summary, classical economists counted on price flexibility to help restore full employment in *two* ways. First, there was general price flexibility. A fall in the average price of goods and services would increase the purchasing power of money, and thus encourage buying. Second was the flexibility of a specific price; namely, the rate of interest. A fall in the interest rate would bring investment demand into line with full-employment saving (Figure 10-14).

SAY'S LAW

There was also a third, less precise proposition in classical theory, known as *Say's law*, after nineteenth-century economist J.B. Say. Say put forward the disarmingly simple idea that *supply creates its own demand*. When people sell a good or service, they do so in order to be able to buy some other good or service. The very act of supplying one good or service thus creates a demand for some other good or service. There can be too much supply for some specific product, such as shoes, but, if so, there is too much demand and not enough supply of some other product. Surpluses and shortages can exist in an *individual* market. Nevertheless, for the economy as a whole, there cannot be an excess of supply over demand.

Keynes put his finger on the problem with Say's simple idea. It is true that, when people create goods and services, they earn income. The income from the production of all the goods and services is sufficient to buy those goods and services. The problem is that people do not spend all their incomes; they save part. Therefore, demand can fall short of production. This shortfall may be offset by investment demand. However, if investment demand is less than full-employment saving, there will be an overall inadequacy of demand, and unemployment will result.

Therefore, Say's simple idea is a weak foundation on which to build the idea that the economy will provide full employment. Say's law simply assumes full employment. It provides no mechanism whereby aggregate demand can be brought into equality with aggregate supply at the full-employment quantity of output.

Furthermore, Say's law is inconsistent with the main body of classical economics. According to Say's law, there can be no excess of supply over demand, *regardless of the general price level*. But, according to the more sensible version of classical theory presented in Chapter 9, supply can exceed demand if the average level of prices is above equilibrium (for example, at P_1 back in Figure 9-3).[4]

Although Say's law has been prominent in economic literature, it should not be considered the main idea in classical macroeconomics. In particular, it does not constitute the central pillar of the classical proposition that full employment will exist in equilibrium. Rather, this proposition depends on the two points explained earlier, namely: (1) the increase in the quantity of goods and services demanded that results when the general level of prices falls (the demand curve in Figure 9-3 slopes downward to the right) and (2) the increase in investment demand, and the decrease in saving, caused by a fall in the interest rate (Figure 10-14).

[4]The inconsistency between Say's law and the main body of classical economics is explained in detail in Don Patinkin, *Money, Interest, and Prices*, 2nd ed. (New York: Harper & Row, 1965).

APPENDIX 10-B

CHANGES IN THE DESIRE TO SAVE: THE PARADOX OF THRIFT

Keynesian theory explains how equilibrium national product NP changes if there is a change in investment demand—as we saw in Figure 10-10. Now let's consider what happens if the saving function shifts upward—or, what amounts to the same thing, the consumption function shifts downward.

Suppose that people become more thrifty; they save more out of any given income. This causes the saving function to shift upward from S_1 to S_2 in Figure 10-16. Consider what happens at the initial national product, A, as a result. The leakage into saving (AG) now exceeds the injections in the form of investment demand (AE_1). Aggregate demand falls short of NP, and unsold goods pile up. Orders are cancelled, and NP decreases to its new equilibrium, B. In this simple case where investment demand is horizontal, an increase in the desire to save has no effect on the equilibrium quantity of saving or investment. The amount saved and invested is the same at BE_2 as it was originally at AE_1. The only effect is a decrease in output.

However, that is not the worst of it. In order to make the analysis simple, the demand for investment so far has been assumed constant. Clearly that need not be the case. Desired investment can change. Specifically, investment demand may increase as NP in-

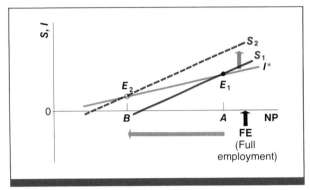

Figure 10-17   The paradox of thrift.
With the investment demand function sloping upward to the right, an increase in the desire to save results in a movement from E_1 to E_2. In equilibrium, the quantity of saving decreases, since E_2 is not as high as E_1.

creases. As more and more goods are produced, there is a need for more machines and factories. In this case, investment demand is an upward sloping function, as shown in Figure 10-17.

Now a shift in the saving function becomes particularly potent. An increase in the desire to save, moving the saving function from S_1 to S_2, causes a very large decrease in equilibrium national product from A to B. Furthermore, the effects on the equilibrium amount of saving and investment are paradoxical. *As a result of the upward shift in the saving function,* observe that *the amount of saving and investment in equilibrium falls,* from distance AE_1 to BE_2. This is the **paradox of thrift.**

> The *paradox of thrift* occurs when an *increase* in the desire to save (a shift from S_1 to S_2) causes a *fall* in actual saving (from AE_1 to BE_2).

What happens is this: Beginning at the initial equilibrium E_1, an increase in the desire to save causes an increase in leakages from the spending stream. Aggre-

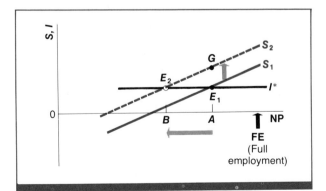

Figure 10-16   An increase in the desire to save.
An increase in the desire to save does not increase equilibrium saving. Instead, it results in a decrease in output.

gate demand and NP fall. As they fall, businesses decide that they need fewer machines and factories. There is a decline in the quantity of investment as the economy moves to the left along the investment demand function. Equilibrium is restored only when national product has fallen enough so that people are content to save an amount which is no more than the *diminished* quantity of investment demand, at point E_2. Because the quantity of investment decreases as national product falls, and because national product must fall by enough to bring saving into equality with investment, saving declines in the move from E_1 to E_2.[5]

The paradox of thrift is an illustration of one important way in which macroeconomic conclusions—covering the economy as a whole—may be quite different from conclusions for a single individual. If a single individual becomes more thrifty—saving more out of any level of income—then he or she will end up with more saving. But we cannot conclude that, just because this is true for a single individual, it will also be true

for the economy as a whole. Such a conclusion would be an illustration of the *fallacy of composition*. Figure 10-17 shows a case in which the results for the society as a whole are exactly the opposite to the results for an individual: For the society, a stronger effort to save means less actual saving.

> The *fallacy of composition* involves the unwarranted conclusion that a proposition which is true of a single individual or single market is necessarily true for the economy as a whole.

The paradox of thrift grows out of Keynesian theory, whose underlying assumptions should be re-emphasized at this point. The Keynesian analysis *deals with the situation in which there is large-scale unemployment and prices are downwardly rigid; changes in aggregate demand lead to changes in output and no change in prices.* In short, changes in aggregate demand cause the economy to move along the horizontal section of the aggregate supply function. If, on the other hand, the economy is experiencing booming demand conditions, and is in the inflationary vertical range of the aggregate supply function, the Keynesian analysis of thrift must be completely reversed. The macroeconomic problem is eased by an increase in the desire to save; that is, by a downward shift in the consumption function. As consumption and aggregate demand fall, inflationary forces are weakened. Furthermore, since the economy is at full employment and is therefore fully utilizing its resources, a decrease in consumption releases resources from the production of consumer goods. These resources become available for the production of capital goods. Thus, an increase in the willingness to save indeed adds to the amount of factories and machinery produced; the real saving of society is augmented. *In a world of inflationary excess demand, the paradox of thrift does not hold.*

---

[5]When investment changes with national product, the multiplier becomes larger; national product changes more as a result of any vertical shift in the investment or saving function. Thus, for example, national product changes more in Figure 10-17 than in Figure 10-16.

The reason is that, as the economy moves to the left from E_1 (in response to the shift of saving from S_1 to S_2), the gap between S and I^* closes more slowly. (The rate at which it closes depends on the difference between the slopes of the S and I^* functions.) In other words, closing a vertical gap between S and I^* requires a greater change in NP; thus, the multiplier is greater. It can be shown that the multiplier in this case is:

$$\text{Multiplier} = \frac{1}{(\text{MPS} - \text{MPI})} \qquad (10\text{-}14)$$

where MPI, the marginal propensity to invest, is the change in investment demand divided by the change in national product. (It is the slope of the I^* function.) Thus, if the MPS = 0.20, as before, while MPI = 0.15, then the multiplier is 20.

Part Three

AGGREGATE DEMAND POLICIES

Part 2 has laid the basis for macroeconomics. Chapter 7 explained how we measure national product and changes in the average level of prices. Chapter 8 surveyed the macroeconomic history of recent decades, paying particular attention to fluctuations in economic activity. The last two chapters focused on aggregate demand and aggregate supply.

One important message came out of those last two chapters: Recessions and depressions are caused by a fall in aggregate demand. Inflation is caused by too much aggregate demand. In Part 3, we look more closely at the several factors that influence aggregate demand, and at the way these factors can be manipulated by governments in order to combat the problems of inflation and unemployment.

Government spending and *taxation* are two important influences on aggregate demand. *Fiscal policy*—that is, deliberate changes in spending and taxation—represents one way in which the government can control aggregate demand. The fine points are explained in Chapter 11, but the main idea is simple. If, during a depression, government increases its spending for such projects as roads or dams, it thereby increases the demand for cement, steel, and other materials. Some people are put to work producing cement and steel, and others start to work directly on the construction of the roads or dams. As a result, the unemployment rate will fall. The taxation side of fiscal policy works more indirectly. When the government cuts taxes, people have more income left after taxes, and they tend as a consequence to buy more—more clothing, more washing machines, more vacations, and more of a whole host of goods and services. Again, people will be put to work producing clothing, washing machines, and all the other goods and services that are being bought.

Aggregate demand is also influenced by exports and imports. When foreigners demand more of our exports, such as newsprint and subway cars, more people are put to work producing these goods. Imports, on the other hand, are a subtraction from aggregate demand. For example, if Canadian consumers switch their purchases from Canadian-produced goods to foreign goods, there is a reduction in aggregate demand in Canada, and national income falls. This relationship between aggregate demand and international trade is also discussed in Chapter 15.

Monetary policy involves changes in the rate of growth of the money stock held by the public. In our economy, there are two types of money. Most obviously, the dollar bills and coins that you have in your wallet are money; you can use them to buy lunch or go to a movie. But many purchases are not paid for with "pocket money." In fact, payment by cheque is much more important than payment with currency: Most large purchases are made by cheque. Because cheques are commonly used to make purchases, the balances that people hold in their chequing accounts are counted as part of the money stock. Because much of our money is held in the form of chequing accounts in banks, Chapter 12 explores how the banking system operates, as a background for studying monetary policy.

Chapter 13 presents a detailed explanation of how monetary policy works. Once again, it is possible to summarize the general idea behind monetary policy. When individuals and businesses have more money in the form of either cash or balances in their chequing accounts, they are encouraged to spend more. By taking steps to increase the quantity of money, the authorities can encourage spending.

Much macroeconomic theory dates from the Great Depression of the 1930s, when aggregate demand was too low and many workers were consequently unemployed. But problems can also exist on the opposite side. Aggregate demand can become too high. If people try to buy more than the limited available supply of goods, the result is inflation. Again, aggregate demand tools may be used by the authorities to combat the problem. Fiscal and monetary policies can be adjusted, this time to restrain aggregate demand.

Part 3 will explain the basic theory of how fiscal and monetary policies can be used to manage aggregate demand. This is an important topic in macroeconomics. By using aggregate demand tools, we have achieved a much better economic performance during the past four decades than in the years between the two world wars. But we repeat our warning in Chapter 2: *Theory necessarily involves simplification.* And when it is presented to beginning students, theory must be especially simple. Thus, the theoretical "road map" of Part 3 has been drawn with the bumps and potholes removed. But bumps and potholes do exist.

The bumps and potholes will provide the topics for Part 4 (chapters 14 to 19). In Part 4, we will look at the real-world complications that make demand management so difficult. We will search for the reasons for a disturbing fact: While the performance of the economy in recent decades has been good by historical standards, it has not become better and better. In particular, the recession of 1981–82 was more severe than any of the recessions since World War II. We clearly have not solved the problem of economic instability.

In searching for the reasons for recent macroeconomic problems, we will broaden our horizon. We will go beyond the problems of demand management, with which economists were preoccupied in the decades immediately following the Great Depression. We will also look in more detail at the other side of the picture—aggregate supply. How do producers respond to changes in the average level of prices? What is the capacity of our economy to produce goods and services? Why does capacity grow more rapidly during some periods than it does during others?

But first, we look at the fundamentals of demand management.

Chapter 11

GOVERNMENT AND FOREIGN TRADE IN THE KEYNESIAN MODEL

Fiscal policy has to be put on constant . . .
alert. . . . The management of prosperity is a
full-time job.

Walter W. Heller,
New Dimensions in Political Economy

In Chapter 10, we considered a very simple economy where the only components of aggregate demand were consumption and private investment. In this chapter, we take the analysis closer to reality by bringing into the picture two further determinants of aggregate demand and income: government spending and international trade. Having done this, we can then discuss how the government can use expenditure and tax changes as tools for improving the economy's performance.

FISCAL POLICY: The Basic Principles

In his *General Theory*, Keynes argued that chronic depression might be the outcome of a policy of laissez-faire. The market mechanism does not ensure full employment. Furthermore, even if the economy were to reach a high rate of employment, this happy situation would probably not last. The market economy tends to be unstable, either slowing down into a recession or speeding up into an inflationary boom.

However, in spite of the defects of the market economy, Keynes was not pessimistic. We are not, said he, inevitably condemned to suffer the economic and social costs of high unemployment or the disruptive effects of inflation. The government can deal with the root causes of these problems. Unemployment is the result of too little aggregate demand; people are thrown out of work when nobody buys the goods they can produce. Inflation is the result of too much aggregate demand; prices rise when too much demand is chasing the available supply of goods. By taking steps to increase aggregate demand during a recession or depression, the government can increase the amount of national product and put the unemployed back to work. By restraining aggregate demand during periods of inflation, the government can slow down the rate of increase of prices.

This, then, was the policy message of the Keynesian revolution: The government has the ability—and the responsibility—to manage aggregate demand, and thus ensure a continuing prosperity without inflation. The government can affect aggregate demand with **fiscal policies**—that is, by changes in government spending or tax rates.

Government Purchases

In the bare-bones economy discussed in Chapter 10, the government was completely ignored; there was no government spending or taxation. In order to proceed in simple steps, we will first introduce the effects of government spending, and ignore taxes until a later point.

Government expenditures for goods and services are a component of aggregate demand. People are employed building roads, teaching school, and maintaining parks. The roads, educational services, and upkeep of parks are included in national product. When government demand is added to the bare-bones economy of Chapter 10, then:

> **Aggregate demand (AD) =**
> **consumption expenditures (C) +**
> **investment demand (I*) +**
> **government purchases of goods**
> **and services (G)**

Thus, government purchases of goods and services (G) can be added vertically to consumption and investment demand, to get the aggregate demand line shown in Figure 11-1. Note that when government purchases of $10 billion are added vertically to consumer demand plus investment demand, the equilibrium moves from point D to point E. The increase in national product, measured by the $50 billion distance AB on the horizontal axis, is a multiple of the $10 billion of government spending. The multiplier process works on government spending just as it worked on investment expenditures. For example, when workers receive income from building roads, a whole series of spending and respending decisions is set in motion. The workers spend most of their wages for consumer goods such as clothing and cars. Additional employees are hired by the clothing and automobile industries, and these employees also spend more as a consequence of their rising incomes. The process is similar to that illustrated earlier for the investment multiplier (Table 10-3).

In spite of government spending, aggregate demand in our economy may nevertheless still fall short of what is needed for full employment. Such was the case during the Depression of the 1930s. There were some

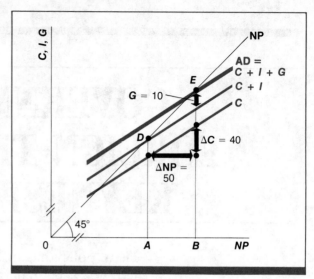

Figure 11-1 The addition of government spending.
Government spending is added vertically to consumption and investment demand in order to get aggregate demand: AD = C + I* + G. Observe that the multiplier process works on government demand. Without government spending, the equilibrium would be at point D (as we saw in Chapter 10). With government spending, the equilibrium is at E. The increase in national product (AB = $50 billion) is a multiple of the $10 billion of government spending. As people's incomes rise, they move along the consumption function, consuming $40 billion more.

Source: Department of Finance. Reprinted by permission of the Minister of Supply and Services Canada.

government expenditures, yet the unemployment rate was very high—reaching almost 20% of the labour force. This situation is illustrated in Figure 11-2, where equilibrium E is far to the left of the full-employment national product.

In order to get to full employment, the government should spend more. The question is, how much more? Observe that at the full-employment quantity of national product (F), the aggregate demand function (AD₁) lies below the 45° line. This shortfall of aggregate demand below the 45° line—distance HJ—is known as the **recessionary gap**.

> A *recessionary gap* exists when the aggregate demand function is below the 45° line at the full-employment quantity of national product. The gap is the vertical distance from the 45° line down to the aggregate demand function,

measured at the full-employment quantity of national product.

The *output gap*—or *GNP gap*—is the amount by which national product falls short of the full-employment quantity. It is measured along the horizontal axis. The output gap (*BF* in Figure 11-2) is larger than the recessionary gap (*HJ*).

In order to get to full employment, the aggregate demand function must be shifted up by the amount of the recessionary gap, *HJ*. Thus, *HJ* is the amount of additional government purchases that are needed.

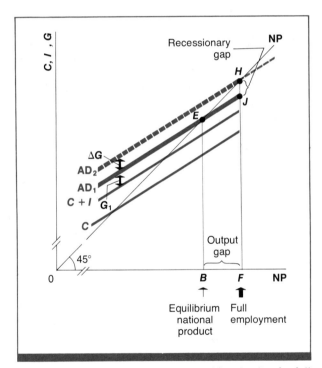

Figure 11-2   The recessionary gap, and fiscal policy for full employment.
At initial equilibrium *E*, there is large-scale unemployment. (National product *B* falls far short of the full-employment national product at *F*.) To reach full employment, government spending (*G₁*) should be increased by *HJ*, the amount of the recessionary gap. This will shift aggregate demand up to AD₂ and move the economy to a full-employment equilibrium at *H*. Note that *HJ*, the recessionary gap, is the vertical distance between the aggregate demand line (AD₁) and the 45° line, measured at the full-employment national product.

Hence, we come to the first and most important rule of thumb for fiscal policy:

By increasing its purchases of goods and services by the amount of the recessionary gap, the government can eliminate the gap, and move the economy to full employment.

When the government increases its spending, once again the multiplier process is put to work. In Figure 11-2, note that an increase of government spending equal to the recessionary gap (*HJ*) causes output to increase by an even larger amount, *BF*; that is, by enough to eliminate the **output gap** and restore full employment.

One final point should be emphasized. For the full impact of the multiplier to occur, *it is essential that taxes not be increased to pay for the additional government spending.* As we shall see shortly, an increase in taxes would remove purchasing power from the hands of the public, and thus act as a drag on consumption. With consumption discouraged in this way, the increase in aggregate demand would be smaller than it would be if tax rates were kept stable.

This, then, is a key policy conclusion of Keynesian economics: During a depression, when a large increase in aggregate demand is needed to restore full employment, *government spending should not be limited to the government's tax receipts.* Spending should be increased without increasing taxes. But if taxes are not raised, how is the government to finance its spending? The answer: by borrowing. That is, by adding to the public debt. Keynes argued that *deficit spending is not unsound during a recession or depression.* On the contrary, it is just what is needed to stimulate aggregate demand and reduce unemployment.

Restrictive Fiscal Policy: The Suppression of Inflationary Pressures

During the 1930s, aggregate demand was too low; the economy was depressed. At other times, aggregate demand has been too high—for example, during World War II and the early post-war period; the result was strong upward pressure on prices. Similarly, aggregate demand was too high in the early years of the 1970s as the government tried to maintain the conditions of low unemployment and high economic growth that had marked most of the 1960s. This set off an inflationary

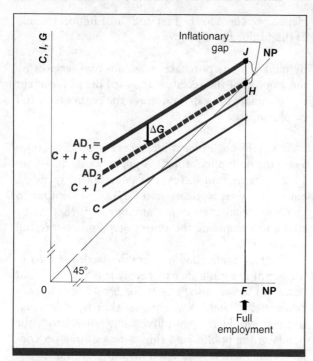

Figure 11-3   The inflationary gap.
At the full-employment quantity of output, aggregate demand may exceed the amount that the economy is capable of producing. (J is above H.) The excess demand will cause inflation. To restrain inflation, aggregate demand should be brought down to AD_2. This can be done by a cut in government spending (ΔG) equal to the inflationary gap.

spiral that lasted for the rest of the decade.

The situation where aggregate demand is too high is illustrated in Figure 11-3. At the full-employment national product, aggregate demand AD_1 is above the 45° line. With existing productive capacity, businesses cannot fill all the orders for goods. There is an **inflationary gap** (HJ); the excess demand will cause a rise in prices.

> An *inflationary gap* exists when aggregate demand is above the 45° line at the full-employment quantity of national product. It is the vertical distance from the 45° line up to the aggregate demand function, measured at the full-employment quantity of national product.

In such circumstances, the appropriate fiscal policy is a sufficient *reduction* in government spending to

bring aggregate demand down to AD_2. Specifically, the second rule of thumb for fiscal policy is this:

During a period of inflation, excessive aggregate demand can be eliminated by a decrease in government purchases equal to the inflationary gap.

TAXES

There is one difference between a tax collector and a taxidermist—the taxidermist leaves the hide.

Mortimer Caplin

Government spending is only one side of fiscal policy; the other is taxation. Although taxes do not show up directly as a component of aggregate demand, they do affect aggregate demand indirectly. When people pay taxes, they are left with less disposable income, and they consequently consume less. Thus, the consumption component of aggregate demand is reduced.

Tax policies can also affect investment. For example, investment may be stimulated by the investment tax credit, which permits those who buy equipment to reduce their taxes by a portion of the cost of the equipment. In this chapter, we concentrate on the effect of taxes on consumption.

A Lump-sum Tax

In order to introduce tax complications one by one, we initially make an unrealistic but very simple assumption—that taxes (T) are levied in a *lump sum*. That is, the government collects a fixed amount—say, $10 billion—in taxes *regardless of the size of national product*.

How does this tax affect consumption? The answer is shown in Figure 11-4. After the tax, people have $10 billion less in disposable income. As a consequence, their consumption declines. By how much? With a marginal propensity to consume (MPC) of 0.8, they consume $8 billion less. They also save $2 billion less. Thus the $10 billion fall in disposable income is reflected in a $2 billion decline in saving and an $8 billion decline in consumption.

This $8 billion decrease in consumption is carried over to Figure 11-5. Point B on the after-tax consumption function C_2 is $8 billion below A. Similarly, every other point on the original consumption function also shifts down by $8 billion. The new after-tax function

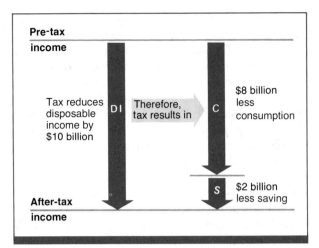

Figure 11-4 A tax depresses consumption.
If the MPC is 0.8, a $10 billion tax reduces consumption by
$8 billion and saving by $2 billion.

is parallel to the original consumption function, but
$8 billion lower. In general:

**A lump-sum tax causes the consumption function to
shift down by the amount of the tax times the MPC.**

When taxes are increased and the consumption function shifts downward, aggregate demand likewise shifts
downward. Thus, when aggregate demand is too high
and prices are rising, an *increase* in taxes is the appropriate policy step. On the other side, a *cut* in taxes
represents a *stimulative* policy; the reduction in taxes
will increase disposable income and shift the consumption function and aggregate demand *upward*.

Note that a change in taxes is almost as powerful a
tool for controlling aggregate demand as a change in
government purchases of goods and services. Almost,
but not quite. An increase of $10 billion in govern-
ment purchases causes aggregate demand to shift up
by the full $10 billion. However, a decrease in taxes of
$10 billion shifts aggregate demand up by only $8
billion—that is, $10 billion times the MPC.[1]

---

[1]Like taxes, a $10 billion change in transfer payments is less power-
ful than a $10 billion change in government spending for goods and
services. When the government purchases road-building equipment
or other goods or services, it provides jobs directly. However, transfer payments—such as Old Age Security benefits—do not provide
jobs directly. Like taxes, they affect demand only indirectly, by

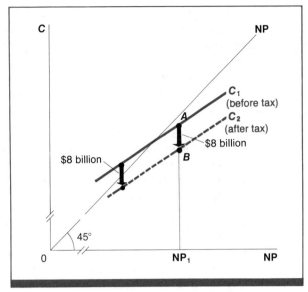

Figure 11-5 Effect of a $10 billion lump-sum tax.
If the MPC is 0.8, a lump-sum tax T of $10 billion causes
the consumption function to shift down by $8 billion
($T \times$ MPC).

Because government purchases of goods and services are more powerful, dollar for dollar, than a change
in taxes, there is reason to turn to government purchases when major changes are desired in aggregate
demand. During the early Keynesian period, economists did concentrate on government purchases in their
fiscal policy recommendations. However, since the late
1950s, tax changes have become a more prominent
way to manage aggregate demand. Thus, substantial
tax-rate reductions were used to counteract rising
unemployment in 1958–59, and as inflationary pressures grew in 1968–69, tax increases were the main
tools used to reduce the size of the inflationary gap. In
the 1970s, major tax cuts were employed to combat
the 1974–75 recession, and as unemployment again
inched upward in 1977–78, further tax cuts were
made.

There were three reasons why tax changes became
more important as a component of fiscal policy, beginning in the late 1950s.

---

changing disposable income. Specifically, a $10 billion increase in
transfer payments raises disposable income by $10 billion, and thus
causes an upward shift of the consumption function by $10 billion
times the MPC.

1. A tax cut is generally *less controversial* than an increase in government spending as a way of stimulating the economy. This is true in part because of skepticism over the ability of the government to spend money wisely, and because of fears that the government will grow bigger and bigger.

2. Tax changes may be put into effect *more quickly* than changes in government spending. Increases in spending for highways, government buildings, dams, or other public works require considerable planning, and this takes time.

The problem of delays in changing government programs were well illustrated by the attempts of Finance Minister Marc Lalonde to counteract the 1981–82 recession by an increase in government spending. His "Special Recovery Program" was not ready to be introduced in Parliament until April 1983, and by the time substantial spending on the program actually began in late 1983 and early 1984, the recovery was already well underway.

3. Tax changes are *more easily reversed* when conditions change.

It is true that the public may be unhappy when previously cut taxes are reimposed. However, they may be even more unhappy if government spending programs are eliminated. Furthermore, some government spending—for example, for roads, buildings, or dams—cannot be stopped without considerable waste. A half-finished bridge or dam is no good to anybody.

To summarize our policy conclusions thus far:

1. To *stimulate aggregate demand*, and thus combat unemployment, the appropriate fiscal policy is an increase in government spending and/or a cut in taxes; that is, steps that increase the government's deficit or reduce its surplus.

2. To *restrain aggregate demand* and thus combat inflation, the appropriate fiscal policy is a cut in government spending and/or an increase in taxes; that is, steps which move the government's budget toward a surplus.

A government deficit acts as a stimulus to aggregate demand. A surplus acts as a drag.

Adding Realism: A Proportional Tax

These two important policy conclusions have been illustrated by looking at a simple lump-sum tax that was $10 billion no matter what national product might be. But this tax isn't realistic. In fact, tax collections rise and fall with national product. This is obviously true of income taxes. The more people earn, the more taxes they pay. It is also true of sales taxes. If national product and total sales rise, government revenues from sales taxes likewise rise.

We may take a giant step toward realism by discarding the lump-sum tax and studying instead a tax that does rise and fall with national product. The one we consider is a proportional tax; that is, a tax that yields revenues which are a constant percentage of national product.

As we saw in Figure 11-5, a lump-sum tax shifts the consumption function down by a constant amount. However, this is not true of a proportional tax. If national product doubles, tax collections likewise double, and the depressing effects on the consumption function also double. To illustrate, suppose there is a 20% proportional tax. At national product NP_1 in Figure 11-6, this tax depresses consumption from point B to D. But if national product is twice as great, at NP_2, this same tax depresses consumption by twice as much—from K to L.

Of course, a 30% tax depresses consumption even more than a 20% tax. Thus, consumption function C_3 lies below C_2. In general, the heavier the tax, the more the consumption function rotates clockwise, as shown in Figure 11-6.[2]

Note two important effects of a proportional tax:

1. The higher the tax rate, the more disposable income is reduced and the more the consumption function is lowered. Thus, an increase in the tax rate lowers the aggregate demand function, and a cut in taxes raises the aggregate demand function.

On this first point, then, the effects of a propor-

---

[2]Note that the consumption function rotates around point A. Why is this so? By assumption, taxes are proportional to national product. Therefore, in the limiting case where national product is zero, taxes are likewise zero. Consumption is therefore unaffected. Thus, point A is on every consumption function, regardless of how high the tax rate is.

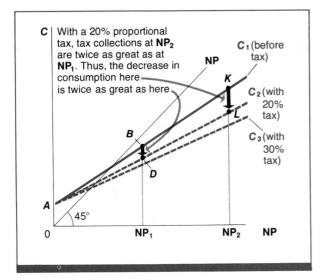

Figure 11-6 A proportional tax: Effect on consumption. When a proportional tax is imposed, the consumption function rotates clockwise around point A. The higher the tax rate, the more the consumption function rotates. As the tax rate rises from 20% to 30%, the consumption function becomes lower and flatter.

tional tax are similar to those of the lump-sum tax considered earlier. (But on the next point, they differ.)

2. In an economy with proportional taxes, the consumption function is *flatter* than in a tax-free economy. And the higher the tax rate, the flatter the consumption function becomes. However, as we saw in Chapter 10, the flatter the consumption function, the lower the multiplier. Moreover, the effect of a proportional tax in lowering the multiplier can be very substantial. Recall that, with no taxes and an MPC of 0.8, the multiplier was 5. When a 25% proportional tax is introduced, the multiplier drops sharply, to only 2.5. (The appendix to this chapter explains how to compute the multiplier when taxes and other things change.)

EXPORTS AND IMPORTS

Adding government spending and taxes to the bare-bones picture of the economy in Chapter 10 brings us a long way toward a more realistic view of the Cana-

dian economy. But to bring the picture even closer to reality, we must also take into account foreign trade. As we saw in Chapter 7, exports and imports are large in relation to Canada's GNP, and they are important in determining aggregate demand.

When exports and imports are included, the expression for the aggregate demand for Canadian goods and services becomes

> Aggregate demand (AD) =
> consumption expenditures (C) +
> investment demand (I^*) +
> government purchases of goods
> and services (G) + export demand
> (X) − demand for imports (M)

Exports to foreign countries add directly to the aggregate demand for Canadian goods and services. Furthermore, as we export more forest products or subway cars, workers in the forestry or transport equipment industries have larger incomes, and consequently they step up their consumption expenditures. Thus, an increase in exports sets the multiplier process in motion in the same way as an increase in investment demand or government spending.

Imports, by contrast, are a subtraction from the aggregate demand for Canadian goods and services. If part of the consumption expenditures of Canadians is spent on imported goods, such as shirts from Korea, that part of consumption does not become income of Canadian workers or firms. (The value of the shirts is part of Korea's national product, not Canada's.) Or, if a large firm spends one million dollars investing in an imported data processing system, that part of investment demand does not become income of Canadians. To account for this the spending on imports must be *subtracted* from aggregate demand.

Notice that there is a similarity between imports and taxes in their effect on aggregate demand: A switch by Canadian consumers toward purchases of imported goods will shift the aggregate demand schedule downward, just as an increase in taxes would do. Moreover, just like taxes, imports are likely to be large when national product is large. (When people have high incomes and high expenditures, their spending on imports is also likely to be high.) Therefore, the depressing effect of imports on aggregate demand will be larger at higher levels of national product.

The combined effect of imports and exports on aggregate demand is illustrated in panels (*a*) to (*c*) of Figure 11-7. Panel (*a*) shows how imports increase when national product increases. For example, at NP_1 imports are $50 billion; at NP_4 they are $75 billion. However, exports are assumed to remain constant (at $60 billion) for all levels of Canadian national product. (The demand for our exports depends on national product and income in *foreign* countries, not in Can-

ada.) **Net exports**—that is, exports minus imports—are shown in panel (*b*). When exports are higher than imports, net exports are positive. (For example, at NP_1 net exports are $10 billion and are shown by the black arrow. But as imports grow larger with a higher national product, net exports become negative. (At NP_4, net exports are −$15 billion, as shown by the coloured arrow.) In panel (*c*), we add net exports to aggregate demand. Notice that the aggregate demand curve (AD_2) in an **open economy** is flatter than it would be in an economy with little or no international trade—a **closed economy** (AD_1). This happens because net exports become smaller and smaller as national product rises. Indeed, beyond NP_2 they turn negative; thus AD_2 lies *below* AD_1 to the right of NP_2.

> An *open economy* is an economy where exports and imports are large relative to domestic national product.
>
> A *closed economy* is an economy where exports and imports are very small relative to national product.

Because the aggregate demand curve becomes flatter as a result of international trade, the multiplier becomes smaller. In the previous section, we saw that introduction of a proportional tax would cause the

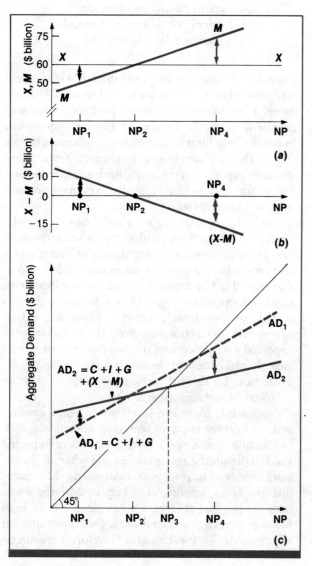

◀ **Figure 11-7 Adding net exports to aggregate demand.**

(*a*) Imports are an increasing function of national product: The higher the national product, the higher the imports. Exports are assumed to be constant at $60 billion and independent of national product.

(*b*) Net exports are found by vertically subtracting imports from exports. Thus at NP_2, net exports in panel (*b*) are zero: Import spending is equal to export earnings. In panel (*a*) we saw that at a small national product such as NP_1, imports are smaller than exports; thus net exports at NP_1 are positive, as shown by the left arrow in panel (*b*). Conversely, at NP_4, imports are greater than exports by an amount shown by the coloured arrow. Net exports are negative.

(*c*) The AD_1 line shows the sum of consumption, investment, and government spending. When foreign trade is taken into account, we must add net exports (from panel (*b*)) vertically to AD_1, which gives us the AD_2 line showing aggregate demand in an open economy. Equilibrium national product, as usual, occurs where AD_2 cuts the 45° line; equilibrium national product in this economy is NP_3.

multiplier to be smaller than in the simple economy with neither taxes nor foreign trade. In an economy with foreign trade, the multiplier becomes smaller yet, as we also show in the appendix to this chapter.

Notice that in panels (b) and (c) of Figure 11-7, net exports are shown as negative at the equilibrium national product NP$_3$, where the aggregate demand curve AD$_2$ crosses the 45° line. As the figure has been drawn, Canada exports less than it imports at the equilibrium national product. But there is no reason why that should always be true. For example, if there is an increase in American demand for our exports, the horizontal export curve in panel (a) would shift upwards, as would the net export curve in panel (b) and the aggregate demand curve AD$_2$ in panel (c). If the increase in exports were large enough, there would be positive net exports at the new equilibrium. As we saw in Figure 7-5, this is in fact what happened in 1984 when our exports exceeded imports by some $1.6 billion.

INJECTIONS AND LEAKAGES: AN ECONOMY WITH GOVERNMENT AND FOREIGN TRADE

The previous chapter explained a very simplified economy, with only consumption and investment and no government sector. Such an economy *reaches equilibrium when the injections* into the spending stream, in the form of investment demand, *are just equal to the leakages* from the spending stream, in the form of saving.

When government spending, taxation, and international trade are introduced, a similar proposition still holds. *Equilibrium exists when injections and leakages are equal.* But now there are three injections and three leakages (Figure 11-8).

Specifically, *government spending* is an *injection* into the spending stream, similar to investment demand. When the government spends more for roads, buildings, etc., the producers of these roads and buildings earn higher incomes, and their consumption consequently rises. The circular flow of expenditures broadens as a result of this government spending. Similarly, *exports* are an injection into the income stream: If our exports of wheat to foreigners rise, Canadian wheat farmers will have higher incomes, and therefore they will spend more on consumption. Thus, the circular

flow of expenditures broadens as a result of the extra government spending or the increased exports.

On the other side, *taxation* is a *leakage*, similar to saving. Income taken in taxes cannot be used by the public for consumption expenditures. As consumption falls, the circular flow of expenditures narrows. *Imports* of goods from foreign countries are also a leakage from the income stream. If Canadian consumers spend part of their money on imported goods and services, that part does not become income of other Canadians; it is a leakage that goes to foreigners. Only the part of consumption expenditures that is used to purchase goods and services produced *in Canada* continues around in the circular flow of expenditure.

Equilibrium occurs when the injections working to broaden the spending stream are equal to the leakages working to narrow it. Specifically, in an economy with government spending, taxes, and foreign trade:

Equilibrium occurs when the injections (investment demand plus government spending plus exports) are equal to the leakages (saving plus taxation plus imports). That is, equilibrium occurs when:

$$I + G + X = S + T + M$$

AUTOMATIC STABILIZERS

Because taxes and imports lower the size of the multiplier, they add to the stability of the economy. For example, in an economy with large leakages into taxes and imports, the multiplier is small. Therefore, a fall in investment demand or exports causes only a moderate decline in national product. On the other side, a runaway boom is less likely in an economy with large imports and taxes. Much of the increase in income is taxed away before people get a chance to spend it; and part of the extra spending that does occur goes to the purchase of imports and thus leaks out of the domestic economy.

Tax revenues and import spending that vary with national product are therefore **built-in stabilizers** or **automatic stabilizers**. As an example, Figure 11-9 illustrates the way that taxes act to stabilize the economy. In this diagram, taxes (T) are just adequate to cover government expenditure (G) when the economy is at the full-employment national product NP$_1$; the budget is balanced (G = T). Now suppose the economy slips into a recession, with national product decreasing to NP$_2$. Tax collections fall, and the budget automatically moves into deficit. This fall in tax collections helps to keep up aggregate demand: Disposable income is left in the hands of the public, and consumption therefore falls less sharply. Thus, the downward momentum in the economy is reduced. Similarly, the tax system acts as a restraint on an upswing. As national product increases, tax collections rise. The government's budget moves toward surplus, and the upward movement of the economy is slowed down.

Similarly, imports help stabilize the economy, as

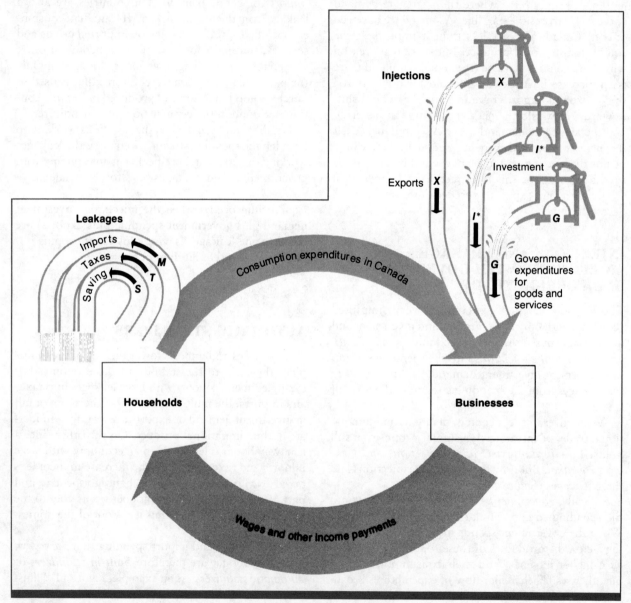

Figure 11-8 The circular flow, with government spending and taxes, and exports and imports.
When the government sector and foreign trade are added, there are three injections (investment, government spending, and exports) into the circular stream of spending. And there are three leakages (saving, taxes, and imports). Equilibrium is reached when injections are equal to leakages.

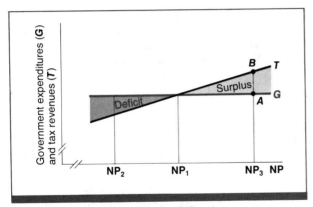

Figure 11-9   Automatic fiscal stabilization.
As national product increases from NP_1 toward NP_3, the government's budget automatically moves into surplus. This slows down the expansion. Conversely, the budget automatically moves into deficit during recessions as national product decreases from NP_1 toward NP_2. The government deficit helps to keep up disposable income and consumption and thus alleviates the recession.

we may see by referring back to Figure 11-7(*a*). Suppose again that the economy is moving into a recession. As national product decreases, imports fall. With a smaller leakage into imports, net exports will be larger, and the decline in aggregate demand and national product is moderated. Conversely, when the economy swings upward, imports rise and the upswing is restrained.

> An *automatic stabilizer* is any feature of the economic system which reduces the strength of recessions and/or the strength of upswings in demand, without policy changes being made. (Thus, an automatic stabilizer should be distinguished from a discretionary policy action, such as a cut in tax rates or the introduction of new government spending programs.)

The degree of automatic stabilization depends on how strongly tax collections and import spending respond to changes in national product. That is, it depends on the marginal tax rate for the economy as a whole, and on the **marginal propensity to import**—the fraction of extra income which is spent on imports.

The marginal propensity to import (MPM) =
$$\frac{\text{Change in imports}}{\text{Change in national product}}$$

The greater the marginal propensity to import, the steeper are the import and net export functions in Figure 11-7, and the stronger is the automatic stabilization. Similarly, the greater the marginal tax rate, the steeper is the taxation function (T) in Figure 11-9, and the stronger the stabilizing effect of taxes. (The stabilizing effect of a high marginal tax rate and a high marginal propensity to import is explained further in the appendix to this chapter.)

There are also automatic stabilizers on the government expenditures side (not shown in Figure 11-9). As the economy slides into a recession, there is an automatic increase in government spending for unemployment insurance benefits and social assistance. The additional government spending sustains disposable income, and therefore slows the downswing.

Automatic stabilizers reduce the severity of economic fluctuations. But they do not eliminate them. The objective of discretionary fiscal policy is to reduce the fluctuations even more.

FISCAL POLICY: SOME COMPLICATIONS

The tendency for the government's budget to swing automatically into deficit during recessions, and into surplus during inflationary booms, helps to stabilize the economy. It may therefore be looked on as a plus. But it also introduces two important complications into fiscal policy.

1. Measuring Fiscal Policy: The Full-Employment Budget

Because the government's budget swings *automatically* toward deficit during recessions and toward surplus during booms, the state of the budget cannot be taken as a measure of how fiscal policy has changed. For example, when the budget moves into deficit during recession, this does not demonstrate that policymakers have accepted the teachings of Keynesian economics and have acted to stimulate the economy and offset the recession. They may have done nothing. The deficit may merely reflect a decline in the government's tax revenues as a result of the recession.

In order to determine whether fiscal policy is moving in an expansive or restrictive direction, some measure other than the actual budgetary deficit or surplus is therefore needed. The ***full-employment budget*** provides such a measure. The full-employment budget indicates what the surplus or deficit would be if the economy were at full employment.

The full-employment budget (B_{FE}) is defined:

$$B_{FE} = R_{FE} - G_{FE}$$

where:

R_{FE} represents full-employment receipts; that is, receipts that the present tax laws would yield if the economy were at full employment

G_{FE} stands for full-employment government expenditures; that is, actual expenditures less expenditures (payments to the unemployed, etc.) that would be avoided if full employment existed.

The point of the full-employment budget is illustrated in Figure 11-10. Suppose the economy starts at NP_1, a position of full employment. With the existing tax rate, represented by line T_1, government revenues are equal to government expenditures G; the actual budget is in balance. (So is the full-employment budget. When the economy *is* at full employment, the two budgets are exactly the same.) Now suppose that the economy slips down into a recession; national product falls to NP_2. Tax revenues decline to C, and the actual budget automatically swings into deficit BC. To the unwary, it might seem that the government has acted to stimulate the economy by creating a budget deficit. But this is not so. The government has not yet made any policy change. All it has done is to let automatic stabilizers work.

In contrast to the actual budget, the full-employment budget accurately reflects what has happened to fiscal policy: nothing. The full-employment budget is measured at the full-employment national product NP_1, regardless of what the actual national product may be. The full-employment budget is still in balance at A; it has not been affected by the onset of the recession.

The full-employment budget *is*, however, affected by a change in fiscal policy. Suppose that, with the economy at NP_2, the government takes discretionary steps to combat the recession by cutting the tax rate to T_2. How does this show up in the full-employment budget measure? At the full-employment national product, NP_1, the new, lower tax rate T_2 would yield revenues of only E. Thus, the tax cut causes a full-employment budget deficit of AE. (It also causes an increase in the actual budget deficit, from BC to BD.) Similarly, an increase in government spending—which would be shown by an upward shift of G—would cause the full-employment budget to move into deficit, and the actual budget to move into greater deficit.

In summary, then:

1. A downward swing in the economy automatically causes the actual budget to move toward deficit. However, the full-employment budget does not automatically move toward deficit.

2. A cut in tax rates or an increase in government spending causes both the actual and the full-employment budgets to move toward deficit.

3. Because the actual budget responds both to (1) changes in economic activity and (2) changes in

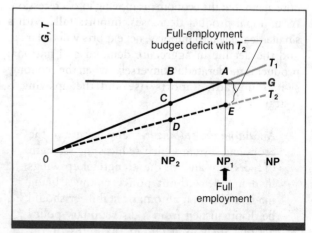

Figure 11-10 The full-employment budget.
A decrease in economic activity from NP_1 to NP_2 causes the actual budget to move into deficit BC. Because the full-employment budget's tax receipts are measured at full-employment national product NP_1, regardless of the actual quantity of output, the full-employment budget is not affected by the recession. However, it does move into deficit (AE) as a result of a cut in tax rates, shown by the fall from T_1 to T_2.

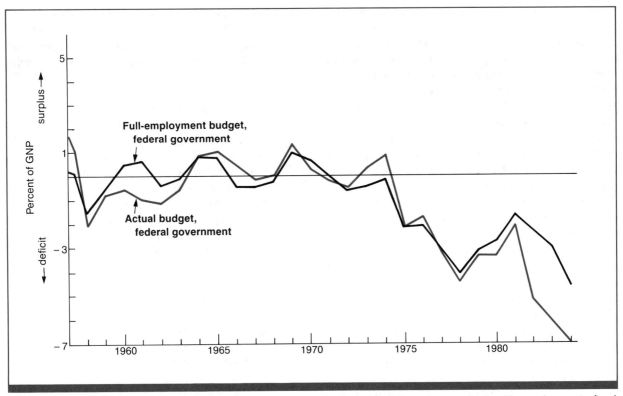

Figure 11-11   The full-employment (or cyclically adjusted) budget and the actual budget, 1957–1984.
When the economy is operating below the full-employment level, tax revenues are depressed and the actual budget shows a larger deficit (or smaller surplus) than the full-employment budget. The full-employment budget shows changes in fiscal policy.

Source: Adapted from Department of Finance, *Economic Review* (April 1985).

policy, it is a misleading measure of policy alone. On the other hand, the full-employment budget is unaffected by changes in economic activity, and it does measure policy changes. In the example in Figure 11-10, the reduction in tax rates from T_1 to T_2 moved the full-employment budget into deficit *AE*. This movement indicated that the government had changed fiscal policy in an expansionary direction.

The full-employment budget, 1957–84. The comparison between the federal government's actual budget and its estimated full-employment budget in Figure 11-11 gives several illustrations of how misleading the actual budget can be as a measure of fiscal policy. For example, the actual budget shows an increase in the deficit during the 1959–61 period. However, the full-employment budget shows a move from a deficit to a surplus during the same period; the deficits in 1960 and 1961 were due to the economy's weak performance, rather than to an expansionary policy. The change in the full-employment budget shows that policy was actually becoming tighter, not more expansionary. From 1972 to 1974, the actual budget shows a large change from a deficit to a surplus. But according to the full-employment budget (which remained in deficit throughout), there was little change in policy. The large surplus in 1974 was primarily due to the 1973–74 inflationary export boom. Finally, both the actual and full-employment budgets show increased deficits in 1982 and 1983. However, the full-employment budget shows that to a large extent, the huge deficits in those years were caused by the recession.

The estimated full-employment budget also shows how fiscal policy has been used on several occasions to try to counteract economic fluctuations. For example, during the second half of the 1960s as inflationary pressures were building up (partly in response to huge U.S. government spending to pay for the war in Vietnam), the Canadian government gradually tightened fiscal policy. And as the U.S. economy slid into a deep recession in 1974–75, Ottawa enacted large tax reductions and spending increases which provided needed stimulus. (Partly as a result of this policy, the recession in Canada was much less severe than in the United States.) Finally, the full-employment budget shows how the government was willing to try to fight the 1982 recession by moving the federal budget toward more stimulus, even though the deficit was already very large.

At the same time, Figure 11-11 shows some disquieting aspects of our recent fiscal history. Consider first the 1970–73 period. Between 1970 and 1971, the full-employment budget indicates that fiscal policy was changed (somewhat belatedly, since the recession occurred in 1970) from restraint to stimulus. However, during 1970–73 the economy was recovering nicely, and unemployment gradually fell; by 1974, severe inflationary pressures were developing. Yet according to Figure 11-11, the government continued to change fiscal policy in the direction of more stimulus throughout the 1970–73 period: While the actual deficit turned into a surplus under the influence of the buoyant economy, the full-employment budget showed a growing deficit. In retrospect, the expansionary fiscal policy during this period contributed substantially to the inflationary spiral that started in the early 1970s.

Again, following the end of the 1974–75 recession, the economy gradually recovered through 1979. The recovery was slow, however, and the unemployment rate did not come down significantly. In an attempt to accelerate the recovery, the government moved the budget toward more stimulus, even though it was starting from a large deficit in 1975. As a result, both the actual and full-employment budgets showed growing deficits throughout. Then when recession occurred in 1980 and again in late 1981, the government was caught on the horns of a dilemma. On the one hand, the deficit was already very large, and there was considerable political pressure on the government to reduce it. On the other hand, there were calls for tax reduc-

tions and increased expenditures to fight the recessions.

Why wasn't fiscal policy used in a more precise way to combat recessions and inflation, in line with the theory of this chapter? There are two major reasons why fiscal policy has not been strongly stabilizing in practice:

1. At any particular time, there will always be some disagreement over what the thrust of fiscal policy should be. In part, this is because there is disagreement on what should constitute a realistic full-employment target. As we saw in Chapter 8, most economists now agree that it was not realistic to expect unemployment rates in the 1970s to go as low as they had been in the 1950s and 60s without causing strong inflationary pressures. But this may not have been clear to the politicians who were making the decisions concerning fiscal policy at that time. For example, during the 1970–73 period, the expansionary policy that was pursued can be seen as an attempt to reach the Economic Council's target of 3.8% unemployment. The research which established that this target was unrealistic did not become available until much later.

   A related problem is that some policymakers tend to be more concerned with fighting inflation, while others consider unemployment a much more serious problem. This conflict became especially severe during the late 1970s when the unemployment and inflation rates *both* increased. The difficulty in deciding what the stance of fiscal policy should be during those years is reflected in several budget statements in which the Finance Minister announced that his budget proposals were designed to "fight the twin evils of inflation and unemployment". As we will discuss in detail in Chapter 17, in the short run price stability and high employment are likely to be conflicting goals, so that fiscal policy cannot simultaneously promote both.

2. Even if agreement can be reached about the direction in which fiscal policy should be changed, there are often sharp disagreements about *how* the change should be accomplished. For example, suppose it is agreed that government should move fiscal policy in a more restrictive direction, reduc-

ing the budget deficit. Those politicians who think that the government is already too big and the tax burden on Canadians too high will insist that the proper way to reduce the deficit is to cut expenditures. However, once it comes down to actually specifying particular programs where cuts are to be made, there will be vociferous opposition from the beneficiaries of those programs; they will suggest that the deficit should be reduced through tax increases instead.

An example of how this type of disagreement reduces the flexibility of fiscal policy was provided by the first budget of Finance Minister Michael Wilson in May 1985. During the 1984 election campaign, the Conservatives had promised decisive action to reduce the deficit. However, in spite of a projected deficit of around $36 billion in 1984–85, the net impact of the new tax measures introduced in the budget was estimated to be a revenue increase of no more than $250 million in 1985–86 and $1.8 billion in the following year. While the proposed expenditure cuts were somewhat larger, the overall result was still to leave an estimated deficit of more than $30 billion in 1986–87. (Furthermore, in the face of strong public opposition, the government quickly backed down from some of the proposed spending cuts.)

2. A Policy Trap:
The Annually Balanced Budget

Because the actual budget swings automatically into deficit during recessions, it sets a trap for the unwary policymaker. Suppose that the government tries to balance the actual budget every year. As the economy enters a recession, tax collections decline, causing budgetary deficits. If policymakers are determined to balance the budget, they will have two choices: they can cut government spending, or increase tax rates. Either step will depress aggregate demand and make the recession worse. By raising taxes or cutting expenditures, the government will offset the automatic stabilizers built into the tax system. Trying to balance the budget each year is a policy trap.

One reason this trap deserves emphasis is that the Canadian government (the Conservatives led by R.B.

Bennett) seemed to fall into it during the most serious years of the Great Depression in the 1930s.[3] The government was convinced that deficits had to be avoided so as not to add to the national debt and diminish international confidence in the economic soundness of Canada. Large increases in the rates of sales tax, corporate income tax and personal income tax were introduced in 1932 and 1933—the worst years of the Depression.[4]

The change in fiscal policy was precisely the opposite of what was needed to promote recovery. Rather than the needed stimulus, the country got a large dose of restraint: In attempting to deal with the Depression, the government was making it worse. Ironically, the policy of raising taxes did not even succeed in balancing the actual budget. Because of the gradual collapse of the economy, government *revenues* actually fell in spite of the increases in tax rates; the automatic stabilizer was creating a deficit even though the government was trying to raise taxes. (The government also tried various measures to decrease expenditures, such as disbanding the Air Force and reducing civil service salaries, but expenditures on unemployment relief and public works obviously had to rise.) In the government's defence, it should be noted that it was following the course that most people at the time thought correct. The Liberal opposition under Mackenzie King, far from urging the government to provide more stimulus, concentrated its criticism on what it regarded as excessive spending: ". . . this vast expenditure and waste."

The accepted wisdom of the day, which led to the government's blunder in recommending a huge tax increase, set the stage for the Keynesian revolution with its important message: Spending and tax policies

[3]For a description of fiscal policy during the Depression, see Irving Brecher, *Monetary and Fiscal Thought and Policy in Canada, 1919–1939* (Toronto: University of Toronto Press, 1957), pp. 199–200.
[4]In the United States the story was much the same, with President Hoover recommending, and Congress passing, one of the largest tax increases in peacetime history in 1932.

In the presidential campaign that year, Roosevelt took his strongest stand for fiscal conservatism in a Pittsburgh speech on October 19. This speech became something of an embarrassment as the deficits mounted during his first administration. And it inspired a story which circulated in Washington. When Roosevelt was returning to Pittsburgh several years later, he turned to one of his speech writers for advice on how to explain away his earlier stand for a balanced budget. The reply was, "Deny you were ever in Pittsburgh."

should be aimed at the goals of full employment and price stability, and not at the goal of balancing the budget. *Fiscal policy should be designed to balance the economy, not the budget.*

However, the wide acceptance of Keynes' message has left two nagging worries. (1) If the government is not held accountable for balancing the budget, how can it be expected to show restraint in its spending and taxing decisions? (2) If the government runs large deficits, will we not eventually end up with a crushing burden of public debt? Isn't the government in danger of going bankrupt?

THE ISSUE OF RESTRAINT

Keynesian economists attacked the old rule of an annually balanced budget. But to keep the budget under control, many people long for something to put in its place. If the government does not have to live within its tax revenues, its spending may escalate out of control, or it may cut taxes without corresponding restraint on spending. We may warn of the dangers of excess, but can we really expect restraint?

Concerns have grown with the increase in government deficits during the 1980s. Particularly worrisome were the huge deficits of 1983 and 1984, which occurred even though the economy was well on the road to recovery. Many people felt that getting the deficit under control should be the highest priority in fiscal policy.

In recent decades, a number of alternative guidelines have been suggested to provide restraint, while avoiding the destabilizing fiscal policies that can occur if the government tries to balance the actual budget every year.

1. Balance the full-employment budget every year

Remember why the old balanced-budget rule was destabilizing. As the economy moves into recession and a budget deficit automatically appears, the balanced-budget rule requires an increase in tax rates, or cuts in government spending. These can make the recession worse. Such destabilizing actions can be avoided if the government aims at balancing the *full-employment* budget. Since this budget does not automatically swing into deficit during recessions, it does not give a false

signal that a tax increase or spending cut is needed. Thus, the full-employment budget has two major uses: as a *way of measuring* fiscal policy; and as a *guide* to fiscal policy.

However, in a severe recession, balancing the full-employment budget may be inadequate. All it does is to allow the automatic stabilizers to combat the recession. It does not allow the government to go one step further and actively fight the recession by introducing fiscal stimulus. (Such stimulus—for example, a cut in tax rates—would violate the rule, since it would put the full-employment budget into deficit. Recall that precisely this case was illustrated in Figure 11-10). Thus, this first rule represents an unambitious strategy. Its aim is to avoid destabilizing actions, not to actively stabilize the economy. It is therefore reminiscent of the doctor's motto: *Primo non nocere*, or "First, do no harm."

2. Balance the full-employment budget, but only when the economy achieves full employment

This alternative approach is more ambitious. It allows a government to take the initiative in managing the economy. During a recession, tax rates *can* be cut or spending increased in order to speed the return to full employment. In other words, the full-employment budget can be shifted into deficit during recessions. But the government is still subject to restraint. It has to return to a balanced budget when the economy reaches full employment.

3. The cyclically balanced budget

Either of the first two guidelines permits the government to have an *actual* budget which is in deficit on the average. The reason is that, whenever the economy falls short of full employment, either guideline allows a deficit in the actual budget. There is no call for offsetting surpluses during periods of full employment.

More long-term restraint can be provided by *balancing the actual budget over the business cycle*. According to this approach, there should be sufficient surpluses during good times to cover the deficits of the recessions. But, unlike the annually balanced budget, the cyclically balanced budget is consistent with active fiscal management. Tax rates can be cut and spending increased to combat recessions.

4. Built-in spending restraints

Experience in Canada and elsewhere, especially since the mid-seventies, has led a number of observers to wonder whether any of these principles can be used as a realistic guideline for fiscal policy. In practice, while it appears to be relatively easy to increase spending during a recession, governments seem to have found it difficult to reduce their deficits even when they have announced that this has been their objective. Therefore, more attention has been given to attacking the problem on the expenditure side, by building direct restraints into the administrative process where spending decisions are made. In past years, the federal government has introduced measures aimed at monitoring the productivity of civil servants, to ensure that government departments are reasonably *efficient* in carrying out their various activities. (Obviously, the government should always try to carry out its own functions at the lowest possible cost, even when the economic situation calls for a deficit. There are better ways for a government to create a deficit than wasting money; for example, it can reduce taxes.) The Operational Performance Measurement System (OPMS) and the technique of Management by Objective (MBO) are examples of measures introduced to increase the productivity of government departments. Other techniques, such as Program Planning and Budgeting Systems (PPBS), have been used to evaluate entire government programs.

The 1985 budget of the Mulroney government outlined several new approaches to the problem of giving incentives to government officials to restrict spending and improve management efficiency. They included:

- Abolition of the past practice of automatically increasing departmental budgets to compensate for inflation

- A commitment to gradual reduction in the number of federal public service employees according to a fixed schedule (starting with a 2% reduction in 1985–86)

- A substantial reduction in the contingency funds usually included in departmental budgets

In addition, plans were outlined for more extensive use of the user-pay principle under which private firms pay the government for special services it provides.

For example, firms may, for a fee, contract to have Statistics Canada provide them with unpublished data. Together, these efficiency-enhancing initiatives were forecast to recover more than $2 billion in the 1985–86 fiscal year.

In the United States, there have been a number of radical proposals to force governments to reduce their spending. In a referendum a few years ago, residents of California voted in favour of a proposal (known as Proposition 13) to impose strict limits on the amounts that cities and municipalities were allowed to collect in property taxes. And in recent years, there has been an active campaign to call a constitutional conference for the purpose of amending the U.S. constitution to force Congress and the president to balance the federal budget every year (see Box 11-1).

THE PUBLIC DEBT

Whenever the government runs a deficit, it must borrow the money to pay for expenditures in excess of its revenues. Thus, the adoption of Keynesian fiscal policies (with deficits whenever needed to get the economy back to full employment) created fears of a rising public debt that would become a crushing burden on future generations. The apparent inability of the government to bring the federal deficit under control following the economy's recovery from the 1982 recession has again brought this issue to the fore. To try to answer the question whether the fears of a growing debt are justified, we discuss a specific issue: Who bore the burden of the enormous government deficits during World War II, when Canada's public debt expanded at its most rapid rate ever? Was the burden borne by the people of the time, or by their children who inherited the huge debt?

In order to explain and weigh the problems with a rising government debt, it is helpful to divide the discussion into two parts, looking first at the deficit spending, and then at the consequences of the debt itself.

Deficit Spending: What Is Its Opportunity Cost?

When the government spends, it makes a claim on productive resources. *If the economy is at full employment, an increase in government purchases must*

BOX 11-1

THE U.S. BALANCED BUDGET AMENDMENT

Some critics of government spending in the United States argue that it is unrealistic to expect the government to be restrained by any of the guidelines or rules discussed in the text. No matter what policy they proclaim, the administration and Congress are likely in practice to choose the path of least resistance. They will give in to those clamouring for bigger spending programs, and cut taxes in order to increase their popularity at the polls. Because the administration and Congress are unable or unwilling to show restraint, these critics argue that restraint should be imposed from the outside, in the form of a constitutional amendment requiring a balanced budget.* Not surprisingly, the U.S. Congress does not look favourably on such an amendment, which would limit its powers. Despite the support of the Reagan administration, Congress has been unwilling to pass a balanced-budget amendment and submit it to the states for ratification.

Proponents of the balanced-budget amendment are therefore trying to bypass Congress by having a constitutional convention called. This will happen if two-thirds (34) of the American states petition for a convention. By 1984, 32 states had submitted such petitions, and proponents of the amendment were hoping that two more would be added.

Opponents of a balanced-budget amendment put forth a number of objections:

1. As noted in the text, the government would fall into the same trap as Prime Minister Bennett in Canada and President Hoover in the United States if it tried to balance the budget every year. As the budget automatically went into deficit during a recession, the government would raise tax rates or cut expenditures, making the recession worse.

2. A balanced-budget requirement would limit the power of Congress to deal with unforeseen emergencies in the future.

3. A balanced-budget amendment would raise numerous technical complications. One problem is exactly how to define the budget. The easiest way to balance the budget is to change accounting methods to move deficit items out of the budget.

Proponents have tried to go at least part way toward meeting the first two of these objections. The proposed amendment would allow a deficit if it were approved by a 60% majority in Congress.

* The case for an amendment is explained by Milton Friedman and Rose Friedman, *Tyranny of the Status Quo* (New York: Harcourt Brace Jovanovich, 1984).

---

involve a reduction in production for the private sector of the economy. For example, if a firm like Canadian General Electric was making navigational equipment for warships during World War II, it couldn't make refrigerators at the same time.

Thus military (or other government) production in 1943 came at the opportunity cost of giving up consumer goods in 1943. Therefore, in a fundamental sense, the burden of the war fell on the people at the time, since it was they, and not we, who had to do without new refrigerators. They were the ones who suffered, not only in terms of lives lost, but also in terms of consumer goods foregone.

But to conclude that the burden of the war fell on the people of the early 1940s would be only 90% correct. An element is missing. If Canada had been at peace, we could not only have produced more consumer goods, but *more capital goods too.* Instead of turning out guns and ammunition, Canadian industry could have produced more machines and built more factories. And if it had, the rising capital stock would have benefitted not only the people of the 1940s, but future generations also. Thus, because our capital stock has been lower, future generations *have* borne some of the burden of World War II.

Quite a different set of conclusions follows if we look at deficit spending during a depression. Producing more goods for the government does not then cause a reduction in private consumption and investment. On the contrary, because of the operation of the multiplier, we produce more consumer goods too. As more consumer goods are produced, investment demand is stimulated; to produce more cars and refrigerators, businesses need more machines and factories. Thus, deficit spending by the government *during a depression* generates benefits rather than burdens for both present and future generations. It stimulates the production of more consumer goods for the current generation, and more capital stock for future generations.

Effects of the Public Debt

The government finances deficit spending by borrowing (selling bonds), and thus increasing the public debt. What about the debt itself? Does it create a burden for future generations?

To answer this question, consider the government debt that existed in 1955 because of the deficit of 1943. The first important point is that interest payments on this debt were not made by the people of 1955 to the people of 1943. Rather, they were made by some people in 1955 to other people in 1955. Specifically, the government collected taxes from the general public, and used some of the taxes to pay interest to bondholders. Thus, government debt—indeed, any debt—transfers funds *from one group now to another group now*. It does not transfer funds from people in one time period to people in an earlier period.

However, this transfer from one group to another is neither costless nor unimportant. It causes a number of problems:

1. The transfer may lead to an *undesirable redistribution of income*. This depends on who has to pay the taxes, and who holds the bonds and receives the interest. (It also depends on what we consider a "desirable" distribution of income.)

2. When Canadian government debt is held *by foreigners*, some of the foreign money that we earn through exports must be used to pay interest to foreign bondholders. As a result, there is less left to pay for imports of goods and services. The reduction in the amounts we can import is the real burden of the foreign-held part of the debt.

3. When the government collects taxes to pay interest on the debt—whether held at home or abroad—there is another cost: the **excess burden** of taxation. When taxes are imposed, the public has an incentive to alter its behaviour to avoid paying taxes. For example, people have an incentive to hire lawyers to search for tax loopholes,

and to divert their savings into tax-sheltered investments—that is, investments on which little or no tax is paid. As a result, the efficiency of the economy is reduced.

The *excess burden* of taxes is the decrease in the efficiency of the economy that results when people change their behaviour to avoid paying taxes. It should be distinguished from the primary burden, which is measured by the amount of taxes people actually pay.

4. The need for the government to make interest payments on a large debt may contribute to *inflation*. For example, inflation may result if the government decides to finance interest payments, not by collecting taxes, but instead by borrowing and thus running up its deficit. The rising deficits stimulate aggregate demand, and add to inflationary pressures. The inflationary effects are particularly strong if the Bank of Canada (our central bank) creates new money and lends it to the government in order to help the government make its interest payments.

5. The national debt can *feed on itself*. As the debt rises, the government's interest payments also rise. But, as these interest payments are part of the government's expenditures, they make it more difficult to get the expenditures under control in the future.

This fifth problem has caused great concern during the 1980s. Recent deficits have been very different from the large deficits of the early 1940s, which were caused by a temporary wartime crisis. When the war ended, military spending plunged, automatically eliminating the deficits. In contrast, deficits of the 1980s have arisen because the government has committed itself to long-run spending programs that substantially exceed its tax revenues. If the government can't keep deficits down now, how will it be able to do so in the future, when it must make much larger interest payments? Because of a large debt and high interest rates, interest payments are now much larger, compared to GNP, than they have been in the past, and they are growing rapidly (Table 11-1, column 5).

6. The danger of the debt "feeding on itself" has

Table 11-1
Federal Government Debt and Interest Payments, 1929–84
(billions of current dollars)

1 Year	2 Government Debt	3 Interest Payment on Government Debt	4 Government Debt as Percent of GNP	5 Interest Payment as Percent of GNP
1929	2.28	0.12	37	2.0
1940	5.15	0.14	77	2.0
1946	16.00	0.44	135	3.7
1954	14.26	0.48	55	1.9
1960	16.88	0.75	44	2.0
1966	20.26	1.15	33	1.9
1969	22.87	1.59	29	2.0
1973	29.13	2.52	24	2.0
1975	37.18	3.71	22	2.2
1978	59.66	6.41	26	2.8
1980	79.49	9.90	27	3.3
1981	91.96	13.74	27	4.0
1982	110.60	16.68	31	4.7
1983	136.68	17.41	35	4.5
1984	162.24	21.32	39	5.1

SOURCE: Compiled by authors from data in F.H. Leacy, M.C. Urquhart, and K.A.H. Buckley, eds., *Historical Statistics of Canada*, 2nd ed. (Ottawa: Statistics Canada, 1982), *Bank of Canada Review*, and Statistics Canada, *CANSIM Databank*. Statistics Canada figures reproduced by permission of the Minister of Supply and Services Canada.

become so severe that some economists fear that we may have *lost our ability to use fiscal policy to combat future recessions*. If the deficit is $36 billion in the relatively prosperous year of 1985, what will happen if we use fiscal policy vigorously to combat the next recession? With even larger deficits, won't we generate an unstoppable tide of debt, and even greater interest payments and deficits in the future?

This danger has added urgency to the issue of restraint. If we can't control the budget during normal times, such as 1985, won't we paint ourselves into a corner, where we can't call on fiscal policy when it is needed to fight a recession?

Could the Government "Go Broke"?

If it gets more and more deeply into debt, could the federal government, like a business corporation, go bankrupt? The answer is no, but the reason why it won't "go broke" should be carefully stated.

First, consider one common, but inaccurate, argu-

ment. It is frequently asserted that the government cannot go bankrupt because it has the authority to tax. Thus, it has the power to extract from the public whatever amounts are necessary to service the debt. But there is surely something wrong with this argument. Provincial and local governments also have the power to tax, yet they can, theoretically, go broke. In a democracy, the government must face elections. Even dictatorships depend on public support. As a result, there are political and practical limits to taxes. The holder of a government bond does not have a guarantee of repayment merely because the government has the right to tax.

The federal government cannot go broke for quite a different reason. It has a power even more potent than the power to tax. Bonds are repayable in money. The government has the power to print money to pay interest or principal—either directly or, more subtly, by pressuring or coercing the central bank (the Bank of Canada) to create money and lend it to the government to avoid default. In other words, a national government does not go bankrupt because bonds are repayable in something—money—which national governments can create.

However, if large quantities of money are created to help make payments on the public debt, the consequence will be a rise in prices. (Recall what happened in the prisoner-of-war camp when large quantities of cigarette "money" suddenly came on the scene.) Thus, an excessive national debt has quite different consequences from an excessive corporate debt: It causes excess demand and inflation, not bankruptcy.

However, there is one situation in which even a national government may default on its debts—namely, if it has borrowed in terms of a foreign currency. If the

Canadian government issues bonds repayable in Canadian dollars, it can, in an extreme case, print the money to repay the debt. But suppose that it borrowed large amounts in a foreign currency, such as U.S. dollars, German marks, or Japanese yen. In such circumstances, default would be possible. No matter how desperate our situation might become, the Canadian government could not print foreign currency. Similarly, other national governments that borrow large amounts in foreign currency may run the risk of default. Indeed, in the early 1980s, the danger of default was a severe problem for a number of governments that had borrowed heavily in U.S. dollars—for example, Argentina, Brazil, Mexico, and Poland.

KEY POINTS

1. An increase in government spending causes an increase in equilibrium national product. An increase in taxes causes a decrease in equilibrium national product.

2. Net exports (that is, exports minus imports) are added to consumption, investment, and government spending in determining aggregate demand. An increase in our exports to foreign countries increases Canada's GNP. An increase in Canadian imports from foreign countries decreases GNP.

3. When aggregate demand is low and the rate of unemployment is high, fiscal policy should be expansionary; that is, the government should increase spending and/or cut tax rates. These steps tend to increase the government's deficit.

4. When excess aggregate demand is causing inflation, fiscal policy should be restrictive; the government should cut spending and/or increase tax rates. These steps will move the government's budget toward surplus.

5. Tax collections automatically rise as national product increases, and fall as national product falls. Thus, the government budget automatically tends to move into deficit during a recession, and into surplus during expansions. This tendency helps to reduce the amplitude of cyclical swings in aggregate demand, and thus provides built-in stability to the economy.

6. Because the government's budget automatically

responds to changes in national product, the actual budget cannot be taken as a measure of fiscal policy actions. The appropriate measure is the full-employment budget, which indicates what the surplus or deficit would be with current tax and spending legislation, if the economy were at full employment.

7. Imports also tend to change automatically in the same direction as national product. Imports are a leakage from the circular flow of income, just as taxes are. Therefore, this tendency for imports to rise and fall as national product fluctuates also helps to reduce the swings in aggregate demand, and to stabilize the economy.

8. If the government attempts to balance the actual budget every year, it will fall into a policy trap, and take destabilizing actions. During a downturn in economic activity, when the budget automatically tends to move into deficit, the government will cut expenditures or raise taxes in an effort to balance the budget, thereby making the downturn worse. The Bennett government fell into this policy trap in 1932 when it initiated legislation for a large tax increase.

9. This trap can be avoided if the full-employment budget, rather than the actual budget, is used as a policy guide. The full-employment budget has no tendency to swing automatically into deficit during recessions, and therefore it does not erroneously suggest that taxes should be

234 PART THREE AGGREGATE DEMAND POLICIES

raised. Thus, the full-employment budget has two major functions: (1) as a measure of fiscal policy, and (2) as a guide for fiscal policy.

10. Wars must be fought with the resources available at the time. In a fundamental sense, then, the burden of a war—or other deficit spending by the government—must be borne at the time the expenditures are made. Nevertheless, future generations may be adversely affected. Insofar as deficit spending shifts resources away from investment, future generations will inherit a smaller capital stock.

11. A large government debt involves transfers from one group (taxpayers who finance the interest payments) to another group (domestic or foreign bondholders who collect interest). The interest payments on a large government debt can cause a number of problems:

   (a) They may cause an undesirable redistribution of income within a country.

   (b) Insofar as the debt is held abroad, people at home will be taxed to pay interest to foreigners.

   (c) When taxes are imposed to pay the interest, there will be a loss of economic efficiency as people look for ways to avoid taxes. This loss of efficiency is called the "excess burden of taxes."

   (d) If the government pays interest by borrowing rather than taxing, it can add to inflationary pressures.

   (e) The debt can "feed on itself." A large debt requires large interest payments. This makes it difficult to avoid future deficits, which add to the size of the debt.

   (f) Since a large debt requires large interest payments, it can cause such large deficits that the government feels that it has lost the ability to fight recessions with additional deficit spending.

KEY CONCEPTS

aggregate demand management	closed economy	actual budget
recessionary gap	taxes as a leakage	full-employment budget
output gap or GNP gap	imports as a leakage	full-employment receipts
inflationary gap	marginal propensity to import	full-employment government
budget surplus	government spending as an injection	expenditures
budget deficit	exports as an injection	annually balanced budget
lump-sum tax	deficit spending	cyclically balanced budget
proportional tax	automatic stabilizers	public debt
open economy	discretionary policy action	excess burden of taxes

PROBLEMS

11-1 Using a diagram, explain the difference between the recessionary gap and the output gap. Which is larger? How are these two measures related to the multiplier?

11-2 During the Great Depression, Keynes argued that it would be better for the government to build pyramids than to do nothing. Do you agree? Why or why not? Are there any policies better than pyramid building? That is, can you think of any policies that would give

all the advantages of pyramid building, plus additional advantages? Explain.

11-3 During the Great Depression, the following argument was frequently made:

A market economy tends to generate large-scale unemployment. Military spending can reduce unemployment. Therefore, capitalism requires wars and the threat of wars if it is to survive.

What part or parts of this argument are correct? Which are wrong? Explain what is wrong with the incorrect part(s). Rewrite the statement, correcting whatever is incorrect.

11-4 (a) When the United States experiences an upswing in economic activity, American demand for Canadian exports generally rises. Explain why this increase in the demand for our exports is likely to increase Canada's national product.

(b) If price inflation in Canada is higher than in the United States, Canadian goods will begin to be more and more expensive compared with U.S. goods. What effect do you think this would have on the import function in panel (a) of Figure 11-7? on the net export function in panel (b) of the same figure? How would it affect aggregate demand and the equilibrium national product in Canada?

11-5 In 1965 and 1974, when the government wanted to stimulate aggregate demand, it cut tax rates. What are the advantages of cutting tax rates, rather than increasing government spending? What are the disadvantages? When restraint is needed, would you favour increases in taxes, cuts in government spending, or a combination of the two? Why?

11-6 Assume that full employment initially exists and that the actual budget is in balance.

(a) If the economy then slips down into a recession and there are no policy changes, will the actual budget and the full-employment budget behave in the same way? Explain why or why not. (For help with this question, refer to figures 11-10 and 11-11.)

(b) Suppose, as an alternative, that the government takes strong fiscal policy steps to combat the recession. Will there be a difference in the behaviour of the actual budget and the full-employment budget? Explain.

11-7 Attempting to balance the budget every year can set a trap for policymakers. It leads to incorrect policies during a depression. Does such a balanced-budget rule also lead to incorrect policies during an inflationary boom? Why or why not?

11-8 (a) Explain why a large increase in the government debt may impose a burden on future generations even if it is entirely held by Canadian residents, and even if the total amount of productive capital inherited by future generations is the same as it would have been without the government debt. (Hint: Consider the possible role of foreign ownership of capital.)

(b) Suppose the government prohibited all foreign ownership of capital in the Canadian economy. Would this change your answer to the question in (a), above?

APPENDIX

INTERNATIONAL TRANSACTIONS AND THE MULTIPLIER PROCESS

In the domestic economy, we have seen that there are two major injections (investment and government spending) and two main leakages (saving and taxes). International transactions make things more complicated. There is one more injection, and one more leakage.

Exports are the injection. Larger exports of wheat or subway cars increase Canadian national product. Farmers and workers in the subway car factory have larger incomes, and they consequently step up their consumption expenditures. Thus, the multiplier process is set in motion by additional exports, just as it is set in motion by an increase in investment or government spending.

Once we consider international transactions, the multiplier process is more complicated. Consider what happens if Canadair exports a jet aircraft. This is the initial injection. In the "first-round," national product goes up by the full amount of the value of the airplane. What is the "second-round" effect?

Because the government takes a slice in taxes—of, say, 25%—only 75 cents of each dollar of aircraft sales gets into the hands of consumers as disposable income. Of this 75 cents, consumers save, say, one-fifth (15 cents), leaving only 60 cents in consumption. But not all of this is spent on Canadian-produced goods and services. A portion—say, 10 cents—goes to purchase imported goods. As a result, the "second-round" increase in national product is only 50 cents for each initial injection of $1.

At this second round, one-half of each $1 in income again leaks out into taxes, saving, and imports; only 50 cents is spent by consumers for domestically produced goods. Similarly, one-half is consumed, and one-half leaks out of the domestic spending stream in each later round. For each $1 in initial injection, this gives a sum of all rounds equal to:

$$\$1(1 + 0.5 + 0.5^2 + 0.5^3 + \ldots)$$

Using equation 10-8, we find:

$$\text{Sum} = \$1 \left(\frac{1}{1 - 0.5} \right) = \$2.00$$

Therefore, the multiplier is 2.[5]

Thus, in an economy with international transactions, the multiplier is smaller because of the additional leakage into imports.

---

[5]In an economy with taxes and international trade, the general formula for the multiplier is:

$$\text{Multiplier} = \frac{1}{s + t + m - st}$$

where

s is the marginal propensity to save
t is the marginal tax rate
m is the marginal propensity to import (that is, the fraction of national product that is imported)

Chapter 12

MONEY AND THE BANKING SYSTEM

You can't appreciate home till you've left it,
[or] money till it's spent.

O. Henry

Fiscal policy is the first major tool for managing aggregate demand. Monetary policy is the second. Monetary policy involves control over the quantity of money in our economy. If the quantity of money is increased, spending is encouraged; aggregate demand tends to rise. Similarly, if the quantity of money decreases, aggregate demand tends to fall. By adjusting the quantity of money, the authorities can affect aggregate demand.

However, there is also another reason why money is an important topic in macroeconomics. Money not only provides a way to stabilize the economy; it can also represent a source of problems. Indeed, monetary disturbances have been associated with some of the most spectacularly unstable episodes in economic history. Two examples stand out. One occurred in the years following World War I, when Germany went through a period of hyperinflation. In December 1919, there were about 50 billion marks in circulation. Four years later, this figure had risen to almost 500,000,000,000 billion marks—an increase of 10,000,000,000 times! Because money was so plentiful, it became practically worthless; prices skyrocketed. Indeed, money lost its value so quickly that people

were anxious to spend whatever money they had as soon as possible, while they could still buy something with it. (For a more recent case of hyperinflation, see Box 12-1.)

The second illustration involves the North American experience in the Depression of the 1930s. Economists are still debating how important monetary disturbances were as a cause of the Depression. But there is little doubt that the misbehaviour of the monetary and banking system played some role, particularly in the United States.[1] As the U.S. economy slid down into depression, the quantity of money fell from $26.2 billion in mid-1929 to $19.2 billion in mid-1933—that is, by 27%. By the time Roosevelt became U.S. Presi-

---

[1] As we saw earlier in Chapter 9 (especially in Figure 9-4), those in the classical tradition argue that a fall in the quantity of money was a major cause of the collapse into the Depression. For details, see Milton Friedman and Anna Schwartz, *A Monetary History of the United States, 1867–1960* (Princeton, N.J.: Princeton University Press, 1963), chap. 7. Keynesians tend to be more skeptical. See, for example, Peter Temin, *Did Monetary Forces Cause the Great Depression?* (New York: W.W. Norton, 1976). The disagreements between Keynesians and classicists over the importance of money will be explained in more detail in Chapter 14.

dent in 1933, many banks had closed their doors, and many people with large deposits had been wiped out. In Canada, there were no major bank failures during the Depression, but the quantity of money fell in this country, too; it declined about 15% between 1928 and 1932. In the 1980s, many institutions in the North American financial system were once more in difficul-ties; in Canada, several trust companies went under, and in 1985 two small chartered banks went bankrupt. But in the 1980s, the money stock continued to increase in spite of these problems in the financial system, and we avoided the sort of economic collapse that occurred in the 1930s.

In the coming chapters, we will investigate the

BOX 12-1

WHEN THE INFLATION RATE IS 116,000%, PRICES CHANGE BY THE HOUR*

In Bolivia, the Pesos Paid Out Can Outweigh the Purchases;
  No. 3 Import: More Pesos

LA PAZ, Bolivia, 6 February 1985—A courier stumbles into Banco Boliviano Americano, strug-gling under the weight of a huge bag of money he is carrying on his back. He announces that the sack contains 32 million pesos, and a teller slaps on a notation to that effect. The courier pitches the bag into a corner.

"We don't bother counting the money anymore," explains a loan officer standing nearby. "We take the client's word for what's in the bag." Pointing to the courier's load, he says, "That's a small deposit."

At that moment the 32 million pesos were worth only $500. Today, less than two weeks later, they are worth at least $180 less.

Bolivia's inflation rate is the highest in the world. In 1984, prices zoomed 2,700%, compared with a mere 329% the year before. Experts are predicting the inflation rate could soar as high as 40,000% this year. Even those estimates could prove conser-vative. The central bank last week announced Janu-ary inflation of 80%; if that pace continued all year, it would mean annual inflation of 116,000%.

Prices go up by the day, the hour, or the customer. Julia Blanco Sirba, a vendor on this capital city's main street, sells a bar of chocolate for 35,000 pesos. Five minutes later, the next bar goes for 50,000 pesos. The two-inch stack of money needed to buy it far outweighs the chocolate.

Bolivians aren't yet lugging their money about in wheelbarrows, as the Germans did during the legen-dary hyperinflation of the Weimar Republic in the 1920s. But Bolivia seems headed in that direction.

Tons of paper money are printed. Planeloads of money arrive twice a week from printers in West Germany and Britain. Purchases of money cost Bolivia more than $20 million last year, making it the third-largest import, after wheat and mining equipment.

The 1,000 peso bill, the most commonly used, costs more to print than it purchases. It buys one bag of tea. To purchase an average size television set with 1,000 peso bills, customers have to haul money weighing more than 68 pounds into the showroom. (The inflation makes use of credit cards impossible here, and merchants generally don't take checks, either.)

"When it comes to inflation, we're the interna-tional champs," says Jorge von Bergen, an execu-tive with a paper-products company, who lugs his money around in a small suitcase. His wife has to take the maid along to the market to help carry the bales of cash needed for her shopping. But all that money buys so little that Mrs. von Bergen easily carries her purchases back home on her own.

Because pesos are practically worthless, dollars now are being demanded for big-ticket purchases. People get their dollars from the 800 or so street-side money vendors who line Avenida Camacho, long La Paz's Wall Street. Banking, in effect, has moved outside.

*Abridged, from the *Wall Street Journal*, 7 February 1985, p. 1.

problems and *opportunities* which the monetary system presents. Specifically, we will explore the following questions:

1. What are the forces that cause disturbances within the monetary system? What has been done in the past and what can be done in the future to reduce the disturbances and make the monetary system more stable?
2. How can money be managed to stabilize aggregate demand and reduce fluctuations in economic activity?

In this chapter, we explain how the monetary system works, and begin to sketch an answer to the first question. Future chapters (especially 13, 14, and 15) will provide greater detail on this question (the problems) and explain the second (the opportunities).

THE FUNCTIONS OF MONEY

Without money, specialized producers would have to resort to barter. Because barter is so cumbersome, a monetary system will naturally evolve, even in the absence of a government—as the development of cigarette money in the prisoner-of-war camp so clearly illustrated (Chapter 3).

Money has three interrelated functions:

1. First, money acts as the **medium of exchange**. That is, it is used to buy goods and services.
2. When money is used as a medium of exchange, it also becomes the basis for quoting prices. For example, a car is priced at $10,000, and a pair of shoes at $50. Thus, money acts as the **standard of value**.
3. Finally, money serves as a **store of value**. Because it can be used to buy goods or services whenever the need arises, money is a convenient way of holding wealth.

Of course, money is not a perfect store of value, because its purchasing power can change. As we saw in Chapter 1 (Figure 1-4), prices of goods and services have risen, and the purchasing power of money has consequently declined.

MONEY IN THE CANADIAN ECONOMY

If it waddles like a duck,
And quacks like a duck,
Then it is a duck.

Anonymous

Money is what money does. To define money, we should begin by looking at *what is actually used* to buy goods and services. What is used by the householder paying the hydro bill? by the customer at the supermarket? by the child buying candy? by the employer paying wages?

Coins and paper currency (quarters, $1 bills, $10 bills, etc.), which together are known as **currency**, are used in many transactions—but certainly not in all. Indeed, most payments are made by cheque. When you write a cheque, it is an order to your bank to make a payment out of the balance in your account.

Until the mid-1970s, most of the money held in bank accounts that were used for writing cheques was held in the form of **demand deposits**—that is, deposits which the owner has the legal right to withdraw without prior notice, and on which the banks usually pay little or no interest. Consequently, until a few years ago, economists usually defined money as currency plus demand deposits in the chartered banks. This concept of money—which is denoted by **M1**—is the one we will usually refer to in later chapters when we discuss monetary policy in Canada.

In recent years, banks have been offering several other kinds of deposits which are close substitutes for demand deposits. For example, they issue "daily interest chequable savings accounts" on which interest is calculated on the actual balance each day, and which can be used for writing cheques. (Technically, savings deposits are referred to as *notice deposits*, because the chartered banks have the formal right to demand a few days' notice before the funds can be withdrawn; however, in practice they routinely waive this right.) Further, notice deposits held by large corporations ("non-personal" notice deposits) can effectively be used for making payments, since the chartered banks will automatically transfer funds from these accounts to the demand deposits on which the corporations' cheques are drawn.

Since many individuals and corporations have switched from demand deposits to chequable daily interest savings accounts or notice deposits, economists at the Bank of Canada have argued that M1 may have become too narrow a definition of money. As an alternative, they have suggested a definition of money which includes daily interest chequable savings deposits and non-personal notice deposits as well as currency and demand deposits. Since the early 1980s, this concept of money—referred to as **M1A** has become more commonly used in discussions of money and monetary policy in Canada.[2]

M1 = currency + demand deposits in chartered banks

M1A = M1 + daily interest chequable deposits + non-personal notice deposits

Of the total quantity of money M1A shown in Figure 12-1, observe that the bank deposit component is by far the largest: It was more than $50 billion in December 1985, compared to $14 billion in currency.

Several complications should be noted about the basic definitions of money, M1 and M1A. In either definition, "money" has been identified as the items which are used in making transactions. But something seems to have been left out: When shopping, people often use credit cards rather than either currency or cheques. Yet, there is no mention of credit cards in the definition of money. There are two related reasons. First, in a fundamental sense, people don't "pay" with credit cards. They simply defer the payment for a few weeks or months. When the credit card bill comes, it must be paid by cheque (or, conceivably, with currency). Thus, it is the final payment with a cheque, rather than the initial charging with a credit card, that represents the fundamental payment. It is the balance in the bank account which is money, not the credit card. Second, people *own* currency and bank accounts. Credit cards, on the other hand, represent an easy way to run up debt. If, as the result of a sudden windfall, I acquire an extra $1,000 which I deposit in my bank account, I will be very much aware of the fact, and will clearly be better off as a result. On the other hand, if the credit card issuer informs me that I can

charge an extra $1,000, I will not necessarily be better off. Indeed, I may scarcely notice. When we are calculating the quantity of money, we should not mix together *assets*—such as currency and bank deposits—with the **lines of credit** available to holders of credit cards.

A *line of credit* is a commitment by a lender to lend up to a specific amount to a borrower. For example, if I have a $2,000 line of credit

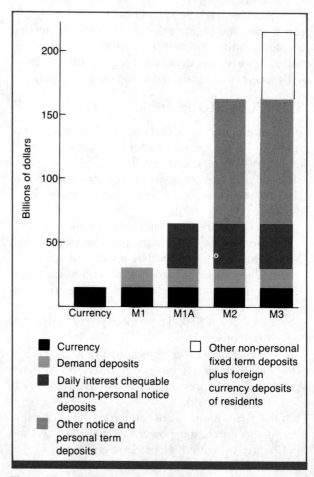

Figure 12-1 Measures of money.
Deposits with the chartered banks constitute the largest component of "money," whether "money" is defined as M1 or M1A. The still more broadly defined concepts of money M2 and M3 (explained later in the text) are much larger than M1 or M1A.
Source: *Bank of Canada Review.*

[2]Here and elsewhere in the discussion of money definitions, we skip over some of the details. For example, M1 also includes an item referred to as "net float," consisting mainly of Bank of Canada cheques issued to the public (but not yet deposited in a chartered bank), net of outstanding cheques drawn on chartered banks for deposit in the government account with the Bank of Canada. For an excellent and readable account of this and other technical issues relating to monetary statistics, see Peter Martin, *Inside the Bank of Canada's Weekly Financial Statistics: A Technical Guide* (Vancouver: The Fraser Institute, 1985).

with a credit card company, the company is committed to letting me charge up to $2,000.

The second complication is a technical point regarding the data in Figure 12-1. Coins are issued by the Government of Canada through the Royal Canadian Mint. Paper currency is issued by the **Bank of Canada**, our government-owned central bank. (Look at a dollar bill and you will see the Bank's name written across the top.) The bank deposits shown in Figure 12-1 are liabilities (debts) of the chartered banks. When the quantity of money is calculated, currency and deposits are counted only when they are held by the public; that is, by individuals and non-bank institutions. Holdings by the federal government, the Bank of Canada, and chartered banks are not included in the money stock, since these are the institutions that create money. This exclusion makes sense. For example, if the Bank of Canada has a million $1 bills printed up and stored in its vaults, it makes little sense to say that the money stock has gone up by $1 million. That currency gains significance and becomes "money" only when it passes out of the hands of the Bank of Canada and into the hands of the public.

M2, M3, and Liquid Assets
Money is important because it is used in transactions; it makes the exchange of goods and services work much more smoothly and efficiently than a barter system. But money is also important because it can affect aggregate demand. When people have more money, they are likely to spend more.

Once we concentrate on the effect of money on spending, it is even less clear precisely how we should define money. For example, the line between M1A and other similar assets is a fine one. Consider savings deposits against which cheques cannot be written. It is true that such deposits cannot be used directly to make payments. But they can easily be switched into chequable deposits, which in turn can be spent. The spending patterns of someone with $10,000 in a non-chequable savings account may not be very different from the spending of a person with $10,000 in a demand deposit account, or a daily interest chequable savings account.

Thus, when economists are investigating the effects of the banking system on aggregate demand, they go even further, beyond the narrowly defined M1 or M1A.

Specifically, they often use an even broader definition of "money," **M2**, which includes non-chequable notice deposits and other close substitutes for M1A:

$$M2 = M1A + \text{all other notice deposits} + \text{personal term deposits}$$

In this definition, *non-chequable* personal savings accounts are included in "other notice deposits." A *term deposit* is similar to a notice deposit, except that it has a specific time to maturity. For example, if you have a term deposit that matures in three months, your asset is tied up until that date. If you want to withdraw it sooner, you must pay a penalty.

Large term deposits (over $100,000) are generally held by businesses, in the form of "Certificates of Deposit" (CDs). These can be sold on the financial markets, just as government securities can be sold, thus enabling the depositor to liquidate a CD at any time prior to maturity. These large term deposits are included in an even broader definition of money, **M3**, which also incorporates foreign-currency deposits (mostly in U.S. dollars) held in chartered banks by Canadian residents.

$$M3 = M2 + \text{non-personal term deposits} + \text{foreign-currency deposits of Canadian residents in the chartered banks}$$

In studying what determines spending, one can go even further and consider other **liquid assets** or "near monies"—such as Canada Savings Bonds, deposits in trust companies, and short-term marketable securities issued by government or large non-bank corporations.

> A *liquid asset* is an asset that can be converted quickly into money (M1A) with little fuss and cost, and at a stable dollar value.

(An example of an asset which is generally not liquid is real estate. It may be very difficult to sell, and its price may be quite uncertain, particularly if the owner is eager to sell quickly.)

BANKING AS A BUSINESS

Because chequable deposits in chartered banks constitute a large share of the money used in everyday purchases, banks occupy a strategic position in the economy. But, in addition, they also have a particular significance to a small fraction of the population: the shareholders of banks. Banks, like manufacturing corporations or retail stores, are privately owned, and one of their major objectives is to make profits for their shareholders. Therefore, two questions are relevant in an analysis of banking operations: (1) How do banks earn profits? and (2) How can banks be used by the authorities to stabilize the economy?

The Goldsmith: The Embryonic Bank as a Warehouse

The quest for profits led to the development of the modern bank. How this happened can be illustrated by dipping briefly into the history of the ancestors of banks—the mediæval goldsmiths.

As their name implies, goldsmiths worked and shaped the precious metal. But they also undertook another function. Because gold wares were extremely valuable, customers looked to the goldsmith for safe storage of their treasures. In return for the deposit of a valuable, the goldsmith would provide the customer with a warehouse receipt—the promise to return the valuable to the customer on demand. Thus, the goldsmiths performed a service for a rich elite that was basically similar to the service that a baggage checkroom performs for you or me. They stored packages for a fee, and returned them to the owner on demand.

When unique gold ornaments were deposited, the customer naturally wanted to get back precisely the item which had been left with the goldsmith. But goldsmiths held not only unique items for their customers; golden bars and golden coins were also deposited. In these cases, it was not essential to the depositor to get back *exactly* the same gold that had been deposited. Thus the basis for the development of banks was laid.

Fractional-Reserve Banking

To see how the banking business developed, let us look at the goldsmith's business in more detail. To do so, the balance sheet is a useful device. Recall the fundamental balance sheet equation presented in Chapter 6:

Assets = liabilities + net worth

Consider an early goldsmith who had 10,000 "dol-lars" of his own funds invested in a building. This investment showed up as a building on the left-hand asset side of the goldsmith's balance sheet, and as net worth on the right-hand side (Table 12-1). Now, suppose the goldsmith accepted $100,000 in gold coins for safekeeping. As the coins were in his possession, they appeared on the asset side. But the owners of the gold had the right to withdraw them at any time upon demand. The goldsmith had **demand deposit liabilities** of $100,000; he had to be prepared to provide the depositors with this much gold whenever they requested it. Thus, the early goldsmith had the balance sheet shown in Table 12-1.

Table 12-1
Balance Sheet of the Early Goldsmith

Assets		Liabilities	
Gold coins	$100,000	Demand deposit	
Building	$ 10,000	liabilities	$100,000
		Net Worth	$ 10,000
Total	$110,000	Total	$110,000

The early goldsmith operated a warehouse, holding $1 in gold for every $1 in deposits.

At this stage, a fundamental question arose regarding the goldsmith's business. If it operated simply as a warehouse, holding the $100,000 in gold coins which the customers had deposited, it would not be very profitable. Its sole source of profits would be the small amount charged for safeguarding gold.

After some years of experience holding gold for many different depositors, the goldsmith might have noticed something interesting. Although he was committed to repay the gold of the depositors on demand, he did not actually repay them all at once in the normal course of events. Each week some of the depositors made withdrawals, but others added to their balances. There was a flow of gold out of the warehouse, but there was also an inflow. While there was some fluctuation in the goldsmith's total holdings of gold, a sizeable quantity remained on deposit at all times.

Sooner or later a question therefore occurred to the goldsmith. Why not lend out some of this gold that was just sitting in the vaults, "collecting dust"? Since

Table 12-2
The Goldsmith Becomes a Banker

Assets		Liabilities and net worth	
Reserve of gold coins	$ 40,000	Demand deposits	$100,000
		Net worth	$ 10,000
Loans	$ 60,000		
Building	$ 10,000		
Total	$110,000	Total	$110,000

When loans are made . . .

. . . reserves decline . . .

. . . and are now only a fraction of deposit liabilities.

Once the goldsmith had begun to lend the deposited gold and kept gold reserves equal to only a fraction of demand deposit liabilities, the business ceased to be a simple warehouse and became a bank.

the depositors did not all try to withdraw their gold simultaneously, he did not need to have all the gold on hand. Some could be put to work earning interest. We can therefore imagine the goldsmith beginning to experiment by making loans. Undoubtedly he started cautiously, keeping a relatively large quantity of gold in his vaults. Specifically, suppose that he kept a large reserve of $40,000 in gold to pay off depositors in the event that a group of them suddenly demanded their gold back. He lent the remaining $60,000 in gold, with the borrowers giving him promissory notes stating their commitment to pay interest and repay the principal after a period of time. Then the goldsmith's balance sheet changed to the one shown in Table 12-2. The only difference was on the asset side: The goldsmith had exchanged $60,000 of gold for $60,000 in promissory notes (shown simply as "Loans").

In making loans, the goldsmith went beyond warehousing and entered the **fractional-reserve banking** business. That is, *he held gold reserves that were only a fraction of his demand deposit liabilities*. In normal times, everything worked out well. He kept enough gold to pay off all depositors who wanted to make withdrawals. And he earned interest on the loans he had made.

As time passed and goldsmiths gained confidence in the banking business, they experimented by keeping gold reserves that were lower and lower fractions of their deposit liabilities. Sometimes they had only 20% in reserve, or even less. They had an incentive to reduce reserves, because each additional dollar taken out of reserves and lent out meant that additional interest could be earned. But, while the entry into

fractional-reserve banking allowed goldsmiths to prosper, they faced two major risks in their new banking business:

1. Their loans might go sour. That is, goldsmiths might lend to businesses or individuals who became unable to repay. Clearly, then, the evaluation of credit risks (the estimation of the chances that borrowers would be unable to repay) became an important part of goldsmithing—and of modern banking.

2. Because they kept reserves equal to only a fraction of their demand deposit liabilities, the goldsmith-bankers were counting on a reasonably stable flow of deposits and withdrawals. In normal times, these flows were indeed likely to be stable. But the goldsmith-banker could not count on times being normal. If for some reason depositors became frightened, they would appear in droves to make withdrawals; in other words, there would be a *run* on the bank.

Bank Runs and Panics

During business downturns, people were particularly likely to become frightened, and look for safety. What could be safer than holding gold? In crises, then, the public tended to switch into gold—that is, they withdrew gold from their banks. But the banks, operating with gold reserves equal to only a fraction of their deposits, did not have enough gold to pay off all their depositors. A panic, with a run on the banks, was the result. Since banks could not possibly pay off all their deposit liabilities, every individual depositor had an incentive to withdraw his or her deposit before the bank ran out of gold and was forced to close. For all depositors as a group, this was self-destructive behaviour: The run could push banks into bankruptcy, with some depositors losing their money forever. But individual depositors could not be expected to commit financial suicide for the common good; they could not be expected to stay out of a lineup of those making withdrawals. Indeed, each depositor had a personal interest to be *first* in line to get back his or her gold.

THE MODERN CANADIAN BANKING SYSTEM

This account obviously has been an extremely simplified version of the history of banks. But it does help to explain the crises that occurred in the Canadian and U.S. banking systems during the nineteenth century, and why monetary problems contributed to the Great Depression in both Canada and the United States.

In the United States, following a crisis in 1907, a National Monetary Commission was set up to study monetary and banking problems. As a result of the commission's recommendations, the Federal Reserve System was established in 1914, giving the United States a central bank. In Canada, a Royal Commission on Banking and Finance was appointed during the Great Depression; it concluded that the authorities needed more powers to resolve the monetary problems that had arisen during the Depression. Following the commission's recommendations, the *Bank of Canada* was founded in 1935.

The Bank of Canada

The Bank of Canada is our central bank. It is the Canadian equivalent of foreign central banks such as the Bank of England, the Deutsche Bundesbank of Germany, and the U.S. Federal Reserve (sometimes known only as "the Fed"). As our central bank, the Bank of Canada:

1. Has the responsibility to *control the quantity of money* in Canada.
2. *Issues paper currency* (dollar bills).
3. *Acts as a "bankers' bank"*. (While you and I keep our bank deposits in the chartered banks, the chartered banks in turn keep deposits in the Bank of Canada. While you and I—and business corporations—can go to the chartered banks for loans, chartered banks in turn can borrow

from the Bank of Canada. The Bank of Canada also helps the chartered banks make the system of payments by cheque work smoothly and inexpensively.)
4. *Supervises the chartered banks* and collects detailed data on all aspects of their operation. (The formal responsibility for ensuring that the chartered banks comply with the provisions of the Bank Act, however, rests with the Inspector General of Banks, who is appointed by the federal government and is an official in the Department of Finance, not in the Bank of Canada.)
5. *Acts as the federal government's bank.* The government keeps some of its deposits in the Bank of Canada, and the Bank administers the sale of government bonds and their repayment when they come due. The Bank also acts on behalf of the government in buying and selling foreign currencies, such as U.S. dollars or German marks.

How the Bank of Canada carries out these responsibilities will be major topics in future chapters.

The Chartered Banks

In contrast to the banking system in the United States, where there are about 15,000 separate banks, Canada has a highly concentrated banking system. If we exclude foreign banks operating here through subsidiaries, Canada has no more than a dozen chartered banks (that is, banks that have received a "charter" permitting them to do banking business under the provisions of the Bank Act). The five largest ones (the Royal Bank, Canadian Imperial Bank of Commerce, Bank of Montreal, Bank of Nova Scotia, and Toronto Dominion Bank) account for about 90% of the total assets of chartered banks. Each of these banks operates a large number of branches throughout the country. (A branch is a building, other than the head office, where the bank accepts deposits.) This contrasts with the situation in the United States, where some states confine each bank to a single building, and where interstate branching has not been permitted. (In the formative years of U.S. banking, politicians feared that large banks might become too powerful, and set up regulations that hindered their expansion across the country. However, the regulations against banking in more than one state are currently being relaxed.)

The two functions at the heart of banking show up clearly in the combined balance sheet of the Canadian chartered banks in Table 12-3: accepting deposits (items 7 and 8), and making loans to businesses and individuals (item 2). As we have already seen, chartered bank deposit liabilities constitute the largest component of the money stock M1A in Canada.

A number of other items on the balance sheet are also worthy of note, beginning with the first entry—reserves. Unlike the goldsmiths and the early banks, modern banks do not hold gold as reserves; gold is no longer the basic money of Canada or of other countries. Instead, banks hold two kinds of *cash reserves*: deposits in the Bank of Canada, and currency. Banks are *required by law* to keep cash reserves equal to certain percentages of their deposits. The present Bank Act stipulates that the chartered banks have to hold reserves equal to 10% of demand deposit liabilities, and an additional amount equal to 3% of notice deposit liabilities. Note that reserves, which appear on the *asset* side of the balance sheet, must meet the required percentages of the deposits (items 7 and 8) on the *liabilities* side of the bank's balance sheet. (For example, if the required reserve ratio were set at 10% of all deposits, a bank with $50 million in deposit *liabilities*

would have to hold $5 million of its *assets* in the form of reserves.)

Required reserves are reserves that chartered banks are required to hold in order to meet their legal obligations. These reserves are specified as percentages of deposits. Required reserves are held in the form of currency or deposits in the Bank of Canada.

Continuing down the asset side of the balance sheet, note that $177 billion of assets are *loans* that banks have extended to businesses and individuals (item 2). The banks also hold substantial amounts of *securities* issued by the federal and provincial governments or by corporations (item 3). An individual bank may also hold *deposits in foreign banks*, or other foreign currency assets (item 4). It may also have borrowed money from foreign banks or have accepted deposits denominated in U.S. dollars (rather than in Canadian dollars). The banks' foreign liabilities are shown in item 9. Finally, "other assets" of banks (item 5) include the value of bank buildings, computers, and other equipment.

Secondary reserves. Even though bankers may gener-

Table 12-3
Combined Balance Sheet, Chartered Banks, December 1985
(billions of dollars)

Assets			Liabilities	
1. Reserves			7. Demand deposits	19.3
(Currency and deposits in			8. Notice and term deposits	164.8
Bank of Canada)		5.6	9. Foreign currency liabilities	204.9
2. Loans		177.0	10. Shareholders' equity	18.8
Short-term loans	(1.6)		11. All other liabilities	35.9
Real estate mortgages	(44.9)		12. Total liabilities and net worth	443.7
Other loans	(130.5)			
3. Securities		27.6		
Treasury bills	(12.3)			
Government bonds	(2.6)			
Canadian securities	(12.7)			
4. Foreign currency assets		201.9		
5. All other assets		31.6		
6. Total assets		443.7		

SOURCE: *Bank of Canada Review.*

ally count on a reasonably steady inflow and outflow of deposits, they must still protect themselves against temporary surges of withdrawals. The reserves that banks hold to meet the reserve requirements laid down by the Bank Act do not provide an adequate cushion against such withdrawals. Suppose, for example, that the required reserve ratio is 20%, and that a bank holds just barely enough reserves to meet this requirement. Then assume that owners of deposits withdraw $100,000 in currency. With a required reserve ratio of 20%, required reserves fall by $20,000 as a result of the $100,000 withdrawal. But the bank's actual reserves fall by a full $100,000 when it pays out the currency, since currency is counted as part of total reserves. Thus, with actual reserves declining by $100,000, and required reserves declining by only $20,000, the bank's reserves are now $80,000 short of the legal requirement.

There are three ways in which a bank can protect itself against this danger. First, it may regularly hold **excess reserves** of currency and Bank of Canada deposits. For example, if the bank initially held $90,000 in excess reserves, this sudden withdrawal would create no problem. The holding of excess reserves is, however, expensive: currency earns no interest, nor is interest paid on reserve deposits in the Bank of Canada. As a result, banks generally hold only small amounts of excess reserves. (Typically, excess reserves are less than 1% of total reserves.)

> *Excess reserves* are reserves, in the form of currency or deposits in the Bank of Canada, that are in excess of those required by law.
>
> Excess reserves =
> total reserves − required reserves

Another way for the bank to protect itself is to hold other kinds of **secondary reserves**; that is, assets that do not count as part of required reserves, but that can be liquidated (converted into cash) on short notice. If the bank needs cash to deal with a surge in withdrawals by its depositors, it can quickly get it by selling off secondary reserves. The Canadian chartered banks usually maintain relatively large amounts of secondary reserves, not only as a protection against sudden deposit withdrawals but also because they are forced to. Under the Bank Act, the Bank of Canada can require the chartered banks to hold secondary reserves (defined as short-term Treasury bills, day-to-day loans to invest-

ment dealers, and any excess cash reserves) equal to a specific minimum percentage of their deposit liabilities.

As a precautionary measure, the banks usually maintain a cushion of secondary reserves over and above the legal minimum: Because they earn interest on their secondary reserves, it is not as expensive to maintain excess secondary reserves as it would be to have large excess cash reserves.

The third protection against a shortfall in cash reserves is the banks' ability to borrow. A bank in difficulty may replenish its reserves by borrowing from the Bank of Canada. Or it may turn to the **short-term money market**; that is, a market for short-term loans in which banks with inadequate reserves can borrow them from other institutions.[3]

BANKS AND THE CREATION OF MONEY

The public's use of bank deposits as money would be reason enough to look carefully at the operation of banks. But banks require attention for an additional reason—and one of great economic importance. In the normal course of their operations, they create money. Most people have heard of this power in a vague and imprecise way. Banks are consequently looked on with a mixture of awe and resentment. How did they acquire this magical ability, and why should they have such extraordinary power? These attitudes reflect a lack of understanding of banking. There is, in fact, nothing magical in the process whereby money is created. Your local bank does not have a magical fountain pen with which it can create unlimited amounts of money out of thin air.

The operations of banks, and how they create money, can be understood most easily by looking at the balance sheets of individual banks. An individual chartered bank, like the aggregate of chartered banks shown in Table 12-3, has a list of assets and liabilities.

---

[3]The chartered banks are not the only firms that are allowed to borrow from the Bank of Canada: *authorized investment dealers* may also do so. Thus, when the banks need cash reserves, they may call in the loans they have made to investment dealers. If the dealers pay off these loans by borrowing from the Bank of Canada, the chartered banks' cash reserves will increase. (The dealers' cheques drawn on the Bank of Canada will be credited to the chartered banks' accounts with the Bank of Canada.) (Investment dealers will be discussed further in Chapter 13.)

Table 12-4
Changes in Assets and Liabilities when Chartered Bank Receives Deposit

Chartered bank A			
Assets		**Liabilities**	
Reserves of currency	+$100,000	Demand deposits	+$100,000
Required $20,000			
Excess $80,000			
Total	$100,000	Total	$100,000

When you deposit $100,000 in currency . . .

. . . bank reserves also rise by $100,000.

Your balance sheet			
Assets		**Liabilities**	
Currency	−$100,000	No change	
Demand deposit	+$100,000		
Total	0	Total	0

When chartered bank A receives your $100,000 deposit, its assets and liabilities both rise by $100,000. But your holdings of money do not change. You have merely switched from one type of money (currency) to another (a demand deposit).

To avoid being burdened with detail, we simplify the following tables by showing only the *changes* in the balance sheet of a bank. (Like the whole balance sheet, changes in the balance sheet must balance.) To avoid untidy fractions, we assume that the required reserves of banks are a nice round figure—20% of their deposit liabilities—even though requirements are not, in fact, this high. To simplify further, we assume that all deposits are chequable demand deposits, and that banks initially have just enough reserves to meet the legal reserve requirement.

Now, suppose that you find $100,000 left in a shoe box by your eccentric old uncle when he died. In a state of bliss, you rush to your local bank to put the $100,000 into your chequing account. As a result, your bank—call it bank A—has $100,000 more in currency on the asset side of its balance sheet (Table 12-4). It also has $100,000 more in liabilities, since you have a $100,000 claim on the bank in the form of a chequing account deposit. (This $100,000 deposit represents an *asset* to you; it is something you own. However, this same $100,000 deposit is a *liability* to the bank; the bank must be prepared to pay you $100,000 in currency if you ask.)

As a result of this deposit, what has happened to the quantity of money? The answer is: nothing. You initially held the $100,000 in currency; you exchanged the currency for $100,000 in deposit money. Once the deposit is made, the $100,000 in dollar bills ceases to be counted as part of the money stock, since it is held by the bank. (Remember the technical point regarding the data in Figure 12-1: Currency and deposits are included in the money stock only when they are held by the public, but not when they are held by the Bank of Canada, the federal government, or the chartered banks themselves.) The *composition* of the money stock has changed—there is now $100,000 more in deposits and $100,000 less in currency in the hands of the public. However, the total amount has not changed.

But this is not the end of the story, because the bank now has excess reserves. Its deposit liabilities have gone up by your $100,000. Therefore, its required reserves have risen by $20,000 (that is, $100,000 times the required reserve ratio of 20%). But its total reserves have risen by the $100,000 in currency that you deposited. Therefore, it now has $80,000 in excess reserves. Like the goldsmith of old, it is in a position to make loans to businesses and other customers.

Suppose that a local shoe store wants to expand its operations, and approaches the bank for a loan of $80,000, an amount that just happens to equal the excess reserves of the bank. The bank agrees. Mechan-

Table 12-5
Bank A Makes a Loan

Assets		Liabilities	
Reserves of currency	$100,000	Demand deposits	
		yours	$100,000
Loan†	+$ 80,000	shoe store's†	+$ 80,000
Total	$180,000	Total	$180,000

— When a bank makes a loan . . .

. . . demand deposits increase.

When the bank lends $80,000, demand deposits increase by $80,000. This represents a net increase in the money stock.

†Items resulting from the loan.

ically, what happens? The bank could, presumably, hand over $80,000 in dollar bills to the store owner, in exchange for the promissory note that commits the store to repay the loan. However, the bank does not normally operate this way. Instead, when it makes the loan, it simply adds $80,000 to the deposit account of the borrower. This is entirely satisfactory to the borrower, who can write a cheque against the account. As a result of this loan, the balance sheet of the chartered bank is modified, as shown in Table 12-5.

Now, what has happened to the money supply? Observe that when *the bank makes a loan, the stock of money in the hands of the public increases*. Specifically, there now is $80,000 more in demand deposit money. But what has the bank done? Nothing extraordinary. It has merely lent its excess reserves. That is, it has lent less than was placed in its safekeeping when you made your original deposit.

How a Cheque Is Cleared
So far, so good. However, our story has just nicely begun. The shoe store borrowed from the bank in order to buy inventory, not to leave its money sitting idly in a chequing account. Suppose that the shoe store orders shoes from a Montreal manufacturer, sending a cheque for $80,000 in payment. The shoe company in Montreal deposits the cheque in its bank (bank B). This sets in motion the process of **cheque clearing—** which straightens out accounts between bank A in your home town and bank B in Montreal (Figure 12-2). Bank B sends the cheque along to the Bank of Canada, receiving in exchange a reserve deposit of $80,000. Bank B's accounts balance, since its assets in the form of reserves have gone up by the same amount ($80,000)

as its demand deposit liabilities to the shoe manufacturer. (The $80,000 reserve deposit represents an *asset* to bank B and a *liability* to the Bank of Canada.)

The Bank of Canada, in turn, sends the cheque along to bank A, subtracting the $80,000 from bank A's reserve deposit. Bank A balances its accounts by subtracting the $80,000 from the deposit of the shoe store that wrote the cheque in the first place.

Why a Bank Can Safely Lend No More Than Its Excess Reserves
When the effects of the cheque clearing (in Figure 12-2) are added to bank A's earlier transactions (shown in Table 12-5), the net effects on bank A's balance sheet may be summarized in Table 12-6. Observe that, as a result of the cheque clearing, bank A's excess reserves have completely disappeared. (Its currency reserves rose by $100,000 when you deposited the original $100,000. Its reserve deposit in the Bank of Canada fell by $80,000 when the shoe store's cheque cleared. Thus, its net change in reserves is $20,000, just the amount required as a result of its $100,000 demand deposit liability to you.) This was the result of bank A's lending the shoe store an amount equal to its excess reserves. Thus, we come to a fundamental proposition:

A bank may prudently lend an amount up to, but no greater than, its excess reserves.

The Multiple Expansion of Bank Deposits
We have seen how bank A's excess reserves are eliminated when the shoe store's $80,000 cheque clears. But observe (in Figure 12-2) that bank B now has

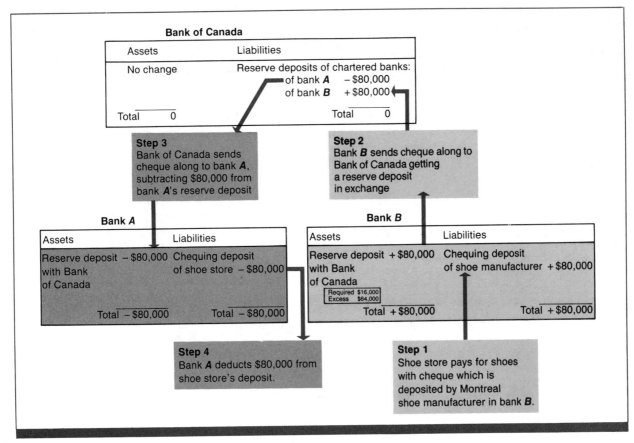

Figure 12-2 The clearing of a cheque.
In the cheque-clearing process, the bank in which the cheque was deposited (bank B) acquires
reserves, while the bank on which the cheque was drawn (bank A) loses reserves.

Table 12-6
Net Effects on Bank A
(cheque clearing combined with earlier transactions)

Assets		Liabilities	
Reserves	+ $ 20,000	Demand deposits	
Required $20,000		yours	+ $100,000
Excess 0			
Loan	$ 80,000		
Total	$100,000	Total	$100,000

This table gives the combined effect on bank A of cheque clearing (Figure 12-2) and earlier
transactions (Table 12-5). After the cheque is cleared, bank A has no excess reserves.

Table 12-7
Bank B Lends to Camera Store

Assets		Liabilities	
Reserve deposit	$ 80,000	Demand deposits	
		shoe manufacturer's	$ 80,000
Loan†	+ $ 64,000	camera store's†	+ $ 64,000
Total	$144,000	Total	$144,000

When bank B lends $64,000 . . .

. . . demand deposits increase by $64,000.

As a result of the second round of lending, the money stock increases by $64,000.

†Items resulting from the loan.

Table 12-8
The Creation of Money: After the Second Round

	Bank B		
Assets		Liabilities	
Reserves	$16,000	Demand deposits	
Required $16,000		of shoe manufacturer	$80,000
Excess 0			
Loans	$64,000		
Total	$80,000	Total	$80,000

	Bank C		
Assets		Liabilities	
Reserves	$64,000	Demand deposits	
Required $12,800		of Kodak	$64,000
Excess $51,200			
Total	$64,000	Total	$64,000

When bank C receives deposits and reserves of $64,000, it can prudently lend $51,200. And so the process continues.

excess reserves of $64,000; that is, the difference between the $80,000 increase in its actual reserves and the $16,000 increase in its required reserves. ($16,000 = 20% of the $80,000 increase in its demand deposit liabilities.)

Bank B may prudently lend up to the $64,000 of its excess reserves. In Table 12-7, we suppose that it lends this amount to the local camera store. When the loan is made, $64,000 is added to the demand deposit of the camera store. Because the amount of demand deposits held by the public goes up by $64,000, *the money stock increases by this amount.*

Suppose that the camera store has borrowed the $64,000 to buy film, cameras, and equipment from Kodak. To pay for its purchases, it writes a cheque to Kodak. Kodak deposits the cheque in its Toronto bank—bank C. Once again, the cheque-clearing mechanism is set in operation. When bank C sends the cheque to the Bank of Canada, it receives a reserve deposit of $64,000 (Table 12-8). But when the cheque is sent along to bank B (the camera store's bank), that bank loses $64,000 in reserves, and no longer has any excess reserves.

Observe, however, that bank C now has excess

Table 12-9
The Multiple Expansion of Bank Deposits

A. The chain reaction

Bank	(1) Acquired reserves and demand deposits	(2) Required reserves (2) = (1) × 0.20	(3) Excess reserves = loans that banks can make (3) = (1) − (2)	(4) Changes in money stock (4) = (3)
A	$100,000 (yours)	$20,000	$80,000	$80,000
B	$80,000 (shoe manufacturer's)	$16,000	$64,000	$64,000
C	$64,000 (Kodak's)	$12,800	$51,200	$51,200
D	$51,200	$10,240	$40,960	$40,960
•	•	•	•	•
•	•	•	•	•
•	•	•	•	•
Maximum sum	$500,000	$100,000	$400,000	$400,000

B. Effects on consolidated balance sheet of all chartered banks (with maximum permissible expansion)

Reserves	$100,000	Demand deposits	$500,000
Required $100,000			
Excess 0			
Loans	$400,000		
Total	$500,000	Total	$500,000

The banking system as a whole can do what no single bank can do. It can transform the original deposit of $100,000 in currency into as much as $500,000 in demand deposit money.

reserves of $51,200, which it can lend out. When it does so, it will create a new demand deposit of $51,200, thus increasing the money stock once again. And so the process continues. As a result of your initial deposit of $100,000, there can be a chain reaction of loans, as shown in Figure 12-3 and Table 12-9. At each stage, the amount of loans that can be made (and the amount of deposits that can thereby be created) is 80% of the amount made in the previous stage. The total increase in deposits is the sum of the series: $100,000 + $100,000 × 0.8 + $100,000 × 0.8². . . . If this series is taken to its limit—with an infinite number of rounds—then, by a basic algebraic proposition,[4] the

sum is equal to $100,000/(1 − 0.8) = $500,000.

Thus, when the banking system acquires additional reserves, it can increase deposits by a multiple of the initial reserve increase. The deposit multiplier D is equal to the reciprocal of the required reserve ratio R:

$$D = \frac{1}{R}$$

In our example:

$$D = \frac{1}{20\%} = 5$$

The initial acquisition of $100,000 in reserves made

[4]Mathematically, this is the same theorem used in the derivation of the multiplier in Chapter 10 (footnote 2). But the economic issues are quite different in the two cases. In the multiplier, the total ef-

fects of various rounds of spending are derived. Here, changes in the stock of money are calculated.

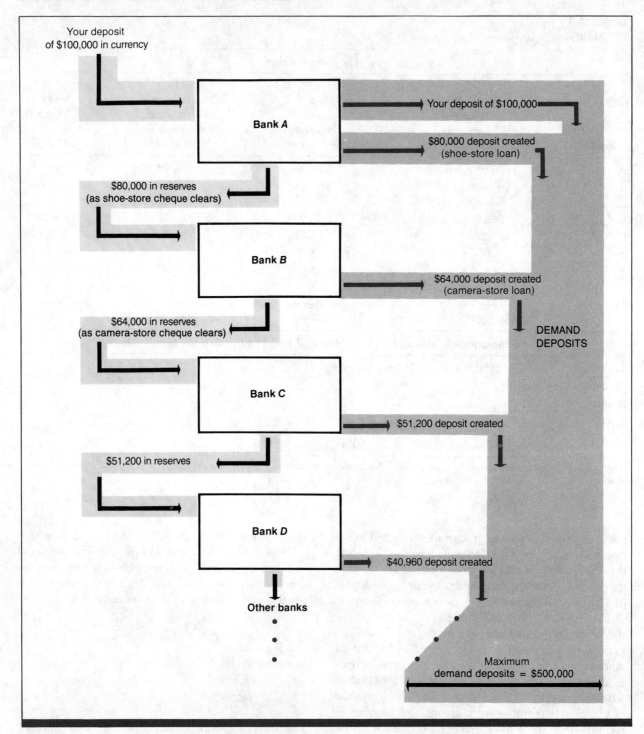

Figure 12-3 The multiple expansion of bank deposits.
The banking system as a whole can do what no single bank can do. It can transform the original deposit of $100,000 in currency into as much as $500,000 in demand deposit money.

possible an increase in demand deposits of $500,000 (that is, $100,000 × 1/0.2). Alternatively, if the required reserve ratio were only 10%, the banking system would have been capable of creating up to $1,000,000 (that is, $100,000 × 1/0.1) in deposit money on the basis of $100,000 in reserves. Thus, *when there is a change in the required reserve ratio, there is a powerful effect on the amount of loans that the banks can make, and on the amount of deposit money that they can create.*

A few pages earlier, we emphasized that required reserves provide a bank with little cushion in the event of a withdrawal of deposits. That is not their primary purpose. Rather, the requirement that banks hold reserves is a way of *controlling the amount of loans they can make and the amount of money they can create.*

During the multiple expansion of deposits, *the banking system as a whole does something which no single bank can do.* The banking system as a whole can create deposits equal to a multiple of the reserves which it acquires. But any single bank can create deposits (by lending its excess reserves) in an amount equal to only a fraction (80% in our illustration) of the reserves that it acquires.

Two Complications

With a required reserve ratio of 20%, $500,000 is the *maximum* increase in demand deposits following a $100,000 acquisition of reserves by the banking system. In practice, the actual increase in deposits is likely to be considerably less, because of two complications:

1. Banks may decide not to lend out the maximum permitted, but to hold some excess reserves instead. During prosperous times, this is not an important complication. Because of the strong incentive to make loans and thus increase their interest earnings, they prefer to hold only small amounts of excess reserves.

   But during a depression, bankers may become panicky. They may be afraid to make loans because they doubt the ability of borrowers to repay. They may decide to keep their funds secure by holding them as excess reserves. Thus, during the Great Depression, Canadian banks held large excess reserves. (So did U.S. banks.) This unwillingness of the banks to lend tended to keep down the amount of money in the hands

of the public, and slowed the recovery from the Depression.

2. As loans are made and people get more deposit money, they may want to hold more currency, too. In other words, they may withdraw currency from their deposits. Insofar as this happens, the reserves of the chartered banks are reduced; the initial deposit of currency that started off the expansion is partially reversed. As a consequence, the total amount of monetary expansion is reduced.

When currency is held by the public, it is, in a sense, just ordinary money. The dollar I hold in my pocket is only a dollar. On the other hand, when currency is deposited in a bank, it becomes "high-powered." Although the dollar ceases to count directly in the money stock (since chartered bank holdings of currency are excluded from the definition of money), that dollar bill is a bank reserve. On this reserve base, the banking system can build a superstructure of as much as $5 of demand deposit money if the required reserve ratio is 20%. The large amount of demand deposit money, built on a much smaller base of reserves, can be represented graphically by an inverted pyramid (Figure 12-4).

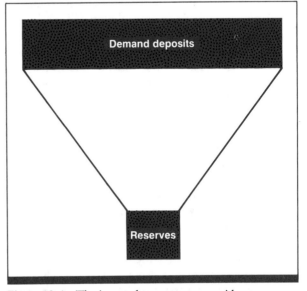

Figure 12-4 The inverted monetary pyramid.
On their reserve base of currency and reserve deposits, the chartered banking system can build a superstructure of demand deposits—of as much as $1/R$ times the base.

WHEN BANKS PURCHASE SECURITIES, THE MONEY SUPPLY ALSO INCREASES

Thus far, we have assumed that a chartered bank with excess reserves lends these excess reserves to its customers in order to earn interest. Alternatively, banks can use these funds to purchase securities, such as bonds issued by federal, provincial, and local governments or by private corporations. The effect on the money stock is similar, whether the banks use their excess reserves to make loans or purchase securities.

To illustrate this point, suppose that, in the nth round in the monetary expansion chain, bank N acquires $10,000 in demand deposits and reserves. If the required reserve ratio is 20%, it then has $8,000 in excess reserves. Suppose that it uses these reserves to purchase $8,000 in government bonds owned by the XYZ Corporation. Bank N pays for the bonds by writing a cheque, which the XYZ Corporation deposits in bank O. Then the money stock as a consequence rises by $8,000; that is, by the $8,000 demand deposit which the XYZ Corporation now owns. The change in the money stock is thus exactly the same as it would have been if bank N had used these excess reserves to make a loan rather than to buy a bond. Moreover, as a result of this transaction, bank N loses its $8,000 of excess reserves, while bank O gains $8,000 of reserves. It is now bank O that finds itself with excess reserves ($6,400, to be precise). When it uses these reserves to make a loan or buy securities, the process of money creation continues.

KEY POINTS

1. Money is important in the study of macroeconomics because:
   (a) The authorities can take steps to alter the quantity of money, and thus affect aggregate demand. *Monetary policy* is the second great tool, along with fiscal policy, that can be used to manage aggregate demand. The details of monetary policy will be explained in Chapter 13.
   (b) At times, strong disturbances have occurred in the monetary system; for example, during the Depression of the 1930s. Such disturbances can make the economy unstable.
2. Money has three interrelated functions. It acts as:
   (a) the medium of exchange
   (b) the standard of value
   (c) a store of value
3. The traditional definition of money (M1) includes only currency and demand deposits. Because certain types of notice deposits have also come to be commonly used for transactions, they are included in the somewhat broader money concept (M1A) which has been used by the Bank of Canada since the early 1980s. Deposit money constitutes the largest component of M1A.
4. Non-chequable personal notice deposits and term deposits are not included in M1A. However, they are relatively close substitutes for the types of deposits that *are* included. When studying how money and the banking system affect aggregate demand, economists thus sometimes focus on another alternative definition of money, M2, which includes all notice deposits and personal term deposits in chartered banks. A third concept, M3, includes large non-personal term deposits, as well as foreign-currency deposits of Canadian residents.
5. The Bank of Canada is our central bank. As such,
   (a) It has the responsibility to control the quantity of money.
   (b) It issues paper currency.
   (c) It acts as the "bankers' bank."
   (d) It supervises and inspects the chartered banks.
   (e) It acts as the federal government's bank.
6. Banks have two principal functions: to accept deposits and to make loans. When a bank makes a loan or purchases a bond, it increases the stock of money.
7. Chartered banks are required to hold reserves in the form of currency or reserve deposits in the Bank of Canada. These reserves must meet required percentages of the chartered banks'

deposit liabilities. The purpose of required reserves is to control the quantity of money that banks can create.

8. When a *single* bank acquires additional deposits and reserves, it can safely lend out only a fraction of these reserves—specifically, its excess reserves. However, the banking *system* (all chartered banks taken together) can create deposits that are a multiple of any new reserves that it acquires.

9. The maximum increase in deposit money that can be created by the banking system is:

$$\frac{1}{R} \times \text{the acquisition of reserves}$$

where R is the required reserve ratio.

10. In practice, the increase is likely to be less than the maximum, since:
   (a) Banks sometimes hold substantial excess reserves, especially during a depression. (During the 1930s, the unwillingness of banks to lend their excess reserves kept down the quantity of money, and slowed the recovery from the Great Depression.)
   (b) As people get more deposit money, they are likely to want to hold more currency, too. When they withdraw currency from their deposits, the reserves held by the banks are reduced.

KEY CONCEPTS

monetary policy	M1	central bank
medium of exchange	M1A	chartered bank
standard of value	M2	cash reserves
store of value	M3	required reserve ratio
purchasing power	liquid assets	required reserves
currency	credit card	excess reserves
Bank of Canada note	line of credit	secondary reserves
demand deposit	fractional-reserve banking	cheque clearing
notice deposit	balance sheet	multiple expansion of bank
daily interest chequable notice deposit	deposit liability	deposits
	promissory note	deposit multiplier
non-personal notice deposit	loan	"high-powered" reserves
term deposit	bank run	monetary pyramid
certificate of deposit (CD)	Bank of Canada	

PROBLEMS

12-1 (a) Suppose that a corporation that previously paid its workers in cash decides to pay them by cheque instead. As a result, it decides to deposit $10,000 which it has held in currency in its safe. Show how this deposit will affect the balance sheets of (1) the corporation, and (2) its bank (the Bank of Nova Scotia).

(b) Does this deposit of $10,000 affect the money stock? Why or why not?

(c) How much can the Bank of Nova Scotia now lend if there is a required reserve ratio of 10%? If it lends this amount to a farmer to buy machinery, show the direct effect of the loan on the bank's balance sheet. Then show the Bank of Nova

Scotia's balance sheet after the farmer spends the loan to buy machinery and the farmer's cheque is cleared.

(d) As a result of the original deposit (in part (a) of this problem), what is the maximum increase in demand deposits that can occur if the required reserve ratio is 10%? What is the maximum amount of bank lending? the maximum increase in the money stock?

12-2 Suppose that a bank receives a deposit of $100,000 and decides to lend the full $100,000. Explain how this decision can get the bank into difficulty.

12-3 If all banks are required to keep reserves equal to 100% of their demand deposits, what will be the consequences of a deposit of $100,000 of currency in bank A?

12-4 During the 1930s, banks held large excess reserves. Now they hold practically none. Why? If you were a banker, would you hold excess reserves? How much? Does your answer depend on the size of individual deposits in your bank? on interest rates? on other things?

12-5 Suppose that there is a single huge chartered bank that holds a monopoly on all banking in Canada. If this bank receives $100,000 in deposits, and if the required reserve ratio is 20%, how much can the bank safely lend? Explain. (Hints: (1) Study Table 12-9, Part B. (2) In Figure 12-2, bank A lost reserves to bank B. If there is only one bank, will it lose reserves in this way?)

12-6 During the 1930s, the banking systems in Canada and the United States did not work well. Banking disturbances contributed to the depth and duration of the Depression.

(a) Explain how, during a financial crisis, individual bank depositors have an incentive to behave in a manner that makes the crisis worse. Do you think that an educational campaign to teach depositors the dangers of such actions would help to solve this problem? If so, explain how. If not, explain why not.

(b) Explain how, during a depression, individual banks have an incentive to behave in a manner that makes the depression deeper and longer-lasting. Do you think that an educational campaign to teach bankers the dangers of such actions would help to solve this problem? If so, explain how. If not, explain why not.

Chapter 13

THE BANK OF CANADA AND THE TOOLS OF MONETARY POLICY

There have been three great inventions since
the beginning of time: fire, the wheel, and
central banking.

Will Rogers

The Bank of Canada is our central bank, acting as the federal government's bank and the bankers' bank. As the central bank, it has one responsibility of prime importance: to see that monetary conditions are consistent with the achievement of the goals of high employment and stable prices. If business is getting worse and the economy is sliding into a recession, the job of the Bank of Canada is to expand the money stock, and thus support aggregate demand. And when business is booming and inflation threatens, the job of the Bank is to exercise restraint, to prevent an excessive monetary growth from fueling the fires of inflation.

The principal purpose of this chapter is to explain:

1. **Open market operations**, that is, purchases or sales of government securities by the Bank of Canada. Through open market operations, the Bank of Canada can control the quantity of reserves held by the chartered banks, and thereby control the quantity of deposit money that the chartered banks can create.

 Open market operations constitute the main policy tool in the hands of the Bank of Canada. In this chapter, we will also look at other actions which influence chartered bank reserves, namely:

2. **Purchases or sales of foreign currencies** by the Bank of Canada, and
3. **Transfers of federal government deposits** between the Bank of Canada and chartered banks.

We will also study other monetary policy tools that the Bank of Canada has used at various times in the past; specifically, we will discuss:

4. **Changes in the Bank Rate**, that is, the interest rate at which the Bank of Canada lends to chartered banks.
5. **Changes in required reserve ratios** that specify the reserves that banks must hold, as percentages of their demand and other deposit liabilities.

But before turning to these topics, let us look briefly at the origins of the Bank of Canada.

ORIGINS AND ORGANIZATION OF THE BANK OF CANADA

The establishment of a Canadian central bank was a controversial step. While the need for some form of central control and regulation of banking was recognized by many economists and political leaders long before the Great Depression, there was also strong opposition, in part based on the fear of centralized financial power. And there was opposition from the existing private banks: they feared that a central bank would become an instrument for political manipulation of the banks. There was also another reason for the existing banks' lack of enthusiasm: Until the 1930s, the Canadian chartered banks were allowed to issue their own bank notes. (These notes circulated in the economy as currency, side by side with the government-issued "Dominion notes.") Since the note issue was a profitable part of their business, the banks were opposed to a central bank which would get a monopoly on the issue of currency.

The fact that the banking system was dominated by a small number of well organized large-scale banking institutions made it less susceptible to crises than the U.S. system. (In the United States, many banks went under during the Depression, and bank failures have continued to be fairly common there. In contrast, no Canadian bank failed during the Depression, and the only bank failures since the 1920s involved two relatively small western institutions, the Canadian Commercial Bank and the Northland Bank, both of which went bankrupt in 1985.) The smaller number of banks in Canada also made it easier for the authorities to influence banking conditions without using a formal system of regulation through a central bank. As a consequence, there was no central bank in Canada until 1935, more than 20 years after the Federal Reserve was set up in the United States. By 1935, however, the government had come to recognize that it had to take more complete responsibility for the control of banking conditions, and the Bank of Canada was established. At the beginning of its life, the Bank was privately owned, but the government bought out the last private shareholders in 1938. The Bank of Canada is now wholly owned by the Canadian government.

The affairs of the Bank of Canada are managed by a board of directors appointed by the government; the directors then appoint the governor and the deputy governor of the Bank, but these appointments also have to be approved by Cabinet.

The division of responsibility for monetary conditions between the government and the Bank of Canada has on occasion given rise to conflicts, most notably in 1959-60 when the Bank stuck to a tight monetary policy in spite of a high rate of unemployment and slow economic growth. The government objected to the tight policy, and asked the Bank of Canada's governor, James Coyne, to resign when he rejected suggestions that the policy be changed. At first, Coyne refused. However, after considerable government pressure, he finally did resign in June 1961. Partly as a result of this affair, however, the Bank Act has been clarified and now explicitly states the duty of the governor to resign in the case of a fundamental conflict with the government. The principle of the government's ultimate responsibility was described by Governor Louis Rasminsky (who replaced Governor Coyne in 1961) in the following way:

> If there should develop a serious and persistent conflict between the views of the government and the views of the central bank . . . , the government should be able formally to instruct the Bank what monetary policy it wishes carried out and the Bank should have the duty to comply.

In the United States, economic policy is much less centralized than in Canada. For example, both the executive and legislative branches have responsibility for taxation and other policies. In addition, the Federal Reserve has a considerable degree of independence from the U.S. administration; it does not have to follow the suggestions of the president. The Federal Reserve also has a somewhat complex and untidy organizational structure, in part because there was opposition to the idea of a central bank when the Fed was established. Technically, there is not a single central bank in the United States, but 12 regional Federal Reserve banks and a board of governors in Washington. The important policy decisions, however, are made by committees acting for the Federal Reserve System as a whole.

We now turn to a discussion of the Bank of Canada's principal policy tools; the most important one is open market operations.

OPEN MARKET OPERATIONS

The Bank of Canada can increase the quantity of chartered bank reserves—and thereby increase the quantity of deposit money the banks can create—by purchasing government securities on the *open market*. That is, it puts in a bid on the securities market;

Table 13-1
An Open Market Purchase: Initial Effects
(thousands of dollars)

Bank of Canada			
Assets		**Liabilities**	
Government securities	+ 100	Reserve deposits of bank A	+ 100
Total	100	Total	100

Chartered Bank A			
Assets		**Liabilities**	
Reserve deposit with Bank of Canada	+ 100	Demand deposits of Algoma Steel	+ 100
Required 20			
Excess 80			
Total	100	Total	100

The open market purchase increases A's reserves by $100,000. At this stage the money supply has also increased by $100,000, because Algoma Steel has a demand deposit of that amount.

Chartered bank A has excess reserves, and therefore a further expansion of the money supply can take place.

the seller may be any bank or any member of the general public who holds government securities and is willing to sell. Who the actual seller will be, the Bank does not know. But whether the government security is sold by a chartered bank or by the public, the results are similar.

Suppose the Bank of Canada puts in a bid for a $100,000 Treasury bill (a short-term form of government debt, usually issued with a maturity of 90 days) and that Algoma Steel Limited is the seller. Algoma delivers the Treasury bill and gets a cheque for $100,000 in return. It deposits this cheque in its chartered bank (bank A). In turn, bank A sends the cheque along to the Bank of Canada, and has its deposit with the Bank of Canada increased by this amount. In other words, bank A's reserves increase by $100,000. The changes in the balance sheets of the Bank of Canada and chartered bank A are shown in Table 13-1.

At this initial step, the money supply has gone up by $100,000; Algoma Steel's demand deposit is counted as part of the money stock. And the stage is set for a further expansion because of the new reserves held by

bank A. Specifically, bank A now has $80,000 in excess reserves that can be lent. And a whole series of loans, similar to those already described in Chapter 10, can take place. Thus, with a 20% required reserve ratio, the $100,000 open market purchase makes possible a maximum increase of $500,000 in deposit money—that is, an increase of $500,000 in the money stock. (Again, as explained in Chapter 12, this is a maximum. In practice, the actual increase will be less, insofar as the public decides to hold more currency along with its higher bank deposits, and insofar as chartered banks hold excess reserves.)

This, then, is the power of the Bank of Canada's open market operations. The Bank carries out the simple transaction of buying a government bond or Treasury bill, and the reserves of the banking system increase as a result. Thus, the Bank makes possible a multiple increase in the nation's money supply.

Now suppose that the Bank of Canada buys the $100,000 Treasury bill from a chartered bank rather than from Algoma Steel. The result is the same: The maximum increase in the money stock is once again

Table 13-2

An Open Market Purchase: When a Chartered Bank Is the Seller (initial effects, in thousands of dollars)

Bank of Canada			
Assets		**Liabilities**	
Government securities	+100	Reserve deposits of Bank of Commerce	+100
Total	100	Total	100

Bank of Commerce			
Assets		**Liabilities**	
Government securities	−100	No change	
Reserve deposit	+100		
Required 0 Excess 100			
Total	0	Total	0

If the Bank of Canada buys the government security from a chartered bank (say, Bank of Commerce), no change takes place in the money stock at this initial stage. However, the Bank of Commerce now has a full $100,000 in excess reserves, which it can lend out.

$500,000, although the mechanics are slightly different. Table 13-2 shows the initial effects of an open market operation if the Bank of Canada buys the Treasury bill from the Canadian Imperial Bank of Commerce. The Bank of Commerce sends the Treasury bill to the Bank of Canada and gets a reserve deposit in the Bank of Canada in exchange. At this initial stage, no change has yet taken place in the money stock. But note that the Bank of Commerce now has a full $100,000 in excess reserves, since its total reserves have gone up by $100,000, while its deposit liabilities—and therefore its required reserves—have not changed. The Bank of Commerce can safely lend out the full $100,000 in excess reserves, creating a $100,000 demand deposit when it does so. Once again, the maximum deposit expansion is the series $100,000 + $80,000 + $64,000 + . . . , giving a total of $500,000.

In both examples of an open market purchase (tables 13-1 and 13-2), note that when the Bank of Canada acquires an asset (the government security), its liabilities also go up. This is scarcely surprising, since the balance sheet must balance. The increase in the Bank's liabilities takes the form of chartered bank deposits, which act as the reserves of the chartered banks. Thus, we have a fundamental rule:

When the Bank of Canada wants to increase chartered bank reserves and thus make possible an expansion of the money supply, it acquires assets.

Restrictive Open Market Operations

Just as the Bank of Canada purchases securities when it wants to increase the money supply, so it sells securities when it wants to decrease the money supply. The numbers on the balance sheets are the same as in tables 13-1 and 13-2, but the signs are the opposite.

However, an actual open market sale might lead to very tight monetary conditions. We live in a growing economy, in which productive capacity increases. It is appropriate that the money stock grow through time, in order to encourage aggregate demand to grow and keep the economy at full employment. Thus, restrictive policies by the Bank of Canada normally do not involve actual sales of securities. Rather, a *reduction in the rate of purchases of securities* aimed at reducing *the rate of growth* of the money stock generally provides monetary conditions that are as tight as the Bank wishes in its fight against inflation.

OPEN MARKET OPERATIONS AND INTEREST RATES

When the Bank of Canada goes on the market to buy government bonds or shorter-term securities, it increases the demand for these securities. As a result, it puts upward pressure on their prices.

There is an important relationship between security prices and interest rates, which may be clarified by looking at Treasury bills more closely. Unlike a government bond, which provides semiannual interest payments, a Treasury bill involves no such explicit interest payment. It simply represents a promise by the government to pay, say, $100,000 on a specific date, usually three months after the date of issue. The purchaser obtains a yield by purchasing the bill at a discount; that is, for less than the full $100,000 face value. For example, a buyer who pays $97,000 for a three-month bill gets back $3,000 more than the purchase price when the bill reaches maturity. Thus, the interest or yield on that bill is approximately 3% for the three-month period—that is, 12% per annum. (By convention, interest is quoted at an annual rate, even for securities with less than one year to maturity.)

Now, suppose that the Bank of Canada enters the market, bidding for bills and pushing up their price to $98,000. What is the gain of a purchaser who buys a bill at this price? Only $2,000, or about 2% for the three months; that is, 8% per annum. Thus, we see that:

Security prices and interest rates move *in opposite directions*. A "rise in the price of Treasury bills" (from $97,000 to $98,000 in our example) is just another way of saying "a fall in the interest rate on Treasury bills" (from about 12% to 8% in our example). Similarly, a fall in the price of securities involves a rise in the interest rate.

Thus, when the Bank of Canada purchases government securities on the open market and bids up their prices, it is thereby bidding down interest rates. The proposition that a rise in security prices means a fall in interest yields also holds for long-term bonds. (See Box 13-1).

Secondary Effects

The secondary effects of the open market purchase also work toward a reduction of interest rates. As chartered bank reserves rise, the banks will purchase securities and step up their lending activities. The purchase of securities once again tends to push up security prices and push down interest rates. And, in their eagerness to make additional loans, banks may reduce the interest rate they charge. Specifically, they may shave their **prime rate**.

> The *prime rate* is the interest rate charged by banks on their least risky loans.

Thus, an open market purchase by the Bank of Canada has three important, interrelated effects: (1) it increases the money stock; (2) it makes more funds available for the chartered banks to lend; and (3) it lowers interest rates. The way in which these three forces can stimulate aggregate demand are considered in detail in Chapter 14.

SALES AND PURCHASES OF FOREIGN CURRENCIES BY THE BANK OF CANADA

According to the Bank of Canada Act, one of the responsibilities of the Bank is to "control and protect the external value of the national monetary unit." ("External value" means the price of the Canadian dollar in terms of foreign monetary units such as the U.S. dollar or the Japanese yen. Such a price—of one currency in terms of another—is known as an **exchange rate**. For example, $1.00 (one Canadian dollar) = $0.75 (75 cents U.S.) is an exchange rate.)

In order to carry out this responsibility, the Bank of Canada buys or sells foreign currencies (particularly U.S. dollars) in the markets for foreign currencies. In Chapter 15, we will discuss in detail how exchange rates are determined, and how they are affected by the foreign exchange transactions of the Bank of Canada. However, the important point to be made here is that Bank purchases and sales of foreign currencies will

BOX 13-1

BOND PRICES AND INTEREST RATES

The relationship between bond prices and interest rates can be seen most easily by considering a *perpetuity*—that is, a bond that has no maturity date and is never paid off. It represents a commitment by the government of the issuing nation to pay, say, $80 per year forever. Just as the semiannual interest or coupon payments on an ordinary bond remain fixed regardless of what happens to market interest rates after the bond has been issued, so the commitment of the government to pay $80 per year forever to the holder of the perpetuity remains in force, regardless of what happens to current interest rates in the financial markets.

Like other bonds, perpetuities may be sold by their initial owners. A buyer willing to pay $1,000 for such a perpetuity would obtain an interest rate or yield of 8%; that is, $80 per year on the purchase price of $1,000. But if the price fell, and the buyer could get the perpetuity for $800, the annual $80 payment would provide a yield of 10%. Again, we see that a fall in the price of a security means a rise in the interest rate or yield that the security offers.

A bond with a specific maturity of, say, 10 years involves a much more complex calculation. As a background, note that if $100 is deposited in an account paying 10% per annum, the deposit will be worth $110 at the end of the first year. During the second year, 10% interest will be paid on this $110. That is, $11 interest will be added, raising the deposit to a total of $121 by the end of the second year.

This can be expressed:

$$\$100(1 + 0.10)^2 = \$121$$

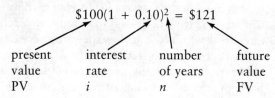

present value PV | interest rate i | number of years n | future value FV

In general, this can be rewritten:

$$PV(1 + i)^n = FV$$

This relationship is often written in the alternative form:

$$PV = \frac{FV}{(1 + i)^n}$$

In our example:

$$\$100 = \frac{\$121}{(1 + 0.10)^2}$$

This tells us that, if the interest rate is 10%, an asset that has a future value or payoff of $121 is worth $100 today.

For many assets, the payoff is strung out over many years. In other words, there are many terms on the right-hand side of the present value equation. For example, a bond with a ten-year maturity and coupon payments of $8 per year will have a payoff of $8 each year until the tenth year, when the owner receives a final payoff of $8 plus the face value of $100. If the market interest rate is, say, 9%, the present value of this bond (the price at which it can be bought or sold today) is calculated as follows:

$$PV = \frac{\$8}{1.09} + \frac{\$8}{(1.09)^2} + \frac{\$8}{(1.09)^3} +$$
$$\cdots + \frac{\$8 + \$100}{(1.09)^{10}} = \$93.58$$

Or, in general,

$$\text{Price (PV) of bond} = \frac{C}{1 + i} + \frac{C}{(1 + i)^2}$$
$$\cdots + \frac{C + \$100}{(1 + i)^n}$$

where C is the coupon payment.

From this equation, we can calculate the price if we know the rate of interest (i), or we can calculate the interest rate if we know the price of the bond. The higher the one, the lower the other. Thus, once again we see that the higher the price of bonds, the lower the interest rate.

influence chartered bank reserves and therefore the stock of money in Canada.

Suppose as an example that the Bank of Canada buys U.S.$100,000 at a price of C$1.40 per U.S. dollar, and that the seller is Abitibi-Price Inc. (Abitibi may have earned the U.S. dollars by exporting paper products to the United States.) The Bank pays for the U.S. currency by issuing a cheque for C$140,000 to Abitibi; this cheque is then deposited in Abitibi's chartered bank account with, say, the Royal Bank. The Royal Bank sends the cheque back to the Bank of Canada and its reserve deposit is increased by $140,000. If the reserve requirement is 20%, the Royal now has excess reserves of $112,000 (= $0.8 \times \$140,000$), and it can expand its lending. When it does this, it will create new demand deposits, and the money stock will expand through the process described in the previous section.

The effects of this transaction on the Canadian money stock are similar to the effects of a purchase by the Bank of Canada of $140,000 worth of Treasury bills (rather than foreign currency) from Abitibi: In either case, Abitibi's Canadian-dollar deposits increase by $140,000, and Abitibi's bank has $112,000 in excess reserves. In either case, there can be an increase in chartered bank lending, and the money supply can expand by a multiple of $140,000. Conversely, if the Bank of Canada were to sell foreign currency, the chartered banks would lose reserves, and the money supply would be reduced in the same way as when the Bank of Canada sells Treasury bills. We may therefore conclude:

When the Bank of Canada buys foreign currencies, the stock of money in Canada will increase in precisely the same way as it does when the Bank buys an equivalent amount of government securities. When the Bank sells foreign currencies, the money stock contracts in the same way as it does with an open market sale of government securities.

As we will discuss in detail in Chapter 15, the effects on the money supply of Bank of Canada sales and purchases of foreign currencies sometimes create a problem. The foreign currency transactions may be undertaken for the purpose of stabilizing exchange rates—that is, the external value of the Canadian dollar. But the resulting effects on the Canadian money supply may destabilize the domestic economy.

*A Bookkeeping Complication: The Exchange Fund Account

Even though the Bank of Canada sometimes buys and sells large amounts of foreign currencies, the Bank's balance sheet rarely shows any substantial sums of foreign currency assets. The reason for this is that Canada's foreign currency reserves are not held by the Bank of Canada, but by the federal government in the *Exchange Fund Account* (EFA). When the Bank of Canada buys and sells foreign currency in order to stabilize exchange rates, it technically does so on behalf of the federal government: When it buys foreign currency, the Bank immediately resells it to the EFA, and when the Bank sells foreign currency, the foreign funds come from the government's EFA reserves.

When the government is acquiring foreign currency reserves that have been bought for it by the Bank of Canada, how does it pay for these reserves? The answer is that *it generally pays by issuing an equivalent amount of government securities to the Bank*. Thus, when $100 million worth of foreign currency is bought by the Bank of Canada for the EFA, we can think of it as a transaction involving two steps:

1. The Bank of Canada buys $100 million worth of foreign currency. The $100 million in foreign currency is added to the asset side of the Bank's balance sheet; on the liability side of the balance sheet, the transaction results in an increase of chartered bank deposits with the Bank of Canada by $100 million, as explained previously. As chartered banks now have increased reserves, the money stock can expand.

2. The Bank of Canada then sells the foreign currency to the EFA, in return for $100 million in securities issued by the government. The Bank's foreign currency assets are decreased by $100 million, but $100 million in government securities is added to the Bank's assets. The Bank's liabilities are not affected in this step: Thus, step 2 does not affect chartered bank reserves or the money stock.

Table 13-3 shows the changes in the balance sheets of the Bank of Canada and the EFA when both steps have been completed.

Notice that the effect on chartered bank reserves, and therefore on the money stock, would have been

---

*Starred sections are optional. They may be omitted without loss of continuity.

Table 13-3
The EFA Acquires Foreign Currency Reserves
(millions of dollars)

Bank of Canada			
Assets		Liabilities	
Government securities	+100	Deposit of chartered banks	+100

Federal Government (EFA)			
Assets		Liabilities	
Foreign currencies	+100	Government securities	+100

When the Bank of Canada has bought $100 million in foreign currency, it immediately re-sells it to the EFA. The foreign currency disappears from the Bank's assets but is replaced by $100 million in new government securities.

the same even if step 2 had not taken place. The transaction between the Bank and the government is purely a matter of bookkeeping, and has no effect on the money stock or the rest of the economy. The effects on the economy of Bank of Canada sales and purchases of foreign currency would be exactly the same even if the EFA didn't exist and Canada's foreign exchange reserves were held by the Bank as part of its assets.

*TRANSFERS OF GOVERNMENT DEPOSITS

As we noted in Chapter 12, the Bank of Canada acts as the government's banker: the government maintains a substantial account with the Bank, and public revenues and expenditures are channelled through the government's account with the Bank of Canada. The government also maintains deposits in the chartered banks.

In its role as the government's principal bank, the Bank of Canada *can transfer government funds into or out of chartered banks*. It thereby has another powerful tool for influencing chartered bank reserves and the money stock. Suppose, for example, that the Bank of Canada wants to increase chartered bank reserves. It can do this by buying government securities in the open market, as explained earlier. As an alternative, the Bank may instead transfer part of the government's deposits with the Bank of Canada to the chartered

banks. When the Bank of Canada transfers, say, $10 million in government funds to the chartered banks, the banks receive $10 million in reserves, as shown in Table 13-4.

The transfer of government deposits does not directly increase the money supply: Remember that deposits owned by the government are not counted as part of the money supply, whether they are held with the Bank of Canada or the chartered banks. But it does create excess reserves in the chartered banks. (For example, if the required reserve ratio is 20%, the chartered banks in Table 13-4 now have excess reserves of $8 million). As a result, the chartered banks can expand their lending, and create new demand deposits in exactly the same way as described in the section on open market operations. Thus, by transferring government deposits to the chartered banks, the Bank of Canada can cause the money stock to increase. Conversely, if the Bank wants to decrease the money stock, it can do so by transferring government deposits from the chartered banks to the government's account with the Bank of Canada. This will reduce chartered bank reserves, forcing them to reduce their lending and thereby reduce the stock of deposit money.[1]

[1] A comprehensive discussion of government deposit transfers and other tools of monetary policy can be found in Thomas J. Courchene, *Money, Inflation and the Bank of Canada: An Analysis of Canadian Monetary Policy from 1970 to Early 1975* (Montreal: C.D. Howe Research Institute, 1976).

Table 13-4
The Bank of Canada Transfers Government
Deposits to the Chartered Banks
(millions of dollars)

Bank of Canada		
Assets	**Liabilities**	
(No change)	Deposits of the federal government	− 10
	Deposits of chartered banks	+ 10

Chartered Banks		
Assets	**Liabilities**	
Deposits with Bank of Canada + 10	Deposits of the federal government	+ 10

As the Bank of Canada transfers $10 million of government deposits to the chartered banks, chartered bank reserves increase by $10 million. They now have excess reserves and can expand their loans.

While deposit transfers can be used to control the money stock, it could equally well be controlled by open market operations. Why, then, does the Bank sometimes use government deposit transfers rather than open market operations? The answer may be that the Bank may want to influence the money stock without bringing about sharp changes in securities prices and interest rates. Suppose, for example, that the Bank wants to *reduce* the money stock. If it tries to do this by selling government securities, the prices of securities will fall and interest rates rise, as we discussed above. But if the Bank instead reduces the money stock by transferring government deposits from the chartered banks, it will not directly affect the market for securities: There will be no direct impact on securities prices or interest rates.

However, most economists believe that in the end, the effects of the deposit-transfer method will be similar to the effects of open market operations. While the deposit transfers do not directly influence securities prices and interest rates, they will do so indirectly: As chartered banks lose reserves, for example, they will begin to sell securities, thereby depressing security prices and raising interest rates. And the banks may increase the interest rates they charge on loans, in order to cut back on lending. In other words, the indirect effects of controlling the money stock through deposit transfers will be similar to the secondary effects of open market operations which we described in the previous section. Thus, economists look on the deposit transfer method as essentially equivalent to open market operations as a tool for controlling the money stock.

CHANGES IN THE BANK RATE

The Bank of Canada acts not only as the government's bank, but also as the banker of the chartered banks. Just as chartered banks lend to the general public, so the Bank of Canada may lend to chartered banks. In exchange for such a loan (or "advance") from the Bank of Canada, the chartered bank gives the Bank of Canada its promissory note. The interest rate on these advances is known as the **Bank Rate.**

> The *Bank Rate* is the interest rate charged by the Bank of Canada on its loans to chartered banks.

In Chapter 12, we saw how a chartered bank provides its customer with a bank deposit when it makes a loan. The transaction between the Bank of Canada and a chartered bank is similar. When the Bank of

Table 13-5
The Bank of Canada Grants a Loan
(thousands of dollars)

Assets		Liabilities	
Chartered bank borrowings	+100	Reserve deposits of chartered bank	+100
Total	100	Total	100

When the Bank of Canada lends to a chartered bank, bank reserves are increased.

Canada grants an advance to a chartered bank, it increases that bank's reserve deposit in the Bank of Canada, as shown in Table 13-5. Thus, *such loans add to the total reserves of the banking system.*

Unlike open market operations, Bank of Canada lending is done at the initiative of the chartered banks, rather than the Bank of Canada. However, the Bank of Canada is able to influence the amount that the chartered banks borrow. For example, if the Bank of Canada increases the Bank Rate, borrowing will become more expensive for the chartered banks. Thus, they will try to avoid borrowing; rather, they will try to meet their required reserve ratios in other ways, such as selling securities or calling in loans. Unlike borrowing from the central bank, these alternative ways do not increase the total reserves of the chartered banking system. Therefore, an increase in the Bank Rate is a restrictive move: It discourages borrowing, holds down total chartered bank reserves, and restricts the total quantity of money in the system.

From time to time, the Bank of Canada has adjusted the Bank Rate as one of its tools of monetary policy—for example, in the decade following World War II, and again in the period from 1962 to 1980. Particularly in the earlier period, Bank Rate changes took place infrequently, and when they were announced, they were interpreted as strong indicators of Bank policy. (That is, an increase was important not only because of its direct effect in discouraging chartered bank borrowing, but as a signal of the Bank of Canada's intention of following a tighter policy.)

At other times, however, the Bank of Canada has not used Bank Rate policy as an active tool of monetary policy. Between 1956 and 1962, the Bank of Canada had a *floating Bank Rate*. That is, it continuously adjusted the Bank Rate to keep it at a fixed margin (1/4 of 1%) above the market rate of interest on Trea-

sury bills. Since 1980, the Bank of Canada has again used a floating rate. Thus, even though the weekly changes in the Bank Rate are prominently announced in newspapers and on television, they do not in themselves reflect changes in the Bank of Canada's policy. Rather, they reflect an adjustment of the Bank Rate to what has already happened in the market for Treasury bills. (Of course, what happens in this market may depend on Bank of Canada sales and purchases of Treasury bills—that is, on the Bank of Canada's open market operations.)

Because the Bank Rate is kept at a *penalty rate*—that is, it is kept above market interest rates—chartered banks have an incentive not to borrow. In practice, Bank of Canada loans to the chartered banks have normally been very small and of short duration. Thus, a penalty Bank Rate is a way for the Bank of Canada to back up the constraints which it sets on chartered bank reserves through its open market policies: The chartered banks do not escape discipline by borrowing from the Bank of Canada.

Loans to Investment Dealers

In addition to the chartered banks, there is another group of firms that has access to credit from the Bank of Canada: the *authorized investment dealers*. These are firms that buy and sell short-term money market securities, and finance a large part of their securities holdings with *call loans* from the chartered banks. Since the chartered banks can demand repayment of these loans ("call" the loans) at very short notice (usually one day), the banks will normally lend out any excess reserves they have to the dealers. As soon as they need more reserves to meet the legal reserve requirement, they can simply call the loans. The dealers will then have two options: They can either sell some of their securities in order to get the funds to repay their loans from the banks, or they can borrow from the Bank of Canada. If they borrow from the Bank of Canada to repay the chartered banks, the reserves of the chartered banks will increase (just as they increase when the chartered banks themselves borrow from the Bank of Canada): The dealers will repay their chartered bank loans with cheques drawn on the Bank of Canada. However, the rate charged by the Bank of Canada on loans to investment dealers is usually very close to the Bank Rate, and has always been held above the Treasury bill rate. This means that if the dealers hold Treasury bills or other assets with similar rates of interest, they have an incentive to repay their loans to the Bank of Canada as quickly as possible.

Bank of Canada lending to chartered banks and investment dealers has sometimes been criticized. For example, it has been argued that it reduces the effectiveness of open market operations. Suppose, for example, that the Bank wants to restrain the growth of the money stock. To do this it may sell securities in the open market, causing chartered banks to lose reserves. However, by borrowing from the Bank of Canada, the chartered banks may replenish their reserves. Thus, the Bank of Canada with its left hand (loans to chartered banks) may pump back the reserves it is extracting with its right hand (open market operations). Bank of Canada loans to investment dealers have a similar effect.

In response, it is argued that advances to chartered banks act as a safety valve, allowing the Bank of Canada to follow tighter policies than it would otherwise dare. If there were no lending of this kind, the Bank would have to tread lightly in restrictive open market operations, taking care not to put too much pressure on the chartered banks. Even though Bank of Canada lending involves some slippage, it may indirectly make it possible to pursue tighter policies than in the absence of such lending: the Bank can safely push harder on the open market lever.[2]

---

[2]In the United States, where loans by the Federal Reserve are known as "discounting" and the "Bank Rate" is known as the "discount rate," the discount rate has from time to time been below market rates of interest. This has led to the criticism that discounting involves hidden subsidies to the "commercial banks" (the U.S. equivalent of chartered banks). This criticism was particularly strong in 1974 when the discount rate was far below most short-term interest rates, and when a single New York bank (Franklin National) borrowed over $1 billion from the Fed.

CHANGES IN RESERVE REQUIREMENTS

The quantity of deposits that the chartered banks can create depends on the size of their reserves and on the required reserve ratio. In the last chapter, we saw, specifically, that deposits can be created up to the amount of the reserves times $1/R$. Thus, an *increase* in R (the required reserve ratio) will *decrease* the amount of deposits that can be created.

Before 1967, the Bank of Canada had the legal power to change the required reserve ratio within certain limits. Clearly, this is a very powerful tool. With total reserves of, say, $100 million, an increase in the required reserve ratio from 10% to 12.5% would reduce the maximum quantity of deposit money from $1,000 million to $800 million. In part because this tool would have a very strong impact on financial markets, and also because other tools such as open market operations or transfers of government deposits already give the Bank a high degree of control over the stock of money, the power to change the reserve ratio was never used by the Bank. When the Bank Act was revised in 1967, the power was therefore abolished, and between 1967 and 1980, required reserves were fixed at 12% of demand deposits, and 4% on notice deposits. However, the 1980 Bank Act revision provided for a gradual reduction in the required ratios to 10% and 3%; and since 1985 the ratios have been fixed at those levels. Note that reduced reserve ratios work to increase chartered bank profits: The banks can hold less reserves (on which they earn no interest) and more loans and other assets (on which they do earn interest). (The effect of changes in reserve requirements on chartered bank profits may also be one explanation why the Bank of Canada never chose to use this tool even when it had the power to do so.)

Secondary Reserve Ratios

Since 1967, the Bank of Canada has had the power to require the chartered banks to hold a specified portion (between 0% and 12% of their Canadian-dollar deposit liabilities) in the form of *secondary reserves*. Secondary reserves are defined as the sum of their holdings of Treasury bills, loans to investment dealers, and cash reserves in excess of required reserves. The Bank of Canada made use of this tool on several occasions in the 1970s. (Because the banks earn interest on most secondary reserves, they find this tool less objectionable than the primary reserve requirement.)

What happens to the stock of money when the Bank of Canada increases the secondary reserve ratio? The answer is that nothing much is likely to happen. The chartered banks may be forced to buy more Treasury bills, thus increasing their secondary reserves, by selling long-term securities that do not qualify as a secondary reserve asset. Such transactions do not affect the public's bank deposits. Thus, there will be no effect on the stock of money.

Most economists now believe that the most important way in which the Bank of Canada can influence the economy is by controlling the stock of money. Thus, they tend to be skeptical about the usefulness of changes in the secondary reserve ratio as a tool of monetary policy: Changes in the ratio may force the chartered banks to rearrange their assets, but they do not affect the stock of money.

OTHER MONETARY TOOLS: MORAL SUASION

The Bank of Canada may reinforce its control over the monetary and financial system with *moral suasion*— that is, requests to chartered banks and other financial institutions that they take certain actions, or refrain from others.

The Bank of Canada has exerted moral suasion on many occasions. During the 1950s, for example, it requested the cooperation of the chartered banks in limiting the growth rate of their total lending, and of their long-term loans to private borrowers. At various times, there have been requests to the banks to increase their lending to specific groups of customers, such as small businesses or borrowers in the less prosperous areas of Canada (for example, the Maritime provinces).

The Bank also has tried at times to influence interest rates through the use of moral suasion. One famous example was the *Winnipeg Agreement* of 1972. The Bank of Canada had become concerned about what it considered to be overly aggressive competition between chartered banks for large corporate deposits. In their efforts to attract these deposits, the banks had been offering such high interest rates that foreign companies had begun transferring large amounts of their funds from U.S. banks to Canadian banks. Many Canadian firms were also selling other assets in order to increase their deposits, and this led to unsettled conditions in the markets for these other assets. To stabilize markets and reduce the inflow into Canada of foreign funds, the Bank of Canada met with representatives of the chartered banks, and an arrangement was worked out under which the banks agreed to limit the interest rates offered on corporate term and notice deposits to 5.5%. (The Winnipeg Agreement remained in force throughout 1973 and 1974.)

On occasion, the Bank of Canada and the government have tried to use moral suasion as a way of dealing with disturbances in the financial system, especially when fast action has been needed to prevent a problem from developing into a major crisis. A recent example was the government's attempt to persuade the major chartered banks to contribute to the effort to save the Canadian Commercial Bank from bankruptcy in March 1985. On that occasion, the strategy was not successful: the CCB did go under in September of the same year (see Box 13-2).

In this and other episodes, moral suasion was used to persuade chartered banks to do certain things that they would otherwise have preferred not to do, such as increasing their lending for house building, limiting their loans to large firms, or lending money to a bank that was expected to go bankrupt. But, as the critics of moral suasion point out, there is no reason to expect that all banks will respond with equal willingness to the persuasion of the Bank of Canada or the government. The result may then be that only some banks will, for example, reduce their loans to large firms. This may mean that the large firms will switch their business to the other banks. Thus, the chartered banks that try to "act responsibly" and obey the instructions of the Bank of Canada may end up with less business and lower profits. Or again, those chartered banks that agreed to participate in the 1985 attempt to rescue the CCB ended up with a potential loss of $60 million; those that did not participate lost nothing. For these sorts of reasons, some people argue that moral suasion is often either ineffective or unfair, or both. Thus they believe that the Bank of Canada should concentrate its efforts on achieving effective control over the money stock through its general tools (most notably, open market operations). Moral suasion

Table 13-6
Balance Sheet of the Bank of Canada, December 1985
(billions of dollars)

Assets		Liabilities		
1. Government of Canada securities	15.7	5. Notes outstanding		16.7
2. Loans to chartered banks		6. Deposits		2.9
and investment dealers	3.5	Chartered banks	(2.2)	
3. All other assets	1.9	Government	(0.3)	
4. Total assets	21.1	Foreign and other	(0.4)	
		7. All other liabilities		
		and net worth		1.5
		8. Total liabilities		21.1

SOURCE: *Bank of Canada Review*.

should be used only temporarily as a device to deal with short-term disturbances in financial markets, and not to do the job of the general policy instruments. Furthermore, other objectives such as stimulating the housing industry or the small business sector are political ones and are therefore more appropriately dealt with by the government and Parliament. Control of the overall quantity of money and credit is difficult enough, and should not be complicated by asking the Bank of Canada to perform other quite different functions such as controlling how credit will be allocated among different sectors of the economy.

THE BALANCE SHEET OF THE BANK OF CANADA

Some actions of the Bank of Canada do not show up directly on its balance sheet (for example, moral suasion, or changes in secondary reserve requirements). But other actions do—for example, its open market operations. Thus, the balance sheet of the Bank of Canada can provide insights into some of the Bank's activities.

The balance sheet of the Bank of Canada is shown in Table 13-6. Two entries on the right-hand side are particularly worth noting. First is the large amount of Bank of Canada notes outstanding. This is the result of the public's desire to hold more currency as its overall holdings of money have increased. (While open market operations and other Bank policies affect the *amount* of money in the economy, the public is free to

choose the *form* in which it wants to hold its money.) When the public withdraws currency from the chartered banks, these banks in turn can get more from the Bank of Canada by withdrawing some of their reserve deposits.)[3]

The second noteworthy item on the right-hand side is the small net worth of the Bank of Canada. If the Bank were a private corporation, this would be cause for alarm. The slightest reversal in its fortunes might cause the value of its assets to dip below the amount of its liabilities, wiping out its net worth and threatening bankruptcy. But the Bank is no ordinary corporation. It is a part of the government, and a very special part, as it has the power to create money. Because of this special power, the Bank has an assured high flow of profits, and need not worry about building up its net worth. (The Bank of Canada is very profitable because it earns interest on the large holdings of government

---

[3]When the public decides to hold more currency, chartered bank reserves are reduced; the process is the opposite of the one described in Chapter 12, where a $10,000 deposit set the stage for a multiple expansion of bank deposits.

The large amount of Bank of Canada notes outstanding means that our earlier warning (in Chapter 12, in the "Two Complications" section) should be re-emphasized. As the money stock is increased, there is a large leakage of currency from bank reserves into the hands of the public. As a consequence, actual money creation following an open market operation is generally much less than given in the formula for the maximum increase in deposits:

$$D = \frac{1}{R}$$

BOX 13-2

DOUBLE FLIPS AND LOAN WORKOUTS: ARE THE REGULATORS KEEPING UP?

In the United States, government regulation of financial institutions is an issue that has always been high on the political agenda. On the one hand, many have called for more regulation, to reduce the frequency of failures among banks and other financial institutions. Others have opposed this call: They have seen regulation as something that has tended to inhibit competition, and that has made it hard for businessmen to attract capital to finance risky but potentially profitable investment projects.

In Canada, there were no bank failures between the 1920s and the mid-1980s. (The last time a bank failed before 1985 was in 1923, when the Toronto-based Home Bank went under, following large losses on bad loans.) Thus few people saw any need for strengthening the existing regulatory legislation, or tightening the relatively loose and informal system of enforcement that had evolved over the years. In comparison with the U.S. context, some economists have argued that, if anything, the existing regulatory framework is too restrictive, discouraging entry of new firms and competition in the financial system. (Partly in response to this criticism, the 1980 Bank Act revision included provisions that gave foreign banks direct access to the Canadian market.)

In reply, however, the defenders of the existing system of regulation could point to several signs that competition was alive and well in the Canadian financial system. In Alberta, for example, the dominant position of the big Eastern chartered banks was being challenged in the mid-1970s by two newly founded chartered banks, the Canadian Commercial Bank and the Northland Bank. In Toronto, entrepreneur Leonard Rosenberg was aggressively expanding his Greymac Trust Company; ultimately, his aim was to merge several trust companies and a bank, to form a giant new financial institution that would be able to compete head to head with the dominant chartered banks.

Starting in the early 1980s, it gradually became clear that there might be severe weaknesses in the regulatory system. In late 1982, both the federal and provincial governments began looking more closely at Rosenberg's affairs. The federal government was concerned about the attempts of Rosenberg and his associates to take control of the Canadian Commercial Bank, in violation of "the spirit" of the Bank Act provisions intended to prevent an individual or firm from controlling more than one financial institution. The Ontario provincial government became involved after Rosenberg arranged a $500 million real estate transaction (that he estimated yielded him a $43 million profit): It appeared that the deal might have violated a regulatory provision that limits the amount that a trust company is allowed to lend for financing any one transaction. (The province was interested in the deal for another reason as well: It involved a "double flip," that is, a sale and subsequent repurchase at a higher price, of a large apartment complex, undertaken primarily for the purpose of making it possible to get regulatory approval to raise rents for the apartments.) In fact the parties to the deal had found a disarmingly simple way of circumventing the regulation limiting the amount that any one trust company could lend to finance a transaction: Technically, the money was lent to 50 separate companies, each one handling one-fiftieth of the entire deal.

After examining the books, an investigator appointed by the Ontario government concluded that the money of the depositors in Rosenberg's trust companies was in danger, and in January 1983, the provincial government simply took over Greymac and two other trust companies controlled by Rosenberg and his associates. The lawsuits resulting from this action had not yet been settled in late 1985.

That there were problems at the Canadian Commercial Bank was known to the federal government as early as 1982, when the office of the inspector general of banks became worried about the extent to which the CCB had concentrated its lending in the risky real estate business, and in the energy sector, which was being severely hurt by the weakening international market for oil. The problems were compounded when a California bank, in which the CCB had earlier bought a controlling interest, began to have difficulties in 1983. In early 1985, the CCB was faced with a loss of about $90 million on its American holdings, and it was clear that it was going to have trouble with many of its Canadian loans as well. (Some of the potential losses were being concealed by giving loans a "workout": lending more money to a borrower in trouble so as to avoid having to explicitly write off the original loans.)

In an attempt to stave off bankruptcy, the CCB turned to Ottawa for help. In March 1985, on the recommendation of the inspector general of banks, the federal government persuaded the six largest chartered banks, as well as the governments of Alberta and British Columbia, to contribute to a $255 million effort to rescue the CCB. The effort failed. In early September, after nervous depositors had withdrawn more than $1.5 billion from the CCB, the federal government ordered its liquidation. Later in 1985, the government stated its intention to liquidate a second Alberta bank, the Northland Bank, that faced problems similar to those of the CCB.

In an interview with *Maclean's* magazine, William Kennett, the inspector general of banks, defended the actions of his officials in the CCB/Northland affairs. In this interview, Kennett referred to the "limited powers" of his department, and the fact that it has "traditionally relied on 'moral suasion' (rather than compulsion) to convince companies to change what it thinks are unsafe business practices".

Courtesy Canapress Photo Service

Kennett also told *Maclean's* "that government banking regulators have traditionally left detailed examination of accounting transactions and valuations in the auditors' hands" rather than undertaking evaluations of their own.

The final cost of the CCB/Northland failures will be high. The Canada Deposit Insurance Corporation is reported to be responsible for some $420 million in guarantees to insured depositors. In addition, in a controversial move, the federal government voluntarily undertook to reimburse unsecured depositors; this could potentially involve a cost of as much as $875 million. In another ironic twist, the six chartered banks that were persuaded by the government to commit funds in the abortive attempt to shore up the CCB in March of 1985 have threatened to sue the government to retrieve the $60 million they stand to lose from the CCB's failure. (The banks argue that they were not given an accurate picture of the CCB's status when they agreed to join the rescue effort.) Another creditor, finally, is the Bank of Canada: As depositors withdrew funds from the troubled banks, the Bank of Canada ended up lending the two banks as much as $1.8 billion before the government pulled the plug.

In the wake of the Rosenberg affair and the CCB/Northland failures, there were many calls for strengthened regulation of banks and trust companies. Barbara McDougall, Minister of State for Finance in the Mulroney government, quickly made proposals for reforms that would make it possible for regulators to intervene more forcefully when they felt that a financial institution was making decisions that were threatening its solvency.

Ironically, the actions of the federal government in these affairs were also criticized for being too interventionist. By raising the limit on insured deposits to $60,000 in the middle of the Rosenberg affair, and by unilaterally offering to protect uninsured depositors in the CCB and the Northland Bank, the government reduced depositors' incentive to check the reputation of institutions like the CCB and Northland, which were trying to attract funds by paying higher interest rates than others. In the words of Toronto Dominion's president Robert Korthals, this action "says that people who have taken imprudent risks are smart and those who have taken lower rates are the fools." As a result, the government may also have discouraged the managers of financial institutions from being conservative in their lending practices. The consequence of this, the critics charge, may be more non-performing loans and more instability in the financial system.

securities on the asset side, while it pays no interest on most of its liabilities—in particular, chartered bank reserve deposits and Bank of Canada notes). Instead of building up a large net worth, the Bank simply turns over its profits to the federal government.

On the asset side of the Bank of Canada's balance sheet, Government of Canada securities are by far the largest entry; these securities have been accumulated through past open market operations. Chartered bank borrowings and loans to investment dealers were $3.5 billion at the end of 1985. Normally, these items are very small, although they occasionally shoot up when the chartered banking system as a whole is short on reserves. The $3.5 billion worth of such loans in 1985 represents an exceptionally large amount, however, and have a special explanation: They were a part of the Bank of Canada's efforts to avert the failure of the CCB and Northland Banks (Box 13-2).

WHAT BACKS OUR MONEY?

Money is debt. The largest component of the money stock (namely, bank deposits) is debt of the chartered banks. And Bank of Canada notes—the currency of everyday use—are liabilities of the Bank of Canada.

In a sense, the money supply is backed by the assets of the banking system. Bank deposits are backed by the loans, bonds, and reserves held by the chartered banks. And Bank of Canada notes are backed by the assets of the Bank, mainly Canadian government securities. What, in turn, backs the government securities? The government's promise to pay, based in the first instance on its ability to tax, but in the final analysis on its ability to borrow newly created money from the Bank of Canada or to print money directly. (Recall the section in Chapter 11 entitled: "Can the Government Go Broke?")

Clearly, we have gone in a circle. Currency is backed with government debt; and government debt is ultimately backed by the ability of the federal authorities to print more currency. In a sense, the whole game is played with mirrors; money is money because the government says it is. Until a few years ago, Bank of Canada notes boldly proclaimed that "the Bank of Canada will pay to the bearer on demand" the face value of the note. And what would happen if an individual submitted a $1 bill and demanded payment? He or she would receive another $1 bill in exchange. This does not make much sense, and the bold proclamation has now been eliminated from Bank of Canada notes. Now, we can say simply: A dollar is a dollar is a dollar.

What, then, determines the value of a Bank of Canada note? Dollar bills have value because of (1) their relative scarcity compared to the demand for them, and (2) their general acceptability. So long as the Bank of Canada keeps the supply of money in reasonable balance with the demand for it, money retains its value even though it has no explicit backing with precious metal or any other tangible commodity.

Dollar bills are generally acceptable by such diverse people as the taxi driver, the house painter, and the dentist. They all know they can turn around and buy other goods and services with the dollar bills. In part, general acceptability is a matter of convention (as in the case of cigarettes in the POW camp). But convention and habit are reinforced by the status of currency as *legal tender*. Creditors *must* accept dollar bills in payment of a debt. (Coins are also legal tender, but only up to reasonable limits. The electric utility company is not obliged to accept 4,562 pennies if a customer offers them in payment for a bill of $45.62.)

> *Legal tender* is the item or items that creditors must accept in payment of debts.

The Canada Deposit Insurance Corporation

But how about bank deposits? What protects their role as part of the money stock? Unlike currency, bank deposits are not legal tender. A gas station is not obliged to accept a personal cheque, and usually won't do so.

People are willing to hold money in the form of bank deposits because of the convenience of paying many types of bills by cheque, and because they are confident that they can get currency for the deposits when they want it. But what assurance do depositors have of actually being able to get $100 in currency for every $100 they hold in bank deposits?

The first assurance lies in the assets of the banks—their reserves and interest-bearing loans and securities. If a bank finds that people are withdrawing more than they are depositing, it may cover the difference by selling securities on the financial markets, or using the proceeds of its loans or bonds as they come due. But bank assets may not always be enough; in the United States, for example, they proved to be woefully inadequate during the Depression of the 1930s. As the economy collapsed, many businesses could not repay their bank loans, and the value of bank assets shrank. As their assets fell to less than their deposit liabilities, the banks were driven into bankruptcy, and many depositors suffered heavy losses.

This situation clearly was dangerous because bank runs are contagious. In early 1933, the contagion spread like wildfire, and the U.S. banking system collapsed. In order to prevent a repetition of the 1930s, an important additional backing was therefore provided for bank depositors. The U.S. government set up the Federal Deposit Insurance Corporation (FDIC) to insure bank deposits up to a sizeable limit.

Even though the Canadian banking system has generally been much more stable than the U.S. system throughout most of this century, Canada nevertheless followed the U.S. example, and since 1967, deposits in Canadian chartered banks and trust companies have been insured through the *Canada Deposit Insurance Corporation* (CDIC). The maximum amount covered per deposit has been changed several times; in the mid-1980s the limit was $60,000 per deposit.

In return for the insurance coverage that it provides, banks and trust companies pay premiums to the CDIC, and part of the backing for the deposit insurance consists in the premium reserves that the CDIC has accumulated over the years. In addition, however, the CDIC is authorized to borrow as much as it needs from the federal government, so that, indirectly, the insurance is in fact backed by the government.

In the mid-1980s, the system of deposit insurance came under renewed debate. As Box 13-2 explains in more detail, some critics of the system argued that the existence of insurance had made it easier for institutions like the Ontario trust companies controlled by Leonard Rosenberg, or the Canadian Commercial Bank and the Northland Bank in Alberta, to attract deposits with which to finance the kind of speculative real estate deals that ultimately got them into trouble. According to this view, putting stricter limits on the extent to which deposits are insured would reduce the flow of deposits to institutions engaged in these sorts of practices, and thus reduce the amount of funds wasted on speculative ventures that ultimately fail. Thus, while everyone agrees that some type of deposit insurance is needed (to help prevent the kind of financial instability that contributed to the Depression in the 1930s), the events of the mid-1980s brought attention to the problems that may arise if too much insurance is provided, and reform of the system of deposit insurance moved higher on the political agenda.

Why Not Gold?

There is an obvious problem with *fiat money*—that is, money that is money solely because the government says it is. The government or central bank can create such money at will. What, then, is to restrain the authorities from creating and spending money recklessly, generating runaway inflation?

It is this question that provided a rationale for the *gold standard* to which many countries adhered prior to World War I, and which was briefly resurrected during the interwar period. If the currency issued by the government and the central bank is convertible into gold, the authorities will not be able to create money recklessly. Like the goldsmith of old, they will have to keep a gold backing equal to a reasonable fraction of their currency liabilities.

> A country is on the *gold standard* when its currency is convertible into gold; that is, when the government and/or central bank stands ready to buy or sell gold at a fixed price (for example, 1 ounce of gold = $20.00). When a country is on the gold standard, gold coins may circulate as part of the money stock.

How did the monetary system function under the gold standard? The system formed a large inverted pyramid built on a base of gold. On the base of its gold

holdings, a central bank could build a structure of deposits and currency, the maximum size of which depended on the gold reserves that the central bank kept. This structure, in turn, formed the base for an even larger superstructure of chartered bank deposits, the maximum size of which depended on the required reserve ratio of banks (Figure 13-1).

While the gold standard fulfills its objective of restraining reckless money creation, it has two serious flaws. First, the quantity of money tends to fluctuate as a result of changes in the quantity of gold. When the central bank buys gold flowing into the country from abroad—or from domestic gold mines—the effects are similar to those of an open market operation: Chartered bank reserves increase. Moreover, the gold improves the reserve position of the central bank itself. Therefore, the central bank is able to lend more to the chartered banks or buy more government securities on the open market. Thus, chartered bank reserves can be increased in this indirect way as well. Consequently, a gold inflow can lead to a large increase in the money stock. Similarly, a gold outflow can have a very powerful contractionary effect. There is no assurance that a monetary system that responds to gold flows in this manner will provide the quantity of money needed for a full-employment, non-inflationary economy.

The second difficulty is even more severe. Because of the fractional-reserve system applying to both the chartered banks and the central bank under the gold standard, any tendency for the public to demand items lower in the pyramid has a powerful contractionary effect on the size of the money stock. We saw in Chapter 12 how your deposit of $10,000 in currency permitted a monetary expansion; a withdrawal of currency by the public likewise has a contractionary effect. But if the public withdraws gold (for example, during a depression), it is withdrawing the item at the base of the whole pyramid. In this case, the contractionary effect is particularly great: Reserves have been removed from the central bank itself, and the bank must take restrictive steps (such as reducing its loans to chartered banks) in order to meet its own required reserve ratios. In short, the money supply shrinks as part of the gold base is withdrawn.

During the Great Depression, people became frightened as unemployment and business bankruptcies shot upward. Being frightened, they tried to get their assets in the safest form possible. In the United States, they withdrew currency from banks and switched from paper currency into gold. (Canada had effectively left the gold standard already in 1928, but the United States stayed on the gold standard even while its economy collapsed.) The U.S. monetary system thus came under strong contractionary pressures when the economy was already headed downward. When things became bad enough, the rules of the game were changed:

The U.S. government suspended the convertibility of currency into gold in 1933.

The problem with the gold standard, then, is that it does not provide a *steady* and *measured* restraint. Rather, it exerts restraint in the form of a *threat of disaster*: If too much money is issued, there will be a crisis of confidence, a switch by the public away from paper money and into gold, and a collapse of the monetary structure. So long as the authorities are lucky (with gold flowing in from mines or from foreign countries), and so long as they follow farsighted policies

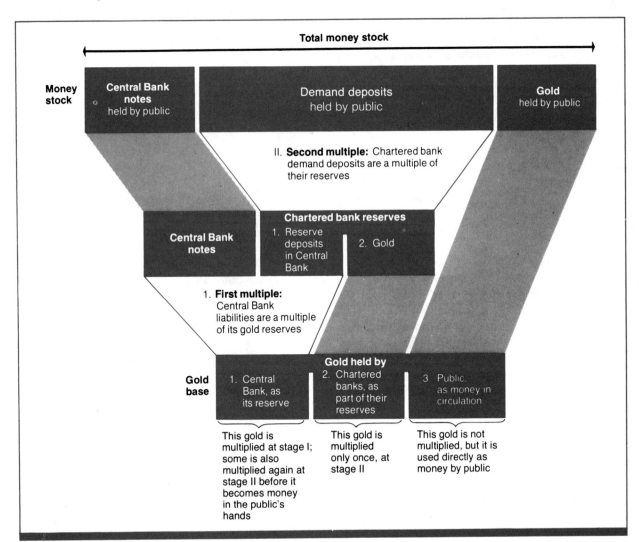

Figure 13-1 The gold standard pyramid (simplified).

aimed at avoiding any crisis of confidence, it is possible that the system will work reasonably well. But in the period between the two world wars, the authorities were neither farsighted nor lucky. The gold standard added to the disaster of the 1930s. Any system that "kicks an economy when it is down" is basically destructive and should be discarded.

The history of the gold standard, and, in particular, the role of gold in the Great Depression in the United States and Europe, has become an issue of some importance in the last several years. With the apparent unwillingness or inability of governments and central banks to exercise enough restraint to control inflation, some observers, especially in the United States, have concluded that the only way to restore a sound monetary system is to re-establish some link to gold, and thus impose an external constraint on monetary policy.

While we grapple with the intractable inflation of our time, we should be aware of the problems in some of the proposed solutions—including a return to the gold standard. In particular, we should remember how the gold standard contributed to the Depression of the 1930s. And we might remember the words of British economist D.H. Robertson, who, looking back at the economic wreckage of the period between the two world wars, wrote:[4]

> The value of a yellow metal, originally chosen as money because it tickled the fancy of savages, is clearly a chancy and irrelevant thing on which to base the value of our money and the stability of our industrial system.

[4]D.H. Robertson, *Money*, rev. ed. (Cambridge: Cambridge University Press, 1948), p. 144.

KEY POINTS

1. The Bank of Canada is responsible for controlling the quantity of money in the Canadian economy. It has several major quantitative tools at its command:
   (a) open market operations
   (b) transfers of government deposits
   (c) changes in the Bank Rate

2. While the Bank of Canada is owned by the government, it has been organized in such a way that it has considerable freedom from political influence in its day-to-day operations. However, the government retains ultimate responsibility for the Bank's policy: If there were a fundamental disagreement between the government and the governor of the Bank of Canada, the governor would be obliged to resign.

3. When the Bank of Canada purchases securities on the open market, it creates chartered bank reserves; when it sells securities, it eliminates reserves. Changes in reserves affect the amount of deposit money that chartered banks can create.

4. A purchase of securities by the Bank of Canada tends to bid up security prices. When this happens, the yields (interest rates) on securities are bid down.

5. Purchases and sales of foreign currencies are sometimes made by the Bank of Canada in order to stabilize the exchange rates between the Canadian dollar and foreign currencies. Foreign currency sales and purchases by the Bank of Canada affect the money stock in the same way as sales and purchases of government securities.

6. The Bank of Canada can also influence the money stock by transferring federal government deposits between itself and the chartered banks. Such transfers create or eliminate chartered bank reserves and thereby affect the money stock.

7. An increase in the Bank Rate discourages borrowing by the chartered banks and investment dealers from the Bank of Canada. Such a decrease in borrowing reduces chartered bank reserves. In recent years, the Bank Rate has

been floating: It has been tied to the Treasury bill rate, and has not been used actively as an instrument of Bank policy.

8. Less important tools of the Bank of Canada include *moral suasion*. For example, the Bank may try to persuade chartered banks to restrict certain types of lending, or increase credit to particular groups of borrowers.

9. In the final analysis, there is nothing backing our currency: "A dollar is a dollar." Money retains its value because it is scarce. Even though it doesn't cost the Bank of Canada anything to create reserve deposits, and the costs of printing currency are small, the Bank does not create money recklessly. If it did so, there would be wild inflation.

10. Under the old gold standard, there was a restraint on irresponsible money creation. But the gold standard had two enormous defects. First, the amount of money that could be created on the available gold base was not necessarily the quantity needed for full employment with stable prices. The second defect was even worse. In a crisis of confidence, people exchanged other forms of money for gold. This caused a sharp contraction of the money supply. Because of its defects, the gold standard was abolished.

KEY CONCEPTS

open market operation	Bank of Canada board of directors	legal tender
foreign currencies	governor of the Bank of Canada	acceptability
exchange rate stabilization	Treasury bill	fiat money
transfers of government deposits	prime rate	gold standard
Bank Rate	penalty rate	monetary pyramid
required reserve ratio	moral suasion	

PROBLEMS

13-1 What are the major tools that the Bank of Canada has for controlling the quantity of money? Which of these tools affect the quantity of reserves of the chartered banks?

13-2 Suppose that the Bank of Canada purchases $100,000 in Treasury bills from chartered bank A. Explain how the balance sheets of the Bank of Canada and chartered bank A are affected. How much can chartered bank A now safely lend? (Assume that bank A's reserves were just adequate prior to the purchase by the Bank of Canada.)

13-3 Suppose that the price of a three-month, $100,000 Treasury bill is $96,000. What is the yield on this bill? (Following the conventional practice, quote the yield at an annual rate.) Now suppose that the price of three-month bills falls to $95,000. What happens to the yield?

13-4 The Bank of Canada makes loans at the initiative of the chartered banks and investment dealers. In what way do such loans reduce the control of the Bank of Canada over the money supply? In what way might the power of the Bank to change the Bank Rate increase its control over the money stock?

13-5 "Counterfeiting is generally an antisocial act. But when there is a depression, all counterfeiters should be let out of jail." Do you agree or disagree? Explain why.

13-6 What backing do Bank of Canada notes have? Why are these notes valuable?

Part Four

GREAT MACROECONOMIC ISSUES OF OUR TIME

Part 3 of this book has introduced the two major tools of demand management: fiscal policy (involving changes in government spending and in tax rates) and monetary policy (open market operations, transfers of government deposits, changes in the Bank Rate). By changing monetary and fiscal policies, the authorities can influence aggregate demand, aiming for the objectives of full employment and stable prices.

In the introduction to Part 3, the reader was warned that an effort would be made to keep the explanations simple. The "potholes" in the road map of economic policy were left out. But, while theory may be simplified, the real world remains complex. Although substantial progress has been made during the past 40 years in managing the economy to provide for full employment and stable prices, there have also been failures in the form of periodic recessions and stubborn inflation. We have done much better than our grandparents did in the decades between the two world wars. But we do not seem to be moving on from one success to ever greater successes. The problem of recession has not been licked. In fact, the recession of 1981–82 was the most severe in the past four decades. Whether measured by the rate of unemployment, the rate of inflation, or the rate of growth of real national product, the Canadian economy has performed less well since 1970 than it did during the 1960s.

Nor is there unanimity on how we should proceed from here. On the contrary, there are sharp controversies on some of the most basic issues of macroeconomics. The chapters in Part 4 will deal with six of the great macroeconomic issues of our time.

1. Monetary Policy or Fiscal Policy: Which Is the Key to Aggregate Demand?

Most economists believe that *both* fiscal policy and monetary policy are important tools for controlling aggregate demand. But there are substantial disagreements over which should be made the centrepiece of aggregate demand policy. Those in the Keynesian tradition often emphasize fiscal policy, while those in the classical tradition see money as the key to changes in aggregate demand. This controversy is the subject of Chapter 14. We will conclude that the best approach generally involves a combined, cooperative use of both fiscal and monetary policies.

2. Fixed or Flexible Exchange Rates?

In earlier chapters, we have seen that economic conditions in Canada are highly sensitive to economic fluctuations in foreign countries. This sensitivity reflects the great importance of foreign trade and capital flows in the Canadian economy. Since most of our international transactions are with the United States, fluctuations in the U.S. economy are particularly likely to spill over into Canada.

In trying to give a complete answer to the question of how monetary and fiscal policies affect the Canadian economy, one must take into account that either policy will affect our international trade and capital flows; the changes in trade and capital flows will then in turn further influence the economy. In other words, in addition to their direct effect on aggregate demand, monetary and fiscal policy have an indirect effect which results from the influence of either policy on international transactions. In Chapter 15, we extend the analysis of Chapter 14 to consider how the choice between monetary and fiscal policy is affected by these international factors.

An important facet of this topic is the *exchange rate system*. Should exchange rates between Canadian and foreign currencies be *pegged* by the government, or should they be allowed to *fluctuate* in response to changes in supply and demand?

(An exchange rate is the price of one national currency in terms of another. For example, the price of the British pound in terms of Canadian dollars is an exchange rate, as is the price of the Canadian dollar in terms of the U.S. dollar. An exchange rate is pegged when it is kept fixed by a national government; for example, between 1962 and 1970, the Canadian government pegged our dollar at 92.5 U.S. cents.)

3. How Actively Should Aggregate Demand Be Managed?

Some economists are very concerned with the instability of aggregate demand, particularly the investment component. They believe that it is important for the fiscal and monetary authorities to manage demand actively, in order to combat recessions and inflationary booms. Other economists are very skeptical that policymakers know enough to stabilize aggregate demand. They believe that, in practice, active policy management is more likely to destabilize than to stabilize aggregate demand. They therefore recommend that the authorities follow a set of stable policy settings. In particular, they argue that central banks such as the Bank of Canada and the U.S. Federal Reserve should aim at a stable, moderate rate of growth of the money stock. This controversy, which is perhaps the most important single macroeconomic debate of our time, is studied in Chapter 16.

4. Aggregate Supply: How Can Inflation and Unemployment Coexist?

Chapter 9 introduced a relatively simple set of aggregate supply functions: (1) the vertical aggregate supply function of classical theory; (2) the aggregate supply function of basic Keynesian theory, which forms a reversed L; and (3) the curved, upward-sloping aggregate supply curve which is useful in explaining how an increase in aggregate demand may be reflected partly in an increase in real output, and partly in an increase in prices.

However, in order to explain some of the puzzles of recent years, it is necessary to consider aggregate supply in more detail. In particular, none of the three simple aggregate supply functions is adequate to explain an important problem that has cropped up over the last decade and a half: How can a high rate of inflation and a high rate of unemployment exist *together*? This question will be considered in Chapter 17.

5. How Do We Adjust to Inflation?

The problems of high unemployment are obvious: With many people out of work, the society foregoes the goods and services that otherwise could have been created. The loss of a job often brings both economic hardship and demoralization.

The problems with rapid inflation are less clear. But they are important because of the rapid inflation both here and abroad during the past decade. They are studied in Chapter 18. One of the major, lasting consequences of our inflation has been that people trying to buy their first homes find great difficulty in doing so.

6. Supply-side Economics: Productivity Problems and Policies

Traditionally, macroeconomics has concentrated on the "demand side"—that is, aggregate demand policies designed to achieve high employment and stable prices. But there is also a "supply side," involving the productive capacity of the economy.

The supply side has attracted increasing attention over the past several years. The main reason for this has been the poor productivity performance of the Canadian economy in the late 1970s and the first half of the 1980s: The average rates of increase in productivity per hour worked during the five decades before 1975 were much higher than in the decade 1975–85. A similar worsening of productivity performance occurred in the United States. In Chapter 19, we consider possible explanations for changing productivity growth rates; we also discuss some policies that have been suggested as methods for stimulating productivity in Canada and the United States.

Chapter 14

MONETARY POLICY AND FISCAL POLICY: WHICH IS THE KEY TO AGGREGATE DEMAND?

Nothing in excess.

Ancient Greek adage (Diogenes)

In the previous chapters, we have dealt with the two major tools with which aggregate demand can be controlled: fiscal policy and monetary policy. When we have two tools, the question naturally arises: "On which one should we rely?"

Views on that question have changed considerably in recent decades. The Keynesian revolution not only emphasized the responsibility of government to manage aggregate demand. It also identified fiscal policy as the primary tool to be used in doing so. Monetary policy was considered much less important. Keynes and his followers argued that, in the deepest pit of a depression, expansive monetary policies might be completely useless as a means of stimulating aggregate demand. An increase in the money stock might have no effect on spending. In more normal times, Keynes was less skeptical regarding the effects of monetary policy. In fact, he emphasized the importance of money in his earlier works, especially in *Monetary Reform* (1924) and *A Treatise on Money* (1930). Nevertheless, the *General Theory* left a strong legacy in its emphasis

on fiscal policy as the primary tool to control aggregate demand.

In the two decades between 1945 and 1965, when Keynesian theory dominated macroeconomic analysis in North America, fiscal policy was at the centre of attention, and monetary policy was considered much less important. Some Keynesians went as far as Warren Smith, who in 1959 dismissed the control of aggregate demand through monetary policy as "a mirage and delusion."[1]

During the 1960s, there was a resurgence of interest in monetary policy, and in the classical theory which had identified money as the key determinant of aggregate demand. The most prominent role in this revival of classical economics was played by Milton Friedman,

[1] In *Staff Report on Employment, Growth, and Price Levels* (Washington: Joint Economic Committee, U.S. Congress, 1959), p. 401. Smith was writing about general monetary controls, such as open market operations, that affect the quantity of money. He was less skeptical of the effectiveness of selective controls, such as those on consumer instalment credit.

then a professor at the University of Chicago. Friedman summarized his position: "Money is extremely important for nominal magnitudes, for nominal income, for the level of income in dollars. . . ." Furthermore, Friedman was skeptical about the effectiveness of fiscal policy as a tool for controlling aggregate demand. He of course recognized that the government budget has an important influence on the allocation of resources: The budget determines how much of national product is spent by the government, and how much is left for the private sector. But Friedman doubted that fiscal policy has an important effect on aggregate demand: "In my opinion, the state of the budget by itself has no significant effect on the course of nominal income, on inflation, on deflation, or on cyclical fluctuations."[2]

While Friedman and other *neoclassical* macroeconomists have had a profound effect on the way economic problems are perceived, neoclassical theory has not attained the predominant position enjoyed by Keynesian theory in the decades following World War II. Most macroeconomists are eclectic, agreeing with some parts of Keynesian analysis, and with some parts of classical economics. In response to the question posed back in the first paragraph, most present-day macroeconomists would answer: "Both monetary and fiscal policies are important. We should not rely exclusively on either."

To understand current thinking on monetary and fiscal policies, it is important to study both Keynesian and classical theories. Each theory provides a sensible framework for the orderly investigation of macroeconomic developments. Each can heighten our understanding of how the economy works. Chapter 11 explained the Keynesian view of how fiscal policy can affect aggregate demand. In this chapter, we consider the relation between monetary policy and aggregate demand, and the question of whether fiscal or monetary policy should be the principal tool of economic policy. Specifically, this chapter will explain:

1. The Keynesian view of how monetary policy can affect aggregate demand, and the circumstances in which the effect may not be very strong.
2. The classical view on how monetary policy can affect aggregate demand, and why those in the

classical tradition expect the effects of monetary policy to be both strong and predictable.
3. The reasons why some of those in the classical tradition have doubts about fiscal policy; specifically, why they doubt that fiscal policy has the strong and predictable effect on aggregate demand suggested by the Keynesian theory outlined in Chapter 11.
4. The advantages of using a combination of monetary and fiscal policies as part of an overall strategy for stabilizing aggregate demand.

In order to keep the discussion from becoming too complicated, we will concentrate in this chapter on the *domestic* effects of monetary policy. But from the viewpoint of a Canadian policymaker, this means that the analysis is seriously incomplete. In an economy such as ours where international trade and capital flows play such an important role, the overall effectiveness of both monetary and fiscal policies depends a great deal on how those policies influence our transactions with foreign countries. A detailed discussion of these issues is postponed until the next chapter. In the meantime, it is important to keep in mind that as we lay the groundwork for understanding monetary policy in this chapter, we are only telling half the story of how monetary policy works in Canada.

THE EFFECTS OF MONETARY POLICY: THE KEYNESIAN VIEW

In his *General Theory*, Keynes identified a three-step process by which a change in monetary policy could affect aggregate demand (Figure 14-1):

1. An open market operation and a change in the money stock can affect the rate of interest. For example, an open market purchase of bonds by the central bank will raise bond prices; that is, lower the interest rate.
2. A change in the interest rate can affect investment demand. With a lower interest rate, business executives are encouraged to borrow money to buy new machines or to build new factories.
3. Higher investment demand will have a multiplied effect on aggregate demand and national product.

The third step involves the familiar multiplier explained in Chapter 10. Here, we will look at steps 1 and 2.

[2]Milton Friedman and Walter Heller, *Monetary vs. Fiscal Policy: A Dialogue* (New York: W.W. Norton, 1969), pp. 46, 51.

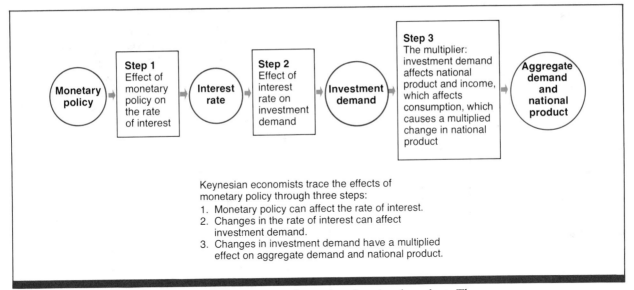

Figure 14-1 How monetary policy affects aggregate demand and national product: The Keynesian approach.

Step 1: Monetary Policy and the Interest Rate: The Stock of Money, and the Demand for It

The first step in the process—how an open market operation can affect interest rates—was discussed briefly in Chapter 13. Because this step is important in the Keynesian evaluation of monetary policy, we consider it in more detail here.

In Keynes' theory, the interest rate reaches equilibrium when the demand and supply of money are equal; that is, *when people are willing to hold the amount of money that exists in the economy.*

People hold money in order to buy goods and services. As a result, the demand for money *depends on national income.* The reason is straightforward. The higher the national income, the more purchases people will plan to make, and the more money they will consequently want to hold.

The demand for money also *depends on the interest rate.* Whenever money is held rather than used to buy a bond or other interest-bearing security, the holder of money gives up the interest that could have been earned on the security. Suppose that interest rates are high. The treasurers of corporations will try to keep as little money on hand as is conveniently possible, putting the rest into interest-bearing securities. At an interest rate of 15% per annum, for example, $10 million earns $30,000 in interest per week—a tidy

sum. On the other hand, if interest rates are very low, people do not need to be so careful about cash management; they do not forego much interest by holding money rather than securities. Therefore, more money will be held.

This willingness of people to hold more money at a lower rate of interest is illustrated by the downward-sloping demand curve in Figure 14-2. Now, suppose that $20 billion of money has been created by the banking system. S_1 illustrates this money supply. The equilibrium interest rate is 8%, at the intersection of the demand and supply curves.

Consider next what happens if the Bank of Canada purchases securities on the open market, causing an expansion of the money stock to $30 billion, as shown by S_2. At the old 8% interest rate, there is a surplus of money shown by the gray arrow; people have more than they are willing to hold at this interest rate. What do they do with the excess? They buy interest-bearing securities. Bond prices are bid up; that is, interest rates are bid down. The interest rate falls to its new equilibrium, 6%.

Step 2: The Interest Rate and Investment Demand: The Marginal Efficiency of Investment

Having seen how an increase in the stock of money can lead to a fall in the interest rate, we now turn to

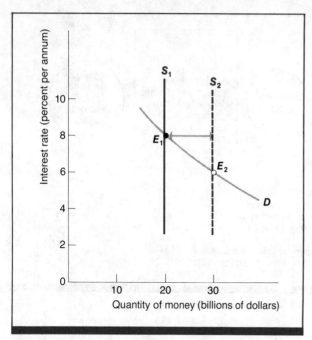

Figure 14-2   The stock of money, and the demand for it. The quantity of money demanded increases as the interest rate falls. The equilibrium interest rate occurs where the quantity of money demanded is equal to the stock in existence.

the second step: How a fall in the interest rate can lead to an increase in investment. But, before we take this step, we should consider how the decision to invest is made.

Business executives are interested in acquiring equipment or buildings because of the stream of returns such investments will provide. Consider a very simple illustration, an imaginary machine costing $100,000 that will last forever. With it, a manufacturer expects to produce and sell $50,000 more in goods each year. If the wages paid to workers to run the machine, plus the cost of material inputs, plus administrative costs, add up to $40,000 per year, the machine will provide a return (R) of $10,000 per year. In other words, the machine will provide a *rate of return* (r), or *yield*, of 10% per annum on the initial investment of $100,000.

Alternatively, consider quite a different machine, which also costs $100,000 but completely wears out in one year. Suppose that this machine generates enough in sales to cover labour, material, and administrative costs, plus an additional $110,000. Then this machine also provides a rate of return of 10%. That is, it pro-

vides enough to cover the $100,000 purchase price of the machine, and leave 10% over.

Both these illustrations are very simple. But they do provide examples of how the percentage rate of return may be calculated by taking into account:[3]

1. the initial price and expected life of the machine
2. the addition to sales expected as a result of the machine
3. costs associated with running the machine, for labour, materials, etc.[4]

In making plans for capital expenditures for the coming year, the business executive will look first at the equipment or building that provides the highest expected rate of return. For a dynamic company in a growing industry, this rate may be very high—20% or 30% per annum, or even more. In such cases, a corporation that is able to borrow will find it profitable to do so to acquire the new equipment.

It will be profitable to continue to borrow and invest, *as long as the rate of return (r) from the investment exceeds the rate of interest (i) paid on the borrowed funds.* As long as this is so, the new plant or equipment will provide a flow of returns sufficient to cover the interest payments, and leave something over to add to profits. On the other hand, it would be a mis-

---

[3] The formula for calculating the rate of return r is a close cousin of the bond formula in Box 13-1. Specifically, if a machine has a life of n years, then:

$$\text{Price of machine} = \frac{R_1}{1 + r} + \frac{R_2}{(1 + r)^2} + \cdots \frac{R_n + S}{(1 + r)^n}$$

where

R_1 is the return in the first year, measured in dollars; R_2 is the return in the second year; etc.

S is the scrap value of the machine at the end of its life in year n

r is the rate of return (measured as a percentage or fraction)

If we know the price of the machine and estimate the R's and S, we can solve for r.

In the simple example of a machine with a one-year life (in which we implicitly assumed a scrap value of zero at the end of the first year), this calculation is:

$$\$100,000 = \frac{R_1}{1 + r} = \frac{\$110,000}{1 + r}$$

Therefore,

$$r = 0.1 = 10\%$$

[4] Interest paid on funds borrowed to buy the machine is not included in these costs. Interest comes into the decision-making calculation at a later point, as we shall soon see.

take to invest in plant or equipment with an expected rate of return below the rate of interest. More would be paid out in interest than would be contributed by the machine or building, and profits would suffer as a result. Even if the firm has excess funds from retained profits and has no need to borrow to finance new plant and equipment, it would be a mistake to undertake investments with low rates of return. The money could more profitably be used to buy bonds and earn interest. Thus, to determine whether to undertake an investment project, the business executive calculates *whether the expected rate of return on the plant or equipment is greater than the rate of interest.*

Of course, the executive lives in an uncertain world, and cannot be confident that the estimated rate of return will prove accurate. Therefore, the prudent executive will adjust expected yields downward by some amount to compensate for risks, and be on the safe side in making investment decisions.

Other businesses make similar calculations. Thus, for the economy as a whole, those investment projects will be undertaken whose risk-adjusted rates of return (r) exceed the rate of interest (i).

This decision-making process is illustrated in Table 14-1 and Figure 14-3. In Table 14-1, all investment projects for the economy are ranked according to their expected rates of return. For example, the highest-ranked $13 billion in projects are expected to yield returns of 12% or higher, and so all these projects will be undertaken if business can borrow at 12% or less. The next $3 billion in projects (for a cumulative total of $16 billion = $13 billion + $3 billion) are expected to yield at least 10%, and so on. This schedule, commonly called the **marginal efficiency of investment** (MEI), is graphed in Figure 14-3. It shows how investment increases as the interest rate falls. For example, if the interest rate is 8%, $20 billion of investment is undertaken. (The first $20 billion of investment yields a return of at least 8%.) Then, if the interest rate falls to 6%, investment will increase to $25 billion at point *D*. Thus, a drop in the interest rate from 8% to 6% causes a $5 billion increase in investment.

> The *marginal efficiency of investment* is the schedule or curve that shows possible investment projects, ranked according to their expected rates of return. It shows how much businesses will want to invest at various inter-

Table 14-1
Expected Return on Investment

	(1) Expected rate of return (r) (percent per annum)	(2) Amount of investment expected to yield at least the return in (1) (in billions)
A	12%	$13
B	10%	$16
C	8%	$20
D	6%	$25

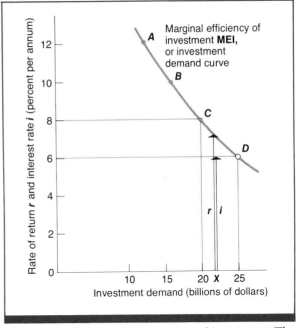

Figure 14-3 The marginal efficiency of investment: The investment demand curve.
The investment demand (or marginal efficiency of investment) curve slopes downward to the right. At a lower interest rate, more investment projects are undertaken.

est rates. It is also sometimes known as the *investment demand* schedule or curve.

The advantage to businesses of undertaking additional investment when the interest rate falls from 8% to 6% may be seen more precisely by considering a specific project that ranks between C and D; for example, project x, which ranks in the 22nd billion dollars of investment. The rate of return (r) on this project is just over 7%, as shown by the height of the MEI curve. When the interest rate was 8%, this project was not undertaken, because the 8% cost of borrowing money exceeded the 7% return. However, when the interest

rate fell to 6% (arrow i), the project was undertaken. It added to profits because the 7% return now more than covered the interest cost. Similarly, the other projects between C and D become profitable when the interest rate falls from 8% to 6%.

We may now summarize how monetary policy affects aggregate demand (in Figure 14-4).

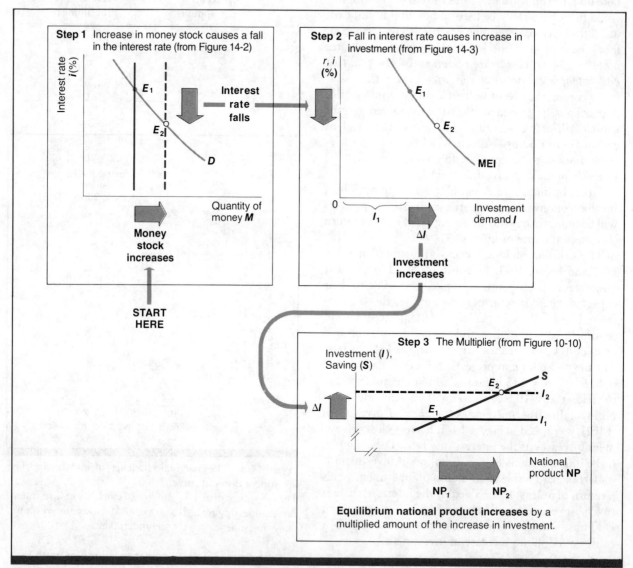

Figure 14-4 How monetary policy works: Details on the Keynesian approach.
This figure fills out the details in Figure 14-1. In step 1, the fall in the interest rate depends on the amount of additional money and the slope of the money demand function. In step

2, the amount of extra investment that is generated by a reduction in the interest rate depends on the MEI curve. In step 3, the investment has a multiplied effect on aggregate demand. In the simple economy, the multiplier equals 1/MPS.

An expansive monetary policy operates as follows:

Step 1	**Step 2**	**Step 3**
Open market purchase →	Interest rate down →	Investment up →	National product up by a multiplied amount

With a restrictive policy, the signs are the opposite:

Step 1	**Step 2**	**Step 3**
Open market sale →	Interest rate up →	Investment down →	National product down by a multiplied amount

Problems with Monetary Policy

By this three-step process, open market operations can affect aggregate demand. Why, then, were early Keynesians skeptical regarding the possible effectiveness of monetary policy as a tool for managing demand? The answer is: We cannot be certain that the effects at either of the first two steps will be very strong.

Keynes himself was particularly concerned that an expansive monetary policy might be ineffective at the very first step, and therefore could not be counted on as a way of getting out of the deep depression that existed when the *General Theory* was written. During a deep depression, interest rates may be very low—for example, in the 2% to 3% range that prevailed during much of the Depression of the 1930s. In such circumstances, the ability of the Bank of Canada to push the rates down even further is not very great. Clearly, interest rates cannot be pushed all the way down to zero. (At a zero interest rate, nobody would be willing to hold bonds. They would be giving up the use of their money, and getting nothing in return. It would be better to hold money in the bank instead.) Thus, when interest rates are already very low, it may become impossible for the Bank of Canada to move them much lower. Expansive monetary policy cannot have much effect on interest rates; it fails at step 1.

In more normal times, open market operations can significantly affect the interest rate, and the second step becomes the principal concern in the operation of monetary policy.

The Responsiveness of Investment to a Change in the Interest Rate

As Figure 14-3 is drawn, investment is quite respon-sive to a change in the rate of interest. For example, a fall in the interest rate from 8% to 6% will cause a 25% increase in investment demand, from $20 billion to $25 billion. An alternative possibility is illustrated in Figure 14-5. Here, the investment demand (MEI) curve falls much more steeply than it did in Figure 14-3. Now, even with a sharp drop in the interest rate from 8% to 6%, investment does not increase very much—only by $1 billion. This, then, is the second reason why monetary policy may be ineffective.

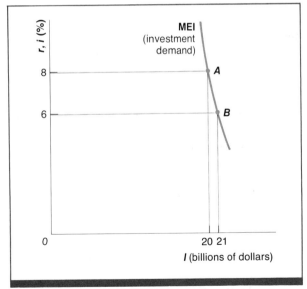

Figure 14-5   Monetary policy is ineffective at step 2 if an interest rate reduction has little effect on investment.
If the MEI curve is steep, investment will not increase much when the interest rate falls. Therefore, the effect of monetary policy on aggregate demand is not very powerful.

During the 1940s and 1950s, economists were concerned about this very possibility: that businesses might not increase their investment much when the interest rate fell. Early studies of the MEI schedule suggested that it might, in fact, be almost vertical. Thus, in contrast with Keynes, who believed that monetary policy might be ineffective during a depression because of the central bank's inability to lower interest rates (step 1), some of his followers developed even broader skepticism regarding monetary policy. Even if interest rates could be changed, they doubted that investment would be greatly affected (step 2). Thus, they doubted that monetary policy could be counted on to play much more than a secondary, supporting role to the main tool, namely, fiscal policy.

An Effective Monetary Policy

During the last two decades, there has been a movement back toward a more central position. The early fears—that monetary policy is ineffective—have been dissipated. As we have seen, these fears were partly based on the early evidence that investment does not respond much to changes in interest rates. However, the early studies did not provide a conclusive case for believing that monetary policy is ineffective, for two major reasons.

1. Statistical problems in measuring how much investment responds to changes in interest rates. First, it is not clear that the early studies were correct in concluding that interest rates do not affect investment demand very much.

It is surprisingly difficult to identify the effects of interest rates on investment because so many other important changes are occurring at the same time. If investment doesn't fall much as the interest rate rises, there are two possible explanations: (1) The interest rate has little effect on investment—as the early studies concluded; or (2) investment is influenced by the interest rate, but there are other offsetting influences. For example, investment may remain high or even rise during a period when rising interest rates are tending to depress it, because at the same time investment is being stimulated by increasing business optimism. More recent statistical work indicates that the early studies did not adequately deal with such complications, and consequently did not provide good estimates of how much investment responds when the rate of interest changes.

2. Credit rationing: The availability of loanable funds. It is possible that investment might be affected by monetary policy even when investment demand is very unresponsive to changes in the rate of interest. This is illustrated in Figure 14-6, which repeats the steep MEI curve of Figure 14-5.

Suppose that the initial equilibrium is at A, with $20 billion in investment. The central bank introduces a restrictive monetary policy. By selling securities on the open market, it pushes up interest rates and reduces chartered bank reserves. If banks initially have little or no excess reserves, they will be forced to cut back on their loans and other earning assets.

However, we are assuming that even with higher interest rates—of, say, 10% rather than the original 8%—businesses are still quite eager to borrow and to invest. At B, businesses want to invest almost as much as at A. However, this is what businesses want, not what they get. Banks can't lend as much as businesses want. To protect their reserve positions, banks **ration**

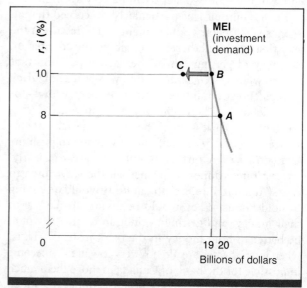

Figure 14-6 Credit rationing.
When the Bank of Canada reduces the quantity of chartered bank reserves by an open market sale, chartered banks *must* reduce their loans or other earning assets to meet reserve requirements. As a consequence, they may ration credit, lending less than borrowers want and less than the banks would be willing to lend if they had ample reserves. Because of an inability to borrow, businesses are forced to cut back on investment. The effects of credit rationing are shown by distance BC.

their available funds, lending less than credit-worthy customers want to borrow.

> *Credit rationing* occurs when banks and other lenders are short of loanable funds. They lend less than they would like if they had the funds, and less than credit-worthy borrowers want to borrow.

When this happens, investment decreases from *B* to *C*, to the *left* of the marginal efficiency of investment (MEI) curve. Investment declines, not because of a lack of desire to invest, but because businesses are unable to obtain financing. The distance *CB* reflects investment that doesn't occur because of the *unavailability of funds*. Thus, restrictive monetary policy works not only because of (1) the discouraging effect of higher interest rates on investment (shown by the movement from *A* to *B*), but also (2) the inability of businesses to invest because they cannot get funds (the movement from *B* to *C*).

However, a question arises as to why credit rationing can occur in the first place. If there are eager borrowers and limited funds, why doesn't the price of funds (the interest rate) rise to bring demand and supply into equality? In other words, why doesn't the price rise in this market, just as the price of wheat would rise if the quantity demanded exceeded the quantity supplied?

Historically, one important reason has been a government-imposed ceiling on the interest rate that chartered banks were allowed to charge on their loans: Before 1967, the Bank Act limited loan interest rates to no more than 6%. Rising demands for bank credit therefore showed up only partly in terms of rising interest rates, and partly in terms of shortages and rationing.[5] During the 1960s and early 1970s, the Bank of Canada sometimes used "moral suasion" to discourage banks from raising interest rates even when

the Bank wanted to bring about monetary restraint. For example, in late 1969 and early 1970 the Bank was trying to fight inflation by limiting the growth in chartered bank reserves; at the same time it was trying to keep Canadian interest rates down in order to discourage a capital inflow. The result was substantial credit rationing. Since the mid-1970s, however, interest rates have been much freer to move upward in times of monetary restraint. Consequently, credit rationing has become much less important, and high interest rates have become more important, as mechanisms for discouraging borrowers during periods of tight money.

Whether it is better for restrictive monetary policy to work through high interest rates or credit rationing has been a matter of heated debate, particularly during 1981 and 1982 when interest rates were very high. Unfortunately, this debate is quite complex. The case for allowing interest rates to rise to their equilibrium levels—that is, the case against interest rate ceilings—will be explained in detail in Chapter 35. The main point is that high interest rates allocate the available funds in the most efficient manner, to the borrowers who are most willing to pay. These are generally the borrowers with the most productive investment opportunities. On the other side, it may be argued that rationing is preferable. It is true that severe rationing—the so-called "credit crunches"— can be acutely painful, but crunches do help the Bank of Canada to suppress demand effectively and quickly. Consider, in contrast, what happens when interest rates are free to move up, and little or no credit rationing takes place. Some financial analysts fear that interest rates might have to reach "murderous" levels, threatening mass bankruptcy, before effective monetary restraint could be achieved.[6] According to this view, rising interest rates work more slowly and more dangerously than restraint through credit rationing.

We repeat the main points. Credit rationing is a

---

[5] In the earlier discussion of rent controls (Box 4-1), we have already seen how a government-imposed price ceiling can cause a shortage. In that example, buyers could not rent all the apartments they wanted at the controlled market price, and they therefore ended up at a point to the left of their demand curve. For similar reasons, borrowers can end up to the left of their demand curve, at point *C* in Figure 14-6, when there is a shortage of funds and credit is rationed.

[6] Rising interest rates can increase the danger of collapse of financial institutions in at least two ways. (1) Rising interest rates cause a decline in the prices of bonds and other securities (as explained in Box 13-1). This depresses the value of the assets of banks and other financial institutions. (2) High interest rates increase the difficulties that developing countries face in meeting their debt payments to banks. Particularly in 1983–84, banks had trouble collecting on their large foreign loans.

controversial topic. However, until the mid-1970s, it provided an important way in which restrictive monetary policy could suppress aggregate demand.

The Asymmetrical Effect of Monetary Policy

While credit rationing can contribute to the effectiveness of monetary policy, it also adds to the list of reasons why *restrictive* monetary policies may have a stronger and quicker effect on aggregate demand than *expansive* policies. Specifically, there are three reasons why restrictive monetary policies may be more effective than expansive policies:

1. The Bank of Canada can be more confident of its ability to push interest rates up than of its ability to push them down. If interest rates are already low, the Bank may be unable to push them down further. On the other hand, there is no limit on the height to which interest rates can be pushed by restrictive monetary policies.
2. When the Bank of Canada follows an easy money policy by purchasing securities on the open market, it increases chartered bank reserves and thus makes additional bank loans and an increase in the money stock *possible*. But the Bank of Canada cannot force the chartered banks to lend. Indeed, when banks were frightened during the Depression of the 1930s, they held large quantities of excess reserves. On the other hand, consider a restrictive policy of open market sales. Chartered bank reserves are reduced below the legal minimum. In this case the banks *must* respond by reducing their holdings of loans and securities, thus cutting back on the money stock.
3. A tight monetary policy can work by causing credit rationing. Businesses may be unable to borrow to finance investments, and thus may be pushed to a point to the left of the MEI curve (Figure 14-6). However, the opposite is not true. No matter how expansive monetary policies become, businesses cannot be forced to borrow more than they want; they cannot be forced to a point to the right of the MEI curve.

Because of these asymmetries, monetary policy is sometimes compared to controlling aggregate demand with a string. If restrictive policies are adopted, the string tightens; investment is firmly drawn back. However, the effects of expansive policies are much less certain. An expansive "push on the string" makes an increase in investment possible. If the demand for investment is strong, investment in fact does respond, keeping the string taut. In this case, monetary policy is powerful. However, if business executives are pessimistic, they may not respond much to easier monetary conditions. They borrow little more, if any. Investment remains stagnant. The string goes limp. Monetary policy aimed at stimulating aggregate demand has little effect. In short, monetary policy may be more effective as a tool for restraining aggregate demand during periods of inflation than it is for stimulating the economy during periods of recession or depression.

MONETARY POLICY: THE CLASSICAL VIEW

In contrast to Keynes, who started his analysis of aggregate demand by looking at its components (consumption, investment, government purchases of goods and services, and net exports), classical economists began from quite a different point. Their analysis was based on the *equation of exchange*

$$MV = PQ \qquad (14\text{-}1)$$

where

M = quantity of money in the hands of the public
P = average level of prices
Q = quantity of output; that is, real national product or real national income[7]

Thus,

PQ = national product, measured in nominal (dollar) terms

and

V = **income velocity of money**; that is, the

---

[7]In basic theoretical discussions, the distinction between national product and national income is ignored, and the two terms are used interchangeably.

Besides Equation 14-1, there is another version of the equation of exchange. This alternative version focuses on total transactions, including intermediate sales, rather than just on the final transactions included in national product. Here we concentrate on the final-payments or income version of the equation of exchange, as it leads to the simplest comparisons between the classical and Keynesian theories.

average number of times that the money stock (M) is spent to buy final output during a year. Specifically, V is defined as being equal to PQ/M.

Suppose that the money stock is $20 billion. Assume that, in the course of a year, the average dollar bill and the average demand deposit are spent six times to purchase final goods and services. In other words, V is 6. Then, total spending for final output is $20 billion times 6, or $120 billion. In turn, this total spending (MV) equals the total quantity of goods and services (Q) times the average price (P) at which they were sold.

But how can the same dollar be used over and over to purchase final goods? Very simply. When you purchase groceries at the store, the $50 you pay does not disappear. Rather, it goes into the cash register of the store. From there, it is used to pay the farmer for fresh vegetables, the canning factory for canned goods, or the clerk's wages. The farmer or the clerk or the employee of the canning factory will in turn use the money to purchase goods. Once more, the money is used for final purchases. The same dollar bill can circulate round and round.

The Quantity Theory of Money

The equation of exchange, by itself, does not get us very far, because it is a *tautology* or truism. That is, it *must* be true because of the way the terms are defined. Note that velocity is defined as $V = PQ/M$. Thus, by definition, $MV = PQ$. (Just multiply both sides of the first equation by M.)

However, in the hands of classical economists, the equation of exchange became more than a tautology; it became the basis of an important theory. This theory— the **quantity theory of money**—was based on the proposition that *velocity (V) is stable*.

> The *quantity theory of money* is the proposition that velocity (V) is stable. Therefore, a change in the quantity of money (M) will cause nominal national product (PQ) to change by approximately the same percentage.

If, for example, the money stock (M) increases by 20%, then as a consequence, nominal national

product (PQ) will also rise by about 20%. In other words, the old classical economists and their modern neoclassical followers put forward the following central proposition:

1. A change in the quantity of money (M) is the key to changes in aggregate demand. When people have more M, they spend more on the nation's output.[8] Specifically, an increase in M will cause an approximately proportional increase in nominal national product (PQ).

In Chapter 9, we encountered several other important classical propositions:

2. *In the long run*, real output (Q) moves to the full-employment, capacity level. Therefore, the long-run effect of a change in M is on P, not on Q. Most notably, a rapid increase in the quantity of money causes rapid price inflation.

3. *In the short run* (over periods of months or quarters), a change in M can have a substantial effect on both P and Q. For example, a decline in the quantity of money can cause a decline in output (Q) and the onset of a recession. During a recession, growth of M can cause a short-run increase in Q, moving the economy back toward full employment.

4. Monetary disturbances are a major cause of unstable aggregate demand and of business cycles. If M is kept stable, a market economy will be quite stable.

5. Thus, the major macroeconomic responsibility of the authorities is to provide a stable money supply. Specifically, the money supply should be steadily increased at a rate that is adequate to buy the full-employment output of the economy at stable prices. As the capacity of the economy grows gradually, economists in the classical tradition argue that the authorities should adhere to a *policy rule*, increasing the money stock at a slow, steady rate of about 3% per year.

Why Should Velocity Be Stable?
The Demand for Money

The quantity theory may be traced back over 200 years, at least as far back as the writings of philoso-

---

[8]In other words, the aggregate demand curve shifts when the money stock changes, as already illustrated back in Figure 9-4.

pher David Hume in the eighteenth century. The early quantity theorists attributed the inflation of the time to the inflow of gold and silver from the New World. The exact mechanism by which money affected aggregate demand and prices was not spelled out in detail by these early theorists. They believed that it was self-evident that, when people have more money, they spend more. When they spend more—with more money chasing a relatively fixed quantity of goods—prices rise.

More recently, particularly in response to the criticisms of Keynesians, neoclassical economists have been more explicit about their theory. Velocity is stable, they argue, *because the demand for money is stable.* The demand for money arises because of the usefulness of money in purchasing goods and services. Money is held only temporarily, from the time people receive income until they spend it to purchase goods and services. The higher people's incomes, the more money they will need to make purchases. Therefore, the quantity of money demanded depends on the size of national income. And it is national income in current dollars (that is, PQ rather than simply Q) that is important in determining the demand for money: If prices rise, people will need more money to pay for the more expensive goods and services. Thus, neoclassical economists focus on nominal national income as the principal determinant of the demand for money.

Figure 14-7 illustrates this relationship. The higher the current-dollar, or nominal, national product (measured up the vertical axis), the greater the quantity of money demanded (measured along the horizontal axis). Suppose that the actual amount of money in the economy is initially at S_1, and the current-dollar national product is at A_1. Then the supply S_1 and demand for money will be in equilibrium at point E_1. The quantity of money demanded, measured by the distance $A_1 E_1$, will be equal to the quantity of money (S_1) actually in existence.

Now, suppose that an expansive monetary policy is followed, with the money supply increasing to S_2. At the existing national product (A_1), the stock of money that people have ($A_1 B$) is greater than the amount they want to hold ($A_1 E_1$); there is a temporary surplus of money of $E_1 B$. With more money than they want, people spend it to buy more goods and services. In other words, aggregate demand goes up. If the economy is initially in a depression, with large amounts of

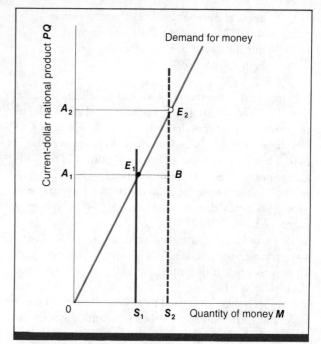

Figure 14-7 The demand for money: A classical view.
Those in the classical tradition argue that the demand for money is stable and depends primarily on current-dollar national product. If the stock of money which people hold exceeds the demand for money, then people will increase their spending.

excess capacity, output (Q) will respond strongly to the increase in money. But if the economy is already at or near full employment, then Q can't increase substantially, and higher aggregate demand will cause a rise in prices (P). In either case, current-dollar national product (PQ) will increase. As this happens, people become willing to hold more money. The process continues until current-dollar national product rises to A_2, where the quantity of money and the demand for it are again in equilibrium at E_2. In this way, a change in the quantity of money causes an approximately proportional change in national product PQ. But this in turn means that V is stable. (If a 10% increase in PQ occurs whenever there is a 10% increase in M, then the ratio PQ/M is constant. That is, V is constant.)

Thus, the theoretical underpinning of the quantity theory of money—the proposition that V is stable—is this: There is a stable demand for money, similar to the straight line shown in Figure 14-7.

CLASSICAL DOUBTS ABOUT FISCAL POLICY: CROWDING OUT

Classical economists were united in emphasizing the importance of money as a determinant of aggregate demand. However, their views on fiscal policy were less unanimous. During the Great Depression of the 1930s, some of them recommended substantial increases in government spending as a way of increasing demand, output, and employment. Others were quite skeptical about the effects of fiscal policy. For example, the British Treasury opposed additional government spending on the ground that it would do no good, since it would merely displace or **crowd out** an equivalent amount of private investment demand. (One of Keynes' principal objectives in writing the *General Theory* was to combat this view.)

Expansive fiscal policies may crowd out investment demand in the following way. When the government increases its expenditures or cuts taxes, its deficit rises. To finance its deficit spending, the government sells new bonds or shorter-term securities. That is, it borrows from the financial markets. The additional borrowing pushes up interest rates. Higher interest rates

in turn cause a movement along the marginal efficiency of investment (MEI) curve; the amount of investment decreases (Figure 14-8).

> *Crowding out* occurs when an expansive fiscal policy causes higher interest rates, and these higher interest rates in turn depress investment demand.

There is little doubt that some crowding out takes place. The question is how much. Keynesian economists—and particularly early Keynesians—have often argued that investment is not very responsive to interest rates. This view is illustrated back in Figure 14-5, where investment decreases only a little in a move from B to A. As a result, not much crowding out of investment takes place. Consequently, fiscal policy is a powerful tool for controlling aggregate demand (and monetary policy is weak). Monetarists, on the other hand, generally believe that the MEI curve is quite flat, as shown in Figure 14-8, and that deficit spending by the government tends to crowd out a relatively large amount of private investment.

In casting doubt on the effectiveness of fiscal policies, monetarists make one important qualification. If the central bank buys any of the additional bonds being issued by the government, it will be engaging in an expansive open market operation. New money will be created and this will have a powerful expansive effect on aggregate demand. But monetarists attribute the higher demand to a change in the money stock, not to the government deficit itself. They see **pure fiscal policy** as having little effect on aggregate demand.

> *Pure fiscal policy* involves a change in government spending or tax rates, unaccompanied by any change in the rate of growth of the money stock.

FISCAL POLICY AND NET EXPORTS

There is a second reason why fiscal policy may sometimes become ineffective: Its effect on aggregate demand may be partially offset by opposite changes in net exports. Consider again the case where the government is increasing the budget deficit as a way of stimulating the economy. As we explained above, as the

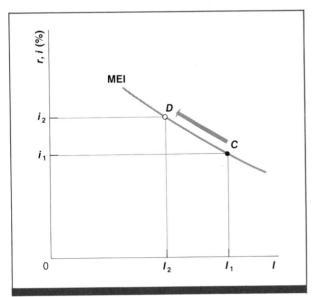

Figure 14-8 Crowding out: The monetarist view.
Government deficits may push up the interest rate—from i_1 to i_2, for example. This causes a movement along the MEI curve from C to D, and investment demand decreases from I_1 to I_2.

government has to increase its borrowing in the capital market to finance the larger deficit, there will be a tendency for interest rates to rise. But not only will rising interest rates lead to a reduction in private investment (that is, cause some crowding out of investment); it will also tend to increase the rate of capital inflow into Canada as foreign investors move their funds here in order to take advantage of the higher interest rates. An increased inflow of capital will cause a rise in the value of the Canadian dollar; the higher value of the Canadian dollar, in turn, will cause exports from Canada to fall and imports into Canada to rise. But this implies a reduction in the net export component of aggregate demand, partially offsetting the initial stimulative fiscal policy.

This argument may be summarized:

> Taxes down or government spending up → government deficit up → interest rate up → purchase of Canadian assets by foreigners → rise in price of Canadian dollar in terms of foreign currencies → fall in exports and rise in imports

Even though foreign trade and capital flows usually play a much less important role in the United States than in Canada, during the mid-1980s the relation between the budget deficit and net exports became an issue of considerable concern in the United States, too. Because of the very large U.S. government deficit under the Reagan administration, federal borrowing was very large, and interest rates in the United States reached unprecedented highs. In response, there was a large capital inflow into the United States, and the value of the U.S. dollar increased substantially in terms of currencies such as the German mark and the Japanese yen, especially in 1983 and 1984. As a result, there was a large reduction in U.S. net exports. Indeed, weak exports and rapidly growing imports were major concerns of U.S. policymakers in the mid-1980s.

DOUBTS ABOUT THE EFFECTS OF POLICY: AGGREGATE DEMAND AND AGGREGATE SUPPLY

The two complications we have just studied—regarding "crowding out" and net export demand—explain why fiscal policy may have a weak effect on *aggregate demand*. However, insofar as fiscal policy is aimed at affecting real output, we should also look at the limits on fiscal policy because of the nature of *aggregate supply*.

This will be illustrated in Figure 14-9, which represents an elaboration of earlier Figure 10-13b. Consider first the simplest case, where fiscal policy has its maximum effect. There are no complications to detract from its strength. Specifically, (1) there is no crowding out of investment; (2) there is no negative effect on net exports; and (3) the aggregate supply curve is horizontal, which means that any increase in aggregate demand will show up entirely in terms of an increase in output, and not at all in terms of higher prices. In this simple case, an expansive fiscal policy causes a strong rightward movement in aggregate demand, from AD_1 to AD_2 in Figure 14-9 (left panel). Equilibrium moves from E to H with real national product increasing sharply from Q_1 to Q_2.

The left panel also illustrates what happens when some investment demand is crowded out, and net exports decline. In this case, the effect of fiscal policy on aggregate demand is weakened. The aggregate demand function shifts only from AD_1 to AD_3, with equilibrium national product increasing to Q_3. Thus, distance $Q_3 Q_2$ shows the combined effect of crowding out and a decline in net exports.

Finally, the right panel also includes complications on the supply side. Now, as aggregate demand increases from AD_1 to AD_3, both prices and real national product increase. The economy moves upward along the aggregate supply curve AS_2 to the new equilibrium K, where output is Q_4. The distance between Q_4 and Q_3 represents the output that isn't produced because of a rise in prices.

This last complication—the failure of output to rise because of the upward slope of the aggregate supply function—applies equally to monetary policy. Thus, the debate studied in this chapter—over the relative effectiveness of monetary and fiscal policies—has to do only with their relative effectiveness *in changing aggregate demand*. If the aggregate supply function is steep, then *neither* an expansive monetary policy *nor* an expansive fiscal policy will have much effect in promoting an increase in real output.

STATISTICAL EVIDENCE

To summarize the major debate in this chapter: Monetarists argue that velocity is stable. Money is the key to changes in aggregate demand. An increase in the

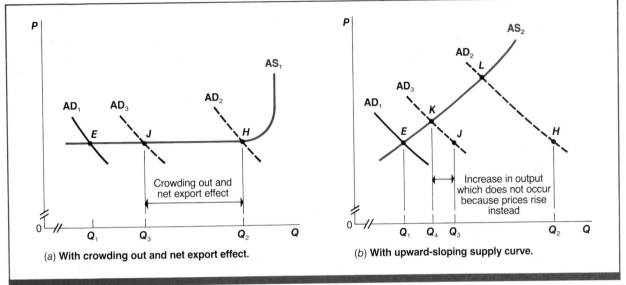

Figure 14-9 **The effects of fiscal policy.**

In the left panel, aggregate supply is horizontal. In the absence of crowding out and a decline in net exports, expansive fiscal policy has a strong effect on real output. However, if crowding out occurs and net exports decline, aggregate demand shifts only to AD_3 rather than AD_2. The effect of fiscal policy is weaker.

The right panel introduces an upward-sloping aggregate supply curve. In this case, some of the increase in demand goes into higher prices, rather than greater output. With aggregate demand AD_3, the new equilibrium is at K, not J.

quantity of money causes an increase in national product, measured in dollars. Some monetarists are skeptical about pure fiscal policy, arguing that it will have little effect on aggregate demand. In contrast, Keynesians believe that fiscal policy has a powerful impact on aggregate demand. Some Keynesians argue that monetary policy is less effective, particularly as a way of getting an economy out of a depression or recession.

It would seem easy to settle this dispute— simply look at the facts and see which theory is more in line with the observations of the real world. Unfortunately, this is easier said than done, for reasons that may be best understood by considering the full-scale counterattack which monetarists launched against Keynesian economics during the 1960s.

This counterattack was supported by two major statistical studies in the United States, the first by Milton Friedman and David Meiselman, and the second by a group of economists at the Federal Reserve Bank of St. Louis.[9] Friedman and Meiselman argued that

Keynesian economics had been accepted and classical economics rejected on the basis of the theoretical case put forward by Keynes in his *General Theory*. Yet nobody had stopped to study the facts seriously. Nobody had done a *comparative study* to find out which was more consistent with the facts—the classical theory or the Keynesian theory. The time had come, said Friedman and Meiselman, to conduct such a study.

The centrepiece of classical theory was the velocity of money; classical theory was based on the premise that velocity is stable. The central theoretical tool of Keynesian analysis was the marginal propensity to consume (MPC) and its algebraic cousin, the multiplier. For Keynesian demand-management policies to be useful, the MPC and the multiplier must be reasonably stable and predictable. According to Friedman and Meiselman, therefore, the debate came down to a basic question: Which is more stable, velocity or the multiplier?

[9]Milton Friedman and David Meiselman, "The Relative Stability of Monetary Velocity and the Investment Multiplier in the United States," in *Commission on Money and Credit, Stabilization Policies* (Englewood Cliffs, N.J.: Prentice-Hall, 1963), pp. 168-268; and Leonall C. Andersen and Jerry Jordan, "Monetary and Fiscal Actions: A Test of Their Relative Importance in Economic Stabilization," *Federal Reserve Bank of St. Louis Review*, (November 1968): 11–16.

Looking at the statistical evidence for 1897 through 1958, they found the results to be "remarkably consistent and unambiguous." The velocity of money was found to be decidedly more stable than the multiplier throughout that six-decade period—with one notable exception: the decade of the depressed 1930s. The conclusion indicated by the Friedman-Meiselman results: Keynes' theory was not a "general" theory at all. Rather, it was a special theory with relevance to the thirties. (Keynes had called his theory "general" because it dealt not only with conditions of full employment, but also with those of large-scale unemployment. In contrast, he considered the classical theory "special," since it applied only to a fully employed economy.)

In the test between Keynesian and classical economics, Friedman and Meiselman declared the classical theory to be the clear winner. Similar results were obtained by the St. Louis Fed.

Problems of Interpretation

Needless to say, these results did not persuade Keynesian economists to give up the contest; the monetarist studies were themselves vulnerable to attack. Most important, perhaps, was a fundamental problem that bedevils *any* statistical test of a theory. A theory is usually in the form of a cause-and-effect statement: "If the money stock is increased, this will cause an increase in aggregate demand"; or, to take an illustration from simple microeconomic theory, "If the price of a good rises, then consumers will, as a consequence, buy a smaller quantity." Yet, statistical evidence is merely a series of observations. The observed facts regarding money, aggregate demand, prices, and quantities purchased tell us simply *what* has happened, not *why* it has happened. Statistics do not show what caused what; they show only what things have happened together.

For example, if we observe that two items (A and B) are closely related, both rising and falling together, this observation does not, in itself, permit us to decide whether (1) A caused B, or (2) B caused A, or (3) both A and B were caused by a third item, C.

Now consider the Friedman-Meiselman and St. Louis statistical results, which indicated that changes in the quantity of money (M) and changes in nominal national product (PQ) moved together closely. Friedman and Meiselman concluded that the quantity theory was upheld, that changes in the stock of money *cause*

a powerful and predictable change in aggregate demand. What was the response of their critics? That no such powerful causal relationship had been demonstrated. While aggregate demand and changes in the quantity of money do indeed move together, a significant part of this relationship may be the result of forces working in the opposite direction. That is, *changes in aggregate demand can cause changes in the money supply*.

How could that be so? Consider an important, and relatively volatile, component of aggregate demand, namely private investment. Suppose that businesses become optimistic regarding their future prospects, and decide to order new equipment. In order to finance their investment, they go to their banks, which respond by granting loans. The statistics will show an increase in the money stock. But the driving force is the decision of businesses to invest, not the decision of the banking system to increase the quantity of money. So say the critics of Friedman and Meiselman.

(In this illustration, where the desire of businesses to invest causes an increase in the quantity of money, it is possible that the money stock will grow *before* the investment takes place; businesses may line up financing before the construction actually gets under way. Thus we cannot tell which is the cause by looking at which happens first. The unwarranted conclusion that, if A happens before B, A caused B is known as the *post hoc ergo propter hoc* fallacy [literally, "after this, therefore on account of this"]. An example of this fallacy: The rooster crows. The sun rises. Therefore, the rooster's crowing causes the sun to rise.)

THE UNCERTAIN LESSON OF RECENT HISTORY

The difficulty of deciding which theory is more correct is increased by the conflicting lessons that may be drawn from recent Canadian history.

If one looks at the first half of the 1970s, there would appear to be considerable support for the monetarist explanation of fluctuations in economic activity. Monetary policy seemed to be the key influence: The recession of 1970 was accompanied by a sharp reduction in the growth rate of Canada's money supply, and occurred in spite of a relatively sharp shift toward a more expansionary fiscal policy. (The contractionary budget surplus in 1969 was greatly reduced in 1970.) Moreover, there was more apparent support for the monetarist position in 1973 and 1974. In those years, fiscal policy became contractionary as the government budget shifted into large surplus positions. According to the Keynesian view, this should have had a strong dampening effect on aggregate demand, and the inflation rate should have been reduced. But inflation accelerated instead, and the monetarists were not surprised, since the Bank of Canada had pursued a very expansionary monetary policy, with high rates of increase in the money supply, during those years. Up until the mid-1970s, the monetarist position seemed strongly supported: Monetary policy seemed to be the key to aggregate demand.

But the evidence from the late 1970s and early 1980s was much less clearly in favour of the monetarist position. While the Bank of Canada steadily reduced the growth rate of M1, and actually allowed M1 to *fall* for a period in 1981–82, the inflation rate did not come down: The increases in the consumer price index in 1981 and 1982 were as high as they had been during the worst years in the mid-1970s. To an orthodox Keynesian, this would not have come as a surprise: Fiscal policy was highly expansionary during the period, with large and growing federal budget deficits.

Figure 14-10 shows one reason why inflation did not come down even though M1 grew relatively slowly: The velocity of M1 kept rising, and increased especially quickly during the period of monetary contraction in 1981–82. In other words, if we use M1 to represent the money stock in the equation of exchange, the increase in PQ was largely attributable to an increase in V, not an increase in M. The data did not support the monetarist view that V is stable.

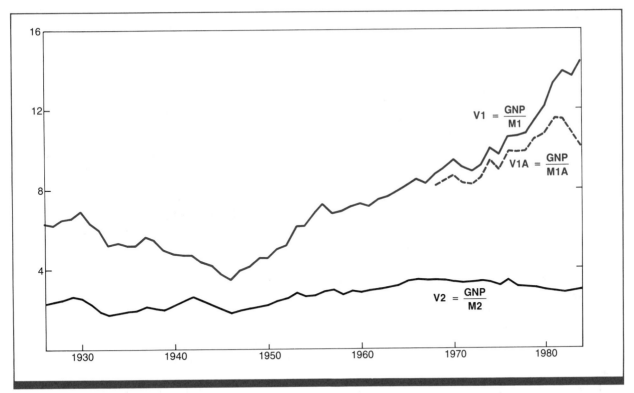

Figure 14-10   The income velocity of money.
The income velocity of money is the ratio of national product to the quantity of money. If either M1 or M1A is taken as the definition of money, then there has been a strong upward trend in velocity, especially in the decade since 1975. If M2 is taken as the definition of money, then velocity has been quite stable for the past three decades.

Source: Compiled from Statistics Canada, *CANSIM Databank* and K. Buckley and M. Urquhart, eds., *Historical Statistics of Canada*, 1st ed. (Toronto and Cambridge: Cambridge University Press and Macmillan of Canada, 1965). Statistics Canada figures reprinted by permission of the Minister of Supply and Services Canada.

As we noted in Chapter 12, since the early 1980s Bank of Canada economists have been using a somewhat broader definition of money, M1A, as an indicator of monetary policy. But as Figure 14-10 shows, the velocity of M1A also changed substantially in the late 1970s and early 1980s. The velocity of M2, finally, *did* remain quite stable. Thus, if one uses the M2 definition of money, the data look much more consistent with the monetarist hypothesis. Accordingly, a monetarist could argue that the high rate of inflation in the early 1980s *was* in fact due to a high rate of growth of the money supply M2.

But if monetarists have to switch back and forth from one definition of money to another in order to defend their position, their defence is questionable: If there is uncertainty about whether it is M1 or M1A or M2 that explains aggregate demand, which one is the policymaker supposed to increase slowly and steadily?

The history of the past two decades has not been kind to doctrinaire economists, whether monetarist or Keynesian.

The Recent Reliance on Monetary Policy

The difficulty in identifying a well-defined concept of money with stable velocity has weakened the case for monetarism in the past decade. Nevertheless, the emphasis on monetary policy has been substantially greater in the past decade than in previous years.

Particularly notable was the policy announced by the Bank of Canada in late 1975. The new policy involved a significant step in the direction of the monetarist position: From November 1975, the Bank would follow a policy of letting M1 grow at a rate that would lie somewhere in a pre-announced "target range". The target range would be revised from time to time, but the Bank made clear its intention of gradually lowering the target growth rate in order to reduce inflationary pressures. The announcement was particularly significant in that it implied a change in the Bank's earlier policy of using interest rates and credit availability as the criteria by which to judge monetary tightness or ease: The new policy put the money supply, and the rate of growth of money, at centre stage.

There are several explanations why the Bank made this decision in 1975. The velocity of M1 had remained relatively stable before that time. Furthermore, the decision seemed an appropriate response to the policy problem facing the government and the Bank of Can-

ada in the mid-1970s. Inflation had been accelerating rapidly, from about 3% in 1970–71 to well over 10% in 1974 and 1975. People were wondering how far the inflationary spiral would go. Fears of even higher inflation in the future were themselves contributing to inflation. For example, unions were demanding higher wages in the expectation that prices would continue to rise. In turn, businesses were raising prices further in order to cover their higher wage costs. Contrary to the experience in the United States, Canada had escaped the 1974–75 recession relatively lightly, and it seemed that cooling inflation and breaking inflationary expectations should be the highest priority of economic policy. The federal government had just announced a program of wage and price controls as a short-run response to high inflation, and the time seemed ripe for making it clear that monetary policy would provide effective support in bringing inflation down.

Monetarism, with its focus on price stability as a policy goal, provided an appropriate framework for this campaign. By declaring its intention to lower the rate of growth of the money stock, the Bank of Canada hoped to convince the public that it meant business. Furthermore, emphasis on the supply of money could reduce the Bank's political problem. An anti-inflationary, tight monetary policy would lead to an increase in interest rates, at least in the short run. By emphasizing its responsibility for controlling the money supply, the Bank hoped to reduce the political pressures on it to keep interest rates down.

As it turned out, even though the Bank did restrict money supply growth to within the successive target ranges for most of the rest of the 1970s, the target rates of growth were initially so high that inflationary pressures subsided only very slowly. But by the early 1980s, money supply growth had been brought down to a very low rate. In late 1982, the Bank formally announced that it was no longer setting specific targets for the money supply. But by that time, the battle against inflation had finally been successful: In 1983 and 1984, the annual inflation rates were 5.8% and 4.4%, respectively.

Since the late 1970s, there has been another reason for the emphasis on money and monetary policy. The federal tax cuts and increases in transfer payments since 1974 resulted in very large deficits in the federal budget. Although many political leaders believed that it was important to reduce deficits, there was little agreement on how to do so. Each spending program had its supporters, and tax increases were unpalatable. Fiscal policy was caught in a political gridlock: Conflicting pressures made it very difficult to cut spending or raise taxes substantially. Because it was so difficult to make major adjustments in fiscal policy, monetary policies seemed to be the only macroeconomic "game in town." Monetary policy was left at the centre of the stage by default.

THE CASE FOR USING MONETARY AND FISCAL POLICIES TOGETHER

It can be argued that the exclusive concentration on monetary policy has in some respects been undesirable. A substantial case can be made that the best macroeconomic policy includes both fiscal and monetary policies, used in combination.

The controversy covered in this chapter provides the first reason. Although the profession may have moved away from the extremes and toward the centre,

there is still a difference of opinion over the relative strengths of monetary and fiscal policies. Statistical evidence does not provide a sharp, clean resolution to this dispute. Continuing uncertainties about the effectiveness of monetary and fiscal policies provide a case for using both. It's unwise to put all our eggs in one basket, particularly when we're not sure which basket it should be.

Furthermore, there are other reasons for favouring a combined monetary-fiscal strategy. During a boom in aggregate demand, restrictive steps are desirable. Such steps are painful. Cuts in government spending hurt various groups in the economy. Nobody wants an increase in their taxes. A tighter monetary policy and higher interest rates can put a squeeze on housing construction and other types of investment. By using a combination of policies, the effects of each may be kept moderate and the adverse impacts diffused. Thus, we may avoid placing a very heavy burden on any single segment of the economy.

KEY POINTS

1. Most present-day economists take a central position, believing that both fiscal and monetary policies have substantial effects on aggregate demand. However, some economists have taken polar positions. Early Keynesians not only focused on fiscal policy; some also believed that monetary policy might have little effect on aggregate demand. On the other side is the monetarist view that money is the predominant force determining aggregate demand, and that fiscal policy has little effect.

2. Keynes proposed that the effects of monetary policy be analysed by looking at three steps:
   (a) the effect of monetary policy on the rate of interest
   (b) the effect of the interest rate on investment
   (c) the effect of a change in investment on aggregate demand (the multiplier)

3. Keynes himself believed that expansive monetary policies could not be counted on to get the economy out of the Depression of the 1930s because of a problem at the very first step. Interest rates were already very low, and could

not be pushed down much further by an expansive monetary policy.

4. Some early followers of Keynes had more general doubts about the effectiveness of monetary policies—not just in a depression, but also in more normal times. Specifically, they argued that a problem would arise at the second step because investment is not very responsive to changes in the rate of interest. That is, the MEI schedule is steep, as illustrated in Figure 14-5.

5. However, even if the MEI schedule is steep, restrictive monetary policies may reduce investment and aggregate demand by forcing banks to ration their loans.

6. Monetary policy may be more effective in restraining aggregate demand than in raising it. Using monetary policy has been compared to controlling aggregate demand with a string.

7. Classical macroeconomics was based on the equation of exchange ($MV = PQ$) and on the proposition that velocity V is stable (the quantity theory). If velocity is stable, a change in money M will cause current-dollar national

product (PQ) to change by approximately the same percentage.

8. Classical economists believed that, in the long run, the principal effect of a change in the rate of growth of M would be a change in the price level P. In the short run, however, changes in the growth of M could also affect real national product Q.

9. Indeed, those in the classical tradition believe that monetary disturbances are one of the principal causes of fluctuations in real output.

10. The view that velocity is stable is based on the belief that there is a stable demand for money. If, after a period of equilibrium, people get more money, their holdings of money will exceed their demand for it (Figure 14-7). They will use the surplus to buy goods and services, thus increasing current-dollar national product (PQ).

11. Some of those in the classical tradition doubt that fiscal policy will have a substantial effect on aggregate demand unless the fiscal policy is accompanied by changes in M. That is, they have doubts about the effectiveness of pure fiscal policy. These doubts are based on the belief that an increase in deficit spending will push up interest rates and therefore crowd out private investment.

12. Statistical evidence does not give a clear, unambiguous confirmation of either the strong Keynesian or the strong classical view. At times the evidence supports the quantity theory, and at other times—such as in the late 1970s—the evidence tends to contradict it.

13. Because of this—and for other reasons, too—it is undesirable to place exclusive reliance on either monetary or fiscal policy. Instead, it is wiser to use a combined monetary-fiscal strategy.

14. Nevertheless, there has been a very heavy reliance on monetary policy since the mid-1970s. One reason has been the desire of the Bank of Canada to restrain the high rate of inflation that started in 1973–74. Another has been the great difficulty in changing fiscal policy during the 1980s.

KEY CONCEPTS

demand for money	credit crunch	monetary rule
marginal efficiency of investment (MEI)	availability of loanable funds	crowding out
rate of return	pushing on a string	investment responsive to a change in the interest rate
investment unresponsive to a change in the interest rate	equation of exchange	change in the interest rate
credit rationing	income velocity of money (V)	pure fiscal policy
	quantity theory of money	cause-effect relationship

PROBLEMS

14-1 In the Keynesian framework, there are three separate steps in the process by which monetary policy affects aggregate demand.
  (a) What are these three steps?
  (b) Keynes argued that expansive monetary policy would be ineffective in getting the economy out of the Depression of the 1930s because of a problem at one of these three steps. Which step? What was the nature of the problem?

  (c) Some of the followers of Keynes argued that monetary policy is generally a weak and ineffective tool for controlling aggregate demand. They foresaw a problem at another one of the steps. Which step? What was the nature of the problem?

14-2 The Keynesian theory of the demand for money (shown in Figure 14-2) was developed at a time when no interest was paid on chequable deposits. There was an obvious cost in holding money: namely, the interest that could otherwise have been earned by buying a security.

Now banks and other institutions are permitted to pay interest on chequable deposits, as we saw in Chapter 12. When banks pay interest on such deposits, how would you expect the demand for money to be affected as a result?

14-3 Suppose that a machine that will last forever costs $100,000 and yields a return of 10%. Now suppose that the price of the machine doubles to $200,000, while the amount that such a machine will produce remains the same, and the prices of outputs and inputs also remain unchanged. What happens to the yield on the machine?

14-4 The marginal efficiency of investment shows the expected rates of return of possible investment projects. For what reasons might expected rates of return on investment projects change through time? How would each of these reasons affect the MEI curve?

14-5 How do strong Keynesians and strong monetarists disagree on the way in which the MEI curve should be drawn? How does the way a strong Keynesian draws the MEI curve cast doubt on the effectiveness of monetary policy? How does the way a strong monetarist draws the MEI curve cast doubt on the effectiveness of fiscal policy in controlling aggregate demand?

14-6 Why might a restrictive monetary policy have more effect on aggregate demand than an expansive monetary policy?

14-7 "I accept the equation of exchange as valid. But I do not accept the quantity theory of money." Is it consistent for an economist to hold such a position? Why or why not?

14-8 Suppose that the demand for money is initially equal to the quantity of money in existence. Then suppose that the quantity of money is doubled because of action by the central bank. According to a Keynesian economist, what will happen? According to a classical economist, what will happen?

14-9 Explain how a budget deficit might cause a trade deficit. (A trade deficit is an excess of imports over exports.)

Chapter 15

STABILIZATION POLICY AND INTERNATIONAL TRANSACTIONS: SHOULD CANADA HAVE FIXED OR FLEXIBLE EXCHANGE RATES?

Cecily, you will read your Political Economy
in my absence. The chapter on the Fall of
the Rupee you may omit. It is somewhat too
sensational. Even these metallic problems
have their melodramatic side.

Miss Prism, in Oscar Wilde's

The Importance of Being Ernest

Economic efficiency requires specialization. It is efficient to grow wheat on the Prairies and corn in southern Ontario. And the scope for specialization goes far beyond the boundaries of any single country. Even such a large nation as the United States can gain by international specialization. It is efficient for the United States to export wheat and import oil and bananas. For the smaller and resource-rich Canadian economy, the gains from specialization are even more important.

While the United States exports less than one-tenth of its national product, almost 30% of the goods and services produced in Canada are exported to foreign markets—products such as wheat, newsprint, automobiles, and various other manufactured goods. In return, we import such things as coffee, fresh fruits and vegetables, automobiles, computers, and other manufactured goods.

The way in which international specialization can

contribute to a high standard of living fits into the study of economic efficiency in Part 6; we therefore defer the detailed consideration of international trade and efficiency to that part. In this chapter, we study the relationship between macroeconomic conditions and international transactions. How can we use monetary and fiscal policies to prevent international business cycles from spilling over into Canada? If there are large government deficits and high interest rates in the United States, must interest rates rise in Canada too? Does the relative effectiveness of monetary and fiscal policy depend on the way these policies influence foreign trade and capital flows? Should Canada and other countries have fixed or flexible exchange rates? Since international transactions play such a large part in Canada's economy, the answers to these questions are of great importance to our policymakers.

EXCHANGE RATES

In many ways, international trade is like domestic trade; it adds to economic efficiency because of comparative advantage and economies of scale. But there are two major complications that make international transactions different from domestic trade:

1. Domestic trade involves a single currency. For example, when a Manitoban buys a bottle of British Columbia wine, both the consumer and the producer want the payment to be made in the same currency—namely, Canadian dollars. But consider a British importer of Canadian wheat, who has British pounds to pay for the wheat. The Canadian exporter wants to receive payment not in pounds but in Canadian dollars. Therefore, the British importer will go to the **foreign exchange market** in order to sell pounds and buy the dollars needed to pay for the wheat, as illustrated in Figure 15-1. (Foreign exchange markets are located in financial centres, such as London, New York, Montreal, and Toronto.)

> *Foreign exchange* is the currency of another country. For example, U.S. dollars, British pounds, and Japanese yen are foreign exchange to a Canadian. Canadian dollars are foreign exchange to a Briton, a German, or an American.

> A *foreign exchange market* is a market in which one national currency (such as the Canadian dollar) is bought in exchange for another national currency (such as the British pound).

> An *exchange rate* is the price of one national currency in terms of another national currency. For example, the price £1 = $2 is an exchange rate, and so is $1 = 175 Japanese yen.

2. International trade is complicated by *barriers* that do not exist in trade between regions, provinces, or cities within the same country. Most notably, *tariffs* (also called *duties*) protect domestic producers of many goods by giving them an advantage over foreign competitors. The consumer, however, suffers: Prices of imports are increased by tariffs. And, when the prices of imported goods rise, domestic producers may also raise their prices, since they can now do so without losing business to foreign competitors.

> A *tariff* is a tax imposed on a foreign good as it enters the country.

Other barriers also impede international trade. For example, the Canadian government sometimes imposes a *quota* on the amount of beef that can be imported, in order to protect domestic beef producers.

> A *quota* is a limit on the quantity of a good that can be imported.

Tariffs and other restrictions on trade will be studied in Chapter 32. Here, we concentrate on the first point—foreign exchange transactions, and the complications they raise for domestic stabilization policies.

THE FOREIGN EXCHANGE MARKET

Because there are more than a hundred countries in the world, the foreign exchange markets involve many currencies, and transactions can be complicated. In

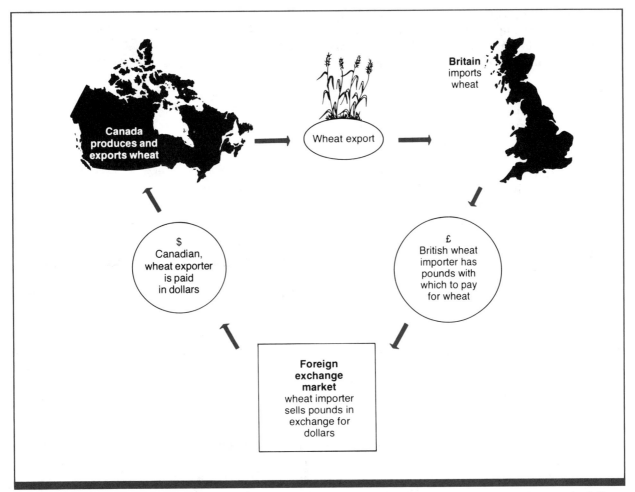

Figure 15-1 International trade and the foreign exchange market.
International trade normally involves more than one national currency. The British importer wants to pay in pounds; the Canadian exporter wants to receive payment in dollars. Consequently, the British import results in a transaction on the foreign exchange market, with pounds being sold for dollars.

order to keep the discussion simple, let us first concentrate on transactions between just two countries, Canada and the United States. Just as the price of wheat is determined in the market where wheat is bought and sold in exchange for money, so the exchange rate between the Canadian dollar and the U.S. dollar is determined in the foreign exchange market where Canadian dollars are bought and sold in exchange for U.S. dollars. And just like the market for wheat, the foreign exchange market can be studied by looking at demand and supply. The demand for Canadian dollars (C$) by those originally holding U.S. dollars (U.S.$)

arises from three types of transactions:

1. *American imports of Canadian goods;* that is, Canadian exports of goods to the United States. For example, when an American firm buys Canadian newsprint, a demand for Canadian dollars is created. (The American firm has U.S. dollars, but the Canadian firm wants Canadian dollars. Thus, either the American or the Canadian firm has to buy Canadian dollars in exchange for U.S. dollars).

2. *American imports of Canadian services.* For example, an American tourist may stay in a Canadian hotel or travel on a Canadian airline. When the Cana-

dian hotel or airline receives payment in U.S. dollars, it sells these dollars in order to obtain the Canadian dollars it wants. In other words, spending by the tourist creates a demand for Canadian dollars in exchange for U.S. dollars.

(What is the difference between international trade of a good and trade of a service? When an American imports a good from Canada, the good physically leaves Canada and enters the United States; the newsprint is unloaded at an American railroad terminal. In the case of most services, there is no such physical transfer of a good; obviously, the hotel room stays in Canada. But in either case, a demand for Canadian dollars is created.)

3. *American acquisitions of Canadian assets.* For example, if an American corporation wants to invest in Canada by building a new factory here, it will need Canadian dollars to pay the firm that constructs the factory.

The demand for Canadian dollars, like the demand for wheat, depends on the price. Suppose, for example, that for some reason the price of the Canadian dollar rises in terms of U.S. dollars from U.S.$0.80 to U.S.$1.10. What would this mean? Because the Canadian dollar has become more expensive to Americans, Canadian goods and services also become more expensive to Americans. To illustrate, suppose a Canadian hotel room costs C$50 per day. When the price of the Canadian dollar was U.S.$0.80, that room would cost $40 in U.S. money. But when the price of the Canadian dollar rises to U.S.$1.10, that same room would cost an American $55 in U.S. money. Notice that the price that an American pays for a Canadian hotel room depends on two things: (1) the Canadian price for the room (C$50 in the example); and (2) the exchange rate between the U.S. dollar and the Canadian dollar. Therefore, with a more expensive Canadian dollar, American tourists would be less likely to go to Canada, and American firms would be less likely to buy Canadian goods. Thus, when the Canadian dollar costs U.S.$1.10, the quantity of Canadian dollars demanded is less than when a Canadian dollar costs U.S.$0.80, as illustrated by the demand curve (D) in Figure 15-2.

Now consider the other side of the market, the supply of Canadian dollars to be exchanged for U.S. dollars. Whenever those who hold Canadian dollars

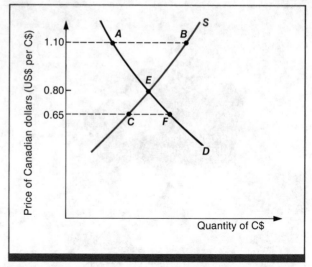

Figure 15-2   The demand and supply of Canadian dollars in the foreign exchange market.
The equilibrium exchange rate is determined by the intersection of demand and supply. The demand for Canadian dollars in terms of U.S. dollars depends on (1) U.S. imports of Canadian goods; (2) purchases of Canadian services by Americans; and (3) purchases of Canadian assets by Americans. The supply of Canadian dollars depends on (1) Canadian imports of U.S. goods; (2) Canadian purchases of U.S. services; and (3) Canadian purchases of U.S. assets.

want to buy something that has to be paid for in U.S. dollars, a supply of Canadian dollars is created: The firms and individuals who want to buy American goods and services, or American assets, have to offer Canadian dollars in the foreign exchange market in order to get U.S. dollars. Thus, the supply of Canadian dollars depends on:

1. Canadian imports of U.S. goods
2. Canadian imports of U.S. services
3. Canadian acquisitions of U.S. assets; that is, Canadian investment in the United States.

The supply of Canadian dollars to the foreign exchange market also depends on price. If the price of the Canadian dollar falls, that is another way of saying that the price of the U.S. dollar rises. Thus, American goods and services become more expensive to Canadians. (For example, suppose the price of the Canadian dollar falls from C$1.00 = U.S.$1.00 to C$1.00 = U.S.$0.80. This means that Canadians will now have to pay C$1.25 for one U.S. dollar. Thus, a Canadian car dealer would now have to pay C$12,500 for an American car costing U.S.$10,000. But before the fall in the price of the Canadian dollar, the dealer would have had to pay only C$10,000.)

When the price of the Canadian dollar falls on the exchange markets, Canadians will therefore reduce their purchases of American goods and services, and this will tend to reduce the amount of Canadian dollars supplied to the foreign exchange market. A rise in the price of the Canadian dollar has the opposite effect: It will make American goods and services cheaper in terms of Canadian money. As a result, Canadian buyers will increase their imports from the United States, and this tends to increase the quantity of Canadian dollars supplied to the foreign exchange market, as the supply curve S in Figure 15-2 illustrates.[1]

While the example we have been discussing deals with the market where Canadian dollars are exchanged for U.S. dollars, there are also markets where Canadian dollars are exchanged for German marks, Swiss francs, Japanese yen, British pounds, and so forth. Clearly, some of these markets are more important than others, because they involve countries with which Canada has large transactions. Specifically, the largest volume of foreign exchange transactions by far takes place in the market in which Canadian dollars are exchanged for U.S. dollars. The main reason for this, of course, is that the largest part of our international transactions are with the United States.

However, another reason is that many transactions between Canada and other foreign countries (say, Mexico) take place using U.S. dollars (rather than Mexican pesos or Canadian dollars). For example, a Mexican firm that imports lumber from a Canadian sawmill may pay for the lumber in U.S. dollars. Or a Canadian tourist may pay for hotel expenses in Acapulco with a U.S. dollar traveller's cheque bought in Canada. Note that although these transactions are with Mexico, rather than with the United States, they still involve the market where Canadian dollars are exchanged for U.S. dollars.

Thus, demand and supply in the market where Canadian dollars are exchanged for U.S. dollars depend not only on our transactions with the United States: They also depend on our transactions with other foreign countries. To keep the discussion simple, we can let the supply and demand for Canadian dollars in exchange for U.S. dollars represent our total transactions with *all* foreign countries. Using this simplification, we can interpret Figure 15-2 as saying that a fall in the value of the Canadian dollar in terms of the U.S. dollar will increase the quantity of Canadian dollars demanded by *all* foreigners because it will make our goods less expensive in world markets, and thus induce foreigners to increase their purchases of our exports. A fall in the exchange value of the Canadian dollar will make all foreign goods and services more expensive in Canada. Therefore, Canadians will want to import fewer goods and services from foreign countries; accordingly, the quantity of Canadian dollars supplied to the foreign exchange market will tend to fall.

CANADA'S BALANCE-OF-PAYMENTS ACCOUNTS

Canada's balance-of-payments accounts provide a record of transactions between residents of Canada and those of other countries. The accounts are constructed with a positive or "credit" side, and a negative or "debit" side. With one important exception (which we will explain later), the credit side corresponds to the *demand* for the Canadian dollar on the foreign exchange market, and the debit side to the supply. Thus, on the credit side, one records transactions that give rise to a foreign demand for Canadian dollars; for example, Canadian exports of goods and

---

[1]Actually, the quantity of Canadian dollars supplied to the foreign exchange market will not *necessarily* increase when the price rises. Suppose that, when C$1.00 = U.S.$1.00, Canadians buy one million units of U.S. goods, each worth U.S.$1.00. Then to buy these goods worth U.S.$1 million, Canadians must supply C$1 million. Now, suppose that the price of the Canadian dollar rises to C$1.00 = U.S.$1.11; that is, the U.S. dollar falls to U.S.$1.00 = C$0.90. Suppose that, as a result of the fall in the prices of U.S. goods as measured in Canadian dollars, Canadians now buy only slightly more U.S. goods — 1,050,000 units, worth U.S.$1,050,000. Then the cost in Canadian dollars is only C$945,000 (that is, 1,050,000 × 0.90 = 945,000). In this example, the increase in the quantity of Canadian imports is not enough to outweigh the lower value of the U.S. dollar; Canadian expenditures on imports fall, measured in Canadian dollars. That is, the quantity of Canadian dollars supplied to the foreign exchange market *decreases*. Normally, however, a rise in the exchange value of the Canadian dollar will increase imports by a sufficiently large amount so that there is an increase in the quantity of Canadian dollars to the foreign exchange market.

Table 15-1
Canada's Balance of Payments, 1984
(in billions of dollars)

Credits (+)		Debits (−)	
A. CURRENT ACCOUNT			
I. Merchandise trade			
1. Exports of Goods	112.1	1. Imports of Goods	91.5
II. Other Current Accounts			
1. Exports of Services	19.2	1. Imports of Services	38.2
(a) Travel 4.4		(a) Travel 6.5	
(b) Interest and dividend receipts 1.8		(b) Interest and dividend payments 13.1	
(c) Other service receipts 13.0		(c) Other service payments 18.6	
2. Unilateral transfers (receipts)	3.3	2. Unilateral transfers (payments)	2.4
B. CAPITAL ACCOUNT			
III. Capital Flows, Excluding Changes in Official Reserves			
1. Long-term capital inflows	14.8	1. Long-term capital outflows	12.1
(a) Foreign direct investment in Canada 2.2		(a) Canadian direct investment abroad 3.8	
(b) Long-term portfolio investment in Canada 12.6		(b) Long-term portfolio investment abroad 8.3	
2. Short-term capital inflow	2.3	2. Short-term capital outflow	2.4
		3. Net Errors and Omissions	6.2
IV. Change in Official Reserve Assets			
		1. Net increase in Canada's foreign exchange reserves	− 1.1

SOURCE: *Bank of Canada Review.*

services to foreign countries, and acquisitions of Canadian assets by foreigners. On the debit side, we find transactions which represent a *supply* of Canadian dollars to the foreign exchange market: Canadian imports of goods and services, and Canadian acquisitions of foreign assets.

Canada's balance of payments is divided into two main accounts. In one of these— the **capital account**— statisticians enter changes in foreign-owned assets in Canada, and changes in Canadian-owned assets in foreign countries. That is, *international investment* is entered in the capital account. All other items—that

is, those which do not represent changes in the ownership of assets—are put in the **current account**, shown at the top of Table 15-1.

The Current Account

The current account is subdivided into two main categories. First are the figures for *merchandise trade*: exports and imports of goods from and into Canada (category I). Observe that in 1984, Canadian exports of merchandise ($112.1 billion) were larger than imports of merchandise ($91.5 billion). Thus, Canada had a **merchandise trade surplus** of $20.6 billion.

A country has a *merchandise trade surplus* (or, more simply, a *merchandise surplus*) when its exports of goods exceed its imports of goods. When imports of goods exceed exports of goods, a country has a *deficit* on merchandise trade.

Category II is made up principally of exports and imports of *services*. In addition to services mentioned earlier—expenditures by foreign tourists for hotels or airline tickets—the service category includes interest and dividends; they represent payments for the services rendered by capital. Note that *returns* from investments (in the form of interest and dividends) appear in the current account, even though investments themselves appear in the capital accounts. The reason is this: If Northern Telecom builds a new plant in Germany, Canadian-owned assets abroad rise. Therefore, this investment belongs in the capital accounts. But when Northern Telecom receives dividends from this foreign subsidiary, there is no change in ownership. Northern Telecom receives the dividends, but still owns the foreign subsidiary. Thus, the dividends go in the current account (Item II.1.b). Similarly, interest from a foreign bond appears in the current account. (But, if the foreign bond were paid off, that would represent a change in asset holdings, and would appear in the capital accounts.) In addition to services, category II also includes **unilateral transfers**—items such as remittances by Canadian immigrants to foreign relatives and Canadian aid to less developed countries on the debit side; and inheritances by Canadian citizens from relatives abroad, on the credit side.

While Canada had a substantial merchandise surplus in 1984, the services and transfers category showed a deficit ($18.1 billion). This pattern, which has been typical in the Canadian balance-of-payments accounts in recent years, is explained partly by the large income earned by foreigners on their past investments in Canada—earnings that appear on the debit side of the services account. Taken together, the merchandise surplus and the deficit on services and transfers produced a small *current account surplus* of $2.5 billion in 1984.

The Capital Account

On the credit side of the capital account are shown foreign acquisitions of Canadian assets, also referred to as **capital inflows** into Canada. On the debit side, we find Canadian acquisitions of foreign assets—also referred to as **capital outflows**.

> Acquisitions of Canadian assets by foreign residents are referred to as *capital inflows*.
> A *capital outflow* occurs when Canadians acquire foreign assets.[2]

The capital account is divided into two main parts: Category IV, "Change in official reserve assets" explained below), and Category III, which includes all other capital flows. Category III is subdivided into *long-term* capital flows and *short-term* capital flows, depending on whether the asset acquired has a maturity of more or less than one year. (A bond and common stock are examples of long-term assets; bank deposits and Treasury bills are short-term assets.) In turn, long-term capital flows are subdivided into **direct investment** and **portfolio investment**.

On the credit side, *direct investment* by foreign residents in Canada represents the foreign acquisition of a controlling interest in a firm which operates in Canada, or foreign financing of new Canadian production facilities owned by firms that foreign residents control. As an example, when Volvo of Sweden establishes a Canadian subsidiary and constructs an assembly plant in Canada, this appears as a direct investment (part of the $2.2 billion figure shown in Table 15-1).[3] Other kinds of capital inflow are referred to as *portfolio investment*. In other words, the distinction between direct investment and portfolio investment depends on whether foreigners control the operation (as in the case of Volvo's direct investment), or whether they are simply *providing financing* for Canadian-

---

[2]Capital inflows are also sometimes called *capital imports*. But be wary of this terminology. Note that a capital *import* appears on the same side of the balance of payments as an *export* of goods. Why is this? Because both result in a demand for Canadian dollars.

[3]When Canadian residents purchase a controlling interest in firms which operate in Canada under foreign control, this is recorded as a negative direct investment on the credit side of the capital accounts. For example, in the second quarter of 1981, following the introduction of the government's National Energy Program, there were takeovers by Canadian investors of some large Canadian subsidiaries of foreign oil companies. For that quarter, the balance of payments statistics show a foreign direct investment of −$3.5 billion.

controlled businesses or for other Canadian borrowers (such as provincial governments).

Canadian investments abroad are put on the debit side. Thus, if Northern Telecom builds a plant in the United States, this appears on the debit side, as a direct investment. And if you or I were to buy a British government bond, this would appear on the debit side, as a portfolio investment.

The final category (IV), known as "change in official reserve assets" or "net official monetary movements," reflects purchases and sales of *foreign exchange reserves* by Canadian monetary authorities—that is, by the Bank of Canada and the Exchange Fund Account. These reserves include foreign currencies—mainly U.S. dollars—plus two other assets that are readily exchanged for foreign currencies; namely, gold, and Canada's balance held in the *International Monetary Fund* (IMF).

> *Foreign exchange reserves* are foreign currencies, gold, and balances in the IMF which are held by the government or central bank.

Acquisitions of foreign exchange reserves by the Canadian monetary authorities appear on the debit side of the accounts, just like acquisitions of foreign assets by Canadian corporations. (When Canada's foreign exchange reserves *decrease*, as they did in 1984, a negative entry is made on the debit side.)

Theoretically, this should be the end of our story; we should now have finished with the complete balance-of-payments accounts. To see why, note that the credit side in the balance-of-payments accounts provides a record of all transactions in which Canadians acquired foreign currencies (export sales of goods and services, and sales to foreigners of Canadian assets). The debit side of the accounts, on the other hand, tells us what the foreign currencies were used for: Some were used to pay for imports of goods and services into Canada, while others were used by Canadian firms or individuals to increase their holdings of foreign assets. Whatever was left over must have ended up as part of our official foreign exchange reserves. When changes in our official reserves are included, it is a straightforward logical conclusion that the balance-of-payments accounts should balance; that is, the two sides should add to the same total.

And the accounts would in fact balance, if government statisticians had perfect information. But they do not. For example, government officials do not tag along with tourists to see just how much they spend. And the government has only imperfect information on how many foreign assets are acquired. Furthermore, even the statistics on exports and imports of goods are imperfect. In order to compensate for the measurement inaccuracies, government statisticians calculate "errors and omissions." This item—which is whatever number is needed to make the two sides of the balance of payments add to the same total—is entered in the capital account (item 3 on the debit side), because it is believed that this is where the greatest problems of measurement occur.

The Concept of the Balance of Payments

But if the two sides of the balance-of-payments accounts must be equal (because of the way the accounts are constructed), what do we mean when we talk of the balance of payments being in "deficit" or "surplus"? The answer is that a deficit or surplus can exist only when certain items in the accounts are excluded. The standard concept of the balance of payments is the difference between the credits and debits in categories I, II, and III; that is, the balance of payments is calculated by *excluding* the changes in reserves shown in category IV. If the credits in the first three categories exceed the debits, we have a *balance-of-payments surplus*. The quantity of Canadian dollars demanded by foreigners in order to buy Canadian goods, services, and assets exceeds our supply of Canadian dollars to buy foreign goods, services, and assets. The difference ends up in our official reserves (that is, in category IV). In other words, the Bank of Canada or the Exchange Fund Account (EFA) are supplying the shortfall of Canadian dollars, and are acquiring foreign currencies in exchange. Thus, when Canada has a balance-of-payments surplus, we are acquiring reserves; when we have a deficit, we are losing reserves.

> A country has a *balance-of-payments surplus* when it is acquiring foreign exchange reserves; that is, when the sum of its credits in categories I, II, and III exceeds the sum of the debits.
>
> It has a balance-of-payments *deficit* when it is losing reserves.

In an important sense, changes in foreign exchange reserves are a balancing item in the balance-of-payments accounts: The authorities acquire (or sell) reserves to mop up the surplus (or shortage) of foreign currencies on the exchange markets. This observation allows us to tie up a loose end from the earlier discussion: All the items in the balance of payments *except for changes in reserves* are normally considered part of the demand and supply of Canadian dollars on the foreign exchange markets. (Strictly speaking, the Canadian authorities create a demand for Canadian dollars when they sell reserves to buy Canadian dollars. However, this is not considered part of normal demand, but rather the result of action by the authorities to eliminate a surplus of Canadian dollars and thus stabilize the price of the dollar. In this chapter, we use the terms "demand" and "supply" in the standard way. That is, we exclude the authorities' purchases or sales of Canadian dollars in exchange for foreign reserves when we refer to the demand or supply of the Canadian dollar in the exchange market.)

Thus, a balance-of-payments deficit and a loss of reserves, for example, means that the supply of Canadian currency to the foreign exchange market exceeds the demand for Canadian currency, as would be the case at the exchange rate C$1 = U.S.$1.10 in Figure 15-2. At that exchange rate, the amount AB by which the supply of C$ exceeds the demand is equal to the balance-of-payments deficit and loss of reserves, expressed in Canadian dollars. Similarly, at an exchange rate of C$1 = U.S.$0.65, the demand for C$ would exceed the supply, and the amount CF of excess demand would measure the surplus in the balance of payments and gain of reserves.

DISEQUILIBRIUM IN THE EXCHANGE MARKET

Suppose we start with an exchange rate of, say, C$1.00 = U.S.$0.80. It is possible that at this exchange rate, the quantity of Canadian dollars demanded in the foreign exchange market exactly equals the quantity supplied. Thus, the demand and supply curves intersect at C$1.00 = U.S.$0.80, as shown at the initial equilibrium E in Figure 15-3.

But we live in a changing world. Even if the demand and supply are initially in equilibrium at the price C$1.00 = U.S.$0.80, one or both curves may shift as time passes. Suppose that the demand for Canadian dollars decreases from D_1 to D_2. It might do so for any number of reasons; anything that decreases the Ameri-

can (or any other foreign country's) demand for Canadian products will cause a leftward shift of the demand curve. An example would be a reduction in the U.S. demand for Canadian nickel. Similarly, a reduction of foreign purchases of Canadian assets would also shift the demand curve to the left.

As a result of the leftward shift, the initial price of C$1.00 = U.S.$0.80 is no longer an equilibrium. In the face of this change, the Canadian government has the option of taking any one (or a combination) of the following steps:

1. Intervention in the foreign exchange market. In the example in Figure 15-3, the Canadian authorities can keep the price of the Canadian dollar stable by selling foreign exchange reserves in order to buy up the oversupply GE of Canadian dollars. (As we noted earlier, GE would then show up as a deficit in the balance-of-payments accounts. For example, if the dis-

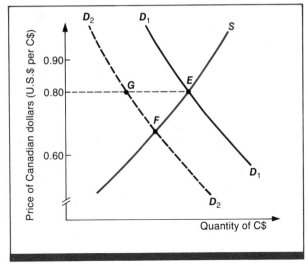

Figure 15-3 Disequilibrium in the foreign exchange market.
If the demand for Canadian dollars shifts to the left from D_1 to D_2, there will be an oversupply (GE) at the old exchange rate. The Canadian government can eliminate this oversupply by one or a combination of the following steps: (1) The purchase of Canadian dollars in exchange for U.S. dollars by the Canadian authorities. (This will only work temporarily, however, because Canadian reserves of U.S. dollars are limited.) (2) A reduction in the supply of Canadian dollars by Canadian restrictions on imports and other international transactions. (3) Restrictive aggregate demand policies in Canada, which also reduce Canadian imports and capital outflows, and hence the supply of Canadian dollars to the exchange market. (4) A change in the exchange rate to its new equilibrium F.

tance *GE* were $500 million per year, this would be the loss of reserves that would show up in the accounts.)

The initial disturbance may be only temporary. The U.S. demand for our nickel may pick up, or foreign investors may decide to acquire more Canadian assets; demand will then shift back from D_2 to D_1, and E will again become the equilibrium. In this event, official intervention in the foreign exchange market is no longer necessary; it has successfully smoothed out the temporary aberration. But not all shifts in supply and demand are temporary. For example, the U.S. demand for nickel may be permanently lower. In this case, the Canadian authorities cannot maintain the original exchange rate of C$1.00 = U.S.$0.80 indefinitely by selling reserves of U.S. dollars on the foreign exchange market. Why? Because our holdings of U.S. dollars and other reserve assets are limited; sooner or later we will face the prospect of running out of reserves.

Thus, in the face of a permanently reduced foreign demand for Canadian dollars, the Canadian government must move to one of its other options:

2. Imposing direct restrictions on international transactions. In order to maintain the initial exchange rate, the Canadian government may reduce the supply of Canadian dollars by taking direct action affecting international transactions. That is, it may shift curve *S* to the left so that it passes through *G*, and thus again make $0.80 the equilibrium price. For example, the government can do this by limiting the amount of foreign assets that Canadians are legally permitted to acquire (as it did during World War II). Or it may limit Canadian imports of foreign goods by the imposition of additional tariffs or quotas (as it did during the exchange crisis of 1962).

3. Altering domestic monetary and fiscal policies. The Canadian government may indirectly reduce the supply of Canadian dollars coming onto the foreign exchange market (that is, shift *S* to the left) by adopting restrictive monetary and fiscal policies. For example, tighter monetary or fiscal policies will slow down economic activity and reduce incomes. As a result, consumption will fall, including the consumption of imported goods. Furthermore, the tighter policies will reduce Canadian inflation. And, as our goods become more competitive in price, Canadian consumers will be encouraged to buy domestic goods instead of imports. (Moreover, tight economic policies also tend to increase exports: More competitively priced

Canadian goods may capture a larger share of U.S. and other foreign markets. As foreigners buy more Canadian goods, the demand for Canadian dollars will increase, helping to eliminate the gap *GE* between the demand and supply for Canadian dollars at the exchange rate C$1.00 = U.S.$0.80.)

4. Allowing the exchange rate to adjust. The Canadian government may allow the exchange rate to move to the new equilibrium *F*, where the price of the Canadian dollar is lower, at U.S.$0.70.

Since the end of World War II in 1945, the central debate in international finance has been over which of these four options should be used by countries facing disequilibrium in their exchange markets. In the early postwar period, most countries leaned toward the second option (direct restrictions). This tool, however, has a grave defect: By interfering with international transactions, it reduces the efficiency of the world economy.

Thus, most of the discussion in recent decades has focused on the other three options. In particular, there has been a debate whether countries should rely primarily on option 1—the maintenance of a stable exchange rate through official intervention—or option 4, changes in exchange rates.

FIXED OR FLEXIBLE EXCHANGE RATES?

Since 1973, most of the world's industrialized nations have used option 4; that is, they have followed a policy of *flexible* (or *floating*) exchange rates, allowing exchange rates to fluctuate in response to changing conditions of supply and demand. Historically, however, many countries tried to maintain a system of *fixed* exchange rates. Before World War I, the world's major industrialized countries adhered to the **gold standard**. Under the gold standard, gold coins circulated as part of the money stock, and paper currency could be converted into gold. But when the values of different currencies were kept stable in terms of gold, this meant that the exchange rates between currencies were kept stable as well.

During World War I, the gold standard broke down. In the face of huge government budgets, inflationary monetary policies, and huge expenditures for imports, governments were unable to maintain convertibility of their currencies into gold. Then, during the 1920s, steps were taken to restore the gold standard. For example, Britain re-established gold convertibility in 1925, and Canada in 1926. But the World War had greatly weakened the international financial system, and the gold standard collapsed for good a few years later; Canada and Britain suspended gold convertibility in 1931, and the United States did the same in 1933. During the rest of the Depression, currencies fluctuated widely; for example, within a few months in 1932, the price of the Canadian dollar fell from U.S.$1.00 to about U.S.$0.80; by 1934, it had once again risen to U.S.$1.00.

The Depression gave flexible exchange rates a bad name, and at the end of World War II, an international conference was held at Bretton Woods, New Hampshire, to establish a stable international monetary system. A system of *pegged-but-adjustable* exchange rates was established. Specifically, countries were generally expected to keep their exchange rates stable within a narrow *band* of ±1% around an officially declared *par value*. (Countries generally pegged their currencies to the U.S. dollar; for example, Canada initially pegged its dollar at C$1.00 = U.S.$0.909, the same rate that had prevailed during the War.)

However, in the event of substantial pressures on a currency—reflected, in part, by large changes in reserves—a country could change the par value of its currency. (For example, as you can see in Figure 15-4, in 1946 Canada *revalued* its dollar, to C$1.00 = U.S.$1.00; and we *devalued* our dollar in 1949, back to C$1.00 = U.S.$0.909.) A new organization—the *International Monetary Fund* (IMF)—was established to lend reserves to countries in balance-of-payments difficulties, and to supervise changes in par values. (A second organization—the International Bank for Reconstruction and Development (IBRD), or World Bank—was also established at Bretton Woods. Its major function now is to help less developed countries (LDCs) finance economic development projects.)

The *par value* of a currency (under the IMF system prior to 1973) was the official price of the currency, generally specified in terms of the U.S. dollar.

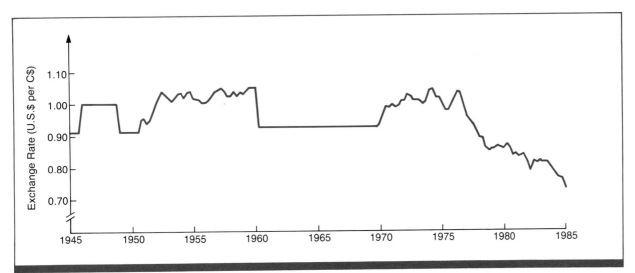

Figure 15-4   The exchange rate between the Canadian and U.S. dollars, 1945–1985 (U.S.$ per C$).
At the end of World War II, the Canadian dollar was pegged at a value of U.S.$0.909. It was revalued in 1946, but devalued again in 1949. During 1950–1962, Canada allowed the exchange rate to float; during most of the period, the dollar remained fairly stable in value at around C$1 = U.S.$1.00. However, the Canadian dollar began to fall in 1960, and following an exchange crisis in 1962, the government decided to peg the exchange rate at C$1 = U.S. $0.925. In 1970, the dollar was again allowed to float. In the mid-1980s, it reached its modern-era low value of around C$1 = U.S.$0.70.

Source: Compiled from Statistics Canada, *CANSIM Databank*. Reprinted by permission of the Minister of Supply and Services Canada.

A country *devalues* when it lowers the par value of its currency.

A country *revalues* when it raises the par value of its currency.

Between 1945 and 1973, most of the world's countries belonged to the system of pegged-but-adjustable exchange rates. However, there were some exceptions. Canada found that a system of pegged rates sometimes created difficulties in the management of monetary policy, and the Canadian dollar was allowed to float during the period 1950–1962, and again in 1970. By the early 1970s, other countries were also finding it difficult to maintain pegged exchange rates. (The problems with the system are discussed in detail in the Appendix to this chapter.) Ultimately, the pegged-rate system also broke down: Since 1973, most major industrial countries have had floating exchange rates—although a number of the LDCs keep their currencies pegged to the currency of a major industrial country.

As we explain in the Appendix, under the Bretton Woods system countries were expected to rely primarily on a combination of option 1 (intervention in foreign exchange markets) and option 3 (changing domestic monetary and fiscal policies) to deal with disturbances in their balance of payments. Because the rules of the system *did* allow for exchange rate adjustments in certain circumstances, it was not, strictly speaking, a system of *fixed* exchange rates. Nevertheless, those who supported the Bretton Woods system did so because they expected devaluations or revaluations to occur only in exceptional circumstances, and they hoped that it would work very much like a system of fixed exchange rates. As it turned out, however, devaluations and revaluations occurred fairly frequently under the pegged-but-adjustable system, and the problems caused by these exchange rate adjustments ultimately turned out to be an important part of the reason why the system ultimately collapsed in the 1970s.

Fixed Exchange Rates: The Case For . . .

Those who are in favour of fixed exchange rates argue that they have two major advantages over floating rates:

1. A system of fixed exchange rates provides a more stable environment for international trade and investment because it eliminates (or at least greatly reduces) the *exchange risk* in international transactions. Exchange risk is important for international trade and investment because trade and investment decisions are influenced by expectations about the future values of foreign currencies. For example, suppose a Canadian firm contracts to sell equipment to a Mexican mining company at a price of U.S.$1 million, with payment to be made six months hence. With a fixed exchange rate, the Canadian exporter knows how many Canadian dollars he will eventually get in exchange for the U.S.$1 million. But if rates are flexible, the exporter runs the risk of a fall in the price of U.S. dollars and therefore a reduced payment in Canadian dollars. The advocates of fixed exchange rates often point to the unprecedented expansion of international trade and investment which took place in the decades before World War I, when the gold standard kept exchange rates stable, and under the pegged exchange rate system of 1945–73.

2. Fixed or pegged exchange rates exert an important *anti-inflationary discipline* on monetary and fiscal policy-makers, which is lost if exchange rates are allowed to fluctuate. For example, under the IMF system of pegged exchange rates, a country following highly inflationary policies will find that its goods are being priced out of world markets. Its balance of payments will move in a negative direction, and it will lose reserves. The fear of further reserve losses will act as a restraint; unless it is prepared to devalue its currency, the country will have to follow less inflationary domestic policies. (Under the old gold standard, the discipline was even more direct. A balance-of-payments deficit led automatically to a loss of gold. But as we saw in Chapter 13, a reduction in the amount of gold in a country would automatically force a reduction in its money supply.)

. . . And the Case Against

Advocates of flexible or floating exchange rates make a number of points:

1. The *discipline* imposed on policymakers by fixed exchange rates is a *two-edged sword*. True, the fear of losing foreign exchange reserves may sometimes be a healthy thing: In an inflationary

period, it may force policymakers to tighten monetary and fiscal policies. But at other times, *it may induce the authorities to carry out restrictive policies when there is little inflationary pressure*, or even when a country faces a high rate of unemployment. This was particularly true during the early part of the Depression of the 1930s: A number of countries (such as Britain and the United States) ran balance-of-payments deficits, and tightened policy in order to protect their gold reserves. When they did so, they made the collapse into the Depression more severe.

The perverse effect of the gold standard during the depression was the reason why it was abandoned in the 1930s. And when the time came to design the post-World War II system, the alternative that was chosen was a system of adjustable pegs rather than one of rigidly fixed rates.

2. Once a system of pegged-but-adjustable exchange rates became the alternative to floating rates, it was no longer clear that floating rates created greater exchange risk. True, pegged exchange rates were normally stable. But then, from time to time, very large, sudden changes occurred when a country picked a new par value. In short, a pegged rate brings less risk of frequent small changes than a floating rate. But it brings a greater risk of occasional large, highly disruptive changes.

3. *Speculation* can be a major problem in a system of pegged exchange rates.

> A *speculator* is anyone who buys or sells a currency (or any other asset) in the hope of profiting from a change in its price.

Consider, for example, what happens with pegged exchange rates if the British begin to run a large balance-of-payments deficit; that is, they start to lose large quantities of reserves. Speculators may begin to wonder whether the U.K. will be forced to devalue its currency—and they will therefore have an incentive to sell pounds and buy dollars. (For example, if speculators sell pounds for dollars at a price of $2.80 per pound, and buy them back later for $2.40 per pound—

after the U.K. has devalued—they will make a tidy profit of $0.40 on each pound.) But when speculators do sell pounds, the British government will either have to devalue at once, or use up some of its dollar reserves as it buys up these "speculative pounds" that are being dumped on the foreign exchange market. Thus speculators can virtually force a deficit country to devalue.

Speculation can also be a problem for a surplus country. In fact, an inflow of speculative capital in the third quarter of 1950 induced the Canadian government to abandon the pegged exchange rate system, and adopt a flexible exchange rate. What happened was this. Oil had been discovered in Alberta, and Americans had begun to invest in Alberta oil fields. Moreover, with the outbreak of the Korean war in 1950, the U.S. demand for Canadian raw materials shot upward. For both reasons, the Canadian balance of payments moved strongly into surplus. Speculators began to wonder if the Canadian dollar would be revalued. Their interest was kindled by an incautious statement by C.D. Howe, Minister of Trade and Commerce: "It is true, at the moment, that Canadian funds are at a 10 per cent discount, but that is a temporary situation. The historic position of the Canadian dollar is at par with the United States (that is, C$1.00 = U.S.$1.00)."[4] The result was a large capital inflow: The rush to buy cheap Canadian dollars was on. To keep the value of the Canadian dollar down, the Canadian authorities had to sell a large amount of Canadian dollars in exchange for U.S. dollars.

This, in turn, created a major problem in the management of monetary policy. When the Bank of Canada bought U.S. dollars, it paid for them with newly created Canadian dollars. As we saw in Chapter 13, Bank of Canada purchases of foreign currencies increase chartered bank

---

[4]Note that the term "par" has two meanings: (1) In the IMF system, it means the officially chosen exchange rate, regardless of what that exchange rate may be. (2) In Canada, the word "par" often means the specific exchange rate C$1.00 = U.S.$1.00. (This Canadian meaning of the word "par" is the result of an historical accident: Both the Canadian and U.S. currencies are called a "dollar," and the exchange rate between the two currencies has usually been fairly close to C$1.00 = U.S.$1.00.)

reserves. Hence, the Bank's actions eased monetary conditions. But, because of the threat of renewed inflation brought on by the Korean war, the Bank of Canada was trying at the time to move in exactly the opposite direction—toward a more restrictive monetary policy. Therefore, in order to cancel out the expansionary monetary effects of the purchases of foreign reserves—in other words, in order to *sterilize* the increase in Canada's reserves of U.S. dollars—the Bank of Canada engaged in the tight monetary policy of selling bonds on the open market.

> The Bank of Canada *sterilizes* an increase in its holdings of foreign exchange reserves when it offsets the effect of this increase on the money stock. It does this by engaging in open market sales. The expansionary effect of an increase in the Bank's holdings of foreign exchange reserves is offset by the contractionary effect of a reduction in its holdings of government bonds, leaving the money stock unchanged.

But the result of this Bank of Canada sale of bonds was lower bond prices (higher interest rates) which made Canadian bonds more attractive to Americans; this in turn created an even larger capital inflow, adding once again to Canadian bank reserves and the Canadian money supply. Thus, the attempt to sterilize failed: Canada had lost control of its monetary policy. Accordingly, in 1950 the Canadian authorities abandoned the pegged exchange rate and opted instead for a floating rate. But this experience taught the Canadian government an important lesson which is often cited by those who favour flexible exchange rates and oppose pegged rates:

4. A country with a pegged exchange rate may *lose control of its monetary policy.* Observe that the loss of control of monetary policy in 1950 arose because the Bank of Canada's responsibility to peg the Canadian dollar forced it to invervene in the foreign exchange market to purchase foreign currency (U.S. dollars), and because of the high degree of capital mobility between the United States and Canada. Thus

Canada was the first country to discover point no. 4. But, as the international mobility of capital increased elsewhere, others discovered it too— particularly Germany. In 1961 and again in 1969, Germany faced the same problem as Canada in 1950: It could not keep its existing exchange rate pegged and still follow an anti-inflationary monetary policy. Accordingly, in 1969 it temporarily let the mark float. And by the early seventies Germany was sympathetic to the new era of exchange rate flexibility.

EXCHANGE RATES AND FOREIGN INFLATION

As we have just seen, a commitment to a fixed exchange rate limits the authorities in using monetary policy to stabilize the domestic economy because the money supply is influenced by balance-of-payments pressures. During the late 1960s and early 1970s, when many of the world's industrialized nations began to experience rapid inflation, this raised an important question: Is it possible for a small country (like Canada or Sweden) to insulate its own economy from a world inflationary trend, while still maintaining a fixed exchange rate?

The answer, most economists now agree, is no: A commitment to fixed exchange rates effectively ties a small country to world inflation rates. To see why, suppose there is a sudden increase in U.S. inflation. Some of this inflation is quickly imported into Canada, because of the higher prices we must pay for U.S. goods. As U.S. goods are priced out of the Canadian market, Canadian imports will fall and the Canadian balance-of-payments will move into surplus. The surplus will increase if the Bank of Canada tries to use restrictive monetary policy as a way of counteracting the inflationary tendencies: As we saw in the discussion of the 1950 episode, higher Canadian interest rates will attract U.S. capital. But a balance-of-payments surplus will lead to an increase in Canada's money supply as the Bank buys U.S. dollars to keep the exchange rate stable. This in turn will put upward pressure on the Canadian price level—a pressure that will continue until the Canadian rate of inflation rises to roughly the world rate. Therefore:

With a fixed exchange rate, a small country such as Canada cannot protect itself from international infla-

tion. In the long run, Canada would have about the same inflation rate as the countries with which we trade.

On the other hand, if Canada's exchange rate is *floating*, our rate of inflation need not be dictated by inflation elsewhere—in particular, by inflation in the United States. Under a floating rate, any pressure toward a balance-of-payments surplus would have no effect on the Canadian money supply (since there would be no intervention by the Bank in the foreign exchange market). Instead this pressure would result in an **appreciation** of the Canadian dollar—that is, a reduction for Canadians in the cost of a U.S. dollar, and therefore in the cost of imports from the United States.

A flexible or floating currency *appreciates* when its price rises in terms of other currencies. (Note that a pegged currency is *revalued*; a floating currency *appreciates*.)

A floating currency *depreciates* when its price falls in terms of other currencies. (When the price of a pegged currency is decreased, it is *devalued*.)

Because the Canadian dollar appreciates, the price in Canada of imported goods wouldn't rise much after all. (For Canadians, the falling cost of the U.S. dollar would offset the increase in U.S. prices.) In short, a floating Canadian dollar helps to *insulate the domestic Canadian economy from externally generated inflation.*[5]

However, the independence from foreign inflation that a floating rate gives us may sometimes represent a disadvantage: *A floating rate also makes it easier for a country to generate its own inflation.* Just as a floating rate allows the authorities to follow policies that result in a *lower* rate of inflation than elsewhere, it also allows them to follow policies that result in a *higher* rate of inflation than elsewhere. With a commitment to fixed exchange rates, such policies would sooner or later have to be abandoned, since they would ulti-

mately result in a large excess of imports over exports and a loss of foreign exchange reserves. With floating rates, the authorities are not subject to this discipline. If the government is prepared to accept a continuing depreciation of the exchange rate, inflationary policies can be continued.

Notice that the relationship between inflation and depreciation of a country's currency involves a bit of the classic problem of the-chicken-or-the-egg. For example, a high rate of inflation in Canada will tend to make the Canadian dollar depreciate. But this depreciation will raise the cost of imported goods, which in turn contributes to more inflation. Thus a country may be caught in a **vicious circle**, with domestic inflation causing a depreciation, the depreciation in turn adding to domestic inflation, and the higher inflation leading to even more depreciation.

But note also that this process may work the other way; a country may move in a *virtuous* circle. Suppose a country (Germany, for example) manages to bring down its inflation to a lower rate than the countries it trades with. In response to the lower German inflation, sooner or later the Deutschmark will begin to *appreciate* against other currencies. Once this happens, the inflationary momentum in Germany is further reduced: The appreciation of the Deutschmark will lower the cost of imports, which will contribute to lower inflation.

HOW MONETARY AND FISCAL POLICY INFLUENCE THE BALANCE OF PAYMENTS

In Chapter 14, we raised the question: Which of the two main macroeconomic policy instruments—monetary policy or fiscal policy—is likely to be more effective in stabilizing aggregate demand and national income? The discussion in this chapter suggests that in answering this question, one must consider not only the impact of monetary and fiscal policies on domestic conditions, but also their impact on international transactions. Moreover, the answer may depend on the choice of exchange rate regime. (An alternative way of stating point no. 4 above is: Under a fixed exchange rate, monetary policy becomes very ineffective.)

The question of how the effectiveness of monetary policy on the one hand, and fiscal policy on the other, is influenced by the choice of exchange rate regime is

---

[5]Under a system of pegged-but-adjustable rates, it would be possible for the government to counteract foreign inflation by continually revaluing the domestic currency. But such a policy would essentially be equivalent to a floating rate.

particularly important for a country like Canada, where international trade and capital flows play such a large role in the economy. In answering it, we first consider the effect of monetary and fiscal policy on Canada's foreign trade (the current account); then we examine the effect of each policy on capital flows (the capital account).

Monetary and Fiscal Policies and the Current Account

Any *restrictive* policy (monetary or fiscal) that reduces aggregate demand and income will tend to move the current account toward a *surplus*. There are two reasons for this.

1. As we saw in Chapter 11, there is a high *marginal propensity to import* (MPM) in Canada: Whenever there is an increase in national income, a substantial proportion of this increase goes into additional purchases of imported goods and services; similarly, a decrease in aggregate de-

mand and national income causes a substantial decrease in imports. Therefore, a restrictive policy that *reduces* aggregate demand and income will reduce imports and therefore move the current account toward a surplus.

2. A restrictive monetary or fiscal policy reduces Canadian inflation. This will tend to make Canadian-produced goods more attractive relative to imported goods; it will also make Canadian export goods more competitive in foreign markets. These effects on the prices of Canadian goods will reinforce the tendency for the current account to move into surplus.

Similarly, any *expansive* monetary or fiscal policy will move the current account toward a *deficit*.

Monetary and Fiscal Policies and the Capital Account

As we have seen, the inflows and outflows of capital which appear in the balance-of-payments accounts rep-

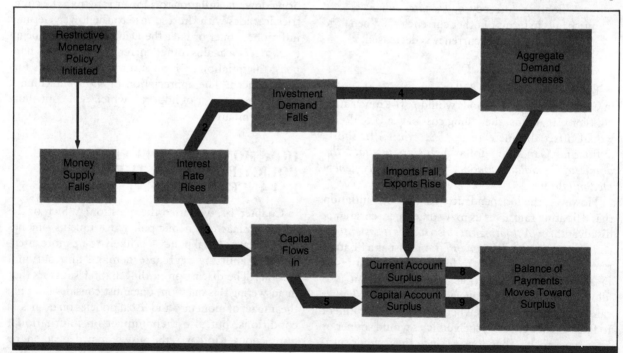

Figure 15-5 Effects of restrictive monetary policy on the balance of payments.

A restrictive monetary policy raises domestic interest rates (arrow 1). This affects the balance-of-payments accounts in two ways:

(a) Because investment and aggregate demand decrease (arrows 2 and 4), there is a tendency for imports to de-

crease and exports to increase (arrow 6). Thus, the current account moves toward a surplus (arrow 7).

(b) A higher domestic interest rate causes a capital inflow (arrow 3), and the capital account moves toward a surplus (arrow 5).

Thus, the overall balance of payments moves toward a surplus (arrows 8 and 9).

resent purchases and sales by foreigners of Canadian assets, or transactions by Canadians in foreign assets. The main determinant of these purchases and sales of assets is the difference in the rate of return that an investor can expect to get by buying Canadian rather than foreign assets. Financial institutions and other corporations are constantly trying to invest their short-term assets where they yield the highest return, and will quickly move their funds into Canada if interest rates in Canada rise above foreign interest rates—and move them out again as quickly, if Canadian rates fall below world levels.

To see what happens to capital flows under a restrictive *monetary* policy, note that this policy will make interest rates in Canada rise relative to U.S. rates. This encourages both Canadian and American investors to sell U.S. assets in order to buy the Canadian assets that are now yielding a higher return. Thus the result of this tight monetary policy is a capital inflow into Canada, that is, a movement in the capital account toward a surplus. Similarly, an easy money policy that lowers Canadian interest rates will move the capital account toward a deficit.

Fiscal policy also has an impact on the capital account. The reason is that fiscal policy affects interest rates. For example, if the government moves toward a tighter fiscal policy by decreasing expenditure or raising taxes, the result is a smaller government budget deficit (or even a budget surplus). Hence, there is a reduction in the amount that the government has to borrow in the bond market. But as we saw in Chapter 14, decreased government borrowing will tend to push down Canadian interest rates; and this will cause a capital *outflow* from Canada.

To sum up the last two sections:

Whereas a tight monetary policy and a tight fiscal policy have the *same* effect on the current account (they move it toward a surplus), they have *different* effects on Canadian interest rates and therefore on the capital account. A tight monetary policy *raises* interest rates and therefore results in a capital *inflow*, whereas a tight fiscal policy *lowers* interest rates and results in a capital *outflow*. Figures 15-5 and 15-6 illustrate these effects.

With the preceding discussion as a background we can now return to the important policy issue: How does the relative effectiveness of monetary and fiscal

policy depend on whether Canada has a fixed exchange rate or a flexible exchange rate?

EXCHANGE RATES AND THE EFFECTIVENESS OF MONETARY POLICY

1. With a fixed exchange rate. Figure 15-5 showed a restrictive monetary policy having a favourable effect on both the current account (arrow 7) and on the capital account (arrow 5). The resulting move toward a surplus in the balance of payments is shown as arrow 2 in Figure 15-7. Under a fixed exchange rate, the Bank of Canada must buy foreign currencies in order to prevent the Canadian dollar from rising (arrow 3). But as we have seen, this expands chartered bank reserves and therefore the money supply (arrow 5). This tends to offset the original restrictive monetary policy. In other words, Figure 15-7 confirms what we have already seen: Under a fixed exchange rate (shown in Figure 15-7 by the "inner loop" of arrows 3, 5, and 7) international complications make it difficult for the authorities to use monetary policy effectively.

2. With a floating exchange rate. Again assume a restrictive monetary policy, with a resulting balance-of-payments surplus. With a floating exchange rate, the Bank of Canada simply lets the Canadian dollar rise in value (arrow 4 in Figure 15-7). Because the Bank makes no attempt to hold the Canadian dollar down by buying foreign exchange, there is no complication in the form of an expansion of the money supply. But a rise in the Canadian dollar *does* affect our exports and imports: The higher-priced Canadian dollar makes our goods more expensive relative to foreign goods, and thus reduces our exports and increases our imports (arrow 6). The resulting reductions in Canadian output—in both our export and import-competing industries—augment the restrictive effects of the initial tight money policy. Thus, the "outer loop" of Figure 15-7 (arrows 4, 6, and 8) shows how a floating exchange rate *strengthens* the traditional domestic impact of a tight monetary policy.

While fixed exchange rates may cause a country to lose control of its monetary policy, flexible exchange rates *reinforce* the effectiveness of monetary policy.

(As an exercise, recast figures 15-5 and 15-6 to

show the effects on the balance of payments of easy monetary policies; and then change Figure 15-7 to show that the boldfaced conclusion above still holds.)

In Chapter 14 we saw that much of the early debate in Britain and the United States about the potential effectiveness of monetary policy focused on the lack of responsiveness of investment to changes in the rate of interest. However, the reasoning in this chapter shows that in an open economy with interest-sensitive capital flows, monetary policy may potentially be very powerful even if investment is not very interest-sensitive: If exchange rates are flexible, monetary policy may have a very strong effect on aggregate demand because it influences net exports as well as investment. As we will discuss in more detail in Chapter 16, the

Bank of Canada appears to consider the link between monetary policy and the exchange rate a very important part of the mechanism through which money affects aggregate demand. Indeed, during the early 1980s the Bank appeared to use exchange rate movements as the most important indicator in making monetary policy decisions.

Finally, recall again that exchange rate flexibility adds to the *freedom* of the monetary authorities to follow an expansive policy when they consider it desirable: They do not have to worry about running out of reserves, and therefore do not have to tighten monetary policy on that account. However, this conclusion—that a flexible exchange rate adds to the freedom of the central bank to pursue domestic objectives—

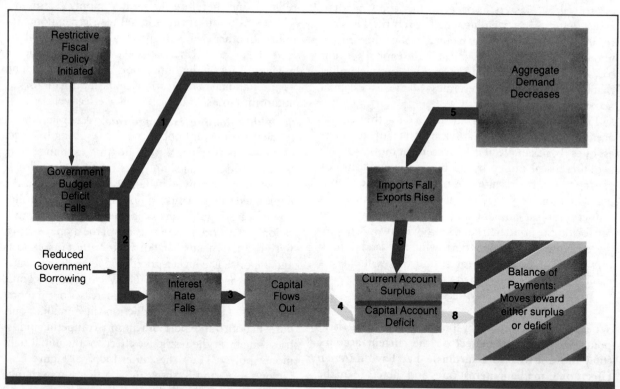

Figure 15-6   Effects of restrictive fiscal policy on the balance of payments.

A restrictive fiscal policy decreases domestic aggregate demand (arrow 1); furthermore, it reduces the government's need to borrow, and therefore tends to lower domestic interest rates (arrow 2). There are two kinds of effects on the balance of payments:

(a) The reduced aggregate demand causes imports to de-

crease and exports to increase (arrow 5), moving the current account toward a surplus (arrow 6).

(b) The lower interest rate causes a capital outflow (arrow 3), moving the capital account toward a deficit (arrow 4).

Because the current and capital accounts move in opposite directions, we cannot tell whether the overall effect (arrows 7 and 8) will be to move the balance of payments toward a surplus or a deficit.

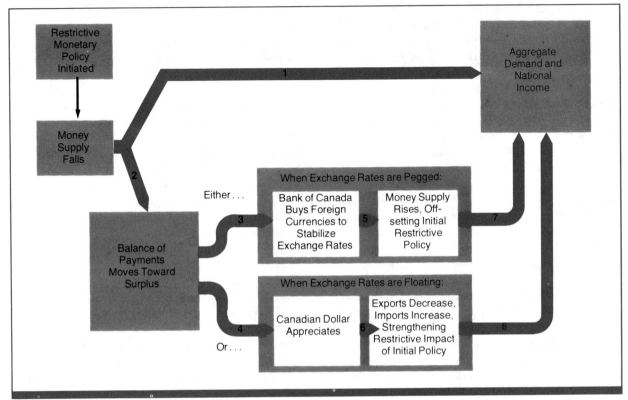

Figure 15-7   Monetary policy is more effective with floating exchange rates than with fixed rates.
Arrows 1 and 2 summarize the effects of a restrictive monetary policy from Figure 15-5. With fixed exchange rates (arrow 3), Bank of Canada purchases of foreign currencies tend to increase the Canadian money supply (arrow 5); this increase in the money supply tends to offset the initial restrictive policy (arrow 7). With floating exchange rates (arrow 4), the balance-of-payments surplus causes an appreciation of the Canadian dollar. As a result (arrow 6), Canadian net exports tend to decrease, which further reduces aggregate demand (arrow 8).

should not be overstated. Freedom is a matter of degree; there is no absolute policy freedom in a world of close international economic relationships. To illustrate: Although the Bank of Canada can pursue an easy monetary policy without fear of running out of exchange reserves (it lets the Canadian dollar fall instead), its freedom may be constrained by the fear of the inflation that will be generated by a falling dollar.

EXCHANGE RATES AND THE EFFECTIVENESS OF FISCAL POLICY

As shown in Figure 15-6, a restrictive fiscal policy results in a positive move in the current account (arrows 1, 5, and 6) and a negative move in the capital account (arrows 2, 3, and 4). Because of these conflicting pressures, we cannot be certain of the overall effects on the balance of payments. However, in a country where capital is very mobile, even small changes in the rate of interest lead to large capital flows. In such a country the capital account effect may well dominate; in this case, the balance of payments will move in a deficit direction in response to a restrictive fiscal policy. If this happens we get the following effects on fiscal policy under each exchange rate regime:

1. With a fixed exchange rate. Because of the balance of payments deficit, the authorities will lose foreign exchange reserves, thus reducing the chartered banks' reserves and the money supply. In other words, the original restrictive fiscal policy will induce monetary restrictiveness, and will thereby be strengthened. Similarly, an expansionary fiscal policy indirectly induces monetary expansion, which reinforces the fiscal policy. Thus, under a fixed exchange rate, the effectiveness of fiscal policy is *increased*.

Notice that this conclusion can be related to the discussion of "crowding out" in Chapter 14. Crowding out potentially reduces the effectiveness of an expansionary fiscal policy, say, because an expansionary policy increases the government's need to borrow, and this tends to drive up interest rates which in turn reduces private investment. Thus, the initial stimulating effect of a larger deficit is partially offset by reduced investment demand. However, with fixed exchange rates, there will be less of a tendency for interest rates to rise: As the extra government borrowing begins to put upward pressure on interest rates, capital will begin to flow in, forcing the central bank to buy foreign exchange and thereby expanding the reserves of chartered banks and thus the money supply; this induced expansion in the money supply will limit the increase in interest rates, so that there will be less crowding out of private investment.

2. With a flexible exchange rate. In this case, the balance-of-payments deficit that results from a restrictive fiscal policy does not result in a loss of foreign exchange reserves, but instead causes a depreciation of the country's currency. As noted earlier, this depreciation tends to raise aggregate demand for the country's goods and services, and therefore offsets some of the restrictive effects of the tighter fiscal policy. Thus fiscal policy is *weakened* under a flexible exchange rate.

The overall conclusions in the last two sections may be summarized thus:

Monetary policy is weakened by a fixed exchange rate, but strengthened by a flexible exchange rate.

When international capital is sufficiently mobile, the reverse is true for fiscal policy: Fiscal policy is strengthened by a fixed exchange rate, but weakened by a flexible rate.

EXCHANGE RATES, MONETARY POLICY, AND INFLATION, 1970–1985

In Chapter 14, we discussed some reasons why monetary policy has been more important than fiscal policy as a tool for economic stabilization during the late 1970s and 1980s. The fact that the Canadian dollar has been floating since 1970 is another reason: As we

have just seen, with floating exchange rates monetary policy becomes a relatively more effective tool for managing aggregate demand. Canadian experience during the last two decades provides an interesting illustration of the complex interactions between monetary policy, inflation, and exchange rate movements in an open economy with interest-sensitive capital flows.

In 1968–69, inflationary pressures were building up in the United States. To prevent the U.S. inflationary trends from being imported into Canada, the Canadian authorities abandoned the pegged exchange rate in early 1970, allowing the Canadian dollar to float upward. (Refer back to Figure 15-4). Soon, however, the Bank of Canada became concerned that the appreciation was too fast: The rising value of the Canadian dollar was making Canadian goods more expensive on world markets, and was thus creating difficulties for our export and import-competing industries. Accordingly, the Bank bought up large amounts of foreign exchange (sold large amounts of Canadian dollars) in order to limit the rise in the Canadian dollar. We therefore had a **managed float** or **dirty float**: The Canadian dollar wasn't floating completely freely since the authorities were intervening in the exchange market.

A currency is *freely flexible* or *freely floating* if there is no official intervention in the foreign exchange markets. A *free float* is also sometimes spoken of as a *clean float*.

A float is *managed* (or *dirty*) if the government intervenes in the foreign exchange markets, buying or selling reserves in order to influence the exchange rate.

The accumulation of foreign exchange reserves by the Bank of Canada continued in 1971 and 1972, and resulted in a high rate of growth in the Canadian money supply. This monetary expansion set the stage for the rapid increase in inflation which took place in 1973–75.

Thus, the floating of the dollar in 1970 provided the *opportunity* to insulate Canada from the world inflationary trend of the 1970s. But it was an opportunity that was missed because the authorities intervened to stabilize the exchange rate, thereby getting a result partway between a pegged and a freely flexible rate. By the mid-1970s, it became clear that we had indeed missed the opportunity: Canada's inflation rate had risen to the inflation rate in the United States.

The deep recession in 1974–75 led to a substantial reduction in the inflationary pressure in the U.S. economy. In Canada, both monetary and fiscal policies were set to provide a strong stimulus to aggregate demand, and our recession was much less severe than in the United States. However, inflationary pressures in Canada also remained strong: We had double-digit inflation (that is, the rate of inflation exceeded 10%) both in 1974 and 1975, and the Canadian dollar depreciated sharply in relation to the U.S. dollar (by more than 7% between March 1974 and September 1975). By late 1975, reducing inflation became the government's top priority. The Bank of Canada announced that it would begin fighting inflation by gradually decreasing the rate of growth of the money supply, and the Trudeau government created the Anti-Inflation Board to supervise the wage and price controls that were applied in October 1975. Following these measures, the Canadian dollar appreciated substantially between 1975 and 1976, and inflationary pressures moderated somewhat. However, the Canadian inflation rate continued to remain well above the U.S. rate throughout the rest of the decade. Beginning in late 1976, the Canadian dollar started to fall; by mid-1979 it had gone as low as 83 U.S. cents. The resulting steady increase in import prices helped fuel the inflationary spiral, offsetting much of the Bank of Canada's efforts at reducing inflation by gradually decreasing the growth rate of M1.

In 1979, the U.S. Federal Reserve Bank moved its monetary policy sharply toward contraction, driving U.S. interest rates to record levels. The Bank of Canada was now faced with a dilemma. If it decided to stick with its previous policy of reducing the growth rate of the money supply only gradually, the high interest rates in the United States would almost certainly cause a large outflow of capital from Canada, and the Canadian dollar would depreciate even further. With inflationary pressures already high, adding further to these pressures by allowing a continued fall in the dollar was the last thing the Bank of Canada wanted to do. But the alternative was not very attractive either: The very high interest rates in the United States were coming under criticism for the hardships they created for farmers, small businesses, and homeowners whose mortgages were coming up for renewal. If the Bank of Canada decided to follow the policy of the Federal Reserve and move to a highly restrictive policy, the same problems would arise in Canada.

In the event, the Bank of Canada decided that the battle against inflation would take precedence. It put on the monetary brakes sharply in 1979, sending short-term interest rates above 16%. In 1981, U.S. interest rates rose sharply once more as the economy recovered from the mini-recession in 1980. In Canada, the Bank again refused to allow our dollar to depreciate; it continued tightening monetary policy until short-term interest rates at one point went above 20%, even higher than U.S. rates. Criticism of the Bank became louder, and many observers feel that the extreme restrictiveness of monetary policy in 1981 contributed to the severity of the 1981–82 recession; while Canada had escaped the 1974–75 recession much better than the United States, the 1981–82 recession was, if anything, *more* severe in Canada than south of the border. And while the Bank succeeded in its objective of preventing the Canadian dollar from depreciating, this did not seem to be enough: The rate of inflation remained high well into the recession.

Starting toward the end of 1982, however, Canada's inflation rate finally began coming down. By 1984, it was less than 5%. The Bank of Canada had finally proved its point: It had shown that with a sufficiently restrictive monetary policy, inflation can be beaten. But the price had been very high, with punishing interest rates, and a degree of monetary restriction that aggravated and prolonged the deepest Canadian recession since the Great Depression.

Many observers have been highly critical of the Bank's policies during this period. While they recognize that the sharp monetary restraint and the stabilization of the exchange rate certainly helped beat inflation, they argue that the policy of gradual reduction in monetary growth that the Bank was following before 1979 would in the end have accomplished the same thing, and at a substantially lower cost in terms of the depth of the recession. And while allowing some depreciation of the Canadian dollar in 1982 would have added somewhat to inflationary pressure in Canada in that year, the addition would not have been large: The rate of increase in the Canadian prices of goods imported from the United States depends *both* on the depreciation of the exchange rate *and* on the rate of increase in the U.S. prices of these goods, and U.S. prices in 1982 were relatively stable.

As the inflationary pressure abated, the Bank of Canada began moving in the direction of an easier policy, and in spite of the low rate of inflation, the

Canadian dollar once again depreciated in terms of the U.S. dollar, falling below 70 U.S. cents in 1986. One reason why the Bank was prepared to allow this depreciation was the fact that the *American* dollar had *appreciated* very substantially against other currencies such as the Deutschmark and the British pound. This meant that even though the Canadian dollar was falling relative to the U.S. dollar, it was actually *rising* in terms of these other currencies.

KEY POINTS

1. International trade is different from domestic trade because:
   (a) Imports are often subjected to special taxes (tariffs).
   (b) International trade involves more than one national currency.
2. A foreign exchange market is a market where the currency of one nation (for example, the Canadian dollar) is exchanged for the currencies of other nations. The supply of a nation's currency to the world's foreign exchange markets depends on
   (a) the nation's imports of goods
   (b) its imports of services
   (c) its acquisitions of foreign assets
   Similarly, the demand for a national currency in the world's foreign exchange market depends on:
   (a) the nation's exports of goods
   (b) its exports of services
   (c) foreign acquisitions of assets from the nation
3. A country's balance-of-payments accounts provide a record of transactions in the foreign exchange market between residents of that country and residents of foreign countries. For example, the debit side of Canada's balance-of-payments accounts show the transactions that give rise to a supply of Canadian dollars in exchange for foreign currencies (imports of goods and services, and capital outflows); the credit side shows the transactions that cause a demand for Canadian dollars in the foreign exchange markets (Canadian exports of goods and services, and capital inflows into Canada).
4. Exports and imports of goods and services are shown in the current account. Capital inflows and outflows are recorded in the capital account, which shows Bank of Canada transactions in official reserve assets, as well as private transactions in non-reserve assets. The surplus or deficit in the balance of payments is calculated by taking the net amount of all credits and debits in both the current and capital accounts, but excluding transactions in official foreign exchange reserves.
5. Suppose that after a period of equilibrium, Canada's balance of payments begins to move toward a deficit—that is, the demand and supply curves in the foreign exchange market shift so that the demand for Canadian dollars decreases relative to the supply. The Canadian government can deal with this change in the relationship between supply and demand by one or a combination of the following steps:
   (a) By intervention in the foreign exchange market; that is, by selling foreign currencies (from its foreign exchange reserves) for Canadian dollars;
   (b) By devaluing the Canadian dollar (or permitting it to depreciate in response to market forces, if exchange rates are floating);
   (c) By reducing the supply of Canadian dollars through restrictions on imports or other international transactions;
   (d) By restricting aggregate demand in Canada, and thus reducing Canadian imports and the supply of our dollars to the foreign exchange market.
6. When a country belongs to a system of fixed or pegged exchange rates, the authorities are committed to buying and selling the country's currency in exchange for foreign currencies in order to maintain stable exchange rates. With flexible or floating exchange rates, the authorities do not have to intervene in the foreign

exchange market: Instead, they can simply let the country's currency appreciate or depreciate in response to changing supply and demand factors.

7. Before the Great Depression, many countries belonged to the international gold standard. Under the gold standard, the value of each currency was fixed in terms of gold, which meant that the exchange rates between currencies were fixed as well.

    The international gold standard collapsed during the Great Depression. However, at the end of the Second World War, most countries joined in the IMF system which involved pegged (but adjustable) exchange rates. Most countries continued to belong to the adjustable peg system from 1945 until 1973, when it broke down and was replaced by the present system of flexible, or floating, exchange rates. But during a large part of the adjustable-peg period, Canada was an exception: We followed a system of floating exchange rates during the 1950–1962 period.

8. Flexible exchange rates have a number of advantages, and a number of disadvantages. There are two main arguments for flexible exchange rates:
    (a) It is not clear that there is a good alternative. (The IMF system ultimately broke down.)
    (b) With flexible rates, countries gain freedom to tailor their aggregate demand policies to the domestic objectives of full employment and stable prices, rather than to the balance of payments.

9. Criticisms of flexible exchange rates include the following:
    (a) Changes in exchange rates may disrupt trade.
    (b) If they don't have to worry about keeping the exchange rate fixed, central bankers and governments may follow overly inflationary policies.
    (c) A depreciation of the currency will make imports more expensive, and thus add to inflation.

10. The effectiveness of monetary and fiscal policy as tools for stabilizing a country's domestic economy depends on whether the country is on a fixed or flexible exchange rate. With a fixed exchange rate, monetary policy may be relatively ineffective, particularly if capital is highly mobile across borders. A floating rate, on the other hand, tends to increase the effectiveness of monetary policy. When capital is very mobile, the reverse conclusion holds for fiscal policy: It tends to be more effective under a fixed than under a flexible rate.

11. If a country decides to peg its exchange rate, it becomes virtually impossible for it to prevent foreign inflation from spilling over into the domestic economy. If a country wants to insulate itself against foreign inflation, it has to be prepared to let its currency appreciate. While such possible insulation from foreign inflation may sometimes be an advantage of a flexible rate, it may at other times be a disadvantage: It may permit the country to pursue policies that lead to a substantially faster rate of inflation than in foreign countries.

KEY CONCEPTS

exchange rate
foreign exchange market
imports of goods and services
tariff acquisition of foreign assets
  (that is, investment in foreign
  countries)
long-term capital inflow/outflow

direct investment
foreign exchange reserves
official intervention in the
  exchange market
current account deficit or surplus
balance-of-payments deficit
  or surplus

changes in official reserve assets
sterilization of reserve changes
gold standard
adjustable peg
International Monetary Fund
  (IMF)
par value

KEY CONCEPTS (cont'd)

devaluation/revaluation
speculation
appreciation/depreciation of
   a currency
flexible or floating exchange rate
fixed or pegged exchange rate

clean (or dirty) float
international mobility of
   capital
exchange risk
monetary policy under
   fixed exchange rates
monetary policy under
   floating exchange rates

fixed exchange rates and
   imported inflation
fiscal policy under fixed
   exchange rates
independent stabilization
   policy

PROBLEMS

15-1 Suppose that, after a period of equilibrium, there is a fall in the demand for Canadian dollars in the foreign exchange market. What alternatives does the Canadian government have for dealing with this change?

15-2 With fixed exchange rates, why does a balance of payments surplus usually cause an increase in a country's money supply?

15-3 "Under the old IMF adjustable-peg system, the finance minister of a deficit country would be unwise to admit that a devaluation was being considered." Explain this statement. Was Canada's trade and commerce minister similarly unwise to admit that a revaluation was being considered in 1950?

15-4 In early 1982, reports in some Canadian newspapers stated that the government was considering a major devaluation of the Canadian dollar. (Finance Minister MacEachen immediately denied these reports in Parliament). Explain to your friend (who is a journalist) what was wrong with the terminology in the press reports. (Hint: Was Canada on pegged or flexible exchange rates in early 1982?) What do you think the reports actually meant to say?

15-5 In early 1973, speculators bought marks, correctly anticipating a rise in its exchange value. Explain how they gained at the expense of the German government when the mark was allowed to rise on the exchange markets.

15-6 Because the balance-of-payments accounts must always balance, each international transaction gives rise to two entries, one on the credit side and one on the debit side. As an example, consider a single transaction, namely the sale of a Canadair Challenger airplane to a U.S. buyer. The effects on Canada's balance of payments are shown in Table 15-2.
Since each international transaction affects both sides of the balance of payments equally, the two sides of the balance of payments always sum to the same total.

Table 15-2
An International Transaction

Positive Items (Credits)	Negative Items (Debits)
Export of Canadian-made airplane $1 million	Increase in Canadian-owned bank account in the United States $1 million

For each of the following transactions, construct a simple balance of payments like the one shown in Table 15-2, showing how each transaction results in the same dollar entry on each side of the balance sheet:

(a) Canada imports $100 million in goods, and pays for these goods with $100 million of exports.

(b) Northern Telecom buys a factory from a foreign cable manufacturer, and the foreign company deposits the proceeds in a Montreal bank.

(c) A Canadian company pays a U.S. resident dividends of $500. The U.S. resident deposits the dividends in a Canadian bank.

(d) Later, the U.S. resident makes a trip to Canada, spending the $500 previously deposited for motels, meals, and other similar expenses.

(e) A Canadian manufacturer exports a $100,000 machine. The importer does not pay now, but promises to pay in 3 months.

15-7 The purpose of Problem 15-6 was to help you keep straight on which side of the balance of payments various items are entered. Now go back to Problem 15-6, and identify which of the items are included in the capital account, and which in the current account.

15-8 Explain why monetary policy is a more powerful instrument under floating exchange rates than under fixed exchange rates.

*15-9 Suppose Canadian capital is very mobile internationally. Try to draw a diagram similar to Figure 15-7 to illustrate why fiscal policy is relatively more effective under fixed exchange rates than under floating exchange rates.

*15-10 Consider a country where capital is very immobile, so that the capital account effects of a tight fiscal policy are dominated by the current account effects. Would a restrictive fiscal policy be more effective under a fixed or floating exchange rate?

*15-11 Some observers have suggested that in 1981–82, the Bank of Canada was engaged in a "managed float" of the Canadian dollar, because it was influencing its value not so much by intervention in the foreign exchange market (although it did some of this) as by raising interest rates in Canada to attract and hold international capital. Explain why you agree or disagree.

APPENDIX

SYSTEMS OF FIXED OR PEGGED EXCHANGE RATES: THE PROBLEMS OF ADJUSTMENT AND LIQUIDITY

An important aspect of a system of exchange rates is the way it brings about *adjustment* when changing conditions in the international economy cause disequilibrium in foreign exchange markets.

For example, suppose a disequilibrium arises in the international market for the British pound, because of a fall in the international price of oil. Recall from the text that there are only four major ways for Britain to deal with a disturbance in the foreign exchange market. It may:

1. Keep the price of pounds stable by buying surplus pounds with gold or foreign exchange reserves, or selling pounds in the event of a shortage.

2. Change tariffs or other restrictions on imports or other international transactions.

3. Change domestic aggregate demand policies in order to shift the supply curve for pounds in terms of dollars.

4. Change the exchange rate.

It is widely agreed that option 2 should be used as little as possible because direct restrictions hinder efficient trade and capital flows. Therefore, in a system of *fixed* exchange rates, the burden of adjustment will fall on methods 1 and 3, since exchange rates aren't supposed to change. In a system of *pegged-but-adjustable* exchange rates (such as the Bretton Woods system), the *major* burden of adjustment is also supposed to fall on methods 1 and 3. However, in *some* situations, exchange rate adjustments (devaluations or revaluations) may be called for. Thus, in designing a system of fixed or pegged exchange rates, two important issues must be considered:

(a) How should countries use methods 1 and 3 to bring about adjustments in foreign exchange markets?

(b) In a system of pegged-but-adjustable exchange rates, in what circumstances are countries allowed to change their exchange rates (i.e., to devalue or revalue their currencies)?

Under the classical gold standard, adjustments took place automatically as a country's money supply changed in response to balance-of-payments deficits or surpluses. But as we saw in the text, the automatic adjustment mechanism provided by the gold standard had major defects. During the 1930s, it created monetary contractions in countries that were already in a depression, making the depression worse. It could also lead to very *unstable* monetary conditions. Under the fractional-reserve system of banking, a large quantity of money was built on a relatively small base of gold. The monetary system was therefore vulnerable to a crisis of confidence and a run on the gold stock.

The IMF adjustable peg system organized in 1945 was designed to provide some of the exchange-rate stability of the old gold standard, while avoiding its major defects. It represented a compromise, with each of the four possible adjustment methods playing a part. Increases in tariffs or other restrictions on imports (option 2) were considered undesirable, since they reduced international trade and made the world economy less efficient. However, they were permitted in emergencies, including the severely disrupted period after World War II.

To deal with temporary exchange market disturbances, countries were expected to use foreign exchange reserves to intervene in the foreign exchange market (option 1). However, because temporary swings might be quite large, the IMF was empowered to lend foreign currencies to deficit countries in order to help them stabilize their currencies on the exchange markets. Thus, "Fund" is an important part of the title of the IMF. The member countries of the IMF provided it with the funds to lend to deficit countries.

If the balance-of-payments disequilibrium persisted, countries were expected to turn to option 3, changes in domestic aggregate demand. However, as the experience of the Depression showed, an adjustment in domestic demand is not always a desirable way of dealing with an international payments problem. For example, restrictive aggregate demand policies to solve international payments problems might make a recession worse.

In circumstances where the first three options had been ruled out or proved inadequate, the country was in a **fundamental disequilibrium**, and the Bretton Woods system approved the only remaining option: Change the exchange rate. In other words, under the IMF system exchange rates were *pegged, but adjustable*.

For several decades, the IMF system worked reasonably well—well enough to provide the financial framework for the recovery from World War II, and for a very rapid expansion of international trade. But it contained major flaws that caused a breakdown in the early 1970s.

In practice, there were defects in the policy of changing the par value of a currency to deal with a "fundamental disequilibrium." When a country begins to run a deficit or surplus, it is uncertain whether the deficit or surplus is only temporary—in which case it can be dealt with by buying or selling foreign currency rather than by changing the exchange rate—or whether it represents a fundamental disequilibrium, in which case a change in the par value is appropriate. The IMF agreement itself provided no help in this regard. At no place did it define a fundamental disequilibrium.

Since a fundamental disequilibrium involves a surplus or deficit that will persist, one simple test is to wait and see whether in fact it does persist. But waiting can be a nerve-wracking experience. In particular, deficits cause the loss of foreign exchange reserves. And as we saw in the text, speculation may add to the problem. To dissuade speculation, the authorities may try to proclaim firmly their determination to defend their currency. But once government leaders have staked their reputations on the defence of the currency, it is very difficult for them to back down and change its par value. Therefore, in practice, devaluations tended to be infrequent and long delayed under the IMF system. And, once they came, they tended to be large, so that the government would not have to go through the painful experience again in the near future. Thus, the system of adjustable pegs did not work out as hoped. For long periods the system was one of rigid pegs as officials committed themselves firmly to the existing exchange rates. Then, when pressures became intolerable and changes had to be made, jumping pegs were the result, with drastic adjustments being made.

The lack of a smooth and effective adjustment process was not the only shortcoming of the old IMF system. Another problem was caused by the special role of the U.S. dollar in the system, and the difficulties this created for the United States.

Under a pegged exchange-rate system, countries are not all equal. It is not possible for every country to have control over its exchange rate. The reason is that there are fewer independent exchange rates than there are countries. In a very simple world of two countries, say the United States and Britain, there is only one exchange rate. (Of course, this rate may be quoted either way. For example, $1 = £0.50$ is just another way of stating that £1 = $2.) In general, in a world of n countries, there are only $n - 1$ independent exchange rates.[6]

This fundamental fact posed two interrelated questions for the designers of the IMF system:

1. If an exchange rate—such as the rate between the British pound and the U.S. dollar—begins to rise or fall, does Britain or the United States have the responsibility of intervening in the foreign exchange market to keep it close to the official par value?
2. In the case of fundamental disequilibrium, the par value might have to be altered. Does the United States or Britain make the decision to alter the par value? And which country chooses the new par?

The IMF solution to the first question was as follows. Other countries tied their currencies to the U.S. dollar, and the United States in turn undertook to keep the dollar convertible into gold. This determined the entire set of exchange rates between countries. As far as exchange rates were concerned, the

United States was the odd man out. Every other country was responsible for an exchange rate. As the nth country, the United States had no such responsibility.

The answer to the second question followed from the answer to the first. Since Britain was responsible for keeping the pound pegged in terms of dollars, the ball was in the British court when the decision came to change the parity. However, Britain was to consult other members of the IMF regarding the new parity.

Thus, the United States had a unique role in the IMF system. The dollar was the **key currency**. Other countries kept their currencies pegged to the dollar. The United States was thus placed squarely in the centre of one of the thorniest problems of the IMF system—that of **international liquidity**. What volume of reserves should there be, and how should additional reserves be created?

> *International liquidity* is the total amount of reserves held by the various nations.

Under the old adjustable peg system, a country held its international reserves in the form of:

1. gold
2. foreign exchange, especially dollars
3. the country's reserve position in the IMF (that is, the contributions that the country had made to the IMF. Each country had an unconditional right to withdraw its past contributions)

For the United States—with its responsibility to keep the dollar convertible into gold—gold formed the primary reserve. Other countries had the responsibility of stabilizing their currencies relative to the dollar, and they therefore kept sizable amounts of dollars to be used as needed to intervene in the exchange markets. In his 1960 book, *Gold and the Dollar Crisis*, Robert Triffin of Yale University argued that there was a fundamental problem with the IMF system. As international trade expanded, countries would want more reserves. How could reserves be increased? By digging more gold, or by increases in foreign holdings of U.S. dollars.

The prospects for large increases in the supply of gold were not promising. Thus, if countries were going to get the reserves they needed, their holdings of dollars would have to increase. But how does a foreign country get more U.S. dollars? By running a surplus with the United States. *In other words, if other countries were*

---

[6]In a three-country world—Britain, France, and the United States—it may seem that there are three independent exchange rates: between the pound and the dollar, between the franc and the dollar, and between the franc and the pound. But in reality, there are only two (that is, $n - 1$). Any two exchange rates determine what the third will be. For example, if the price of the pound is $2 and the price of the franc is 20 cents, it follows that the pound is worth 10 times as much as the franc. That is, £1 = 10 francs.

to accumulate dollar reserves, the United States would have to have deficits. But, as American deficits continued and foreign dollar holdings became larger and larger compared with the relatively stable U.S. stock of gold, the ability of the United States to convert the dollar into gold would increasingly come into question. There would inevitably be a crisis of confidence, a run on U.S. gold by foreign governments, and a collapse of the IMF system.

In brief, the IMF system could not last. The United States could eliminate its deficit, giving the world a *liquidity crisis*, with inadequate reserves. Or the United States could continue to run deficits, with the predictable result of a *crisis of confidence* and a run on U.S. gold. Triffin suggested a solution. The IMF should be turned into an international central bank, capable of creating an international reserve that would supplant the U.S. dollar. This reserve could be methodically created to meet growing needs for liquidity.

Toward the end of the 1960s, an international consensus developed that something had to be done about this problem, along the lines outlined by Triffin. After a series of hard negotiations, the IMF was empowered to create **Special Drawing Rights** (SDRs), which could be used by nations to cover balance-of-payments deficits.

SDRs consist of bookkeeping accounts in the IMF owned by national governments, somewhat similar to the deposits that individuals hold at chartered banks. But the mechanism for creating SDRs is much simpler than the open market operations by which a central bank creates money within a domestic economy. The IMF creates SDRs in the easiest possible way: It directly adds SDRs to the accounts of the various nations within the IMF. Nothing is received in exchange. The SDRs are simply *allocated* to the various member nations of the IMF. SDRs can be used by a nation to cover an international deficit.

However, the strengthening of the role of the IMF was not enough to save the adjustable peg system. In August 1971, the United States suspended the convertibility of the dollar into gold, and imposed tariff surcharges in order to pressure foreign countries into raising the prices of their currencies—that is, into lowering the value of the dollar. In the uncertainty that followed, a number of countries abandoned their fixed pegs and allowed their currencies to float on the exchange markets.

In December 1971, an attempt was made to patch up the pegged exchange-rate system at a conference at the Smithsonian Institution in Washington. The new pegged rates chosen by most of the participants involved higher prices of their currencies. Thus, the United States achieved its goal of dollar devaluation. But the Smithsonian patchwork did not last. In 1972, the British let the pound float. Stresses on the exchange-rate system increased. There were such large amounts of internationally mobile money that an exchange rate could not be held in the face of speculation. In an unsuccessful attempt over a four-day period to keep the mark from rising, West German authorities sold enough marks to speculators to buy 2 million Volkswagens. In early 1973, countries abandoned the pegs of the Smithsonian Agreement, and most major currencies were allowed to float. The era of the adjustable peg system was at an end.

Chapter 16

FINE TUNING OR STABLE POLICY SETTINGS?

> If something works,
> don't fix it.
> American proverb

In the study of macroeconomics, better policies are the ultimate goal. No matter how elaborate our theories, and no matter how much progress we make in understanding detailed macroeconomic relationships, our work has not succeeded if it cannot be translated into better policies. And the ultimate test of macroeconomic policies is the degree to which they help in the achievement of high employment and stable prices.

It is not clear whether we should judge the policies of the past 25 years as a success or a failure. In part, the answer depends on the question: Successful compared to what? Certainly, compared to the depressed decade of the 1930s, the economy has performed well during the past quarter-century. The unemployment rate has never come anywhere close to the levels it reached during the 1930s. However, we have not been doing better and better as time passes. The recession of 1981–82 was much more severe than any during the preceding 30 years, with the unemployment rate rising to 12.8%, the highest rate since the Great Depression. With respect to inflation, the experience of the past two decades has also been worse than that of the preceding period. Bursts of inflation occurred during the mid-1970s and the early 1980s, with inflation hitting a peak of 12.7% in 1981. Although inflation was brought under much better control in the early 1980s, it still remained at about 4% to 5% per year in 1983–84, substantially above the average annual rate of 1.8% between 1955 and 1966.

The mediocre performance of the economy in the past two decades has revitalized an old debate that goes back to the early days of the Keynesian-classical controversy in the 1930s. On the one side are those in the Keynesian tradition, who argue that aggregate demand policies should be *actively managed* in pursuit of the goals of high employment and stable prices. As the economy heads toward recession, expansive policies should be adopted. As the economy heads toward an inflationary boom, restraint should be exercised.

On the other side are the monetarists, who argue that activist, discretionary policies are more likely to do harm than good, no matter how well-intentioned policymakers might be. Consequently, they argue that *discretionary* policies should be avoided. Instead, permanent policy settings should be chosen and maintained regardless of the short-term fluctuations in economic activity. That is, a *policy rule* should be followed. It is of course important that the rule be chosen carefully and, in particular, that it be consistent with economic stability. For example, it would be a mistake to adhere to the rules of the old gold standard.

Because banks under that system kept fractional reserves in the form of gold, a large superstructure of money could be built on a relatively small base of gold reserves. This made the banking system vulnerable to runs.

However, monetarists suggest that there is a policy rule that *is* consistent with a high degree of economic stability. Specifically, they suggest that the Bank of Canada should aim at a slow, steady increase in the money supply, at something like 3% or 4% per year. This increase would provide the money needed to purchase the expanding national output at stable prices.

> *Discretionary* fiscal and monetary policies are policies that the government and the central bank adjust periodically in order to deal with changing conditions in the economy.

As in Chapter 14, the sharp contrast between Keynesians and monetarists may be illustrated by comparing the statements of Keynesian Warren Smith and monetarist Milton Friedman. The flavour of the activist, hands-on-the-helm Keynesian view was given by Smith:[1]

> The only good rule is that the budget should never be balanced—except for an instant when a surplus to curb inflation is being altered to a deficit to fight deflation.

Friedman explicitly criticized the activist policy of attempting to "fine-tune" the economy:[2]

> Is fiscal policy being oversold? Is monetary policy being oversold? . . . My answer is yes to both of those questions. . . . Monetary policy is being oversold. . . . Fiscal policy is being oversold. . . . Fine tuning has been oversold.

We introduce this debate over the active management of demand by looking more closely at the Keynesian approach, in which aggregate demand policies are adjusted in pursuit of the goals of full employment and stable prices. In later sections of this chapter, we will explain criticisms of that policy, and problems with the alternative of following a monetary rule.

---

[1] Warren Smith, statement to a meeting of Treasury consultants, as quoted by Paul A. Samuelson in *Economics*, 11th ed. (New York: McGraw-Hill, 1976), p. 222.

[2] Milton Friedman and Walter Heller, *Monetary vs. Fiscal Policy* (New York: W.W. Norton, 1969), p. 47.

AIMING FOR A STABLE, HIGH-EMPLOYMENT ECONOMY: THE ACTIVE KEYNESIAN APPROACH

As we have seen—especially in Chapter 10—Keynes believed that a market economy would suffer from two major diseases. The economy would move toward an equilibrium where there would probably be inadequate aggregate demand and high unemployment. And, even if the economy did get to a position of full employment, it would be unlikely to stay there, primarily because of the instability of investment demand. In short, demand would tend to be both *inadequate* and *unstable*.

In the early days of the Keynesian revolution, inadequate aggregate demand was considered a more important problem than instability. This was scarcely surprising, because of the depth and persistence of the Great Depression. However, since the late 1940s, the emphasis of Keynesian thinking has shifted away from the problem of stagnation and toward the problem of instability. The economy did not lapse back into depression in the period after World War II as many economists feared it would. In the past four decades, it has gone through bouts of inflation, as well as periodic recessions. There has been no long-run lack of aggregate demand, although demand has been unstable.

Nevertheless, concern continued over both the adequacy and the stability of aggregate demand. Therefore the policy problem, as seen by Keynesian economists, was (1) to stimulate aggregate demand to the full-employment level, and then (2) to adjust or *fine-tune* it whenever needed to combat business fluctuations.

This Keynesian strategy is illustrated in Figure 16-1. Suppose that the economy in year 1 begins at a position of high unemployment. The actual production of the economy, at *A*, is well below the potential at full employment (*B*). Of course, the potential output of the economy does not remain constant. As time passes, the labour force grows, the capital stock increases, and technology improves. Thus, the path of full-employment or potential GNP has an upward trend. The objective of policy in year 1 should be to aim the economy toward the full-employment path. However, full employment cannot be achieved immediately; there are lags in the implementation and effect of policy. Thus, policy in year 1 should be aimed at stimulating the economy so that it approaches full employment at

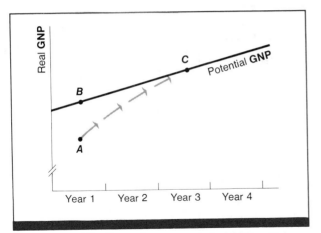

Figure 16-1 The Keynesian strategy: An active policy.
The activist Keynesian strategy is to move to the potential GNP path. Fiscal and monetary policies should then be fine-tuned to combat instability and keep the economy as close as possible to potential GNP.

years; by 1964, the economy was pretty much on target. What remained now was to fine tune the economy, keeping it as close as possible to the potential growth path.

There were, of course, problems. One was the tendency of prices to rise before full employment was achieved, a problem which will be considered in detail in the next chapter. The second was the well-recognized problem of lags: How do you adjust policies when the actions taken today do not affect the economy until some future time, when they may no longer be appropriate? Keynesians believed that they had an adequate—although far from perfect—answer. By forecasting, policymakers can get a fairly good idea of where the economy is headed. Thus, they should be able to "lead" their moving target.

Details of economic forecasting are deferred until a later section in this chapter. Here, we turn to the way in which lags are used as an argument against an active demand-management policy.

some time in the reasonably near future, as shown by the arrows in Figure 16-1.

An Example
By going back to the early 1960s, we can find a very clear and explicit illustration of this Keynesian strategy. By early 1961, the recession that started in 1960 had produced an unemployment rate in excess of 7%, the highest rate in Canada since the Second World War. As a consequence, a large GNP gap estimated at more than 6% of potential GNP had emerged, as shown in Figure 16-2. The policy problem was to try to eliminate the GNP gap fairly quickly, by making actual GNP follow a path like the thin line A. On the other hand, if the policymakers failed to stimulate the economy, it might follow a path like B: Along this path, the GNP gap would remain as wide in 1963–64 as it was in 1961.

The policies actually pursued in 1962–63 were intended to stimulate demand: The federal and provincial governments together ran substantial deficits, and the Canadian dollar was devalued. (Recall that a reduction in the value of the Canadian dollar stimulates Canadian exports and reduces our imports; it therefore stimulates aggregate demand for Canadian goods.) The results of the policy are shown by the coloured curve in Figure 16-2. Although the GNP gap was not eliminated very quickly, it was eliminated within four

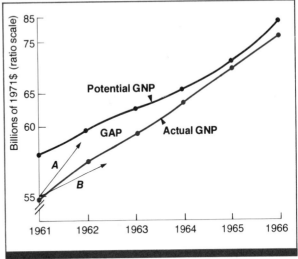

Figure 16-2 The Keynesian strategy in practice, 1961–1966.
The diagram shows the estimated paths of potential and actual GNP during the first half of the 1960s, and illustrates how different policies might have affected the large GNP gap existing in 1961. Path A would have eliminated the gap quickly, but would have called for very expansionary policies. If policies would not have been expansionary enough, the economy might have followed path B: Along this path, a large GNP gap would have persisted for a long time.

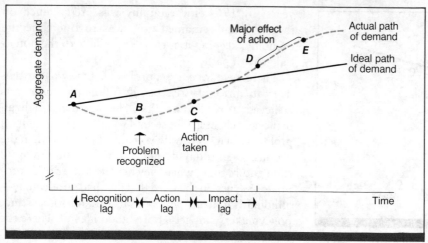

Figure 16-3 Lags and economic instability.
Because of the recognition, action, and impact lags, it is possible that policy changes will make
things worse. Expansive steps aimed at fighting the recession at point *C* may add to a later
inflationary boom at *E*. Similarly, policies aimed at restraining an inflationary boom may make
the next recession worse.

THE CASE AGAINST ACTIVISM: LAGS

The core of the case against activism is the argument that active policies are more likely to destabilize than to stabilize the economy. The first reason that monetary and fiscal policies may cause instability is that they may be badly timed. They may fight the battles of last year, and be inappropriate to deal with the problems of the present and, more important, those of the future.

There are *three lags* between the time that aggregate demand should be changed and the time when the change actually occurs. To illustrate, suppose that the economy begins to slide down into a recession. This fact may not be recognized for some time. It takes time to gather statistics on what is happening. Initial signs of weakness may be dismissed as temporary disturbances; not every little jiggle in economic activity grows into a recession or boom. Thus, the first lag is the *recognition* lag, which occurs between the time the weakness in the economy begins and the time when it is recognized. Furthermore, even after the decline is recognized, policymakers take some time to act; this is the *action lag*. For example, spending programs must be designed before they can be implemented. Finally, after action is taken, there is some delay before the major *impact* on the economy is felt.

For example, when government spending is finally increased, the various rounds of consumer spending in the multiplier process take time. For monetary policy, there is a lag between the open market purchase that pushes down interest rates and the actual investment that is stimulated as a consequence. These, then, are the lags that occur before aggregate demand actually changes: the **recognition lag**, the **action lag**, and the **impact lag**.

Consider how these lags can lead to incorrect policies and add to the instability of the economy. Suppose, for example, that the ideal path of aggregate demand is shown by the solid line in Figure 16-3. But actual demand follows the dashed curve. Starting at point *A*, aggregate demand starts to slip below the desired level; the economy begins to move into a recession. However, this problem is not recognized for some time—not until point *B*. Even then, taxes are not cut immediately; action does not take place until point *C*. By this time, it may be too late. There is a further lag before the action affects demand (between points *D* and *E*), and by then the economy has already recovered. Fuel is added to the inflationary fire. Then, as the severity of inflation is recognized, policies are shifted in a restrictive direction. But once again there are lags; the policies can come too late, making the next recession worse. Rather than trying to adjust to changing conditions, it might be better to follow a stable set of policies. So argue those in the classical tradition.

The Helmsman's Dilemma

The slowness of the economy to respond, and the momentum that can accumulate in the downswing or upswing, mean that the problem of the policymaker can be compared with that of the helmsman of an ocean-going ship. The helmsman may turn the wheel, but a large ship does not respond immediately. Suppose a ship heads out of Halifax harbour, with plans to go due south past the eastern tip of Cuba on the way to the Panama Canal. If the helmsman finds his course drifting to the east, he can correct it by turning the wheel to starboard.

The problem is, how much? If he turns the wheel just slightly, the ship will continue on its easterly course for some time; it does not respond quickly. In his anxiety, he may then turn the wheel more sharply. Clearly, the more sharply the wheel is turned, the more quickly the ship will return to its course. But, if the wheel is swung hard to starboard, a new problem will arise. Once the ship points in the right direction, it will be turning with considerable momentum; the ship will move in a westerly direction. In his panic, the helmsman may be tempted to swing the wheel back hard to port. We can imagine the voyage of the anxious mariner—zigzagging down the Atlantic Ocean.

Of course, ships do not zigzag all over the ocean. With some practice, the helmsman learns not to lean too hard on the wheel. He learns to move the wheel back to the centre *before* the ship gets back to its intended course; the ship's momentum will complete the turn. Policymakers face the same type of problem. They must try to switch toward restraint *before* an economic expansion turns into an inflationary boom. As a former chairman of the U.S. Federal Reserve once sadly observed, central bankers have an unpopular task: to take away the punch bowl just when the party really gets going.

Not only do policymakers have the helmsman's problem; they also face a few more which provide extra excitement. One of the additional complications is that the helm and the rudder of the economic ship are connected by elastic bands and baling twine. Unlike the mechanism connecting the ship's wheel to the rudder, the mechanism connecting monetary and fiscal policies to aggregate demand does not work in a precise, highly predictable manner. Furthermore, the economic policymaker may have to chart a course across turbulent and stormy seas. Between 1965 and 1982, there were large shocks to the Canadian economy: first, a sustained export boom from 1966 to 1968 (caused partly by the high level of economic activity in the United States as a result of the Vietnam War); then the inflationary pressures in food prices stemming from Soviet crop failures and large-scale North American grain exports during the years 1972-75, and also from the effects of the quadrupling of world oil prices in 1973 and 1974; then the second big jump in oil prices in 1979–80; and, finally, the high U.S. interest rates and recession in 1980–82. If the ship is being guided across placid seas, the policymaker has the luxury of turning the wheel meekly and slowly so as not to overcorrect. But in stormy waters, this is not good enough. A meek application of policies will be overwhelmed by other forces. This, then, is the helmsman's dilemma: How hard should the wheel be swung, and how soon should it be moved back toward centre?

THE CASE AGAINST ACTIVISM: THE OVERESTIMATION OF POTENTIAL

The danger of overreaction is increased by a fourth type of lag. The three lags in the previous section represented delays *before* aggregate demand changes. The fourth lag occurs *after* aggregate demand changes. It involves the differing speeds with which real GNP and prices respond to changes in demand. Specifically, when aggregate demand rises, the short-run effect on real output is generally powerful. Unless producers are already straining hard against their capacity limitations, they respond to an increase in demand by producing more. However, as time passes, the higher demand is reflected more and more in terms of higher prices, and less and less in terms of real output. Thus, *when aggregate demand is stimulated, the favourable output effects come quickly; the unfavourable price effects are delayed.* This creates a temptation to stick with expansive fiscal and monetary policies too long, in order to gain their short-term benefits in terms of higher output.

Figure 16-4 illustrates this lag. Note that the response of prices in the lower panel comes after the change in output shown in the top panel. Figure 16-4 also illustrates some of the criticisms directed at the activist

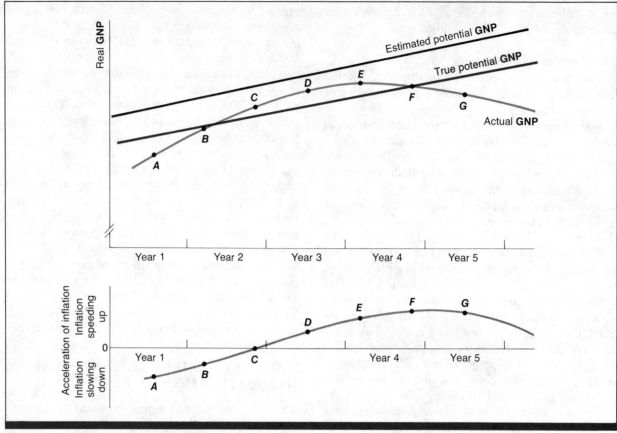

Figure 16-4 Policy activism: The case against.
Because of the delayed response of prices and overly ambitious goals, aggregate demand will
be overstimulated, say the critics of active demand management. When inflation finally does
become an obvious problem, then policymakers will overreact.

Keynesian approach. The first step in the Keynesian approach is to estimate potential GNP. Policymakers tend to be optimistic, overestimating potential GNP and the amount by which unemployment can be reduced by expansive demand policies. Such an overly optimistic estimate is shown by the black estimated potential GNP line in Figure 16-4. The red line shows the true potential path that can be followed without causing an overheating of the economy and an acceleration of inflation.

Now let us see what the critics fear if activists are in charge. Beginning at *A*, the economy is recovering from a recession. Monetary and fiscal policies are set for the expansion of aggregate demand. Real output is rising briskly, the unemployment rate is falling, and

inflation—with its delayed response—is still slowing down because of the previous period of slack. Everything seems to be going well. The expansive policy settings are retained. But, without anyone noticing, the economy moves past *B*, crossing the true potential path. The error in estimating the potential path means that policymakers incorrectly believe that aggregate demand is still too low. (GNP is still below the optimistic black estimate of potential.) As a result, expansive policies are continued. In reality, however, aggregate demand is too high, since the economy is above the true potential path shown in red. Therefore, a less expansive policy is appropriate.

As the economy crosses the true potential path, the seeds of a more rapid inflation are being sown, although the inflationary result does not appear for some time. As the curve in the lower diagram illustrates, inflation does not begin to accelerate until time C.

If the error in estimating the black potential GNP path has been large, the economy may never actually reach it. The expanding demand shows up increasingly in terms of inflation, and less and less in terms of real output. The expansive fiscal and monetary policies cause an increase in aggregate demand, but they do not control the extent to which the higher demand will cause higher output, and the extent to which it will show up in the form of higher prices.

Between C and D, a sharp policy debate is likely. Those focusing on the optimistic black path argue that to reach it, aggregate demand should be increased even more. But, as inflation is by now accelerating (to the right of point C in the lower part of the diagram), others urge caution. As time passes and inflation gets worse and worse, those urging restraint eventually win the debate. With inflation by now rising rapidly, the policy adjustment may be abrupt.

As a result, the economy may fall into a sharp recession. But, as always, inflation responds with a lag. *It remains serious even though tight policies have been introduced. As a consequence, everything seems to be going wrong during the period between E and G*—just as everything went right during the expansion between A and B. The economy is headed into a recession and unemployment is rising, yet inflation is still getting worse. As the unemployment rate rises higher and higher while inflation continues stubbornly, more and more people argue that demand restraint simply won't stop inflation. Inflation has become "built in," and skeptics charge that nothing much can be done about it with monetary and fiscal policies. Aggregate demand policies are therefore turned in an expansive direction quite quickly, in order to increase output and reduce unemployment. A new upswing begins. But inflation has accelerated more as a result of the extended period of excess demand than it has fallen as a result of the shorter period of slack. Thus, each upswing begins with a higher rate of inflation than the previous one. This, then, is the case against activism.

Just as the case in favour of activism can be supported with real-world evidence (most notably from the early 1960s, as shown in Figure 16-2), so the critics can point to evidence of failures of discretionary policies. First, they note that most recent recoveries

have in fact begun with higher and higher rates of inflation. The inflation rate was less than 1% in the early recovery year of 1961; between 4% and 5% in the recovery of 1972; about 10% in the early recovery of 1975; and well over 10% as the economy came out of the mini-recession in 1980. (The recovery from the 1981–82 recession was an exception: During the 1983–84 recovery, inflation fell below 5%. But even if the recession of 1981–82 broke the inflationary spiral, it can hardly be taken as an example of successful discretionary policy.)

Second, the 1970s and early 1980s provide a real-world illustration of the principal point of Figure 16-4; that is, how an overestimation of potential GNP can lead to policy problems. With the benefit of hindsight, it seems clear that Canadian policymakers in the 1970s substantially overestimated potential GNP because they were using an unrealistically high full-employment target. The target used by the Economic Council of Canada at that time was an unemployment rate of no more than 3.8%. But later studies show that a realistic target in the 1972–75 period would have been between 5% and 6% unemployment.[3] Nor is there a consensus concerning what a realistic full-employment target should be in the 1980s. A study carried out by Peter Dungan and Thomas Wilson of the University of Toronto shows the full-employment rate *declining* from about 6% in the mid-1970s to 5% in the mid-1980s; in contrast, a study by Ernie Stokes of the Conference Board of Canada suggests that the attainable full-employment target *increased* from 6% in 1975 to roughly 7.5% in the first half of the 1980s.[4]

In Figure 16-5 we show several simplified estimates of the gap between actual and potential GNP based on alternative full-employment targets. Curve A traces the gap if one takes the Economic Council's 3.8% unemployment as a target. Curves B and C show the estimated gaps between actual and potential GNP if

[3]The reasons given for these changes in the full-employment rate include the increase in the share of young workers and women workers in the labour force during those years. Because these groups traditionally have higher unemployment rates than other groups, the studies argue that the unemployment target has to be raised when this share increases.

[4]D. Peter Dungan and Thomas A. Wilson, *Potential GNP: Performance and Prospects* (Toronto: Institute for Policy Analysis, University of Toronto, 1982), and Ernie Stokes, *Canada's Output Growth: Performance and Potential, 1966–92* (Ottawa: The Conference Board of Canada, April 1983).

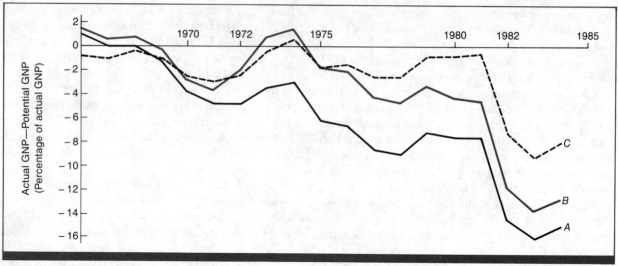

Figure 16-5   Estimates of the gap between actual and potential GNP, 1966–1984.

With a full-employment target of 3.8%, the target used by the Economic Council of Canada in the mid-1970s, the estimated gap between actual and potential GNP remained large throughout the 1970–73 period (the solid black curve). Accordingly, expansionary policy settings were followed in order to close the gap. Later estimates (red curve and broken black curve) based on more realistic full-employment targets show that the gap decreased during 1970–73, and that in 1973, actual GNP was *above* potential. Hence, restric-

tive policies to contain the inflationary pressure would have been the appropriate policy stance.

In the late 1970s, estimates of the gap between actual and potential GNP based on the relatively optimistic full-employment targets of Dungan and Wilson (the red curve) indicate that GNP in those years was well below potential. However, the gap estimated on the basis of Stokes' full-employment target indicate that GNP was quite close to potential during those years, and that policy may have been too expansionary.

Source: Estimates by authors.

one uses the more realistic estimates of Dungan/Wilson (curve *B*) or Stokes (curve *C*).

Consider now the situation in the early 1970s. The estimates actually used by the policymakers at that time would have been close to those shown by curve *A*. According to these estimates, the gap between potential and actual GNP remained almost as high through 1973 as it had been during the recession year 1970. To close the gap, the policymakers moved toward expansionary monetary and fiscal policy settings; monetary policy especially was expansionary, with M1 growing at nearly 15% per year in both 1972 and 1973.

But in retrospect, GNP was *not* substantially below its potential in 1973. Using later estimates of a realistic full-employment target, the unemployment rate in 1973 had fallen well below the full-employment target. In other words, actual GNP was *above* potential GNP. As a result, the stage was set for the outburst

of double-digit inflation in the second half of the 1970s.

In the early 1970s, potential GNP was overestimated mainly because the policymakers had an unrealistically low target for the unemployment rate. In the late 1970s and early 1980s, it was overestimated for another reason as well: the economy's declining productivity performance. For reasons that will be discussed in Chapter 19, the rate of productivity growth fell sharply in the mid-1970s. Once again, the policymakers were slow to recognize that potential GNP was growing less rapidly than expected; consequently, the gap between actual and potential GNP was overestimated. Partly because of this, the policymakers did not adequately restrain aggregate demand, even though inflation was running at a high level. Fiscal policy in particular was highly expansionary from 1975 to 1978; had we recognized that the gap was far smaller than we thought, policy might have been more restrictive and inflationary pressures less severe.

In the United States, a number of policy errors were made in the 1970s, for similar reasons as in Canada. The 1980 Annual Report of the Council of Economic Advisors summarizes the problem: "Projecting potential GNP growth into the future is subject to large errors." But this conclusion throws into question the whole strategy of active aggregate demand management which is based on the assumption that potential GNP can be accurately forecast and taken as a target at which aggregate demand policy should be aimed.

THE CASE FOR A MONETARY RULE

There are many doubts about how well discretionary demand-management policies have worked. However, discretionary policies cannot be considered in a vacuum. We should also look at the alternative suggested by monetarists, that the quantity of money be increased at a steady, moderate rate. There are several elements in this monetarist case:

1. The desirable path of aggregate demand is one of steady, moderate growth, which will make possible the purchase of the growing output of the economy at approximately stable prices.

2. The best way to ensure a steady, moderate increase in aggregate demand is with a steady, moderate increase in the money stock. Velocity is, of course, not perfectly constant, and therefore even a perfectly stable growth of money would not lead to a perfectly stable growth in demand. But, say the advocates of a monetary rule, the amount of instability would be less than the instability caused by discretionary policies. Furthermore, a rule involving a slow growth of the money stock would avoid the strong inflationary tendencies that have resulted from discretionary policies during the past two decades. That is, monetarists have two objectives: to reduce the *instability* of aggregate demand, and to avoid an inflationary *trend* in demand.

3. Some of the proponents of a policy rule base their case on political as well as economic considerations. They believe that a policy rule will result in less interference by government officials in the free-enterprise system.

Several decades ago, Henry C. Simons of the University of Chicago made rules a cornerstone of his *Economic Policy for a Free Society*:[5]

In a free enterprise system we obviously need highly definite and stable rules of the game, especially as to money. The monetary rules must be compatible with the reasonably smooth working of the system. Once established, however, they should work mechanically, with the chips falling where they may. To put our present problem as a paradox—we need to design and establish with the greatest intelligence a monetary system good enough so that, hereafter, we may hold to it unrationally—on faith—as a religion, if you please.

Moving toward a rule: Canadian monetary policy in the 1970s. During the second half of the 1970s, support for the monetarist position grew in Canada. Our experience with fine tuning during the first half of the 1970s had not been encouraging: The contractionary monetary and fiscal policies initiated in 1968–69 to counteract the threat of inflation almost certainly contributed to the high unemployment rates in the 1970 recession. The attempt at fighting the persistently high unemployment during 1971–73 through a very expansionary monetary policy resulted mainly in accelerated inflation, without accomplishing any significant reduction in unemployment rates. Similarly, while the expansionary fiscal policy in 1975 may have reduced the severity of the 1974–75 recession, it also created a huge government deficit which turned out to be very difficult to reduce. In retrospect, it seems fairly clear that smaller and more gradual changes in the settings of both monetary and fiscal policy would have lessened the severity of the subsequent inflation problem, without necessarily aggravating the unemployment problem.

The most significant step in the direction of monetarist policy based on rules was taken by the Bank of Canada in November 1975. At that time, the Bank announced that it would follow a policy of establishing given target ranges for the growth of the money supply (narrowly defined as M1). When a target range

[5]Henry C. Simons, *Economic Policy for a Free Society* (Chicago: University of Chicago Press, 1948), p. 169.

was first adopted, it allowed for relatively high rates of monetary growth; the Bank announced that M1 would grow no faster than 15% at an annual rate, but no slower than 10%. But the Bank also made it clear that it intended to reduce the target rates gradually, so that there would be a gradual reduction of the inflationary pressures in the Canadian economy. The first decrease in the target growth rate came in less than a year: In August 1976, the Bank announced that M1 would be growing between 8% and 12% per year. Subsequent decreases brought the target growth down to a range of 4% to 8% by early 1981.

THE CASE AGAINST A MONETARY RULE

On behalf of discretionary policy making, we will examine several major criticisms of a fixed monetary rule.

1. The proponents of a monetary rule generally aim for a slow rate of increase in aggregate demand, in order to ensure price stability. The critics argue that, in practice, the result may be an unnecessarily high rate of unemployment. That is, *the trend of demand may be too low* if the monetarist proposal is followed.

2. In practice, it is not possible to have a policy rule that will be followed forever, *regardless of the consequences*. No government will continue to stick blindly to a policy rule if it turns out that the effects of the rule are very different from what was originally expected, or if adherence to the rule makes it impossible to attain important policy objectives other than those that the rule was intended to serve. For example, as we shall see, part of the reason why the Bank of Canada departed from its anti-inflationary monetary targets in 1979–80 was to prevent sharp changes in the exchange rate. (For another practical problem that may arise in adopting a rule, see Box 16-1.)

3. Even though there is much to be said for a stable rate of growth of aggregate demand, a monetary policy rule will not provide it. *Velocity is not stable*. In other words, there are substantial non-monetary sources of disturbance in the economy. In reality, policies must be changed from time to time to combat these disturbances, and smooth aggregate demand. (Non-monetary

sources of instability are studied in the appendix to this chapter.)

We now consider each of these points in more detail.

1. Insufficient Aggregate Demand?

Monetarists generally propose a monetary rule designed to allow aggregate demand to rise no more rapidly than the productive capacity of the economy. If successful, the rule would result in long-run price stability.

It is not altogether clear whether it is desirable to have a trend in aggregate demand which is just barely adequate to buy the growing output of the nation at stable prices. It depends in part on the nature of aggregate supply. If the aggregate supply curve slopes upward before full employment is reached—as illustrated by the intermediate range of the Keynesian aggregate supply curve back in Figure 9-5—then a case can be made for increasing aggregate demand somewhat more rapidly than the productive capacity of the economy. By accepting a moderate upward movement in prices, we can achieve greater output and employment.

If, on the other hand, the aggregate supply curve is vertical, as in the classical theory illustrated in Figure 9-3, then a non-inflationary trend is just fine. Output and employment will be just as high as with an inflationary trend. Thus, the monetarist proposals for aggregate *demand* depend in part on their belief in the vertical aggregate *supply* of classical theory.

A detailed study of aggregate supply must be deferred until the next chapter. However, the main point can be summarized. Critics of a monetary rule fear that monetarists would keep the trend of aggregate demand too low, creating high unemployment. Monetarists believe that discretionary policymakers will create too much demand, causing a persistent inflation.

2. Rules Can't Be Followed Regardless of the Consequences

Monetarists argue for a policy rule that should be followed regardless of current conditions. In Simons' view, it should be followed regardless of how the chips fall. However, this rigid position can scarcely be taken literally. After all, evidence regarding economic institutions and economic behaviour should be taken into account in establishing any rule; not to do so would be foolish. Yet these institutions and patterns of behaviour change. When they do, any rule based on them should be reconsidered—not held to steadfastly, like a religion.

BOX 16-1

POLICY RULES: THE PROBLEM OF TRANSITION

The decision by the Bank of Canada in 1975 to keep money supply growth within a predetermined target range was clearly in the spirit of the monetarist prescription. However, the decision to smooth the transition to the new policy by initially allowing relatively high rates of growth was criticized by some monetarists. In the critics' view, the right policy would have been to directly reduce monetary growth to a rate that would be consistent with price stability.

The Bank's decision to reduce the rate of monetary growth only gradually was an implicit recognition of an important point: *A sudden and sharp policy change may cause severe disruption in the economy.* For this reason, the proper way to introduce a policy rule may well be to opt for a *gradual* change toward a rule, even if this implies that the desired objective (such as price stability) is not reached as quickly.

In the United States, the Federal Reserve faced the problem of transition in 1979. Since the beginning of the 1970s, the Fed had followed a policy of trying to stabilize both interest rates and growth of the money supply. However, following the deep recession of 1973–75, which was accompanied by a very slow growth in money, Congress urged the Fed to pay more attention to money growth targets. Then came the announcement in October 1979 that the Fed would focus more on money growth targets, and less on interest rates.

The issue arose as to how the transition to a new policy would take place. There is an inherent problem in adopting the monetarist prescription in an inflationary period like 1979, with high inflation and relatively rapid increases in the money stock. (The U.S. money supply was increasing at about 8% per year.) If the objective is to have money grow at a slow, steady rate of, say, 3% per year, how is this new policy to be introduced? If the Fed immediately moves to a 3% money growth path, a sharp change will have occurred: The growth of the money stock will have been very unstable during the transition. On the other hand, if the Fed simply stabilizes money growth at the existing rate of 8%, the anti-inflationary goal will never be achieved.

In practice, the Fed compromised, picking a goal somewhat less than the prevailing 8%. By the middle of 1980, the narrowly defined money supply was only 5% higher than a year earlier. Thus, a rather sharp change in policy had taken place—although not so sharp as would have occurred by moving immediately to a money growth rate of 3%. However, the sharp deceleration in the rate of growth of money was accompanied by record-high interest rates in 1980–81 and the two recessions in 1980 and 1981–82. Thus, even with this degree of compromise, the transition to a policy based on a monetary rule may have been very costly: It may have contributed substantially to the severity of the 1981–82 recession.

There used to be a monetary "religion" based on the gold standard. However, it contributed to the disaster of the 1930s. As Simons himself observed, "The utter inadequacy of the old gold standard, either as a definite system of rules or as the basis of a monetary religion, seems beyond intelligent dispute."[6] But that is exactly the point—the evidence indicated that the gold standard was a bad rule. Rules should not be maintained regardless of the evidence, regardless of how the chips fall.

The difficulties that may arise in following a rule were well illustrated by Canadian monetary policy in the early 1980s. During the 1975–79 period, the policy followed by the Bank of Canada was reasonably consistent with the intentions announced in 1975. M1 remained close to the predetermined target ranges and grew at a reasonably steady rate. (During the postal strikes in late 1975 and in 1978, the Bank allowed M1 to grow very rapidly for short periods. However, these

[6]Simons, *Economic Policy for a Free Society*, p. 169.

episodes can be seen as deliberate exceptions to the main thrust of the Bank's policy: By allowing the money supply to expand rapidly during the strike, the Bank was making it easier for businesses to borrow money in order to cover the strike-induced shortfall in their cash flow.)

However, following the sharp increase in U.S. interest rates in 1979 and early 1980 (in response to the tighter policy being followed by the Federal Reserve), the Bank began departing from its announced rule. It tightened monetary policy by sharply restraining the growth of M1. By mid-1980, M1 was substantially lower than it would have had to be in order to stay within the target range that the Bank had announced. Then, as U.S. interest rates fell during the 1980 recession, the Bank sharply reversed itself and allowed a very high rate of growth in M1 during the second half of 1980; in late 1980 M1 was *above* the Bank's target range. By the end of 1981, it looked as though the Bank had all but abandoned its policy rule: M1 was sharply reduced and fell some 10% below the lower end of the target range. It remained well below the target range throughout the 1982 recession. And in November 1982, the Bank confirmed what by then had become obvious: It announced that it was no longer controlling M1 according to specific targets. Thus ended—at least temporarily—the Canadian experiment with a monetarist rule.

In retrospect, it is not difficult to find the main reason why the Bank departed from its earlier policy beginning in 1979. With the record-high interest rates in the United States, there would have been a large capital outflow from Canada if the Bank had not driven up Canadian interest rates as well. Such an outflow would have led to a depreciation of the Canadian dollar, which would have added to our inflation rate. It was precisely in order to prevent this that the Bank started following a policy of trying to keep Canadian interest rates relatively close to U.S. rates.

Not surprisingly, the supporters of the monetarist position were critical of the Bank. While they agreed that the Bank's policy may have reduced capital outflows, and therefore stabilized the exchange rate, they noted that it also resulted in Canadian interest rates following the wild gyrations of U.S. rates during 1980–82. Critics believe that a better policy would have been for the Bank to stick more closely to its original monetary growth target, even if this would have meant a bit more fluctuation in the exchange rate. In the words of the University of Western Ontario's Tom Courchene,[7]

> This [policy] is not [a monetary rule. It] is pegging the exchange rate, or essentially equivalently, following U.S. monetary policy. The Bank of Canada may express concern that U.S. policy is forcing some unattractive options on Canada. The fact is that this is the Bank's own doing, since it has effectively tied Canada's fortunes to U.S. monetary policy.

The Bank's policy, its critics argued, gave monetarism a bad name. The record high interest rates in 1981–82 gave rise to a public outcry against monetarist policies. But, say the Bank's critics, those interest rates were not the result of the Bank's long-run strategy of following a monetary rule; instead, they resulted from the Bank's departure from a rule as it tried to stabilize the exchange rate.

3. Would a Monetary Rule Make the Growth of Aggregate Demand More Stable?

In 1982 when the Bank of Canada announced that it was no longer keeping M1 within a specific target range, it also referred to another important reason why a stable rate of monetary expansion could no longer be considered the best policy: the instability of velocity. Clearly, a stable rate of monetary expansion makes most sense if velocity is stable: It will then lead to a stable rate of expansion of aggregate demand as well. But as we already saw in Chapter 14, the velocity of M1 (the narrowly defined concept of money that the Bank was controlling) was highly unstable during the late 1970s and early 1980s. And while the velocity of M2 appears to have been more stable during those years, the critics of monetarism rightly observe that we cannot be sure how long it (or any other velocity) will *remain* stable.

However, although the recent changes in velocity in Canada (and also in the United States) have weakened economists' confidence in the quantity theory of money, we should be very careful not to come to sweeping conclusions.

[7]Thomas J. Courchene, *Money, Inflation and the Bank of Canada*, (Montreal and Calgary: The C.D. Howe Institute, 1981), vol. II, *An Analysis of Monetary Gradualism, 1975–80*, p. 194.

In particular, we should recognize that the debate is over the relative merits of two options: (1) a monetary rule; (2) discretionary demand-management policies. The evidence of the past 15 years suggests a rather disconcerting conclusion. As compared to where we were 15 years ago, we can have less confidence in a good macroeconomic performance *regardless of whether* option (1) *or* option (2) is chosen. We have just seen that, because of recent changes in velocity, we have less reason to be confident that stable money growth will lead to a stable growth in aggregate demand. The early pages of this chapter showed why we have less reason to be confident about discretionary policies. In the early 1960s, discretionary policies seemed successful. The period since 1970 leads to harsher judgements, as explained in the discussion of Figure 16-5.

With both options looking rather unattractive, it is not clear what has happened to the *relative* merits of the two. It's not clear whether discretionary policies or a monetary rule will make aggregate demand more stable. We seem to be left with only one straightforward conclusion, which we don't much like. It's less fun to be a macroeconomist now than it was in 1970.

THE OUTCOME OF THE DEBATE

While monetarist rule makers remain in the minority, significant changes in attitude have occurred since the 1960s and early 1970s as a consequence of their criticisms of activist policies and as a consequence of the disappointing results with aggregate demand management:

1. There has been increased awareness that demand management itself may be a cause of economic instability. Overly ambitious demand management may cause accelerating inflation. Furthermore, substantial lags may result in actions that are too late and that add to the magnitude of cyclical swings.
2. There is more widespread recognition of the importance of paying attention to the long-term consequences of policies. In particular, because aggregate demand has a lagged effect on prices, there is a general recognition that anti-inflation policies should be made with the long run in mind.

FORECASTING

If a little knowledge is dangerous, where is the man who has so much as to be out of danger?
Thomas Huxley

The proponents of rules have made significant contributions to macroeconomic policy debates, but they have not swept the field. Monetary and fiscal policies are still adjusted from time to time. However, the debate over discretionary policies has highlighted the dangers of managing aggregate demand.

In particular, lags mean that policies adopted today will not have their full effect until some months in the future. The problem is this: Will the effects of the policy be appropriate at that time? In deciding whether or not to change policy, the Bank of Canada and fiscal policymakers have *no alternative but to forecast*. The question is not *whether* to forecast or not, but *how*. Anyone who thinks that forecasting can be avoided is, in fact, forecasting in a naïve way. By implying that policy should be designed for the needs of the moment, such a person is making the simple forecast that the problems of the future will be the same as those of today. Even the proponents of a monetary rule are forecasting in a sense. Their case is based on the forecast that velocity will be stable in the future.

Forecasting with a Model

In developing a forecast for the coming months, economists in and out of government use a number of techniques, most of them with computers. Typically, past information on consumption, income, etc., is used to estimate how the economy behaves. For example, how is consumption related to income? Based on past relationships, future consumption is estimated. Typically, forecasters also estimate future investment, government expenditures, and net exports. The path of investment is forecast on the basis of current and expected future interest rates and other important influences. The budget is used to estimate the probable course of government spending. Exports are estimated on the basis of expected economic activity abroad; the more prosperous foreign economies are, the more likely they are to buy our exports. Such pieces are fitted together to make a statistical—or *econometric*—model of the economy. With such a model, it is possible to make a projection of GNP.

A simple example will give a general idea of how this is done. We begin with the fundamental equation of an earlier chapter:

$$GNP = C + I_g + G + X - M$$
$$(16\text{-}1, \text{ repeat of } 7\text{-}2)$$

Suppose that statistical evidence indicates that consumers in the past have spent 90% of their disposable incomes, and that two-thirds of GNP flows through to consumers in the form of disposable income. That means that consumption is 60% of GNP (that is, 90% × 2/3):

$$C = 0.6GNP \qquad (16\text{-}2)$$

Suppose, also, that businesses are expected to invest $90 billion in the coming period:

$$I_g = \$90 \qquad (16\text{-}3)$$

The budgets of the federal, provincial, and local governments commit them to $120 billion in purchases of goods and services:

$$G = \$120 \qquad (16\text{-}4)$$

Exports are expected to amount to $100 billion:

$$X = \$100 \qquad (16\text{-}5)$$

Finally, past experience indicates that imports are about 25% of GNP:

$$M = 0.25GNP \qquad (16\text{-}6)$$

Substituting the last five equations into equation 16-1, we can solve for GNP:

$$GNP = 0.6GNP + \$90 + \$120 + \$100$$
$$- 0.25GNP$$
$$GNP = 0.35GNP + \$310$$

That is:

$$GNP = \$476.92 \qquad (16\text{-}7)$$

We thus forecast GNP to be $477 billion.

In practice, of course, economists use substantially more complicated equations. For example, consumption expenditures depend not only on consumers' disposable income, but also on their wealth (such as stocks and bonds). When forecasting, economists pay particular attention to the time element, for example, *how*

quickly consumption responds to changing levels of disposable income. Taking these two complications into account, we get a more sophisticated consumption function:

$$C_t = 0.5DI_t + 0.2DI_{t-1} + 0.05W_t \qquad (16\text{-}8)$$

where:

DI stands for disposable income
W   stands for wealth

and the subscripts stand for time periods; specifically,

$t - 1$ is the quarter before t.

In plain English, equation 16-8 says that consumption expenditures in any quarter (C_t) depend on disposable income in that quarter (DI_t) and in the previous quarter (DI_{t-1}), and also on wealth in that quarter (W_t).

Although equation 16-8 is still relatively simple, it is beginning to resemble the consumption function used in actual econometric models. The appendix to this chapter will introduce some of the basic ideas used to explain investment in such models.

By the mid-1980s, a substantial number of econometric models of the Canadian economy had been developed.[8] Several of them are used primarily for short-term forecasting. Well-known models in this category include the Data Resources of Canada Model, The Informetrica Model (TIM), and the Medium Term Forecasting Model (MTFM) of the Conference Board of Canada. Because of the close links of the Canadian and U.S. economies, several of these models are linked with similar forecasting models for the United States, so that the effects of changing U.S. economic conditions can be directly incorporated into the Canadian forecasts. (Other models, such as the Economic Council of Canada's CANDIDE model, the Bank of Canada's RDX2, or the FOCUS model of the Institute for Policy Analysis at the University of Toronto, are used primarily to investigate the medium-term effects of policy changes, rather than for short-term forecasting of the business cycle.)

These models provide a useful starting point for forecasts, and are particularly helpful in cross-checking

[8]A useful recent summary of Canadian econometric models is provided in Ronald G. Bodkin, Lawrence R. Klein, and Kanta Marwah, "Canadian Macroeconometric Modelling, 1947–1979 and Beyond," Research Paper #8502, University of Ottawa, July 1985.

the various components of aggregate demand (consumption, investment, government spending, and net exports) to make sure that they are consistent. However, models have a major limitation. Essentially, they project the future on the basis of relationships which have held in the past, but which may change. The future of the economy depends on many forces, some of which are not easy to incorporate into formal econometric models. Thus, forecasters generally adjust the initial results of their econometric models to allow for additional factors that they consider important. The final result is a "judgemental" forecast—using the results of models, but with modifications.

In adjusting the raw output of econometric models, forecasters use the results of various surveys of future intentions, for example, the Conference Board's questionnaires regarding business investment intentions and surveys of consumer attitudes.

Turning points. One of the hardest problems in forecasting is to tell when a turning point will take place— when an expansion will reach a peak and a decline will begin, or when a recession will hit the trough and a recovery begin. One of the weakest features of econometric models is that they do not forecast turning points very accurately. But turning points are very important. If an upswing will end in the next several months, now is the time to consider more expansive policies.

What is needed, then, is something that will signal a coming turn. To fill this need, economists have tried to construct indexes of **leading indicators**. Since the 1970s, such indexes have been published on a regular basis by several chartered banks, and (since 1981) by Statistics Canada. While each of the indexes is somewhat different, they are all computed on the basis of economic variables that tend to turn up or down well in advance of turning points for GNP. Variables that usually behave in this way include stock prices, new orders for durable goods, and the number of job vacancies in business firms.

> A *leading indicator* is an economic variable that reaches a turning point (peak or trough) before the economy as a whole changes direction. (New orders for durable goods are an example.)

As we saw in Chapter 8, business fluctuations in Canada often occur simultaneously with fluctuations in the United States. For this reason, several of the leading-indicator indexes used in Canada take account of the U.S. Department of Commerce leading-indicator index as well, so that our indexes include both the leading indicators in the domestic economy and information on variables that will affect future demand by foreigners for Canadian goods and services.

As Figure 16-6 shows, leading indicators may be helpful. The Trendicator index published by the Royal Bank of Canada correctly forecast the recessions in 1970, 1974, and 1980, as well as earlier slumps. But the figure also shows that leading indicators may sometimes give confusing signals. In 1966, the index predicted a recession that failed to materialize. In late 1983 it again indicated a coming downturn; however, the economy grew at a healthy rate through 1984 and 1985. However, even when leading indicators correctly signal a future recession, they may not tell very precisely *when* it will occur; they don't provide the same period of advance warning each time. For example, the Trendicator usually predicts a downturn with a lead time of about two quarters. But the 1980 recession did not occur until about a year after the index first indicated a downturn was coming, and more seriously, the deep 1981–82 recession occurred with almost no lead time at all.

The record: How well can we forecast? To evaluate the accuracy of various forecasting methods, economists have compared a number of forecasts with actual outcomes. In a 1979 study, a group of economists at the University of Ottawa found that during the 1970s, the quarterly changes in GNP predicted by several forecasting models were much more accurate than the changes that would have been predicted on the basis of some "naïve" procedure, such as extrapolating from recent trends, or assuming that the increase over the next year will be the same as the average increase for the past few years.[9] More recent studies in the United States have found a similar result. These conclusions are reassuring. Businesses and governments pay millions for forecasts. They are not wasting their money.

Less reassuring, however, is the record of forecasters during the recession of 1981–82. Forecasters in

[9]Ronald G. Bodkin, Victoria Cano-Lamy, et al., "*Ex ante* Forecasting with Several Econometric Models of the Canadian Economy," *Journal of Post-Keynesian Economics* (Spring 1979): 16–40.

the United States largely failed to predict this recession, even though it was the most severe one in decades. Partly as a result, there was little or no advance warning of the recession in Canadian forecasts as well.

In defence of the forecasters, one can argue that forecasting was particularly difficult during 1981–82 both in the United States and Canada, because in both countries, fiscal policy was set for expansion while monetary policy was contractionary. This reinforces the point made at the end of Chapter 14. When mone-

tary policy is pushed in one direction, and fiscal policy in another, the path of the economy becomes particularly uncertain.

Nevertheless, it is worrisome that forecasters are not able to anticipate recessions better. If discretionary policies are to be successful, it is particularly important that policy be moved in an expansive direction as the economy is approaching a recession. But this can only be done if we can rely on forecasts to give us advance warning of coming recessions.

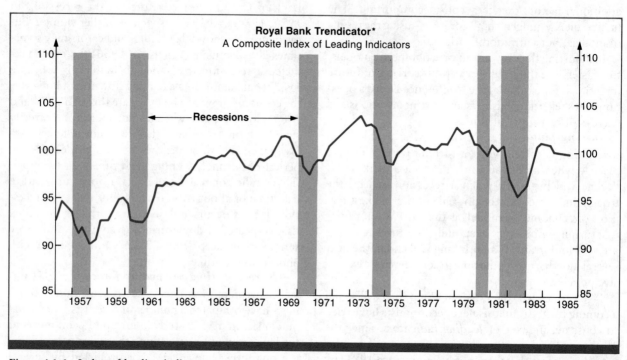

Figure 16-6   Index of leading indicators.
The curve shows the behaviour of the Royal Bank Trendicator* index since 1956. Note that the index correctly predicted the downturns in 1970, 1974, and 1980. But it has not always been reliable. In 1966 it turned down sharply, but there was no recession at that time. Similarly, in late 1983 the index predicted a coming recession, yet the economy continued to expand through 1984 and 1985. And

even though the index turned down sharply *during* the 1981–82 recession, it provided no advance warning: The downturn of the index did not come until mid-1981 when the recession had already started.

Source: Adapted from Royal Bank Trendicator,* *Royal Bank Trendicator* Report*, vol. 12, no. 5 (August 1985). (*Trademark)

KEY POINTS

1. The mediocre record of monetary and fiscal policies in recent years has enlivened an old debate: Should aggregate demand policies be actively adjusted in the quest for high employment and stable prices? Or should monetary and fiscal rules be followed?

2. The activist Keynesian approach involves several steps. First, the full-employment or potential path of GNP is estimated. Second, if actual GNP is significantly below potential GNP, aggregate demand should be expanded until the potential path is approached. Thereafter, fiscal and monetary policies should be adjusted as needed to combat fluctuations.

3. This strategy was followed with success during the first half of the 1960s. However, aggregate demand became too high and inflation accelerated in the last half of the decade.

4. The existence of time lags makes it difficult to design countercyclical policies. Actions taken today may not be appropriate to the economy of tomorrow, when they will have their major effect.

5. There are *three lags* between the time that aggregate demand should be changed and the time that the change actually occurs. The *recognition lag* is the interval before changes in economic conditions are recognized. The *action lag* is the interval between the time a problem is recognized and the time when fiscal and monetary policies are adjusted. The *impact lag* is the interval between the time when policies are changed and the time when the major effects of the policies occur. Because of lags, policies implemented today will have their effects at some time in the future, and then it may be too late.

6. There is also another important lag. When aggregate demand changes, the effects on prices lag behind the effect on output. That is, when aggregate demand increases, output generally responds quickly, with inflation increasing only after a lag. When aggregate demand falls, output generally falls quickly, with the economy sliding into a recession. Inflation begins to fall only after a lag.

7. Monetarists believe that discretionary policies are likely to do more harm than good. They recommend a *policy rule*—that the money stock be increased by a fixed percentage, year after year, regardless of current economic conditions. Monetarists believe that discretionary adjustments in aggregate demand policies are likely to do more harm than good because:

   (a) There are lags before aggregate demand can be adjusted, and between changes in demand and the effect on prices.

   (b) People tend to be overly optimistic in estimating the potential path of real GNP (Figure 16-5).

   (c) Because of the lags and overoptimism, expansive policies are generally continued too long. Then, when inflation becomes a clear and present danger, policymakers generally overreact, causing a fall in aggregate demand and a recession. However, inflation does not respond quickly to the lower aggregate demand. The restrictive policies are therefore deemed a failure, and another round of expansive policies is begun. Consequently, discretionary policies are likely to cause instability and an inflationary bias in the economy. Each recovery tends to begin with a higher rate of inflation than the previous one.

   (d) Policy rules will result in less interference by the government, and therefore in more economic freedom.

8. The economy can be destabilized when policymakers pursue what seem to be plausible goals. A number of examples have been provided:

   (a) Chapter 11 explained how policymakers can fall into a trap and destabilize the economy if they attempt to balance the budget every year.

   (b) This chapter has explained the problems that arise if policymakers aim at an unattainable estimate of potential GNP.

9. A number of arguments can be made against a monetary rule and in favour of discretionary policies:

(a) In practice, no government will follow a policy rule regardless of the short-run consequences (how the chips fall) and competing objectives (such as wartime finance).

(b) Rulemakers tend to propose a rule that will keep the trend of aggregate demand too low. An unnecessarily high rate of unemployment will be the result. (Compare this with key point 7(c), the monetarist view that activist policies will give the economy an inflationary bias.)

(c) A monetary rule does not ensure a stable increase in aggregate demand.

(d) Efforts to follow stable policies may paradoxically lead to abrupt policy shifts (Box 16-1).

10. In spite of these counterarguments, important changes in attitudes have occurred as a consequence of the monetarist criticisms of fine tuning and the disappointing results with aggregate demand management:

(a) The problem of lags is more clearly recognized.

(b) The importance of keeping long-term objectives in mind is more widely recognized.

11. Because policies have their major effect on aggregate demand some months in the future, a forecast of future conditions must be made—explicitly or implicitly—whenever policy is changed. To forecast, economists use econometric models, supplemented with survey data and "judgemental" adjustments. The experience of recent years suggests that it is particularly difficult to forecast recessions.

KEY CONCEPTS

policy activism	recognition lag	productivity of labour
discretionary policy	action lag	econometric model
policy rule	impact lag	turning point
fine tuning	lag between output changes	leading indicator
potential GNP	and price changes	
GNP gap		

PROBLEMS

16-1 Explain the various steps in the activist Keynesian strategy.

16-2 What case do monetarists make against the activist approach?

16-3 If discretionary policies are followed, what are the consequences of overestimating potential GNP growth? Use the Canadian experience since 1960 in your answer.

16-4 What case can be made against a monetary policy rule?

16-5 In 1981, as interest rates rose to record highs in the United States, the Bank of Canada reduced the growth rate of M1 well below the target range that it had previously announced. As a result, interest rates in Canada rose rapidly as well.

Some critics of the Bank argued that by not sticking to its own target range, the Bank *destabilized* the economy. In defence of the Bank, others argued that if the Bank had stuck to its target range, the economy would have been even less stable in than it was. Try to explain the possible reasoning underlying these conflicting views.

16-6 In the section describing the possible overestimation of potential GNP, we observed that output and prices do not respond at the same rate to changes in aggregate demand. In such circumstances, why do the statistics sometimes give policymakers conflicting signals about the appropriate way to adjust aggregate demand? How do the conflicting signals add to the "recognition lag"?

16-7 Why must future economic conditions be forecast when monetary or fiscal policies are changed? If policymakers do not believe they are forecasting, why may we conclude that they are in fact using implicit forecasts? If someone argues for no change in monetary and fiscal policies, is he or she making any forecast about the future? Why is it particularly important to forecast turning points? Can you think of any reason why it is difficult to forecast turning points accurately?

APPENDIX

THE ACCELERATOR: A NON-MONETARY EXPLANATION OF BUSINESS FLUCTUATIONS

If business cycles were primarily the result of monetary disturbances, a smooth growth in the money stock would make the economy more stable. However, the stronger non-monetary disturbances are, the less the economy can be smoothed by a monetary policy rule, and the stronger is the case for discretionary policies to offset the disturbances—provided that the authorities can act quickly enough in the presence of lags.

Separating monetary from non-monetary disturbances is not a simple matter. "Non-monetary" theories of business cycles generally focus on the investment sector of aggregate demand, since this is the most unstable. The theory of investment presented in this appendix will be "non-monetary" in the sense that money is not an integral part of the theory. However, we cannot demonstrate that it is completely "non-monetary." In fact, we will see later that monetary issues are lurking in the background.

INVESTMENT DEMAND: THE SIMPLE ACCELERATOR

Suppose that we put ourselves in the business executive's shoes. Why should we want to invest? Why, for example, should we want to acquire more machines?

The simplest answer is that businesses want more machines because they want to produce more goods. *The desired stock of capital depends on the amount of production.* This fundamental proposition lies behind the **acceleration principle**, illustrated in Table 16-1 and Figure 16-7. In the first two years of this example,

a bicycle manufacturer sells 200,000 bicycles per year. Suppose that one machine is needed for every 10,000 bicycles produced. Assume also that the manufacturer initially has the 20 machines needed to produce the 200,000 bicycles. So long as the demand for bicycles remains stable (as shown in Table 16-1, Phase I, years 1 and 2), there is no need for additional machines; there is no net investment.

That does not mean, however, that machine production is zero. Suppose that a machine lasts for 10 years, with 2 of the original 20 machines wearing out each year. So long as the demand for bicycles remains constant at 200,000 per year, gross investment will continue to be 2 machines per year. (That is, 2 machines will be purchased to replace the 2 that wear out each year.)

Now, suppose that the demand for bicycles starts to grow in Phase II. In the third year, sales increase by 10%, from 200,000 to 220,000. As a consequence, the manufacturer needs 22 machines; 2 additional machines must be acquired. Gross investment therefore rises to 4 machines—2 replacements plus 2 net additions. An increase in sales of only 10% has had an *accelerated* or magnified effect on investment. Gross investment has risen from 2 to 4 machines, or by no less than 100%. (This magnified effect on investment provides an important clue as to why investment fluctuates so much more than GNP.) Then in the fourth year, with the growth of sales remaining constant at 20,000 units, gross investment remains constant at 4 machines per year.

Table 16-1
The Acceleration Principle

Time	(1) Yearly sales of bicycles (in thousands)	(2) Desired number of machines (column 1 ÷ 10,000)	(3) Net investment (change in column 2)	(4) Gross investment (column 3 + replacement of 2 machines)
Phase I: Steady sales				
First year	200	20	0	2
Second year	200	20	0	2
Phase II: Rising sales				
Third year	220	22	2	4
Fourth year	240	24	2	4
Phase III: A levelling off				
Fifth year	250	25	1	3
Sixth year	250	25	0	2
Phase IV: Declining sales				
Seventh year	230	23	−2	0
Eight year	210	21	−2	0
Phase V: A levelling off				
Ninth year	200	20	−1	1
Tenth year	200	20	0	2

Investment fluctuates much more than consumption. Net investment depends on the *change* in consumption.

Next, see what happens in Phase III. In the fifth year, demand begins to level out. As growth slows to 10,000 bicycles, only one additional machine is needed. Both net and gross investment *decline* as a result of *slowing* of the growth of bicycle sales. We emphasize: *An actual decline in sales is not necessary to cause a decline in investment.* (Sales did not decline in the fifth year; they merely grew more slowly than in the fourth year.) Then, when the demand for bicycles levels out in the sixth year, there is no longer a need for any additional machines; net investment drops to zero, and gross investment falls back to 2. Then, if bicycle sales begin to decline in Phase IV (year 7), the number of machines the manufacturer needs will decline; the machines that are wearing out will not be replaced. Net investment becomes negative, and gross investment can fall to zero.

This example of the acceleration principle (or "accelerator") illustrates a number of important points:

1. Investment (in machines) fluctuates by a much greater percentage than output of the goods for which capital is used (bicycles).

2. Net investment depends on the *change* in the production of the goods for which capital is used.

3. Once output begins to rise, it must continue to grow by the same amount if investment is to remain constant. A reduction in the growth of output will cause a *decline* in investment (year 5). But a very rapid growth of sales may be unsustainable. Therefore, a rapid upswing in economic activity contains the seeds of its own destruction. As the growth of consumption slows down, investment will fall.

4. It is possible for gross investment to collapse, even though there is only a mild decline in sales (year 7).

5. For investment to recover, it is not necessary for sales to rise. A smaller decline in sales is sufficient (year 9). Thus, a decline in economic activity contains the seeds of recovery.

This illustration is simplified, but the validity of its major points may be shown in a few examples. If business slackens off and fewer goods are shipped, the amount of trucking declines. Consequently, the demand for new trucks will decline sharply. Or consider what happens when the birthrate declines. Construction of schools is cut back. (New schools are needed primarily to accommodate an increase in the student population.) Note how the accelerator applies not only to machines, but also to other forms of investment such as school buildings and factories.

The accelerator can also apply to inventory investment, and this can add to the instability of the economy. Merchants may attempt to keep their inventories in proportion to sales. Thus, if sales increase by, say, 10%, orders to the factory may be increased by perhaps 20% in order to bring inventories up into line with the higher sales. Nevertheless, inventory investment does not always act as a destabilizing force. There

is no need for retailers to keep any rigid relationship between their sales and inventories. On the contrary, the effects of temporary spurts in sales may be cushioned by the existence of inventories: Retailers may meet the increased sales by running down their inventories.

MODIFICATION OF THE SIMPLE ACCELERATOR: LAGS IN INVESTMENT

Even in the case of a manufacturing operation, it is an oversimplification to assume that a rigid relationship exists between sales and the number of machines. In practice, the firm does not need exactly one machine for every 10,000 bicycles produced. Instead of acquiring new machines, a firm can run its factories overtime when demand increases. In this way, it can change

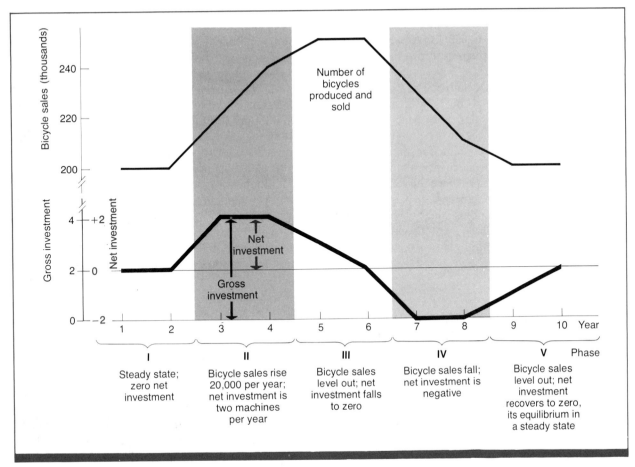

Figure 16-7 The acceleration principle.

its *capital-output ratio*. Furthermore, at the end of ten years, an old machine does not suddenly disintegrate; it wears out gradually. During a boom, older machines can be kept in use beyond their normal retirement age.

> The *capital-output ratio* is the value of capital (machines, factories, etc.) divided by the value of annual output.

What should be taken into account by businesses in deciding whether to buy new machinery or to "make do" by patching up old machinery or scheduling overtime? One important consideration is how long an increase in sales is expected to last. If it is just a temporary spurt and will quickly subside, expensive new machines should not be ordered. They may not be received quickly enough to meet the bulge in demand, and may add to idle capacity during the next downturn. Thus, the immediate response to increases in sales may be to schedule overtime, and to wait and see before ordering new machines. As a result, there are significant delays in the response of investment to changes in sales.

In the short run, these delays add to stability. Businesses do not rush out to buy new machines with every little increase in sales. However, over longer periods, lags can add to the force of an upswing or a downswing. If high sales continue for some time, businesses conclude that prosperity is permanent. Orders for new machines are placed. Once this happens, competitors may become concerned. If they don't jump on the bandwagon, they may lose their place in a growing market. A boom psychology can develop. Although investment demand is initially slow to respond, it can gain momentum.

INTERACTIONS BETWEEN THE ACCELERATOR AND THE MULTIPLIER

Interactions between consumption and investment add to the momentum of the economy. As more machines are ordered, incomes rise in the machinery-producing industries. As incomes rise, people consume more. As they buy more consumer goods, business optimism is confirmed—the rising sales are "for real." As a consequence, orders for plant and equipment increase even

more. Once again, the higher incomes resulting from higher investment stimulate consumption; the multiplier process makes the expansion stonger. Thus, increases in investment demand and increases in consumer demand reinforce one another.

Eventually, however, a strong expansion must slow down. Economic resources—land, labour, and capital— are limited, and national output cannot expand indefinitely at a rapid pace. Output begins to increase more slowly. Because of the accelerator principle, investment turns down. Because of the multiplier, national product declines by several times as much as the decrease in investment. A recession is underway. Thus, the interaction of the accelerator and multiplier helps to explain not only (1) the *strength* of cycles, but also (2) *why turning points occur*—why, for example, a boom does not continue indefinitely, but instead reaches a peak and turns into a recession.

However, an expansion does not *inevitably* turn into a recession. If the increase in demand and output can be kept moderate and steady, the natural rebound into recession may be avoided. For this reason, *moderate growth can be more healthy and lasting* than a business boom.

The downswing and lower turning point. When the lessons of the simple accelerator model (listed earlier as points 1 through 5) are modified to take account of time lags and the interaction between the multiplier and accelerator, the following sequence occurs as a result of a reduction in the growth of sales:

1. In the short run of a few weeks or months, there is little if any decline in investment in plant and equipment. This is because investment in plant and equipment is cushioned from the effects of changing sales in a number of ways:
   (a) Inventories are temporarily allowed to increase, with the result that factory orders hold up better than final sales.
   (b) Overtime is reduced.
   (c) The opportunity is taken to retire machines that have been kept in service past their normal lifetimes.
2. If sales continue to be weak, business executives begin to fear the worst. Rather than accumulate higher and higher inventories, firms cut back sharply on their orders. As production falls, factories slash new orders for machines. (These are the effects of the accelerator.) Momentum is

added to the downswing as laid-off workers reduce their consumption (the multiplier).

3. However, consumption demand does not continue to decline indefinitely. While some purchases may easily be postponed, consumers try to maintain their expenditures for food and other necessities. Furthermore, as automobiles and other consumer durables wear out, consumers become increasingly anxious to replace them. As the decline in consumer spending moderates, investment in machinery and buildings begins to recover. (However, the recovery may be delayed by the desire of retailers, wholesalers, and manufacturers to work off excessive inventories.)

Each of these three stages is important, and each contains its own valuable lesson. These lessons are, respectively:

1. Investment is not volatile in the face of small and temporary reductions in the rate of growth of sales.

2. If sales remain weak for some time, investment falls. The downswing gathers momentum because of feedbacks between falling investment and falling consumer demand—that is, because of the interaction of the multiplier and the accelerator.

3. However, the downward movement does not continue forever. Even in the worst depressions, economic activity does not collapse toward zero. The accelerator process generates natural forces of recovery even before consumption bottoms out.

In deciding whether or not to invest, business executives compare the advantages of new machinery with the alternative of "making do" by scheduling overtime and keeping old machines in production. In this decision, a relevant consideration is the cost of new machines. There are two important costs: (1) the price of the machine itself; and (2) the price of the financing—that is, the interest rate. Here is an important place where money comes into the picture. For example, open market purchases can be used to push down interest rates, and thus lower the cost of acquiring new machines, buildings, and inventories. Thus, the Bank of Canada can encourage the recovery from a recession. Similarly, open market sales (or less-than-normal purchases) and higher interest rates discourage investment, and thus can help prevent a healthy expansion from turning into an unhealthy boom.

KEY POINTS

12. Investment fluctuates more widely than other segments of GNP. The accelerator principle illustrates why. Investment depends on the change in output, and investment demand can change by a large percentage in the face of relatively small percentage changes in sales. The accelerator also helps to explain why turning points occur in the business cycle. Investment can fall even in a growing economy if the *growth* of sales slows down. An actual decline in sales is not necessary. During a recession, investment can recover when sales decline at a slower rate. An actual upturn in sales is not necessary.

13. While the acceleration principle illustrates important forces that help to determine investment demand, it represents a simplification. In practice, there may be delays in the response of investment to changes in sales. These delays contribute to the stability of the economy in the face of small disturbances. However, they mean that, once an expansion or contraction gets going, it can gather momentum.

14. The interaction between the accelerator and the multiplier also adds to the momentum of an upswing or downswing. When investment demand falls, incomes and consumption demand also fall, causing a further decline in output (the multiplier). This decline in output in turn depresses investment (the accelerator).

PROBLEMS

16-8 Complete the table below illustrating the acceleration principle. Assume that one machine is needed to produce every 1,000 automobiles. Assume that a machine lasts 10 years. Assume also that one-tenth of the initial number of machines is scheduled for retirement in each of the next 10 years.

Year	(1) Yearly sales of autos	(2) Desired number of machines	(3) Net investment	(4) Gross investment
1	100,000			
2	100,000			
3	90,000			
4	80,000			
5	80,000			
6	80,000			
7	90,000			
8	100,000			
9	100,000			

16-9 Suppose, alternatively, that there is a lag in investment. The number of machines desired in any year is calculated by taking the average number of autos produced in that year and the previous year. In other respects, follow the assumptions of Problem 16-8. Then recalculate the table in Problem 16-8. Does this change in the assumption make investment demand more or less stable?

16-10 Suppose you are in business, and demand for your product has recently increased. You now have to choose among (1) turning away some of your new customers, (2) scheduling overtime, (3) adding a new shift, or (4) expanding your factory and the number of your machines. Explain the important considerations in choosing among these four options.

Chapter 17

AGGREGATE SUPPLY: HOW CAN INFLATION AND UNEMPLOYMENT COEXIST?

The first panacea for a mismanaged
nation is inflation of the currency;
the second is war. Both bring a
temporary prosperity; both bring a
permanent ruin. But both are the refuge
of political and economic opportunists.

Ernest Hemingway

In the three decades following the Great Depression, macroeconomists were preoccupied with aggregate demand. How could we prevent a repeat of the Depression, with its decade-long inadequacy of demand? How and to what extent could we hope to manage aggregate demand in order to reduce short-run fluctuations in the economy? Then, beginning in the 1960s, macroeconomists also began to pay close attention to aggregate supply. Any study of macroeconomics is now incomplete without an investigation of *both* demand and supply.

The last five chapters have dealt in detail with the demand side, and, in particular, with the use of monetary and fiscal policies to affect aggregate demand. In this chapter, we turn to aggregate supply.

Chapter 9 introduced the aggregate supply function of Keynesian theory, repeated here as Figure 17-1. According to this view, if there is initially a deep depression at *A*, with output falling far short of the economy's full-employment potential, then an increase in aggregate demand will cause the economy to move toward *B*. In the horizontal range *AB*, the increase in demand will be reflected entirely in an increase in output, and prices will remain stable. At the other end, if an economy begins on the vertical section at *F*, an increase in demand will be reflected entirely in terms of higher prices, as the economy moves upward from *F*. Finally, there is an intermediate range, between *B* and *F*. As

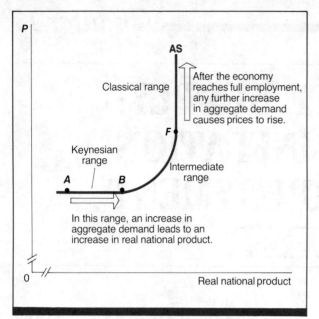

Figure 17-1   The Keynesian aggregate supply function.
This figure repeats the aggregate supply function of earlier chapters. If the economy begins at a point of depression, such as *A*, an increase in demand will increase real output. The economy will move from *A* toward *B*, with prices remaining stable. Once full employment has been reached at point *F*, a further increase in aggregate demand will cause inflation, with the economy moving upward from *F*.

the economy approaches full employment, an increase in demand will be reflected partly in terms of higher output, and partly in terms of higher prices.

(We re-emphasize a point already encountered several times. A change in *demand* causes a movement *along* a *supply* curve. For example, an increase in aggregate demand causes a movement along the aggregate supply curve from *B* to *F* in Figure 17-1. In Chapter 4, we similarly saw how a shift in demand for an individual product would cause a movement along the supply curve for that product.)

In all probability, the reader has become increasingly uncomfortable with the view of the world represented by Figure 17-1. It doesn't seem to fit the facts very well. In particular, it suggests that, whenever inflation rates are high, the economy should be at full employment, at *F* or above. On the other hand, prices should be stable whenever the unemployment rate is high, to the left of *B*. Yet there have been times when *both* the unemployment rate and inflation have been

high. In 1980, for example, the inflation rate exceeded 10% at a time when unemployment averaged 7.5%. In 1982, both unemployment and inflation had risen to about 11%. While Figure 17-1 has been useful as an introduction to the idea of aggregate supply, it is too simple. It is not consistent with what has happened in recent decades. The time has come to look closely at the facts.

To do so, economists use a slightly different approach from Figure 17-1. Instead of looking at how prices and output change, they use a diagram with the two central macroeconomic problems—inflation and unemployment—on the axes, as shown in Figure 17-2. In this diagram, the three general ideas behind Figure 17-1 can be illustrated:

1. First is the idea that prices will be stable in a deep depression. This is illustrated by points *A* and *B*. When *prices* are *stable*, the *rate of inflation* is zero. Thus, points *A* and *B* are on the

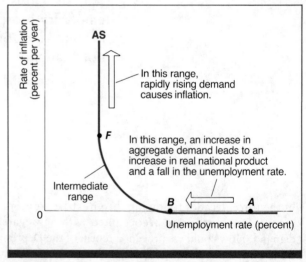

Figure 17-2   The aggregate supply function: An alternative presentation.
The major ideas in Figure 17-1 are repeated in this diagram. Starting from a point of depression, such as *A*, an increase in demand will leave prices stable. The rate of inflation will be zero. Output will increase. Unemployment will fall, as illustrated by the leftward movement to *B*. In the intermediate range from *B* to *F*, an increase in aggregate demand is reflected partly in inflation, and partly in output and employment. Once full employment has been established at *F*, a more rapid growth in aggregate demand is reflected entirely in terms of inflation, with no change in the unemployment rate.

horizontal axis of Figure 17-2. If, starting from a point of severe depression at *A*, aggregate demand rises, output will increase and the rate of unemployment will fall. The decrease in the unemployment rate shows up as a *leftward* movement from *A* to *B* in Figure 17-2. This corresponds to the *rightward* movement when output increases in Figure 17-1.

2. Second is the idea that whenever there is rapid inflation, the economy is at full employment. This idea is illustrated by the vertical range above *F* in Figure 17-2. Because of frictional unemployment, there is some unemployment—of something like 5% or 6%—even at points of "full employment." In the range above *F*, a

faster growth in aggregate demand will mean more inflation, with no change in output or employment.

3. Third is the intermediate range, between *B* and *F*. An increase in demand is reflected partly in higher prices, and partly in terms of rising output and falling unemployment.

THE FACTS

Historical observations are plotted in Figure 17-3, where each point shows the inflation rate and the unemployment rate in one of the years since 1961. Two major points stand out:

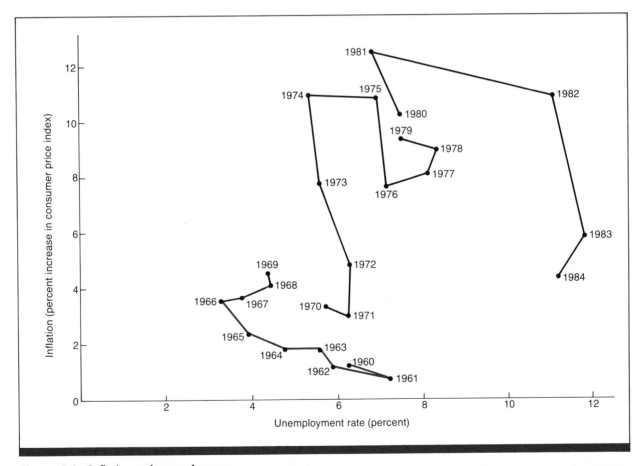

Figure 17-3 Inflation and unemployment.
The points for most of the 1960s trace out a Phillips curve. Points for the 1970s and 1980s are higher and further to the right, reflecting higher inflation *and* larger unemployment rates.

Sources: Compiled from F.H. Leacy, M.C. Urquhart, and K.A.H. Buckley, eds., *Historical Statistics of Canada*, 2nd ed. (Ottawa: Statistics Canada, 1982) (reprinted by permission of the Minister of Supply and Services Canada) and *Bank of Canada Review* (January 1986), Table A1.

1. During most of the 1960s, the data form a smooth curve, similar to the intermediate range of the aggregate supply function in Figure 17-2. Such a curve is known as a **Phillips curve**, after British economist A.W. Phillips, who found that British data for 1861–1957 fitted a similar curve.[1]

> When the rate of inflation (or the rate of change of money wages)[2] is put on the vertical axis and the rate of unemployment on the horizontal axis, historical data sometimes trace out a smooth curve bending upward to the left—for example, the curve traced out by the Canadian data for most of the 1960s. Such a curve is known as a *Phillips curve*.

2. The observations since 1968 are above and to the right of the Phillips curve traced out earlier in the 1960s. In the 1970s and 1980s, we have frequently suffered from high rates of both inflation and unemployment. To use an inelegant but common term, we have suffered from *stagflation*.

> *Stagflation* exists when a high rate of unemployment (stagnation) and a high rate of inflation occur at the same time.

In the rest of this chapter, we will look closely at these two points. First, we will look at why the economy might move along a Phillips curve, as it did during the 1960s. Second, we will look at the puzzle presented by the 1970s and 1980s. Why did things get worse after the 1960s, with higher inflation *and* higher unemployment?

The importance of answering the second question can scarcely be exaggerated. Suppose we cannot figure out what is happening. Suppose the economy does not behave in a predictable manner—it does not move along a predictable aggregate supply curve or Phillips curve in response to a change in aggregate demand. Then the basis for the demand-management policies discussed in earlier chapters is undercut. If expansive fiscal and monetary policies are introduced during a recession, can we count on an increase in output? Or will we get more inflation instead? On the other hand, if we apply restraint during an inflationary boom, can we count on a reduction in the rate of inflation? Or will we merely get less output? In other words, demand management policies require both a knowledge of how monetary and fiscal policies affect aggregate demand, and a knowledge of how the economy responds to changes in aggregate demand. Making sense of what has happened since 1970 is therefore one of the major tasks of macroeconomic theorists. But, before turning to this central question, we lay the foundations of the discussion by looking at the Phillips curve traced out in the 1960s.

THE PHILLIPS CURVE OF THE 1960s

During the 1960s, available empirical evidence—particularly from the United States and Britain—pointed strongly toward the conclusion that increases in aggregate demand move the economy along a smooth, stable Phillips curve. Increases in aggregate demand had an effect partly on output and employment, and partly on prices. And, as the economy moved further and further to the left up the Phillips curve, this curve became steeper and steeper. In other words, each additional increase in demand caused more and more inflation, and a smaller and smaller decline in the unemployment rate. Why might the economy move along such a curve in response to changes in demand?

Consider, first, the position of businesses. When there is large-scale unemployment of the labour force, plant and equipment are also likely to be used at much less than capacity. If demand increases in these circumstances, the primary response of businesses is to increase output rather than prices. An increase in output

---

[1] A.W. Phillips, "The Relation between Unemployment and the Rate of Change of Money Wages in the United Kingdom," *Economica* (November 1958): 282–99. For a readable account of the controversies over the Phillips curve (on which this chapter concentrates), see Robert M. Solow, "Down the Phillips Curve with Gun and Camera," in David A. Belsley et al., eds., *Inflation, Trade and Taxes* (Columbus: Ohio State University Press, 1976), pp. 3–32.
[2] The original Phillips curve showed the rate of change of money wages—rather than inflation—on the vertical axis. Since money wages rise rapidly during periods of high inflation, a similar curve is traced out whichever measure is put on the vertical axis.

will allow the fuller utilization of plant and equipment and result in rising profits. Furthermore, businesses may be skeptical about their ability to make price increases stick. If they raise prices rapidly, their competitors—who also have excess capacity—will be only too eager to capture a larger share of the market.

As the expansion continues and plant and equipment are used more fully, businesses respond differently to an increase in demand. They have less excess capacity. Therefore, as demand increases, they have less opportunity to raise profits by increasing output rapidly. At the same time, they are increasingly in a position to raise prices. Higher prices involve less risk of a loss of markets to competitors, since the competitors are also approaching capacity and are in no position to expand output rapidly to capture additional sales. Furthermore, as the unemployment rate falls, businesses find it harder to hire and keep workers. As the labour market tightens, businesses become increasingly aggressive in their bidding for workers, offering higher wages. As wage rates move upward, the costs of production rise. Businesses respond by raising the prices of their products.

Similarly, labour responds differently to increases in aggregate demand as employment increases. When the unemployment rate is high, the first concern of workers is with jobs. If they are offered work, they are generally quick to take it without too much quibbling over pay. However, as economic expansion continues, the situation gradually changes. Workers become less concerned with getting and keeping a job, and more aggressive in demanding higher pay.

These changing conditions, which affect both business and labour, do not come about suddenly at some well-defined point of full employment. On the contrary, they occur gradually. When demand increases, the economy may consequently move smoothly up a Phillips curve like the coloured curve in Figure 17-3, with successive increases in demand being reflected more in terms of inflation, and less in terms of output and employment.

Thus, there were two reasons for policymakers to believe that they faced a well-defined, stable Phillips curve during the 1960s. (1) It seemed plausible from a theoretical viewpoint. (2) It conformed to the facts—most notably, Phillips' historical study, and the unfolding situation in the United States.

In Canada, the evidence of a well-defined Phillips curve was not as clear-cut as in the United States and Britain. This should not be surprising. With the very important role of international trade in our economy, Canada's rate of price inflation is not only influenced by the prices set by Canadian firms, or the cost of labour in Canada: Our inflation rate also depends on price changes in foreign countries. For example, if Canada is on fixed exchange rates, foreign inflation would quickly lead to rising prices here because the prices of our imports would rise—and this could happen even if Canada had a high rate of unemployment. (The fact that the observations for 1968 and 1969 in Figure 17-3 lie to the right of the other observations during the 1960s can be explained in this way. During 1968–69, Canada was on fixed exchange rates, and inflation in the United States was relatively high.) Nevertheless, as Figure 17-3 shows, the data for *most* of the 1960s pointed to a fairly stable Phillips curve in Canada as well. Statistical studies confirmed this: After allowing for the influence of foreign price increases on Canadian inflation, there was still a strong tendency for low unemployment rates to go with high rates of price inflation.

The Policy Dilemma of the 1960s: The Trade-off between Inflation and Unemployment

This belief by policymakers—that they faced a well-defined Phillips curve—presented them with a *policy dilemma*. By adjusting aggregate demand policies, they could move the economy along the Phillips curve. But what point should they try to pick? A point like G in Figure 17-4, with low inflation and a high rate of unemployment? Or a point like H, with low unemployment but a high rate of inflation? Or some point in between? Facing a *trade-off* between the goals of high employment and price stability, what relative importance should they attach to the two objectives?

Faced with this dilemma, the response of both the Canadian and U.S. governments was to emphasize the objective of high employment. After all, unemployment represents a clear and unambiguous loss to the economy, whereas the costs of inflation are much more difficult to identify. In the United States, where Kennedy had just become president, the decision was gradually made to pursue an expansionary policy. The policy was successful—in the latter half of the 1960s, U.S. unemployment averaged well below 4%.

In Canada, the unemployment rate also fell rapidly

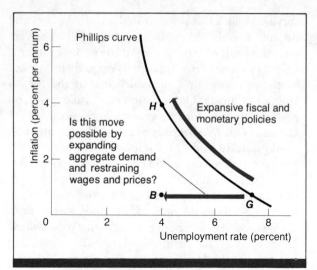

Figure 17-4 The problem of the sixties: The inflation-unemployment trade-off.

The Phillips curve presents policymakers with a dilemma. By adjusting aggregate demand, they can choose a point on the Phillips curve. But what point should they choose? *G* provides a low rate of inflation but high unemployment. *H* provides high employment but at the cost of substantial inflation. In 1961, the economy was at point *G*. The objective of the government was to reduce unemployment—but without increasing inflation. By restraining wage and price increases as aggregate demand expanded, the government hoped to move the economy toward point *B*.

during the first half of the 1960s. One important reason for this was the decision in 1962 to peg the Canadian dollar at the relatively low value of 92.5 U.S. cents; this action increased aggregate demand by stimulating exports and discouraging imports. Another important factor was the sizeable government deficits during the early 1960s.

As you can see from Figure 17-3, the unemployment reduction during this period was accomplished at the cost of some increase in the inflation rate. (The observations for the 1963–67 period are to the northwest of those from the early 1960s.) But prices were not rising very fast. By and large, it still seemed possible to attain a fairly low rate of unemployment (around 4%) without much inflation (also about 4%).

However, by 1968–69, there were signs that trouble was ahead. In those years, under the restrictive influence of a rising government budget surplus and sluggish monetary expansion, unemployment rose con-

siderably. But in spite of this, the rate of inflation did not come down. Thus, as the 1970s began, the prospect of avoiding inflation without a high cost in the form of unemployment suddenly appeared much less bright.

THE RECORD SINCE 1970: HIGHER INFLATION AND HIGHER UNEMPLOYMENT

In comparison with the 1960s, the performance of the economy in the 15 years after 1970 was extremely disappointing. During that period, we had the worst of both worlds. High rates of unemployment and inflation have occurred simultaneously. What went wrong? Two principal explanations have been offered.

Cost-push vs. Demand-pull Inflation

The age of Keynesian economics is over; the macroeconomic revolution in fiscal and monetary management we owe to Keynes has run afoul of the microeconomic revolution in trade union and corporate power.

John Kenneth Galbraith

The first explanation involves the distinction between *demand-pull* and *cost-push* inflation. This distinction can be illustrated most easily with the simple aggregate demand and aggregate supply curves shown in Figure 17-5. The left panel shows what happens when aggregate demand increases—that is, when the aggregate demand curve shifts to the right. Output increases, and unemployment declines. But the rising demand also pulls up prices. The economy moves upward to the right, from *G* to *H*. This is the typical demand-pull inflation—rising prices are accompanied by rising output.

> *Demand-pull* inflation occurs when demand is rising rapidly. Buyers bid eagerly for goods and services, "pulling up" their prices.

Now suppose that strong labour unions and monopolistic companies have the power to influence wages and prices. Even during a period of slack in the economy, when the demand for labour is low and the unemployment rate is high, a strong union may be able to use the threat of a strike to negotiate higher wages.

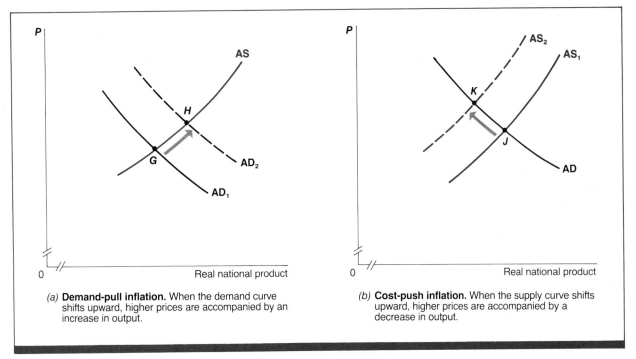

(a) **Demand-pull inflation.** When the demand curve shifts upward, higher prices are accompanied by an increase in output.

(b) **Cost-push inflation.** When the supply curve shifts upward, higher prices are accompanied by a decrease in output.

Figure 17-5 Demand-pull inflation vs. cost-push inflation.

Furthermore, a firm with few competitors may raise its prices even though demand is sluggish. If this firm is producing basic materials, parts, or other intermediate goods, its higher prices will push up the costs of other companies using its products. Businesses with higher costs of labour and material inputs may pass them along to the consumer in the form of higher prices. In other words, there is **cost-push** inflation.

> *Cost-push* or *supply-side* inflation occurs when wages or other costs rise and these costs are passed along in the form of higher prices. Prices are "pushed up" by rising costs. Cost-push inflation is also sometimes known as *market power* inflation.

This possibility is illustrated in the right-hand panel of Figure 17-5. As costs rise, the aggregate supply curve shifts upward, from AS_1 to AS_2. As the economy moves from J to K, rising prices are accompanied by a *decline* in output and a rise in the unemployment rate.

In the late 1950s, cost-push was used to explain why inflation and unemployment were both increas-

ing. This early round in the cost-push debate was heated. In particular, it invited a search for culprits. Business executives blamed inflation on the aggressive and "irresponsible" bargaining of labour unions for higher wages that had forced businesses—so they claimed—to pass along their higher labour costs in terms of higher prices. On the other hand, labour blamed powerful corporations for pushing up prices in their greed for "fantastic profits."

Oil. While labour and management blamed each other for cost-push inflation during the late 1950s, one cost-push culprit stood out in the 1970s: the Organization of Petroleum Exporting Countries (OPEC). In a brief period during 1973 and 1974, OPEC doubled and then redoubled the prices that importers had to pay for oil. In 1979–80, oil prices more than doubled again.

Because of the importance of oil as a source of power for industry, as a fuel for our transportation system, and as a source of heat for our homes and factories, the skyrocketing price of oil had a powerful effect on all oil-importing countries—including the United States, which still had to import roughly half the oil it used. (Japan was perhaps the hardest hit of all, because practically all of its oil must be imported.)

Canada was not as badly hurt as the large oil importers. While we had to pay more in the world market for the oil we import into the Eastern provinces, we also received higher prices for the oil, natural gas, and electricity we exported. Furthermore, the government's policy in 1973–74 was to keep the domestic Canadian oil price well below the world price. However, indirectly the cost-push pressure of higher oil prices spilled over into Canada as well. Because prices rose in countries such as the United States and Japan, the prices of goods imported into Canada from these countries rose rapidly. Rising prices of imported goods contribute to inflation both directly (as people have to pay more for imported consumer goods) and indirectly (as businesses pass on the higher cost of imported inputs in the form of higher prices for the goods they produce). These international cost-push pressures contributed to the double-digit inflation rates in Canada in the mid-1970s, and even higher rates in 1980 and 1981.[3]

The cost-push idea can be illustrated by an upward shift of the aggregate supply curve (as shown in Figure 17-5b), or, alternatively, by an upward shift of the Phillips curve from PC$_1$ to PC$_2$ in Figure 17-6. Earlier, we saw that even a stable Phillips curve—such as PC$_1$ in Figure 17-6—presents the authorities with a dilemma. They can choose low inflation, but this will mean high unemployment (at point G). Alternatively, they can choose low unemployment, but this will mean high inflation (at point H). Or they can pick an intermediate point, such as J. Observe how much more difficult the situation becomes when cost-push forces are strong, and the Phillips curve shifts upward. If the authorities keep aggregate demand stable, both unemployment and inflation will increase, as illustrated by the move from J to K. If they decide to prevent any increase in inflation, regardless of the cost, they will have to restrain aggregate demand. The result will be a move from J to L. While inflation will be no higher at L than it was at J, there will be a large increase in unem-

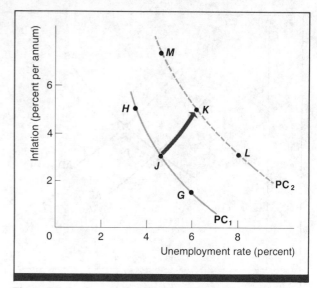

Figure 17-6   Cost-push inflation: The policy problem.
Cost-push shifts the Phillips curve upward, from PC$_1$ to PC$_2$. If demand is restrained in order to fight inflation, the unemployment rate will increase, from J to L. If demand is expanded in order to keep the unemployment rate from rising, the rate of inflation will increase, from J to M.

ployment. On the other hand, if the authorities aim at preventing any increase in unemployment, they will stimulate aggregate demand, and the rate of inflation will go even higher as the economy moves to M.

In Canada, the international cost-push pressures in 1973–74 and 1979–80 showed up primarily in terms of inflation. On the first occasion, there was some increase in the unemployment rate—from 5.5% in 1973 to 6.9% in 1975—but the increase in the inflation rate was substantially larger, from 7.7% in 1973 to 10.8% in 1975. During 1979–81, unemployment stayed almost constant at about 7.5%, and the cost-push forces were reflected almost exclusively in prices—inflation rose from 9.2% in 1979 to 12.5% in 1981.

In summary, this first explanation of stagflation depends on disturbances from the cost side. The Phillips curve can be shifted up by aggressive wage and pricing activities by unions and businesses, or by shocks from abroad, such as increases in the prices of imported goods. When such a shift occurs, the economy is likely to suffer an increase in inflation (the move from J to M) and perhaps also in unemployment (J to K).

[3]As we saw in Chapter 15, rising prices of foreign goods need not cause inflationary pressure in Canada if the Canadian dollar is allowed to appreciate. However, while there was some appreciation of the Canadian dollar relative to the U.S. dollar in 1974, it was not nearly enough to offset the effects of the increasing world price levels. During 1979 to 1981, the effects of rising world prices were reinforced by a *depreciation* of the Canadian dollar.

PRICE EXPECTATIONS AND THE WAGE-PRICE SPIRAL: THE ACCELERATIONIST ARGUMENT

The second explanation of simultaneous high rates of inflation and unemployment goes further, throwing into question the whole concept of a permanent curve such as the one discovered by Phillips. According to this line of argument, the Phillips curve is inherently unstable. *It shifts whenever people's expectations of inflation change.* In particular, it shifts upward as inflation gathers momentum. If the managers of monetary and fiscal policies aim for a low rate of unemployment, inflation will accelerate to higher and higher rates. Hence, this is known as the **accelerationist** argument.

The easiest way to explain this argument is to assume initially that prices have been stable for a long period of time. On the basis of past experience, they are expected to remain stable into the indefinite future. The economy rests at a stable equilibrium at G on the initial Phillips curve (Figure 17-7), where the inflation rate is zero. Now suppose that the government decides that the unemployment rate at G is unacceptable. Expansive fiscal and monetary policies are introduced in order to increase aggregate demand and reduce the unemployment rate to a target of U_T.

What happens? To meet the higher demand, producers need more workers. Job vacancies increase, and those looking for jobs get them easily and quickly. Production increases and unemployment falls. In the face of higher demand, producers gradually begin to raise prices. But in the early stages of inflation, little change takes place in money wages. Most collective bargaining contracts are for three years, and union wages change only slowly as a result. Non-union wages are also sticky. People may work on individual contracts that run for one year or more. Even where there is no written contract, it is customary to review wages only periodically—say, once a year. Thus, the initial reaction to the increase in demand is a relatively large increase in output, only a moderate increase in prices, and an even smaller increase in wages. The economy moves along the Phillips curve to point H (Figure 17-7).

However, *point H is not stable.* The initial Phillips curve (PC_1) reflects wage contracts *that were negotiated on the assumption of stable prices.* But prices are

no longer stable, and the contracts do not last forever. As new contract negotiations begin, workers observe that their real wages—the amount of goods and services their wages will buy—have been eroded by inflation. They demand a cost-of-living catch-up. So long as aggregate demand rises rapidly enough to keep the economy operating at full blast, the unions are in a good position to get their demands. With booming markets, employers capitulate to strike threats. Non-union employees are likewise granted raises to keep them from quitting to look for more highly paid work. Because demand is high and rising, businesses can

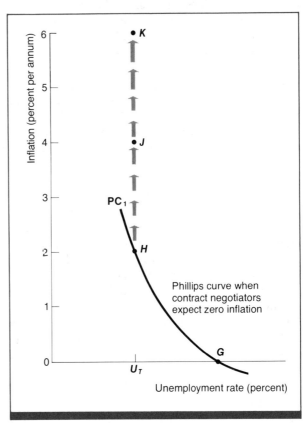

Figure 17-7   The acceleration of inflation: The wage-price spiral.
If demand is continuously increased by whatever amount is necessary to maintain the low target rate of unemployment U_T, the result is an ever-increasing rate of inflation. The economy moves successively to points H, J, K, and higher. (The original Phillips curve PC_1 shows how the economy responds to changes in aggregate demand during the short-run period *when the initial wage contracts remain in force.*)

easily pass along the higher wages in the form of higher prices, and they do so. The rate of inflation accelerates; the economy moves to point *J*, above the original Phillips curve. But, with a higher rate of inflation, workers find that once again they have been cheated by inflation; once again their real wages are less than expected. At the next round of wage negotiations, they demand a larger cost-of-living catch-up. The **wage-price spiral** gathers momentum. So long as demand is expanded enough to keep unemployment at the low target rate of U_T, inflation will *continue to accelerate*, from *H* to *J* to *K*, and so on.

Thus, the Phillips curve gives the wrong impression. It creates the illusion that there is a simple trade-off between inflation and unemployment, that a low rate of unemployment can be "bought" with a moderate, steady rate of inflation. But, in fact, the cost of trying to achieve a low rate of unemployment is much more serious: *an ever accelerating rate of inflation*. Wages and prices spiral upward, with higher prices leading to higher and higher wage demands, and higher wages being passed along in the form of higher and higher prices.

Limiting the Rate of Inflation

An ever-accelerating rate of inflation is intolerable. If prices rise faster and faster, sooner or later the whole monetary system will break down and the economy will revert to an inefficient barter system. (The rate required for a complete breakdown is very high indeed— thousands of percent per annum. Nevertheless, severe disruptions may be caused even by rates of inflation of 10% or 20%.) At some time, therefore, the monetary and fiscal policymakers will decide to draw the line; they will refuse to increase aggregate demand without limit.

To keep this illustration simple, assume that (1) the monetary and fiscal line is drawn sooner rather than later, and (2) aggregate demand policies can be adjusted quickly and precisely. As soon as the economy gets to point *H*, the government recognizes the danger of an ever-accelerating inflation. It therefore switches aggregate demand policies. Instead of increasing aggregate demand by whatever amount is necessary to maintain a low target rate of unemployment, the authorities limit aggregate demand to whatever degree is necessary to prevent inflation from rising above the 2% reached at *H*. In other words, the authorities *change*

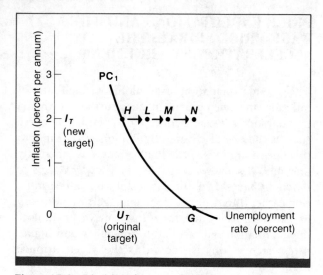

Figure 17-8   Limiting the rate of inflation.
If the managers of monetary and fiscal policies switch targets, limiting demand to prevent inflation greater than I_T, then the economy will begin to move to the right.

the policy target. Their objective is no longer to keep the unemployment rate low at U_T, but instead to keep inflation from rising above the 2% target level I_T (Figure 17-8).

What happens? Workers still push for higher wages because the 2% rate of inflation is still eroding their purchasing power. But employers are now in a bind. They cannot easily pass along higher wages because of the restraint on demand. Furthermore, the restraint on demand means that output begins to fall and unemployment rises. The economy moves to the right.

The Vertical Long-run Phillips Curve

As demand is restrained, the economy moves to the right. But how far? Suppose demand is controlled in such a way as to keep inflation permanently at a rate of 2%. Where will the ultimate equilibrium be in Figure 17-8? At *L*? At *M*? further to the right? There are reasons to believe that the economy will stop at *N*, directly above the original equilibrium *G*.

To see why, let us go back to the initial point, *G*. This represented a stable equilibrium. It was the result of an extended experience with a zero rate of inflation. Both businesses and labour had a chance to adjust completely to the stable price level. If they now get a chance to adjust completely to a 2% rate of inflation—

and this may take some time—then the new equilibrium should be at N, where both labour and business are in the same *real* position as at G. At G, prices were stable. Now, at N, prices are rising by 2%. However, workers are just as well off as at G because they are receiving enough additional money income to compensate for the inflation. Their real wage is unaffected by the inflation. Consequently, they should be neither more nor less eager to work. Businesses are also in the same real situation at N as at G. They pay 2% more

for labour and for material inputs each year than they would have paid at G, but they are compensated by the average increase of 2% in their prices. Their profits are the same in real terms. Therefore, they should hire the same number of workers at N as they did at G. Thus, N lies directly above G, and the unemployment rate is the same at N as at G.

With a steady 2% rate of inflation, the economy moves eventually to N, where the unemployment rate, real wages, and real profits are the same as at G. Alternatively, if the rate of inflation rises to 4% before monetary and fiscal policymakers draw the line to prevent more rapid inflation, the economy eventually moves to R (Figure 17-9); or with a steady 6% rate of inflation, to T. All these are points of stable equilibrium. In each case, people have adjusted completely to the prevailing rate of inflation. (In contrast, point H was unstable because workers had not yet had a chance to renegotiate their wages to reflect the new inflation.)

In other words, the points of long-run equilibrium trace out a vertical line; the **long-run Phillips curve** (PC$_L$) is *perfectly vertical. In the long-run, there is no trade-off* between inflation and unemployment. By accepting more inflation, we cannot *permanently* achieve a lower rate of unemployment. Expansive demand policies cause a lower rate of unemployment *only during a temporary period of disequilibrium*—at H, for example. During the temporary disequilibrium, workers and others are committed to contracts they would not have accepted if they had correctly anticipated the rate of inflation. As people have time to adjust, unemployment gravitates toward the equilibrium or **natural rate.**

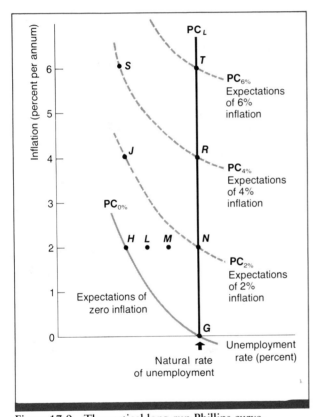

Figure 17-9 The vertical long-run Phillips curve.
The economy gravitates toward the vertical long-run Phillips curve (PC$_L$) as the negotiators of wages and all other contracts adjust to the prevailing rate of inflation. There is no long-run trade-off between unemployment and inflation.

However, the short-run Phillips curve is *not* vertical. For example, once contracts have adjusted completely to a 4% rate of inflation at R, then an unexpected disturbance in aggregate demand will cause the economy to move along the short-run Phillips curve (PC$_{4\%}$) running through R. Thus, a spurt in demand will cause an increase in output, a fall in unemployment, and an increase in inflation as the economy moves from R to S.

The *long-run Phillips curve* is the curve (or line) traced out by the possible points of long-run equilibrium; that is, the points where people have adjusted completely to the prevailing rate of inflation. At such points, actual inflation is the same as expected inflation.

The *natural rate of unemployment* is the equilibrium rate that exists when people have adjusted completely to the prevailing rate of inflation. (Alternatively, it may be defined as the equilibrium rate that exists when the inflation rate is accurately anticipated by the public.)

The accelerationist argument includes the following related propositions:

1. The long-run Phillips curve is vertical. There is an equilibrium or "natural" rate of unemployment which is independent of the rate of inflation.

2. If demand is stimulated by however much is needed to keep the unemployment rate below the natural rate, the result will be a continuous acceleration of inflation.

Through each of the long-run equilibrium points—such as N, R, or T in Figure 17-9—there is a *short-run Phillips curve*, each reflecting contracts based on the prevailing rate of inflation. For example, the short-run Phillips curve (PC$_{4\%}$) running through R is based on the expectation by contract negotiators that there will be a continuing rate of inflation of 4% per year. Suppose that after a number of years at R, the authorities adjust monetary and fiscal policies to make aggregate demand grow more rapidly. Faced with a high demand, businesses increase output, hire more workers, and begin to raise prices by more than 4% per annum. Their profits temporarily shoot up because workers are committed to the old labour contracts, based on expectations of 4% inflation. The economy moves along the short-run Phillips curve PC$_{4\%}$ to a point such as S, with a low rate of unemployment. But S is unstable for the same reason that H was unstable. Point S results from wage contracts that were agreed to when inflation was expected to be 4%. But actual inflation is 6%. Therefore, contracts will be adjusted during the next round of negotiations. When wage contracts are adjusted upward, an accelerating wage-price spiral will result if the authorities continue to follow expansive aggregate demand policies. Alternatively, if demand managers take steps to prevent any further increase in inflation, the economy will move to the right, back toward the long-run Phillips curve and the natural rate of unemployment at T.

Note that there is a similarity between this accelerationist or natural rate theory and the earlier explanation of inflation based on cost-push. In each case, the Phillips curve shifts upward, and in each case, higher wage contracts can play an important role in the shift. But here the similarity stops. While cost-push theorists see higher wages as a major *cause* of inflation, accelerationists believe that wage and price increases are *both* the result of a *single* underlying cause: excess demand. The government should not go looking for culprits in the form of powerful unions or powerful businesses or OPEC. Rather, the culprit is right in Ottawa: the government itself (including the Bank of Canada), which has generated the inflationary demand in the first place with excessively expansionary policies.

The vertical long-run Phillips curve brings us back to the view of classical quantity theorists. *In the long run*, changes in aggregate demand affect prices (P) and not the quantity of output (Q) or employment. Thus, the vertical long-run Phillips curve turns out to be the same as the vertical aggregate supply curve of classical economics (originally shown in Figure 9-2), but in another guise.

Because we are brought back to the classical view, it is not surprising that the case for the vertical long-run Phillips curve—together with other aspects of the accelerationist argument—came from the pen of one of the leading monetarists, Milton Friedman. (Another early proponent was Edmund Phelps of Columbia University.)[4] Friedman wrote, "There is *always* a *temporary tradeoff* between inflation and unemployment; there is *no permanent tradeoff*." The short-run Phillips curve slopes downward to the right; the long-run Phillips curve is vertical.

During the 1970s, the idea of a vertical long-run Phillips curve became widely accepted by those in the Keynesian and classical traditions alike. Now, it would be difficult to find any economist who believes that the original, curved Phillips curve represents a stable, long-run relationship. By 1975, economist Arthur Okun was willing to concede on behalf of the original Phillips curve school: "We are all accelerationists now."[5]

Nevertheless, two matters of controversy remain:

1. Some economists in the Keynesian tradition argue that the long-run Phillips curve bends to

[4]Milton Friedman, "The Role of Monetary Policy," *American Economic Review* (March 1968): 1–17; and Edmund S. Phelps, "Phillips Curves, Expectations of Inflation and Optimal Unemployment over Time," *Economica* (August 1967): 254–81.

[5]Okun, "Inflation: Its Mechanics and Welfare Costs," *Brookings Papers on Economic Activity* 2 (1975): 356. Okun was paraphrasing an earlier concession of Friedman: "In one sense, we are all Keynesians now." (Friedman had, however, tacked on the qualification that "in another [sense], no one is a Keynesian any longer." From Milton Friedman, *Dollars and Deficits* (Englewood Cliffs, N. J.: Prentice-Hall, 1968), p. 15.)

Okun pointed out that the data fit a Phillips curve "like a glove" during the 1960s. However, he observed that, since 1970, "the Phillips curve has become an unidentified flying object."

the right as the rate of inflation gets very low, even though it may be vertical throughout most of its length. This view is explained in Box 17-1. Furthermore, some Keynesians argue that the acceleration of inflation in the 1970s had little to do with excess demand, as the accelerationists claimed. Instead, it resulted primarily from "supply shocks," most notably the two major increases in the international price of oil.

2. At the other end of the intellectual spectrum, some go beyond the views of Phelps and Friedman to argue that there is no trade-off between inflation and unemployment at all, *even in the short run*. This will be explained later, in Box 17-2.

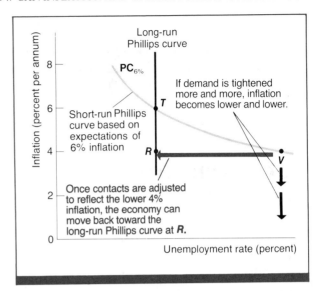

Figure 17-10   High unemployment while inflation is being unwound.
Once inflation becomes built into contracts, it is painful to unwind. The short-run Phillips curve shown here reflects contracts based on the expectation of 6% inflation. It takes a period of high unemployment at *V* before wage contracts are adjusted downward.

THE PROBLEM OF UNWINDING INFLATIONARY EXPECTATIONS

The short-run Phillips curve represents another trap for policymakers. Those who decide on monetary and fiscal policies may think that they can achieve low rates of unemployment to the left of the long-run Phillips curve by expansive demand policies. In fact, they will be able to maintain such a low rate of unemployment only if they allow inflation to spiral higher and higher.

Furthermore, the problem is even worse than that. Once inflation becomes ingrained in negotiators' expectations, it can be eliminated with demand-management policies only at the cost of a high rate of unemployment, to the right of the long-run Phillips curve.

This is illustrated in Figure 17-10. Suppose that the economy has reached point *T*, with inflation consistently running at 6% year after year. This point is stable; inflation will neither rise nor fall, and the unemployment rate will remain steady. Now, suppose that policymakers decide that an inflation rate of 6% is too high. They are determined to reduce it by restrictive monetary and fiscal policies.

As aggregate demand is restrained, businesses find their sales falling. Production is cut back and workers are laid off. The unemployment rate rises. Because of intensifying competitive pressures as businesses scramble to make sales, businesses no longer insist on such high price increases and the rate of inflation begins to slacken off. However, this does not happen quickly. Businesses are still committed to pay the hefty wage

increases under the old labour contracts; their costs continue to rise even though demand is slack. As a result, the short-run effect of the restrained demand shows up most strongly in a fall in output and a rise in unemployment, and only to a limited extent in lower inflation. The economy moves to point *V*.

The high short-run costs of an anti-inflationary aggregate demand policy—in terms of greater unemployment—have been emphasized by many economists. For example, Arthur Okun presented the following grim prospect in testimony before the U.S. Congress:

> Each dollar trimmed from [nominal] GNP means a loss of about 90 cents of output, and the saving of about a dime on price level. Any anti-inflationary proposal that relies solely on balancing the budget and tightening money is, in reality, a proposal for an encore of that experience. And it should carry a truth-in-packaging label.[6]

Because point *V* is off the long-run Phillips curve, it is unstable. It is on the short-run Phillips curve running through point *T*, reflecting wage contracts negotiated

[6]Testimony before the Joint Economic Committee, U.S. Congress, 30 April 1979.

on the expectation that inflation would continue at 6% per year. But actual inflation is now only 4%. Because of the lower inflation rate, workers are willing to settle for more moderate wage increases at the next round of wage negotiations. This willingness is reinforced by their desire to protect their jobs during a period of high unemployment. Furthermore, employers take a strong bargaining stance because of disappointing sales and low profits.

When wage settlements become more moderate,

BOX 17-1

A CURVED LONG-RUN PHILLIPS CURVE?

"We are all accelerationists now." At least, we are all accelerationists during periods such as the past two decades, when inflation has consistently been above 3%. Most economists acknowledge that even more expansive demand policies would not reduce the unemployment rate in the long run. Above an inflation rate of 2% or 3%, the long-run Phillips curve is vertical.

However, some economists—particularly those in the Keynesian tradition—still believe that the long-run Phillips curve bends to the right as the economy approaches and crosses the horizontal axis. If aggregate demand were held to little or no increase year after year, then the result would be a high rate of unemployment year after year. This is illustrated by point *B* in Figure 17-11.

There are two grounds for this belief. First is a theoretical argument which can be traced back to Keynes' *General Theory*. Second is the evidence of the Great Depression.

Consider first the theoretical argument. As we have already seen, the case for the vertical Phillips curve can be explained by looking at what happens as inflation begins to rise. Workers are concerned with their real wages, and demand additional money wages to compensate for the inflation. As a result, the short-run Phillips curve shifts upward.

Suppose, however, that demand is slack, creating downward pressures on wages. In such circumstances, said Keynes, workers are concerned not only with their *real* wages. They are also concerned with *money* wages. If prices are falling, then workers would be able to maintain their real standard of living even if they accepted cuts in their money wages. However, they will resist such cuts. In his *General Theory* (p. 14), Keynes suggested a reason: People who accept an outright cut in money wages will find their *relative* positions deteriorating, compared with those who do not accept nominal wage cuts. A cut in the money wage represents a humiliation that workers will resist strongly, regardless of what is happening to the level of prices and to real wages.

Why should this unwillingness to accept lower money wages matter? After all, we live in a growing economy. In most years, productivity increases, and the trend of real wages is upward. Thus, even in an economy with zero inflation, the average nominal wage should increase.

However, not all industries are average. Even in a growing economy, some industries decline. As their demand falls, they will discharge workers, adding to the rolls of the unemployed. This process may be slowed down if the industry cuts its prices relative to other prices. Its ability to do so depends in part on the wage it pays. If the rate of inflation is zero and average wages in the economy are going up by 1% per annum, the declining industry gains a wage advantage of only 1% by giving its workers no increase at all. On the other hand, if the inflation rate is 2% and the average money wage increase is 3%, the declining industry may gain a 3% advantage by keeping nominal wages constant. The workers will not like their declining real wages. They may grumble. But they will go along rather than face unemployment. However, they would not have acceded to a cut in nominal wages.

Thus, by permitting workers to accept some decline in real wages gracefully without the humiliation of a nominal wage cut, a modest rate of inflation tends to maintain employment in declining industries. Consequently, there may be a less seri-

the economy moves from point V. If monetary and fiscal policies are kept tight, the rate of inflation will continue to drop. The economy will move down from V to progressively lower points. The argument here is similar to that in Figure 17-7, except that everything is operating in the opposite direction.

On the other hand, if monetary and fiscal restraint is eased as the economy reaches 4% inflation, sales will begin to revive, the unemployment rate will fall, and the economy will move back toward the long-run

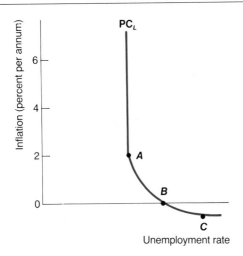

Figure 17-11 A curved long-run Phillips curve?

ous unemployment problem with a 2% rate of inflation (at point A in Figure 17-11) than with a stable price level (at B). In short, the unwillingness to accept lower nominal wage rates provides a reason for believing that the long-run Phillips curve bends to the right as it approaches the axis.

It also means that, in the face of a collapse in demand, the unemployment rate may rise very high, and may stay for an extended time at a point such as C. Because firms find that they can cut nominal wages very little, if at all, they resist cuts in their prices. The very low aggregate demand shows up primarily in terms of low output and high unemployment, and very little in terms of falling prices.

Some fragmentary evidence from recent decades suggests that money incomes as well as real incomes may indeed be important. For example, during the 1970s, the real incomes of many professors fell, since their salaries failed to keep pace with infla-

tion. If prices had been constant, and if administrations had tried to bring about exactly the same real cuts by reducing dollar salaries, it is likely that professors would have objected much more strongly.

However, it is to the Great Depression that we must go for comprehensive evidence regarding downward wage rigidity. Suppose, for the moment, we assume that prices and wages *do* adjust downward, and that the long-run Phillips curve as a consequence is vertical right down to the axis and beyond. Suppose, then, that aggregate demand is slack, causing unemployment in excess of the "natural rate." Not only should inflation be wrung out of the economy, but prices should start to fall *at an accelerating rate*. (The argument is similar to that in Figure 17-7, except that prices are now falling rather than rising. Workers are willing to accept lower and lower money wages as prices fall.) In fact, nothing of the sort happened during the Depression. Prices did fall between 1929 and 1933. However, they then stabilized. Between 1933 and 1937, prices actually rose, even though the unemployment rate consistently exceeded 10%. This evidence is flatly inconsistent with the accelerationist hypothesis. If that hypothesis were correct, the prices should have fallen faster and faster, as long as unemployment remained above the natural rate.

Not surprisingly, this complication has not been a major preoccupation of economists in the past quarter-century, when the pressure on prices has been upward, not downward. But it is of considerable historical interest. Moreover, if anti-inflationary policies are successful, it may become relevant once more. The implication of a diagram such as Figure 17-11 is that, once inflation has been reduced to 1% or 2%, we should be satisfied, and declare victory. Any attempt to stabilize prices further may raise the problem of a trade-off, in terms of higher unemployment.

Phillips curve at point R. This argument corresponds to the earlier one in Figure 17-8, again operating in the opposite direction.

This theory provides another possible explanation for the simultaneous high rates of unemployment and inflation in the period from 1974 to 1981 (as an alternative to the explanation based on the cost-push forces arising in the international oil market). During the late 1960s and early 1970s, aggregate demand was overstimulated, and inflation allowed to gather steam. Then, as inflation became more and more of a concern to the government and the Bank of Canada, the Bank followed the example of the U.S. Federal Reserve and in 1980 moved to a very tight monetary policy. The result of the sharp contraction in aggregate demand was the deep recession in 1981–82. By 1984, inflation had finally been "wrestled to the ground" (in the words of Prime Minister Trudeau), but at a very high cost: an unemployment rate that remained above 10% for over three years.

POLICIES TO DEAL WITH UNEMPLOYMENT AND INFLATION

The accelerationist theory raises three important policy issues:

1. What are the implications of this theory for demand-management policies?
2. What can be done to reduce the natural or equilibrium rate of unemployment in the economy? That is, what can be done to shift the long-run Phillips curve to the left?
3. Can anything be done to ease the transition to a lower rate of inflation? That is, are there other policies available to reduce inflation, without causing the high unemployment that normally accompanies a tough restrictive demand policy (illustrated by V in Figure 17-10)?

1. Aggregate Demand: The Importance of Steady Growth

The vertical long-run Phillips curve implies that the *trend* of aggregate demand has no effect on the unemployment rate. A consistent inflation will lead to no gains in terms of lower unemployment. However, there is a strong advantage in a *stable* rate of growth of aggregate demand.

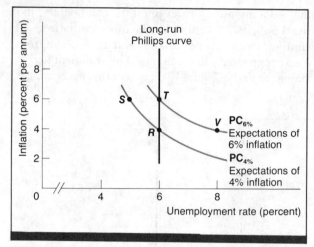

Figure 17-12   Instability and the average rate of unemployment.

In a stable economy, the economy stays at R, at the natural rate of unemployment (shown here as 6%). In an unstable economy, moving from R to S, T, V, and back to R, the average rate of unemployment is greater. This is because the employment gain (of 1% less than the natural rate) in moving to S is less than the unemployment penalty (2% greater than the natural rate) while inflation is being unwound at V.

This point is illustrated in Figure 17-12, which brings together the argument of Figure 17-10 and the top part of Figure 17-9. With a stable increase in aggregate demand, we would expect to stay at a point—such as R—on the long-run Phillips curve, with a stable rate of inflation (4% in this example). Consider, now, the unstable situation, where periods of rapid expansion in aggregate demand alternate with periods of recession.

During the period of rapid expansion of demand, output increases, the unemployment rate falls, the inflation rate accelerates, and the economy moves to a point such as S, to the left of the long-run Phillips curve. (This repeats the argument we have already covered in Figure 17-9.) If, then, the rapid expansion of demand is slackened, the economy moves back toward the long-run Phillips curve, to a point such as T. But the higher rate of inflation (6%) is by now built into the economy: T is on short-run Phillips curve $PC_{6\%}$ reflecting expectations of 6% inflation. Now, suppose that the growth of aggregate demand is restrained in order to bring inflation back down to its original 4% rate. The economy slides down $PC_{6\%}$ to point V, with a high rate of unemployment. (Again, we have already encountered this argument in Figure 17-10.) As contracts are renegotiated to recognize the 4% inflation, the economy can revive toward R with a stable 4% rate of inflation—provided, of course, that the growth of aggregate demand also revives.

Which of these patterns is better—an economy consistently at R, or one that moves consecutively from R, to S, T, V, and back to R in the face of unstable demand? The answer is: the stable pattern. *Because the short-run Phillips curves are curved*, the unemployment penalty in moving to V (2% in our example; that is, from 6% to 8%) is greater than the amount by which unemployment is eased in moving to S (1% in the example; that is, from 6% to 5%). Thus, we come to an important conclusion: *Instability causes a higher average rate of unemployment*. It further follows that if we want to avoid the necessity of fighting inflation with points such as V, we should also be careful not to let aggregate demand expand so rapidly as to push the economy to points such as S. We have already noted Okun's grim analysis of points such as V. As the other half of the argument, he warned against overexpansion of demand (that is, points such as S):

> We should set our fiscal and monetary policies to accept some down-side risks on output and unemployment in the short run. We didn't accept enough of these risks in 1977–1978. It turned out in retrospect that fiscal-monetary policy was too stimulative. We must do better in the future to establish a safety margin against overly strong markets.[7]

Because of the importance of stability, we cannot put "virtuous" anti-inflationary conduct in the bank. If we decide to follow a very restrictive demand policy and live with a high rate of unemployment, we will not acquire a "right" to an equivalent amount of compensating employment during an expansionary period in the future. Whatever the trend of demand, there is an advantage in *stability* of demand.[8]

[7]Testimony before the Joint Economic Committee, U.S. Congress, 30 April 1979.
*[8]In addition to Figure 17-12, there is a second argument leading to the conclusion that stability is desirable. According to this argument, the economy operates best when it is in equilibrium, along the vertical Phillips curve. People have had a chance to adjust. Workers make their best choices. They weigh the real wage against the risk of unemployment in deciding whether or not to accept job offers. Because this is the best outcome, any deviation from the

2. What Can Be Done to Reduce the Equilibrium Rate of Unemployment?

Even if we were to achieve a perfectly smooth growth of aggregate demand, our macroeconomic problems would not be solved. Although cyclical unemployment would be eliminated, there would still be a sizeable amount of "natural" unemployment due to frictional and structural causes. Not all of this represents voluntary unemployment while people search for appropriate jobs. Some workers—particularly teenagers—have trouble finding jobs no matter how hard they look. Accordingly, it is appropriate to study ways of reducing the natural rate—that is, ways of shifting the long-run Phillips curve to the left.

The increase in the natural rate in the past 25 years.
In fact, however, we have been going in the opposite direction. As we discussed in Chapter 16, estimates of the equilibrium or natural rate of unemployment—below which inflation will begin to accelerate—have been revised upward substantially during the last 25 years. In the middle of the 1960s, the Economic Council of Canada suggested that it should be possible to achieve an unemployment rate as low as 3% without unleashing inflationary pressures; by the late 1970s and early 1980s, most analysts were estimating that the natural rate may have been as high as 7%.

While it is impossible to get precise estimates of the natural rate, the main message is clear: There was a substantial increase in the natural rate in the 1970s. Particularly disconcerting was the experience in 1977–78. Even though these were not recession years, unemployment in Canada was above 8%, the highest value since the war. But in spite of this, and even though there were no major inflationary impulses from the world oil market, inflation still did not come down; in

long-run Phillips curve represents a loss—whether the deviation is to the right or to the left. The loss to the right—in terms of high unemployment—is obvious. But there is also a loss at a point such as S, to the left of the long-run Phillips curve. The reason is that workers are working more than they would be willing to work if they had anticipated inflation. They have been tricked into working too much. The lower unemployment rate represents a loss, not a gain.

This second argument in favour of stability has been put in a footnote because we do not entirely agree with it. Because of the difficulty which some people have in finding jobs, we do not subscribe to the view that it is necessarily bad for unemployment to fall below the "natural" rate. However, we do recognize that there can be circumstances where people work more than they want to.

BOX 17-2

THE THEORY OF RATIONAL EXPECTATIONS: NO TRADE-OFF, EVEN IN THE SHORT RUN?

Friedman and Phelps argued that the long-run Phillips curve was vertical, and thus cast doubt on whether there is a *long-run* trade-off between inflation and unemployment. Recently, some economists have taken an even stronger position, casting doubt on whether policymakers face a trade-off *even in the short run*. The chief doubters are members of the **rational expectations** school, an offshoot of monetarism.

To introduce the general idea of rational expectations, we consider the accelerationist argument in more detail. We have already seen that, according to this argument, an attempt to hold unemployment at U_T—less than the natural or equilibrium rate, U_N—leads to an ever-accelerating inflation. To summarize briefly: From an initial point of equilibrium, G (Figure 17-13), an increase in aggregate demand causes unemployment to decrease and prices to rise. The economy moves to H. But H is not a stable equilibrium. H is on the short-run Phillips curve $PC_{0\%}$ which is based on the expectation of zero inflation. However, actual inflation is running at 2% per annum. Contracts are adjusted upward to compensate for the 2% inflation, causing the short-run Phillips curve to shift up to $PC_{2\%}$. If the government wants to keep unemployment at the low target rate of U_T, it will have to increase aggregate demand more rapidly, moving the economy from H to J in the next period.

Suppose we have arrived at J in this manner, with actual inflation at 4%. The question is, on what rate of inflation will the next round of contracts be based? What rate of inflation will people expect in the next period?

The answer, according to the original accelerationist argument, is that the expected rate for the future will be the same as the *actual* rate today—in

our example, the 4% rate of inflation at point J. (This is an example of *adaptive expectations*; people's expectations adapt to past inflation.) If people adjust to inflation in this way, the short-run Phillips curve will shift up to $PC_{4\%}$. By increasing aggregate demand enough, the authorities can move the economy to K, keeping unemployment at the low rate U_T.

However, this is not necessarily the correct answer. Rational expectations theorists point out that the public has already been fooled twice. They expected zero inflation, but got 2% inflation at H instead. Then they expected 2% inflation, and were wrong again. Inflation was 4% as the economy moved to J. It is therefore not rational for people to expect that they will necessarily get the same inflation next period that they have today. Once people figure out the authorities' strong commitment to a low rate of unemployment, they will come to expect that future inflation will be *worse* than inflation today. Hence, at J, a *rational expectation* would be that inflation in the future will be higher than the 4% that exists today. Suppose that the public has learned this lesson while the economy is at J, and sets new contracts on the expectation of 6% inflation. In other words, when the economy is at J and people have a chance to renegotiate contracts, the short-run Phillips curve shifts up from $PC_{2\%}$, not to $PC_{4\%}$, but rather all the way up to $PC_{6\%}$.

> *Rational expectations* are based on available information, including information about the policies being pursued by the authorities. The public does not make systematic mistakes. (In this example, they learn not to keep underestimating future inflation.)

There are now two possibilities:

1. The authorities remain determined to keep unemployment at the small percentage U_T, and expand aggregate demand at an increasingly rapid rate in order to do so. The economy moves from J to M, leapfrogging over K. The rate of inflation has jumped from 4% at J all the way to 8% at M.

The public has once again been fooled. (They expected 6% inflation, but got 8%.) No matter what inflation they anticipated in the past, the actual inflation they got exceeded what was expected. Next time, how much inflation will they anticipate? 15%? 20%? more? The next jump in the inflation rate may be huge.

Thus, so long as demand-management authorities attempt to keep unemployment at less than the natural rate U_N, *rational expectations make inflation even more severe*. Indeed, the lid may be blown right off the inflation rate *as soon as the public figures out what the authorities are up to*.

2. The second possibility at point J is that the authorities recognize the danger of runaway inflation, and accordingly do not expand aggregate demand so rapidly. In this case, the economy moves from J to L, where the inflation rate is at least stable. At L, equilibrium exists: The public expects 6% inflation, and gets it.

Rational Expectations Make Unwinding Inflation Easier

Now consider what happens if the authorities take a further step, and try to unwind inflation by following restrictive demand policies. We shall see that rational expectations make it *easier* to lower inflation.

Reconsider the traditional argument, based on the assumption that people expect the current rate of inflation to continue. With the tighter aggregate demand policy, the economy moves from L to R. Inflation drops from 6% to 5%. With people expecting current inflation to continue, contracts are now written on the expectation of a 5% inflation rate. Thus, the short-run PC curve shifts down to $PC_{5\%}$.

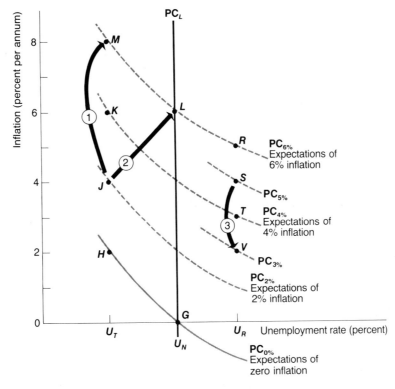

Figure 17-13   Rational expectations and the acceleration of inflation.

If the authorities continue to pursue tight enough policies to keep the unemployment rate at U_R, substantially greater than the natural rate, the economy will move to S in the next period, then to T, and so on. Thus, the inflation rate is reduced—but very painfully. The unemployment rate is high, while inflation comes down only 1% each time period.

However, this traditional argument is once more based on irrational expectations. People expect that inflation will be the same in the future as it is now. But that's not what's happening. The inflation rate is coming down each period.

Once people learn that the authorities are firmly committed to reducing inflation, even at the cost of heavy unemployment, they develop the rational expectation that inflation will be *less* in the future than it is now. When they sign contracts based on this assumption, the *PC* curve shifts down even more rapidly. Therefore, if the economy is at S, they will sign contracts based not on the assumption that inflation will stay at its current rate of 4%, but will instead be lower, say 3%. Thus, just as rational expectations caused inflation to leapfrog up from J to M in response to continuing expansionary policies, so rational expectations will cause the economy to leapfrog from S to V (arrow 3). In short, rational expectations make it possible to bring inflation down more rapidly. *Long periods with high unemployment may not be necessary to unwind inflation.*

Note that the **credibility** of an anti-inflationary policy becomes its key to success. Paradoxically, the way to stop inflation *without* long periods of high unemployment is to convince the public that you *will* tolerate long periods of high unemployment. They will be willing to sign contracts based on lower inflation rates only if they believe that inflation will, in fact, come down.

Rational Expectations and Discretionary Policy

Let us sum up the rational expectations argument thus far:

1. A consistently expansionary policy can quickly lead to very rapid inflation.

2. A consistent, credible policy of restraint can lead to a rapid unwinding of inflation.

In other words, a policy aimed at a low unemployment rate can lead to an inflationary disaster. But a policy aimed at stable prices can be successful without an unemployment disaster. The best choice: Follow a consistent policy aimed at stable prices. Since rational expectations theory is an offshoot of monetarism, it argues that the way to do this is with a steady increase in the quantity of money.

However, this is not the end of the case that rational expectations theorists make against discretionary policies. Thomas Sargent and Neil Wallace of the University of Minnesota also claim that it is *useless to follow a policy of fine tuning the economy by introducing expansive aggregate demand policies each time the economy goes into a recession.* Briefly, the argument is this. The ultimate effect of more demand is higher prices. If demand is

fact, the inflation rate even rose slightly. These events suggest that the natural rate in those years may have been even *higher* than 7%.

Such increases in the natural rate, and similar increases in the United States, do not conflict with the accelerationist theory that the long-run Phillips curve is vertical. According to that theory, *demand management* does not affect the equilibrium rate of unemployment; the rate of unemployment cannot be permanently reduced by a more inflationary policy. However, the natural rate of unemployment *can* be changed if conditions in the labour market change. That is, the whole long-run Phillips curve can shift to the right or left.

Three explanations have been put forward for the apparent increase in the natural rate of unemployment; that is, the rate to which unemployment can be reduced without causing an acceleration of inflation.

The first is based on the change in the composition of the labour force. Compared with the sixties, the labour force in the 1970s contained a larger percentage of teenagers, who have higher unemployment rates than adults. As teenagers became a larger fraction of the labour force, the overall unemployment rate tended

increased each time the economy moves into a recession, people will come to *anticipate* the inflationary consequences. Anticipating higher prices, they will press for higher wages. Eager borrowers will bid up interest rates. Businesses will increase the prices of their products. Thus, the increase in aggregate demand will go into higher prices, not higher output and employment. *When the public anticipates the effects of expansive demand policies aimed at reducing unemployment, it renders these policies ineffective.* Systematic fine tuning of aggregate demand is useless. The central bank can affect output and employment only by trickery; that is, by following erratic policies. (The economy may move from G to H during a brief period if the bank tricks the public by a sudden, unexpected increase in the money stock.) Whenever the central bank follows a consistent policy, the public will figure it out; the only effect will be on prices, not output. In effect, the authorities *face a vertical Phillips curve* in either the long run or the short. No consistent policy will have any effect on output. (Output may, however, still deviate from the natural rate because of random disturbances which neither the central bank nor the public can anticipate.)

This argument has attracted much attention among economists because it may help to explain the disappointing results from the stabilization policies of the 1970s. Even though the authorities frequently attempted to reduce unemployment with expansive policies, the unemployment rate remained high, and inflation accelerated. It may also help to

explain the speed with which the rate of inflation declined during the recession of 1980–1982.

However, the rational expectations argument has been challenged by advocates of demand management, such as MIT's Franco Modigliani, winner of the 1985 Nobel prize in economics. In his 1976 presidential address to the American Economics Association, Modigliani observed that the rational expectations model is inconsistent "with the evidence: if it were valid, deviations of unemployment from the natural rate would be small and transitory—in which case [Keynes'] *General Theory* would never have been written."*

Modigliani's point is this. Within the rational expectations framework, the unemployment rate departs from the natural rate only when there are surprises. According to the rational expectations theory, people are perceptive; they do not consistently make the same mistake. Therefore, while the unemployment rate might fluctuate around the natural rate because of random disturbances, the theory suggests that the unemployment rate should not be *consistently* above or consistently below the natural rate for any extended time. In fact, it was far greater than the natural rate *throughout* the 1930s. The rational expectations theory is inconsistent with the facts.

*"The Monetarist Controversy, or Should We Foresake Stabilization Policies," *American Economic Review* (March 1977): 6.

---

to rise. However, this should be a smaller problem in the future. Because of changes in the birthrate, the percentage of teenagers in the labour force has been declining in recent years, and this drop should reduce the natural rate of unemployment. (In fact, Peter Dungan and Thomas Wilson of the University of Toronto have suggested that, because of this and other factors, the natural rate had already dropped well below 6% in the early 1980s.)[9]

[9]D. Peter Dungan and Thomas A. Wilson, *Potential GNP: Performance and Prospects*, report no. 10 (Toronto: Institute for Policy Analysis, University of Toronto, 1982).

Second, increases in legislated minimum wages may have worked toward a higher equilibrium rate of unemployment, because employers are discouraged from hiring low-productivity workers. This is particularly true of teenagers with limited training and work experience. Because the minimum wage can make it difficult for teenagers to get that first job and acquire work experience, proposals have been made to exempt teenage employment from the minimum wage, or, alternatively, to have a lower minimum for teenagers than for adults. These proposals have been opposed by those who fear that employers would simply replace adults with lower-wage teenagers. However, in some Canadian provinces, the minimum-wage laws *do* in fact provide for a lower minimum for young people.

The third explanation is that improvements in unemployment insurance and welfare help to maintain the incomes of the unemployed. As a consequence, they are less desperate to take the first job that comes along. Frictional unemployment rises as those out of work engage in a more leisurely search for jobs. According to several studies, the substantial increase in benefits under the government's Unemployment Insurance program in 1971 may have added anywhere between 0.5 and 1.3 percentage points to the unemployment rates in the 1970s.[10] Dungan and Wilson attribute more than half of the increase in the natural rate between the late 1960s and late 1970s to this factor. It is not clear what, if anything, should be done about this effect of unemployment insurance, since there is a conflict of objectives. It is desirable to reduce the hardship of the unemployed by providing unemployment insurance. But their incentive to take unattractive jobs is thereby lessened, and this makes it more difficult to achieve the goal of lower unemployment. However, one thing is clear. Government programs should be designed, insofar as possible, to maintain incentives to get a job.

Steps to reduce the equilibrium rate of unemployment. In addition to the two measures just suggested—exempting teenagers from the minimum wage and taking care to retain incentives when designing unemployment insurance—what else might be done to reduce the equilibrium rate of unemployment? First, a reduction in discrimination against women would help to reduce the relatively high female unemployment rate. Second, government training programs might help the chronically unemployed prepare themselves for useful work. The *Adult Occupational Training Act* of 1967 was intended to speed up the retraining of unemployed workers, to provide them with the skills needed for new jobs. Increased resources were provided to the Canada Manpower Centres, to assist them in their task of matching people looking for jobs with firms

looking for workers. By filling vacancies more quickly, the Centres could reduce unemployment. Furthermore, the Department of Regional Economic Expansion (DREE) was set up in 1969, with the purpose of creating jobs in those areas of Canada where unemployment is traditionally high. By moving the jobs to the unemployed, it was hoped to reduce the unemployment rate faster than by waiting for the unemployed to move to where the jobs are.

(In recent years, some economists have been criticizing these programs because they are so expensive. The alternative solution of assisting people to move to where the jobs are involves only a once-and-for-all relocation cost. But moving the jobs to the unemployed may mean a continuing cost. For example, inducing an industry into an unfavourable location that is far distant from its markets may mean it continues to face high transportation costs. Thus, unless it is provided with a very large subsidy, it may eventually leave or collapse.)

The government as the employer of last resort? Government programs that provide jobs for the unemployed might be made more ambitious. The government might act as the **employer of last resort.** That is, the government might stand ready to provide jobs to all those who want work but are unable to find it in the private sector.

Proposals to make the government the employer of last resort are very controversial. On the positive side, government projects might give the unemployed something useful to do. For example, the unemployed might do maintenance jobs in the cities, or carry out conservation and public works projects such as reforestation. If people are unemployed, it would certainly seem worthwhile for the government to hire them for, say, $4 to produce $2 worth of services; society at least gets the $2 worth of services, rather than the nothing at all that they would produce if they remained jobless. However, critics of public employment programs argue that this logic may be misleading. Without last-resort government jobs, people might look harder for jobs in the private sector. Thus, over time, public employment could come to include some people who would otherwise have been employed in the private sector, where workers typically produce at least as much as they earn. Consequently, public employment could be a drag on the overall output of the economy.

There seems to be no simple, painless, and un-

[10]Ronald G. Bodkin and Andre Cournoyer, "Legislation and the Labour Market: A Selective Review of Canadian Studies," in H.G. Grubel and M. Walker, eds., *Unemployment Insurance: Global Evidence of Its Effects on Unemployment* (Vancouver: The Fraser Institute, 1978).

controversial way to lower the high natural rate of unemployment.

3. Bringing the Inflation Rate Down: Proposals to Ease the Transition

A high natural rate of unemployment can be painful. But even more painful are the transitional periods when the inflation rate is being wound down, and the unemployment rate exceeds the natural rate (for example, at point *V* back in Figure 17-10). It is only through the hardship of unemployment—or the threat of it—that the market persuades individuals and institutions to reduce their demands.

A number of suggestions have been made to reduce wage and price increases in a less painful manner:
1. direct restraints on wages and prices
2. the *indexation* of labour contracts (that is, providing for changes in wages during the contract period in response to changes in the level of prices)
3. steps to increase productivity and thus lower the cost of goods and services (this was a prominent element of the "supply side" strategy of the Reagan administration in the United States and of Margaret Thatcher in the United Kingdom)
4. the pursuit of a strong, definite, credible anti-inflation policy so that expectations of inflation will be quickly adjusted downward.

Each of these proposals is controversial. The issue of credibility was raised in Box 17-2. Indexation is deferred to Chapter 18, and supply-side economics to Chapter 19. Here we look at direct restraints.

DIRECT RESTRAINTS ON WAGES AND PRICES: INCOMES POLICIES

Policies aimed at controlling inflation by direct restraints on money wages and prices are sometimes known as *incomes policies*. Wage restraints affect the money incomes of workers. Price restraints affect other incomes, such as profits and rent.

> An *incomes policy* is a policy aimed at controlling inflation with the use of guidelines or other restraints on money wages and prices. (Wage restraints affect labour incomes. Price restraints affect other incomes, such as profits and rents.)

Price and wage controls have often been introduced during wartime to suppress the inflationary pressures unleashed by excess demand. For example, they were used during World War II, when aggregate demand rose rapidly because of huge increases in military spending. In the four decades since the war, controls have also been used from time to time, in North America and elsewhere.

International Experience with Incomes Policy
Many European countries have continued using incomes policy on a more or less regular basis. The policies have usually involved negotiations between the governments and representatives of the major labour unions concerning guidelines for wage negotiations. In countries such as the United Kingdom and in Scandinavia, incomes policy is made easier because of the highly centralized organization of the trade union movement, which means that a small group of union representatives can negotiate on behalf of very large numbers of unionized workers. But at the same time, the political influence of the workers' representatives has sometimes made the negotiations difficult. Thus, in 1972, the Conservative government in the United Kingdom was firmly committed to a set of wage guidelines which the labour representatives would not accept. After a series of strikes disrupting the British economy, the government was finally forced to call a general election in which it went down in defeat. In Sweden, the first general strike in decades took place in 1980 as the government intervened in the annual wage negotiations between the Swedish trade unions and the employers' association.

In the United States, the Kennedy administration experimented with an incomes policy in the early 1960s. The government announced two basic "guideposts":
1. On average, prices should not rise.
2. In general, money wages should not rise by more than the increase in labour productivity in the economy as a whole, estimated at 3.2% per year in the early 1960s.

These two guideposts are consistent. If wages increase by no more than productivity, no inflation need result. Labour can be paid more because labour produces more. Employers can afford to pay the higher wages and still keep prices constant on average.

According to the guideposts, the increase in wages should be no more than the 3.2% increase in productivity in the economy *as a whole*—not the increase in productivity in a specific industry. In some industries—such as computers—productivity rises very rapidly, by as much as 20% per year. Such industries do not have to pay workers 20% more each year; they can get all the workers they want with much more moderate wage increases. With productivity rising much more rapidly than wages, costs per unit of output fall, and prices should accordingly be adjusted downward. On the other side, industries with little or no increase in productivity have to pay wage increases in line with the economy as a whole. Otherwise, they are unable to hire and retain workers. But, with wages rising and productivity stable, these industries find their costs rising. They have to raise their prices. Thus, the Kennedy guideposts recommended that prices *on average* remain stable, but prices were expected to rise in industries with small increases in productivity, while prices should fall in industries with large gains in productivity.

The guideposts came under severe strain in the mid-1960s when the rapid expansion of aggregate demand began to pull prices up strongly. In these circumstances, workers could scarcely be expected to stick to a 3.2% wage increase. If they did so, their real wages would fall; they would not get a share of the rising national product. One way to deal with this problem would have been to protect labour's real income by permitting the money wage to increase by the estimated 3.2% productivity increase plus the rate of inflation. But this larger wage increase would have perpetuated inflation, not cured it. After 1965, less and less attention was paid to the guideposts. They became irrelevant.

A second major attempt at an incomes policy in the United States was made in August of 1971, when the Nixon administration imposed a 90-day freeze on wages, prices, and rents, followed by less rigid controls which lasted through 1972. These wage and price controls were accompanied by expansionary monetary and fiscal policies aimed at reducing the rate of unemployment.

In one way, the controls seemed to work very well—the inflation rate dropped sharply in late 1971 and 1972, and the unemployment rate declined slightly. But inflation quickly spiralled up again after the controls were relaxed. Consequently, there are two conflicting views of this episode:

1. The wage-price controls worked, breaking the inflationary momentum and laying the basis for stable prices without going through the costs of an extended period with high unemployment. But the initial success was wiped out when monetary and fiscal policy became too ambitious.

2. The controls were not really a success at all, but merely a short-run illusion. They temporarily suppressed price increases but did not improve underlying trends. When the freeze was ended, prices quickly regained lost ground.

Canada's Experience with Incomes Policy

Unlike the Kennedy-Johnson administration, the Canadian government refrained from attempting specific incomes policies until the late 1960s. While there was a "suggestion" by the government that wage increases should not exceed a specific figure (6% per year) as early as 1966, the first real attempt to intervene in wage negotiations did not come until 1969 when the federal government created a *Prices and Incomes Commission* under the chairmanship of British Columbia economist John Young. The approach of the Commission was supposed to be based on *voluntary* agreements by unions and firms to limit wage and price increases. In the early discussions with labour representatives, however, it quickly became clear that there was no support from labour for voluntary restraints and, in the end, no attempt was made to impose specific guideposts such as the ones used in the United States. The Prices and Incomes Commission continued in existence as a government advisory body until 1972; in its final report (drawing on studies of wage and price controls in other countries), it concluded that, despite the problems involved, Canadians should consider an incomes policy on a temporary basis if inflationary forces became strongly entrenched.

At the time of the 1974 election campaign, inflation had reached double-digit figures (more than 10% annually). The Conservatives under Robert Stanfield argued strongly that some kind of incomes policy was needed, but the Liberals argued against, pointing to the disappointing experience with those policies in the United States, Britain, and elsewhere. The electorate sent the Conservatives down to defeat.

A little more than a year later, in October 1975, the Trudeau government nevertheless instituted a program of wage and price controls, under which most wages, salaries, and professional fees were not allowed to rise faster than 10% per year. This figure was to be gradually reduced: The program was to last for three years, and goals were set which would provide for a gradual reduction in the rate of inflation.

Because of the difficulty in predicting trends in labour productivity and in the prices of imported goods and services, no specific figures were given for the allowable rates of price increases by firms. But the general rule was to be that price increases would be subject to approval by a new *Anti-Inflation Board* (AIB), which would only allow firms to raise prices at the rate of increase of their cost of production.

It remains very much a matter of controversy whether the 1975–78 controls program had any appreciable effect on inflation in Canada. Initially, there seemed to be some grounds for optimism: Most wage settlements in 1976 were not very far out of line with the target set by the AIB, and the rate of inflation in 1976 was considerably below the 1975 figure. But difficulties also began to appear as the AIB approved a number of wage settlements well above the guidelines for the allowable wage increases, causing bitterness among those labour unions that had complied with the guidelines. Thus, as the program wore on, fewer unions were willing to go along with it. And following the initial success in reducing the inflation rate in 1976, the rate became higher again in 1977 and 1978—rather than lower as foreseen in the program. In 1978, price inflation was back up at about 9% per year, rather than down to 4% as planned. Since wage increases were no higher than 6% to 7% on average, real wages were falling, and it is difficult to imagine labour unions going along with continued controls in these circumstances.

What was perhaps even more disappointing than the failure of the inflation rate to come down was that the main objective of the controls program—to shift the Phillips curve back toward the origin—was not realized. Indeed, in 1977–78 the inflation rate was rising *and* Canada's unemployment rate had increased to a level which was higher than at any time since World War II. As an attempt to get rid of the problem of stagflation, the AIB was a failure.

Thus, the conclusions of those who have studied Canada's experience under the AIB are similar to the assessments made in the United States of the Nixon wage-price freeze. On the positive side, the advocates of the anti-inflation program point to the initial success of the AIB in moderating the very strong inflationary forces that had appeared in 1974–75. The critics, by contrast, point to the failure of the program to achieve the gradual reduction in the inflation rate which was hoped for at the outset. They also point out that whatever reduction in the inflation rate *did* take place can equally well be explained by the relatively restrictive monetary policy of the Bank of Canada and the high rate of unemployment that prevailed in those years.

The experience with controls in Canada and the United States have led some economists to propose a more flexible type of incomes policy, under which wages and prices would not be directly controlled, but in which the government would use the tax system to encourage compliance.

The proposals for a *Tax-Based Incomes Policy* (or TIP) were first made in the United States, and attracted considerable attention there during the Carter administration in the late 1970s. But it was never tried out: Critics doubted that TIP would be effective enough to justify the complications it would introduce into the administration of the tax system. In a book published in 1979, Toronto economists Arthur Donner and Douglas Peters argued that Canada should seriously consider using some form of TIP.[11] In their view, the strategy of reducing Canada's inflation through monetary restraints had been a failure. It produced high unemployment rates, but did not bring much of a reduction in the inflation rate. Therefore, they argued, Canada should once again try an incomes policy, in spite of the administrative difficulties that such a policy entails. The Donner-Peters proposal was widely discussed in the press, and was said to be under serious consideration by the Liberal government in 1981; the reason for this was the consistent support for some form of incomes policy in public opinion polls. Even some economists who are generally opposed to wage and

[11]Arthur W. Donner and Douglas D. Peters, *The Monetarist Counterrevolution: A Critique of Canadian Monetary Policy 1975–1979* (Toronto: James Lorimer and Company in association with the Canadian Institute for Economic Policy, 1979), pp. 45–50.

price controls gave TIP some support. In the words of University of Ottawa's Ronald Bodkin, ". . . one might regard as the strongest feature of tax-based incomes policies their role in taking the place of an even more objectionable set of policies".[12] But many observers, including some former AIB officials, remain unimpressed: Even if TIP is more flexible than other kinds of incomes policies, it still has many of the same disadvantages as the other policies, and would be particularly difficult to administer.

In the end, the Liberal government decided against renewed imposition of a comprehensive incomes policy. Instead, the June 1982 budget of Finance Minister MacEachen introduced a controls program that was essentially limited to the public sector. Under this program (which became known as the "6 and 5" policy), the government committed itself to holding down the wage settlements in the federal public sector to a maximum of 6% in 1982–83 and 5% in 1983–84; it also announced that prices of goods and services subject to government regulation (such as transportation, many agricultural commodities, and so on) would not be allowed to rise by more than these same percentages. The federal government appealed to the provinces to follow similar guidelines for that part of the public sector subject to provincial jurisdiction. There was no attempt at formally regulating wages and prices in the private sector, though the government tried to put some pressure on private-sector unions and firms to voluntarily comply with the guidelines.

Like other control programs, 6 and 5 was also controversial. In particular, labour unions in the federal and provincial public sectors complained that they were being unfairly singled out, since the program effectively nullified their right to collective bargaining while other unions were not affected. But many other observers were sympathetic to 6 and 5. Because it was limited to the public sector, the difficulties of enforcement were far less severe than they are with a comprehensive program. Also, many economists had been critical of incomes policy in the past because these policies were being used to make up for the government's unwillingness to fight inflation by restricting aggregate demand. In 1982, by contrast, a combina-

tion of earlier restrictive policies and the international recession had already driven unemployment to its highest level since the Great Depression. Thus the 6 and 5 program was not seen as a substitute for restrictive aggregate demand policy: It was seen instead as a way of speeding up the process through which the high unemployment would ultimately break the wage-price spiral.

By 1984, the actual inflation rate in Canada was less than 5%: The ultimate goal of the 6 and 5 program had been realized. However, those who are skeptical about incomes policy are quick to point out that with unemployment exceeding 10% since the beginning of 1982, inflation probably would have come down anyway. (In support of their view, they also point out that in the United States, the inflation rate came down even faster, even though American unemployment rates were lower than in Canada and there were no wage and price controls in the United States during this period.)

INCOMES POLICY: CONTROVERSIAL ISSUES

The case in favour of incomes policies has been neatly summarized by John Kenneth Galbraith: "Any idiot can argue the case against controls in the abstract. It is only that there are no alternatives." If direct action is not taken to restrain wages and prices, there is only one way to stop inflation—restrain aggregate demand, and allow a painfully high rate of unemployment, as happened in 1981–82.

But many economists remain skeptical. Incomes policies are controversial for five major reasons.

1. *Limited workability.* If the government proclaims guideposts, business and labour leaders can scarcely be expected to cooperate voluntarily. Labour leaders have to answer to union members, who want higher wages, and business executives have to answer to their shareholders, who want higher profits. Indeed, guideposts may be counterproductive. If the government has approved a 6% wage increase, how can any self-respecting labour leader settle for less? The 6% may thus become the floor from which bargaining begins. Furthermore, guideposts may also be counterproductive on the price side. Fearing that guideposts may simply be a warning of more stringent controls to come, businesses may decide to "jump the gun." If

---

[12]Ronald G. Bodkin, "The Challenge of Inflation and Unemployment in Canada during the 1980s: Would a Tax-Based Incomes Policy Help?" *Canadian Public Policy*, Supplement to vol. 7 (April 1981): 213.

prices are about to be frozen, won't a business try to raise them now, while there is still time?

Moreover, price controls require a major bureaucracy. But even a large bureaucracy can't keep up with the complex interactions among markets. If costs of inputs rise, businesses may quit producing goods if they are not allowed to raise prices. Thus, price controls may result in shortages. Goods in high demand may be channelled into *black markets*, where prices are above the legal limits. Because sellers are breaking the law, they may charge higher prices to compensate for their risk of being fined or imprisoned. In such circumstances, price controls might make the inflation worse.

Finally, governments that use incomes policies may suffer from the illusion that they can indeed control prices in this way, and that they are therefore free to increase aggregate demand rapidly. If they do so, the incomes policies will collapse under the intense pressures of excess demand, and prices will shoot up.

2. Allocative efficiency. Opponents of guidelines and controls point out that they interfere with the function of the price system in allocating production. As we saw in Chapter 4, prices provide information and incentives to producers. When goods are scarce, prices rise, encouraging producers to make more. If prices are controlled, they no longer can perform this important role.

A particular problem arises because controls or guideposts may be enforced erratically. Responding to political pressures, the government may enforce price restraints most vigorously for goods that are considered essential. As a result of the relatively low prices, businesses will switch to the production of more profitable items. Thus, *price controls may end up by creating shortages of the very goods the society considers particularly important.* (Recall the discussion of rent control in Box 4-1.)

Proponents of incomes policies recognize this danger, but believe that it can be dealt with. Advocates of guideposts or controls generally propose that a government agency be given the authority to grant exemptions, permitting higher wages and prices in industries where there is a threat of shortages.

3. The problem of import prices. As we saw in Chapter 7, imported goods and services play a very large role in Canada's economy: The value of imports in 1984 amounted to nearly one-third of the total value

of personal consumption, investment, government spending, and exports. Because imports are so large, the prices of imported goods have a large weight in Canadian price indexes such as the CPI.

But the prices of goods imported into Canada cannot be controlled by a Canadian government agency such as the AIB: the AIB could not control the prices charged by California producers for fresh vegetables imported into Canada, or the prices set by Japanese manufacturers for their cars. Because imported commodities have such a large weight in our CPI, it is difficult for the agency in charge of enforcing an incomes policy to set a specific target for the overall inflation rate. And if the agency cannot control the overall rate of price inflation, it is difficult to ask workers to accept firm limits on maximum permissible wage increases, since labour will be reluctant to go along voluntarily with a program that may result in a reduction in workers' real wages.

With flexible exchange rates, changes in the prices of imported goods in Canada also depend on the price of the Canadian dollar. As we saw in Chapter 15, an appreciation of the Canadian dollar will make imports less expensive; a depreciation of our dollar will contribute to increasing the prices of imports. Thus, if our dollar appreciates because of factors such as a strong world demand for Canada's exports, or because tight Canadian monetary policy leads to high interest rates and a capital inflow, the government's job will be easier: As our dollar appreciates, import prices will decline (or at least not rise as quickly), which will moderate the increase in our CPI (and also make it easier to control the prices of goods produced in Canada but using imported inputs). But if our dollar depreciates (because of a weak world demand for our exports, or because of an easy Canadian monetary policy), an incomes policy will be less effective in limiting inflation—it will have to fight the inflationary momentum of rising import prices.

The actual experience of our anti-inflation program during 1975–78 confirms the importance of the exchange rate as a factor which helps explain Canada's inflation rate. In 1975–76, the Canadian dollar appreciated slightly relative to the U.S. dollar; during those years, our inflation rate came down. In 1977–78, the Canadian dollar *depreciated* by some 14% in terms of U.S. dollars. This depreciation, together with strong inflationary pressures in the United States, led to a substantial increase in the prices of imported goods, contributing to the higher inflation rates in 1977 and 1978, in spite of the anti-inflation program. (In the mid-1980s, import prices did not rise as much, even though the Canadian dollar continued to depreciate. The reason was that the prices *in U.S. dollars* of the goods we imported were relatively stable in the mid-1980s as inflation abated in the United States.)

Because of the importance of the prices of imported goods in Canada, most economists agree that an incomes policy will be much better able to control inflation if monetary and fiscal policy are tight enough to avoid "imported inflation" (inflation caused by rising import prices). But some critics of controls go even further. In their view, tight monetary and fiscal policies will not only make it easier to control wages and prices: They will bring inflation down even if there are no wage and price controls in the first place.

4. *Economic freedom.* Because of the need for flexibility, any kind of incomes policy requires a government agency (such as the AIB) with authority to approve exceptions to the maximum price or wage increases allowed under the policy. The need for such an agency is viewed with alarm by the opponents of incomes policies, because of the economic power it places in the hands of government officials. If officials are allowed to decide whether a firm will be able to raise its prices, they may gain the power to decide whether the firm will survive or not. Price and wage controls restrict the freedom of businesses and labour.

Proponents of controls tend to downplay these dangers and argue that they must be put in perspective. If no restraint is applied to wage and pricing decisions, the control of inflation will involve high rates of unemployment. The unemployed will be used as "cannon fodder" in the war against inflation. Thus, the freedom of business executives and labour leaders to do as they please must be weighed against the right of workers to have jobs.

5. *Equity.* Price guideposts tend by their very nature to be complicated; it is difficult to impose any general standard on all prices. Prices must be allowed to rise by more than average in industries with less than average increases in productivity, as we have already seen. Wage guideposts, on the other hand, can be more specific, and applied across-the-board. For example, a guidepost of 3% may be proclaimed for all workers.

Labour leaders in Canada and other countries have complained that, as a consequence, wage-price guideposts tend to be unfairly enforced. Most of the attention is directed toward the relatively simple wage guideposts. Thus, labour leaders sometimes argue that they don't object to a general policy covering all incomes, but they do object to a policy that *only* controls wages. Incomes policies should not be used to redistribute income away from labour and toward profits.

The enforcement of price guidelines may also lead to complaints about unfair treatment of specific businesses. In pressing for compliance, the government may find politically unpopular businesses to be especially inviting targets for public ridicule and official harassment.

The first two of these issues become particularly important when we address the question of how long incomes policies should last. Some proponents argue that such policies should be used only temporarily to slow down specific inflationary spurts. If they are soon removed, allocative problems are unlikely to be severe. (Again, recall from the discussion of rent control in Box 4-1 that the shortage of apartments becomes more acute as time passes.) However, if controls are removed quickly, prices may simply bounce up to where they would have been in the absence of restraint; there may be no lasting effect. Some economists—most notably John Kenneth Galbraith—argue that the problem of reconciling high employment and stable prices is a permanent one. Therefore, *permanent* restraints on wages and prices should be imposed.

Incomes policies: A final word. A discussion of incomes policies would be incomplete without noting that governments also follow policies that raise prices. For example, government-sanctioned marketing boards keep up farm prices, while restraints on imports reduce competition and raise the prices of products such as home computers and Japanese cars. In the face of strong political lobbies, it is easy for the government to take the line of least resistance, and extend such price-raising policies. But to do so is to sabotage its fight against inflation. Thus, in evaluating an administration's anti-inflationary policies, we should keep in mind two related questions: What policies have they been following to benefit specific industries or specific groups of workers? To what extent have these policies raised prices and wages?

KEY POINTS

1. Data for most of the 1960s trace out a *Phillips curve*. Observations since 1968–69 are above and to the right of this curve.

2. Two major explanations have been offered for the simultaneous high rates of inflation and unemployment of the 1970s—that is, for the upward shift in the short-run Phillips curve:
   (a) cost-push, particularly in the form of higher oil prices
   (b) higher wage settlements, which workers demand in order to compensate for higher prices (in other words, a wage-price spiral causes an upward shift in the short-run Phillips curve)

3. Because inflation affects wage and other contracts, the short-run Phillips curve is unstable. There is a different curve for every expected rate of inflation.

4. Phelps and Friedman argue that people adjust completely to a steady, expected rate of inflation. As a consequence, there is *no long-run trade-off* between inflation and unemployment. The long-run Phillips curve is a vertical straight line.

5. The equilibrium rate of unemployment, where the Phillips curve is vertical, is known as the *natural rate* of unemployment. The natural rate has increased in the past quarter-century.

6. Proposals to bring the natural rate of unemployment back down include:
   (a) steps to combat discrimination against women and minorities

   (b) training programs for the unemployed
   (c) a program in which the government acts as the employer of last resort

7. When restrictive monetary and fiscal policies are used to bring down the rate of inflation, the result can be a very high rate of unemployment. Several proposals have been made to ease the transition to a lower rate of inflation:
   (a) *incomes policies*, in the form of wage-price guidelines or controls
   (b) the pursuit of a firm, *credible* policy (Box 17-2)
   (c) indexation of labour contracts (studied in Chapter 18)
   (d) steps to increase productivity (Chapter 19)

8. Incomes policies have been used in an attempt to ease the transition to a lower rate of inflation. In the 1970s, the Trudeau government created the Anti-Inflation Board to enforce wage-price guidelines in an attempt to contain inflationary pressures. In 1982, a more limited set of guidelines was used in the "6 and 5" program.

9. Incomes policies are controversial on five principal grounds:
   (a) Are they effective?
   (b) Do they adversely affect allocative efficiency?
   (c) Can they be effective in an economy with large imports?
   (d) Are they consistent with economic freedom?
   (e) Are they fair?

KEY CONCEPTS

Phillips curve
stagflation
policy dilemma
the trade-off between inflation and unemployment
demand-pull inflation
cost-push inflation

shift in the Phillips curve
acceleration of inflation
accelerationist theory
wage-price spiral
long-run Phillips curve
natural, or equilibrium, rate of unemployment

government as employer of last resort
incomes policies
guidelines
wage-price freeze
import prices
tax-based incomes policies (TIP)

PROBLEMS

17-1 Why does the (short-run) Phillips curve bend more and more steeply upward as it goes to the left? That is, why isn't it a straight line?

17-2 Explain why expansive demand policies aimed at a low rate of unemployment might cause a wage-price spiral and an accelerating rate of inflation.

17-3 A steady increase in aggregate demand will result in a lower average rate of unemployment over an extended period of time than will a stop-go policy, which involves alternate periods of restrictive and expansive policies. Why?

17-4 For each of the following statements, state whether you agree or disagree, and explain why. If the statement is incorrect, fix it.

(a) On each short-run Phillips curve, there is one and only one stable point, namely, the point at which the short-run Phillips curve intersects the long-run Phillips curve.

(b) According to the Phelps-Friedman theory of the vertical Phillips curve, there is no trade-off between the objectives of high employment and stable prices in the short run. Such a trade-off occurs only in the long run, after the economy has had a chance to adjust to the prevailing rate of inflation.

(c) The Kennedy-Johnson wage guideposts in the United States provided for an increase of wages of approximately 3%. The objective of this wage increase was to provide labour with a gradually increasing share of national product, in order to make up for past exploitation of workers.

17-5 Guidelines and wage-price controls are often opposed both by labour unions and by business executives. Why do labour leaders oppose them, when their objective is to make possible a combination of low inflation and low unemployment? Why do business executives oppose them, when one of their main objectives is to restrain nominal wage increases without having to put the economy through a period of recession and falling profits?

17-6 In the text it was explained how a depreciation of the Canadian dollar would make it hard to control inflation through an incomes policy, because it would tend to make import prices rise.

A depreciation of the Canadian dollar also tends to increase the prices received by Canadian *exporters* for the goods they sell in foreign markets. Explain what effect (if any) this tendency might have on Canadian inflation.

*17-7 If the Phillips curve—such as that shown in colour in Figure 17-3—is stable only in the short run, how was it possible for Phillips to find a curve for Britain that was stable for almost a full century?

*17-8 Would you favour the government's acting as the employer of last resort? Why or why not? If you are in favour, what jobs would you give to those hired under a last-resort program? How much would you pay them? Would you place any time limit on how long they could work for the government under this program?

*Questions marked with asterisks are more difficult than the others.

Chapter 18

HOW DO WE ADJUST TO INFLATION?

Inflation is the time when
those who have saved for a
rainy day get soaked.

Together with unemployment, inflation is one of the two major macroeconomic diseases. Each trip to the supermarket or department store is a nagging reminder of how much the value of the dollar has shrunk.

Not so many years ago, inflation was considered a problem of secondary importance—and with good reason. It is true that there had been an inflationary burst in the 1940s and early 1950s, associated with the Second World War and the conflict in Korea. But, following the end of the Korean war in 1953, the price level remained quite stable for more than a decade. In 1965, prices on average were only 18% higher than in 1953, reflecting an average rate of inflation of less than 2% per year.

Furthermore, from a longer historical viewpoint, rapid inflation had been an exceptional disease associated with war, as Figure 18-1 illustrates. During wars, governments typically resort to the printing press, creating money to help finance their military expenditures. As a consequence, prices shoot upward. (During the U.S. Revolutionary War, the quip "not worth a continental" reflected the sharp decline in the value of the currency issued by the new "continental" government of the United States.) During peacetime periods,

in contrast, there had been no strong upward trend of prices. In 1914, the average level of prices in Canada was no higher than at the turn of the century. On the eve of the Second World War in the late 1930s, the average level of prices was *below* the peak of 1920.

In the 1970s, a fundamental change took place. The rapid inflation of the period from 1973 to 1981 was new; it cannot be attributed to military spending. Like Canada, a number of other industrialized countries— such as Britain and the United States—also suffered high rates of inflation in spite of extended peace.

Starting in late 1982, the inflation rates in North America and elsewhere were brought down sharply, largely as a result of the severe recession; in 1984 and 1985 Canadian inflation was below 5% for the first time since 1970. Nevertheless, we seem to have entered a new era. Rates of inflation above 5% can no longer be considered abnormal events, associated simply with war (Box 18-1).

In the early discussion of inflation in Chapter 8, we emphasized the distinction between *expected* and *unexpected inflation*. When inflation is unexpected, it causes an arbitrary redistribution of income and wealth. Debtors gain. Bondholders lose, as do people working for fixed money wages. But when inflation persists, people come to expect it, and they adjust their behaviour to protect themselves. In Chapter 17, we studied one of the ways in which people adjust to continuing, expected inflation. Specifically, inflation is taken into account by wage negotiators, who may be able to adjust money wages in such a way as to leave workers with the same real wages that they would have achieved in the absence of inflation. The argument that there is a vertical long-run Phillips curve is based on the view that negotiators will in fact adjust completely to continuing, steady rates of inflation.

In this chapter, we will consider some of the other ways in which individuals and the government respond to persistent inflation. We will also look at the ways in which markets—particularly those for bonds—may *fail to adjust*, even over extended periods, with the result that inflation has a continuing impact on real incomes and other real variables. While unexpected inflation has the strongest effects on people's real incomes and wealth, there can be continuing effects even when people come to anticipate the inflation. Finally, we will look at the complications that infla-

tion creates for a government trying to develop a coherent macroeconomic strategy.

Specifically, in this chapter we shall:

1. Illustrate the ways in which the bond market may adjust to a continuing inflation, and the ways in which this market may not adjust completely, even in the event of a steady, perfectly anticipated inflation.
2. Illustrate how *taxes* can be a major reason why inflation has a substantial, continuing effect on the bond market, even when the inflation is anticipated perfectly.
3. See that when inflation is rapid, it tends to be *highly variable* from year to year. Consequently, it is *difficult to anticipate* what the inflation rate will be during a rapid inflation. This is one reason why rapid inflation has serious consequences.
4. Study the causes and effects of *indexation*—the provision in contracts for automatic adjustments (in wages, etc.) in response to inflation. In particular, we will see how indexation can have unpredictable effects, sometimes making it easier to re-establish price stability, but often contributing to high and volatile inflation.

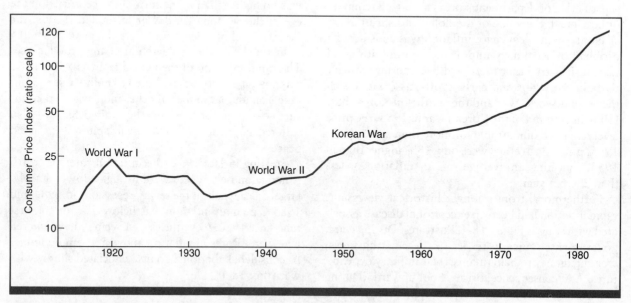

Figure 18-1   Inflation.
Rapid inflation has usually been associated with wars or their immediate aftermath. The rapid inflation during the last half of the 1970s and early 1980s was a notable exception.

BOX 18-1

POCKET MONEY

By Russell Baker*

A curious side effect of inflation is the psychological change that occurs in the human attitude toward money. Recently, for example, without even noticing it, I abandoned the habit of carrying all paper money in my wallet and took to stuffing bills of $1 and $5 denominations into my trouser pocket, which in the past had been habitually reserved for items of small value, like coins.

In my rigidly organized psychological system, the wallet was the repository for things of value—paper money, credit cards, permits issued by the more terrifying bureaucracies, and so forth. The pants pocket, more easily, more thoughtlessly accessible to the right hand, has always been the place

for things whose loss would not be a disaster. Toothpicks collected from the delicatessen counter, coins, chewing gum wrappers, lint, and messages to telephone editors, lawyers, and agents immediately.

A year or so ago, I began noticing dollar bills turning up among the coins and lint. Then, a couple of months ago, reaching in the pocket for a dollar to buy a magazine that used to cost 25 cents, I was startled to come up with a $5 bill. At first, somewhat alarmed, I stuffed the big bill into the wallet, but it left me uncomfortable. What, after all, was a $5 bill anymore? Did it deserve the dignity of a wallet? At the rate people were demanding $5 bills, you could wear out a wallet in two weeks if you had to manhandle it for each demand.

The $5 bill went permanently to the pants pocket along with the lint, toothpicks, the ridiculous pennies and quarters, and the wretched, bloodless, decaying, unworthy one-dollar bills.

This created immense psychological relief. When one stopped thinking of $5 bills as "real money," the pain and outrage occasioned by being charged $1.25 for a copy of *Newsweek* and $6 for a pound of veal became almost tolerable. I no longer look with awe upon fellow New Yorkers who pay $110 a month for parking space for their cars. The people across the street who rent two-bedroom apartments for $2,200 a month still leave me agape in such wonder as will be dispelled, I suppose, only when I shift the $20 bills from wallet to pocket.

*Abridged from his column in the *New York Times*, 14 February 1979.

---

5. Study the effects of high inflation on the government's budget, and see why it becomes so difficult to determine which macroeconomic policies are most appropriate during periods of rapid and changing inflation.

Throughout this chapter, one recurring theme will be the effects of inflation on the cost of home ownership. Housing not only represents a major expenditure for the typical Canadian family; it is also the most important way most families save. (The largest asset the typical family acquires is its home, and paying off the mortgage is one way to save.) The significance of the housing market scarcely needs to be emphasized to undergraduates. During the next decade, many of you will acquire your first homes. The more rapid the inflation, the more difficult it will be for you to buy a home—even if your money income completely keeps up with inflation.

ADJUSTING TO STABLE, CONTINUING INFLATION

Consider first a stable, continuing, predictable inflation. Such inflation is a nuisance: Workers, bondholders, homeowners, and others have to adjust dollar amounts for inflation if they want to calculate their real incomes or wealth. However, it is not obvious how the fundamental performance of the economy is changed. In fact, there is a traditional argument in economics that the real quantities in an economy—such as real incomes and real wealth—will be affected little, if at all, by a steady, predictable inflation. We have already seen in Chapter 17 how real wages may remain unaffected by steady inflation.

A similar argument suggests that the *relative* prices of various goods may be unaffected by *stable, predictable* inflation (of, say, 6% per annum). Typically, with a zero rate of inflation—where prices *on average* are stable—some prices will rise while others will fall. To the degree that a steady, predictable inflation leaves fundamental conditions in the economy unchanged, then relative prices need not be affected. The price of a good which, for a variety of reasons, would have risen in the non-inflationary situation by 2%, will in this inflationary situation rise by 8%—that is, 6% to compensate for inflation, plus 2% for the other reasons. Similarly, prices that would have fallen in the non-inflationary situation will rise by less than the rate of inflation.

The Real Rate of Interest

Because inflation has such a strong effect on borrowers and lenders, it affects the interest rate that lenders charge and borrowers pay. We've already seen in Chapter 8 how inflation harms lenders; they are repaid in money whose value has declined. Consequently, inflation makes lenders reluctant to make loans. The supply of loanable funds decreases, as illustrated by the move from S_1 to S_2 in Figure 18-2. At the same time, inflation benefits borrowers. People are therefore eager to borrow, and the demand for loanable funds by businesses, home buyers, and others increases from D_1 to D_2. Equilibrium moves from E_1 to E_2. There is an increase in the price of loans (the interest rate).

The question is, how much does the interest rate rise? One common argument—traced back a half-century to the work of Irving Fisher of Yale—is that the

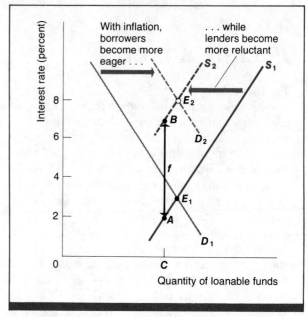

Figure 18-2   Inflation and the demand and supply of loanable funds.

As a result of inflation, people are eager to borrow; the demand for funds increases to D_2. Lenders are reluctant, causing the supply of loanable funds to decrease to S_2. As a result, the rate of interest rises.

interest rate will rise by the amount of inflation, thus leaving borrowers and lenders in the same real position as before. That is, borrowers and lenders will face the same **real rate of interest** as before, with this real rate calculated in a manner similar to that used for the real wage in Chapter 7. Specifically:[1]

The *real rate of interest* $\simeq$
the nominal rate of interest
– the expected rate of inflation   (18-1)

---

[1]As in the case of the real wage (equation 7-10), this is only an approximation. Once again, we have to divide to get the precise answer:

$$i_r = \frac{1 + i_n}{1 + \text{expected rate of inflation}}$$

where

i_r is the real rate of interest, and
i_n is the nominal rate of interest.

Figure 18-2 illustrates the reason for believing that the nominal rate of interest will include a full compensation for inflation, bringing the real interest rate back to its original level. The non-inflationary equilibrium is at E_1, with a nominal rate of interest of 3%. With zero inflation, the real rate of interest is likewise 3%.

With a steady, expected inflation of 5% per year, how much does the supply of loanable funds (S_1) shift? Point A on supply curve S_1 shows us that, *before inflation*, lenders had to receive 2% interest to induce them to provide C units of loanable funds. This suggests that, once there is an inflation of 5%, those lenders will be willing to lend the same C units only if they receive an interest rate of 7%, at point B. This provides them with a 5% compensation for inflation— shown by arrow f—and the same 2% real rate of interest as before. No matter what point we consider on S_1, the corresponding point on S_2 is 5% higher. Thus, the entire supply curve shifts up by the amount of the inflation arrow f.

A similar argument applies to borrowers. With inflation, their enthusiasm for borrowing increases, since they will repay with money whose value has declined. Their demand for loans shifts up by 5%: No matter how much they borrow, they will be willing to pay 5% more for it, because this is the benefit they get from inflation. With both curves shifting up by the same 5%, new equilibrium E_2 is 5% above original equilibrium E_1. In this simple case of a stable, predictable inflation, the nominal rate of interest therefore should rise to 8% to compensate for the 5% inflation, leaving the real interest rate unaffected at 3%. Of the 8% total, 3% can be looked on as a net payment to lenders, while the other 5% compensates them for the decline in the value of the money they have loaned (Figure 18-3).

INFLATION AND INTEREST RATES IN CANADA

In Figure 18-4, we can see that over the past two decades, there has been a tendency for nominal interest rates to rise during periods when the rate of inflation has increased. Thus nominal rates rose gradually during the second half of the 1960s, as inflationary pressures were increasing in Canada and the United States. Again, as inflation picked up momentum during the 1970s, nominal rates increased sharply, especially after 1977. Conversely, there has been a significant *decrease* in nominal rates between 1981 and 1984 as inflation fell back from over 10% to below 5%. Generally speaking, these movements in nominal rates are consistent with the theory just explained.

Unfortunately, it is difficult to go further, and determine whether the nominal interest rates have changed enough to give full compensation for inflation. The problem is that people look to the *future* when they borrow or lend; the theory says that nominal interest rates should include compensation for *expected* inflation. The difficulty is that we do not live in the simple world we have thus far assumed, where the rate of inflation is stable and perfectly predictable. In the real world, we don't know the *expected* rate of inflation with any degree of precision, and therefore we have no straightforward way to calculate the real rates of interest that bond buyers and other lenders expect to receive.

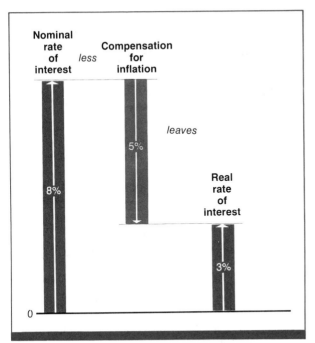

Figure 18-3 Nominal and real rates of interest, with 5% inflation.
On a $100 loan, $5 is required to compensate the lender for the yearly loss of value of the $100 loaned. With a nominal payment of $8, this leaves the lender ahead by $3. Thus, the real rate of interest is 3%.

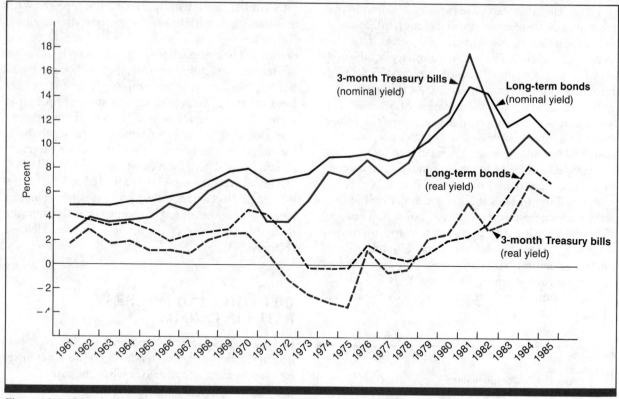

Figure 18-4   Nominal and real yields on long-term government bonds and Treasury bills.
Market yields have risen sharply since the early 1970s. However, before 1980, the increases
could be largely explained by more rapid inflation. Real rates of interest did not exceed 4%
until the early 1980s.
Source: Compiled from *Bank of Canada Review.*

The situation is not hopeless, however. Expected future inflation surely depends in part on what is happening currently. One very simple approach is to assume that people expect the current rate of inflation to continue into the future. This rate of inflation can then be used in equation 18-1 to estimate the real rate of interest.

This has been done in Figure 18-4. When calculated in this way, long-term real interest rates were quite stable, between 2% and 3%, until 1973. Until that time, economists were quite confident that real long-term interest rates would remain quite stable in the face of inflation.

However, the estimates of real yields on bonds became very low during the mid-1970s, actually falling below zero. That is, nominal yields were less than the current rate of inflation. The most plausible ex-

planation of the negative rates is that there is something wrong with the assumption that people expected current inflation to continue. In the mid 1970s, the public did *not* seem to expect the high prevailing inflation to continue. The high inflation could be attributed in part to the oil price shock, whose inflationary effects might be expected to peter out through time.

It is less easy to explain the high estimates for the real rate of interest since 1980. Nominal interest rates remained very high, even though the rate of inflation declined from 12.5% to less than 5%. One logical possibility is that people considered the low rate of inflation an aberration, and were skeptical that inflation would be kept down in the future. Again, they may have doubted that the current rate of inflation would continue. Another possibility is that real interest rates were in fact very high, in part because of the large government budget deficits in both Canada and the United States. At any rate, economists are now much less confident than they were a decade ago that nominal interest rates will compensate fully for inflation, leaving the real rate stable. In an American study, Lawrence H. Summers of MIT has concluded that "the data suggest some tendency for interest rates to adjust to changes in expected inflation, but far less than is predicted by theory."[2] In other words, inflation *may* have some continuing effect on the real rate of interest. If this is so, inflation can have substantial and continuing effects on borrowers and lenders.

We now turn to three complications: (I) how inflation causes a "front loading" of debt; (II) how inflation and taxation interact; and (III) why high inflation is generally variable and unpredictable inflation. In each case, we consider how bond contracts may be adjusted in an effort to reduce the effects of inflation—and how and why these efforts may not be completely successful.

I. HOW INFLATION CAUSES A "FRONT LOADING" OF DEBT

Even if nominal interest rates rise enough to compensate completely for inflation, the inflation may still have real consequences. Borrowers face a problem. To see why, suppose a family buys a home. They take out a mortgage of $100,000, to be repaid over a 30-year period.

First, consider their situation in a non-inflationary world, with nominal and real interest rates at 4%. Their payments are approximately $475 per month for 30 years. This monthly payment covers both interest and the repayment of the $100,000 loan. Because there is no inflation, the burden of the debt is spread evenly over the 30-year period. The $475 they pay in the last month has the same purchasing power as the $475 paid in the first month.

Now, consider what happens with 10% inflation. If the real interest rate remains at 4%, the nominal rate will be 14%. This will mean payments of approximately $1,500 per month over the 30 years. This $1,500 represents a *huge* burden at first, since prices

[2]Lawrence H. Summers, "The Nonadjustment of Nominal Interest Rates," in James Tobin, ed., *Macroeconomics, Prices and Quantities* (Washington: Brookings Institution, 1983), p. 232.

have not yet risen very much. However, by the final year, the $1,500 will be trivial. It will represent less purchasing power than $100 in the first year. (With 10% inflation, prices double every 7 years. Prices will therefore increase more than sixteenfold within the 30-year period. See Box 18-2.)

Thus, inflation and high nominal rates of interest result in the burden of mortgages being shifted forward to the early years. The mortgages are *front-loaded.*

> A debt is *front-loaded* if the payments, measured in real terms, are greater at the beginning than at the end of the repayment period.

Many people who could buy a home in a non-inflationary situation find they cannot do so if inflation is rapid, because of the heavy burden they face during the early years. This is an important real effect of inflation—*even if the real interest rate remains unchanged.*

Graduated-Payment Mortgages

Why not remove front loading by starting with low payments, increasing them gradually as prices rise? In our example, in which prices rise steadily at 10% per annum, home buyers would have an initial payment of approximately $480 at the end of the first month, when prices have risen only a little. The monthly payment would then rise gradually, in line with inflation, to reach $8,300 by the time the final payment was made at the end of the 30th year. In this way, the burden would be the same in every month—*provided that inflation continued at a steady 10% per year.* (The figures are correct. With 10% inflation, $8,300 at the end of 30 years has the same purchasing power as $480 at the end of the first month.)

However, if inflation slowed down, a family would be in trouble if it had a mortgage whose payments rose in this way. With money retaining much of its value, the rising dollar payments would become a larger and larger burden, and home owners might be unable to meet their payments. A rapid inflation may indeed slow down, as it did in the early 1980s. This means that it would be risky for banks and trust companies to make loans with **fully graduated** payments, that is, loans whose payments would remain constant in real

BOX 18-2

THE RULE OF 70: HOW LONG DOES IT TAKE FOR PRICES TO DOUBLE?

Consider the effects of a steady inflation at 10%. During an initial base year, the index of prices is 100; in the second year, it becomes 110. During the third year, the index rises again by 10%. That is, it rises to 110% of the previous year's height, or to 121 (= 110 × 110%). Because the index grows at a compound rate, it increases by a larger number each year. As a result, the index reaches 200 in less than 10 years. But how long does it take? The answer is: about 7 years.

This answer is found by using the *rule of 70*:

Approximate number of years required to double =

$$\frac{70}{\text{percentage rate of growth per year}}$$

In our example, where the rate of growth was 10% per year:

Approximate number of years required to double =

$$\frac{70}{10} = 7$$

Because it is a general formula, the rule of 70 has broad applicability. It can be used to estimate not only how long prices take to double, but also how long your interest-bearing bank account takes to double, or how long a GNP growing at a constant real rate takes to double. For example, if GNP grows at 3.5% per year, it will double in about 70/3.5 = 20 years.

The rule of 70—reflecting the underlying phenomenon of compounding—would lead to spectacular results if inflation were to continue at 7%, the average annual rate during the decade from 1975 to 1985. Between 1985 and 1995, prices would double, and then redouble by year 2005. By 2015, they would be 8 times their 1985 level; by 2025, 16 times. If you wanted to earn $32,000 in 1985 dollars by the time of your retirement in 2035, you would have to bargain for a million bucks a year. But that would be just a hint of things to come. If all prices were to rise at the same average rate, by 2060 your grandchildren would be paying $80 for a cup of coffee. It would cost them $2.5 million to send one of their kids to a private college for one year!

terms if the present rate of inflation were to continue: Some of their borrowers might not be able to pay back their loans.

A *graduated-payment* mortgage is one whose money payments rise as time passes. A *fully graduated* mortgage is one whose money payments will rise enough to keep real payments constant if the present rate of inflation continues. (Such fully graduated mortgages are not available.)

To ease the burden on young home buyers, the Canadian government (through the Canadian Hous-

ing and Mortgage Corporation, CMHC) began to experiment with graduated-payment mortgages in the high-inflation years in the late 1970s. However, the experiment was not particularly successful; even though the CMHC guaranteed repayment, mortgage-lending institutions such as banks and trust companies were reluctant to issue mortgages of this type. Furthermore, a mortgage which was graduated according to the schedule suggested by the CMHC fell far short of the degree of graduation that would have been needed to level out the real burden, and thus leave the pattern of real payments unaffected by inflation. As a consequence, most home buyers continued to face the necessity either to settle for a more modest home than they could afford in the longer run, or to take on a crushing short-term burden of mortgage payments.

II. INFLATION AND THE TAX SYSTEM

Inflation can introduce three major complications into the tax system: (1) in the past, inflation has pushed people into higher tax brackets; (2) inflation greatly complicates the taxation of interest; and (3) inflation introduces quirks and inequities into the taxation of businesses.

1. The Tax Bracket Creep: Inflation and the Increasing Burden of Taxes

Until 1974, inflation meant that, as dollar incomes rose, taxpayers were pushed up into higher and higher tax brackets. The general idea may be illustrated by referring back to the 1984 tax schedule in Table 5-3. A low-income couple with taxable income of about $13,000 would have an income tax liability of about $3,200, or 25% of their income. Suppose that the average level of prices doubles, and so does the couple's taxable income. It is now $26,000, which barely keeps up with inflation. If the tax schedule were to remain unchanged, taxes would now take $7,511, or 29% of their income. Although they are earning no more in real terms, taxes take a larger share. Similarly, inflation can cause taxes to rise for other families, both rich and poor, whose incomes barely keep up with inflation. While all are affected, the problem is most severe for the middle class. The poor do not pay much income tax. The rich are already in the highest marginal tax bracket. It is the middle class whose taxes rise most if the tax schedule is not adjusted for inflation.

In order to eliminate this effect, the federal government introduced provisions for the income tax to be **indexed**, beginning in 1974. Indexation means that tax brackets and exemptions rise with inflation. If prices double, so does the nominal income at which the various tax brackets begin. For example, the 34% bracket begins at $36,000 instead of $18,000. Thus, if your money income doubles when prices double, you stay in the same place in the tax table. Your income remains the same in real terms, and so does your tax.

If the income tax is *indexed*, the law provides for exemptions, tax brackets, and other dollar measures in the tax code to increase automa-

tically, in the same proportion as the increase in the price index.

The 1974 indexation reform meant that the federal government's share of GNP no longer increases automatically when there is inflation. In addition, because individuals' provincial income-tax liabilities are generally specified as a percentage of the federal tax liability, provincial income taxes in provinces where this is done have also in effect become indexed. (For example, if the provincial income tax payable is specified as 48% of federal tax payable, when the federal tax is reduced by indexation, so is the provincial tax liability. Other federal and provincial taxes—such as the federal manufacturers' sales tax, or the provincial sales taxes—are specified in constant percentages that are unaffected by inflation.)

In the United States, the federal income tax remained un-indexed through the high-inflation period in the 1970s and early 1980s. When indexation was finally passed in 1981, its implementation date was delayed until 1985, more than 10 years after it had been introduced in Canada. While indexation was not part of Reagan's early tax proposals, he ultimately came to support it strongly. When there were opposing suggestions in 1983 and 1984 that indexing be deferred or eliminated as a way to reduce the large U.S. budget deficits, he summarized the case for indexing:

> Let's not kid ourselves. Government has found inflation a very handy method for getting additional revenues without having to face the public and demand a tax increase. It is a tax. Government gets a profit from inflation. And I would like to see indexing put in place to permanently take away from government the incentive to create inflation in order to get more money.

In Canada, the *principle* of indexing is by now firmly established. Recently, however, the principle has been partially compromised as the government has been trying hard to increase revenues and reduce the federal deficit. In 1982, Finance Minister MacEachen put a "cap" on indexing as part of his "6 and 5" restraint program: The maximum increase in tax brackets and exemption levels would be 6% even if the rate of price inflation turned out to be more than this. And in the 1985 budget of the Conservative government, the indexing provisions were substantially modified: Brackets and exemptions were raised by *three percentage*

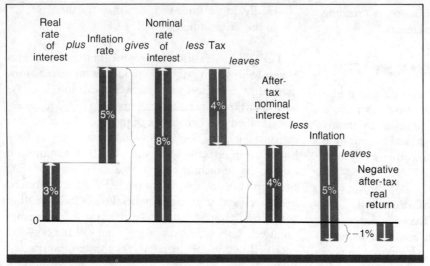

Figure 18-5   Effect of 50% tax, with 3% real rate of interest.
When inflation is 5% per year, the individual or corporation in the 50% tax bracket is not left with enough to compensate for inflation. The real after-tax interest rate is negative.

points less than the rate of inflation in the 1986 taxation year. (For example, an inflation rate of 5% would only cause the brackets and exemptions to rise by 2%.) Thus, with an indexing system that adjusts only partially for price changes, inflation has a real effect on the economy, since it increases the percentage of Canadian income that is paid in taxes. (As a further move to reduce the deficit, the Conservatives also proposed to abandon the principle of raising transfer payments such as Old Age Security benefits and family allowances to compensate for inflation. However, these proposals ran into strong opposition and were subsequently modified.)

2.   Inflation and the Taxation of Interest

Inflation has another real effect on taxpayers—it imposes a tax penalty on bondholders. To illustrate, consider a non-inflationary situation where the interest rate is 3% in both nominal and real terms. (To keep matters simple, we disregard the rule that exempts the first $1,000 of interest earnings from income tax.) A bondholder in the 50% tax bracket pays one half of the interest in taxes, leaving an after-tax return of 1 1/2% in both nominal and real terms.

Now suppose that there is a continuing rate of inflation of 5%, which gets built into the interest rate. The

results are shown in Figure 18-5. The nominal interest rate rises to 8%, leaving a constant pre-tax real rate of interest of 3%. The bondholder in the 50% tax bracket pays half the 8% interest in taxes, leaving 4% after taxes. Note what has happened to the ***real after-tax return***. Subtracting the 5% inflation rate, we find that the real after-tax return has not only disappeared; it has in fact become negative. The reason is that the tax is collected, not just on the 3% real rate of interest, but rather *on the whole 8% of nominal interest.*

However, while the tax system adds to the woes of bondholders and other lenders, it lessens the interest burden borne by borrowers. The reason is that interest payments reduce the taxable incomes of many borrowers. (Interest payments represent a business expense for corporations; they are subtracted as a cost in calculating taxable profits. Similarly, farmers and small businesses may deduct interest payments on borrowed money in calculating taxable income.) Just as the lender includes the full 8% of nominal interest as part of income, so the borrower can subtract the full 8% in nominal interest in calculating taxable income. Thus, the calculations of Figure 18-5 also apply to a borrower in the 50% tax bracket. With 8% paid in nominal interest, half of this is saved in taxes, leaving a net nominal cost of 4%. But this is less than the rate of inflation. The after-tax real burden on the borrower is negative.

Because inflation and high nominal interest rates increase both the tax advantages to borrowers and the tax penalties on lenders, why aren't the shifts of demand and supply in Figure 18-2 even greater? Why doesn't the nominal interest rate rise by even more than the rate of inflation, in such a way as to stabilize the *after-tax* real rate of interest? The problem is that it is not clear just how this could happen. While borrowers and lenders are all affected by inflation, not all are subject to tax. For example, pension funds pay no tax on interest earnings. Other borrowers and lenders are subject to widely different marginal tax rates. If nominal interest rates were to respond to taxes, it is not clear to *which* tax rate they would respond.

3. The Inflation-Taxation Combination: The Effects on Business

In some respects businesses lose from inflation, while in other respects they gain.

How businesses lose: They pay taxes on artificial profits. Consider what happens when a business uses materials bought several years ago in producing goods today. Their accounting cost—that is, the cost at which the materials were acquired—is less than the current cost of similar materials. Thus, the costs of production tend to be understated, and profits consequently overstated. Some of the profits that appear on the business statement are artificial. But they are still taxed.

What is true of material inputs is also true of machinery. Of course, a machine is not used up all at once. Rather, it is "used up"—depreciated—over a number of years. Suppose a machine is depreciated over, say, five years. According to present tax law, the price at which the machine was originally acquired is used in calculating depreciation. But, after several years of inflation, the price of the machine is higher. When the original price is used to calculate depreciation, the current costs of production are once more understated. Profits are accordingly overstated. Once again, artificial profits are taxed.

These artificial profits can be very large, particularly during periods of rapid inflation, as calculations by a number of large companies have shown. General Motors estimated that $1.1 billion of its total 1979–80

profits of $2.9 billion were the result of inflation. In 1980, a large steel company found that, when account was taken of inflation, its reported profit of $121 million became a *loss* of about $200 million.

Many business executives suggest that they be allowed to depreciate buildings and equipment more heavily, to take account of inflation, so that there will be fewer artificial profits for the government to tax. Specifically, they advocate **replacement-cost depreciation.** Depreciation would be calculated using the current replacement cost of the machine, rather than its original price.

> With *replacement-cost depreciation*, the current replacement costs of buildings and equipment are used in calculating depreciation, rather than the actual acquisition costs.

How businesses gain from the inflation-taxation combination: They borrow. If inflation is unexpected, businesses get a windfall because the funds they have borrowed at low interest rates can be repaid with lower-valued money. If inflation is expected, interest rates are higher in compensation. But businesses still get the tax advantage—explained earlier—which comes to borrowers in the event of inflation. This advantage is particularly great for businesses with large real estate holdings. Real estate can often be mortgaged for a large percentage of its value. Furthermore, land and buildings generally rise in price during inflationary periods.

Because inflation offers this advantage to business, the proposal to allow replacement-cost depreciation is controversial. Critics charge that it would give an unfair break to business by removing the disadvantages while leaving the advantages they gain from inflation. The case for replacement-cost depreciation is further weakened by the other tax breaks enjoyed by businesses that invest—for example, accelerated depreciation and the investment tax credit.

Inflation introduces many quirks and peculiarities into the tax system, which was developed on the assumption that the average level of prices would remain reasonably stable. It would be *very* complicated to rewrite the tax laws to remove the effects of inflation. One of the best ways to limit tax inequities is to keep the rate of inflation down.

III. INFLATION AND UNCERTAINTY

The chief evil of an unstable
dollar is uncertainty.

Irving Fisher

Thus far, the main focus has been on the effects of
continuing, stable, anticipated inflation and on the
ways in which the economy does and does not adjust
to such inflation. We have seen that, even in this case,
inflation has real effects. But when it is unexpected,
inflation has much stronger effects. These can be very
serious when the average rate of inflation is high,
because rapid inflation generally has a large, erratic,
unexpected component. A country with a very rapid
inflation may, for example, find that inflation bounces
from 100% one year to 50% the next, and to 90% the
next. On the other hand, a country with a low average
rate of inflation will find that the inflation rate is also

quite stable from year to year. Thus, observe in Figure
18-6 that the year-to-year change in the Canadian rate
of inflation was quite small during the 1960s and early
1970s when the average rate was low. Between 1972
and 1982, inflation was more rapid *and* more erratic.
Let us consider the effects of erratic inflation on the
issuers and buyers of bonds, and on wage earners and
employers.

Erratic Inflation and the Debt Market

Bonds are generally bought by people interested in a
stable income; those who are willing to take risks are
more likely to go into the stock market. While increases
in nominal interest rates help compensate bond buyers
for *predictable* inflation, unpredictable inflation makes
the real return on bonds very uncertain. If the rate of
inflation shoots up above the nominal interest rate,
the bondholder will be "soaked"; the interest won't

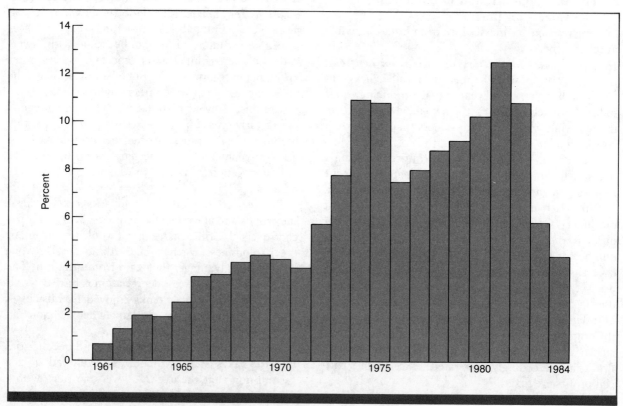

Figure 18-6   The rate of inflation, 1961–1984.
When inflation was relatively low, in the 1960s and early 1970s, there was little change in its
rate from year to year. Between 1972 and 1982, the rate of inflation was higher on average,
and it also varied considerably from year to year.

even cover the dollar's loss of value through inflation. On the other hand, if the inflation rate unexpectedly comes down, the bondholder will receive a windfall.

Because bond buyers are generally interested in stability and safety, they tend to withdraw from the market if inflation becomes erratic. Similarly, potential borrowers are reluctant to issue bonds; they are also uncertain whether erratic inflation will make them winners or losers. Thus, erratic inflation tends to dry up the traditional long-term bond market. Bond buyers are reluctant to buy, and corporations are reluctant to issue bonds. For example, in 1983, there was great uncertainty as to whether inflation would come down, and, if so, by how much. For this reason (and also because of the recession), the number of new bonds issued in Canada fell sharply. Because uncertainty over the future rate of inflation disrupted the bond market, businesses found it more difficult to finance long-term projects. This inflicted a real cost on the economy.

Innovations in the mortgage market.   Like the bond market, the market for residential mortgages may also be severely affected by uncertainty about the inflation rate. Because buying a home represents a very large investment for most people, they need a mortgage to cover a large proportion of the purchase price, and most people will want to pay back the mortgage over a long period, perhaps 20 or even 30 years. But with uncertainty about inflation, the borrower and the lender may be reluctant to commit themselves to a constant interest rate for such a long time.

Because of this problem, most lending institutions in Canada currently issue mortgages that provide for renegotiation of the interest rate periodically, say every one to five years. If the inflation rate and the interest rate on other debt instruments change, the interest rate on the mortgage will be adjusted correspondingly. Therefore, with such **renegotiable** mortgages, real interest payments can be stabilized in the face of changing conditions.

Other adjustments to uncertainty about inflation are possible. In Britain, the building societies (which are similar to our trust companies) have used ***variable-rate mortgages*** since the end of World War II. Such mortgages have added to the financial stability of the building societies: During periods of high inflation and high market rates of interest, they automatically receive high nominal interest on the mortgages they own. Since the early 1980s, Canadian banks and trust companies have also begun offering variable-rate mortgages.

> A *variable-rate mortgage* has an interest rate that is adjusted periodically in response to changes in the market interest rate.

But mortgages with interest rates that have to be periodically renegotiated, or with variable interest rates, have a disadvantage to borrowers: They face the risk that the interest rate will become so high that they cannot afford the payments, and they may lose their homes. (Many Canadian families were forced to sell their homes when mortgage interest rates rose to more than 20% in late 1981.) Because of this risk, families may shy away from the long-term commitment of buying their own home. This depresses the market for houses and leads to decreases in new construction. Once again, we see that erratic inflation can have serious effects on the economy: It discourages all kinds of long-term investment, by corporations and families alike.

INDEXED WAGES

Inflation is like toothpaste. Once it's out,
you can hardly get it back in again.
   Karl-Otto Pohl, President of the West
                          German Central Bank

Unforeseen changes in the rate of inflation also affect the real returns from other contracts, such as wage contracts. As already noted, the real wages of workers on long-term contracts decline when inflation accelerates unexpectedly.

One way for workers to protect themselves during periods of erratic inflation is to negotiate shorter-term contracts; for example, contracts covering one year rather than the three years that are standard for union contracts in North America. However, frequent negotiation is time consuming for business executives and labour leaders. Furthermore, it raises the possibility of more frequent strikes.

An alternative is to arrange in the contract for increases in the money wage to compensate for inflation. In other words, wage contracts can be **indexed**. During the 1970s, when the rate of inflation was accelerating rapidly, contracts that were indexed by the inclusion of an *escalator clause* became common in Canada.

> An *indexed wage* contract contains an *escalator clause* that provides workers with additional money wages to compensate for inflation, generally as measured by the consumer price index (CPI). The additional wage is often referred to as a *cost-of-living allowance* (COLA).
>
> Often, there is a *cap* on the indexation, which limits indexation to no more than a specified percentage.

Indexed Wages: A Way of Easing the Transition to Lower Inflation?

The primary reason for wage indexation is to reduce workers' uncertainty over their real wage. But it is also sometimes recommended as a help in unwinding the inflationary spiral discussed in Chapter 17. We noted there that a vicious circle can exist. Because people expect inflation, they build it into their wages and other contracts. As a consequence, costs continue to rise and continuing upward pressure is exerted on prices. To a considerable degree, inflation exists because people expect it, and people expect it because it exists. Karl-Otto Pohl's toothpaste has gotten out of the tube.

If wage contracts are not indexed, the process of unwinding inflation may be very slow and painful, as we noted in Chapter 17. It may take a number of years of abnormally high unemployment (at points such as V in Figure 17-10) before expectations of inflation can be reduced and inflation sweated out of the system. Some economists have suggested indexing wages as a way of breaking the inflationary spiral. Instead of negotiating a 10% wage increase during a period of 8% inflation, workers might settle for a 2% real wage increase; that is, an increase of 2% plus the increase in the price index. If initial success were achieved in reducing the rate of inflation (by, say, 3%), then indexing would *automatically* reduce the increase in nominal wages (from 10% to 7%). Upward pressures on prices would be reduced further, and the inflationary spiral broken in a relatively rapid and painless way.

However, two major difficulties arise when indexed contracts become common:

1. If inflation gets worse, indexation makes the spiral worse still. Wages respond more quickly, generating even faster price increases. Thus while indexing means that inflation can be wound down more quickly, it also means that inflation can accelerate more quickly. Prices become more erratic. (The natural tendency of negotiators to index contracts during periods of high inflation is one reason why high inflation tends to be erratic. Put another way, the desire of people to protect themselves from erratic inflation makes inflation even more erratic.)

   The danger of indexation causing an acceleration of inflation is particularly great if the increase in productivity slows down. Consider an extreme example. Suppose that all wage agreements and other contracts (such as bonds and contracts for the delivery of materials and parts) are fully indexed, with no caps. In other words, all contracts are set in real terms. Suppose that productivity has in the past been rising at 3% per annum, and that labour contracts include a 3% real wage increase for the future. Then suppose that the growth in productivity slows down to 1%. Something has to give. Contracts promise people 3% more per year in real terms. These contracts cannot be fulfilled, since only 1% more is being produced each year. Money wages will be continuously increased in a vain attempt to provide the 3% real wage increase. The result of such unfulfillable contracts will be an explosion of money wages and prices.

   In fact, as indexation increased in the 1970s, the rate of productivity growth declined (for reasons which will be studied in Chapter 19). The combination of indexation and weak productivity growth added to the acceleration of inflation during that decade.

2. Indexing leads to a quick response of wages and other prices to an external shock, such as an increase in the prices of imported goods in response to a rise in the price of the U.S. dollar. Somebody has to pay the higher cost of imports. If wages and other incomes remain unchanged in Canadian dollar terms, then each of us will bear the burden of higher import prices. But if we are protected by indexing, then our wages and the prices of what we sell will increase automatically. The burden will be passed along

to someone else who is not protected—such as a retired person with a private pension fixed in dollar terms.

Thus, in the face of an external shock, indexing leads to two problems: a speeding up of the inflationary effect, and an even heavier burden on those "at the end of the line" who are not protected from inflation. In this regard, Britain had a particularly unfortunate experience with indexation. In 1973, Prime Minister Edward Heath's Conservative government encouraged the inclusion of escalator clauses in wage contracts, in the belief that they would make it easier for labour leaders not to demand overly large nominal wage increases. The timing could not have been worse. The new indexation clauses added to the inflationary effect of the first explosion in the international price of oil in late 1973 and 1974.

Because of such problems, some early advocates of indexing (such as Milton Friedman) have become less enthusiastic about it in recent years. While wage indexing undoubtedly contributed to the rapid fall in the rate of inflation in Canada in 1982–84, it often seems to have made inflation worse, not better. Most sobering, perhaps, has been the experience of Israel, where indexing is widespread. Inflation increased from about 40% in 1974 to 130% in 1980 and 425% in 1984. Ezra Sadan, of the Finance Ministry, compared indexation to a drug: "Once you've got used to it, you have to keep it up." Of course, indexing is not solely, or even primarily, responsible for the acceleration of inflation. Israeli problems are compounded by very high military expenditures. Like high oil prices, they must be borne by somebody.

As we saw above, in Canada the government has begun moving away from full indexing of the tax system as a way of reducing government deficits and thus reducing aggregate demand and inflationary pressures. The "6 and 5" restraint program introduced by the Liberal government in 1982 also involved an attempt at bringing down inflation by reducing the extent of indexing in the labour market. Wage increases of government employees were to be limited to 6% in 1982 and 5% in 1983, even if the inflation rate was more than that. Furthermore, the government tried to put pressure on unions and employers in the private sector to hold wage settlements within these limits.

Other countries, too, have tried to fight inflation by decreasing the amount of indexing, or avoiding it in the first place. West Germany has had legal prohibitions against wage indexation. In Greece, Andreas Papandreou's government combined a wage freeze with a delay in the indexing of pensions. In Brazil, France, and Italy, governments have tried to reduce the inflationary spiral by changing the indexes used to compensate workers and others for inflation. In Brazil, the cost of imported oil was excluded from the index, thus reducing the inflationary effects when oil prices were rising and dealing with problem no. 2, above. In order to combat inflation, the French government of François Mitterrand in 1982 decided to link wages and pensions, not to the actual rate of inflation (14% in 1982), but to the *target* rate for the coming year—8% for 1983 and then 5% for 1984. In this way, the indexing system was transformed into a method of restraining wages and pensions. Such moves sometimes meet severe resistance. In Italy, when Prime Minister Cossiga took office in 1978 with the announcement that he would fight inflation by adjusting the wage escalator (*scala mobile*) downward, the reaction of the unions was so strong that he quickly backed down. (However, this was just one round in a continuing fight. In 1984, Prime Minister Bettino Craxi took steps to curb the *scala mobile*, and his actions were upheld in a national referendum in 1985.)

MACROECONOMIC POLICY IN AN INFLATIONARY ENVIRONMENT

Inflation not only creates problems for home buyers, businesses, and labour negotiators. It also means that policymakers have difficulty in figuring out what is going on, and what policies are most appropriate. In particular, inflation changes the value of outstanding government debt, and therefore complicates the measurement and evaluation of fiscal policy.

To see why, let's reconsider some of the major facts about the federal government's finances in a recent year. At the end of 1981, the government's total outstanding debt was $94 billion. During that year, government expenditures were $76 billion, receipts were $58 billion, and the cash deficit was accordingly $18 billion. The deficit necessitated additional government borrowing, which raised the national debt to $112 billion by the end of 1982. That is, the debt rose by the amount of the deficit. Of the government's expenditures, about $13 billion were interest payments on the national debt. The inflation rate was approximately 11%.

Calculating the "Real" Deficit

Here's one possible interpretation of these facts. With 11% inflation, the beginning debt of $94 billion could grow by a similar 11%—or by about $10 billion—without its real size changing at all. Thus, the first $10 billion of the deficit is not really a deficit. It does not add to the government's obligations in real terms; it simply offsets the effects of inflation. Thus, the true deficit was not the $18 billion commonly reported. Rather, it was $10 billion less, or only $8 billion. That is, the **real deficit** was only the amount by which the real debt of the government rose. According to this line of argument, the standard figures greatly overstate the real deficit, and therefore greatly overstate the stimulus coming from the fiscal side.

> The *real deficit* of the government is measured by the increase in the real debt of the government. If the debt falls in real terms, then the government has a *real surplus*.

Proponents of this interpretation include John Bossons and Peter Dungan of the Institute for Policy Analysis at the University of Toronto. When they recalculated the total deficit of all governments (federal, provincial, and local) as the increase in the real value of government debt, Bossons and Dungan found that this greatly altered the picture of fiscal policy. Rather than sizeable deficits—as shown in the standard figures—they estimate that the real budget of the total government sector was in approximate balance in 1979 and 1980.

Even more striking are their calculations for 1983. According to the Department of Finance estimate, the full-employment deficit of the overall government sector in 1983 was about $7.5 billion; that is, fiscal policy was providing a substantial stimulus to aid the recovery. The Bossons-Dungan picture of the fiscal policy stance is quite different. Their estimates imply that the *real* full-employment budget was in *surplus* by about $1 billion. They concluded that when correctly measured, fiscal policy was actually *restrictive*,

and that this had "contributed to the magnitude of the current economic depression."[3]

An Alternative View

An alternative view is that it is a great mistake to measure fiscal policy in real terms, even though it is of course perfectly correct that inflation lowers the real value of outstanding government debt.

According to this alternative view, it is reasonable and desirable for individuals and corporations to recalculate their debt and other liabilities and assets in real terms, to get a better idea of how they are doing. Individuals and corporations may *adjust* and *respond* to inflation in this way. However, the government is fundamentally different. The government should not simply respond to inflation. Through its monetary and fiscal policies it is primarily *responsible* for inflation. If it keeps its accounts in real terms, it is not only more likely to ignore inflation; it is also likely to make inflation worse. By keeping accounts in real terms, it can *destabilize the economy*.

To see why, consider what happens if the economy enters a period of inflation. As a result, the real value of the debt falls. As calculated by Bossons and Dungan, the real budget automatically swings into surplus. Measured in this way, fiscal policy is becoming more restrictive. To offset this unexpected restraint, the government may cut taxes or increase spending. But this will add to the inflation.

Similarly, if the government focuses on the real deficit or surplus, it may destabilize the economy during a deflationary period such as the early 1930s. Between 1929 and 1933, prices fell approximately 20%. As a result, the real value of the government debt rose. In real terms, the government's budget was moving into deficit. If a government were to focus on a real deficit like this, it might erroneously assume that it was already providing a large stimulus, and fail to make the needed shift toward expansion. It might even introduce budget cuts to limit the increase in the real debt. But such cuts would make the depression worse.

---

[3]John Bossons and D.P. Dungan, "The Government Deficit: Too High or Too Low?", *Canadian Tax Journal* (January–February 1983): 1–29. (The quote is from p. 23.)

Monetary Policy in an Inflationary Environment

Similar issues arise with respect to monetary policy. The real quantity of money in the economy is important; it helps to determine the quantity of goods and services that people will buy. What would happen if the Bank of Canada were to concentrate on the real quantity of money? To make things simple, suppose that the Bank follows a policy of slowly increasing the real money stock, in line with the slow increase of the productive capacity of the economy.

Again, the focus on real magnitudes could have destabilizing results. Consider again an economy entering a period of inflation. The nominal quantity of money has undoubtedly been rising. However, when we adjust it for inflation, we may find that the real amount of money has not been rising much. It may even have been falling.[4] If the central bank is focusing on the real quantity, it may conclude that monetary policy is too tight, and create more money. This is precisely the wrong way to respond to inflation.

Similarly, concentrating on the real quantity of money can be the wrong thing to do during a period of deflation. Again, consider what happened between 1929 and 1933. Prices fell approximately 20%, while the nominal quantity of money fell by less than 15%. Thus, in real terms, the quantity of money actually *increased*. A central bank focusing on the real quantity might conclude that there was only a small problem with monetary policy. But, in fact, the large decline in the nominal quantity of money was having catastrophic effects. The central bank should not focus on the real quantity of money. Furthermore, outside observers should not use changes in the real quantity of money as the primary way of judging the tightness or looseness of monetary policy.

In brief, real accounting—which makes sense for individuals and corporations—does not make nearly as much sense for the government and central bank, since they are responsible for the overall operation of the economy. Real accounting can lead to destabilizing actions. A somewhat similar point may be made about indexation. For individuals or unions, it makes sense; it provides some protection from the uncertainty of inflation. But the government is fundamentally different. It has responsibility for the system as a whole. It may reasonably oppose indexation, because of the destabilizing effects on the price level.

It is going too far to argue that real magnitudes are not important. They are. But the use of real magnitudes as guides for macroeconomic policy is problematic, to say the least. Even in the best of times, policymakers face difficulties in determining the best macroeconomic policies. When inflation is rapid, it greatly adds to their difficulties.

KEY POINTS

1. During periods of inflation, people are eager to borrow and reluctant to lend. This causes nominal rates of interest to rise.

2. The *real* rate of interest is (approximately) the nominal rate less the expected rate of inflation. Real interest rates cannot be calculated precisely because we do not have direct observations of the *expected* rate of inflation. However, they may be estimated by assuming that the expected rate of inflation equals the current rate.

3. When real rates are calculated in this way, we find that the real rate of interest has been much more stable than the nominal rate, which has risen with inflation. However, real interest rates have not remained perfectly stable in the face of inflation. For example, real rates were low in the mid-1970s.

4. When inflation pushes up nominal rates of interest, the effect is that in real terms, borrowers have to repay loans more quickly. For example, the normal mortgage, with the same dollar payment each month, becomes "front-loaded." This makes it more difficult to buy a home, since higher real payments are required in the early years.

5. One way to deal with this problem would be

*[4]This is a likely outcome if the inflation is rapid. Because money is losing much of its value, people have an incentive to spend it more quickly. This will drive prices up even more. Prices may rise more than the nominal quantity of money, resulting in a decline in the real quantity.

with graduated-payment mortgages, whose money payments rise over the life of the mortgage, thus lessening the front loading. However, graduated-payment mortgages are very rare, and even in the few cases where they are available, the amount of graduation falls far short of the amount that would be needed to level out the real burden on the borrower.

6. Without indexing, inflation causes people to move into higher income tax brackets, even if their real incomes are stable. To eliminate this effect of inflation, the Canadian income tax has been indexed since 1974.

7. The combination of high inflation and taxation means that lenders in high tax brackets end up with negative after-tax returns. Borrowers in high tax brackets end up gaining in real terms. Thus, during periods of rapid inflation, well-to-do people and corporations are discouraged from lending, and encouraged instead to borrow.

8. Inflation complicates the taxation of businesses. For example, it raises the question of whether historical costs or current replacement costs should be used as the basis for depreciation.

9. High inflation tends to be erratic inflation. One way that people may use to protect themselves from erratic inflation is with indexed contracts. However, such contracts make inflation even more erratic. It is possible that indexation might aid in a relatively painless unwinding of inflation. In practice, it has more frequently been associated with accelerating inflation.

10. According to some estimates, if the government's deficit or surplus is measured as the increase or decrease in the *real* value of government debt outstanding, there was a full-employment surplus, rather than a full-employment deficit, in the overall budget of the government sector in 1983, delaying the recovery from the 1981–82 recession.

11. It is, however, questionable whether fiscal policy should be measured in this way, as the change in the real debt. In particular, governments that focus on this real measure may engage in destabilizing fiscal actions. Similarly, a central bank may destabilize the economy if it focuses on what is happening to the real quantity of money.

KEY CONCEPTS

nominal rate of interest	indexation of the income tax	escalator clause
real interest rate	real after-tax return from bonds	cost-of-living allowance
front-loaded mortgage payments	replacement-cost depreciation	cap on indexation
graduated-payment mortgage	variable-rate mortgage	government's real debt
tax-bracket "creep"	indexed wages	real quantity of money

PROBLEMS

18-1 How does inflation make it difficult for people to acquire their first homes, even if they have assurance that their future incomes will rise with the general price level? Why are the problems less severe for those who already own a home, but are selling it to move into a larger one?

18-2 Suppose that, after a period of stable prices, inflation rises gradually to a rate of 10% per annum. At 10%, it hits a peak, and then gradually disappears.
   (a) How will this affect homeowners who acquired their homes before the inflation began?

(b) How will those who acquire homes when inflation peaks at 10% be affected as inflation decreases?

18-3 What problem can be reduced with graduated-payment mortgages? What problem with variable-rate mortgages?

18-4 Do you favour "indexation" of the income-tax code? Why or why not? What is the best case to be made on the other side?

*18-5 Would full indexation make the income tax a more or less powerful "automatic stabilizer"? (Refer back to the section on built-in stabilizers in Chapter 11. And be careful. This is not an easy question. You should consider what happens both during a strong upswing and during a recession.)

18-6 In the early 1970s, the maximum marginal tax rate on unearned income (including interest) was 98% in Britain. (Top marginal rates have since been reduced.) During that period, the rate of inflation in Britain rose to more than 20% per annum.

(a) With 20% inflation and 98% tax rates, what would the nominal interest rate have to be to leave the high-income bondholder with a zero real after-tax return? with a 3% real after-tax return?

(b) Without looking up the facts, can you make an educated guess as to whether nominal interest rates in Britain rose by enough to leave high-income individuals with a positive after-tax real return? If you looked at the list of holders of bonds of a British corporation, would you expect to find many high-income individuals?

18-7 Explain why the government's deficit or surplus may be calculated as the change in the real value of the debt. Calculated in this way, is the government more or less likely to have a deficit than it does with standard calculations? Why?

18-8 What difficulties arise if the government's deficit or surplus, as calculated in question 18-7, is used as a guide in making fiscal policy decisions? Does the same problem arise if the real stock of money is used as a guide by the central bank? Why or why not?

*18-9 Do you favour allowing businesses to use replacement-cost depreciation in calculating taxable income? Why or why not?

Chapter 19

PRODUCTIVITY AND GROWTH: WHY HAVE THEY BEEN DISAPPOINTING?

Not to go back, is somewhat to advance,
And men must walk, at least, before they dance.

Alexander Pope

In previous chapters, we have focused on the goals of high employment and price stability. There is also a third macroeconomic objective that is especially important in the long run: economic growth.

PRODUCTIVITY AND ECONOMIC GROWTH

The key to growth is an increase in productivity. When the typical worker produces more in an hour—that is, when the *average productivity of labour* increases—then total output grows. This follows from the basic relationship:

Total output (Q) =

labour hours (L)   (19-1)
× average productivity of labour (Q/L)

In other words, total output depends on:
1. the total number of hours worked

2. the average productivity of labour. (This is often known as "labour productivity" or, even more simply, as "productivity.")

The three curves in Figure 19-1 show the average annual rates of change of the three items in equation (19-1) above—namely, the quantity of output (Q), labour hours (L), and labour productivity (Q/L). (The dates on the horizontal axis indicate the beginning and end of each period. Thus, the leftmost point of the black curve in Figure 19-1 shows that total output rose at an average annual rate of 2.6 percent over the period 1926 to 1940.)

During the 15 years before World War II, labour productivity grew by less than 2% per year, as the coloured curve shows. (This relatively slow growth is not surprising, since the period includes the Great Depression during the 1930s.) During the next 20 years, productivity grew very quickly (at over 4% per annum). However, the disappointing performance in the second half of the 1970s also stands out very clearly

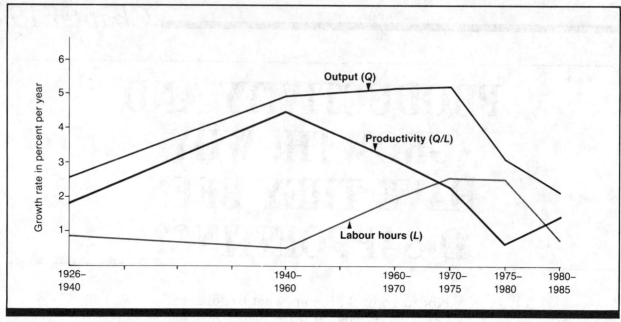

Figure 19-1 Average annual rates of change of output, labour hours, and productivity, Canada 1926–1985.
Between 1926 and 1960, there was a strong upward trend in the rate of growth of labour productivity (Q/L). This trend coincided with a downward trend in the rate of growth of total labour hours worked (L). But since the 1960s, the rate of productivity growth has been falling, while labour hours have been increasing more rapidly. Note also the sudden slowdown in productivity growth in the second half of the 1970s.

Source: Compiled from Statistics Canada, *CANSIM Databank*. Reprinted by permission of the Minister of Suppiy and Services Canada.

in the figure. In particular, between 1975 and 1980, labour productivity increased by no more than 0.5% per year, compared to the average annual increase of 3% to 4% during the peak period in the 1950s and 1960s. Observe also the somewhat more rapid increase in productivity in the first half of the 1980s; as we shall see later, the increase has been especially noticeable since the end of the 1981–82 recession.

These big changes in the rate of productivity improvement raise four major questions:

1. Why did productivity increase so rapidly in the period following World War II?
2. Why was productivity performance so poor in the latter half of the 1970s?
3. Are the productivity problems of the 1970s behind us? Do the figures for the mid-1980s represent the beginning of a new upward trend?
4. Is it desirable for the government to promote productivity and growth? What policies has the government used?

These questions will provide the main topics for this chapter. But before looking at them in detail, we will consider the relationship between labour hours and productivity.

Increases in Labour Hours and Productivity
Observe in Figure 19-1 how the increase in labour productivity generally has moved in the opposite direction to the increase in labour hours. When the input of labour hours has risen slowly, productivity has generally increased rapidly. In particular, the most rapid increase in productivity (1940–60) coincided with the slowest rate of increase in labour hours.

There is a good reason for this inverse relationship. The fewer workers entering the labour force, the more capital each one has to work with. With more capital, each worker can produce more.

Therefore, one of the explanations for the slow increase in productivity in the 1970s is straightforward. The labour force grew rapidly. As a result, there was only a slow increase in the amount of capital at the disposal of the average worker, and productivity likewise increased slowly.

The two reasons for the rapid growth in the labour force were:

1. The "baby boom" after World War II. Following a long depression and war, many people felt free for the first time to have children. By the late 1960s, these children were reaching working age.
2. The increasing participation of women in the labour force. In 1966, no more than 35% of women over 15 were in the labour force (that is, were either employed or looking for work). By 1980, the figure had risen to more than 50%.

As a result, *employment increased rapidly during the 1970s.* The number of civilians with jobs rose from less than 8 million in 1970 to over 10.5 million in 1980.

Thus, the slower increase in productivity in the 1970s was partly attributable to the normal working of the economy. More people wanted jobs. On the whole, the economy was successful in providing these jobs. The result was less capital for each worker than there otherwise would have been, and consequently a less rapid increase in productivity. To the extent that this was the explanation for the slower growth in productivity, there is no cause for alarm. On the contrary, the economy worked well, because it provided jobs for new entrants into the labour force. However, a rapid growth in employment was *only partly* responsible for the disappointing productivity performance. There were other, less reassuring, forces at work, as we shall see later in this chapter.

THE INCREASE IN PRODUCTIVITY, 1960–1973

The question of what makes productivity grow has preoccupied economists for a long time. Much of the modern work on the subject has used the framework developed by U.S. economist Edward F. Denison in his study of the sources of growth in the American economy between 1929 and 1957. Studies of productivity growth by economists at the Economic Council of Canada and elsewhere owe a great deal to the methods developed by Denison for trying to sort out the

contributions of various factors to economic growth.[1]

In a comparative study of productivity growth in various countries, J.W. Kendrick has analysed the sources of Canadian growth for the periods 1960–73 and 1973–78. His findings for the 1960–73 period are summarized in Column 1 of Table 19-1.

Between 1960 and 1973, real national income and output in Canada grew on average by about 5.8% per annum. Out of this increase, Kendrick attributed 1.6 percentage points to an increase in the number of hours worked. The increase in the number of persons employed would have contributed 2.3 percentage points. However, there was another factor that *reduced* labour's contribution to growth—a decrease in the number of hours worked each week by the typical worker. This acted as a drag on growth. The effect of shorter hours was large by historical standards: it reduced growth by 0.7 percentage points. The difference of 4.2 percentage points between the growth rates of output and labour input (5.8 − 1.6 = 4.2) represents growth that was due to increased labour productivity.

One possible source of increasing labour productivity is changes in the *quality* of the workforce. During 1960–73, there were two offsetting trends that affected labour quality: more education, which *increased* the average worker's productivity; and an increased proportion of recent entrants to the labour force which *decreased* average productivity (because of the new workers' lack of experience). The estimated net effect was zero: more education added 0.5 percentage points to the growth rate, but this was offset by the growth-reducing change in the composition of the labour force.

Increases in physical capital contributed 1.5 percentage points to the growth rate; this was three times as much as the amount attributable to increases in "human capital" in the form of education. An improved allocation of resources—which may result from such

[1]The original study by Denison was, *The Sources of Economic Growth in the United States and the Alternatives Before Us* (New York: Committee for Economic Development, 1962). Denison has subsequently updated his study several times.

Canadian studies of productivity growth include Dorothy Walters, *Canadian Growth Revisited, 1950–67,* staff study no. 28 (Ottawa: Economic Council of Canada, 1970), and Economic Council of Canada, *A Climate of Uncertainty: Seventeenth Annual Review* (Ottawa: Minister of Supply and Services Canada, 1980), Chapters 4–7.

Table 19-1

Sources of Growth in Real Income, Canada 1960–73 and 1973–78

(percent per year)

	1 1960–73	2 1973–78	3 (2-1) (Difference)
Growth of real national income	5.8	3.3	− 2.5
Contribution to growth by:			
Increase in labour hours	1.6	1.8	0.2
Increase in persons employed	2.3	2.8	0.5
Decrease in average hours worked	− 0.7	− 1.0	− 0.3
Increase in labour productivity	4.2	1.5	− 2.7
Improvement in quality of labour force	0.0	0.3	0.3
Education	0.5	0.6	0.1
Age-sex composition	− 0.5	− 0.3	0.2
Increase in capital	1.5	1.5	0.0
Improved resource allocation	0.2	− 0.1	− 0.3
More economies of scale	0.6	0.3	− 0.3
Change in capacity utilization	0.2	− 0.8	− 1.0
Advances in knowledge; residual	1.7	0.3	− 1.4

SOURCE: Adapted from John W. Kendrick, "International Comparisons of Recent Productivity Trends," in Sam H. Schurr, Sidney Sonenblum, and David O. Wood, eds., *Energy, Productivity, and Economic Growth* (Cambridge, Massachusetts: Oelgeschlager, Gunn & Hain Publishers, 1983), pp. 86–87.

factors as (1) lower barriers to international trade and (2) a gradual transfer of resources out of agriculture, where their productivity was lower than elsewhere— added 0.2 percentage points.

Increased economies of scale were estimated to have added 0.6 percentage points to the growth rate. The gains in real income from larger-scale production can come about in several ways. It may result from a larger Canadian demand for various products, so that each existing plant produces a larger volume of output. Or it may result from consolidation of production for the Canadian market in a smaller number of large-scale plants. Or again, the gains may come about as more and more Canadian firms try to take advantage of economies of scale by producing for the world market, rather than for the smaller Canadian market only. More intensive capacity utilization contributed another 0.2 percentage points.

Finally, "advances in knowledge," which includes a residual not explained elsewhere, accounted for as much as 1.7 percentage points, more than a third of the total growth. A significant source of growth in-

cluded in the residual is an **improvement in technology**; that is, new inventions, better designs of machinery, and better methods of production.

The most important conclusion from Kendrick's estimates is that growth resulted from a *combination* of causes. *No single determinant held the key to growth*, nor could any simple strategy—such as increasing investment in plant and equipment—hold out hope for a major acceleration of growth. Commenting on similar findings in a study of productivity in the United States, Denison observed: "The tale of the kingdom lost for want of a nail appears in poetry, not in history."

THE PUZZLE OF THE 1970s:
Why Was Growth So Disappointing?

As columns 2 and 3 in Table 19-1 show, the growth in labour productivity in the 1973–78 period was much less rapid than before 1973: the growth rate fell from 4.2% per year in 1960–73 to 1.5% per year in 1973–78. Kendrick's study shows that a similar slowdown occurred in most industrialized countries, including the United States, where productivity growth fell from an annual rate of 2.9% in 1960–73, to 1.2% in 1973–78. The poor productivity performance continued into the early 1980s both in Canada and the United States. What went wrong?

Part of the answer lies in cyclical factors. In 1973, aggregate demand and capacity utilization were high; in 1978 they remained weak following the worldwide recession in 1975 and the restrictive monetary policies of the Bank of Canada. As we shall see in more detail shortly, there is a tendency for productivity to vary systematically over the cycle. It tends to rise rapidly as the economy approaches a cyclical peak, and then to fall (or at least rise less rapidly) during recessionary periods. This kind of cyclical effect shows up in the "capacity utilization" item in Table 19-1: While rising capacity utilization contributed 0.2 percentage points to productivity growth during 1960–73, Kendrick estimates that *falling* capacity utilization *reduced* productivity growth by 0.8 percentage points during 1973–78.

Structural Shifts

The cyclical effect explains why *actual* productivity will fall when demand is weak, but it does not explain why *potential* productivity (after correcting for short-term cyclical factors) falls. What are the additional reasons for the decline in productivity?

One of the explanations appears to be that during 1973–78, we were less able than in earlier periods to increase productivity by reallocating resources from low-productivity industries to others in which their productivity was higher. For example, during earlier periods, there was a steady transfer of labour from low-productivity agriculture to other higher-productivity sectors. As a consequence, the nation's overall productivity improved. But in the 1970s, the structural shift of resources out of agriculture became much less important (in part because agriculture was already a relatively small part of the economy.) A more significant trend in the 1970s was the transfer of labour into the service industries; but in these industries, labour productivity tends to be *lower* than elsewhere in the economy.

Capital Accumulation and Economies of Scale

There is little disagreement that a high rate of capital accumulation will contribute to high productivity growth. Similarly, productivity will increase if firms

are able to take advantage of the economies of large-scale production. (Recall from Chapter 2 that economies of scale means that if labour and other inputs grow by 4%, say, output will grow by more than 4%.)

While the contribution of capital investment to growth in labour productivity remained the same (1.5 percentage points) during 1973–78 as in the earlier period, the contribution of scale economies to productivity appears to have fallen, according to Kendrick's estimates. This decline contributed 0.3 percentage points to the slowdown.

Changes in the Quality of the Labour Force

Increasing education of the labour force continued to make a substantial contribution to productivity growth during 1973–78. Similarly, the composition of the labour force continued to change, with more women and young people entering the labour force; their relative inexperience resulted in a reduction of productivity growth.

Recently, questions have been raised concerning the importance of the age-sex composition of the labour force as an explanation of productivity. The traditional analysis is based on the assumption that workers are paid according to their productivity. Since teenagers and women are paid less on average than prime-age males, it is therefore assumed that they produce less. There is something to this: Teenage males, for example, obviously have less experience than 40-year-old men, and if they make up a larger proportion of the labour force, this is likely to act as a drag on output per worker. But even here, we must be careful. The higher incomes of older men reflect not only experience (which contributes to productivity), but also seniority provisions which are common in employment contracts, and which may have little to do with productivity. (People get higher wages simply because they have been on the job longer, not because they produce more.) To the degree that the higher prime-age wage reflects seniority rather than greater productivity, the traditional estimates may be in error.

Similarly, to the extent that women's lower incomes are due to discrimination (rather than to differences in productivity), there is a second source of error. Similar arguments may be applied to the effect of increasing education on economic growth. Estimates of its contribution (such as those shown in Table 19-1) have been based on the assumption that people with more education are paid more because the skills thay have learned make them more productive. But some economists have suggested that the educational system has another function that is equally important—to provide employers with some way of telling which individuals are bright, and have the capacity and diligence to learn quickly on the job.

But to the extent that education merely serves to identify those individuals who are highly productive to begin with, rather than to *increase* the productivity of those receiving the education, the overall productivity of the labour force is not increased by having people spend more time in school. Because the traditional analysis is based on the assumption that more education increases an individual's productivity, it may overestimate the contribution of education to growing productivity.

The Mysterious Residual

The most striking aspect of the estimates in Table 19-1 is that *they leave a large part of the slowdown in productivity growth unexplained*. Comparing the 1960–73 period with 1973–78, productivity growth decreased by 2.7 percentage points. Out of this decrease, cyclical variation in capacity utilization accounted for 1 percentage point. Together, the other factors discussed above explain another 0.3 percentage points. The remaining decline of 1.4 percentage points is just a decline in the largely unexplained residual item "advances in knowledge." In a similar study of the productivity slowdown in the United States, Edward Denison was able to explain no more than 30% of the decline by looking at the traditional factors discussed above; over 70% of the slowdown was left unexplained.[2] Ruefully, Denison concluded: "What has happened is, to be blunt, a mystery".

SOME OTHER EXPLANATIONS

Because the traditional factors do not seem to explain much of the slower rate of productivity growth in

the 1970s, a number of alternative ones have been suggested.

First, some economists have suggested that part of the explanation lies in the *imperfect way in which we measure productivity*. For example, when we measure real output (the numerator of the productivity index), we usually measure the money value of the goods and services produced, and then deflate this value by a price index, to correct for price inflation. But, the critics point out, price increases for different goods and services may to a large extent reflect quality improvements. (For example, the price of a new car has increased a great deal since the 1960s. But some of this represents not inflation, but rather a higher payment for a higher-quality car that is safer and more fuel-efficient.) By failing to account for quality improvements, we overestimate inflation, which means that we underestimate real output increases and productivity growth.

This argument is certainly correct as far as it goes. But while it explains why we might generally underestimate real productivity growth, it does not explain why the rate of productivity growth *declined* in the 1970s. (There is no convincing evidence that the rate of quality improvement for various goods and services became faster during the seventies than it was in earlier decades.)

Another similar explanation for the disappointing productivity growth is the *increasingly stringent environmental regulations* that were introduced in the 1960s and 70s. These regulations have required the use of more of the nation's labour and capital for reducing pollution and increasing safety. But the benefits in terms of a better environment do not show up in measured GNP. Thus, our productivity in creating the good life may be increasing, even though our productivity in terms of measured GNP is falling.

While much of the environmental regulation has improved the quality of life, and thus has probably been worth the cost, there are other forms of regulation that may not have been as beneficial. They include numerous types of price and entry regulation (studied in detail in Chapter 27) in different industries and occupations. These regulations have been costly and may have reduced productivity growth, even though they have little effect on the quality of life.

Apart from regulation, there are two other factors that have frequently been mentioned as causes of the

---

[2]Denison's analysis was based on *potential* output (with the cyclical effects removed), while the estimates in Table 19-1 are based on *actual* output, which includes cyclical effects. If cyclical effects are excluded, the factors shown in Table 19-1 would have explained less than 20% of the Canadian productivity slowdown.

productivity slowdown: a decrease in the *rate of technological improvement*, and the *rise in world energy prices*.

Research and Development

In the United States, the suggestion that a decline in the rate of technological improvement may be to blame for slower productivity growth has been largely motivated by an observed decline in the rate of spending on research and development (R&D). However, Denison, in a study of the U.S. productivity slowdown in the 1970s, is skeptical that smaller R&D explains much of the disappointing U.S. performance. As a percentage of U.S. GNP, R&D expenditures did decline, from a peak of 3.0% in 1964 to 2.3% in 1977. But this decline was gradual, and it is hard to see how it could account for the abrupt deterioration in the growth of output per U.S. worker in 1973–74. Furthermore, the decline in R&D was concentrated in the government category, mostly for weapons and space research. Private R&D expenditures—that is, expenditures by industries and universities, which make the greatest contribution to higher output—remained relatively stable from 1970 to 1977 as a percentage of GNP.

Canada also had a decline in R&D expenditures relative to GNP: From a peak of almost 1.3% of GNP, R&D expenditures had fallen to less than 1% of GNP by 1980. But again, it seems unlikely that this decrease was a major explanation of the sharp drop in Canada's productivity growth during the 1970s, partly because the decrease was so gradual, and partly because R&D spending is less important relative to GNP in Canada than in the United States.

A related explanation of slowing productivity growth has been advanced by U.S. economist F.M. Scherer. His suggestion is that the *payoff* from R&D expenditures has become lower because the underlying scientific base has already been substantially exploited. As evidence, Scherer cites the decline in the number of new patents issued to U.S. domestic corporations since 1971.[3]

In Canada the total number of new patents issued each year also fell during the 1970s, from over 30,000 in 1970 to less than 25,000 in 1978. However, it is interesting to note that the number of Canadian patents

issued to *domestic* residents remained relatively stable (at about 2,000 per year). Most of the decline in the total number of patents was due to a fall in the number of Canadian patents issued to foreign (mostly U.S.) residents. Hence, part of the explanation for slower productivity growth in Canada may be a decrease in the contribution to Canadian growth of new technology imported into Canada from foreign countries.

The Increase in Energy Prices

The rise in energy prices is perhaps the most interesting of the remaining possible explanations for slower productivity growth in the 1970s. Energy prices are an obvious scapegoat, since they could explain the timing of the sharp deterioration after 1973–74 when the price of oil skyrocketed. Moreover, the higher oil price might explain why the growth rate declined abruptly in *many* countries at about this time.

In a study of productivity in the 1970s, the Economic Council of Canada did indeed find that in the mid-1970s, following the 1973–74 price increases, the amount of energy per unit of output declined in a majority of industries. But the Council was skeptical of the suggestion that this was a major cause of the overall productivity slowdown. The principal reason was that the amount of energy per unit of output did not decrease by very much. (If it had fallen sharply, this would have indicated the adoption of different and probably less productive methods of doing business. But, since oil use did not fall much, it is difficult to explain the productivity deterioration in this way.)

In spite of the Council's findings, many economists continue to believe that the large increases in energy prices must have been one of the most important explanations for the disappointing Canadian productivity performance in the 1970s. After all, not only did productivity growth slow down sharply in 1974 in Canada and the United States (and in the rest of the world as well); it also fell dramatically again in 1979–80, following the second sharp increase in OPEC's oil prices. The coincidence is too strong to ignore.

This raises the question of whether oil prices could have had greater effects on productivity than the Economic Council (and others) estimated. There are several reasons for believing that this may have been the case. In the first place, considerable new investment was required in response to the higher oil prices—for example, in the automobile industry, which had to go

---

[3] F.M. Scherer, "Technological Maturity and Waning Economic Growth," in *Arts and Sciences*, Northwestern University (Fall 1978).

through a complete retooling to produce smaller cars. Such investments do not show up in large current reductions in oil consumption by industry. Yet they do make a major claim on capital resources. Furthermore, business executives spent much time and effort trying to figure out how best to respond to higher energy prices.

In summary, we have a fair idea of what some of the important factors are that explained Canada's poor productivity performance in the 1970s. And circumstantial evidence suggests that rising oil prices may have been a more important factor than formerly believed. But *we simply do not know with any degree of confidence the reasons for the drastic deterioration in the productivity performance of the Canadian economy during the 1970s.*

THE 1980s: A RENEWAL OF VIGOROUS GROWTH?

If we had a more precise idea of what happened a decade ago, we would be in a better position to interpret the recent signs of an upturn in productivity, shown in Figure 19-2. For example, if we knew that spiralling oil prices really were the major culprit in the productivity slowdown, we would expect productivity to have rebounded with the falling oil prices in the mid-1980s.

However, it is not just our lack of knowledge of what happened in the 1970s that makes it hard to tell whether the early 1980s mark the beginning of a new period of vigorous growth. We should avoid coming to firm conclusions from *any* brief period, because year-to-year changes in productivity can be strongly affected by the business cycle.

Cyclical Swings in Productivity
During cyclical recoveries, productivity generally increases very rapidly. During recessions, it generally increases very slowly, or even declines. Why?

A major reason is that employment is sticky in the face of fluctuating demand. Many white-collar workers are on annual salaries, and cannot easily be laid off during recessions. Nor is it costless to lay off production-line workers. They may get jobs elsewhere and be unavailable when the company wants to expand.

Because of the costs of hiring and training, a company's labour force represents an investment which may be lost if workers are laid off. As the economy slides into a recession, firms therefore reduce their employment less than their output. Because underemployed workers are retained, productivity suffers. Then, as economic conditions improve and output recovers, the slack is picked up. Firms can increase their output rapidly without adding many new workers. As a result, productivity rises rapidly during the recovery from a recession.

Figure 19-2 shows how productivity declined or stagnated during the recessions of 1974–75 and 1980. And while 1977–79 were not recession years, the weak productivity performance in these years can be explained partly by the fact that they were years of weak demand and slow growth of real output.

However, not all recessions have an equal effect on productivity. The recession of 1982 was much more severe than that of 1980. Yet productivity actually increased during 1982. One reason was that many firms had already been weakened by the recession of 1980. In order to survive in the face of the severe recession of 1982, they felt that they had to give up their practice of retaining underutilized workers, and they cut their workforce. The 1982 recession was tough for white-collar workers, as well as for those on the production line. Many lost their jobs. There were two major results. The unemployment rate rose unusually rapidly. However, because labour input was being cut drastically, productivity was stronger than usual for a deep recession. In brief, business cycles can have strong, but uneven, effects on productivity.

What, then, are we to make of the large increase in productivity during the years 1983–85? Is it just the result of the cyclical expansion from the depths of the 1982 recession? Or should we come to the more optimistic conclusion that it is the beginning of a new upward trend? While it may be too early to tell yet, some observers argue that there are several reasons for optimism: falling energy prices, a tendency toward reduced regulation, and the emergence of promising computer-based technology in many sectors of the economy. However, predictions concerning future productivity growth should be interpreted cautiously: Past experience does not inspire confidence in our ability to predict productivity performance.

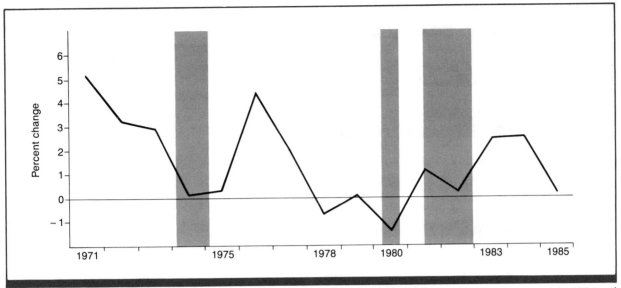

Figure 19-2   Annual changes in labour productivity, 1974–1985.

During recessions, productivity is weak. Notice how productivity stagnated or actually declined during the recessions of 1974–75 and 1980. On the other hand, productivity expands rapidly during cyclical expansions, as in 1976 and 1983–84.

Source: Compiled from Statistics Canada, *CANSIM Databank*. Reprinted by permission of the Minister of Supply and Services Canada.

INTERNATIONAL COMPARISONS

Figure 19-3 confirms that the slowdown in productivity growth that occurred in Canada and the United States also affected other industrialized countries. But Figure 19-3 also illustrates another important fact that has raised some concern. While Canada had a faster rate of productivity growth than the United States in the 1960s and 1970s, productivity grew considerably faster in European countries such as Germany and France, and especially in Japan, than in either the United States *or* Canada.

Three principal explanations have been offered for the slower productivity improvement in North America in the 1960s and 1970s: (1) Countries that are catching up can copy North American technology, (2) capital investment in North America is low by international standards, and (3) cultural differences give an advantage to some countries, particularly Japan.

Borrowed Technology?

Paradoxically, one reason why countries such as France, Germany, and Japan had higher rates of productivity growth in the past was that their economies were less technologically advanced than those in North America. In the countries that are already using the most advanced technology, further technological improvement is costly: It requires a flow of new inventions. Although some ideas come in a brilliant flash, most research and development is painstaking, expensive, and yields results only gradually. Consequently, productivity improvement from this source is relatively slow. For less advanced countries, however, productivity growth depends not only on the development of new technology; it can also result from *copying* of technology that has already been developed in more advanced countries. Since this can be done more easily and yields faster results, productivity growth in less advanced countries tends to be faster.

However, this explanation was much more valid 20 years ago than it is today. Although North America retains the lead in many areas of technology, other countries have closed much of the gap. Japan is ahead in robotics, and productivity in Japanese automobile factories surpasses that in the United States. It is American car manufacturers who are now copying the

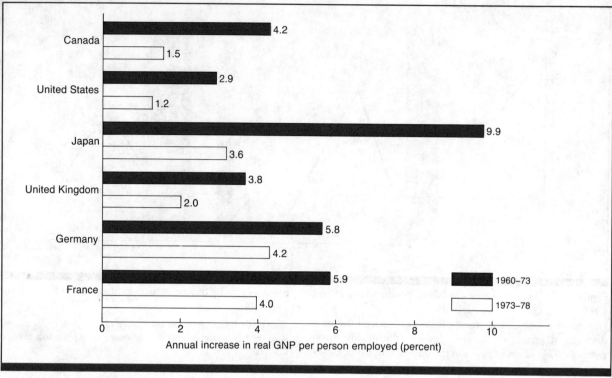

Figure 19-3 Productivity changes: International comparisons.

Productivity increases in Canada have been faster than in the United States. However, productivity in Japan, Germany, and France has been growing substantially faster than in either the United States or Canada.

Source: John W. Kendrick, "International Comparisons of Recent Productivity Trends", in Sam H. Schurr, Sidney Sonenblum, and David O. Wood, eds., *Energy, Productivity, and Economic Growth* (Cambridge, Massachusetts: Oelgeschlager, Gunn & Hain Publishers, 1983), pp. 86–87.

Japanese. Furthermore, the position of North America, and particularly the United States, as the leader in developing new technology, has been eroded in recent years. Twenty years ago, other countries could copy North American technology, and they could grow rapidly in spite of their lower R&D expenditures. However, as the technology gap has closed, foreign R&D has grown rapidly, particularly in Germany and Japan. These countries are counting more and more on domestic technology to maintain their high rates of growth.

Low Investment

Investment is one of the major sources of growth, and low investment is frequently cited as a major reason for lagging productivity in North America. According to Kendrick's comparative study on which Figure 19-3 is based, a low rate of investment was a particularly important factor in explaining slow productivity

growth in the United States. In Canada, the investment rate has been higher than in the United States, but in Canada too, the contribution of investment to productivity growth has been much lower than in countries such as Germany and Japan. One secret of Japan's success is really no secret at all: The Japanese have put a large percentage of their GNP into investment.

Cultural Differences?

The Japanese, it is sometimes argued, have a major advantage because of their strong cultural traditions. In their crowded islands, individuals are continually reminded of their duties to society. This gives Japanese businesses an advantage, because they have a committed labour force which is willing to pay meticulous attention to quality.

It is hard to know how much of the Japanese reputation for quality is the result of cultural differences, and how much is due to management practices. Major Japanese firms are committed to provide lifetime employment for many of their workers. Workers have a greater stake in their company's future, and this may explain their attention to quality. However, in its U.S. plant, Honda has been able to maintain Japanese-level quality, suggesting that it is management, rather than culture, which provides the primary explanation for quality.

WHY GROW?

Slow growth in North America has led to a search for ways to promote growth. But, before turning to policies designed to increase productivity and growth, we consider an even more fundamental issue: *Should* we strive for a higher rate of growth?

A Rising Material Standard of Living

At first glance, it might seem obvious that growth is desirable. Higher output makes possible a higher material standard of living. Even small changes in rates of growth can compound into large differences over long periods of time. If output increases by 1% a year, it doubles every 70 years. But if it rises by 2% per year, it doubles every 35 years, and *quadruples* every 70. (The growth rate in the average standard of living also depends on the rate of growth of the population; the trade-off between population and economic growth is briefly discussed in Box 19-1.)

However, we should not simply assume that the faster the economy grows, the better. If our overriding goal is faster growth, we may sacrifice other important goals, such as *current consumption*, a *cleaner environment*, and *leisure*.

1. The cost of investment: Current consumption foregone. As we noted in Chapter 2, one way to grow faster is to invest more. But when we invest more, we give up the consumer goods we alternatively could have produced today. Even though investment now will make it possible for us to produce more consumer goods in the future, there is a limit to how far we should pursue a high-growth policy. At some point, it makes no sense to reduce our current consumption further, just so our children or grandchildren can live in splendour in the future.

2. The environment. E.J. Mishan, formerly of the London School of Economics, has argued that growth—as usually measured by GNP—is a mirage, since goods and services are included, but the degradation of the environment and the "uglification" of the countryside are ignored.[4]

One way to increase the rate of growth of GNP would be to eliminate government regulations to improve the environment and increase safety. The expenditures on these objectives could then be used for investment, thereby increasing our output. But, while GNP would grow faster, we would not necessarily be better off. Even though clean air is not included in GNP, it is nevertheless important.

3. Leisure. As we saw in Chapter 7, GNP also excludes leisure. During the twentieth century, the average work week has become substantially shorter. We *could* have had more growth by taking less leisure. But we would not necessarily have been better off.

CHANGING ATTITUDES TOWARD GROWTH

During our early history, the common attitude was that the government should assist in the opening of the new land. The Dominion Land Act of 1879 reflected this view. It gave the right to any settler to claim 160 acres of Crown land for farming purposes, and the settler was given permanent title to the land if he could show that he had been using at least part of it for food production. And, during the nineteenth century, the government granted extensive subsidies and substantial blocks of land to the Canadian Pacific Railway, providing not only the right-of-way needed for its lines, but also additional lands whose value would rise as new western territories were opened up.[5]

The prevailing view into the twentieth century was that growth was obviously a worthwhile goal, which business and government should pursue in partnership. In the United States, the government's role in stimulating growth was initially seen as fairly limited; its main function was to provide a favourable milieu in which private enterprise would bring about growth. In Canada, on the other hand, the government has always

---

[4]E.J. Mishan, *Technology and Growth* (New York: Praeger, 1969).
[5]For a fascinating history of the CPR, see Pierre Berton, *The National Dream: The Great Railway, 1871–1881* (Toronto: McClelland and Stewart, 1970) and Pierre Berton, *The Last Spike: The Great Railway, 1881–1885* (Toronto: McClelland and Stewart, 1971).

been more active in promoting growth, by subsidizing private projects, or by investing public money in specific enterprises considered beneficial to growth. The federal involvement in rail and air transportation, through Crown corporations such as the CNR and Air Canada, or the provincial governments' investment in industries such as hydroelectric power genera-

tion or telephone services, are examples of this more active role. (In the United States, these industries are generally in private hands.)

During the 1930s and 1940s, the objective of raising the economy's productive capacity was pushed into the background, for obvious reasons. During the Great Depression, the problem was not to raise pro-

---

BOX 19-1

POPULATION GROWTH AND ECONOMIC GROWTH: THE BIG TRADE-OFF

Growth may result from an increase in production *per capita*—an increase which makes possible a rising standard of living. It may also result from an increase in population. In examining how population and growth are related, one must consider the difficult issue of whether there is an "optimal" population. Clearly this involves fundamental social values which go well beyond economics, but the size of the population also has economic implications.

If the population grows, there are two conflicting effects on per capita output. Most obviously, there is a depressing effect. With more people and a larger labour force, there are less capital and fewer natural resources at the disposal of the typical worker. On the other hand, a larger population and a larger market may raise the standard of living by making possible economies of large-scale production.

For some countries in some periods of history— for example, Canada before the twentieth century— population was small, while resources were abundant. In these cases, economies of scale were the more important influence. A rising population contributed to an increase in per capita income. But such cases are rare. In most countries, certainly in modern times, the population is large enough to be pressing on resources, especially in some less developed countries where limited agricultural resources make it difficult to feed the population, but also in industrialized countries where the depletion of resources such as timber or fresh water is posing

increasing problems. Resource restraints are the more important of the two influences. While a 10% increase in population causes an increase in production, the increase is less than 10%. Therefore, the additional population depresses *per capita* output.

Hence, a question arises: Do we want a larger population if it holds down per capita output and income? In, say, 50 years, is it desirable to have a larger population than today, even though our standard of living may be held in check by the population growth? Or would it be better to have about the same population as today, with a much higher income per capita? Would it be better yet to have a declining population, with a *very* much higher income per capita? This is not a question for an economist, but for a moral philosopher. There is nothing in economic analysis that allows us to answer the question of whether one life is "worth" more or less than two lives with a lower income per capita.

One answer that is sometimes suggested is that there is an "optimal" population, namely that population where *per capita income is at a maximum*. But this argument is based on the implicit judgement that additional lives have no value if they depress per capita income. It is not clear what the basis for this judgement might be. Most families reject it whenever they decide to have a child, since their per capita income is reduced as a result. And if individual families prefer children rather than a higher per capita income, shouldn't society as a whole do the same? On the other hand, we may ask: Do families really take properly into account that their decisions (and those of other families) to have additional children may ultimately put intolerable pressure on global resources? There are no easy answers to these questions; perhaps they are better answered by moral philosophers than by economists.

ductive capacity, but rather to put the existing capacity to work and reduce unemployment. Then during the war years, all available capacity had to be used for the war effort. But during the 1950s and 1960s, growth again became an important policy goal, for several reasons. For one thing, there was the perceived challenge of the Communist nations. To use the catchwords of the time, the North American economies were in a race to "keep ahead of the Russians," to prevent the Soviet Union from using a more rapid rate of growth to increase its political influence among the less-developed countries (LDCs), and attain superiority in armaments production. In retrospect, these arguments were based on an exaggerated estimate of Soviet growth. In spite of the fears of 1960, the mixed economies of Western Europe, Japan, and North America remain substantially ahead of the Soviet Union, particularly in the mass production of consumer goods, in the development of high-technology products, and in agriculture.

But there were also other strong arguments for growth: The 1960s were years of rapid expansion of services provided by the federal and provincial governments in education and health care and in strengthening our social welfare programs. All these policies required resources that could be provided only by a strong growth performance. During the years of the Pearson administration in the mid-sixties, we also began to take seriously our commitment to help people in the LDCs by increasing foreign aid. This, too, required resources and growth. In the United States, Kennedy and his advisors considered a rapid rate of growth highly desirable for many reasons. Not only would greater investment promote high employment; but some of the increase in production could also be used to improve the lot of "The Other America"[6]—that is, the relatively invisible Americans who live in poverty.

But by the 1970s, many Canadians and Americans were having doubts that faster growth was desirable. In part, this seemed to be a retreat from the ambitions and enthusiasm of the 1960s. The rapid expansion of health, education, and other social programs was proving increasingly expensive, and in spite of large amounts of foreign aid, economic and social conditions in the

LDCs did not seem to improve very quickly.

There were also more direct doubts that growth should be a prime objective. Increasing attention was given to the environment and other competing goals. And, after the first great increase in the price of oil in 1973–74, there was concern that a growth in output might put intolerable pressures on natural resources.

However, as the 1970s drew to a close, the pendulum was beginning to swing back toward productivity and growth as national objectives. Faster growth was desired not only for the additional goods and services that would be available, but also because the greater supply of goods and services would reduce inflationary pressures.

"SUPPLY-SIDE" ECONOMICS: A NEW GROWTH POLICY?

The new concern with growth in the late 1970s and early 1980s represented a major change in emphasis in macroeconomics. Since the "Keynesian Revolution," the major preoccupation of macroeconomists had been with demand management—that is, with the adjustment of fiscal and monetary policies to provide enough aggregate demand to ensure a low unemployment rate, but not so much as to cause inflation. But the poor productivity performance of the late 1970s drew attention to the fact that output depends not only on aggregate demand, but also on the ability of the economy to supply goods and services.

Some changes in Canadian federal tax laws in the early 1980s can be seen as a reflection of an increasing emphasis on *supply-side* policy. Marginal tax rates in high-income brackets were reduced, and capital gains were exempted from personal income tax (up to a specified maximum). Tax credits were given to individuals who invested in firms undertaking research and development. These tax changes were aimed at promoting growth in three ways: (1) by encouraging savings and investment, (2) by encouraging people to work more, and (3) by promoting innovation and technological change.

In the United States, the change of policy was more dramatic, especially in the early Reagan administration, when massive supply-side tax reductions were implemented. Personal income taxes were cut by almost one-quarter, and corporate taxes were reduced, both directly (through lower tax *rates*) and indirectly (through

---

[6] *The Other America*, by Michael Harrington (Baltimore: Penguin Books, 1962), described the bleak existence of the poor in the United States.

changes in the rules according to which firms may depreciate new investments); corporations were also given tax credits for research and development expenses.

Proponents of these tax changes not only expected that they would increase the capacity of the economy to supply more goods and services. They also hoped that the tax changes would enable the government to control inflation in a relatively painless way.

Reducing Inflation without Recession?

As we saw in Chapter 17, macroeconomic policymakers face a cruel dilemma, at least in the short run. If demand is suppressed in order to fight inflation, the unemployment rate may shoot up. Figure 19-4 illustrates how supply siders hoped to escape from this dilemma. If the aggregate supply curve can be shifted to the right, from AS_1 to AS_2, the economy will move from A to B. Rising output will go hand in hand with success in fighting inflation.

There is no doubt that a rightward shift in aggregate supply makes it easier to suppress inflation without causing unemployment. The question is, how strong is this favourable effect? How much can the aggregate supply curve be shifted? Over any short-term period, the answer is: not much. It is very difficult to raise the growth rate by as much as 1% per year. Yet this causes only a small shift in aggregate supply in any one year.

In practice, shifts in aggregate supply were completely overshadowed by shifts in demand during the early 1980s. Inflation was reduced substantially, from 12.5% in 1981 to 4.4% in 1984. However, the major reason for the lower inflation was not a shift in aggregate supply. Instead, the major reason was a decline in aggregate demand and the deep recession of 1981–82.

Cutting Taxes without Losing Revenue?

Some of the more enthusiastic supply-side economists not only believed that inflation could be licked without causing unemployment. They also believed that tax rates could be cut without the government losing revenue.

This idea was put forward most explicitly by Arthur Laffer of the University of Southern California, who drew the *Laffer curve* shown in Figure 19-5. This curve illustrates the relationship between tax rates and total government revenues. If the tax rate is zero, no

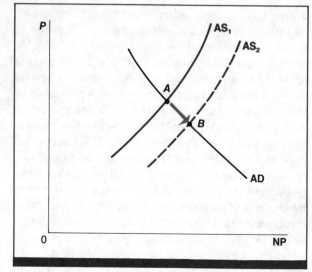

Figure 19-4   A supply-side tax cut.
Supply-side economists expect that a cut in taxes will lead to a rightward shift in the aggregate supply curve, as illustrated by the shift from AS_1 to AS_2. If aggregate demand remains stable, equilibrium will move from A to B. There will be two favourable effects: Output will be greater, and inflation lower.

revenues are collected. On the other hand, if the tax rate is 100%, once again revenues are zero; nobody will work to earn income if the government taxes it all away. People will either loaf, or, more likely, spend their time finding ways—legal or otherwise—to avoid the tax.

At some intermediate tax rate, T_m, revenues are at a maximum. If the tax rate is below this level, say at T_1, a tax increase will cause little change in work effort and tax avoidance. Therefore, a tax increase will cause a rise in government revenues. For example, as taxes rise from T_1 to T_2, revenues increase from R_1 to R_2. On the other hand, if taxes are initially *above* T_m —at T_3, for example—then a further increase in the rate to T_4 will cause enough idleness and tax evasion that the total taxes collected by the government will decrease, from R_3 to R_4.

The question is whether the initial tax rate is above or below the maximum revenue rate, T_m. Although we know that revenues are zero if the tax rate is either zero or 100%, we do not know how high T_m is. For example, the curve could be the dashed L_2 rather than L_1. Laffer believed that the U.S. economy was already above T_m in 1980, in the range where a tax increase

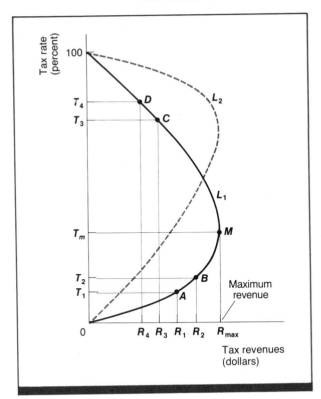

Figure 19-5   The Laffer curve.
The Laffer curve illustrates the relationship between tax rates (T) and government revenues (R). If the tax rate is zero, no revenues are collected. If the rate is 100%, revenues are likewise zero, since nobody will earn income for the government to confiscate. At some intermediate point, M, tax revenues are maximized.

leads to a fall in government revenue. In other words, a *cut* in the tax rate would lead to an *increase* in revenues. Thus, a tax cut would be a painless policy, benefitting the public while reducing the government's deficits.

Laffer's claim was implausible. Suppose, for example, that personal income is initially $300 billion, and the average tax rate is 20%. The government collects $60 billion. If the tax rate is now cut by one-quarter, to 15%, personal income will have to increase to $400 billion if government revenues are to remain stable ($400 × 15% = $60). It is not clear how a cut in the tax rate could cause such a huge increase in income.

In practice, things did not turn out as supply-siders hoped. The Reagan tax cuts of 1981 did not generate

additional tax revenues. Instead, government deficits ballooned.

Do Tax Cuts Promote Growth? Incentives vs. Crowding Out

When supply siders predicted that tax cuts would lower inflation and generate more revenues, they touched off a lively debate. But there is an even more fundamental issue: Do supply-side tax cuts in fact promote investment and growth?

At first glance, the answer would seem to be an obvious "yes." Tax incentives— such as accelerated depreciation—promote investment, and investment promotes growth. But unfortunately, the answer is not quite so simple. Tax cuts set in motion other forces that can depress the rate of growth.

Specifically, the larger deficits caused by the tax cuts can "crowd out" investment, as explained in Chapter 14. In order to finance its deficit spending, the government borrows on the financial markets. This creates upward pressures on interest rates. In turn, higher interest rates discourage investment.

Thus, tax cuts create two conflicting forces. The direct effect of tax incentives is to increase investment. But investment is discouraged by the indirect effects, working through higher deficits and higher interest rates. It is not clear which of these effects is stronger.

COOPERATION BETWEEN BUSINESS AND GOVERNMENT

In the business community, it is a widely held belief that one of the principal explanations for our disappointing productivity performance is the increasing cost and effort that has to be devoted by business to dealing with various levels of government. A common attitude is that business could be much more productive if only government would leave it in peace.

One major source of aggravation is regulation. While most businessmen, both in large corporations and small firms, understand and sympathize with the need for health, safety, and environmental regulation, they are upset at the complications and delays that arise because of confusion in the regulatory process. In a study on Canadian regulation, businessmen complained about "time consuming delays in obtaining approvals and . . . excessively finicky requirements for documentation and testing, and . . . expressed frustration at the number of agencies and levels of government involved in regulatory situations."[7]

Some tension is, of course, inevitable when government regulations impose costs on businesses. But both the government and the business community have become concerned about the degree of tension, and the feeling of business executives that they are being harassed.

Partly in response to these concerns, some steps toward regulatory reform were taken in the first half of the 1980s. An important part of the reform process was a comprehensive study by the Economic Council of Canada of all forms of regulation by the federal and provincial governments. In its 1981 report, the Council made wide-ranging proposals for regulatory reform. However, deregulation is not a simple matter. One problem is how to streamline the regulatory process and eliminate excessively detailed and inconsistent regulation, while still giving appropriate weight to other social goals, such as safety and cleaner air. Another major issue is how to protect the interest of various groups in society (such as farmers) through regulation, without reducing the productive efficiency of the industries in which they work. These issues are discussed more fully in Part 6.

An Industrial Strategy?

Some proponents of growth want to achieve even closer co-operation, and do more than simply reduce tension between business and government. One common suggestion is for Canada to develop an *industrial strategy*. An attempt would be made to identify the most promising products for future development. Research grants or other government programs could then be used to encourage resources to move into the future "winners," and out of declining industries.

Although the proposal to "pick winners" seems attractive, such a policy poses substantial risks. It may be as difficult for governments as for racetrack bettors to pick winners. Governments may in fact be less able than capital markets to pick winners. Before investing in a company, private individuals or firms have a great

incentive to investigate it carefully, until they are convinced that it is a likely winner. But, in deciding how to invest the public's money, a politician has two separate objectives: to "pick winners" with a high economic payoff, and to "pick winners" that gain votes. Thus, rather than picking the economic winners (as the Japanese sometimes—but not always—do), the Canadian government might end up picking losers, as the British and Italian governments sometimes do. The government might come to the aid of corporations in danger of collapse. Consequently, an industrial strategy might lead to "lemon socialism"—that is, government ownership and support of dying companies.

One problem is that proposals for an industrial policy are motivated by two quite different objectives:

1. to encourage new, high-productivity industries
2. to help declining industries

Those who focus on the second objective express alarm that the North American economies are "de-industrializing" as fewer and fewer workers find employment in the older, heavy industries. A number of business leaders have jumped on the industrial policy bandwagon, hoping that it will lead to protection from foreign competition. But the more attention is paid to propping up declining industries, the less likely it is that an industrial policy would add to the dynamism and productivity of the economy.

Conclusion: Uncertainties about Growth and Productivity

If one thing stands out in this chapter, it should be this: Growth and productivity are complex phenomena. We understand their causes only imperfectly—as illustrated by the large, mysterious residual in studies of the sources of productivity growth. And there is great uncertainty about the best policies to stimulate productivity. In particular, the relatively simple policies offered by some supply-side economists and industrial policy advocates seem to be based on weak foundations. There is no single, simple key to unlock the door to higher productivity; there is no "horseshoe nail" to save our "kingdom."

[7]Economic Council of Canada, *Reforming Regulation* (Ottawa: Minister of Supply and Services Canada, 1981), p. 123.

KEY POINTS

1. The growth of output depends on the combined effect of increases in (1) the number of hours worked, and (2) labour productivity.

2. Productivity grew most rapidly in the 1940–60 period. This corresponded to the slowest rate of growth of labour hours. Productivity growth was slow during the second half of the 1970s when labour hours were increasing rapidly.

3. Studies of productivity growth have shown that a number of factors contributed to rapid productivity growth before the mid-1970s. No single cause was the "key" to rapid growth.

4. A large part of the deterioration in Canada's productivity performance since 1973 cannot be accounted for by traditional factors. However, those who have analysed this problem may have underestimated the effects of R&D and the increase in the price of oil.

5. Productivity improved rapidly in 1983–85, and the economy grew vigorously. It is unclear how much of this was due to the recovery from the recession, and how much was due to an increase in the underlying growth trend of the economy. It is too early to say whether or not we are on a new, vigorous growth path.

6. We should not simply assume that the faster the growth rate, the better. If we single-mindedly pursue the growth objective, we may give insufficient attention to other goals, such as current consumption, a clean environment, and leisure.

7. There has been a cycle in attitudes toward growth. The policies of the 1950s and 1960s emphasized growth. Then doubts about growth increased in the late 1960s and early 1970s. By the late 1970s and early 1980s, the growth issue regained the attention of policymakers.

8. Supply-side economists advocate tax cuts as a way of increasing the capacity of the economy to supply goods and services. They believe that tax cuts will shift the aggregate supply curve to the right by promoting saving, investment, hard work, and efficiency. They also suggest that tax cuts provide an escape from difficult trade-offs. When the supply curve shifts to the right, inflation may be reduced without creating unemployment. Some enthusiastic supply-siders suggest that tax rates may be cut without losing any government revenue; the lower rates may be offset by higher incomes on which taxes are collected. The large U.S. deficits of recent years suggest that this view is too optimistic.

9. Tax cuts increase the profitability of investments, and thus encourage businesses to invest. However, there is also a force working in the opposite direction. Tax cuts increase government deficits. When the government borrows, it puts upward pressure on interest rates, and the higher interest rates discourage investment (the "crowding-out" effect). It is not clear whether the net effect of these two forces is an increase or a decrease in investment.

10. Another proposal for stimulating growth is for government to adopt an industrial strategy to help "winners." One risk in this policy is that the government might in practice slip into "lemon socialism," helping losers and keeping resources in low-productivity industries.

KEY CONCEPTS

average productivity of labour
technological improvement

supply-side tax cuts
Laffer curve

industrial policy
lemon socialism

PROBLEMS

19-1 Why might a rapid increase in population cause a drag on productivity? Are there any circumstances in which a rapid increase in population might encourage a rapid increase in productivity?

19-2 Observe in Figure 19-1 that the rate of growth of labour hours in the 1926–40 period was almost as slow as in 1940-60. But the rate of growth of productivity was substantially less rapid. That is, productivity did not grow as rapidly between 1926 and 1940 as we might expect simply by looking at the low rate of growth of labour hours. Were there any events during this period that acted as a drag on productivity? Explain how they acted to keep productivity from increasing more rapidly.

19-3 During recessions, productivity generally expands very slowly, or even declines. On the other hand, it generally expands very rapidly as the economy recovers from recession. Explain why. The 1982 recession was more severe than that of 1980, but productivity nevertheless held up better in 1982 than in 1980. How can this be explained?

19-4 How might an increase in energy prices cause a slowdown in productivity? Which of your explanations will show up in a reduction in the quantity of oil used? In 1985–86, oil prices *fell* rapidly. Do you think that this will cause productivity growth to increase? Why or why not?

19-5 Opponents of an industrial strategy fear that government aid to specific industries would end up by helping the "losers." Can you think of possible examples of this danger in recent Canadian history? Can you think of any ways an industrial strategy might be designed to reduce this danger?

19-6 Explain how supply-side policies might make it possible to achieve both higher output and lower rates of inflation at the same time. Illustrate your answer with a diagram.

19-7 One of the ideas behind supply-side economics is that, if taxes are cut and people are left with more disposable income, they will work more. Some evidence on this point is provided in Figure 1-1, which shows how the work week has changed as living standards have risen. Since 1900, has the work week increased or decreased as incomes have risen? Is this also true in the period since 1950? How do you explain the way in which the work week has changed? What tentative conclusion can we come to about the relationship between people's incomes and their willingness to work?

Part Five

MICROECONOMICS: IS OUR OUTPUT PRODUCED EFFICIENTLY?

Parts 2, 3, and 4 have focused on unemployment and inflation, the two great problems in macroeconomics. Now that we have taken this broad overview of the economic "forest," we turn to a more detailed examination of the "trees." Thus, the microeconomic analysis that follows in parts 5, 6, and 7 will involve an examination of the individual producers of goods and services—such as Northern Telecom or the Nova Scotia apple grower—and the individual consumers who purchase telephones and apples. This study of the economy "in the small" is directed to the three questions introduced in Chapter 4: *What* is produced? *How* is it produced? *For whom* is it produced? In parts 5 and 6 we will deal with the first two questions, just introducing the question of *for whom,* which will be taken up in detail in Part 7.

In Part 5 our focus will be on efficiency. One might well ask: "Because Parts 2, 3, and 4 were concerned with unemployment, were they not also devoted to the question of efficiency?" The answer is a clear yes. Historically, unemployment has been a major source of economic inefficiency. Idle labour and idle capital have meant the loss of output that could have been produced. We have also seen that severe inflation causes inefficiency. If the price system breaks down because of inflation and no longer gives the clear signals on which business planning must be based, decision making deteriorates and the nation's output is less as a consequence.

Recognizing that these sources of inefficiency are important, we now turn our attention in Part 5 to the additional reasons why our economy may be inefficient. To isolate these new sources of difficulty, we shall assume away the two great macroeconomic problems of inflation and unemployment. In other words, *we now assume that there is no general rise in prices or large-scale unemployment.* Even if these extremely favourable assumptions were realized, there would still be reasons why we might not be making the most of our productive ability. Specifically, we might be producing too much of one good and not enough of some other. That is one of the major problems to be studied in Part 5.

In this study of microeconomics, we begin by picking up the demand and supply curves devel-oped in Chapter 4. A brief review of those curves is provided in the following box, entitled "Re-member?" If you don't remember, we strongly recommend that you reread Chapter 4.

REMEMBER?

Demand . . .

The quantity of apples demanded depends on the price of apples . . .

. . . and other influences, such as the price of bananas, changing tastes, or changing consumer income.

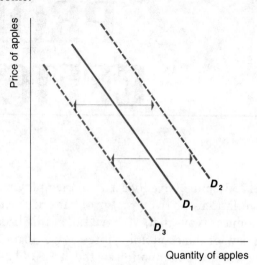

In this panel, we see that if the price of apples rises, the quantity demanded becomes smaller. Such a movement along a given demand curve is described as a "decrease in the quantity demanded."

In this panel, we see that if one of the other influ-ences changes, the demand curve shifts. For exam-ple, if income rises, the demand curve shifts from D_1 to D_2.

On the other hand, if income falls, the demand curve shifts to D_3. This leftward shift in the curve is described as a "decrease in demand."

Supply

The quantity of apples supplied depends on the price of apples . . .

. . . and other influences such as the weather, the price of fertilizer and other inputs, changing technology, and the prices of alternative outputs like wheat.

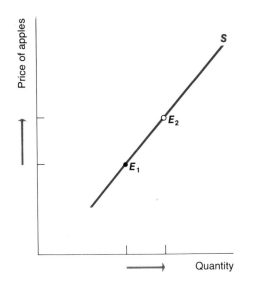

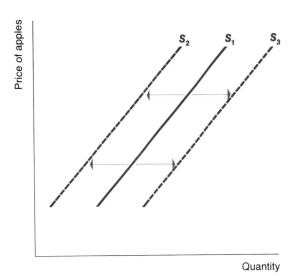

In this panel, we see that if the price of apples increases, equilibrium moves up the supply curve. Such a movement is referred to as an "increase in the quantity supplied."

In this panel, we see that if one of these other influences changes, the supply curve shifts. For example, if the price of fertilizer or some other input rises, the supply curve shifts from S_1 to S_2.

On the other hand, if there is particularly good weather, then the supply curve shifts to S_3. Such a shift in the supply curve is described as an "increase in supply."

Supply and Demand Together Determine Price

Equilibrium price and quantity occur at E, where the supply and demand schedules intersect.

Note: Neither curve shifts so long as other influences on supply and demand do not change ("other things remain equal"). However, . . .

. . . suppose that other influences do change. For example, suppose that consumer income rises, so that demand shifts from D_1 to D_2. Then equilibrium moves from E_1 to E_2, with more sold at a higher price.

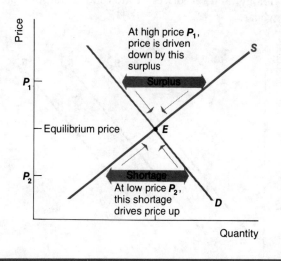

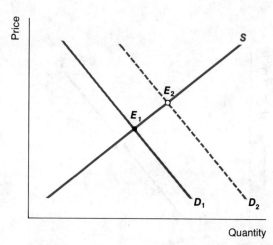

Chapter 20

DEMAND AND SUPPLY: THE CONCEPT OF ELASTICITY

When you have nothing else to wear
but cloth of gold and satin rare,
for cloth of gold you cease to care—
up goes the price of shoddy.

Gilbert and Sullivan, *The Gondoliers*

There isn't a farmer in the country who complains when he has a good wheat crop. But some thoughtful ones may be concerned if everyone else, including farmers in Russia, the United States, and other countries, also have good crops. The reason is simple: A good crop worldwide will reduce the price, and that may hurt farmers more than the benefit they get from increased sales. Whether or not they will benefit or lose on balance depends on the **elasticity of demand**. This chapter is devoted to developing this concept and showing how important it is in answering such widely diverse questions as: Will a bumper crop result in higher or lower farm income? Does the consumer or the producer bear the burden of a sales tax? Why are agricultural prices unstable?

THE ELASTICITY OF DEMAND: HOW MUCH DOES THE QUANTITY DEMANDED RESPOND TO A CHANGE IN PRICE?

Suppose you are managing the university drama club. Your play has a week to run, and the theatre is run- ning half empty for each performance. You consider lowering the ticket price by 20%, from $10 to $8. This policy will be a great success if it fills a lot of those empty seats. But it will be a failure if the public doesn't respond and you get very few extra sales.

These two possibilities are illustrated in Figure 20-1. To explain this diagram, we must first identify total revenue geometrically. For example, if the initial equilibrium is at E_1 in panel (*a*), what is total revenue? The answer is $10,000, that is, the base Q of 1,000 tickets times the height P of $10 a ticket. However, base times height is the area of a rectangle—in this case, rectangle 1, shaded in colour. Similarly, we can sketch in gray rectangle 2 that measures the total revenue at the different point E_2 on the demand curve.

The *total revenue* of sellers is the area of the rectangle to the southwest of the point of equilibrium on the demand curve. It is the quantity sold (the base of the rectangle) times the price (the height of the rectangle). This rectangle also represents the total cost of this good to buyers, that is, their total expenditure on this good.

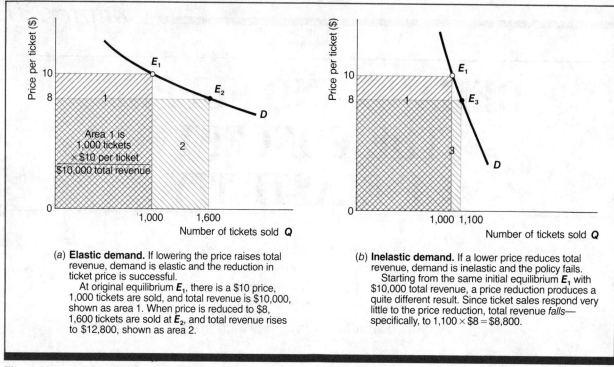

(a) **Elastic demand.** If lowering the price raises total revenue, demand is elastic and the reduction in ticket price is successful.
    At original equilibrium E_1, there is a $10 price, 1,000 tickets are sold, and total revenue is $10,000, shown as area 1. When price is reduced to $8, 1,600 tickets are sold at E_2, and total revenue rises to $12,800, shown as area 2.

(b) **Inelastic demand.** If a lower price reduces total revenue, demand is inelastic and the policy fails.
    Starting from the same initial equilibrium E_1, with $10,000 total revenue, a price reduction produces a quite different result. Since ticket sales respond very little to the price reduction, total revenue *falls*—specifically, to $1,100 \times \$8 = \$8,800$.

Figure 20-1   Pricing theatre tickets: The elasticity of demand and total revenue.

Now let us return to the original question: Can you increase your total revenue by lowering the price? If you look at the demand curve shown in panel (a), the answer is yes. The quantity demanded is very responsive to the reduction in price; demand is described as *elastic.* As you lower price from $10 to $8 and move down the demand curve from E_1 to E_2, total revenue rises from the $10,000 of area 1 to the $12,800 of area 2. (This $12,800 represents 1,600 tickets at $8 each.)

On the other hand, if you look at the demand curve shown in panel (b), the price cut fails. Attendance increases very little as you lower price. As you move down the demand curve from E_1 to E_3, total revenue decreases from $10,000 to $8,800. Because the quantity demanded is relatively unresponsive to the change in price, demand is described as *inelastic.* Thus, elasticity is a measure of how strongly the quantity responds to a change in price:

Elasticity of demand, ϵ_d =
$$\frac{\% \text{ change in quantity demanded}}{\% \text{ change in price}} \quad (20\text{-}1)$$

If ϵ_d is greater than 1, demand is *elastic.*
If ϵ_d is less than 1, demand is *inelastic.*
If ϵ_d is equal to 1, then demand has *unit elasticity.*

Reconsider, now, the theatre example in Figure 20-1. In both panels, the price reduction is the same: $2, or 20%. In panel (a), quantity increases sharply, from 1,000 to 1,600. Since this represents a larger percentage increase in quantity than the 20% decrease in price, demand is elastic. Furthermore, the large increase in quantity more than offsets the reduction in price, resulting in an increase in total revenue. This leads us to a rule of thumb for judging whether a demand curve is elastic or not: If a fall in price causes an increase in total revenue as in panel (a), demand is elastic. However, if a fall in price causes a reduction in total revenue—as in panel (b)—demand is *inelastic.* Finally, if revenue remains unchanged in the face of a change in price, elasticity is 1.

A number of calculations of elasticity are provided in Box 20-1. Less formal illustrations are provided in the demand curves shown in Figure 20-2. In panel (a)

the elasticity of the completely vertical demand curve is zero. The reason is that price has no effect whatsoever on the quantity demanded, which remains 10 regardless of how the price may change. Thus, the elasticity ratio in equation 20-1 is zero because the change in the quantity demanded in the numerator is zero. At the other extreme, the completely horizontal demand in panel (e) has infinitely large elasticity because even the smallest drop in price would result in an unlimited increase in the quantity demanded.

In the intermediate case in panel (c), quantity increases at the same percentage rate as price falls. Hence, the numerator and denominator in equation 20-1 are the same and elasticity is 1. Note how total revenue remains constant in this case.

In Figure 20-2, as we move farther to the right, the slope gets smaller. (For a review of the concept of slope, see the appendix at the end of Chapter 1.) While the slope is getting smaller and smaller, the demand curve is becoming more and more elastic. Can we conclude that this relationship between slope and elas-

ticity always holds? The answer is yes, *if the curves being compared pass through the same point,* such as E_1 in the two panels of Figure 20-1. Thus, we have another rule of thumb for elasticity:

If two demand curves pass through the same point, the one with the smaller slope is more elastic.

This idea is important. However, it is also important to recognize that when two demand curves do *not* pass through the same point, elasticity *cannot* be judged merely by slope. An illustration is provided in Figure 20-3, which shows the demand for bananas in the small Swedish economy and the large U.S. economy. Although U.S. demand has less slope, both curves have exactly the same elasticity. In both cases, the quantity demanded increases by 100% when price falls by 20%.

Another example where slope is not a good measure of elasticity is provided in panel (c) of Figure 20-2. As we move down this curve, its slope changes.

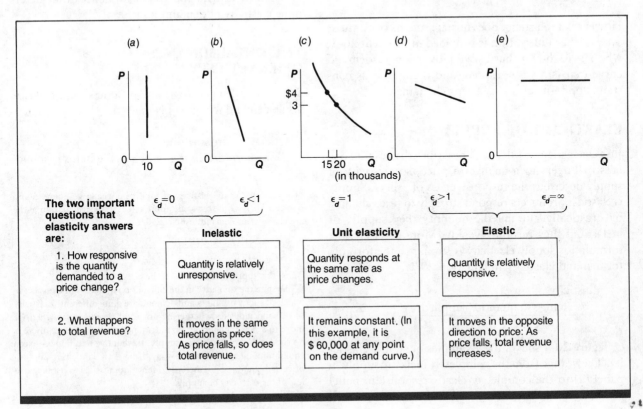

Figure 20-2 Varying degrees of elasticity.

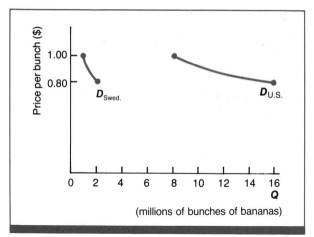

Figure 20-3   Why slope alone does not indicate elasticity. The U.S. demand curve for bananas has less slope than the Swedish demand, but the elasticity of the two curves is identical. The reason is that if the price falls by 20%, the quantity doubles in both cases. In Sweden, it increases from 1 to 2, whereas in the United States, it increases from 8 to 16.

However, its elasticity does not; it remains constant at 1. A further illustration is provided in problem 20-5, where it is shown that as we move along a demand curve that is a straight line—and therefore has constant slope—its elasticity keeps changing.

ELASTICITY OF SUPPLY

Just as elasticity of demand describes the responsiveness of buyers to a change in price, so elasticity of supply describes the responsiveness of sellers. Supply is elastic if producers respond strongly to price changes by drastically altering the quantity they supply, or inelastic if they respond weakly. More precisely, the formula for supply elasticity is similar to the formula for demand elasticity in equation 20-1:

$$\text{Elasticity of supply, } \epsilon_s = \frac{\text{\% change in quantity supplied}}{\text{\% change in price}} \quad (20\text{-}3)$$

Figure 20-4 shows five examples of supply elasticity. They range from the completely inelastic supply in panel (a) to the completely elastic response in panel

(e).[1] Once again, as in the case of demand, there is a simple rule of thumb for relating slope to elasticity: *If two supply curves pass through the same point* (such as the common point at the lower left end of each supply curve in Figure 20-4), *the one with the smaller slope is the more elastic*. But otherwise, elasticity cannot be judged merely by slope.

In contrast with demand—which traces out a curve if the elasticity is one—supply with unit elasticity is a straight line. If extended, it would pass through the origin 0. Note that this is true of the supply curve with unit elasticity in panel (c) of Figure 20-4. On such a line, P always changes by the same percentage as Q; in our example, when P doubles, Q also doubles. Since the numerator and denominator in equation 20-3 are equal, the elasticity of supply is 1.

So far we have calculated elasticity assuming that the location and slope of the demand and supply curves are known. However, usually they are not; the problems involved in estimating them are described in the appendix to this chapter.

We now turn to the broad influences that determine elasticity of demand and supply.

THE DETERMINANTS OF ELASTICITY

Why is the demand for some products highly elastic while demand for others is inelastic?

Elasticity of Demand

1. Importance in the budget. Big items in a bud-

[1] To calculate the arc elasticity of supply between two points A and B in panel (d), we use the same approach as in the calculation of the arc elasticity of demand in Box 20-1:

$$\epsilon_s = \frac{\Delta Q / \overline{Q}}{\Delta P / \overline{P}} = \frac{100 / [(100 + 200)/2]}{2 / [(5 + 7)/2]} = 2$$

Thus, this supply is confirmed to be elastic.

Despite the similarity in the calculations, there is one respect in which elasticity of supply and demand are quite different. Elasticity of demand indicates whether or not total revenue rises when we move to a new equilibrium on a demand curve. However, there is no similar interpretation for supply. If we move to a higher-priced equilibrium on a supply curve—say, from A to B in Figure 20-4c—price and quantity both increase. Hence, total revenue rises regardless of the elasticity of supply.

BOX 20-1

CALCULATION OF ELASTICITY

In this box we show how elasticity between two points on a demand curve can be calculated. If we let ΔQ represent "change in Q," then the percentage change in quantity in equation 20-1 may be written $(\Delta Q/Q) \times 100\%$. If we similarly rewrite the percentage change in price as $(\Delta P/P) \times 100\%$, our elasticity formula becomes

$$\epsilon_d = \frac{(\Delta Q/Q) \times 100\%}{(\Delta P/P) \times 100\%} = \frac{\Delta Q/Q}{\Delta P/P}$$

Applying this formula in a straightforward manner to the move from E_1 to E_2 in panel (a) of Figure 20-1, we get a first approximation of the elasticity of demand:

$$\epsilon_d = \frac{600/1,000}{2/10} = 3.0$$

(Actually, ϵ_d is negative, since the change in quantity is positive, while the change in price is negative. However, the negative sign on ϵ_d is often omitted.)

Unfortunately, there is a problem with this straightforward "first approximation." We used the initial E_1 values of $Q = 1,000$ and $P = 10$. But now suppose we had moved in the reverse direction along the demand curve, from point E_2 to point E_1. The initial values would now be those at E_2; that is, $Q = 1,600$ and $P = 8$. You can confirm that this would result in the different calculation of $\epsilon_d = 1.5$. This raises a problem because we would like an elasticity measure that is the same whether we start at E_1 or E_2. Therefore, rather than taking either E_1 or E_2, we take the average of the two; that is, we use the average quantity $\overline{Q}$ and average price $\overline{P}$. Thus, elasticity of demand is calculated to be

$$\epsilon_d = \frac{\Delta Q/\overline{Q}}{\Delta P/\overline{P}} \qquad (20\text{-}2)$$
$$= \frac{600/[(1,000 + 1,600)/2]}{2/[(10 + 8)/2]} = 2.1$$

As we expected, this falls between our two previous calculations of 3.0 and 1.5. Because this value is more than 1, demand is elastic.

Since equation 20-2 provides a way of calculating elasticity between two points separated by an arc of the demand curve, it is commonly referred to as the *arc elasticity* formula.

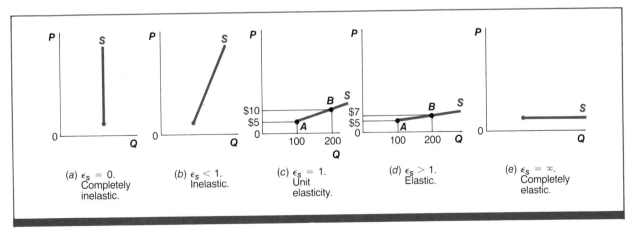

Figure 20-4   Different elasticities of supply.

get tend to have a more elastic demand than small items. For example, the demand for cars is more elastic than the demand for salt. Car purchasers may spend hours trying to negotiate a 3% price reduction on a new car; if they don't get it, they may not buy the car. But they won't even notice a 30% drop in the price of salt. For such a small item, consumers are very insensitive to price.

2. Substitutability. Items that have good substitutes generally have a more elastic demand than those that do not. To illustrate, consider sugar and salt, both of which are small items in any budget. Yet sugar has a more elastic demand than salt because its substitutes—like honey—are better than the substitutes for salt. (Can you think of any?)

3. Luxuries versus necessities. Whereas essentials such as electric power or bread have a relatively inelastic demand because purchasers can scarcely avoid buying at least some of them, luxuries generally have a more elastic demand. For example, luxuries like foreign vacations have an elastic demand because purchasers can stop buying them if their prices rise. (However, if we go all the way up to the category of superluxuries, demand may become inelastic again. The reason is that these goods are bought by those who are so rich that they aren't affected by a change in price—indeed, they may not even notice it. There is no better illustration than John Pierpont Morgan's comment that anyone who has to ask the cost of a yacht can't afford one.)

4. Time. Over time, demand becomes more elastic. For example, if the price of gasoline rises, there is very little immediate reduction in the amount the public purchases. It takes some time for drivers to switch to smaller cars and longer yet for the auto companies to design and build more fuel efficient cars. However, when they do, the public's purchases of gasoline are reduced. Thus, demand is more elastic in the long run than in the short.

Elasticity of Supply

Supply is elastic if producers are able to back away from the market if prices fall, and are able and willing to expand sales if prices rise. Thus, elasticity of supply depends upon:

1. The feasibility and cost of storage. Goods that spoil quickly must be put on the market regardless of price; their elasticity of supply is low. The same tends to be true of goods that are costly to store.

2. The characteristics of the production process. Does an item have a close substitute in production? That is, can the labour, land, and equipment used to produce the item be readily switched into the production of another good? If the answer is yes, supply will be elastic. For example, the elasticity of supply is greater for an individual grain—such as corn—than for all grains taken together. The reason is that, in the face of a fall in the price of corn, a producer is able to shift production into a substitute grain such as wheat or barley. This ability of producers to respond to a change in price makes the supply of corn elastic. On the other hand, if the prices of *all* grains fall, a farmer will have much more difficulty in shifting out of grain production altogether because there aren't close substitute activities. For example, if the farmer were to try to move into, say, dairy farming instead, this would be a very costly switch because it would require different kinds of capital equipment. Thus, with farmers less able to respond to a change in price, the elasticity of supply of grain will be less. In short, products like corn with a close substitute in production have a more elastic supply than products without a close substitute in production.

In contrast to substitutes in production—like corn and wheat—other goods may be *joint products,* like beef and hides: When you produce one, you get the other. The decision to butcher a steer is influenced by the price of beef but hardly at all by the price of hides. Once the steer has been butchered, the relatively unimportant hide will be sold regardless of its price. In other words, the supply of hides is inelastic because hides are a relatively unimportant joint product.

3. Time. Just as time makes demand more elastic, it also makes supply more elastic. In fact, this idea has already been encountered in our discussion of rent control in Chapter 4. It is only with the passage of time that the supply of apartments becomes more elastic. Figure 20-5 provides another example used by the English economist Alfred Marshall in his discussion of the influence of time on supply almost a century ago.

Suppose demand for a perishable commodity like fresh fish suddenly rises from D_1 to D_2. The immediate effect on the first day in panel (*a*) is that price rises to P_2. Note that the quantity supplied is not influenced by price. Whatever quantity has been caught that day—in our example, Q_1—is put on the market,

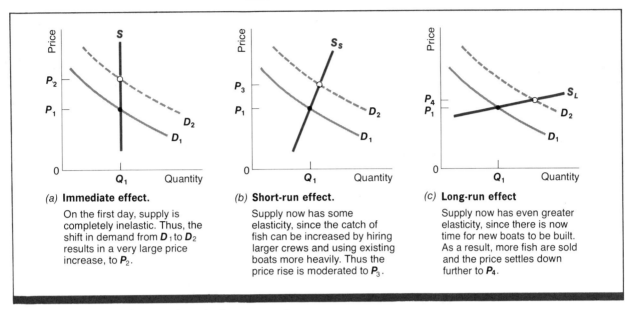

(a) Immediate effect.

On the first day, supply is completely inelastic. Thus, the shift in demand from D_1 to D_2 results in a very large price increase, to P_2.

(b) Short-run effect.

Supply now has some elasticity, since the catch of fish can be increased by hiring larger crews and using existing boats more heavily. Thus the price rise is moderated to P_3.

(c) Long-run effect

Supply now has even greater elasticity, since there is now time for new boats to be built. As a result, more fish are sold and the price settles down further to P_4.

Figure 20-5 How the elasticity of supply changes over time.

regardless of price. (In Marshall's day, refrigeration was inadequate. Thus, there was no way suppliers could respond to a changed price by putting more or less on the market.) Consequently, the immediate supply S in panel (a) is completely inelastic.

However, in the days that follow, the higher price induces fishing boat captains to increase their crews and bring retired boats back into service. The quantity of fish caught and offered for sale increases. Thus, supply becomes more elastic in panel (b), and price settles down somewhat to P_3. But this is not the long-run equilibrium. As more time passes, new boats can be built and even more fish caught. Thus, in the long run, supply is even more elastic, as shown in panel (c). The result is a further moderation of price, to P_4.

With this discussion of the elasticity of demand and supply in hand, let's show how useful elasticity can be in answering two important policy questions: First, who bears the burden of a sales tax? Second, what are the special problems of agriculture?

APPLYING ELASTICITY: WHO BEARS THE BURDEN OF A SALES TAX?

To answer this question, consider the supply and demand for a good shown in panel (a) of Figure 20-6.

The initial equilibrium before the tax is at E_1, with 10 million units sold at a price of $3. Suppose that the government now imposes a sales tax of $1 per unit, to be collected from sellers. Who bears the burden of this tax?

The effect of this tax is to shift the supply curve upward from S_1 to S_2 by the full $1 amount of the tax. To confirm this, consider any quantity supplied—say, 12 million units. Point A on the supply curve S_1 shows that before the tax, sellers would have to receive $4 per unit to induce them to sell these 12 million units. This means that *after* the tax, they must receive $5—at point B—in order to enable them to pay the government the $1 tax and still have the same $4 left. Thus, point B is on the new after-tax supply curve S_2. And no matter what point we consider on S_1, the corresponding point on S_2 is always $1 higher. Thus, the entire supply curve shifts upward by the amount of the tax.

As a result of the tax, the equilibrium moves from E_1 to E_2, and the price rises from $3 to $3.20. Thus, buyers bear 20 cents of the burden; they pay 20 cents more per unit. What happens to sellers? The price they receive rises by 20 cents—from $3 to $3.20; but $1 of this must go to the government, so the seller gets only $2.20 after tax. Because the seller ultimately receives $2.20 rather than the original $3, the seller

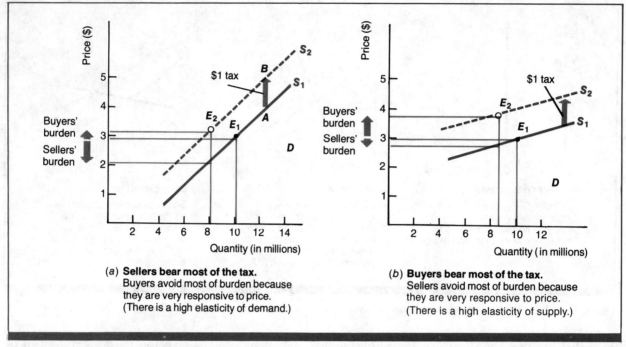

Figure 20-6 How the burden of a sales tax depends on the elasticity of demand and supply.

In part (a), equilibrium of S_1 and D results in a before-tax price of $3. When the $1 tax is imposed, supply shifts from S1 to S2 and the new equilibrium price is $3.20. Buyers pay 20 cents more; this is the burden of the tax that they bear.

Sellers receive $2.20—that is, the $3.20 market price less the $1 tax that they must pay the government. Thus they receive 80 cents less than the original $3, and this 80 cents is the burden they bear. In part (b), supply is more elastic than demand, and the after-tax price rises to $3.80. In this case, buyers bear 80 cents of the burden and sellers only 20 cents.

bears 80 cents of the burden. To sum up, the two gray arrows on the far left show how the $1 tax is split up into the 20-cent burden on buyers and the 80-cent burden on sellers.

Buyers bear a lighter share of the burden in this case because they respond more to changes in price than do sellers; that is, demand is more elastic than supply. However, in panel (b) the reverse is true. Here, sellers are more responsive to changes in price; supply is more elastic than demand. As a result, sellers bear the lighter burden of the tax.

These conclusions can best be summarized if we think of two groups in a market, one buying, the other selling. Suppose one group—it doesn't matter which—takes the view: "We aren't keen to stay in the market. If the price moves against us, we can back away. In responding to price changes, we're flexible, sensitive, *elastic*." Suppose the other group feels: "We have no

choice; we must stay in the market. Even if price moves against us, we can't back away. We're inflexible, unresponsive, *inelastic*." It is no surprise that this second group will bear most of the burden of a tax and will, in other situations as well, be in the more vulnerable position.

APPLYING ELASTICITY: WHAT ARE THE SPECIAL PROBLEMS OF AGRICULTURE?

The two decades between World War I and World War II were times of distress for Canadian agriculture. Farm prices and land values fell sharply and bankruptcies were common. In response, the government greatly expanded its policies of assistance to farmers. Over the decades that followed, these policies have been modified and extended, and new ones added.

Today, Canadian governments are deeply involved in agriculture, through a wide range of policies designed to raise farm incomes.

One of the most important of these is the policy of supporting the price that the farmer receives for a number of commodities. Since the 1930s, the federal and provincial governments have intervened in the market to support the prices of many farm products. In the mid-1980s, various kinds of government support programs existed in the markets for wheat, barley, oats, eggs, dairy products, cattle, hogs, sheep, and turkeys, and in other markets as well. In the simplest kind of program, the government announces a support price, and stands ready to buy at that price. When market prices are weak, and farmers cannot get a higher price by selling on the private market, they can sell instead to the government at the support price. (For example, in the late 1950s, and again in the mid-1970s, the government had to buy large amounts of eggs and skim milk powder because it was offering relatively high support prices for these products.[2])

Why does the government offer price guarantees to farmers, but not to other producers? One reason is that agriculture has historically suffered from two special problems. Agricultural prices have been *unstable,* fluctuating up and down from year to year; and they have shown a tendency to *fall,* compared to the prices of other goods. To understand each of these problems, we first ask: "What would happen to agricultural prices if there were no government intervention in these markets?" As we shall see, the concept of elasticity is very important in providing an answer.

Year-to-Year Price Instability

In Figure 20-7, we show the problems that arise because agricultural demand and supply are inelastic in the short run. Demand for farm products is relatively inelastic because people must satisfy their appetite for food no matter what happens to price. Supply is also inelastic in the short run for several reasons. In some cases the product is perishable; in other cases, the crop is already planted and it is too late for farmers to respond much to a change in price.

As an example, suppose Figure 20-7 represents the Ontario market for a perishable product like tomatoes. In a normal year with demand D and supply S_1, equilibrium is at E_1 with price P_1. But with a bumper crop, the resulting supply curve shifts to S_2. Because the product is perishable and expensive to transport, the whole crop has to be quickly sold in the Ontario market, no matter what the price. As a result, equilibrium shifts to E_2, and the price falls all the way to P_2. In this example, a bumper crop cuts price by a third! Worse yet for Ontario's tomato farmers: The inelasticity of demand has meant that their income has been reduced (from the rectangle enclosed to the southwest of E_1 to the smaller rectangle to the southwest of E_2). Similarly, you can confirm that a poor crop that results in equilibrium at E_3 will raise farmers' income. In short, because both demand and supply are inelastic, relatively small variations in crop yield result in large price fluctuations. Moreover, the better the crop, the lower farm income may be as a result. (This point is illustrated further in Box 20-2.)

If we consider a product that can be relatively eas-

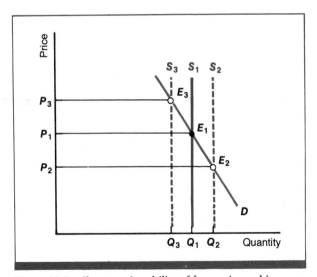

Figure 20-7 Short-run instability of farm price and income.
In a normal year, inelastic demand D and supply S_1 result in equilibrium at E_1. However, if there is a bumper crop and Q_2 is put on the market, equilibrium is at E_2 and price falls from P_1 to P_2. Because demand is inelastic, farm income is lower at E_2 than at the normal equilibrium E_1. But if there is a poor crop Q_3, equilibrium is at E_3 and farm income is higher than normal.

---

[2]In recent years, the government has tried to avoid large direct purchases of farm products; instead, it has used different and more complicated methods for supporting farm prices. We will discuss some of these alternative methods in Chapter 24.

BOX 20-2

TO FLORIDA CITRUS GROWERS, A FREEZE IS A BLESSING

Cold Eases the Fears of a Bumper-Crop Surplus Resulting in Money Loss

The freezing weather in Florida's citrus belt will reduce this year's previously predicted bumper crop. . . . but ironically it will ease the worries of growers who had feared they would lose money because of the surplus.

"Nature has bailed us out of a bumper crop," a spokesman for the Florida Citrus Commission said yesterday in a telephone interview. "The growers were going to lose money, but now the problem has been taken care of and an oversupply situation has been corrected."

This was the story in 1977*; and in 1981, 1983 and 1985, history repeated itself. For example, in 1981 a freeze destroyed about 20% of the Florida

*Rona Cherry in *The New York Times*, 23 January 1977. Reproduced with permission.

Courtesy Canapress Photo Service

orange crop. The wholesale price of concentrated orange juice immediately rose by 30%.

What do these events imply about the elasticity of demand for citrus fruit, and oranges in particular?

---

ily transported all over the world (such as wheat or soybeans), we can let Figure 20-7 represent the whole world market for the product.[3] For example, D may represent the (relatively inelastic) world demand for wheat, and S_1 the world supply from all producing countries. A large wheat crop in one or more of the world's wheat-growing areas will shift the world supply curve to the right (S_2); because world demand is inelastic, the result is a large decline in the world price

[3] If a good can be easily transported, its price will not fluctuate very much in response to variations in the local crop in a province or even a country. For example, a large corn crop in Canada need not lead to low corn prices here: If the price in Canada falls even slightly below the world price, Canadian farmers will start selling this corn in foreign markets instead. By doing so, they will prevent the Canadian price from falling below the world price. However, the world price of goods such as grains may fluctuate substantially in response to variations in the total worldwide crop.

of wheat. (This is the case that concerned the thoughtful farmer in the introduction to this chapter.) On the other hand, a poor harvest in an important wheat-growing nation (such as the Soviet Union, for example) may send the world price of wheat sky-rocketing, as happened in 1973 and 1974.

Long-Run Downward Trend in Price

The second farm problem is best understood by considering our economic history. If we go back far enough, farming was our largest activity, with the majority of the population working on the soil. With old-fashioned techniques of agricultural production, an individual family could do little more than produce enough for itself.

However, with improvements in agricultural methods and technology, productivity increased. A typical farm family could produce more and more food: enough for two families, then three, then four, and so on. As that happened, the number of people required on the farm to produce food fell to a smaller and smaller fraction of the population. This decline has had effects that have reached far beyond agriculture. In fact, one of the essential requirements for North America's industrial development has been the ability of farmers to produce more food than they consume. Without this capability, the labour force necessary for a developing industry would never have been released from the task of grubbing a bare living out of the soil. It was no accident that the Industrial Revolution in Britain in the eighteenth century was preceded by a revolution in agricultural productivity. And that agricultural revolution has continued at a rapid pace: A typical Canadian or American farm family today supplies food for itself and over twenty non-farm families as well.

However, this huge increase in agricultural productivity has been a mixed blessing for the farmers who have achieved it. Once again, elasticity is the key to understanding why. In panel (*a*) of Figure 20-8, E_1

represents the initial equilibrium in an earlier period, at the intersection of long-run supply S_1 and demand D_1; demand is relatively inelastic because food is a necessity. Over many decades, D has been shifting to the right from D_1 to D_2 because of (1) the increase in the total food-consuming population and (2) the rising income of that population. However, the effects of rising income have been fairly modest. Although consumers purchase more of almost everything as their incomes rise, their expenditures on food rise less rapidly than their expenditures on many other goods. With rising income, people may double their expenditures on clothes and triple their expenditures on vacations, but they increase their food consumption by only a small amount. After all, how much more can anyone eat? Technically, we say that the ***income elasticity*** of demand for food is low; that is, food purchases respond weakly to an increase in income. (For more on income elasticity and other kinds of elasticity, see Box 20-3).

On the other hand, over these same decades there has been an even greater shift in supply (from S_1 to S_2 in panel (*a*) of Figure 20-8) because of rapid improve-

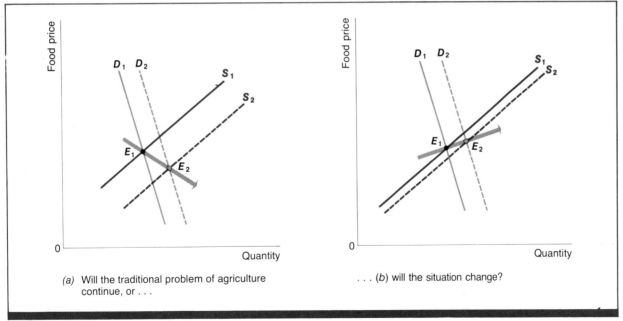

(a) Will the traditional problem of agriculture continue, or . . .

. . . (b) will the situation change?

Figure 20-8   The long-run trend in agriculture.
The classic problem of agriculture in part (*a*) has been that supply has shifted to the right more rapidly than demand. Hence, price has fallen. This situation may repeat itself in

the future or it may, as some people predict, change to the situation shown in part (*b*). There, shifts in supply do not keep pace with shifts in demand and price rises.

BOX 20-3

OTHER ELASTICITY MEASURES

The demand for any good is affected not only by its price but also by many other influences, such as consumer income. In this box we show how the elasticity concept can be used to measure the strength of these other influences as well.

Income Elasticity of Demand

Just as price elasticity measures how the quantity demanded responds to price changes, income elasticity measures how the quantity demanded responds to income changes. Formally,

$$\text{Income elasticity of demand} = \frac{\% \text{ change in quantity demanded}}{\% \text{ change in income}} \quad (20\text{-}4)$$

Notice how this definition is similar to that of price elasticity in equation 20-1. (Incidentally, when economists use the simple term "elasticity," they generally mean "price elasticity.")

The North American automobile is an example of a good with a high income elasticity of demand. Various estimates place its value between 2.5 and 3; in other words, a 1% increase in income results in an increase in auto purchases of 2.5% to 3%. On the other hand, the income elasticity of gasoline

is about 1 and of tobacco even less—perhaps as low as 0.6. Thus the demand for tobacco is described as "income inelastic"; when income rises, tobacco purchases rise less rapidly.

Income elasticity has another important interpretation. Recall that income is a "demand shifter"; when income rises, the demand—for autos or tobacco—shifts to the right. Income elasticity of demand measures the magnitude of that shift. In the case of automobiles, the shift is important, while in the case of tobacco it is far less so. (For a small category of goods—inferior goods—an increase in income shifts the demand curve to the *left*; purchases decline as income rises. In such cases, the income elasticity of demand is negative. An exam-

---

ments in farm productivity. With supply shifting to the right more rapidly than demand, price has fallen to a new equilibrium at E_2. However, as price falls, farmers—and even more important, their children—leave the farm to pursue more highly paid careers in the city. Because they do, the proportion of the population on the farm falls. This outflow of people from the farm also means that there is a less rapid increase in farm output than would otherwise occur. In other words, agricultural supply S_2 shifts less rapidly to the right. In turn, this means a less severe price reduction.

This, in a nutshell, is the history of North American agriculture: Because productivity has outrun demand, the proportion of the population on the farm has fallen. By becoming more and more productive,

farmers are doing a great service to the public in terms of providing large quantities of food at a very low price. But their very success has meant that farmers are producing themselves—or their neighbours—out of jobs.

Will the Future Bring Food Scarcity?

Prices in North American agriculture would be even more depressed were it not for our large exports of food products to other parts of the world. These exports became particularly important in the early 1970s as a result of crop failures in the Soviet Union and elsewhere. Indeed, the buoyant demand for agricultural goods on world markets pulled up the international prices of wheat, soybeans, and other items, drawing

ple is low-quality food: When income rises, people buy less, since they are now able to afford better food.)

Cross Elasticity of Demand

The quantity of a good demanded depends not only on its own price but also on the prices of other goods. For example, the demand for cars depends on the price of gasoline, The *cross elasticity of demand* measures the strength of this effect.

Courtesy Miller Services Limited

Specifically:

$$\text{Cross elasticity of demand} = \frac{\% \text{ change in quantity demanded of } X}{\% \text{ change in the price of } Y} \quad (20\text{-}5)$$

If the cross elasticity is positive, the goods are *substitutes*. For example, beef and pork are substitutes: A 1% increase in the price of pork causes an increase of about 0.3% in the quantity of beef demanded; that is, it causes the demand curve for beef to shift to the right by 0.3%. As another example, a 1% increase in the price of butter causes an increase of about 0.8% in the quantity of margarine demanded. Thus butter and margarine are even closer substitutes than beef and pork.

On the other hand, if cross elasticity is negative, the goods are *complements*. For example, as a result of an increase in the price of gasoline, people drive less; the demand for cars is reduced. Thus the price of gasoline is a demand shifter, moving the demand for cars to the left. Cross elasticity—which is negative in this case—measures the magnitude of this shift.

To sum up: The *sign* of cross elasticity determines whether goods are substitutes or complements, that is, whether an increase in the price of one shifts the demand for the other to the right or left. The *numerical value* of cross elasticity measures the strength of this effect.

up North American food prices as well. (In Canada, the index of food prices rose by more than 30% in 1973 and 1974 alone; this was a substantially higher rate of increase than in the overall consumer price index.)

The question is: Was this period of scarcity and high price just an early warning of a new era of food shortage rather than surplus? Specifically, will the traditional problem of supply outrunning demand and downward pressure on price shown in panel (*a*) of Figure 20-8 be replaced by the new problem shown in panel (*b*), where supply shifts less than demand and food prices rise rather than fall?

Some of the reasons put forward for expecting food supply to lag behind demand are not very convincing—

for example, the claim that we are facing a food crisis because the world is running out of land. In fact, studies indicate quite the contrary: Only about half of the world's arable land is now being used, and much of the unused acreage has good agricultural potential. Moreover, recent advances in technology have allowed us to increase output by expanding our use of other inputs—like fertilizer—rather than land. If this trend continues, our future requirements for additional land may not be as great as is often supposed.

However, there are other reasons that food supply may lag behind demand that are not so easy to dismiss. For example, there is the continuing question of how much damage is being done to the environment by the heavy use of fertilizers and pesticides. More-

BOX 20-4

ANOTHER PERSPECTIVE ON AGRICULTURE: IS FALLING PRICE THE SIGN OF A SICK INDUSTRY?

Not necessarily. To see why, suppose that the price of a good you are producing has fallen by 50%. But suppose that your productivity has risen, so that you are now producing three times as many units. Even though you are selling these units at half the price, your income is *increasing*.

For a real-world example, consider IBM. Computer technology has developed at an incredible rate over the past three decades. As already noted, a computer that once filled a room has now been replaced by a tiny chip that can be held on the tip of your finger. As a result, IBM and other computer manufacturers have been able to cut prices drastically. Yet, in spite of rapidly falling prices, IBM's profits have increased. Lower prices and higher profits have *both* been possible because of the large increase in productivity.

For the Canadian farmer, prices have also fallen—at least compared to the prices of other goods. Specifically, the prices farmers receive for their products like wheat and corn have risen far less rapidly than the prices they must pay for consumer goods and for their inputs such as fertilizer and machinery. And because demand for farm products has been growing relatively slowly, the farm buiness has become a much smaller share of the total economy than it once was. (In the 1920s, farm families accounted for more than one-third of Canada's population; by the 1980s, the farm population was less than 5% of the total.)

But despite the falling prices and the relative decline in the importance of the farm sector, farmers have not become poorer and poorer. In a study published in 1981, agricultural economist George Brinkman estimated that in the first half of the 1970s, the returns to the labour and capital resources employed on the average commercial farm in Ontario were almost the same as the returns earned by comparable resources in other industries.* (Brinkman defined commercial farms as farms with annual gross sales over $15,000. When he looked at the larger farms, with gross sales over $50,000 per year, he found that the resources used on those farms yielded *larger* returns than they would have earned outside farming.) Because the returns on resources in farming have kept up with returns elsewhere in the economy, there was little difference between the average incomes of farm and non-farm families.

The reason why farmers' incomes have managed to grow as fast as incomes elsewhere while farm prices have been falling, is that the productivity of the individual farmer has increased many times over since the beginning of the century. The increase in productivity has made it possible for consumers of food to enjoy lower prices, *and* for farmers to enjoy higher incomes. Thus, the fall in the prices of farm products has been a poor indicator of what has been happening to farm incomes—just as a low price on computers was a poor indicator of IBM's income.

(While studies of this kind show that *average* farm income has kept up with the rest of the economy over the years, this is certainly not to deny that farming has sometimes been facing severe problems. Thus in the 1930s, Prairie farmers were hit exceptionally hard by both low farm prices and drought. Moreover, studies consistently show that a large number of small-scale farmers in various parts of Canada have incomes below Statistics Canada's poverty line. And in the mid-1980s, slumping world prices and drought, as well as continued high interest rates, once again combined to create severe financial hardship for many western grain farmers.)

*George L. Brinkman, *Farm Incomes in Canada* (Ottawa: Economic Council of Canada and the Institute for Research on Public Policy, 1981).

over, in some parts of the world (including the southwest United States) there is a problem of the depletion of ground water because so much has been drawn off for irrigation purposes. The deforestation of many areas—particularly in the developing world—has interfered with a steady supply of water and made soil erosion worse. Finally, some observers believe that the serious crop failures in foreign countries in the last 15 years have been the result of unfavourable trends in the world's climate.

To decide whether the future situation will be the one shown in panel (*a*) or panel (*b*) of Figure 20-8 requires projecting not only world food supply but also demand. This projection requires an answer to the difficult question: Will the rapid population increase

in the developing countries continue, or will these countries begin to show the lower birthrate patterns observed in the industrialized parts of the world?

In the mid-1980s, it is impossible to predict whether, in the next century, we will face a continued surplus in agriculture or a severe world scarcity. All we can say for sure is that by the mid-1980s, the major agricultural problem facing governments both in North America and Europe was not food scarcity. Quite the contrary: The problem was what to do about large surpluses.

The problems of agriculture, and the various policies that the government has introduced in response, are so important that we examine them in more detail in Box 20-4 and return to them in Chapter 24.

KEY POINTS

1. Elasticity of demand is a measure of the responsiveness of quantity demanded to price: the more responsive, the more elastic.
2. Elasticity of demand also indicates what happens to total revenue as price changes. If demand is elastic, a reduced price will raise total revenue. However, if demand is inelastic, a reduced price will lower total revenue. Goods with high demand elasticity include large-budget items and items with close substitutes.
3. If two curves pass through the same point, the one with less slope is the more elastic. However, if they do not pass through the same point, there is no such simple relationship between slope and elasticity.
4. Elasticity of supply measures the responsiveness of quantity supplied to a change in price; again, the more responsive, the more elastic.

Goods with high elasticity of supply include items that can be easily and cheaply stored and goods with close substitutes in production.

5. The elasticities of demand and supply are less in the short run than in the long run.
6. Year-to-year fluctuations in food prices are made more severe by inelasticity of demand. This same inelasticity means that a bumper crop may lower farm income, while a poor crop may raise income.
7. The downward trend in farm prices relative to other prices has occurred in the past because of rapidly improving farm technology and our relatively stable demand for food. As a consequence, supply has tended to outrun demand. It is not clear whether this will continue or whether the situation will be reversed, with food prices rising in the future.

KEY CONCEPTS

elastic demand
inelastic demand
unit elasticity of demand
total revenue as $P \times Q$
   rectangle

relationship of elasticity
   to total revenue
elasticity of supply
burden of a sales tax

joint products
why low elasticity leads to
   price instability

PROBLEMS

20-1 At a time when the price of gasoline was 30 cents a gallon, a newspaper editorial stated that a 15-cent increase in its price would lower gasoline consumption by an estimated 10%. What does this imply about the elasticity of supply or of demand?

20-2 Suppose you are the manager of Maple Leaf Gardens, home of the Toronto Maple Leafs. You have been selling tickets for $15 each, but for reasons that you cannot understand, recent games have not been sellouts, and you are losing money. The owner who has employed you may be a millionaire, but he has large expenses, and is pressing you to take action to increase your total revenue. Specifically, he suggests that you raise the ticket price to $20. This suggestion bothers you—particularly when it leaks out to the press. Not only do the sportswriters denounce the "greed" of the owner; they also argue that higher prices will backfire, causing even more fans to stay away from the games. As a consequence, gate receipts will be even lower, or so the sportswriters say.

In this controversy, what role does the elasticity of demand play? What assumptions is the owner making about elasticity? What assumptions are the sportswriters making?

20-3 Fill in the blanks with reference to the figure below:

The curve with the greatest elasticity is _____

The next greatest elasticity is _____
The next greatest is _____
The lowest elasticity is _____
Unit elasticity is _____

20-4 (a) Why don't we define elasticity much more simply, as just the slope of a curve; that is, elasticity = (the change in Q)/(the change in P)? *Hint:* Plot exactly the same demand curve as in Figure 20-1 (a) but change the scale in which you measure price. Specifically, measure price in quarters, not dollars, so that the height of E_1 and E_2 are now four times as great. What happens to the slope of D?

(b) "Slope is a poor measure of elasticity because it depends on the arbitrary scale in which P (or Q) is measured." Is this statement true or false?

20-5 "Heating oil for homes has a greater elasticity of demand in the long run than in the short." Do you agree? Explain.

20-6 Using equation 20-2, calculate the elasticity of section AB in the demand curve shown below. Do the same for section CE. Consider the following statement: "Since AB and CE have the same slope, but different elasticity, this shows once again that slope does not necessarily reflect elasticity." Is this true or false?

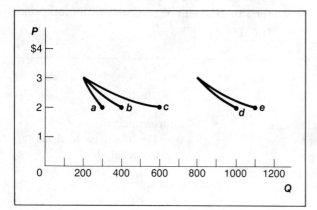

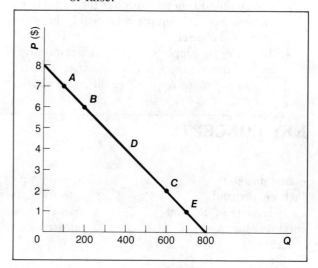

20-7 The supply curve in panel (c) of Figure 20-4 is reproduced as S_1 in the diagram below. Its elasticity has already been calculated to be 1. Which of the other two supply curves—S_2 or S_3—also has an elasticity of 1? What is the elasticity of the other? Does this confirm our statement that slope does not necessarily measure elasticity? Extend S_3 downward and to the left. Which axis—the P or the Q axis—does it intersect? Is the following statement correct? If not, correct it.

"If a straight-line supply curve, when extended, passes through the P axis, it is inelastic. If it passes through the Q axis, its elasticity exceeds 1."

20-8 Would you expect the income elasticity of food to be higher or lower than that of restaurant meals? Explain.

*20-9 Redraw Figure 20-6(a) on the assumption that buyers, rather than sellers, initially pay the tax. Does this change affect the way the two groups bear the eventual burden?

20-10 This problem is based on Boxes 20-1 and 20-4. In the diagram below:
(a) What is the elasticity of demand curve D_1 as price falls from $20 to $10? As price rises from $10 to $20?
(b) How does the elasticity of D_1 compare with that of D_2?
(c) Now suppose income has doubled and that demand has consequently shifted from D_1 to D_2. Calculate the income elasticity of demand.

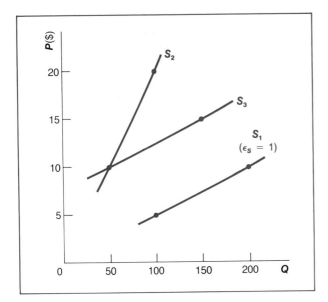

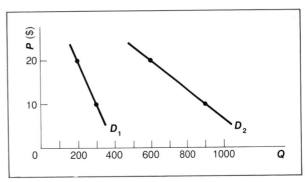

APPENDIX

STATISTICAL DIFFICULTIES IN ESTIMATING DEMAND AND SUPPLY: THE IDENTIFICATION PROBLEM

To understand the problem of discovering the shape and location of demand and supply curves, first consider demand. One method of estimating it is to observe how much of the good has been purchased in the past at various prices. For example, the 1985 dot in panel (*a*) of Figure 20-9 tells us that quantity Q_1 was purchased in that year at price P_1. If we are lucky we will observe a "scatter" of observations like the one shown in this diagram. A straight line fitted to these observations provides our estimated demand curve.

In panel (*b*), we examine the underlying demand and supply curves that gave rise to these four "lucky" observations. Through the entire period of observation, the demand curve remained stable at *D*. But the supply curve shifted. For example, the 1982 observation was the result of the intersection of the demand curve and the 1982 supply curve S_{82}, while the 1983 observation was the result of the intersection of that same demand curve and supply, which had now shifted to S_{83}.

The reason that we were lucky in our scatter of observations in panel (*a*) was that they were generated in panel (*b*) in precisely this way—by the intersection of a *stable* demand curve and a *shifting* supply curve. We have been able to "identify" demand because of shifts in supply. (As an exercise, set up an example where supply is identified by shifts in demand.)

In the more typical case shown in Figure 20-10 we are not so fortunate. Since both supply and demand have shifted from year to year in panel (*b*), the resulting scatter of observations in panel (*a*) gives us neither demand nor supply but some apparently incomprehensible combination of both.

To emphasize the difficulty in this problem, in panel (*c*) we show a completely bogus supply and demand system that could equally well have generated the scatter in panel (*a*). When all we have to work with is what we see in panel (*a*), how can we decide whether this scatter has been generated by the true, inelastic supply and demand system in panel (*b*) or the com-

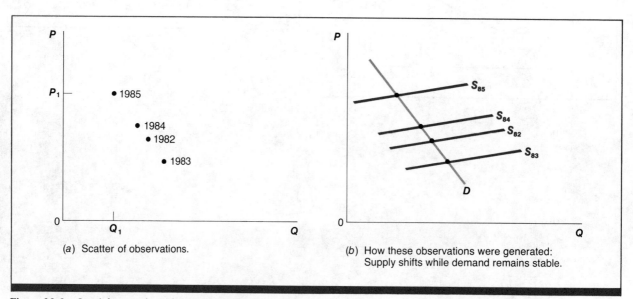

(a) Scatter of observations.

(b) How these observations were generated: Supply shifts while demand remains stable.

Figure 20-9 Special case where demand is easily estimated.

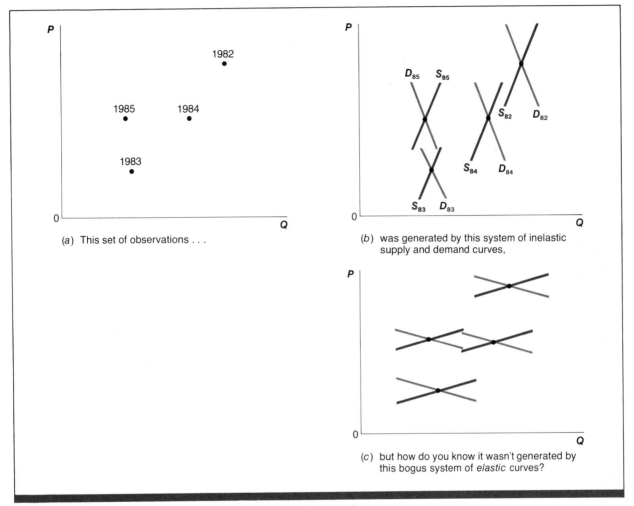

(a) This set of observations . . .

(b) was generated by this system of inelastic supply and demand curves,

(c) but how do you know it wasn't generated by this bogus system of *elastic* curves?

Figure 20-10 When demand estimation requires a special approach.

pletely bogus elastic system in panel (*c*)? Or by some other bogus system? The answer is that the problem is indeed hopeless unless we can get more information. Specifically, we require information on how supply shifts and on how demand shifts. The way in which such information can be used is illustrated in the highly simplified example in Figure 20-11—a figure that initially seems just as puzzling as Figure 20-10. (As an exercise show how this scatter could have been generated by several supply and demand systems.)

Now let us see how we *can* identify the true underlying supply and demand system if we have additional information on how each curve shifts. First, suppose we know that an increase in income causes a parallel

shift to the right of the demand curve. We examine the figures on income and discover that it was the same in 1983 and 1984, but did indeed increase in 1985. This implies that the demand curve remained in the same position in 1983 and 1984, but shifted to the right in 1985.

Next consider supply. What might have caused it to shift? On investigation, we discover that there was a strike in 1984; this reduced the quantity supplied, shifting the supply curve temporarily to the left in 1984. Accordingly, we conclude that the supply curve was in the same position in 1983 and 1985 (when there were no strikes) but temporarily shifted to the left in 1984.

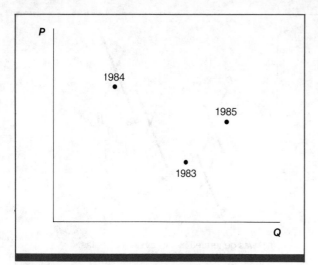

Figure 20-11 Can demand be identified?
This scatter seems hopeless. Without further information, it is.

Of course, this simplified illustration can provide only a "feel" for the identification problem. In practice, estimating supply and demand—like estimating most other economic relationships—involves additional complications. For example, each curve may shift in response to several influences rather than just one. Thus, the demand for beef shifts not only with income but also with the price of pork. This sounds like "too much" information. But it isn't: All of it can be used to estimate demand and supply by an econometrician (economic statistician) using the appropriate statistical techniques.

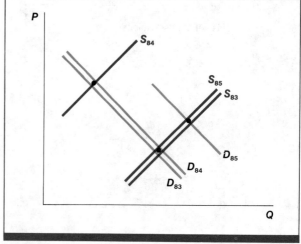

Figure 20-12 How demand (and supply) can be identified.
With knowledge that there was a parallel shift to the left in supply in 1984 and a parallel shift to the right in demand in 1985, this supply and demand system is the only one that can be fitted to the three observations in Figure 20-12.

This additional information allows us to eliminate all bogus supply and demand systems from further consideration. There is now only one supply and demand system that could have generated the observations in Figure 20-11, and that is the true one. As an exercise, you should try to discover it yourself before looking at the solution in Figure 20-12.

To sum up: We started out with an apparently incomprehensible scatter of observations that seemed to reveal neither demand nor supply. However, with some additional information on what causes demand and supply to shift, we were able to estimate both in Figure 20-12.

PROBLEM

20-11 Using Figure 20-12, illustrate our claim that shifts in supply identify demand and that shifts in demand identify supply. In particular, show graphically the scatter we would have observed, and what we would—or would not—be able to identify if
(a) there had been no income increase in 1985;
(b) there had been neither an income increase in 1985 nor a strike in 1984.

Chapter 21

DEMAND

"Producers dance to the consumers' tune."
Reprise from Chapter 4

What is the tune that consumers play? Why do they demand certain products but not others? In this chapter we will examine the demand curve in detail in order to clarify what it tells us about consumers' behaviour. While we will be developing many important ideas, there will be several that we will emphasize in boldface type as being essential for an understanding of future chapters. For example, we will show graphically how much consumers are hurt when the price of a good rises. To illustrate, we will demonstrate the damage to consumers from an increase in the price of oranges following a Florida freeze.

In Chapters 4 and 20 we described and used the *market* demand curve. In this chapter, we will go behind this curve to examine its fundamental characteristics. The first step is to see how the market demand curve is related to the *individual* demand curves of the many consumers who buy a product.

MARKET DEMAND AS THE SUM OF INDIVIDUAL DEMANDS

The total market demand for a good or service is found by summing the demands of all individual consumers, as illustrated in Figure 21-1. (In this example, two individuals represent the millions of consumers in the economy.) Mike Wilson's demand, illustrated in panel (*a*), shows how much he is willing and able to buy at various prices. Similarly, Flora McDon-

nell's demand is shown in panel (*b*), indicating her quite different willingness to buy the same product. At any given price, say $1, we horizontally add the quantities demanded by each consumer in order to get the corresponding point on the market demand schedule in panel (*c*). Observe that individual demand curves are labelled with a small *d*, and the market demand with a capital *D*.

Let us now consider the behaviour of an individual consumer in detail.

THE INDIVIDUAL CONSUMER'S DECISION: THE CHOICE BETWEEN GOODS

The consumer chooses between goods: for example, food and clothing. Should the consumer use a given income to buy more clothing and less food, or more food and less clothing? This choice between goods is a key decision, and we will return to it later.

However, it is also useful to view the consumer as choosing, not between food and clothing, but between food and *all* other goods; in other words, choosing between food and money (since money can be used to buy all other goods). This decision between food and money is described by the individual's demand curve: At each price, the demand curve tells us how much food the consumer will choose.

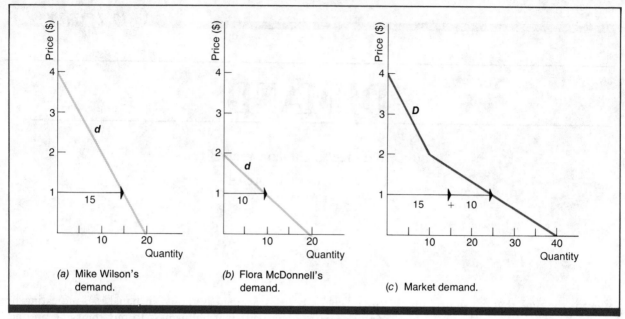

Figure 21-1   How individual demands combine to make up market demand.
To find total quantity demanded at each price—for example, $1—horizontally add the quantities demanded by all individual consumers.

BEHIND THE DEMAND CURVE: SUBSTITUTION AND INCOME EFFECTS

Consider a very simple example: an individual's demand for apples. The demand curve indicates that the consumer will buy more apples when their price falls. There are two reasons for this:

1. Apples become a better buy, compared to other goods. Remember from Chapter 4: When we draw a demand curve for a good, we assume that "other things" remain unchanged—including the prices of all other goods. Thus, a fall in the price of apples means that they become cheaper relative to other items. Consequently, the consumer *switches* from other goods—such as pears and oranges—and buys more apples instead. The increase in the number of apples bought because of such switching is called the **substitution effect.**

2. The other reason concerns income. When we draw a demand curve, we assume not only that the prices of other goods remain unchanged but also that *money* income is constant. For example,

the consumer continues to have an income of, say, $10,000. But when the price of apples falls, money goes further. More can be bought with the $10,000; that is, the consumer's *real income* rises. The consumer is now able to buy more goods, *including* more apples. This is called the **income effect.**

The substitution effect and the income effect combine to make the consumer willing and able to buy more of a good when its price falls.

For most goods, there is little income effect. For example, items like pepper, apples, or even shoes are such a small part of the consumer's budget that a fall in the price of any of these would have little or no discernible effect on anyone's real income. Thus, for most goods, we do not have to pay much attention to the income effect. However, there are a few items—such as cars, clothing, and housing—that are such an important part of people's budgets that a reduction in their price would significantly increase the real income of consumers. Furthermore, if we deal with a broad class of goods—for example, all food rather than just a single item like apples—this becomes a large part of our budget and the income effect becomes more important. (At the same time, the substitution effect becomes less important: There is no good substitute for food as a whole.)

In the balance of this chapter we will examine specific, relatively small items such as apples, where the income effect is not very important, and defer to the appendix the analysis of broad classes of goods—such as food and clothing, where the income effect is more important.

HOW THE DEMAND CURVE REFLECTS MARGINAL BENEFIT

Thus far, we have viewed the demand curve in the way it is shown in panel (*a*) of Figure 21-2. We considered the various possible prices of apples. For each of these prices, a *horizontal* arrow indicates how much the consumer will buy.

In panel (*b*) we reproduce *exactly the same demand curve* with exactly the same points on it. However, we now take a slightly different point of view. In this case, we begin by considering the various possible quantities that may be purchased. For each of these quantities, a *vertical* arrow indicates the maximum price the consumer is willing to pay. For example, the arrow on the left indicates that the consumer is willing to pay $7 for the fourth box of apples. If the price is above $7, the consumer won't buy that fourth box.

The reason it is important to examine demand from this slightly different viewpoint is that the consumer's willingness to pay in panel (*b*) reflects how much benefit or satisfaction he or she gets from this good. For example, we've seen that a consumer who already has three units will pay a maximum of $7 for a fourth unit. In other words, $7 is the consumer's own evaluation of the additional benefit—that is, the **marginal benefit**—derived from that fourth unit. (The word "marginal" is frequently used in economics to mean *additional* or *extra*.) Similarly, the marginal benefit from the fifth unit is $6. Thus:

> The *marginal benefit* is the amount of money that an individual would be willing to pay for having an additional unit of a good or service, per unit of time.

Notice how the individual's marginal benefit declines as more and more is acquired. This makes sense. An individual might get a lot of benefit from the first box of apples. But with more and more apples, the con-

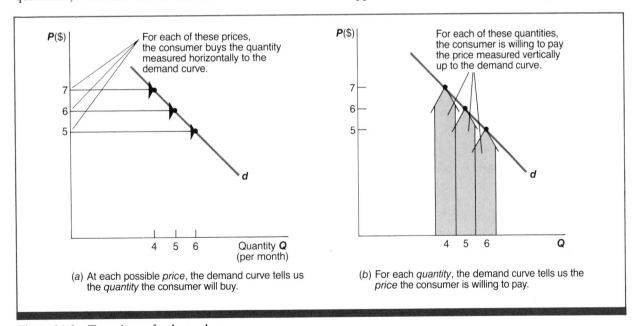

(a) At each possible *price*, the demand curve tells us the *quantity* the consumer will buy.

(b) For each *quantity*, the demand curve tells us the *price* the consumer is willing to pay.

Figure 21-2   Two views of a demand curve.

sumer's appetite for apples is satisfied; that is, the consumer gets less satisfaction—or *utility*—from each additional box. Since eventually this must be true for any good, it is called the *law of diminishing marginal utility*, or the *law of diminishing marginal benefit*.[1]

Be careful with this "law." Although marginal utility must *ultimately* fall, it may rise at first. For example, if the apples are an exotic variety, for which a taste is acquired only slowly, the consumer may get more pleasure out of a second box than the first. But eventually, as more and more apples are acquired, the individual's desire for these apples must decline.

CONSUMER EQUILIBRIUM: HOW MUCH OF A GOOD TO BUY?

In Figure 21-3, the consumer's demand schedule is reproduced from the previous diagram, with more detail added. If the market price is $6 as shown, the demand curve tells us the individual will decide to buy five units. Another way of describing this decision is to note that the first unit will obviously be purchased, since the consumer values it at $10 (the first marginal benefit arrow), while its price is only $6. Since the second, third, and fourth units are also valued above their price of $6, the consumer will also buy them. The fifth will be the last one purchased because the $6 benefit it provides is just equal to its $6 price. The consumer will then be picking the best point and will be in equilibrium.

A consumer does best—that is, reaches equilibrium—by buying additional units of a good until the marginal benefit it provides falls to the level of its price, that is, until

$$MB = P \qquad (21\text{-}1)$$

It is easy to confirm that the consumer should not go beyond this point to purchase more. For example, it would be a mistake to purchase the sixth unit because the $6 price of that unit exceeds the $5 benefit from it. In Box 21-1, equilibrium for a consumer is examined

[1]If we measure utility in terms of dollars, then the law of diminishing marginal utility and the law of diminishing marginal benefit are the same thing. For some purposes, however, money may not be a good yardstick for measuring utility. The reason is that the utility obtainable from one dollar may change. Because of this problem, most advanced texts do not make use of the concept of diminishing marginal utility.

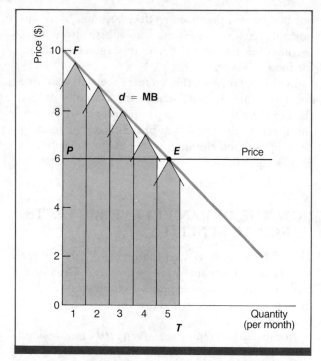

Figure 21-3   Diminishing marginal benefit and consumer equilibrium.
Willingness to pay—as shown by each arrow under the demand curve—reflects the marginal benefit the consumer receives from this good. Eventually, as more is bought, this marginal benefit must decline.

The consumer continues to buy more of this good as long as the marginal benefit from it exceeds the price. Equilibrium occurs at E, where marginal benefit equals price.

using an approach that emphasizes how the consumer chooses *between* goods.

WHY MARGINAL AND TOTAL BENEFIT MUST BE CLEARLY DISTINGUISHED: ADAM SMITH'S PARADOX OF VALUE

We've seen the importance of *marginal benefit* (MB) to the consumer making a decision on how much to purchase. Now we consider the *total benefit* the consumer gets from the *entire* purchase. For example, the total benefit for the consumer who purchases five units in Figure 21-3 is the shaded area *FET0*. The first arrow shows the benefit from the first unit; the second arrow shows the benefit from the second unit; and so on, giving a sum equal to the shaded area.

The *total benefit* a consumer receives from a good is the sum of the marginal benefits it provides—that is, the shaded area under the demand curve and to the left of the quantity purchased.

This distinction between marginal and total benefit is essential to solve a puzzle first posed in 1776 by Adam Smith in the *Wealth of Nations*. One of the most valuable commodities in the world is water; we simply cannot do without it. If necessary, we would be prepared to sell everything we own to acquire it. Yet it sells at a very low price. In contrast, we could easily do without diamonds or champagne; yet they sell for very high prices. Is the world upside down?

To show why the answer to this question is no, we bring together the supply and demand curves for water and champagne in Figure 21-4. In the case of water in panel (*a*), the price P_W is very low because water is so plentiful; a huge quantity can be supplied at a very low price. We consume a huge quantity of it, using it even in ways in which it has very little value, such as washing the car or watering the lawn. Thus, its low price reflects the low *marginal* benefit it provides, shown by arrow Q_1E.

On the other hand, in panel (*b*), we see that the demand for champagne is far less than the demand for water. But champagne sells at a high price because it is very scarce and costly to produce; that is, it can be supplied only at a relatively high price. Consequently, only the most enthusiastic buyers consume it, and on the last unit they consume they enjoy a marginal benefit GE—shown by the higher arrow—equal to the price P_C. We conclude that the higher price of champagne is

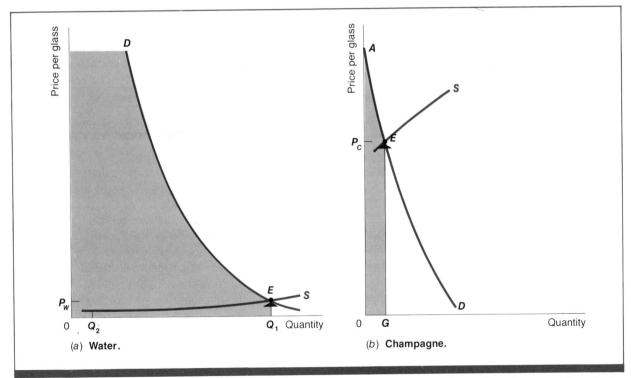

Figure 21-4   How can the price of a necessity like water be so low while the price of an unnecessary luxury like diamonds or champagne is so high?

In panel (*a*), D and S result in equilibrium at E, with price at P_W and the low marginal benefit of water shown by the arrow Q_1E. On the other hand, in panel (*b*) the high cost of supplying champagne means that its price and marginal benefit are

at the much higher level P_C. Thus, if we consider *only the last unit consumed*, champagne has a higher value. However, if we consider *all units consumed*, this conclusion is reversed. The total benefit from water—the shaded area in panel (*a*)—greatly exceeds the total benefit from champagne, the shaded area in panel (*b*).

BOX 21-1

EQUILIBRIUM FOR THE CONSUMER: HOW TO CHOOSE BETWEEN GOODS

Figure 21-3 shows how much of a single good a consumer buys. An important alternative approach addresses the question at the beginning of the chapter: How does a consumer choose *between* goods? How should a consumer's food budget be divided between oranges and cherries? The answer is: The quantities of the two goods should each be adjusted (either increased or decreased) until a dollar's worth of oranges yields the same marginal utility as a dollar's worth of cherries. To see why, suppose that the consumer is initially out of equilibrium. Specifically, the marginal utility of $1 of cherries is greater than $1 of oranges. In this case, income will provide more satisfaction or utility if the consumer buys $1 more of cherries and $1 less of oranges. The utility received from the additional cherries will exceed the utility lost on the oranges. The total satisfaction obtained from the consumer's income

will continue to increase if purchases are switched in this way until the marginal utilities are equalized. And they will indeed equalize because the law of diminishing marginal utility tells us that eventually the marginal utility of cherries will fall as more are bought, while the marginal utility of oranges will rise as fewer are bought.

We can state this as a theorem in general:

A consumer will be in equilibrium if purchases of each good are adjusted to the point where *the marginal utility from the last dollar of expenditure on one good is the same as the marginal utility from the last dollar spent on each of the other goods*. In this way, the individual maximizes the total utility from a given income.

If you wish, you may pursue this basic idea further. This conclusion may be restated: Consumer equilibrium requires that:

$$\frac{\text{marginal utility from a basket of cherries}}{\text{price of cherries}} = \frac{\text{marginal utility from a basket of oranges}}{\text{price of oranges}}$$

$$(21\text{-}2)$$

telling us that, *at the margin*—where we look at only the last unit consumed—*champagne has higher value than water*.

However, this is only part of the story. The *total* benefit from water includes not only the value of the last glass we use, but of *every* glass, and the ones that keep us from dying of thirst are very valuable indeed. In fact, the marginal benefit of one of those first glasses of water, say at Q_2, is so high that we don't have enough room at the top of the diagram to show it. In other words, the total benefit from water—the shaded area in panel (*a*)—is so large that there isn't room to show it in full. Compare this to the relatively small total benefit from champagne—the shaded area in panel (*b*). Thus we conclude that, *overall,* water is much more valuable to us than champagne, even though its price is lower; that is, even though its value *at the margin* is less. The paradox is resolved.

Throughout our study of microeconomics we'll be looking at what happens when people decide to con-

sume or produce one more unit; that is, we will be focusing on what's happening "at the margin." Looking at the margin is the best way to evaluate *how well markets are working*. However, this champagne/water example should remind us that the units *before* we get to the margin may be very important.

Finally, observe that the total shaded area of benefit people get from champagne in panel (*b*) exceeds the rectangle $0P_CEG$ that they pay for it. (This rectangle to the southwest of E is the quantity $0G$ that consumers buy times the price $0P_C$ that they pay per bottle.) The excess of consumer benefit over cost—that is, the triangular area P_CAE—is sometimes referred to as *consumer surplus.*

Consumer surplus is the difference between the maximum amount the consumer *would be willing* to pay for all units consumed of a good, and the amount *actually* paid in the market. Thus, it is the net benefit (measured

In symbols:

$$\frac{MU_{cherries}}{P_{cherries}} = \frac{MU_{oranges}}{P_{oranges}} \qquad (21\text{-}3)$$

To illustrate, suppose a basket of cherries is twice as expensive as a basket of oranges; for example, suppose that $P_{cherries}$ is \$8 while $P_{oranges}$ is \$4. Then equation 21-3 tells us that in equilibrium the consumer will get twice as much marginal utility from the last basket of cherries as from the last basket of oranges. Suppose this is indeed the case: The last basket of cherries provides 24 units of utility, and the last basket of oranges provides 12 units. Thus we confirm that equilibrium exists because equation 21-3 checks out:

$$\frac{24 \text{ units of utility}}{\$8} = \frac{12 \text{ units of utility}}{\$4}$$

Note from the left side of this equation that the consumer is spending \$8 on the last basket of cherries to get 24 units of satisfaction. In other words, each dollar spent on the last basket of cherries yields a marginal utility of $24/8 = 3$ units. On the right side, each dollar spent on the last basket of oranges

provides the same utility; specifically, $12/4 = 3$ units. Thus we confirm that equation 21-3 is just a recasting of the basic principle in boldface. In equilibrium, the consumer gets the same amount of utility—in this example, three units—from the last dollar spent on cherries as from the last dollar spent on oranges.

Alternatively, we can rearrange equation 21-3 to get another statement of the consumer's equilibrium:

$$\frac{MU_{cherries}}{MU_{oranges}} = \frac{P_{cherries}}{P_{oranges}} \qquad (21\text{-}4)$$

In our example:

$$\frac{24 \text{ units of utility}}{12 \text{ units of utility}} = \frac{\$8}{\$4}$$

This is just a restatement of the same simple idea. In equilibrium, the consumer must get twice as much marginal utility from the last basket of cherries (on the left side of this equation) because cherries are twice as expensive (on the right side). The appendix confirms in a more formal way that equation 21-4 does indeed describe consumer equilibrium.

in dollars) that a consumer gets from being able to purchase a good at the market price.

Geometrically, consumer surplus can be approximately measured by the area under the demand curve and above the price (the area FPE in Figure 21-3).

It is important to note that the geometric measure of consumer surplus is an approximation only. But even though it is only approximately correct, we will often make use of it in the following chapters. The main reason is that it makes the analysis much simpler; and furthermore, it is usually a close approximation.[2]

[2]To see why it is an approximation, consider, for example, the fourth unit. According to Figure 21-3, the consumer is willing to pay \$7 for that unit. But \$7 *is the maximum amount she is willing to pay for the fourth unit if she can buy all four units for no more than \$7 each.* If we make her pay *more* than \$7 each for the first three units, she probably would *not* be willing to pay as much as \$7 for the fourth unit: She would then have less money left to spend

HOW IS THE CONSUMER AFFECTED BY A CHANGE IN PRICE?

In Figure 21-5, we reproduce the consumer's demand for apples from Figure 21-3, along with the equilibrium at E if the price is \$6. Now suppose the price of apples falls to \$2 with the new equilibrium at E_2. How much does the consumer gain because the price is lower?

To answer this question, first note that the consumer saves \$4 on each of the first five units because

on other things, and therefore would probably be less keen to buy a fourth unit of this good. But this reasoning applies to the other units as well, so that the area under the demand curve and above the price in Figure 21-3 is a little bit of an overestimate of the total consumer surplus on all units together.

A very useful discussion showing how close the approximation is likely to be, may be found in Robert D. Willig, "Consumer Surplus without Apology," *American Economic Review* (September 1976): 589–97.

the price is $2 rather than $6. This gain is shown by the first five shaded segments in Figure 21-5—that is, by the rectangle $PERP_2$. However, there is also a second source of gain because, in response to the lower price, the consumer increases purchases from five to nine units; and the consumer enjoys a gain on these additional units as well. For example, the sixth unit

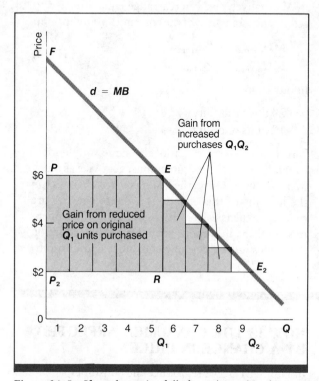

Figure 21-5 If market price falls from $6 to $2, the consumer gain is the shaded area.

At the initial $6 price, the consumer purchases 5 units at E. When price falls by $4, the consumer gains by being able to obtain these 5 units more cheaply. The gain on these 5 units is $4 × 5 = $20, shown as the shaded rectangle P_2PER.

However, the consumer also obtains a second gain. Because of the price reduction, more units are purchased, as shown by the movement from E to E_2. On these additional units, there is a gain of shaded triangle REE_2. To illustrate, consider one of these additional units, the sixth. The $5 the buyer would be willing to pay for this unit is shown by the height of the demand curve. But since this unit costs only $2, the buyer enjoys a shaded gain of $3. All similar shaded areas in triangle EE_2R represent gains on the *new* purchases.

When both of these sources of gains are considered, the consumer's benefit from the price reduction is the entire shaded area.

yields a gain of $3. This is the $5 the consumer would have been *willing* to pay for this unit—as given by the height of the demand curve—less the $2 *actually* paid.

There are similar shaded gains on other new units purchased. Thus, the gain from the additional purchases is shown as the triangle EE_2R. Taking both these sources of gain into account, we conclude that a decrease in price from P to P_2 yields a consumer gain equal to the entire shaded area.

This area of gain may also be looked on as the *increase in consumer surplus*. Initially, consumer surplus is the triangular area PFE. With the lower price, it becomes the larger triangle P_2FE_2. The difference in these two is the shaded area. This increase in consumer surplus is the consumer's gain from the price reduction.

In Figure 21-5, we visualized demand as a series of distinct marginal benefit bars. As we go from an individual demand curve to a market demand curve, the diagram must represent a large number of such bars. (Remember, market demand is just the sum of the demands of all individuals.) Because each bar will be very narrow, we can approximate demand by a smooth curve—such as in Figure 21-6—which shows how much *all* consumers in a market gain together if the price of a good falls from $10 to $6 and they move from equilibrium E_1 to E_2. First, they enjoy a benefit of area 1 (equal to $1600) because they can now buy the 400 units they originally purchased, at a price of $6 rather than $10. Second, they also enjoy a consumer surplus of area 2 (equal to $400) on the 200 additional units they are now purchasing, for a total increase in consumer surplus of $2000.

Thus, to summarize:

If the market price *falls*, there is an *increase* in consumer surplus equal to the horizontal area between the old and new price, and to the left of the demand curve.

Of course, the same proposition applies to a price increase:

If the market price *rises*, there is a *decrease* in consumer surplus equal to the horizontal area between the new and the old price, and to the left of the demand curve.

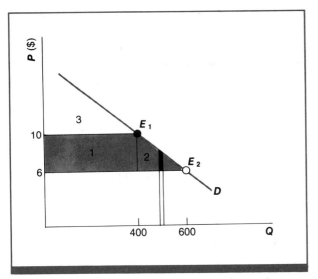

Figure 21-6 **If the market price falls from \$10 to \$6, consumer surplus for all consumers together increases by shaded area 1 + 2.**

On the 400 units that they originally bought, consumers gain area 1 because of the \$4 price reduction. On the additional 200 units they buy at the lower price, they gain area 2. (To illustrate, we show the gain on the five-hundreth unit. The \$8 that the buyer would be willing to pay for this unit is shown by the height of the demand curve; that is, by the white bar plus the black bar. Since each unit only costs the buyer \$6 [the white bar], there is a consumer surplus of \$2 [the black bar].)

THE FLORIDA FREEZE: APPLYING THE ANALYSIS OF CHAPTERS 20 AND 21

As noted in the previous chapter, cold waves in 1977, 1981, 1983, and 1985 froze part of the Florida citrus crop. The effects of a freeze are illustrated in Figure 21-7. (To simplify this illustration, picking, shipping, and other costs of getting the oranges to market are ignored.) The harvest coming onto the market is reduced from the normal supply S to S_2. This in turn means that prices are higher, with equilibrium at E_2 rather than E_1. Several groups of people are affected, as follows:

Producers benefit. Because demand for citrus fruit is inelastic, producers' revenue increases. As a group, they gain more from the higher price than they lose from the reduced harvest. Of course, those who lose their entire crop are worse off, but their loss is less

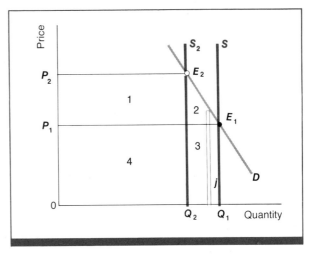

Figure 21-7 **How Florida citrus freeze benefits producers but damages consumers and the nation as a whole.**
The normal crop of S would have resulted in equilibrium E_1 with price P_1. But because of a freeze, the supply coming to the market is reduced to S_2. Consequently, equilibrium is at E_2 with price P_2.

Without the freeze, producers' total revenue would have been the rectangle 4 + 3 to the southwest of E_1, that is, the number of units sold Q_1 times the price of each P_1. However, with the freeze shifting equilibrium to E_2, revenue is area 1 + 4 instead. Since area 4 is common to both, producers gain area 1 from the freeze but lose area 3. Consumers lose area 1 + 2 as a result of the increased price. For the nation overall, we must consider the effect on both groups:

Consumers	lose 1	lose 2	
Producers	gain 1		lose 3
Sum indicates nation will		lose 2	lose 3

This overall loss to the nation of area 2 + 3 is easily confirmed. Consider j, one of the cases of fruit that freezes. The marginal benefit it would have provided is the height of the thin bar at j. If we sum all the similar bars throughout the range of lost output between Q_2 and Q_1, the result is area 2 + 3, the total damage to the nation as a whole because those oranges froze.

Warning: Area 1 is a loss to consumers and a gain to producers. In cancelling it out in the tabled calculations above, we assume that area 1 is valued similarly by the consumers losing it and the producers receiving it—or at least similarly enough not to upset our conclusions. Although this is a reasonable enough assumption, it represents a complication that we will return to in Chapter 25.

than the gain of the other producers who can sell their crop at a higher price.

Consumers lose. Because the price rises, consumers lose areas 1 + 2.

With producers benefitting and consumers losing, it is not immediately obvious how the economy as a whole is affected, on balance. However, a moment's reflection leads us to the following conclusion:

On balance, there is a net loss. When oranges freeze, there are fewer oranges to eat. The economy as a whole—that is, taking producers and consumers together—is worse off.

The various effects of a crop loss may be summarized. Because demand is inelastic, producers as a group gain; their total revenues increase. (If demand were elastic, total revenues would fall, and producers as a group would be worse off.) However, regardless of demand elasticity, consumers and the economy as a whole, suffer a loss.[3]

Now let us examine more carefully our conclusion that producers benefit from a freeze. If you are an individual producer, it will not be in your interest to let your crop freeze. Nothing you can do as an individual affects price. Whatever the price may be, the more you have to sell, the better. However, a freeze benefits

producers as a group, because the resulting scarcity *does* affect price. This raises the question: If producers cannot get Mother Nature to restrict their supply, is it not in their interest to work together to do it themselves? The answer is yes. However, in practice they may have difficulty in organizing to restrict supply. In turn, this may lead them to look instead to the government to introduce and enforce collective supply restrictions—for example, a government restriction on the number of acres that a farmer may plant. Such a limitation raises price and may also raise farm income, but what it does to consumers and the nation as a whole is quite another matter.

EXTENSIONS OF DEMAND THEORY: TRANSACTIONS AND TIME COSTS

Time is Money.

Ben Franklin

In deciding to buy another unit of a product, the consumer compares the benefit the unit provides with its cost. However, cost is a broad term, covering more than just the purchase price. For example, someone considering the purchase of a car will be concerned with not only its price but also the expected cost of gasoline, insurance, service, and repairs. Informed buyers also take account of **transactions costs**.

Transactions Costs

To illustrate such costs, suppose that, after careful consideration of the profit prospects of Hiram Walker & Sons Limited, you buy 100 shares of that company's stock from a "discount" broker. In addition to the cost of the stock itself, you incur two transactions costs:

1. *The commission charged by the broker.* Discount brokers provide only one service: buying or selling stocks. For this, they charge a fee or commission. They do not give advice or provide information on companies. As a consequence, you also face a second cost.

2. *Search cost*, also called *information cost*. This is the cost in collecting the information necessary to make a sensible decision. This cost includes not only the time you spend in your study of Hiram Walker, but also any out-of-

---

[3]Some of the oranges grown in Florida are sold here in Canada; hence, part of the consumers' loss from a Florida freeze is borne by *Canadian* (rather than American) consumers. If this part were large enough, this may mean that if we look at the effects of a Florida freeze from a strictly American point of view, there *may* be a net *gain* from a freeze. True, part of the gain to U.S. orange producers is offset by the losses of American consumers. But since some of the losses to consumers are borne by *foreign* consumers, it is possible that a Florida freeze may cause a net gain to the *U.S.* economy. As another example of a net gain from a crop reduction, consider the case of Brazilian coffee (most of which is exported from Brazil to foreign countries). When frosts in Brazil reduced coffee supplies in 1977, the world price of coffee soared. Brazil as a nation gained. In cases of this kind it may be in the national interest to artificially restrict supply, as Brazil did during the 1930s by dumping coffee into the ocean.

Such supply restrictions should, however, be approached cautiously, even if a narrow national viewpoint is taken. In the long run, the demand elasticity may be much higher than in the short run. In other words, if coffee prices are kept high for a long period, people may switch to tea and decide that they prefer it. Furthermore, competing producers (in Africa or elsewhere) may be encouraged to increase production in response to higher prices.

pocket expenses you may incur. For example, you may subscribe to publications that provide information on corporations. The cost of gathering information may be larger than the commission you pay the broker.

You may, of course, play your cards differently the next time by going to a traditional broker. You will pay more, but you will get more in return. The broker will not only buy the stock for you, but also provide you with information on corporations and suggestions on what stocks to buy or sell.

> *Search cost*, or *information cost*, is the time and money spent in collecting the information necessary to make a decision to buy or sell stocks or any other item.

The Business of Providing Information

It's not just traditional stockbrokers who are in the information business. As another example, real estate agents provide information to both buyers and sellers. They give buyers information about houses that are available. They provide sellers with advice on pricing of a home and information on possible buyers.

If you are selling a house, should you go to a real estate agent—to whom you will have to pay a commission if the house is sold—or should you place an ad in the paper and try to sell the house on your own? You will usually do better by going to an agent; agents are in the business of making contact with potential buyers. Specialization in marketing may be just as important as specialization in other skills, such as law or medicine.

Nevertheless, you should beware. Whenever you deal with people who provide information or advice, it's important to ask: Is the information or advice really in *your* interest, or are the agents being influenced—consciously or subconsciously—by quite different interests of their own? For example, is your real estate agent suggesting that you accept a low price on your home in order to make the sale and earn a commission? Does your stockbroker have the same motive in encouraging you to buy or sell stocks?

How Do Search Costs Influence Market Price?

The more information auto buyers have, and the more willing they are to bear search costs by seeking out alternative sellers, the less car dealers will be able to overcharge; that is, the less dealers will be able to raise their prices above the level of their competitors. Thus, search tends to reduce the average price the public pays and also the variation in prices. Moreover, the percentage variation in price will be less for expensive items like cars—where it pays the consumer to search hard for the best buy—than for small-ticket items where it's not worth the trouble. A grocer may be able to raise the price of salt by 10% without anyone noticing, but a car dealer who tries to charge 10% more than the competition will soon be out of business.

Search efforts undertaken by the public provide several benefits. Individuals who search generally purchase products that better satisfy their requirements. Moreover, the benefits go beyond the individual. As the public searches and acquires more information, it becomes less likely that a poor product will survive in the marketplace. In addition, as we've already seen, prices tend to be lower and have less spread. If all these things happen, it becomes less necessary for a single buyer to incur large search costs. There will be less risk of being overcharged or ending up with a poor product. Thus, paradoxically, the more searching the public does, the less any individual buyer needs to search.

Time represents a major part of search costs—for example, the time a consumer spends shopping around at various car dealers. But time can be expensive, not only in searching for products, but also in consuming them after they have been purchased.

Time Costs in Consumption

Examples abound. Car or TV buyers seek out a reliable product because, once they have made their purchase, they don't want to waste a lot of time getting it repaired. Time may be a critical consideration in deciding not only on goods but also on services. For example, a train trip from Toronto to Winnipeg costs only about half as much as an airline ticket, but most people don't take the train because it takes more time. In particular, people with high incomes incur high time costs in travelling by train; the time they waste is very valuable. Consequently, the rich fly.

Time cost helps to explain consumption patterns, not only within Canada but also among countries. In North America we buy costly home appliances because they save valuable time. In poorer countries, the laundry is more likely to be done by hand; the time required is of little consequence where incomes are low and time is therefore less valuable.

Throughout the balance of this book, we refer simply to price; but remember that "price" should be interpreted broadly to include transactions and time costs.

KEY POINTS

1. Marginal benefit is the satisfaction derived from consuming one more unit of a good or service. It is measured by the height of the demand curve, which shows how much the consumer is willing to pay for an additional unit.

2. When you see a demand curve, you should visualize the vertical marginal benefit bars beneath it.

3. To reach equilibrium, a consumer increases the purchase of a product until its marginal benefit falls to the level of its price.

4. When price falls, consumers gain by the horizontal area to the left of the demand curve and between the old and the new price.

5. When a crop is damaged (by spoilage, frost, or whatever), producers may be better or worse off, depending on whether demand is elastic or not. But consumers and the nation as a whole lose.

6. Price should be interpreted broadly, to include transactions and time costs.

KEY CONCEPTS

individual demand
market demand
choice among goods
substitution effect
income effect
marginal benefit (MB)
law of diminishing marginal utility

relationship of demand to
   marginal benefit
consumer equilibrium, where
   marginal benefit equals price
consumer surplus
gain to consumers from a fall
   in price

effect of lost output on
   consumers, producers, and
   the nation as a whole
transactions cost
time cost
search cost (information cost)

PROBLEMS

21-1 Suppose each of three individuals has unit elasticity of demand for a particular good. Without drawing any diagrams, can you guess what the elasticity of the total market demand for this good will be? Now draw diagrams showing each of the individual demands, and how the market demand should be constructed. How does the slope of market demand compare with the slope of the individual demands? Is market demand therefore more elastic? Explain.

21-2 Using your own example, explain why marginal benefit must eventually fall.

*21-3 If the price of oranges rises and the price of cherries remains constant, show in either equation 21-2 or 21-3 (in Box 21-1) why the consumer is no longer in equilibrium. What action does the consumer take to get to a new equilibrium?

21-4 Suppose that a substantial part of a lettuce crop spoils en route to market because of the producers' negligence. Will these producers suffer a loss as a consequence? Explain. How will consumers and the nation as a whole be affected? Would your conclusion be changed if the producers were insured?

21-5 (a) Suppose that, without even looking at the new products available, a buyer has decided to purchase a new camera rather than a new TV. Show how this decision might be reversed if, for the first time, the buyer realizes that these two alternative purchases involve different search costs.

(b) Repeat question (a), replacing search costs with time costs in consumption.

21-6 What do you estimate the time cost of your education to be?

21-7 Consider two individuals—one who is retired and one who is not. Both are wealthy and therefore equally able to purchase the world's most reliable and most expensive car. Which one is more likely to do so? Why?

APPENDIX

THE THEORY OF CONSUMER CHOICE: INDIFFERENCE CURVES

In this appendix, we develop an important principle introduced in Chapter 2 and emphasized in Box 21-1: Economic behaviour involves a *choice between alternatives*. To illustrate, consider an individual consuming unit—a single individual or household. Suppose for simplicity that the household is consuming only two goods, food and clothing. To analyse the decision it faces, we introduce the concept of an **indifference curve** in Figure 21-8 and Table 21-1.

To illustrate this concept, suppose that the household begins at a point chosen at random in Figure 21-8; say, point *A*, where it is consuming three units of clothing and two units of food. Then, to draw the indifference curve through *A*, we ask the following question: What other combinations of clothing and food would leave the household equally well off?

The household may inform us that it would be equally satisfied at point *B*, with two units of clothing and three units of food. In other words, if the household starting at *A* were asked if it would give up one unit of clothing in return for one more unit of food, it would respond that it doesn't care whether such a

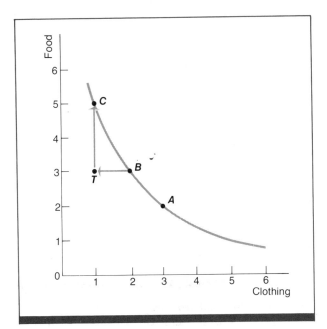

Figure 21-8   An indifference curve.
An indifference curve joins all points where the household has the same level of total utility or satisfaction.

Table 21-1
Combinations among Which the Household Is Indifferent

Combi-nation	Clothing	Food	Amount of additional food required to induce household to give up 1 unit of clothing (the marginal rate of substitution of food for clothing)
A	3	2	
B	2	3	1
C	1	5	2

change takes place or not: The household is indifferent between points *A* and *B*.

> On an *indifference curve*, each point represents the same level of satisfaction or utility. A household is indifferent among the various points on its indifference curve.

Now let us continue the experiment, asking the household under what conditions it would be willing to give up one more unit of clothing. In moving upward and to the left from point *B*, the household recognizes that it is getting short of clothing and already has a lot of food. It states that it is willing to give up another unit of its very scarce clothing only in return for a large amount (two units) of food. Consequently point *C*, representing one unit of clothing and five of food, is on the same indifference curve as *A* and *B*. Because the household is increasingly reluctant to give up clothing as it has less and less, the indifference curve has the bowed shape shown.[4]

THE MARGINAL RATE OF SUBSTITUTION: THE SLOPE OF THE INDIFFERENCE CURVE

In moving from *B* to *C*, notice that the slope of the indifference curve is 2.[5] This geometric concept has an important economic meaning. It is the amount of food ($TC = 2$) that is required to compensate for the loss of 1 unit of clothing ($BT = 1$); that is, it is the **marginal rate of substitution** of food for clothing.

> The marginal rate of substitution (MRS) of food for clothing is the amount of food required to compensate for the loss of one unit of clothing, while leaving the consuming unit

equally well off. Geometrically, it is the slope of the indifference curve.

THE INDIFFERENCE MAP

The indifference curve in Figure 21-8 is reproduced as u_1 in Figure 21-9. Recall that our starting point, *A*, was a point chosen at random. We might equally well have started at point *F* or *G*; there is an indifference curve that passes through each of these points as well. In other words, there is a whole family of indifference curves which form the **indifference map** in Figure 21-9.

While all points on a single indifference curve represent the same level of satisfaction, points on another indifference curve represent a different level of satisfaction. Observe that, at point *G*, the family has more clothing and more food than at *F*. Thus, the family prefers *G* to *F*. Because other points on u_3—such as *H*—are equivalent to *G*, they must also be preferred to *F* and to every other point on u_2. Therefore, indifference curve u_3 represents a higher level of satisfaction or utility than u_2. The farther the indifference curve is

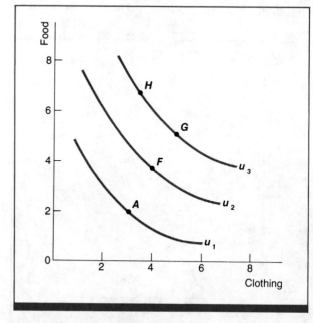

Figure 21-9   An indifference map.
There is a whole set of indifference curves for the household, each curve representing a different level of utility. Thus, u_2 represents a higher level of utility than u_1, and u_3 a still higher level.

---

[4]Although indifference curves usually have a changing slope, this need not always be the case. For example, a two-car family might be indifferent among the choices of (a) two Hondas, no Ford; (b) one Honda, one Ford; or (c) no Hondas, two Fords. Then, with Hondas on one axis and Fords on the other, the indifference curve joining points *A*, *B*, and *C* would be a straight line. The reason is that this particular family considers the two cars to be *perfect substitutes* for each other.

[5]Actually the slope of a line between *B* and *C* is −2. (The vertical change is +2, while the horizontal change is −1.) For simplicity, we ignore the negative signs that apply to all slopes in this appendix.

away from the origin (to the northeast), the greater the level of satisfaction.

Incidentally, this illustrates how three variables can be shown in a diagram with only two dimensions. The three variables are the quantity of food, the quantity of clothing, and the household's utility. We can visualize this system of indifference curves as mapping out a utility hill, with each curve representing a contour line showing points with equal utility, just as a geographer's contour line shows points of equal height above sea level. A geographer's contour lines do not cross, and the indifference curves of a household do not cross either.

As the household moves from the origin to the northeast, it moves up the utility hill to higher and higher levels of satisfaction.[6]

THE BUDGET LIMITATION

As we have seen, the indifference map reflects the household's *desires*; the household prefers G to F in Figure 21-9 and is indifferent between H and G. However, the household's behaviour depends not only on what the household *wants,* but also on what it is *able* to buy.

What the household is able to buy depends on three things: its money income, the price of food, and the price of clothing. If the household's income is $100, while the price of food is $10 per unit and clothing is $20, the various options open to the household are illustrated by the **budget line** KL in Figure 21-10.

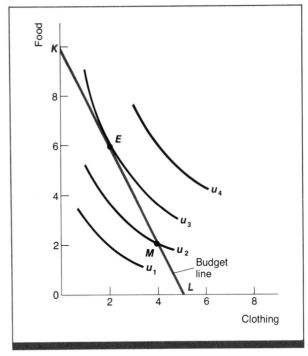

Figure 21-10   The equilibrium of a household with a budget limit.
KL represents the household's budget limit. Each point on this line represents a combination of food and clothing that can be purchased, and that just barely exhausts the household's budget. Equilibrium involves moving along this budget line to the point E of tangency with the highest achievable indifference curve.

> The *budget line*—sometimes called an *income line* or *price line*—shows the various options of a household with a given money income and facing a given set of prices.

If the whole $100 is spent on food at $10 per unit, the household can buy 10 units, as shown by point K. At the other extreme, if the household spends its whole $100 on clothing at $20 per unit, it can buy five units, as shown by point L. Similarly, it can be shown that any other point on the straight line KL will exactly exhaust the budget of $100. (As an exercise, show that this is true for point M.)

The slope of the budget line between K and L is

$$\frac{\text{Vertical distance } OK}{\text{Horizontal distance } OL} = \frac{10}{.5} = 2$$

[6]One advantage of the indifference curve approach is that we don't have to worry about the units of measurement as we move up the utility hill. We know that curve u_3 represents more utility than curve u_2, but we don't need to know *how much* more. Specifically, with indifference curves, we are only making statements such as: "F is preferred to A, G is preferred to F, and G and H are equally desirable."

Thus, the indifference map involves simply an *ordering* of various consumption packages. This is called **ordinal measurement** (for example, F is better than A) in contrast to **cardinal measurement** (for example, F is 25% better than A). Cardinal measurement is not necessary with the simple ordering represented by indifference curves.

Avoiding the problems in cardinal measurement of utility was one of the main reasons why Nobel prizewinner J.R. Hicks developed the indifference curve approach in his *Value and Capital* (London: Oxford University Press, 1939).

This is the same as the price ratio of the two goods; that is,

$$\frac{P_{\text{clothing}}}{P_{\text{food}}} = \frac{\$20}{\$10} = 2 \qquad (21\text{-}5)$$

Since this is always true,

The slope of the budget line is equal to the price ratio of the two goods.

THE HOUSEHOLD'S EQUILIBRIUM

Faced with the budget limit KL, the household purchases the combination of food and clothing shown at E; that is, it moves along the budget line to the point where that line touches the highest possible indifference curve, in this case u_3. Any other affordable purchase, like M, is less attractive because it leaves the household on a lower indifference curve—u_2 rather than u_3.

Consumers maximize their satisfaction or utility by moving along their budget line to the highest attainable indifference curve. This is achieved at a point of tangency such as E in Figure 21-10.

A point of tangency, of course, is a point where the slope of the indifference curve (MRS) is equal to the slope of the budget line (the price ratio of the two goods). That is,

$$\text{MRS} = \frac{P_{\text{clothing}}}{P_{\text{food}}} = 2 \text{ in this example}[7] \qquad (21\text{-}6)$$

[7]For readers who have studied marginal utility in Box 21-1, it can be shown that MRS—with its value of 2 in this case—is also the ratio of the marginal utilities of these two goods. That is,

$$\text{MRS} = \frac{\text{MU}_{\text{clothing}}}{\text{MU}_{\text{food}}} = 2 \qquad (21\text{-}7)$$

We can see why from our example. Since the household is willing to give up only one unit of clothing to get two units of food, it values clothing twice as highly as food; that is, its marginal utility of clothing is double its marginal utility of food.

When we substitute equation 21-7 into 21-6, the result is

$$\frac{\text{MU}_{\text{clothing}}}{\text{MU}_{\text{food}}} = \frac{P_{\text{clothing}}}{P_{\text{food}}} \qquad (21\text{-}8)$$

which is a confirmation of the basic relationship, equation 21-4, introduced in Box 21-1.

In conclusion, we re-emphasize that the budget line and the indifference map are independent of one another. The indifference map shows the household's preferences; in defining the indifference map, no attention is paid to what the household can actually afford. What it can afford is shown by the budget line. When the indifference map and the budget line are brought together, the choice of the household is determined.

DERIVING A DEMAND CURVE FROM AN INDIFFERENCE MAP

The indifference curve/budget line analysis is used in panel (a) of Figure 21-11 to show how the household responds to a fall in the price of clothing. When clothing was originally priced at $20 per unit, we have seen that the budget line was KL and the equilibrium was E_1—both reproduced from the previous figure. Now suppose that the price of clothing falls to $10, but the price of food remains unchanged. Because the price ratio has changed, the slope of the budget line changes. Specifically, the budget line rotates from KL to KR. (If all $100 is spent on clothing, the household can now buy 10 units at point R. But because the price of food does not change, the new budget line still ends at point K, as before.)[8]

Faced with the new budget line KR, the household again searches for its highest possible indifference curve, finding it at the point of tangency E_2. The two points of equilibrium, E_1 and E_2, define the two points on the demand curve of the household, shown in panel (b) of Figure 21-11. Thus, the individual's demand curve can be derived from his or her indifference map.

THE RESULTS OF A PRICE CHANGE: SUBSTITUTION AND INCOME EFFECTS

We have already seen that, in the event of a decrease in the price of clothing, the consumer will increase purchases because of the substitution effect and the income effect. In Figure 21-12 we begin with a decrease in

[8]Because our simple example has only two goods—food and clothing—food may be interpreted as representing all goods other than clothing. In showing the relationship between the indifference curve diagram and the demand curve for clothing, it is customary to write "all other goods" on the vertical axis, as we have done in panel (a) of Figure 21-11.

price that moves the consumer from E_1 to E_2—thus increasing clothing purchases from Q_1 to Q_2. We shall now show how this increased purchase can be broken

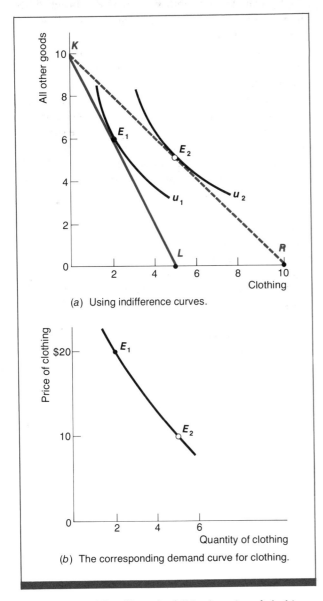

(a) Using indifference curves.

(b) The corresponding demand curve for clothing.

Figure 21-11   The effect of a fall in the price of clothing. As the price of clothing falls from $20 to $10, the budget line rotates counterclockwise from KL to KR. As a result, the quantity of clothing purchased increases from 2 to 5 units. In panel (b) we graph exactly this same information about price and quantity; again we move from point E_1 to E_2. However, in panel (b) these points define the consumer's demand curve.

down into a substitution and income effect. To look at the effects of substitution alone, we keep the consumer on the original indifference curve u_1. This means that we are holding real income constant. At the same time, we allow the slope of the price line to change to reflect the lower price of clothing. Thus, we find a new price line ST parallel to KR—thus reflecting the new price—but tangent to the original indifference curve u_1 at point V. The **substitution effect** is the quantity change Q_1Q_3 associated with the move from E_1 to V, as shown by arrow 1.

However, the consumer does not actually move from E_1 to V, but from E_1 to E_2. The rest of the move—

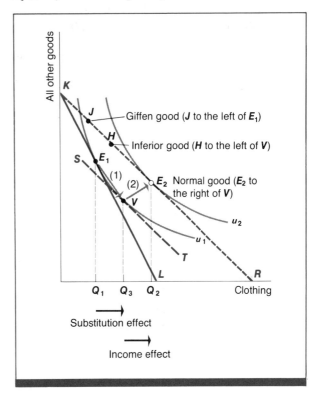

Figure 21-12   The substitution and income effects of a price reduction: A detailed description of the move from E_1 to E_2 (in Figure 21-11a).
With the fall in the price of clothing, there is a move from equilibrium E_1 to E_2, which can be decomposed into two parts: Move (1) from E_1 to V shows the substitution effect by holding real income constant. (V is on the same indifference curve as E_1.)

Move (2) from V to E_2 shows the income effect by holding relative prices constant. (The slopes at V and E_2 are the same.)

from V to E_2, shown by arrow 2—represents the **income effect.** Observe that a shift in the price line from ST to KR results from a change in real income alone; that is, it involves no change in relative prices, since the slopes of ST and KR are the same.

> The *substitution effect* is the change in the quantity purchased which would occur as a result of a change only in relative prices, with real income held constant. In Figure 21-12, it is the distance from Q_1 to Q_3.
>
> The *income effect* is the change in the quantity purchased which would occur as a result of a change only in real income. In Figure 21-12, it is the distance from Q_3 to Q_2.

When the price of clothing falls, the shape of the indifference curve guarantees that the substitution effect will lead an individual to buy more clothing and less of other goods; that is, arrow (1) points to the southeast in Figure 21-12. However, the sign of the income effect is not certain. For the vast majority of goods—the normal goods—the income effect will lead an individual to buy more of both clothing and other goods; arrow (2) points to the northeast, as shown in Figure 21-12. However, for the few goods that are *inferior*, the income effect is different; an increase in income alone—that is, a move from budget line ST to KR—

reduces the quantity purchased. In such a case, the tangency of an indifference curve to KR occurs not at E_2 but instead at a point such as H, *to the left of* V. (To illustrate this possibility, draw in this other indifference curve, ensuring that it is tangent to KR at H.) Note that in this case, arrow (2) no longer points to the northeast but instead points to the northwest: The increase in income reduces the quantity of clothing purchased.

Economists have been fascinated with the logical possibility that this sort of unusual income effect might be sufficiently strong to more than offset the substitution effect; in other words, that an indifference curve might be tangent to KR at a point such as J, *to the left of E_1.* Then the reduction in the price of the good would lead to a move from E_1 to J and a *reduction* in the purchase of that good. Such a case would be extremely rare. One example has been attributed to Victorian economist Giffen, involving the purchase of potatoes in a very poor economy. In such a special case, a fall in the price of the basic staple—potatoes—would so increase people's real income and their purchases of meat and other expensive foods that they would buy *fewer* potatoes. Notice that such a peculiar good—a so-called *Giffen good*—would have a strange demand curve; it would slope downward and *to the left.*)

PROBLEM

21-8 Gasoline is a normal good. Show the substitution and income effects of a price increase.

Chapter 22

COST AND PERFECTLY COMPETITIVE SUPPLY: THE SHORT RUN

"... and consumers dance to the producers' tune."

Reprise from Chapter 4

In the last chapter, the consumer was king, deciding which goods would be produced and which would not. But in fact, it's a joint regency: The producer is also a king. Goods aren't produced unless the consumer wants them *and* the producer can deliver them at a price that both covers costs and is acceptable to the consumer. In this chapter, we begin our study of producers.

In the last chapter, we stressed the *choices* open to consumers, specifically, the choice of which goods to consume. The producer likewise faces fundamental choices:

1. *Which* goods will the firm produce? And *how many* units of each?
2. *What combination of inputs* will the firm use in the production of these goods? For example, will a manufacturer of home appliances use a highly automated assembly line that can be operated by only a few workers or use less automated equipment and more workers? Will a wheat farmer use a great deal of fertilizer on

each acre or produce the wheat using more land and less fertilizer?

While these are the fundamental choices, in practice producers are constrained by their decisions of the past. For example, Massey-Ferguson is committed to the production of farm machinery by its huge investment in plant and equipment, most of which can be used only to make farm machinery. Thus it does not have the choice next month of producing aircraft or shoes instead. Furthermore, Massey-Ferguson's short-term commitment for next month is not only to the *kind* of equipment it will have—that is, equipment to produce tractors and combines. It is also committed to the existing *quantity* of equipment; it is now too late to order new machines or build new factories to use in next month's production. With its stock of plant and equipment already determined, Massey-Ferguson has only a narrow set of production decisions for next month: *How many tractors, combines, etc., will it produce, and how many workers and how much material will it use* to produce these machines?

THE SHORT RUN AND THE LONG

The narrow decisions just referred to are the ones that Massey-Ferguson faces in the **short run**, when it cannot change the quantity or type of capital it has inherited from past investment decisions. However, if the firm is deciding what it will be doing five or ten years from now, it will have far more flexibility. It will have time to acquire more capital. Or, it can contract its capital stock by deciding not to replace its worn-out plant or equipment. Thus, in the **long run**, the firm can pick from a wide range of choices. It can choose to produce in a **capital-intensive** manner—with many machines and few workers—or in a **labour-intensive** manner, with many workers and few machines. It can enter new businesses or drop certain products altogether.

> The *short run* is the period during which the firm cannot change the quantity or type of its plant and equipment.
>
> The *long run* is the period during which the firm is able to change the quantity or type of its plant and equipment.

The short run is *not* defined as any specific number of weeks, months, or years. Instead, it is whatever time period plant and equipment are fixed. In some industries, the short run may last many years. That much time is needed to design and construct a large electric power plant, for example. In other industries, the short run may be just a matter of days. To illustrate, a student entrepreneur can quickly buy a word processor and thereby acquire the capital equipment to set up business typing term papers. Furthermore, the short run may be briefer for an expanding firm than for a firm that is contracting its operations. An expanding firm may be able to acquire new equipment quickly, while a contracting firm may be able to reduce its capital stock only slowly. There may be no market in which it can sell its used machinery, and its capital stock may take years to wear out.

In the next few chapters, we will be looking at the decisions of producers. We begin in this chapter by considering a specific case. How many units will a firm produce if (1) it is making a *short run* decision and (2) it is in a *perfectly competitive* industry? In Chapter 23, we will turn to the long run, still looking

at a perfectly competitive industry. Chapters 25 through 27 will consider monopolies, oligopolies, and other types of imperfectly competitive industries.

Through all these chapters, we will assume that business executives try to maximize their firm's profits. Of course, executives may also have other motives—for example, ensuring the security of their jobs or increasing their own importance by expanding their operations and the number of people who work for them. However, to keep things simple, we focus on the important objective of profit maximization. Specifically, we assume that if a firm can increase its profits by making more of a good, it will do so. Or if it can increase profits by producing less, that's what it will do.

If it is trying to maximize profits, how much output will a firm produce and supply in the short run? That's the central question in this chapter. We begin with production costs, which have a major influence on supply.

COSTS IN THE SHORT RUN

A firm's total costs of production may be subdivided into two components: (1) **fixed costs** and (2) **variable costs.**

1. Fixed costs or *overhead costs.* Fixed costs (FC) are the costs that do not vary as output changes. Indeed, they are incurred *even if no output is produced at all.* This is illustrated in Table 22-1, which shows the costs of a hypothetical manufacturer of shoes. Observe that fixed costs in column 2 are constant at \$35, regardless of the quantity of output q in column 1.

Because the firm cannot change the quantity of plant and equipment in the short run, many of the costs associated with such capital are fixed. For example, interest must be paid on the funds originally borrowed to buy the equipment, and *depreciation* occurs whether or not any output is produced. Similarly, buildings must be protected with fire *insurance* regardless of how much is produced.

2. Variable costs. On the other hand, variable costs (VC) *do* change as the firm increases the quantity of output. For example, the firm hires more labour and buys more electricity, leather, and other materials. In Table 22-1, column 3 illustrates how variable costs rise as quantity increases.

Table 22-1
Short-Run Costs of a Hypothetical Firm Producing Shoes

(1) Quantity produced (pairs) q	(2) Fixed cost FC	(3) Variable cost VC	(4) Total cost TC = FC + VC = (3) + (2)	(5) Marginal cost MC = change in total cost
0	35	0	35	
1	35	24	59	59 − 35 = 24
2	35	40	75	75 − 59 = 16
3	35	60	95	95 − 75 = 20
4	35	85	120	120 − 95 = 25
5	35	115	150	150 − 120 = 30
6	35	155	190	190 − 150 = 40
7	35	210	245	245 − 190 = 55
8	35	295	330	330 − 245 = 85

Fixed costs are those costs that do not change as output increases.

Variable costs are those costs that *do* increase as output increases.

Total cost (TC) in column 4 of Table 22-1 is the sum of fixed and variable costs. For example, we see that, if the firm is producing eight pairs of shoes, it incurs $35 of fixed costs and $295 of variable costs, for a total cost of $330.

Marginal cost (MC) is the additional cost as output increases by 1 unit. Business executives often refer to marginal cost as "incremental cost."

> *Marginal cost* is the increase in total cost because one additional unit is produced.

In Table 22-1, marginal cost is calculated in column 5. For example, if the firm increases its output from seven to eight units, its total cost in column 4 increases from $245 to $330; that is, its total cost increases by $85. This is the marginal cost of the eighth unit.

The costs in Table 22-1 are illustrated in panel (*a*) of Figure 22-1. As output increases and we move to the right in this panel, we see that fixed cost remains the same. However, variable cost—shown as the upper white arrow—rises. Total cost also increases since it is

the sum of the two—that is, it is the combined height of the two white arrows.

Observe that each red bar or "stairstep" in this diagram represents marginal cost MC because it shows how total cost rises with each additional unit of output.

The red marginal cost bars in panel (*a*) are shown separately in panel (*b*). For example, the first marginal cost bar in panel (*b*) is $24 high. This is just a reproduction of the first red bar in panel (*a*), which shows total cost rising by $24—from $35 to $59—when output increases from zero to one unit. Similarly, the second bar in panel (*b*) is a reproduction of the second red bar in panel (*a*), with its value being $75 − $59 = $16. Thus the whole set of MC bars in panel (*b*) can be viewed as "what would be left" if the supporting gray bars in panel (*a*) were removed and the red MC bars were allowed to settle down to the base line.

THE LAW OF DIMINISHING RETURNS

As output increases, marginal cost may fall at first, but eventually it *must* rise (as indeed it does in Figure 22-1(*b*)). The reason is the **law of (eventually) diminishing returns**. To understand this law, consider the short-run situation of the firm producing shoes with a given stock of capital. Suppose it has only one vari-

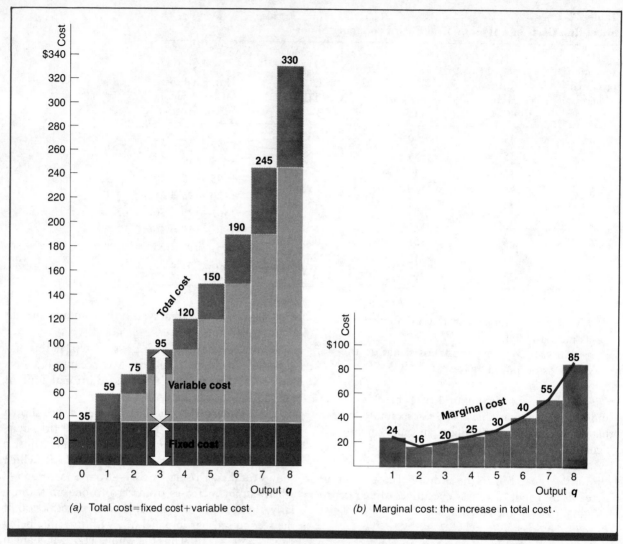

Figure 22-1 Short-run costs of the shoe manufacturer in Table 22-1.
In panel (a), total cost is the sum of fixed cost and variable cost. Marginal cost indicates how much total cost is increasing, and is shown by the set of coloured bars in panel (a) or in panel (b).

able factor, labour. As it initially hires more labour, each additional worker increases the firm's output by a substantial amount. But ultimately, as its labour force grows and its capital equipment is operated closer and closer to capacity, an additional worker will add only a small amount to the firm's output. All the new employee can do is work on odd jobs or stand around waiting for one of the machines to be free. In other words, the **marginal product of labour** must eventu-

ally decrease. This illustrates the law of eventually diminishing returns.

The *marginal product of labour* is the number of additional units of output which result from using one more worker.

The *law of (eventually) diminishing returns*: If more of one factor (labour) is employed while all other factors (like capital) are held constant, eventually the marginal product of that one factor (labour) must fall.

This law is easily confirmed in agriculture. As more and more workers are added to a constant amount of land—say, 100 acres—the marginal product of labour *must* eventually fall. If it did not, the entire world could be fed from this single farm—or, for that matter, from your back garden.

In Part 7 of this book, we shall see that the law of diminishing returns is a key to explaining wages and other income payments. For now, it is important because it explains why marginal costs must ultimately rise. In our example, the law of diminishing returns means that eventually an extra worker in the shoe factory is able to do only odd jobs and produce very little. Most of his time is wasted. True, the firm can still produce another unit of output; but when it's done by a worker like this who is wasting most of his time, this unit of output comes at a very high marginal cost.

The law of diminishing returns ensures that marginal costs must eventually rise.

The law of diminishing returns is illustrated in more detail in Box 22-1.

Figure 22-2 reproduces the rising portion of the marginal cost curve from Figure 22-1(*a*). We shall show that this is the key to deriving the firm's supply curve. However, in order to do so, we must first answer the important question: How will the firm maximize its profits?

PROFIT MAXIMIZATION: MARGINAL COST AND MARGINAL REVENUE

To determine how much the perfectly competitive firm will produce to maximize its profit, we must also know the price at which it can sell. Suppose this price is $40, as shown in Figure 22-2. Because the perfectly competitive firm has no control over price, the $40 price is shown as a horizontal line: Price remains at $40, regardless of what this firm does. This price line is also the firm's marginal revenue, which, as you can by now guess, is defined:

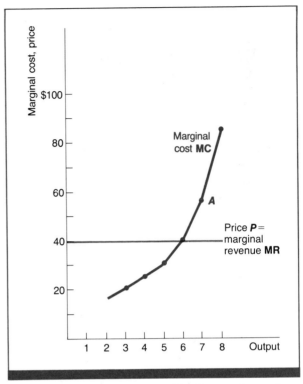

Figure 22-2   A perfectly competitive firm produces where MC = price (marginal costs are for the shoe producer shown in Figure 22-1).
Marginal cost MC is equal to price *P* at an output of six units. This is the amount that will be supplied by the profit-maximizing firm if the price is $40.

Marginal revenue (MR) is the increase in total revenue from the sale of one more unit.

It is easy to confirm that marginal revenue will be this constant $40 price. The reason is that total revenue will be $40 from the sale of one unit, $80 from the sale of two, $120 from three, and so on. No matter how many units the firm may be selling, its total revenue will always increase by $40 if it sells one unit more.

Given this $40 price and the marginal cost schedule shown in Figure 22-2, how many units will the firm produce? The answer is six. The reason is that any decision to produce at a greater output, say seven, would be a mistake, since the $55 marginal cost of producing that seventh unit exceeds the $40 in additional revenue which it brings in. On the other hand,

BOX 22-1

DIMINISHING RETURNS: THE SHORT-RUN PRODUCTION FUNCTION

To study the idea of diminishing returns in more detail, it is helpful to look at the *short-run production function*, which shows how physical output increases because of an increase in variable input. As an example, Table 22-2 shows the short-run production function of a hypothetical bicycle producer whose only variable input is labour. Because we are looking at the short run, the quantity of capital is fixed.

The first line in this table shows the number of workers this firm may employ, while the second line shows the resulting number of bicycles produced in a week. For example, if the firm uses three workers, it is able to produce 18 units of output. Line 3 shows the marginal product of labour, that is, the number of additional bicycles produced when one more worker is added. For example, when the fifth worker is added, production increases from 21 to 23 bicycles, and the fifth worker's marginal product is therefore two bicycles. Finally, the fourth line shows average product—that is, total product TP in line 2 divided by the number of workers in line 1. The data from this table are illustrated in Figure 22-3.

This example illustrates the law of eventually diminishing returns. Although marginal product rises at first—the marginal product of the second worker (seven bicycles) is greater than that of the first worker (five bicycles)—marginal product then begins to fall, to six bicycles, three, two, and then one. Again, the explanation is that the firm's machinery becomes more and more fully used, and the

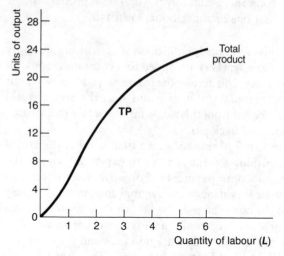

(a) **Total product.**

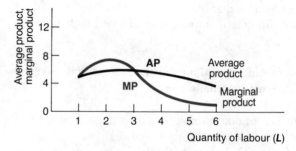

(b) **Average and marginal product.**

Figure 22-3 Total and marginal product curves for the bicycle firm.
The curves in this diagram correspond to the data in Table 22-2. The marginal product MP curve must eventually decline because of the law of (eventually) diminishing returns.

new workers therefore don't have much machinery at their disposal.

The marginal product MP for the fourth, fifth, and sixth workers in Table 22-2 is reproduced in

Table 22-2
The Short-Run Production Function for a Bicycle Manufacturer
(The quantity of capital is fixed. Product is measured in
number of bicycles per week.)

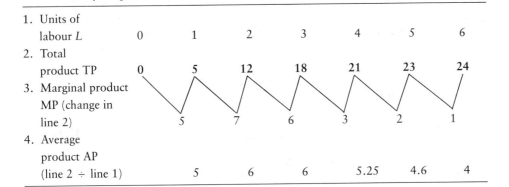

1. Units of labour L	0	1	2	3	4	5	6
2. Total product TP	0	5	12	18	21	23	24
3. Marginal product MP (change in line 2)		5	7	6	3	2	1
4. Average product AP (line 2 ÷ line 1)		5	6	6	5.25	4.6	4

line 2 of Table 22-3. This can now be used to calculate the marginal cost of bicycles in line 4—provided we know the wage rate; suppose it is $300 per week, as shown in line 3. To illustrate how marginal cost can be calculated, note that the fourth worker has a marginal product of three bicycles. Since it cost $300 to hire that worker, and he produces three bicycles, the marginal cost of each of those bicycles is $100, as shown in line 4. Continuing these calculations, we see that when the fifth

Table 22-3
Declining Marginal Product and
Rising Marginal Cost

1. Units of labour L	4	5	6
2. Marginal product MP	3	2	1
3. Wage per worker	$300	$300	$300
4. Marginal cost (line 3 ÷ line 2)	$100	$150	$300

worker is hired at a cost of $300, the result is only two more bicycles, for a marginal cost of $150 per bicycle. Observe how diminishing returns—that is, the declining marginal product of labour in line 2—results in rising marginal cost in line 4.

Finally, once we calculate marginal cost in this way, and if we know fixed cost, we can calculate other costs. Returning to our earlier example of the shoe company in Figure 22-1, we see that knowledge of marginal cost in panel (b) plus knowledge that fixed cost is $35 is all that is needed to reconstruct the *complete cost diagram in panel (a)*. To confirm this, cover panel (a) and reconstruct it for yourself. All that is necessary is to start with the dark gray $35 of fixed cost as a base, and build up the red marginal cost "stairsteps" on top of this, one by one.

We can therefore sum up, for any such firm whose only valuable input is labour. All its costs can be derived from its short-run production function, once its wage and fixed costs are known.

if the firm is at an output below six, say four, expansion will be in its interest. Why? The marginal cost of the fifth unit is $30, and it can be sold for $40; consequently, it's in the firm's interest to produce that unit. But at six units, there is no tendency to expand or contract production because marginal cost MC has risen to the level of price (that is, marginal revenue). This is the equilibrium output for the firm because at this point its profit is at a maximum.

To maximize profits, a firm will expand its production until it reaches the output where its marginal cost has risen to the level of its marginal revenue, that is, to the point where

$$MC = MR \qquad (22\text{-}1)$$

For a perfectly competitive firm, MR = price P.
   Such a firm will maximize profit where

$$MC = MR = P \qquad (22\text{-}2)$$

This can be confirmed in Table 22-4. The first three columns show some of the costs of the perfectly competitive shoe producer described earlier. Column 4 shows how the firm's total revenue rises $40 for each additional unit sold, giving the constant marginal revenue of $40 shown in column 5. Profits are calculated in the last column as total revenue minus total cost. We confirm that this firm's maximum profit is $50, and this is realized if its output is six. The arrow on

the right marks this as the output the firm will produce. (Profit is also a maximum at five units of output, but in cases like this economists typically assume that the firm produces the larger output.) Note that, at this profit-maximizing output of six, marginal cost in column 3 is equal to the $40 of marginal revenue (price) in column 5. This confirms our conclusion that this firm maximizes its profit where its marginal cost is equal to its marginal revenue. For an alternative view of profit maximization, see Box 22-2.

THE SHORT-RUN SUPPLY OF THE PERFECTLY COMPETITIVE FIRM

While the firm facing a $40 price in Figure 22-2 responds by producing six units, what does it do if the price rises to $55? To answer this question, visualize the horizontal price line shifting up from the $40 shown to this new, higher, $55 level. The firm will respond to this higher price by increasing its output to seven units, where MC is again equal to price. Or, if price falls to $30, it will supply five units (as confirmed in Table 22-7 in the appendix to this chapter). Notice that, in showing how much output the firm will supply at various prices, we are defining the firm's supply curve. As price rises, the firm simply follows its marginal cost curve up; or if price falls, it follows its MC curve down. Thus, MC defines the supply curve of the indi-

Table 22-4
Profit Maximization by a Perfectly Competitive Shoe Producer Facing a $40 Price†

(1) Quantity of output q	(2) Total cost TC	(3) Marginal cost MC	(4) Total revenue TR	(5) Marginal revenue MR = price P	(6) Profit or loss (6) = (4) − (2)
0	35		0		−35
		24		40	
1	59		40		−19
		16		40	
2	75		80		5
		20		40	
3	95		120		25
		25		40	
4	120		160		40
		30		40	
5	150		200		50
		40		40	
6	190		240		50 ←
		55		40	
7	245		280		−35
		85		40	
8	330		320		−10

†The first three columns in this table are cost figures reproduced from Table 22-1.

BOX 22-2

ANOTHER VIEW OF PROFIT MAXIMIZATION: TOTAL REVENUE AND TOTAL COST

Graphing a firm's marginal revenue and marginal cost curves in Figure 22-2 is not the only way we can visualize its profit maximization. We can alter-natively graph its *total* revenue and *total* cost curves in Figure 22-4, and show its profit-maximizing out-put on this diagram. Specifically, we first plot the firm's red total cost curve, taken directly from Fig-ure 22-1(*a*). (In that figure, it was plotted as a series of bars, but here we draw it as a curve.) The firm's total revenue is also plotted. Note that it is a straight line from the origin because of our earlier observa-tion: Given the $40 price the firm faces, the first unit it sells yields $40 of total revenue, the first two units yield $80, and so on. Note that the slope of this line is equal to the price—that is, to the firm's marginal revenue.

Initially, if the firm produces only one unit of output, it operates at a loss of $19, shown by arrow *d* in Figure 22-4: Its $59 total cost exceeds its $40 total revenue. However, as it increases its output, the firm moves upward to the right out of the red loss area into the gray profit range where total cost is below total revenue. Finally, at eight units or more of output, total cost rises above total revenue, and the firm again operates at a loss.

Where in the range between two and seven units of output does the firm maximize profits? The answer is at six units, the output where its profit—the vertical distance *c* between the total revenue and total cost curves—is greatest.*

This is also the output where the slopes of the total revenue and total cost curves—specifically, the slopes of line segments *a* and *b*—are the same. We have already seen that the slope of the total revenue line is marginal revenue. Likewise, the slope of the total cost curve is marginal cost.† Thus, equat-ing these two slopes is, in fact, equating marginal cost and marginal revenue— just as we did in Fig-ure 22-2.

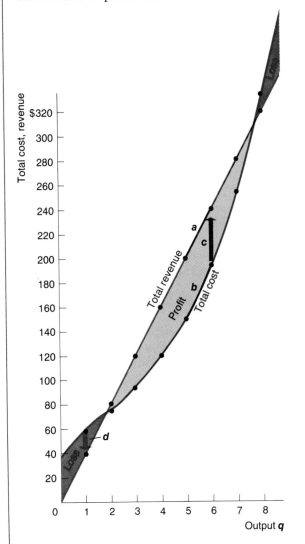

Figure 22-4 Another view of profit maximization by the perfectly competitive shoe producer.

*As noted earlier, profits are also at a maximum at five units, but in such cases, economists assume that the larger output is sold. We also assume here that the firm can't produce a fraction of a unit; for example, it can't produce 5 1/2 units.

†This is easily confirmed by referring back to Figure 22-1. Each marginal cost stairstep in that diagram becomes the slope of the corresponding segment of the total cost curve in Figure 22-4. Readers familiar with calculus will now see why it is a valuable tool in economics. Marginal cost is simply the first derivative—that is, the slope—of the total cost curve.

vidual firm—subject to one important qualification.

The Shutdown Point
The qualification is that it is not certain the firm will produce anything at all. If it does, MC does indeed determine the quantity supplied. However, if the price falls low enough, the firm will close down. The next important question therefore is: How far can price fall before the firm closes down and stops producing altogether?

To throw light on this question, more information on costs is required. In Table 22-5 we reproduce, for reference only, the earlier cost calculations for the shoe firm in Table 22-1 and now add three additional columns of cost calculations, as follows:

1. *Average cost* (AC) or *average total cost* (ATC), defined as total cost divided by output. For example, suppose the firm produces five units of output; reading over to column 4, we see that its total cost is $150. Therefore its average cost is $150/5 = $30, as shown in column 6.

2. *Average variable cost* (AVC), defined as variable cost divided by output. For example, if the firm produces five units of output, its variable cost is $115 in column 3. Therefore, its average variable cost is $115/5 = $23, as shown in column 7.

3. *Average fixed cost* (AFC), defined as fixed cost divided by output. If the firm is again producing five units of output, its fixed cost is $35 in column 2; therefore its average fixed cost is $35/5 = $7 in column 8.

Each of these concepts, along with the MC curve, is graphed in Figure 22-5. Note that the MC curve cuts the AC curve where AC is at a minimum. This must be so for reasons explained in Box 22-3, where we also explain the significance of AFC.

Now consider what happens if the price falls to $30. To identify its best output, the firm finds the point where MC equals the $30 price; this is *H*, where five units are produced. Observe that, at this point, average cost AC is at a minimum and is equal to price. Since the price received for selling each unit barely covers the average cost AC, the firm's profit is zero. The best the firm can do is **break even**.

> The *break-even point* is the lowest point on the AC curve. When the price is at this height, the firm makes zero profit.

Next, suppose price falls below $30, to say $25. If the firm produces at all, its output will be four units, at point *J* where MC equals the $25 price. At this point, the firm will suffer a loss, since *J* lies below the AC curve: The $25 price does not cover the $30 aver-

Table 22-5
Short-Run Costs of a Hypothetical Firm Producing Shoes†

(1) Quantity produced (pairs) q	(2) Fixed cost FC	(3) Variable cost VC	(4) Total cost TC = FC + VC = (3) + (2)	(5) Marginal cost MC = change in total cost	(6) Average cost‡ AC = TC ÷ q = (4) ÷ (1)	(7) Average variable cost‡ AVC = VC ÷ q = (3) ÷ (1)	(8) Average fixed cost‡ AFC = FC ÷ q = (2) ÷ (1)
0	35	0	35				
1	35	24	59	59 − 35 = 24	59 ÷ 1 = 59	24 ÷ 1 = 24	35 ÷ 1 = 35
2	35	40	75	75 − 59 = 16	75 ÷ 2 = 38	40 ÷ 2 = 20	35 ÷ 2 = 18
3	35	60	95	95 − 75 = 20	95 ÷ 3 = 32	60 ÷ 3 = 20	35 ÷ 3 = 12
4	35	85	120	120 − 95 = 25	120 ÷ 4 = 30	85 ÷ 4 = 21	35 ÷ 4 = 9
5	35	115	150	150 − 120 = 30	150 ÷ 5 = 30	115 ÷ 5 = 23	35 ÷ 5 = 7
6	35	155	190	190 − 150 = 40	190 ÷ 6 = 32	155 ÷ 6 = 26	35 ÷ 6 = 6
7	35	210	245	245 − 190 = 55	245 ÷ 7 = 35	210 ÷ 7 = 30	35 ÷ 7 = 5
8	35	295	330	330 − 245 = 85	330 ÷ 8 = 41	295 ÷ 8 = 37	35 ÷ 8 = 4

†The first five columns are reproduced from Table 22-1.
‡Rounded to the nearest dollar.

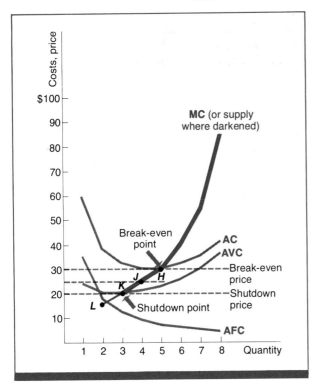

Costs, price

MC (or supply where darkened)

Break-even point

AC
AVC

Break-even price

Shutdown price

Shutdown point

AFC

Quantity

Figure 22-5 **The firm's cost curves and how they define its short-run supply.**
Marginal cost is reproduced from Figure 22-2. Average cost AC, average variable cost AVC, and average fixed cost AFC are taken from the last three columns in Table 22-5. The firm's short-run supply curve is shown as the heavy curve. It is that portion of its MC curve that lies above its AVC curve.

age cost of producing each unit. It sounds as though this firm will close down. But it does not. *Even though it is operating at a loss, it continues to produce at J in the short run.* The reason is that its $25 selling price more than covers its average *variable* cost; that is, point J is above AVC. Therefore, the firm can completely cover its variable cost and still have some revenue left over to cover part of its fixed costs. It is better to cover part of these fixed costs than to shut down and cover none at all. (To confirm this conclusion, note that if it closes down, its loss will be equal to its fixed cost of $35. However, if it produces four units, its loss will be only $20—that is, the difference between its total revenue of $100 and its total cost of $120.)

Thus, so long as a firm is at least covering its variable costs, it continues to produce. That remains true so long as price is above the **shutdown point**, K. If the

price falls below this, the firm will close down because it will not even be able to cover its variable costs. For example, suppose the price falls to $16. If the firm produces at all, it will be two units at point L. But at this point the $16 price is below AVC. Since the firm can't cover even its variable costs, it will shut down. If it were to insist on producing two units, its revenue would be $32, its cost $75, and its loss $43. This is more than the loss it incurs by closing down—namely, the $35 of fixed cost it still must pay. Therefore, the firm does better by shutting down.

> The *shutdown point* is the point where the MC curve cuts the AVC curve. If price is below this point, the firm produces nothing.

By trying various prices we have established that the firm will supply the quantity given by its MC curve—*unless* the price falls below the shutdown point K, in which case the firm will supply nothing. In other words: *In the short run*—in the period when the firm is working with a fixed capital stock—the firm reacts to any given price by supplying a quantity that can be read off its marginal cost curve, *provided it is at a point above AVC*. This then allows us to specify the firm's short-run supply curve:

> The firm's *short-run supply curve* is that part of its marginal cost curve MC that lies above its average variable cost curve AVC.

The idea that supply is derived from the marginal cost of the producer is just as important as the idea in Chapter 21, that demand represents marginal benefit to the consumer. Just as we visualized a set of marginal benefit bars or arrows beneath the demand curve, so we arrive at a similar idea on the supply side:

Whenever you see a supply curve, you should visualize the set of marginal cost bars enclosed beneath it.[1]

THE ECONOMIST'S CONCEPT OF COST: OPPORTUNITY COST

Before we turn in detail to the long run in the next chapter, there is one important final point to clarify:

---

[1]Just as a set of marginal cost bars is enclosed beneath the curve in panel (*b*) in Figure 22-1.

BOX 22-3

TWO IMPORTANT INFLUENCES ON AVERAGE COST

In this box we examine how a firm's average cost curve is influenced by its marginal cost curve and its average fixed cost curve.

Courtesy Canapress Photo Service

The Influence of Marginal Cost: Why a Firm's Costs Are Like a Baseball Player's Average

Late in the 1980 season, Kansas City's George Brett had the best chance to hit the magic .400—that is, 40 hits in each 100 times at bat—since the Boston Red Sox' Ted Williams did it with .406 in 1941. The numbers on the right show Brett's batting performance during one week in September. In the first three games against Chicago and Detroit he batted a disappointing .250 (one hit in each four times at bat). Since this marginal performance shown in red was below his average in the .380s, it pulled his average down. However, in the next three games, his fortunes improved: He batted .500 or better. Since this marginal performance was above his average, it pulled his average up.*

So too with marginal and average costs. Until they reach their point of intersection *H* in Figure 22-5, marginal cost is below average cost; hence, it is pulling AC down. But to the right of *H*, MC is above AC and hence is pulling AC up. Since AC is falling until it reaches *H* but rising beyond, it must be at a minimum at *H*, where it meets MC.

*Did Brett hit .400? Although the last three games shown here started him on a hitting streak that carried him over .400 for a week in late September, he couldn't maintain the pace and finished the season with .390.

The economic definition of cost is not the same as the accounting definition. To illustrate the broader economic definition, suppose a friend who operates a store has asked you to analyze her business. Her breakdown of costs in column (*a*) of Table 22-6 seems to confirm her view that she is being successful. With revenue of $122,000 and costs of $74,000, she is earning an accounting profit of $48,000.

However, you dig more deeply. You discover that she could earn a $44,000 salary by accepting a job from an insurance company. This is an *implicit cost*—or *imputed cost*—because it is not paid out of pocket. However, we must include it, as we have done in

column (*b*); otherwise, we would not have an adequate picture of the true economic costs in operating this business—that is, the cost of all the resources used, including her own time. And we would not be able to judge whether she is doing as well in this business as she could in another activity, namely, working for the insurance company.

This implicit cost for her own time illustrates the concept of **opportunity cost**, that is, the alternative foregone.

> The *opportunity cost* of an input is the return that it could earn in its best alternative use.

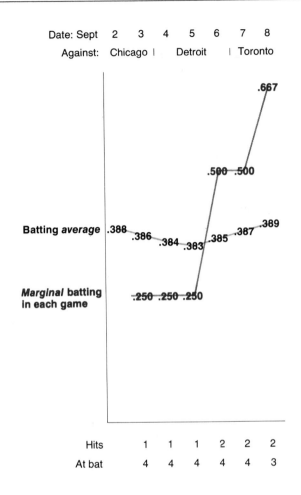

Date: Sept	2	3	4	5	6	7	8
Against:	Chicago		Detroit			Toronto	

Batting *average* .388 .386 .384 .383 .385 .387 .389 .500 .500 .667

Marginal batting in each game .250 .250 .250

Hits	1	1	1	2	2	2
At bat	4	4	4	4	4	3

The Influence of Average Fixed Cost

To show how average cost is influenced by average fixed cost AFC, note that as output increases and we move to the right in Figure 22-5, AFC gets smaller and smaller. It must; after all, a fixed overhead cost—in this case the constant $35—is being divided by a larger and larger output. As business executives know, increased volume means that overhead can be spread over a larger number of units of output. Consequently, the overhead cost that has to be charged to each unit shrinks.

This is important because average cost AC in column 6 of Table 22-5 is the sum of two components: average variable cost AVC plus average fixed cost AFC in columns 7 and 8.† When AVC ceases to fall—in our example, at two units of output—AC continues to fall for a while because it is pulled down by its other component, the always-falling AFC. Moreover, the larger the fixed costs, the more influential AFC will be; that is, the longer it will continue to pull AC down. (To confirm, do the simple calculations in problem 22-2 at the end of this chapter.) Thus, high overhead industries—such as the telephone companies that require very heavy investment—tend to have falling average costs over a wide range of output.

†This is easy to confirm: Just divide all terms in the equation TC = VC + FC by the quantity of output q.

Opportunity cost also indicates *how much an input must be paid to keep it in its present use*. For example, if your friend doesn't earn her opportunity cost—that is, her potential salary in insurance—she has an incentive to shift out of her present activity into the higher-return insurance business. This illustrates a point made early in this chapter. Producers make a *choice* as to what goods or services to produce. In this case, your friend chooses between retailing and insurance services. (Incidentally, if your friend has strong non-monetary reasons for preferring her own retail business—such as the freedom she gets from self-employment—she may not take the other higher-paying job after all.

Such non-monetary motives are often important. However, in the simplified story described here, we ignore such motives.)

You also discover that your friend has other opportunity costs which must also be included in column (b). For example, she has a substantial amount of her own funds tied up in this business. What would be her best alternative use of these funds? She indicates that she would lend out part, getting $1,000 in interest. She would use the rest to buy part ownership of a company in which she could reap a $2,000 profit. This last item—the opportunity cost of capital—is called **normal profit**.

Table 22-6
The Evaluation of Costs and Profit

(a) By accountants			(b) By economists		
Total revenue		$122,000	Total revenue		$122,000
Costs (out-of-pocket)			Explicit (out-of-pocket) costs		
Labour	$10,000		Labour	$ 10,000	
Materials	59,000		Materials	59,000	
Rent	5,000		Rent	5,000	
Total	$74,000	$ 74,000			
			Implicit costs (income foregone)		
			Owner's salary	$ 44,000	
			Interest	1,000	
			Normal profit	2,000	
			Total costs	$121,000	$121,000
Accounting profit		$ 48,000	Economic (above-normal profit		$ 1,000

We emphasize that whenever we draw a cost curve in this book, we include not only explicit out-of-pocket accounting costs, but also implicit costs such as normal profit. Therefore, in our example, costs are the full $121,000 shown in column (b) of Table 22-6. This broad definition means that costs tell us how much all the resources employed by the firm could be earning elsewhere. Since her $122,000 of revenues exceed this $121,000 cost, she has earned above-normal profit of $1,000. (In economics, the word "profit" means *above-normal* profit unless otherwise stated.) It is this $1,000 "bottom-line" profit that allows you to judge that your friend is indeed successful. Her business not only provides her with an appropriate $44,000 income for her own time, and an appropriate return for the capital she has invested. It also provides her an additional $1,000. If present firms in an industry are making such above-normal profits, there is an incentive for other entrepreneurs to move their capital into this business to get in on a good thing.

Economic profit is above-normal profit; that is, profit after the opportunity costs of capital have been taken into account.

Now suppose that salaries in other jobs increase. Specifically, suppose the insurance company increases its offer to your friend from $44,000 to $47,000. This increases the $44,000 owner's salary item by $3,000; and when column (b) is accordingly recalculated, the $1,000 of (above-normal) profit becomes a $2,000 loss. Your friend is no longer able to earn as much in this enterprise as in her best alternative activity. So long as she views this alternative line of work as equally interesting, she has an incentive to move.

Thus, *economic profit* (or loss) *provides a signal, indicating whether resources will be attracted to* (or repelled from) *an activity*. Accordingly, economic profit exerts pressure on the firm, directing it toward "what" to produce.

KEY POINTS

1. The producer has a number of fundamental choices:
   (a) which good should be produced,
   (b) how many units should be produced, and
   (c) what is the best combination of inputs to use.
2. In this chapter we have described the short run, when the firm can change only the quantity of labour it uses. It cannot change its quantity of plant and equipment; it is committed by past decisions. In the next chapter we will consider the long run, when the firm can change its capital stock.
3. *For any firm*, profits are maximized at the output where MC = MR.
4. *For a perfectly competitive firm*, the price is given; price is not affected by how much the firm produces. For such a firm, MR = P and the firm will maximize its profits at the output where MC = P, as shown in Figure 22-2.
5. In turn, this means that a firm's short-run supply is determined by its short-run marginal cost curve—provided the price is at least high enough to cover the firm's variable costs.
6. By cost, economists mean "opportunity" cost. Thus, economists include not only explicit accounting costs, but also implicit costs such as the normal profit on capital invested in the enterprise.
7. After all such opportunity costs have been covered, any remaining profit—that is, above-normal profit—provides an indication of how much more is being earned in this activity than in the next best alternative. If present firms are making such a profit, resources are attracted into this industry. On the other hand, if present firms are not covering their opportunity costs—that is, if they are suffering an economic loss—resources are encouraged to move out.

KEY CONCEPTS

short run
long run
fixed cost
variable cost
total cost
marginal cost
law of diminishing returns
marginal product of labour

marginal revenue
average cost
relationship of marginal cost to
   average cost
average variable cost
average fixed cost
break-even point
shutdown point

how supply is determined
   by marginal cost
economic versus accounting
   definitions of cost
explicit versus implicit costs
opportunity cost
normal versus above-normal
   (economic) profit

PROBLEMS

22-1 Recalculate Table 22-4 and find the profit-maximizing output for the firm if the price is:
(a) $50,
(b) $35.

22-2 Suppose the fixed cost of the firm in Table 22-1 were $10,000 instead of $35, while variable cost remained the same. What happens to MC? to AC? Is it correct to say that, as fixed overhead costs increase in importance, AC tends to fall over a wider range of output?

22-3 To understand the problem of operating at a point like *J* in Figure 22-5, suppose you have inherited a house in another city which you wish to rent. You have to pay $80 a week of fixed costs such as taxes, whether or not it's rented, and another $40 a week of variable costs such as utilities if you do rent it. If you can get only $100, should you rent the house or leave it vacant? Explain why.

22-4 Explain why economists define costs to include normal profit. If additional profit exists, what does this tell us?

22-5 Suppose a farmer in Manitoba provides a statement of his costs to his income tax accountant. Are there any opportunity costs he may miss? Explain.

22-6 "In the long run, all costs are variable." Do you agree? Explain, using machinery as an example of a fixed cost.

*22-7 In Box 22-1, we claimed that once you know marginal costs in panel (*b*) of Figure 22-1, along with fixed cost of $35, you can cover up panel (*a*) and reconstruct it. As an alternative demonstration, cover up all the figures in Table 22-5 except the fixed cost in columns 1 and 2 and the MC figures—24, 16, 20, etc.—in column 5. Can you then fill in columns 3 and 4? If so, can you go on to fill in columns 6, 7, and 8? If not, what additional information would you require?

APPENDIX

SHORT-RUN PROFIT CALCULATIONS FOR A PERFECTLY COMPETITIVE FIRM

The costs of the hypothetical firm in Table 22-1 are reproduced in the first five columns of Table 22-7. In the other columns we show how this firm selects its output to maximize profit—or minimize loss—if it is faced with various market prices such as $40, $30, $25, and $20.

Columns 6 and 7 repeat our earlier calculation in Table 22-4 of how the firm responds to a $40 price. Total revenue is shown in column 6 as the $40 price times the number of units. Profit is calculated in column 7 from the figures in columns 4 and 6. For example, if output is two units, total revenue is $80 in column 6, and total cost is $75 in column 4. Thus, profit is $5. Alternatively, if output is one unit, total revenue is $40 and total cost is $59, resulting in a loss of $19—that is, a profit of −$19. The result of all such calculations in column 7 confirms our conclusion in Figure 22-2 that an output of six units maximizes profits.

If price is $30, the arrow in column 9 shows that the firm will produce five units of output at a zero profit: Its total cost in column 4 is $150, exactly the same as its total revenue in column 8. Since the firm facing a $30 price can do no better than break even with a zero profit, $30 is its break-even price.

If the price is $25, the best the firm can do is to minimize its loss at $20 by producing four units. It does not close down because its total revenue of $100 more than covers its variable cost of $85 in column 3, thus leaving $15 to partly cover its fixed cost. This result is better than shutting down and not covering *any* of its fixed cost.

If price is $20, the firm has two equally unattractive options. It can produce three units at a loss of $35, with its $60 in revenue just barely sufficient to cover its $60 of variable costs. Or it can close down completely, in which case it would run the same $35 loss—that is, the $35 of fixed cost that it cannot avoid. Twenty dollars is its "shutdown" price. At any price below this, it cannot even cover its variable costs, and it will close down.

Table 22-7
How a Perfectly Competitive Firm Will Select Its Profit-Maximizing (or Loss-Minimizing) Output in Response to Four Hypothetical Prices

(1)	(2)	(3)	(4)	(5)	(6)	(7)	(8)	(9)	(10)	(11)	(12)	(13)
								Best output (shown by arrow) if:				
					Price = $40		Price = $30		Price = $25		Price = $20	
Quan-tity q	Fixed cost FC	Vari-able cost VC	Total cost TC	Mar-ginal cost MC	Total reve-nue TR	Profit (+) or loss (−) TR − TC	Total reve-nue TR	Profit (+) or loss (−) TR − TC	Total reve-nue TR	Profit (+) or loss (−) TR − TC	Total reve-nue TR	Profit (+) or loss (−) TR − TC
1	35	24	59	24	40	−19	30	−29	25	−34	20	−39
2	35	40	75	16	80	5	60	−15	50	−25	40	−35
3	35	60	95	20	120	25	90	− 5	75	−20	60	−35←
4	35	85	120	25	160	40	120	0	100	−20←	80	−40
5	35	115	150	30	200	50	150	0←	125	−25	100	−50
6	35	155	190	40	240	50†←	180	−10	150	−40	120	−70
7	35	210	245	55	280	35	210	−35	175	−70	140	−105

†Profit is also at a maximum at five units of output. In cases like this, we assume that the firm selects the larger output.

Chapter 23

COST AND PERFECTLY COMPETITIVE SUPPLY: THE LONG RUN

Variability is the law of life.

Sir Walter Osler

Chapter 22 explained costs and supply in the short run, when there is no opportunity to change the quantity of plant and equipment. In the long run, the quantity of capital can change for two reasons:

1. Existing firms may acquire new plant and equipment, or decide not to replace plant and equipment that wears out.

2. *New* firms may enter the industry, bringing in additional plant and equipment, or old firms may leave.

In this chapter, we will explore how these two changes in the capital stock can affect costs and supply. First, we will look at how an existing firm's decision becomes more complicated in the long run. It has to decide not only on how much labour it will employ, but also how much capital it will install. Its plant and equipment which were *fixed* in the short run, become *variable* in the long run.

This presents business executives with one of their most important and challenging questions: Should they expand by acquiring new machines and building new factories, or should they contract by deciding not to replace old capital as it wears out and becomes obsolete?

LONG-RUN COSTS OF A FIRM

To find the firm's long-run costs, we begin with the short-run cost curves AC and MC in Figure 22-5 and reproduce them here as SAC_A and SMC_A in Figure 23-1. S designates the short run, and the subscript A represents the fixed amount of capital the firm has been using in the short run.

Suppose this firm has been producing shoes at output q_1 and it wishes to produce a larger number, say q_3. It could do so by hiring more labour while continuing to use its present small capital stock A. In other words, it could continue to operate on cost curves SMC_A and SAC_A. However, if it does this, the cost of producing shoes would become very high. As we saw earlier, the new workers would spend a lot of their time standing around waiting for one of the available machines to become free. This problem is shown in Figure 23-1 as the extremely high marginal cost of producing a pair of shoes at point c—and the very high average cost at point d.

This strategy doesn't make sense. If the firm wants

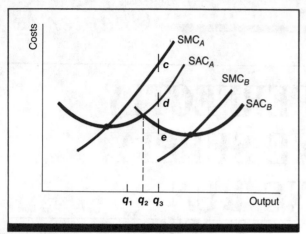

Figure 23-1   Costs in the short and long run.
SAC_A shows short-run average cost with a given fixed capital stock A. If the firm wishes to produce more than q_2 in the long run—say q_3—it can reduce its average cost by expanding its capital stock and moving to short-run average cost curve SAC_B. This reduces its average cost from d to e.

to produce quantity q_3, it has an incentive to install more equipment and perhaps build a new factory. By providing workers with more machines, the firm will be able to cut costs. In other words, the firm makes the *long-run* decision to expand its capital to a new larger amount B. Then it will be able to operate on the new short-run average cost curve SAC_B. (Each short-run AC curve applies to a specific amount of capital. When the firm's stock of capital changes, so does its short-run AC curve and the corresponding MC curve.) Note how successful this is. Since the firm is now operating on SAC_B rather than SAC_A, its average cost of producing q_3 units is only e, rather than d.

If the firm expects to produce any output greater than q_2, the larger capital stock B is better than A; it will mean lower average costs. That is, for any output exceeding q_2, SAC_B lies below SAC_A. However, for a small output less than q_2, it is *not* desirable to have large capital stock B, because in this range SAC_B lies *above* SAC_A. The reason is that a large capital stock means high overhead costs. If very little output is produced, the high overheads will be spread over few units; average costs will be high. Unused capacity is expensive.

To sum up so far: A firm starting with capital stock A follows SAC_A as it expands output. However, when output expands beyond q_2, the firm acquires more

capital and moves to SAC_B. Thus the lowest average cost it can achieve in the long run—when it can choose between capital stock A and stock B—is given by the thicker, scalloped curve in Figure 23-1.

The Envelope Curve
In Figure 23-2 we reproduce SAC_A and SAC_B and add two more cost curves, SAC_C and SAC_D, that apply when the capital stock is even larger. If the firm making a long-run decision wishes to produce output q_4, it chooses capital stock C and operates on short-run curve SAC_C at point R. This is the lowest possible average cost at which the firm can produce q_4. Alternatively, if it wishes to produce q_5, it chooses larger capital stock D and operates on SAC_D at point S—the lowest average cost at which it can produce q_5. If we join all points like R and S, the result is the heavy long-run average cost curve LAC. This is called an *envelope curve* because it encloses all the short-run SAC curves from below. (While it seems quite easy to draw this curve, the economist who introduced the idea had difficulty, as explained in Box 23-1.)

To draw the smooth envelope curve LAC, we assume that there are many quantities of capital from which the firm can choose, not just the four illustrated. You can imagine many intermediate SAC curves in Figure 23-2. (Nevertheless, it should be recognized that in some cases, capital may be "lumpy." For example, a firm can't acquire half a machine. The "lumpy" case was illustrated in Figure 23-1, where there were no feasible quantities of capital between A and B, and where the envelope curve was scalloped, not smooth.)

We emphasize that LAC shows the *lowest* average cost at which each output, such as q_4 or q_5, can be produced in the long run, when producers have the opportunity to adjust their quantity of capital. Because the decision to acquire capital depends on expectations regarding future sales, LAC is sometimes called a *planning curve*. Points in the light area below LAC cannot be achieved with present technology and with present prices of factors of production. Points in the darker area above LAC can be chosen. However, a technically efficient firm rejects any such point in favour of a lower-cost point on the LAC.

ECONOMIES OF SCALE

Observe that, until point R in Figure 23-2 is reached, long-run average cost falls as output increases. The question arises: How can that be? How can the cost

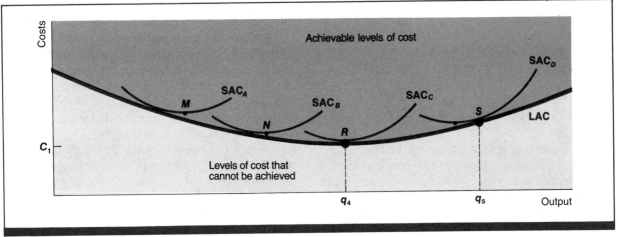

Figure 23-2   The long-run envelope cost curve.

The SAC curves are the short-run average cost curves that apply if capital stock is fixed at various levels, *A*, *B*, etc. LAC is the long-run average cost curve that encloses all of them from below. It is the appropriate curve for a firm in its long-run planning when it is free to select any quantity of capital. For example, to produce q_4, it would select capital stock *C*, thus operating on SAC_C at point *R* and keeping its average cost down to the lowest possible level—that is, the height of *R*. Similarly, to produce q_5, it would select capital stock *D*, thus operating on SAC_D at point *S* and keeping its cost down to the lowest possible level at *S*.

per unit fall when output is increased from, say, 1,000,000 units to 2,000,000?

The answer lies in *economies of scale*. Recall from Chapter 3 that economies of scale exist if an $x\%$ increase in the quantity of *all* inputs results in an increase of more than $x\%$ in the quantity of output.

The way in which economies of scale lead to falling average costs may be illustrated with an example. Suppose that a firm faces fixed input prices: It won't bid up the wage rate, regardless of how many workers it hires, nor will it bid up the price of any other input like steel or machinery, no matter how much it buys. Because input prices are constant, an increase of, say, 100% in the quantity of all inputs raises total costs by the same 100%. However, because of economies of scale, output rises by more than 100%; that is, output rises faster than total costs. Consequently, there is a decrease in the cost per unit; in other words, average cost falls.[1] Thus we arrive at an important conclusion: Economies of scale mean falling long-run average costs—as long as input prices are constant.

[1] To illustrate, suppose it initially costs $3,000 to produce two units of output; average cost (LAC) is $3,000/2 = $1,500. Now suppose costs double to $6,000, and because of economies of scale, output increases even faster—it triples to six units. LAC falls to $6,000/6 = $1,000. In short, LAC falls because output increases faster than cost.

In turn, another question arises: Why do economies of scale exist? There are a number of reasons. Improvements in technology, such as the development of the word processor, may create economies of scale if this new equipment is very expensive. For example, in a very small office with a small output, it may be impossible to justify the expense of a word processor; one ordinary typewriter will do. In a much larger office with much larger output, a word processor may replace several typewriters, at a substantial cost savings. In a factory, greater output may mean that workers can become adept at specialized tasks—like the workers in Adam Smith's pin factory, described in Chapter 3. It also means that more highly specialized machinery can be used in an assembly-line operation. Furthermore, with a greater output, a firm may be better able to use its talent. If a production line supervisor is able to direct 20 workers but is in charge of only 10, output and the number of workers employed can be doubled without requiring another supervisor. Similarly, the firm's executives may be able to handle more work and responsibility; as the firm grows and output increases, new managers are initially not required. Therefore, there is less management cost for each unit of output and average costs tend to fall.

With all these reasons for economies of scale, why are there ever *diseconomies of scale*? Why does LAC

*Jacob Viner, "Cost Curves and Supply Curves," 1931; reprinted in George J. Stigler and Kenneth E. Boulding, *Readings in Price Theory* (Homewood, Ill.: Richard D. Irwin, 1952), p. 214.

BOX 23-1

IF YOU HAVE HAD TROUBLE DRAWING CURVES IN ECONOMICS, YOU ARE NOT ALONE

The discerning reader will notice in Figure 23-2 that LAC touches the lowest short-run curve (SAC$_C$) at its minimum point. However, it doesn't touch any other SAC curve at its minimum. For example, it touches SAC$_A$ slightly to the left of its minimum point M.

This is such a subtle problem that it was missed by Jacob Viner, the Canadian economist who first developed the idea of the "envelope" curve. He asked his draftsman to draw an envelope curve to pass through the minimum point on each SAC curve. His draftsman knew that this couldn't be done, and said so. Viner insisted. So the draftsman presented him with a long-run curve that went through the minimum points on each SAC. But it clearly wasn't an envelope curve. (To confirm this, sketch a curve through the minimum points such as M and N, and you will see that it is not the envelope curve LAC at all.) Viner permitted the erroneous diagram to appear in his article, complaining that his obstinate draftsman "saw some mathematical objection which I could not succeed in understanding."*

There was a sequel. In the 1930s, Viner was unimpressed by Keynes's new theory of unemployment and income. On his arrival in North America, Keynes was asked to name the world's greatest living economist. He reportedly replied that modesty prevented him from naming the greatest, but the second greatest was surely Viner's draftsman.

ever begin to rise, as it does at point R in Figure 23-2? The supervisor example provides a clue. Suppose output and employment, which have already doubled, now increase by another five times. In addition to the original supervisor, five new ones must now be hired. So far, it seems that average cost need not change, since there has been the same proportionate increase in both output and costs. However, another person may now be required just to coordinate activities among the six supervisors. Thus, as a company grows, new tiers of management may have to be created. Eventually, a point is reached where management becomes too costly and unwieldy, and decision making becomes too cumbersome and slow. There are just too many people between the vice-president who makes the final decisions and the workers on the line who carry them out. Consequently, average costs tend to increase.

The point where decision making becomes unwieldy generally occurs much earlier in agriculture than in industry. Therefore point R, where LAC begins to rise, is encountered in agriculture at a relatively small output. One reason is that, on a relatively small farm, the owner-operator has the opportunity and incentive to make crucial decisions with great speed. When the sun shines, the farmer makes hay. When crops are ripe and the weather is threatening, the farmer drops secondary activities and works very hard to harvest the crop. On the other hand, if the farm were part of a huge company, the crop could be lost by the time decision making worked its way through several echelons of management.

Economies of Scale and Diminishing Returns

We shall now show that it is possible for a firm to be facing both economies of scale—as described here—*and* diminishing returns, as described in the last chapter. Since economies of scale mean falling costs and diminishing returns mean rising costs, we might well wonder: How is this possible?

The answer is that the law of diminishing returns is a short-run concept that applies if only one factor (labour) can change, while economies of scale is a long-run concept describing a situation where all factors are variable.

In Figure 23-3 we show a firm that is facing both diminishing returns and economies of scale. *In the short run*, as more and more labour is applied to the constant capital stock, marginal costs rise, as shown by arrow *f*. These rising costs are a reflection of diminishing returns. However, as capital increases *in the long run*, costs fall as the firm moves down along LAC (arrow *e*). There are economies of scale. (Economies of scale and diminishing returns are considered in further detail in Appendix 23-A, where we examine the firm's long-run and short-run production functions. Its long-run production function is then used in Appendix 23-B to provide more detail on how a firm maximizes its long-run profit.)

SUPPLY IN THE LONG RUN: THE PERFECTLY COMPETITIVE INDUSTRY

The discussion of long-run costs in the previous section applies in general to firms selling in any type of market—whether it be monopoly, perfect competition, or any other form of market. However, when we come to drawing a supply curve, we must narrow our focus and look at perfectly competitive suppliers.

The Definition of Perfect Competition

The time has come for a more precise description of perfect competition. Thus far, we have emphasized only one of its characteristics:

*1. **Each individual buyer and seller is a price taker.*** That is, no firm can influence the price by deciding to increase or decrease its production, and no buyer can influence the price by deciding to increase or decrease purchases. Because each buyer and seller takes the market price as given, each concentrates on the *quantity* to buy or sell; there is no pricing decision for the individual market participant to make.

This first characteristic follows from two underlying assumptions:

(a) **There are many buyers and sellers**, with each buying or selling only a trivial fraction of the total market transactions.

(b) **The product is standardized**; that is, the product is the same regardless of where or by whom it is produced. For example, one farmer's wheat is the same as another's; it doesn't matter to buyers whether wheat is produced in Minnesota or in Manitoba. In contrast, autos are not standardized. It makes a lot of difference whether you get a Hyundai Pony or an Oldsmobile. This is one reason why the auto industry is not perfectly competitive.

The second characteristic of a perfectly competitive market is important in any study of long-run supply:

*2. **An absence of barriers to entry.*** That is, firms are free to enter the industry. An example of a barrier to entry exists in the trucking industry. In most provinces, the law requires truckers to have licences, and the government grants new licences only after a cumbersome application process. Other examples of barriers to entry will be discussed in later chapters.

> In a *perfectly competitive industry*, there are many buyers and sellers of a standardized product, with no single buyer or seller having any influence over its price. New firms are free to enter the industry because there are no barriers, such as restrictive government licensing.

The Importance of Entry

Figure 23-4 shows how the entry of new firms affects supply. Initially, with 200 similar firms in the industry, each supplying 10 units at price P_1 in panel (*a*), there are 2,000 units supplied to the market in panel

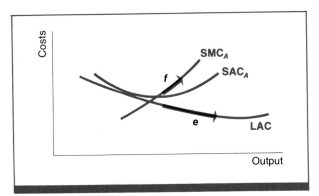

Figure 23-3   How a firm can face both economies of scale and diminishing returns.
This firm faces diminishing returns, as shown by arrow *f*; its marginal cost curve SMC_A rises in the short run, so long as its capital stock is fixed at level *A*. For this firm, there are also economies of scale, as shown by arrow *e*; its average cost LAC falls in the long run as it is able to increase its use of *all* factors.

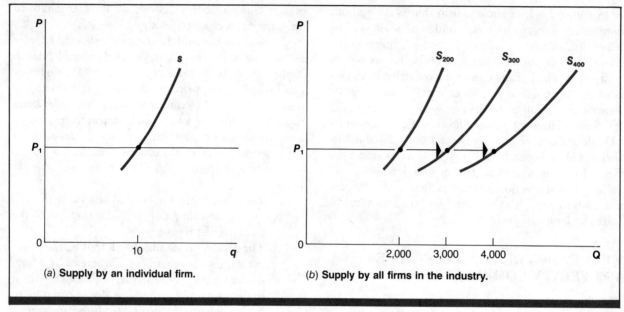

(a) **Supply by an individual firm.**

(b) **Supply by all firms in the industry.**

Figure 23-4 **With no barriers to entry, industry supply shifts as new firms enter.**
In a perfectly competitive industry, suppose there are 200 firms like the one shown in panel (a); then industry supply in panel (b) is S_{200}. If the number of firms increases to 300, the supply becomes S_{300}; and so on.

(b). Indeed, at any price such as P_1, the quantity supplied to the market is found by multiplying the supply s of the individual firm in panel (a) by 200. In other words, to derive the industry's supply curve S_{200} in panel (b), we horizontally sum the 200 supply curves of the individual firms in panel (a). (At the beginning of Chapter 21, a market demand curve was derived in a similar manner, by summing individual demand curves.)

If 100 similar new firms enter, increasing the number to 300, then 3,000 units are supplied at price P_1; the supply curve shifts from S_{200} to S_{300}. Finally, if the number of firms increases to 400, industry supply shifts to S_{400}.

Supply in the Long Run

As price rises in a perfectly competitive industry, new firms are encouraged to enter, increasing the quantity supplied. We now ask: How many firms will enter, and what will the equilibrium price be in the long run? Two possibilities should be distinguished.

Case A: Perfectly elastic long-run supply. In this first case, every input is uniform, or *homogeneous*. All land is identical, all entrepreneurs are equally skillful, all workers have the same talents, and so on. In

addition, the industry is not very large in the economy. As a result, the expansion or contraction of the industry causes no change in the prices of its inputs. In other words, new entrants can obtain the same quality of inputs as existing firms, and inputs are available at stable prices. In these circumstances, the long-run supply curve will be perfectly horizontal.

Figure 23-5 shows why. Panel (a) describes an individual firm, while panel (b) shows the demand and supply for the whole industry. Initially, the industry is at point E_1 in panel (b); price is P_1, and output is 5,000 units. There are 1,000 firms, each producing an output of five units at break-even point H in panel (a).

Since the individual firm is producing at its break-even point, P_1 is just sufficient to cover the firm's average cost. Because existing firms are earning no (above-normal) profit, there is no incentive for new firms to enter. Thus, point H in panel (a) is a long-run equilibrium for the firm, and point E_1 in panel (b) is the corresponding long-run equilibrium for the industry.

Now consider what happens in panel (b) if demand increases to D_2. In the short run, the higher demand causes equilibrium to move to E_2, with price rising to

P_2. In response to this higher price, each firm in panel (a) moves up its supply curve to T, where it is producing seven units and making a temporary profit shown by the shaded gray rectangle.

To explain this profit rectangle, note that the firm's profit *per unit* is TU—the difference between its selling price at T and its cost per unit at U. Its *total* profit is this per unit profit of TU—the height of the rectangle—times the seven units it sells—the base of the rectangle. That is, its total profit is the area of this rectangle. (We re-emphasize that this is *above-normal* profit. Remember, normal profit is included in the average cost curve.)

Because of the absence of any barriers to entry, this profit will attract new entrants. As the number of firms increases from 1,000 to 1,500, supply in panel (b) shifts from S_{1000} to S_{1500}. This influx of new firms continues until there are 2,000 firms in the industry, with the new supply curve S_{2000} moving the industry to new equilibrium E_3. In the process, price drops all the way back to P_1, and the individual firm in panel (a) responds by moving back to H. Since it no longer

makes a profit, there is no longer any incentive for new firms to enter. Thus, E_3 is the new long-run equilibrium for the industry in panel (b), and H is the long-run equilibrium for the individual firm in panel (a).

We now construct the long-run supply curve S_L in panel (b) by joining points of long-run equilibrium like E_1 and E_3. Unlike supply curves S_{1000}, S_{1500}, and S_{2000}—each of which is drawn on the assumption of a specific number of firms—the supply curve S_L applies to the long run when there is time for the number of firms to change. Observe that this long-run supply S_L is horizontal—that is, perfectly elastic; in the long run, price doesn't rise at all. Increased demand doesn't raise price because any increase in demand can be satisfied by new firms entering the industry, producing at the same cost as existing firms. It is possible for new firms to produce at this same cost because they have access to inputs of the same quality, at stable prices.

A similar argument applies if demand declines from D_1 to D_3 as in Figure 23-6. The industry in panel (b)

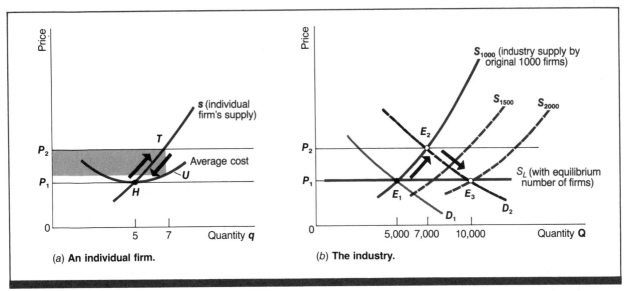

(a) An individual firm.

(b) The industry.

Figure 23-5   Long-run adjustment to an increase in demand. In this diagram, both the individual firm and the industry are initially in equilibrium at price P_1. The firm in panel (a) is at H, producing 5 units. The industry in panel (b) is in equilibrium at E_1, with 5,000 units sold. (There are 1,000 firms like the one in panel (a).)

Now suppose that demand increases from D_1 to D_2. In the short run, the price rises to P_2 and firms make temporary profits shown by the shaded area in panel (a). New firms

enter, shifting supply to the right in panel (b). The price falls. In the long run, the number of firms in the industry increases to 2,000, with supply shifting to S_{2000}. The new equilibrium is at E_3, with price dropping all the way back to P_1. Faced with price P_1, the individual firm in panel (a) moves back to H; it no longer makes profits, and there is no further incentive for new firms to enter. With each of the firms in panel (a) producing 5 units, the 2,000 firms in the industry produce the 10,000 units shown in panel (b).

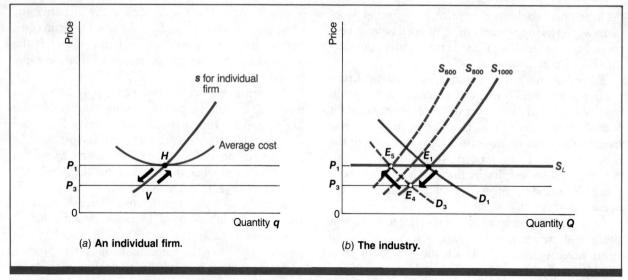

Figure 23-6   Long-run adjustment to a decrease in demand.
In this diagram, the initial long-run equilibrium (H for the firm, E_1 for the industry) is the same as in Figure 23-5. Now, however, demand decreases from D_1 to D_3 in panel (b). In the short run, the price falls to P_3, and each firm in panel (a) suffers a loss because this price is too low to cover its average cost. Some firms leave the industry, shifting supply to the left in panel (b). The price recovers. In the long run, the price rises all the way back to P_1 at new long-run equilibrium E_5. Each of the individual firms that remains in the industry moves back to H in panel (a) and no longer suffers losses. Therefore, there is no further tendency for firms to leave.

moves from E_1 to a new short-run equilibrium at E_4, with price depressed to P_3. In response to this lower price, each individual firm in panel (a) moves down its supply curve from H to V, where it suffers a loss because the new price P_3 is less than its average cost. Therefore, in the long run, firms leave the industry. As a consequence, the supply curve in panel (b) shifts to the left from S_{1000} to S_{800} and eventually to S_{600}, at which point the number of firms in the industry has been reduced from 1,000 to 600. E_5 is the new long-run equilibrium; price has gone back up to P_1, and each individual firm in panel (a) has responded by moving back up to H. At this point the firm no longer suffers a loss and there is therefore no further incentive for firms to leave. Again, we see that the long-run industry supply, defined by joining long-run equilibrium points E_1 and E_5, is the horizontal line S_L.

Case B: A rising long-run supply curve. The long-run supply curves S_L of many industries are not horizontal; they slope upward to the right. This happens if costs rise as new firms enter, either because these firms bid up the prices of inputs or because they have to use inputs of lower quality. As an example, new wheat growers may find that the highest-quality land is already being used by existing producers; the only land still available may be less productive.

Such a case is illustrated in Figure 23-7, where the initial long-run equilibrium is at E_1. An increase in demand from D_1 to D_2 causes a move to a new short-run equilibrium at E_2. At high price P_2, profits of existing firms encourage new entrants. As the number of firms increases from 100 to 150, supply shifts from S_{100} to S_{150} and the new long-run equilibrium is established at E_3. In this case, price does not drop all the way back to P_1. Instead, it falls only part way, to P_3. At this price, a new firm producing on the best land that's left—relatively poor land on which costs of production are relatively high—is just able to cover its costs. There is no further incentive for firms to enter. This is why E_3 is the new long-run equilibrium. Therefore, the long-run supply curve S_L, constructed by joining long-run equilibrium points E_1 and E_3, slopes

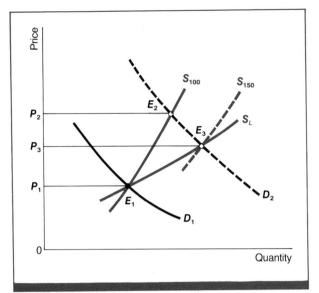

Figure 23-7   Long-run adjustment with a rising supply curve.
In this diagram, factors of production are not uniform in quality; some land is more suitable for growing wheat than other land. When demand increases from D_1 to D_2, the price rises to P_2 in the short run. The resulting profits to existing producers encourage new entrants into the industry. As the number of firms increases from 100 to 150, the industry supply moves from S_{100} to S_{150}. As a result, equilibrium moves from E_2 to E_3 and price declines from P_1 to P_3. However, it does not fall all the way back down to P_1 because the new entrants are using land less well suited to wheat, and their costs are accordingly higher than P_1.

upward. It is not perfectly elastic. (Another view of the adjustment of the industry in this case is provided in Appendix 23-C.)

HOW MUCH DO PRODUCERS GAIN FROM A HIGHER PRICE?

Just as we examined how a price change will affect consumers in Chapter 21, we now consider how a price change will affect producers.

In Figure 23-8, suppose price is initially $500, with producers responding by producing 30 units at R. Their total revenue is rectangle 1—that is, the 30 units (the base of the rectangle) times the $500 price for each unit (the height of the rectangle). If price increases to $700, producers move to new equilibrium T with

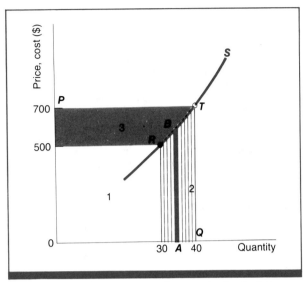

Figure 23-8   As price rises, producers gain the shaded area.
At initial price $500 and equilibrium R, 30 units are supplied for a total revenue of 30 × $500 = $15,000, shown as area 1. At a price of $700, equilibrium moves from R to T and 40 units are sold, for a total revenue of $28,000, or areas 1 + 2 + 3. Total revenue thus increases by area 2 + 3. Of this increase, area 2 represents the additional cost of producing the 10 more units, while area 3 is the gain to producers.

their total revenue increasing to rectangle $0PTQ$, that is, area 1 + 2 + 3. In this move, their total revenue increases by area 2 + 3. However, only area 3 is a net gain because area 2 represents increased costs. To clarify area 2, note that it is made up of a whole set of marginal cost bars enclosed under the supply curve. For example, the marginal cost of the 34th unit is bar AB. Area 2 is simply the sum of all such marginal cost bars as output is increased from 30 to 40 units. It represents the increase in total cost. Therefore, in this case we confirm that area 3 is the net gain to producers.

If price rises, the gain to producers may be estimated as the horizontal area to the left of the supply curve between the old and the new prices.[2] If market price falls, producers are worse off by a similar amount.

[2]This gain is sometimes spoken of as an increase in *producer surplus*. It is analogous to the increase in consumer surplus when the price falls.

Appendix 23-D explains why this sort of area may be only an approximate measure of the effect on producers.)

This conclusion applies either in the long run or the short—depending on whether we draw the long- or short-run supply curve[3] in Figure 23-8.

[3]However, those who ultimately receive this gain may be quite different in the short and long run. In the short run, the firms already in the industry—for example, the original wheat farmers—capture most or all of this gain in the form of profits. This is true whether they own or rent the land. But in the long run, this gain goes to the owners of the wheat land. The reason is that, as new farmers enter wheat production, they have to use less suitable land. Farmers therefore bid up the rent on the more productive original wheat land. (It doesn't matter to them whether they pay a high rent for productive land or less rent on lower-productivity land.) Owners of the original highly productive land therefore get a windfall in the form of higher rental income—or a higher price when they sell the land. Thus, in the long run, the gain from an increased price goes to factors—such as land—which are particularly suited to the good being produced. These ideas will be developed in more detail in Chapter 35.

KEY POINTS

1. In the long run, a firm's average cost curve is the "envelope" of all its short-run average cost curves. The long-run envelope curve indicates how average costs change as the firm changes its capital stock.

2. If input prices are constant, economies of scale cause the long-run average cost curve to slope downward.

3. It is possible for a firm to face both economies of scale (that is, a falling long-run average cost curve) and diminishing returns (a rising short-run marginal cost curve).

4. In a perfectly competitive industry, there are so many buyers and sellers of a standardized product that none can affect price. In addition, there is an absence of barriers to entry by new firms.

5. An industry's long-run supply is more elastic than its short-run supply. One important reason is that, in response to a higher price, new firms enter. As a result, industry output increases.

6. If new firms can enter an industry without facing higher costs, long-run supply is horizontal. However, if new firms face higher costs, long-run supply slopes upward.

7. A price increase provides a gain to producers roughly equal to the area to the left of the supply curve between the old and the new price. A price decrease makes producers worse off by a corresponding amount.

KEY CONCEPTS

envelope cost curve
economies of scale
diseconomies of scale
economies of scale occurring
   with diminishing returns

standardized product
barriers to entry
homogeneous inputs
long-run supply

entry and exit of producers
effect of a price change on
   producers

PROBLEMS

23-1 (a) Consider a firm operating at point R on the SAC_C and LAC curves in Figure 23-2. Does its short-run supply extend below R? If so, how far? Why?

(b) Suppose price falls below C_1 on the left axis. Explain how the firm, with the benefit of hindsight, would view its original decision to enter this industry. What would its output be in the short run? in the long run? Is this another illustration of why supply is more elastic in the long run than in the short run?

23-2 "A firm that is facing diminishing returns (rising costs) cannot be facing economies of scale (falling costs)." Do you agree? Explain.

23-3 In Figure 23-5, the shaded gray area measures the temporary profits that firms make as a result of an increase in demand. In Figure 23-6, demand decreases, and each firm suffers a short-run loss, which was not shown in this diagram. Redraw this figure, showing this temporary loss area.

23-4 Suppose demand increases from D_1 to D_2 in Figure 23-7 and the industry moves from E_1 to new equilibrium E_3. Since new P_3 is above the original P_1, does this mean that all new entering firms will earn an excess profit? Explain.

*23-5 At new equilibrium E_3 in Figure 23-7, would you expect that the original firms renting the most productive land would be able to hang onto their excess profit? Or might at least some of it be captured by the owners of that very productive land?

APPENDIX 23-A

THE LONG-RUN PRODUCTION FUNCTION

Because the firm can change the quantity of capital in the long run, the options open to it are much broader than in the short run. The broader options are shown in its **long-run production function**. An example is given in Table 23-1.

Because the firm is varying the quantity of capital as well as labour, this production function has two dimensions. From left to right, the quantity of labour increases. In the upward direction, the quantity of capital increases. For each combination of capital and labour, the corresponding number in the production function table indicates the maximum quantity of output that the firm can produce. For example, if the firm uses 3 units of capital (K) and 5 units of labour (L), it can produce 39 units of output. (For the moment, ignore the fact that some numbers in Table 23-1 are shown in colour. The reason for this is explained in Appendix 23-B.)

Table 23-1 is the long-run production function of the firm whose short-run production function was shown in Table 22-2. That earlier table now appears as the bottom row of Table 23-1. In fact, the long-run production function is made up of a *whole set* of rows, with each representing a different short-run production function. Once the firm chooses how much capital it will use, it is confined in the short run to operate along the corresponding row of this table. For example, if it chose six units of capital, it is confined in the short run to the top line of the production function.

However, in the long run, it can move anywhere in Table 23-1.

The long-run production function—or, more simply, the production function—shows vari-

Table 23-1
A Hypothetical Firm's Production Function

This simplified production function shows the number of units of output a firm can produce from various combinations of inputs. For example, if it combines 2 units of labour with 1 unit of capital, the second element in the bottom row indicates that it can produce 12 units of output.

Units of Capital (K)

	1	2	3	4	5	6
6	24	35	42	47	51	54
5	23	32	39	44	48	51
4	20	28	35	40	44	47
3	17	24	30	35	39	42
2	14	19	24	28	32	35
→ 1	5	12	18	21	23	24
	1	2	3	4	5	6

Units of Labour (L)

ous combinations of inputs and the maximum output that can be produced with each combination of inputs. For a simple firm with only two inputs (labour and capital), the production function can be shown by a two-dimensional table like Table 23-1.

The production function in Table 23-1 can be used to illustrate economies of scale. To do so, we look at what happens when *both* inputs are increased in the same proportion. Suppose the firm doubles its input of labour from 1 to 2 workers, and also doubles its capital from 1 to 2 units. As a result, its output more than doubles, from 5 to 19. Since its output increases by a greater percent than its inputs, it enjoys econo-

mies of scale in this range.

However, in the short run, the same firm faces diminishing returns. To see this, consider what happens when only *one* input—labour—is increased, while the quantity of capital is fixed at, say, 1 unit. The firm is therefore confined to the bottom row in the production function. As it increases the input of labour, the second worker has a marginal product of 7 units (that is, 12 minus 5 units) while the third has a marginal product of 6 units (18 minus 12). Since marginal product is falling, the firm is facing diminishing returns. We therefore conclude that a firm enjoying economies of scale may also face diminishing returns; this confirms the point made in Figure 23-3.

APPENDIX 23-B

THE FIRM'S LONG-RUN PRODUCTION FUNCTION AND ITS PROFIT-MAXIMIZING CHOICE OF INPUTS

In this appendix we study in more detail a question posed at the beginning of Chapter 22: How does a profit-maximizing firm decide which combination of inputs to use? For example, does it use a great deal of labour and little capital, or a great deal of capital and only a small amount of labour? Put this way, the decision applies to the long run, since it is only in the long run that the firm's capital can be changed. The question is: What is the best point for it to select in its long-run production function in Table 23-1? (The same type of decision is made in the short run when there are several variable inputs; for example, if the farmer is deciding on whether to use a lot of fertilizer and only a little labour, or vice versa.) To decide what combination of inputs to use, the first step is to graph the production function.

STEP 1. GRAPHING THE PRODUCTION FUNCTION: EQUAL-OUTPUT CURVES

First, note that several input combinations in Table 23-1 yield 24 units of output. These appear in colour

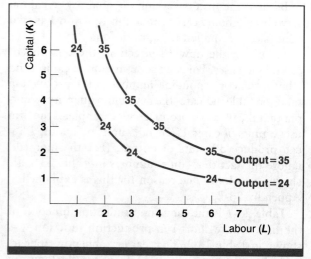

Figure 23-9 The production function in Table 23-1 graphed as a set of equal-output lines.
To graph the production function, we extract the red numbers from Table 23-1. For example, each of the input combinations that yield 24 units of output in Table 23-1 is graphed in this diagram. When joined, they become the "output = 24" curve.

and are reproduced to form the "output = 24" curve in Figure 23-9. Similarly, the "output = 35" curve is also extracted from Table 23-1. These equal-output curves—often called *isoquants*—are similar to the indifference (or equal-utility) curves that were shown earlier in Figure 21-9. Just as the indifference map in that earlier diagram showed a whole family of indifference curves, each representing a higher level of utility as the household moved northeast from the origin, so the production function provides a whole set of equal-output curves that also forms a hill. As the firm moves to the northeast, using more inputs, it reaches higher and higher output levels.

In one respect, however, the equal-output curves of the producer contain more information than the indifference curves of the consumer: Each equal-output curve represents a *specific number* of units of output. On the other hand, all we know about indifference curves is whether they represent "higher" or "lower" levels of satisfaction. We don't know how many "units of utility" they represent.

STEP 2. GRAPHING THE PRICE OF INPUTS: EQUAL-COST LINES

Maximizing profits requires not only the production function information we have just graphed but also information on the price of inputs. How is this graphed? If the price of labour is $20 per unit, and the price of capital is $30, straight line c_2 in Figure 23-10 is an *equal-cost line*. This shows all the combinations of labour and capital that can be purchased for a total cost of $120. (For example, this is the cost the firm will incur at A if it buys four units of capital at $30 per unit and no labour. For more detail, see the caption for Figure 23-10.) Similarly, c_1 represents the input combinations that would cost the firm $60. You can visualize a whole family of parallel lines showing successively higher costs for the firm as it moves to the northeast.

MAXIMIZING PROFIT

Figure 23-11 brings the previous two diagrams together. Curves q_1 and q_2 are from the firm's production function in Figure 23-9, while the straight lines are equal-cost lines of the type drawn in Figure 23-10. If the

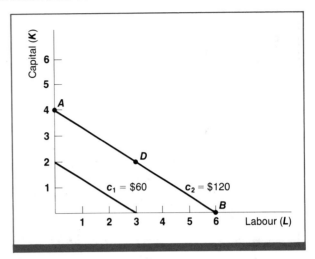

Figure 23-10   Equal-cost lines.
If the price of labour is $20 per unit and the price of capital is $30, c_2 is the equal-cost line that shows all combinations of these two inputs that can be purchased for $120. For example, combination D of 3 units of labour and 2 of capital costs $3(\$20) + 2(\$30) = \$120$. Similarly, combination B costs $6(\$20) + 0(\$30) = \$120$. Parallel line c_1 is also an equal-cost line, but it shows all input combinations that would cost $60. There is a whole family of similar parallel lines, each representing a different cost. If the price of labour relative to capital changes, there is a whole new family of parallel lines with a different slope.

firm wishes to produce 24 units of output, it will do so at the least cost by using the input combination shown by E_2—that is, two units of capital and three of labour. In general:

The firm selects the point on its equal-output curve that is tangent to an equal-cost line.

Any other way of producing this quantity is rejected because it would be more costly. For example, the firm does not use input combination E_4 because this lies on higher cost line c_4.

Just as E_2 is the best point for a firm wishing to produce 24 units of output, so E_5 is the best point if it wishes to produce 35 units of output. The final step for the firm is then to examine all points such as E_2 and E_5 and select the one that will maximize its profits. This, then, is the way one can answer our original question: "What point in Table 23-1 does the firm select to maximize its profit?"

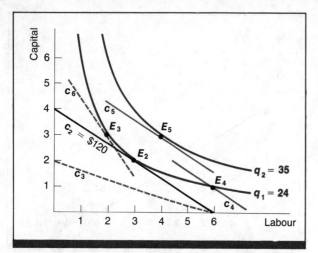

Figure 23-11   The firm's equilibrium is determined by its equal-output curves and its equal-cost lines.
The least cost way of producing 24 units of output is to select input combination E_2 where the equal-output and equal-cost lines are tangent. The firm then calculates its profit at E_2 by comparing its $120 cost with its revenue (24 units of output times whatever its selling price may be). Similarly, to produce 35 units of output, the firm selects tangency point E_5 and evaluates its profit there. Of these tangency points, it selects the one with the greatest profit.

THE EFFECT OF A CHANGE IN THE PRICE OF INPUTS

If the relative price of labour and capital changes, there is a new family of equal-cost lines with a different slope. For example, if the price of capital rises from $30 to $60 while the price of labour is unchanged, flatter line c_3 is now the new $120 equal-cost line. You can visualize the whole family of new equal-cost lines parallel to it. Thus:

The slope of the family of equal-cost lines depends on the relative price of the firm's inputs.

Thus, an equal-cost line for the firm is similar to a consumer's budget line; its slope depends on the relative price of the items being purchased.

Now suppose that capital has become *less* (rather than more) expensive relative to labour, and the equal-cost lines have therefore become steeper. Specifically, suppose the new set of equal-cost lines is c_6 and the family of lines parallel to it. To produce 24 units of output, the firm no longer uses input combination E_2. Instead it picks E_3, the point of tangency with one of its new equal-cost lines. This type of move to the northwest will also occur along q_2 and all the other equal-output lines. Thus, no matter what its initial profit-maximizing point, the firm moves northwest, substituting an input that has become relatively less expensive (capital) for the one that has become relatively more expensive (labour).

PROBLEM

23-6 With capital at $30 and labour at $20, how much less is the cost incurred by the firm that operates at E_2 rather than E_4 in Figure 23-11?
    With capital at $20 and labour at $30, how much less is its cost if it operates at E_3 rather than E_2?

APPENDIX 23-C

LONG-RUN SUPPLY IN A PERFECTLY COMPETITIVE INDUSTRY WITH NON-UNIFORM FACTORS OF PRODUCTION

The first three panels of Figure 23-12 display the long-run marginal cost curves of three wheat-producing firms. (For every long-run average cost curve, we may draw a corresponding marginal cost curve.) These three firms represent the large number that are either producing wheat or are willing to start producing if the price rises enough.

At price P_1, the only firm willing to produce wheat is firm A. It is the firm with the land that is most suitable for wheat and is the only one that can produce with an average cost as low as P_1. Thus, total industry supply in the last panel is just arrow f, the quantity supplied by firm A.

Although price P_1 is not high enough to induce firms B and C to enter the industry, suppose price rises. At P_2, industry supply is substantially augmented as firm B starts to produce and supplies the quantity indicated by arrow g. As price rises above P_2, market supply becomes the horizontal sum of the individual supplies of firms A and B. Finally, at price P_3, firm C is attracted into production, and market supply is shown by the three arrows representing the supplies of all three firms. Thus, the industry supply curve is the heavy line in the last panel, representing the horizontal sum of the supplies of the individual firms. It has an upward slope because differences in the quality of wheat land cause differences in the costs of the three wheat-producing firms.

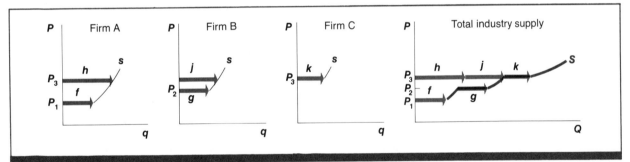

Figure 23-12   A rising long-run industry supply.
At P_1, market supply is arrow f from firm A, the only firm able to produce at that low price. At P_2, A's supply is augmented by arrow g from firm B, since B is barely induced into production. At price P_3, firm C also starts to produce (arrow k). Thus, at any price, industry supply S in the last panel is the horizontal sum of the supplies of all individual firms.

APPENDIX 23-D

USING THE INDUSTRY SUPPLY CURVE TO MEASURE THE GAIN TO PRODUCERS: SOME COMPLICATIONS

As we have seen in Figure 23-7, the long-run industry supply curve may slope upward because of different qualities of factors of production, such as different qualities of wheat land. In this case, a rise in the price of the product results in a gain for those who provide the factors of production. Specifically, the owners of the better qualities of land receive higher rents. These gains were measured in Figure 23-8 by the area to the left of the supply curve between the old and the new price. In this appendix, we consider other forces that may affect the long-run slope of the supply curve, and may therefore make this area of gain to producers an imperfect measure. For example:

Case 1. First, the long-run supply curve may slope upward even if all factors of production are of uniform quality. To illustrate, the supply of trucking services may slope upward even if the factors of production (drivers, trucks, etc.) are of equal quality. The reason is that, as more and more trucks are operated, the roads become congested. Trucks move more slowly, and as a consequence the costs of the trucking companies rise. This makes the supply curve of trucking services slope upward.

In this case, an increase in the demand for trucking may cause an increase in the long-run equilibrium price *without* any gain for producers—in particular, without any benefit to *any* factor of production in the trucking industry. The higher price may simply be dissipated in the higher costs resulting from road congestion.

Case 2. It is even possible for the long-run supply curve to slope *downward* if all factors of production are of uniform quality. Consider the case of a metal-fabricating industry made up of a number of competitive firms located in a small city near Montreal. As the industry grows, the costs facing each firm may fall. This may occur, for example, because the Hamilton supplier who is shipping unprocessed steel to this industry is now delivering much more. There are economies of scale in shipping, and the resulting savings may be passed along to the firms buying steel.

Case 3. Finally, there may be a combination of forces at work. For example, the long-run supply curve of the metal-fabricating industry may be horizontal because two sets of forces are balanced: As this industry expands, the fall in the price of unprocessed steel may be just offset by the rise in rents on land being used by this industry. In this case, an increase in output does provide a gain to those who supply factors of production—specifically, a gain to the owners of land. This gain occurs even though the supply curve is horizontal and therefore provides no indication whatsoever of any gain for producers from expansion of this industry.

To sum up: Case 1 shows that the area to the left of the supply curve may *exaggerate* the gain for producers in an expanding industry; it may suggest a gain where none exists. On the other hand, case 3 illustrates how the area to the left of the supply curve may *understate* the gain to producers. In that case, there *was* a gain, but it couldn't be shown to the left of the supply curve because the supply curve was horizontal.

Because of such complications, the supply curve can be used only as a rough first approximation in measuring how producers gain from an increase in price.

Chapter 24

PERFECT COMPETITION AND ECONOMIC EFFICIENCY

> Under perfect competition, the
> business dodoes, dinosaurs and
> great ground sloths are in for a
> bad time—as they should be.
>
> R.H. Bork and W.S. Bowman, Jr.

In Chapter 21, we examined how consumers in a perfectly competitive market respond to the price they face. In chapters 22 and 23, we studied how producers on the other side of such a market respond. In this chapter, we bring these two sides together, in order to *describe how a perfectly competitive market operates.* This will then be used to *evaluate its performance* from the point of view of society as a whole. How well does a perfectly competitive market deliver the goods and services the public wants?

We shall see that, *if two important assumptions are satisfied,* a perfectly competitive market does provide an efficient result: Neither too much nor too little output is produced. In future chapters, we shall see why other market structures typically do not result in allocative efficiency. For example, we shall see in the next chapter that monopoly is not efficient: Too little output is produced.

TWO IMPORTANT ASSUMPTIONS

Thus far, we have made no distinction between the *private benefit* a good provides to those who buy it and the benefit it provides to society as a whole—its *social benefit.* Often the two are the same. For example, when someone buys beefsteak, the only benefit that goes to society is the benefit received by that individual. There is no additional benefit to anyone else. However, private and social benefit don't always coincide in this way. For example, the benefit to society of services provided by professional gardeners may include not only the benefit enjoyed by those who buy these services, but also some benefit to other individuals in the neighbourhood.

But for now, we assume away this complication. We assume that the purchaser gets all the benefit from the good; that is, the benefit received by the purchaser represents the total benefit to society. Thus:

Assumption 1. Social benefit is the same as private benefit. More precisely, the marginal benefit of a good to society as a whole—which we shall call MB_S—is the same as MB, its marginal benefit to those who consume it. Either can be measured by the height of the market demand curve.

$$MB_S = MB \text{ to consumers} \qquad (24\text{-}1)$$

We make a similar assumption about cost:

Assumption 2. The cost of a good to society is the same as the private cost incurred by producers of this good. More precisely, the marginal cost of a good to society as a whole—which we shall call MC_S—is the same as MC, its marginal cost to producers. Either is shown by the height of the market supply curve.

$$MC_S = MC \text{ to producers} \qquad (24\text{-}2)$$

For example, the cost to society of producing wheat is generally just the cost incurred by wheat farmers. However, there are again exceptions. The cost to society of paper may be not only the private cost incurred by the firms producing it, but also the cost to those people living downstream who suffer if these firms dump polluting wastes into the river.

Exceptions to these two assumptions are important, and will be the focus of attention in chapters 26, 27, and 28. But until then, we limit ourselves to the large number of cases where they can be taken as valid.

With these assumptions in hand, we now turn to a detailed description of a perfectly competitive market.

HOW A PERFECTLY COMPETITIVE MARKET WORKS

Figures 24-1 and 24-2 illustrate the decisions of many consumers and many producers in a perfectly competitive market. In the middle panel of Figure 24-1, note that supply and demand are equal at an equilibrium output of 100 units and a $10 price. At this equilibrium, the quantity purchased by each consumer is shown in the panels on the left, while the quantity sold by each producer is shown in the panels on the right. (Just as in Figure 21-1, we use only a few consumers to represent the very large number who participate in

this market, and we do the same for producers.)

In Figure 24-1, the central panel showing S and D is so important that it is reproduced in Figure 24-2. In panel (a) we show what's happening to consumers, as originally described in Figure 21-3. Consumers make the decision that is best for them by continuing to purchase until *their marginal benefit equals their marginal cost*. Their marginal cost is what they have to pay for each additional unit of the good; that is, its price P. Thus, consumers purchase 100 units where their marginal benefit equals the price:

$$\text{For consumers: } MB = P \qquad (24\text{-}3)$$

In panel (b) we show what's happening to producers, as originally described in Figure 22-2. Producers make the decision that is best *for them* by continuing to produce and sell this good until *their marginal benefit equals their marginal cost*. In perfect competition, the marginal benefit that they get from selling one more unit is the price P. Therefore they produce 100 units where

$$\text{For producers: } P = MC \qquad (24\text{-}4)$$

From these last two equations, it follows that

$$\text{consumers' } MB = MC \text{ to producers} \qquad (24\text{-}5)$$

as we see in panel (c). Finally, recall the two key assumptions introduced earlier (24-1 and 24-2). Because of these two assumptions, the equation above becomes:

$$MB_S = MC_S \qquad (24\text{-}6)$$

that is, the marginal benefit to society equals the marginal cost to society. This is the condition that provides an efficient outcome for society as a whole, as we will confirm in the next section.

The efficient outcome for society is where

$$MB_S = MC_S$$

This occurs in perfect competition, if social benefits are the same as benefits to consumers and social costs are the same as costs to producers.

To sum up so far: Under perfect competition, with consumers making *their* best decision by equating *their* marginal benefit and marginal cost in panel (a), and producers making *their* best decision by equating *their* marginal benefit and marginal cost in panel (b), the

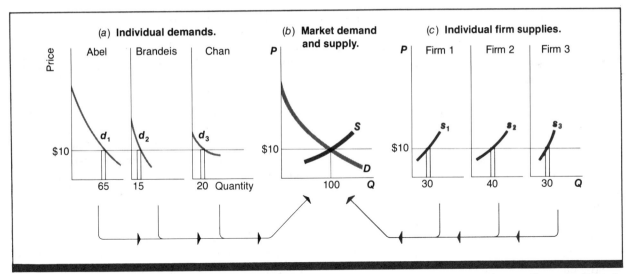

Figure 24-1   Individual consumers and producers in a perfectly competitive market.

In panel (*b*), market demand *D* reflects the individual demands in panel (*a*), while market supply *S* reflects the supplies of individual firms in panel (*c*). The perfectly competitive solution, where *S* and *D* intersect, is at a price of $10 and an output of 100 units. The bars in panel (*a*) show how each consumer continues to purchase until marginal benefit MB equals the $10 price, and the bars in panel (*c*) show how each firm produces to the point where its marginal cost MC is equal to this $10 price. Since each consumer's MB is therefore equal to each producer's MC, any change in production or consumption would result in an efficiency loss.

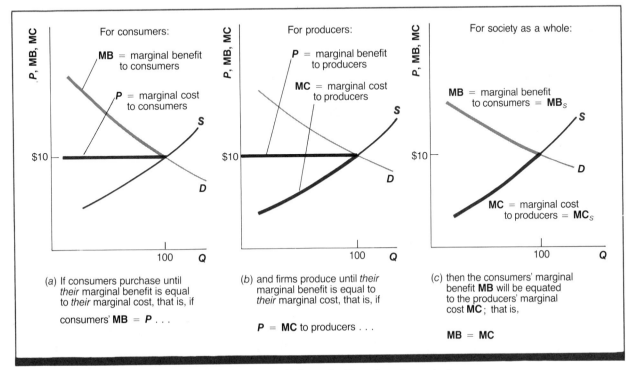

Figure 24-2   The competitive market: The equalization of marginal benefit and marginal cost.
This is an elaboration of panel (*b*) in Figure 24-1.

result in panel (*c*) is an efficient output for society as a whole.

This is such an important conclusion in economics that we emphasize it in Box 24-1 and now illustrate it with two examples.

DEMONSTRATING WHY PERFECT COMPETITION IS EFFICIENT

It has been shown that under specified conditions perfect competition equates the marginal benefit to society MB_S and the marginal cost to society MC_S. We will now demonstrate that, because $MB_S = MC_S$, this outcome is efficient; we can't do better.

In Figure 24-3 we reproduce the market supply and demand curves from panel (*c*) of Figure 24-2. Now suppose output is expanded beyond the perfectly competitive quantity of 100 units, where marginal benefit

to society equals marginal cost to society. Specifically, suppose the quantity is the 140 units shown in panel (*a*). This outcome is inefficient, as we can see by considering a single unit, *c*, of this additional output. Its benefit is shown by the white bar, the height of the demand curve. However, its cost is even larger, as shown by both the white bar and the red bar—that is, the height of the supply curve. Thus the net loss on this unit is the red bar. The sum of all similar losses on all the other excess units of output in the range between 100 and 140 is shown by the red triangle. This is the efficiency loss from producing too much.

On the other hand, suppose that for some reason output is less than 100 units—say, the 60 units shown in panel (*b*). This outcome is also inefficient, as we can see by considering one of the units that is no longer produced, say *d*. Since its cost would have been the white bar under the supply curve and its benefit

---

BOX 24-1

CONDITIONS THAT RESULT IN AN EFFICIENT SOLUTION

Since MB and MC represent marginal private benefits and costs, and MB_S and MC_S represent marginal social benefits and costs, then:

If social and private benefits are the same,	$MB_S = MB$	(24-1)
and if consumers in a perfectly competitive market act in their own self-interest by purchasing up to the point where their marginal benefit equals price	$MB = P$	(24-3)
and if producers in a perfectly competitive market act in their own self-interest by producing up to the point where their marginal cost equals price,	$P = MC$	(24-4)
and if private and social costs are the same,	$MC = MC_S$	(24-2)
then Adam Smith's "invisible hand" works; the pursuit of private interest by both consumers and producers yields a result that is in the interest of society as a whole	$MB_S = MC_S$	(24-6)

That is, there is an efficient solution.

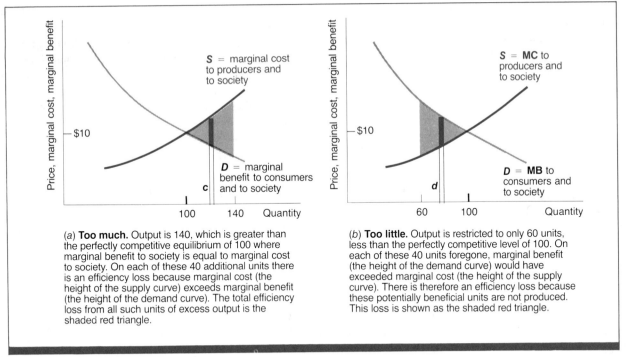

(a) **Too much.** Output is 140, which is greater than the perfectly competitive equilibrium of 100 where marginal benefit to society is equal to marginal cost to society. On each of these 40 additional units there is an efficiency loss because marginal cost (the height of the supply curve) exceeds marginal benefit (the height of the demand curve). The total efficiency loss from all such units of excess output is the shaded red triangle.

(b) **Too little.** Output is restricted to only 60 units, less than the perfectly competitive level of 100. On each of these 40 units foregone, marginal benefit (the height of the demand curve) would have exceeded marginal cost (the height of the supply curve). There is therefore an efficiency loss because these potentially beneficial units are not produced. This loss is shown as the shaded red triangle.

Figure 24-3   Inefficient quantities of output.

the white bar plus the red bar under the demand curve, the net benefit to society of producing it would have been the red bar. Or to put the same point another way, society incurs the loss of this red bar because this potentially beneficial unit is not produced. The sum of all such losses through the range of restricted output from 100 down to 60 is the red triangle. This is the efficiency loss from producing too little. An example is the rent control program described earlier in Box 4-1. When the government sets a low price, suppliers reduce their output. This decline in quantity results in an efficiency loss from producing too little, just like in panel (b).

Since there is an efficiency loss if either more or less is produced than the perfectly competitive output where marginal benefit and cost to society are equal—in our example, 100 units—this is the output that is efficient. Only if output is at this level do we avoid a red efficiency loss.

This idea of an efficiency loss—sometimes called a deadweight loss—is so important in the study of microeconomics that you should be sure you have mastered Figure 24-3 before proceeding. In particular, we emphasize:

An efficiency loss—or deadweight loss—occurs whenever there is a move away from the output where the marginal benefit to society is equal to the marginal cost to society. Such an efficiency loss from producing too much or too little can be shown graphically by one of the red triangles in Figure 24-3.

Finally, as an alternative demonstration of why efficiency occurs at the perfectly competitive output—where marginal benefit and cost to society are equal—return to Figure 24-1, where we first described the market we have been studying so far in this chapter. Suppose you are an all-powerful bureaucrat or czar and think you can do better than this perfectly competitive solution. Specifically, suppose that you arbitrarily order that, instead of the equilibrium quantity of 100 units, 40 more units are to be produced. Try as you like, you cannot avoid a social loss on those additional units. On the one hand, they must cost more than $10 to produce. Regardless of the firms you select to produce them in panel (c), those firms will have to move to the right, up their supply curves to a higher marginal cost. At the same time, those additional units will be consumed by individuals in panel (a) who value them at less than $10. No matter who gets to consume these units, those individuals will move to the right, down their demand curves to a lower marginal benefit. Because the cost of each additional unit is greater than $10, and the benefit it provides is less than $10, there is a net social loss; that is, an efficiency loss. You thought you could do better. In fact, you did worse.

A further discussion of efficiency is provided in Box 24-2 and in Appendix A at the end of this chapter.

FREE ENTRY AND ECONOMIC EFFICIENCY

In defining perfect competition, one of the key requirements is the absence of barriers to entry. We shall now show that, if this condition is not met, inefficiency will result. To illustrate, suppose that the third firm in Figure 24-1 has been blocked out of this market for some reason; for example, suppose it's a firm that needs a government licence, and it has been turned

down. Because its supply s_3 would not exist, total market supply in the centre panel would be less, that is, it would lie to the left of S. You can visualize (or sketch in) this new supply curve. Note that the equilibrium output where this new supply intersects D is less than the efficient output level of 100, and a triangular efficiency loss would therefore result: Potentially beneficial units of output would not be produced, because this third firm would have been unable to enter this market and produce them.

OTHER TYPES OF EFFICIENCY

Thus far we have only shown how a perfectly competitive market can provide *allocative efficiency*. How does this market measure up in terms of *technical* and *dynamic* efficiency?

Technical or Technological Efficiency

This kind of efficiency means avoiding outright waste.

BOX 24-2

PARETO AND THE ELIMINATION OF DEADWEIGHT LOSS

With a bit of extra effort and imagination, we can increase our understanding of the important idea of efficiency.

A change that will make one individual better off without hurting anyone else is called a *Pareto-improvement*, after Italian Vilfredo Pareto, who originated the idea. If we have made all such Pareto-improvements, we arrive at a **Pareto-optimum**. This is exactly what economists mean by an efficient solution. It means that all deadweight losses have been eliminated—that is, all possible Pareto-improvements have been made.

The idea of a Pareto-improvement can be illustrated by referring back to Figure 24-1. Suppose that initially Brandeis gets 1 less unit than we have shown there (namely, 14 units), while Chan gets 1 more (21 units). A Pareto-improvement is now possi-

ble because we can make Chan better off without hurting anyone else—that is, without hurting Brandeis, the only other person involved. Here's how. Let Chan sell that 1 unit to Brandeis for $10. Chan benefits from this transaction: Because he values his twentieth unit at $10, he values his twenty-first unit—the one he is giving up—at less than $10; so he benefits when he receives $10 for it. At the same time, Brandeis has not been hurt because he values the unit he receives—his fifteenth—at exactly the same $10 that he pays for it.

This Pareto-improvement is possible because, initially, all producers and consumers did not value their last unit equally. But with this transaction, we have reached the perfectly competitive solution in Figure 24-1, where all consumers and producers *do* value their last unit equally, at $10. That is, the marginal benefit MB for every consumer is equal to the MB for every other consumer, and is also equal to the marginal cost MC for every producer. Consequently, any further Pareto-improvement is impossible. Therefore this perfectly competitive solution is Pareto-optimal, that is, efficient.

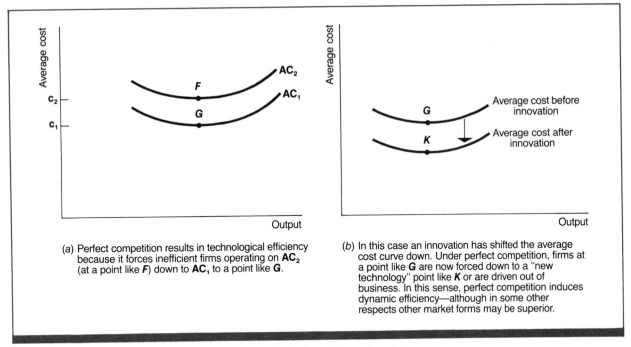

(a) Perfect competition results in technological efficiency because it forces inefficient firms operating on **AC₂** (at a point like **F**) down to **AC₁** to a point like **G**.

(b) In this case an innovation has shifted the average cost curve down. Under perfect competition, firms at a point like **G** are now forced down to a "new technology" point like **K** or are driven out of business. In this sense, perfect competition induces dynamic efficiency—although in some other respects other market forms may be superior.

Figure 24-4   How perfect competition promotes technical and dynamic efficiency.

Thus, a restaurant is technically inefficient if it produces a standard meal using twice as much beef and twice as much labour as other restaurants. A construction firm is technically inefficient if it destroys its machinery because it fails to keep it oiled. In brief, technical inefficiency exists if there is poor management, and unnecessarily high costs. To illustrate in panel (a) of Figure 24-4, technical inefficiency raises the firm's average cost curve up to AC₂, compared to the average cost curve AC₁ of a technically efficient firm.

Perfect competition works toward technical efficiency as well as allocative efficiency. If a firm is inefficient and is therefore producing at a high-cost point such as F, it won't be able to survive in competition with technically efficient firms that produce with average costs at G. Thus, there is a tendency for inefficient old firms to go the way of the dinosaurs—to be driven out of business by their existing competitors, or by new firms with lower costs. (Note how perfect competition puts pressure on firms to produce at the lowest point on their average cost curves. We also saw this in our earlier example in Figure 23-6 where the firms that survive in the long run all produce at the lowest point, H.)

In contrast to the firm in perfect competition, a monopoly firm may be protected from the pressures of competition. If it has a stranglehold on a market—because of a patent, for example—it can survive even if management is sloppy; it doesn't have to worry about facing new competitors. But even though monopoly does not *have* to achieve technical efficiency, it still has an incentive to do so; greater technical efficiency means greater profits. Therefore, in later chapters we will generally show monopoly firms producing on their technically efficient average cost curves.

Dynamic Efficiency
This exists when changes are occurring at the best rate—for example, when new technology is being developed and adopted at the best rate. While a competitive market gets high marks for promoting allocative efficiency and technical efficiency, its superiority is less clear in terms of dynamic efficiency.

In some ways, perfect competition does indeed promote dynamic efficiency. Suppose, for example, that a new process or new invention has been discovered that reduces costs. This shifts the average cost curve down as shown in panel (b) of Figure 24-4. Firms that do not lower their costs by adapting to this new technology will be left producing at a point such as *G*, at a disadvantage in competing with firms using the new technology and producing at a point such as *K*. Thus, firms that ignore new technology and are consequently unable to compete will also go the way of the dinosaurs. We conclude that, by forcing firms to *adopt* new technology, perfect competition generates dynamic efficiency.

However, let's go one step further and ask the question: What sort of market does the best job of *creating* new technology in the first place? There is considerable debate over this question, with many contending

that, in this respect, some other market forms are superior. One argument is that it is easier for a large monopolistic firm to finance the research necessary for many innovations. Furthermore, a large firm has more incentive to engage in research, since it is large enough to reap many of the gains. In contrast, no individual farmer has much incentive to try to develop a new strain of wheat; most of the gains would go to other farmers.

In conclusion, the competitive market scores high in two of the three aspects of efficiency— including allocative efficiency, which will be our focus in the next few chapters.

MARKET PRICE AS A SCREENING DEVICE

Every economy must have some device to determine who will consume a scarce good and who will not. In our economy, market price plays that role by acting as a barrier that must be overcome by buyers. In panel (*a*) of Figure 24-5, we see a competitive market in which 1,000 units are sold at a $15 price. In panel (*b*), we see that this price has blocked out consumers who aren't willing to pay at least this $15 price. In panel (*c*), we see that this same price also acts as a barrier, blocking out all high-cost producers who are unable to sell this good for $15. Thus, a perfectly competitive price screens out unenthusiastic buyers and high-cost sellers; both groups are excluded from the market because of one simple criterion—they are unwilling or unable to meet the market price.

PREVIEW: PROBLEMS WITH THE COMPETITIVE MARKET

Thus far, we have provided a very rosy picture of how well perfectly competitive markets work. The examples of inefficient outcomes occurred when the government intervened to overrule the workings of a competitive market. When the government czar dictated output, too much was produced. When the government set a rent ceiling, too little housing was produced. Indeed, up to this point, the analysis has had a strong laissez-faire message: The government should leave the market alone, its wonders to perform.

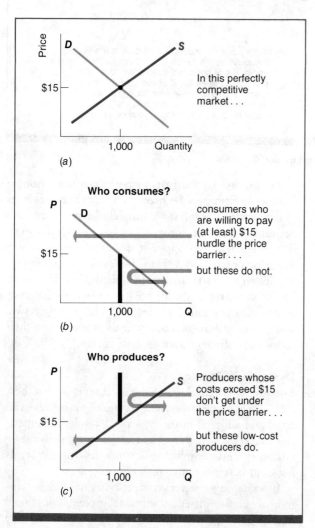

Figure 24-5 Price as a barrier that screens buyers and sellers in a competitive market.

Table 24-1
How the Four Basic Conditions That Lead to Efficiency Can Be Violated

	Condition	Will be violated if:	Considered in Chapter(s):
(24-1)	$MB_S = MB$	There are benefits to others than purchasers; for example, neighbours enjoy a well-kept garden.	30
(24-2)	$MB = MC_S$	There is pollution or other costs not borne by producers.	28, 29
(24-3)	$MB = P$	A single buyer has some influence over price. This may occur if there are only a few buyers.	34
(24-4)	$P = MC$	A single seller has some influence over price. This may occur if there are only a few sellers.	25, 26

However, this gives a distorted view of the Canadian economy. In particular, all four basic conditions listed in Table 24-1 must be met if the free market is to lead to an efficient outcome.

In practice, these conditions are often violated; in Table 24-1 we show how they may be violated, and the chapters that deal with each case. When they are violated, a laissez-faire economy will operate inefficiently. In this case, government intervention may make the economy work more efficiently, not less. Furthermore, *even when all four conditions are met*, the outcome will not necessarily be quite as good as this chapter has so far suggested, as we shall now see.

A RESERVATION ABOUT THE PERFECTLY COMPETITIVE SOLUTION: IT DEPENDS ON THE DISTRIBUTION OF INCOME

Let's now return to Figure 24-1. Suppose that Abel has a higher income than Brandeis, and this is the reason why he has greater demand for this good. (Remember, demand depends both on desire for the product and ability to pay. And with his higher income, Abel has a greater ability to pay.) In Figure 24-6 we reproduce Figure 24-1, making only one change: We suppose that the incomes of Abel and Brandeis are reversed. Brandeis now has the high income and hence high demand, while Abel has the low income and low demand, as shown in the section shaded in gray in this diagram. Since nothing else need change,[1] the rest of Figure 24-6 is the same as before. In this diagram, just as in Figure 24-1, a perfectly competitive market yields an efficient solution. However, it is quite a different solution. There is no way that economists can judge which of the two solutions is better. All we can say is that both are efficient.

Abel and Brandeis, of course, will each have a clear opinion on which is better: Abel prefers Figure 24-1, where he gets most of this good (65 units), while Brandeis will prefer Figure 24-6, where *he* gets the lion's share. However, from the point of view of society as a whole, there is no way to judge. True, if we could put an imaginary measuring device into the heads of these two individuals and thus be able to say that, in moving from Figure 24-1 to Figure 24-6, Brandeis's gain in satisfaction or utility exceeds Abel's loss, we might judge the pattern in Figure 24-6 to be superior. But this we cannot do, since *there is no known way of comparing the utility or satisfaction one person gets from a good with the utility someone else gets*.

To sum up: For each possible distribution of income, there is a different perfectly competitive solution. Each

[1] Market price need not be exactly the same $10 as in Figure 24-1; but this is an unimportant detail that does not affect the argument.

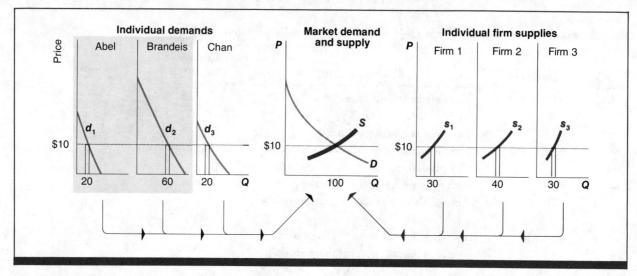

Figure 24-6 Another efficient, competitive solution.
This figure is similar to Figure 24-1, except that Brandeis now has a greater income and demand than Abel, and consequently consumes the greater quantity (60 units). This diagram also shows a perfectly competitive solution just like the one in Figure 24-1. Both solutions are efficient, but

of these solutions is efficient; but we cannot demonstrate that one is better than the rest. The question of how income should be distributed is one that economists alone cannot answer, although we will shed more light on it in Chapter 36.

ANOTHER RESERVATION: WHEN BUYERS OR SELLERS ARE MISLED BY PRICE SIGNALS

We have now dealt with the basic features of perfectly competitive markets. However, there are a number of additional complications. For example, a market price acts as a signal to which both consumers and producers react; but what happens if they get the wrong message?

To illustrate this problem, we consider a case where producers may misread the price signal. Recall from Figure 20-7 how a small shift in the supply of an agricultural product—perhaps because of crop failure or disease in a herd—will result in a substantial change in price. We shall now show that this instability may be made worse if there is a time lag between the decision to produce an agricultural good and its eventual

which is better? The individuals concerned will have conflicting views. Abel prefers Figure 24-1 and Brandeis prefers this figure. However, an economist examining this from the point of view of society as a whole cannot judge, because in the move from Figure 24-1 to this figure it is impossible to compare Brandeis' utility gain to Abel's utility loss.

delivery to the market. There are many examples of this sort of delay: Wheat must be planted in the fall or spring for harvest in the summer, and the decision to breed cattle is made several years before the beef is eventually sold.

In such situations, an initial disturbance may set off a cycle of price fluctuations, with price high one year, low the next, high the next, and so on. To illustrate, suppose that, due to some initial disturbance, hogs become very scarce; perhaps a large number are lost because of disease. As a result, the price of hogs is unusually high. Seeing this high price, farmers are induced to expand hog production. When these hogs come to market at a later date, the result will be an oversupply, and the price will fall. In turn, this depressed price will induce farmers to switch out of hogs, and this shift will lead in the next period to scarcity, raising the price again to an abnormally high level. Thus the cycle continues as long as producers misread the market price signals and erroneously use today's price in making their production decisions. Even though this market is perfectly competitive, it follows a cyclical pattern and therefore does not work well, as we shall see in more detail in the next section.

*SPECULATION AND PRICE INSTABILITY

There are several ways in which a cycle of fluctuating prices may be broken. First, after perhaps two or three sharp changes in price, more and more farmers recognize what is happening and accordingly stop making the erroneous assumption that today's price provides a good prediction of tomorrow's price. As they do, the price cycle is moderated. The second way that price fluctuations may be reduced is if others in the economy—speculators—recognize what is happening and take action.

Speculation as a Stabilizing Influence

The public often views speculators as gamblers who take risks, whose profits or losses have little or no effect on the general well-being of society. However, the actions of speculators may be beneficial to the economy as a whole, as we will now demonstrate. Then, in the next section we will show how speculation can be damaging.

To illustrate how speculation works, suppose that price in a hog cycle was high last year, and is accordingly low this year. Now a number of people realize: "This has happened before. This is that hog cycle again. Because price is low this year a lot of farmers will be getting out of hogs. Next year pork will be scarce and the price will go way up again. Let's buy some of this year's cheap pork, refrigerate it, and sell it next year."

This will be a profitable venture—if the costs of storage, etc., are not too high—because it puts into practice the advice any stockbroker will give: Buy cheap and sell dear. The remarkable thing is that this action benefits not only those who undertake it, but also society as a whole, because it moderates the price cycle. Why? The purchase of pork when it is cheap creates an additional demand that prevents its price from falling quite so far. And when the speculators sell pork later at a high price, this creates an additional supply that prevents the price from rising quite so far. Thus the cycle is moderated by *speculation*.

Speculation is the purchase of an item in the hope of making a profit from a rise in its price; or the sale of an item in the expectation that its price will fall.

Basically, the case for speculation is as simple as that: It tends to stabilize price. But the argument isn't complete until we show that stabilizing price is beneficial from the viewpoint of society as a whole. We demonstrate this by considering the case where speculators buy pork this year when price is low, and then sell it next year when its price is high.

Panel (*a*) of Figure 24-7 shows the demand curve for pork. In the absence of speculation, initial equilibrium is at E_1, with low price P_1 because of high output Q_1. Panel (*b*) shows next year with the same demand curve, but with lower production Q_2. In the absence of speculation, equilibrium is at E_2, and the price is a high P_2.

Now consider the behaviour of speculators. This year in panel (*a*), they buy $Q'_1 Q_1$ units when the price is low, store them, and sell them next year when the price is high. This year their purchases reduce the available supply from Q_1 to Q'_1. Therefore price is raised from P_1 to P'_1. Next year, their sales increase the supply from Q_2 to Q'_2. This lowers the price from P_2 to P'_2. Note that the cyclical swing in price has been almost eliminated: Speculation has changed price in the two years to P'_1 and P'_2, and there is very little difference between the two. The only reason that there is a difference at all is that speculators have to earn a return to cover their storage and interest costs[2]—and to compensate them for the risk they have to run in a situation in which a wrong guess can cost them dearly.

This sort of speculation not only provides an adequate return for speculators; it is also beneficial for society as a whole. True, reduced consumption this year takes away benefits from the public now, as shown by the red area in panel (*a*). To confirm this loss, note

[2]The necessity of earning a return in order to cover interest and storage costs explains why speculators stop when they do; any more speculation would further reduce the price difference in the two years and thus no longer leave them with an adequate return. For an examination of how storage can benefit not only consumers—as we will demonstrate here—but also producers, see Brian D. Wright and Jeffrey C. Williams, "The Welfare Effects of the Introduction of Storage," *Quarterly Journal of Economics* (February 1984): 169–92.

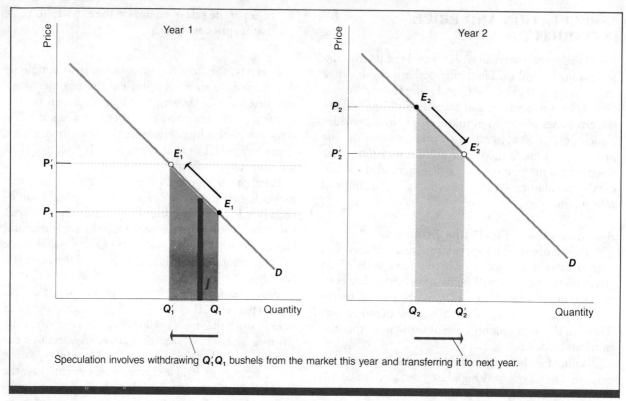

Figure 24-7 How speculation may have the beneficial effect of stabilizing price.
Without speculation, equilibrium this year is at E_1 and next year at E_2. Speculation involves reducing the available supply on the market this year from Q_1 to Q'_1 (as shown by the arrow) and transferring it to next year, thus increasing the supply then by this same amount, from Q_2 to Q'_2. This raises price this year and lowers it next year until the two are almost equal. The loss from reduced consumption this year is the light red area in panel (*a*). However, the gain from increased consumption next year will be the gray area in panel (*b*). The difference in these two areas is the beneficial effect of the speculation.

that since typical unit j is no longer consumed, the marginal benefit to consumers shown by the dark red bar is eliminated; and the total loss because all such benefits are eliminated in the range $Q'_1 Q_1$ is the total red area. However, this year's loss to consumers in panel (*a*) will be more than offset by an even greater gray increase in benefit to consumers next year in panel (*b*).

The reason for this difference is that, in this year of plenty when there is a glut, the public is losing units that it doesn't care that much about because its appetite is already reasonably satisfied. But next year when there is a scarcity, a "relatively hungry" public will be getting back these units when they mean a lot. The difference between the red and gray areas therefore indicates the net benefit to society from this speculation.

In short, speculation reduces the fluctuation in price. It also reduces the fluctuation in the quantity consumed: Without speculation, different quantities—Q_1 and Q_2 —would be consumed each year; with speculation, roughly the same quantities are consumed—Q'_1 and Q'_2. By ironing out the fluctuation in quantities—that is, by moving some of this good from a year of glut to a year of scarcity—speculation provides a benefit to society.

Moreover, this conclusion—that there is a benefit from eliminating a price cycle—means that there is a loss from having a price cycle in the first place. A pattern of stable prices would be better for society. This then leads us to our second major reservation about a perfectly competitive market: It may lead to unstable prices if there is a failure in the timing and signalling mechanism. If this unstable price pattern is not ironed out by speculators, the public loses; the free movement in price allowed by a perfectly competitive market becomes a disadvantage. This is true *even though a free movement in price can offer advantages in other circumstances*. For example, when an unexpected freeze drives up the price of oranges, people are encouraged to use the scarce oranges carefully.

Speculation as a Destabilizing Influence

So far, speculators emerge from this discussion very much the heroes of the piece, but only because we have assumed that they predict the future correctly. However, they may guess wrong, and if they do, their actions can result in a loss both to themselves and to society. For example, suppose they purchase and store pork this year in the expectation that there will be a greater shortage and higher price next year, and they are wrong; there is a glut and lower prices instead. In this case, speculators lose because the pork they hold falls in price. Moreover, society as a whole also loses, because speculators move some of today's supply into next year's period of plenty, when pork is needed even less. Thus, the individual success of speculators *and* their potential benefit to society depend on their ability to predict the future correctly.

There is another possible problem with speculation: The speculators we have described so far operate in a perfectly competitive way. Although all of them together influence price, none of them individually can. The story is quite different for a speculator who attempts to **corner a market.**

> *A market is cornered* when someone buys enough of the good to become the single (or at least dominant) seller, thus acquiring the power to resell at a higher price.

To see why cornering a market is quite different from perfectly competitive speculation, note that the perfectly competitive speculators who buy today to sell next year are *hoping* for a future shortage and higher price. On the other hand, the speculator who tries to corner a market is trying to *create* a future shortage and higher price: If he can succeed in becoming the only seller, he can then create a future shortage by, say, cutting his sales in half. In this case, society loses. Because of the artificially created shortage, there is less of this good for the public to consume.

Even if the speculator doesn't succeed in cornering the market, just the attempt to do so may be damaging for society because of the price gyrations that result. An example was provided by U.S. billionaire Bunker Hunt and his brothers, who bought silver heavily, pushing up the price from about $10 an ounce in the summer of 1979 to a record level of more than $50 in January 1980. It has been estimated that, by that time, the Hunt group held about *one-sixth* of the Western world's stock of silver. Improbable though it might seem—and although the Hunts still had a long way to go—it appeared they might be trying to corner the world market in silver. (One investigator later was not so sure; he suggested that they were just playing around in a game of monopoly with real money.) In any case, their adventure turned into disaster. The silver market turned down, in part because of the slack demand caused by the 1980 recession. A wave of selling drove the price back down to about $10 an ounce. Estimates of the Hunt's losses during this collapse ran as high as $1 billion. No one would pretend that such price gyrations were beneficial to the economy as a whole; indeed, they dislocated industries, such as photography, that use silver. Thus we conclude that this type of speculation is costly to society, *whether or not* the speculator succeeds in cornering the market.

*GOVERNMENT AGRICULTURAL PRICE SUPPORTS

One of the arguments for agricultural price supports is that the government thereby acts like the stabilizing speculators in Figure 24-7, preventing the severe fluctuations in price that would otherwise occur. The problem of price instability is particularly serious in agriculture not only because producers may misread price signals—as we saw in our earlier example of a pork cycle. In addition, prices may be unstable because agricultural goods are sold in perfectly competitive markets where supply and demand are relatively inelastic and supply may shift dramatically because of changes in the weather; this case was illustrated in Figure 20-7. For example, without government intervention, the prices of wheat and other grains could rise by 50% in a year of drought and fall by 50% in a year of glut. This does not happen elsewhere in the economy: The prices of cars or clothing simply do not gyrate in this way. Moderating such fluctuations in price is desirable not only for farmers, but for the economy as a whole.

However, it is difficult to evaluate farm price supports, because they can have two quite different objectives.

Objective 1. To Stabilize Price and Consumption

And let them gather all the food of those good years that come, and lay up corn under the hand of Pharaoh, and let them keep food in the cities.

And that food shall be for store to the land against the seven years of famine, which shall be in the land of Egypt; that the land perish not through the famine.

Genesis 41:35–36

To see how a government price support program can have the same favourable effect as the successful, perfectly competitive speculation in Figure 24-7, suppose that the government commits itself to maintaining price at a support level of P_1' in panel (a). In a bumper-crop year, it buys up quantity $Q_1' Q_1$, thus keeping price up to the P_1' support level. Then in the poor crop year in panel (b) when there is a shortage, the government sells the accumulated stock, thus keeping price down. In short, the government moderates price fluctuations just as stabilizing speculators might, by moving goods from a period of plenty in panel (a) to a period of crop failure in panel (b). As a consequence, the nation realizes an efficiency gain.

This idea of an "ever-normal granary" has had a renewed appeal in recent years because of international developments. It is not only a North American crop failure that can send our food prices shooting skyward. A crop failure in some other part of the world can do the same thing. Thus, rapidly rising food prices in the early 1970s were a result of crop failures in the Soviet Union and elsewhere. As grain prices began to fall again in the latter half of the 1970s, both the Canadian and U.S. governments started to rebuild their inventories of wheat and other grains. Thus, the total inventory of unsold wheat in Canada at the end of each crop season rose from around 8 million metric tonnes in the mid-1970s to nearly 15 million tonnes at the end of the 1978–79 season,

primarily as a result of relatively low export sales by the **Canadian Wheat Board**, the government agency responsible for the marketing of all wheat grown in the Prairie provinces.

> The *Canadian Wheat Board* (CWB) is a government agency that has a monopoly on the marketing of all wheat (as well as oats and barley) grown in the Prairie provinces. That is, farmers who want to sell these grains can only sell them to the CWB; the CWB in turn resells the grain either in the domestic market or in the export market.

In 1980 and 1981, international wheat prices again came under upward pressure. However, the increase in the world price was moderated as the United States and Canada increased their exports and allowed their inventories to run down once again. And when prices began to fall again in 1982 and 1983, partly as a result of record North American harvests, a huge inventory build-up in the United States helped stabilize the price.

While one can make a case for such government action to reduce price fluctuations, some questions remain. For example: Since a government price stabilization program has much the same effect on price and quantity as successful private speculation, why can't private speculators do the job? If they can see a future shortage developing, why wouldn't they buy at low prices now in order to sell at high prices in the future period of scarcity—in the process moderating the fluctuation in price and quantity consumed?

To some degree, the question of who can do the better job of stabilizing price—private speculators or the government—reduces to the question of whether the government can predict future price as well as speculators can. If it can, then a government price support is the better way to stabilize price. The reason is that a government guarantee to farmers at planting time of the price they will eventually receive is the best way to induce the right production response—and private speculators cannot provide such a guarantee.

But even though this answer has merit, some economists remain skeptical. In order for price stabilization to be effective, the government has to accurately predict the future price of the product. (If the government can't do this, it may buy *high* and sell *low*, thereby *de*stabilizing the market rather than stabilizing it.) And, say the critics, it is unlikely that the government will be as good at predicting future prices as private speculators. (Private speculators *have to* be good at predicting: Those that aren't, lose money and therefore will no longer be able to speculate in the market.) Furthermore, there is another problem with government price stabilization: The government may become entangled in the pursuit of a second objective.

Objective 2. To Raise Average Price

To isolate one issue at a time, assume that the problem of price instability does not exist; food is being produced at an efficient rate, and the government has already stored away an ever-normal granary to cover the risk of bad crops here or abroad. In these circumstances, suppose the government introduces a price guarantee designed to *raise price rather than stabilize it*. Farmers respond to this higher price by producing more. There are two major effects. First, farm output has been increased beyond its initial perfectly competitive, efficient level, so that there is an efficiency loss. At the same time, there is also a transfer of income to farmers who receive a higher price, from taxpayers who must pay the subsidy necessary to raise the price.

How, then, does one defend the idea of a price guarantee designed to raise farm income? One argument is that it will help cure farm poverty. But a program of price guarantees that subsidize the production of farm products such as eggs, rather than a program

that subsidizes the income of poor farmers, is a very ineffective method of curing poverty. The reason is that a price guarantee subsidizes the wealthy, high-volume farmer much more than the poor, low-volume farmer. This raises the question: Wouldn't it be better to subsidize the poor farmers directly, simply because they are poor, rather than subsidize *all* farmers according to how many eggs (or other farm products) they produce?

We conclude that in government farm policies, the reason for a price guarantee is a key issue. If the price guarantee is designed only to stabilize price by accumulating an ever-normal granary, then a substantial argument can be made in its favour. However, if it is also designed to raise average farm prices, it becomes more difficult to justify. Moreover, this issue is complicated by the fact that the real objective of price supports is often to raise price, but they are promoted on the grounds that they would stabilize price. How, then, does one determine which objective is being pursued? While there is no sure-fire way of answering this, here's one important clue. If the government surplus grows beyond the amount that is necessary to cover future crop failures, then price guarantees have been raising farm income. But if farm income is judged a desirable objective, shouldn't we be developing far more appropriate policies—policies that would more successfully cure farm poverty, without further enriching the already affluent farmer?

KEY POINTS

1. The efficient quantity of output from the point of view of society as a whole is where marginal social cost is equal to marginal social benefit.

2. If social costs are the same as private costs and social benefits the same as private benefits, a perfectly competitive market results in an efficient output. Thus, perfect competition eliminates deadweight loss; it allocates resources efficiently.

3. While the first two points above relate to allocative efficiency, perfect competition also tends to encourage technical efficiency, by putting pressure on firms to operate on their lowest possible average cost curve.

4. In terms of dynamic efficiency, perfect competition may or may not be the best market form to induce new innovations. However, it does rate highly in ensuring that, once new innovations exist, they will be rapidly introduced.

5. For each distribution of income, there is a different perfectly competitive result. Economics cannot tell us clearly which one is best.

6. Another problem with a perfectly competitive market is that its price signals may be misread, and price may fluctuate as a result. An example is the hog cycle that occurs if producers erroneously assume that price this year is a good indication of what price will be next year.

7. Private speculation or government price guarantees may be beneficial in a perfectly competitive market if on balance they reduce price fluctuations. Competitive speculators, if successful, tend to stabilize price. However, those with larger resources who attempt to "corner a market" can have a destabilizing influence.

8. If government price supports are designed to raise, rather than just stabilize price, they become more difficult to justify. They introduce inefficiency into the system, and they are a high-cost, relatively ineffective way of curing farm poverty.

KEY CONCEPTS

private versus social benefit
private versus social cost
allocative efficiency
technical efficiency
dynamic efficiency
why perfect competition provides
   allocative efficiency

why perfect competition provides
   technical efficiency
efficiency loss, or deadweight loss
how price rations scarce goods
efficiency and the distribution
   of income
when market signals mislead

*speculation
*when speculation is efficient,
   when not
*cornering a market
*agricultural price supports
*how farm subsidies transfer
   income

PROBLEMS

24-1 By showing what happens to individual consumers and producers in panels (a) and (c) of Figure 24-1, confirm that a reduction of output to below 100 units must result in an efficiency loss.

24-2 "A perfectly competitive price that all buyers and sellers take as given is the key link in orchestrating production and consumption in an efficient way." Do you agree? If so, illustrate. If not, explain why not.

24-3 According to Adam Smith, the pursuit of private gain leads to public benefit. Under what circumstances is this not true?

24-4 Suppose existing firms in a perfectly competitive industry are all producing in panel (a) of Figure 24-4 at technically inefficient point F, with price also at this level. Show how they will be driven out of business by technically

efficient new entrants producing at G. In your answer make sure you address the following questions: Is there initially a profit to be made by new entrants producing at G? Why? Do new firms therefore enter? What does this do to industry supply? What then happens to industry price? Can the old firms at F remain in business?

24-5 In our discussion of speculation, we stated that if speculators guess wrong, they lose and so does society. Using a diagram like Figure 24-7, confirm that this statement is correct. In answering this, assume that speculators buy a good in one year, but in the next year when they sell it, it is even more plentiful and cheap.

24-6 What are some of the pros and cons of government-guaranteed prices for farmers?

APPENDIX 24-A

ILLUSTRATING THE EFFICIENCY OF PERFECT COMPETITION WITH INDIFFERENCE CURVES

This chapter has shown that perfect competition results in efficiency—provided that social and private benefits are the same, and social and private costs are equal. To illustrate this point, demand and supply curves have been used. The same conclusion can be shown in an alternative way, using the indifference curves explained in the appendix to Chapter 21, and the production possibilities curve introduced in Chapter 2.

Figure 24-8 illustrates how producers maximize their income. Suppose that they are initially at point A on their production possibilities curve, making 500 units of clothing and 1,300 units of food. Suppose also that the prices of food and clothing are both $10 per unit. Then producers' income totals $18,000; that is, ($10 × 500) + ($10 × 1,300). Producers are now on the $18,000 income line L_1, whose slope reflects the relative prices of the two goods, just like the slope of the equal cost lines in Figure 23-10. Just as there was a whole family of equal-cost lines in that earlier diagram, we can visualize a whole set of parallel income lines such as L_1 and L_2 in Figure 24-8, each indicating successively higher income levels as producers move to the northeast. The objective of producers is to reach the highest one possible. To illustrate, producers operating at point A on the $18,000 income line can do better by moving along the PPC to point E, which is on the $20,000 income line. (At E, they produce 1,000 units of each good for a total income of $20,000.) This is the best they can do—it is the highest income line they can reach.

Producers maximize their income by producing at the point on the production possibilities curve that is tangent to the highest attainable income line.

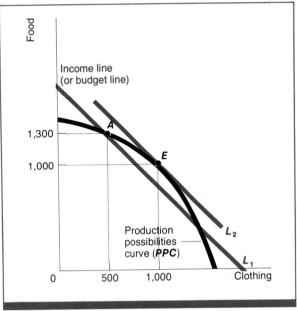

Figure 24-8 How producers maximize their incomes. The line representing producers' income goes through the point (A) at which production is taking place. The slope of this line depends on the relative prices of the two goods. Producers attain the highest income line by producing at tangency point E, where the slope of the production possibilities curve is the same as the slope of the income curve.

In Figure 24-9, we put this theory of producer behaviour together with our earlier theory of consumer behaviour, in which we described consumer preferences with a set of indifference curves such as U_1, U_2 and U_3. In a perfectly competitive economy, in which every producer and every consumer take prices as given, equilibrium is at E in Figure 24-9. On the one hand,

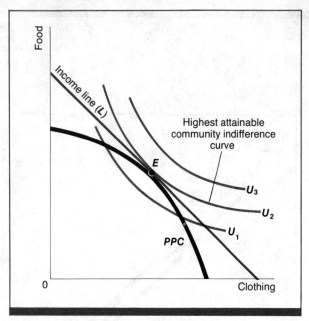

Figure 24-9 The competitive equilibrium.
The competitive equilibrium occurs at E. Producers pick the point where the PPC is tangent to the highest attainable income line. Consumers pick the point where the income line is tangent to the highest attainable indifference curve. At this point, E, the production possibilities curve and the indifference curve are tangent. The maximum level of utility U_2 is achieved, given the productive capacity of the economy as shown by the PPC.

producers maximize their income by selecting point E on the production possibilities curve because this point is tangent to the highest attainable income line L. At the same time, consumers maximize their utility by also selecting point E—because this is the point of tangency between their highest attainable indifference curve U_2 and the income line L. Thus, the community as a whole achieves an efficient solution, because at E it is producing the combination of food and clothing that lifts it to its highest attainable level of utility U_2. Given the community's ability to produce, as given by its PPC, there is no way it can reach a higher level of satisfaction than U_2. For example, it's not possible to reach U_3.

This, then, is our alternative illustration of the proposition established in Figure 24-2: A competitive economy leads to an efficient solution.[3]

[*3]It may seem that there must be a catch somewhere. According to this analysis, there seems to be a single (unique) efficient solution at

We emphasize again that this efficient solution results from producers on the one hand and consumers on the other responding independently to the competitive market prices reflected in the slope of the income line L.[4] This, in turn, raises the final question: Why does the competitive market generate the relative prices shown by L? To answer this question, suppose that initially the relative prices are different; specifically, suppose that they are shown by line L_1 in Figure 24-10. (The lower slope of L_1 reflects a lower relative price of clothing.) Facing these relative prices, producers maximize their income by producing at A, the point of tangency between the PPC and income line L_1. But consumers try to consume at B, the point of tangency between income line L_1 and indifference curve U_3. However, they are in fact unable to reach point B, since the economy is incapable of producing this combination of food and clothing. (B is outside the PPC.) As a consequence, markets are out of equilibrium. The quantity C_B of clothing demanded by consumers exceeds the quantity C_A supplied by producers; the price of clothing consequently rises. At the same time, the quantity F_B of food demanded is less than quantity F_A supplied; the price of food falls. As the relative prices of food and clothing change, the income line moves from L_1 toward L. In response, producers move from A toward E, while consumers move from B toward E. This movement continues until the income

E—and we have already seen in Figure 24-6 that there is not: For each income distribution there is a different efficient solution. This puzzle is resolved by noting that in Figure 24-9 we have drawn a set of indifference curves for the community as a whole, rather than for an individual household. There are problems in defining such a community indifference system; there is no simple way of "adding up" the preferences of all the individuals in the nation. To illustrate, consider the simple, extreme case of a two-person economy. If I have all the income, then my preferences are the ones that count; if you have all the income, then it is your preferences that count. In other words, a community's preferences depend on who has the income. This means that there is no unique community indifference system; the community's indifference map can change every time there is a change in the distribution of income. Nor, as a consequence, is there a unique, efficient equilibrium; the equilibrium depends on how the nation's income is distributed. This is exactly the conclusion we reached earlier.

[*4]To illustrate what can go wrong if producers do not act as perfect competitors, suppose that the producers of clothing form a monopoly, and restrict the supply of clothing. In other words, the economy moves to the left of E in Figure 24-9, and it is no longer possible to reach indifference curve U_2. Consequently, the nation's utility is less than a maximum, that is, less than U_2.

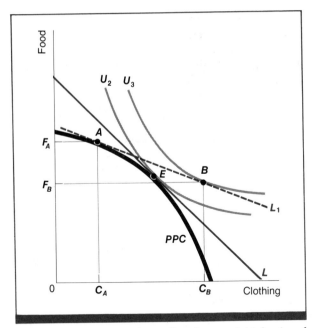

Figure 24-10 How markets adjust from an initial point of disequilibrium.
If the relative price of clothing is originally below its equilibrium—that is, if prices are those reflected in L_1 rather than L—producers will want to produce at A and consumers will want to consume at B. As a result, there will be a shortage of clothing equal to $C_B C_A$ and a surplus of food equal to $F_A F_B$. Consequently, the price of clothing will rise and the price of food will fall until these prices reach their equilibrium values, reflected in the slope of the income line L.

line actually becomes L, and producers and consumers have moved all the way to E. It is only then that demand and supply are brought into equilibrium. Thus, the equilibrium prices are indeed those reflected in line L.

APPENDIX 24-B

FORMS OF FARM ASSISTANCE

Before World War II, family incomes in farming were generally below the average for the economy as a whole. Farmers were especially hard hit during the Depression: Cash income of farmers fell by some 60% from 1928 to 1932, while wages in manufacturing fell by less than 45% over a comparable period. However, by the 1970s, even though many farmers were still poor, average farm incomes had caught up and were roughly the same as incomes elsewhere (see Box 20-4).

Part of the reason for the improvement in farm income was a wide variety of government assistance programs. Most important were programs aimed directly at raising farm prices.

SUPPORT PRICES AND DEFICIENCY PAYMENTS

In the absence of any government action, equilibrium in the market for milk is shown at E_1 in each of the panels of Figure 24-11. Income of dairy farmers is equal to the rectangle to the southwest of E_1—that is, price P_1 times quantity Q_1. The three panels illustrate three different ways the government may raise the price the farmer receives.

(a) Price supports. In panel *(a)* the government supports the price of milk at a higher level P_2. Farmers respond to this price incentive by moving up their supply curve from E_1 to E_2. At the same time, con-

sumers are discouraged by this higher price and move back up their demand curve from E_1 to E_3. Thus, at this higher price there is now an oversupply equal to $E_3 E_2$ which must be purchased by the government at a cost to the taxpayer equal to the shaded area; this taxpayer cost is the number of litres the government must buy up—the base of the rectangle—times the

price it must pay for each litre— the height of the rectangle. However, this government program has increased farm income from the original rectangle to the southwest of E_1 to the larger rectangle to the southwest of E_2; that is, farmers now receive price P_2 on the Q_2 litres they sell.

(b) *Deficiency payments.* This alternative policy,

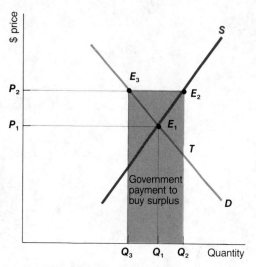

(a) **Price support at P_2.** The government must buy this surplus.

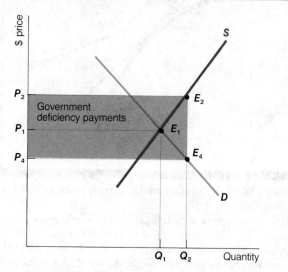

(b) **Deficiency payment.** The government pays farmers $P_2 P_4$ for each litre sold.

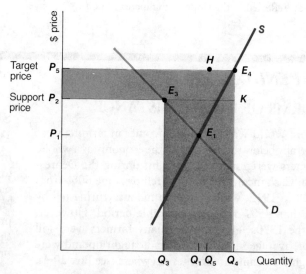

(c) **Policies a and b combined.** The government buys this surplus $Q_4 Q_3$ and makes a deficiency payment $P_5 P_2$.

shown in panel (b), is of equal benefit to the farmer. In this case, the government again guarantees the same price P_2 to farmers, who again respond in the same way by moving up their supply curve from E_1 to E_2, and thus, as before, produce Q_2. However, in this case the government makes no attempt to maintain the market price at P_2 by buying up the surplus. Instead, it lets the market price "find its own level." Because Q_2 is coming into the market, price falls to P_4. (Point E_4 on the demand curve tells us that large quantity Q_2 will be purchased only at low price P_4.)

Dairy farmers are guaranteed P_2 per litre by the government, but they are only getting P_4 from the market. The government must therefore put up the difference; in other words, it must pay a subsidy P_2P_4 to farmers for each litre of milk they sell. Multiplying this by Q_2, the number of litres sold, yields the shaded area—the total subsidy paid by the government to farmers.

How do policies (a) and (b) compare? Note that each of these policies involves an efficiency loss because the government is inducing farmers to produce Q_2, which is more than the efficient, perfectly competitive quantity Q_1. (We reemphasize: Here we are considering policies that permanently increase the price received by farmers, not policies that smooth out fluctuating prices.) As a consequence, there is triangular efficiency loss E_1E_2T in panel (a). The efficiency loss in panel (b) is likely to be even greater: If the quantity Q_1Q_2 that

the public doesn't get is simply thrown away, the loss may be as much as $Q_1E_1E_2Q_2$.

Which policy do farmers prefer? The answer is that they generally favour the price support policy (a). They view it as providing a fair price for their milk whereas they sometimes regard the deficiency payment in panel (b) as a subsidy from the public purse. However, in fact, the two policies benefit farmers equally: Under either scheme their income increases from the area to the southwest of E_1 to the area to the southwest of E_2. Moreover, under either scheme, the large area to the southwest of E_2 also represents the total cost of milk to the public. This includes both the shaded rectangle that the public pays in taxes for the government support program, and the unshaded rectangle that consumers pay when they buy milk. (Specifically, consumers pay the unshaded area to the southwest of E_3 in panel (a), and the unshaded area to the southwest of E_4 in panel (b).) In short, under either program, farmers receive the same amount for their milk while the taxpaying/ consuming public pays the same amount for milk.

There is, however, one good reason for the public to prefer the deficiency payment policy: It gets more milk—Q_2 in panel (b), rather than the Q_3 in panel (a). Public preference for this policy clearly holds as long as the surplus farm produce bought by the government is not needed to build up adequate buffer stocks, or simply cannot be stored, so that it will either spoil or have to be sold at give-away prices.

◀**Figure 24-11 Alternative farm assistance programs.**
Under either program (a) or (b), the government guarantees that farmers will receive P_2 per litre. They consequently move up their supply curve from equilibrium E_1 to E_2.

In panel (a), the government provides a *price support* by fixing the market price at P_2. Consumers move up their demand curve from E_1 to E_3. The difference in the amount produced at E_2 and consumed at E_3 must be purchased by the government, at a cost shown by the shaded area.

In panel (b), the government still guarantees farmers' price P_2, but makes no attempt to keep up the price paid by consumers. As a consequence, this price falls to P_4, the highest price consumers will pay if they are to buy the large quantity Q_2 that is produced. Since farmers have been guaranteed a price P_2 and are receiving only P_4 from buyers, the government pays them the difference, that is, a *deficiency payment* of P_2P_4 on each litre. Since farmers are producing Q_2 litres, the total payment they receive from the government is the shaded area.

Thus in either panel (a) or panel (b), the large unshaded rectangle is what consumers pay when they buy the milk, while the shaded rectangle is the cost to taxpayers. In either case, the taxpaying-consuming public pays the same total amount for milk—that is, the entire area to the southwest of E_2.

In panel (c), the government combines the two policies. The *support price* is set at P_2; this becomes the market price. In response, consumers buy Q_3. The government then makes a deficiency payment to farmers of P_2P_5 to reach the *target price* of P_5 that farmers receive. In response, farmers produce Q_4. The government must purchase the resulting surplus of Q_3Q_4 at P_2 per litre, with this part of the program therefore costing the taxpayer rectangle $E_3KQ_4Q_3$. In addition, the government makes a deficiency payment of P_2P_5 on Q_4 litres of milk, for an additional cost to the taxpayer of rectangle $P_5E_4KP_2$.

Because of the problem of unwanted surpluses that occurs under policy (*a*), many Canadian farm support programs now rely principally on deficiency payments (method (*b*)). However, method (*a*) is still used for products such as eggs and milk. To avoid overproduction leading to unwanted surpluses, the marketing boards administering these programs have put strict limits on the amounts that each producer is allowed to produce. (A farmer is not allowed to produce more eggs or milk than is specified in the *quota* issued to him by the marketing board.) By controlling the total amounts produced, the government tries to limit total output to Q_3 in panel (*a*), the amount that consumers want to buy at the support price.

But sometimes the marketing boards miscalculate, and a surplus emerges. This can place the government in an embarrassing position. For example, in 1975 Canadian industrial buyers had to pay the support price of 38 cents/lb. for powdered milk. At the same time, the government was selling surplus powdered milk to foreign buyers for 6 cents/lb. And in the middle of the 1970s, between 20 and 30 million eggs, many of which had been stored so long they were rotten, simply had to be thrown away. To the consumers who were paying good money for eggs in the supermarket, this seemed an absurd situation.

Other countries with price supports of the type shown in panel (*a*) have had similar difficulties. Faced with the prospect that an accumulated butter surplus would otherwise spoil, the European Common Market sold it to the Russians for roughly one-quarter the support price its own citizens were paying.

Programs of price supports and deficiency payments are at least as extensive in American agriculture as they are in Canada. For products such as cotton, rice, and wheat, the U.S. government has not only fixed the market price, but has also given farmers deficiency payments on top of this price (that is, it has paid a production subsidy on top of the support price). As farmers have responded to the higher prices, the government has been forced to buy up increasing surpluses. The cost of these purchases to the public treasury grew especially rapidly in the early 1980s. The reason was that the target price—that is, the inducement to farmers to produce—had been set to increase automatically each year with inflation, at a rate that turned out to be unrealistically high and that therefore induced an unexpectedly large supply. In addition, demand was disappointing because export markets were less than expected. Thus, in the early 1980s, the government purchased large surpluses. Moreover, the annual increases in the target price led to increasing deficiency payments.

In an attempt to limit the costs of these programs, the U.S. government used two types of incentives to induce farmers to take acreage out of production and thus cut back on their output. First, deficiency payments were only made available to farmers who agreed to cut back acreage. Second, outright payments were made to farmers who reduced production. While some of this payment was in the form of cash, the administration didn't like the idea of paying farmers cash for not producing. Therefore, beginning in 1983, the government introduced payments in kind (the PIK program). Instead of money, the government paid farmers bushels of wheat, or whatever else they had been producing.

Another U.S. government policy that indirectly helps farm income is the *food stamp* program. Under this program, the poor are eligible to receive food stamps, which can be exchanged for food. But even though they can be exchanged only for food, food purchases don't increase much. True, the poor use the stamps they receive to buy food. However, they then take most of the money they previously spent on food and use it to buy something else. This is why, for every $100 of food stamps that are issued, it is estimated that food purchases increase by only about $12. Thus, whether or not food stamps are effective as an anti-poverty measure, they are relatively ineffective in increasing the consumption of farm products.

PROBLEM

24-7 If you are working for the government, and your only concern is to minimize the money the government has to pay to farmers, would you prefer the program in panel (*a*) or panel (*b*) of Figure 24-11:

(a) if the demand curve passing through *E* is very elastic?

(b) if demand is very inelastic?

Chapter 25

MONOPOLY

The monopolists, by keeping the market constantly understocked . . . sell their commodities much above the natural price.

Adam Smith,
Wealth of Nations

At one end of the market spectrum, there is perfect competition, with many sellers. At the other end of the spectrum, there is monopoly, with only one seller. (The Greek word *monos* means "single," and *polein* means "to sell.") The last chapter showed that, under certain conditions, perfect competition is efficient. This chapter will demonstrate why monopoly is not. A case can therefore be made for government intervention in the marketplace. But in what way should the government intervene?

To begin, consider the conditions that lead to monopoly.

WHAT CAUSES MONOPOLY?

There are four major reasons why there may be only one firm selling a good:

1. *Monopoly may be based on control over an input or technique.* A firm may control something essential that no other firm can acquire. One example is the ownership of a necessary resource; an oft-cited illustration was Alcoa's control over bauxite supplies that allowed it to monopolize the sale of aluminum before World War II. Another example is the ownership of a patent, which allows the inventor exclusive control over a new product or process for a period of 17 years. (Patents are designed to encourage expenditure on research by allowing the inventor to reap a substantial reward.) When an existing firm owns an essential patent or exclusive control over a resource, new firms might like to enter the industry, but they cannot; the industry remains monopolized.

2. *Legal monopoly.* It is sometimes illegal for more than one company to sell a product. For example, under provincial law a private trucking firm may be given the exclusive right to service a community. Similarly, before 1984 it was illegal for a private company to set up in competition with Canada Post in the delivery of letters. (Since 1984, private couriers *are* allowed to deliver letters, but the law forces them to charge much higher rates than Canada Post.)

3. *Collusive monopoly.* If permitted by law, several producers may get together to form a single firm, or a single unified marketing operation in order to charge a higher price and increase their profits. However, once these firms have created a monopoly, it may not be easy to maintain. They may have difficulty in keeping out new firms attracted by the high price.

4. *Natural monopoly.* A natural monopoly exists when economies of scale are so important that one firm can produce the total output of the industry at lower cost than could two or more firms. An example is the local telephone service. It obviously costs less to string one set of telephone wires down a street than two.

The prevalence of monopoly depends partly on the

way in which a market is defined. For example, suppose you live in a small town with only one furniture store. If the relevant market is defined as the market for furniture *bought in that town*, the store has a monopoly: It is the only seller in the market. (Sometimes the term *local monopoly* is used to emphasize that one is talking about a local market only.) But if people are able to shop for furniture in nearby cities without incurring high transportation costs, it is more reasonable to define the relevant market as including nearby towns and cities as well. With this broader definition of the market, your hometown furniture dealer is no longer a monopolist. Similarly, even though B.C. Sugar Refining is the only company that sells sugar *refined in British Columbia*, it doesn't make sense to classify it as a monopolist: In the market for all sugar sold in British Columbia, it has to compete with sugar refined in other provinces. And if we look at the market for large harvester combines *produced in Canada*, Massey-Ferguson is a monopolist. But if we look more generally at the overall Canadian market for large harvester combines, Massey-Ferguson is not a monopolist, since it has to compete with combines brought in from other countries.

The extent of monopoly also depends on how broadly one defines the range of products that are considered a part of the market. For example, in the early 1970s, Boeing had a temporary monopoly in the world market for jumbo jets; the 747 still had no competition from other jumbo jets. But Boeing did not have a monopoly in the broader market for airliners, since it still had to compete with McDonnell-Douglas and other firms in the sale of smaller aircraft. (Even in jumbo jets, Boeing's monopoly was short-lived, as other manufacturers developed similar planes.) The telephone company has a monopoly of local telephone service, but not of the broader market for communications where it must compete with the mails and telegraph companies. Indeed, in the very broadest sense, every producer competes with every other producer for the consumer's dollar. If you buy a new hi-fi, you may cut down on long-distance telephone calls to help pay for it. Thus, in a very broad sense, the telephone company is in competition even with the producer of hi-fi equipment.

But if markets are defined in a reasonably limited way, significant areas of monopoly exist. Examples include telephone services and local gas and electricity

services. Note that these kinds of services must be locally produced: A resident of Winnipeg can't very well have his home hooked up to the natural gas distribution system in Regina if he is unhappy with the service of the local gas distributor. Thus, competition from distant sellers is effectively eliminated, and it makes sense to define the relevant market in this relatively narrow way.

Nonetheless, the overall importance of monopoly should not be exaggerated. **Oligopoly**, where the industry is dominated by only a few sellers, is much more important in our economy. Some of the largest industries in North America are oligopolies: automobiles, computers, aircraft, farm implements, large electrical generators, and steel. In spite of the importance of oligopoly, it is appropriate to consider monopoly first. Monopoly is the simpler form, and it provides a necessary background for the study of oligopoly.

NATURAL MONOPOLY: THE IMPORTANCE OF COST CONDITIONS

When discussing the problems that arise from the monopolization of an industry and the appropriate government policy, it is essential to answer the question, "Is this industry a *natural* monopoly?" In other words, "Can this good be produced less expensively by one firm than by two or more firms?" As we shall see, many of the questionable decisions by the government and the courts in dealing with monopoly have been the result of a failure to address this question.

The cost conditions that lead to natural monopoly are shown in panel (*b*) of Figure 25-1, and are contrasted with conditions that do not in panel (*a*). The two products shown are assumed to have identical demand curves in order to highlight the difference in their costs—the central issue in explaining natural monopoly.

In the industry shown in panel (*a*), a typical firm's long-run average cost curve AC reaches a minimum at only 10 units of output, a very small portion of the total market. As a consequence, total demand cannot be satisfied by one firm operating at its minimum cost. Instead, the least costly way of servicing this market is to have many small firms producing just 10 units each. If a firm tries to produce at higher volume, say 20 units, it will incur a relatively high cost that will leave it unable to compete with smaller, lower-cost firms.

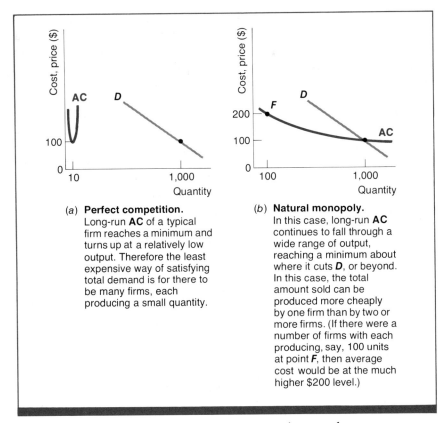

Figure 25-1   How cost conditions can lead to natural monopoly.

With many small firms surviving, the result is perfect competition.

In panel (b), AC reaches the same minimum value of $100, but the big difference is the much larger volume of output necessary for a firm to achieve this low cost. Unlike the AC curve in panel (a) that reaches a minimum and turns up at a very small volume, AC in panel (b) continues downward. The least expensive way of servicing the market is with one firm, and the stage is set for monopoly. By definition:

> *Natural monopoly* occurs when the average cost of a single firm falls over such an extended range of output that one firm can produce the total quantity sold at a lower average cost than could two or more firms.

Why might costs continue to fall through much or all of the range needed to satisfy total market demand? The answer may be high fixed cost, that is, high over-

head. Local electric, telephone, water, and gas services are all natural monopolies, because the fixed cost in running electric or telephone wires, or in laying water or gas pipes, is very high relative to variable cost. To illustrate what happens when fixed costs dominate, set fixed cost in Table 22-1 at $1,000, rather than just $35, and recalculate average cost. Notice how AC continues to fall as this $1,000 of fixed overhead is spread over a larger and larger number of units of output.

To verify that the cost curve in panel (b) in Figure 25-1 leads naturally to a monopoly, suppose that initially a few firms are each producing 100 units at point F. This low volume results in a high average cost of $200 for each firm. An aggressive firm will discover that by increasing its output, it can lower its cost, and hence offer its product at a lower price than its competitors. Thus, it can squeeze them out of business. In such a case of natural monopoly, competition tends to drive all firms but one out of the market. Small firms, with their relatively high costs, simply cannot compete with the single large firm operating at—or near—minimum cost.

There is an obvious attraction to the consumer of such price competition during the period in which the industry is being "shaken down" and the number of firms reduced. However, this favourable situation for the consumer is likely to disappear once the successful firm has eliminated all its competitors and has emerged as a monopoly. It now has to worry little about the entry of new competitors: With its high volume—and therefore low cost—the monopoly can greet any new entrants with whatever price cutting is necessary to drive them into bankruptcy. With little fear of present or future competition, the monopoly can then raise its price. Thus consumers of this product are at the mercy of the monopolist, except insofar as they are prepared to cut back their purchases in the face of a higher price—or insofar as the government regulates price. The question is: If the monopoly is free to set its price, how high will the price be? But before answering this question, we need to make one more distinction between perfect competition and monopoly.

THE DIFFERENCE IN THE DEMAND FACING A PERFECT COMPETITOR AND A MONOPOLIST

A perfectly competitive firm must take the market price as given. For example, an individual farmer never thinks of asking 10 cents a bushel more for his wheat, because he knows he won't get it; and he never offers to sell his wheat for 10 cents less, since he can sell all of it for the going market price. The farmer has no *market power*: As an individual producer among many, he is unable, by reducing the quantity he supplies, to have any noticeable influence on price.

> The *market power* of a firm is its ability to influence its price, and thereby its profit.

To confirm that a farmer has no market power, suppose that the price of a bushel of wheat is $2, as determined by market supply and demand in panel (*b*) of Figure 25-2. In panel (*a*) we show the response of the individual farmer to this price.
Because his supply curve is *s*, he produces 2,000 units. Now suppose he tries to influence the price. Specific-

ally, suppose he cuts his supply in half from 2,000 to 1,000 units in the hope of making wheat scarce and raising its price. His move will reduce market supply in panel (*b*), shifting S to the left, but by such a trivial amount—only 1,000 units—that this action won't even be noticed in the market; if you try to draw the new supply curve, you will find that you are essentially just drawing a line over the old supply S. Consequently market price, as determined in panel (*b*), will remain the same. The farmer has tried to raise the price, but this attempt to exercise market power has failed miserably. As an individual seller, he has no influence whatsoever over price, and this is reflected in the completely elastic demand curve he faces in panel (*a*). In short, he has to take the market price as given.

The situation facing a monopoly is quite different, as shown in panels (*c*) and (*d*). In panel (*d*), total market demand is exactly the same as in the competitive case above. The only difference is that this market demand is now being satisfied by a single monopoly firm; in other words, *the demand facing the individual firm in panel (c) is exactly the same as the total market demand in panel (d)*.

As a result, the monopoly can indeed affect price. To confirm this, suppose that it is initially selling at a $2 price. Because it is the only seller, this firm alone is supplying all the 2 million units sold, shown at point A in both panel (*c*) and panel (*d*). Now suppose the monopoly tries to influence price by cutting its sales in half, from 2 million to 1 million units. The demand curve tells us that price rises to $3: This is the price that buyers will pay if there are only 1 million units available. Thus, the firm moves from A to B on the demand curve. By restricting its output, the monopoly is able to make this good scarce and thus raise its price. (Alternatively, the firm could have made exactly this same move from A to B by quoting a $3 price, in which case buyers would purchase 1 million units.)

In short, the monopoly firm has market demand within its grasp. It can move along the market demand curve from a point like A to B, selecting the one that suits it best. On the other hand, the perfect competitor has no control over market price; instead, the individual firm faces its own completely elastic demand curve, and all it can do is select the quantity to sell. While the monopolist can raise the price, the perfect competitor must take price as given. The monopolist is a *price maker*; the perfect competitor is a *price taker*.

WHAT PRICE DOES THE MONOPOLIST SELECT?

As we saw in Chapter 22, any firm—whether a monopolist or perfect competitor—maximizes profit by selecting the output where its marginal cost MC equals its marginal revenue MR. (See statement (22-1).) In that earlier chapter we also saw that *marginal revenue for the perfectly competitive firm is the given market price at which it sells*. In our present example,

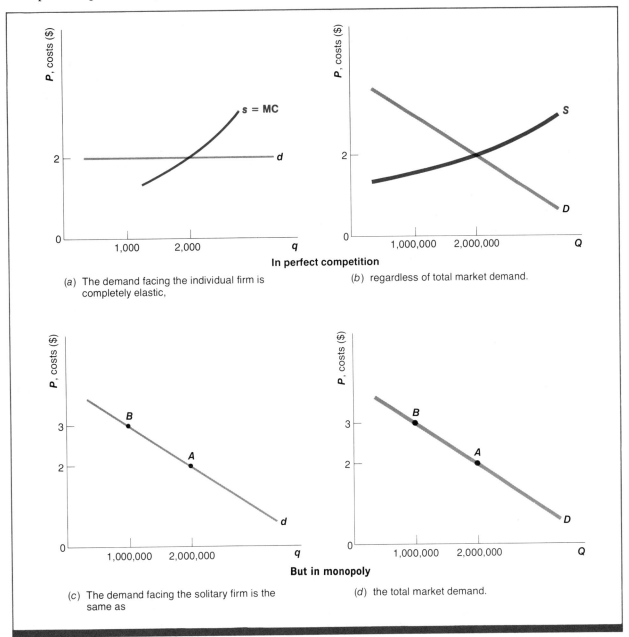

(a) The demand facing the individual firm is completely elastic,

(b) regardless of total market demand.

In perfect competition

(c) The demand facing the solitary firm is the same as

(d) the total market demand.

But in monopoly

Figure 25-2   The difference in the demand facing the monopolist and the perfect competitor.
On the left-hand side, the demand facing an individual firm is shown with a light line and marked with a small *d*. Market demand is shown on the right-hand side with a heavy line and is marked with a capital *D*.

marginal revenue for the perfectly competitive firm in panel (*a*) of Figure 25-2 is the $2 selling price; no matter how many units the firm sells, its revenue will increase by $2 if it sells one more. In other words, its marginal revenue schedule is identical to its completely elastic demand curve. However, *for the monopolist, marginal revenue is not equal to the selling price.* This is such an important point that it deserves a detailed explanation.

What Is the Marginal Revenue of a Monopolist?

Suppose the monopoly firm in Figure 25-3 moves from *B* to *C* along its demand curve. At *B* it was selling 1 unit at a $50 price, but now at *C* it is selling 2 units at a price of $45 each; in other words, at *C* its average revenue AR is $45. What is its marginal revenue for that second unit, that is, the additional revenue it receives because it is selling 2 units rather than 1? To calculate the answer, note that the monopoly's total revenue from selling 1 unit was $50; but when it sells 2, its total revenue is $90. Thus, its revenue has risen by $40; this is its marginal revenue from the sale of the second unit. We conclude that the firm's marginal revenue of $40 is less than the $45 price. This point is worth emphasizing:

For a monopolist, marginal revenue MR is *less than* price P.

Table 25-1 shows the monopolist's calculation of marginal revenue at each output. Total revenue is given

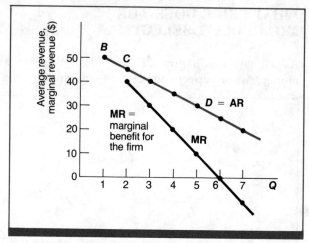

Figure 25-3 Why a monopolist's demand (AR) and marginal revenue (MR) differ.
Numbers are drawn from Table 25-1. At point *B*, the monopoly sells 1 unit for $50. At point *C*, it sells 2 units for $45 each, for a total revenue of $90. The sale of the second unit increases its total revenue by $90 − $50 = $40. Thus its marginal revenue from increasing its sales from 1 to 2 units is $40. Another way to calculate this is to note that the monopoly receives a $45 price on the sale of the second unit; but from this it must deduct the $5 "loss" it must take on the first unit because it is getting only $45 for this, rather than the original $50.

in column 3, while column 4 shows how this total revenue changes for each successive unit sold. This is the marginal revenue schedule MR that is graphed along with the demand curve in Figure 25-3. This

Table 25-1
How Marginal Revenue for a Monopolist Is Derived from Demand (Average Revenue) Information

(1) Quantity (Q)	Demand (2) Price P (average revenue)	(3) Total revenue (P × Q)	(4) Marginal revenue (MR)
1	$50	$ 50	
2	45	90	(90 − 50) = $40
3	40	120	(120 − 90) = 30
4	35	140	(140 − 120) = 20
5	30	150	(150 − 140) = 10
6	25	150	(150 − 150) = 0
7	20	140	(140 − 150) = −10

diagram emphasizes how the monopoly's marginal revenue curve lies below its demand curve.

The demand and marginal revenue curves now become the stepping stones needed to answer the question: How high does a profit-maximizing monopoly set its price?

Monopoly Output and Price

Like any other firm, the monopoly maximizes profit by equating marginal cost MC with marginal revenue MR. An illustration is provided in panel (a) of Figure 25-4, where the monopolist's D and MR curves are reproduced from the preceding diagram, along with its MC and AC curves. The monopoly selects output

Q_1 where MC and MR intersect. This is the output that maximizes its profit. If the firm selects any other output—whether greater or smaller—its profit will be less, as confirmed in the caption to this diagram.

A monopolist—like a perfect competitor—maximizes profit by selecting the output where
    marginal cost MC = marginal revenue MR
However, for the monopolist—unlike the perfect competitor—MR is not the same as price.

With its output thus determined at Q_1, what price does the firm then charge? In other words, what is the maximum price the monopoly can charge, and still

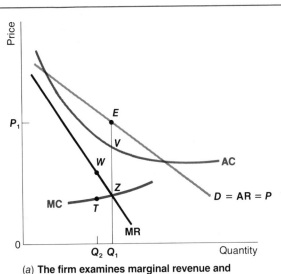

(a) **The firm examines marginal revenue and marginal cost, and equates the two.** To confirm that profit is maximized at output Q_1, where **MR = MC**, we use the familiar method of showing that any other output is inferior. For example, suppose the monopoly is producing at smaller output Q_2. It can increase its profit by producing one more unit, since the additional cost of this unit is only T, while it provides a marginal revenue of W. Consequently, the monopolist produces this additional unit—and continues for the same reason to expand output so long as **MR** lies above **MC**; in other words, up to output Q_1, where **MR** and **MC** are equal. Similarly, if the monopoly is producing an output greater than Q_1, it will contract. Only at Q_1, where **MC = MR**, is there no incentive to expand or contract.

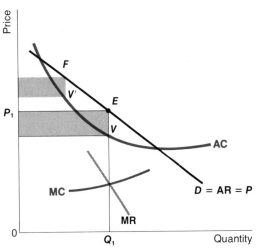

(b) **The firm examines average revenue and average cost, and maximizes the gray profit area.** This is exactly the same firm as in part a. In this case its average curves are darkened, because it is concentrating on these. At **E**, the firm earns the profit shown by the gray area, because it is producing P_1E units at a profit of **EV** on each. (Since average revenue is **E**, and average cost is **V**, average profit is **EV**.) The firm selects the point **E** on its demand curve that maximizes this gray profit area; the selection of any other point, such as **F**, leads to a smaller profit area.

Figure 25-4 Two equivalent views of the profit-maximizing equilibrium of a monopoly.
A third view is illustrated in problem 25-4. This uses the *total* revenue and *total* cost curves in the same way that they were used to show the profit maximization of a perfect competitor in Figure 22-4.

sell quantity Q_1? The answer is given by the demand curve, which indicates at point E that the firm can charge a price as high as P_1 and still sell those Q_1 units. This choice by the monopolist of output Q_1 and price P_1 is often referred to as its selection of the *profit-maximizing point* (E) on its demand curve.

A monopoly, like any other firm, must address another important question: Should it be in business at all? For the firm shown in this diagram, the answer is yes. In selling Q_1 units, it makes an above-normal or monopoly profit of EV on each unit. This is the difference between the price it gets for selling each unit—the height of E on the demand curve—and its average cost of producing each unit, that is, the height of V on the AC curve. The monopoly will remain in business as long as it can cover its costs, including a normal profit; that is, as long as its selling price E is at least as high as its average cost V. (Recall from Chapter 22 that the average cost curve includes normal profit.) However, if the demand curve lies below the average cost curve throughout its range, it is not possible for the monopoly to cover its costs, and it will leave this business in the long run.

If distance EV is the monopoly's per unit profit, what is its total profit? The answer is the large shaded area in panel (*b*)—that is, the per unit profit EV times P_1E, the number of units sold. This area is shaded in gray to represent above-normal profits, in contrast to losses which will appear later in red.

These two panels show in two equivalent ways how the monopoly firm maximizes profit: In panel (*a*), it equates MC and MR. Alternatively, in panel (*b*), it arrives at the same output Q_1 by selecting the point E on its demand curve that maximizes the shaded profit area. That is, it selects the point E that creates a larger profit rectangle than would be created by selecting *any* other point on its demand curve, such as F.

We shall use these two approaches interchangeably. For now, we concentrate on the MC = MR approach in panel (*a*); however, we will later use the approach in panel (*b*) because it clearly shows the profits that the firm is attempting to maximize. Moreover, panel (*b*) demonstrates both conditions that a firm must satisfy: It ensures (1) that the marginal condition MC = MR is met, and (2) that the firm is operating at a profit—or, more precisely, that the firm is not operating at a loss that would drive it out of business in the long run.

Although the monopoly's decision to equate MC and MR results in the profit-maximizing output *for the firm*, a question remains: Is this the efficient output for *society as a whole*?

IS MONOPOLY EFFICIENT?

The answer is no. The analysis developed so far will allow us to show that monopoly results in *allocative* inefficiency: The firm produces too little output, and the nation's resources are misallocated as a consequence. However, before we show this, let us consider monopoly from the viewpoint of technical and dynamic efficiency.

A monopoly may be *technically* inefficient; the firm may not be operating on its lowest possible cost curve. Because it has no competition, a monopoly may be careless in its cost controls, and resources may be wasted as a consequence. In drawing our diagrams, we have been assuming away this kind of inefficiency. However, in doing so we should not forget: *Technical inefficiency in monopoly industries may be a very important cost to society.*

The relationship between monopoly and dynamic efficiency is less clear. As noted in the previous chapter, large, profitable monopolistic firms may have a greater financial capacity and incentive to engage in research and development than smaller, perfectly competitive firms. This research and development may lead to new techniques of production that will lower the firm's cost curves. And any firm has an incentive to develop a distinctive new product that will put it in a monopoly position. (For example, Bombardier Ltd. had an incentive to develop the snowmobile, because it provided the firm with a temporary monopoly in the market for snowmobiles. Thus monopoly is the payoff for innovation, and innovation is a source of growth.) The next chapter will deal with the dynamic effects of monopoly in more detail.

Consider now the central concept of efficiency studied by economists: allocative efficiency—or just "efficiency," for short. As we have seen earlier, a good is being produced efficiently if its marginal social benefit is equal to its marginal social cost. To see whether or not monopoly passes this test, we extract the demand curve D from Figure 25-4 and reproduce it in Figure 25-5. It is now labelled the marginal benefit to society, since it shows the benefit this good provides to con-

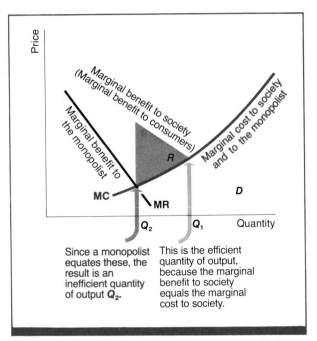

Since a monopolist equates these, the result is an inefficient quantity of output **Q₂**.

This is the efficient quantity of output, because the marginal benefit to society equals the marginal cost to society.

Figure 25-5 Monopoly results in allocative inefficiency. The invisible hand goes astray.
Monopoly results in output Q_2, which is less than the efficient output Q_1; each of the units of reduced output between Q_1 and Q_2 offers a higher marginal benefit to society (shown by the height of the D curve) than their marginal cost to society. It would therefore be beneficial to produce these units, and the efficiency loss from monopoly occurs because these potentially beneficial units are not produced. This loss is shown by the red triangle.

sumers. (We continue to make the assumptions from the last chapter that the marginal benefit to society $MB_S = MB$ to consumers, and the marginal cost to society $MC_S = MC$ to the producer.) We also reproduce the monopoly's marginal revenue curve MR and its marginal cost curve MC. With MC being the marginal cost of this good to the only firm producing it, it is also the marginal cost of this good to society as a whole. Since this curve intersects society's marginal benefit curve at R, the efficient quantity of output is Q_1.

However, this is not the output that the monopoly produces. Instead, as we have seen, it produces the smaller and therefore inefficient output Q_2 where MC = MR. The reason that it produces too little is that the firm equates marginal cost MC not with the

marginal benefit to *society* (D) but instead with MR, the marginal benefit to the *firm itself*. Thus Adam Smith's invisible hand goes astray. The pursuit of benefit by an individual firm does *not* result in maximum benefit for society.

The efficiency loss that results because monopoly produces too little (Q_2 rather than Q_1) appears as the red triangle. Note its similarity to the triangle in Figure 24-3(b), which also showed the efficiency loss from too little output.

An Example: Collusive Monopoly

The analysis above applies to any profit-maximizing monopoly, that is, any of the four types described at the beginning of this chapter. Now let us consider in more detail one of these types—specifically, a collusive monopoly.

Figure 25-6(a) illustrates an industry that is perfectly competitive: The least expensive way of producing this good is with many small firms. As long as this industry remains perfectly competitive in panel (a), total output of the industry is the efficient quantity Q_1 where supply—reflecting marginal costs—is equal to demand, reflecting marginal benefits. The price of the product is P_1.

Now suppose in panel (b) that these small firms get together to form a monopoly. Specifically, suppose they collude to form a single marketing agency to raise price. (In the 1930s, all the firms in Canada producing cardboard boxes did precisely this: The only seller of cardboard boxes in Canada was Container Materials Ltd., the industry's marketing agency. A more recent example is the Canadian Egg Marketing Agency which regulates all sales of eggs in Canada; monopolistic marketing agencies for farm products such as eggs are discussed in more detail in Appendix 25-A.) Further suppose that the marketing arrangement leaves costs and demand unchanged; in other words, the MC and demand curves in panel (b) are the same as in panel (a). What price and quantity does the marketing agency select in order to maximize the profits of the producers?

The agency will follow the monopolist's strategy of calculating its marginal revenue curve MR from its demand curve D. It then restricts output from Q_1 to Q_2 where MC = MR, and raises price from P_1 to P_2. In other words, as a monopoly, the agency will select point E_M on the demand curve.

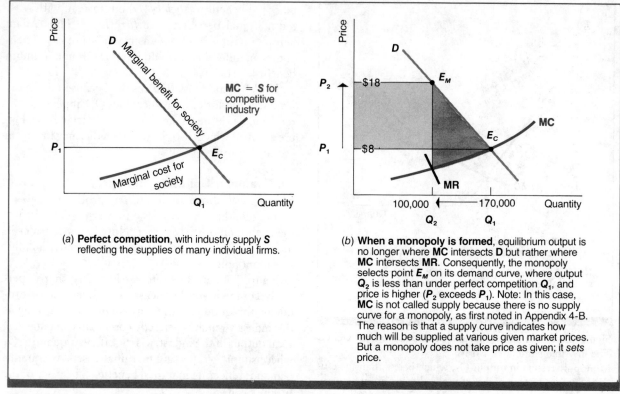

(a) **Perfect competition**, with industry supply **S** reflecting the supplies of many individual firms.

(b) **When a monopoly is formed**, equilibrium output is no longer where **MC** intersects **D** but rather where **MC** intersects **MR**. Consequently, the monopoly selects point E_M on its demand curve, where output Q_2 is less than under perfect competition Q_1, and price is higher (P_2 exceeds P_1). Note: In this case, **MC** is not called supply because there is no supply curve for a monopoly, as first noted in Appendix 4-B. The reason is that a supply curve indicates how much will be supplied at various given market prices. But a monopoly does not take price as given; it *sets* price.

Figure 25-6   When a perfectly competitive industry in panel (*a*) is monopolized in panel (*b*), the result is a red efficiency loss and a gray transfer of income.

The monopolization of a perfectly competitive industry raises price from P_1 to P_2 in our example, and reduces output from Q_1 to Q_2. This reduction in output means that too little is being produced and there is the red triangular efficiency loss shown in panel (b).

The monopolist's policy of restricting output is designed to make the good scarce, so that its price can be raised. For producers who form a monopoly, it is this ability to raise price that provides them with an opportunity for profit that wasn't available to them when they were perfect competitors.

THE TRANSFER EFFECT OF A MONOPOLY

The previous discussion seems to lead to the clear judgement that society is harmed if a perfectly competitive industry is monopolized. While this conclusion is generally correct, it's not absolutely airtight,

for two reasons. One is described in Box 25-1. The other arises because of the *transfers* associated with monopoly.

To illustrate, when monopoly raises price from P_1 to P_2 in panel (b) of Figure 25-6, consumers suffer while the monopolized producers benefit. In other words, there is a transfer from consumers to producers, equal to the $1 million area of the gray rectangle. (The price increase that consumers pay and producers receive is $10 per unit on each of the 100,000 units purchased.)

This gray area cancels out in dollar terms; the monopolized producers gain this $1 million while consumers lose it. However, it may not cancel out in terms of satisfaction. That is, the gain in satisfaction to producers who receive this extra $1 million may conceivably be greater than the reduction in satisfaction to consumers who lose it. For example, suppose that the item is something like the grapes from which champagne is made; the farmers who produce the

BOX 25-1

THE THEORY OF THE SECOND BEST

The conclusion that the monopolization of an industry results in inefficiency—that is, a misallocation of resources—is generally correct, but not always.

To understand why, consider industry X in an economy where all other industries are perfectly competitive. If X is monopolized, not enough of X's output is produced, and too much of all the other goods is produced. There is allocative inefficiency: Too few of the nation's resources are going into the production of X. This is the standard conclusion.

However, now suppose that all the other industries are themselves monopolized, but X is perfectly competitive. In this case, there will be too little output of all the other goods; in other words, there will be too much X. What happens if industry X is now monopolized? This will reduce its output, moving it in the right direction by bringing it back closer into line with the other industries; thus, the allocation of the nation's resources may actually be *improved*.

This is known as the *problem of the second best*. The first-best economy is one in which all industries behave in a competitive way. If one industry is

then monopolized, the economy becomes less efficient. However, in a second best world—one in which some industries are *already* monopolized—it is unclear whether monopoly in yet another industry will make the economy more or less efficient. There is no simple answer to this question; the **theory of the second best** is quite complex.

> The *theory of the second best* is the theory of how to get the best results in remaining markets when one or more markets have monopoly or other imperfections about which nothing can be done.

A second-best argument is sometimes made in support of government policies to allow producers of various agricultural products to form monopoly-like marketing boards such as those described in Appendix 25-A. Since the rest of the economy is pervaded by monopoly influences, so the argument goes, monopolizing agriculture may improve the nation's resource allocation. By and large, economists remain unimpressed with this argument and continue to recommend that we aim at the "first-best" solution by reducing monopoly influence wherever it may be found. Hence, the theory of the second best is introduced here, not as a reason for encouraging monopoly in any specific sector, but rather as a warning that the economic world is seldom as simple as we might hope.

---

grapes get together to set up a marketing board that raises the price. The consumers of champagne are so wealthy they hardly notice the increase in price. However, if the farmers who produce the grapes have low incomes, they may get very great satisfaction from the additional $1 million they receive. In this case, most people would conclude that the act of transferring income provides a net benefit. Moreover, it is conceivable that such a benefit might offset the red efficiency loss that arises because output declines from Q_1 to Q_2. In this case, one could argue that the monopolization of the industry would be desirable.

While this argument is logically possible, it is also somewhat strained; we have picked a very special case. Therefore, most economists would be prepared to stick

with the conclusion that the monopolization of an industry typically results in a net loss to society.[1]

Note that this problem of whether the $1 million is of equal benefit to buyers and sellers arises in evaluating almost every economic policy, whether it is controlling monopoly price, limiting pollution, or opening

[1] Any full evaluation of monopoly involves examining several other issues as well. For example, to the degree that firms hire lawyers to help them establish or strengthen a monopoly position, then it's reasonable to argue that, from society's point of view, these legal resources are being wasted. For a discussion of this and other costs of monopoly not discussed here, see for example, Anne Krueger, "The Political Economy of the Rent-Seeking Society," *American Economic Review* (June 1974): 291–303; and Richard Posner, "The Social Costs of Monopoly and Regulation," *Journal of Political Economy* (August 1975): 807–28.

trade with foreign countries. Most policies result in a change in some market price, and hence a transfer of income between buyers and sellers. Thus, any normative conclusion as to whether the policy is desirable or not, requires a reasonable working assumption of how people compare in their valuation of income.[2] Anyone unprepared to make such an assumption is restricted to positive economics—to an analysis of economic events, policies, and institutions, without any judgement on whether or not they have been beneficial to the community as a whole.

GOVERNMENT POLICIES TO CONTROL MONOPOLY

We shall now explain our earlier claim that, in formulating policies to protect the public from monopoly, the government should begin with the question: "Is the industry in question a natural monopoly or not?" Suppose it is not; suppose the monopoly is the result of collusion. In this case, we've already seen that there is a strong argument for preventing monopolization—or if it has occurred, for breaking it up. To achieve this objective, "anti-combines" legislation has been passed in Canada and "anti-trust" laws in the United States; this legislation will be considered in Chapter 27.

In the balance of this chapter we will concentrate on the other case, which we illustrate in Figure 25-7. Here economies of scale—that is, an average cost curve AC that keeps falling over a wide range of output—makes the industry a natural monopoly: The least expensive way for market demand to be satisfied is by one large producer. Breaking the monopoly up into a number of smaller firms would be counterproductive. We don't need more than one set of electrical wires running down a street; nor do we need more than one set of gas pipes. If we had several firms in any of these activities, they would be duplicating the investment—

<hr>

[2]The same issue arises in macroeconomics. During any period in which the nation's per capita income increases, most Canadians benefit, but a few are hurt. Any judgement that such an income increase has been of benefit to the nation overall involves a reasonable assumption about how people compare in their valuation of income: The assumption normally used is that losers get roughly the same satisfaction from $1,000 of income as winners do. For more detail, see Arnold Harberger, "Three Basic Postulates for Applied Welfare Economics: An Interpretive Essay," *Journal of Economic Literature* (September 1971): 785–97.

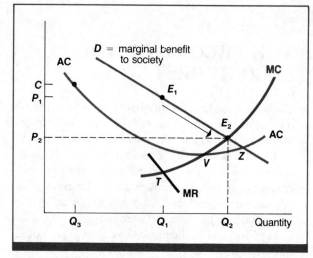

Figure 25-7 Natural monopoly: Regulating price rather than breaking up the firm.

Without price regulation, the monopoly firm maximizes its profit by selecting point E_1 on its demand curve: At this point, output is Q_1, where the firm's MR = MC. If the government sets maximum price at P_2, the firm is forced down its demand curve to point E_2, with its output increasing to Q_2. This is the efficient output where the marginal benefit to society (D) is equal to marginal cost MC. The efficiency gain from this policy comes from the elimination of the original "triangle" of monopoly inefficiency E_1E_2T; this triangle is the same sort of efficiency loss as the red triangle in Figure 25-5. This policy also reduces monopoly profit: Since initially the monopolist maximized profit by selecting point E_1, any other point on the demand curve—including E_2—involves less profit.

that is, the fixed costs—of the existing monopoly, and this would involve a waste of resources.

Graphically, breaking the natural monopoly in Figure 25-7 up into a number of small firms, each with output Q_3, would raise average cost to C; the benefits from economies of scale would be lost. In the case shown here, everyone would lose. The monopoly would lose its monopoly profit. Moreover, consumers would also be damaged: Even if the new, perhaps highly competitive firms were to earn no economic profit, they would still have to sell at a high price C, just to cover their high costs; and that price would be higher than the price P_1 that consumers were paying before the monopoly was broken up.

Thus, breaking up a natural monopoly is no solution at all. Indeed, reducing the output of the firm by breaking it up is a move in the wrong direction, because this raises costs. Instead, the government should force the firm to expand. Specifically, it should force the firm to move from E_1 down its demand curve to the efficient point E_2 where the marginal benefit to consumers (and to society) is equal to the marginal cost to producers (and to society).

How does the government force the monopoly to do this? The answer is: Set the maximum price that the firm can charge at P_2, the price at which its MC curve intersects the demand curve. This is called *marginal cost pricing.*

> *Marginal cost pricing* is setting price at the level where MC intersects the demand curve.

Since the monopoly is now prohibited from raising price, it is forced to act like a perfectly competitive firm, taking price P_2 as given. Like the perfectly competitive firm, it will produce to point E_2, where its MC curve rises to the level of its given price P_2. Because E_2 is the efficient output where MC intersects demand, this policy has eliminated the original efficiency loss due to monopoly.[3] We emphasize that, in forcing the move to the efficient point E_2, the government has *not* broken up this natural monopoly. It has simply *removed the monopoly's market power*—that is, the power of the monopoly to set a high price. In practice, there are two ways the government can do this:

1. It may take over and operate the monopolized activity, setting the price of its output at P_2. Provision

of utilities such as water and electricity by city governments is an example of this type of solution.

2. Alternatively, the government may let the monopoly continue as a privately owned firm but will set up a regulatory agency to control its price. This is the way telephone service is provided in most of Canada. (The prairie provinces are an exception: There the government owns the telephone companies.) The regulatory agency then dictates price P_2.

In summary, consider how well marginal cost pricing solves the monopoly abuse of producing too little at too high a price. The monopoly is forced to reduce its price, and consequently it sells more, that is, its output increases. In addition, its monopoly profit has been reduced, though not necessarily eliminated; in our example, a per unit profit of E_2Z remains.

Unfortunately, dealing with monopoly in practice is often not so easy. Although marginal cost pricing still allows a profit in the example shown in Figure 25-7, in other circumstances it may lead to a loss. In such a case, marginal cost pricing is not a satisfactory policy, since the government would be setting the price too low to allow the firm to stay in business. Such a monopoly requires some other form of price regulation. This more difficult situation is dealt with in Box 25-2.

THE SPECIAL CASE OF DISCRIMINATING MONOPOLY: LETTING A MONOPOLIST ACT LIKE A MONOPOLIST—IN SPADES

The argument so far is that a monopolist should not be allowed the freedom to set a high price. However, this general rule has an interesting exception which can be illustrated in the special case of a dentist thinking of offering her services in a small town that currently has no dentist.

Figure 25-9 shows the demand she faces; some individuals are willing to pay more than others for the service she offers. This diagram also shows her average costs, which, as always, include her opportunity costs—the income she could earn elsewhere. If she must quote a single price to all patients, she will not stay in this community. The reason is that the average cost curve AC is always above the demand curve D, regardless of the price charged. Consequently, there is no single price she can select that will cover her costs. The best

---

[3] The original efficiency loss under uncontrolled monopoly was triangle E_1TE_2, because the monopoly chose equilibrium E_1 rather than the efficient equilibrium E_2.

This example presents a puzzle: A government price ceiling increases efficiency here, but in other circumstances a government price ceiling—such as the ceiling on rents described earlier—reduces efficiency. How is this possible? The answer: The ceiling on rents moved an industry away from an efficient, perfectly competitive equilibrium. On the other hand, the price ceiling in Figure 25-7 moves an inefficient monopoly at E_1 toward an efficient equilibrium at E_2.

Clearly, government intervention can be a powerful tool, since it can move a market away from its free-market equilibrium. While this can be damaging if the free market is initially competitive, it can be beneficial if the free market is initially monopolized. For this reason, economists oppose price regulations in some circumstances, but favour it in others.

BOX 25-2

UNFORTUNATELY, DEALING WITH NATURAL MONOPOLY IS OFTEN NOT SO SIMPLE

In Figure 25-7, average cost reached a minimum and turned up at point V *before* it reached the demand curve, that is, it turned up to the left of the demand curve. In Figure 25-8 we now consider the case where the average cost curve AC keeps falling until *after* it has crossed the demand curve. In this instance, the regulation of monopoly price involves substantial problems.

To see why, suppose that we try to apply the policy that worked so well in Figure 25-7, and again try to drive the monopoly firm down its demand curve from its original profit-maximizing equilibrium at E_1 to the efficient point E_2, where marginal cost intersects demand. As before, suppose we attempt to do so by regulating price at P_2. This policy will not work here, because it will turn the monopoly into a money-loser and eventually drive it out of business. The reason is that at E_2 it is operating below its average cost curve AC. Thus, the price P_2 that the firm receives is not enough to cover its average cost at G. The firm's per unit loss is GE_2, and its total loss is the red area.

A different approach is required; we now consider three possibilities.

Average Cost Pricing

The lowest price the government can set without eventually forcing the firm out of business is P_3, which will result in a new equilibrium at E_3. Here price is barely high enough to cover average cost; the firm just breaks even. This policy is called **average cost pricing**. Once again, the regulatory agency takes away the monopoly's power to select a point on its demand curve; the agency makes the decision on the appropriate point and makes it stick by regulating price.

> *Average cost pricing* is setting price at the level where AC intersects the demand curve.

In theory, break-even price P_3 should be easy for the agency to find. If the firm is earning an (above-normal) profit—as it would, for example, at E_1—then price is too high; so lower it. If the firm is operating at a loss, at a point like E_2, then price is too low; raise it. This simple rule of thumb will bring the regulators to P_3, the price that just covers costs, including a fair return on the capital the owners have invested. *In practice*, however, P_3 is very difficult to determine, largely because of problems in defining (1) a fair percentage return to capital, and (2) the amount of capital invested—problems examined in Appendix 25-B.

Finally, the effect on efficiency of average cost pricing is shown in panel (*b*) of Figure 25-8. If it were possible to move the monopoly all the way down its demand curve from E_1 to E_2 the result would be the now familiar triangular efficiency gain shown as area 4 + 5. However, average cost pricing allows us to move this firm only part way, from E_1 to E_3. Therefore the gain is limited to area 4.

We conclude that since this policy of average cost pricing increases monopoly output from Q_1 to Q_3, it results in a gain in *allocative efficiency*. (Remember that unless we state otherwise, the word "efficiency" means "allocative efficiency.") Unfortunately, however, this policy, and any of the others discussed in this box, may lead to a *loss in technical efficiency*—that is, the firm may not operate on its lowest possible cost curve. After all, why should the firm in Figure 25-9 strive hard to lower its costs, when a reduction in costs will cause the regulatory agency to correspondingly lower price? Why shouldn't the firm's executives be allowed generous expense accounts, since such costs are simply passed on to consumers in the form of higher prices? No matter what the firm does, it isn't allowed to make an above-normal profit; so why should it tightly control its costs? (At best, the firm can earn an above-normal profit only temporarily, between the date it reduces its costs and the date the regulatory agency gets around to reducing its price.)

Government Subsidy (with Marginal Cost Pricing)

Another possible government policy to deal with the monopoly in Figure 25-8 is to force it all the

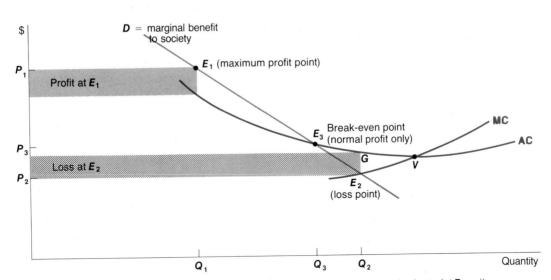

(a) **Average cost pricing.** An unrestricted monopoly would maximize profit by selecting point E_1 on its demand curve. (The profit it would earn is shown by the gray area.) Average cost pricing involves driving the monopoly down its demand curve to E_3, by setting a price ceiling at P_3. At this point the firm just breaks even, earning only the normal profit necessary to keep it in business. Marginal cost pricing—that is, setting price at P_2 in order to drive the monopoly further down its demand curve to E_2—is not feasible, because price P_2 is below average cost. Thus the firm would incur the loss shown by the red area, and eventually go out of business.

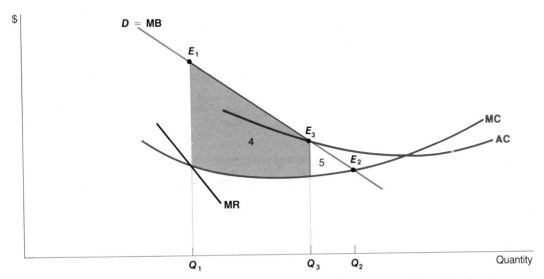

(b) **Efficiency gains that are achieved (4), and those that are not (5).** If it were feasible to drive the monopoly firm all the way down its demand curve from E_1 to E_2, then there would be an efficiency gain 4 + 5. But since the firm can be driven down only to E_3, the efficiency gain is limited to area 4.

Figure 25-8 Regulating monopoly price: The difficult case.

way down its demand curve from E_1 to efficient point E_2 by marginal cost pricing, while at the same time paying the firm whatever lump-sum subsidy is necessary to cover its loss. In other words, a regulated price of P_2 drives the firm down its demand curve to point E_2 (thus capturing the entire possible efficiency gain 4 + 5), while a subsidy equal to the red area in panel (a) keeps the firm in business.

Although this policy may be attractive in theory, it raises such serious problems in practice that it is seldom used. One reason is that it is difficult for the public to understand why a government committed to controlling the market power of monopoly should end up subsidizing it. The point that the government is also regulating price—and thus eliminating the profit of the monopoly—is difficult to explain to the public. Moreover, the policy of taking money out of the monopolist's pocket with one hand (the regulated price) while putting it back with the other (the subsidy) may strike the public as being inconsistent, even though it is not. In addition, the general problem in price regulation reappears here. So long as the government is committed to subsidizing the costs of a monopolist, how can those costs be controlled? A firm may be very successful in holding costs down so long as it has to meet the test of the marketplace where failure means bankruptcy; but it may be far less successful in controlling its costs if it knows it will receive a subsidy for any loss it incurs. Finally, a government that has to get a subsidy passed in a political system where there is log-rolling ("I'll vote for the subsidy in your riding if you'll vote for the subsidy in mine") may end up with a compromise subsidy that has little relationship to the original efficiency objective.

Government Ownership

The political problems involved in granting a subsidy are less severe if the government owns the monopoly, which it can then operate in the public interest at efficient point E_2. Again, taxpayers must subsidize the loss that results. Government-owned mass transit systems are often cited as examples; government subsidies often cover a large portion of the costs of large urban public transportation system.

However, there is no guarantee that such a publicly owned enterprise will be operated at the most efficient point E_2, since the objective of the government-appointed management may not be to increase efficiency so much as to redistribute income. For example, the government may be trying indirectly to provide income—in the form of low-cost fares—to those who use the urban transport system.

Finally, we re-emphasize that the same problem arises here as with the other policies discussed in this Box: So long as the firm's management receives whatever subsidy is necessary to cover its costs, it has inadequate incentive to keep costs down. There is a good reason why this may become a particularly serious problem in a public enterprise. Even in a private enterprise, the owners (shareholders) may have problems in controlling a management that is inefficient, wasteful, or pursuing its own interests at the expense of the owners' interests. However, in a public enterprise this is even more difficult, because of the layers of government bureaucracy separating the managers of the enterprise from its owners—in this case, the taxpayers. (Problems of a bureaucracy are examined further in Chapter 30.)

she could do would be to select a point like E_1 on the demand curve, setting her fee at P_1 and selling quantity Q_1. However, she would still suffer a loss: Specifically, her total loss, compared with what she could earn elsewhere, would be areas 1 + 2; that is, Q_1 units sold at a loss of CP_1 on each.

Under such circumstances, this community loses its dentist. The question is: Isn't there some way she could be allowed to charge more, and thus find this town attractive after all? The answer is yes. Indeed

she can charge more in a way that will not only benefit her, but the community as well. Here's how: by discriminating among patients, selling her service at a higher price to some than to others. To illustrate, suppose she starts at initial position E, charging one price P_1 to all her patients and incurring losses 1 + 2. She can do better by charging her wealthy patients a higher fee P_2 for the Q_2 of services they require. This increases her income by areas 1 + 3, more than offsetting her original losses 1 + 2. Therefore, she is now able to more than cover her costs. With a higher income here than she could earn elsewhere, she decides to stay in town.

In short, if she cannot discriminate, she won't be able to earn as much here as elsewhere, and will leave. However, if she is allowed to discriminate, she will be able to earn a higher income, and stay in town. This is

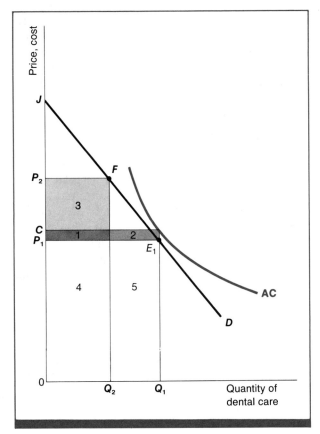

Figure 25-9 When discriminating monopoly may be justified.
If the dentist—the potential monopolist—can charge only one price, she will not move into this town, because the demand D is not substantial enough to overlap AC. Any point such as E that she might select on D would thus leave her operating at a loss, shown by area $1 + 2$, and she would stay away. On the other hand, she will move into town if she is allowed to discriminate, charging low fee P_1 to the poor and high fee P_2 to the rich. On her Q_2 of services sold to the rich, she increases her income by area $1 + 3$ which is more than enough to offset her original loss $1 + 2$. Thus, she can earn a profit—her benefit from discriminatory pricing. At the same time, her patients also benefit because they get a dentist whom they would not have been able to attract otherwise.

beneficial not only for her, but for her patients as well. They get area JEQ_10 of benefit from her services, which is more than the area $3 + 1 + 4 + 5$ that they pay for these services. (Her wealthy patients pay price P_2 for Q_2 of her services, for a total of area $3 + 1 + 4$. At the same time, her less wealthy patients pay price P_1 for Q_2Q_1 units, for a total of area 5.) Price discrimination is justified in this case, because it benefits everyone concerned.

However, even when price discrimination is desirable, it may not be possible. To make different prices stick, the discriminating monopolist must be able to divide the market, thus preventing individuals who buy at the low price from turning around and selling to those who are charged the higher price. In our example, the dentist is able to divide her market: A poor patient who is able to buy a root-canal job at a bargain price cannot turn around and sell it to a friend with a toothache. On the other hand, a bus company may not be able to divide its adult market, charging some customers $10 and others $20. The reason is that those who are able to buy cheap $10 tickets may sell them to the others for some price like $15 that benefits both groups. (However, the bus company *can* divide its market between adults and children, since an adult can't buy a cheap ticket from a child and use it on a bus. The company may also give a discount to senior citizens, since they are also relatively easily identified, and those who are not 65 usually don't want to pretend that they are.)

Finally, it should be re-emphasized that it is possible to defend price discrimination by the monopolist in Figure 25-9 because D does not overlap AC and she would be out of business otherwise. However, price discrimination cannot be so easily justified in the normal case of monopoly where D does overlap AC and the monopolist can therefore at least cover costs by quoting a single price. This is the type of monopoly that we shall concentrate on hereafter in this book.

DO FIRMS REALLY MAXIMIZE PROFITS?

The best of all monopoly profits is a quiet life.
J.R. Hicks.

So far, it has been assumed that producers maximize profits. However, they may occasionally pursue quite different objectives. Sometimes, they may decide on a policy because it makes them look good to their shareholders. Sometimes, with the objective of expanding their market share, they may increase output beyond the profit-maximizing point, provided they achieve some reasonable level of profit. (It is often not clear whether this is simply expansion for its own sake, or whether firms are giving up profit in the short run in order to increase it in the long run: For example, firms may want to grow in order to generate public confidence and thereby make it easier to sell their products in the future.) Alternatively, in order to avoid risk, producers may swing in the other direction, and "think small," only undertaking expenditures that will yield an assured high profit. Or they may follow a policy of "no change" solely because they enjoy the quiet life. For example, if they are earning large profits, why should they worry about changing their output and price just because their cost curves have shifted slightly? Or why should they worry about the minor loss incurred if they hire a few relatives?

Why not construct our economic theory using one of these other assumptions instead? The answer, in some cases, is that these other assumptions would not be specific enough. For example, 10 business executives in identical circumstances, each pursuing the quiet life, might come up with 10 different decisions on output and price; you can't construct much of a theory with that. Even in those cases where a theory can be constructed, it will have the same flaw as profit maximization: It will not describe all economic decision making. Accordingly, we use profit maximiza-

tion because this assumption is simple and precise enough to allow us to "get off square one" and construct a theory, and because it generally describes economic decision making at least as well as any alternative simple assumption. However, we recognize that in some cases it may not be as accurate a description of reality as we would like. And it is often only part of the story, since other objectives may also influence the decision-making process.[4] So we should be appropriately guarded in making claims of generality for our conclusions.

Of course, if we have evidence that certain firms are pursuing some other objective such as rapid growth, we may be able to adjust our profit-maximization conclusions in some reasonable way. For example, since high-growth firms tend to produce a larger output than profit-maximizing firms, we might ask: What does this greater output imply about price to the consumer? What are its effects on efficiency? How would producers respond to price regulation? And so on. The answers to some of these questions are straightforward, but others are not so clear. If we wanted to clarify them, we might even go one giant step further and construct a whole new theory from scratch, based on some other assumption than profit maximization. But that's a story for a more advanced course.

[4] For more detail on alternative theories of decision making by the firm, see H.A. Simon, "Rational Decision Making in Business Organizations," *American Economic Review* (September 1979): 493–513; and Robin Maris, *The Economic Theory of Managerial Capitalism* (New York: Basic Books, 1968).

KEY POINTS

1. Monopoly means that there is a single seller. This situation may occur when a firm controls something essential to the production or sale of a good—such as a patent, resource, or government licence. Or it may occur if a number of firms collude in order to be able to quote a single industry price.

2. Another important reason for monopoly is that a firm's costs may fall over such a wide range of output that total market demand can be most inexpensively satisfied by a single firm. This is a *natural monopoly*. Even if there are initially

many firms in such an industry, they will tend to be eliminated by competition, with the single large firm that emerges able to undercut any present or future competitors.

3. A monopoly can do something a perfectly competitive firm cannot: Because it faces a demand curve that slopes downward to the right, it can quote the price at which it will sell.

4. Whereas marginal revenue MR for a perfect competitor is the same as price, MR for a monopoly is less than price. That is, a monopoly's MR curve lies below its demand curve.

5. A monopolist maximizes profit by equating MC with MR, not with price. As a consequence, monopoly results in an inefficiently low output. It also results in a transfer of income from consumers to the monopolist.

6. If the monopoly is not a natural monopoly—but instead is, say, the result of collusion—the government has available anti-combines legislation to break up the collusive arrangement or prevent a monopoly from being formed in the first place. These laws will be described in Chapter 27.

7. If the monopoly is a natural monopoly, then breaking it up would raise costs. A preferred gov-

ernment policy is to set the maximum price the monopolist can charge. Facing this given price, the monopolist is forced into the price-taking role of the perfect competitor, and consequently increases output to a more efficient quantity.

8. A case can sometimes be made for allowing a monopoly to price-discriminate, that is, to charge a higher price to one group than to another. Our example was a dentist in a small town who charged a higher price to her wealthy patients. Such discriminatory pricing may be justified if the good or service could not otherwise be produced.

KEY CONCEPTS

patent
legal monopoly
collusive monopoly
natural monopoly
oligopoly
market power
price maker

price taker
monopolist's demand
monopolist's marginal revenue
monopoly inefficiency
how monopoly raises price
   and reduces output
transfer effect of monopoly

theory of the second best
marginal cost pricing
average cost pricing
discriminating monopoly
   (when justified, when not)
objectives other than
   maximizing profit

PROBLEMS

25-1 Which is closer to being a monopoly, American Motors or Rolls Royce? Answer the same question for the producer of bread in a small town or the producer of the wheat used in it. In each case, explain your answer.

25-2 Consider an industry in which the discovery and development of advanced machinery and technology mean that, as time passes, average costs for a firm tend to drift lower and lower. That is, through time the average cost for an individual firm moves from AC_1 to AC_2 in the following diagram. What do you think would happen in such an industry? Explain why. From the point of view of society as a whole, does the falling cost involve any advantages? Any disadvantages? In your view,

how do these compare?

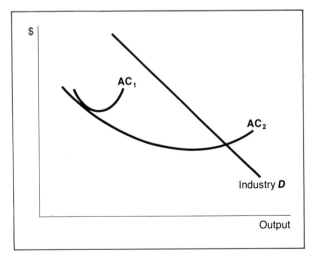

25-3 (a) If the firm with AC_2 in the diagram above is not regulated, would you expect that all the monopoly profits would go to the firm's owners? If not, who else do you think might eventually capture a share of these profits?

(b) Draw in the marginal cost curve that corresponds to AC_2. Show the best level at which to set regulated price. Explain why it is best.

*25-4 This provides another way of viewing a monopolist's profit maximization, in addition to the two set out in Figure 25-4. In the diagram below, note that the TC and TR curves for a monopolist are the same as for a perfect competitor (shown in Figure 22-4 in Box 22-2) except for one important difference: Because a monopoly faces a downward-sloping demand curve, its TR is a curved rather than a straight line. Using that earlier approach, describe how the profit-maximizing output of this monopolist is determined. In particular, show geometrically why MC = MR.

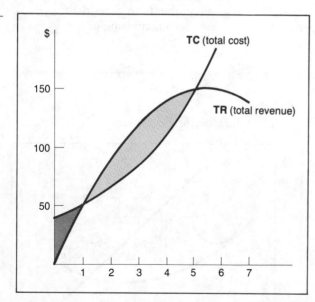

25-5 Given the cost conditions in the following diagram, name the price that would be set by a monopoly that is:

(a) maximizing its profit

(b) operating as a non-profit organization

(c) run by the government at an efficient output

If (a) and/or (b) are not efficient, explain why.

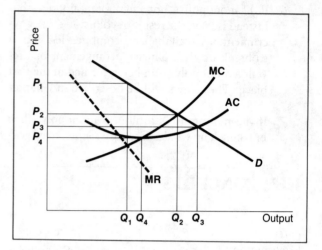

25-6 Does output Q_1 in Figure 25-4(b) yield the monopolist the largest profit per unit of output? Explain why or why not.

25-7 Consider the following statement: "Monopolies should be subject to price control. Competitive industries should not. Every owner has a monopoly in the renting of his or her building. Therefore, the government should control rents." Do you agree in part or in whole with this statement? Explain.

25-8 We have seen that the uncontrolled monopoly in Figure 25-7 is inefficient. Which of the conditions for efficiency in Box 24-1 has been violated? Hint: What is the marginal cost of the uncontrolled monopoly? What is its price?

25-9 The following diagram shows the demand and the costs the government faces in providing a public utility service (say electricity) in a certain city.

(a) If the government is interested only in maximizing the utility's profit—or minimizing its loss—show the price it will set and how much it will produce and sell. Also show its profit or loss.

(b) Is this output the best from the view-

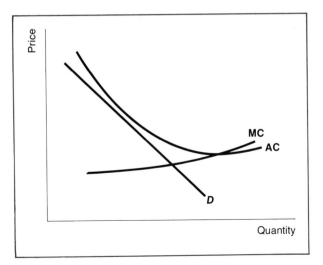

point of allocative efficiency? If so, explain why. If not, show what the most efficient output is and explain why. What price does the firm set to achieve this output and what is its profit or loss at the efficient output?

(c) Suppose that this public utility is allowed to set discriminatory prices. It decides to charge the public a higher rate for its initial purchases, while for any additional purchases it continues to charge the rate it set in question (b). Could the public utility sell an efficient output and still make profits by following a policy of price discrimination?

(d) Do you see now why public utilities are sometimes allowed to set discriminatory rates?

(e) In the section "The Special Case of Discriminating Monopoly," it was observed that for successful discrimination, a firm must be able to segregate its market and prevent resale among buyers. The dentist has no great problem in segregating her market. How about the public utility selling electricity?

*25-10 Suppose the government owns the two monopolies shown in figures 25-7 and 25-9. In the interests of efficiency, how should their prices be set? Would each firm operate at a profit or a loss? What government subsidy(ies) would be required? Would two such monopolies taken together necessarily require a subsidy? Explain.

*25-11 Evaluate the following policy recommendation: "The sole objective in dealing with monopoly is to eliminate excess profits. And this is easy to do. Just examine the firm's current operations, calculate its average cost (including normal profit), and set price at this level."

APPENDIX 25-A

GOVERNMENT MARKETING PROGRAMS: HELPING COMPETITORS TO ACT LIKE A MONOPOLIST?

Things are seldom what they seem,
Skim milk masquerades as cream.

Gilbert and Sullivan,
H.M.S. Pinafore

We have seen how a government agency set up to regulate a monopoly will force the firm to act like a perfect competitor, in the process driving it down its demand curve. However, in some cases, the government has acted in the opposite direction. A competitive industry has been provided with a marketing organization—that is, a single agency that can quote price for all the firms, and thus allows these competitive firms to act like a monopolist. Specifically, by quoting a higher price, the agency can move these firms up their market demand curve—something they cannot do by acting individually.

In panel (a) of Figure 25-10, point E_1 is the equilibrium in a competitive industry before any attempt is made to create a monopoly. The market price is $80, with 1,000 units being sold. At the same time, the situation of one of the 100 individual firms in the industry is shown in panel (b). The firm is in equilibrium at F_1, producing 10 units and just covering its costs. (As an aside, note that panel (a) will be picking up much of the argument developed for the industry in Figure 25-6, while panel (b) will be detailing what happens to an individual firm.)

When a marketing association is formed, all producers speak with one voice and quote a higher price. Suppose the price the association decides on is $140, well above the competitive $80 level. The industry consequently moves up its demand curve in panel (a)

from E_1 to E_2. To make this higher price stick, the association must, like any monopolist, reduce sales from 1,000 units to 600. This cut implies that the individual firm in panel (b) must decrease its output from 10 to a quota of 6. Therefore, the firm moves from F_1 to F_2. Despite the fact its output has been reduced, its increased price now allows it to earn the profit shown as the shaded gray area.

The monopolization of this industry has had the expected results. Producers benefit from their newfound profit, while consumers lose because of increased price. On balance, there is an overall efficiency loss shown by the red area in panel (a).

However, there are strong pressures for such associations to come apart. While it is in the collective interest of all firms to restrict their output in order to raise price to $140, at this high price it is in the interest of the individual firm to *expand* output. In fact, at the $140 price set by the association, the firm in panel (b) has an incentive to produce, not at F_2, but at B where MC intersects the given price. The problem, then, for the industry association is how to compel each individual firm to operate in the collective interest at F_2, rather than attempt to pursue its own interest at B. This discipline is essential: If some firms start to produce more than their quota, more than 600 units will come onto the market, and price will fall. Moreover, getting existing firms to stick to their quotas is not the

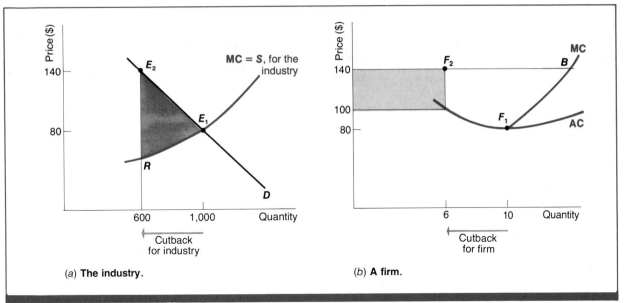

(a) **The industry.**   (b) **A firm.**

Figure 25-10   Effect of a producers' association or government marketing board on an industry, and on an individual firm.

Panel (a) illustrates a competitive industry. Market equilibrium is at E_1 where $D = S$. When this industry is monopolized by a producers' association or government marketing agency, equilibrium moves from E_1 to E_2. The association raises price from $80 to $140, and this reduces industry sales from 1,000 units to 600.

In turn, the sales of the individual firm in panel (b) must

be reduced from 10 units to a quota of 6. This means that the firm moves from F_1 to F_2 where it makes the $240 profit shown by the gray area: On each of its 6 units, it earns a $40 profit. Although this reduction in output has generated profits, each firm facing the given $140 price would like to *increase* its output, by moving from F_2 to B, where MC = price. However, such additional output would drive market price down; the industry in panel (a) would slide down its demand curve from E_2 toward E_1, with the individual firm in panel (b) moving from F_2 to the no-profit point F_1.

only problem: The entry of new firms, attracted by the gray above-normal profits, would also drive price down.

The problems of enforcing quota limitations on production and restricting entry would make it difficult for private marketing associations to monopolize their industries, even if it were legal for them to do so. Moreover, Canadian law generally makes it illegal for private firms to form an organization to control production and prices in an industry. (We will discuss this legislation in more detail in Chapter 27.) However, in some sectors of agriculture, the law allows producers to form **marketing boards** which may be given government authority to fix prices and impose quota limits on the output that each producer is allowed to market. (A marketing board can be established by a majority vote of all producers of a particular commodity in a province. Once the majority have voted for a marketing board, all producers must join, even

those who voted against the board.) Thus, through the marketing boards, producers in agriculture are able to do what marketing associations in other industries cannot legally accomplish: They get a measure of control over prices and output in their industry.

Marketing boards have become very common in recent years in Canada. A study prepared for the Canadian Consumer Research Council[5] listed 95 provincial marketing boards in 1974; the commodities they covered ranged from eggs, milk, cheese, and hogs, to apples, asparagus, blueberries, and mushrooms. While most marketing boards are provincial in scope, federal legislation has helped the provincial boards co-ordinate their activities in several markets, thereby in effect creating a set of nationwide marketing agencies.

Since production controls may lead to substantial

[5]The study is quoted in Christopher Green, *Canadian Industrial Organization and Policy* (Toronto: McGraw-Hill Ryerson, 1980), pp. 286–87.

increases in price to the Canadian public, and to an efficiency loss like the red area in Figure 25-10(a), why does the government allow the formation of marketing boards with the power to fix prices and control output? In support of marketing boards, farmers point to the special problems facing agriculture discussed in Chapter 20. Supply and demand forces would lead to highly unstable prices and incomes in the markets for many farm products if there were no government policy to support farm prices. Since the support policies we discussed in Appendix 24-B tend to become very expensive for the government, relying on marketing boards may appear as an attractive alternative. The boards can stabilize prices at a level that is satisfactory to producers; and since production is controlled, the government does not have to buy up large quantities of farm products to support the price. However, the effect of the boards on consumers is of course quite a different matter.[6]

In recent years the Canadian marketing board system has come under increasing criticism. Opponents

have argued that the system has become very costly to consumers, and that the efficiency losses are becoming unacceptably large. Furthermore, the critics fear that the political power of the marketing boards may ultimately become so strong that the boards will begin to function as independent monopolies over which the government has little control. Speaking about the operation of the marketing board system in the poultry sector, the authors of a recent study on Canadian farm policy state:

> . . . the excesses [of marketing boards] in the egg and broiler chicken industries have long been known, but the responsible statutory regulatory agencies have maintained a thunderous silence. In the final analysis, the situation portrayed is also an indictment of the policy process and parliamentary control of it. For it is doubtful if earlier policy makers intended, or if present legislators could now justify to their constituents, a regulatory regime for eggs and chickens that transfers over $100 million a year to 4,600 individuals . . .[7]

---

[6]Many Canadian marketing boards are allowed by the government to fix prices at a level that depends on the farmers' cost of production. For example, when the prices of inputs such as fertilizer or fuel oil go up, the boards are *automatically* allowed to charge higher prices to consumers.

[7]J.D. Forbes, R.D. Hughes, and T.K. Warley, *Economic Intervention and Regulation in Canadian Agriculture*, a study prepared for the Economic Council of Canada and the Institute for Research on Public Policy (Ottawa: Minister of Supply and Services Canada, 1982), p. 49. Reproduced by permission of the Minister of Supply and Services Canada.

PROBLEMS

*25-10 Show the profit that the firm in Figure 25-10(b) would capture if it could get away with producing at point *B*. Is this an equilibrium if all firms try to do the same? Explain.

*25-11 How might an agricultural marketing board be defended by using the theory of the second best?

*25-12 The British Columbia Milk Marketing Board sells milk at a price more than 10 percent above the free-market level. The board has also made it illegal to sell reconstituted milk, that is, powdered milk mixed with water and fresh milk. The reason given for this action is to protect the consumer from an inferior product. Yet, in tests, consumers cannot distinguish this milk from fresh milk, and it would cost far less. Is the marketing board protecting consumers or some other group?

APPENDIX 25-B

AVERAGE COST PRICING: PUBLIC UTILITY REGULATION

Several problems arise when the theory of average cost pricing is put into practice in regulating or operating a *public utility*.

> A *public utility* is a natural monopoly in which many decisions—particularly pricing decisions—are regulated by a government agency. (Some public utilities are owned by the government.) A public utility typically provides an essential service to the public and often has high overhead costs because of the heavy equipment it requires to deliver its product to the consumer. Examples include the provision of telephone services (via phone lines), natural gas (via pipelines), electricity (via transmission lines), and railroad transport (via rail).

HOW IS AVERAGE COST CALCULATED?

Recall from Figure 25-8 that average cost pricing involves setting a price that will barely cover average costs, including normal profit. In other words, the objective is to keep the price low enough to prevent excessive monopoly profits, but high enough to provide the normal profit that will keep the firm in business. Estimating a fair or normal profit for the owners involves estimating the amount of capital they have invested, and a fair percentage rate of return to be applied to that capital.

(a) *What is a fair percentage rate of return on capital invested?* The answer to this should be: the opportunity cost of capital—the percentage rate of return it could earn elsewhere in the economy. Although regulatory agencies have given some consideration to earnings in other sectors of the economy, their rates of return have not matched rates elsewhere, perhaps because of tradition and a feeling that it is their responsibility to the public to keep their prices down. This problem of a relatively low rate of return in public utilities has been made worse by a squeeze that results from inflation. It raises the costs of inputs to utilities, but there is a regulatory time lag before the utilities are allowed to compensate by raising their price. In turn, relatively low rates of return in privately owned public utilities make it difficult for them to attract capital.

(b) *What is the value of the capital invested (the "rate base")?* Should it be the *original cost* of the machinery and other capital bought by the firm, or the *present replacement cost* (less depreciation in either case)? Because of inflation, this makes a lot of difference. The cost of replacing most equipment far exceeds its original cost years ago. Thus far, there is no clear consensus among the regulatory agencies on which method to use.

OTHER PROBLEMS AND REFORM PROPOSALS

Few would argue that regulation of a public utility should be abolished. Such regulation is the most reasonable way of getting the low costs offered by a natural monopoly while avoiding the worst monopoly abuses. However, it is far from being problem-free; it can be argued that regulation can be improved, both by making it more consistent, and by speeding up regulatory decisions (so capital-starved utilities are caught less in an inflation squeeze). It is also important to ensure that regulation is being applied only to a natural monopoly and not to a (perhaps closely related) activity that is not a natural monopoly at all. For example, the provision of telephone service is a natural monopoly and requires regulation. But certain other closely related activities—such as the production of telephones and telephone terminal equipment—may not be. (In a 1980 decision, the Canadian Radio-television and Telecommunications Commission (CRTC) ruled that Bell Canada could no longer force its subscribers to use only telephones supplied by Bell. Almost immediately, a number of new suppliers entered the market for telephones in competition with Bell.)

PROBLEM

*25-13 Some recently installed nuclear power plants in the United States have been so expensive to build, that covering this cost would require the regulatory agencies to raise electricity prices by 40% to 60%. Moreover, this 40–60% price increase has been calculated on the assumption that even this sort of "rate shock" would not change the quantity of electricity demanded. Explain why a regulatory agency that passed this full 40–60% price increase on to the public might find that the utility could still not cover its costs. (If you can, include some reference to overhead [fixed] costs in your answer.)

Chapter 26

MARKETS BETWEEN MONOPOLY AND PERFECT COMPETITION

> People of the same trade seldom meet
> together, even for merriment and
> diversion, but the conversation ends
> in a conspiracy against the public,
> or in some contrivance to raise
> prices.
>
> Adam Smith,
> *Wealth of Nations*

Monopoly represents the clearest form of market power; the monopoly firm is alone in the marketplace and has the power to choose its selling price. But even though there are some markets that are controlled by a single monopoly firm, most of the giants in Canadian business are not monopolists. Air Canada competes with CP Air and several regional carriers in the market for domestic air travel; and Canadian National competes with CP Rail in railroad transport. In the market for telecommunications equipment, Canada's Northern Telecom faces competition from international firms like the ITT Corp., Western Electric, and Sweden's L.M. Erickson; General Motors of Canada has to contend with Ford, Chrysler, Toyota, Hyundai, Volkswagen, and others. In the market for petroleum products, Imperial Oil has to compete with Shell, Texaco, and other foreign-owned companies—as well as with government-owned Petro-Canada. *Oligopoly—*

where a market is dominated by a *few* sellers—is more significant in the Canadian economy than outright monopoly.

This chapter initially deals with oligopoly, concentrating on the difficult policy questions it raises, and the various measures the government can use to control it. In addition, it describes another of the many kinds of market that lie between monopoly and perfect competition: monopolistic competition, which has been used to describe firms engaged in retail trade. This will complete our discussion of the basic market forms.

OLIGOPOLY

The degree to which an industry is dominated by a few sellers may be measured by a *concentration ratio*. Two such ratios are in common use: The four-firm

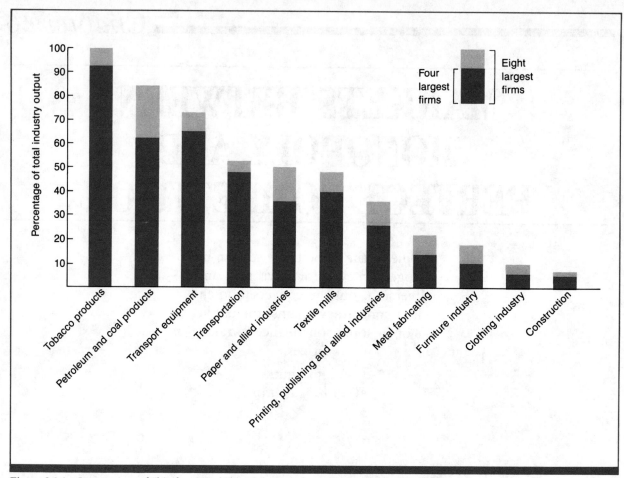

Figure 26-1   Importance of "big four" and "big eight" in selected industries, 1982. (Shares of output sold by domestic firms.)

Source: Compiled from Statistics Canada, *Annual Report of the Minister of Supply and Services under the Corporations and Labour Unions Returns Act 1982 (CALURA)* (Ottawa: Statistics Canada and Minister of Supply and Services Canada, 1985), Part I, *Corporations*. Reprinted by permission of the Minister of Supply and Services Canada.

concentration ratio measures the proportion of an industry's sales made by its four largest firms, while the eight-firm ratio measures the sales of its eight largest firms. Figure 26-1 shows that the tobacco products, transport equipment (which includes motor vehicles), and petroleum and coal products industries are dominated to a considerable degree by the few largest firms. But also notice that there are many industries which are not, such as the furniture, clothing, and construction industries. Moreover, the figure shows the relative importance of the four or eight largest firms in sales *by domestic producers*; the degree of concentra-

tion in *total* sales in the Canadian market is much smaller in many industries where imports account for a large share of sales.

Have these concentration ratios been getting larger or smaller over time? The answer is that there has been no strong tendency for Canada's largest firms to eliminate their competitors and emerge as monopolists from the competitive struggle. (Studies of American industrial concentration have shown that this holds true in the United States as well.)

In the past decade, the overall competitiveness in the North American economy may, if anything, have been getting somewhat *greater*, because of the rise of new industries such as microcomputers, with many small, highly competitive firms; and because of the increasing importance of service industries, where firms are generally small. In addition, reductions in transport costs and other barriers to international trade, as well as the growing economic strength of countries such as Japan and South Korea has exposed Canadian manufacturing to greater competition from imports. For example, import competition has made the auto industry far more competitive than its high concentration ratio in Figure 26-1 suggests. (However, in some cases the government has limited this competition by barriers to international trade, such as the limits on the imports of Japanese cars.) Failure to take imports into account limits the validity of any measure of concentration, including the two shown in Figure 26-1 or the "Herfindahl index" in Box 26-1.

Because there is no strong tendency for industries to become monopolized, oligopoly seems to be a stable form of market organization. It is not merely a temporary stop on an inevitable road to monopoly. What accounts for this stability? Why do a few firms grow so large, while none goes all the way to become a monopolist? In other words, why are there several firms in an industry, rather than just one?

Part of the answer lies in the nature of costs. In many industries, there are advantages of large-scale production; there is a decline in average cost as output rises. A plant designed to produce 500,000 cars per year can operate at a much lower average cost than a plant designed to produce 50,000. But costs do not continue to fall forever. Once a plant is producing a million units, doubling its output won't significantly reduce its costs further. When costs cease to fall, there is no longer this incentive for firms to continue to grow into a monopoly position.

The result is *natural oligopoly:* In panel (*b*) of Figure 26-2 we see that this market form falls somewhere between the extremes of perfect competition and natural monopoly. Note that average costs for an individual firm continue to fall over a considerable range, up to an output of 300 units. If existing firms are producing less than this, there is a tendency for them to expand. However, at an output of 300 units—still far short of satisfying total market demand of 1,000

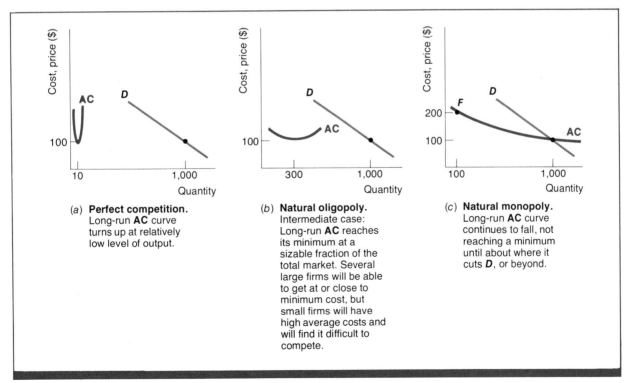

(a) **Perfect competition.**
Long-run **AC** curve turns up at relatively low level of output.

(b) **Natural oligopoly.**
Intermediate case: Long-run **AC** reaches its minimum at a sizable fraction of the total market. Several large firms will be able to get at or close to minimum cost, but small firms will have high average costs and will find it difficult to compete.

(c) **Natural monopoly.**
Long-run **AC** curve continues to fall, not reaching a minimum until about where it cuts **D**, or beyond.

Figure 26-2 Natural oligopoly compared with perfect competition and natural monopoly.

BOX 26-1

ANOTHER MEASURE OF INDUSTRY CONCENTRATION: THE HERFINDAHL INDEX

To understand this index, first consider a monopoly—an industry with the maximum possible degree of concentration. One hundred percent of the industry's output is sold by one firm. That is, the market share of this firm is 100% = 1.0. In this case, the Herfindahl index value is

$$(1.0)^2 = 1.0, \text{ the largest value the index can take.}$$

Next, consider a nearly monopolized industry. One firm produces 90% of the output, while the only other firm produces 10%—that is, their market shares are 0.9 and 0.1. In this case, the index becomes

$$(0.9)^2 + (0.1)^2 = 0.82, \text{ still a very high value.}$$

Notice that the value of the Herfindahl index falls as the number of firms in the industry increases.

As our final example, suppose that there again are two firms in the industry, but the first one no longer dominates. Instead, they both sell the same amount; their market shares are 0.5 and 0.5. Following our procedure of squaring market shares, we get a Herfindahl index of

$$(0.5)^2 + (0.5)^2 = 0.50$$

Thus, the index also falls as the market shares of the firms become more nearly equal.

Formally, the Herfindahl index is defined as the *sum of the squared market shares of all the firms*. It does a good job of taking into account the number of firms in an industry, and how close their market shares are to being equal. These are two characteristics that are critical in any evaluation of whether or not an industry is too concentrated.

---

units— costs stop falling. At this point, existing firms no longer have a "falling cost" incentive to expand into a monopoly position.

> *Natural oligopoly* occurs when the average costs of individual firms fall over a large enough range so that a few firms can produce the total quantity sold at the lowest average cost.

Comparisons between concentration ratios in Canadian and U.S. manufacturing generally show a higher degree of industrial concentration in Canada. This should not come as a surprise: The Canadian market for most goods and services is less than one-tenth as large as the U.S. market. This smaller market can support fewer firms—especially in industries where firms tend to be relatively large because of cost conditions (economies of scale).

However, it is not just cost conditions that account for the persistence of oligopoly. Oligopoly represents a balance of forces that encourage concentration and those that work against it.

One of the strongest forces working toward larger and larger corporations is the incentive such firms have to acquire market power. The larger a firm becomes by internal growth or by buying out and absorbing its competitors, the greater is its power to set price. (The fewer and smaller its competitors, the fewer sales they will be able to take away if the firm raises its price.) For this reason, a firm in natural oligopoly, with no further opportunities to cut costs by expanding, may nonetheless still seek to expand in order to push competitors out of the market and thus acquire more power to set price.

On the other side, the government provides a countervailing force that deters the expansion of firms, and discourages the monopolization of an industry. Specifically, the government has passed anti-combines laws as a countervailing force. Anti-combines laws prohibit such practices as *predatory pricing*— that is, attempts by large firms to drive a smaller competitor out of business by temporarily charging very low prices. By prohibiting this, the anti-combines law tries to protect the small competitors of large firms, in order to protect consumers against the higher price that large firms might charge if they were to become like monopolists.

Another factor which also works to protect the consumer against monopoly is the threat of competition from imported goods. Even if a large firm establishes a monopoly-like position in the *Canadian* market, it may still face competition from foreign firms, so that it cannot raise its price above the price of comparable imported goods.

The **product differentiation** which exists in many oligopolistic markets also discourages monopolization. A car is not just a car; there are many kinds—it's a differentiated product. For many years, American Motors has been very successful in the production of a special kind of vehicle—a four-wheel-drive jeep. The profits it obtained by its strength in producing this highly differentiated product saved it from bankruptcy, and thus prevented the broader auto industry from becoming even more concentrated. Likewise, product differentiation is important in many other oligopolistic industries. Electrohome Ltd. sells colour televisions which are similar but not identical to RCA's. Beer brewed by Labatt's is not the same as that produced by Molson's (though some people can't tell the difference). However, the product differentiation that is so important in many oligopolistic markets, may not be significant in others. In the basic steel industry, for example, one company's product is much the same as another's.

THE OLIGOPOLIST AS A PRICE SEARCHER

We have seen that oligopoly lies in the broad area between the extreme cases of monopoly and perfect competition. At either of these two extremes, the firm does not have to worry about how its competitors will react if it changes its price or output. By definition, the monopolist has no competitors worth worrying about.

On the other hand, the perfectly competitive firm has so many competitors that none will even be aware of any change it may make in its price or output. Since it provides such a miniscule part of the total market supply, its competitors won't even notice if it reduces the amount it is supplying. In contrast, in an oligopoly, each firm is very much aware of the other firms. Each recognizes that the others will notice any action it takes, and it must therefore be concerned about how they will react. If it reduces price, will its competitors follow? Will its action set off a price war? Where might this lead? In an oligopoly, the firms are mutually *interdependent*; each is very sensitive to the reactions of its competitors.

The three different types of market can be distinguished in a simple way. In perfect competition, firms are **price takers**. The individual firm has no influence over price, since it is determined by the impersonal forces of demand and supply. In monopoly, the firm is a **price maker**. It is able to select a point on the market demand curve, that is, it is able to choose the price at which it will sell. In oligopoly, the firm is a **price searcher**. Although it has some influence over price, it can't set a price in the simple way that a monopolist can. Instead, in its pricing decisions it must take into account a major complication: How will its competitors react?

Because an oligopolistic firm is in competition with several other large firms capable of vigorously responding to its actions, it must develop a marketing strategy. The world of oligopoly can resemble a chess game, with move and countermove. And, like a chess game, the outcome may be unpredictable. Once we enter the world of oligopoly, we leave behind the simple, definite solutions of both monopoly and perfect competition. Ever since Augustin Cournot's nineteenth-century study of duopoly (two sellers), it has been recognized that when there are just a few sellers, the search for an equilibrium price can be quite complex. Oligopoly is one of the least satisfactory areas of economic theory.

For this reason, it is not possible here to do more than emphasize a few highlights. The first topic involves the situation where oligopolists recognize their common interest in raising prices and collude to act as though they were a monopoly. The second topic is the case where oligopolists abandon this common interest in pursuit of their own individual interests and the collusive arrangement comes apart.

Collusion

In both Canada and the United States, collusion is against the law. The reason for such laws may be seen by looking at the economic effects of a **cartel**, the most formal type of collusion, where firms get together to gain the advantages of monopoly.

> A *cartel* is a formal agreement among firms about price and/or market sharing.

As a simple example, consider a market in which there are three similar firms. Suppose that, while maintaining their separate corporate identities with their own plants and sales forces, they get together to agree on a common price. In their collective interest, what is the best price to choose? The answer: the price that

a monopolist would pick; that is, the price that will maximize their combined profits. Specifically, this price is determined in Figure 26-3 as follows. The gray arrows show how the marginal cost curve for the industry in panel (*b*) is derived, as always, from the marginal cost curves of the individual firms. The highest profit in panel (*b*) is earned at an output of 600 units, where the MC curve for the industry cuts the industry's marginal revenue curve MR. (MR may be calculated from the demand curve for the industry, just as it was for the firm in Table 25-1.) Point *E* on the demand curve indicates that, to sell the profit-maximizing output of 600 units, price can be raised all the way up to $100.

Thus, the collusive oligopoly maximizes profits by behaving as if it were a monopoly. However, it faces a problem that the monopolist doesn't have to worry about: How is the restricted production of 600 units divided among the three firms? The simplest solution

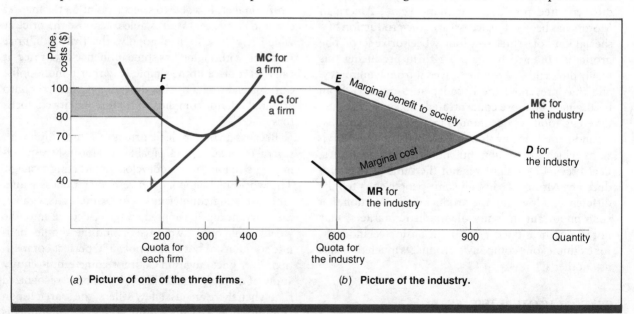

(a) **Picture of one of the three firms.**   (b) **Picture of the industry.**

Figure 26-3 Collusion by three oligopolists.
In panel (*b*), MC for the industry is shown as the horizontal sum of the MC curves for the three individual firms on the left, and MR for the industry is calculated from the industry's demand *D*. The maximization of industry profit requires that output be set at 600 units (where the industry's MC = MR) and that price be set at $100. In other words, the colluding firms select point *E* on the market demand curve. Each firm is then allowed a quota of 200 units of output in

panel (*a*) where it earns the gray profit area. The problem is that the individual firm facing the given $100 price would prefer to sell more than its 200-unit quota. (It can sell an additional unit for $100, while its cost of producing it is only $40.) If it does so, more than 600 units will be produced, and the industry's price in panel (*b*) will begin to fall. If firms thus forget their *collective* interest in favour of pursuing their *individual* interest, the price-fixing arrangement comes apart.

is to set a quota of 200 units for each, as shown in panel (*a*). Each firm sells at point *F*, where it makes a profit of $4,000, illustrated by the gray area; that is, it sells 200 units at a profit of $20 each. (The $20 profit is the difference between the $100 selling price and the $80 average cost.)

While this collusive arrangement benefits the three firms, it is harmful to the economy as a whole. Just as in the case of monopoly, too little is produced, as we see in panel (*b*). For an efficient allocation of resources, output should not be at 600 units. Instead it should be at 900, where marginal cost equals the marginal benefit to society; that is, where the marginal cost curve intersects the demand curve. The efficiency loss from collusion is shown by the red triangle—another example of the triangular loss from producing too little, first explained in panel (*b*) of Figure 25-6. In a cartel, just as in a monopoly, Adam Smith's "invisible hand" fails, as Smith himself recognized in the quote at the beginning of this chapter.

There are a number of ways that participants in a cartel can agree to limit sales. The market may be divided equally among all members of the cartel, as in the example here. Another way to divide the market is to use historical market shares—or, even more simply, geographical areas. For example, two European firms agreed in the 1920s to carve up the market for explosives. Dynamite was allowed exclusive rights in certain continental European markets, in exchange for leaving British Empire markets to Nobel, a firm established by a Swedish industrialist who later donated the funds from which the annual Nobel prizes are awarded.

Another form of collusion is a *bidding cartel*. For example, in isolated cases, some antique dealers in Britain have met together before the auction of a valuable item to set the price at which all of them but one would drop out of the bidding. This meant that their designated member who was left in the bidding was able to buy the antique for a bargain price at the expense of the seller. Why were the other dealers prepared to stop bidding at a low price? The answer: They knew that they would get their turn to make a bargain purchase.

The Breakdown of Collusion: The Incentive to Cheat

Market-sharing arrangements tend to be unstable, whether the firms have agreed on equal shares or not. Each firm in the cartel has an *incentive to cheat* by producing more than its alloted share.[1] To see why, note in panel (*a*) of Figure 26-3 that an individual firm producing 200 units of output could produce another unit at a marginal cost of only $40. If it could sell it for the going price of $100 by stealing away a sale from one of its competitors, the firm's profit will increase by $60. Thus, it has an incentive to step up sales efforts, or give secret price rebates in order to win customers. (Even if a firm grants a 30%, 40%, or 50% rebate on the selling price of $100, it will still receive more from this sale than its marginal cost.) Thus, the cartel's problem is this. The members have a *collective* interest in restricting sales in order to keep the price up. However, each member firm has an *individual* interest in selling more than its allotted share. If individual interests come to dominate, with firms producing beyond their quotas, industry output in panel (*b*) will increase beyond 600 units, and there will be a move down the demand curve to a lower price. In other words, a struggle by firms to increase their market share will lead to a price war that destroys the cartel. Because of the strength of the individual interest, cartels have often collapsed after short and stormy histories.

Moreover, when there is a complete breakdown in a cartel, the struggle over markets may intensify. This is particularly true if the cost advantages of large-scale production have been increasing as a result of technological change. In this case, a natural oligopoly may be evolving into a natural monopoly. In the absence of government intervention, only one firm will ultimately survive. The question is, which one? Each firm wants to be the victor; each has an incentive to try to gain an advantage over its rivals by expanding rapidly to gain the lower costs from large-scale production. Excess production is likely, with firms pushing frantically for sales. The result may be ***cut-throat competition***; that is, selling at a price below cost in order to drive rivals out of business. In this struggle, the prize sometimes goes to the firm with the "deepest pockets" (the largest financial resources), which enable it to sustain the short-term losses while it is cutting the throats of its rivals.

---

[1] It is "cheating" as viewed by the other members of the cartel, but not as viewed by the public. More production will lower price and reduce the red efficiency-loss triangle.

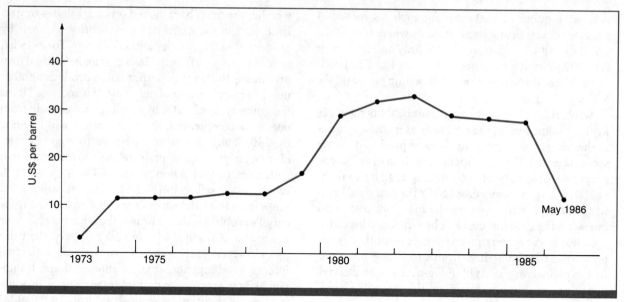

Figure 26-4 How OPEC raised the world oil price.
There have been two periods of very rapid increases in the world price of oil: 1973–74 and
1979–80. But in between, the oil price rose by less than the rate of inflation. (OPEC's real income per barrel of oil declined.) In early 1986, the price fell dramatically.

Sources: 1793–85: International Monetary Fund, *International Financial Statistics*, various issues; May
1986: *Oilweek*, 12 May 1986.

A CASE STUDY OF COLLUSION: OIL

The most conspicuous collusive arrangement of recent
decades has been the Organization of Petroleum Exporting Countries (OPEC), made up of many major
oil exporters, including a number of Middle Eastern
nations, along with Indonesia, Nigeria, and Venezuela.
The prime objective of OPEC was to raise the price of
oil, and in less than a decade—between 1973 and
1982—that price rose from less than $3 a barrel to
$34, as shown in Figure 26-4. The result was far and
away the greatest peacetime transfer of wealth among
nations in history. Why was OPEC this successful in
the 1970s? And why did it seem to be losing control
as the price of oil fell dramatically in the mid-1980s?

OPEC's success in 1973–74 was particularly surprising because a number of experts thought it would
fail. However, in those early days, OPEC had one
great strength: Oil buyers had to deal with its members,
since they were by far the largest international source
of oil, as Figure 26-5 illustrates. In particular, note the
pre-eminent position held by Saudi Arabia. Because of

their position as the dominant suppliers of internationally traded oil, OPEC leaders were able to meet from
time to time to decide on the price that they would
charge—the world price of oil.

However, OPEC had an apparent weakness: While
it was raising the price, it had no effective system of
production quotas to restrict its output and supply.
How then was it able to make its high prices stick?
There were several special reasons; one of the most
important is described in the next section, while the
others are discussed in Box 26-2.

The Rising Price in the 1970s:
The Key Role of the Saudis
Although the OPEC countries collectively had no effective way of controlling production, one OPEC member—Saudi Arabia, the largest producer for the world
market—had such enormous sales that during the early
years of OPEC success, it was able to keep the oil
price up. Specifically, whenever it appeared that a price-
depressing glut (overproduction) was developing on
the world oil market, Saudi Arabia would cut back its

own production. This maintained the world oil short-age that kept the price from falling. Thus OPEC was able to maintain a high price during the 1970s without enforcing production quotas.

Saudi Arabia was willing and able to cut back its production of oil because of its very special circumstances. With its small population, it had accumulated huge assets from past oil sales. Therefore, unlike some of the heavily populated OPEC countries such as Nigeria, Saudi Arabia wasn't desperate to raise money by large-scale oil production; it could comfortably "keep its black gold in the ground." To illustrate, by early 1975, Saudi production was little more than half of capacity, and it was this restricted production that helped make the rapid price increase of 1973–74 stick. Thus, Saudi Arabia stood ready to cut back its sales by whatever amount was necessary to allow other OPEC members to sell about what they wanted, at the going price. This reduced the incentive for other OPEC members to cut price.

The Saudis stabilized price not only by keeping it up, but also by keeping it down; or, more precisely, by keeping it from rising even farther and even faster during periods of strong demand. Why did the Saudis want to do this? One reason was that they recognized that a high price of oil would encourage countries such as the United States to develop substitute forms of energy, and this would weaken the future demand for Saudi oil. The future has always been a greater concern for Saudi Arabia, with its very large oil reserves, than it has been for some of the other OPEC countries with smaller reserves but large populations, and therefore heavy immediate financial requirements.

How did Saudi Arabia keep the price from rising even faster than it did? The answer is that, on some occasions, the Saudis threatened to increase their sales; and on other occasions, they actually did increase them. Thus, for example, the Saudis threatened to sell more in 1977. And in 1979–80 they actually did, in an attempt to offset the upward price pressures caused by

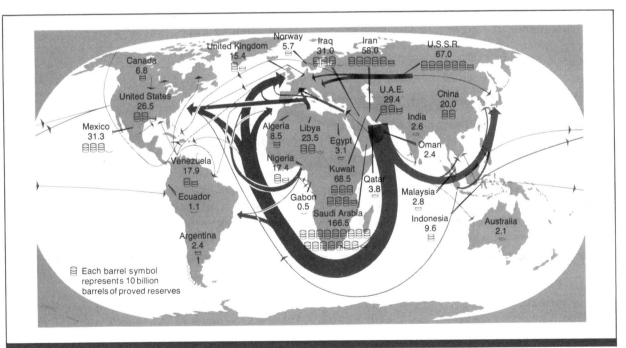

Figure 26-5 If you wanted to buy oil on the international market in the 1970s, OPEC was the place to go.
This map illustrates how important the OPEC countries were in determining the supply of oil *on the international market*. The width of arrows indicates the volume of international flows of oil in 1978. (This figure shows only inter-national flows, and does not include domestic flows. Two of the largest domestic flows were from producers to users within the United States, and within the U.S.S.R.)

Source: Energy Information Agency, U.S. Department of Energy, *Annual Report to Congress*, 1979, vol. 2, pp. 37, 72.

BOX 26-2

WHY OPEC WAS INITIALLY ABLE TO RAISE PRICE WITHOUT EFFECTIVE PRODUCTION QUOTAS

When everything went wrong in the 1980s it was a severe shock for OPEC, because in the 1970s everything had gone right. There were several reasons for OPEC's good fortune in those early days.

1. International oil companies such as Exxon and Royal Dutch Shell were very concerned about the future scarcity of oil. Therefore, in order to ensure their own future oil supplies, they made a major effort to maintain good relations with OPEC members. In particular, they were hesitant to encourage price cutting by switching away from a country with a high price to one with a somewhat lower price (although they did this to some degree).

Furthermore, the major oil companies had no strong incentive to encourage price cutting and a break-up of OPEC since their profits soared as a result of higher oil prices. At the same time that the OPEC countries were getting a price increase on the oil they were producing in the Middle East, the oil companies were getting a price increase on the oil they were producing in their existing wells in Canada, the United States, and elsewhere.

2. Oil demand was inelastic in the short run; that is, it was insensitive to price. It is true that, in the long run, oil demand *is* sensitive to price; for example, the high oil price has led to the development of fuel-efficient cars and thereby reduced the

quantity demanded. However, in the early 1970s, there wasn't yet time for such long-run adjustments. This meant that OPEC could raise price without a large short-run reduction in the quantity demanded; thus, its total revenues increased sharply when its price was raised. Because of the huge increases in their revenues, the members of OPEC had relatively little temptation to "rock the boat" by squabbling over market shares.

There were several reasons why the short-run demand for OPEC oil was inelastic. For many users, oil and gasoline were necessities. Factories were willing, if necessary, to pay a much higher price for oil, rather than shut down. The person who had to drive to work continued to buy gasoline, even when its price rose sharply.

Another reason why the demand for OPEC oil was insensitive to price was that in countries such as Canada and the United States, governments kept the price of oil from rising as fast as the world price quoted by OPEC. Therefore oil buyers faced less "price shock." It was no surprise that they responded less strongly, in terms of cutting back their consumption of oil. In other words, because of the governments' price controls, it seemed—at least from OPEC's point of view—that North Americans were willing to keep on buying oil without being sensitive to the price OPEC was charging. So why shouldn't OPEC raise price further? (In the 1980s, as the U.S. and Canadian governments allowed the domestic price of oil to rise toward the world price, consumers *did* face the full price shock, and there were greater conservation efforts. As a result, OPEC could no longer sell the same large quantities of oil to North America at the previous high price; this

speculative buyers who feared that the Iranian revolution might make oil scarce in the future. However, this Saudi action wasn't enough, and the price more than doubled in 1979–80.

To sum up so far: During the seventies, OPEC was a cartel in the sense that its members fixed price. But it was not a cartel in the sense of fixing and enforcing formal production quotas to limit the sales of each member country. Instead, the price was maintained by the leadership of Saudi Arabia, which, as the domi-

nant supplier, was prepared to adjust its own sales. For this reason, some experts view OPEC in the seventies less as a traditional cartel than as a market characterized by Saudi leadership.

The Falling Price in the 1980s: The Attempt to Enforce Production Quotas
By the early 1980s, however, there was strong downward pressure on the price OPEC could charge, because

was one of the reasons the world price fell.)

3. Not only was the short-run elasticity of demand for oil low. In addition, during the critical 1973 period when OPEC began its rapid price increases, the demand curve for oil was shifting out rapidly because of the boom conditions that existed then. Accordingly, when OPEC began hiking the price, demand was both inelastic and growing. (In the early 1980s, in contrast, oil demand was sluggish because economic growth was slowing.)

4. At the same time, the quantity of oil sold by OPEC was curtailed for non-economic reasons. Because of the Arab embargo on sales to the United States and other countries supporting Israel in the 1973 Yom Kippur War, OPEC's oil exports fell by about 25%. This "political" restriction in supply helped to make the price increase stick in 1973.

Courtesy Miller Services Limited

demand for OPEC oil was falling. There were several reasons:

1. The deep international recession of 1981–82 reduced the demand for oil.
2. Substitute supplies of energy, whose production was stimulated by the high price of oil, came on the market in substantial volume. These substitutes included coal and natural gas. The production of nuclear power also rose significantly in some countries, such as France.
3. Conservation efforts, also stimulated by the high oil price of the seventies, began to have substantial effects by the early 1980s. For example, aging gas-guzzlers were replaced on the road by smaller cars, and fuel-efficient equipment was introduced in industrial plants.
4. The process of conservation was accelerated by the removal of U.S. price controls on oil and gasoline. This decontrol meant that Americans had to pay the high world price of oil, and they

responded by buying less. In Canada, prices were also allowed to rise gradually toward the world price. As a result, oil use in North America grew less rapidly than before.

5. North Americans, Europeans, and other oil importers not only used less oil. The oil they did import increasingly came from new, non-OPEC sources, such as Mexico and the North Sea; it was less risky to buy from these sources than the war-torn Persian Gulf. Moreover, these non-OPEC countries were frequently willing to sell at a price below that of OPEC. Thus, the Persian Gulf tended to become the residual source of supply. North American purchases of Persian Gulf oil fell about 75% between January 1981 and May 1983. Although Japanese purchases remained relatively strong, the massive flow of oil out of the Persian Gulf shown in Figure 26-5 had fallen by about 50%. By 1985, more oil was being pumped out of the North Sea than Saudi Arabia, and OPEC's sales had fallen from two-thirds of world-traded oil to one-third.

In the face of falling sales, each OPEC member came under increasing pressure to cut its price to prevent its sales from falling further. For example, Iran and Iraq were desperate for funds to finance their war; they couldn't afford to lose oil sales. Even the Saudis felt that they had to keep their sales from falling even more, because the cost of their rapidly increasing imports was outrunning their oil revenues. Besides, they had already cut their production to the bone. By 1985, the Saudis were producing at a rate substantially less than one-third of their capacity. Therefore, OPEC's problem of overproduction and price cutting could no longer be solved by a large reduction in Saudi output. Even if the Saudis had reduced their output to *zero*, the other OPEC countries—along with non-OPEC suppliers— would still have been able to over-supply the world market.

In these circumstances, one, or both, of two things had to happen: (1) the world price of oil had to fall; or (2) OPEC had to convert itself into a *bona fide* cartel by enforcing effective production quotas on its members. In the early 1980s this was the key question: Could OPEC, a loose price-fixing organization that had prospered in the 1970s when market demand was moving in its favour, now turn itself into a disciplined price- and output-fixing cartel as market pressures turned against it?

The set of new OPEC quotas introduced in March 1982 was not very successful. There was widespread cheating; Iran and Libya simply disregarded their quotas. With OPEC unable to control supply, competitive price cutting began. In less than a year, the world price of oil fell from U.S.$34 to less than $30. Then there followed a series of meetings in which new agreements were reached, only to be broken. By 1985, the Saudis' output was so far reduced that they were no longer willing to act in this way to support price. In order to recapture a larger share of the market, they increased production. In the face of this increased supply, the price of oil fell rapidly in early 1986 to about U.S.$10 a barrel, and it seemed unlikely that the oil-exporting countries would be able to piece together another pricing agreement in the near future.

OPEC's history in the 1980s made it a classic case study in the two problems that make it so difficult to hold a cartel together: (1) How can the cartel keep individual members from producing more than their quota? and (2) How can the cartel prevent outside producers—in this case, producers such as those in the North Sea and Mexico—from entering the industry and destroying the production restraint on which the high price depends?

PRICING BY CANADIAN OLIGOPOLIES

We have seen that one of the ways oligopolists can try to avoid price wars is to form a cartel and agree formally on price and market shares; we have also seen how difficult this is to enforce. In Canada, the United States, and many other countries, there is an additional problem: Collusion is illegal. How, then, do oligopolists reduce the pressure of price competition? How do they avoid price wars and arrive at a reasonably profitable price?

One explanation is that each firm faces a "kinked demand curve." Although this concept is controversial, it provides important insights into how each oligopolist must take the others' responses into account.

The Kinked Demand Curve

The best way to understand this idea is to put yourself in the position of one of the three large oligopolists in an industry. The demand you face will have a kink, if your competitors behave in the following way:

1. If you cut your price, the firms competing with you take your act as a challenge. They will not

want you to take customers away from them, and therefore they will meet your price cut with a price cut of their own.

2. On the other hand, if you raise price, your competitors consider this a golden opportunity. By keeping their own selling price stable, they will be able to capture a share of your sales.

In short, your competitors behave in a non-symmetric way: If you drop your price they will follow you, but if you raise your price they will not.

Figure 26-6 shows how this behaviour leads to a kinked demand curve and to price stability. This figure illustrates an industry with three firms of similar size. Each initially has one-third of total sales, with point E_1 showing your initial price and sales. If you change price and *if* your competitors follow, you may

expect to retain your present one-third of the market. Thus you will move along the relatively steep demand curve labelled d_F. (Note that at any price, say P_2, the quantity you sell on d_F is one-third of the total sales shown on the market demand curve D.)

However, d_F is relevant only if you quote a price *below* the existing price at E_1. If you quote a price *above* this—say P_3—your competitors will *not* follow. Instead, they will stand pat. Because you will now be quoting a higher price than they are, you will lose part of your market to them, as shown by the red arrow.

Therefore, if you drop your price below E_1, you face demand d_F, while if you raise your price above E_1, you face demand d_N. In other words, the behaviour of your competitors presents you with the **kinked demand curve** shown by the heavy lines.

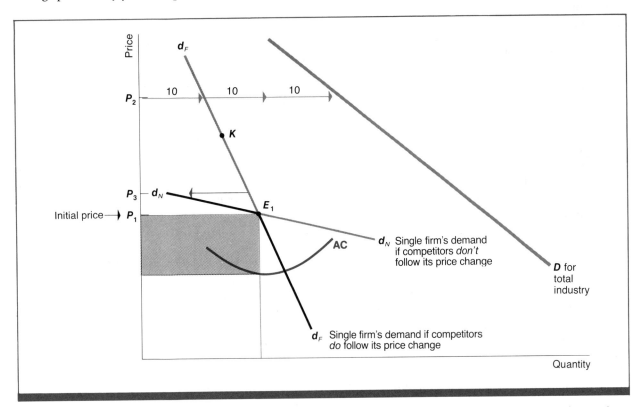

Figure 26-6 A kinked demand curve.

Suppose that you have two equally large competitors, and your initial position is at E_1. If your competitors were to follow any price change you might make, you would face demand curve d_F. Regardless of the price you might quote, you would retain one-third of the market. (For example, if you were to quote price P_2, you would sell 10 units.) Unfortunately, you do not face d_F throughout its entire range,

because your competitors will only follow you if you reduce price. Thus, the only portion of d_F that is relevant is the heavily lined section below E_1. If you raise price, your competitors will not follow, and you will face demand curve d_N. (Since they don't raise their prices, your competitors will cut into your share of the market, as shown by the red arrow.) In short, if your competitors follow your price change down but not up, you will face the heavy, kinked demand curve.

The *kinked demand curve* shown by the heavy lines in Figure 26-6 is the demand the oligopolistic firm faces if its competitors follow its price down but not up.

Faced with this demand curve, how do you maximize profit? The likely answer: Select point E_1 where the kink occurs. Thus, you don't rock the boat. You continue to quote the price P_1 that you and your competitors have been quoting, and you retain your safe, traditional share of the market. Your profit is shown as the shaded rectangle. (Experiment with other points on the kinked demand curve above and below E_1; note that in each case the resulting profit rectangle is less. Moreover, also shift your cost curve AC up or down a bit, and notice that E_1 remains your profit-maximizing point. Thus you tend to keep your price stable at P_1 even if your costs change.)

The idea of a kinked demand curve was first developed in the 1930s, and it has had continuing appeal as a way of explaining why oligopoly prices are stable, and, in particular, why they often remain firm during recessions when demand declines. There are, nevertheless, important exceptions. In 1974, 1980, and 1982, some auto manufacturers offered rebates—in effect, price reductions—in order to increase their lagging sales.

The theory of the kinked demand curve is controversial. In the first place, it is incomplete. While it may explain price stability, it does not explain how price is established in the first place. For example, in Figure 26-6, price remains at P_1 because it started out at P_1 and that is where the kink occurs. But how did price get to be P_1 in the first place? It has no explanation, like the "smile without the cat" in *Alice in Wonderland*. The second difficulty is that prices are not nearly as rigid as the theory suggests. As already noted, automobile prices have occasionally fallen. And they have frequently risen. The same is true of steel prices. Over the years, the prices of computers have been cut many times, leaving them at a small fraction of their earlier level.

Thus, the theory of the kinked demand curve explains too much; it explains something (price stability) that frequently does not exist. Rather than try to explain why oligopoly prices are stable—when often they are not—it makes more sense to ask why oligopoly prices

change in a reasonably orderly way. One answer is provided by the theory of *price leadership*.

Price Leadership

Where collusion is illegal, the simplest way for firms to achieve an orderly change in price is for one firm to take the initiative with the others following.

To illustrate this price leadership concept in Figure 26-6, suppose that you are the price leader, in the sense that you know you can quote a different price and your competitors will follow you. Then the demand curve you face is no longer kinked. Instead, *it is the line d_F throughout its entire length*, because your competitors will follow your price change either down *or* up. In these circumstances, you will be able to lead the industry up to a new, higher price at a point like K, provided you are correct and the other firms will indeed follow your lead.

If your leadership is thus assured, the result may approach that of a cartel. As leader, you will have selected the price at point K that will maximize your own profits. Moreover, this price should be approximately the one that will maximize profits for the industry as a whole; this is why the other firms may be willing to accept your leadership. The outcome at K is the same monopoly-like solution that would result from collusion. Therefore, although collusion does not formally exist, the result may be the same: Firms arrive at the collusive profit-maximizing price, not by illegally agreeing on it beforehand, but simply by following the leader. This is sometimes called "tacit collusion."

However, because there is no formal agreement, your leadership may not be assured after all; the problem of "cheating" may be substantial. The leader may find others shaving prices (or providing rebates) in order to increase their market shares. A good example of this problem was provided by the market for electric light bulbs during the 1950s. Canadian General Electric, with 45% of the market, acted as a price leader. But other firms, while claiming that they were following the lead of CGE, tried to increase their market shares by giving discounts to specific customer groups, or to buyers of large quantities of bulbs. (In the end, a formal agreement was struck among the three larger companies to end price competition. But because such an agreement was illegal, the firms were convicted in 1976 of price fixing, following a long trial.)

Sometimes, the best strategy for the price leader is to ignore price cutting by smaller firms: The alternative for the leader is to retaliate, but this may provoke industry-wide price cutting, leaving all firms, including the largest one, with lower profits. But if the small firms are allowed to do this, the market share of the price leader may be eroded. An example from the United States was giant U.S. Steel which sometimes acted as a price leader, but did not always react to under-the-table price cuts by smaller firms. Consequently, these smaller firms were able to take advantage of U.S. Steel's price umbrella to cut into its markets. In 1910, U.S. Steel held almost half the market, but by the 1950s, its share had fallen to about one-third. Similarly, in the Canadian cement industry, Canada Cement Ltd. held as much as 80% of the market at the end of World War II, and acted as the undisputed price leader in this industry. But because it was the price leader, it did not compete aggressively by reducing prices when other firms expanded their market shares. Therefore, in a ten-year span after the war, its market share fell to less than 50%. Thus, while the giant in an industry may have a decided advantage from lower costs, the smaller firms may also have a major advantage: They may be able to compete aggressively without provoking competitive responses from the giant.

In practice, it may be quite difficult to identify any clear pattern of price leadership. There may be no consistent price leader; first one company may take the initiative in changing prices, then another. General Motors does not always announce its new model prices first; the initiative is sometimes exercised by Ford. Furthermore, price leadership may be quite tentative. One firm may announce a price increase to see if others follow. If they don't, the price change may be rescinded. This sort of "trial and error" pricing may just be a way for the firm to test whether or not it can in fact act as a price leader.

Firms in an oligopolistic industry may sometimes also end up quoting the same price even though there is no price leadership. For example, many Canadian oligopolies face competition from imports. This may make it easier for firms to guess at the price that other firms will set, and hence quote the same price. All of

them are likely to set a price below—but not too far below—the price of imports. In such an industry, the Canadian price of the good will rise when the foreign price increases, or when the cost of imports is raised by other factors such as a depreciation of the Canadian dollar, or an increase in the customs duty charged by the government on imports of the good.

Finally, even when oligopolists follow a pattern of price leadership, we cannot be certain that they are exerting monopoly power. If costs have generally risen by, say, 10%, an oligopolist may raise price by about 10% in the expectation that others will follow. Price leadership has apparently occurred; yet the firms may merely be defending themselves against rising costs, rather than exploiting monopoly power at the expense of the public.

There are many ways in which oligopoly price may be set, with no single pattern followed in all cases. For a sample of several other patterns of oligopoly price determination, see Box 26-3.

NON-PRICE COMPETITION

Price is not the only way in which oligopolistic firms compete; they also compete, for example, by advertising and by attempting to provide a better product. These ways of competing are often preferred to price competition because they don't risk setting off a price war in which all participants lose.

Advertising

The firm that advertises has a simple objective: to make people want its product and buy more. That does not mean, however, that the more advertising the better. Since advertising must be paid for, it also makes the cost curve shift up. At some point, the firm will find that enough advertising is enough; any further advertising would involve a cost that can no longer be justified by increased sales.

In an oligopoly, the primary goal of advertising is often to capture the competitor's market. Thus, for example, the primary objective of Labatt's advertising is to take sales away from Molson's and other brewers. For its part, Molson's advertises to take sales away from Labatt's.

Advertising also increases the total market demand for the product. A monopoly firm will sometimes advertise, not to take sales away from competitors (since it has none), but instead to increase the demand for its product. For example, Bell Canada advertises to increase the demand for long-distance calls. Some associations of perfect competitors also advertise to increase total market demand, even though no single producer would find it profitable to do so. For example, the Ontario Egg Marketing Board advertises to encourage people to eat more eggs. However, the most heavily advertised products lie in the battleground between

---

BOX 26-3

THE DETERMINATION OF OLIGOPOLY PRICE

In this box, we consider several other ways in which oligopoly price may be determined. For the first, we return to Figure 26-6 to see how a different assumption about competitors' reaction will lead to a different price.

1. Nash Equilibrium

In Figure 26-6, we have seen that being a price leader means facing demand curve d_F throughout its entire length. Such a firm is fortunate; any change in its price will lead to the same change in price by all its competitors. Therefore the firm is able to raise its price above the "kinked value" P_1.

Now suppose, at the other extreme, that the firm assumes that none of its competitors will react at all to any price change it makes, in either direction. Such a firm will face demand curve d_N throughout its entire length, with the subscript N meaning "No response by competitors." If a firm is initially facing the kinked demand curve and producing at point E_1, and now finds itself facing demand curve d_N through its entire length, the firm will maximize its profits by moving from E_1 down d_N to the southeast. That is, the firm will increase its output and reduce its price.*

If all firms make the same assumption that competitors won't react, then they will all behave in the same way; they will all reduce their price and increase their quantity. The new **Nash equilibrium** will be to the southeast of E_1.

> A *Nash equilibrium* is the equilibrium that results when each firm assumes that none of its competitors will react to any change it makes.

In fact, the Nash equilibrium is a more complicated concept than this single example suggests, with possible applications beyond an analysis of oligopoly. In its application to oligopoly, it has been criticized because it is often unrealistic for a firm with only a few competitors to assume that they will ignore a change in its policy. For example, if Zenith lowers the price of TV sets, is it reasonable to assume that RCA won't respond? If Atari offers a discount on its home computers, won't Commodore be under pressure to follow?

2. Conjectural Variation

A broader approach to the problem of oligopolistic pricing is to assume that a firm's decisions are based on *conjectural variation*. The firm makes an assumption (a conjecture) as to how its competitors will respond. One example is the firm with the kinked demand curve in Figure 26-6; it conjectures that its competitors will follow its price change down, but not up. Another example is the price leader that assumes its competitors will follow its price change in either direction. Still another is the firm we've just described that moves to a Nash equilibrium.

The problem, of course, is that there is a whole

---

*Why will it move in this direction? To answer this, note that we are considering a firm that selected point E_1 when it faced the kinked demand curve. But now it is facing d_N; that is, it can move to a point anywhere on d_N. To maximize its profit, which way will it move? It won't move to the left; it could have done that when it faced the kinked demand curve, and it chose not to do so. Therefore it will move to the right. (If E_1—the firm's profit-maximizing point when it faced the kinked demand curve—also happens to be its profit-maximizing point when it faces d_N, the firm won't move at all. However, this is a very special case.)

perfect competition and monopoly, where a firm like General Motors may benefit from advertising both because it increases the total demand for automobiles and, more particularly, because it takes sales away from its rivals.

There is some controversy over the social value of advertising. On behalf of their industry, advertising agencies make the following points:

1. Advertising helps the consumer to make better decisions. It informs the public of new products

---

whole multitude of such conjectures. Another example would be a firm that assumes that half of its competitors will follow it down, but none will follow it up. (You can sketch this case in Figure 26-6. The firm's demand curve is d_N down to point E_1, and thereafter a demand curve lying midway between d_N and d_F.) In short, the concept of conjectural variation is useful, but *only if* the firm can make a reasonable and specific assumption about its competitors' reactions.

3. Focal-Point Pricing

Harvard University's Thomas Schelling gives the following non-economic example to illustrate how independent firms may end up quoting the same price even though there is no price leadership, nor any collusion, nor even a pre-existing price:

> You are to meet someone in New York City. You have not been instructed where to meet; you have no prior understanding with the person on where to meet; and you cannot communicate with each other. You are simply told that you will have to guess where to meet and he is being told the same thing and that you will just have to try to make your guesses coincide. You are told the date but not the hour of this meeting; the two of you must guess the exact minute of the date for meeting. At what time will you appear at the chosen meeting place?†

Of the thousands of possible choices, Schelling discovered that most people selected the information booth at Grand Central Station, at high noon. Both are "focal points" because they provide the best guess of what the other person will do. So, too, with price: A retailer who wants to guess the price

that competitors will charge for a new product in the range of, say, $11.20 to $12.40, may well select the focal point $11.98. This price is based on the familiar tradition of "charging $12 but making it seem like $11." Thus, without any communication whatsoever between firms, this focal point of $11.98 becomes the industry price.

4. Cost-plus Pricing

With cost-plus pricing, a firm determines its price by adding a specified mark-up of, say, 20% to its average cost. Economists have been uncomfortable with this concept because it raises a couple of nagging questions: Why does the firm pick 20%, rather than some other figure? How does the firm know its average cost without first knowing its output? (In Figure 26-6, observe how the firm's average cost AC changes as its output increases.) In practice, firms that use this approach may solve this problem by arbitrarily specifying a target output of, say, 80% of capacity; then at this specified output level, their average cost is determined by the height of the AC curve. Finally, by adding on their fixed percentage mark-up, they arrive at a price.

This approach presumes that a firm pricing this way will be able to sell roughly its target quantity, using the target mark-up. However, if it is under pressure from price-cutting competitors, it may have little hope of doing so. To prevent its sales from falling substantially, it may have to reduce its mark-up. Although such a firm may view itself as engaged in fixed-mark-up (cost-plus) pricing, it's not doing this at all. Instead, it is adjusting its price in response to market pressures like any other profit-maximizing firm. Its percentage mark-up isn't fixed at all.

---

†Thomas C. Schelling, *The Strategy of Conflict* (Cambridge Mass.: Harvard University Press, 1960), p. 56.

and of improvements in old ones. By informing consumers of what is available, it reduces search costs. For example, advertising may tell consumers where the bargains are, so they can save time and effort in shopping.

2. Advertising helps new producers to compete. By informing the public of a new product, it helps the producer to expand sales toward a high-volume, low-cost level.

3. Advertising stimulates research. If new products could not be advertised and sold in huge quantities, the cost of their research and development could not be covered.

4. Advertising supports the communications industry. Radio and TV are financed by advertising revenues. If we didn't pay for our entertainment this way, we would have to pay for it in some other way. Even the mundane classified ads play a significant role in the support of newspapers.

5. Advertising results in higher-quality products: The goodwill built up from past advertising of a brand may be an asset of great value for a firm—an asset it will be careful not to damage by turning out a shoddy product.

On the other side, critics respond:

1. Most advertising represents a waste. The heaviest advertising takes place in oligopolistic markets where firm A's major motive is to steal customers from firm B, and B advertises to cancel out the effects of A's advertising. After advertising, A and B share the market in roughly the same way as before. Little has changed, except that costs have gone up. Consumers pay more for this product merely because it is advertised. (Firms can't opt out of this wasteful game, because then they *would* lose market share to competitors.)

2. Where advertising is not a self-cancelling waste, it is often pernicious, creating frivolous wants, distorting tastes, and increasing the materialism of a materialistic society. Advertising of products such as liquor and cigarettes has drawn especially sharp criticism, and regulations have been passed to limit it, particularly in radio and television. (Canadian cigarette manufacturers have in fact voluntarily agreed among themselves to stop all radio and TV advertising of cigarettes, partly to avert this type of criticism.)

3. Advertising often misinforms, and leads to lower-quality products. This occurs, for example, if firms are able to sell inferior products by falsely implying in their advertising that they are better. In this case, the cost of advertising includes both the waste in resources that go into making this claim *and* the cost to the public because it gets an inferior product.

4. Much advertising is offensive. We cannot listen to radio or TV without being bombarded with tasteless ads. Worse yet, advertising may lead to distorted news coverage. It may be difficult for a newspaper to provide a balanced treatment of a labour dispute if it is getting a great deal of advertising revenue from the firms involved, but none from the labour union. (However, if a lot of workers buy the paper, the pressures may even out.)

Since it is difficult to compare these conflicting claims, our conclusion is that the statement that advertising involves "*all* loss" is too extreme, and so is the statement that advertising involves "*no* loss whatsoever." What do you think?

Other Ways in Which Firms Compete

In addition to advertising, there are other forms of non-price competition. A firm can hire a larger sales staff in order to beat the bushes for customers. Or it can spend more on research, development, or design to improve the quality or attractiveness of its product. The typical oligopoly, such as an auto or appliance company, is locked in a struggle to match its competitors' price, advertising, sales force, and improvements in design and quality. Little wonder that the world of the oligopolist seems more competitive than that of the farmer, who may operate in a "perfectly competitive" market, but who never even thinks of a neighbour as a competitor. (But remember: According to the economist's definition, farming is the more competitive industry, since a single farmer has no influence whatsoever over price.)

BARRIERS TO ENTRY

Non-price competition often creates barriers to entry. For example, if several large oligopolistic firms such as the auto companies have been competing in the past by making huge expenditures on advertising, it may be almost impossible for a new firm to break into the industry unless it, too, has vast sums to spend. Existing producers may be associated with widely recognized brand names, either because of past advertising, or because their product has been used for many years. In some countries, the brand name "Kodak" is almost synonymous with "camera," and how do you compete with that?

There are also other barriers to entry. Existing producers may get more favourable treatment from retailers. A new entrant may be caught in a vicious circle: It can't sell unless retailers give it shelf space; but retailers won't give it shelf space until it can prove it can sell. This is a particularly serious problem for the large number of new manufacturers of microcomputers. How do they get their products into the stores, when most stores can comfortably stock no more than eight or ten models? (Sales staffs find it difficult to keep track of the detailed performance of more models.) One option is to sell through their own stores, as Tandy (Radio Shack) does. However, this is very expensive, and the large financing required is itself a barrier to small entrants. (Tandy was already in the retail business, selling CB radios and other electronics before it developed its computers.)

But the single most important barrier to entry is the fact that, in most oligopoly industries, costs fall over a wide range of output. In other words, economies of large-scale production make it very difficult for a small firm to compete. In order to get started, a new firm must have "deep pockets"; it must have the financial resources to set up a productive facility large enough to move it quickly into the high-volume, low-cost range of production. For this reason, new competition in oligopolistic markets often comes, not from struggling new firms, but rather from giants in other industries. For example, Xerox was faced with new competition when IBM, Kodak, and several Japanese firms entered the market for office copiers.

If such barriers to entry are low or non-existent, new firms freely enter. The result is no longer oligopoly (with a few sellers), but instead a quite different market form: monopolistic competition. This is the last type of market we will describe. As we do so, you can compare it with other markets in summary Table 26-1.

Table 26-1
Types of Market Structure

Type of market	Number of producers and type of product	Entry	Influence over price	Advertising	Examples
Monopoly	One producer; product with no close substitute	Difficult or impossible	Substantial (price maker unless price is regulated by government)	Only to increase market demand	Local telephone service
Oligopoly	(a) Few producers; little or no product differentiation	Difficult	Some (price searcher)	Yes, although less than if there is product differentiation, as in case (b)	Steel Aluminum
	(b) Few producers; differentiated product	Difficult	Some (price searcher)	Heavy	Autos Computers Cigarettes
Monopolistic competition	Many producers; differentiated product	Easy	A little	Yes	Retail trade
Perfect competition	Many producers; undifferentiated product	Easy	None (price taker)	None, except perhaps through a marketing board	Some agricultural products

MONOPOLISTIC COMPETITION:
Low Barriers to Entry

If the average cost curve stops falling and starts to rise when the firm is producing only a small fraction of the total sales of the industry, there is no cost advantage in being a giant, and many competitors enter the industry. This situation sounds like perfect competition, but it is not if firms are producing a *differentiated product*. In this case, the result is *monopolistic competition*. Because each firm is selling a somewhat different product, it has some control over price; if it raises its price slightly, it won't lose all its customers. Thus, it does not face the perfect competitor's perfectly horizontal demand curve. Instead, its demand curve slopes downward to the right. But because of the existence of many competitors, its control over price is not great. In other words, the demand curve facing the individual producer is quite elastic, as illustrated in Figure 26-7.

> *Monopolistic competition* exists when there are many sellers of a differentiated product in an industry without barriers to entry. The

demand curve facing the individual competitor is quite elastic, but not completely so; thus, the firm has very limited control over its price.

Even if products are physically identical, they can still be differentiated in other respects. As an example, consider tubes of Crest toothpaste sold in stores in different locations. Although the products are physically the same, the consumer will view the closer store's toothpaste as "better," and will consequently be willing to pay a few cents more for it. Thus, location gives each store some control over its price; it can charge a few cents more and not lose all its customers. However, it doesn't have much control. If it charges a much higher price, buyers will bypass it to go to one of its less expensive, though less convenient, competitors.

Small retail stores in a large metropolitan area are often viewed as monopolistic competitors. They have very little control over price, and don't need to be greatly concerned about the responses of their competitors. However, the three grocery stores in a small village are local oligopolists; each has to consider carefully the responses of its competitors if it cuts prices.

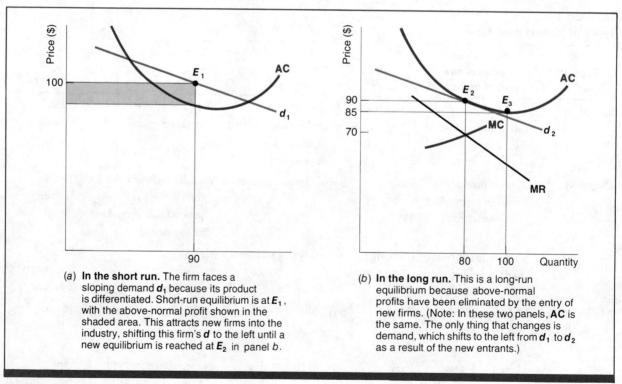

(a) **In the short run.** The firm faces a sloping demand d_1 because its product is differentiated. Short-run equilibrium is at E_1, with the above-normal profit shown in the shaded area. This attracts new firms into the industry, shifting this firm's d to the left until a new equilibrium is reached at E_2 in panel b.

(b) **In the long run.** This is a long-run equilibrium because above-normal profits have been eliminated by the entry of new firms. (Note: In these two panels, **AC** is the same. The only thing that changes is demand, which shifts to the left from d_1 to d_2 as a result of the new entrants.)

Figure 26-7 Equilibrium for a typical firm in monopolistic competition.

Similarly, Woolco and K-Mart are local oligopolists, rather than monopolistic competitors, because each is a significant participant in the local retail market, and each has to give some thought to how the other will respond.

It is relatively easy to get into small-scale retailing; a vast pool of funds is not necessary to buy a single drugstore. Where existing firms are making above-normal profits, new entrants will come in, tending to eliminate these excess profits, as illustrated in Figure 26-7. Initially, the typical firm shown in panel (a) is operating at E_1 and earning a profit shown by the shaded area. But as new competitors enter and capture some of its sales, the demand curve it faces shifts to the left. (It gets a smaller share of the total market.) This process continues until its demand becomes tangent to the average cost curve, as shown in panel (b). Faced with this new demand curve, the best the firm can now do is to select the point of tangency E_2, where it earns no excess profit. (Any other point on the demand curve would leave it operating at a loss.) Thus, free entry tends to eliminate above-normal profits for the run-of-the-mill firm in monopolistic competition.

Observe in panel (b) that monopolistic competition seems to be inefficient. At the firm's output of 80 units, MC ($70) is not equal to price ($90), so there is no reason to expect an efficient allocation of resources. It is often claimed that there is "excess capacity," that is, too many firms in the industry. Consumer demand could be satisfied at lower cost if there were fewer firms, each producing more—that is, if the typical firm in panel (b) were to move from E_2 to E_3, by increasing its output from 80 units to 100, and thus lowering its average cost to the minimum of $85. If the industry were reorganized in this way, wouldn't the result be a more efficient allocation of resources?

The answer is: not necessarily. True, cost would be lower, and this would be an advantage for society. However, there would also be a disadvantage: Since there would be fewer firms, consumers would have less choice. For example, a reduction in the number of retail stores would mean that those remaining could sell a larger volume, thus reducing their costs (and prices). But it would also mean that some customers would have to travel further to shop. Perhaps the convenience of local stores is worth the slightly higher price we have to pay.

In short, if you drive the typical firm down from E_2 to E_3 in Figure 26-7, it would produce at lower cost

and this would be a benefit to society. However, because its output would be increased, the number of firms would be reduced and consumers would get less variety; this would be a loss. On balance, it is not clear that this move would be beneficial. Thus, when a product is differentiated, it becomes difficult to pin down the idea of efficiency as simply as we did with an undifferentiated product (in Box 24-1). As a practical matter, no economist argues that the government should undertake broad regulation of firms operating in monopolistic competition. It is difficult to make a federal case out of the inefficiences—if any—that arise from monopolistic competition.

But this is not true of monopoly or oligopoly. For such markets, the case for government intervention through anti-combines legislation is much stronger, as we explain in the next chapter.

As already noted, Table 26-1 provides a summary of market structures, with perfect competition and monopoly on the two extremes, and monopolistic competition and various forms of oligopoly in the broad spectrum in between. In reviewing this table, an important word of warning is in order.

DON'T JUST COUNT NUMBERS: THE CONCEPT OF CONTESTABLE MARKETS

When one observes an activity in which there is only a single firm, there is a natural tendency to conclude that it is a monopoly, with all the problems that this raises. For example, how much does it restrict output below the efficient quantity? How much is its product overpriced? Should this firm be split up, or should its price be controlled? And so on.

However, even if a firm is technically a monopolist—in the sense that it is the only seller in a particular market— it may not always be able to behave like one by restricting its output and raising price. The reason is that by doing this, the firm runs the risk that it will attract a competitor: That is, another firm may move in to "contest" the market, attracted by the high price. If this threat is strong enough, the fact that there is only a single seller in the market may not give rise to the usual problems of monopoly.

An example of the limited monopoly power of firms that operate in contestable markets was provided when the airline industry was deregulated in the United States some years ago. Many people feared that deregulation of price and entry would lead to substantial price increases on those routes between small and medium-sized cities that were served by only a single airline. With no regulation of ticket prices, the argument went, such an airline would exercise its monopoly power and raise price. After deregulation was implemented, however, it quickly became clear that the ability of an airline to exercise this kind of monopoly power was very limited: If it tried to raise ticket prices, other airlines would start serving these cities. Thus, to stave off potential competition, an airline flying such a route was forced to behave like a competitive firm even though it may have been the single seller in its market. The moral is this. In analysing any market—and in particular, in analysing what appears to be a monopoly—don't just count the number of *actual* sellers. Emphasis must also be placed on freedom of entry; that is, on the number of *potential* new sellers. How *contestable* is the market?

An airline route perhaps provides the best example of a contestable market, because it is so easy to shift planes from one route to another. But other examples might be cited. There may be only two or three contractors building houses in a small town. If they can restrict entry of new competitors in some way—for example, by getting special zoning restrictions or acquiring all the available land—then an oligopoly model with long-run profits may be the best way to describe their behaviour. But if they can't restrict entry and local carpenters can start to build houses, then there may be enough potential competition to keep the two or three existing firms from earning above-normal profits. Similarly, the only carpenter in a village may not be able to charge high prices, because this will simply cause somebody else to take up carpentry. In contrast, people can't simply "take up" medicine; they must go to medical school and be licensed. Thus, the doctor has more market power than the carpenter. Once again, we see the importance of ease of entry. It is *potential* competition that matters.

KEY POINTS

1. Many Canadian markets are oligopolies, dominated by a few firms. In any such market, there is an incentive for firms to collude so that they can act like a monopolist in raising price and restricting output. Such monopoly-like behaviour would lead to an inefficient allocation of resources. One deterrent to such collusive behaviour is the difficulty of establishing and enforcing the production quotas or market sharing that is typically required to maintain a high price. Even more important are the prohibitions against collusion in the Canadian anti-combines law.

2. An important example of a collusive agreement is OPEC, the Organization of Petroleum Exporting Countries. Between 1973 and 1981, OPEC increased the world price of oil by more than 12 times. The result was the greatest peacetime transfer of wealth in history. OPEC was remarkable because for very special reasons it did not enforce formal production quotas during the 1970s when it was raising price. However, during the 1980s, in an attempt to resist downward market pressure on price, it tried to establish an effective quota system. By early 1986, it appeared that this attempt was a failure, as oil prices fell dramatically.

3. While anti-combines laws prohibit firms from engaging in overt collusion that restricts competition, there are forms of tacit collusion—such as price leadership—that are difficult to prosecute, but that may allow oligopolists to exercise some degree of monopoly-like power.

4. Oligopolists often prefer to compete in ways other than cutting price. They may try to capture sales from rivals by extensive advertising campaigns, or by expenditures on research to develop better products.

5. When there are no barriers to entry—such as patents or economies of large-scale production—and many small firms enter an industry, the result is monopolistic competition. This is similar to perfect competition except that each firm is selling a differentiated product. For this reason, each firm has some small control over price: It faces a slightly sloping demand curve rather than

the completely flat demand facing a perfect competitor. Because of free entry, above-normal profits for the run-of-the-mill firm tend to disappear in the long run.

6. Price *could* be reduced below the level that occurs in monopolistic competition, but only at the cost of providing consumers with less choice.

Therefore, little case can be made for government regulation.

7. In analysing any market, counting the number of competitors is not enough. One must also examine the freedom of entry; is the market "contestable"? If it is, then even a single producer may have little monopoly power.

KEY CONCEPTS

concentration ratio
Herfindahl index
natural oligopoly
differentiated product
collusion
cartel
bidding cartel
incentive to cheat
cut-throat competition

Organization of Petroleum
    Exporting Countries (OPEC)
kinked demand
price leadership
tacit collusion
Nash equilibrium
conjectural variation
focal-point pricing

cost-plus, or mark-up,
    pricing
competition by advertising
competition in product
    quality
barriers to entry
monopolistic competition
contestable markets

PROBLEMS

26-1 Suppose there is a monopoly in the production of good X.

(a) For this firm, what is the four-firm concentration ratio, like the dark red bars shown in Figure 26-1? What is the Herfindahl index?

(b) Repeat question (a) for an industry in which there are three equal-sized firms.

(c) Do the four-firm concentration ratio and the Herfindahl index both take account of all firms in the industry? In your view, which does a better job of describing the degree of industry concentration? Why?

26-2 If there are only four large firms in your industry, explain why collusion would be in your economic interest as a producer. Explain how consumers of your product would be affected. Describe the problems involved in arranging a collusive agreement and in making it stick. Would the agreement be legal?

26-3 What do you think would happen to the world price of oil if

(a) OPEC countries were able to enforce a quota system?

(b) non-OPEC producers were to reduce their production?

(c) the North Sea producers were to cut price by $5 a barrel?

(d) large new deposits of oil were discovered in the Canadian Arctic?

(e) large new deposits of oil were discovered off the Saudi Arabian coast?

(f) Saudi Arabia were to withdraw from OPEC?

(g) there were major developments in nuclear technology, with fusion power expected to become a major source of electricity by 2010?

(h) the U.S. government were to impose an additional tax of $1.00 per gallon on gasoline?

26-4 "In early 1985, when the Saudis were

operating at less than 40% of their oil-production capacity, they could no longer hold oil price up by reducing their supply. However, the Saudis were able to keep oil price up by forcing the other OPEC members to restrict their supplies. The Saudis did this by threatening to drive the price lower." Explain. Could the Saudis really have driven price lower? If not, why? If so, how? When the price of oil fell dramatically in 1986, was it because the Saudis (a) further restricted their supply, or (b) gave up their previous policy of restricting supply?

26-5 "Agricultural prices are unstable, but other prices are stable." Evaluate this statement in light of our discussion of kinked demand and our earlier analysis of agriculture in Chapter 20. To what degree do you believe this difference justifies agricultural price supports?

26-6 On balance, do you think that advertising is beneficial or damaging to society?

26-7 Canadian governments derive large amounts of revenue from excise taxes on liquor and tobacco; they also pay most of the cost of providing health care to Canadians. With this (and other factors) in mind, argue the case for and against a ban on advertising of liquor and tobacco products.

In 1972 when Canadian tobacco manufacturers agreed among themselves to stop radio and TV advertising, their decision was widely applauded as a sign of increasing social responsibility in the industry. Can you think of some reason other than a sense of social responsibility why the firms agreed to put this restriction on themselves?

26-8 In this chapter, we noted that some people have tried to justify advertising because it helps new competitors enter the market. However, others have argued that advertising provides a major advantage to established firms, and thus is a barrier to entry. Is it possible for both these views to be correct? If so, explain how. If not, which case do you think is the stronger, and why?

26-9 At one time, American lawyers who cut their fees below the level allowed by their state bar association could be disbarred. How would you evaluate this regulation from an economic point of view? If you were a lawyer, how would you view it?

*26-10 What is the difference between the monopoly-like collusion of the cartel in Figure 26-3, and the monopolization of the milk industry in Figure 25-10? Why should the monopolization of an industry be outlawed in the first case, yet condoned—in fact, organized—by the government in the other?

ECONOMIC EFFICIENCY: ISSUES OF OUR TIME

Part 6 will deal with a number of microeconomic issues, such as the best way to protect the environment and the effects of barriers to international trade. While studying these issues, we will continue to ask the fundamental questions addressed in Part 5: When do free markets work well, and when do they work badly? When they work badly, what forms of government intervention should be considered?

In Chapter 27, some of the ways that government intervenes to regulate business are examined. Through its anti-combines laws, the government discourages the monopolization of industry and forbids price-setting conspiracies among oligopolists. While such policies have often made the economy more competitive and efficient, the government has also used policies that have had the opposite effect. For example, it has reduced competition and efficiency in some industries by restricting the entry of new firms.

The government also intervenes in the marketplace to improve the quality of life by regulating safety, health, and working conditions. In Chapter 28 we examine in detail one of the major quality-of-life issues—controlling pollution of the environment. What policy is the government now using to control pollution and what alternative methods are available?

Chapter 29 deals with a quality-of-life issue of particular importance to future generations. At what rate should we use our natural resources? Are we facing a future "doomsday" when our expanding resource requirements will collide with shrinking resource supplies?

The focus of Chapter 30 will be on "public goods"—those goods and services which cannot be adequately delivered by a free market. One example is police protection: A privately owned, profit-maximizing firm cannot be relied upon to protect the public at large. If we are to have adequate police protection, it must be provided by the government. However, special problems arise. One of the most important is the problem of determining how much the government should spend on each of the goods and services it provides. The public has much more difficulty in signalling to the government what it wants—via the ballot box—than in telling private firms what it wants when it"votes"in the marketplace, purchasing certain goods and ignoring others.

The last two chapters in this part deal with international trade. Chapter 31 describes how countries benefit from such trade. For example, Canada gains by specializing in such products as wheat and telecommunications equipment, exporting these items in exchange for coffee, TV sets, and shirts. Other countries likewise gain from specialization. Trade also makes our economy more efficient by increasing competition. The Canadian auto market is more competitive because of imported Japanese and European cars. In addition to showing how trade increases efficiency, this chapter also explains how trade redistributes income. Who are the winners and losers?

Finally, Chapter 32 describes the ways in which governments intervene in the international marketplace, by imposing barriers to trade. For example, the Canadian government restricts the imports of Japanese cars, which makes the auto market less competitive. Such restrictions generally reduce the income of the nation as a whole, although they do benefit certain groups, such as the producers of cars. An issue of particular importance to Canada concerns restrictions imposed by the American government on Canadian exports to the United States. In Chapter 32 we also discuss one possible way for Canada to resolve this problem: Negotiating a free-trade agreement with the United States.

Chapter 27

GOVERNMENT REGULATION OF BUSINESS: HOW MUCH IS ENOUGH?

Government . . . promotes our happiness . . . by
restraining our vices.

Thomas Paine,
Common Sense

One of the principal ways the government influences the economy is by regulations on private business. For example, the government enforces rules that limit the exercise of market power by large firms. It has also imposed regulations in other sectors, such as transportation and farming, in order to protect producers against wide price fluctuations and to ensure consumers of a regular supply of farm products and transport services. And government regulation has been used to promote safety and health in our workplaces, highways, and the environment.

The growth in government regulation was especially rapid, both in Canada and the United States, during the 1960s and 1970s. In this chapter, we discuss questions such as: What forms of regulation developed during this period? How successful was it in accomplishing what it was designed to do? In the United States, there has been a strong trend toward less regulation since the late 1970s; in some sectors, there has even been a dismantling of existing regulation. In the mid-1980s, there were some signs that this trend was

spreading to Canada. Will this trend toward deregulation continue?

Government regulation of business falls into three major categories:

1. Laws to prevent firms from reducing competition by such acts as collusion, or driving competitors out of business through means such as cut-throat pricing.
2. Regulatory controls over an industry's price and conditions of entry. Within this broad category, two quite different kinds of regulation should be distinguished:
   (a) Regulation of natural monopoly in sectors such as production of electric power or telephone services. Since this form of regulation has already been studied in Chapter 25 (especially Box 25-2 and Appendix 25-B) we will concentrate here on type (b).
   (b) Regulation of naturally more competitive industries such as trucking or dairy farming.
3. Quality-of-life regulation of health, safety, and

working conditions. This type of regulation grew rapidly during the 1970s.

We will look at each of the three types of regulatory policies in turn, beginning with the policy followed by the government to safeguard competition, sometimes referred to as the government's *competition policy*. The most important element of Canada's competition policy is our **anti-combines legislation**, the legislation that outlaws various strategies that business firms could use to lessen competition in an industry. (Another very important special area of regulation is discussed in a later chapter: the regulation of foreign investment, in Chapter 35.)

Before studying the anti-combines law itself, we consider the difficult economic questions that must be considered in developing a sensible competition policy.

I. COMPETITION POLICY: SOME PROBLEMS

The task of developing policies to deal with the market power of monopolists and oligopolists is not an easy one. One difficult problem is how to effectively prevent large firms in an oligopolistic industry from entering into agreements or understandings that reduce price competition: How does the government know when such agreements exist? Another problem has to do with the role of large firms in the economy. In an industry with only a few large firms, each firm is likely to have substantial market power. If the industry had a larger number of small firms, it would probably be more competitive: Individual firms would be more likely to behave as price takers. But even though competition generally promotes efficiency, there are many industries in which small firms simply cannot produce as efficiently as large firms. Therefore, it is not certain that preventing firms from acquiring a large share of the market will improve the performance of the economy. In business, big isn't necessarily bad.

We now look at these problems in more detail.

What Constitutes Collusion?

In order to protect the consuming public, the present **Combines Investigation Act**, the Act that sets out the rules of Canada's anti-combines policy, prohibits *collusive agreements* (or "conspiracies") by oligopolists to raise prices. But proving that collusion has taken

place in a particular instance is easier said than done. There may be exceptional cases, of course, where collusion is easy to establish (see Box 27-1). For example, competitors may have formal meetings with the specific intention of fixing a common price and splitting up the market. If this can be proved, they can be fined—or perhaps even sent to jail—for their efforts. But consider a more complex case, such as a group of building contractors in a city who have an understanding that they will inform each other when they are bidding on major construction projects, and who take turns submitting the lowest bid. Such collusion may be difficult to prove: After all, each firm may submit a different bid. Or consider the case where oligopolists with a common interest end up setting the same price without even so much as a wink or a nod because all firms follow a price leader. Certainly we cannot make it illegal to quote the current market price. If a firm is only "meeting the (price) competition," how can it be condemned? After all, doesn't a perfectly competitive producer (like the wheat farmer) sell at the going market price? Similar prices do not prove collusion.

A further complication is that collusion between firms in an industry isn't always a bad thing. For example, those who are critical of advertising would argue that the 1971 agreement among Canadian tobacco companies to stop advertising cigarettes on radio and TV was a good thing. (Similarly, the current ban on advertising of hard liquor in the electronic media originated in a voluntary agreement among distillers to stop such advertising.) Or as another example, if North American auto producers were allowed to "collude" by sharing their research, they might develop pollution-control and safety equipment more quickly and cheaply. However, because they are afraid that any form of collusion is going to attract the attention of the regulators, they have been reluctant to get together in their research.

Thus, proving collusion and deciding how vigorously it should be fought are difficult issues that complicate the tasks of framing the rules of competition policy, and of enforcing those rules once they have been set. Even more difficult problems arise when we consider the other major way in which competition in an industry may be reduced: There may be a reduction in the number of firms in the industry as some firms are driven out, or are taken over by others.

BOX 27-1

LONG DISTANCE: THE NEXT BEST THING TO BEING THERE

A price-fixing agreement does not necessarily require extensive negotiations; sometimes a simple phone call will do. A report in *Time* magazine (7 March 1983) describes an apparent attempt by American Airlines' Robert Crandall to strike a price-fixing deal in a call to Braniff Airline chairman Howard Putnam. This excerpt—which Putnam taped without telling Crandall—picks up a discussion of how difficult it was for the two airlines to make a profit when they were both flying the same routes and cutting prices.

Crandall: . . . there's no reason I can see, all right, to put both [our] companies out of business.

Putnam: But if you're going to overlay a route of American's on top of . . . every route that

Braniff has—I can't just sit here and allow you to bury us without giving our best effort.

Crandall: Oh, sure, but Eastern and Delta do the same thing in Atlanta and have for years.

Putnam: Do you have a suggestion for me?

Crandall: Yes, I have a suggestion for you. Raise your [expletive] fares 20%. I'll raise mine the next morning.

Putnam: Robert, we . . .

Crandall: You'll make more money and I will too.

Putnam: We can't talk about pricing.

Crandall: Oh [expletive] Howard. We can talk about any [expletive] thing we want to talk about.

In this case, no price fixing actually occurred because Putnam didn't take the bait. However, if he had, this tape could have put them both in jail.

Although competition may be reduced as the remaining large firms begin to dominate the market, allowing large firms to merge may be advantageous for other reasons.

Are There Advantages to Large Size?

In a number of industries, there are advantages to large size, for several reasons:

1. Large firms can better afford research and development. Because of their very large sales, big firms may be able to finance large research and development (R&D) projects that could not be undertaken by small firms. These expenditures benefit not only the firms that are thereby able to develop the profitable new products. Society as a whole also benefits as these new products become available. In his classic defence of large firms, Joseph Schumpeter wrote:

> As soon as we go into details and inquire into the individual items in which progress was most conspicuous, the trail leads not to the doors of those firms that work under conditions of comparatively free competition but precisely to the doors of the large concerns—which, as in the case of agricul-

tural machinery, also account for much of the progress in the competitive sector—and a shocking suspicion dawns upon us that big business may have had more to do with creating that standard of life than keeping it down.[1]

Although large firms with their heavy R&D expenditures are often the source of innovation, their role should not be exaggerated. Many innovations come not from firms that are already large, but from firms that are small and seeking to become large. For example, the snowmobile was originally developed by Bombardier, a relatively small Montreal-based company. And the personal computer was introduced by upstart Apple, not by the giants of the computer industry.

2. Large firms can capture economies of scale. In many industries, economies of scale can be realized only by very large firms. As we have already noted, in any decision whether to use anti-combines legislation to try to prevent a firm from becoming a monopoly in an industry, a crucial question arises: Is this a natural

---

[1] Joseph Schumpeter, *Capitalism, Socialism and Democracy*, 3rd ed. (New York: Harper, 1942), p. 82.

monopoly based on economies of large-scale production? If the answer is yes, then by preventing a firm from becoming a monopoly, you also prevent production from taking place at minimum average cost. A better solution may be to allow the monopoly to form, but to regulate the monopolist's price. On the other hand, if the industry is not a natural monopoly, it is appropriate to use anti-combines legislation to prevent a single firm from becoming a monopolist.

In the present Combines Investigation Act, there is no explicit reference to economies of scale as a reason for allowing a firm to dominate the market for a particular good. However, the Economic Council of Canada has put forward proposals under which a large firm would be allowed to increase its market share (by taking over one of its smaller rivals) if its increased size would make possible a "substantially" reduced cost of production. On the other hand, if average cost would not be "substantially" reduced, a takeover would not be allowed if it would increase the large firm's market share beyond, say, 20%. The Council's compromise between the views that "monopoly is bad" and "big is better" is reflected in the new competition bill that the government introduced in Parliament in 1985.

In constructing an anti-combines policy it is clearly an error to ignore economies of scale; but it may also be a mistake to place too much emphasis on them. To see why, consider an industry where a few competing firms have been able to capture most, but not all, economies of scale. If economies of scale are the only consideration, then the policy should be "hands off"; allow one firm to buy up other firms, monopolize the market, and capture even more economies of scale. But if this is allowed, the new monopoly will have to be regulated—with the whole new set of difficulties this will involve. Better to keep a few firms in beneficial competition than to try to capture the last nickel of economies of scale by allowing the monopolization of the industry.

A very important postscript should be added to the discussion of this aspect of Canada's anti-combines policy. In industries that are subject to intense foreign competition, there should be far less objection to the emergence of a few very large Canadian corporations. There are two reasons:

1. A Canadian firm may simply be unable to compete with imports unless it is large enough to capture economies of scale. (This will be especially true if Canada enters into some type of free-trade agreement with the United States; abolition of tariffs and other barriers against trade with the United States would increase exposure of Canadian firms to competition from U.S. firms. We will discuss this issue further in Chapter 32.) Even in the U.S. auto market, it is recognized that there is a need to have large-scale domestic producers in order to compete with imports. With the flood of Japanese auto imports in the 1980s, nobody was talking about the earlier proposals to increase competition by breaking up General Motors.

2. Because of competition from imports, the market power of large Canadian firms is reduced: They are not as free to raise prices as they would be without import competition.

What Is Unfair Competition?

In many cases, it is difficult to tell whether a firm that is taking a growing market share in an industry is deliberately trying to create a monopoly for itself, or whether it is just growing because it is more efficient than other firms. However, the *method* by which it is increasing its market share may give an indication. For example, a firm that already has a large market share may try to increase it by actions that are systematically designed to drive its smaller competitors out of the industry. This raises a general question: How aggressively should a big firm be allowed to compete with smaller ones? Sometimes the large firm doesn't compete aggressively—but instead provides a high price umbrella under which its small, less efficient competitors can survive. (Some U.S. observers believe that General Motors during the 1960s priced cars high enough to protect Chrysler, fearing that a Chrysler bankruptcy would lead the government to try to break up G.M.) On the other hand, the large firm sometimes does compete aggressively, by **cut-throat competition** designed to force its small competitors out of business. If successful, this puts it in a monopoly position, in which it can then turn around and raise price.

Cut-throat competition (sometimes called *predatory pricing*) is pricing below costs in order to drive competitors out of business.

The classic Canadian case of cut-throat competition was the Eddy Match Company, which succeeded in driving several potential competitors out of the market for wooden matches between 1928 and 1949. In each case, Eddy Match subsequently bought up the company it had driven bankrupt. In 1951, however, Eddy was convicted of violating the anti-combines legislation through its predatory pricing practices.

It is very difficult to draw a line between fair competition and unfair, cut-throat competition. One might think, for example, that a fair price to charge might be one that just covers the firm's costs (including a normal profit). But it's not that easy. One reason is that a firm typically produces many products, and it's not clear how some costs (in particular overhead) should be allocated among them. Furthermore, pricing below costs may not always reflect cut-throat competition aimed at eliminating competitors. In the early 1980s, both G.M. and Ford suffered large losses (that is, they priced below average costs). But they weren't trying to "cut Chrysler's throat." Rather, they were frantically trying to hold their shares of the North American market in the face of stiff Japanese competition. Because of such real-world complexities, it is very difficult even to define—let alone control—"unfair" competition.

The Difficult Problem of Mergers

Another way in which a big firm may become even bigger is through a *merger* or *take-over* of another firm. How to deal with mergers is perhaps the most difficult issue of all in competition policy.

The nature of the problem is most clearly seen in the case of a **horizontal merger** involving the union of two firms which previously competed with one another. On the one hand, it is obviously anti-competitive: the remaining firm will now have the market share of the one that it acquired, as well as its own original share. On the other hand, the merger or takeover may make it possible for the firm to take advantage of previously unexploited economies of scale. For example, production may now be concentrated in one plant. Or it may be possible to achieve cost reductions in marketing, management, and research and development.

A **vertical merger**—in which company A merges with its supplier B—need not greatly reduce competition, as long as neither A nor B has very large shares of the market. But sometimes vertical mergers may be a way in which companies indirectly manage to reduce

competition. Thus, between 1945 and 1960, a group of Canadian cardboard box manufacturers (who had already been convicted for a price-fixing agreement before World War II) proceeded to merge vertically with container board firms that supplied them with cardboard. Thus, the cardboard box producers were able to consolidate their hold on the market for boxes: By supplying cardboard only to firms inside the group, they made entry of new firms difficult, and were able to get together in a new scheme to raise prices without much fear of competition. (In 1966, they were again convicted for price fixing.)

The third type of merger is a **conglomerate merger** where a firm joins another in a completely different activity. Whether such mergers adversely affect competition—and if so, by how much—is a controversial issue. A conglomerate merger may invigorate a weak company in an industry by providing it with new capital and more aggressive management. In such cases, competition can be enhanced. But a merger may help an already strong company to increase its dominance of an industry. The issue of conglomerate mergers has become increasingly important in both Canada and the United States during the last two decades, and we discuss it in some detail in the appendix to this chapter.

> A *horizontal merger* involves a union of firms in the same competing activity.
>
> A *vertical merger* involves a union of a firm and its supplier.
>
> A *conglomerate merger* involves a union of firms in unrelated activities.

CANADA'S ANTI-COMBINES LAW: A SUMMARY

Because the anti-combines legislation is so complicated, it is not possible to do more than note the most important provisions.

As early as 1889, a House of Commons committee was appointed to investigate monopolistic activities in a number of Canadian industries. Following the committee's report, provisions that outlawed various practices to limit competition were put into Canada's Criminal Code. Even though these provisions have been modified and extended on many occasions and are now incorporated into a separate Combines Investigation Act, these 1889 provisions are still the core of our anti-combines legislation.

1. Collusive Agreements

Section 32 in the Combines Investigation Act prohibits agreements or conspiracies to fix prices, or to limit output in order to raise prices. It provides both for fines (of up to one million dollars) and for imprisonment of the persons responsible for the conspiracy or agreement. Over the years, the government has won a number of cases against firms that had agreed to fix prices in their industry. (One of the most famous convictions under this section was won in 1976 against Canadian General Electric and other firms who had fixed prices on electric lightbulbs). But the government has also lost several cases, and many economists believe that the wording of section 32, and the courts' interpretation of it, has made it too difficult for the government to prevent price fixing. There are two main difficulties.

(a) Section 32 only prohibits conspiracies or agreements under which firms "unduly" limit production, or in which price fixing by a group of firms "unduly" lessens competition in the market. Canadian courts have long struggled with the question of what "unduly" means, but by and large, they have interpreted it narrowly, making it difficult for the government to prosecute price fixing: In order for the government to be sure of winning a case, the price-fixing agreement has to be a flagrant one and involve virtually all firms in an industry.

(b) Because the Combines Investigation Act is part of our criminal law, the rule that a defendant is presumed innocent until proven guilty applies, and the government can only win a case if it can prove "beyond reasonable doubt" that a conspiracy or an explicit agreement exists among the participating firms. As we have seen above, this may be difficult because competing firms may very well quote similar prices without an explicit agreement (for example, in an industry with a price leader).

2. Monopoly and Merger

Section 33 of the Act prohibits actions of a firm to create a monopoly position for itself in a market: "Every person who is a party or privy to or knowingly assists in, or in the formation of, a merger or monopoly is guilty of an indictable offence and is liable to imprisonment for two years." The Combines Act here uses the term "merger" in a somewhat unusual sense: It is defined in the Act not just as an acquisition by a firm of another firm (a competitor, supplier, or customer), but an acquisition which implies that competition in the market "is or is likely to be lessened to the detriment or against the interest of the public." The Act's definition of "monopoly" is also somewhat restrictive. In order for a monopoly to be illegal under the Act, it must be "operated . . . to the detriment or against the interests of the public." Because of these restrictive definitions, the government has again had difficulty in consistently preventing large firms from acquiring and maintaining a monopoly position. In one of the few cases where the government did win a conviction (the case against Eddy Match) the firm had systematically tried to eliminate its rivals through blatant cut-throat competition. But unless a monopolist engages in practices of that sort, it is difficult to prove that the firm is using its position to the detriment of the public.

As an example of the government's lack of success in making its charges stick, in 1977 New Brunswick industrialist K.C. Irving was acquitted (after an appeal to the Supreme Court of Canada) of a merger charge after he had obtained a monopoly in the New Brunswick market by buying all of the five existing English-language newspapers. The Supreme Court's acquittal was based on the argument that the Crown had failed to prove that the formation of the monopoly was detrimental to the public.

3. Price Discrimination

The Combines Investigation Act (like U.S. anti-trust legislation) has a section that outlaws certain forms of *price discrimination*. (As we saw in Chapter 25, price discrimination occurs when a seller charges different prices to different buyers.)

In the U.S. law against price discrimination, the Robinson-Patman Act, the objective appears to have been to protect smaller buyers (such as individual retail stores) against larger competitors (such as chain stores): Specifically, U.S. law makes it illegal for manufacturing firms to sell their goods to chain stores at substantially lower prices than they charge smaller retailers. One can argue that the prohibition of this type of price discrimination is desirable, because it makes it easier for many small firms to survive in retailing, and therefore it promotes competition. But one can also argue that the main effect of the law is to protect small and inefficient retail firms: Because small firms pay the same price as large firms, many more small-scale retail stores will survive, and the average costs of distribution will be higher.

In Canada, however, the Combines Investigation Act states that price discrimination is illegal only if it involves different prices to buyers who buy goods of like quality *and quantity*. Therefore, it *is* in fact legal in Canada for a producer to charge lower prices to buyers (such as chain stores) that purchase a large quantity. Thus, in contrast to the U.S. legislation, Canada's anti-combines law has not substantially hindered the development of efficient large-scale firms in the retailing industry.

4. Other Provisions

Resale price maintenance. In Canada, it is against the law for a manufacturer to fix the price at which retailers sell their goods to the public. Even though a manufacturing firm may "suggest" a list price (a price at which the firm would like to see its product sold in stores), it cannot force retailers to maintain that price, nor can it refuse to supply retailers who offer to sell the product to the public at a lower price.

The effect of these provisions has been to stimulate price competition in the retail sector, by allowing the development of discount outlets (such as Consumers' Distributing).

Misleading advertising and tied selling. The Combines Investigation Act also has certain minor provisions prohibiting *misleading advertising* and some cases of *tied selling*. (Tied selling, sometimes also called *full-line forcing*, means that a firm with one particularly appealing product forces retailers who want to carry that product to also carry the firm's full line of related products. A good example of this is the practice of oil companies to force their service station distributors to carry the full line of the company's automotive products, such as tires and batteries.) The prohibition against tied selling is enforced by the ***Restrictive Trade Practices Commission*** (RTPC), part of Consumer and Corporate Affairs Canada. (The RTPC is also the agency in charge of investigating firms suspected of having violated other provisions of the Combines Investigation Act.)

REFORMING CANADA'S COMPETITION POLICY

The weaknesses of the present anti-combines legislation have been recognized for a long time, and various reform proposals have been made. In recent times, the most important set of suggestions for reform are contained in the ***Competition Act*** that was introduced by the government as far back as 1971. One of the main features of the reform package contained in this Act was to move many of the provisions in the anti-combines laws from criminal to civil law, which would have the effect of making it easier for the government to obtain convictions. In addition, it also removed some of the restrictive provisions of the Combines Investigation Act, such as the provision that the government had to prove a "detriment" to the public in order to invalidate a merger.

The Competition Act became highly controversial right from the beginning, and partly as a result of this, the actual process of reform turned out to be very slow. However, some important changes were made in 1976, when some of the minor provisions in the Combines Investigation Act (such as the provisions relating to tied selling) were removed from criminal law, and the RTPC was empowered to enforce these provisions by issuing remedial orders to firms that were found to have violated these provisions. (The CRTC decision in 1980 to stop Bell Canada from requiring its customers to use only equipment supplied by its subsidiary Northern Telecom, came after an investigation by the RTPC.) In 1985, after years of intensive consultations and lobbying, the government finally brought in a bill calling for approval of the Competition Act by Parliament. A major thrust of this proposed new legislation is the recognition that, in industries where goods and services flow freely across the border, international trade is an important way to ensure that the Canadian domestic market will remain competitive. Moreover, in determining whether to allow a reorganization of a Canadian industry (for example, through a major takeover), the authorities should take into account whether or not this reorganization would result in efficiency gains that would improve Canada's trade performance. In addition, in order to allow Canadian firms to compete more effectively in the world market, they would be given more freedom to enter into cooperative export agreements.

Final Observations: How to Achieve Workable Competition

When Canada's anti-combines legislation and U.S. anti-trust laws were introduced in the late nineteenth century, support for these laws was strong. There was much public resentment of the growing U.S. business giants and their predatory methods, and of the anti-competitive cartels that were formed in Canada by domestic firms protected against competition from imports by the government's high-tariff policy. But since the days of the "robber barons," there have been relatively few black and white situations. Anti-combines history is largely the story of difficult gray areas.

From the beginning, it was clear that Canada could not simply try to preserve competition by trying to ensure that there would be many small firms competing with each other in every industry. Economies of large scale production, and the small Canadian market, necessarily mean that in many industries there is room for, at most, only a few firms of efficient size. (Furthermore, a market may be highly competitive even if there are only a few producers in Canada: As long as their products have to compete with imports, there is a definite limit to the exercise of market power by any Canadian firm.) Thus, the law *sometimes* has to allow an industry to be dominated by a few firms. This is one of the reasons why the existing anti-combines law is written in such a flexible, qualified way. For example, we have seen that mergers are prohibited only if they reduce competition "to the detriment or against the interest of the public," and agreements to restrict price competition are illegal only if they lessen competition "unduly." But standards have been changing, and if Parliament passes the tougher proposals in the new Competition Act, the government will be in a better position to intervene successfully against firms with real market power.

In the face of the need to balance the complex considerations of market power and tacit collusion, and the need to achieve economies of scale in the limited Canadian market, it may be too much to hope for a simple solution. Perfect competition is the perfect answer only in textbooks. In the real world, we must settle for "workable competition," where we gain many of the advantages of large-scale business, but curb the more flagrant abuses. One analyst has compared competition legislation with traffic laws. Going 84 kilometres an hour in an 80-kilometre zone represents no calamity. But the police are there to catch the speeder who goes 100. The fact that we might get caught makes most of us drive a little more carefully. Similarly, the cases that have been won by the government remind business executives that there are stiff fines (and adverse publicity) awaiting the flagrant offender; they are likely to be more careful as a result.

II. REGULATION OF PRICE AND ENTRY

. . . [In the U.S. airline industry] it appears that the prime obstacle to efficiency has been regulation itself and the most creative thing a regulator can do is remove his or her body from the market entryway.

Alfred Kahn, former chairman of the
U.S. Civil Aeronautics Board.

In Chapter 25, we examined in detail the strong case that can be made for government regulation of a natural monopoly such as the local telephone company. (Regulation forced the firm to act more like a perfect competitor facing a given market price.) Here we discuss a policy that is much more difficult to justify: government regulation of a naturally more competitive industry, such as the trucking industry. As will become evident, regulation in this case typically allows firms to act in a less competitive way. For example, regulation may reduce competition by blocking the entry of potential new firms. Therefore, it is no surprise that this form of regulation is often welcomed by the firms that are already in the industry. (A preview of some of the problems that arise is given in Box 27-2.)

A Case History: Regulation of Commercial Trucking

An interesting example of price and entry regulation is provided by the Canadian trucking industry, which has been extensively regulated in all provinces except Alberta.

Regulation of the for-hire trucking industry in Canada had its beginnings in the 1930s during the Great Depression. However, to understand the reasons why regulation was introduced into this industry, one has to go back in history and look at government regulation of the railroad industry.

A particularly important motive for railway regulation in Canada has always been to ensure that low-cost and reasonably efficient service would not be restricted to large cities and to the more densely populated parts of Canada: Smaller localities and remote areas, it has been argued, deserve good rail service too. But service to small communities in thinly populated areas can be provided only at a high average cost. (The heavy fixed costs of this industry—track, locomotives, and other equipment—must be spread over a small traffic volume.) As a solution to this dilemma, the regulatory authorities allowed a certain amount of **cross-subsidization**, that is, allowing the railroads to recoup their losses on the unprofitable low-volume traffic to small cities by letting them charge rates well above average cost on the profitable high-volume routes.

> *Cross-subsidization* by a firm or a public agency means that the firm or agency uses revenues generated in profitable lines of activity to offset losses in other less profitable lines of activity.

Cross-subsidization has played a particularly important role in the system of grain transport from the prairie provinces (see Box 27-3).

As long as railway transport constituted the only really practical method of shipping, the system of regulation and cross-subsidization was relatively easy to maintain. However, during the 1920s and 1930s more efficient trucks were developed and better roads were being built thoughout Canada. As a consequence, the railroads began facing increasingly intense competition from commercial trucking, in particular, on high-volume, short-haul shipments of high-value commodities. (Few truckers were interested in serving the transport needs of sparsely populated areas, even though trucking would have been an efficient alternative to railroad freight in such areas; the truckers could not compete because the government regulators had forced the railways to maintain low rates on these routes.)

Thus a serious problem developed: competition from trucking on the most profitable (short-haul, high-volume) routes tended to squeeze out the railroads' profits on these routes, and thus reduced their ability to cross-subsidize their less profitable activities. The railroads, therefore, began to lobby intensively for extending the system of regulation to the trucking indus-

try as well. Truckers' representatives also supported the proposals for regulation of their own industry: Because of the Depression, competition among truckers had intensified, and many new firms were entering the trucking business. By agreeing to regulation, the truckers hoped to reduce competition from new entrants and diminish what they saw as tendencies toward cut-throat competition in the industry. With support from both the railroads and the trucking industry, several provinces introduced trucking regulation.

Since the 1930s, regulation of the trucking industry has become more widespread and increasingly detailed. All provinces except Alberta now control entry into both intraprovincial and interprovincial trucking, and grant trucking licences subject to a wide variety of restrictions. Thus, a licence may specify what kinds of goods the firm may ship, what routes it may follow, and whether or not the firm is allowed to unload or pick up goods on the way. The frequency of service to different communities may also be specified, just as it is in the federal regulation of railroads. And several provinces regulate trucking rates within their borders.[2] Moreover, in all the provinces, the trucking industry maintains tariff bureaus which provide advice and information to trucking firms on various matters, including the rates charged by other firms. This tends to lessen competition, because it makes it easier for all firms to quote the same price. (It can be argued that such "cartelizing" activity by the tariff bureaus is in violation of the Combines Investigation Act. But the government can't prosecute the truckers because the Act does not apply to regulated industries.)

The Effects of Trucking Regulation

There is no doubt that the provincial regulation of trucking has had extensive effects on the transport industry in Canada. It has also been a costly process. Apart from the substantial costs of paying for the personnel and other expenditures of the regulatory agencies themselves (costs that have been borne by the provincial taxpayers), there have also been heavy costs incurred by the trucking firms in dealing with the agencies. In a study done for the Economic Coun-

---

[2]Manitoba and Saskatchewan have effective rate regulations; in other provinces trucking firms can change their rates simply by filing a notice to the provincial Highways Board (which is the regulatory authority).

BOX 27-2

THE PARABLE OF THE PARKING LOTS

Producers have a natural interest to narrow the market and raise the price.

Adam Smith,
Wealth of Nations

Henry Manne, professor of law at the University of Miami, tells a simple parable to illustrate the problems of government regulation which protects existing firms by blocking the entry of new firms.*

Once upon a time in a city not far away, thousands of people would crowd into the local football stadium on a Saturday afternoon. The problem of parking was initially solved by a number of big commercial parking lots whose owners formed the Association of Professional Parking Lot Employers (APPLE). But, as time passed and crowds grew, every plumber, lawyer, and schoolteacher who owned a house in the neighbourhood went into the

parking business on Saturday afternoon, and cars appeared in every driveway and on most lawns. Members of APPLE viewed the entry of these "amateurs" into their business with no great enthusiasm, especially since some were charging a lower fee. Stories began to circulate about their fly-by-night methods, and the dents they had put in two cars (although, on investigation, it was discovered that denting was an equally serious problem in the commercial lots).

At a meeting of all members of APPLE, emotions and applause ran high as one speaker after another pointed out—in some cases, in a very statesmanlike way—that parking should be viewed, not as a business, but as a profession governed by professional standards. In particular, cut-throat price competition with amateurs should be regarded as unethical. The one concrete proposal, quickly adopted, was that APPLE members should contribute $1 per parking spot "to improve their public image, and put their case before the proper authorities."

No accounting was ever made of this money, but it must have been spent wisely, since within a few months the city council passed an ordinance to regulate industry price and to require that anyone parking cars must be licensed. However, it turned

**"The Parable of the Parking Lots," *Public Interest* no. 23 (Spring 1971): 10–15. Abbreviated with the author's permission.*

cil of Canada, Norman Bonsor of Lakehead University estimated that the firms' costs of preparing and presenting applications for licence extensions, responding to other firm's applications for new licences, and so on, amount to at least $40 million annually. Those costs are borne either by the firms themselves, or passed on to their customers in the form of higher prices.

But more important than these direct costs are the indirect effects of regulation on the cost and efficiency of firms in the industry. In another study for the Economic Council, James McRae and David Prescott found that the highest trucking rates are in Ontario, Quebec, and British Columbia: In those provinces, trucking is regulated—in particular, entry into the industry is regulated—but there are no effective controls on rates. In Alberta where there is no regulation, and entry into the industry is not restricted, rates are con-

siderably lower. But in spite of the higher rates, profits of trucking firms in Ontario, Quebec, and B.C. are no higher than in Alberta. Therefore, McRae and Prescott conclude, regulation in Ontario, Quebec, and B.C. has resulted in inefficiency—that is, higher costs of trucking. (As an example of this inefficiency, regulation makes it difficult for firms to reduce either the number of miles that their trucks have to run empty, or the amount of idle truck time.)

Regulation in Other Canadian Industries

The trucking industry is not the only example of a regulated industry in Canada. For example, the airline industry is subject to detailed federal controls on both entry and fares. Local governments control entry in the taxi business in most municipalities. The oil and gas industry has become more and more extensively

out to be difficult for an independent house owner to get a license; it required passing a special driving test to be "professionally administered" by APPLE, a $27,000 investment in parking facilities, and $500,000 in liability insurance. Since every commercial lot found its costs consequently increasing by 20 percent, the city council approved a 20 percent increase in parking fees. (Within a year, APPLE had requested that the city council guarantee the liability insurance, so that people would have no fear of parking in commercial lots. One argument put forward by an APPLE spokesman was that this idea was similar in its intent to recent congressional legislation setting up an insurance scheme for stockbrokers.)

On the next football afternoon, a funny thing happened on the way to the stadium. Since police were out in large numbers to enforce the ordinance, driveways and lawns were empty and long lines of cars were backed up waiting to get into each commercial lot. The snarl was even worse after the game. Some people simply gave up waiting for their cars and had to return to retrieve them next day. (There was even a rumour that one car was never found.) In response, APPLE decided to go ahead with a "statistical-logistic study of the whole socio-economic situation" by two computer science pro-fessors at the local university. Their report cited the archaic methods of the industry and pointed out that what each firm needed was fewer quill pens and more time on a computer.

As the parking lots began to computerize their operations it became quite clear that in the face of these rising costs, a further increase in parking fees was required. The increase was quickly approved by city councillors, relieved that, in the modernization of the industry, they had finally found a solution. But, unfortunately, it was no solution after all. The problem, it turned out, was not so much deciding which car should be moved where, as actually moving it—and that continued to be done by attendants who had become surly and uncooperative because of the pressure they were facing.

Relief, however, did appear in two forms. First, many people got fed up with the hassle and started watching the game on TV. Second, small boys who lived in the houses closest to the stadium went into the car wash business on Saturday afternoon. They charged $5, but it was worth the price, since they guaranteed a top-quality job. (In fact, they guaranteed that they would spend at least 2 hours on it.) And they always had as many cars as they could handle, even on rainy days—in fact, especially on rainy days.

regulated in the 1970s and 1980s (see Chapter 29), and entry into the broadcasting industry is federally controlled by the Canadian Radio-television and Telecommunications Commission (CRTC). The growth of regulation has been especially rapid in agriculture, where provincial marketing boards now control both the output and prices of a large variety of agricultural products.

Another area where regulation has been multiplying rapidly is in government licensing and certification requirements for specific occupations: Legislation in various provinces sets standards of practice and entry qualifications for a wide variety of occupational groups, ranging from doctors, lawyers, and architects to interior decorators, music teachers, and timber scalers. (As an example of the trend in this direction, the Economic Council cites the instance of Quebec, where during a two-year period in the mid-1970s no fewer than 23 occupational groups applied for status as "professional corporations" under the province's regulatory legislation.)

The motives for regulating these various industries are different. In the case of the airline industry (and also in trucking) there was fear that unregulated firms would provide inadequate service to areas of low population density, or would engage in unfettered competition that could lead to destructive price wars and periodic disruption of the industry. In the case of agriculture, one reason for regulation was the belief that without it, prices of farm products would be highly unstable. In the broadcasting field, one of the main motives for regulation has been the fear that unregulated firms would not produce an adequate supply of distinctively Canadian programming and news reporting. In the occupations and professions that have been regulated, the argument has been that the public needs to be protected against fraudulent or harmful practices. (Some forms of occupational or professional licensing, for example, in medicine, are more justified than others such as interior decoration: If doctors aren't licensed—and anyone can enter the profession—patients who can't tell which "doctors" are competent, and which are not, may make life-and-death mistakes.)

Although regulation may help to solve the problems cited above, it may also create a whole set of new problems: Regulation raises prices because it raises costs—or because it provides firms with monopoly power (as in the case of profitable trucking firms that hold the exclusive license to specific routes). Because price and entry regulation introduces the possibility of monopoly profits and reduces the competitive pressure on inefficient producers, it is generally supported by the majority of producers who are already in the regulated industry. In some cases, regulation increases the possibility that the industry may become like a private price-fixing cartel—except that, because it is regulated by the government, it is exempt from the penalties of the anti-combines law. (Some economists argue that many agricultural marketing boards in Canada have begun to resemble private cartels.) Similarly, occupational regulation is strongly supported by those already in the regulated professions, not only because it protects the public, but also because it sometimes gives the professional associations the opportunity to legally reduce price competition by restricting entry and enforcing uniform fee schedules. Thus, for the public, the result is not just higher-quality service, but also higher prices.

A Trend toward Deregulation?

While regulation grew rapidly in the 1960s and early 1970s, by the late 1970s many people were becoming disillusioned with some of the results. It seemed that regulation had been shifting more and more toward

---

BOX 27-3

ORIGINS OF CANADIAN TRANSPORT REGULATION: Railroads

It was almost inevitable that the Canadian government should become heavily involved both in supporting and regulating the railroads during the 1800s: Because of the enormous expense of building the railroad network necessary to serve the expanding economy (particularly the wheat-based economy of the Prairies), the railroad companies needed both direct financial support and assurance that they would be able to earn a reasonable return on their investment.

To meet the latter requirement, the government often granted a monopoly to individual railroad companies on the service between specific areas or localities. But the government, in turn, had to be sure that the companies did not abuse this monopoly position by overcharging railroad users. Therefore, the government generally maintained control over the freight rates that the companies could

charge, and also regulated other aspects of the railroads' activities, such as frequency of service.

As noted in the text, a subsidiary purpose of regulation was to ensure good rail service to remote areas, a policy that was achieved by cross-subsidization. Another example of cross-subsidization has been the low rates charged in transporting grain from the prairie provinces to the seaports at Vancouver, Churchill, and the Lakehead, from which much of the grain is exported. The so-called statutory rates which the railroads are allowed to charge on such grain shipments were originally set in an 1897 agreement between CP Rail and the Canadian government (the Crowsnest Pass Agreement), and subsequently became part of the Canadian Railway Act. Despite numerous attempts by the railroads to have the rates renegotiated, they have remained unchanged over the years, with the result that the railroads can now cover only a fraction of the *variable* costs of shipping this grain (covering the rest of their costs by charging higher rates on more profitable routes).

In 1982, the federal government announced that it intended to reduce the Crowsnest subsidy in order to release funds for overdue improvement of

restriction of competition, with a resulting increase in prices and loss of economic efficiency: Regulatory officials seemed to be increasingly preoccupied with the welfare of the regulated firms, rather than with the welfare of the public. At a conference of Canada's First Ministers in February 1978, provincial governments voiced concerns about the problem of overlapping responsibilities of the federal and provincial governments in the regulation area, and about the mushrooming of regulation in general. Following the conference, the federal government instructed the Economic Council of Canada to undertake a wide-ranging investigation of the effect of regulation in Canada, and between 1978 and 1981, the Council commissioned a large number of studies of regulation in specific industries. In the final report the Council made sweeping recommendations for abolishing or reducing regulation in many Canadian industries (particularly in trucking, air transport, telecommunications, and agriculture).

By the mid-1980s, the government appeared to be moving decisively in the direction of deregulation in some sectors. In July of 1985, the Minister of Transport, Don Mazankowski, issued a discussion paper on deregulation in transportation, which incorporated many proposals similar to the recommendations by the Economic Council. For example, the paper recommends that current restrictions on entry in the airline industry be abandoned and that any firm "fit, willing, and able" to provide air service on a particular route be allowed to do so; it also recommends abolition of current restrictions on rate setting. For railways, it is proposed to allow confidential contracts between a railroad company and a shipper (under current rules railroads must make their rates public and are not allowed to offer rebates to shippers). The paper also advocates a reduction in the use of cross-subsidization in cases where transportation firms are asked by the government to serve communities or shippers that they would prefer not to service: In any such case of

the railroad track. By this time, Westerners were divided on the question of whether or not they wanted the Crowsnest subsidy to continue. Grain farmers said yes because it increased the price they received for their grain (after they paid for the reduced transport costs). But this higher value of grain in the West led to opposition from Western beef farmers because of the higher price they had to pay for the grain they feed their cattle. Furthermore, the higher price of grain—and smaller beef industry—made it more difficult for the West to attract food-processing firms away from their traditional location in the East.

Courtesy Canapress Photo Service

"imposed public duties," a direct payment by the government is seen as a better way than cross-subsidization to compensate the firms.

The federal government has also come out in support of initiatives to deregulate trucking. In February 1985, an agreement was struck between federal and provincial transport ministers to move toward less restrictive entry regulation by shifting the burden of proof from the new applicants to the existing firms in the industry. (That is, rather than the applicant having to prove that serving a new route would be in the public interest, it would be up to any existing firm opposing the application to prove that entry of the new firm would *not* be in the public interest.) The agreement also calls for reduced regulatory control over trucking rates.

It is difficult to tell how fast these and other proposals for deregulation will be implemented; the process of actually changing the rules is slow and cumbersome, and there will be vociferous opposition from the firms and consumers who benefit from the current rules. But some loosening of regulatory restrictions now seems likely.

In the United States, the trend toward deregulation started earlier, and has proceeded further than in Canada. Trucking was largely deregulated in 1980, and air travel as far back as 1978. In trying to forecast the effects of deregulation in Canada, the experience of the U.S. air travel industry since 1978 provides an interesting case study (Box 27-4).

III. "QUALITY-OF-LIFE" REGULATION TO IMPROVE HEALTH, SAFETY, AND WORKING CONDITIONS

The price/entry regulation described in the previous section is imposed in a single industry. By contrast, quality-of-life regulation of health and safety standards is usually applied economy-wide, on all industries. There is also another significant difference between the two types of regulation: Price/entry regulation (for example, in trucking or airlines) often comes to promote the interests of the firms being regulated; on the other hand, quality-of-life regulation is often opposed by regulated firms because it typically raises their costs and is considered a nuisance. Thus, quality-of-life agencies tend to reflect the views, not of the regulated firms, but instead of those who worked hard

to have the regulations imposed. For example, the regulations in the Canada Labour (Safety) Code, and the provincial laws on occupational safety tend to reflect the view of organized labour; and the agencies in Environment Canada tend to reflect the views of environmental groups. (Pollution and the role of Environment Canada in controlling it are studied further in the next chapter.)

Since quality-of-life regulation is introduced to promote important social objectives such as health, safety, and a better environment, it might be concluded that any regulation which contributes to these objectives is in the public interest. Many regulations probably do; but in some cases, the costs of a regulation may exceed its benefits, so that, on balance, it is not in the public interest.

Problems with Quality-of-Life Regulation: Inadequate Cost-Benefit Analysis

The improved health, safety, and environmental standards that are designed to provide obvious benefits to society also involve substantial costs. For example, when firms are required to purchase safety equipment, their costs rise. While the economy-wide evidence is that some of these higher costs are borne by the firms' owners or labour force in the form of lower income, much of the burden is passed on to customers in the form of higher prices. But in one way or another, the public pays for the health and safety benefits it receives.

Under what circumstances are we buying too little safety, and when are we buying too much? The answer is: We are buying too little whenever there are additional safety regulations that would cost less than the benefit they would provide. And we are buying too much if we have introduced safety standards with costs that exceed their benefits.

Examples of buying too little safety may be found by going back to the 1950s, when there were inadequate restrictions on the use and disposal of dangerous chemicals or radioactive wastes. An example of buying too much safety may be the proposed system of inflatable airbags intended to protect people in passenger cars in a crash: Even though the system has been extensively tested and has been shown to be effective in some cases, the regulatory agencies have judged that its benefits are not yet large enough to justify its considerable costs.

Thus, a new regulation *cannot be justified simply*

BOX 27-4

AIRLINE DEREGULATION IN THE UNITED STATES

Deregulation of airline fares in the United States occurred in early 1978. By the end of the year, U.S. air travellers were benefitting from lower fares. In turn, lower prices resulted in more airline travel. In 1978, passenger travel increased by 40% as airline fares fell by 20%. At the same time, the airline industry was entering a state of competitive flux. The major airlines did indeed drop some of their previous cross-subsidized service to small cities. However, between 1978 and 1983, 14 new airlines moved into the industry, not only to "fill the gap" by serving the small-city routes discontinued by the major airlines; they also provided the majors with severe competition on the big-city trunk routes. In the shakeout that often occurs when an industry becomes more competitive, several long-established airlines faced bankruptcy. While some narrowly escaped, one notable casualty was Braniff. With deregulation, Braniff had gone deeply into debt to buy new planes, in the hope of gaining a much larger share of the market.

The airline shakeout was complicated by a combination of unlucky events. Jet fuel prices doubled in 1979–80. Following a crash, DC-10s were grounded for more than a month in 1979 by the Federal Aviation Administration. Airline travel was further disrupted by a strike of air traffic controllers in 1981, and the recessions of 1980 and 1981–82 reduced the numbers of people flying.

In response to these external pressures, the airlines—now free to compete—tried to fill the empty seats by cutting prices. This was beneficial to travellers. It became possible to travel one way between New York and Los Angeles for $99. Moreover, passengers were now taking advantage of a much wider variety of discount fares; three out of four passengers travelled on a discount, compared to one in three before deregulation. However, this discounting added to the losses for the airlines.

Consequently, during this shakeout period the question arose: "How much of the financial difficulty of the airlines is due to deregulation, and how much is due to other pressures on the industry?" A number of airline executives, including some who had originally opposed deregulation, expressed the view that the airline companies—as well as passengers—had benefitted on balance from deregulation. For example, deregulation was allowing the airlines to move their equipment around quickly into more efficient routing patterns. Moreover, with the recovery during 1983 and 1984, with some of the shakeout complete, and with falling fuel prices, the airlines' profit-and-loss statements improved.

However, not all problems were solved. Deregulation allowed airlines to fly whenever and wherever they wished. Many of them scheduled flights for the rush hours along the trunk routes. The resulting traffic jams at the major airports left travellers late and angry. A simple market solution—auctioning off the right to each specific landing time—was resisted because it would make it prohibitively expensive for private planes to land and take off. Pressures were finally eased when the airlines were permitted to get together to discuss their scheduling problems. Some observers argued that this was much inferior to an auction of landing rights. There was a danger that the airlines might use an agreement over schedules as a way of limiting competition and working toward a private cartel.

---

because it promotes a desirable goal such as health, safety, or a better environment. Instead, it should be subjected to some kind of **benefit-cost** test.

Benefit-cost analysis involves estimating both the benefits and costs of a policy. A *benefit-cost test* is the requirement that the benefits of a policy be at least as great as its costs.

Obviously, this rule is sometimes difficult to apply because the costs, and especially the benefits, of a policy are hard to measure: How, for example, do you evaluate the benefit to workers and their families of a reduction in the number of accidents at the workplace, or the benefit to a community of architectural regulations which make new factories less of an eyesore? Yet, some attempt should be made. Often regulations

are introduced with no attempt whatsoever to estimate either their benefits or their costs. Most of the
fault for this does not lie with the regulatory agencies
themselves, but rather with the terms of reference they
have been given by the federal and provincial governments: Few agencies are required to do explicit benefit-
cost tests of their own regulations.

The Costs of Quality-of-life Regulation

*1. The payment of salaries and other costs of oper-
ating the regulatory agencies.* Although no comprehensive estimate of these costs exists for Canada (partly
because they are spread out over many agencies both
in the federal and provincial governments, and even
to some degree in municipal governments), evidence
from other countries suggests that these costs in Canada are likely to amount to several hundred million
dollars per year. While this represents a significant
sum, it is nevertheless relatively unimportant compared to other costs of regulation.

*2. Costs of regulation incurred by firms and con-
sumers.* These include the costs to business firms of
having to purchase health and safety equipment for
the workplace (such as protective enclosures for machines). These also include the increases in the cost of
production which result when products have to meet
higher standards of safety or freedom from pollution.
(For example, cars have become much more expensive in the 1970s and 1980s because higher standards
of crash protection have been imposed, and stricter
pollution limits have been set on exhaust emissions.)
Another cost of regulation that has become significant
in some industries is the manpower and other resources
that must be used in dealing with the paperwork required by regulatory agencies. This cost tends to be an
especially important item for firms planning to start
up production facilities in new areas: They must often
go through a long process of satisfying governments
at several levels that the proposed project will not have
an adverse environmental impact. It is also an important cost for small business firms that frequently don't
have the specialized manpower needed to deal with
the regulating agencies' requests for information of
various sorts.

A particularly frustrating effect of increasingly complex quality-of-life regulation is the delay that often
occurs in the regulatory process. For example, a company planning to introduce a new drug or food additive

may have to face a long delay before Health and Welfare Canada is satisfied that it meets the standards of
the Food and Drug Act. (Decisions on new drugs can,
of course, be made much more quickly if the drug has
already been tested in other countries, and the test
results are available to the Canadian authorities. But
that does not always solve the problem: The average
time required for testing and approval of a new drug
by the U.S. FDA [Food and Drug Administration] now
is roughly five to seven years. And reports of faked
test results in private companies that have investigated
chemicals for the American FDA may make Health and
Welfare Canada less willing to accept U.S. evidence in
approving new drugs.)

There may also be long delays in approval of projects
for which extensive environmental impact studies are
required (such as large-scale industrial developments or
energy projects in the Arctic). Such delays may involve
very significant costs to firms—especially those that
cannot begin to earn revenue from the new products
or projects until regulatory approval has been given.

Some of the costs of excessive delay may be borne
by the consumer. For example, if a new drug can save
the lives of people with a serious disease, a long delay
in introducing it will mean a loss of lives it could have
saved. (Because the regulators tend to be more severely
criticized for releasing a drug that turns out to be
unsafe than for delaying approval of a safe drug, they
tend to err on the side of delay. Consequently, some
economists have argued that regulators are now using
testing standards that are too strict.)

In both Canada and the United States, many observers attribute at least a part of the apparent slowing
down of productivity growth to the rising costs of
regulation. Many important investment projects that
could have raised productivity have been delayed or
abandoned altogether because of regulatory delays.
Moreover, critics argue, the more funds that must be
channelled into investment in safety and antipollution
equipment, the less that remain for other investments
in the equipment that produces increased output in
the future. Thus, lost output in the future is the opportunity cost of investment in antipollution and safety
equipment today.

Even though any estimate of the overall costs of
regulation must necessarily be subject to considerable
error, existing figures suggest that the costs of quality-
of-life regulation are now substantial. The question

is: Have these regulations provided benefits sufficient to justify this high cost?

Benefits of Quality-of-Life Regulation

Whereas most of the costs of quality-of-life regulation can be expressed in terms of a decrease in GNP or a slower rate of economic growth, the benefits of regulation cannot easily be expressed in terms of an increased GNP. (Benefits such as improved health or safety or a cleaner environment cannot be included in GNP, given present methods of measurement.) Instead, benefits have to be measured in a piecemeal fashion, for one type of regulation at a time. Past studies estimating benefits have yielded mixed results. For example, in 1981 the Economic Council estimated the effects of increasingly detailed federal and provincial regulation of safety in the workplace. The evidence was disappointing: In spite of the more stringent safety rules (and even though a growing proportion of the labour force was working in the relatively safe service sector), the number of reported work injuries was slightly higher at the end of the 1970s than at the beginning of the decade. The incidence of occupationally induced illness also did not seem to be declining (but this may have been due in part to previous underreporting of such diseases).

On the other hand, some regulations did seem to generate substantial benefits. For example, federal and provincial regulation to reduce air and water pollution has apparently not only ended a trend toward a more polluted environment, but in some cases has even reversed it (as we detail in the next chapter). Moreover, U.S. and Canadian regulation giving more stringent specifications for the construction of cars to make them safer, together with laws lowering speed limits and making it mandatory for drivers to wear seatbelts, have all contributed to a reduction in auto injuries and fatalities. This is even more impressive because, during the 1970s and 1980s, cars were becoming smaller and lighter—and for this reason less safe. Therefore, just preventing the safety record from getting worse represented substantial success.

Thus, while quality-of-life regulations have come at high cost, their benefits have been mixed: important in some areas, disappointing in others. Accordingly, by the early 1980s, some regulatory agencies were under pressure to reduce existing regulations and to be more selective in introducing new ones.

How Can the Regulatory Process Be Improved?

Because of the problems in estimating both the costs and the benefits of quality-of-life regulation, it is difficult to judge whether or not present regulation has gone too far. The recent Economic Council study also raises the question of whether the whole process of regulation is seriously flawed. Time and again, the large and small business firms interviewed in the study complained of the confusion and delays that had resulted from overlapping jurisdiction and responsibility among various regulatory agencies—and also among the agencies of different levels of government. (In the case of a proposed new steel plant in Nanticoke, Ontario, the Steel Company of Canada had to report on the project's environmental impact to seven major regulatory agencies: two federal departments, four Ontario ministries, and one International Joint Commission. Stelco claimed that both the construction and operating costs were substantially increased by the delays and changes required by these agencies; and that the required changes didn't improve the environmental impact after all.) Many of the Council's recommendations, therefore, focus on improving the regulatory process. By reducing the bureaucratic confusion and overlapping federal and provincial responsibilities, we might hope to gain the same quality-of-life benefits at a lower cost.

But the most promising suggestion is likely to be a requirement that any new regulation pass a benefit-cost test. However, benefit-cost analysis is difficult, not only for the reasons noted already, but for others as well: For example, it is difficult enough to estimate that the cost of a certain regulation will be $4 million and its benefit will be the saving of 20 lives. But that is only half the job: Before these two figures can be compared, it is necessary to put a dollar value on the human lives that are saved. And how do you do that? (For some suggestions, see Box 27-5.)

Thus benefit-cost analysis must, by its very nature, remain imprecise. Nonetheless, despite its limitations, it will still be far superior to the system used in the late 1970s when regulations were sometimes being introduced with little evidence of benefits and little regard for costs. As an example of how this may result in "too much regulation," consider the case of saccharin, a very mild carcinogen that had to be banned temporarily in the United States because of a law that prohibited adding artificial carcinogens to food. Accord-

BOX 27-5

THE ETERNAL PUZZLE:
What Is a Human Life Worth?

Thief (holding a gun): "Your money or your life."
Jack Benny (pausing): ". . . I'm thinking . . . . I'm thinking."

The simple answer to the question in the title is: Any life is worth an infinite amount. The miner trapped underground has a life which is priceless. Yet, we don't value our own lives this way. Were they to have infinite value, safety concerns would dominate all others. We would live as close as possible to our work and never drive a car, let alone take a trip to earn something as trivial as a few thousand dollars.

Society doesn't place an infinite value on a life either. To illustrate: Lives can be saved by installing crash barriers down the middle of roads. Yet we don't do this on every country road. We simply aren't willing to spend the billions of dollars this would cost. This then raises the critical question: "How much are we willing to spend to save a human life?" This is really just a recasting of the original question: "What is a human life worth?" However, this new question is one that everyone—including even those who philosophically refuse to place a money value on a human life—will recognize should be asked if we want to make a sensible decision on, say, whether a crash barrier will be built or not.

Why not then just ask people: "What would you be willing to pay to save your life?" Unfortunately, we wouldn't be able to get a sensible reply to this question because almost everyone would say "An infinite amount if I could get my hands on it." However, we can estimate how much people value their lives by observing those who actually "put their lives on the line." Thus we may ask, for example: "How much more than the average wage must be paid to induce a worker to take a high-risk job like that of a lumberjack?"

Although this is probably the most promising way of evaluating a human life, several difficulties remain.* For example: (1) This estimate includes only the valuation of the person's own life. But isn't an additional value placed on this life by family and friends? (2) The higher wage paid in high-risk jobs only indicates how the workers who actually take these jobs value their lives. But isn't this far less than the valuation of the vast majority of the population who won't take such risky jobs because they value their lives more highly? (3) How much of the higher wage is compensation for the risk of death, and how much for the risk of injury? The higher wage compensates for both, but we are only interested in evaluating the risk of death. (4) These esti-

*It is certainly an improvement over one of the early methods which has frequently been used in legal judgements—namely, evaluate a life by asking: "How much would the individual have earned over the rest of his or her lifetime?" This yields a poor measure because it implies that the value of the life of a disabled person unable to work is zero.

ing to this law, the enormous benefits of saccharin could not even be considered. (As a sugar substitute, it helped people keep their weight down, and thus reduced death from heart failure.) So the U.S. ban on saccharin—followed by a similar ban in Canada—may have saved some lives from cancer but lost at least as many more from overweight.

This saccharin example illustrates the final respect in which regulation requires reform. It should be made more consistent. Why should saccharin have been banned outright because it was a food additive, when there was no similar ban against natural foods that

had cancer-inducing effects? And why stop at foods, and thus exclude tobacco, one of the strongest carcinogens humans contact?

CONCLUDING OBSERVATIONS:
Regulatory Conflicts and the Shift in Economic Decision Making

Federal and provincial politicians are faced with a wide array of problems which involve large expenditures of their own time and public funds. It is no surprise, therefore, that whenever they encounter a problem that can apparently be solved by passing a

mates are meaningful only if the people taking these jobs understand the risks they are taking.

In a recent study, Martin Bailey of the University of Maryland looked at how workers act in risky situations. Their behaviour suggests that they estimate the value of their own lives somewhere in the $200,000 to $700,000 range.† The imprecision of this estimate illustrates how difficult it is to place a value on a human life.

Courtesy Miller Services Limited

†Martin J. Bailey, *Reducing Risks to Life: Measurement of the Benefits* (Washington: American Enterprise Institute, 1980).

Rachel Dardis uses a different approach, examining how much consumers are willing to pay for fire detectors that reduce the risk to their lives. She concludes that the value of a human life is between $200,000 and $500,000—that is, in the bottom half of Bailey's range. See Dardis, "The Value of Life: New Evidence from the Marketplace," *American Economic Review* (December 1980): 1077–82.

new law or setting up a regulatory agency, they are inclined to do so. (Although this involves spending a minimum of taxpayers' money, the public still pays. But payment occurs in hidden ways, for example in a higher price for autos because of pollution controls. The public does not pay very much in the form of taxes that are easy to blame on the politicians.)

Because the costs are hidden in this way and because politicians at all levels of government are continually being urged by various interest groups to introduce more regulation, the pressure toward more and more comprehensive and detailed regulation will remain.

The final observation is that the rapid growth of regulation has resulted in a substantial shift in decision making away from the economic marketplace: Business decisions that were once determined in the marketplace are now increasingly being influenced by the regulatory agencies, the federal and provincial governments, and the courts. The question arises: Could we not have done a less expensive and more effective job of pursuing the praiseworthy objectives of these agencies by continuing to rely on the market, but in a specially modified form? Answering this question is one of our major objectives in the next chapter.

KEY POINTS

1. Federal and provincial governments regulate business in three principal ways: (a) through anti-combines law which is designed to keep markets competitive by limiting the amount of market power that a firm or a group of firms can accumulate; (b) through regulatory agencies which control price and conditions of entry into certain industries—including both natural monopolies (such as local phone companies or railroads) and more naturally competitive industries such as trucking, airlines, or milk and egg production; and (c) through other agencies which are responsible for health, safety, and working conditions economy-wide (across all industries).

2. Anti-combines legislation (and other kinds of competition policy) raise difficult questions. For example, when is price cutting unfair or "predatory"? How do you know when firms are colluding? How effective is import competition in limiting market power of Canadian oligopolists?

3. The Combines Investigation Act has strengthened competition in the Canadian economy, because violations can lead to fines and damaging adverse publicity. The main sections of the Act deal with price fixing and "monopoly and merger"; other important sections deal with price discrimination, resale price maintenance, and misleading advertising and tied selling.

4. Although government regulation may be appropriate for dealing with natural monopolies, its usefulness in naturally more competitive industries such as trucking, air transport, or agriculture is less clear. Many economists have charged that government regulation in such industries has increasingly become a legal way of limiting competition and raising the market price. By the mid-1980s, there was a trend toward some reduction of regulation, especially in the transport sector.

5. A particular quality-of-life regulation cannot be justified simply because it is imposed in pursuit of a desirable goal—even if the goal is saving lives. Instead, regulations should be subjected to at least some sort of benefit-cost test. But estimating benefits and costs is often difficult, and judgement must sometimes be substituted when good estimates are not available.

6. Growing regulation and a larger economic role for the government has meant that economic decision making in Canada is gradually shifting from the marketplace to the political arena or the courts. The question whether the scope of regulation should be extended or reduced will continue to be an important topic of debate in Canada in future years.

KEY CONCEPTS

competition policy
Combines Investigation Act
advantage of large firms
how import competition reduces
  market power
cut-throat or predatory
  competition
collusion
price fixing
resale price maintenance

Restrictive Trade Practices
  Commission
horizontal merger
vertical merger
conglomerate merger
workable competition
Competition Act
laws that restrict competition
regulated industries and
  anti-combines law

price/entry regulation
cross-subsidization
quality-of-life regulation
the value of a life
direct and indirect costs
  of regulation
benefit-cost analysis
overlapping regulation
  responsibilities

PROBLEMS

27-1 It sounds like a good idea to forbid any firm from predatory price cutting if this would drive its competitors out of business. But consider the two examples below. In each case, do you think that the price-cutting action should be judged illegal (as it sometimes has been)?

(a) An efficient firm with lower cost charges a lower price, and thus drives its less efficient competitors out of business. This is an example of how our competitive system works: The more efficient take business away from the less efficient. Do you think this is a good system? If the less efficient are not driven out of business, what happens to the cost of producing goods?

(b) In a natural monopoly with economies of scale, the large expanding firm finds its costs are falling; hence, it lowers its price and drives its small competitors out of business.

Do you see now why enforcing the Combines Investigation Act may be difficult?

27-2 Which of the following agreements between firms in an industry do you judge desirable? undesirable?

(a) an agreement to reduce output by 10 percent to end a glut on the market

(b) an agreement to quote the same price

(c) an agreement by the CN and CP railroads to lay the same width of track

27-3 Suppose that, for the last 10 years, a government agency had regulated the prices of hotel rooms, thus preventing price competition among big companies like Holiday Inn and CP Hotels. Suppose, also, that in return, these companies had maintained hotels in many smaller cities. Suppose the government is now considering an end to this regulation. As an advisor to this industry, draw up a brief on how dangerous this action would be. Now switch roles, and criticize the brief. In your view, which is the stronger case? Do you think this example is similar to trucking regulation? (In fact, this analogy was used by the opponents of airline regulation in the United States.)

*27-4 To understand cross-subsidization better, consider a simplified example in which there are two individuals: A lives in a large city, B in a small one. Initially, in an unregulated situation, A gets airline service at price P_1, while B gets none. Draw the demand curves for both individuals. Show how it may be possible to get a collective benefit (an increase in the combined consumer surplus of both) by the following policy of cross-subsidization: B is forced to pay a price above P_1 (and has consumer surplus reduced) in order to allow A for the first time to have airline service (and thereby enjoy a consumer surplus). Show how this policy may provide a collective benefit (an increase in the combined consumer surplus of both individuals taken together).

27-5 Provincial regulation in Ontario stipulates that a person can be fitted with dentures only by a dentist or by somebody working under the direct supervision of a dentist. In recent years, Ontario denturists (technicians who construct dentures) have asked for a change in the law, so that it would allow them to fit a patient with dentures without supervision. Ontario dentists have opposed this regulatory change.

(a) What argument do you think the dentists have used in opposing the regulatory change?

(b) Can you think of some other reason why dentists were opposed to the change?

27-6 Supporters of more strict government regulation of the Canadian economy have on occasion used the following argument: "A clean environment is a necessary precondition for any economic activity. Similarly, safety for the labour force is a necessary precondition for manufacturing. Thus these objectives must be achieved regardless of what their benefits and cost may be." Do you agree? Explain why or why not.

27-7 Should a careless driver whose car is destroyed when he runs into a railroad train be able to sue the auto maker for producing a car that involves an unreasonable safety risk? Should he be able to sue the auto company if he has bumped into another car at very slow speed and his engine has exploded as a consequence? If your answer differs in these two cases, how do you draw the line?

APPENDIX

MERGERS, BREAK-UPS, AND COMPETITION

In this appendix, we discuss two important issues in competition policy that were only briefly touched on in the main text.

The first is the issue of conglomerate mergers. While the possible anti-competitive effects of horizontal and vertical mergers are fairly obvious, whether conglomerate mergers and takeovers adversely affect the national interest, is a much more controversial question.

As a first step toward providing an answer, we discuss the pros and cons of mergers and takeovers from three different points of view: (1) the acquiring firm; (2) the "target" firm; and (3) society as a whole. We also consider various strategies that can be used when there is a "takeover battle" such as occurred recently when Unicorp of Toronto took over Union Gas, a southern Ontario natural gas distributor and resource company.

Second, we briefly discuss the strategy of *breaking up* large corporations. The logic of this strategy is simple. If preventing firms from acquiring a monopoly or a monopoly-like position is beneficial because it increases competition and protects the public against the exercise of market power, doesn't it follow that it may also be beneficial to break up a large firm that has somehow already managed to become dominant in a market? In the United States, the strategy of ordering the break-up of large firms has in fact been followed on a number of occasions. Should Canada follow this U.S. example?

MERGERS: THE INTERESTS OF THE ACQUIRING FIRM

What are the incentives for one firm to acquire another?

In the main text, we focused on one possible incentive: the desire to acquire a bigger market share. But this is not the only reason for mergers and takeovers. In particular, it does not explain conglomerate mergers or takeovers where the firms that are merged are in different industries.

Sometimes, mergers may be motivated by tax considerations. For example, it may pay for a profitable company—firm A—to take over a company—firm B—that has been suffering losses: Firm A may then use the past accumulated losses of B to reduce its taxable income and thus reduce its tax liability. Another example of takeovers induced by tax considerations was the spate of takeovers of foreign-owned firms in the oil and gas industry by Canadian companies (such as Dome Petroleum) in the early 1980s. Under the National Energy Program introduced by the Liberal government in 1979, foreign-owned firms were discriminated against in that they had to pay higher taxes and were not eligible for subsidies that Canadian companies could claim. Thus, energy assets in Canada were worth more if they were owned by Canadians than if they were foreign-owned, and there was an incentive for Canadian-owned firms to acquire the assets of foreign-owned firms. However, tax advantages play a much smaller role in explaining mergers or takeovers in Canada than in the United States. The reason is that in Canada, the system of dividend tax credits, explained in Chapter 6, has effectively eliminated the double taxation of dividend income. In the United States, dividend income is still subject to double taxation. (Before it becomes after-tax income of the shareholder, it has been subject to both the corporation income tax, and the personal income tax of the shareholder.) Therefore, profitable firms in the United

States have more incentive than profitable Canadian firms to use their profits in other ways than paying them out as dividends, and using them to take over other firms is one alternative.

In the case of a horizontal merger, such as the purchase by one steel company of another, the new, higher-volume company may be able to achieve economies of scale simply because its output of steel has increased. In the case of any of the three kinds of merger, the acquisition of another business may be a challenging way for a firm to use underutilized management talent. That is, expanding the firm may be a way of achieving economies of scale in management. There may also be economies of scale in R&D. To illustrate, Saab-Scania, a Swedish conglomerate, produces aircraft, trucks, and automobiles, thereby reducing the design and engineering costs of each. Another incentive for a merger is to diversify by expanding into a new business. For example, if a firm is producing ski equipment with profits in the winter, its management may be interested in acquiring a tennis equipment company to provide profits in the summer.

One of the largest mergers in recent North American history provides an example both of the importance of potential scale economies and diversification as motives for a merger. In the summer of 1985, Genstar Corporation of Toronto acquired control over Canada Trustco Mortgage Company of London, Ontario. Since Genstar already owned Canada Permanent Mortgage Corp., another trust company, its main purpose in taking over Canada Trust was to create a single large trust company. (The combined assets of the two companies were $21 billion, which means that the new company is as large as a major Canadian chartered bank.)

The new corporation will be large enough to take advantage of economies of scale in the production of financial services. In addition, it will be a highly diversified company, in several ways. For example, the Permanent has a strong branch network in the Maritimes, Quebec, and eastern Ontario, while Canada Trust has more branches in southwestern Ontario and the western provinces. The Permanent has developed special expertise in real estate brokerage and lending to medium-sized business, while Canada Trust has concentrated on term loans to large corporations and management of pension funds.

Another factor that plays a role in making a corporation interested in a takeover is the price of the "target firm's" shares. From the viewpoint of the acquiring firm, an attractive target is a firm whose shares are priced low relative to the value of its assets and profit potential. For example, firm A's shares may be priced low in the stock market because it has weak management. If firm B is a well-managed firm with an abundance of talented executives, a takeover will be an attractive strategy: If B takes over A, it can ease out the existing managers of A and install its own managers instead. With better management, the profits of A are likely to rise, and the prices of its shares will rise as well. The market price of the shares of the *acquiring* firm may also play a role in some cases. For example, the price of shares in well-managed company B may be high relative to the value of its fixed assets, or in relation to its actual earnings, simply because the market recognizes the superior competence of its managers. This makes a takeover look like an attractive strategy from the viewpoint of B's managers and shareholders: It can pay for the shares of target firm A by issuing a relatively small amount of its own high-priced shares. Thus, share prices in the stock market may play a role in indicating which firms may be involved in takeovers, either as acquiring firms or as targets.

MERGERS: THE INTERESTS OF THE TARGET FIRM

Shareholders of a firm may welcome a takeover bid by another firm, since they are typically offered more than the current market price of their stock. Thus, one game in the stock market is to try to identify and buy the stock of potential target companies before they actually receive takeover bids.

While the *shareholders* of a target firm may welcome a takeover bid, a quite different view may be taken by its *management*—the president, vice-presidents, etc., who run the company. Why would managers object? After all, they are frequently also large shareholders, and this gives them an incentive for welcoming a takeover. However, *in their role as managers* they often oppose a takeover because the corporate reorganization that follows may place their jobs in jeopardy. In order to protect managers in the event of a merger, they are sometimes offered a "golden parachute" contract—that is, the right to a large financial settlement if they decide to "bail out" of the merged firm, or if they are fired.

If the management of a target firm agrees, the takeover is a "friendly" one, and there may be little fanfare in the press. The highly publicized struggles occur when the takeover is contested, because management decides to resist the acquiring firm, which is then called a "shark" or a "black knight."

Dramatic takeover struggles have been common in the United States for several years. In the mid-1980s, they became more frequent in Canada as well. A spectacular example was the battle that occurred in the summer of 1985 when Unicorp of Toronto took over Union Gas of Chatham, Ontario. It was a classic struggle, with Union's management trying desperately, but ultimately unsuccessfully, to stave off the takeover. (The resistance operation was codenamed "Project Doug Harvey," in honour of a former defenceman on the Montreal Canadiens hockey team.)

WHITE KNIGHTS, GREENMAIL, AND OTHER FORMS OF SHARK REPELLANT

Here are some of the strategies the management of a target firm may use to resist an unfriendly takeover:

1. The target firm may use various legal manoeuvres to block the takeover. In the Unicorp-Union Gas fracas, Union Gas tried to invoke a regulation that no shareholder could hold more than 20% of the shares of a regulated utility, such as a distributor of natural gas. (The attempt failed on a technicality: Formally, Unicorp took over not Union Gas but Union Enterprises, a holding company with 100% ownership of Union Gas and some allied companies. The government ruled that the ownership restriction did not apply to such a holding company.)

2. When a target firm realizes its stock is being accumulated by a "shark," the target firm may buy back this stock by offering the shark a premium price for it, that is, a price above its current market value. Because some view this payoff in the face of a threat as a legal form of blackmail, it is called "greenmail."

   Who bears the cost of this greenmail? The answer is: the other shareholders who don't get paid off; they are left with a company of diminished value because money has been wasted in this payoff. Thus, the payment of greenmail is a way for top executives to save their jobs by using small shareholders' money to pay off big shareholders (the sharks). Sometimes smaller shareholders become so infuriated that they sue the executives for making this payment.

   An interesting variant of this strategy was considered by Union Gas: It was proposed that the firm's employee pension fund would buy back the Union Gas shares that Unicorp had already acquired. In such a case, it would be the employees in the pension plan who would pay the greenmail.

3. Another way of dealing with a shark is the Pac-Man strategy of eating it before it eats you. In the Unicorp-Union Gas battle, it was in fact suggested that Union Gas might turn around and take over Unicorp, paying for the purchase with an issue of Union Gas shares. However, nothing came of this, so Union Gas tried a fourth form of resistance.

4. Find a "white knight," a friendly company with compatible goals and substantial resources that is invited to take over the target company in order to prevent it from falling into unfriendly hands. In the Union Gas case, Redpath Industries was initially considered for the role of white knight; the president of Union Gas, former Ontario Treasurer Darcy McKeough, was also the chairman of Redpath. When this did not work out, Union Gas tried a fifth strategy.

5. Take a poison pill: That is, the target firm takes some action that makes it less attractive to the shark. To make itself a less attractive target, Union Gas bought control of a third corporation, Burns Foods Ltd. of Calgary, paying for the purchase with an issue of $125 million in Union Gas voting preferred shares. As a result of this increase in the number of outstanding voting shares in Union Gas, Unicorp had to buy a larger number of shares than before in order to get voting control of Union Gas. When the takeover was finally accomplished in spite of Union's resistance, Unicorp found itself the unwilling owner of Burns Foods as well.

MERGERS: THE INTERESTS OF SOCIETY

Benefits of mergers. The basic argument for allowing mergers is that they are the result of a search for business profit, and, *provided that competition is not restricted*, this profit is likely to result in an economic gain for society. There are exceptions. For example, the payoff to greenmailers represents a transfer from present shareholders, with no additional income or wealth created. A second example occurs when lower taxes constitute the only gain from a merger.

To illustrate how mergers may indeed lead to economic gains, consider a merger that does not reduce competition or decrease employment. Let's first ask the question: What kind of firm is most likely to be a target for such a merger or takeover? The answer: A firm that, for some reason, is making inefficient use of its assets, so that it earns a relatively low return and its shares therefore sell at a low price in the stock market. Such a firm will look like an attractive target for a firm that expects to be able to make more efficient use of the assets. To the acquiring firm, it is the prospect of increased profits that constitutes the reason for the takeover; to society, it is the more efficient use of the assets that represents the gain. Notice also that while the gain in efficiency may initially be reflected primarily in increased profits of the firm's owners, it may later on (through competition) benefit others in the economy: Workers whose wages rise because their productivity has risen, and consumers who may benefit from lower prices for the firm's products as costs fall when efficiency improves.

Cost of mergers. If a merger restricts competition, then, like any form of monopolization, it is likely to result in private profit for the firms but an efficiency loss to society. This is why the regulators, in evaluating a merger, ask: "Would this merger increase the monopolization of a market?"

For several additional reasons, it has been argued that mergers may be damaging on balance. Size itself may be considered objectionable, especially if one considers the political implications of the concentration of power in the hands of very large firms. For example, the giant American conglomerate IT&T became involved in schemes to try to prevent the election of Salvador Allende as president of Chile.

Mergers may also have a long-term deterrent effect on entrepreneurship. The fear of an eventual takeover may discourage entrepreneurs from setting up and developing their own businesses. While this may be true in some cases, in others it is not. Some entrepreneurs set up a business in the *hope* it will be taken over; they view an attractive takeover offer as their eventual financial reward. They will particularly welcome a takeover if their business has reached a point where it is worth more to sell than to continue to operate it themselves.

BREAKING UP EXISTING FIRMS TO INCREASE COMPETITION

Most of the efforts of those enforcing Canada's anti-combines policy goes toward trying to *prevent* firms from obtaining too large a market share in the first place. But if doing this is a good way of increasing competition, what about the case where we are faced with a firm that has already managed somehow to become the dominant firm in an industry? Wouldn't it be a good idea to try to promote competition by actually *breaking up* such a firm?

The strategy of actually trying to break up large, monopoly-like firms has not played a major role in Canada's competition policy. In the United States, however, the anti-trust regulators have tried this strategy on several occasions, and some of the most complicated and well-publicized anti-trust cases have involved such break-ups.

The strategy has not always worked. For example, on its last business day in early 1969, the outgoing administration of President Lyndon Johnson filed suit against IBM for trying to monopolize the computer business. The case dragged on and on. The government didn't even begin to present its case until 1975, and then took three years to complete it; one witness alone was on the stand for 78 days. Two judges observed that the case was lasting longer than World War II and jokingly suggested that it might cost more. Little wonder that lawyers referred to the case as a "black hole" into which their careers might disappear without a trace. In 1982, the government dropped its case on the grounds that is was "without merit."

The outcome was different in an anti-trust action initiated in 1974 against another giant: AT&T (American Telephone and Telegraph), a company that held a monopoly in the provision of some phone services. AT&T was a huge company with assets greater than those of Exxon, Mobil, and General Motors combined.

Specifically, the U.S. Justice Department sued AT&T to force it to divest itself of Western Electric, its manufacturer of telephone equipment. Because of serious delays, such as the death of the first judge, the case didn't go to trial until 1981. Because both AT&T and the Reagan administration wished to reduce the uncertainty surrounding the future of the company, they reached an out-of-court settlement in 1982 to split up AT&T, not into two companies, but instead into eight. Seven of the new companies each now provide local phone service to a U.S. region. The eighth company— the new leaner (and meaner?) AT&T—still retains Western Electric to produce telephone equipment, along with divisions that provide research and long distance service. An AT&T executive described the break-up as the "largest corporate event in history, like taking apart a 747 and putting it back together again while it is still in the air."

Telephone users who previously dealt with only one phone company—the old AT&T—often found their service deteriorating. Moreover, the rates on local phone services were increased to more fully cover their costs. On the other hand, rates were reduced on long distance services, where AT&T faced competition and where costs had been falling as technology improved. The price of much phone equipment fell as Western Electric now had to face increased competition.

Because the old AT&T had been one of the world's most efficient telephone systems, breaking it up was a clear rejection of the guideline "If it works, don't fix it." It wasn't immediately clear whether the new system would work better or worse than the old. This depended on the answers to a large number of questions, such as: Would economies of scale be lost because of the break-up? On the other hand, would new, more intense competition reduce costs? Would Bell Labs, the research wing of AT&T, lose or retain the excellence that had led to such inventions as the transistor?

PROBLEM

27-3 Explain why the tax incentives for conglomerate mergers are stronger in the United States than in Canada. What other reasons are there for Canadian firms to undertake mergers? Do you think Canadian anti-combines law should take a tougher stand on mergers? Why or why not?

Chapter 28

PROTECTING THE ENVIRONMENT IN A GROWING ECONOMY: HOW SHOULD POLLUTION BE LIMITED?

Nature has been kind to mankind. But nature's response
has limits. Its recuperative powers are finite . . . so
man must learn to respect the laws of nature and live within
their bounds as the earth's other creatures have to do.

Environment Canada

During recent decades, we have become increasingly aware of the pollution of our environment. Air pollution causes the acid rain problem which is destroying life in many lakes in North America and Europe. (In a 1980 report, the Canada Centre for Inland Waters estimated that as many as 4,000 Ontario lakes have become so affected by acid rain that a fish population cannot live in them.) Air pollution also reduces the life expectancy of the residents of big North American cities by an estimated two years.[1]

Water pollution poisons fish and drinking water. In

1970, the Indian community of Grassy Narrows on the English-Wabigoon river system in northern Ontario was severely disrupted when deadly concentrations of mercury were discovered in fish caught in the river. In the Great Lakes region, scientists have identified nearly a thousand different chemicals that enter the lakes from factories, chemical waste dumps, sewage plants, and farm fields. Even very small amounts of highly toxic chemicals, such as PCBs and dioxins, are enough to gradually cause high concentrations in birds, fish, and humans—and these are chemicals that never break down naturally. Warns Pollution Probe, an environmental lobby group based in Toronto: "Unless governments really come to grips with the problem soon, the

[1]Lester B. Lave and Eugene P. Seskin, *Air Pollution and Human Health* (Washington: Resources for the Future, 1977).

water from Lake Ontario will be undrinkable in 10 years."

POLLUTION: THE COSTLY JOB OF CONTROL

Both federal and provincial governments have responded to the pollution problem by passing legislation to protect the environment. The most important federal statutes are the Canadian Water Act, the Clean Air Act, and the Environmental Contaminants Act.[2] However, because constitutional authority for legislation over the environment rests mainly with the provinces, enforcement of these federal statutes also requires separate provincial legislation, and all provinces have their own anti-pollution laws. Most of the time, federal and provincial officials cooperate in enforcing anti-pollution laws; but occasionally the job is made more difficult by disagreements between the two levels of government about the question of who has jurisdiction over a particular area of environmental regulation.

One of the most important roles of federal legislation has been to take the lead in setting acceptable *standards* for the quality of our air and water. The federal government also provides a nationwide system for monitoring pollution, by measuring the concentrations of pollutants in the air and water. Federal tax laws also encourage investment in anti-pollution equipment by private firms: It allows the firms to reduce their corporation tax liability by letting them depreciate the cost of such investments over a short period.

Another role of the government's environmental legislation is to limit the pollution discharged by *products*. This legislation covers such pollutants as emissions from cars and trucks, and radiation from television sets and alarm clocks with illuminated dials.

While pollution continues to be an enormous problem, the government's environmental regulation and the large investments in anti-pollution equipment have nevertheless had considerable success: There has been substantial progress in cleaning up the environment. Today, the air in Canada's cities is less befouled by

[2]Other federal statutes also deal with environmental issues: The Ocean Dumping Control Act, the Northern Inland Water Act, the Arctic Waters Pollution Protection Act, and parts of the Fisheries Act are important examples.

lead, carbon monoxide, and other noxious gases than it was in the early 1970s. The Great Lakes are cleaner and clearer: Commercial fishing is once again allowed in areas where it was previously prohibited, and the beaches of Lake Erie, once closed to swimming because of the polluted water, have now been opened again. There has been progress in the United States too. There are now boutiques in Cleveland along the Cuyahoga, a river that used to be so contaminated with oil and debris that it twice caught fire. In some places, salmon have come back to rivers that were previously dead: People in downtown Bangor, Maine, claim to be catching 20-pounders in the Penobscot River during lunch hour.

But these tales tell only half the story. The environmental laws are to be judged not only by such instances where the environment has improved, but also by a number of instances where the environment has not improved—where the sole "success" has been to keep the environment from getting worse. It is important to recognize that pollution will be a continuing problem, because we will never be able to eliminate it completely. Even if we were to bring industry to a standstill by closing down every plant that did any polluting whatsoever, pollutants from millions of country barnyards and city streets would still wash into our streams. Since it is not possible to *eliminate* pollution, the practical questions are:

How far should pollution be cut back? What costs should we be willing to bear?

Before answering these questions, we should understand the various costs involved in pollution control. No matter how the clean-up is initially financed, the public eventually bears the burden in one way or another:

1. As taxpayers, we pay higher taxes because of the subsidies granted to firms installing pollution-control equipment.
2. Since these subsidies cover only part of the cost of that equipment, some must also be borne by the firms that install it. In turn, they pass on much of this burden to the public by charging more for their products.
3. Alternatively, to the degree that firms "pay for"

pollution control equipment by investing less in other types of capital equipment, our growth of productivity and output are reduced. Thus, the public pays in the future.

4. The most highly publicized cost occurs when jobs are lost because pollution-control standards force a plant to close down, or cause it to lose sales to imports.

In the choice between creating jobs and protecting the environment, job creation often wins, especially in depressed areas. In November 1985, the government of Nova Scotia faced the decision whether to resume local production of coke for its steel mill in Sydney, or to permanently close the coke ovens and import the coke from elsewhere. Federal officials recommended closing. Earlier studies (when the coke ovens were operating) had found elevated levels of carcinogenic chemicals in the air in Sydney, and death rates from cancer and lung diseases were significantly higher among people living downwind from the plant than among those living upwind, or elsewhere in Canada. Nevertheless, the government decided to re-open the ovens: To keep them closed and import coke from elsewhere would have meant a loss of jobs both at Sydney Steel and in the Cape Breton coal fields (where the coal for the local coke production is mined).

In one way or another, the cost of controlling pollution touches us all. It is a large tab—no one really knows how large. It has been estimated that properly cleaning up just one of the leaking chemical dumps in the Niagara Falls area might cost as much as $300 million. With respect to air pollution, American government officials have estimated that a substantial reduction in the acid rain problem alone could cost more than $20 *billion*.

Because it is so costly to control pollution, we should use the least expensive methods. Unfortunately, we have often not used these methods in the past: One of the major criticisms of past pollution-control policies is that they have been far too expensive. This chapter will explain why, and outline a better approach. (A worse policy, but one that is sometimes recommended, is described in Box 28-1.) But first, we consider why government intervention is necessary in the first place. Why does the private market fail? Why can't we count on Adam Smith's "invisible hand" to limit pollution?

POLLUTION: AN EXTERNAL COST

When pollution exists, private and social costs differ. To illustrate why, consider a pulp and paper factory located on a river. The costs of paper to society include not only the private or **internal cost** of production faced by the pulp and paper firm, but also the cost to those who live downstream and must put up with the wastes that the firm releases into the river. While the pulp and paper firm has to pay for internal production costs, any cost downstream is **external** to its operation, since this cost must be borne by others.

> *Internal* or *private* costs are the costs incurred by those who actually produce or consume a good. *External* costs—also known as *neighbourhood* costs or cost *spillovers*—are costs borne by others. Pollution is an example.

Consider a simple illustration. Suppose that each unit of a product is treated with an ounce of a fluid that is then released as waste into a river. Suppose also that each of these ounces of fluid imposes a constant damage to those downstream. Then each unit of output imposes a constant external pollution cost, shown as the short, dark red arrow in Figure 28-1. When it is added to the internal cost borne by producers (the black arrow MC), the result is the tall arrow MC$_S$,

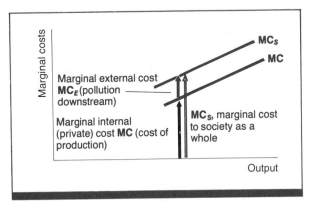

Figure 28-1 With pollution, private and social costs differ. The marginal cost to society of a good, shown by the longest arrow MC$_S$, includes both the marginal *internal* cost to the producing firm (the black arrow MC) plus a marginal *external* cost not borne by the producing firm (the dark red arrow).

BOX 28-1

WHY NOT CONTROL POLLUTION BY ENDING ECONOMIC GROWTH?

A no-growth policy would do no more than *stop the increase* in pollution; it would provide no reduction whatsoever in *existing* pollution. Thus, as a way of reducing pollution, a no-growth policy would be inferior to our present policies. They have allowed us to reduce some kinds of pollution by an esti-mated quarter or a half. To have achieved such a reduction in pollution simply by reducing output would have required a massive reduction in GNP. Instead, we have achieved this reduction while the economy has been growing.

Thus, as a way of reducing pollution, a limit on output would be extraordinarily expensive, yet inef-fective. It is like killing a rat by burning your house down. Even if you cure the problem, the side effects are appalling. Better by far to find a cure specific-ally designed to deal with the problem: If the prob-lem is a rat, get a trap; if the problem is pollution, find a policy that directly reduces it.

Courtesy Miller Services Limited

the marginal cost of this good *to society*. MC_S is a constant height above MC because of our assumption of a constant external cost for each unit of output.

CONTROLLING POLLUTION: THE SIMPLE CASE

When there is such an external cost, even a perfectly competitive market results in a misallocation of re-sources, as shown in Figure 28-2. In this figure, MC and MC_S are reproduced from the previous diagram, and demand D represents this good's marginal benefit—both private and social. S_1 shows what firms are will-ing to supply. This curve measures internal, private costs—the only costs faced by firms making supply

decisions. With demand D and supply S_1, the per-fectly competitive equilibrium is E_1.

For society, E_1 is not an efficient outcome, because it equalizes marginal benefit and marginal *private* cost only. An efficient solution requires that marginal benefit be equal to marginal *social* cost MC_S. This occurs at E_2, at the smaller output Q_2. We conclude that in a free, competitive market, firms produce too much of a polluting good—Q_1 rather than the efficient amount Q_2.[3] It is in society's interest to cut back production of

[3]In terms of our earlier analysis, the market does not lead to an efficient solution because marginal private cost MC is not equal to marginal social cost MC_S, and the condition stated in equation 24-2 (Chapter 24) is violated.

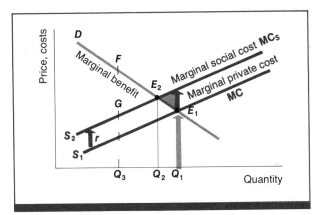

Figure 28-2   Free-market efficiency loss when there is an external cost.

Before the anti-pollution tax, industry supply is S_1, reflecting only the private internal costs of production facing sellers. This supply equals demand at E_1, with output at Q_1. This output is inefficient because marginal social cost exceeds benefit for all units between Q_2 and Q_1. For example, the last unit Q_1 is not worth producing; its benefit, shown by the light red arrow under the demand curve, is less than its two costs to society (the light red arrow plus the dark red arrow under the MC_S curve). The efficiency loss is the sum of all such dark red arrows—that is, the red triangle. *After the tax r*, producers are forced to face both the internal *and* external costs, so that their supply curve shifts up from S_1 to S_2. D and S_2 now yield an equilibrium at E_2, with output Q_2. This is efficient because marginal social cost and benefit are equal. The efficiency gain from reducing output from Q_1 to Q_2 is the elimination of the red triangle.

this good and use the resources to produce something else.

To confirm that Q_1 is an inefficient output, note that the benefit from the last unit produced is the light red arrow under the demand curve. However, its cost is even greater, since it includes both its private cost (this same light red arrow) and its external cost shown by the dark red arrow. Hence, this dark red arrow represents the net loss in producing this last unit Q_1. Since there is a similar sort of loss in the production of each of the other "excess" units between Q_2 and Q_1, the total efficiency loss is measured by the red triangle.

In this instance, a relatively simple cure is possible: Levy a per-unit tax on producers equal to the marginal external cost shown by the red arrow. Note that such a tax imposes a cost on producers equal to the cost of their pollution to others. Thus, the tax "inter-

nalizes" the externality: The producer is forced to face the external cost along with the internal cost. As a result of the tax, the supply curve shifts up from S_1 to S_2; to confirm, recall that supply reflects marginal cost, and this has risen by the amount of the tax that must be paid. The new equilibrium is at E_2, where demand and new supply S_2 intersect. The new output of Q_2 is efficient because marginal benefit equals marginal social cost. Finally, the efficiency gain from this tax policy is the red triangle, the original efficiency loss that has now been eliminated. In brief, as a result of this tax, society gets a benefit that the market would otherwise not deliver—cleaner water.

Several other ways have been suggested for reducing pollution. One is discussed in Box 28-2. Another is to set a limit on the output of polluting firms.

Such a limitation may or may not help to solve the problem; in fact, it may even be worse than doing nothing at all. For example, suppose output is limited to Q_3 in Figure 28-2. As an exercise (Problem 28-1) you can show that too little will be produced and there will be a loss to society of triangle FE_2G. Since this loss will exceed the original loss, the cure in this case will be worse than the original problem. You should also be able to show that an even more severe restriction on output will result in an even greater efficiency loss. Thus, an arbitrary limit on output is not an efficient policy. A much better approach—if the costs of pollution can be estimated—is to impose a tax of this same amount. Then the correct degree of pressure will be applied to the market to push it back from the initial Q_1 to the efficient output Q_2.

CONTROLLING POLLUTION: A MORE COMPLEX CASE

In practice, policymakers face a number of complications omitted from our earlier example. In any particular air space— say, over Toronto—or any particular body of water, such as Lake Erie, the problem is not just the single polluting industry shown in Figure 28-2, but many. Second, pollution and output are not locked together in the fixed way assumed in the earlier diagrams, in which each additional unit of output generated a constant amount of pollution. In the more typical case, the amount of pollution may vary. A good may be produced with a large amount of pollution if wastes are dumped uncontrolled into the water or air. However, if wastes are treated, or if less polluting fuels are used, then there will be only a small amount of pollution.

Consider a firm that begins to treat its wastes, or uses cleaner but more expensive fuels. This firm reduces

pollution, but at a cost. This cost of reducing pollution for all firms in an area is shown in Figure 28-3 as the curve MCR. (R stands for reducing pollution.) It is drawn by first graphing point Q_1, the amount of

---

BOX 28-2

THE POSSIBLE ROLE OF PROPERTY RIGHTS IN DEALING WITH AN EXTERNAL COST

It has been suggested that the problem of too much pollution by upstream firms could be cured by assigning those who live downstream the property right to clean water. Suppose, for example, that they can sue or charge any polluting firm an amount that exactly compensates them for any damage they incur. For example, in Figure 28-2, suppose that those living downstream can charge firms $r per unit of pollution that these firms emit. Polluting firms are now in exactly the same position as they were when the government imposed a tax of $r; the only difference is that they are now paying this "tax" to the residents downstream instead of to the government. In either case they will voluntarily reduce their output from Q_1 to Q_2 where inefficiency has been eliminated. It seems as though proper assignment of property rights over the water is the key.

In an article on "The Problem of Social Cost" (*Journal of Law and Economics*, October 1960), Ronald Coase of the University of Chicago went one step further. He argued that, strictly from the point of view of economic efficiency, it does not matter who holds the property rights. In our example, it does not matter whether those downstream have the property rights and are compensated $r per unit by the upstream polluting firms, or if the upstream firms have the property rights. True, if the upstream firms have the rights, they are free to dump waste into the river. However, it is more profitable for them to limit themselves, charging

those downstream $r for every unit they cut back.*

Thus, according to Coase, an externality such as pollution arises because there is something valuable—in this case, clean water—over which there are no property rights. Consequently, there is no market. That is, clean water can't be bought and sold. Create property rights, and you create a market that makes it possible for Adam Smith's invisible hand to work to reduce or eliminate inefficiency. Some other form of government intervention is not necessary; all the government needs to do is to establish a market, and then let it work. It is enlightening to consider this analysis from another point of view: The problem with pollution is that something that used to be in unlimited supply—clean water—has now become scarce. Unless someone owns it and charges for its use, it will be used in wasteful ways; for example, the water will be used to carry off pollutants, and the river will become a public sewer. On the other hand, if someone does own the water and charges for it, its price will act as a monitoring device to direct it into its most productive uses. Moreover, if markets work perfectly, *it doesn't matter who owns the water*—those living downstream, those firms located upstream, or the public as a whole. (Ownership by the public is the case described in Figure 28-2. On behalf of the public, the government extends its ownership over this water, and charges a fee of $r to firms that use it for waste elimination.) The point is that *someone* owns the water and charges for it. Only

---

*Those living downstream will be willing to pay this $r per unit because this is what pollution costs them; it is therefore what they would be willing to pay to get rid of it. Moreover, since the polluting firms receive a payment of $r per unit for reducing pollution, they will cut back to Q_2—for the same reason that they cut back that far in the face of the government's $r per unit tax. (It doesn't matter whether firms are paid $r per unit for cutting back, or are taxed $r per unit if they do *not* cut back. In either case they have the same incentive to cut back.)

pollution that will occur if it is not restricted in any way. As pollution is cut back, we move to the left up the MCR curve. At first, clean-up costs are low as the easy battles are won. For example, pollution unit Q_2

can be eliminated at the low cost shown by the short red bar. However, the more pollution is reduced, the higher becomes the cost of further clean-up. That is, the MCR curve becomes higher and higher as we move

---

then will the water be used efficiently.

However, it is important to emphasize: Coase's only claim is that it does not matter, *in terms of efficiency*, who owns the water. However, in terms of equity, it obviously does matter: If property rights are held by downstream residents, they collect a fee from the upstream firm. But if the property rights are held by the upstream firms, *they* collect a fee from the downstream residents.

Even though no claim can be made that the result is equitable, the conclusion that property rights and free bargaining may eliminate inefficiency is a very interesting one. It follows—subject to a number of reservations that will be considered directly—because the existence of inefficiency means that the two parties collectively lose. Therefore, it is in their collective interest to get together and make a deal to eliminate this inefficiency. However, this raises an even broader question: Why can't free bargaining remove any *other* form of inefficiency as well, such as monopoly? Since inefficiency makes the two parties collectively worse off, why don't they make a deal to avoid it? Specifically, why can't buyers compensate the monopoly firm to get it to stop acting like a monopolist, that is, to get it to lower its price and increase its output?

The answer is that there are problems ("transactions costs") in making such deals. How do a million buyers of a monopoly product organize themselves to make a payment to the monopolist? How do a thousand residents on a river and the hundreds of polluting firms upstream organize themselves to make and receive payments? To illustrate, suppose the property rights to the water are owned by the polluting upstream firms. How do downstream residents get together to pay these firms to reduce their pollution? Specifically, how do the downstream residents keep some of their members from becoming "free riders," that is, people who are happy to have a payment made—and their pollution thereby reduced—but who won't contribute

themselves?†

Another problem is: How do downstream residents know which firms are polluting the river and which are not? Moreover, if the downstream residents do reach an agreement with the polluting firms, how do they know that these firms have indeed reduced their pollution? Even attempting to solve these problems may involve substantial transactions costs.

For this reason, the existence of property rights and free bargaining would not always lead to an efficient result. Even if it did, the question of equity would not be resolved: Who should pay the fee necessary to achieve efficiency, and who should receive it? Nonetheless, Coase's ideas are important because they help us to understand more clearly why externalities are a problem, and how it may be possible to deal with them in a wide variety of ways.

---

†These problems would be far less serious if the property rights are held, not by the upstream firms, but instead by the downstream residents; and if the payment (fine) to be paid to them by the upstream firms is set by the courts. Polluting firms would then respond to this fine just as they did to the tax in Figure 28-2. In fact, this policy is effectively the same as the pollution tax in that earlier diagram—except for one important respect: The residents downstream, rather than the government, receive the payment from the polluting firms. This sounds very equitable: The people downstream who are hurt by pollution are compensated for it. Unfortunately, this provides an example of why the objectives of equity and efficiency are often in conflict. This very equitable solution introduces a *different* source of inefficiency: Because of the compensation people receive if they locate downstream, more decide to do so, and the pollution they consequently absorb represents a loss to society. In their location decision, people should take pollution into account, and—other things equal—locate away from the river. But they won't take pollution into account if they are fully compensated for it by the polluting firms. Thus too many people locate downstream, and there is an efficiency loss to society. This loss is paid for, not by the new downstream residents who absorb the pollution (since they are fully compensated), but instead by the polluting firms that pay the compensation, and by the public which pays higher prices for the products these polluting firms produce.

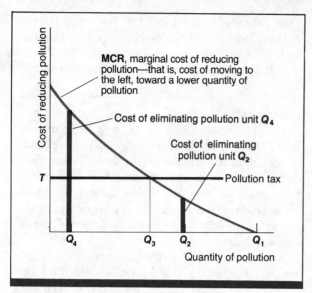

Figure 28-3 The cost of reducing pollution and the effect of a tax.

Q_1 is the amount of pollution that would occur in the absence of any control measure. As we move from this point back to the left along MCR, we see the cost of reducing pollution by one more unit—for example, by installing pollution-control equipment. Thus, if pollution has been restricted all the way back to Q_4, any further reduction would involve very expensive pollution-control measures, with a cost shown by the tall red bar.

If a pollution tax T is imposed, firms voluntarily reduce pollution, moving from Q_1 to Q_3. So long as they are still to the right of Q_3, they will continue to reduce pollution because the cost of doing so (for example, the short red bar) is less than the cost of paying the tax. However, they would not move to the left of Q_3. In this range, it costs them more to reduce pollution (the tall red bar) than to continue to pollute and pay the tax T.

to the left in this diagram.

Until the last few decades, there were few restrictions on pollution. Therefore, firms generally dumped pollutants rather than going to the expense of treating them. The result was pollution Q_1. Some of our lakes and rivers became public sewers.

To prevent this, suppose the government wishes to reduce pollution dramatically. Specifically, suppose it wants to cut pollution in half—from Q_1 to Q_3. Consider the policies that might be used.

Option 1. A Pollution Tax

Assume that the government levies an effluent fee—that is, a tax on each unit of pollution discharged into the environment. Specifically, in Figure 28-3, suppose that tax T is charged for each unit of pollution. Then firms eliminate pollution in the right-hand tail of the MCR curve, where it costs less to stop polluting (for example, the short red bar) than to continue to pollute and pay the tax T. However, pollution is reduced only to Q_3, where the tax line intersects MCR. To the left of this point, the costs of reducing pollution are high, as illustrated by the tall red bar. In fact, they are higher than the tax T. Thus, in this range, firms have an incentive to pay the tax and continue to pollute.

Option 2. A Physical Limit on the Pollution by Each Firm

One might well ask: Why go to all the trouble of setting the pollution tax in Figure 28-3 when pollution could be cut by the same amount by a simple, direct control—specifically, by requiring every firm to cut its emissions by half? The answer is that although this approach would achieve the same reduction in pollution, it would involve heavier clean-up costs, as we shall now show.

Not all firms face the same costs in reducing pollution. With a tax, pollution is cut back by firms that can do so at the lowest cost, that is, by firms to the right of Q_3. Firms to the left of Q_3 continue to pollute. However, if all firms are required to cut their pollution in half, firms to the left of Q_3 must now also participate—at the high cost illustrated by the tall red bar.

Therefore, the advantage of a pollution tax is that it "lets the market work." With firms reacting to the tax, pollution is reduced by those firms that can do so in the least expensive way. Thus society devotes fewer real resources to the clean-up task.[4] The savings can

---

[4]To simplify this illustration, we have assumed that any firm is either completely to the left of Q_3, or completely to the right. In fact, firms typically have some units of pollution on each side. High-cost firms have most of their units to the left of Q_3, and low-cost firms have most of their units to the right. Nevertheless our conclusion still holds: The least costly way of cutting pollution in half is with a tax, with every firm eliminating only its pollution to the right of Q_3. Thus, low-cost firms will be cutting their pollution by more than half, while the high-cost firms will be cutting it by less than half.

be substantial. Based on a number of recent estimates, U.S. economist Wallace Oates has ventured the rough guess that a pollution tax would cost society 75 to 85 percent less than a policy of requiring all firms to reduce pollution by the same fraction.[5]

While economists have long recognized that pollution taxes are more efficient than direct regulation, North American governments have found it politically difficult to introduce such taxes. As a result, economists and environmental officials have recently been considering a third compromise solution that allows the government to set physical limits on pollution, but also "lets the market work," and hence avoids unnecessarily large clean-up costs.

Option 3. Physical Limits on Pollution with Trade Allowed in Emission Permits

In this case, the authorities set a specific limit on the amount of pollution that each firm is permitted to emit. For example, each firm may be given a permit to pollute just half as much as in the past. So far, this is just like option 2. But now a twist is added to let the market work: Firms are allowed to buy and sell pollution permits. It can be shown that in a perfectly competitive market, permits will sell for price T. Firms to the right of Q_3 gain by selling their permits for T, and cleaning up pollution at the low cost illustrated by the short red bar. For firms to the left of Q_3, it is cheaper to buy permits costing T and continue to pollute than to undertake the even higher cost of reducing pollution shown by the tall red bar.[6] Thus, pollution is reduced by those firms to the right of Q_3 which can do

so at the lowest cost. Accordingly, under option 3 with marketable permits, pollution will be reduced in the same low-cost way as in option 1, with a pollution tax. Therefore, options 1 and 3 are superior to option 2. It is only under the second option—in which all firms are required to reduce pollution by a fixed amount— that high-cost cleanup is undertaken by firms to the left of Q_3.

The general principle is this:

Pollution can be reduced at lower cost if the government enlists the power of the market. It can change incentives by imposing a tax or introducing marketable permits and then letting private firms respond. The firms are the ones that know best what their costs are, and thus are best able to select the response that will minimize those costs.

This then is our basic conclusion: Because option 2 does not use the market, it is more costly than options 1 or 3. But in comparing options 1 and 3, which is preferred?

A Comparison between Options 1 and 3

One important practical problem with option 1 is the question of how high a pollution tax should be set. If the government overestimates the ability of industry to reduce pollution, it may set a tax rate that is too low; as a result, the amount of pollution that firms will continue to generate will be more than the government intended. This problem may be particularly difficult in cases where the government has to rely in part on the technical expertise of firms in the industry when it tries to find the tax rate that will reduce pollution to the efficient level: The firms have an incentive to overstate their ability to reduce pollution in order to induce the government to impose a low tax rate. One major advantage with the marketable permits of option 3 is that the government does not face this uncertainty: The government determines the amount of pollution that will actually take place when it sets the number of permits that it issues.

An additional advantage of option 3 is that a system of permits may be constructed in a way that will eliminate the opposition to this policy from the existing firms in the industry. With a tax, as in option 1, existing firms lose: Either they have to pay the tax (to the extent that they continue to pollute), or they have to incur the costs necessary to reduce pollution. But

[5]"Markets for Pollution Control," *Challenge* (May-June 1984): 12. One of the studies on which Oates based his estimate was that of Allen V. Kneese and Charles L. Schultze, *Pollution, Prices, and Public Policy* (Washington: The Brookings Institution, 1975).

Although a tax is generally preferable, there are exceptions. For example, in the case of radioactive wastes that would damage the environment far into the future, it may be simpler and just as effective to impose a physical limit—namely, an outright ban on emitting such materials. If a tax were used to eliminate such wastes, it would have to be set at a prohibitively high level, and thus be equivalent to a ban.

*[6]Why would the price of permits be T? If this is the price, then firms have the same incentive to reduce pollution as if they faced a tax T. In either case, they respond by reducing their pollution to Q_3. Thus, if the permit price is T, Q_3 will be the quantity of permits firms will want. This is exactly equal to the Q_3 of permits provided by the government. Therefore, T is the equilibrium price.

with marketable permits under option 3, existing firms need not lose. For example, suppose the government issues free permits to existing firms. In that case, a firm that is able to reduce its own pollution at a relatively low cost may actually gain. Instead of continuing to pollute up to the amount permitted by its allocation of permits, it may be better off reducing its own pollution and selling some of its permits to other firms less able to reduce their pollution. And those firms that continued to pollute would only have to pay for permits if they chose to pollute *more* than allowed by the permits they were given by the government (rather than pay a tax on *all* of their pollution, as in option 1).

However, while the polluting firms clearly prefer this policy of free permits, such a policy is likely to be unpopular with the general public. Why should businesses that have polluted in the past be granted valuable emission permits, some of which they may sell? In other words, why should some firms be allowed to profit from their past pollution? One way of modifying option 3 to counter this objection would be to charge a price for the permits when they are first issued. While this would not be as favourable to business as giving out the permits free, it would appear more equitable. If there is a charge for permits, this policy becomes very similar to a tax, with the firms being charged in either case for the polluting they do. Nonetheless, there is an important difference: Under option 3, the government retains more direct and precise control over the amount of pollution that actually takes place.

Thus far, we have assumed that the government has set as its target a reduction in pollution by one-half, to Q_3. Why not by a third, or three-quarters, or some other figure? Box 28-3 describes how the target should be set.

Local Pollution: Sag Points and Bubbles

The damage done by pollution may depend on *where it is emitted*. Smoke discharged in a city affects more people than smoke emitted over a wilderness area; pollution dumped into a river above a city is more harmful than pollution below the city. A location where pollution is particularly harmful is sometimes known as a *sag point*. It is especially desirable to reduce pollution in such locations. This may be done by imposing higher taxes on emissions or by having particularly strict emission controls at sag points. Thus, for example, it might make sense to impose stricter standards on the pollution-control equipment of cars used mainly in and around large cities than on cars used mainly in rural areas. Local pollution problems are sometimes dealt with by placing an imaginary *bubble* over a sensitive area, with pollutants being controlled strictly within the bubble. New sources of pollution are permitted only if the firm arranges for an equal reduction of pollution—that is, an *offset*—elsewhere within the bubble.

POLLUTION CONTROL IN CANADA: Which Option Does the Government Use?

Surprisingly, the provincial governments in Canada, which are responsible for enforcing our anti-pollution legislation, rely principally on regulatory controls rather than letting the market work with a pollution tax, or tradeable pollution permits. Specific pollution limits are set and enforced for individual firms—a policy, as already noted, that involves large unnecessary clean-up costs.

Moreover, there is a second problem. Air and water standards are set with little regard for the cost of reducing pollution. Instead, the regulators tend to concentrate on what is *technologically* possible given existing pollution-control knowledge, and some of these measures are extremely expensive. Furthermore, the federal specifications for maximum allowable rates of pollution emission by a plant, which are supposed to be enforced by the provinces, are the same for *all* areas of Canada. The purpose of this uniformity is to discourage a particular province from relaxing its emission standards in order to attract new industry. But as we have seen, uniform emission standards may be inefficient: They mean that the maximum permissible amount of pollution is the same in southern Ontario (where air quality is already relatively low because there are many polluting industries) and in Saskatchewan (which still has relatively clean air). This blocks one avenue for reducing the overall pollution problem, namely shifting firms from overloaded, highly polluted areas into regions with low pollution levels (where at least *some* of the pollutants could be "washed away" by natural processes).

Moreover, because pollution regulations have been so severe, many firms have been in violation of air or water standards. Because firms have thought it possible to persuade the governments to be more lenient, they have been expending more of their efforts in fighting the regulations in private and public battles with provincial governments than in trying to find a pollution cure. And sometimes, the firms have had some success. A classic case is the continuing fight between the International Nickel Corporation in Sudbury, Ontario, and the Ontario Ministry of the Environment. In 1970, INCO (which is North America's largest single source of sulphur dioxide emission) was ordered to gradually reduce its emissions so that by 1978 they would be no more than 15% of the 1970 levels. During the 1970s, INCO repeatedly sought and obtained relaxation of the standards and extensions of the deadline. As a result, emission levels in 1980 were still about 65% of the 1970 level, and a new ministry guideline was set allowing an emission level for 1982 of 30% (rather than the original 15%) of 1970 levels. Such flip-flops have tended, at a minimum, to erode the credibility of the controls. And they have created the impression that standards have not been set in an even-handed way, but instead have been defined by governments under pressure to make last-minute changes.

An Alternative Policy? Subsidizing Pollution-Control Equipment

In the pulp and paper industry, one of the major polluters in Canada, the federal and provincial governments in Ontario and Quebec have announced programs under which they fund capital expenditures for modernization of the industry's anti-pollution equipment. Provincial governments also subsidize pollution-control equipment by paying a large share of the cost of municipal sewage treatment facilities. And as we have seen, the federal government provides subsidies in the form of tax reductions to private firms installing pollution-control equipment. How effective are these kinds of subsidy schemes as a way of controlling pollution?

In the first place, such subsidies are effective only if the equipment that is installed does a good job of reducing pollution. One of the problems has been that, after the government subsidizes the new installation, it pays little or no attention to how efficiently it is operated—that is, how effectively it reduces pollution.

The second problem is that this form of subsidy puts all the emphasis on *end-of-pipe treatment*—that is, on the reduction of pollution as it is about to be discharged into the environment. However, if a subsidy is justified for end-of-pipe treatment, it should be similarly justified for *any* reduction in pollution, regardless of how it may be achieved—for example, by the use of less powerful chemicals or cleaner fuels. Such alternatives may be far less costly.

It may be concluded, therefore, that an end-of-pipe subsidy is too narrow an attack on the problem. Firms may not use the lowest-cost method to control pollution, but instead may switch to the end-of-pipe method solely because it is subsidized. The principle is a simple one. It is better to tell firms *what* to do than to give them detailed instructions on *how* to do it. A regulation made as far back as the eighteenth century B.C. illustrates this principle. Hammurabi, King of Babylonia, set a very simple building code. If a house collapsed and killed an occupant, the builder was put to death. All details for meeting this regulation were left to the builder.

An even narrower approach is a regulation that requires firms to install a *specific kind* of end-of-pipe equipment. For example, consider the requirement that coal-burning electric power plants install "scrubbers" to clean the smoke they emit. This tends to divert them from the more sensible solution of using cleaner coal; so long as the government requires scrubbers, there is no incentive to use the more expensive, cleaner fuel. In turn, the continued heavy use of dirty coal creates a new problem in the form of a liquid sludge generated by the scrubbers. Thus, reducing air pollution creates water pollution. Again we conclude: The lowest-cost policy is to provide firms with a sufficient incentive to clean up, and let them, in the pursuit of profit, decide on the least expensive *way* of doing it.

FUTURE PROBLEMS IN PROTECTING THE ENVIRONMENT

During the 1970s, North Americans attacked the problem of cleaning up the environment with some enthusiasm. It was clear that during earlier decades, we had not paid enough attention to the problem, and most people agreed that we needed firm policies to combat pollution. Many new anti-pollution laws were brought in, and some early successes seemed to justify optimism: It appeared that the battle against pollution was being won.

BOX 28-3

POLLUTION CONTROL: PROBLEMS AND PERSPECTIVES

In Figure 28-3, the target amount of pollution is assumed to be Q_3. In fact, it is not a simple task to determine the target amount.

How Far Should Pollution Be Reduced?

In Figure 28-4 we reproduce MCR from Figure 28-3, and also show MCP, the marginal cost of pollution to society. These two curves should not be confused. MCR is the cost of *reducing* pollution—for example, the cost of pollution-control equipment. On the other hand, MCP is the cost of *having* pollution; that is, the cost to us of foul air and contaminated water. As long as there is only a small amount of pollution—at, say, Q_4—the marginal cost of having this pollution (the height of MCP) is low. The first units of waste that are dumped into a stream generally break down and are absorbed by the environment. Similarly, the smoke from a campfire in a deserted area has no perceptible effect on the air. However, as pollution builds up, additional emissions become increasingly noxious and damaging; that is, as we move to the right in this diagram, the MCP curve rises.

With these two curves, the best target is to reduce pollution to point Q_3 where MCP = MCR. Any other quantity is less desirable, as we can illustrate with the case where pollution is left completely uncontrolled and consequently reaches Q_1. For all units of pollution to the right of Q_3, MCP is greater than MCR, so it is a mistake to let this pollution continue. To evaluate the social cost of this mistake, consider one typical unit of this excess pollution, say unit Q_2. The cost of eliminating this unit of pollution is the height of the MCR curve, as shown by the light red arrow. This is less than the cost of letting this pollution continue (the height of the MCP curve, as shown by the light and dark red arrows). Therefore, the net cost of allowing this

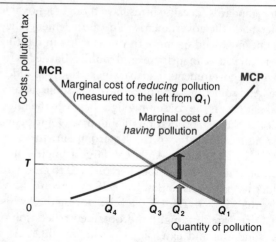

Figure 28-4 Efficiency loss from leaving pollution uncontrolled.
MCR is reproduced from Figure 28-3. We also show MCP, the environmental cost of additional units of pollution. The best target is to restrict pollution to Q_3, where MCR = MCP.

unit to continue is the dark red arrow. If we sum the similar costs on all such units through the range Q_3 to Q_1, the result is the triangular red area—the loss to society from allowing pollution to continue at its uncontrolled level of Q_1 rather than limiting it to Q_3.

On the other hand, a policy of cutting pollution back to the left of Q_3 also causes a loss. For example, if pollution is reduced to Q_4, the cost of the last unit is just the height of the MCP curve above Q_4. However, this last unit is exceedingly costly to eliminate (the height of the MCR curve). Eliminating it is therefore a mistake. We conclude that the best target, Q_3, can be found only by taking into account both the cost of having pollution MCP, and the cost of removing it MCR.

Unfortunately, in practice it is not that easy to estimate the target Q_3, because of the difficulties in estimating MCP and MCR. For example, in trying to estimate the marginal cost of pollution MCP, we simply do not know with any precision how dangerous many pollutants really are. Furthermore, there are many pollutants, and the damage that any one pollutant does may depend on the presence of other types. For example, asbestos in the air is more likely to cause cancer when other pollutants are present, or when people smoke.

Pollution in Historical Perspective

Why are we so concerned now with pollution, while a few decades ago we were almost totally unconcerned? Is the problem worse, or have we just awakened? If it is getting worse, what can we expect 20 or 30 years from now?

Figure 28-5 illustrates how the MCR curve shifts to the right as the economy grows. MCR_{1960} cuts the horizontal axis at Q_{1960}, the level of pollution that would have occurred had it been left completely unrestricted at that early date. Similarly, the other MCR curves indicate uncontrolled pollution levels Q_{1980} and Q_{2000} at those later dates. The red triangle marked 1980 shows the loss from a policy of leaving pollution uncontrolled at that time; it is defined just like the red triangle in Figure 28-4.

Now consider our situation in 1960. At that time, there were fewer factories clustered along any river and fewer cars spewing fumes into the air. Therefore, pollution was less severe. The result of leaving pollution uncontrolled was the relatively small loss shown as the red triangle marked 1960. In those days, people did not think much about this problem.

Now let us look ahead to the future, to the year 2000. If industrial activity keeps growing, unrestricted pollution would grow to Q_{2000}, and the loss from failing to deal with it would be the very large red triangle 2000. There are several reasons why this loss builds up so rapidly. First, as output grows, so too does pollution. Second, pollution may grow even faster, since more powerful chemicals and other materials may be used as technology changes. Thus, MCR shifts rapidly to the right. In addition, in the view of many experts, the MCP curve becomes steeper and steeper: The cost of pollution not only rises, but it does so at an increasingly rapid rate.

We emphasize that Figure 28-5 is not a prediction of the future; it is merely a picture of what the future would have looked like if we had not taken

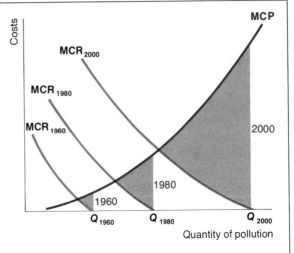

Figure 28-5 Pollution in perspective.
If no attempt had been made to deal with this problem, unrestricted pollution would have increased (with growing GNP) from Q_{1960} to Q_{1980} and eventually to Q_{2000}. As a result, the loss to society of leaving pollution unchecked in each of these years would have been the rapidly growing set of triangles marked 1960, 1980, and 2000.

action—or what it will look like if we give up our efforts to control pollution.* In this respect, pollution is similar to the public health problem in the nineteenth century. With the increase in urban population, lack of adequate sanitation produced a growing health problem that could equally well have been described by a diagram like Figure 28-5. The response to this challenge was the public health programs that prevented the "prophecy" in such a diagram from coming true. Similarly, pollution-control legislation can help to ensure that the prophecy in Figure 28-5 does not come true.

---

*Moreover, we have simplified this diagram, just like any other economic analysis. For example, we have assumed that pollution does not accumulate; in other words, that the cost of pollution depends only on how much occurs in the year in question. But pollution does accumulate. Chemicals dumped in the ground years ago remain a source of water pollution today. Our future problem could therefore be even more severe.

But by the mid-1980s, a certain amount of disillusionment had set in. The public was becoming more aware of the high cost of pollution control: Business firms were complaining loudly that strict anti-pollution laws were reducing profitability, and warning that jobs might be lost if they were forced to close down plants that did not meet anti-pollution standards. Stricter regulations of polluting products were costly too: In the auto industry, controls on exhaust emissions contributed to the squeeze on profits and raised the prices of new cars. Managers of the auto firms, and unions representing the auto workers, had strong incentives to mount lobbying efforts against the tighter standards, and they could expect sympathetic voices from buyers of new cars. On the other hand, those who benefit from better pollution control cannot be expected to be as vocal in their support of the measures. True, everybody benefits from something like cleaner air. But there is only a small benefit *to any individual person* from a small reduction in air pollution. In cases where the benefits are thinly spread in this way, the lobbying efforts by the supporters of anti-pollution legislation are likely to be less intensive than the efforts of their opponents.

Another reason why pollution policy is controversial is that it operates in an area of relative scientific ignorance. We *simply don't know* how dangerous many pollutants are. This raises a conflict between the government and industry. Who should bear the burden of proof? (1) Should the government have to prove that a waste product is harmful before restricting it? If so, we may today emit wastes that are in fact dangerous, but have not yet been proved so. Or (2) should business have to prove that a waste product is *not* harmful before emitting it? If this rule were applied, waste disposal would become such an enormous problem that many firms would be unable to survive, and many of those that did would be charging the public far higher prices.

Pollution as a Source of Interprovincial and International Conflict

An additional problem arises when pollution spills over political boundaries. For example, a large part of the sulphur dioxide emissions from coal-fired generating stations in Ontario ends up polluting the air over Quebec. Therefore, while most of the *costs* of stricter emission controls will be borne by people in Ontario, a large part of the *benefits* will accrue to people outside of the province. Because of this, there may be a need for *federal* legislation to make sure that the government of Ontario takes into account the interests of Quebec residents as well as those of residents of Ontario when it sets provincial emission standards.[7] And some kinds of pollution spill over *international* boundaries. For example, chemical pollution of the Great Lakes hurts both Canadians and Americans. If the two governments only take account of the benefits *to their own citizens*, the result will be an inefficiently high level of pollution. (Both governments would underestimate the benefits of pollution control by failing to take into account the benefits to citizens of the other country.) To overcome this problem, Canada and the United States have negotiated a mutual agreement that specifies limits on allowable effluent discharges from either country.

The acid rain problem is a particularly difficult case. While some of Quebec's acid rain pollution results from sulphur dioxide emissions in Ontario, most of the acid rain throughout Canada originates with sulphur dioxide emissions in the United States, particularly from coal-burning electric power plants in the U.S. Midwest. At the same time, little of the damage to the U.S. environment originates in Canada. Thus, in the words of Bruce Forster of the University of Guelph, the acid rain problem is a "unidirectional international externality." This makes Canada's negotiating position very difficult: We are in a situation where we are asking the American government to undertake a costly clean-up operation that will primarily benefit us, rather than them.

Partly as a result of this problem, the actual negotiations have been going very slowly, and so far the result has mostly been commitments by the Americans to allocate more funds to research rather than to undertake actual reductions of emissions. In resisting Canadian demands for more direct action, the Reagan

---

[7]A popular method for controlling air pollution in the 1960s was to require plants to have tall smoke stacks. The main effect of this method was simply to spread the pollution over a wider geographic area, rather than reducing the total amount of pollution.

administration has also put the burden of proof in this case on Canada: If we are expecting the Americans to undertake the clean-up for our benefit, Reagan argues, we must first prove to them that they are in fact the source of the problem. That is difficult or even impossible to do at present, because so little is known about the extent to which emissions are transferred over long distances (such as from the U.S. Midwest to Canada). This U.S. position has infuriated Canadian environmentalists. In their view, there is enough scientific evidence (based in part on computerized models of atmospheric transfer of pollutants) to place the blame squarely on U.S. sources. The issue has also gone to the courts, where Canada experienced an unexpected piece of good luck in 1985: Following a suit brought by the conservationist Sierra Club and the governments of several Northeastern states (which also suffer acid rain damage), a U.S. judge ruled that the U.S. Environmental Protection Agency must order Midwestern states to reduce their sulphur dioxide emissions. However, it is virtually certain that this ruling will be appealed, either by the U.S. government or by the Midwestern power companies.

Concluding Observations

Setting aside these international complications, we can be reasonably sure of one conclusion. As pollution limits continue to be imposed on business by the government, there will be continued conflict between the two. This is a further reason for the government to impose fewer of its own regulations and rely more on the marketplace—that is, replace detailed regulations with a market-oriented system of incentives that requires business to worry about the details. In other words, the government should be spending more of its effort in designing and building "better dams to control pollution" (such as tax incentives or marketable permit systems) and less on "putting a regulatory finger into every leak."

However, when we criticize the government for not always using the most effective pollution-control method, we should not lose perspective. Control should be improved, yes; but abandoned, no. "Where would we be without an agency such as Environment Canada?" is an important question to keep in mind. (See Figure 28-5.)

RECYCLING

One of the most promising ways to deal with pollution is to recycle wastes rather than dump them into the environment. Beer cans do not deface the landscape if they are reprocessed and used again. Wastes that are recycled into the production process do not foul our rivers.

Figure 28-6 illustrates the potential benefits from recycling. The basic idea behind this diagram is the

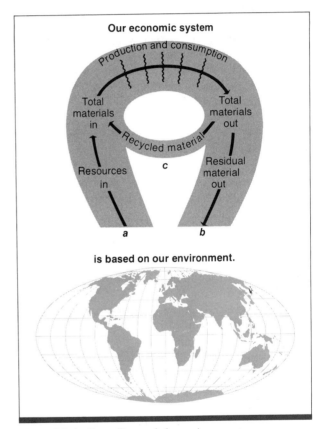

Figure 28-6   Recycling and the environment.
The economic system in the upper half of this diagram uses the environment in the bottom half by extracting resources from it through pipe *a*, and returning residuals back to it through pipe *b*. For any given level of production and consumption, increased recycling—that is, diverting materials from pipe *b* to pipe *c*—provides two benefits: It reduces the residuals dumped into the environment through pipe *b*, *and* it reduces the natural resources that must be drawn out of the environment through pipe *a*.

concept of *material balances*. On the left, production draws in the materials it requires. Included are both new materials drawn up through pipe *a*, and recycled materials returned to the production process through pipe *c*. These materials pass through the production/consumption process and reappear in different form as "total materials out" on the right side of the diagram. Some of these leftover materials, such as chemical wastes, are the result of production. Others—like beer cans—are residuals from consumption.

This figure provides a framework for thinking about two important issues:

1. As our economic system expands, strains on the environment tend to increase both because more material is drawn up through pipe *a*, and because more pollutants are dumped back into the environment through pipe *b*.

2. The pollution problem can be reduced by more recycling, that is, by directing more of the leftover material on the right into pipe *c* rather than pipe *b*. Moreover, any success on this score will have a highly desirable side effect. The more our production/consumption requirements on the left can be satisfied by materials recycled through pipe *c*, the fewer natural resources will have to be drawn from the environment through pipe *a*. In brief, recycling helps to solve two important problems at once: the problem of pollution and the problem of conserving natural resources. In the next chapter we turn to a detailed analysis of the conservation of natural resources.

KEY POINTS

1. Pollution is an example of an external cost, a cost that is borne not by the individual or firm directly involved in the activity, but instead by somebody else.

2. Through environmental legislation, the federal and provincial governments have imposed controls on the amount of pollutants firms can release into our air or water.

3. However, there are two alternative market-oriented systems of control that are more efficient: (a) charging a tax on polluters, or (b) issuing marketable permits to polluters. Both are designed to encourage the reduction in pollution by those firms that can do so at least cost.

4. Either a marketable permit system or a tax is superior to another government policy that has been used: subsidizing firms or municipalities for installing pollution-reducing equipment. Such a subsidy is too narrow an approach to the prob-

lem because it attacks pollution only at the "end of the pipe." Hence, opportunities to reduce pollution in less costly ways may be missed.

5. Pollution policy is sometimes complicated because pollution moves across political boundaries; the problem becomes especially severe when pollution crosses an international boundary. Two of the most critical pollution problems in Canada, acid rain and the chemical pollution of the Great Lakes, are affected by transboundary pollution flows.

6. Recycling production or consumption wastes back into the production process helps solve two problems: First, less polluting waste is dumped into the environment. Second, fewer natural resources need to be extracted from the environment to support our present production and consumption levels.

KEY CONCEPTS

internal (private) cost	inefficiency of free market	marginal cost of reducing
external cost	how a tax may increase efficiency	pollution (MCR)
social cost	internalizing an externality	

KEY CONCEPTS (cont'd)

*marginal cost of having
   pollution (MCP)
pollution tax
pollution limits for
   individual firms
marketable pollution permits
sag points

bubbles
offsets
subsidization of pollution-
   control equipment
end-of-pipe treatment
transboundary pollution
international externality

recycling
material balances
how recycling helps to solve
   the problems of pollution
   and resource conservation

PROBLEMS

28-1 Is output Q_3 in Figure 28-2 efficient? If not, explain why, showing the triangular efficiency loss.

28-2 In 1977, after almost a week of oil spill, an oil blowout in the North Sea was finally capped by a high-priced, high-living American named Red Adair. Draw a diagram like Figure 28-1 to show the various costs involved in offshore drilling for oil. Determine whether the following costs are external or internal: (a) the expenditure by the oil companies on installing and operating drilling rigs; (b) the cost to the companies of hiring Red Adair; (c) the loss of marine life and the damage to beaches if oil spills occur that cannot be capped in time.

28-3 "When faced with a problem, economists have a natural inclination to suggest a solution that somehow utilizes the power of the price system; thus their solution for pollution control is a tax. On the other hand, lawyers have a natural inclination to set up regulations, and pass judgement on a case-by-case basis. And because lawyers make our laws, this is what has happened." Explain why this case-by-case approach of lawyers has increased the cost of pollution abatement.

28-4 Critically evaluate each of the following statements:
  (a) "Pollution taxes are immoral. Once a firm has paid its tax, it has a licence to pollute. And no one should have this licence."

  (b) "Imposing a physical limit on the emission of a pollutant is like saying that you can do just so much of a bad thing and pay no penalty, but the moment you step over this line you will pay a large penalty."

  (c) "There is no point in insisting on crystal-clear discharges into water that is as dirty as in the harbour in Hamilton, Ontario."

  (d) "Since it is impossible (and in any case, undesirable) to eliminate all polluting activities, the cost of pollution can be reduced if some polluting activities are moved into geographic regions where the environment can absorb most of the pollutants without noticeable effect."

  (e) "Whereas a tax discourages a polluting activity, a subsidy to install pollution-control equipment does not. Therefore a subsidy should not be used."

*28-5 Redraw Figure 28-4 to illustrate the two special cases where a pollution tax is not appropriate:
  (a) where pollution is no problem
  (b) where pollution is so costly (as in footnote 5 in the section "Controlling Pollution") that it should be banned outright.

28-6 Use Figure 28-6 to explain the various effects on the environment that occurred when cars were made smaller during the decade of the 1970s.

28-7 It is sometimes suggested that society should not tolerate crime. Do you agree with this suggestion? In other words, do you think we should expand crime prevention and hire police until the crime rate is driven to zero? Explain how your answer can be related to the discussion of the right target rate for pollution.

*28-8 Suppose that, instead of issuing marketable permits to polluting firms, the government sells these permits in an auction sale. Is the following statement true or false? Wherever false, correct it.

> Under an auction sale of permits, the result would still be an efficient one; pollution would still be cut back to its target level, because this is the number of permits the government would auction off. The big difference is that there would be no windfall to past polluters. All proceeds from the auction would go to the public treasury (just like the proceeds from the tax in option 1). In other words, an auction of permits would be as equitable as a tax on polluters, because either would channel the funds raised from pollution control into the public treasury, and thus prevent any of these funds from falling into the hands of past polluters.

*28-9 (Based on Box 28-3.) The most equitable solution for air pollution is to have polluting firms pay a tax, not to the government, but instead to the nearby residents who suffer from pollution. Is this also likely to be the most efficient solution? Why or why not?

APPENDIX 28-A

CONGESTION AND THE AUTOMOBILE

Parking is such sweet sorrow.

Sid Caesar

Congestion can be analysed in much the same way as pollution, since both represent an external cost. An individual who decides to drive a car during congested periods takes into account costs such as gasoline, as well as the personal costs of aggravation and delay. Since the driver must face these costs, they are internal costs. However, the driver does not take into account the external costs—the increased aggravation and delay that *other* drivers encounter because one more car is on the road, making traffic jams a little more dense and parking spots a bit harder to find.

The problem is illustrated in Figure 28-7. During non-rush hours, drivers equate the marginal costs (MC) and marginal benefits of driving (MB_1). Forty-five trips are taken, at equilibrium E_1. Traffic moves smoothly, and drivers face no congestion problems. But during rush hours, drivers put a much higher value on using the highway because they have to get to work, and driving is the most convenient way. Accordingly, the marginal benefit curve shifts up to MB_2, and equilibrium moves from E_1 to E_2, where drivers take 90 trips. Congestion is now a problem for two reasons. First, congestion results in a loss of time and gasoline and consequently increases each driver's own *private* cost of taking a trip; that is, E_2 is on the rising portion of the MC curve. Second, since each additional car makes the congestion worse, other drivers also face an additional burden of aggravation and delay. This is the *external* cost of the trip the driver is taking; it is shown as the dark red arrow in Figure 28-7. When this cost is added to the private cost MC, the result is the marginal cost to society of having one more car on the road (MC_S).

The rush-hour problem is this: The decision by any driver to take a trip is based only on *private* cost MC rather than *social* cost MC_S. Thus, equilibrium is at E_2, with too many cars on the road, and with an efficiency loss shown by the light red triangle (as detailed in the diagram's caption). The way to avoid this loss is to reduce the number of trips being taken from 90 to the efficient number, 80; in other words, move equilibrium from E_2 to E^*. This can be done by imposing a tax or toll T on each trip equal to the gap at E^* between MC and MC_S. Such a toll will raise the private cost MC up to MC^*, with each driver then taking into account not only his or her own private costs, but also the external costs for other drivers. Private decisions equating MC^* with MB_2 will then result in efficient equilibrium E^*. This will eliminate the efficiency loss shown by the light red triangle. (Detail on this triangle is provided in the caption to Figure 28-7.)

This general conclusion should, however, be qualified. This toll will provide a net gain only if the benefit it provides—that is, the elimination of the triangular efficiency loss—exceeds the cost of collecting the toll, including traffic delays at toll booths. To reduce the cost and delays of toll collection, it has been suggested that toll booths be replaced with an electronic device or a TV camera that would read off the licence plate of each passing car, along with the time of day. Then drivers would be sent a bill—like a phone bill—at the end of each month.

Note that, as in the case of pollution, the efficient solution does not require the elimination of congestion, but only its reduction. In Figure 28-7, traffic is

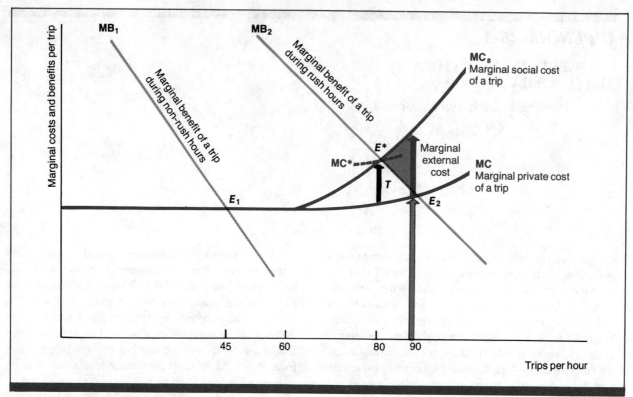

Figure 28-7 Traffic congestion.
During non-rush hours, equilibrium is at E_1, with 45 trips being taken. There are no external costs; MC and MC_S coincide. However, during rush hours, drivers put a higher value on using the highway, so that the marginal benefit MB_1 increases to MB_2, with drivers taking more than the 60 trips where congestion begins to be a problem. Because the highway is now crowded, traffic is delayed and private MC rises; each driver wastes his or her *own* time and gasoline in the traffic jam. In addition, *other* drivers also suffer increased delay whenever one more car is added to the traffic. This external cost must be added to private MC to get marginal social cost MC_S. Private decisions by drivers equating MB_2

and private MC result in equilibrium at E_2, with 90 trips being taken. This is 10 more than the efficient number (80), where MB_2 equals social cost MC_S. The cost of congestion because of these 10 excess trips is the red triangle, for the following reasons: The last trip (the ninetieth) provides the benefit shown by the light red arrow under MB_2. However, the cost of this trip is the height of the MC_S curve—that is, the private cost shown by the light red arrow, *plus* the external cost to the other drivers, shown by the dark red arrow. Thus, the net cost of this excess trip is the dark red arrow. When similar costs for the other 10 excess trips are summed, the result is the red triangular efficiency loss. This can be eliminated by a toll T that moves equilibrium from E_2 to E^*.

reduced to only 80 cars, not 60. Also note that the appropriate toll varies with the time of day: When MB_2 is high, reflecting the desire to travel in rush hours, the efficient toll is T. But when MB_1 is lower, reflecting the more limited desire to travel in non-rush hours, no toll is required. Thus, the appropriate toll is determined by the pressure of drivers to use the highway. Once set, the toll then relieves that pressure.

In describing such a toll, we have considered only

the objective of efficiency. Of course, another objective of a toll may be to raise money to pay for the road. But in a congested area, the toll should not be set just for this money-raising reason. An example will illustrate why: Suppose that there are two bridges into a city, and that they are just barely able to handle the traffic without tie-ups. If a toll is set on each bridge to raise the money to cover its costs, there will be no toll on the old bridge that has already been paid for, but a high toll on the new bridge. As drivers consequently switch from the new to the old bridge, a traffic jam will be created where none existed before.

Finally, there have been a number of other suggestions for reducing auto congestion. Each would reduce the problem, although generally in a somewhat less efficient way than a toll. These include proposals to: (1) Increase the tax on gasoline. This would reduce congestion by reducing the cars on the road anywhere, at any time. But this policy is less effective than a toll because it does not deal directly with the problem of congestion on specific highways at specific times. (2) Induce people to form car pools by levying a toll not on the car, but rather on the empty seats in it. (3) Provide a further incentive for car pools by reserving fast lanes for cars with more than, say, two passengers. (4) Reserve fast lanes for buses, so that some of the people in a hurry will stop driving their cars in favour of a faster trip by bus. (5) Tax downtown parking lots, to discourage drivers from entering the congested area. (6) Charge people a monthly flat-rate licence fee to drive in a congested area, with police imposing fines on non-licensed cars caught in these areas.

PROBLEMS

28-8 Show why completely eliminating congestion by cutting traffic back to 60 cars in Figure 28-7 would be worse than taking no action at all. Is it always true that the complete elimination of an externality is worse than no action whatsoever?

*28-9 Do you see any similarity between rush-hour tolls and peak-load (rush-hour) increases in the price of electricity? What do you think the efficiency effect of setting a high price on peak-load electricity would be?

*28-10 The Communist government of an Italian city subsidized the local public transportation system so that it could offer free rides, but only during morning and evening rush hours. Would such a subsidy work toward an efficient outcome? Why or why not? (Be careful. This is a complicated question.) Could there be objectives other than efficiency in this type of subsidy?

*28-11 In Chapter 27, we saw that there are government regulations which force airlines and railroads to provide service to relatively small cities on lightly travelled routes. Supporters of regulation argued that this small-city service encouraged people to stay in small cities, and thus reduced congestion in big cities. Is this argument valid? Does it (a) reverse, (b) temper, (c) leave unchanged, or (d) strengthen your previous view about the appropriateness of these regulations? Why?

Chapter 29

NATURAL RESOURCES: ARE WE USING THEM AT THE RIGHT RATE?

The . . . economy of the future might be called the "spaceman economy," in which the earth has become a single space ship, without unlimited reservoirs of anything.

Kenneth Boulding

Natural resources are the endowments of nature. Examples include metals, fish, timber, and oil. While natural resources are an important factor of production, they are typically quite different from other essential factors of production, such as labour. The amount of labour that will be available next year will be little affected by whether or not it is used (employed) today. However, this is not true of natural resources such as iron ore and timber, where the amount available next year *does* depend on how much is used today. For this reason, questions of conservation are important. Are we adequately conserving these resources, or are we using them too rapidly? Do the expanding industrial requirements of a growing economy, along with our finite and shrinking resource supplies, put us on a collision course that will eventually bring about a collapse of the economy, as some observers have predicted? And what can economics tell us about when and how the government *should* intervene to limit our use of natural resources?

For Canada, this issue is clearly more important than for most other countries, because so much of our economic activity depends on natural resources. Mining, fishing, and production of timber, wood-pulp, and newsprint, are all examples of important Canadian industries that make extensive use of resources. And in the 1970s and early 1980s, another resource-intensive sector came to the forefront of the economic policy debate: energy, which is supplied from natural resources such as deposits of oil, coal, and natural gas, and from the waterflow in our river systems.

THE INEFFICIENT USE OF A COMMON PROPERTY NATURAL RESOURCE: FISH

To illustrate why we may use a resource too rapidly without adequate concern for conservation, consider fishing. The main reason that too many fish are caught is this: Nobody owns the oceans, rivers, and lakes, or the fish that swim there. That is, fish are a **common property** resource. The result is shown in Figure 29-1. *D* is the market demand for fish. The height of this

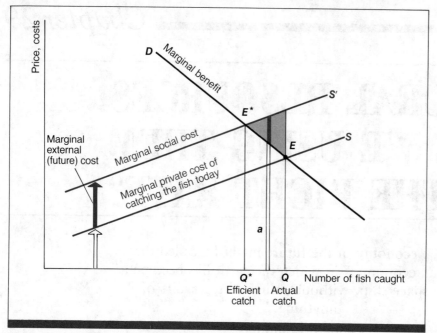

Figure 29-1 Market for a common property resource.
The cost of fishing is shown by the marginal social cost curve. This includes the white arrow of marginal private cost incurred by those who fish today (the cost of labour, mending nets, etc.); and the red arrow of external cost because there will be fewer fish available in the future. The efficient equilibrium is at E^*, where marginal benefit is equal to marginal social cost. However this is not the equilibrium that occurs, because this natural resource is not privately owned. Those who fish take into account only their marginal private cost of fishing today; they ignore the external

future cost. Therefore, their supply curve is S, and the actual equilibrium is at E, where $S = D$. The result is an inefficiently large catch Q, with an efficiency loss shown by the red triangle. This efficiency loss is easily confirmed by considering a, one of the "excess" fish caught. The empty bar under the demand curve represents the marginal benefit of catching a, while its marginal cost—including the effect on future catches—is shown as the empty bar plus the red bar. Thus, the net loss from catching this fish is the red bar, and the sum of the losses on all the other "excess" fish caught over the range Q^*Q is the red triangle.

curve, as usual, reflects the marginal benefits these fish provide to the public that consumes them. S is the supply of fish. The height of this curve reflects the marginal cost faced by those who "produce" (catch) the fish. This cost includes, for example, the expense of hiring crews and mending nets, and is shown by the white arrow on the left. But S does *not* take into account another important cost, shown by the red arrow. This is the *external* cost of fishing done today. The more fish are caught today, the fewer fish will be available for those who fish in the future. Individual boat captains who fish today do not take this into account in calculating this cost. After all, any fish an individual boat catches today will not affect the number it will be able to catch in the future. Thus, each captain has an

incentive to respond to supply curve S, taking no account of how fishing today affects the future fish population. The result is an equilibrium at E where $D = S$ and the catch is Q. However, this is not efficient. Instead the efficient equilibrium is at E^*, with a smaller catch Q^*, where marginal benefit D equals marginal social cost S'. The efficiency loss from the overfishing that occurs at E is shown as the familiar red triangle, reviewed in detail in the caption to the diagram.

Similar problems arise for other common property resources. For example, commonly owned pastures, or **commons**, are likely to be overgrazed.

Note how this problem of overfishing or overgrazing is analytically similar to the problem of overpolluting described in Figure 28-2. In both cases, the problem is that decision makers fail to take an important external cost into account. In the case of pollution, the external cost is the damage to those who live downstream or downwind. In the case of fishing, the external cost is the damage to those in the future who have less of the resource available. (For more detail on how fishing today may reduce future catches, see Box 29-1.)

MEASURES TO INDUCE APPROPRIATE CONSERVATION

There are three approaches that may be used to provide better conservation of a common property resource—that is, there are three ways to reduce the catch in Figure 29-1 from the inefficient overfishing quantity Q to the efficient quantity Q^*, thus eliminating the triangular efficiency loss. We will illustrate these three approaches by considering the problem of conserving the fish population in an offshore fishery such as those off the coast of British Columbia or the Maritime provinces. To simplify matters, we will disregard a difficulty that arises in offshore fisheries because of the fact that fish swim: Even if we try to conserve by reducing the catches that Canadian fishermen are allowed to land, won't the fish just be caught by foreign fishermen operating off our coastlines? (We will briefly consider this problem in Box 29-2.)

1. Place Limits on the Catch
The government may encourage conservation directly by restricting the amount of fish each boat is allowed to land. Or it may shorten the fishing season, only allowing fishing during certain periods during the year. In other cases, more peculiar non-price restraints have been imposed, such as setting a maximum size of the boats that fishing crews are allowed to use.

While this sort of limitation on equipment may indirectly reduce the size of the catch, it is far from clear by how much. To rephrase this point in terms of Figure 29-1, there is no way of pinpointing whether the catch is reduced from Q to more or less than the desired target Q^*. This is important because—just as in the case of pollution—a restriction that is too severe may be worse than no restriction at all. Moreover,

even if the government restriction on equipment *were* to reduce the catch to exactly the desired target Q^*, it would be an expensive way of doing it. The reason is that labour would be wasted because each crew would be able to use only a relatively small boat; therefore, more people would be engaged in fishing. The same problem arises if each fishing boat is limited in the amount of fish it can land: Too much labour or too many boats are expended in the effort.

The problem with this first approach to conservation is that it does not use the market mechanism. We now turn to two alternative approaches that do.

2. A Tax or Fishing Fee
In this case, the government would deal with the externality by using a tax policy similar to the one suggested for controlling pollution in the previous chapter: Impose a tax equal to the external cost. Tax those who catch fish today according to the damage they do to future catches. In other words, tax them or charge them a fishing fee equal to the marginal external cost shown by the red arrow in Figure 29-1. This will raise their supply curve from S to S', thereby internalizing the externality. That is, this tax will force decision makers to take into account the external, as well as the internal, costs of their actions. Accordingly, it will result in an efficient catch Q^* where D intersects the new supply curve S'.

3. Create Property Rights
There may be an even simpler way of achieving efficiency. In certain circumstances, a common property resource may be transformed into private property. For example, a large common pasture may be divided into 50 smaller fields, with one given to each of the families which previously used the commons. Once these fields have been fenced, each family will have an incentive not to overgraze its particular field.

It is not so easy to create property rights in the case of fish. However, in some cases it may be possible. For example, where fish are drawn from a number of small inland lakes, the fishing rights to each separate lake might be granted or sold to an individual, who would then have an incentive to limit the fishing in that lake. (In Box 29-2, we discuss some suggestions of how to introduce property rights in an ocean fishery.)

To see how property rights result in desirable con-

BOX 29-1

THE IDEA OF MAXIMUM SUSTAINABLE YIELD

Our statement that "The more we fish today, the less there will be to catch in the future" is generally true, but it lacks precision. We will now make this idea much more precise.

To begin, note that in certain circumstances, fishing today may have a disastrous effect on future catches; in other cases, it may have little effect. As an example of the disastrous possibility, suppose the fish population is so reduced in number that it can barely survive. Then reducing that population further by fishing today may extinguish the species. In this case, our fishing today would reduce all future catches to zero. At the other extreme, suppose the fish population is so large it cannot grow further. There are no further natural food sources to sustain it, and for every fish that is born, another must die. Then fishing today will have little effect on the fish population, and therefore on future catches. If we don't prevent the fish population from growing by catching some of it, it will be prevented from growing by starvation.

These two cases, and the many other possibilities, are illustrated in Figure 29-2. This diagram shows how the growth in a fish population on the vertical axis depends on the size of the population on the horizontal axis. Point D indicates that the maximum size of the population is 10 million fish. This is the point at which there are so many fish that their population cannot increase further: For each new fish, an existing one will die. If there is no fishing, the fish population will grow toward this number, but not beyond. To confirm this, note that at any point to the left of D, such as K, the fish population will grow (by the height of K). As a result, the population will be greater in the next period, causing a movement to the right, which will continue as long as the yield curve lies above the axis. But once D is reached, there is no further

growth in the number of fish.

There is no reason why a hungry human race should be particularly interested in this "no fishing" solution. There is little satisfaction in knowing that the sea is as full of fish as it can possibly get. Instead, let us consider a point like C that does involve fishing. Here, the fish population is $X_c = 2$ million, and is increasing by $Y_c = 1\ 1/3$ million fish per year. At this point, we can take out the natural increase of $1\ 1/3$ million fish year after year without reducing the 2 million population. Hence, this curve is known as the *sustainable yield curve*, where sustainable yield is the amount of a renewable resource (such as fish) that can be harvested while still leaving the population constant.

The highest point M on this sustainable yield curve represents the maximum sustainable yield. This is a point of particular interest, because it shows the maximum number of fish (in this case, 2 million) that can be caught on a continuing basis without depleting the parent stock. To harvest fish at this maximum rate requires a parent population of 5 million, measured along the horizontal axis. A reasonable objective is to prevent the resource from falling below this 5-million quantity.

Now consider the situation that existed long ago, before there was large-scale commercial fishing. This is illustrated by a point like K, with the ocean almost as full of fish as it could get. As human population and our demands on the seas increased, the fish population was reduced by heavy commercial fishing; there was a move to the left in this diagram. However, so long as the fish population still remained above 5 million (that is, to the right of the maximum sustainable yield at M), there was no conservation problem. As we harvested more, the fish population fell, but it became more able to regenerate itself. That is, the natural increase—as shown by the height of the curve—became greater as we moved from K toward M. It is only at point M, where the fish population is only 5 million, that we encounter the conservation problem. If at this point we continue to harvest more than the natural increase, we will continue to reduce the fish popu-

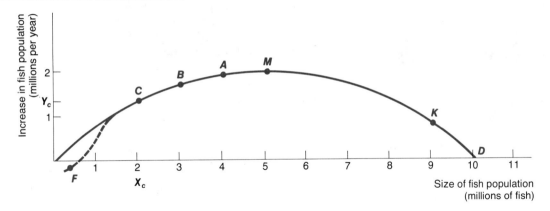

Figure 29-2   Sustainable yield curve.
Point C indicates that if the population of fish on the horizontal axis is 2 million, this will increase by 1 1/3 million per year, measured up the vertical axis. Therefore 1 1/3 million fish can be caught each year, and still leave the population constant at 2 million. As we move to the right along this curve it rises at first: The larger the fish population, the greater its natural increase. However, this increase reaches a maximum at M, where a fish population of 5 million generates an annual increase of 2 million. This 2 million is the *maximum sustainable yield*, the largest number that can be caught per year and still leave the fish population intact. To the right of M, the yield curve falls as the ocean becomes increasingly crowded with fish. When the population of fish reaches 10 million at point D, the ocean can support no further increase.

lation. But now, with each such decline, the fish population becomes less able to regenerate itself. That is, each movement to the left leads to a lower point on the yield curve, closer to the point where the fish population can barely survive. If we do not limit our catches, we may risk extinguishing a whole species, just as we very nearly extinguished the buffalo.

Fishing out an ocean is not just a theoretical possibility. This almost happened with herring in 1969 as a result of the development of larger, more efficient fishing boats. Moreover, the introduction of sonar for chasing down whales has endangered some types of whale.

To understand fully the dangers of overfishing, suppose the yield curve is the dashed curve on the left in Figure 29-2. In this case, heavy fishing may do irreversible damage to the species. This will occur, for example, if we have fished the population down to a quarter-million fish, and are consequently at point F. There are still some fish, but they cannot find other fish to spawn. There is no longer a natu-

ral increase. Instead, there is a natural decrease in population: F lies below the horizontal axis. If we reach a point like F, the population will eventually die out on its own even if we stop fishing altogether. The first rule of conservation should be to prevent such irreversible disasters.

To sum up: Conservation measures should be taken to prevent the population from falling below the level that provides the maximum sustainable yield (M). For plentiful species where unrestricted catches occur far to the right at a point such as K, there is no need to limit catches.*

---

*There are other complications that may move the desired target somewhat to the right or left of M. For example, an influence that tends to pull this target to the right is the fact that, as the fish population gets larger, the fish become easier and cheaper to find. However, because there are other influences that pull in the opposite direction, a target of M is a reasonable first approximation.

servation, consider the case of timber, much of which is in fact held by private owners.

A PRIVATELY OWNED RESOURCE: TIMBER

The market for timber is illustrated in Figure 29-3, with curve S representing the supply curve. Consider a single unit of output, b. The height of the supply curve S shows the price required to induce the owner to cut and sell that unit today. This price, sometimes known as the *reservation price*, covers two costs:

1. The direct cost of harvesting the timber—the wages of lumberjacks, the cost of hauling, etc.; plus
2. The cost to the owner because less timber will be left to cut in the future.

> The *reservation* price of a privately owned resource includes both the cost of harvesting or extracting the resource today *and* the

---

BOX 29-2

MANAGING AN OFFSHORE FISHERY: TWO PROBLEMS

The difficulties and pitfalls that beset the authorities when they try to manage a renewable resource such as an ocean fishery are well illustrated by the Canadian experience with the management of the fisheries off the coasts of British Columbia and the Maritimes. Here we focus on two principal issues. First, which of the three conservation policies discussed in the text have in fact been used, and how effective have they been? Second, fish that swim in an ocean may be caught not only by Canadians but also by foreign fishermen. What measures can we use to protect the fish population in this situation?

1. METHODS OF REGULATION

At present, a variety of different methods are used to control fishing of different species, such as Pacific salmon, cod, herring, and shellfish such as lobster and scallops. In some cases, the government has restricted the number of fishermen permitted to enter the fleet, while in others it has limited the number of days that fishing has been allowed. There have also been controls on the type of gear that fishermen may use. At various times, there have been restrictions on the number of boats that could be used, or on the tonnage of each boat.

According to a recent study by the Economic Council of Canada, the results of these conservation policies have not been entirely satisfactory. On the positive side, the authorities have usually suc-

ceeded in preventing gross overfishing of most species. But their control methods have not been very precise, and from time to time there has been overharvesting. An even more serious problem, however, is that the regulatory methods that have been used have raised the cost of harvesting. For example, the reduction in the legal number of days for fishing has induced fishermen to get large boats and expensive fish-finding equipment. If the fishing season had been longer, it would have been possible to land the same total catch with much less expensive equipment. The Economic Council estimated that the extra costs due to these inefficient harvesting methods might run as high as $750 million to $1 billion a year for Canada's ocean fisheries.

The alternative regulation methods proposed by the Council as a way of overcoming these problems were similar to those discussed in the text. Specifically, the Council proposed a combination of (1) a "landing tax" on the value of the tonnage brought to shore by fishermen, and (2) a system of transferable "stinted landing rights" that would give each fisherman the right to harvest a fixed maximum tonnage each season. Because the government would be able to control the landing rights, it could set a relatively low landing tax without risking problems of overharvesting. One advantage of a low landing tax is that it reduces the opposition of existing fishermen to the regulatory change. Because the landing rights would be transferable, they would not inhibit rationalization in the fishing industry: Efficient fishermen with large catches would be able to buy additional rights from others who wanted to reduce their fishing effort or perhaps leave the industry altogether. (Notice how similar these argu-

amount necessary to compensate the owner for the reduction in the resource available in the future. In other words, it is the height of supply curve S in Figure 29-3.

For more details on reservation price, see Box 29-3.

Observe that Figure 29-3 is very similar to Figure 29-1. In each diagram, there are two upward-sloping curves. The lower curve represents the direct cost of production—what it costs to cut the trees or catch the fish. The vertical distance between the two curves is a reflection of the conservation problem. It measures the cost of having fewer trees or fish available in the future.

However, there is one big difference between the two diagrams. In the case of a common property resource such as fish, in Figure 29-1, the direct costs of production are all that the producers take into account. Therefore, their supply curve is the lower curve, and the result is socially inefficient output Q.

---

ments are to the arguments in favour of transferable pollution permits in Chapter 28.)

2. INTERNATIONAL COMPLICATIONS

While there are several areas where Canadian boats are fishing in competition with foreigners, the particular area that has attracted most attention recently has been the Georges Bank fishing ground located southwest of Nova Scotia, off the coast of Massachusetts.

Until the mid-1970s, most of the fish in the area was caught by long-distance trawlers from the Soviet Union and Eastern Europe. In 1977, however, both the United States and Canada followed the example of many other countries and extended their territorial waters as far as 200 miles offshore, and most foreigners were banned from fishing in the area. But there was a problem: If both Canada and the United States simply define anything within 200 miles of their coastlines as part of their territorial waters, there will be areas in the ocean that fall in the territorial waters of both countries. This problem arises in several places: off British Columbia in the Strait of Juan de Fuca, in the Beaufort Sea (where the Yukon adjoins Alaska); and, in particular, in the sector off the East Coast that includes Georges Bank.

Until 1985, the issue of overlapping claims had not been resolved in any of these areas, and both Canadian and U.S. fishermen fished Georges Bank. Who was responsible for regulating the fishery so as to prevent overfishing? The answer: Canadian fishermen were regulated by the Canadian government, while U.S. fishermen were subject to U.S. regulations. According to the Canadian fishermen, American regulations were much less strict than those imposed on Canadians. As a result, Canadian fishermen lost in two ways. First, they got a smaller share of the total catch in each year. Second, they would suffer in future years because the large catches of the U.S. fishermen would deplete the fish population.

Gradually, both sides came to recognize that the situation was untenable, and a draft fishing treaty was negotiated in 1979. The situation became more complicated when the incoming Reagan administration yielded to pressure from U.S. fishing interests and refused to bring the treaty up for ratification by the U.S. Congress. In the meantime, the boundary problem had been brought up for arbitration in the International Court of Justice in The Hague. In a landmark decision in 1985, the Court came up with a compromise ruling that established boundaries that divided Georges Bank between the United States and Canada. Thus, the question of overlapping jurisdiction has now been decided. But an important question still remains. Since fish populations migrate across Georges Bank, overfishing on one side of the boundary could hurt catches on both sides. In the words of a Nova Scotia fisheries official: "There has to be an equitable arrangement, otherwise one side or the other could massacre the entire stock."

Regulation of fishing is likely to remain a difficult issue in U.S.-Canadian relations for many years to come.

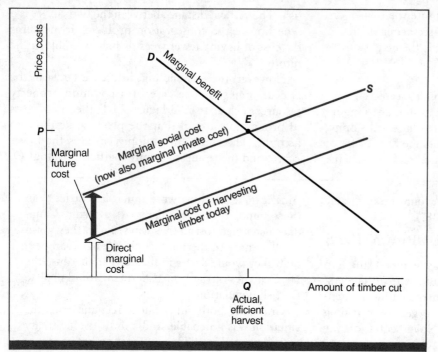

Figure 29-3 Market for a privately owned natural resource.
This is the same as the earlier example in Figure 29-1 except that the resource is now privately owned. In assessing what their harvesting today costs them, the private owners *do* include the red arrow of future cost. Thus their supply is *S*, and equilibrium is at *E*, with an efficient catch *Q*.

Future costs are ignored and there is inadequate conservation. In contrast, timber owners do conserve. They do take into account the red arrow in Figure 29-3, which measures the cost in terms of fewer trees in the future. Therefore, their supply curve is the upper curve. Thus, for a privately owned resource such as timber, equilibrium is at *E* and output is at the socially efficient quantity *Q*.

Of course, private ownership may result in other inefficiencies. For example, if a single firm were to buy up all the timber land, it would be able to exercise monopoly power; that is, it would be able to raise price above *P* by reducing the quantity harvested to even less than *Q*. While this diagram therefore doesn't cover all cases, it does show how a privately owned resource in a perfectly competitive industry can lead to the efficient rate of production.

THE PROBLEM OF THE MYOPIC OWNER

Thus far it has been assumed that private owners of a resource take into account its future value. They do not short-sightedly consider only the present. However, if they do suffer from myopia and fail to see the full implications of their present harvests on the amount of timber available in the future, they will ignore or underestimate the red arrow of future costs in Figure 29-3. Consequently, their supply curve will lie below *S*, and the harvesting of the resource will be more than the efficient quantity *Q*. In this case, private ownership does not provide adequate conservation.

An extreme example of this problem of myopia is aging owners who don't look into the future beyond a few years simply because they don't expect to be alive then. If their philosophy is "Cut the trees now and enjoy the income; who cares about ten years hence?" it's no surprise that they fail to adequately conserve. However, aged owners do not necessarily cause excessive harvesting. They do not, for example, if their objective is to pass on an asset of high value to their heirs. Even if their only concern is to live for the moment, a better option than excessive harvesting is to sell the forest outright to someone who is younger, and can take the long-term view. The sum received will provide the older person with even more money than clear-cutting the land.

BOX 29-3

WHAT INFLUENCES THE RESERVATION PRICE OF A PRIVATELY OWNED RESOURCE?

Some of the major influences on reservation price are:

1. The *expected future price* of the natural resource. The greater the expected price of timber next year, the greater the incentive to leave timber standing "in the bank" so to speak. Therefore, the higher will be the reservation price that owners will require before allowing their timber to be cut today.

2. The *expected future cost of harvesting* the resource. The higher the expected cost of cutting the timber next year, the less incentive the owners will have to leave the timber standing, and the lower will be the reservation price.

3. The *rate of growth of the forest*. If the forest has become fully mature, that is, if it is no longer growing, the owners will acquire no more timber by letting it stand for another year. Some trees may be harvested without substantial adverse effects on future harvests. Therefore, the reservation price will be low.

For simplicity, we have assumed that the owner's decision is only whether to cut the timber this year or next year. But, of course, the issue is not so clear. Instead, the problem is to find the efficient pattern of harvesting over the next *n* years. If the owner is engaged in replanting the forest—rather than simply letting it grow up itself—this is another important cost to be taken into account.

Courtesy Miller Services Limited

THE CONSERVATION OF NONRENEWABLE RESOURCES

Timber and fish are examples of *renewable* resources. They reproduce and grow. A moderate rate of harvesting creates no danger that the forests or fish will disappear.

Other resources, such as oil and copper, are *nonrenewable*. There is a finite quantity of oil and copper in the ground, and if we use a constant amount each year, we will ultimately exhaust the available supply. Moreover, rising population creates pressures to increase the rate of extraction. We may therefore wonder if we are facing a day of reckoning in the not-too-distant future when we will face the exhaustion of our nonrenewable resources.

Simple Projections Spell Disaster

Anyone who projects the present rate of world population growth into the future finds that our requirement for nonrenewable resources is on a collision course with their available supply. Within the next hundred years or so, something must change. A number of models have been developed to show that, on our finite planet, today's trends in population growth and resource use cannot continue long into the future. A decade ago, a group of scholars at the Massachusetts Institute of Technology (MIT) concluded on the basis of a computer-based study that:

If the present growth trends in world population, industrialization, pollution, food production, and resource depletion continue unchanged, the limits to growth on this planet will be reached sometime within the next one hundred years. The most probable result will be a rather sudden and uncontrollable decline in both population and industrial capacity.[1]

If present trends continue, by the middle of the twenty-first century disaster will be upon us—or, more precisely, upon our grandchildren.

But does it make any sense to assume that present trends *will* continue for a century? The assumption that they will has been questioned by Robert Solow, also of MIT:

> The characteristic conclusion of the Doomsday Models is very near the surface. It is, in fact, more nearly an assumption than a conclusion, in the sense that the chain of logic from the assumptions to the conclusion is very short and rather obvious. . . . The imminent end of the world is an immediate deduction from certain assumptions, and one must really ask if the assumptions are any good.

After all, if we are prepared to project present trends, we can project the end of the world very easily, and we don't need a computer to show it. Any simple illustration will do. For example, if we project from a period in which the fruit fly population is growing, we can in a matter of a relatively few years bury the earth three kilometres deep in fruit flies. Any such projection provides an illustration, not of good economics or biology, but of the mathematical magic of mechanically compounding a rate of growth.[2] A far more challenging and rewarding intellectual exercise is to ask: Why will the population of fruit flies eventually stop growing at a constant rate? Why will major changes in our present economic and social system occur?

Adjustments as Resources Become Scarcer
What changes can we expect in our present pattern of life as a growing population presses on a shrinking resource supply?

Change 1. Substitution in production. As demand presses on available supply, the prices of resources rise and producers substitute other inputs. For example, as copper has become more scarce and expensive, construction firms have replaced copper pipe with plastic pipe.

Change 2. Induced innovation. While plastics have been known substitutes for copper for many years, copper may also be displaced by products not yet developed. For example, copper wires are now being displaced in communications systems by far less expensive optical fibres made of glass. We couldn't have predicted this displacement of copper 20 years ago, since we knew almost nothing of fibre-optics then. Even though we can't precisely predict future technology, we can expect that copper will be further displaced in the future by more innovations.

Change 3. Substitution in consumption. As forests have been cut down and quality wood has become scarcer, most consumers have found that solid wood furniture has become too expensive. Therefore they have turned to furniture made with veneers.

Change 4. Changes in population growth. Population growth cannot be projected far into the future because the rate of population increase will be modified by the economic pressures that build up. As our planet becomes more crowded, bringing up children becomes more expensive—and this may influence the typical couple's decision on family size. Moreover, the population growth rate may fall for other reasons that have little to do with economics. In the highly industrialized countries, birthrates have recently been dropping because of changing social attitudes toward the family and children, and because of the development of birth control methods. True, much of the world's population is still in the less developed countries, where the rate of increase remains high. Reasons for this continued high rate include a decline in death rates because of better medical treatment, religious or social objections to birth control, and poverty. (Parents who are so poor that they can't afford insurance may view children as a way of providing for their old age.) However, these influences are likely to weaken. Living standards are rising and death rates cannot be expected to fall as rapidly in the future as in the past.

With the increasing scarcity of resources, there is a major problem. But it is not the problem of some future Doomsday; there are far more plausible rea-

---

[1]Donella H. Meadows and others, *The Limits to Growth* (New York: Universe Books, 1972), p. 29.

[2]To confirm the magic of compound growth, consider this: We will give you a million dollars, if you will give us just 1 cent today, 2 cents tomorrow, 4 cents the next day, and so on, for just one month.

sons than a scarcity of resources for the human race to face Doomsday before the year 2100, particularly if we are unable to control nuclear weapons.

What, then, is the nature of the resource problem? Basically, it is one of *cost* and *technology*. To illustrate, consider one of our most essential resources, but one that we frequently take for granted: fresh, clean water. Suppose that some day we run so seriously short of it that certain areas are forced to tap a new, extremely expensive source of supply: the ocean, where the supply is practically unlimited. The use of seawater would involve the enormous cost of purifying and transporting it. Our problem is to keep these potential future costs in mind when we make decisions today, to ensure that we do not use our resources carelessly and wastefully. The more intelligently we conserve resources, the less the future cost of resource scarcity will be.

The central question, either in the case of resources or fruit flies, is therefore not: What would happen if current trends were to continue for 100 years? but rather: What is the likely process of adjustment? Even more to the point: What is the best path of adjustment? What can we do to make the process of adjustment work smoothly in terms of encouraging the discovery and development of substitutes? Finally, are resources being priced high enough today to protect our interests tomorrow? For a detailed analysis of this question, see Box 29-4.

RESOURCES, THE ENVIRONMENT, AND ECONOMIC GROWTH

In earlier chapters, several arguments for growth have been considered:

1. Unemployment is likely to be less severe in a rapidly growing economy.
2. Growth makes it easier to solve the poverty problem. Growth brings an across-the-board increase in income that lifts many families out of poverty; it is a "rising tide that lifts all boats." Moreover, growth makes it easier to change the *relative* position of the boats—to increase the percentage of the nation's income that goes to the poor. It is far easier to provide for the poor if the total income pie is growing. If it is not growing, then

any gains to the poor will require that someone else's income actually decline.
3. Growth increases not only our own future income, but also the income of our children.

However, as already noted, this third point should not be overstated. If history is any guide, technological improvements will make our children wealthier than we are, no matter what growth policy we follow. As Robert Solow points out: "Why should we poor folk make sacrifices for those who will in any case live in luxury in the future?"

Growth has recently been questioned on other grounds as well: It depletes our resources and increases the pollution in our environment. Do these arguments justify slowing growth—or, as some suggest, setting a target growth rate of zero? Earlier we argued that a no-growth policy would be an extremely costly way to attack the pollution problem. Moreover, it would be relatively ineffective, since it would not deal directly with the problem; it would only prevent pollution from growing, but it would not cut it back. There are similar reasons for being skeptical of a no-growth policy to conserve our resources. It would involve great cost, and it would not directly attack the problem of resource scarcity. Even if we were to end growth completely, we would still need to use resources, and we might still use them in a wasteful way. Better to deal specifically with the resource problem by encouraging the discovery and development of substitutes, and by ensuring that resources are priced high enough to induce us to cut back adequately on their use. In short, a policy of slowing growth is not specific enough to cure any single problem like resource depletion, pollution, or congestion.

Finally, in assessing the growth-versus-anti-growth debate, a helpful question to ask is this: Would the arguments now used against growth have applied equally well a hundred years ago? If so, has our growth over the past century been a mistake? Some people argue that, if we could, we should turn back the clock; but most would disagree. This is a judgement that you will have to make for yourself. However, in comparing the past with the present, don't forget the simple things we take for granted today. Before deciding in favour of the idyllic pastoral life of a few centuries ago, ask yourself this: What would you think of a world with less medical care, food, and the other things that we now view as essential?

BOX 29-4

DYNAMIC EFFICIENCY IN PRICING A NONRENEWABLE RESOURCE*

How high should a nonrenewable resource be priced in order to ensure that our future requirements can be met? Although this is a difficult question, we can isolate some of the issues by considering the following simplified example. Suppose we have a limited quantity of a metal that will be completely replaced in two years by a cheaper plastic substitute of equal quality. The objective, then, is to completely use up the available supply of the metal in the next two years in the most efficient way. (Because cheaper plastic will then become available, there is no need to save any metal beyond this date.) How should it be priced this year and next year to achieve this objective?

The answer is shown in Figure 29-4. Select resource prices P_1 and P_2 in the two years so that the following two conditions are met:

1. The quantities used in the two years should exactly add up to the total available quantity Q. In other words, $Q_1 + Q_2 = Q$.

2. Price P_2 should be higher than P_1 by a gap AB equal to the interest rate. Thus, if the interest rate is 5 percent, P_2 should be 5 percent higher than P_1.

Why does this price pattern result in the efficient allocation of this resource over time? The answer is that efficiency requires that we value the marginal productivity of a tonne of metal to the same extent in both years. (Otherwise, we would be able to increase output by switching a tonne of metal from

*This box is based on Harold Hotelling's classic article that triggered the study of natural resource economics a half-century ago: "Economics of Exhaustible Resources," *Journal of Political Economy* (April 1931): 137–75. For a summary of some of the research that this article has stimulated, see S. Devarajan and A.C. Fisher "Hotelling's 'Economics of Exhaustible Resources': Fifty Years Later," *Journal of Economic Literature* (March 1981): 65–73.

†The different valuation of goods in two years is explained in full in Chapter 35. However, for now you can see intuitively

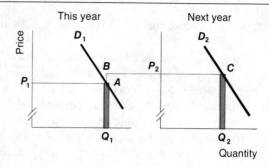

Figure 29-4   Efficient pricing pattern for a nonrenewable resource over two years.
Efficient pricing requires that the gap AB between prices in the two years be equal to the interest rate. Efficiency also requires that the amount of the resource used up ($Q_1 + Q_2$) be equal to the total quantity available. Note that there is no reason for D_1 and D_2 to be the same; in fact, they are quite different in Figure 29-5.

the year of low productivity to the year of high productivity.) But hasn't this efficiency criterion been violated, since the marginal productivity of a tonne of metal this year— as defined under demand curve D_1—is bar Q_1A, while its marginal productivity next year is the higher bar Q_2C? The answer is no: *We value these two marginal productivities equally because they are earned in two different years*, and we value goods this year more highly than goods next year, with the interest rate measuring the difference.† When we accordingly raise the value of this year's Q_1A by the interest rate, we see that it is worth exactly the same as next year's Q_2C. (It was precisely to make these values equal that we separated P_1 and P_2 by the rate of interest.)

To sum up the message of Figure 29-4: The fixed quantity of this resource is efficiently allocated if we use Q_1 this year and Q_2 next. This is what will occur in a competitive market if prices are P_1 and

why things have a higher value this year than next year by asking this simple question: Would you prefer to have $100 of money today or $100 of money next year? Your answer will be "$100 this year; it's worth more." By putting it in the bank and collecting, say, 10% interest, you can make it grow to $110 next year—and that's clearly better than taking $100 next year. Indeed, note that it is better by the amount of the interest rate. As we shall see later, what is true of money is true of other things as well.

P_2 in the two years. We make no claim that this is the price pattern that will necessarily prevail; in fact, it may not. For example, if the supply of this resource is controlled by a small number of producers they may, like any other group of oligopolists, use their market power to set prices above P_1 and P_2. True, higher prices will mean that some of this resource will not be used up by the end of year 2, when it will be displaced by substitutes. However, the oligopolists may still have maximized profits because of the increased price on the amount that they actually do sell. This is just an extension of our conclusion in Chapter 26 that it may be profitable for colluding oligopolists to raise price, even though they sell less as a consequence.

In Figure 29-4, it has been assumed that the resource will be completely replaced by a substitute in two years. Figure 29-5 extends this analysis to the case where the resource is replaced after a longer period.

The resource in Figure 29-5 is replaced by a substitute after year 4. This does not necessarily mean that a substitute eliminates all demand in succeeding years. In fact, there is still demand for the metal in year 5, namely, D_5. However, this demand lies below P_5; the good, inexpensive substitute has "stunted" the demand for this metal. Of course, another reason that demand may be stunted is that public taste has turned against this resource; thus, our use of it could end for this reason as well. An example is coal. Home furnaces were quickly converted away from coal about half a century ago,

not only because oil and gas substitutes were developed, but also because no one wanted to shovel coal.

There are three crucial but highly unpredictable influences that will affect the efficient pricing pattern:

1. If existing deposits of the resource turn out to be less plentiful than expected, there will be less Q to distribute over time, and the whole price "staircase" PP' will shift upwards. (As this happens, note how the quantity used each year is reduced into line with the reduced total quantity Q.) On the other hand, if new deposits are discovered, there will be more Q available, and the price staircase will shift down.

2. Price staircase PP' will shift if there is an unexpected change in demand. For example, if future demand is greater than expected, the price staircase will shift up.

3. The price staircase will fall (or rise) if substitutes are developed more (or less) rapidly than expected. It is very difficult to predict just when the development of substitutes will, in fact, occur. For example, it is very difficult to estimate, when if ever, nuclear fusion—as opposed to present-day nuclear fission—will become inexpensive enough to begin to displace our current sources of energy such as oil and coal.

In practice, therefore, it is very difficult to pin down specifically the efficient pricing and allocation pattern for any resource. But this box has highlighted some of the important considerations that should be taken into account.

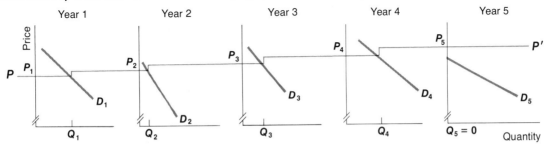

Figure 29-5 Efficient pricing pattern for a nonrenewable resource over a longer period.
This figure extends Figure 29-4. Determining the efficient pattern of price and resource use over time may be viewed as fitting a price "staircase" PP' to the demand curves, with the restriction that $Q_1 + Q_2 + Q_3 \ldots$ be equal to the total fixed available quantity of the resource. As before, the height of each step in this staircase is the interest rate.

OIL: A RESOURCE WITH VERY SPECIAL PROBLEMS

Any discussion of scarce natural resources would be incomplete without some reference to the resource problem that has been an important issue in public policy over the last two decades: oil. Recall that the world price of oil rose from less than $3 a barrel in 1973 to more than U.S.$30 in 1982.

In one sense, the huge price increase may have been a good thing: It put pressure on energy users around the world to conserve a nonrenewable resource. But the main reason why the world oil price rose was not a desire to bring about conservation. Instead, the high price was brought about by OPEC, a cartel of many of the world's oil exporting nations, for the purpose of increasing their revenues from oil exports. And OPEC's gain was other countries' loss: Those countries that have large net imports of oil and other forms of energy were clearly hurt. The effects on a country like Canada were less clear-cut. On the one hand, we were hurt by the higher prices that we had to pay for the oil we imported into Eastern Canada; but on the other hand, we gained from the higher prices we received on our *exports* of oil and natural gas from the Western provinces. (Because natural gas is a close substitute for oil, its price tends to move with the price of oil.) Since Canada's energy exports (in the form of oil, natural gas, and electricity) have typically exceeded its energy imports, Canada as a whole enjoyed a modest net benefit from rising energy prices.

But even though Canada's wealth of energy resources helped protect us from the consequences of the world oil price increase, the developments in the international oil market forced the government to confront several difficult questions. In particular:

1. Should it try to protect all Canadian energy users by preventing energy prices in Canada from rising to world levels, or would it be better to take a hands-off attitude, allowing the price to rise?
2. Should it allow producers of oil, gas, and electricity to cash in on rising world energy prices by raising their exports of Canadian energy resources?

With respect to the pricing question, the government initially chose to keep Canadian energy prices below the world level. To protect Canadian energy users, it froze the Canadian oil price at $3.80 a barrel (far below the world price of more than $10 a barrel). During the rest of the 1970s, the government gradually allowed the domestic price to rise, but not enough to keep up with the increase in world prices: Thus, the Canadian price remained substantially below the world price throughout the last half of the decade.

To support its policy of keeping the domestic oil price below the world price, the government imposed a tax on Canadian oil exports equal to the difference between these two prices. (If it had not, Canadian producers would have received a higher price for exported oil, and would have sold all their oil in the world market.) In addition, the government imposed strict limitations on the quantity of oil that producers were allowed to export.

The Progressive Conservative government under Joe Clark that was elected in 1979 tried to change the low-price policy. In the budget introduced in late 1979 by John Crosbie, provisions were made for an increase in the Canadian oil price toward the world level. However, the Conservatives were defeated after less than a year in office, and in the **National Energy Program** (NEP) introduced by the Liberal government in 1980, the consumer price of oil was again set well below the world price. It was not until the mid-1980s that the Canadian domestic price essentially reached the world price.

The problem of oil and gas pricing in Canada is complicated because of a number of factors, including the fact that many of the firms producing oil and gas in Canada are foreign-owned, and that our oil and gas deposits are concentrated primarily in the three Western provinces. Because of these factors, distributional effects play a very important role in the debate over Canadian energy policy: The fact that a high-price strategy would imply a redistribution of real income from Canadian energy users to foreign-owned oil companies, and from the relatively poor Maritime provinces to resource-rich Alberta, was one of the main arguments against such a policy. These distributional issues are briefly discussed in Box 29-5. Here we concentrate on the aggregative efficiency effects of the pricing policy.

A policy that keeps the domestic price of oil—or

any other internationally traded commodity—below the world price leads to an efficiency loss. The reasons are illustrated in Figure 29-6.

Implications of Keeping the Domestic Canadian Price below the World Price

Without government intervention, the domestic price would be the same as the world price, P_W. At this price, the quantity demanded in Canada would be $P_W C$,[3] of which $P_W B$ would be produced in Canada. The balance, BC, would be imported. Now consider the effect of government controls that kept the Canadian price below P_W, at P_1.

Consumers responded to the lower price P_1 by moving down their demand curve from C to F; thus, consumption increased by arrow 1. In addition, the lower price induced domestic producers to move down their supply curve from B to A; Canadian oil production decreased by arrow 2. With consumption expanded and production contracted, the difference between the two—that is, imports—increased from BC to AF.

This increase in imports was one of the most important effects of this policy of holding down the domestic price of oil. However, there were other effects as well:

1. Because the domestic price was kept below the world price, Canadian oil consumers benefitted. (The "oil price shock" was not as severe for them as it would otherwise have been.) At the same time, Canadian producers were hurt because the price they received (P_1) was not as high as it would otherwise have been. Thus, this policy benefitted consumers at the expense of producers. However, even though the Canadian oil price didn't rise as high as the world price, it nevertheless rose substantially relative

[3]So long as the government doesn't interfere and oil can be freely bought and sold on the world market for P_W, Canadian buyers won't pay more for it than this, and Canadian producers won't sell it for less. Therefore its price in Canada will also be P_W.

As we shall see later, the actual system the government used for reducing price was more complex than the one we now describe in the text; moreover, the story was further complicated by the fact that even though Canada is a net importer of oil, it also exports some oil. To keep the analysis simple, we disregard these complications here.

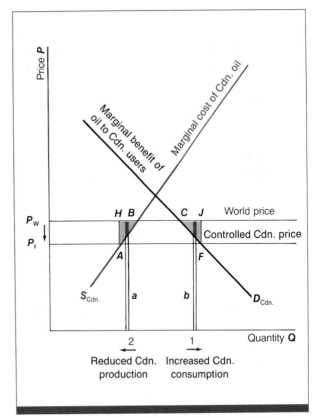

Figure 29-6 The effects of keeping the domestic Canadian price of oil (P_1) below the world price P_W.
The first effect was increased domestic consumption equal to arrow 1 that had to be satisfied by increased imports. The result was an efficiency loss because each of these barrels, such as b, cost more to import (the height of the white bar plus the red bar) than the benefit it provided to consumers (the white bar). Therefore, there was a loss on this barrel equal to the red bar. Adding up the similar losses on all the other barrels over the relevant range CJ of increased consumption, yielded the triangular efficiency loss CJF. At the same time, keeping the domestic price below P_W at P_1 also resulted in arrow 2 of reduced domestic oil production; this also had to be covered by increased imports. The result was an efficiency loss because each of these barrels, such as a, cost more to import (the height of the white bar plus the red bar) than it would have cost if it had been produced domestically instead (the height of the white bar). The result was a loss on this barrel equal to the red bar. Adding up the similar losses on all the other barrels over the relevant range HB of decreased Canadian production, yielded the triangular efficiency loss HBA.

to the early 1970s; between the early 1970s and the time the National Energy Program was established, there had already been a large transfer in the opposite direction, from consumers to producers. Thus, the policy of keeping the domestic price from rising as rapidly as the world price was judged to be a "fair" or equitable one because it prevented this transfer from consum-

---

BOX 29-5

THE INTERNATIONAL INCOME TRANSFER AS THE WORLD PRICE OF OIL INCREASED: OPEC AS A "CONSERVING MONOPOLIST"?

What we are witnessing in . . . oil and raw material prices is virtually the same as what is going on between trade unions and employers associations on the national level. It is a struggle for the distribution and use of the national product, a struggle for the world product.

> Helmut Schmidt, then Minister of Finance and later Chancellor of the Federal Republic of Germany

So far in this book we have considered several kinds of changes in the economy that may cause income transfers within Canada. For example, if a marketing board restricts supply and drives up the price in a previously competitive agricultural industry, there is a transfer from Canadian consumers to Canadian farmers. Or if the provincial government raises the excise tax on beer, there is a transfer from Canadian beer drinkers to taxpayers. While these transfers represent losses to some Canadians (consumers of farm products or beer drinkers), these losses are in large measure offset by the gains of others (farmers, provincial taxpayers).

As Canada and other countries allowed domestic oil prices to gradually rise toward world prices, following the huge OPEC-induced increase in the world oil price in the 1970s, there was a large transfer of real income from energy users in those countries. Who were the gainers? In countries that were more or less self-sufficient in energy, the gainers were domestic energy producers. But for countries such as Japan and some European countries who depend on imports for a large part of their energy needs, the transfers from energy users were not offset by gains to domestic producers. Instead, many of the gains from a higher oil price went to foreign producers—in particular, producers in the OPEC nations. From the viewpoint of the citizens in an importing nation like Japan, such transfers were a dead loss.

What about the Canadian case? Because Canada is largely self-sufficient in energy, increases in energy prices in Canada mostly result in a transfer from Canadian energy users to firms that produce energy from Canadian resources. But there is a catch: Many of these firms are not owned by Canadians, but instead by foreigners. From the viewpoint of the well-being of Canadians, therefore, the transfers are to some extent a dead loss: a substantial part of any increase in energy prices is transferred from Canadians to foreign owners of the multinational oil companies that operate in Canada.

In reality, the issue is more complicated because governments collect taxes and royalties from the energy sector. Thus, while higher energy prices in Canada during the 1970s meant higher profits for foreign-owned oil companies, some of these profits were taxed away, and thus went to Canadian taxpayers. However, here we have yet another complication. Because much of the taxation of energy resources has been under the jurisdiction of the province in which the oil and gas is extracted, much of the transfer went from energy users all over Canada to taxpayers in the Western provinces where most of our oil and gas resources are located.

To sum up: While the argument in the text in favour of letting the Canadian oil price rise to the world level is correct as far as it goes, it must be modified to take into account the fact that a transfer from domestic oil users to domestic producers represents a loss to Canada if the producing firms are owned by foreigners. Moreover, in actual policy making, one must also take into account the political problems that arise because an increase in oil and gas prices results in a transfer between provinces.

ers to producers from becoming even bigger. As we show in Box 29-5, the issue of transfers was particularly sensitive because many of the producing firms were foreign-owned.

2. Canadian oil consumers were not encouraged to conserve. Instead their oil consumption was higher, as shown by arrow 1. The result, as detailed in the caption to the diagram, was an efficiency loss of red triangle *CJF*—reflecting the fact that imported oil was costing more (the world price P_W) than the benefit consumers were getting from it (the height of the demand curve *CF*).

3. The reduction in domestic oil production shown by arrow 2 resulted in another efficiency loss—red triangle *HBA*, also described in detail in the caption to Figure 29-6. The reason for this efficiency loss is that we were importing oil at high cost P_W rather than producing it domestically at the lower cost shown by the height of the supply curve *AB*. (An important warning is required here. This conclusion need not follow if producers were "myopic"—that is, if they failed adequately to take into account the fact that extracting oil reduced the availability of oil in the future. If they were thus inadequately concerned with conservation, then an argument can be made for measures that would have induced them to conserve. The price reduction from P_W to P_1 had this effect, since it induced producers of oil to reduce their output by arrow 2.)

   4. It was very expensive for the government to make such a simple price-control system work. Importers had to pay P_W to buy oil on the world market. In forcing them to sell it at the lower price P_1, the government had to pay them the difference—that is, a subsidy of $P_W P_1 = AH$ per barrel. Thus, the total subsidy that the government had to pay on the *AF* barrels imported was $AH \times AF$ = area *HAFJ*.

To reduce problems 3 and 4, the government's National Energy Program actually used a more complex system than the one described so far.

The Blended Price System

Instead of fixing a single domestic price of oil, the government specified a number of prices, falling into three basic categories:

1. The relatively high price paid for "new oil"—that is, oil from newly drilled wells. (Under the 1981

version of the NEP, negotiated between the federal government and the producing provinces, this price was close to the world price P_W.)

2. A lower price P_1 that producers could charge for "old oil," that is, oil from wells already in production.

3. A "blended price" that domestic *buyers* had to pay. This blended price was lower than the high producer price for new oil, but not as low as the producer price of old oil; the difference between the blended price and this producer price took the form of a tax that the government collected on the domestic sale of old oil. The revenue from this tax—and from the tax on oil exports—was enough to pay for the subsidy on oil imports. Thus, problem 4 above was solved; the policy did not involve massive government expenditure. Moreover, by allowing producers to charge essentially the world price P_W for new oil, the government avoided problem 3. Producers responded to this high price by operating at point *B* in Figure 29-6. Thus, there was no reduced production (arrow 2); nor was there any efficiency loss associated with it. Because old oil was already in production and would be produced anyway—or so it was hoped—keeping its price at the lower level P_1 would not significantly affect production.

In theory, it was an ingenious solution. However, in practice it created a number of problems. To illustrate, consider just two: First, because there was no way of physically distinguishing between old and new oil, illegal operators were given an incentive to use complex transactions to disguise the source of old oil. This would allow them to sell it as new oil at a higher price. Second, even though the government had raised the price of new oil and was subsidizing exploration, there was a substantial decrease in drilling activity in the early 1980s, with many companies moving their equipment out of Canada. Toward the mid-1980s, there was less and less enthusiasm for the system of price controls in the energy sector. By 1985, the Conservative government had moved to dismantle much of the control system. (In the United States, the earlier system of controls over oil and gas pricing had also been abandoned, consistent with the Reagan administration's general philosophy of deregulation.)

Oil Pricing, Conservation, and Energy Security

In the discussion of oil pricing so far, we have focused

on the issues of efficiency and transfers between consumers and producers. Looking at efficiency alone, the discussion has pointed to the conclusion that the best policy is to simply allow the domestic Canadian price to follow the world price. By adopting this policy, we would have eliminated the efficiency losses (illustrated by triangles *CJF* and *HBA* in Figure 29-6) that arose when Canada had to increase oil imports to make up for the shortfall in domestic production.

However, another important issue in Canadian energy policy is the problem of potential instability in the world oil market. In particular, the volatile political situation in the Middle East, which supplies a large portion of the oil traded in the international market may lead to a sudden disruption of oil supplies. How should we take this problem of instability into account in formulating Canadian energy policy?

Surprisingly, the answer is that when we allow for the instability problem, the best strategy may be to set the Canadian domestic price even higher than the world price. The logic is this: A sudden disruption in world oil supplies may involve very high costs to Canada, especially if oil-using industries are forced to cut back production, or if we run out of oil for home heating. (Any disruption of supplies of imported oil to Canada would affect the United States as well, so there is little possibility that we could import American oil in a crisis.) The risk of having to bear the costs of emergency measures can be viewed as an additional cost of depending on oil imports, rather than being self-sufficient. This risk-related cost should be added to the world price P_W that we have to pay for oil, in order to arrive at its true cost. According to this argument, efficiency requires that the domestic Canadian price should fully reflect this cost and therefore also be above P_W. (Efficiency requires that the domestic price faced by consumers and producers provide a clear message of *all* the costs of a good.) Therefore, oil should be taxed to raise its price *above P_W*.

(The case for raising the domestic price above the world price applies even more strongly in the United States, since it is more dependent than Canada on imported oil. It has also been argued that reduced American dependence on oil imports may contribute to stabilizing international politics, because it would reduce the risk that the United States would get involved militarily in the Middle East.)

Non-Price Measures to Reduce Oil Imports

There are other ways of reducing our dependence on imported foreign oil, in addition to raising the domestic oil price. The National Energy Program introduced a number of non-price measures that gave consumers incentives to cut back on oil use. For example, to reduce the amount of oil used for residential heating, the government offered to pay part of the cost of improving the insulation in private homes. It also offered to pay up to $800 toward the cost of converting oil heating systems to other forms of heating (such as natural gas or electric heat pumps). The NEP also proposed a low price for natural gas to encourage home owners to switch to gas. In addition, it outlined a plan for extending the system of natural gas pipelines in order to make gas heating available in more places in Canada. The NEP also established mandatory fuel-efficiency standards for cars used in Canada, similar to the standards that had existed in the United States since 1975. Furthermore, it called on provincial governments to reduce the speed limits in their provinces. (Lower speed reduces the gasoline used for a given trip; moreover, it tends to reduce the number of trips taken because each trip takes longer.)

CONSERVING OIL BY DEVELOPING SUBSTITUTE FORMS OF ENERGY

While oil still plays a crucial role, Canada relies on other important sources of energy as well, for example, natural gas, hydro power, nuclear fission, and coal. (Other sources that currently play a less important role include solar power, wind, and waste products from the forest industry.)

There are two major questions to ask about any alternative energy source: (1) What are its costs of production? and (2) What costs does it impose on the environment? The second question has been very important in the case of coal and nuclear energy: Environmental (or external) costs have deterred the development of these otherwise promising sources of energy. But while we should be concerned about the environmental cost of these other forms of energy, we should also recognize that oil itself has such costs. For example, burning oil in the form of gasoline in cars has serious environmental effects in a large city like Toronto, Montreal, or Vancouver. Worse yet, the burning of fossil fuels such as oil or coal may affect the environment in all locations. Some scientists fear that the carbon dioxide that is emitted may cause a "greenhouse effect" that may eventually alter the world's climate. If this theory is confirmed, the use of these fuels may have to be reduced long before the world's reserves begin to run out.

Natural Gas

While burning natural gas also produces carbon dioxide, its overall environmental costs are relatively low. It produces much less air pollution than either coal or oil. Unlike nuclear power, it presents no major safety risk or disposal problem. Unlike coal, its extraction from the ground does little damage to the environment.

Fortunately, Canada has large reserves of natural gas, principally in Alberta and British Columbia. (Conventional *oil* reserves in Alberta have been falling steadily, as extraction has outstripped new discoveries. But Alberta's *total* energy reserves have not been falling, because of large new gas discoveries.) The policies in the NEP which encouraged users to switch to natural gas from other sources of energy increased Canadian consumption of natural gas. Nevertheless, estimates by the National Energy Board indicate that our gas reserves in the Western provinces are large enough to meet increased Canadian demand and leave room for substantial exports to the United States, at least until 1990, and almost certainly beyond that date. In addition, there have been recent finds of natural gas in frontier areas such as the Arctic Islands and off the coast of Newfoundland; thus, many analysts believe that our reserves will be large enough for our domestic requirements well into the twenty-first century.

Nuclear and Hydro-electric Power

Hydro power has several advantages: It is perfectly clean and indefinitely renewable. Its only disadvantages are the high initial costs of tapping the resource, and its environmental effect. Large hydro projects generally require large dams, which change the natural flows of rivers and may put valuable land under water. True, the environmental impact may affect relatively few people if the hydro development is in a wilderness region far from densely populated areas.(An example is the large James Bay project in northern Quebec.)

But when the power stations are located in remote wilderness areas, there are high costs of transmitting the power to the distant centres of population. In addition, in the case of the James Bay project, the area to be flooded included Cree and Inuit communities and hunting grounds whose loss represented a high cost to the local residents. Nevertheless, as the price of energy rises, the capacity to increase Canadian hydro power production through such projects is there. Some additional hydro power can also be produced on a more modest scale by using small dams that have already been built, or by exploiting the rivers close to population centres more intensively.

Coal

The increased price of oil has placed coal in a strong position for a comeback from its declining role as an energy source in the twentieth century. However, coal's growth has been disappointing, because of the problems encountered both in mining and burning it.

1. Problems in mining. Underground mining, as in our Cape Breton coal industry, involves many problems: acid drainage, and the risk of black lung disease or fatal accidents underground. Strip mining, which is done mainly in the Western provinces, involves a different problem: it leaves land scarred and unproductive, as has happened in the past in southern Saskatchewan. To avoid this, coal producers are now required—often at substantial cost—to reclaim and reconstruct the landscape after a mine shuts down.

2. Problems in burning coal in power plants. The principal pollutant that is produced when coal is burned is sulphur dioxide, which is emitted into the air and eventually comes down in the acid rain that has destroyed life in thousands of lakes in North America and Europe. To reduce this problem, the government has required some coal-burning plants to reduce their emissions by installing scrubbers. (Since this creates a sludge, air pollution is being traded, to some degree, for water pollution.)

Nuclear Fission

While our capacity to produce nuclear power is increasing, the growth of this form of energy production in the 1970s fell considerably short of earlier expectations. As the rapid expansion of nuclear power began in the mid-1960s, it was hailed as the cheapest of all sources of energy, and—in response to OPEC—the key to reducing North American dependence on off-shore oil imports. Yet by 1985, nuclear power produced only a small fraction of our energy needs.

The relatively slow growth reflected unexpectedly high plant costs, slower than expected growth in electricity demand, tough regulations, and some public opposition, which became much stronger after the Three Mile Island (3MI) accident near Harrisburg, Pennsylvania, in 1979.

However, even despite the 3MI experience, the industry feels that it has a good safety record. Nuclear power has exposed the public to much less radiation than an equivalent use of coal, since coal contains traces of radioactive materials which are released into the atmosphere when it is burned. Moreover, while lives have been lost in accidents in coal mines, there have been no fatal accidents in commercial power plants. Consequently, the debate on safety has focused less on the past than on three questions for the future: What is the chance of a much more serious accident than 3MI? (Indeed, a second, more serious accident did take place at Chernobyl in the Soviet Union in April 1986.) Will a worldwide use of nuclear power contribute to the proliferation of nuclear weapons? And what will we do with nuclear wastes?

Increasingly, nuclear *fusion* is seen as the process that will provide a virtually inexhaustible source of energy. Whereas present-day fission splits atoms apart, fusion joins atoms together in a controlled, repeated version of what happens in an uncontrolled way when a hydrogen bomb explodes. It is a miniature copy of what is happening all the time in the sun.

While fusion releases enormous heat, the problem is that it requires enormous heat to accomplish. The first big milestone to watch for in future fusion research is the *energy break-even point*, where the output of heat energy released by fusion exceeds the input of heat needed to cause the fusion. At this point the process will at least be able, on balance, to create energy. But that energy will at first be extremely expensive. Therefore, the next step to watch for will be the *economic break-even point*, where energy output exceeds energy input by enough to make nuclear fusion economically competitive with other forms of energy.

If scientists succeed in developing fusion to this point, it would offer great advantages over fission because it would have less external cost. Fusion would be safer than fission, as very little radioactive waste results from the fusion process itself; however, there could be waste from the materials surrounding and containing the process, and "heat pollution" could be a problem. Furthermore, fusion is still a long way off; the best estimate is that it will not become economic until early in the next century. In looking ahead along the uncertain path to fusion, we should remember: Thirty years ago there was great optimism about nuclear fission as an energy source.

KEY POINTS

1. In extracting common property resources, such as fish, that are publicly owned, fishing crews do not take into account how this year's harvest will affect future harvests. The result is an efficiency loss; too much is harvested today.

2. In an attempt to solve this problem by reducing the current catch of fish, the government may impose various restrictions, such as fishing licences or off-season limits on fishing. In the case of ocean fishing, some governments have extended their territorial waters to limit the catch obtained by foreign vessels. However, it is difficult to sort out how much of this territorial extension is a desire to conserve and how much is a desire to protect domestic vessels from foreign competition.

3. Another way to reduce the harvest to an efficient level is to establish property rights. Once the resource becomes privately owned, its supply will reflect not only the current cost of harvesting it, but also the amount necessary to compensate the owner for the adverse effect of present harvests on future resource supplies.

4. Special problems arise when a resource is nonrenewable. If current rates of consumption continue, such a resource must someday be exhausted. This simple observation has led to a number of "Doomsday studies" that predict the

collapse of our economic system. However, a problem with many of these studies is that they do not account adequately for price adjustments: As such resources become scarcer, their prices rise; this encourages conservation and stimulates the search for substitutes. An important question is: Are today's prices of nonrenewable resources high enough to ensure that existing supplies will not be used up too quickly and that the development of new substitutes will be encouraged?

5. The policy of keeping the domestic Canadian oil price below the world price led to two kinds of efficiency loss: (1) It reduced conservation efforts by oil users and (2) discouraged production by domestic producers. It has also resulted in a large transfer from the oil companies to oil users.

6. Non-price measures that have been used to encourage conservation include tax incentives for insulating buildings and converting to natural gas heating, and regulations requiring auto manufacturers to produce cars with improved gas mileage.

7. Important current substitutes for oil include hydro power, coal, natural gas and nuclear fission. There are a number of other promising sources of energy, such as solar power and nuclear fusion. Although we are a long way from developing an economic fusion process, it could become a very important source of energy in the future.

KEY CONCEPTS

common property resource
privately owned resource
reservation price
territorial limits
*sustainable yield curve
*maximum sustainable yield
creation of property rights

renewable resource
nonrenewable resource
induced innovation
producer myopia
blended price system
new oil vs. old oil

environmental problems
  with coal
environmental problems with
  nuclear fission
nuclear fusion
energy break-even point
economic break-even point

PROBLEMS

29-1 Suppose that 50 boats are fishing in an ocean area. Would there be any reason for the government to allow the boat owners to sign an agreement restricting the amount each catches? Is it possible that restricting the catch, which began as a conservation measure, could become a means of exercising market power? Explain. Can you think of any other examples of people who become conservationists because it is a way of providing themselves with more market power? If those who already have their ski chalets in British Columbia become conservationists and prevent new ski runs and chalets from being built, what would this do to the value of their chalets?

29-2 Explain why a "myopic monopolist" might sell an inefficiently large or inefficiently small amount of a resource.

29-3 The problem of efficient timing in harvesting timber is illustrated in the diagram on the next page. For example, point A indicates that if we wait 15 years before harvesting again, an acre will yield 10 units of timber. Which point represents a forest in which there is no longer any timber growth? Would you cut timber every 15, 30 or 66 years? Explain. (Assume that cutting and replanting costs are negligible.)

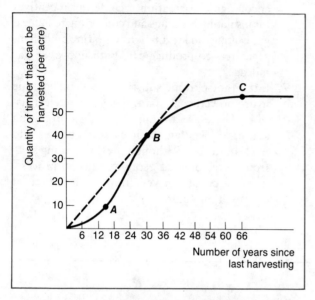

29-4 Doomsday models typically project a constant rate of growth of population and resource usage, and hence forecast disaster. What economic forces tend to cause a change in the use of raw material resources? What forces affect the rate of population growth?

29-5 Equity among generations seems to suggest that we should not sacrifice much for our children, since they are likely to be wealthier than we are, regardless of what we do. How would you evaluate the following counterargument? "Historically, each generation has sacrificed for the next. Is it fair for any generation to opt out of this process and thus become a 'free rider,' receiving benefits from the previous generation, but making no attempt to pass on benefits to the next?"

29-6 Using Figure 29-5, explain how conservation measures may be taken too far. Specifically, explain why it would be a mistake to cut back consumption one unit below Q_1 in year 1 in order to conserve that unit for use in year 5. Also, show why it would be a mistake to ignore conservation concerns and use one unit more than Q_1 in year 1.

29-7 Karl Marx recommended that the forests should no longer be privately owned; they should be made public property. In terms of conserving this resource, what would be the effect? Would this change the distribution of income? Explain both answers.

*29-8 (a) Did holding the Canadian oil price down in the 1970s increase or reduce the international transfer from Canada to oil exporting countries? In your answer, explain the effect of holding the price down on domestic production and consumption, and therefore the effect on Canadian oil imports.

(b) Explain why you agree or disagree with the statement: "To reduce a domestic transfer (from domestic users to domestic producers) the Canadian government followed a policy that made the international transfer worse."

29-9 What would you expect to happen to the price of oil if scientists were to announce that the economic break-even point for nuclear fusion had been achieved? In your answer, explain what would happen to the reservation price of oil producers. Would your answer change if scientists announced only that the energy break-even point had been achieved? If so, explain why.

Chapter 30

PUBLIC GOODS: WHAT SHOULD THE GOVERNMENT PROVIDE?

> There are certain goods that have the peculiarity that once they are available no one can be precluded from enjoying them whether he contributed to their provision or not. These are the public goods.
>
> Robert Dorfman

Throughout this text, we have studied government intervention in the economy. For example, the government imposes regulations that prevent collusion between business firms (Chapter 27), that limit pollution (Chapter 28), and that conserve natural resources (Chapter 29). In these cases, government intervention is designed to influence the behaviour of private firms and individuals. However, the economic decisions on what will be produced and how it will be produced are still made by private firms and individuals, subject to whatever constraints or incentives the government imposes. Although the market is *influenced* by government policies, it still delivers the goods.

In this chapter we consider instances where the free market does not adequately deliver the goods—or fails altogether—and there is a case for government intervention. As we study these goods, we will see once again that externalities are the key. However, the kind of externalities that are important now are not external costs such as pollution, but rather external *benefits* such as the two cited earlier: the benefits neighbours get when a homeowner hires a gardener, or the protection from disease that others receive when an individual gets a vaccination. To begin, consider the simplest possible analysis of such cases.

EXTERNAL BENEFITS AND RESOURCE MISALLOCATION

If there are any external or spillover effects, whether they be harmful or beneficial, the free market will not allocate economic resources efficiently. For example, because the good in Figure 28-2 had an external cost, a free, perfectly competitive market resulted in too much output. Accordingly, we might guess that, if a good has an external *benefit,* a free competitive market will result in *too little* output.

Figure 30-1 confirms that this guess is correct. The supporting argument can be stated briefly because it runs parallel to the argument used earlier in analysing external costs. The key is to recognize that, instead of the external costs that were added to the *supply* curve in Figure 28-2, there are now external benefits to be added to the *demand* curve. Specifically, in Figure 30-1 the marginal external benefit shown by the arrow is added to the marginal private benefit MB, to yield the marginal social benefit MB$_S$. An example might be flu shots. These provide both a private benefit MB to those who acquire them and an external benefit to others who become less likely to pick up the disease. Both these must be added to calculate the social benefit (MB$_S$) of the shots.

If this marginal social benefit MB$_S$ is equated to the marginal cost MC, the result is an efficient outcome

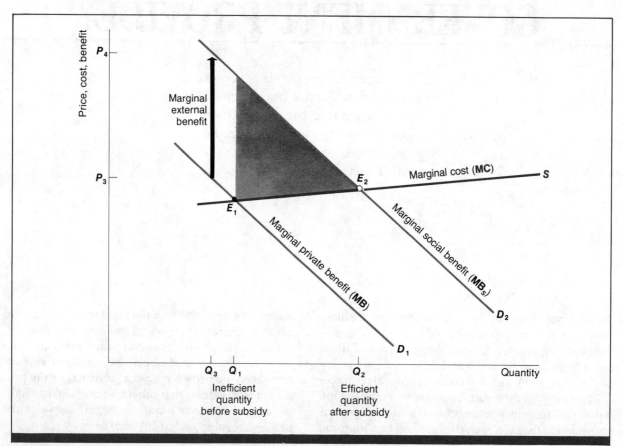

Figure 30-1 Efficiency loss for a product with an external benefit such as vaccinations.

The height of the market demand D_1 shows the marginal benefit of vaccinations to the people vaccinated—that is, their own internal benefit because they don't get the disease. The black arrow shows the external benefit enjoyed by others because the disease isn't passed on to them. When these two benefits are taken into account, the result is the marginal social benefit MB$_S$. In a free market, equilibrium is at E_1, where marginal cost is equal to marginal *private* benefit.

(This private benefit is the demand curve D_1 because it is the only benefit taken into account by those who make the decision to get vaccinations.) The result is an efficiency loss shown by the red triangle. To confirm, note that all units of output between Q_1 and Q_2 have a benefit—the height of MB$_S$—that exceeds their cost shown by the height of MC. Thus, producing them would result in a net benefit. In other words, because they are not produced, there is a net loss—as shown by the red triangle. This efficiency loss from "producing too little" is the same as the triangle in Figure 24-3(*b*).

at E_2. However, in the absence of government interference, a free competitive market will reach equilibrium at E_1 instead, where marginal cost is equal to marginal *private* benefit. (This is the only benefit taken into account by those buying the flu shots; thus, it is their demand curve, and is marked D_1.) With equilibrium at E_1 rather than E_2, the free market generates too little output—specifically, Q_1 rather than Q_2.

One Solution: A Subsidy

One way of getting to the efficient equilibrium E_2 is to provide buyers with a per unit subsidy equal to the external benefit arrow, thus shifting the demand curve up from D_1 to D_2. (Demand shifts in this way because, for example, the individual initially willing to pay only P_3 for unit Q_3 is now prepared to pay P_4—that is, the original P_3 plus the subsidy received from the government shown by the black arrow.) With this shift in demand, a competitive market does the rest. Its new equilibrium is at E_2, where supply and new demand D_2 intersect. Thus, efficient output Q_2 is achieved.

However, such an increase in efficiency alone does not necessarily justify a subsidy or any other form of government intervention. One must also examine the administrative costs of that intervention. Thus, for example, the government does not subsidize each homeowner for planting a garden, because the efficiency gains aren't sufficient to cover the costs of administering such a widespread subsidy program. On the other hand, in the case of many vaccinations, the efficiency gains do outweigh the costs of administration and a subsidy is justified.[1]

Notice in Figure 30-1 that efficiency is achieved by subsidizing a product with an external benefit, just as a product with an external cost was taxed in Figure 28-2. In either case, the government "internalizes an externality." In Figure 28-2, polluting firms that paid the tax were made to "feel internally" the external damage they were causing, so they did less. On the other hand, purchasers of the sort of product we are now considering receive a subsidy that allows them to "enjoy internally" the external benefits it provides; thus, this product is encouraged. In either the tax or

the subsidy case, *private firms or individuals act only after taking external effects into account.* This is as it should be.

Externalities may sometimes be internalized even without government action, but simply as a result of private market forces.

Private Market Transactions That Internalize an Externality

One example is provided by the private real estate firm that purchases a whole block of houses in a run-down neighbourhood. Its renovation expenditure on each house raises the value of that house, and also provides a spillover benefit by raising the value of the other houses in the block as well. Once the firm has renovated all the houses in the block, it can capture both the internal and external benefits. Specifically, when it sells each house, it will enjoy *two* types of price increase: (1) the price increase because that particular house has been renovated, and (2) the additional price increase because the neighbourhood has improved as a result of the renovations to the other houses. Thus, while the firm may not be able to make a profit by purchasing and renovating a single house, it may be able to do so if it purchases and renovates the whole block, simply because it is able to capture the spillover effects.

As another example, if a firm constructs a ski lift on a mountain, it will be able to sell tow tickets. These receipts will be an internal benefit to the firm. At the same time, the ski lift will also generate an external benefit in the form of greater pleasure for those eating at a nearby restaurant who enjoy watching people ski. The internal benefit to the ski-lift company from ticket sales may be insufficient to justify constructing the lift. But suppose the firm can buy the restaurant and, once the ski lift is built, start charging customers more. It can then capture (internalize) the external benefit it has created. It now becomes profitable to build the lift. The nation's output of ski-lift services is no longer too low. It has now been increased to an efficient quantity because external benefits have been internalized. They are now being realized by the firm.

(This suggests an alternative approach to externalities: Allow firms to merge into large enough units so that decision makers will take such spillovers into account. However, this raises a conflict for policy makers. Mergers to internalize externalitites should be

---

[1] In the interests of simplicity, the government subsidy for vaccinations is typically in the form of a reduction in their cost (often to zero), rather than a grant paid to those who acquire them. However, either form of subsidy has a similar effect in encouraging people to acquire more.

allowed. But mergers to accumulate market power should not. The problem is that mergers often do both.)

Now let's pursue the issue of positive externalities further by considering a flood-control dam in a river valley. If a single farmer were to build such a dam, he would enjoy an internal benefit, since his own crops and buildings would be protected from floods. However, such a benefit would be trivial compared to the enormous cost of constructing the dam. As a result, no individual farmer builds it—even though its construction might be easily justified by the large external flood-control benefits it would provide for the thousands of other farmers in the valley. If the dam is to be built at all, it will have to be built *collectively*—by a large group of farmers acting together, or by the government. Thus we come to the idea of a **public good**.

PUBLIC GOODS

The simplest definition of a public good is "anything the government provides." But this is too broad a definition for our purposes, for two reasons: (1) It includes all sorts of government payments such as housing subsidies or family allowance payments that are designed to achieve an equity objective by transferring income from one group to another. Such policies to achieve equity will be discussed in Chapter 37. For now, we continue to concentrate on efficiency; (2) "Anything the government provides" includes all sorts of activities that *could* be undertaken by private firms but are provided by the government instead; public health insurance, public transport systems, and Canada Post are examples. Since we are not interested in so broad a definition, we begin with the narrower idea of goods—such as dams—that cannot be provided by private firms.

Since the idea of external benefits is important to our definition of a public good, we return to a detailed comparison of two of our previous examples. The first is hiring a gardener. Most of the benefits are internal, that is, they go to the family that hires the gardener to work on its own property. Therefore the private market works, at least to some degree: Individuals *do* have gardening done (although the amount is less than socially optimal).

Compare this to our example of a flood-control dam in a river valley. There are two important differences. In the case of the dam, a free market will not work at all. No dam will be built, because there is no individual farmer who will do it. The reason is that the internal benefits of flood control to that individual would be relatively small. Most of the benefits would be external—the protection from floods provided to other farmers in the river valley. Since no individual farmer will do it, any dam that is built will have to be constructed by the government. The second difference is more subtle: Once the government has built the dam, an individual farmer's benefit from it is the same as if he had built it himself.[2] Indeed, many economists use this as their definition of a public good: *It provides an individual with a benefit that does not depend on whether or not that person is the actual purchaser.* Another illustration is the lighthouse mentioned in Chapter 5. Once it is built, no sailor can be excluded from using its services. All sailors are protected from the rocks whether or not they helped to pay for it.

> A *public good* provides benefits that are available to everyone. No one can be excluded from enjoying this good, regardless of who pays for it.

The distinction between a public good and an ordinary private good is shown in figures 30-2 and 30-3. A private good is illustrated in Figure 30-2. The first two panels show the marginal benefit (demand) of two individual consumers. Each consumer would actually have to purchase and acquire the good in order to realize this benefit from it. As we saw in Figure 21-1, a horizontal summation of the individual demands (marginal benefits) in panels (*a*) and (*b*) provides the total market demand in panel (*c*) (the marginal social benefit).

Figure 30-3 shows the alternative case of a public good, where all individuals can benefit from each unit produced. For example, consumer A gets benefit a_1 from the first unit. But this same unit also provides consumer B with benefit b_1. Since both individuals benefit from this first unit—both can, for example, see the warning beam from the same lighthouse—the benefit provided by this first unit is a_1 *plus* b_1, as

---

[2]Notice that this is not true of gardening, where the benefit to an individual does depend on who has the gardening done—himself, his neighbour, or someone far down the street.

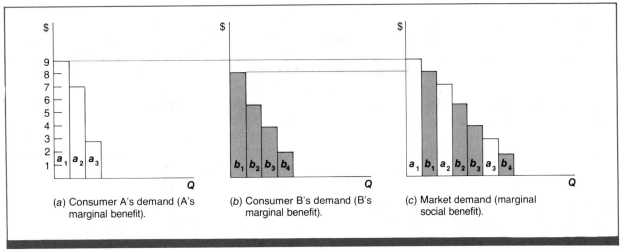

Figure 30-2 A private good.
Individual demands in panels (*a*) and (*b*) are horizontally summed to get market demand in panel (*c*). (At a price of $9, A buys one unit. If the price falls to $8, B also buys a unit. If the price falls to $7, A buys a second unit; and so on.) For such a private good with no external benefits, the market demand curve in part (*c*) represents marginal social benefit.

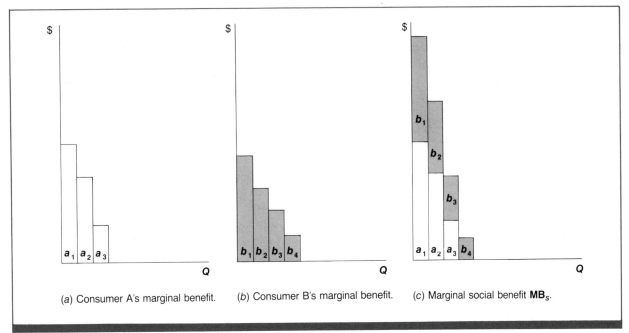

Figure 30-3 A public good.
For a public good, we *vertically* add the individual marginal benefits in panels (*a*) and (*b*) to get the marginal social benefit in panel (*c*). For example, in panel (*c*), b_1 is stacked on top of a_1 to show that *both* consumers get a benefit from this first unit. (There may be some individuals who get zero, or even negative, benefit from a public good such as the army. While most people place a positive value on the defence service it provides, some place a negative value on it. Any such negative valuations should be taken into account, thus reducing MB$_S$ in panel (*c*).)

shown in the last panel. Thus, for such a public good, marginal social benefit (MB_S) is found by *vertically* adding the individual benefits (in contrast to the horizontal addition for a private good).[3]

It is important to recognize that the resulting marginal social benefit (MB_S) is not a demand curve. Nobody would buy the first unit if its price were $a_1 + b_1$. However, if it can be produced at this cost or less, the first unit should be produced. Moreover, if the second unit can be produced for $a_2 + b_2$ or less, it should be produced too; and so on.

PROBLEMS IN EVALUATING THE BENEFITS OF A PUBLIC GOOD

Suppose that the final panel of Figure 30-3 shows the benefits of building a system of flood-control dams on a river; further suppose that the first dam would indeed cost less than $a_1 + b_1$, so that it should be built. Let us now examine in more detail our earlier claim that this public good can be provided only by the government. Why can't it be provided by private enterprise instead? After all, since the two farmers value it at $a_1 + b_1$, why doesn't some entrepreneur collect this amount from them and build the dam? (The entrepreneur would be collecting more than the cost of the dam and therefore could pocket a profit.)

To answer this question, note that our two farmers A and B represent thousands of farmers in the valley. (For other public goods as well, there are very large numbers of consumers.) Thus, you can visualize MB_S as the vertical sum, not of two individual marginal benefit curves, but instead, of thousands of them—with each individual curve being relatively insignificant. Now suppose that you are one of these individuals and the private entrepreneur who is promoting this project asks you for your valuation of the dam. Specif-

ically, he asks how much you would be willing to contribute to its construction.

What would you reply? Clearly, you would have a strong incentive to understate your benefit, because you realize that it is very unlikely that your answer will influence the decision as to whether the dam will be built. You will either get a dam or not, depending on how the thousands of other farmers in the valley respond. All your reply will do is determine the amount that you will be contributing—and it's in your interest to minimize this. So you reply that you believe a flood-control system is exactly what this valley needs, and you believe your neighbours will value it very highly. However, it will provide little value for you; you personally are willing to pay very little for it.

Now, if the dam is built—as you secretly hope—it will cost you very little. Yet you cannot be excluded from enjoying its services: If the dam prevents a flood, your buildings and land will be protected. You get to be a *free rider*, enjoying the benefits while paying little of the costs. The problem, of course, is that you will not be the only one with an incentive to ride free. Every other individual in the valley also has exactly the same incentive, so that the entrepreneur gets a seriously biased response from everyone.

> A *free rider* is someone who cannot be excluded from enjoying the benefits of a project, but who pays nothing (or pays a disproportionately small amount) to cover its costs.

Accordingly, the dam does not get built by the private entrepreneur. It is natural, therefore, to turn to the government, which can solve the free rider problem by forcing everyone to pay taxes to build the dam.

Although it can collect enough taxes to build the dam, the government still faces the problem of evaluating the benefits of the dam in order to decide whether or not it should be built in the first place. In evaluating the benefits, the government, just like the private entrepreneur, encounters problems: It cannot simply ask people how highly they value the dam. If it were to ask you, and you believe that the government will build the dam without noticeably increasing your taxes, it will be in your interest to overstate your valuation in order to increase the chance that the dam will be built. Therefore, even though you previously told the private entrepreneur that the dam is worth almost nothing to

[3] In figures 30-2 and 30-3, we have dealt only with the two extreme cases: a "pure" private good, which provides benefit *only* to the purchaser, and a "pure" public good, which provides each individual with a level of benefit that does not depend *at all* on who purchases the good. There are, of course, many intermediate cases where a good provides benefit to the purchaser *and* to others as well, but where the level of benefit for each individual *does* depend on who purchases the good. (If I purchase it, I'll get more benefit from it than if you purchase it.) Such intermediate cases were illustrated earlier in this chapter in our examples of gardening and vaccinations.

you, you now turn around and tell the government it is worth $1 million to you since you know you won't actually have to pay the $1 million. In short, estimates by individuals of what the dam is worth are unreliable, regardless of who is collecting them.[4]

Another approach is to forget about canvassing people for their views and instead estimate benefits of the dam in some other way. For example, by examining past records, the government can estimate the value of the crops that are likely to be saved from floods. Such benefits can then be compared with the estimated cost of the dam.

There are, however, two potential problems with such a **benefit-cost analysis**. First, unless it is treated with care, it may be used simply as an economic justification for projects that the government has already decided to build for political reasons. For example, a dam may have been promised to a key group of voters in the last election campaign. A politically motivated official with the task of evaluating this dam may estimate its construction costs on the low side, and add more and more benefits until the project is justified. Such benefits might include the recreational services of the new lake and the human lives saved by flood control. While these may be important benefits, there is a wide range of values that can be placed on them, as we have already seen in our discussion of the evaluation of a human life (Box 27-5).

Another reason why it may be difficult to get an accurate estimate is that the engineers who expect to construct the dam may also be the ones who evaluate its benefits. There may be a real temptation for them to estimate the benefits on the high side in order to

justify the dam, and thus create future income and employment for themselves.

OTHER PROBLEMS WITH GOVERNMENT EXPENDITURE DECISIONS

Decision making by a government raises five problems that do not arise—or are less serious—when decisions are made by private firms.

1. The Difficulty in Reversing a Public Expenditure

In the private market economy, if we don't want big cars, we stop buying them and they are no longer produced. The reason is that an auto company would sooner admit its mistake than continue to produce large cars and lose money on them; hence, the saying: "Don't throw good money after bad." In short, business executives will admit their mistakes to save their jobs. Not so in the public sector, where admitting mistakes may *cost* politicians their jobs: If a government expenditure program is dropped, the opposition party may be able to use this "admission of error" to defeat the government in the next election. Furthermore, politicians do not personally suffer out of pocket when they continue questionable expenditures. This also makes them less likely to admit a mistake and reverse an expenditure decision.

2. Voting Politically for Products Is Not Specific Enough

Our auto example suggests another important difference in public vs. private decision making. When you buy a small car, you register a clear vote for its production. However, in the public sector, you vote for a dam—at least in theory—by voting for a candidate committed to building it. Unfortunately, in practice it is not this simple; in fact, you may not get to vote on this issue at all. The reason is that in an election, you vote for a candiate who advocates a whole set of policies. Like most other voters, you may choose among candidates on the basis of their positions on some other completely unrelated issue, such as minority language rights or abortion laws, or even on the basis of the personality of the candidate. It is therefore quite possible that the voters who have elected a candidate promising a dam don't really want the dam at all.

---

[4]Devising ways to get a better evaluation of public goods has become an important area of inquiry. One imaginative suggestion: Inform people that they will be taxed, but only if their individual valuation tips the scale in favour of building the dam; for such an individual, the tax would be the cost of the dam minus the sum of everyone else's valuation. Putting the question this way makes it less likely that people will provide a wildly inaccurate evaluation. In particular, it would prevent you from making your wild overestimate of a million dollars. Think about it: The more you exaggerate, the more likely it is that your answer will tip the scales in favour of the dam, and you will be taxed. In addition, the more you exaggerate, the higher your tax bill could be.

For more detail on this sort of tax—and in particular on the proposal of Edward H. Clarke, see T. Nicolas Tideman and Gordon Tullock, "A New and Superior Process for Making Social Choices," *Journal of Political Economy* (December 1976): 1145–59.

While the issue is not quite this simple—the public can also express its preferences via campaign contributions, by supporting pressure groups, and so on—it is nonetheless true that the political process is a relatively poor method for the public to express its preferences. The public does not vote often enough and specifically enough to provide a clear message to the government of who wants what. Compare this with the private market, where communication is much more effective: Each day millions of messages on millions of products are communicated to producers by consumers when they buy—or do not buy—those products.

3. The Incentive for Politicians to Support "Special Interest" Groups

In making decisions, our elected representatives have a number of motives. For example, they may honestly be trying to promote the public interest, or at least what they believe to be the public interest. (Unfortunately, it is often not clear what the public interest may be; see Box 30-1.) Frequently their desire to serve the public is their reason for going into politics in the first place. However, once they enter politics, they can't accomplish anything without being elected. Thus, of necessity, all politicians—no matter how noble—must be concerned with getting elected or re-elected. One of the best ways to get re-elected is to gain the backing of organized constituencies—or "special-interest" groups—who are able to deliver votes and/or financial support. In turn, the best way to get such backing is to support programs that are of intense interest to such groups, but which are of far less concern to the public that has to pay. The special interest of most people is their job—the goods or services they are producing. (The source of our income is of intense interest to each of us.) Politicians seeking special-interest support therefore pay particular attention to people as producers rather than as consumers, as we shall see, for example, in our discussion of international trade policy in Chapter 32.

4. Short-run, Crisis-oriented Decision Making

The desire to be re-elected also leads politicians to favour policies with a cost that is hidden and a benefit that is obvious and will be realized quickly, before the next election. Why should politicians promote policies that the public won't understand, or policies that will provide benefits after the next election—and thus may help to re-elect their successors? One of the reasons that politicians can take this limited short-run view, is that a busy public cannot be adequately informed about the hundreds of issues on which politicians must decide. Thus, politicians tend to put off tough, long-run decisions; and when they finally do take action, it is often in response to a crisis.

5. The Problem of Government Bureaucracy

Even if Parliament or a provincial legislature, with great foresight, has made a decision that should benefit the province or nation overall, this policy must be introduced and enforced by the appropriate government department (for example, Transport Canada, the RCMP, or a provincial Ministry of Health). Each of these institutions is a "bureau." That is, it receives its income from a granting agency (Parliament or a provincial legislature), rather than as a private firm does—from the sale of a product in the marketplace.[5]

(a) Difficulties in controlling a bureau's performance and cost. The government bureau typically is a monopolist in the provision of its service to the public; indeed, the reason the government may have taken over this activity may be that it is a natural monopoly. For precisely this reason, it is difficult for Parliament to judge its performance: There is no equivalent private agency providing the same service with which the government bureau might be compared. Another difficulty is that a bureau's output can't be measured. Thus, for example, Agriculture Canada can't be judged, like a private firm, on the number of bushels of wheat it produces, because it doesn't produce any. (This problem reaches right down through the ranks of the bureau. Difficulties in measuring output make it difficult for senior members in a bureau to evaluate the productivity of their juniors.)

This difficulty in evaluating performance is only one of the reasons why a bureau's costs are hard to

---

[5]Departments of large private firms may develop many of the characteristics of a bureaucracy, and, to the extent that they do, the difference between the operation of a government department and a business is diminished.

control. Another reason is that a bureau's officials sometimes feel under pressure at the end of the year to inflate costs by spending any remaining funds in their budget: If they don't, their budget may be cut for the next year. Then there are the problems of bureaucratic waste that apply year-round, and that arise because a bureau is in a different situation than a private firm under pressure to sell its product in the marketplace. The private firm has great incentives to cut costs. These incentives come in the form of both a carrot (the desire to make profits) and a stick (the fear of bankruptcy if costs aren't kept in line). On the other hand, a bureau need not fear going broke. It is therefore under far less pressure to keep its costs down. Moreover, because officials in a bureau are not spending their own money, they may lose track of what it is worth. They simply don't "pay attention" in the same way that entrepreneurs do when they have their own money on the line. The result is sometimes substantial waste. For example, in his 1985 Annual Report, Canada's Auditor General noted that since 1982, the Canadian Air Traffic Administration (CATA) had continued to employ several hundred more air traffic controllers than were needed to staff existing control centres and towers at airports. The salaries paid to this surplus staff exceeded $20 million in 1984. In that same year, CATA paid $6 million to two community colleges for providing initial training for almost 200 *new* controllers. As another example, the report cites an expenditure of about $800,000 by the Department of External Affairs to purchase memberships in an exclusive private club in Hong Kong in order to provide recreational opportunities for 34 Canadian diplomats. The Auditor General estimated that membership in a less expensive fitness club could have been bought for less than $25,000.

These examples illustrate waste that is the result of a lack of cost controls, leading to technical inefficiency, that is, unnecessarily high costs. Waste may also come about because officials in a bureau have a tendency to be less careful than managers of private firms in estimating the benefits of proposed expenditures. Thus the Auditor General cites the case of a new airport that was built in the Vancouver region in 1982. When CATA first proposed the project in the late 1970s, traffic forecasts suggested that the area would need a new airport within a few years because existing airports would soon be used to capacity. However, by 1981 it was becoming clear that lower-than-expected traffic volume had essentially eliminated the need for the project: Existing airports had more than enough capacity to handle projected traffic for years to come. Nevertheless, CATA decided to go ahead with the project, and in 1982, the new airport was built—at a cost of $10 million—even though there was no need for it in the foreseeable future.

In the absence of a profit motive, what incentives are there in a bureau? Government officials tend to substitute two other objectives: (1) the public interest (at least as they perceive it), and (2) their own interest, including establishing a public reputation, accumulating the power and perquisites of office, and—often most important—increasing the size of the bureau.[6]

(b) The tendency for the government bureau and its budget to expand. There are several reasons why a government official might try to increase the size of a bureau. By increasing the number of employees, the official will seem to have more responsibility and thus may gain prestige. More employees may also mean more echelons of management—just as in a private firm—and therefore more jobs at the top; this in turn means improved prospects for promotion. Government officials may also seek more funds in order to serve the public or their constituents better; for example, the more funds going to Agriculture Canada, the more benefits it can provide to Canadian farmers. And the more its constituents are thereby satisfied, the more they will put pressure on Parliament if any attempts are made to cut the bureau's budget.

(c) Monopoly inefficiency: Public vs. private. Both a private monopoly and a monopolized public activity may operate in a technically inefficient way—that is, with unnecessarily high cost. One reason is that both have less incentive than a competitive firm to keep costs down. Both monopolies also result in allocative inefficiency—that is, the wrong amount of output. However, this kind of inefficiency appears in two dif-

---

[6]The objectives and behaviour of officials in a bureau are discussed in detail by Albert Breton and Ronald Wintrobe in *The Logic of Bureaucratic Conduct* (New York: Cambridge University Press, 1982).

BOX 30-1

PUBLIC CHOICE: WHAT'S "IN THE PUBLIC INTEREST"?

Majority rule is a basic principle of democracy. We may take this simple and well accepted principle as a straightforward way of determining what is in the public interest, right? Not necessarily—for several reasons.

1. The Problem of the Oppressive Majority

Under majority rule, if 51% of the public want a certain policy they can get it. It doesn't matter how small a value they attach to the benefit—as long as they get *some* benefit. Nor does it matter how heavy the cost of this policy may be to the minority. Thus it is possible for majority rule to leave society as a whole worse off, with the benefits to the majority falling short of the costs imposed on the minority.

To illustrate, consider the following modified version of an example first suggested by Professor Gordon Tullock. There are 100 farmers in a community. Each requires a small connecting road to get access to a main highway. It is in the interests of 51 of these farmers to vote to have access roads put into their own farms only, using taxes collected from all 100 farmers. However, this will involve a loss to society if the 49 losers who don't get roads suffer a great deal from the tax they have to pay, while the 51 winners who do get roads get a benefit that barely exceeds the tax they pay. Therefore, majority rule may be defective. Like private decision-making, it may result in inefficiency—an overall loss to society.*

*Majority rule can be inefficient not only because such undesirable policies *are* introduced, but also because *desirable* policies are *not* introduced. For example, a desirable policy that benefits the minority a great deal may be rejected if it hurts the majority even slightly. Fortunately, majority rule may not be as inefficient in practice as these arguments might lead us to expect. The best evidence comes from Switzerland where many issues are decided by a referendum in which the public votes yes or no on a single issue. In a study of 100 such votes, Eli Noam concluded that

Is there a better voting procedure than majority rule? The answer is that there are a lot of alternatives, but each involves some weakness or other.† For example, one could avoid the problem of the oppressive majority by requiring unanimous consent; then no policy could hurt anyone. But this rule is hopeless. By providing a veto to each individual, it paralyzes the government. Any policy that damaged even one voter would be vetoed. Rather than searching for a voting system that might conceivably be better than majority rule, a more common and reasonable approach is to protect minorities from an oppressive majority with a consitition, either written or unwritten.

Our example of the oppressive majority illustrates two additional points. (1) The government can redistribute income without transferring any cash. Suppose the 51 farmers who get roads receive more benefits than we have so far assumed. Specifically, suppose their net benefits are roughly equal to the loss borne by the minority. In this case, the majority receives a large transfer from the minority—even though no cash transfer takes place between the two. (2) Members of a minority have a strong incentive to try to break down the existing majority coalition in order to form a new ruling coalition including themselves. For example, the 49 excluded farmers are likely to try to get 2 farmers to leave the present majority and join them. Then the newly formed coalition can turn the tables on the 49 who were in a majority but now find themselves out of power. (Of course, the new coalition may then come under the same pressure from outsiders as the old; there may be a cycle of changing coalition patterns.)

2. The Voting Paradox: Why Majority Rule May Lead to No Clear Winner

To illustrate this second problem, consider a population of only three individuals, faced with a choice

there were only a few instances in which the result was inefficient —that is, the minority lost more than the majority gained. See "The Efficiency of Direct Democracy," *Journal of Political Economy* (August 1980): 803–810.

†For a discussion of some alternatives, see Dennis C. Mueller, *Public Choice* (Cambridge, Mass.: Cambridge University Press, 1979), especially pp. 49–58.

Table 30-1
The Voting Paradox: Preferences of Three
Individuals for Alternative Policies A, B, and C

Choice	Individual		
	I	II	III
First choice	A	B	C
Second choice	B	C	A
Last choice	C	A	B

among three options, A, B, and C. Suppose that Table 30-1 shows how each individual ranks each of these options. For example, the first column tells us that individual I prefers option A to option B, and B to C. Which of these options is the will of the majority?

If these individuals choose first between options A and B, a majority (individuals I and III) will vote for A. With A the choice so far, the only remaining question is how it compares to C. In voting between these two, the majority (individuals II and III) prefer C. So C is the final choice, reflecting the apparent will of the majority.

However, suppose instead that these individuals vote first between B and C. In this case, C is immediately rejected because individuals I and II prefer B. Thus, the preference of the majority isn't clear at all; C may be the final choice or immediately rejected, depending on how the voting is set up.

We conclude that in a world in which individual preferences differ, an important determinant of the final choice may be the political process itself (in this example, the political decision on which options will be voted on first). Thus, the individual who sets a committee's agenda or controls its voting procedure may be able to control the result.‡

3. Logrolling

Logrolling occurs when several politicians agree: "You support my policy, and I'll support yours."

‡This voting paradox, first described over a century ago, was extended by Kenneth Arrow in *Social Choice and Individual Values* (New York: John Wiley, 1951).

Table 30-2 shows how it works in a simple case with three voters.

The first row in this table indicates that policy A provides a benefit of 3 to individual I, and a cost of 2 to each of the other two voters.

In a simple majority vote, both policies are defeated. (Individuals II and III vote against policy A, and I and III vote against B.) However, I and II have an incentive to get together first: II agrees to vote for I's pet policy A, if I will vote for II's pet policy B. Because of this logrolling agreement, both policies pass. As shown in the bottom row of this table, individuals I and II both benefit; indeed that was the reason that they engaged in logrolling in the first place. However, III loses—and by even more than the combined gains of I and II. Thus, logrolling hurts the community overall, even though it benefits the "special-interest" groups who engage in it—in our example, individuals I and II.

This is the classical example of logrolling; but there is another possibility. Change the two entries of +3 in this table to +5. As before, in the absence of logrolling, neither policy will pass. Logrolling occurs again for exactly the same reason as before, and once again I and II benefit while III loses. The difference this time is that the combined gain of I and II exceeds III's loss; thus logrolling results in a net overall benefit for this community. Therefore, logrolling isn't necessarily bad. In some cases, it may be the only way of achieving a socially desirable result.

Table 30-2
Logrolling: Benefits (+) or Costs (−) of Each
Policy to Each Individual

	Individual		
	I	II	III
Policy A	+3	−2	−2
Policy B	−2	+3	−2
Net effect on each individual if *both* policies are passed because of logrolling:	+1	+1	−4

ferent forms. On the one hand, a private monopoly produces too little output and therefore employs too few resources. On the other hand, a public monopoly—a bureau—has natural tendencies to expand; thus it often tends to employ too *many* resources.[7]

IS THE ENVIRONMENT A PUBLIC GOOD?

In Chapter 28 we concluded that, in a private market without government intervention, decisions by private firms may seriously damage the environment; and we considered ways that the government may prevent such damage.

However, suppose that the environment is deteriorating of its own accord; no firm or individual is at fault in any way. For example, suppose that a species of wildlife is dying off in the wilderness. In this case, the proper approach is to recognize that the preservation of this species is a public good, just like the construction of a dam in our example earlier in this chapter. Since no individual values the species highly enough to incur the cost of personally preserving it, the private market generally won't deliver. Although private conservation organizations may act, the ultimate decision on whether to save the species—and how much to spend in the effort—is likely to rest with the government. If the government does act, everyone can enjoy the resulting benefits.

How large would these benefits be? This question is not easy to answer. While most people would put some value on the preservation of a wildlife species, it is very difficult to say how much. As Harvard's Richard Caves has put it: "How highly should we value wombats, if they are so far from civilization that no one will ever see them, let alone eat them?" One answer is that we may place some value on them, even though we don't ever see them, just as we may place a value on an air-conditioning system even though we may

not actually turn it on this year. This phenomenon is described as *option demand*—the desire to have an option, whether or not we exercise it. Thus we may want to keep open the option of seeing a species, or drawing on it for medical research, even though we may never in fact exercise this option. Similarly, we may have an option demand for national wilderness parks which we may or may not actually visit. Option demand should be taken into account in the evaluation of environmental benefits.

Yet Caves' point is well taken: In discussing environmental protection, it is important to take a hardheaded view of the benefits and costs involved. For example, consider a caribou population that would be disturbed by the construction of an oil pipeline. A major cost would be involved in the extreme event that the pipeline were to cause the caribou to become extinct, since this could not be reversed by future generations. But if there is no such risk of extinction, what is the difference between reducing the population of caribou by 5 percent and reducing the population of cattle by 5 percent by slaughtering them for meat? Both policies provide obvious benefits: killing cattle provides food, while laying pipelines is essential to provide heat and power.

Again we conclude, as in Chapter 28, that keeping environmental damage down to an appropriately low level makes more sense than trying to avoid any damage whatever.

PUBLIC GOODS VS. PRIVATE GOODS: A REVIEW OF MICROECONOMIC MARKETS

In this section we compare the market for a public good described in this chapter with the other markets described in earlier chapters. Although a complete comparison would take us beyond the scope of this book, we can get a better understanding of how these markets compare by asking the following important question: In each market, how does the cost curve of a single producer compare to the total market demand curve?

In panel (*a*) of Figure 30-4, we answer this question for a perfectly competitive market; in the next three panels, the same question is answered for three other markets. In each case, we see that the market that develops depends heavily on *how far the firm's average costs continue to fall*. To highlight this point, we

[7]In *The Affluent Society* (Boston: Houghton Mifflin, 1958) John Kenneth Galbraith argues that the government is not too large a part of the economy. Indeed, he argues that in some respects the government is too small; compared to a private business, it provides too few goods and services. One reason: Goods such as autos that are provided by private firms have their sales increased by advertising. However, goods such as roads that are provided by the government are not advertised. Therefore, we overspend on autos, but underspend on roads.

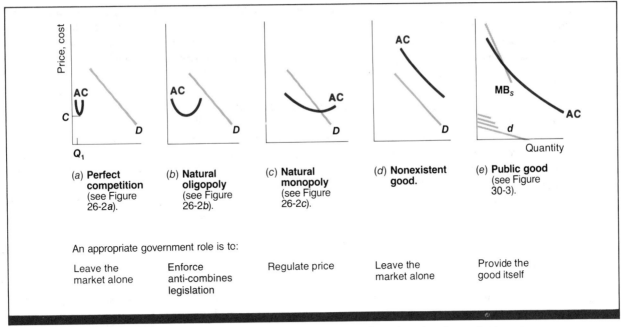

Figure 30-4 **The relationship between the costs of a single producer and total market demand.**

have assumed that the four products shown are similar in other respects. For example, total market demand is exactly the same for each, and the average cost AC of each reaches a minimum at the same height, C. The only difference in these four products is that, as we move from left to right from panel to panel, AC reaches a minimum at an increasingly large output. Thus, in panel (a), AC reaches a minimum at a very small output Q_1, while in panel (d), AC reaches the same minimum height C at such a large level of output—that is, so far to the right—that it cannot even be shown in the diagram.

In the case of perfect competition in panel (a), market demand can be satisfied at minimum cost by a large number of producers. There is little role to be played by the government, since this market is generally efficient when left to its own devices. (We assume here that there are no complications, such as serious price fluctuations over time, or important externalities.)

Panel (b) illustrates the case of natural oligopoly, where market demand can be satisfied at minimum cost by just a few firms. In such a market, a strong case can be made for the vigorous enforcement of anti-combines laws to prevent collusion or the merger of these firms into a monopoly.

In the case of natural monopoly in panel (c), mar-

ket demand can be satisfied at lower cost by one firm than by more than one. Here, the application of anti-combines legislation to prevent any firm from becoming a monopoly makes little sense, since not allowing a monopoly would entail higher costs. A preferred approach is price regulation, which prevents the firm from charging a high monopoly price, while allowing it to become large enough to gain the cost advantages of large-scale production, even though this implies that it becomes a monopoly.

In panel (d) costs have finally outrun demand. At no point do D and AC overlap, so there is no single price a firm can charge and still cover its costs. The product will not even appear on the market; there is no economic justification for its production.[8] The appropriate government policy is "hands off."

Finally, consider panel (e), which shows a public good. In this case, the good is not produced by private firms; there is no standard market demand D (as the

---

[8] An exception occurs in the case of the discriminating monopolist. If the gap between D and AC is small enough, a discriminating monopolist such as the dentist in Figure 25-9 may be able to cover her costs if she is able to charge different prices to different buyers. In this special case, the product does appear on the market, and its production can be justified by the benefits it provides to the public that would otherwise have to do without.

horizontal sum of individual demands d). However, the marginal social benefit (MB_S) of this good *does* exist. It is the *vertical* sum of the individual demand curves. If the MB_S curve overlaps the AC curve, it is in the public interest for the government to provide this good.

We conclude by noting that in some cases, government intervention in the marketplace is not justified. But in other circumstances, when there is private market failure, a case can be made for such intervention. However, a word of warning is in order. Even in cases of private market failure, it should not be assumed that government intervention is a simple, fool-proof solution; it may also fail. Recall, for example, our earlier discussion in this chapter of the difficulties that arise in bureaucratic decision making, and the problems the government encounters in reversing a bad decision or in controlling its costs. Just because government intervention *could* increase efficiency, doesn't mean that it necessarily *will*; the government may improve things, or it may make them worse.

Now that we have completed our discussion of public goods, where the strongest case can be made for government intervention, we will turn in the next chapter to international trade where the case for government intervention is far weaker. In fact, economists have historically been extremely critical of government interference in this area.

KEY POINTS

1. If a good provides an external benefit, a perfectly competitive market will provide less than the efficient level of output. The government can induce the expansion of output to the efficient level by subsidizing buyers of this good by the amount of the external benefit. This "internalizes the externality" because buyers then personally enjoy not only the benefit the good provides to themselves, but also an amount equal to the benefit it provides to others.

2. No individual farmer would ever consider building a flood-control dam, because of its high cost and the fact that the benefits he himself would receive would be trivial compared to the benefits that would go to thousands of neighbouring farmers. This, then, is the general idea of a public good: It is a good that will not be produced by the private market; if it is to exist at all, it must be produced by the government.

3. A more precise and narrow definition is that a public good is one that can be enjoyed by everyone, regardless of who pays for it. For example, once a flood-control dam has been built, no one can be excluded from enjoying its flood-control services.

4. Building such a dam will be justified if its cost is less than the sum of its benefits to all the public.

5. In practice, there may be major problems involved in evaluating these benefits. Even if people have a clear idea in their own minds of what the benefits would be, they are unlikely to tell any government official (or, for that matter, any private entrepreneur). Therefore the alternative approach of benefit-cost analysis is often used. For example, the benefit of flood control is estimated by looking at past records of how often floods have occurred and the damage they have done to crops. But it still remains extraordinarily difficult to estimate some of the benefits, such as saving human lives.

6. When the government provides goods and services to the economy, a number of problems arise that are typically not encountered by private firms. For example, it is more difficult for the government to reverse an error; politicians fear losing votes if they admit mistakes.

7. When the public buys privately produced goods such as certain model cars, producers have a clear-cut indication that this is what the public wants. But when the public votes for a candidate who has promised to, say, build a dam, it's not clear whether the public wants the dam or not. It may have voted for the candidate for foreign policy or other reasons.

8. Politicians often make economic decisions not so much in the interests of the general public

as in the interests of their specific constituency (or some special-interest group within that constituency). Moreover, they tend to favour policies with a payoff that is obvious and will be realized quickly—in particular, before the next election.

9. There is a natural tendency for a bureau and its budget to expand. One reason is that a bureau is typically not under the same cost-cutting pressures as a private firm which must sell its output on a competitive market.

10. There are two important ways to protect the environment. When it is being damaged by, say, polluting firms, the proper approach is to impose a tax or issue marketable emission permits (as described in Chapter 28). But when the environment is deteriorating of its own accord—for example, if a wildlife species is becoming extinct—the preservation of the environment may be viewed as a public good. Thus, government protection of the environment is justified if the costs of this protection are less than the benefits it provides to all individuals in society.

KEY CONCEPTS

external benefits
how a subsidy affects efficiency
internalizing an external
   benefit
internalizing an external cost
a public good
marginal social benefit for a private
   good and for a public good
the free rider problem

benefit-cost analysis
private versus public decisions
difficulty in reversing public
   expenditures
why a political vote may not
   indicate what the public wants
a politician's constituency
special-interest groups
lack of competitive pressures to
   cut costs in government

why government bureaucracies
   tend to expand
technical and allocative
   inefficiency in government
   departments
the environment as a
   public good
option demand

PROBLEMS

30-1 (a) In panel (c) of Figure 30-3, draw a completely horizontal marginal cost curve at a height just above the top of bar a_2. Now show the number of units of this public good that the government should provide. For example, how many dams should the government build in a flood-control network?

(b) In panel (e) of Figure 30-4, extend MB_S downward and to the right. Also extend curve AC to the right until it reaches a minimum, and then draw in the corresponding MC curve. How many units of this good should the government provide?

30-2 If a four-lane highway is to be built into a city, discuss the benefits and costs that you think should be estimated. Explain why preparing such an estimate might be a difficult task.

30-3 Do you think national defence is a public good? Why? Would estimating its benefits be difficult? Why?

30-4 Suppose you are working for a government in the tropics, and a proposal is being considered to spray a wide area of territory for malarial mosquitoes. A critic states that, if such an expenditure were justified, a private entrepreneur would already have seized this opportunity. What position would you take?

30-5 Equilibrium E_1 in Figure 30-1 is inefficient. Which, if any, of the efficiency conditions in Box 24-1 is violated?

30-6 Suppose the only three individuals who would benefit from a public good have the demand (marginal benefit) schedules shown below. Assume also that each unit of this good involves a production cost of C and an external cost of K. Should this good be produced? If so, at what output level? (Note: This problem is based on both chapters 29 and 30.)

30-7 Suppose that, instead of the per unit subsidy to the *buyer* shown as the black arrow in Figure 30-1, the government provides exactly the same subsidy to the *seller*. Show the effect. Does this subsidy increase output to the efficient quantity? How does this policy compare with the policy of subsidizing the buyer?

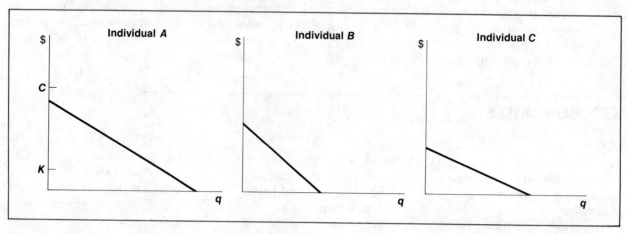

Chapter 31

WHAT ARE THE GAINS FROM INTERNATIONAL TRADE?

Instructed ships shall sail to quick commerce
By which remotest regions are allied
Which makes one city of the universe
Where some may gain and all may be supplied.
John Dryden (1631–1700)

Economic gains come from specialization. One of the reasons for the high material standard of living in Canada is our high degree of specialization. Pulp and paper are produced near the great forests of northern Ontario, Quebec, and British Columbia; wheat is produced in the Western provinces, and petrochemicals, cars, and car parts are manufactured in southern Ontario. By such specialization we are able to increase our total output of goods.

Just as specialization within Canada increases output and efficiency, so too does specialization between Canada and other countries. Specifically, international trade and specialization among Canada and other countries bring the same benefits as domestic specialization, first noted in Chapter 3: namely, the gains from comparative advantage and economies of scale. International trade also exposes domestic producers to increased competition and thus reduces their market power. Because of international trade, we are not only able to buy relatively inexpensive foreign goods. We can also get goods more cheaply from domestic producers who must keep their prices down in order to meet foreign competition.

The major objective of this chapter will be to consider in detail each of these benefits from trade. But before doing so, we ask two questions.

WITH WHOM DO WE TRADE? WHAT DO WE TRADE?

The answers are provided in Table 31-1. From the first column, it is evident that Canada's most important trading partner is the United States. This of course is no surprise, since distance and transport costs—natural deterrents to trade—are at a minimum in our trade with the United States. (Many Americans don't realize the importance of their trade with Canada. The reason is that U.S. purchases from Canada include

Table 31-1
Merchandise Trade Pattern of Canada in 1984 (In Billions of Dollars)

With Whom Do We Trade?		What Do We Trade?	
Exports: 1984 Canadian sales to:		*Exports:* 1984 Canadian sales of:	
U.S.A.	85.4	Farm and fish products	12.2
U.K.	2.5	Forest products	15.5
Other E.E.C.	4.5	Metal and minerals	28.3
		(of which crude petroleum and natural gas: 8.3)	
		Chemicals and fertilizers	5.4
Japan	5.5	Other manufactured goods	50.7
		(of which motor vehicles and parts: 29.4)	
Other OECD	2.1		
All other countries	12.1		
TOTAL	112.1	TOTAL	112.1
Imports: 1984 Canadian purchases from:		*Imports:* 1984 Canadian purchases of:	
U.S.A.	65.7	Energy materials	6.1
U.K.	2.3	Industrial materials	15.7
Other E.E.C.	5.8	Construction materials	1.6
Japan	5.5	Motor vehicles and parts	25.7
		Other transportation	
		Equipment and parts	3.7
Other OECD	2.3	Producers' equipment	22.7
All other countries	9.8	Consumer goods	15.9
TOTAL	91.4	TOTAL	91.4

SOURCE: *Bank of Canada Review*

raw materials [base metals] and manufactured goods [telecommunications equipment] that are not as familiar to the U.S. public as the consumer goods [watches, cars, and radios] that Americans buy from Europe and Japan.) Japan is also a key trading partner of ours, as are the large countries in the European Economic Community (EEC) and Latin America.

The right-hand side of the table indicates that we trade a wide variety of goods. Our exports to other countries include such diverse items as grain from the prairies, and mining equipment from London, Ontario.

And our imports include computers and other equipment essential to Canadian industry, as well as consumer goods such as tropical foodstuffs, shirts, and shoes. For a nation on wheels, cars and trucks account for an important part of our trade: Our purchases of cars and car parts made up more than 25% of our total imports. (Of course, we also have large *exports* of transportation equipment, including both cars and car parts.)

This, then, describes *what* and *with whom* we trade. Now let us return to the advantages we reap from trade. We consider three basic sources of gain: (1) increased competition, (2) economies of scale, and (3) comparative advantage.

MARKETS BECOME MORE COMPETITIVE AND HENCE MORE EFFICIENT

Consider the monopoly firm illustrated in Figure 31-1. Initially, without international trade, this firm has the Canadian market all to itself in panel (a). If it is not subject to government regulation, it will be able to set a monopoly price. In panel (b), we see what happens when trade is opened up. The potential demand facing the Canadian producer is much larger, as shown by the total world demand curve. Therefore, the firm is now able to go after foreign markets as well as the domestic Canadian market. But it is no longer able to take the domestic market for granted, since it faces stiff competition here from foreign producers. Thus, foreign trade can transform a natural monopoly in the domestic market in panel (a) into a natural oligopoly in the world market in panel (b). In the process, this

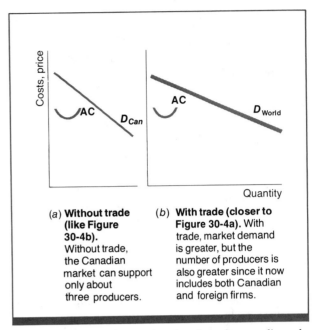

(a) **Without trade (like Figure 30-4b).** Without trade, the Canadian market can support only about three producers.

(b) **With trade (closer to Figure 30-4a).** With trade, market demand is greater, but the number of producers is also greater since it now includes both Canadian and foreign firms.

Figure 31-2 How international trade makes an oligopoly more competitive.

firm's monopoly control of the Canadian market is broken, and its ability to exercise market power (charge a high price) is reduced. As shown earlier, a lower, more competitive price results in an improved allocation of resources, with a corresponding efficiency gain.

On the other hand, if the industry is originally a natural oligopoly, international trade can make it substantially more competitive. To illustrate, consider the Canadian firm in Figure 31-2 that, before trade, has about one-third of the domestic market. After trade is opened up in panel (b), this firm will have a much smaller fraction of the market, because the market is now the whole world. Again, increased competition will tend to keep price down, with Canadian consumers benefitting. Furthermore, they gain in other ways, if the domestic producer is forced to compete in non-price aspects, such as quality or design. Thus, the North American auto industry has been pressured into producing smaller cars as a result of competition, first from European firms in the late 1950s and, more recently, from Japanese auto-makers.

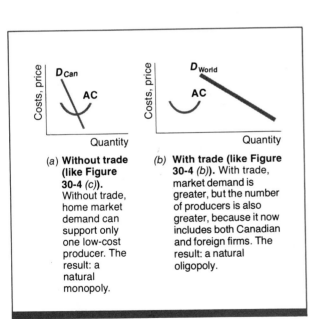

(a) **Without trade (like Figure 30-4 (c)).** Without trade, home market demand can support only one low-cost producer. The result: a natural monopoly.

(b) **With trade (like Figure 30-4 (b)).** With trade, market demand is greater, but the number of producers is also greater, because it now includes both Canadian and foreign firms. The result: a natural oligopoly.

Figure 31-1 How international trade breaks down monopoly power.

ECONOMIES OF SCALE

In the face of economies of scale (falling average cost as output expands), there are two additional potential gains from trade.

New Products Become Available

Specifically, international trade may make it profitable to produce goods which otherwise would not be produced at all. Panel (*a*) in Figure 31-3 illustrates such a product. Demand is too low in the domestic economy to allow this good to be profitably produced. But when the foreign market becomes available, demand becomes large enough to cover average costs (the rightward shift in *D* makes it now overlap AC) and the item is introduced.

An outstanding example is Toronto-based Northern Telecom. Toward the end of the 1970s, Northern Telecom began to invest heavily in developing digital switching technology for use in office communications networks and by phone companies. (This technology is especially useful when communications systems are used both for voice communications and transfer of data between computers.) By the mid-1980s, Northern Telecom had become the world leader in this field. Most of its sales were outside Canada: In 1983, foreign sales were twice as large as domestic sales, and it was expected that by 1988 sales in foreign markets would outpace domestic sales by five to one. If Northern Telecom had not been able to count on foreign sales, there would have been little prospect of recouping the enormous research and development costs for the new technology; most probably, this would have meant that the lead would have gone to an American firm such as AT&T which has a much larger domestic market.

Existing Goods Can Be Produced More Efficiently

Where there are economies of scale, trade results not only in the introduction of new products, but also in the more efficient production of old products. For example, European producers have been able to manufacture automobiles at larger volume and lower cost since the establishment of the European Economic Community. Because tariff barriers have been eliminated within the EEC, a manufacturer in any member country can sell freely to buyers in all member countries.

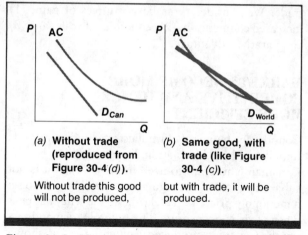

(a) Without trade (reproduced from Figure 30-4 (d)).

Without trade this good will not be produced,

(b) Same good, with trade (like Figure 30-4 (c)).

but with trade, it will be produced.

Figure 31-3 How international trade may create new products.
The AC curves in these two figures are identical. But because of trade, the demand curve in part (*b*) is much farther to the right.

COMPARATIVE ADVANTAGE

Now suppose that there are no economies of scale; instead, suppose costs are constant. (The average cost curve is horizontal.) The theory of comparative advantage tells us that even in these circumstances, gains can be realized from international trade.

The basic idea of comparative advantage has already been introduced in Chapter 3. Even though the lawyer cited there may be more skillful (that is, may have an absolute advantage) in both law and gardening, she does not do her own gardening. Instead, she concentrates on law, the activity in which she has a comparative advantage. By specializing in this way, she can acquire more gardening service than if she were to take the time to do it herself.

Internationally, the idea is exactly the same: Even though Canada may be better—that is, have an absolute advantage—in producing both snowmobiles and radios, it may be in our interest to concentrate on snowmobiles and other products in which we have a comparative advantage, and leave radios to other countries. By specializing in snowmobiles, we may be able to acquire more radios through trade than we could produce ourselves.

The idea of comparative advantage was developed in the early nineteenth century by David Ricardo, an English economist, financier, and member of Parliament. In his simplified illustration of this idea, Ricardo assumed that markets were perfectly competitive, that there were no transport costs, that all production costs were constant, and that the only input was labour. He also assumed that there were only two countries (we shall call them Canada and Britain) producing two goods (we shall call them food and clothing).

Absolute Advantage

As a preliminary, Table 31-2 shows the case where each country has an *absolute advantage* in the production of one good. In the first column, we see that a clothing worker in Britain can outproduce a worker in Canada (4 to 3), so by definition Britain has an absolute advantage in clothing. Similarly, in the second column we see that Canada has an absolute advantage in food, since a Canadian worker can outproduce a

Table 31-2

Illustration of Absolute Advantage

Hypothetical Output per Worker in Britain and Canada

	Clothing	Food
Canada	3 units	2 units
Britain	4 units	1 unit

In the first column, Britain has an absolute advantage in clothing production because a worker can produce 4 units compared with only 3 in Canada. In the second column, Canada has an absolute advantage in food, because a worker here can produce 2 units, compared with only 1 in Britain. Both countries together can produce more total output when Canada specializes in food and Britain specializes in clothing.

To confirm, suppose specialization has not occurred; in other words, suppose that each country is initially producing both goods. Now suppose that they begin to specialize—Canada in food, Britain in clothing. Therefore, a worker in Canada is switched out of clothing and into food production. At the same time, a worker in Britain is switched in the opposite direction (out of food and into clothing). As a result of these two switches:

	Clothing output changes by	Food output changes by
In Canada	− 3	+ 2
In Britain	+ 4	− 1
Therefore, net world output changes by	+ 1	+ 1

British worker (2 to 1). The most efficient allocation of resources is to have Canada specialize in food and Britain in clothing, as the calculations at the bottom of Table 31-2 confirm.

So far, it seems that each country specializes in the good in which it has an absolute advantage. But this is not always so. We shall now show that the key to specialization is *comparative* advantage, rather than absolute advantage.

Comparative Advantage

Table 31-3 illustrates the more difficult case where one country, Canada (like the lawyer in Box 3-2), has an absolute advantage in the production of both goods:

Table 31-3

Illustration of Comparative Advantage

Hypothetical Output per Worker in Britain and Canada

Product	Clothing	Food
Canada	6 units	3 units
Britain	4 units	1 unit

In the bottom row, one British worker can produce either 4 units of clothing or 1 unit of food. Thus, the opportunity cost of 1 unit of food in Britain is 4 units of clothing. In the row above, we see that a Canadian worker can produce either 6 units of clothing or 3 of food. The opportunity cost of food in Canada is therefore 6/3 = 2 units of clothing. (Notice how we calculate this opportunity cost by taking the ratio of the figures in the Canadian row, just as we calculated the British cost (4/1) from the figures in the British row.) Since the opportunity cost of food in Canada is less than in Britain, Canada has a comparative advantage in food and specializes in this good.

To confirm that this specialization will increase total world output, again suppose that each country is initially producing both goods. Now suppose they begin to specialize: Canada switches one worker out of clothing and into food, and Britain switches two workers out of food and into clothing. Then:

	Clothing output changes by	Food output changes by
In Canada	− 6	+ 3
In Britain	+ 8	− 2
Therefore, net world output changes by	+ 2	+ 1

A Canadian worker outproduces a British worker in both clothing (6 to 4) and food (3 to 1). Nonetheless, Canada—like the lawyer in Chapter 3—will not try to satisfy its requirements by producing both goods itself. Instead, it will specialize in one and buy the other from Britain, as we shall now explain.

Our first step is to calculate the opportunity cost of food in each country. First, in Britain: The second row of Table 31-3 tells us that a British worker who is now producing 1 unit of food could, instead, be producing 4 units of clothing. In other words, in Britain *the opportunity cost of 1 unit of food is 4 units of clothing*. Since prices tend to reflect costs, we would expect these two goods to exchange in Britain for the same 1:4 ratio. That is, in the absence of international trade, 1 unit of food will exchange in Britain for 4 units of clothing.

On the other hand, what is the opportunity cost of food in Canada? The first row of Table 31-3 tells us that a Canadian worker who is producing 3 units of food could instead be producing 6 units of clothing. In other words, in Canada the opportunity cost of a unit of food is 6/3 = 2 units of clothing. Consequently, we would expect the two goods to exchange in Canada at this 1:2 ratio. That is, before trade, 1 unit of food will exchange in Canada for 2 units of clothing.

Since the opportunity cost of food in Canada is less (2 units of clothing versus 4 in Britain), we say that Canada has a *comparative advantage* in food. By definition:

> A country's *comparative advantage* is the good that it can produce relatively cheaply; that is, at lower opportunity cost, than its trading partner.

A similar set of calculations, again using the figures in Table 31-3, shows that in clothing, Britain has a lower opportunity cost and hence a comparative advantage.[1]

With this concept of comparative advantage in hand, we shall now see how both countries will benefit if they specialize in their product of comparative advantage and trade for the other—at any price ratio between the 1:2 price ratio which would prevail in an isolated Canada and the 1:4 in Britain. Suppose this price ratio— often called the "terms of trade"—is 1:3; that is, 1 unit of food exchanges internationally for 3 units of clothing. The determination of this price ratio depends not only on the cost conditions that we have been describing, but also on demand in these two countries. For example, the more strongly Britons demand food—the Canadian export good—the higher the price of food will be.

Faced with an international price ratio of 1:3 (1 unit of food exchanging for 3 units of clothing) let's first show how Canada can benefit by specializing in its product of comparative advantage, food, and trading to satisfy its clothing needs. Specifically, for each Canadian worker taken out of clothing production, Canada loses 6 units of clothing. However, that worker instead now produces 3 units of food, which can then be traded (at the 1:3 international price ratio) for 9 units of clothing—for a clear gain of 3 units of clothing. Similarly, Britain also gains by specializing in its product of comparative advantage—clothing—and trading it for food.[2]

To sum up this example, both countries gain from trade. Canada benefits by specializing in food (its comparative advantage) and trading for clothing. At the same time Britain benefits by specializing in clothing (its comparative advantage) and trading for food. The reason that there are gains from trade is that the cost ratios in the two rows of Table 31-3 (namely 6/3 and 4/1) are different. If these ratios (that is, opportunity costs) were the same, there would be no comparative advantage and no gain from trade.

The gain to Canada from trade may be illustrated in another way. Figure 31-4 shows the Canadian production possibilities curve (PPC), derived from the Canadian figures in the first row of Table 31-3, assuming that there are 20 million workers in Canada. For example, if they all work at producing clothing, each

---

[1]In Britain the opportunity cost of clothing is 1/4 of a unit of food; that is, 1/4 of a unit of food must be given up to acquire 1 unit of clothing. Similarly, in Canada the opportunity cost of clothing is 3/6 = 1/2 unit of food. With its lower opportunity cost of clothing, Britain has a comparative advantage in clothing. Notice in this simple two-country, two-good example that if Canada has a comparative advantage in one good (food), Britain *must* have a comparative advantage in the other (clothing).

[2]In switching a worker from food to clothing production, Britain loses 1 unit of food. But that worker produces 4 units of clothing instead, and this output can be traded (at the 1:3 international price ratio) for 4/3 = 1 1/3 units of food—for a gain of 1/3 units of food.

BOX 31-1

WAGES AND TRADE

In our example, will wages be higher in Canada or Britain?

The answer is: In Canada, because labour is more productive here. (Remember, in Table 31-3 Canada has an absolute advantage in the produc-

tion of both goods.) Because they can *produce* more goods, Canadian workers can be *paid* "more goods," that is, a higher real wage. Moreover, Canadians will have a higher real income whether or not the two countries trade. What trade and specialization make possible is an increase in real income in both countries.

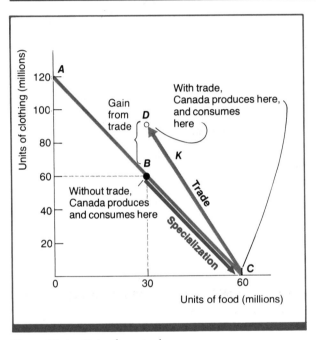

Figure 31-4   Gains from trade.
Canada's production possibilities curve AC is derived from the first row in Table 31-3, on the assumption that there are 20 million workers in Canada. Suppose that, without trade, Canada produces and consumes at point B. When trade is opened, Canada can (1) *specialize* in food, by shifting production from B to C, and (2) *trade* 30 units of food for 90 units of clothing at the prevailing 1:3 international price ratio. Thus, Canada can move from C to D. The Canadian gain from trade is the increase in clothing consumption from the original 60 units at point B to the 90 units at point D.

of the 20 million workers will produce 6 units for a total of 120 million units of clothing, as shown at point A. Or, if they all work at producing food (3 units each) they will produce 60 million units of food and no clothing at point C. Finally, if half the workers

produce food and half clothing, then the 10 million workers in clothing will produce 60 units (6 units each), while the other 10 million workers in food will produce 30 units at point B. In this simple Ricardian example, the constant figures in the first row of Table 31-3 ensure that the production possibilities curve AC is a straight line. The opportunity cost of food in Canada remains constant as we move down this curve: No matter how much food we may be producing, we must give up 2 units of clothing in order to produce 1 more unit of food.

Before trade, Canada will produce and consume at a point on the production possibilities curve, such as B. With trade, Canada can benefit by taking the following two steps.

1. *Specialize.* Shift production from B to C, as shown by the red arrow. That is, produce 30 more units of food by giving up 60 million units of clothing. Thus Canada concentrates on food, the good in which it has a comparative advantage.

2. *Trading.* Trade these 30 million additional units of food at the 1:3 international price ratio for 90 million units of clothing. This second step is shown by the gray arrow.

As a result of this specialization and trade, Canada's consumption can rise from point B to point D. In other words, there are 30 more units of clothing available for consumption; this is Canada's *real income gain*, or efficiency gain from trade.

In panel (*a*) of Figure 31-5, we show that such a gain from trade exists even when opportunity costs are not constant; that is, in the more usual case when the production possibilities curve is not a straight line. This diagram also shows that, although trade induces a country to specialize, it will often not specialize

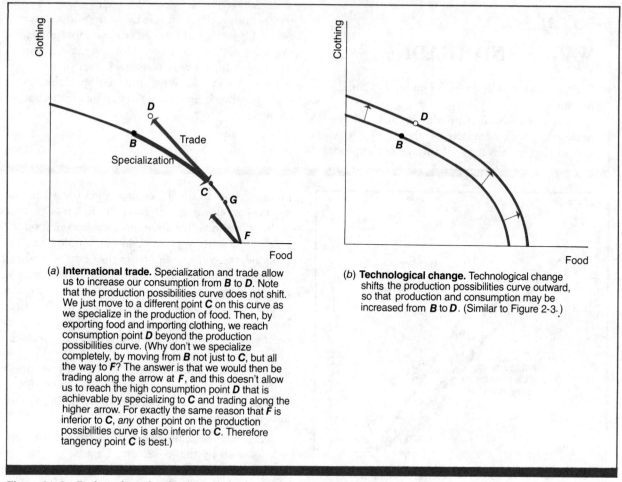

(a) **International trade.** Specialization and trade allow us to increase our consumption from **B** to **D**. Note that the production possibilities curve does not shift. We just move to a different point **C** on this curve as we specialize in the production of food. Then, by exporting food and importing clothing, we reach consumption point **D** beyond the production possibilities curve. (Why don't we specialize completely, by moving from **B** not just to **C**, but all the way to **F**? The answer is that we would then be trading along the arrow at **F**, and this doesn't allow us to reach the high consumption point **D** that is achievable by specializing to **C** and trading along the higher arrow. For exactly the same reason that **F** is inferior to **C**, *any* other point on the production possibilities curve is also inferior to **C**. Therefore tangency point **C** is best.)

(b) **Technological change.** Technological change shifts the production possibilities curve outward, so that production and consumption may be increased from **B** to **D**. (Similar to Figure 2-3.)

Figure 31-5 Both trade and technological change allow us to increase consumption.

completely: Canada moves from *B* to *C*, but not all the way to complete specialization at *F*. And one frequently observes this pattern: A country not only specializes in and exports its product of comparative advantage—in this case, food. It produces other goods as well—in this example, it produces *some* clothing at point *C*. (For details on why such a country will not specialize completely, see the caption to this diagram.)[3]

[3]Figure 31-5(*a*) can be used to show how demand also influences specialization and trade. (In this elementary treatment we have emphasized the other side of the coin: the importance of costs, as reflected in the production possibilities curve. But demand is important too.) Suppose there is an increase in both countries in the demand for food; as a consequence, its price rises. Therefore, less food is needed to buy a given quantity of clothing. In other words, the trade arrow becomes steeper. Consequently, it is no longer tan-

Comparative advantage thus leads to gains from trade. But why does comparative advantage exist? Why does Canada have a comparative advantage in wheat? One important reason is our large endowment of highly productive land, especially in the Prairie provinces. Similarly, the reason that Saudi Arabia specializes in oil is its huge endowment of this resource. On the

gent to the production possibilities curve at point C, but instead at a point to the right, say G. G is therefore the best production point for this country. (The reason the point of tangency is best is given in the caption to Figure 31-5(*a*).) Thus, this country specializes even more, by moving from B not just to C, but to G. (And, of course, from point G, it trades up to the northwest along its new, steeper trade arrow.) To sum up: In response to increased demand, this country's production pattern changes; by producing even more food, it specializes to an even greater degree than before.

other hand, a country like India, with its huge pool of unskilled labour, tends to have a comparative advantage in activities that require a great deal of labour. Comparative advantage depends not only on such resource endowments, but also on skills and technology. For example, our highly developed technology gives us a comparative advantage in producing items such as telecommunications systems.

TRADE AND TECHNOLOGICAL CHANGE: THEIR SIMILARITIES

Panel (a) of Figure 31-5 has shown how trade allows a country to consume at a point such as D, that is beyond its production possibilities curve (PPC). True, *production* is always limited by a country's PPC, but consumption can be greater because of the gain from trade. In other words, international trade is the way for countries to break out of their production limitation and reach a point of consumption beyond it.

In panel (b) we see that technological change has the same effect of allowing us to move from point B to a higher point of consumption D. But it does so by shifting the production possibilities curve outward.

Trade and technological change are also alike in another significant respect. Although they generally provide a benefit to the nation as a whole, they do not necessarily benefit *every* group within the nation. Thus, there are often groups that object vehemently to trade or to technological change. For example, during the first period of rapid technological change in the textile industry about two centuries ago, workers feared that the new machinery being introduced would eliminate their jobs. (Some workers did indeed lose their jobs, even though machinery has ultimately made possible jobs with much higher productivity and pay.) This fear of job loss led some workers at that time to throw their wooden shoes—in French, *sabots*—into the machinery; hence, the word "sabotage" was coined. Similarly, international trade may displace textile workers if production is shifted from textiles—where some markets have been lost to imports—to newsprint or transport equipment, where we have a comparative advantage and export. Once again, those who are harmed may strongly object. In this case, they need not throw their shoes into the machinery; restrictions on imports are the way to seek protection. Note that trade restrictions and sabotage are similar in one

respect: Both prevent a general improvement in the standard of living in order to protect a specific group.

The temporary unemployment that follows either trade or technological change is a problem, but one that is frequently exaggerated. Workers displaced by technological change tend to be fairly quickly absorbed elsewhere, as are workers displaced by imports. For example, this was true in Europe, when the Common Market (the European Economic Community) opened up trade among countries on a very large scale, and temporary unemployment was less than expected. And even though many jobs in traditional North American industries were lost as imports from Japan and other southeast Asian countries grew rapidly after World War II, this was accomplished without any secular increase in unemployment. (Since the late 1970s, however, unemployment in North America has risen substantially in comparison to earlier periods. While many factors have contributed to this increase in unemployment, many observers blame it at least in part on import competition, especially in the United States where the high value of the U.S. dollar in the 1981–85 period led to a dramatic increase in imports. And the fear of increased unemployment is a key factor in the Canadian debate over the issue of free trade with the United States, which we discuss in the next chapter.)

While there are striking similarities between trade and technological change, there is an important difference. Technological change is permanent: Once the production possibilities curve shifts outward in panel (b) of Figure 31-5, it doesn't shift back. In contrast, a trade gain is not necessarily permanent. If trade is sharply reduced—for example, because of the imposition of high tariffs—then most of the gains from trade are lost, that is, the country in panel (a) moves from D back toward point B.

THE VARIOUS EFFECTS OF INTERNATIONAL TRADE ON EFFICIENCY

While this analysis illustrates the general case for trade, it is somewhat abstract, since it lumps all Canadian exports into a single food category and all imports into a single clothing category. Moreover, the only prices that exist are relative, barter-like prices; for example, the price of 1 unit of food is 3 units of

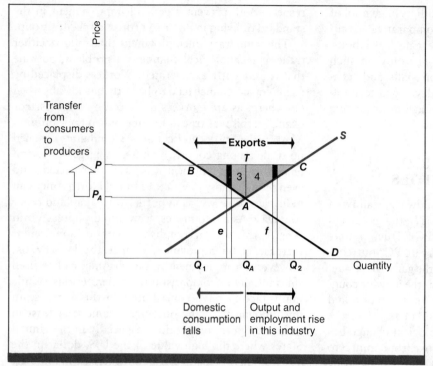

Figure 31-6 Detailed effects of the export of an individual good—wheat.
With trade, price increases from P_A to P with Q_1Q_2 exported. In part, these exports come from reduced consumption (Q_1Q_A); the net gain on these units is area 3. The other part of these exports comes from increased production (Q_AQ_2); the net gain on these units is area 4. Thus, the total efficiency gain from exporting is the entire gray area. There is a transfer effect as well, shown by the white arrow on the left: Because price has risen, producers gain at consumers' expense.

clothing. Now let us return to the more familiar world of supply and demand, where goods are sold for dollars. For example, the price of a bushel of wheat may be $4.20. Here, we shall no longer think in abstract terms of only two goods—a collective export (food) and a collective import (clothing). Instead, we examine one specific Canadian export item (wheat) and one specific Canadian import item (woollens). In this more familiar frame of reference, we shall illustrate how trade increases efficiency.

Efficiency Gain on a Typical Export: Wheat
Figure 31-6 shows the Canadian demand and supply curves for wheat. Without trade, equilibrium in the domestic market is at point A, where the nation's supply and demand intersect. Thus, Q_A is produced at price P_A. At the same time, the price in the rest of the world is at the higher level P, reflecting the higher costs of producing wheat in foreign countries.

When trade is opened, Canadian producers discover that they can sell abroad at this higher price P, and they begin to do so. Moreover, since they can sell at P abroad, they will be unwilling to sell at any lower price in the home market. Thus, the domestic price rises to the world level P.[4]

Canadian producers, earning this more attractive price, expand their output. Specifically, they move up their supply curve from A to C, increasing their output from Q_A to Q_2. But, of course, consumers view this higher price quite differently. They move up their demand curve from A to B, thus reducing their consumption from Q_A to Q_1. In short, Q_2 is now pro-

---

[4]More realistically, the Canadian price rises to the foreign price, less transportation costs. However, to keep this illustration simple, we assume that transport costs and other similar complications do not exist.

duced and Q_1 is consumed, with the difference (Q_1Q_2) being exported. Thus, these Canadian exports come partly from increased production and partly from reduced domestic consumption. We now examine each of these effects in turn.

First consider one of the units of reduced consumption Q_1Q_A, say, unit e. The consumer's benefit from this lost unit of consumption is shown as the white bar under the demand curve. (Recall that demand reflects marginal benefit.) But the gain from exporting this unit is the export price P that is received for it, as shown by the white bar plus the black bar above. Hence, the net gain from exporting it, rather than consuming it, is the black bar. The sum of all such solid bars throughout the relevant range Q_1Q_A is the gray triangle 3. This is the gain from switching goods from consumption to a more highly valued use, namely, export.

Next consider one of the units of increased production for export Q_AQ_2, say, unit f. The cost of producing it is the white bar under the supply curve. (Recall that supply reflects marginal cost.) But the benefit from producing it is the export price P received for it, which is the white bar plus the black bar. Therefore, the net gain from producing it for export is the black bar. The sum of all such black bars through the relevant range Q_AQ_2 is represented by the gray triangle 4. This is the efficiency gain from expanding production for export.

The total gain from exporting is shown as the sum of both these effects; in other words, the total gray area in Figure 31-6. In simple terms, this gain indicates that wheat can be sold to foreigners for more than it costs to produce it, or more than is lost by switching it away from domestic consumption.

Of course, this gray area will represent an efficiency *loss* if producers are *not* allowed to export. It demonstrates that interference in a competitive world market may be damaging, in the same way that we have seen that interference in a competitive home market may be damaging.

Efficiency Gain on a Typical Import: Woollens

A parallel analysis illustrates the gain from importing a specific item. Figure 31-7 shows the Canadian supply and demand curves for an import-competing product like woollens. Without trade, equilibrium in the domestic market is at point A, with price P_A and quantity Q_A produced and consumed. At the same time, the price in the rest of the world is at the lower level P, reflecting the lower costs of production there.

When trade is opened, Canadian consumers can buy imported woollens at this lower price P. Since they will be unwilling to buy from Canadian producers at higher price P_A, the domestic price will fall to the world level P. At this lower price, Canadian consumers increase their purchases; they move down their demand curve from A to J, increasing their consumption from Q_A to Q_6. At the same time, domestic producers respond to lower price P by moving down their supply curve from A to H, thus reducing their output from Q_A to Q_5. In short, Q_5 is now produced in Canada, while Q_6 is consumed; the difference (Q_5Q_6) is the amount imported. Thus, Canadian imports result both in decreased production and increased consumption.

First consider one of the units of decreased production Q_AQ_5, say, unit j. The cost of importing it is the price P that must be paid for it, shown as the white bar. But because it is being imported, we save the cost of producing it ourselves, which is the white bar plus the black bar—that is, its marginal cost as defined under the supply curve. Thus, the net gain from importing it, rather than producing it more expensively at home, is the black bar. The sum of all such solid bars over the relevant range Q_5Q_A is gray triangle 1. This is the gain from allowing imports to displace relatively inefficient, high-cost domestic production.

Now consider one of the units of increased consumption Q_AQ_6, say, unit k. Its cost is the import price P shown by the white bar. However, the consumer values it as the white bar plus the black bar—that is, its marginal benefit defined under the demand curve. Therefore, the net benefit from this unit of increased consumption is the black bar, and the sum of all such benefits is the gray triangle 2. This is the efficiency gain from allowing consumption to expand in response to a bargain international price.

The total efficiency gain on both accounts is the whole gray area in Figure 31-7. In simplest terms, this area shows that we can benefit by buying a low-cost import because it allows us to cut back our own inefficient, high-cost production; and it also allows us to increase our consumption of a bargain-priced good.

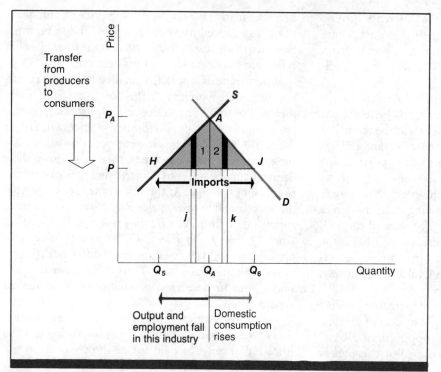

Figure 31-7 Detailed effects of the import of an individual good—woollens.
With trade, price decreases from P_A to P, with HJ imported. This reduces home production by Q_AQ_5; the net gain on these units is area 1. Imports also result in increased con-sumption of Q_AQ_6; the net gain on these units is area 2. Thus, the total efficiency gain from importing this good is the entire gray area. There is also a transfer effect, shown by the white arrow on the left: Because price has fallen, consumers gain at producers' expense.

WINNERS AND LOSERS FROM INTERNATIONAL TRADE

While trade leads to an overall gain in efficiency, it is important to emphasize again that not all groups benefit. For example, in Figure 31-6, trade brings an increase in the price of wheat. As a result, wheat farmers gain, while consumers lose. This transfer is shown by the wide, white arrow to the left of the diagram. (Note: This is an important graphic device that will be used to show transfers throughout the rest of this book.) On the other hand, the import in Figure 31-7 results in the opposite sort of transfer. Because it lowers price, consumers benefit, while producers lose.

These benefits and losses to each group as a result of imports are shown more precisely in the alternative analysis set out in Figure 31-8.[5] Each panel in this diagram reproduces the Canadian supply and demand curves for woollens from Figure 31-7. The gain to the nation's consumers from a lower price is shown by the gray area in panel (*a*) enclosed to the left of the demand curve. At the same time, producers receive a lower price, and lose sales to imports. As a result, producer surplus is reduced by the red area in panel (*b*) enclosed to the left of the supply curve.[6] Because this area 5

[5]*Note to instructors*: To a substantial degree, our analysis of transfer and efficiency effects in the balance of this book will be based on diagrams similar to Figure 31-7. But those who wish to supplement this with diagrams similar to Figure 31-8 will find several such diagrams in the *Instructor's Manual*.

[6]For a review of the basic idea of how consumer surplus changes as price changes, see Figure 21-5. For a similar review of how producer surplus changes—a concept we will also now be using frequently from now on—see Figure 23-8.

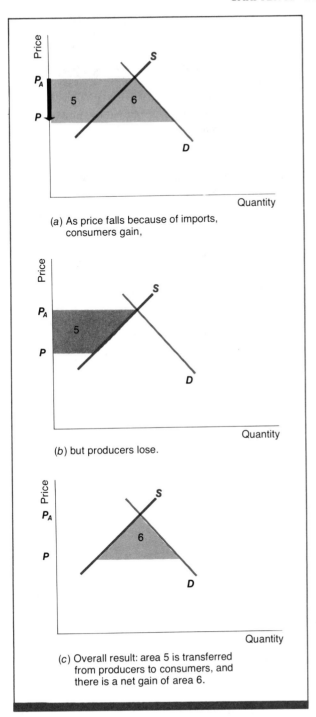

(a) As price falls because of imports, consumers gain,

(b) but producers lose.

(c) Overall result: area 5 is transferred from producers to consumers, and there is a net gain of area 6.

Figure 31-8   Detailed effects of an import of woollens. (An alternative to Figure 31-7).

also appears as a gray gain in panel (*a*), it is a transfer from the producers who lose it in panel (*b*) to the consumers who receive it in panel (*a*). (This technique of identifying a transfer is important because it can be used on a wide variety of problems; for example, see Problem 31-8.) At the same time, area 6 in panel (*a*) is a gray gain not offset by a red loss. This net gain of area 6 is reproduced in panel (*c*). This is, of course, exactly the same gray efficiency gain that appeared in the preceding diagram.[7] Finally, in any such analysis, it's important to repeat an earlier warning: In concluding that there will be an efficiency gain, we have assumed that the consumers' valuation of a $1 increase in income is roughly the same as the producers' valuation of a $1 reduction in income—or at least that they are sufficiently similar that our conclusions are not upset.

As a current example of how imports affect various groups in Canada, consider our imports of textiles from the Far East. The effect on Canadian textile producers is clear. They are damaged because these imports depress the domestic price of textiles and reduce their sales. At the same time, it is clear to Canadian consumers that they benefit from a lower textile price. What is not always clear, however, is the net effect on the nation as a whole. This analysis suggests that the overall effect is favourable, since the benefit to consumers more than offsets the loss to producers.

Finally, note that while output and employment fall in the typical import-competing industry shown in Figure 31-7, they rise in the export industries as shown in Figure 31-6. When both these effects are taken into account, there is no reason to expect either a large increase or decrease in employment as a result of trade— although unemployment may rise during the adjustment period. We emphasize: The principal point of international trade—like technological change—is *not* to increase employment; it is to increase real income.

[7]The method of Figure 31-8 can also be used to explain Figure 31-6 more fully. Specifically, as price rises in Figure 31-6:
  (a) Consumer surplus falls by $PBAP_A$.
  (b) Producer surplus rises by $PCAP_A$.
  (c) Thus, the net effects are a transfer of $PBAP_A$ from consumers to producers, and an efficiency gain of ABC.

KEY POINTS

1. In this chapter, a strong case has been made for international trade; the next chapter will deal with the case for tariffs and other restraints on trade.

2. There are three major sources of benefit from trade: (a) greater competition, (b) economies of scale, and (c) comparative advantage.

3. When trade is opened, countries specialize in certain products, increasing their output of these goods. If there are economies of scale, costs fall as a result of this increase in output.

4. Even if costs do not fall with rising output, trade will be beneficial if countries specialize in the goods in which they have a comparative advantage, that is, in those products in which they are relatively most efficient. We saw this not only in the Ricardian case where cost is constant, but also even in cases such as the one shown in Figure 31-6, where cost (supply) rises as output increases.

5. Because trade lowers the prices of goods we import and raises the prices of goods we export, it hurts some while benefitting others. Consumers of imports benefit, while consumers of exported goods are harmed. To some degree, but not completely, these are the same people, so that this transfer partly cancels out. In addition, producers of exports benefit, while producers of import-competing goods are hurt.

6. International trade is similar in many respects to technological change. Both increase real income by allowing a nation to consume more: Trade allows a country to consume beyond its production possibilities curve, while technological change shifts the production possibilities curve out. Trade and technological change can cause the same sort of short-run unemployment until workers who have lost their jobs shift to new, more productive employment.

KEY CONCEPTS

specialization
increased competition
economies of scale
greater availability of products
absolute advantage

comparative advantage
opportunity cost
gain from trade
trade compared to
    technological change

exports: efficiency and
    transfer effects
imports: efficiency and
    transfer effects

PROBLEMS

31-1 "Foreign competition makes an industry more competitive." Should this result be viewed as an advantage or a disadvantage by (a) consumers of this good? (b) producers of the good? (c) the nation as a whole?

31-2 Suppose that there are economies of scale in the production of both X and Y. If Britain specializes in one and Canada in the other, is it possible for both countries to benefit? Explain your answer. Does this answer still hold if the cost curves for each good are

identical in the two countries? Hint: Review the discussion of economies of scale in Chapter 3.

31-3 Return to Table 31-2, where costs are constant. (a) Change the "northwest" number 3 to 5. Does Britain now have an absolute advantage in either good? A comparative advantage in either? Draw a diagram like Figure 31-4 to show the potential Canadian gain from trade, again assuming that there are 20 million workers in Canada and the international price ratio is 3:1. (b) Now change that same northwest number to 8. Which country now has a comparative advantage in food? in clothing? Are there potential gains from trade? Why or why not?

31-4 In moving from B to D, the country in Figure 31-4 consumes more clothing, but not more food. Therefore, it takes all its gains from specialization and trade in increased clothing. Now suppose that it decides to consume less clothing, that is, it stops trading at point K, with its trade arrow now being only CK, rather than CD. Will all the gains from specialization and trade be in clothing? in food? or in some combination of the two? Graphically show exactly what the gains will be.

31-5 The following diagram shows the situation of Britain corresponding to the Canadian situation in Figure 31-5(a). Identify clearly:
(a) How Britain specializes when trade is opened.
(b) How Britain trades. Fill in details of how much of each good Britain exports or imports.
(c) Are there any lines or curves in this diagram that must be similar to those that appear in Figure 31-5(a)?
(d) Does Britain gain from trade? If so, how much?

31-6 "Economists say that international trade and technological change are similar—but they are wrong. Technological change increases our real income by making us more productive. Trade does not." Evaluate this statement.

31-7 This problem looks ahead to Chapter 32.
(a) Suppose that Canada and Britain become involved in a trade war, with each imposing such heavy restrictions on imports that trade between the two is eventually cut off altogether. Use the diagram on the previous page and panel (a) of Figure 31-5 to show the gains or losses each would suffer. Is a trade war a "zero-sum game" (what one country wins, the other loses)? Or is it like any other kind of war, with losses on both sides?
(b) Use two diagrams like figures 31-6 and 31-7 to show in more detail how Canada would be affected by such a trade war.

*31-8 To see how the analysis of Figure 31-8 can be applied to an entirely different problem, consider the government price-support policy for agriculture set out in Figure 24-11(b).
(a) Use a series of coloured diagrams like the panels in Figure 31-8 to show how each of the following three groups benefit or lose: consumers, producers, Canadian taxpayers. (How much of the taxpayers' money does the government pay out on the program?) By comparing these effects, indicate the transfers that take place, and in a final diagram, show the net, overall efficiency effect of this policy.
(b) Confirm this efficiency effect by noting how this policy affects output, and then applying the analysis of Figure 24-3.

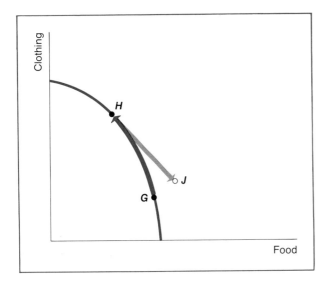

Chapter 32

INTERNATIONAL TRADE: POLICY DEBATES

Park your Japanese car in Tokyo
Detroit bumper sticker

Protectionism is the institutionalization of
economic failure.
Former British Prime Minister Edward Heath

Despite the gains from trade discussed in Chapter 31, no country follows a policy of completely free trade; every nation erects barriers to restrict imports. These barriers include tariffs (taxes imposed on imported goods as they enter a country) and quotas (limits on the number of units that can be imported).

It is true that, since the 1930s, we have made great progress in reducing trade restrictions, especially tariffs. Much of the progress has come as a result of multilateral negotiations, where countries get together to reach agreement on tariff reductions and other trade matters. In the "Kennedy Round" of trade negotiations in the 1960s, most of the non-communist industrial countries of the world agreed to cut their tariffs by about one-third. In the Tokyo Round agreement of 1979, these nations—including Canada—undertook to lower remaining tariffs by another third. And in the automotive industry, most of the barriers to U.S.-Canada trade were abolished following a bilateral agreement in 1965.

However, negotiating tariff reductions has been a long and arduous process. Moreover, as tariffs have been reduced, "non-tariff" barriers, such as quotas, have become more important. Therefore, countries still retain substantial trade restrictions to protect their domestic industries from competition from imports. There are two basic reasons: (1) Trade barriers may be introduced for non-economic reasons. For example, a tariff may be imposed to protect an industry which might be essential to national defence in case of an emergency. (2) A country may restrict imports for special economic reasons, some of which are fallacious, but some of which may contain a kernel of truth.

NON-ECONOMIC EXPLANATIONS OF TRADE BARRIERS

The government may protect an industry for military or political reasons. Consider each objective in turn:

1. An Industry May Be Essential for National Defence

Two centuries ago, Adam Smith argued that national defence is an important goal. He maintained that, in pursuing this objective, we should be willing to protect our defence industries even if such protection involves an economic cost—that is, even if foreign countries have a comparative advantage in producing military supplies. This argument remains powerful more than 200 years later. The general idea is simple. In the event of a war or a major international crisis, a country doesn't want to be dependent on far-away foreign supplies for the things it needs to defend itself.

But for a country such as Canada, the argument that a country's defence industries must be protected has lost much of its importance since World War II, for several reasons. First, because Canada, the United States, and most of the industrialized nations in Western Europe all belong to NATO, it no longer seems as important for each of these countries to have the industrial capability to produce its own military equipment. For example, as long as the West Germans can count on jet fighters from the United States, they need not protect their aircraft industry. The argument that defence industries need to be protected is now heard mostly in the United States, where it is applied to certain "strategic" high-technology industries that are engaged in developing advanced equipment for the space program, or technology for nuclear missiles. (In making this kind of argument, the Americans face an important problem: Where do you draw the line? Do you protect just the industries producing military equipment such as missiles, or do you go one step beyond and protect the aluminum industry because it provides an input essential for missiles? Although the defence argument makes sense in some cases, it can be abused, since almost every industry makes some indirect contribution to national defence.)

2. People Vote for Their Present Jobs

Increased international trade can mean that some jobs are lost in industries whose sales fall because of competition from imports. However, new jobs are created in export industries. The problem is that people are more concerned about the present jobs they may lose than the possibility of new jobs in an export industry. (After all, who knows for sure who will actually get these new export-based jobs?) Therefore, workers who don't want to take risks vote against increased trade; that is, they vote for the tariffs and other trade restrictions that protect their current jobs. As a consequence, too much attention may be paid to the employment that is lost from increased imports, and not enough to the employment that is gained from increased exports.

However, even if we look only at imports, we remember from Figure 31-8 that the losses to producers from increased imports were more than offset by gains to consumers. By pointing this out, why can't a politician sell the idea of allowing imports in more freely?

The answer is that individuals tend to think and vote as producers, not consumers. To illustrate why, suppose that the import is shirts. There may be large benefits to consumers as a group from lower-priced shirts. But this gain is distributed widely among millions of purchasers, with each benefitting by such a small amount that nobody is likely to switch votes on this account. On the producers' side, however, things are different. Here, fewer individuals are affected by increased shirt imports, but the effect on each individual—whether in management or labour—is much greater. For people in this industry, the possible loss of jobs and profits will be important enough to determine how they vote; they become "one-issue" voters. In brief, producers vote for politicians who will protect their jobs with a tariff, while consumers scatter their votes around on a whole variety of issues, with only a few voting against the tariff. Therefore, the interest of consumers in freer trade may be inadequately represented. (For a criticism of a policy that ignores the interests of consumers, see Box 32-1.)

A further, related reason that shirt producers may be able to exert strong political pressure is that they are not spread out all over Canada, as consumers are. Instead, they are concentrated in a few provinces or electoral ridings. For members of Parliament representing such districts, one very good way of getting political support may be to push for import restrictions on shirts. If they do, they will gain many votes from shirt producers, while losing very few from consumers. Moreover, this is not just a political sleight-of-hand. From the narrow point of view of just the shirt-producing communities, tariff-free imports of shirts may in fact be undesirable. The reason is that such communities would bear much of the loss from allowing duty-free imports (the red area in Figure 31-8). At the same time, they would receive little of the benefit (the gray area in panel (a) of that same diagram), because most consumers live elsewhere. For these communities, losses from increased shirt imports would exceed gains.

Therefore, it is no great surprise if the members of Parliament from shirt-producing ridings go to Ottawa

BOX 32-1

WHAT HAPPENS IF THE CONSUMER IS FORGOTTEN: BASTIAT'S NEGATIVE RAILWAY

The absurdity of ignoring the interests of the consumer has never been more eloquently stated than by the French economist Frédéric Bastiat (1801–1850):*

> It has been proposed that the railway from Paris to Madrid should have a break at Bordeaux, for if goods and passengers are forced to stop at that town, profits will accrue to bargemen, pedlars, commissionaires, hotel-keepers, etc. But if Bordeaux has a right to profit by a gap in the line of railway, and if such profit is considered in the public interest, then Angoulême, Poitiers, Tours, Orléans, nay, more, all the intermediate places, Ruffec, Châtellerault, etc., should also demand gaps, as being for the general interest. For the more these breaks in the line are multiplied, the greater will be the increase of consignments, commissions, transshipments, etc., along the whole extent of the railway. In this way, we shall succeed in having a line of railway composed of successive gaps, which we may call a Negative Railway.

*Abridged from Frédéric Bastiat, *Economic Sophisms* (Edinburgh: Oliver and Boyd, Ltd., 1873), pp. 80–81.

Courtesy Miller Services Limited

committed to restricting imports of shirts. When they get there, they meet other members with similar problems: They, too, may be seeking protection for the goods produced in their own ridings. The result is logrolling. The members from shirt-producing ridings agree to support protection for the products of other ridings, in return for the promise of other members to support protection for the shirt industry.

This process leads to continuous pressure in Ottawa for protection of industries that compete with imports. When imports on a wide variety of goods are restricted, the shirt-producing communities may well be damaged after all because of the higher prices of a wide range of imported goods. However, the members from these ridings may still be popular locally because they are remembered for their conspicuous support for the protection of the shirt industry, rather than for their less obvious support for the protection of other goods.

Thus, it is no surprise that some 200 years after the case for free trade was clearly stated by Adam Smith, protection still lives on. In fact, we would have even more severe trade restrictions except for the fact that producers in export industries have a strong interest in international trade, and recognize that foreigners won't buy our exports unless we buy imports from them. Thus, concerted producer-led pressure for freer trade may partially offset the protectionist pressure groups.

ECONOMIC ARGUMENTS FOR PROTECTION

In an attempt to counter the strong case for international trade, advocates of protection have put forward a number of economic arguments. Some are fallacious, amounting to little more than weak rationalizations for protection, while others are stronger. The weakest arguments are considered first.

1. "Buy Canadian because it keeps our money at home."

This argument is sometimes expanded to: "If I buy a personal computer from the United States, I get the computer and the Americans get the dollars. But if I buy a computer made in Canada instead, I get the computer and the dollars stay here." The problem with this argument is that it fails to recognize why the Americans export to us. They do not work hard to produce personal computers for export merely for the joy of holding Canadian dollars. Like you or me, they want to earn money to buy things. To a large extent, they use Canadian dollars to buy such things as subway cars and newsprint from us. In other words, when we import computers, it is subway cars and newsprint that we ultimately give up, not dollars. Similarly, if we buy computers at home, we will *also* be giving up goods such as subway cars and newsprint. (Some of our own resources will have to be diverted from producing subway cars and newsprint to producing computers.) Which way of acquiring computers—from the Americans or ourselves—will cost us fewer subway cars and less newsprint? The answer was given in Chapter 31: Computers will cost us less—in terms of foregone subway cars and other goods—if we buy them from the United States, provided, of course, that the Americans have a comparative advantage in computer production.[1]

2. "We can't compete with cheap foreign labour."

To clarify this issue, it is important first to ask: Why is labour more expensive in Canada than in, say, South Korea? The answer is that wages are higher in Canada than in most foreign countries because labour here is more productive; it can produce more goods. Consequently, it can be "paid more goods", that is, its real wage is higher than elsewhere—a point first illustrated in Box 31-1. When we take into account both our higher wages and our higher productivity, we find that we can compete internationally in some goods, but not others. While we cannot compete with cheap labour in other countries (such as South Korea) in products in which they have a comparative advantage, we can compete in products of our comparative advantage, where our higher labour productivity more than offsets our higher wage. These are the products on which we should be concentrating. (For more on the argument that we will be unable to compete with foreign producers, see Box 32-2.)

In seeking protection from American goods, Canadian producers sometimes turn the above argument around completely. Since they can't argue that U.S. labour is cheaper (in fact, it is typically paid a higher wage), Canadian producers instead point out that U.S. labour is more productive. It is for this reason, say Canadian producers, that they cannot compete and therefore require protection from U.S. competition. Of course, the reply in this case is that, although U.S. labour productivity is higher, American wages are also higher, so U.S. costs are not lower across the board. True, Canadians will not be able to compete in activities where U.S. productivity is particularly great and where the United States consequently has a comparative advantage. But Canadians can compete successfully in those other goods in which we enjoy a comparative advantage (that is, where our wage advantage exceeds the U.S. productivity advantage).

3. "Tariffs should be tailored to equalize costs at home and abroad."

This recommendation may sound plausible, but it misses the whole point of international trade: Gains from trade are based on cost differences between countries; we import bananas or radios precisely because they can be produced more cheaply abroad than at home. Eliminate cost differences and you eliminate the incentive to trade; and when you eliminate

---

[1]As we saw in Chapter 3, for a country that is importing capital, imports of goods and services may be substantially greater than exports. In this case, the argument in this section is no longer so clear-cut; there may be a lag of months or years between our imports and foreign purchases of our goods. Nevertheless, our main point is still valid. The ultimate purpose of countries such as the United States or Japan in selling goods to Canada is to acquire the Canadian dollars to buy goods from us.

BOX 32-2

THE PETITION OF THE CANDLEMAKERS

Sometimes the argument that we can't compete with cheap foreign labour appears in the slightly different form: "We can't compete with cheap foreign goods." This idea has never been more effectively criticized than by Frédéric Bastiat over a hundred years ago. Here is his satirical description of an appeal by French candlemakers to the government to protect them from the free sunlight that was supposedly ruining their business:*

> We are subjected to the intolerable competition of a foreign rival, who enjoys, it would seem, such superior facilities for the production of light, that he is enabled to inundate our national market at so exceedingly reduced a price, that, the moment he makes his appearance, he draws off all custom from us; and thus an important branch of French industry, with all its innumerable ramifications, is suddenly reduced to a state of complete stagnation. This rival is no other than the sun.

> Our petition is, that it would please your honorable body to pass a law whereby shall be directed the shutting up of all windows, dormers, skylights, shutters, curtains, in a word, all openings, holes, chinks, and fissures through which the light of the sun is used to penetrate into our dwellings, to the prejudice of the profitable manufactures which we flatter ourselves we have been enabled to bestow upon the country; which country cannot, therefore, without ingratitude, leave us now to struggle unprotected through so unequal a contest . . .

> Does it not argue the greatest inconsistency to check as you do the importation of coal, iron, cheese, and goods of foreign manufacture, merely because . . . their price approaches zero, while at the same time you freely admit, and without limitation, the light of the sun, whose price is during the whole day at zero?

*Abridged from Frédéric Bastiat, *Economic Sophisms*, pp. 56–60.

---

this, trade disappears. Thus, if we were to follow this recommendation, we would no longer be importing cheap bananas; instead we'd be producing them very expensively at home in greenhouses, with the costs of cheap imports from Central America being equalized by an extremely high tariff. In other words, to the degree that we were successful in the well-nigh impossible task of tailoring tariffs to make costs precisely equal at home and abroad, we would lose the gains from trade we now enjoy. In a word: All that tailored tariffs would do is strangle trade.

While these three arguments for protection are false, the following arguments do contain at least some element of truth.

4. "If we buy steel from Hamilton rather than from Pittsburgh, employment will rise in Hamilton rather than in Pittsburgh."

This statement may be true, particularly if there is large-scale unemployment in Hamilton. Why, then, does it not provide a very strong case for restricting trade, ranking in importance with the efficiency argument for free trade in the previous chapter? Why don't we use import restrictions to raise and maintain Canadian employment? There are two problems with this suggestion.

(a) *If we protect an industry's employment by import restrictions, how can its price be kept from rising rapidly?* If the government becomes committed to providing an industry with whatever trade barrier it needs to protect it from losing sales and employment to foreign firms, this removes a very important restraint on the industry. If it can raise its price without fear of losing sales, it may well decide to do so.

The North American auto industry provides an instructive example. By 1979, it was already losing sales to imports. Nevertheless, labour contracts negotiated that year provided for large wage increases—even though auto wages were already well above the average for other manufacturing industries. The resulting high cost of producing cars was one of the reasons that the U.S. and Canadian companies lost even more sales to Japanese and European imports. Facing large-scale unemployment, auto workers moderated their wage demands in the early 1980s, in some instances accepting wage cuts. At the same time, they exerted great pressure on the government to protect the industry.

In 1981, the U.S. and Canadian governments pressured the Japanese into imposing "voluntary" limits on their auto exports to North America. The resulting reduction in foreign competition led to higher auto prices in the United States and Canada, and thereby imposed a high cost on car buyers. (According to Wharton Econometric Forecasting Associates, restrictions on Japanese cars raised their price in the United States by $920 to $960 in 1981–82 alone.) The reduced competition from the Japanese also led to increased sales and profits to the North American auto companies. This profit, in turn, allowed these companies to pay their executives large bonuses and their labour force increased wages. (However, wage increases were substantially smaller than they had been in earlier years, when competition from foreign cars was still weak.) This raised the question: Why should other workers earning far lower wages be asked to subsidize auto workers and auto executives by paying higher prices for cars? In 1985, the U.S. administration dropped its pressure on the Japanese to continue to limit their auto exports to the United States. However, the Canadian government did not follow this example. As a result, in the mid-1980s, restrictions continued to limit the import into Canada of Japanese cars, especially low-priced models. (Since there was a limit on the total number of cars that they could sell in Canada, importers of Japanese cars concentrated on high-priced models.)

(b) *If employment is protected by import restraints, won't our trading partners retaliate by reducing their imports from us?* To see why this might indeed happen, suppose we restrict steel imports so that Canadian purchases are switched from Pittsburgh to Hamilton. This is often called a "beggar-my-neighbour" policy because we would be trying to solve our unemployment problem by shifting it to the Americans. The problem with this policy is that the Americans may respond by restricting their imports of our goods, and thus shift the unemployment problem back onto us.

In periods of worldwide recession, all countries are tempted to initiate a beggar-my-neighbour policy of increased protection; it is tempting for each of them for exactly the same reason that it is tempting for us. If all countries attempt to solve unemployment in this way, the result will be a general disruption of trade.

Unemployment may consequently rise, not fall. For example, when the U.S. government attempted to protect domestic employment by large tariff increases in 1930, Canada (and other countries) responded by raising their own tariffs. In 1932 we again increased our tariffs against the United States (and other countries not in the Commonwealth) under the so-called Ottawa Agreement. Although this increase in protection was partly offset by a reduction of our tariff on imports from members of the Commonwealth, the net result was still a significant increase in our average tariff level during the 1930s, as you can see in Figure 32-1. There is no doubt that this cycle of tariff increases in one country and retaliation by other countries greatly reduced the amount of international trade and thereby contributed to the worldwide depression in the 1930s.

If there is large-scale domestic unemployment, the cure should be sought in the domestic monetary and fiscal policies discussed in parts 3 and 4, not in mutually destructive beggar-my-neighbour trade restrictions.

5. "Restricting trade will diversify a nation's economy."

This is true. Just as trade leads a country to specialize, restricting trade leads to the opposite: diversification. Isn't it a good thing for a country to diversify—to avoid putting all its eggs in one basket?

The answer is, perhaps. But for countries, like individuals, the risks from specialization are often more than offset by the gains. (The risk of a future oversupply of lawyers or doctors does not prevent individuals from taking up these specialized careers. Their expected gains outweigh the risks they run.)

At the national level, an example of a high degree of specialization is Ghana's dependence on exports of cocoa, a product with a fluctuating price. It is true that Ghana's risks could be reduced by diversification. In turn, diversification may be encouraged by protecting new industries. However, even for a country like Ghana, the argument must be balanced against the advantages of specialization—the gains from trade. Moreover, fluctuations in cocoa price work both ways. There is the risk that price may fall, but there is also the possibility that price may rise. In this case, the greater the degree of specialization, the greater the benefit.

For a country like Canada, a deliberate policy of diversifying the economy by restricting imports is even

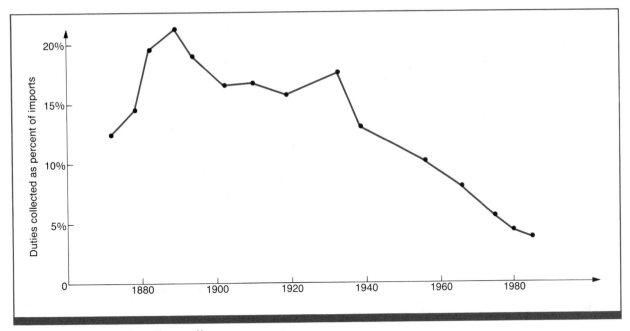

Figure 32-1   Average Canadian tariff rates.
Canada has had high tariffs sometimes and low tariffs at other times. But since the mid-1930s, the trend has been down, so that now our tariffs average less than 5 percent. Increasingly, the focus is on how non-tariff barriers restrict trade.

Sources: Based on H.M. Pinchin, *The Regional Impact of the Canadian Tariff*, A background study for the Economic Council of Canada (Ottawa: Minister of Supply and Services Canada, 1979), and Statistics Canada, *Canadian Statistical Review*, 1972, 1977, 1982, 1985. Reproduced by permission of the Minister of Supply and Services Canada.

harder to justify. While it is true that Canada has large exports of primary products such as wheat, lumber, and natural gas, we export a wide enough range of these products to avoid being highly sensitive to fluctuations in the world price of any single one. Furthermore, even though our primary exports are large, we also export a wide range of manufactured products: In fact, more than half of our merchandise exports are manufactured goods, as Table 31-1 showed.

Even if we move further in the direction of more trade and specialization—indeed, even if we go as far in this direction as entering into a free trade agreement with the United States—our activities are still likely to remain remarkably diversified. The evidence is that we would not give up the production of a whole category of goods (such as industrial products) to concentrate on another (such as agricultural products). Indeed, it would be unlikely that we would completely give up even one industry (say, sporting goods) in order to specialize in another (electrical machinery). Instead, the evidence suggests that trade leads to specialization

in certain *kinds* of sporting goods, and certain *kinds* of electrical machinery. For industrial countries, expanded trade has generally not resulted in a narrow range of products.

6. "We need to protect our infant industries."
The basic idea here is this: A country may not be able to compete with other nations in an industry with economies of scale until this industry is well established and operating at high volume and low cost. This may be true even in an industry where the country will eventually have a comparative advantage and be able to produce very cheaply. This raises a question: Shouldn't such an industry be protected from being wiped out by tough foreign competition during the delicate period of its infancy?

Although this line of reasoning is logically valid, it raises two practical questions: (1) How do you know that the only advantage of the foreign countries is that their industry is already established? For example, if a country is thinking of protecting an infant watch industry, how does it know that the only advantage of the Swiss and Japanese is that their industry is already established? Maybe they enjoy some basic advantage in watchmaking. If so, a watchmaking industry established elsewhere may never be able to compete. (2) When does an infant subsidy become an old-age pension? Industries that receive protection as infants seldom seem to grow up, but instead become forever dependent on their tariffs. Such industries can become a real problem. Once established, they employ many people who vote; thus protection continues to go to them, rather than to the real infants who have not yet hired a large enough labour force to give them voting clout.[2]

7. "Restricting imports may reduce the price we have to pay for them."

This argument applies only to goods in which Canada purchases a large amount of the world's total supply. The idea is this: If Canada imposes a tariff or some other trade restriction on such a good, say coffee, Canadians will buy less on the international market. As a result, the world demand for coffee decreases—that is, shifts to the left—and the price of coffee falls. Thus, by restricting this import, Canada would be able to acquire coffee at a more favourable price.[3] This is sometimes referred to as improving our *terms of trade*, that is, reducing the price of what we buy compared to the price of what we sell.

The difficulty with this argument, however, is that for most internationally traded goods, Canadian demand represents only a very small fraction of world demand. To continue with the coffee example, even if the Canadian government were to prohibit almost all imports of coffee (a frightening thought to many of us), world demand for coffee would drop by less than one-half of one percent. Such a small reduction in

world demand would hardly have a noticeable impact on the world price of coffee. For Canada, the scope for improving our terms of trade through import restrictions is very limited.

8. "Restricting trade will increase our economic independence."

This is true: The less we buy from foreign countries and sell to them, the less sensitive we become to changing conditions and policies there. For example, countries that were heavily dependent on imported oil faced a severe problem when the Arab nations imposed an oil export embargo in 1973, and had to compensate for the sudden cut-off of imports by various painful and costly measures. If oil imports had been restricted to begin with, the embargo would not have had such serious consequences.

While this argument for import restrictions makes sense for a commodity such as oil where a large proportion of the international supply comes from a small number of countries in the politically unstable Middle East, it has less force when we consider commodities that can be supplied from a wider range of countries. For example, if the supply of Canadian imports of machinery and motor vehicles from the United States were to be cut off for some reason, Japan or Western Europe would provide good alternative sources of supply.

International trade also makes us dependent on foreign countries on the export side: Foreign countries are the buyers of our exports as well as the suppliers of our imports. The dependence on foreign markets makes us vulnerable to economic fluctuations in foreign countries (as we discussed in Chapter 8, for example, economic fluctuations in the United States quickly spill over into Canada as U.S. demand for our exports is affected). Moreover, it makes us vulnerable to changes in tariffs and other trade barriers in the countries that make up the market for our exports, especially the United States. By threatening to impose barriers against Canadian exports, the U.S. government can pressure Canada on various international political issues.

However, our vulnerability to outside pressure should not be exaggerated. Just as international trade makes Canada more dependent on foreign countries, it also makes them more dependent on Canada. For example, there are many U.S. industries that are dependent on Canada for raw material supplies, and many

---

[2] A third practical question is this: If such an industry will eventually be a profitable one, why shouldn't its owners cover any initial losses out of their future profits? One possible answer is that the capital markets may not work very well. As a result, firms may be unable to raise the capital necessary to get them through the initial period of losses.

[3] Although Canada as a nation pays a lower price to, say, Brazil, the price paid by individual Canadian coffee buyers rises—because they must pay not only for the coffee, but also for the tariff that goes to the Canadian government. (It is in response to this higher price they are paying that individual Canadian buyers reduce their coffee purchases.)

American firms that have large investments in Canada. To some extent, Canada can therefore neutralize U.S. pressure by threatening to impose policies that would hurt U.S. interests.

FREE TRADE VERSUS PROTECTION: A SUMMARY

This discussion shows that we should never judge an issue by adding up the number of arguments for and against it. There are only a few arguments for free trade, but they are very impressive. A reduction in trade barriers:

- increases competition in our domestic market
- provides consumers with a wider selection of goods
- generates gains because of comparative advantage and economies of scale.

Thus, free trade raises our standard of living.

On the other hand, there is a whole battery of arguments for protection. However, in summing them up, we first note that some are downright illogical. Moreover, even those that do have some element of truth (arguments no. 4 to 8 on the previous pages) don't provide a very strong case for Canadian protection. The principal explanation for tariffs is not economic, but political: In the political process, producers' interests are generally given greater weight than consumers' interests.

THE DEVELOPMENT OF TRADE POLICY IN CANADA AND ELSEWHERE

Figure 32-1 illustrates how Canadian tariff policy has fluctuated in the past. Two trends stand out clearly: A dramatic increase in tariff levels until 1890, and a gradual fall in tariffs since then—except during the Great Depression of the 1930s when the Canadian government raised tariffs in an attempt to protect domestic employment.

The tariff increases of the 1880s were introduced (under the name of the National Policy) by the government of John A. Macdonald in 1879. A high tariff at that time was seen as part of the policy of nation building: By making imports more expensive, the policy would induce Canadian consumers to buy more goods from the industrial firms in Ontario and Quebec,

whose growth would be stimulated; the reduction in north-south trade would stimulate east-west trade between the Canadian provinces. (More east-west trade was also to be encouraged by the Canadian Pacific Railway that was to be built in the 1880s.) But the policy of high tariff protection was controversial then, as it has remained since. It meant higher prices not only for people in Ontario and Quebec, where the industrial growth was concentrated, but also for consumers in the West and the Maritime provinces where there was little industrial growth. In particular, a wheat-exporting province like Saskatchewan received no benefit from a tariff that protected Canadian manufacturing. The only effect of this tariff was to raise prices that residents of Saskatchewan had to pay for manufactured goods.

During the decades before the Great Depression, Canadian tariffs gradually fell from the high levels of the late nineteenth century. As we noted above, however, tariffs were raised substantially in the 1930s, on imports from countries outside the Commonwealth. (Under the system of Commonwealth Preference, members of the Commonwealth imposed lower tariffs on imports from other member countries. The effects of such a system of preferential tariffs are discussed in Appendix 32-B.)

Since the 1930s, the trend in tariff protection has again been downwards. A large reduction in average tariffs took place in 1935, through a *bilateral* (two-way) agreement between Canada and the United States in which both countries agreed to cut tariffs on imports from the other. The downward trend continued after the Second World War. Since 1947, however, there has been less emphasis on bilateral tariff negotiations, under which Canada negotiates tariff reductions with one country at a time. Instead, we have participated in the *multilateral* negotiations in which the many countries belonging to the General Agreement on Tariffs and Trade (GATT) agree to cut their tariffs against all other member countries simultaneously.

> *Multilateral* trade negotiations involve tariff reductions by all participating countries. *Bilateral* negotiations involve only two countries.

The 1965 Auto Pact with the United States was an exception to this trend toward more emphasis on multilateral measures, since the reduction in tariffs on cars and car parts under this agreement initially applied only to trade between the United States and Canada. (For more detail on the Auto Pact, see Box 32-3.) And by the mid-1980s, a bilateral issue had once again moved to the forefront of the trade policy debate in Canada: In 1985, the Mulroney government formally asked the U.S. government to start negotiations concerning a bilateral free trade agreement between Canada and the United States. We will return to this issue below.

The European Economic Community (EEC)

An important development in international trade took place in the late 1950s when the European Economic Community (EEC) was formed. West Germany, France, Italy, the Netherlands, Belgium, and Luxembourg (later joined by Britain and several other countries) agreed to form a *common market*. Its provisions included tariff-free trade among all participating nations; a common tariff against goods coming into the EEC from other countries; and other measures of economic coordination, such as a common policy of agricultural price supports.

One of the reasons for the formation of the EEC was that the member countries eventually wanted to move some distance toward political union. But they also had a strong economic motive: to gain the benefits of freer trade among themselves. Since its formation, the EEC countries have made substantial economic progress, although it is difficult to assess how much has been due to the formation of the EEC, and how much has been due to other causes.

It is also difficult to assess how the EEC has affected outside countries like Canada and the United States. On the one hand, by inducing more rapid European growth, it has made Europe a better potential cus-

---

BOX 32-3

A LIMITED FREE TRADE EXPERIMENT: THE AUTO PACT

Before 1965, Canada maintained a tariff of about 15 percent on imports of motor vehicles and auto parts from all countries. Because of this tariff, the auto makers had found it profitable to supply much of the Canadian market by producing cars in Canada. However, because of the small size of the market and the large numbers of models produced, economies of large-scale production could not be realized, so that costs of production per unit were higher than in the United States. Consequently, car prices were higher in Canada—even though the wages of workers in the Canadian automotive industry were some 25 percent lower than in the U.S. Some of the consequences of mutual tariff reductions and freer trade flows were vividly illustrated when Canada and the United States entered into the 1965 *Automotive Agreement* (the Auto Pact). Under the agreement, both countries abolished all duties on imports of cars or car parts from the other country. (But some protection for Canadian auto production remained: Only the auto companies—but not private Canadian individuals—could import autos into Canada duty-free. And to retain this privilege the auto makers had to maintain certain minimum production levels in Canada.)

The result was a dramatic restructuring of Canada's auto industry. Instead of producing the full range of models sold in the Canadian market, the auto firms introduced specialization so that the Canadian plants would produce only a limited range of models. But since cars produced in Canada could be exported to the United States duty-free, the Canadian plants could now produce each of their selected models on a very large scale (for the U.S. as well as the Canadian market). As a result, unit costs fell rapidly, and the agreement benefitted Canadian auto workers: Wages in the Canadian auto industry reached the same level as in the U.S. within a few years. Factory prices of North American cars in Canada moved closer to the comparable prices in the United States.

The auto pact provides a striking example of the kinds of productivity gains (and therefore real income gains) that can be achieved through increased trade and international specialization.

tomer for North American exports. However, the formation of the EEC has presented two problems for non-members such as Canada:

1. Because Canada is not an EEC member, Canadian firms now face the special problem of being outsiders competing in the European market. For example, before the EEC, Canadian and German firms producing telecommunications equipment faced the same tariff barriers in selling in the French market. But since the EEC has been formed, Canadian firms still face a tariff when going into the French market, while competing German firms do not.

2. The farm subsidies paid under the EEC's Common Agricultural Policy (CAP) have generated European overproduction, which has resulted in agricultural products being sold at distress prices in traditional North American export markets in other countries. Thus, both the quantity and the price of U.S. and Canadian agricultural exports have been reduced. CAP has also been very expensive and divisive for the EEC. Recently, a large percentage of the EEC budget has been going into subsidies to agricultural products. On balance, these subsidies benefit France (with its large farm population) at the expense of more urban countries like the United Kingdom. This has created severe conflicts among member countries of the EEC.

The problem of being outside the EEC was made worse for Canada and other Commonwealth countries when Great Britain became a member of the EEC in 1973. Britain has traditionally been an important market for Canadian exports, since the British imported goods from Canada (and other Commonwealth countries) at low, relatively favourable tariff rates. But since its entry into the EEC, Britain no longer provides Canadian exporters with this preferential treatment. Instead, it now gives preference to its other EEC partners, who can export goods into Britain duty-free. (Further detail on the Canadian problem of being an "outsider" as the Europeans have moved toward free trade is provided in Appendix 32-B.)

The Kennedy and Tokyo Rounds of Trade Negotiations

In the early 1960s, the Kennedy administration in the United States began an international campaign to promote the idea of a new round of multilateral tariff reductions within the GATT. There were several reasons for this U.S. initiative. By reducing all tariffs—and in particular, the U.S. tariff and the new common European tariff—such a move would (1) reduce the U.S. problem of being an outsider (like Canada) in its trade with Europe; (2) promote closer political ties with Europe; and (3) provide the familiar gains from freer trade to all participants. The result of this initiative was the Kennedy Round of negotiations, which resulted in the 1967 agreement to cut existing tariffs on average by about one-third.

Following this major success, a new set of negotiations was begun during the seventies to liberalize trade further—the Tokyo Round. This led to the 1979 agreement to cut tariffs, on average, by another third, in a series of steps during the 1980s. This agreement also provides for tariff-free trade in civilian aircraft.

By 1985, a remarkably high value for the U.S. dollar had made U.S. goods very expensive on world markets. This made it difficult for U.S. industries to compete both in export markets and against relatively inexpensive imports coming into the United States. The result was a U.S. balance-of-trade deficit of almost $150 billion—that is, U.S. imports exceeded exports by this amount—and pressures built up in the United States for protection. Since other countries were also considering protective measures at this time, President Reagan, in his state-of-the-union message in January 1985, called for a further GATT Round to reduce trade barriers, and in 1986, preliminary negotiations began. The objective of this Round was not only to make further cuts in tariffs, but also to greatly extend the "codes of conduct" introduced in the Tokyo Round to limit non-tariff barriers to trade.

Non-Tariff Barriers (NTBs)

We have already described one type of non-tariff barrier (NTB)—a quota that limits the quantity of a good that can be imported. (Appendix 32-A shows why a quota may have many of the same effects as a tariff.) There are also many other, more subtle NTBs. A country may impose complex and costly customs procedures to discourage or delay imports. For example, in 1982, the French were determined to discourage imports of Japanese videocassette recorders (VCRs). They therefore required all imported VCRs to be cleared through the tiny customs office at Poitiers, an inland town far from any main port—ironically, the same small town referred to by Bastiat almost 150 years ago in his illustration of how ridiculous protection could become (Box 32-1).

Alternatively, countries may impose NTBs in the form of stiff quality or health standards that may be difficult for imports to satisfy. If such standards lead to an improvement in the nation's health, they may be justified even though they have the unfortunate side effect of restricting trade. On the other hand, they may have little effect on the nation's health; in this case, the health issue may just be an excuse for introducing measures to reduce imports. For example, at one time the Japanese effectively barred the import of Perrier (a natural sparkling water from France) by the requirement that it be boiled. The key question: "Is a health standard imposed to protect health or to protect domestic industries?" is often difficult to answer.

International negotiations to limit the range of non-tariff restrictions that countries can impose are potentially of great benefit to Canada, because a large portion of our exports go to countries such as the United States and Japan which do impose a wide range of non-tariff barriers and restrictions. For example, the United States indirectly protects a number of industries from foreign competition by means of import quotas; and both U.S. federal and state governments have purchasing policies which specify that U.S. suppliers are to be given preference over Canadian and other foreign suppliers. Since Canadian trade regulations also include a range of NTBs which impede the access of U.S. and other foreign suppliers to the Canadian market, the question of NTBs is also likely to be very important in the forthcoming bilateral free trade negotiations between the United States and Canada.

THE POTENTIAL EFFECTS OF A FREE TRADE AGREEMENT WITH THE UNITED STATES

In the Kennedy and Tokyo rounds, Canada supported the process of multilateral trade liberalization. In part, this support reflects the interest of consumers in freer international trade: The lower the barriers to imports, the easier the access of consumers to relatively low-priced foreign goods. But the support has come not only from consumers. Many people in the business community are also in favour of negotiations leading to freer international trade. The reason is simple. True, such negotiations will lead to a reduction in the protection that many Canadian firms enjoy because of the tariffs and other trade barriers that the Canadian government imposes on imports from foreign countries. But freer international trade also means easier access for Canadian firms to foreign markets, as other countries reduce their tariffs and NTBs. For many sectors of the manufacturing industry in a relatively small country such as Canada, a move toward freer trade is, on balance, likely to be beneficial. In industries where economies of scale are important, a small domestic market may be a severe disadvantage. How can a Canadian producer, with a widely dispersed home market of less than 25 million people expect to compete internationally with producers in the United States, Japan, or Europe, who have access to tariff-free home markets of more than 100 million people? For an American firm, say, that is already producing on a large scale, a small Canadian tariff may not present much of an obstacle: The low unit cost of production of the U.S. firm may be more than enough to offset the tariff, so that the American firm can effectively compete in the Canadian market with Canadian firms that produce on a smaller scale. But for a Canadian firm producing on a relatively small scale for the Canadian market, even a small U.S. tariff may make it impossible to compete in the American market with larger U.S. firms.

Multilateral trade negotiations represent one way in which Canadian producers get better access to the large foreign markets that they need to compete effectively. But such negotiations are slow and cumbersome, and will at best lead to a very gradual process of improved market access. This was part of the reason why the alternative of a free trade agreement with the United States became the focus of Canadian trade policy in the mid-1980s.

The proposals for a U.S.-Canadian free trade agreement go back a long time, and many economists (including two of the authors of this book) have argued strongly in favour of such an agreement. But there has also been strong opposition, and until 1985 there had been no formal move by the Canadian government in this direction. However, in 1985, the prestigious Royal Commission on the Economic Union and Development Prospects for Canada (usually referred to as the MacDonald Commission for its chairman Donald MacDonald, a former Liberal finance minister) made a strong recommendation for such a free trade agreement. In September 1985 Brian Mulroney's Progressive Conservative government asked the Reagan administration to initiate discussions, and in 1986 negotiations began.

In one sense, the timing of this Canadian initiative might have been unlucky. As noted above, by 1986 the United States had experienced several years of dramatically rising imports and growing international trade deficits. As a result, there was increasing pressure on the Reagan administration to impose increased protectionist measures, rather than move toward freer trade. But in another sense, this pressure may explain the timing of the Canadian initiative: Canadian exporters were afraid that unless some type of U.S.-Canadian free trade agreement was struck, they would face increased barriers against their exports to the United States.

Let us now look more closely at the potential effects on Canada of a free trade agreement with the United States. There would be benefits to Canadians in the form of (1) the removal of our own barriers against imports from the United States, and (2) the removal of U.S. barriers against our exports.

The effects of removing our own barriers to imports from the United States. The effects have been detailed in Appendix 32-A, but can be summarized by noting that it would reduce the domestic Canadian price of these imports; as a consequence, Canadians would buy more. Canadians would benefit because we would be using low-cost imports (a) to replace our own inefficient high-cost production and (b) to allow ourselves to increase our consumption of bargain-priced goods.

The effects of U.S. removal of its barriers to our exports. At present, many Canadian industrial exports pay a U.S. tariff at the border, which goes to the U.S. Treasury. With the elimination of this tariff, Canadian exporters would no longer pay this "tax" to Washington. In other words, the U.S. Treasury would no longer collect this income from Canadians. Instead this income would be transferred back from the U.S. Treasury to Canadian exporters and eventually to

Canadian labour and other factors of production.[4] In addition, removal of U.S. trade barriers would make it easier for many Canadian exporters to increase their sales to the U.S. market. The resulting increase in the volume of output of such exporters would reduce manufacturing costs because of economies of scale. This, in turn, would raise Canadian real income.

Thus, an important effect of eliminating barriers against U.S.-Canadian trade would be a rationalization of Canadian production: Canadian firms would specialize in a smaller range of goods, producing each at higher volume and therefore at lower cost. In doing so, Canadian producers would be responding to both a carrot and a stick. The carrot would be free access to the large U.S. market. The stick would be the removal of the Canadian tariff, which would leave many Canadian firms unable to compete with less expensive imports unless they did rationalize and thus reduce their costs. The reductions in Canadian costs (that is, increases in productivity) would allow Canadian producers to reduce their prices and eventually increase their wages. (Indeed, inexpensive imports would force them to reduce their prices.) Thus, because of both lower prices and increased wages, Canadian real income would rise.

A recent set of calculations by Queen's University economists Richard Harris and David Cox indicates that the real income gains to Canada from a bilateral removal of North American trade barriers may be as

---

[4]Since removal of the U.S. tariff would transfer income from the United States to Canada, why wouldn't removal of the *Canadian* tariff transfer income in the other direction—from Canada to the United States? The reason is that, because of the relative size of the two economies, North American prices of industrial goods are set in the United States rather than in Canada. (This is essentially true, but not absolutely so. We overstate slightly to simplify the argument.) Thus, Canadian importers must take the U.S. price as given; therefore, they must raise the price of imports as they come into Canada by the amount of the Canadian tariff. Accordingly, the Canadian tariff that is collected by Ottawa is paid by Canadians (namely, Canadian consumers who pay a higher price). Thus, any change in the Canadian tariff transfers income between groups *within* Canada, not between Canada and the United States.

Technically, we can restate this in terms of our earlier discussion (point 7 above). In North America, it is the United States rather than Canada that determines the terms of trade in industrial goods between the two countries. Therefore, the terms of trade between the United States and Canada are not affected by a change in the Canadian tariff; but they *are* affected by a change in the U.S. tariff.

high as 8%–9% of Canadian GNP.[5] The Harris-Cox calculations confirm that such a move would lead to a very dramatic restructuring and rationalization of Canada's manufacturing industry. With some sectors contracting and some expanding, they estimate that as much as 7% of the labour force would have to be reallocated from one sector to another; if one takes into account that labour within each sector would also be reallocated as production became concentrated in a smaller number of large, efficient firms, the required reallocation would be even greater. But while there would have to be substantial reallocation of labour, the Harris-Cox calculations also indicate that labour as a whole would ultimately reap a large share of the gains from freer trade: Their estimates suggest that about one-fourth of the overall gains would go to Canadian consumers in the form of lower prices, with the remaining three-quarters accruing to labour in the form of substantial real wage increases.

Criticisms of Free Trade with the United States

1. Would Canada lose its independence? While critics generally concede that greater export specialization in a Canada-U.S. free trade area would lower Canadian costs, they also point out that it would make us more dependent—not on foreign markets in general, but on the U.S. market in particular. Thus, once we have rationalized our industry so that it is geared up to serve the North American market, what is to prevent the U.S. government from using the threat of reimposing trade barriers around the U.S. market (on which our industry would then depend) in order to influence Canadian policy in other economic and non-economic areas? In short, wouldn't we lose our political independence?

There is no question that the reimposition of U.S. tariff barriers could severely hurt a rationalized Cana-

dian industry. What is likely to deter Americans from such a threat is the fact that it would severely damage their credibility in future negotiations with Canada and other countries. Furthermore (as we noted above), Americans could also be hurt by a Canadian response (for example, by a Canadian threat to impose a large across-the-board increase in the tax on U.S. investment in Canada). While each country has, from time to time, "shot itself in the foot" in retaliation for some action taken by the other, neither wants anything like an outright economic war; both recognize that this would involve an extremely high cost to both sides. Moreover, for political reasons, neither country wants a hostile neighbour on the other side of the border.

Nevertheless, it does remain true that, no matter what we do, we cannot *guarantee* that new U.S. trade restrictions will not be imposed; and a free trade area would make these more costly for Canada. On the other hand, a free trade area would make such restrictions less likely—not only because it would be more difficult for the United States to impose trade restrictions on a partner in a free trade treaty, but for another reason as well: There is a good chance that in a free trade arrangement the Americans would provide Canada with an exemption from U.S. trade restrictions aimed at third countries (not only in Europe and Japan, but also the rapidly industrializing countries of Southeast Asia whose exports have been growing so rapidly). An example of this occurred when the U.S. tariff was increased in 1971. Although this action was aimed at third countries, it still fell on many Canadian exports—but not on autos, because they were being freely traded under the Canada-U.S. Auto Pact.

In short, having our access to the U.S. market guaranteed in a treaty may well provide us with greater independence than the present system in which Canada must continuously appeal to the U.S. government for exemptions from various new American protectionist measures—at a time when the two countries have on the bargaining table other, perhaps non-economic, disputes on which Canada is expected to make equivalent concessions.

2. Would free trade with the United States reduce Canadians to becoming "hewers of wood and drawers of water"? It is true that removal of only the *Canadian* tariff would move the economy in this direction, at least to some degree. The reason is that the Canadian tariff (like those of other countries) is *escalated*. That is, it provides heaviest protection to manufac-

---

[5]The Harris-Cox estimates are described in Richard G. Harris, "Summary of a Project on the General Equilibrium Evaluation of Canadian Trade Policy," Chapter 8 in John Whalley, ed., *Canada-United States Free Trade*, vol. 11 in the series of research studies written for the MacDonald Commission (Toronto: University of Toronto Press in co-operation with the Royal Commission on the Economic Union and Development Prospects for Canada, and the Canadian Government Publishing Centre, Supply and Services Canada, 1985), pp. 157–77.

Interestingly, this estimate by Harris and Cox is quite close to an estimate published in 1967 by R.J. Wonnacott and P. Wonnacott, in *Free Trade between the United States and Canada: The Potential Economic Effects* (Cambridge, Mass.: Harvard University Press).

tured goods; and if only this tariff were to be removed, Canadian manufacturing would be likely to contract. While it doesn't necessarily follow that the resulting redirection of Canadian activity toward resource extraction would be damaging (as Canadians sometimes assume), few suggest such a policy of removing only the Canadian tariff. Instead the issue focuses on removing both the Canadian and U.S. tariffs; thus we would be getting rid of a U.S. tariff that is also escalated— and that has consequently *deterred* Canadian export and production of highly processed goods. (A high tariff is imposed on these goods at the U.S. border; we tend therefore to concentrate more heavily on exporting unprocessed resources, which enter the United States with low or zero duty.)

> An *escalated* tariff is very low (or zero) on resources, but rises (escalates) as goods become more and more highly processed.

In short, the Canadian tariff encourages us to concentrate more heavily on highly processed goods, while the U.S. tariff pushes us in the other direction, toward concentrating on resources. If both tariffs were removed— with their largely offsetting effects—it's not clear that we would move dramatically in one direction or the other. Indeed, the implication of the Harris-Cox and Wonnacott studies is that, if anything, we would be likely to move slightly toward more concentration on industry and less on resource extraction. The reason is that the existing Canadian industrial corridor between Windsor and Quebec City is a reasonably good location to produce highly processed goods for North American distribution—provided trade is unrestricted. This corridor is at the northern edge of the largest market in North America—that is, the market enclosed in the Chicago/Boston/Baltimore triangle. In this respect, Toronto is in a considerably better location than the "out-of-the-way" Minneapolis–St. Paul area (which, despite its location, has been able to attract and retain considerable industry in free trade competition with other U.S. cities).

3. Could Canadian industry survive the period of adjustment? While some critics argue that there is no way that Canada could compete with the United States, other critics take a more subtle view: They recognize that if we had always had free trade between the two countries, industry would not end at the border; there

would be an industry in Canada, and because of free trade competition, it would be more efficient, specialized, and internationally competitive than at present. But the problem is that we have not in fact had free trade with the United States. Because of a history of North American protection, we have a small-volume industry; and we wouldn't be able to get the long-run benefits of trade liberalization without putting Canadian industry through a painful short-run period of adjustment and rationalization—during which many jobs would be lost as small and inefficient plants closed down and production in some sectors decreased.

In evaluating the potential employment effects of a free trade agreement, however, we should not only consider the jobs that would be lost because of increased competition from imports; we should also take into account the jobs that would be *created* in response to better export opportunities. Studies in which this has been done indicate that the job losses in those plants and sectors that would not be able to compete with imports, would be more than offset by new jobs created by increased exports in those industries that *would* be internationally competitive. Thus, on balance, a Canada–United States free trade agreement would be likely to *increase* employment in Canada.

Nevertheless, even though the *overall* employment effects may be favourable, specific groups of workers would still face adjustment costs because they would have to acquire new skills and, in some cases, move to new communities. How could such adjustment costs be reduced? Two of the recommendations of the Mac-Donald Royal Commission were:

1. The removal of trade barriers should be phased in over a period of several years—perhaps a decade. The experience in other free trade areas is that such a phase-in results in adjustment costs that are substantially lower than expected. Moreover, since the adjustment problem would be more difficult in Canada than in the United States because Canada would start with a large number of relatively inefficient plants, the United States should, if possible, eliminate its barriers more quickly than Canada. Canadian industry would get a bonus period of a few years when it would enjoy free access to the U.S. market while it would still be getting some protection in Canada.

2. The government should create a large program (financed by a reform of the present Unemploy-

ment Insurance system) called the Transitional Adjustment Assistance Program, which should be used to pay part or all of the costs of moving and retraining workers whose jobs would be lost as inefficient plants closed down. Although the Commission recommended creation of such a program to facilitate all kinds of economic adjustment (due to factors such as changing technology, etc.), it is clear that it would have an especially important role to fill if a free trade agreement were negotiated.

Finally, in assessing the extent of adjustment problems under a free trade agreement, we must recognize that adjustment problems will exist even if we *don't* negotiate such an agreement. In particular, in the absence of such an agreement, rising protectionist sentiment in the United States may force us to adjust to a severe employment loss because of higher U.S. barriers against our exports. If this happens, we will suffer twice: First, because we will face the problem of adjusting to reduced access to U.S. markets; and second, because Canadian real income will fall if rising U.S. trade barriers force us into a less efficient pattern of small-scale production for the domestic market.

Nevertheless, the substantial adjustments that will have to occur following a free trade agreement will continue to play a major role in the Canadian debate over trade policy. The debate in 1985 made it clear that there will be considerable opposition against free trade negotiations from those groups or regions who fear that they will end up bearing a large part of those costs. Thus, the reaction of organized labour was generally negative to U.S.-Canadian free trade, and while free trade was supported in the Western provinces (who had always favoured this policy), there were many in Ontario who opposed it, in part because of fear that many of the industrial job losses would take place in that province. While a free trade arrangement with the United States offers considerable promise, it is clear that it does not provide a simple, painless solution to Canada's problems. Such solutions simply do not exist.

IMPORTS FROM THE EMERGING LESS DEVELOPED COUNTRIES

In the mid-1980s, the issue of U.S.-Canadian free trade

dominated the debate on trade policy in Canada. However, there was another issue that was causing concern throughout North America: The rapid growth of imports from a number of rapidly growing less developed countries (LDCs). In the auto industry, for example, where most of the pressure of foreign competition had earlier come from Japan, serious competition emerged from South Korea in the mid-1980s. There were similar examples in other industries as well, especially in those industries where wages made up a large proportion of total production costs; firms in such industries find it particularly difficult to compete with producers in low-wage LDCs.

The export performance of many LDCs has been impressive. Between 1965 and 1976, one group of LDCs (the NICs—the newly industrialized countries) increased their exports almost 10 times. Thus, countries like Taiwan, Hong Kong, and Korea have begun to lift themselves out of the abject poverty that still grips many other countries that are still underdeveloped. But the growth of sales from these countries has raised a clamour for protection by competing industries in the highly developed countries.

While recognizing the problem these industries face, it is far from clear that we should provide them with the protection they seek. Before making any such decision, we should ask: Wouldn't it be better for us to concentrate less on the low-wage industries in Canada that produce cheap clothing, cheap shoes, and the other low-technology products the LDCs are selling to us? Shouldn't we instead be concentrating on higher-wage, higher-technology products (including perhaps more expensive, specialized lines of clothing and shoes)?

Allowing the LDCs to sell to us not only provides us with bargain goods; it may also be the most effective way we can assist them in overcoming their poverty problem. Moreover, it may also be the method that is most effective politically. When LDCs receive grants from Canada or other countries, controversy often arises over the distribution of the grant money among different population groups within the LDCs, and LDC governments may resent it when the Canadian authorities intervene to control the use of the funds. People in the LDCs may instead prefer to have the chance to solve their own problems, by being given greater opportunities to produce and sell in our markets.

KEY POINTS

1. Trade restrictions, such as tariffs or quotas, result in an efficiency loss. (The gains from trade, discussed in Chapter 31, are eroded as trade is reduced.)

2. Trade restrictions on a good also transfer income from consumers to producers. One reason why countries have trade restrictions is that producers generally have more political power than consumers.

3. While many statements on the long list of economic arguments for protection are fallacious, some have a degree of economic merit. A less developed country, now exporting only a natural resource, may protect a domestic industry in order to diversify its economy, thus reducing its economic risks. An even stronger case can be made if the industry in question is a "promising infant," that is, an industry of comparative advantage if only it can be firmly established. (The problem is, however, that such infant support frequently becomes an old-age pension.)

4. A risk of foreign retaliation arises if we impose a tariff to try to cure a Canadian unemployment problem. Since this tariff would simply shift our unemployment problem onto our trading partners, their likely reaction would be to impose their own tariffs, thus shifting the unemployment problem back onto us—in particular onto our export industries.

5. Since Sir John A. Macdonald's National Policy of 1879, Canada has remained a country with high tariffs, relative to our major trading partners. Because Canada has participated in successive rounds of multilateral tariff cutting under GATT, however, there has been a downward trend in tariff levels in Canada, too, since the Second World War.

6. Proposals for a separate free trade agreement between Canada and the United States have a long history. Recent studies have tended to confirm earlier estimates that the efficiency gains to Canada from such an agreement would be substantial. Opposition to a free trade agreement has in large part been based on a fear that it would increase Canada's economic and political dependence on the United States. Although the issue remains controversial, negotiations aiming for a U.S.-Canadian free trade agreement were begun, at Canada's initiative, in 1986.

7. Since the Second World War, imports into North America from Japan have been increasing at a fast rate. More recently, imports from LDCs have also been growing, as LDCs become more competitive with North American producers. The increased availability of low-cost imports has benefitted North American consumers, and for some LDCs, growing exports are reducing their problems of poverty and unemployment. But a rising tide of low-cost imports may create hardship for North American firms who see their sales decline because of competition from imports, and workers in these firms may lose their jobs. Any move toward freer trade could be accompanied by policies to assist the people who are forced into new jobs as imports increase.

KEY CONCEPTS

tariff
quota
military argument for protection
political reason protection
   continues
a tailored tariff
beggar-my-neighbour policy

diversification versus
   specialization
infant industry protection
protection to improve terms
   of trade
tariff retaliation

bilateral versus multilateral
   negotiations
General Agreement on Tariffs
   and Trade (GATT)
European Economic Community
   (EEC)
the Kennedy Round

KEY CONCEPTS (cont'd)

non-tariff barriers
Buy Canadian (or American)
bilateral or multilateral trade
  liberalization

the Tokyo Round
A Canada-U.S. free trade
  agreement
rationalization

adjustment costs
the Auto Pact
tariff escalation

PROBLEMS

32-1 In 1980, United States total exports were equal to about 8.5 percent of U.S. GNP. They are more important for a number of other countries, where they account for even higher proportions of GNP (over 20 percent in Great Britain, Sweden, and Canada).

Do you think the relatively low American percentage makes trade unimportant for the United States? Which of these four countries trades most in absolute terms?

If the United States were, like Europe, split up into several countries, what would happen to the export-GNP ratio of each of these new countries?

*32-2 "The higher the tariff on an import, the more revenue the government collects." Is this statement true or not? Explain.

32-3 "Advertisers can try to persuade consumers to buy a good; but they cannot force them to buy. However, trade barriers involve the coercive power of the state: They can force consumers to buy the domestic product rather than the foreign product (unless the buyers are willing to do without altogether). Therefore, if we wish to protect the sovereignty of the consumer, trade barriers are a greater danger than advertising." Evaluate this statement.

32-4 The following statement was made earlier in this chapter: ". . . in products of our comparative advantage, . . . our higher labour productivity more than offsets our higher wage." Along these same lines, what statement would you make about activities in which a low-wage foreign country has a comparative advantage?

*32-5 (a) Following Figure 31-8, show the effect of a "prohibitive" Canadian tariff that completely eliminates our import of a good.

(b) Using a similar diagram, explain the effects of a foreign tariff that prevents us from exporting a good.

(c) What are the effects if we prohibit our exports of this good? Why, then, might our government impose such a restriction?

*32-6 "Transport costs are like tariffs. Both deter trade. If either were reduced, countries would reap increased benefits from trade. Raising tariffs is much the same as going back to shipping goods in old, expensive clipper ships."

Do you agree? Why or why not? (Hint: don't forget that the government collects revenues from tariffs.)

32-7 Do you think it would pay Australian cement manufacturers to spend a lot of money to promote a tariff on cement? Why or why not?

32-8 For many decades, Canadian and American textile manufacturers have complained that they have been losing out to Japanese manufacturers. More recently, Japanese manufacturers have in turn been complaining of stiff competition from countries like Korea and Taiwan. How would you explain to these

Japanese manufacturers what is happening?

32-9 Explain why you agree or disagree with the following statement: "Because trade between nations provides benefits, a country will benefit from an 'open border in goods.' The same principle applies to fishing. Each nation should have an open border here as well. It should not have territorial rights, since they are just a way of protecting its domestic fishing industry."

APPENDIX 32-A

THE EFFECTS OF A TARIFF OR QUOTA THAT REDUCES IMPORTS

EFFECTS OF A TARIFF

Typically, a Canadian tariff will not cause us to stop importing a good (as in Problem 32-5(a)), but will only reduce it. In Figure 32-2, we consider this case.

Point A is the "no-trade" equilibrium, while J is the free-trade equilibrium, with imports HJ. Now suppose that we impose a tariff t that reduces but does not eliminate this trade. In this case we would (correctly) expect an equilibrium somewhere between A and J, at a point like K. Thus, our tariff t raises price from the free trade level P_w to P_t, shifts our equilibrium from J to K, and reduces our imports from the free trade level HJ to RK.

The effects on all parties concerned are shown in panels (b), (c), and (d). As the Canadian price rises from P_w to P_t, consumer surplus is reduced by the red area enclosed to the left of the demand curve in panel (b), while producers benefit from an increase in producer surplus (the gray area 3 enclosed to the left of the supply curve in panel (c)). But now there is another effect, not encountered before, that is shown as area 4. This is the benefit to Canadian taxpayers because the government is now collecting tariff revenue. (A tariff t, equal to RF, is collected on each of the RK units imported—for a total revenue of area 4.)

Since the two gray benefits in panel (c) also appear as red losses in panel (b), they are transfers. Specifically, area 4 is the transfer from consumers (who pay more) to the government (which collects the duty), while area 3 is a transfer from consumers to producers. But some of the red loss in panel (b) is not cancelled out by gray gains in panel (c). This balance is the net efficiency loss to society, shown as the two red triangles

in panel (d).[6] We conclude that a tariff results in these efficiency losses and a transfer from consumers to producers. Moreover, when a tariff only reduces (rather than eliminates) an import, there is another transfer as well—from consumers to taxpayers.

EFFECTS OF A QUOTA

Trade may be restricted by a tariff, or by a non-tariff barrier (NTB) like a quota. Such a restriction limits the number of units of a good that can be imported, and has many effects similar to those of a tariff. For example, in Figure 32-2(a) we saw that a tariff t raised price in the Canadian market from P_w to P_t, and thus reduced imports from HJ to RK. An equivalent, even more direct way of reducing imports by the same amount would be simply to ban any imports in excess of RK; in other words, impose a quota limit of RK. If we do this, the new equilibrium will again be at the same point K, just as it was with the tariff.

Therefore a quota of RK is sometimes referred to as the "quota equivalent of tariff t." It leads to the same inefficiency in resource allocation as tariff t.

---

[6]These two efficiency effects are marked 1 and 2 because they correspond to the two triangular efficiency effects first encountered in Figure 31-7. (Of course, colours are reversed because in that earlier diagram, trade was being opened [so there were efficiency gains], whereas in this diagram trade is being restricted [so there are efficiency losses]. As an exercise, you should be able to confirm that triangle 1 in Figure 32-2(d) is the efficiency loss that results because inexpensive imports have been replaced by higher-cost domestic production, while triangle 2 is the efficiency loss that results because consumers have been prevented from purchasing this good at the lowest possible price.)

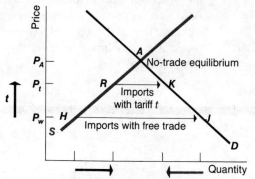

(a) Under free trade, the Canadian domestic price is the same as the world price P_w; equilibrium is at J, with imports of HJ. With tariff t, the Canadian domestic price rises from P_w to P_t; equilibrium is at K, with imports of RK.

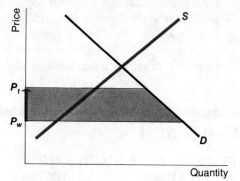

(b) Because price rises, consumers lose.

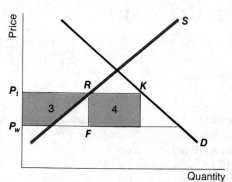

(c) But producers gain 3 and the treasury gains 4. As a result there is a transfer 3 from consumers to producers, and a transfer 4 from consumers to the treasury.

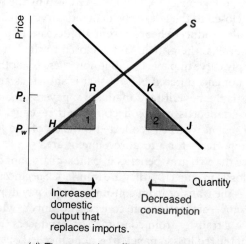

(d) There are also efficiency losses 1 + 2.

◀**Figure 32-2   Effects of a tariff.**

The domestic Canadian supply is S. Under free trade, there is (by assumption) a completely elastic world supply at price P_w. Therefore, the total supply on the Canadian market—from both domestic and foreign sources—is SHJ. This intersects Canadian demand D at point J, the free trade equilibrium involving imports of HJ. But when tariff t is imposed, the world supply shifts up by this same amount t. (Foreign suppliers now require their original P_w plus an amount t to compensate them for the tariff they must pay at the Cana-

dian border.) With this upward shift in foreign supply, the total supply on the Canadian market—from both domestic and foreign sources—becomes SRK. This intersects Canadian demand D at point K, which is the new equilibrium under the tariff. Note that price has increased from P_w to P_t, by the amount of the tariff. Imports have decreased from HJ to RK and Canadian consumption has decreased by the red arrow below the baseline. At the same time, Canadian output has increased by the black arrow; hence, employment in this industry has increased.

Specifically, it raises price in the Canadian market, and so induces high-cost domestic production and decreased consumption. But there is one big difference. With a tariff, the higher price the consumer pays for imports goes to the government in the form of the duty it collects (area 4 in Figure 32-2(c)). But *with a quota, no such revenues are collected.* Therefore, this amount goes not to the government but instead to whomever is lucky enough to acquire the quota right to import (that is, to whomever is able to profit by (1) acquiring this good on the world market at cost P_w, then (2) shipping it into Canada and then (3) selling it there at price P_t). If these rights, or import licences, are granted by the Canadian government to Canadian importers, this windfall income 4 goes to the importers rather than to the government.[7] But if the quota rights somehow end up in the hands of the foreign firms that sell this good in the Canadian market, *this income goes to them rather than to the Canadian gov-*

ernment. Consequently, this is a loss to Canada, and this sort of quota becomes a much more costly protectionist device for Canada than a tariff.

This analysis throws light on an interesting recent policy issue in the United States. Rather than administer tariffs or quotas on their imports of textiles and colour TVs, the United States has pressed hard to get certain countries to agree to impose so-called "voluntary" quotas on their firms exporting to the United States. As a consequence, the Americans have lost income 4 to these foreign firms exporting to them (as well, of course, as efficiency losses 1 and 2 that follow from any form of protection). Why, then, do Americans pressure foreign countries to impose these quotas? Why don't they impose their own import restrictions instead? The reason is that if they were to impose trade restrictions themselves, then according to GATT (the General Agreement on Tariffs and Trade), they would be subject to retaliation by the foreign country.

[7]One solution to ensure against this loss would be for the Canadian government to auction off these quota rights. Since the total revenue raised by the government from this sale would be roughly area 4, such a quota would have effects similar to those of the tariff in Figure 32-2.

APPENDIX 32-B

THE EFFECTS OF COMMON MARKETS AND OTHER PREFERENTIAL TRADE ARRANGEMENTS

In the text, most of the discussion of the effects of a tariff has dealt with the case where the tariff on imports of a particular good into Canada is the same regardless of the country from which it is imported. But in

reality, countries often levy different tariffs on imports from different countries. For example, as we noted in the text, for a long time Canada followed a practice of charging lower tariffs on imports from other Commonwealth countries than on imports from countries outside the Commonwealth. And in other countries of Europe—in the European Economic Community—all tariffs on imports from member countries is zero, while tariffs on imports from non-members continue to be subject to a tariff. (Common markets similar to the EEC have also been created in Africa and Latin America.) And if Canada and the United States do enter into a free trade arrangement with each other, a similar situation will arise: Imports into Canada from the United States, or from Canada into the United States, would have no tariff, but both countries would continue to charge tariff duties on imports from other countries. In this appendix, we discuss what happens when two or more countries form a common market. As an example, we first consider the case of Britain joining the EEC; the effects of this move were hotly debated in the early 1970s before Britain decided to do just that.

ECONOMIC EFFECTS IF BRITAIN JOINS THE EEC

Many of the economic motives for a country joining a common market like the EEC are straightforward and have already been discussed; the expected benefits include those that come from exploiting economies of scale and comparative advantage in a larger market. Such benefits from increased trade flows between market partners are referred to as the benefits from *trade creation*. But because other countries are excluded from this common market, there is now one additional important complication: *trade diversion*. This problem occurs when Britain *switches* its purchases from an excluded country (like Canada) to a country within the common market (like Germany).

Trade diversion occurs because a member country like Britain applies *preferential* (discriminatory) treatment to its imports: Those from its European partners enter duty-free, while imports from outsiders like Canada are still subject to a tariff. We can show why this import tariff may induce the British to switch their purchases from Canada to Germany by adding only one twist to our previous analysis in Figure 32-2. This is done in Figure 32-3, which shows how a country like Britain is affected when it joins the EEC. (So far, we have been drawing diagrams like Figure 32-2 only

for Canada. We emphasize that Figure 32-3 is drawn for Britain.)

Suppose that Britain's cheapest foreign source of supply for this good has always been Canada, at a price of $2 = £1. Under free trade, the British equilibrium in panel (*a*) would have been at *J*, with imports *HJ* from Canada. But suppose that the British historically have had a 50% tariff *t*, so that their equilibrium has been at *K* rather than *J*, with domestic British price at £1.50 and imports from Canada of only *RK*. On these imports, the British Treasury has been collecting *RKBC* of tariff revenue (a per-unit tariff *t* on *RK* units).

As already noted, if the British were to remove their tariff on imports from *all* countries, their new equilibrium would be at *J*, with imports *HJ* from their lowest cost source (Canada.) Moreover, the price in Britain would fall by the full amount of the tariff *t*.

But when they joined the EEC, the British didn't drop their tariff on imports from all countries, but only from EEC countries. Thus, all British imports from Canada must still pay a tariff. Approaching the British dock, the Canadian good has a price tag of £1, which is less than the £1.10 price of the good from Germany (Britain's next cheapest source of supply). That is what these goods cost the British nation as a whole. But that is not how they appear to the individual British consumer, who doesn't get to compare their prices until *after they have gone through British customs*. At this point, the Canadian good has acquired a £1.50 price tag (because of the tariff), while the tariff-free German good still has its original £1.10 price tag. In short, the German good is more expensive for the British nation as a whole, but it is less expensive for the individual British purchaser who makes the decision to buy it. So the British buy from Germany, paying the £1.10 price. The new equilibrium in the British market is shown at *F*. Thus, Britain's membership in the EEC has lowered price in the British market from £1.50 to £1.10, and Britain has now stopped buying from Canada and imports *GF* from Germany instead.

The last three panels in Figure 32-3 show the effects on various groups in Britain. In panel (*b*), the British price reduction is seen to benefit consumers by the gray area enclosed to the left of the demand curve; in panel (*c*), it is seen to damage British producers by

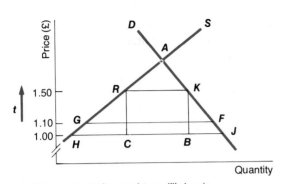

(a) With completely free trade, equilibrium in the British market would be at **J**, with price £1.00 and **HJ** imported from the least cost source — Canada. If the British impose a 50 percent tariff on imports from all countries, equilibrium shifts to **K**, with price £1.50 and **RK** imported from Canada. Finally, when the British join the European Economic Community (EEC) and allow duty-free imports from Europe, but not from Canada, equilibrium shifts from **K** to **F** and price falls from £1.50 to £1.10. This is the price at which Britain can acquire this good from, say, Germany, the cheapest European source. The effects on various British groups of this last step (entry into the EEC) are shown in panels **b**, **c**, and **d**.

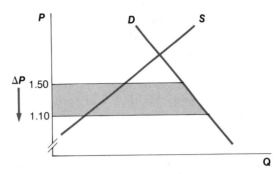

(b) As British domestic price falls by Δ**P**, consumers gain.

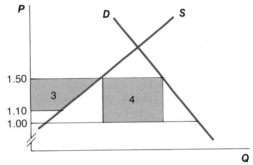

(c) But producers lose 3; and the British Treasury no longer collects tariff revenue 4.

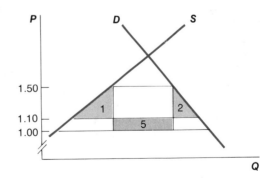

(d) The result is overall efficiency gains 1 and 2, but loss 5.

Figure 32-3   Some of the effects on the British when they joined the Common Market.

red area 3 enclosed to the left of the supply curve. Of course, there is also a loss to the British Treasury (thus, indirectly, to the British taxpayer). Since British imports now enter duty-free, the British Treasury loses its previous tariff revenue of $RKBC$ in panel (a), now shown as red area 4.

The transfers among the British producers, consumers, and Treasury that this policy would bring (that is, those areas that appear both in gray in panel (b) and in red in panel (c)) are left as an exercise. More interesting is the overall effect on efficiency, as shown in panel (d). Areas 1 and 2 are net gains since they appear as a gray benefit in panel (b), but not as a red loss in panel (c). As before, these represent increased efficiency in production and consumption. On the other hand, area 5 is a net loss since it appears as a red loss in panel (c), but does not appear as a gray gain in panel (b). This is the efficiency loss from trade diversion. Specifically, it is the cost to the British nation of acquiring this good from Germany at a cost of £1.10 rather than from Canada, the cheapest source, at a cost of £1. It is a cost that is difficult for the public to see because it only shows up in the form of lost tariff revenue to the British Treasury.

In short, because the British now have a discriminatory tariff, some of their imports are diverted from the least expensive source (Canada) to a more expensive source (Germany), and the British nation as a whole incurs loss 5 as a consequence. But it also reaps benefits 1 + 2 because its domestic price is less distorted than before; in other words, in falling from £1.50 to £1.10, British price has moved at least some distance toward the free trade level of £1. Moreover, the more competitive the price from the partner source (Germany), the greater are benefits 1 + 2 and the smaller is loss 5. (To confirm, redraw panel (d), assuming that the Germans are more competitive, supplying at a price of £1.05. Note how benefits 1 + 2 become larger, and loss 5 becomes smaller.)

EFFECTS ON CANADA OF A U.S.-CANADA FREE TRADE ARRANGEMENT

Clearly, the concepts of trade creation and trade diversion can also be applied to an analysis of what would happen if Canada were to enter into a free trade arrangement with the United States. Because tariffs on imports from the United States would be eliminated, there would be gains from trade creation, corresponding to areas 1 + 2 in Figure 32-3. But there may also be trade diversion. Suppose that for some particular good, Japan is our lowest-cost supplier. Elimination of tariffs on imports from the United States may lead Canadian importers to switch away from the low-cost Japanese suppliers to higher-cost U.S. suppliers, so that we would have a trade diversion loss similar to area 5 in Figure 32-3. It is clear from the previous discussion, however, that if the partner country is already the lowest-cost supplier, there will be no losses from trade diversion when a common market is created. At the present time, a large proportion of Canada's imports already come from the United States, even though there is a tariff on imports of American goods. This means that for a wide range of goods, the United States *is* Canada's lowest-cost supplier, since even with the tariff, U.S. exporters can undersell exporters from other countries in the Canadian market. Therefore, there would be no trade diversion losses for those goods if tariffs were eliminated; there would only be gains from trade creation (such as those measured by 1 + 2 in Figure 32-3).

On the other hand, the lower tariffs charged by Canada on imports from Commonwealth countries under the system of Commonwealth Preferences may have led to substantial trade diversion. Even though the tariffs on imports from the Commonwealth were not zero, they were lower than the tariffs on imports from non-Commonwealth countries such as Japan and the United States. The result was some switching of Canadian imports to sources in Commonwealth countries such as Britain, Australia, and New Zealand, even though imports from those countries were expensive, in part because of high transport costs. If it hadn't been for the preferential tariff, Canadian importers would have bought from less expensive sources in the United States or Japan instead. To the extent that the Commonwealth Preference system led to a switch in Canadian imports from low-cost sources to high-cost sources, it caused losses from trade diversion.

PROBLEM

32-8 Under the provisions of the Canadian Constitution a Canadian province is not allowed to impose tariffs on imports from other provinces. This means, among other things, that the Western provinces (who do not have very much manufacturing industry of their own, and therefore have to import a large quantity of manufactured goods), cannot impose a tariff on imports of manufactured goods from Ontario and Quebec, even though imports of manufactured goods from foreign countries into any province are subject to the Canadian tariff.

Many people in the West have argued that the West would benefit from a lower Canadian tariff on imports from foreign countries, and politicians from the West have often advocated a low-tariff policy for Canada.

Try to show that another policy that could benefit the West would be to give the Western provinces the right to levy tariffs on their imports of manufactured goods from Ontario and Quebec.

Part Seven

MICROECONOMICS: HOW INCOME IS DISTRIBUTED

In Part 7, the central topic will be income distribution: *For whom* is the nation's output produced? We shall be asking questions such as: What determines the income that labour receives in the form of wages? What determines the interest and profit of owners of capital, and the rental income of landowners? Why does such a large proportion of the return to capital in Canada go to foreign capitalists? Why does a rock singer like Bryan Adams earn so much more than a leading dancer with the National Ballet of Canada? And what policies can the government introduce if it wishes to change the nation's distribution of income?

To answer such questions, we shall be turning our attention from the markets for goods and services to the markets for labour, capital, and other factors of production. Fortunately, many of the principles developed in analysing the markets for goods in Part 5 can now be applied (with appropriate modifications) to factor markets. It will be no great surprise to find that factor markets are like product markets. Sometimes they operate efficiently; sometimes they do not. Therefore, while much of Part 7 will be new, much will be the application of the tools developed in Part 5 to a challenging new set of problems.

Before proceeding, we re-emphasize one of the important messages from the preceding chapters.

Almost any government policy, from regulating a monopoly to imposing a tariff, will change a market price. And when a price changes, there are two effects: an *efficiency* effect and a *transfer* from one group to another. (For example, a price rise hurts buyers and benefits sellers; thus it causes a transfer from buyers to sellers.) As we will see, recognition of both efficiency and transfer effects is important in assessing such diverse issues as the role of foreign capital in Canada, or the effects of minimum wage laws.

In the analysis of product markets in parts 5 and 6, the focus was on efficiency. But we have seen that a policy that increases efficiency cannot be judged on this ground alone; its transfer effect must also be recognized. When we shift our major focus to income distribution in Part 7, a similar conclusion is reached: Any policy designed to transfer income cannot be judged only according to this criterion; its effect on efficiency must also be examined carefully. In the box that follows on the next four pages, we illustrate the two concepts of efficiency and income transfer by reviewing several diagrams from parts 5 and 6.

Whether or not you embark on this detailed optional review, you should look at Figures 1 and 2 to get the general idea of their message. Figure 1 shows two policies with exactly the same transfer effects (wide arrows on the left) but completely different efficiency effects (shaded triangles). On the other hand, Figure 2 shows two policies with exactly the same efficiency effects (shaded triangles) but completely different transfers (arrows). Clearly, if we look at either *only* the transfer effect *or* the efficiency effect we may get a very incomplete picture.

WHY BOTH EFFICIENCY AND TRANSFER EFFECTS MUST BE CONSIDERED

AN IMPORTANT MESSAGE FROM PART 5

To see how similar transfer effects can be accompanied by different efficiency effects, we reconsider the commodity tax in Figure 1. Then, to show how similar efficiency effects can be accompanied by different transfer effects, we reconsider monopoly in Figure 2.

REPRISE: THE COMMODITY TAX ON A GOOD THAT POLLUTES AND ON ONE THAT DOES NOT

Panel (*a*) of Figure 1 shows the effect of a commodity tax on a good that creates no pollution and no other externality. Panel (*b*) shows this same tax applied to a good that does involve pollution. Otherwise, these two panels are identical. In both panels, the commodity tax will involve exactly the same set of transfers, shown by the broad white arrows. The reason that the transfers are identical is that, in both cases, the tax shifts supply from S_1 to S_2, and equilibrium from E_1 to E_2. As a consequence, in each case consumers lose because the price they pay rises from P_1 to P_2, and producers lose because the price they receive (after paying the tax) falls from P_1 to P_3. But while consumers and producers lose, the treasury gains in the form of increased tax receipts. Thus, in each panel, the broad upward arrow shows the transfer from consumers to the treasury, and the arrow pointing down shows the transfer from producers to the treasury.

While transfers are the same in these two panels, the efficiency effects are quite different. Without pollution (panel (*a*)), the tax causes a red triangular loss of efficiency. But in the face of pollution (panel

(*b*)), this same tax causes a gray triangular efficiency gain. (We assume the tax is equal to the marginal cost of pollution.) The reasons are detailed in the caption to Figure 1—but the basic idea is simple: In either case, the tax reduces output from Q_1 to Q_2. If there is no pollution (panel (*a*)), this output reduction moves the economy *away from* the efficient output at Q_1, and this results in an efficiency loss. But when pollution exists (panel (*b*)), the efficient output is not Q_1 but rather Q_2. The output reduction caused by the tax moves the economy *toward* this point, thus generating an efficiency gain.

Here is another way of seeing why this policy improves efficiency in panel (*b*) but not in panel (*a*): When pollution exists (panel (*b*)), the tax provides a benefit that does not exist in panel (*a*)—the benefit to the public of having a polluting activity curtailed.

These two panels contain an important message. In two sets of circumstances, a policy can have identical transfer effects but completely different efficiency effects.

REPRISE: THE PROBLEM OF MONOPOLY

Figure 2 illustrates two ways in which monopoly output may be increased, thus increasing efficiency. In panel (*a*), the traditional policy of price regulation is reproduced from Figure 25-7. The monopoly's initial equilibrium is at E_1. A policy of marginal cost pricing (that is, setting maximum price at P_2) will force the monopoly down its demand curve from E_1 to E_2, with the resulting transfer from the monopoly to consumers, as shown by the broad arrow on the left. In the process, monopoly output is increased from Q_1 to the efficient quantity Q_2, with the gray efficiency gain being the result.

Whereas in panel (*a*) the efficiency gain results from controlling the monopoly price, in panel (*b*) exactly the same efficiency gain is achieved by allowing the monopoly complete pricing freedom—including the freedom to charge different prices on

Figure 1
Transfers the same, efficiency effects different: The effects of a commodity tax . . .

(*a*) . . . if there is no pollution (based on Figure 20-6)   (*b*) . . . if pollution does exist (based on Figure 28-2)

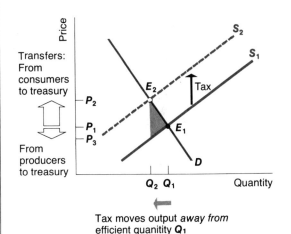

Tax moves output *away from*
efficient quanitity **Q₁**

(a) . . . **if there is no pollution** (based on
Figure 20-6)

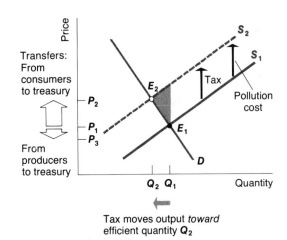

Tax moves output *toward*
efficient quantity **Q₂**

(b) . . . **if pollution does exist** (based on
Figure 28-2)

In both panels: Before the tax, equilibrium occurs at E_1, with price P_1 and output Q_1. The tax shifts supply up to S_2, thus shifting equilibrium to E_2. Consequently, output is reduced to Q_2 and price is increased to P_2.

Panel (*a*)

Transfer effects
The burden of the tax is divided between consumers and producers. Consumers lose because the price they pay rises from P_1 to P_2. Producers lose because the price they receive (after tax) falls from P_1 to P_3. (Producers actually receive P_2, but out of this, they must pay the tax of P_2P_3.) Thus, there are two transfers: (1) the transfer from consumers to the treasury of P_1P_2 per unit (the white arrow pointing up); and (2) the transfer from producers to the treasury of P_1P_3 (the white arrow pointing down).

Efficiency effect
In this case, there are no externalities, so that D represents marginal benefit to consumers *and* to society, while S_1 represents marginal cost to producers *and* to society. Since D and S_1 are equal at output Q_1, this is efficient. Since the tax reduces output to Q_2, it results in an efficiency loss.

Panel (*b*)

Transfer effects
Exactly the same as in panel (*a*).

Efficiency effect
Because pollution costs exist, the marginal cost of this good to society is S_2 rather than S_1. Since S_2 intersects marginal benefit D at E_2, Q_2 is the efficient quantity of output. By reducing output from Q_1 to this efficient quantity Q_2, the tax generates an efficiency gain, shown by the gray triangle.

Figure 2
Efficiency effects the same, transfers different

(*a*) **Regulating monopoly price (based on Figure 25-7)**

(*b*) **Allowing the monopolist to discriminate completely (based on Figure 25-9)**

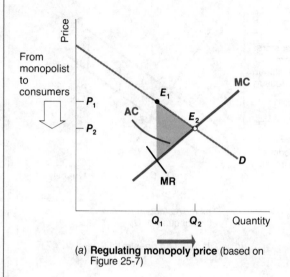

(a) **Regulating monopoly price** (based on Figure 25-7)

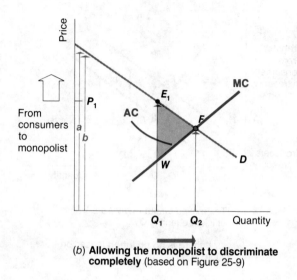

(b) **Allowing the monopolist to discriminate completely** (based on Figure 25-9)

Original equilibrium is at E_1, with the monopoly selling output Q_1 at price P_1.

Panel (*a*)

A price ceiling set at P_2 drives the monopoly down its demand curve from E_1 to E_2.

Transfer effect
Since the price consumers pay is lowered from P_1 to P_2, there is a transfer from the monopolist to consumers shown by the broad white arrow.

Efficiency effect
Output is increased from Q_1 to the efficient quantity Q_2, where marginal cost equals marginal benefit D. The resulting efficiency gain is shown in gray.

Panel (*b*)

This discriminating monopoly prices "right up to its demand curve," charging the first buyer a, the second b, and so on. This allows it to convert its demand D into a marginal revenue curve. Hence, when it works its way down to E_1 it does not stop, since its marginal revenue (Q_1E_1) is still higher than its marginal cost (Q_1W). Instead it continues to produce to F, where these two are equal.

Transfer effect
Since the monopoly is able to squeeze a higher price (a, b, etc.) out of its original consumers, there is a transfer from consumers to the monopoly. (In fact, all the original consumer surplus is transferred to the monopoly.)

Efficiency effect
Exactly the same as in panel (*a*).

different units. Suppose the monopoly is able to divide up its market and thus engage in price discrimination, just like the monopolist in Figure 25-8. However, where that earlier dentist-monopolist could divide the market into just two segments and thus quote only two prices, suppose that this present monopoly is in a strong enough position to quote a different price on each transaction. In other words, in dealing with the very first buyer, this monopoly refuses to sell even one unit unless it receives the maximum price that the buyer is prepared to pay, namely, the thin price arrow a. The monopoly then turns to the next buyer and similarly extracts b, the maximum price that the second purchaser is willing to pay. Thus, the monopoly continues to work its way down its demand curve, exercising the ultimate degree of market power by squeezing every last nickel from every buyer along the way.† Because it can thus price each unit all the way up to its demand curve, it is able to convert its demand curve into a marginal revenue curve. For example, price b on the monopoly's demand curve is also a point on its marginal revenue curve because its additional revenue from selling the second unit is b.

Such a monopoly will not stop at E_1 but instead will continue to F, where its marginal cost MC now equals its new marginal revenue D. (To confirm this, observe that the monopoly selling at point E_1 will receive a marginal revenue equal to Q_1E_1. Since its marginal cost is only Q_1W, it will continue to expand production.) Therefore, in panel (b) the monopoly increases its output from Q_1 to Q_2, the efficient level, just as in panel (a). Hence, there is exactly the same gray efficiency gain.

By now, you may be very uneasy about the way the monopoly in panel (b) is able to benefit from discriminatory pricing. The large transfer from consumers to this monopoly is shown by the broad arrow pointing up. (The height of this arrow is the

average of the price increases the monopoly is now charging its original customers.) Note how this contrasts with the transfer in panel (a), which was in exactly the opposite direction because the monopoly was forced to lower its price. (Note that there is one big difference between the discriminating monopolist discussed here and the discriminating monopolist in Figure 25-9. In that earlier diagram, the dentist-monopolist was not able to produce at all unless she could discriminate. (Her D was always below AC.) And it was better for consumers to be able to buy her services at a high price than not to be able to buy them at all. But there is no such justification for discrimination here, since the monopolist in Figure 2(b) is initially able to produce profitably at E_1 without discriminating.)

Panel (b) also illustrates why *monopoly profits may provide a poor indication of how monopoly distorts resource allocation* (that is, how it reduces efficiency). When the monopoly in panel (b) increases its profit by price discrimination, this does not increase the monopoly distortion in resource allocation. Quite the contrary: It eliminates this distortion altogether.

The message of Figure 2 may be recapped. The outcomes of the two panels involve exactly the same gray efficiency gain. But the transfers are completely different. Whereas the forced reduction in price in panel (a) transfers monopoly profit back to consumers, the unfettered exercise of monopoly power in panel (b) allows the monopolist to profit even more at the expense of consumers.

CONCLUSIONS

Any economic policy can have two effects: a transfer and an efficiency effect. If we consider only one of these effects, we will miss an important part of the total picture. For example, if we were to look only at the transfer effects in Figure 1, we would conclude: There is no difference between these two cases. And we would miss the completely different effects on efficiency. Or, if we were to look only at the efficiency effects of the two policies in Figure 2, we would conclude that they are the same. And we would miss their completely different transfer effects.

---

†Since one individual may appear in several locations on the demand curve, the monopoly must be able not only to quote a different take-it-or-leave-it price to each individual but also, in dealing with one individual, must be able to quote a different price for each purchase. Obviously, no firm does discriminate so completely. But the basic idea in this analysis still holds for firms that price-discriminate to a less complete degree.

Chapter 33

WAGES IN A PERFECTLY COMPETITIVE ECONOMY

Last week a premature blast went off
And a mile in the air went big Jim Goff.

. . .

When the next payday came around
Jim Goff a dollar short was found
When he asked "What for," came this reply
"You're docked for the time you was up in the
sky."

Thomas F. Casey, "Drill Ye Tarriers, Drill"

The wage rate is the price of labour, and the market for labour is somewhat similar to the market for a good, such as wheat. Of course, these two markets are far from being completely the same. Labour is not just a commodity; labour involves people. Thus, there are major policy issues in labour markets which do not arise in the markets for other inputs or for final products. For example, if manufacturers wish to abuse their machines, that is pretty much their own business; the cost will come when the machines wear out quickly, and no major issue of public policy arises. Not so for labour. If a mine owner abuses workers by sending them to hazardous, dust-filled mines, the health of human beings is affected; the government has the right—and the responsibility—to intervene to set health standards. Or consider another example. Some business executives have peculiar quirks with respect to their products. In the early days of the automobile, Henry Ford's attitude was, "You can have any colour

of car you want—so long as it is black." No question of public policy arose; Ford paid for his views with lost sales when competitors were willing to give consumers their choice of colours. In contrast, personal quirks in the market for labour can be pernicious. If an employer just doesn't like women workers, the government may reasonably intervene to enforce non-discrimination. Machines have no rights, but workers do.

Although the labour market is different in these respects from other markets, it may still be analysed with some of the familiar tools we have already developed. What affects labour demand? What affects supply? In what circumstances does a free labour market result in an efficient wage rate and amount of employment and in what circumstances does it not? (An economy cannot be efficient overall unless it has both efficient product markets—as explained in Chapter 24—*and* efficient factor markets, including the labour markets described in this chapter.) Other issues dealt with in this chapter include the policy question: Can the government intervene in the labour market to transfer income to labour, just as it sometimes intervenes in a product market to transfer income from one group to another? When it does, what effect does its intervention have on efficiency?

A PERFECTLY COMPETITIVE LABOUR MARKET

In this chapter, we will study a perfectly competitive market for labour in a specific industry. Such a labour market has characteristics similar to a perfectly competitive product market:

1. Workers are mobile—they are not prevented from moving from one job to another.
2. There are so many buyers of labour services (employers) and sellers (workers) that none has any market power to influence the wage rate.
3. Labour is standardized. All workers are equally skillful and equally productive in the industry being studied.

Since the labour markets we observe in Canada are typically more complicated than this, we will eventually relax each of these simplifying assumptions. For example, later in this chapter we will relax the first assumption, that workers are mobile. Specifically, we will examine the economic effects of sex discrimination, where women are not completely mobile because they are not allowed into jobs traditionally held by men. In the next chapter we will turn our attention to assumption (2) and examine what happens when this condition is not met. What is the result when workers form a labour union in order to bargain for higher wages? or when employers with market power are able to keep the wage down? Finally, in Chapter 35, we will relax the third and most unrealistic assumption—that all workers are equally productive.

Our initial task, however, is to describe a perfectly competitive market, in which all three assumptions do hold. To do so, we first address the question: What determines the demand for labour? Although our main focus in this chapter is on the labour market in a specific *industry* (such as bicycles), we first set the stage by examining the labour demand by a single firm (the individual bicycle producer).

LABOUR DEMAND AND PRODUCTIVITY

In Canada today, real hourly wage rates are approximately four times as high as they were in 1900. They have increased because of rising labour productivity.

> The *real* wage is the nominal (or dollar) wage rate adjusted for inflation. The statement that the real wage is four times as high now as in 1900 means that an hour of labour time will now buy four times as many goods and services as in 1900.

To describe the concept of labour productivity more precisely and to examine its central role in determining the demand for labour, consider the firm in Table 33-1 with a given stock of plant and machinery.

In the first two columns, we see how this firm can increase its physical output in column 2 by hiring more labour in column 1.[1] In column 3, the **marginal physical product** of labour is the increase in total product in column 2 as each additional worker is hired. For example, hiring the second worker increases output from 5 to 12 units in column 2. Thus, the marginal physical product of that second worker is 7 units, as shown in column 3.

However, the firm is even more interested in how its *revenue* increases as it hires each additional worker. This is called its **marginal revenue product**.

> The *marginal physical product* (MPP) of labour is the additional number of units of output a firm can produce because it has hired one more unit of labour.
> The *marginal revenue product* (MRP) of labour is the amount the firm's revenue increases because it has hired one more unit of labour.

The marginal revenue product for the firm in Table 33-1 is calculated in the last column on the assumption that this firm is selling its output in a perfectly competitive market in which it cannot influence price. Specifically, the price of its output remains $20 a unit

---

[1] These figures come directly from the firm's short-run production function in Table 22-2.

Table 33-1
Marginal Physical Product and Marginal Revenue Product of Labour†

(1) Number of workers	(2) Total physical product	(3) Marginal physical product, MPP (change in column 2 because one more worker is hired)	(4) Price per unit of product	(5) Marginal revenue product, MRP (5) = (3) × (4)
0	0			
		5	$20	$100
1	5			
		7	$20	$140
2	12			
		6	$20	$120
3	18			
		3	$20	$ 60
4	21			
		2	$20	$ 40
5	23			

In this hypothetical example, marginal physical product falls, provided that more than two workers are hired (column 3). Thus, beyond the second worker there are diminishing returns to labour.

†Shown for a hypothetical firm with a given capital stock and selling in a competitive market at a constant price.

in column 4, no matter how many units it sells. In this case, we calculate the additional revenue from hiring the second worker to be $140—that is, the 7 additional units that the second worker produces times the $20 price of each unit. Observe that in this example, each marginal revenue product item in the last column is just the marginal physical product in column 3 times the $20 price; that is, it is just the **value of the marginal product.**

Value of marginal product (VMP) = marginal physical product times product price

We emphasize that, as long as there is perfect competition in the product market, with product price being constant—as we assume hereafter—then the firm's marginal revenue product will be the same as the value of its marginal product. (However, when the product is sold in an imperfect market, with the prices in column 4 consequently changing rather than constant, then MRP and VMP are *not* the same. An example is given in Problem 33-3.)

How many units of labour will the firm hire? To answer this question, we first take the marginal revenue product figures in the last column of Table 33-1 and graph them as the black line in Figure 33-1. If the

daily wage paid to each worker is the $60 shown by the red line in Figure 33-1, this firm will stop hiring when it has employed four workers. (The fifth won't be hired because that worker would provide only $40 of additional revenue, but would cost $60 to hire.) Note in Figure 33-1 that in deciding on how much labour to hire, the firm is using a familiar guideline. It is hiring labour up to the point where the marginal benefit it provides (the marginal revenue product of labour) is equal to its marginal cost (the wage rate).

In a perfectly competitive labour market, the profit-maximizing firm hires labour to the point where the marginal revenue product of labour equals the wage rate. (33-1)

It is important to note that what is true of labour is also true of any other factor.

Provided that factor markets are perfectly competitive, the firm hires *each* factor of production to the point where its marginal revenue product equals the payment that must be made for it. A further example of this general principle will appear—in somewhat disguised form—in Figure 35-1. (33-2)

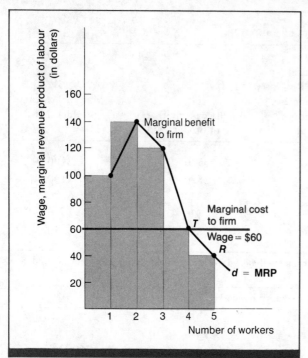

Figure 33-1   A firm's demand for labour is the marginal revenue product of labour (column 5 of Table 33-1).
The points on the MRP curve represent points on the firm's demand curve. For example, point T on the MRP curve is also on the demand curve, because at a wage rate of $60, the firm hires four workers.

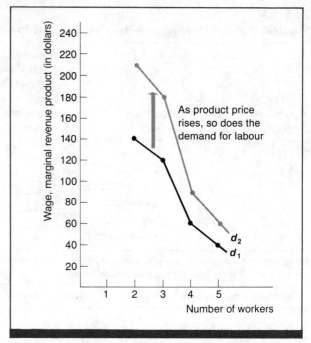

Figure 33-2   The firm's derived demand for labour.
d_1 is the marginal revenue product of labour when product price is $20. (It is calculated in column 5 of Table 33-1, and has already appeared as d in Figure 33-1.) d_2 is the marginal revenue product of labour if product price rises to $30. (This is a recalculation of column 5 in Table 33-1, with $30 replacing $20 in column 4.)

Now let's return to the labour market. So long as the firm is selling its output in a perfectly competitive market—that is, so long as its marginal revenue product is the same as the value of its marginal product—conclusion 33-1, above, can be restated:

The profit-maximizing firm will hire labour to the point where the value of the marginal product equals the wage rate.   (33-3)

The next question is: What is the firm's demand curve for labour? The answer is: its marginal revenue product curve. To see why, note that point T on the firm's MRP curve is also a point on its demand curve (since, at a $60 wage, the firm hires four workers). Similarly, any other point on this MRP curve, say R, is also a point on the firm's demand curve. (At a $40 wage, the firm would hire five workers.) With each point on the MRP curve representing a point on the

labour demand curve, the two curves coincide. Accordingly, the MRP curve in Figure 33-1 is labelled the demand curve for labour.

Whenever you see a demand curve for labour, you should visualize the bars enclosed beneath it, such as the bars shown in Figure 33-1. Each bar shows the marginal benefit of hiring another worker—that is, the marginal revenue product or the value of the marginal product of that worker.

Finally, you should now work through Problem 33-1 to see how the firm's income is divided between the wages it pays to labour and the amount it has left over to pay interest, profit, and rent to other factors of production. This will be a useful introduction to our discussion later in this chapter of how income is divided.

What Causes a Shift in Labour Demand?

Another way of asking this question is: What causes a shift in the marginal revenue product schedule in column 5 of Table 33-1? There are two reasons. First, there may be a change in the price of the firm's output in column 4. For example, if this price rises from $20 to $30, then all the marginal revenue product figures in column 5 will correspondingly rise, causing the demand for labour to shift upward to d_2 in Figure 33-2. Examples of such a shift in demand include the increased demand for carpenters resulting from an increase in the price of houses, and the increased demand for farm labour following an increase in the price of wheat. Both these examples illustrate the **derived demand** for labour. Labour is demanded, not for its own sake directly, but for the goods and services it produces.

> *Derived demand* exists when a good or service is demanded because of its usefulness in producing some other good or service. Thus, there is a derived demand for labour to produce cars, and for land to grow wheat.

The second reason that the demand for labour may shift up—that is, the MRP values in the last column of Table 33-1 may increase—is that the marginal physical product of labour in column 3 may increase. Such an increase can result from an increase in the education or training of the workforce, an expanded use of *capital,* or an improvement in *technology.* For example, if more capital equipment is installed in a factory, the existing workforce may be able to produce more.[2]

If a new type of machine is designed or a better layout for the factory is discovered, technology is improved, and workers consequently may be able to produce more. Often changes in the quantity of capital come hand in hand with improvements in technology. For example, when computers improve, firms may increase the number of computers they use.

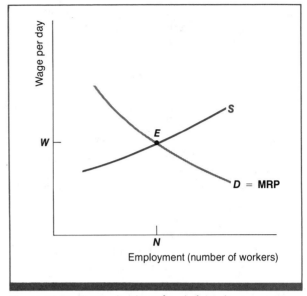

Figure 33-3 Determination of an industry's wage rate.
In a perfectly competitive labour market, the wage rate W is determined by the intersection of the demand and supply curves for labour.

It should be recognized that, in some cases, improvements in technology may result in a short-run *reduction* in the demand for labour. For example, when new weaving machinery was introduced during the Industrial Revolution, some textile workers lost their jobs. However, in the long run, even such "labour-saving" improvements bring increased demand for labour and higher wages in the economy as a whole (as we shall see in Box 34-1).

The Labour Market for an Industry

Now let us turn from the demand for labour by a firm to the demand for labour by an industry. In a perfectly competitive economy, the industry's demand for labour is the horizontal sum of the demands by the individual firms in somewhat the same way that the market demand for a good (see Figure 21-1) is the sum of the demands of individual consumers.[3] Such an industry demand curve for labour (D) is shown in Figure 33-3,

---

[2]For readers who have studied Appendix 23A, suppose the amount of capital employed in Table 23-1 is increased from one unit to two. We now read along the second-last row, rather than the last row. Regardless of how much labour is employed, more output is produced; that is, each output figure in the second-last row is larger than the corresponding figure in the last row.

What happens if there is a technological improvement? The answer: All numbers in the table increase.

[3]In fact, the industry's demand for labour is not exactly the horizontal sum of the demands by the individual firms. To see why, note that if the wage rate falls, each firm hires more workers, as shown by the individual labour demand curves. But this increased hiring results in increased industry output, which depresses the price of that output. This, in turn, shifts the labour demand curve of each

along with the industry supply curve, S, which will be described later. Together, industry S and D determine the industry wage rate W.

The Demand for Labour and the Division of Income

One of our major interests in the rest of this book is to examine how the nation's income is divided. The marginal revenue product of labour curve (the demand for labour) can throw light on this issue. Specifically, in this section we shall show how the income share going to labour and the income share going to other factors of production in an industry can be read off the MRP curve shown in Figure 33-4.

Suppose equilibrium in this labour market is at E, with wage W (reproduced from Figure 33-3). What is the industry's total revenue?[4] The employment of the first worker produces output worth a, the bar on the left in Figure 33-4; that is, the marginal revenue product of the first worker is a. The second worker adds b, and so on to the last worker, who adds j. The total revenue of the industry is the sum of all these bars— that is, shaded areas 1 + 2.

What part of this total revenue goes to labour? The answer is area 2, since wage W is paid to the N workers employed. Thus, if the labour market is competitive, we can summarize how the industry's revenue is distributed in the following two statements:

Labour receives income equal to the wage rate times the number of workers employed. This labour income is the rectangle to the southwest of the equilibrium point on the labour demand curve.

After labour is paid area 2, area 1 remains. This is

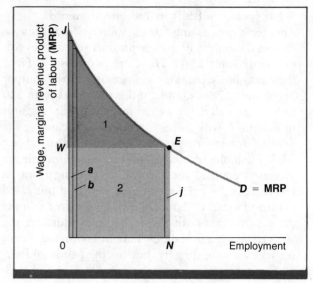

Figure 33-4 An industry's marginal revenue product of labour curve and the distribution of income.
Total income earned by all factors of production is area 1 + 2. Of this, area 2 is paid to labour, and area 1 goes to other factors of production.

what employers have left to distribute to other factors of production: interest and profit to capital, rent to land, and so on. Thus:

After labour is paid, all other factors of production together receive the triangular area enclosed to the northwest of the equilibrium point on the labour demand curve.

AN INDUSTRY'S SUPPLY OF LABOUR IN A PERFECTLY COMPETITIVE ECONOMY

The labour supply for an industry, first shown in Figure 33-3, is now reproduced for more detailed examination in Figure 33-5. As the wage rate rises from W_1 to W_2, the labour supplied to this industry increases from N_1 to N_2 as workers are drawn in from other industries by this increasingly attractive wage rate. As a specific example, the labour supply curve for this industry—say the furniture industry—tells us that when the wage rate rises to W_3, worker a is drawn into this industry.

individual firm. (Remember, each of these curves is drawn on the assumption that output price does *not* change.)

In short, the individual demand curves we are trying to sum do not remain fixed. In ignoring this problem, we recognize that the statements we make from now on will only be approximations. (As one might expect, there are many other such complications in economics.)

[4]More precisely, instead of an industry's total revenue, we mean the industry's value added—that is, the value of the industry's output after deducting the costs of all its inputs purchased from other industries (like the cost of steel to the auto industry). Throughout this analysis we define value of output in this value-added sense.

In order to persuade this worker to move, the wage rate W_3 must be high enough to cover the individual's *transfer price*. Specifically, the wage must be high enough to compensate the worker for:

1. the wage paid in the industry from which the worker is moving, say, the textile industry
2. moving costs, both financial and psychological
3. differences in the attractiveness of working in the furniture industry, compared to the textile industry.

Item 2 need not be very great. It may be zero—if the worker is moving from a textile factory to a furniture factory next door, and needs to make no change in residence or commuting arrangements. Item 3 may be either positive or negative: If the new job in furniture is less attractive than the old job in textiles, a higher wage will be needed to induce the worker to move. If, on the other hand, the new job in furniture is more attractive, then the worker may be willing to come for a *lower* wage than in the old textile job. (More detail on items 2 and 3 will be provided later.)

For the moment, we focus on the first item, which is usually the most important. The wage in the textile industry the worker is leaving was also the value of the worker's marginal product there. (Remember from statement 33-3 that in the perfectly competitive economy we are studying, the wage in any industry is equal to the value of the worker's marginal product there.) Thus, the height of the bar FC represents the value of worker a's output in the alternative activity of producing textiles. This is the opportunity cost of having this worker in the furniture industry. We conclude that:

In a perfectly competitive economy, the height of a single industry's labour supply curve measures the opportunity cost to society of having another worker hired in this industry.

This leads us to the appropriate way to view a labour supply curve:

Whenever you see a labour supply curve for an industry, you should visualize a whole set of bars beneath it, with each representing the value of the output—or the wage—of that worker in another industry.

In most of this chapter and the next, we concentrate on the supply of labour facing an individual industry, leaving to the appendix our description of the supply of labour for the *economy as a whole*. However, note in passing that, when we examine the economy-wide labour supply the question is no longer "As the wage rate rises, how many workers will be attracted in from other industries?" since there are no "other industries." Instead, other questions come to the fore, such as "If the wage rate rises, will workers sacrifice some leisure to work more?"

THE "INVISIBLE HAND" IN A PERFECTLY COMPETITIVE LABOUR MARKET

Does Adam Smith's "invisible hand" work in factor markets as it did in product markets? In a perfectly competitive economy, will market prices result in an efficient allocation of labour?

Panel (*a*) in Figure 33-6 illustrates a labour market in a perfectly competitive economy. The quantity of employment is N_1 and the wage is W_1. This is efficient because it satisfies our criterion: The marginal benefit to society of any activity (in this case, hiring labour) must be equal to its marginal cost to society. The two

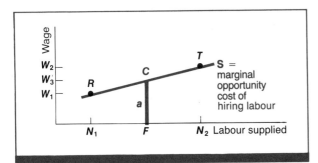

Figure 33-5 Supply of labour for the furniture industry. The rising supply curve for labour shows how an increase in the wage paid by the furniture industry increases the number of workers seeking jobs there. Moreover, in a perfectly competitive economy, the height of the supply curve at any point like C reflects the opportunity cost of hiring another worker a in the furniture industry—that is, the value of his or her marginal product in the previous job in the textile industry. Thus, the supply curve for labour reflects the opportunity cost of hiring one more worker, just as the supply curve for a product reflects the cost of producing one more unit of output.

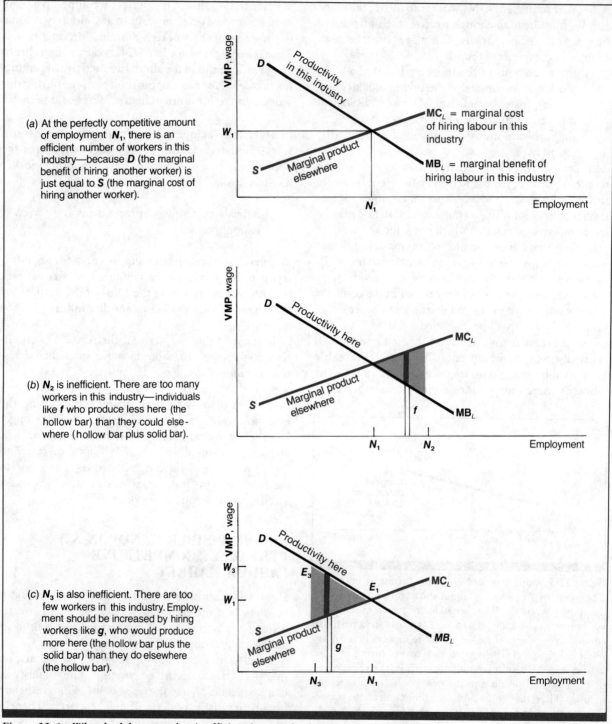

(a) At the perfectly competitive amount of employment N_1, there is an efficient number of workers in this industry—because D (the marginal benefit of hiring another worker) is just equal to S (the marginal cost of hiring another worker).

(b) N_2 is inefficient. There are too many workers in this industry—individuals like f who produce less here (the hollow bar) than they could elsewhere (hollow bar plus solid bar).

(c) N_3 is also inefficient. There are too few workers in this industry. Employment should be increased by hiring workers like g, who would produce more here (the hollow bar plus the solid bar) than they do elsewhere (the hollow bar).

Figure 33-6   Why the labour market is efficient in a perfectly competitive economy.

are equal in panel (a) because demand reflects the marginal benefit of labour, while supply reflects its marginal cost. The efficiency of this result is perhaps most clearly seen by showing in panels (b) and (c) that any other solution is inefficient.

For example, consider panel (b) where, for some reason, employment is greater than N_1. Specifically, suppose it is N_2. Let f represent one of the units of "excess employment." The benefit from employing this worker in this industry is the value of this worker's marginal product (which hereafter will be abbreviated to "marginal product"). This is shown graphically as the white bar under the labour demand curve. However, the cost of employing this worker in this industry is this worker's marginal product in an alternative activity, shown by the white bar plus the red bar under the supply curve. The difference is the red bar, which is the efficiency loss to society because this worker is in this industry rather than in a higher-productivity job elsewhere. The total efficiency loss to society for all such excess workers in the range $N_1 N_2$ is the red triangle.

On the other hand, at employment N_3 in panel (c), there are too few workers in this industry. To confirm, consider one worker g who might be employed in this industry, but is not. The cost of employing this worker here is the value of this worker's marginal product in an alternative activity, shown by the white bar under the supply curve. However, the benefit from employing this worker here is this individual's marginal product in this industry, shown by the white bar plus the red bar under the demand curve. The difference is the red bar, which represents this worker's greater productivity here than elsewhere; this is lost because this individual is not employed here. Finally, the sum of all such losses over the range $N_3 N_1$ is the red triangle which shows the total efficiency loss to society. In brief, this loss occurs because workers are not hired in this industry even though they would be more productive here than elsewhere.

To sum up: There is an efficiency loss if employment in this industry is greater or less than the perfectly competitive quantity N_1 in panel (a). (Further detail on this point is provided in Box 33-1.) Thus, this analysis confirms the clear analogy between the labour market, where perfect competition generates an efficient level of employment in each industry, and

the product market in Chapter 24 where perfect competition generates efficient output.

SOME COMPLICATIONS

As always, we can make no claim that perfect competition necessarily results in the "best of all possible worlds." It satisfies only one of our important objectives: the *elimination of deadweight inefficiency*. However, it does not address the question: How fair is the resulting distribution of income between labour and other factors of production? We will defer this important and difficult question to Chapter 36.

Moreover, in practice there may be a number of departures from the very simple, perfectly competitive model we have described here. For example, there may be external spillover costs or benefits. Externalities can arise in a labour market just as in a product market. For example, the public in a large city may judge that it receives an external benefit when musicians are hired for the local symphony orchestra. This external benefit arises because musicians are thought to make an important indirect contribution to the cultural life of the community merely by living there—in addition, of course, to the direct benefit they provide whenever they play in a concert. This external benefit will mean that a free, perfectly competitive market will result in "too little hiring of musicians"—just as external benefits lead to "too little production" of a good. (Recall that, because of the external benefits in Figure 30-1, equilibrium output Q_1 was "too little"; it was less than the efficient output Q_2.) Now we consider two other departures from the very simple competitive outcome in Figure 33-6: (1) government imposition of a minimum wage, and (2) discrimination against women by employers hiring labour.

THE EFFECT OF A MINIMUM WAGE

Workers in most Canadian industries are covered by minimum-wage laws which stipulate the minimum hourly wages that employers are allowed to pay. For example, in those industries covered by the federal Canada Labour Code, employers had to pay experienced workers at least $3.50 per hour in 1985. Other industries are covered by provincial minimum-wage

BOX 33-1

ADAM SMITH'S "INVISIBLE HAND" IN THE LABOUR MARKET

Our earlier analysis of Smith's "invisible hand" in the product market in Figure 24-2 is now extended to a factor market in Figure 33-7. If all individual employers and employees make decisions that are in their own self-interest, the result will be efficient if perfect competition prevails throughout the econ-

omy. In panel (*a*), employers hire labour up to the point where they maximize their profit—that is, up to the point where *their* marginal benefit is equal to their marginal cost. In panel (*b*), workers pursue *their* self-interest by offering their labour services up to the point where *their* marginal benefit (the wage they can earn here) is equal to their marginal cost—that is, the wage they could earn elsewhere. The result in panel (*c*) is an efficient one for society, made possible because of the key role played by a competitive market wage rate. It is the employers' reaction to a given market wage in panel (*a*) and the worker's reaction to that same wage in panel (*b*)

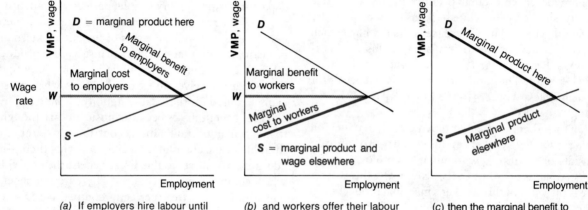

(*a*) If employers hire labour until *their* marginal benefit equals their marginal cost, . . .

(*b*) and workers offer their labour until *their* marginal benefit equals their marginal cost, . . .

(*c*) then the marginal benefit to society (marginal product here) will be equated to the marginal cost to society (marginal product elsewhere) and the resulting outcome will be efficient.

Figure 33-7   How the pursuit of private benefit in a perfectly competitive economy results in the efficient employment of labour. (Compare with Figure 24-2.)

laws. In 1985, provincial minimum wages were generally higher than the federal minimum. For example, in Ontario and Quebec the basic minimum rate was $4.00 per hour, and in Manitoba it was as high as $4.30.

The purpose of the federal and provincial minimum wages has been to raise labour income and thus reduce the poverty problem. But what effect has the minimum wage legislation had? To analyse this question, consider two cases: (1) the effects on an industry if it is the only one covered by the minimum wage; and (2) the effects if the *entire economy* is covered by the

minimum wage. (At present, the Canadian economy is somewhere between these two polar cases, but it is moving closer over time toward case 2.) To keep matters simple, we disregard the difference between the federal and provincial minimum wage rates, and the different rates that apply to certain kinds of workers, and suppose that there is only a single rate which applies in all jurisdictions.

Case 1: Only One Industry Is Covered by the Minimum Wage
This case is exactly described by panel (*c*) of Figure

Courtesy Canapress Photo Service

that ensure in panel (c) that the value of the marginal product of labour will be the same in this industry and elsewhere. Therefore, the nation's output cannot be increased by shifting labour into this industry or out of it. In short, so long as no single individual on either side of the market can influence W, it is the key in orchestrating the actions of employers and employees in an efficient way.

In Figure 33-7, we have assumed that the height of the supply curve for labour measures the value of marginal product in other industries from which labour is being drawn; that is, we have been focusing on item 1 on p. 715. But what about items 2 and 3 which also determine the height of the supply curve; namely, the costs of moving and the pleasantness of the jobs? Do they upset the conclusion that a competitive market is efficient? The answer is no.

Here's why. Costs of moving can be important—for example, if a worker has to relocate in another city in order to get a new job. Resources are used in moving the worker's furniture and other possessions. From the point of view of society, it is not efficient for the worker to move unless that individual's marginal product (and wage) in the new industry are sufficiently higher to compensate for the move. But it must be—otherwise the worker won't move. Accordingly, the operation of the market leads to an efficient result.

Likewise, item 3 does not cause inefficiency. Suppose that the new job is more attractive, and therefore the worker moves even though this individual's wage and productivity are somewhat less here than elsewhere. Since this worker is producing less output, this seems to be an undesirable move. But that is not so. For economic welfare, we should count more than the goods and services produced. It is also important for people to enjoy their jobs. If the pleasantness of the new job at least compensates for the worker's lower wage, no loss of efficiency occurs. And this must be the case: The pleasantness of the new job must compensate for the lower wage—otherwise the worker won't move. Once again, we confirm the efficiency of the competitive market.

33-6. Suppose that there is initially a perfectly competitive, free market wage of W_1 where supply = demand for labour, and the government imposes a higher minimum wage W_3. Employers respond by moving up their demand curve from E_1 to E_3, thus reducing the number of workers they employ from N_1 to N_3. As a result, there is the triangular efficiency loss that follows because there are now too few workers in this industry.

Why, then, does the government introduce this policy? The answer is: to raise labour income and thus help to solve the poverty problem. In fact, this policy does lead to a redistribution of income. The winners are the N_3 workers who still have a job in this industry, and who enjoy a wage increase from W_1 to W_3. The losers are the N_3N_1 workers who lose their jobs in this industry, or are not hired in the first place. They are left in lower-productivity jobs that pay lower wages.

Case 2: All Industries Are Covered by the Minimum Wage

The result in this case is the same in many respects. The winners are those who retain their jobs, while the losers are those who do not. However, there is one important difference. Now, those who lose their jobs do not get jobs elsewhere. Since the whole economy is covered, there are no other jobs for them to get. Because they become unemployed, they lose far more than in case 1. Moreover, the overall efficiency loss to the economy is greater because their lost output is no longer partially offset by their output in another job. They don't get another job.

Since most, but not all, of our employment is covered by the minimum wage, the world in which we live lies somewhere between case 1 and case 2: It is likely that some workers who lose their jobs because of a minimum wage will get jobs elsewhere, but some will not. For those who get a job elsewhere, there is an efficiency loss because they produce less. For those who remain unemployed, there is an even greater efficiency loss because they end up producing nothing.

Some Remaining Issues

Who are the workers who lose their jobs? The answer often is: minority groups who tend to be "last hired, first fired," and teenagers who lack work experience and skills. Because the teenage unemployment rate is usually more than double the rate for adults, a number of economists have argued for a "two-tiered system," with a lower minimum wage for teenagers than for adults. In Canada, the federal government and most provinces have followed this suggestion. For example, in 1985 the provincial minimum wage for employees under age 18 in Manitoba was $3.85, while the adult minimum wage was $4.30.

Such special treatment for teenagers has been opposed by some labour unions on the ground that employers might lay off adults with families to support in order to hire teenagers at a lower wage. Moreover, if teenagers are given special treatment because of their lack of experience, why shouldn't groups facing other disadvantages also be given special treatment to encourage *their* employment? For example, why not also give special treatment—a lower minimum wage—to workers who are near retirement, who may have lost some of their mental or physical sharpness? With a two-tier system giving special treatment only to teenagers, people near retirement face a double problem. They have to convince employers that they are not only worth the standard minimum wage, but also that they should be hired instead of low-wage teenagers.

Another problem with a minimum wage is that the increased income going to workers who keep their jobs may partly be an illusion. This will occur if employers who have to pay the higher wage cover this additional cost by cutting back on some of the other benefits they provide to their labour force—in particular, on-the-job training. Again this has important implications for teenagers. Because of their lack of experience, they have the most to lose if on-the-job training programs are cut back.

On the other hand, there is a good reason why a minimum wage may turn out *better* than we have suggested so far. In panel (*c*) of Figure 33-6, our conclusion that the minimum wage is inefficient depends critically on the assumption that before the minimum wage is introduced, there is a perfectly competitive labour market. In particular, employers have no market power. However, if employers do have such market power, and have used it to depress wages below W_1, our conclusions may be reversed: *A minimum wage that raises wages may lead to greater employment and greater efficiency*, as we shall see in the next chapter.

DISCRIMINATION IN THE LABOUR MARKET: AN INTRODUCTION

In our discussion of the minimum wage, we noted that minorities in the labour market, such as women workers, often bear a relatively heavy burden of any unemployment because they are among the first to be laid off. Worse yet: They may have trouble even before this, in just getting a job in the first place. We shall now show how they may be the victims of discriminatory hiring by employers. In this analysis we will use labour demand and supply curves to identify some of the economic effects. However, it must be recognized that discrimination also has social, moral, and political effects which cannot be dealt with in such a simple framework.

What happens if employers favour one group for the better positions and offer only inferior jobs to women or minorities such as Native Canadians, even when these workers have skill and training equal to those of other workers?

To set the stage, the left panel in part (*a*) of Figure 33-8 shows the situation in an economy in which there is no discrimination. Notice that we are now describing the labour market for the economy *as a whole*, rather than for a single industry; discrimination is an

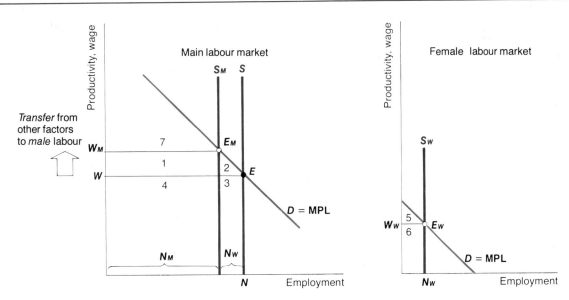

(a) How discrimination effects wages and incomes
In a market *without discrimination*, equilibrium is at E in the left panel. The wage received by all workers is W with N_m men and N_w women employed. *With discrimination*, women are forced into the female market on the right, where equilibrium is E_w. Thus women's wage rates fall from W to W_w and the wage income of women workers falls from area 3 to area 6. Meanwhile the forced departure of women from the main labour market on the left reduced labour supply there from N to N_m, thus raising wages of males from W to W_m, and raising the wage income of men workers by area 1 (that is, from area 4 to areas 4 + 1).

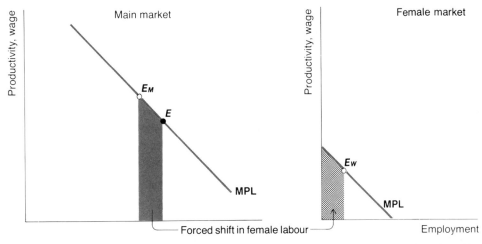

(b) The efficiency effects of discrimination
As a result of the forced departure of female labour from this main labour market, there is lost output of the coloured area under the marginal productivity curve. This is more than . . .

the output (gray area) produced by labour when it is hired in this low-productivity female market. The efficiency loss is the difference in these two areas—the reduced output of female labour because it is shifted from high-to-low-productivity jobs.

Figure 33-8   **An introduction to the economics of labour-market discrimination.**

economy-wide problem. Thus the demand curve D includes the demands of *all* hiring firms in the economy. As a first approximation, we assume that the number of workers in the economy as a whole is given, with the supply curve of labour consequently being vertical.

In the labour market shown in the first panel of part (a) of Figure 33-8, wage W is paid to N workers—N_M men and N_W women. No distinction is made between them; that is, in hiring workers, employers do not discriminate by sex.

What happens if discrimination is introduced into this market? Specifically, consider the extreme case where employers no longer hire women to do the same jobs as men in the main labour market, but hire them instead only for low-productivity, dead-end jobs.

In this extreme case, there is a *dual labour market*. The two quite separate labour markets are shown in the top two panels of Figure 33-8. In the graph on the left, showing the main labour market for men only, supply shifts from S to S_M. The wage rate consequently rises from W to W_M. In the labour market for women on the right, demand for labour D is low, reflecting the fact that the only jobs available are low-productivity tasks. Supply in this market is S_W. The wage rate is W_W, substantially less than the wage W that women received before discrimination.

The effects of such discrimination on each group and on the overall efficiency of the economy may be summarized:

1. *Female workers lose.* Because their wage rate is depressed from W to W_W, their total wage income falls from area 3 to area 6. (They may also suffer higher unemployment, which does not show up in this diagram.)

2. *Male workers gain.* Because their wage rate rises from W to W_M, their total wage income rises by area 1—that is, it increases from area 4 to area 4 + 1.

3. *Owners of other factors of production lose.* Specifically, the income earned by capital and other non-labour factors of production in the main labour market decreases by areas 1 + 2. (According to Figure 33-4, their income before discrimination was area 7 + 1 + 2; but afterwards it is only area 7.) Of this, area 1 is a transfer from other factors to the male workers who receive this wage increase. This suggests that discrimination is not in the interest of employers because it depresses their profits

(included in area 7). In other words, employers have an economic incentive *not* to discriminate; this incentive acts as a market pressure that tends to reduce discrimination. Another way to view this point is to note that there is a profit opportunity for employers who do not discriminate: They can increase their profit by hiring women at their low prevailing wage and putting them in high-productivity jobs. The more employers do this, the more the separate female market shrinks and the greater the upward pressure on women's wages; in other words, the more discrimination is reduced by market pressure.

Yet despite this market pressure, discrimination continues. One reason is that economics is not a controlling influence over long-standing prejudices of employers. A second explanation is that employers may simply be responding to discriminatory pressure from their customers. A car dealership may not hire a female salesperson if its customers are prejudiced against buying from women. The problem is still prejudice, but it may be prejudice in society beyond the hiring firm.

4. *There may be little effect on families with male wage earners.* Because some non-labour factors of production (like capital and land) are owned by families which include male wage earners, there may be little effect on all such families taken together. It is true that male wage earners gain area 1; but this is, in part, a transfer from other factors owned by such families. In addition, many families with male wage earners also include one or more women workers, so that the effect on family income of higher wages for men is partly offset by the lower earnings of women.

5. *There is an efficiency loss.* When we turn from the transfer effects to the efficiency effects shown in part (b) of Figure 33-8, we see that the total product of the economy falls. Because women workers are forced out of the main labour market, the value of output falls by the red area.[5] This is only partially offset by the new gray

---

[5]You can visualize this area as being made up of a whole set of vertical bars, each representing the marginal product that is lost when a woman is forced out of this market and there is one less worker employed here.

output produced in the segregated female market. The difference is the reduced total output of the economy, that is, the efficiency loss that results from discrimination.

6. *This efficiency loss is borne primarily by single women and families with no male wage earner.* Because there may be little net effect on all families with male wage earners taken together, single working women or families headed by a working woman suffer most, and perhaps all, of the efficiency loss from discrimination. To confirm this, notice that the reduction in female income from area 3 to area 6 in panel (*a*) is essentially the same as the efficiency loss (the difference between the red area and the gray area in panel (*b*)).

Empirical studies on the extent and consequences of labour market discrimination in Canada have focused on the problem of discrimination against women, and the debate over legislative proposals to reduce discrimination has centred on this problem as well. (In the United States, the problem of discrimination against blacks has historically been more important; see Box 33-2.) In the next section, we briefly consider the recent Canadian debate on the issue of legislation to reduce discrimination.

Discrimination against Women and Minorities: The Equal Pay Debate

Government legislation to reduce discrimination in the labour market exists in all Canadian provinces as well as at the federal level. When anti-discrimination laws were first passed in the 1950s, the basic principle was that employers had to provide "equal pay for equal work." However, in practice this wording created a problem: How do you define "equal work"? The early legislation took a restrictive view of what constituted "equal work": Even very small differences in the jobs that employees performed were considered sufficient to allow the employer to pay different wages. Furthermore, the legislation usually applied only to employees working for the same firm in a single geographic location.

Because of its restricted applicability, the early legislation came under increasing criticism. The principle of "equal pay for equal work" may have been effective in some cases. As a simple example, it may have forced hospitals to pay the same wages to male and female nurses. But empirical studies have shown

that discrimination in pay against women who perform "equal work" in this restricted sense only amounts to a small proportion of the overall earnings gap between men and women. This early legislation did not deal with a more important reason for the overall earnings gap: differences in pay between men and women who perform different jobs. To see the problem, suppose the government succeeds in getting men and women paid exactly the same salary of, say, $16,000 a year in nursing. Further suppose that the government also succeeds in getting both men and women paid exactly the same salary of, say, $24,000 a year as electricians. Then isn't there still a problem? After all, most nurses are women, while electricians are men. Aren't women being underpaid because their whole profession is underpaid? Isn't there discrimination unless you ensure that people get the same pay not only for the same job, but *also* for different jobs of "equal value" (or "comparable worth") like being nurses and electricians?

The problem with this principle, of course, lies in defining precisely what is meant by "equal value." To determine whether these two jobs do have equal value—or that one has more value than the other—one must address questions like: Which job is more demanding physically and mentally? Which job requires greater qualifications, knowledge, skill, and responsibility? Which involves more hazard or unpleasantness? And so on.

Answers to these questions necessarily involve some arbitrary judgements. Nevertheless, a number of attempts have been made by job evaluation analysts to construct scoring systems that would make it possible to systematically compare different jobs. Studies based on such comparisons have generally found that, on average, women are paid less (perhaps as much as 20% less) for jobs with similar point scores. Many observers have interpreted these findings as conclusive evidence of sex discrimination, and many provinces have broadened their anti-discrimination legislation so that it can be applied in cases where different jobs have been found to be "of equal value" or "substantially similar" on the basis of some type of job evaluation procedure.

But there are still many who believe that the "equal value" principle will prove difficult to apply in practice. The critics ask questions like: How can one possibly evaluate or trade off the greater risks required in washing windows in a skyscraper with the greater academic qualifications required in nursing? A job

BOX 33-2

MEASURING THE EFFECTS OF RACIAL DISCRIMINATION

The analysis of discrimination against women in Figure 33-8 can be applied to the problem of racial discrimination as well. For example, we can reinterpret the diagram and let the graph on the left in panel (a) represent the market for "white workers" (rather than men) and the graph on the right, the market for "black workers" (rather than women). The effects of discrimination against black workers can then be analysed along much the same lines as in the text discussion of discrimination against women.

A number of attempts have been made to estimate quantitatively the effects of discrimination against black workers in the United States. In a paper in the *Journal of Political Economy* (March/April 1971, pp. 294–313), Barbara Bergmann of the University of Maryland estimated that racial discrimination raised the income of white males with less than an elementary school education by 7% to 10%. (This increase corresponds to area 1 in Figure 33-8.) Moreover, the income of poorly educated white females was raised by an even greater amount—between 10% and 15%.

In examining how blacks were affected, Bergmann estimated that discrimination reduced black labour income by about 25% to 40%. In other words, area 6 in Figure 33-8 was about 25% to 40% smaller than area 3. Finally, in evaluating the overall efficiency loss— that is, the difference between the red and gray areas in panel (b)—she estimated that over the economy as a whole, discrimination was unlikely to reduce total national income by more than 1 1/2 percent.

What has happened since the period in the 1960s on which Bergmann's estimates were based? In the 12 years following the 1964 U.S. Civil Rights Act outlawing discrimination in employment, the income difference between black and white males entering the labour force was reduced.

However, some of this observed progress may have been illusory, because of the sort of on-the-job effects noted in the text in the discussion of the minimum wage. In an article in the *American Economic Review* (September 1979, pp. 553–64), Edward Lazear provided evidence that some employers who were legally forced to raise black wages compensated by reducing on-the-job black training. Thus blacks got higher current wages, but in exchange sacrificed future wages. (Notice that some employers seemed to be using reduced on-the-job training as a way to "partially escape" from antidiscrimination laws, just as they might use this policy to try to escape from minimum-wage laws.)

---

that 10% of the population views as pleasant may be viewed by others as downright unpleasant. In this case, do you put rating points on, or take them off? Isn't it best to answer this by looking at workers' willingness to take such jobs, which will be reflected in supply conditions and therefore the wage rate? Do we really want the government overriding labour markets? In particular, if the government, rather than market forces, is involved in determining wages on the basis of the equal value principle, how will the economy adjust when there is a shortage of one kind of labour and an oversupply of another—a problem normally solved by a change in the market wage rate?

In short, critics of the equal value principle argue that it would lead to a great deal of government inter-

ference based on the arbitrary and subjective judgement of those who rank jobs. On the other hand, proponents argue that continuing to rely on the market would allow discrimination to continue, and that's unacceptable.

The controversy over the problem of equal pay are reflected in the 1985 report of the MacDonald Commission.[6] The report concludes that on the one hand, there is a case for stronger legislation to reduce dis-

[6]*Report of the Royal Commission on the Economic Union and Development Prospects for Canada*, vol. II (Ottawa: Minister of Supply and Services Canada, 1985), chapter 15. Much of the discussion in the preceding paragraphs is based on the extensive analysis of the equal pay issue in that chapter.

crimination, given the evidence of substantial pay differentials between men and women in comparable jobs. On the other hand, the possible harmful side effects of more stringent equal pay legislation are discussed at length, and although the Commission comes out in favour of existing federal and provincial policies to promote equal pay for work "of equal value," it does not recommend any new legislative initiatives.

KEY POINTS

1. In a competitive economy, a firm will hire labour until the marginal revenue product (MRP) of labour equals the wage rate. If output markets are perfectly competitive, MRP equals the value of marginal product (VMP), and therefore the demand for labour reflects the marginal revenue product of labour.

2. Demand for labour in an industry, say textiles, may shift because of an increase in the price of textiles. Thus, the demand for labour is "derived" from the demand for textiles. Labour demand may also shift as a result of increased use of capital, or the discovery of a new technique.

3. The supply of labour for an industry reflects the opportunity cost of labour, that is, the value of the marginal product that workers could have produced in other industries. (It also depends on other factors, such as the pleasantness of the job, and costs of moving.)

4. Adam Smith's "invisible hand" works to allocate labour in the most efficient way in a perfectly competitive economy. If all market participants (employers and employees) pursue their individual economic gain, the result is an efficient solution for society as a whole.

5. If labour markets are competitive, the introduction of a minimum wage above the existing wage level will result in an efficiency loss. It will benefit workers who retain their jobs, but hurt workers who become unemployed.

6. Discrimination by employers in hiring women workers will result in an efficiency loss that is borne primarily by women who get segregated into low-wage and low-productivity jobs.

7. To reduce sex discrimination by employers, federal and provincial laws guarantee "equal pay for equal work." It is more difficult to identify and deal with discrimination when men and women hold different jobs. One suggested solution is to require employers to pay women the same as men in jobs "of equal value." Implementing such a policy involves a number of practical problems. However, anti-discrimination legislation at the federal and provincial levels has been moving toward adoption of the principle of "equal pay for work of equal value."

KEY CONCEPTS

real wage
marginal physical product
  of labour
marginal revenue product
  of labour
value of marginal product
  of labour
derived demand

share of income paid to labour
share of income paid to
  other factors
opportunity cost of labour
transfer price of labour
why labour supply reflects
  opportunity cost in a perfectly
  competitive economy
labour market efficiency

minimum wage
discrimination in layoffs
discrimination in hiring
dual labour market
equal pay for equal work
equal pay for work of
  equal value

PROBLEMS

33-1 In Figure 33-1 we concluded that, at a $60 wage, the firm hires four workers.

(a) What, then, is its total revenue? (Use the data in Table 33-1.) What is its total wage bill? How much of its total revenue remains after its wages have been paid? That is, how much does the firm have left over for interest, rent, and profit for its other factors of production?

(b) In that diagram, show the areas that represent:
   (i) the firm's total revenue;
   (ii) the part of this revenue that it pays to labour
   (iii) the part that is left for other factors of production.

33-2 The curve in Figure 33-1 showing the firm's marginal revenue product is drawn on the assumption of a given $20 price for the firm's output. But now suppose that because of decreased consumer demand for this output, its price falls to $10. Show graphically what happens to the firm's MRP curve. Does the firm change its employment? If so, by how much? Is this a further illustration of how "producers dance to the consumers' tune"?

33-3 In this chapter, perfectly competitive labour *and product* markets have been assumed. To see why imperfect competition in product markets is important, return to Table 33-1, but now make the assumption that the firm has influence over its price. Specifically assume that the figures reading down column 4 are $24, $23, $22, $21, and $20. Now, MRP in column 5 does *not* equal the value of the marginal product. Confirm this by calculating
   (a) MRP
   (b) value of marginal product, VMP

33-4 In the early 1980s, the Economic Council of Canada conducted a series of studies which showed that for various reasons, labour productivity in Newfoundland was lower than in other parts of Canada. What consequences would you predict if Newfoundland adopts a minimum-wage rate at the same level as in the rest of Canada? (In fact, Newfoundland's minimum-wage rate *is* about the same as elsewhere in Canada.) Do you know whether provincial unemployment statistics bear out your prediction?

What do you think of the idea of having a minimum wage in Newfoundland low enough to eliminate unemployment there? Would you then achieve the objective of reducing poverty by raising wages?

33-5 Would a minimum wage be more likely to raise the total income of labour if the elasticity of demand for labour is low rather than high? Explain why or why not.

33-6 "The wage rate acts as a screening device that determines where scarce labour will be employed and where it will not be employed." Illustrate this idea, using an argument parallel to the one used in Figure 24-5. Use the example of labour that is hired to build apartment buildings but is no longer hired to hoe field corn.

33-7 The efficiency loss illustrated in Figure 33-8 can be viewed as the result of splitting the labour market into two markets, one for men and one for women, with different productivity in each. Explain why a similar efficiency loss occurs, at least to some degree, in the Canadian labour market because of its geographical divisions. (For example, because workers in the Maritimes find it difficult and costly to move, they often stay in the Maritimes—where productivity and wages are low—rather than moving into higher-productivity areas elsewhere in Canada.) Is it therefore true that barriers to labour mobility impose a cost on the economy? Do you see why a policy of increasing labour mobility increases the efficiency of the economy even when it doesn't reduce unemployment? (In fact, it may also provide another big benefit: It may indeed reduce unemployment.)

APPENDIX

THE ECONOMY-WIDE SUPPLY OF LABOUR

As a first approximation, the economy-wide labour supply might be viewed as a vertical line, reflecting a given labour force for the economy as a whole. This is the quantity of labour that will be supplied if willingness to work is independent of the wage rate. However, there are two reasons why the supply curve may not be completely vertical after all—why the total amount of labour supplied may change if the wage changes:

1. The *labour force participation rate* may change. That is, there may be a change in the proportion of the population in the labour market.
2. There may be a change in the average *number of hours worked* by the existing labour force.

However, it is not certain whether a higher wage will lead to an increase or a decrease in the quantity of labour supplied. This is because a wage increase exerts two conflicting pressures:

1. The **substitution effect**: Since the reward for work (the wage rate) has increased relative to the reward from leisure, people have an incentive to substitute, working more and taking less leisure.
2. The **income effect** works in the opposite direction. A higher wage means higher income, and thus allows workers to acquire more of everything they want: not only more goods, but also more leisure. In acquiring more leisure, they work less.

Which of these two conflicting effects dominates? We cannot be sure. As Figure 33-9 is drawn, the two are exactly balanced at wage W_3, where the quantity of labour supplied is at a maximum. However, if the initial wage is lower than this, the substitution effect dominates. As the wage rate rises from, say, W_1 to W_2, people increase the amount they work from Q_1 to Q_2. On the other hand, at a wage above W_3, the income effect dominates. Workers have now reached a high enough wage that they can say: "Let's use any further increase not only to buy more goods, but also to buy more leisure." In other words, an increase in the wage rate induces them to work less. Specifically, if the wage rate rises from W_3 to W_4 they reduce the quantity of labour they supply. In this range, the labour supply curve is described as "backward bending."

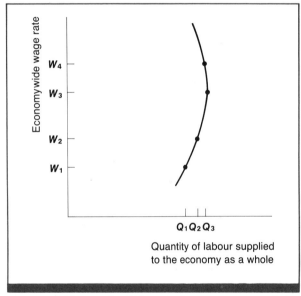

Figure 33-9 The supply of labour in the economy as a whole, rather than just in a single industry.
At low wage W_1, an increase in the wage to W_2 results in an increase in the quantity of labour supplied from Q_1 to Q_2. However, at some higher wage rate (W_3) workers achieve a high enough income level that they can afford to take part of any further increase in income in the form of leisure. Accordingly, they work less; the labour supply curve is backward bending.

Chapter 34

WAGES IN IMPERFECTLY COMPETITIVE LABOUR MARKETS

Trade unionism is not socialism. It is the capitalism
of the proletariat.

George Bernard Shaw

In this chapter we study how the labour market departs from perfect competition. On the supply side, workers in many industries have formed unions in order to influence wage rates and working conditions. On the demand side, employers frequently have some control over the wage rate. An extreme example is a firm that is the only employer of industrial labour in a small town.

When market power exists on both sides of the market, the result is *bilateral (two-way) monopoly*. This is the situation that we eventually want to study in this chapter. However, in order to work up to this complicated subject, we first address two preliminary questions: What happens if there is market power only on the supply side of the labour market? And what happens if there is market power only on the demand side?

First, we will examine unions. Although one of their major functions is to exercise market power to increase wages, they have other significant roles as well.

LABOUR UNIONS: THE BENEFITS OF COLLECTIVE ACTION

It is sometimes said that a perfectly competitive labour market "has no memory and no future." In such a market, people are hired or fired simply on the basis of what they can do *today*. However, in the real world, people work not only for the wage they receive today, but also in order to ensure a secure job for the future. In other words, people have a *stake* in their jobs. An important role of the union is to protect the stake of the workers, to give them a collective voice not only in the setting of wages but also, more generally, in the conditions of employment.[1] With the backing of unions, workers are protected from arbitrary dismissal or changes in the "rules of the game" by management. Because of these assurances, workers are able to com-

[1] This chapter, and in particular, this discussion of labour's voice, draws heavily on Richard B. Freeman and James L. Medoff, *What Do Unions Do?* (New York: Basic Books, 1984).

mit themselves to an occupation more completely than they could in a timeless, impersonal, perfectly competitive market.

Collective Bargaining

When workers gain a voice by getting together in a union, they overcome three disadvantages of "standing alone": (1) A single worker may have difficulty even getting management to listen, let alone negotiate to remove a grievance. (2) Management may retaliate personally against an individual who is complaining. (3) Even if an individual were to succeed in negotiating a change, it is unlikely to be worth the effort. Most of the benefits would go to other workers. In this sense, the resolution of a labour grievance is a public good; *all workers benefit, regardless of who negotiates it*. Negotiations are therefore undertaken collectively—by a union.

> *Collective bargaining* is any negotiation between a union and management over wages, fringe benefits, hiring policies, job security, or working conditions.

In addition to raising wages by negotiating higher pay rates, unions may attempt to raise wages indirectly by negotiating other terms of employment. For example, unions may:

1. Negotiate a shorter work week and early retirement. Such changes reduce the supply of labour, and thus put upward pressure on wages.
2. Negotiate with employers to hire only union members, and then limit union membership by imposing barriers to entry such as high initiation fees or long periods of apprenticeship. This approach also restricts the supply of labour, and thus raises wage rates.

In such negotiations, a union may, of course, have other objectives than just raising wages. For example, a shorter work week may be desired for its own sake, and apprenticeship may be a way of screening bumbling amateurs out of dangerous occupations. Not surprisingly, motives are sometimes mixed. The charge has been made that organized medicine—the Canadian Medical Associaton or the American Medical Association—have acted like unions. For example, the AMA has in the past used its power to limit the number of medical schools, and the number of students admitted to these schools. While the stated reason for

this tough policy was to improve the quality of medical service, it also restricted the supply of graduating doctors and thus increased the incomes of the members of the AMA. In Canada, organized medicine has recently been campaigning against legislation allowing midwives to assist women who want to have their babies at home. The doctors say they consider home births too risky. But skeptics have suggested that the campaign can also be seen as a way to protect the incomes of hospital-based obstetricians.

Another negotiating objective of unions is to establish clear rules on the conditions under which workers can be laid off or discharged. This is particularly important for older workers who would have difficulty finding other jobs. Accordingly, unions work hard to establish **seniority rules** to protect those who have been on the job longest, and who have the most to lose if they are discharged.

> *Seniority rules* give preference to those who have been longest on the job. Individuals with seniority are typically the last to be discharged or laid off, and the first to be rehired.

Without seniority rules, older workers might be in a vulnerable situation. Over the years, their productivity may have declined. In the absence of seniority rules they might be the *first* to be laid off. Thus, union-negotiated rules can be viewed as a way of reducing older workers' vulnerability.

In addition to seniority rules, unions attempt to provide job security in a number of other ways. For example, in the negotiations between the Windsor, Ontario, local of the United Auto Workers and the financially troubled Chrysler Corporation in the early 1980s, the UAW offered to reduce its wage demands in return for an agreement by Chrysler to keep its Windsor plant open. The UAW has also worked hard to get the Canadian government to negotiate with the Japanese government for a limit on the number of cars that Japan exports to Canada, and to get the Japanese to invest in production facilities in Canada.

While unions in the past have focused their attention on wages, job security, and conditions on the shop floor, an important question is whether unions in the future will seek broader areas of influence, such as a voice in the nation's boardrooms. Germany is experimenting with **co-determination**: Labour and management have an equal number of seats on the board of directors, with the owners making the decision in the event of a tie. This experiment has had mixed success. It has improved communication. But both sides have reservations: Management feels that labour representatives sometimes waste time by raising "shop-floor" issues such as plant ventilation and sometimes leak secrets such as proposed plant layoffs. On the other hand, labour members of the board complain that the owners are in control because of the extra vote they get in the event of a tie. Moreover, some rank-and-file workers fear that their board members may begin to think like managers and soften their demands for higher wages and better working conditions.

Before examining the detailed economic effects of unions, we first briefly review the long struggle to establish unions in Canada and the United States.

LABOUR UNIONS: THEIR HISTORICAL DEVELOPMENT

The beginning of the North American union movement dates back to an era when a relatively powerless labour force lived in poverty, or near to it. In the last third of the nineteenth century, the Knights of Labour emerged, hoping to become the one great organization that might speak for all labour in both Canada and the United States. Like the labour movement in England and a number of other European countries, the organization sought to make labour a unified force for radical political change.

The importance of the Knights of Labour as a political force came to an end in the 1880s, partly as a result of the bloody Haymarket Riot in Chicago in 1886, for which the Knights were given responsibility. In Canada, the role as the nation's leading labour organization was taken over by the Trades and Labour Congress of Canada (TLC), founded in 1886. It became affiliated with the American Federation of Labor (AFL) and its objectives and methods closely resembled those of the AFL.

The AFL, following the philosophy of its leader Samuel Gompers, concentrated on the bread-and-butter issues of improving wages and working conditions, rather than on pursuing a political class struggle. When asked what labour wanted, Gompers had a simple answer: "More."

Although the Canadian labour movement continued for many years to follow the bread-and-butter

approach of the AFL and TLC, this has been changing: Unions in Canada have gradually been taking a more active political role, starting with the association formed between labour groups and the Co-operative Commonwealth Federation (CCF) in Saskatchewan in the 1930s, and continuing at the present time through the links between organized labour and the New Democratic Party (the NDP, which succeeded the CCF). But labour still remains uncommitted on many political issues, and workers do not always vote along traditional party lines. This contrasts with the pattern in England and some other European countries, where the labour movement has been a leading political force represented by one of the most powerful political parties.

Following an early rapid increase in membership before and during World War I, the history of Canadian unions can be divided into the four distinct periods shown in Figure 34-1: (1) a period of stagnating membership during the 1920s and 1930s; (2) rapid growth for the next decade; (3) a period of relatively slow growth between 1950 and the early 1960s; and (4) a period of moderate growth since the early 1960s.

The Period before World War II

Until the 1940s, unions in Canada generally developed in a hostile climate. On the one hand, business executives strongly resisted any attempts to unionize their firms, and would frequently retaliate against pro-union workers by firing them and then blacklisting them with other potential employers. They would also sometimes use so-called *yellow-dog contracts*:

> A *yellow-dog contract* required a worker to sign a commitment not to join a union in order to get a job.

An important early question was how the courts would treat labour-management disputes. In particular, in the light of the 1892 amendments to the Criminal Code making it an offence to enter a conspiracy in restraint of trade, would the courts interpret unions as criminal conspiracies? Judgements either for or against unions seemed possible: On the one hand, a union could be viewed as a restraint on trade, since it is a combination of workers seeking to raise wages, just as a collusive monopoly is a combination of sellers seeking to raise price. On the other hand, an argument could be made for treating unions as a different cate-

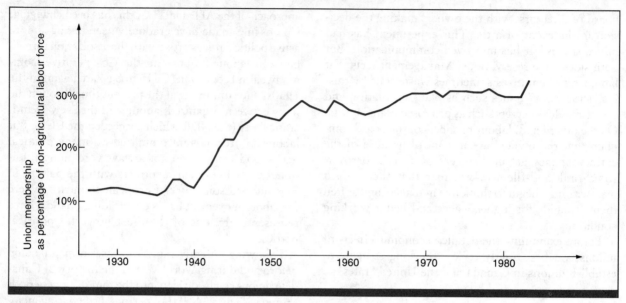

Figure 34-1   Major trends in Canadian union membership (relative to total employment).
Canadian union membership remained low until the beginning of World War II. During the 1940s and early 1950s it rose rapidly. Following decades of stagnation, it started growing again in the mid-1960s.

Sources: Based on data in M. Urquhart and K. Buckley, eds., *Historical Statistics of Canada*, 1st ed. (Toronto and Cambridge: Cambridge University Press and Macmillan of Canada, 1965), and Statistics Canada, *Corporations and Labour Unions Returns Act*, various years. Statistics Canada data reproduced by permission of the Minister of Supply and Services Canada.

gory on the grounds that "labour is not an article of commerce." By and large, the courts' judgements during this early period did not favour labour.

There were several other reasons why union growth was thwarted during the 1920s and early 1930s. The TLC in Canada (like the AFL in the United States) lost ground because it remained committed to the early principle of **craft unions**, that is, unions representing workers with a common skill. Craft unions did not appeal to the increasing number of unskilled workers in mass production industries, such as steel and autos. These workers felt that they would be more effectively represented by **industrial unions** comprising all workers within a given industry.

A *craft union*, such as a plumbers' or carpenters' union, represents a group of workers having a common skill, regardless of the industry in which they are working.

An *industrial union*, such as the United Auto Workers, draws on all workers in an industry or group of industries, regardless of the workers' specific skills.

Moreover, there was growth in employer resistance to unionism. Employers introduced paternalistic schemes providing labour with relatively generous benefits in an attempt to demonstrate that workers would do better outside a union than in. And as a result of growing court hostility toward unions, employers were allowed to use injunctions (court orders) to prevent unions from picketing, striking, or pursuing almost any other activity judged threatening to business.

The Period of Rapid Union Growth during and after World War II
In the latter half of the 1930s, union membership grew quickly in the United States. This was facilitated by several new U.S. laws that improved the climate for unions. In the 1932 Norris–La Guardia Act, yellow-dog contracts were outlawed, and the 1935 Wagner act firmly declared that workers had the legal right to form unions; it also prohibited employers from certain unfair labour practices, such as firing and blacklisting pro-union workers.

In contrast, Canadian union membership grew very slowly during the 1930s: Canadian labour legislation remained relatively unchanged during the Depression. It was not until the beginning of the war that Canadian labour law began to be reformed. In 1939, the Criminal Code was amended so that it became illegal for an employer to dismiss an employee for being a member of a union, and later during the war the government explicitly recognized the right of workers to organize.

An important landmark in Canadian labour law came at the end of 1945, following a long strike by workers of the Ford Motor Company of Canada over the issue of union security. The strike was ended when an arbitration decision was given by Mr. Justice Ivan Rand of Canada's Supreme Court. In his decision, Mr. Justice Rand spelled out a series of rules that have since become known as the **Rand Formula**. Specifically, the Rand Formula made it compulsory for all Ford workers to contribute to the union (through a dues check-off system administered by the company), whether or not they belonged to the union. It also required that a government-supervised vote by all employees had to be held before there could be a strike, and specified penalties for illegal strikes during the term of a collective agreement. The Rand Formula set an important precedent on the question of the rights of unions, and various versions of the formula have been used in a large number of collective agreements; in Ontario, it has recently been incorporated into the province's labour laws.

Apart from the legislative changes strengthening the position of unions, the rapid growth of union membership in Canada and in the United States during the 1940s and early 1950s was also facilitated by the trend toward industrial unions in large sectors such as the steel and automotive industries. In 1936, several U.S. union leaders led by John L. Lewis started this drive by splitting away from the AFL (which continued to concentrate on craft unions) and forming the Congress of Industrial Organizations (the CIO) which was committed instead to industrial unionism. In Canada, a similar split in the labour movement took place three years later when the TLC (which was affiliated with the AFL) expelled the Canadian branches of the American CIO unions; in 1940, these Canadian branch unions formed the Canadian Congress of Labour (CCL) —the Canadian counterpart of the CIO. While the craft-based TLC and the industrial-based CCL operated as separate organizations until the mid-1950s, the advantages of labour unity gradually made them move closer together, and in 1956, they joined forces in a merger which created the **Canadian Labour Congress** (CLC). (In the United States, a merger creating the AFL-CIO had taken place a year earlier.) The CLC now includes most of Canada's large labour unions. (There are some important exceptions, however. For example, the CLC does not include the unions affiliated with the Quebec-based Confederation of National Trade Unions. The fact that the CNTU has chosen to remain outside the CLC is due, in part, to the long tradition in Quebec of unions that are based in Canada, rather than affiliated with the large U.S. unions. On occasion, this tradition leads to jurisdictional strife. For instance, construction of the multibillion dollar hydro-electric project in James Bay was halted for several months in 1974 by a strike that involved this jurisdictional issue.)

The Changing Pattern of Unionism in the 1960s and 1970s

As is evident from Figure 34-1, union membership in Canada has continued to grow, albeit more slowly than before, in the 1960s and 1970s. But during this period, growth has been concentrated in different areas of the labour market. First, relatively rapid growth has occurred in the **national unions**, that is, independent Canadian unions. By contrast, membership in the more traditional **international unions** (sometimes also called *continental unions*), which are affiliated with American unions, has grown more slowly.

> A *national union* is an independent Canadian union that has no formal affiliation with unions outside of Canada.
>
> An *international union* is a union that is affiliated with a foreign (usually American) union.

Second, growth in union membership has been particularly fast in the public sector. (Since public sector unions are national unions, this trend is one of the factors that explains the increasing dominance of national unions in Canada.)

An important factor contributing to increasing unionization among government employees was the passage in 1966–67 of the **Public Service Staff Relations Act**, which gave federal civil servants the right to collective bargaining and the right to strike. Following this legislation, membership in the *Public Service Alliance of Canada* (PSAC) rose steadily, and the majority of federal government employees now belong to the PSAC. Unions representing provincial government employees have also become important. So have organizations such as the *Canadian Union of Public Employees* (CUPE), whose members work for public sector institutions such as municipal governments, hospitals, and provincially owned hydro companies, and the *Canadian Union of Postal Workers* (CUPW), which represents the inside postal employees. (We will discuss further the problems raised by public sector labour relations later in this chapter.)

Turning to the relatively slow growth of union membership *outside* the public sector, there are several explanations. First, during the 1960s and 1970s, there was a decrease in the proportion of workers employed in heavy industry (where union membership is generally high) and an increase in the share of employment in the private service sector (where unions traditionally have been less strong). Second, the share in the labour force of women, part-time workers, and young people, has been increasing. For various reasons, it may be more difficult to attract workers in these groups to the union movement: Unlike the previous generation of workers, they do not remember the 1930s when the labour force felt desperately powerless and had to look to the union for protection. Moreover, recent events have made many younger workers less enthusiastic about unions: the corruption and violence in the American union movement, and a number of unpopular strikes in the public sector (such as strikes by postal workers, school teachers, public transit workers, air traffic controllers, and garbage collectors).

The public's negative attitude toward the union movement has been even more evident in the United States than in Canada: The proportion of workers in the United States who belong to a union is considerably lower than in Canada. (Union members make up roughly a quarter of the U.S. non-agricultural labour force, compared to about one-third in Canada.) Partly, because of public hostility to the union movement, American labour legislation after World War II has been amended in ways that make it more difficult for a union to control the labour force in a company. Thus, the 1947 *Taft-Hartley Act* prohibits strikes due to conflicts between unions over whose members will do specific jobs. It also forbids the "check-off" of union dues unless workers agree to it in writing.

But the most controversial provision of the U.S. Taft-Hartley Act is contained in its famous section 14(b). This recognizes state **right-to-work laws** which forbid compulsory unionism, and thus make the **closed shop** and the **union shop** illegal. About 30 U.S. states— mostly in the South—have passed such laws. Union leaders considered section 14(b) to be overtly anti-union, and they have worked hard for its repeal.

A *closed shop* means that a firm can hire only workers who are already union members.

A *union shop* permits the hiring of non-union members, but requires any workers who are not yet members to join the union within a specified period (such as 30 days).

A *right-to-work law* outlaws the closed shop and the union shop in favour of the *open shop* (in which there is no requirement to join a union).

In Canada, existing labour legislation does not attempt to restrict union practices in this way. On the contrary, under the Rand Formula discussed above, one of the provisions is a compulsory check-off system under which all workers are required to contribute financially to the union, and contracts negotiated under the Rand Formula provide for a form of union shop; closed shop contracts are also legal in Canada.

Because our labour legislation is more favourable to unions, and also because the Canadian public is generally more sympathetic to unions, it is not surprising that the union movement is stronger in Canada than in the United States.

LABOUR UNIONS: THE EXERCISE OF MARKET POWER

Since unions are important actors in the process that determines wages and working conditions in many industries, they must be included in any realistic analysis of the labour market. Evidence from Canadian and American studies indicates that North American unions may be able to raise wages by anywhere from 8% to

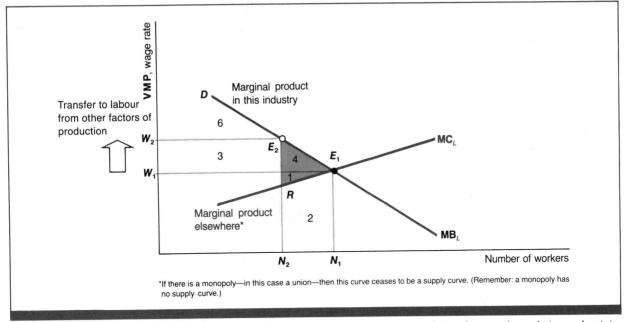

Figure 34-2 The effects of unionizing an industry in a previously competitive labour market.
When a union is formed and raises the wage rate from W_1 to W_2, equilibrium moves from the perfectly competitive point E_1 to E_2; that is, employers respond by reducing employment from N_1 to N_2. The result is the efficiency loss shown by areas 4 + 1. This reflects the fact that N_2N_1 workers don't have jobs in this industry where their productivity would be high, as shown by the height of the demand curve D; instead they have to take jobs elsewhere, resulting in the lower productivity given by the height of the marginal cost for labour curve (the marginal product elsewhere curve). The red triangular wedge between these two curves is the nation's lost productivity—its efficiency loss.

18%; that is, union members earn, on average, 8% to 18% more than non-union workers in comparable activities.[2]

In this section we consider the effects of a union that exercises its market power to raise the wage rate of its members. We also examine what happens when a union bargains to ensure employment for its members.

The Economic Effects When a Union Negotiates Higher Wages: A First Approximation

We begin by assuming a perfectly competitive labour market, with equilibrium at E_1, as shown in Figure 34-2. Employers have no market power, and take the wage rate as given. Workers have no market power, and also take the wage rate as given.

Now suppose that this industry is unionized—that is, the workers who supply labour form a monopoly (a union) that raises the wage rate from W_1 to W_2. The enforcement of this higher wage requires "union discipline"; members must not be allowed to offer their labour services for less than W_2. Faced with this wage, employers react by moving up their demand curve from E_1 to E_2. Because the union has raised wages, employment is reduced from N_1 to N_2.

Efficiency effect. There is the standard deadweight efficiency loss shown by the red triangle. This loss occurs because employment has been reduced from its perfectly competitive, efficient amount at N_1 to N_2, and displaced workers have had to move to industries where their productivity is lower. (This is the effi-

[2]Estimates for Canada, based on Ontario data, are contained in G. Starr, *Union-Non-Union Wage Differentials* (Toronto: Ontario Ministry of Labour, 1973), and in an article by the same author in S. Hameed, ed., *Canadian Industrial Relations* (Toronto: Butterworth, 1975). For American evidence, see C.J. Parsley, "Labour Union Effects on Wage Gains: A Survey of Recent Literature," *Journal of Economic Literature* (March 1980): 20.

ciency loss from too little employment described in detail in Figure 33-6(c).)

Transfer effects. Capital and other non-labour factors of production lose area 3 + 4. (As explained in Figure 33-4, they earned 6 + 3 + 4 at initial equilibrium E_1. After the union is formed and equilibrium moves to E_2, they earn only area 6, for a net loss of 3 + 4.) Of this loss, 3 is a transfer to the N_2 workers who retain their jobs in this industry and enjoy a wage increase of $W_1 W_2$. This is the reason they formed a union: to acquire area 3 of income that the owners of capital and other factors of production would otherwise receive. However, while these N_2 workers in the industry gain, there is a loss to the $N_2 N_1$ workers who would like to work in this industry but who must instead take lower-productivity, lower-wage jobs elsewhere.

In conclusion, we emphasize two important points:

1. In judging that inefficiency results from the unionization of an industry—and from the other labour market changes we examine—we must make assumptions similar to those we made in analysing product markets. For example, we assume that perfectly competitive conditions exist elsewhere in the economy. Moreover, we also keep in mind that although we can make the statement that the move from E_1 to E_2 in Figure 34-2 is inefficient, we cannot make the stronger statement that this move has an adverse overall effect, without making some assumption about how the winners and the losers compare in their evaluation of income. Remember: Efficiency is desirable, but it's not the whole story.

2. Figure 34-2 illustrates once again the similarity of the markets for labour and goods. Specifically, note how the monopolization of a labour market in Figure 34-2 is similar to the monopolization of a product market in Figure 25-5, except, of course, that we are now talking about the wage and employment of labour rather than the price and quantity of a product.[3]

Featherbedding: The Economic Effects

Job security may become the prime objective of a union if employment is shrinking—for example, because of reduced demand for the product, the introduction of labour-saving machines, or the growth of imports. There are three principal ways that a union may try to prevent the loss of jobs. First, it may seek protection from the government in the form of tariffs or quotas on imports. Second, it may negotiate a reduction in the number of hours in a standard work week; if all workers work fewer hours, no worker need be laid off. (Moreover, if the union is able to negotiate a sufficient increase in the per hour wage rate, its members may not suffer any income reduction; they may work less for the same pay.)

The third way that a strong union may deal with falling employment is to use its bargaining strength to negotiate a *featherbedding* agreement. One example is the agreement that standby musicians be hired when non-union musicians are performing. Another was the case of the railroad firemen who had their jobs guaranteed even after coal-burning locomotives were replaced by diesels, which had no fire.

Featherbedding is the employment of labour in superfluous jobs.

What is the effect of such superfluous work? The answer is that it generally keeps employment in that industry higher than in a perfectly competitive labour market.[4] Specifically, it keeps the number of jobs at N^2 in Figure 33-6(b), rather than allowing it to decrease to the competitive number N_1. Moreover, it leads to an efficiency loss which often exceeds the red triangle shown in that earlier diagram. The reason is

---

[3] There is an important reason why we cannot analyse monopoly in a labour market in exactly the same way as we analyse monopoly in a product market. In a product market, a monopoly firm will take into account any loss of sales (reduction in output) that results from its high price. However, in a labour market, it is not clear how fully a union will take into account any reduced employment that results from its high wage. This may be particularly true if the industry is growing and if the high wage does not displace any of the current union members, but instead reduces only the number of new workers coming into the industry. This difficulty prevents us from applying the standard analysis of monopoly to determine precisely how high the union will raise the wage rate.

[4] This is not always the case, however. Featherbedding was a contributing factor in the death of some newspapers in the United Kingdom. In particular, some union contracts required that newspapers receiving typeset copy from advertisers had to reset this copy in "bogus" type, which was not actually used. Featherbedding therefore may have resulted in fewer newspaper jobs even though it may have maintained the existing number of typesetting jobs for a time.

that this triangular efficiency loss is based on the assumption that employers use the extra workers they hire as productively as possible. However, many featherbedding contracts require employers not only to hire more workers, but also to assign them to tasks with low or even zero productivity. This makes the efficiency loss greater.

Is this criticism of featherbedding too severe? Because it protects workers who might otherwise have difficulty in getting another job, isn't it a way of introducing compassion into the economic system? The answer is yes, but it is a bad way to do it. Far better to ease labour's shift into other jobs than to have society carry an overhead of unproductive employment into the future. One compromise way of negotiating the end to a featherbedding contract is for the company to guarantee that all those individuals now holding jobs will continue to be employed; but they will not be replaced. Although this may be a costly solution, it at least guarantees that the problem will disappear as the present work force reaches retirement age. This is far superior to a featherbedding contract, where the inefficiency doesn't disappear when people in non-productive jobs retire, because they keep getting replaced. (More on the relation between efficiency and compassion is provided in Box 34-1.)

HOW UNIONS INCREASE EFFICIENCY: THE OTHER SIDE OF THE COIN

In our analysis so far, we have seen how a union may reduce efficiency by negotiating an increase in wages that reduces employment. But this is only part of the story. A union may also have *favourable* effects on efficiency.

1. Unions can improve the morale of the work force and improve communication between workers and management. This may lead to better decision making.
2. By providing workers with a collective voice, a union makes it possible for them to improve their working conditions rather than quitting.[5]

Because unions reduce "quit-rates" and labour turnover, there is less disruption in the workplace.

3. Even if there are none of these positive "voice" effects, there is another reason why a union that increases wages may still increase efficiency rather than reduce it. This will occur if the labour market is not initially perfectly competitive because market power is held by *employers* on the other side of the market. It will now be shown that in this case the formation of a union may be a counterbalance that increases efficiency.

MONOPSONY: MARKET POWER ON THE EMPLOYERS' SIDE OF THE LABOUR MARKET

Employers typically quote the wage rate they will pay. In doing so, they frequently do not act like perfect competitors who take a market wage as given. Instead, they exercise a degree of market power. In particular, any firm that employs a large fraction of a local labour force will have an influence over the wage rate.

To analyse this situation, we initially assume exactly the same perfectly competitive market that we began with in the previous diagram, with equilibrium at E_1 reproduced in Figure 34-3. This time, instead of introducing monopoly (a single seller, in the form of a union) we introduce **monopsony**—a single buyer, that is, a single employer of labour. What happens if this single employer quotes a lower wage rate, while workers on the other side of the market act as perfect competitors, taking this wage rate as given? Specifically, suppose that the employer quotes a wage W_2 below the perfectly competitive wage W_1. In response to wage W_2, some workers leave this now unattractive industry for other jobs. In other words, they move down their supply curve from E_1 to a new equilibrium at E_2. The result is the red triangular efficiency loss, because employment at N_2 is less than the perfectly competitive amount at N_1. (Details on this move from equilibrium E_1 to E_2 are given in Box 34-2.)

---

[5]The fact that unions exist may even lead to an improvement in working conditions in firms that are *not* unionized. These firms may fear that if they don't improve their working conditions, their workers may form a union. The existence of a union may also benefit non-union workers *in the same firm.* Many firms that sign a contract with a union for higher wages pass on the same increase to

their non-union labour force. However, the conclusion that unions raise non-union wages is still a subject of debate, because in another respect unions exert downward pressure on non-union wages: The higher union wage reduces employment in union jobs; this, in turn, increases the number of workers looking for non-union jobs, and consequently tends to lower wages there.

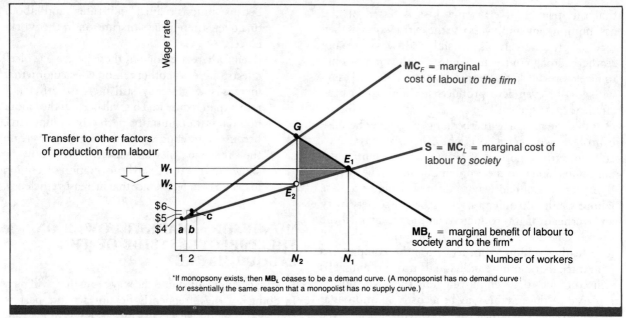

Figure 34-3   Effects when a perfectly competitive labour market is monopsonized.
When a monopsony is formed, equilibrium moves from the perfectly competitive point E_1 to E_2. (Because the monopsonist quotes lower wage W_2, fewer workers offer their labour services and employment falls from N_1 to N_2.) As first ex- plained in Figure 33-6(c), there is the efficiency loss shown by the red triangle because too few workers are employed in this industry. The lower wage also results in a transfer from labour to other factors of production, as indicated by the white arrow on the left.

At the same time, the reduction in the wage paid by the employer results in the transfer shown by the white arrow to the left of this diagram. This transfer is from workers who receive the lower wage, to other factors of production who benefit because more of the firm's income is left for them. (An example of an even stronger exercise of market power by a monopsonist, and therefore an even greater transfer of income is given in Box 34-3.)

Here we see another example of Adam Smith's "invisible hand" gone astray. The monopsonistic employer's pursuit of private benefit does *not* lead to public benefit. Quite the contrary. It leads to the deadweight efficiency loss shown by the red triangle in Figure 34-3.

In reality, there are few cases in which monopsony occurs in its pure form with only *one* buyer. There is more likely to be a small group of employers, that is, an *oligopsony* with a few buyers. In quoting a wage rate, each firm has some latitude; but to a greater or lesser degree it is influenced by the wages quoted by competing firms. On the one hand, competition among these firms may leave each with very little influence over the wage it can quote. In this case, the wage may be close to the competitive level W_1. On the other hand, if the few oligopsonists collude, perhaps in some covert way, they may together lower the wage rate well below W_1 toward the level W_2 that a monopsonist would choose.

Although monopsony rarely occurs in its pure form, with only one buyer, there has been one notable example: the monopsony power that the owners of baseball clubs used to have in buying the services of their players.

Monopsony and Baseball Salaries

I don't understand why grown men play this game anyhow. They ought to be lawyers or doctors or garbage men. Games should be left for kids.

Ted Turner, owner of the Atlanta Braves

One reason grown men play baseball is the high income it offers, especially since the monopsony power of

BOX 34-1

THE CONFLICTING OBJECTIVES OF COMPASSION AND EFFICIENCY

Two centuries ago, at the beginning of the Industrial Revolution in Britain, labour-saving machinery was introduced into the textile industry. Displaced workers in those days had much bleaker prospects than today: It was harder to find another job. Without a job, a worker's family faced severe malnutrition, or worse. Consequently, there were riots in which workers (the Luddites) broke into the factories, destroying the new labour-saving machines. While recognizing their plight, we might ask: Suppose they had succeeded? Suppose labour-saving machinery had been banned and their primitive handcrafting jobs guaranteed? If they and their heirs had been successful in thwarting technological change, wouldn't our situation today be very much like theirs two centuries ago? And if so, what progress would we have made in combatting the problem that concerned them most: poverty?

Although labour-saving machinery may create transitional unemployment, it creates far better jobs in the long run. When bulldozers are introduced, whole armies of workers with shovels lose their jobs. But in the long run, this is highly beneficial both for society and, in most cases, for the workers who initially lose their jobs. This is not only true of the ditchdiggers who get high-productivity, high-pay jobs driving the bulldozers. It is also true of other ditchdiggers who get high-productivity jobs in new, growing industries such as electronics, aircraft, and so on. These jobs exist because the introduction of bulldozers and other machines increases our ability to produce, and therefore raises our income and purchasing power. This, in turn, means that we can afford to buy products that did not exist before.

In brief, society benefits because the labour force is engaged in more productive activities than ditchdigging. Because machines now perform many routine jobs, we produce more. The resulting increase in our income allows us to afford more compassion— that is, we are able to ensure that people do not suffer the extremes of poverty that had to be faced in earlier, less productive eras. The point is a simple one. In protecting people against severe economic adversity, it is important not to use methods that thwart progress by locking in inefficiency.

---

club owners like Ted Turner was broken in 1976. Before this, the "reserve clause" had made each major league owner a monopsonist, since a player could not sign a contract with any other major league team. However, beginning in 1976, a player in certain circumstances could become a free agent and negotiate with other clubs.

Figure 34-4 shows what happened to a few of the players who became free agents. A comparison of their before-and-after salaries indicates the remarkable way that the monopsony power of the reserve clause had depressed players' salaries. Moreover, since 1976, confirming evidence has continued to accumulate. In 1980, the baseball world was astonished when the New York Yankees signed outfielder and free agent Dave Winfield to a contract worth an estimated $1.5 million to $2 million *per year for ten years*. Compare this to his $350,000 salary in San Diego the previous year before

his escape, as a free agent, from the monopsony power of the reserve clause. To get some idea of Winfield's "before-and-after" situation, just increase the height of both bars for Baylor in Figure 34-4 by *ten times*. Further evidence that Winfield's high salary was due to his free agent status was to be found in the much lower salaries of equally good, or arguably better, players still held in the grip of the reserve clause.

The Effects of Unions Reconsidered

We are now in a position to show why our criticism of unions, which was valid if markets were initially competitive, is not necessarily justified if there is monopsony power on the other side of the market.

Figure 34-5 shows how a union that pushes up wages can actually raise, rather than lower, economic efficiency. This will occur, for example, if there has

BOX 34-2

HOW FAR DOES A MONOPSONIST TRY TO REDUCE THE WAGE RATE?

To choose the wage rate that will maximize its profits, the monopsony firm first calculates its marginal cost of hiring labour MC_F from the supply of labour S. This calculation is illustrated in the lower left-hand corner of Figure 34-3: From the S curve we see that the firm must pay $4 an hour at point a to hire one worker, and $5 an hour at point b to hire two. However, the firm's marginal cost MC_F of hiring the second worker is not $5, but is instead $6—the $5 × 2 = $10 it costs to hire the two workers less the $4 it cost to hire one. Thus MC_F, the marginal cost of labour to the monopsony firm,

lies above the supply curve of labour S.

To maximize profit, this firm hires labour to the point G, where its marginal cost of hiring labour MC_F is equal to the marginal benefit it receives from hiring labour. With its desired employment thus being N_2, what's the lowest wage it can quote? The answer is W_2, which is the point on the S curve above N_2. At this wage rate, the supply curve S indicates that just exactly the desired number of workers (N_2) will offer their services to this firm.

Finally, Figure 34-3 provides another view of why a red efficiency loss arises from an employment level of N_2: The private firm equates the marginal benefit of labour MB_L not to society's marginal cost MC_L, but instead to its own marginal cost MC_F. Since the marginal benefit and cost of labour to society are not equated, the solution is not an efficient one.

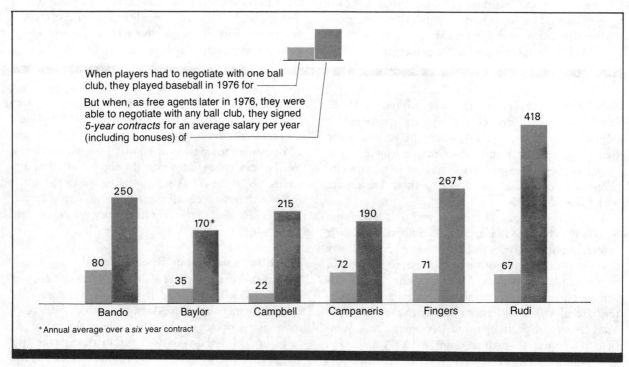

When players had to negotiate with one ball club, they played baseball in 1976 for

But when, as free agents later in 1976, they were able to negotiate with any ball club, they signed *5-year contracts* for an average salary per year (including bonuses) of

*Annual average over a *six* year contract

Figure 34-4   How monopsony (the reserve clause) depressed baseball salaries. (Figures in $000s, rounded.)

been a monopsony firm hiring labour, and this firm has lowered the wage rate from the competitive level W to W_1. At this lower wage, fewer workers have

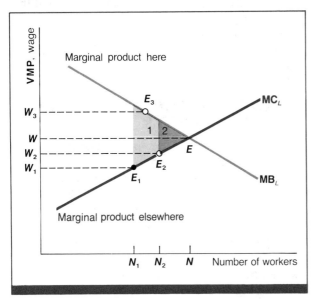

Figure 34-5 How inefficiency may be reduced if a union raises wages in a monopsonized labour market.
Before the union, the monopsonist set the wage rate at W_1; with equilibrium at E_1, there was an efficiency loss of $1 + 2$. When the union is formed it raises the wage to W_2. Equilibrium moves from E_1 to E_2, some employment is restored, and the efficiency loss is reduced to area 2. Consequently, the increased wage improves efficiency by area 1. It also transfers income from the monopsonist to labour. But if the union pushes the wage up past the competitive wage W— for example toward W_3—equilibrium will be shifted away from E toward E_3, and efficiency will be reduced once again.

been offering their labour services to this industry. Therefore, because of monopsony in this labour market, employment has been reduced from N to N_1— that is, equilibrium has moved from E to E_1—with a consequent efficiency loss of areas $1 + 2$. If a union is now formed and raises the wage rate from W_1 to W_2—moving the equilibrium from E_1 to E_2—the efficiency loss is reduced from areas $1 + 2$ to just area 2. In other words, the formation of this union results in an efficiency gain of area 1. Of course, the union also benefits union members by recapturing some of the income previously lost to the monopsonist.

Thus, the following case can be made for unions. When workers form a union in a labour market dominated by a monopsonistic employer quoting a take-it-or-leave-it wage like W_1, they send a representative to the bargaining table who can counter by presenting the same sort of take-it-or-leave-it offer to management: "If you do not accept our wage claim, then we will strike your firm, withdrawing all workers from the job and closing down your operations." Thus, the union allows workers to speak from a position of strength, and the wage will then be negotiated between union and management. Typically, it will lie somewhere between the initial "take-it-or-leave-it" offers of the two parties, that is, somewhere between management's take-it-or-leave-it offer of W_1 in Figure 34-5, and labour's take-it-or-leave-it demand of, say, W_3. Only in this way can labour exercise what John Kenneth Galbraith calls **countervailing power** to prevent the wage from being lowered all the way to management's target level of W_1. Moreover, if labour is able, through such bargaining, to raise its wage from W_1 to, say, W_2,

---

BOX 34-3

MONOPSONY AND DISCRIMINATION IN THE LABOUR MARKET

Monopsonists who use their market power to depress the wage rate of their entire labour force may go one step further and reduce even more the wage paid to a specific subset of their workers, such as a

minority group. To illustrate, consider the monopsonistic firm that has used its market power to depress the wage rate in Figure 34-3 from the perfectly competitive level W_1 to W_2. It may then go one step further and offer the minority group an even lower wage. The firm may discriminate in this way for the same reason that the dentist who was a monopolist in a small town discriminated by charging different fees. In either case, discrimination is a way of increasing profit.

it will not only be promoting its own interest. It will also be increasing overall economic efficiency.[6] Furthermore, union practices like picketing are a means of increasing the union's countervailing power by making it more difficult for the employer to hire strike breakers.

A Complication

Such is the case for unions. However, it does not justify every exercise of market power. If a union gets very strong and pushes the wage up beyond W toward W_3, equilibrium will shift away from E toward E_3 and efficiency will once again be reduced.

Thus, the typical policy problem in the labour market is not that one side has market power and the other does not, but rather, that the relative power of the two may be unbalanced. If the government is pursuing the objective of making labour markets more efficient, it should be careful if it is reducing the bargaining power of one group and not the other. Such government action may sometimes make the situation better; but sometimes it may make it worse. If the government is reducing the market power of the group that is already in the weaker position, this government action will be making the problem of imbalance worse. On the other hand, if the government is increasing the market power of that group, it will be making the situation better.

This discussion also allows us to sharpen up our earlier conclusion about a minimum wage. If a minimum wage raises the wage rate in Figure 34-5 from an existing very low level like W_1 toward the competitive level W, employment and efficiency in this labour market are increased, rather than decreased. On the other hand, if the minimum wage is set at a higher level and therefore raises the wage rate *away from* W and toward W_3, employment and efficiency are reduced. Therefore,

a useful guideline for a minimum wage is to set it near the competitive wage level in most industries. (This guideline is difficult to put into practice because competitive wage rates are difficult to estimate, and they differ among industries. Furthermore, the government may be paying little attention to the objective of efficiency, concentrating on the redistribution of income instead.)

BILATERAL MONOPOLY: RELATIVE BARGAINING POWER

When both sides have market power as in Figure 34-5, they push in opposite directions. While the employer tries to keep the wage rate down close to W_1, the union tries to push it up close to W_3. The outcome depends on the bargaining power of the two sides. We cannot tell by looking at the two curves in this diagram precisely where the final solution will be.

Which Side Has the Stronger Bargaining Position?

To see the importance of bargaining power, suppose that there is only one company in a mining town and that it faces an ineffective union representing only a minority of the workers. In this case, the company will be in a good position to keep the wage low. On the other hand, if there is one union facing a number of employers, the union may have the stronger bargaining position. It has sometimes been suggested that this used to be the situation in the auto industry— although Ford and GM could scarcely be considered weak bargaining adversaries.

If the United Auto Workers judges that its negotiations with the industry are not proceeding in a satisfactory way, it typically threatens to pull its workers out on strike in one of the auto companies, say Ford. If it does so, Ford workers on strike will get income support from a union strike fund drawn from workers from all the auto companies. But the company being struck (Ford) does not get the same sort of support from the other companies in the industry. True, Ford may get moral support from the other firms, but they still go on selling cars and cutting into Ford's market. And therein lies Ford's problem. If it is shut down by a strike and unable to produce cars, it will find that its share of the market is being eroded and that its profits are falling. In fact, a strong union may have the power

[6]This is another example of the *theory of the second best*, first encountered in Box 25-1. If there is only a single firm in a small town, it will be able to exercise monopsony influence over the wage rate. The economist's "first best" efficient solution—with perfect competition on both sides of the market—is simply not possible, no matter how desirable it might be. Instead, we must look for a second best solution. This may involve workers forming a union in order to influence price and thus counterbalance the power that the monopsonist already enjoys on the other side of the market. In his *American Capitalism: The Concept of Countervailing Power* (Boston: Houghton Mifflin, 1952), John Kenneth Galbraith favoured strong unions as a way of balancing employers' power.

to drive a company bankrupt—and sometimes this does happen, although not by design.

Workers rightly regard driving a firm out of business as "overkill," since this would destroy their jobs. Consequently, a union is unlikely to pick as its target one of the financially weak companies in an industry. If a firm is already close to bankruptcy, a strike threat may be very ineffective. It may be met only by the resigned observation: "If we agree to your wage demand, we go bankrupt. If we don't and you strike, we go bankrupt. There is nothing we can do." The negotiations may end there. Consequently, the union will select as its target a company that is reasonably sound financially—one that is both able to afford a sizeable wage increase, and can be hurt a great deal by a strike without being driven bankrupt.

STRIKES

The bargaining position of either side can also depend on its ability to outlast the other in a long strike. For example, the credibility of a strike threat by a union depends in part on the size of its strike fund. If this has been depleted by earlier strikes, the union is in a weak position. The company can play a strong hand, making a low offer near W_1 and sticking close to it, with the knowledge that the union cannot afford to strike. On the other hand, a company will be in a weak bargaining position if it cannot afford a strike. This may be the case for several reasons:

1. A construction company that has to pay heavy penalties for delay in completing a project may be forced to capitulate to a strike threat by the union. As the City of Montreal discovered in 1967, and Vancouver found out in 1985, a city that is playing host to a major international event such as the Olympic Games or an international exhibition (such as Expo 86), is in a particularly vulnerable position.

2. A firm producing a perishable good or service may be in a weak bargaining position because sales and profits lost during a strike may be lost forever. ("Perishable" is used broadly, applying not only to physically perishable goods such as fruit but also to a good that goes out of date. For example, if a newspaper cannot deliver today's edition, the papers become worthless.) Of course, firms producing goods that are not per-

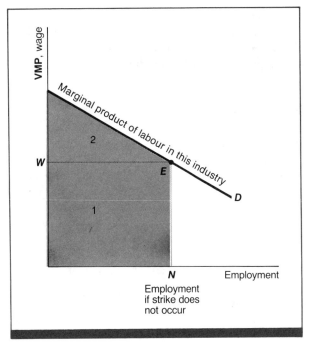

Figure 34-6 Short-run cost of a strike to labour and other factors of production.
Without a strike, the value of total output in this industry is area 1 + 2, as first noted in Figure 33-4. Labour earns area 1, and other factors of production earn 2. But if a strike does occur, both these income areas are lost. (The cost may be less if some of the production lost during a strike can be made up after the strike is settled; or if, in anticipation of the strike, the firm is able to increase its output and inventories.)

ishable are in a much stronger position—especially if these firms have accumulated large inventories, and can consequently keep selling right through a strike. It is no accident that before critical wage negotiations, companies try to build up inventories, just as unions try to build up strike funds.

The Cost of a Strike

Strikes are costly to both sides: to labour in the form of lost wages, to management in the form of lost sales and profits. To illustrate this, suppose that, in the absence of a strike, the wage is W in Figure 34-6, with employment N. Then a strike that reduces employment to zero involves a temporary cost in terms of lost output valued at areas 1 + 2. Labour loses income 1—that is, its wage W times employment N—while the income lost by other factors is the remaining area 2.

Since both parties face a substantial loss in the event

of a strike, it is often assumed that when a strike does occur, it is the result of an error in judgement by at least one of the conflicting parties. However, this need not be the case, as we will now show.

Labour-Management Negotiations to Avoid Strikes

Case (a) in Figure 34-7 illustrates the overwhelming majority of situations: Labour and management should be able to find a wage to agree on, and thus avoid a strike. The range of wages management is willing to pay (arrow M) and the range of wages labour is willing to take (arrow L) overlap through the shaded range W_1W_2. Any wage rate in this positive, shaded "contract zone" is acceptable to both parties. (Remember: The term "wage rate" means total compensation to labour, including fringe benefits and improvements in working conditions.)

The actual negotiations may begin with labour demanding W_4 and management offering W_3. To the public, it appears that they are far apart, and there is little hope of an agreement. However, as the negotiations proceed, both sides compromise, trading off one claim against another. Often neither party will officially concede anything; this may be viewed as a sign of weakness. Instead, each simply remains silent on a claim made by the other, and this "trade" is thereafter mutually recognized. Thus management "moves up its arrow M" and labour moves down its arrow L, until they reach a point of agreement at, say, W_5. In settling on this, management's negotiating team claims success; labour has been negotiated all the way down from its original demand of W_4. The union is also able to claim success; it has negotiated management all the way up from its original offer of W_3.

Most labour negotiations follow this sort of pattern and result in an agreement; a strike is avoided, and there are no stories in the newspapers. The highly publicized cases are those where a strike *does* occur. How does this happen? One answer is shown in panel (b) where L and M do not overlap. There is *no* wage acceptable to both parties, regardless of the negotiating skill they may display. This case will be considered in a moment, but first it is important to explain why a strike may occur even in panel (a) where there *is* a mutually acceptable range of wage rates. Two reasons have been cited:

1. One of the parties may have some extraneous

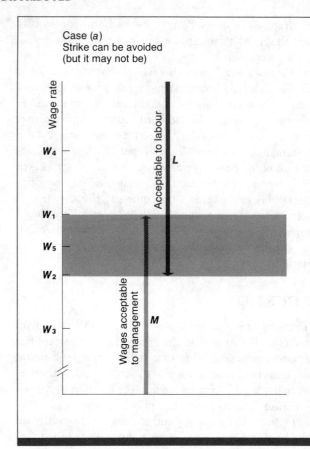

Figure 34-7 Some of the reasons why strikes occur.

objective. For example, a company may want a strike as a means of weakening or destroying workers' support for their union. Alternatively, the union may want a strike in the belief that it will improve labour solidarity and morale. Or, either side may want a strike as a way to increase its long-run credibility—as a means of establishing that when it threatens a strike in future negotiations, it is not bluffing. Credibility is very important for each side, because it makes it possible in future to get a satisfactory settlement simply by *threatening* to strike, rather than having to rely on the far more costly method of *actually* striking.

2. One or both of the parties may engage in poor bargaining strategy. For example, suppose that management's initial offer is far below W_3—in fact, so low that it is viewed by labour as an insult. The anger that results may sour the negoti-

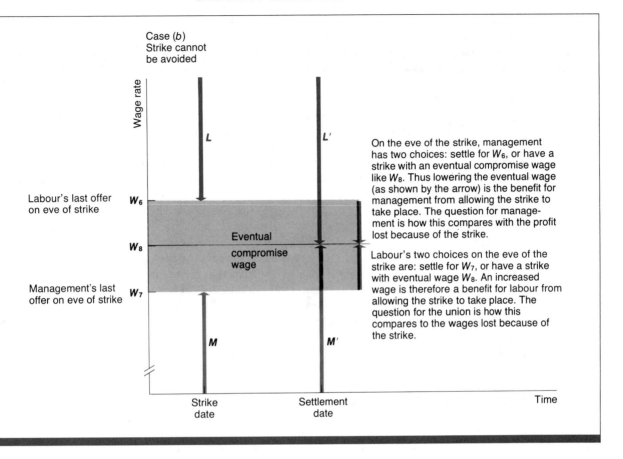

Case (*b*)
Strike cannot
be avoided

Wage rate

L

L'

Labour's last offer
on eve of strike W_6

Eventual

compromise

wage

W_8

Management's last
offer on eve of strike W_7

M

M'

Strike
date

Settlement
date

Time

On the eve of the strike, management has two choices: settle for W_6, or have a strike with an eventual compromise wage like W_8. Thus lowering the eventual wage (as shown by the arrow) is the benefit for management from allowing the strike to take place. The question for management is how this compares with the profit lost because of the strike.

Labour's two choices on the eve of the strike are: settle for W_7, or have a strike with eventual wage W_8. An increased wage is therefore a benefit for labour from allowing the strike to take place. The question for the union is how this compares to the wages lost because of the strike.

ations enough to cause an unnecessary strike. An alternative bargaining error by management may be to make an initial offer that is too *generous*. Specifically, suppose management initially offers W_1, and states that this is its final, best possible offer (which it is; note that W_1 is right at the top of arrow M). The problem is that the union leaders may not believe it. They may view it as a standard opening offer and attempt to negotiate it up. When this attempt fails, a strike occurs because wage W_1 cannot be accepted by the union. It will look foolish to its membership if it has gone through weeks or months of trying to negotiate the company up and has been unable to budge it an inch. It will seem that management has dictated the wage from the beginning, and all that the union has done is to make concessions. Why do the workers need such a union? Thus, although manage-

ment has been very generous in offering W_1, it has inadvertently caused a strike because it has not "played the negotiating game." It has not followed the cardinal rule of "giving the other side a ladder to climb down."

Thus, even when there is a positive contract zone of acceptable wage rates ($W_1 W_2$), an agreement may not be achieved because of inept negotiating. In the words of Lloyd Reynolds of Yale University:[7]

Negotiators may stake out firm positions from which it is later difficult to retreat, may misread the signals from the other side, [or] may be unable to surmount the tactical difficulties of graceful concession.

While economic forces set the background and help to define the limits $W_1 W_2$ within which the negotiated

[7]*Labor Economics and Labor Relations*, 8th ed. (Englewood Cliffs, New Jersey: Prentice-Hall Inc., 1982), p. 447.

wage will fall, collective bargaining has some of the characteristics of a poker game: The wage negotiated is very much the product of the bargaining skills of the participants. Without minimal skills, there may be no bargain at all.

As already noted, the final reason that a strike may occur is that a positive contract zone does not exist—as in case (b) in Figure 34-7. In this situation a strike cannot be avoided, because the positions (arrows) of the two parties do not overlap. On the eve of the strike, there is no wage that is acceptable to both. Each party would rather have a strike than agree to the other side's last offer.

However, the longer the strike goes on, the farther the two parties move to the right in this diagram, and the more likely it is that each side will modify its previous strong position —that is, the more likely it is that the two arrows L' and M' will approach each other. Workers on the picket lines increasingly feel the financial pinch of lost wages. Similarly, management sees its losses mount. Both recognize that the other does, in fact, mean business. Thus L' and M' eventually meet and the strike is settled, at a compromise wage such as W_8. But precisely because W_8 is a compromise wage, it is more attractive for each side than its opponent's last offer before the strike. Thus, achieving a more attractive wage is an incentive for each side to accept a strike rather than to capitulate to the other on the eve of the strike. (Sometimes, one side "loses a strike," and is forced to settle at or very near the pre-strike offer of the other. In this case, it has made a mistake by not settling earlier.)

The Frequency of Strikes

In comparison with other Western nations, labour disputes are relatively frequent and long-lasting in Canada. For example, during 1970–81, Canadian workers on average lost almost twice as many working days to strikes as U.S. workers. In relation to the total labour market, however, the number of workers affected by strikes remains small: As a percentage of total time worked, time lost in strikes in recent years has never been more than about 1 percent, and has averaged one third of one percent. Thus the average Canadian worker spends less than one day a year on strike; time lost to industrial disputes has usually been less than time lost due to industrial accidents and illness.[8]

Nevertheless, strikes may be more costly to the economy than these figures suggest. They may result not only in lost output in the industries where the strikes occur; they may also inflict spillover costs on other industries.

Spillover Costs of a Strike

To illustrate, suppose that when the tire industry is on strike the value of the lost output and income *in that industry* is shown as area 3 in panel (a) of Figure 34-8; this is exactly the same as areas 1 + 2 in Figure 34-6. The loss may not end here: As tire supplies are depleted, auto production may be delayed or dislocated. This disruption involves a cost to the auto industry and inconvenience to the car-buying public. Since these are costs that are not incurred by any firm or individual in the tire industry, they are external, spillover costs of the strike and are shown as area 4. In short, if a strike occurs in the industry, it will involve both internal cost 3 to the industry plus external cost 4 elsewhere in the economy.

In panel (b) we see that the situation could be worse. If one or more auto companies are eventually forced to shut down, the value of the lost output in the auto industry and the inconvenience to the public—shown as area 4—may exceed the value of the lost output in the tire industry, shown as area 3.

Other illustrations abound. When mine workers go on an extended strike, the external cost of a coal shortage to electric power stations and their customers may exceed the costs to owners and labour in the mines. In a 1978 strike by engineers and deck officers on the Great Lakes freighters, lost income of the shipping companies represented only a small part of the cost of the strike. Far more important were the losses to Prairie farmers and the mining and steel companies,

---

[8]Wildcat strikes—sudden walkouts by small groups of workers—are relatively uncommon in Canada. However, they are more frequent in some other countries like Britain, where they have contributed to the decline of several important industries. Such strikes can be more disruptive than a full-scale strike that follows a breakdown in union-management contract negotiations. Wildcat strikes may be the result of unions that are too weak to prevent their members from taking actions that harm the workers in the industry as a whole.

as wheat exports were halted and iron ore could no longer be shipped on the St. Lawrence Seaway. Ultimately, part of the cost was borne by Canadian consumers: As exports were disrupted and our foreign exchange earnings reduced, the price to Canadians of foreign currency rose, increasing the prices of imported goods.

Thus, the general public often has a stake in a strike decision in a specific industry. But the public *is not represented* in the negotiations that lead to a strike. Its attitude is often: "While labour and management in this industry are fighting over how area 3 is to be divided, we are losing area 4. Something is very wrong."

Therefore, a number of ways have been sought to prevent strikes when negotiations between labour and management break down.

Last-Resort Procedures to Prevent Strikes

In cases where major negotiations are deadlocked, the federal or provincial government may appoint an impartial outsider (often a judge) to study the situation and suggest a compromise settlement. This is called **mediation**— or **conciliation**—of the conflict. Although mediators cannot make binding recommendations on how the conflicts will be settled, they may be very helpful in resolving disputes for several reasons: A mediator may be able to (1) discover a solution that the two contending parties have overlooked; (2) find out who is bluffing and who is not, thus reducing the risk of a strike because one side has miscalculated the true position of the other; (3) provide a means of saving face for parties that are otherwise locked into highly publicized positions from which there is no graceful retreat. For example, a union can go back to its members and say: "We didn't capitulate to the

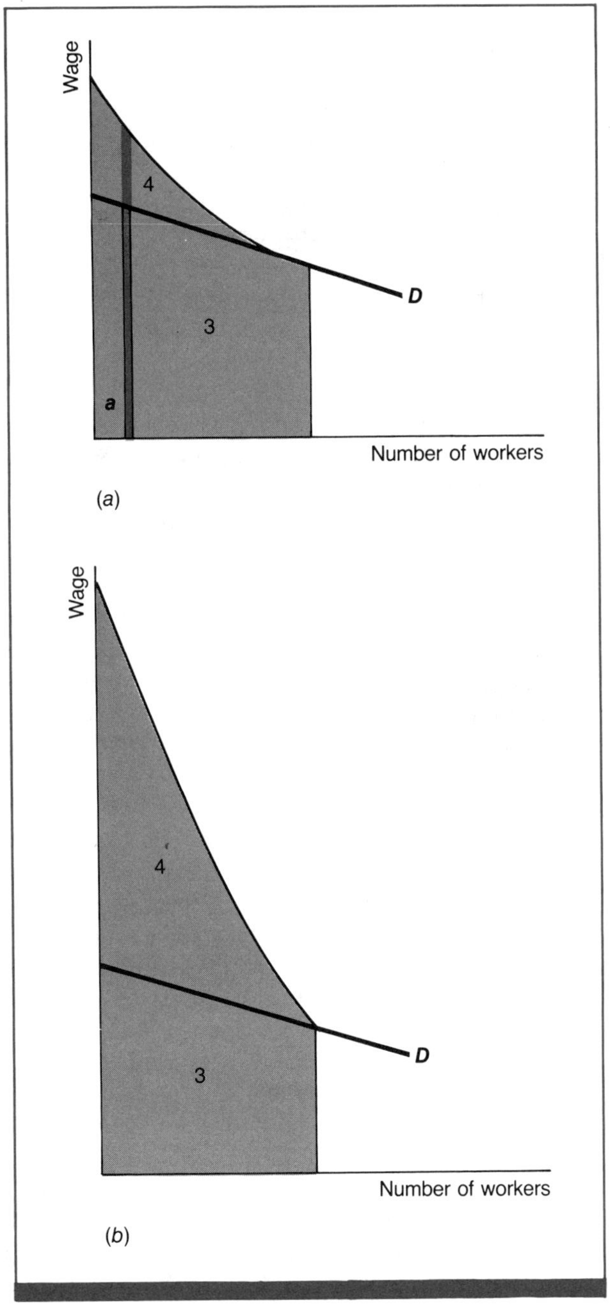

Figure 34-8 Spillover cost of a strike.

(*a*) When a strike occurs in tire production, area 3 shows the internal cost to the industry—the value of the lost output of tires. Area 4 shows the additional external cost to the public, and in particular to the auto industry where production is dislocated because tire supplies have dried up. More specifically, the fact that worker *a* becomes unemployed means that there is a loss of this individual's output of tires, as shown by the light red bar. However, there is a further cost, shown by the dark red bar, because of the dislocation in the auto industry, where car production is delayed because of the shortage of tires. (*b*) If the shortage of tires becomes so severe that auto companies have to lay off workers, area 4 of spillover cost from the strike may be more severe than area 3 of internal cost to the tire industry.

bosses. We accepted the recommendation of an impartial third party." Thus, the two sides may be able to achieve a settlement because they are able to shift the responsibility (blame) onto the mediator.

(In Canada mediators have sometimes been criticized for taking too narrow an approach—for seeking the wage that is most likely to be accepted by both parties, rather than the wage that is acceptable from an overall economic point of view. To illustrate, consider an industry in which a relatively high mediated wage is acceptable to both parties. [Suppose that firms in the industry are able to "pass on" the higher wage to their customers.] If this industry tends to set a pattern for wages elsewhere, the settlement may have unfortunate inflationary consequences.)

If mediation fails, a second, more forceful technique is *voluntary arbitration*: Labour and management submit their conflict to an impartial third party, and *commit themselves in advance* to accept the arbitrator's decision. Provisions for voluntary arbitration are included in many collective bargaining agreements as a way of settling disputes over the interpretation of the terms of the agreement.

A third, and much more drastic, approach is sometimes suggested: *compulsory arbitration*, whereby the government *forces* both parties to submit their dispute to an arbitrator, who then decides on a binding settlement. Although this seems like a simple solution, it has caused bitterness in countries which have relied on it extensively.

DISPUTES INVOLVING PUBLIC SERVICE EMPLOYEES

The most damaging strikes are usually those with large external or spillover costs. These costs—illustrated in panel (*b*) of Figure 34-8—tend to be particularly large in the public sector. When subway workers go on strike, area 3 of lost income of these workers and the transit authority is typically far less than area 4—the spillover cost of tying up the city's economic activity. Serious spillover costs similarly result from a strike of garbage collectors, firefighters, or air traffic controllers. In the case of a police strike, criminals are given carte blanche—although this turned out to be less of a problem than expected when Halifax did have a police strike in 1981.

Public service employees sometimes argue that if they don't have a union, the government, as a monopsony employer, can exercise too much market power in setting their wage rate. They must accept whatever "take-it-or-leave-it" contract the government offers. Accordingly, as we have seen, public service employees have recently been organizing at a rapid rate. However, critics of public service unions have argued that once public service employees do form a strong union, the balance of market power tips too strongly in their favour. They have advanced several reasons for this view:

1. Because public servants—such as the police or transit workers—provide essential services, their threat of a strike becomes a very potent weapon. Whereas a strike in the private sector puts pressure on employers to settle because of the income they will lose, a strike in the public sector (in the post office, for example) puts pressure on the employers (the government) because of the votes it may lose from an irate public suffering from the suspension of an essential service.

2. A government may find it easier than a private employer to raise the funds necessary to pay a higher wage. For example, the government may increase taxes, or borrow. Another way to avoid a strike may be to provide a generous increase in pensions, a relatively painless measure because it commits a future—rather than the present—government to pay employees when they retire. Thus, it has appeal to politicians whose major concern is to win the next election.

3. In private industry a strike may drive a firm out of business. Thus, strikers run the risk that their jobs may disappear, and this prospect acts as a restraint on labour demands. But there is far less restraint of this kind in the public service. True, a strike may cost the government an election. But this is a serious problem only for the government officials who are voted out of their jobs. It is far less of a threat to public service workers, whose jobs are likely to exist no matter who wins the next election. This also puts a public service union in a strong bargaining position.

4. Public employees and their dependents may become a significant percentage of the voting population. This weakens the resistance of elected officials to their demands.

As noted earlier, Canada's federal and provincial laws allow most government employees to strike. But some (such as hospital workers in some provinces) do not have this right. Moreover, in some countries, including the United States, strikes of public service workers are generally illegal. But even when such strikes *are* illegal, workers sometimes resort to them. (Workers may also strike in disguised ways, such as reporting in sick or all resigning at the same time.) The question has therefore been raised, in Canada and elsewhere, whether all public service workers shouldn't have the right to strike.

Many observers have argued that they shouldn't: If garbage collectors go on strike, pollution may threaten public health. If firefighters or policemen go on strike, people may die in fires or be victimized by criminals. In the face of such strike threats, a government may feel almost forced to meet labour demands. Surely no group of individuals should hold this sort of power over a country's elected government.

Unfortunately, however, the problem is not quite that simple. If workers are not allowed to strike, they may reasonably demand some other mechanism for achieving a fair wage, and for negotiating with the employer about working conditions. One approach used by the federal government to deal with the wage issue has been to provide civil servants with salaries equal to those in comparable private sector jobs. But this provides neither a simple nor a complete solution. One difficulty is considered in Problem 34-7; another is the problem of defining what is meant by a "comparable" private sector job. And what downward adjustment, if any, should be made to government salaries because of attractive pensions and greater job security?

Another point, finally, was emphasized by the opponents of public sector unions during the inflationary period in the 1970s: If these unions become too powerful, wage settlements in the public sector may begin to outpace private-sector settlements, and this may make it harder for the government to control inflation. For example, University of Western Ontario economist Thomas Courchene has noted that the 18% wage increase negotiated by government employees in 1975 was well in excess of the 14% average wage increase in the private sector. This 18% increase, together with the subsequent indexing of civil servants' pensions to the cost of living, created demands for catch-up increases in the private sector. As a consequence, it became much more difficult for the Anti-Inflation Board to moderate wage settlements in 1976 and 1977.

WAGE DIFFERENCES: WHY DO THEY EXIST?

In answering this question, we shall draw together and expand on some of the points made in the last two chapters.

1. First, there may be **dynamic differentials** in wage rates. For example, if there is a large increase in the demand for construction workers in Alberta, their wages will rise above wages earned elsewhere; a dynamic differential is created. Eventually, this higher Alberta wage will attract workers from other parts of the country, and this wage will settle back toward the wage level elsewhere; the dynamic differential declines. Such differentials are only temporary; the speed with which they disappear depends on the mobility of the labour force.

> A *dynamic wage differential* arises because of changing demand or supply conditions in the labour market. It declines over time as labour moves out of jobs with relatively low wages and into those that pay a relatively high wage.

2. Some of the wage differential in Alberta may not disappear over time. For example, wages may remain higher in northern Alberta to compensate for some disadvantage of working there such as the colder climate. Similar **compensating wage differentials** may arise in jobs offering less security or less pleasant working conditions.

> *Compensating wage differentials* result if labour views some jobs as less attractive than others. Employers have to pay a higher wage to fill the unattractive jobs.

For example, jobs with high stress generally pay higher wages, and repetitive, boring jobs may also pay higher wages. On the other hand, some unpleasant jobs do not carry the higher wage one would expect. Instead, they have a higher turnover rate. This suggests that there may be a pool of available workers who take jobs without realizing they are unpleasant. When they do realize, they quit.

3. Some wage differences reflect **monopsony or monopoly power.** Thus, workers in a small town facing a monopsony employer may receive a low wage. On the other hand, workers who are exercising market power through a union tend to get higher wages. A particularly high wage may be received by workers who are not only able to exercise market power in their own labour market through a strong union, but who are also employed by a firm with monopoly influence over *its* product market. For example, workers at General Motors have been able to earn a high wage not only because of the strength of the UAW, but also because they work for a company that has been able to earn oligopoly profits in the North American car market. In short, this union has been able to negotiate wage increases out of GM's oligopoly profits in the car market. This was confirmed between 1980 and 1982, when the auto companies' oligopoly power was reduced by competition from imported Japanese cars. When combined with the effects of recession, this resulted not only in losses for the car companies, but also pressure on the UAW to give up some wage increases won in earlier negotiations. The companies were no longer earning oligopoly profits that could be shared with labour.

4. Other departures from perfect competition may result in wage differentials. For example, **barriers to entry** in the form of long apprenticeship requirements may keep wages up in some crafts. **Discrimination** can depress the wages and salaries of ethnic minorities and women.

5. Finally, wage differences exist because people have different **talents, education, and training.** This is a major topic in the next chapter.

KEY POINTS

1. Labour markets are often imperfect. Workers form unions to exercise monopoly power on the supply side of the market. On the other side of the market, employers may exercise monopsony power. Examples include a government that hires public service employees and a private firm that is the only major employer in a small town.

2. Unions provide labour with a collective voice. In collective bargaining, unions promote the interests of their workers by pressing for such improvements as (a) better working conditions; (b) seniority rules to protect long-time workers; and (c) higher wages.

3. If a union is formed in a perfectly competitive labour market without externalities, and uses its market power to raise the wage rate, there is an overall efficiency loss. The reason is that some workers are not hired in this industry even though they would be more productive here than elsewhere. Moreover, by raising the wage rate, the union transfers income to labour from other factors of production.

On the other side of the market, if employers acquire monopsony power and lower the wage below its perfectly competitive level, there will be the same sort of efficiency loss. But while the efficiency effects of monopoly and monopsony will be similar, their transfer effects will be in opposite directions. When a monopsonist lowers wages, the transfer is *from* labour to other factors of production.

4. If a labour market is already monopsonized by a single employer, it no longer necessarily follows that efficiency will be reduced if a union is formed to raise the wage rate. In fact, if the union's market power is used only to offset the market power of the employer, efficiency can be *increased*.

5. A union may increase efficiency in other ways, too. By providing workers with a collective voice, it may improve their performance and reduce costly turnover of the labour force. A union may increase productivity by improving morale and communication between labour and management. On the other hand, a union may negoti-

ate featherbedding rules that reduce efficiency.

6. Bilateral monopoly occurs when market power exists on both sides of the labour market: Unions with monopoly power bargain with employers with monopsony power. The wage that results will fall between the high wage an unopposed union would seek and the low wage an unopposed monopsonist would offer. But, within these limits, it is impossible to predict precisely where the wage rate will be set. However, it will be heavily influenced by the bargaining power of each side. For example, a large union strike fund will increase the union's bargaining power, while a large inventory of finished goods will increase the bargaining power of management.

Bargaining is also affected by the negotiating expertise of labour and management. An incompetent negotiator who won't provide the other side with a face-saving compromise may prevent an agreement from being reached.

7. Membership in public service unions has grown rapidly in recent years. Such a union may have a strong bargaining position, particularly if it provides an essential service. To avoid a strike, a government employer may be willing to tax or borrow to meet a wage claim that would drive a private employer out of business. An important policy issue is whether public employees should have the right to strike.

KEY CONCEPTS

industrial union
craft union
collective bargaining
seniority rules
co-determination
closed shop
union shop
yellow-dog contracts
right-to-work law
open shop

Rand Formula
transfer and efficiency effects
    of a union
featherbedding
transfer and efficiency effects
    of labour monopsony
bilateral monopoly
countervailing power
why a union may decrease or
    increase inefficiency

relative bargaining power of
    union and management
why strikes occur
spillover costs of a strike
mediation
voluntary arbitration
compulsory arbitration
public service unions
dynamic wage differentials
compensating wage
    differentials

PROBLEMS

34-1 Before deregulation of the U.S. airline industry, the American government allowed the airlines to charge high fares, with some of the resulting profit being absorbed by high wage and salary payments. In such circumstances, would you expect that the deregulation that has made the airlines more competitive in setting their fares has affected their labour contracts as well? If so, how?

In light of this, do you think that Canadian unions of airline employees are likely to support the proposals for deregulation of

Canadian airlines that were introduced by the federal government in 1985?

34-2 "Monopsony in the labour market may have exactly the same effect on efficiency as a union." Is this possible? Explain. Would the transfer effects be the same in the two cases? (If you have studied Figure 2 in the introduction to Part 7, show how the two cases in the present example can have identical efficiency effects, but entirely different transfers effects.)

34-3 In the case of monopsony, which efficiency

752 PART SEVEN MICROECONOMICS: HOW INCOME IS DISTRIBUTED

condition in Figure 33-7 has been violated? Explain.

34-4 In Figure 34-5, suppose that the initial wage rate in a unionized labour market is at W_3. If employers form a bargaining association and successfully negotiate a lower wage rate, show how efficiency is affected. Consider two cases: What happens if the association negotiates the wage down to W_2? down to W_1?

34-5 Do you think that, as capital accumulates, the bargaining power of workers vis-a-vis management increases or decreases? Which workers can more effectively threaten to strike: Workers who would be leaving bulldozers idle? Workers who would be laying down their shovels?

34-6 Which union in each of the following pairs has the greater bargaining power? In each case, explain why.

    (a) A union of workers on the Montreal transit system, or a union of workers who build the trains.

    (b) A firefighters' union or a public school teachers' union.

    (c) A public school teachers' union or a university professors' union.

34-7 "Tying wage increases in the public sector to wage increases in private industry will not necessarily equalize wages. All it will do is keep them the same if they start out equal. If public sector wages are initially less than private sector wages, tying wages in this way only guarantees that inequities will be preserved." Do you agree? Do you think it is fair to pay both public and private employees the same wage if public employees have a greater guarantee of job security? If not, explain why and give an estimate of the differential you consider desirable.

*34-8 Use a diagram to show how the theory of the second best applies to labour forming a union in a market that is already monopsonized.

34-9 (a) Why might a union agree to a two-tiered contract, with a lower wage for new workers, provided the old, higher wage continues for existing workers?

    (b) If the lower wage for new workers is equal to the perfectly competitive wage, what will be the effect on efficiency? Why?

    (c) Explain how a two-tiered wage may affect the job security of present high-wage workers.

Chapter 35

OTHER INCOMES

Buy land. They ain't making any more of the stuff.
Will Rogers

Wage and salary payments to labour make up nearly three-quarters of national income. In this chapter, we will deal with the incomes of other factors of production such as capital and land that account for the remaining one-quarter. (However, as we shall see, the statistics may be a little misleading: Some of what is recorded as income to labour can be properly thought of as a return to capital.)

Consider now the income from capital, which comes in several forms. First, interest income is received by those who provide *debt capital*; that is, those who lend money to businesses—or to others—to finance the purchase of machinery or the construction of new buildings. (One way to lend a firm money is to buy its bonds. Another way is to lend money to a bank or other financial intermediary which in turn lends it out to the firm.) Second, profits are earned by those who own *equity capital*; that is, those who own small businesses outright or who own shares of a corporation's stock. Although the individual who buys stocks and bonds may view them quite differently, in this chapter we emphasize their similarity. Both represent a way in which people can contribute to the expansion of the nation's capital stock and receive income in return.

Income is earned not only on physical capital, such as machinery and buildings, but also on *human capital*. An example is the human capital you are now accumulating in the form of an education. Your expenditure of time and money today will increase your productivity in the future and hence increase your

income. Thus, an investment in human capital is like an investment in a machine or some other form of physical capital: It is an expenditure today that is expected to pay off in the future.

INTEREST: THE RETURN TO DEBT CAPITAL

To begin, let's suppose that firms finance investment only by borrowing. Borrowing takes place in the *market for loanable funds,* where lenders who supply funds come together with borrowers who demand funds. Like a competitive commodity market, a perfectly competitive market for loans can be studied with supply and demand curves.

How the Demand and Supply of Loans Determine the Interest Rate

Figure 35-1 shows the demand curve for loans by firms seeking the funds to finance investment projects—for example, funds to acquire new machinery. (People who need loans to buy houses or cars also participate in this market, but in this simple introduction we avoid such complications.) Just as the demand for labour depends on the productivity of labour, so too the demand for loans to buy machinery depends on how productive that machinery will be—that is, on the *marginal efficiency of investment* (MEI) shown in this diagram. Suppose bar *a* on the far left of Figure 35-1 represents the investment in machinery with the high-

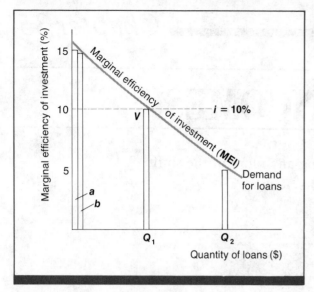

Figure 35-1   The marginal efficiency of investment and the demand for loans.
Investment opportunities are ranked in order, starting with those yielding the highest return on the left. The resulting MEI schedule is also the demand for loans. For example, if the interest rate is 10%, firms will demand Q_1 of loans. They keep borrowing to point V, where the marginal benefit of borrowing (the MEI schedule) is equal to the marginal cost of borrowing (the interest rate).

est return (MEI) of 15%. For example, consider a machine that costs $100,000 and lasts only one year. If this machine generates enough sales to cover labour, materials, etc., and leave $115,000 in addition, it provides a rate of return of 15%. Specifically, this $115,000 repays the firm for its initial $100,000 investment and provides a $15,000 return—that is, a 15% return—on this investment.

The next most attractive investment is b, which yields a 14.5% return; and so on. The result is the marginal efficiency of investment curve (MEI). This curve also represents the demand for investment loans. For example, if the interest rate is 10%, Q_1 of loans will be demanded. Firms will wish to invest in all the high-return opportunities to the left of V, but none to the right, where the return has fallen below the 10% cost of borrowing money. (Further detail on the MEI was given in Chapter 14, in the section entitled "The Effects of Monetary Policy.")

Recall from Chapter 33 that firms hire labour services to the point where the price of labour (the wage

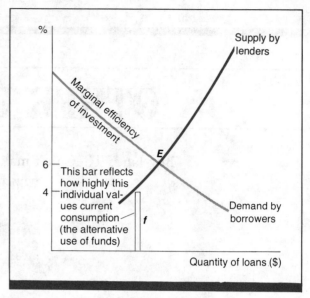

Figure 35-2   The market for loans.
The demand for loans is reproduced from Figure 35-1. It reflects the marginal efficiency of investment. The supply of loans depends on how highly lenders value money in its alternative use—consumption. The equilibrium is at E with a 6% interest rate.

rate) is equal to the marginal revenue product. Similarly, Figure 35-1 shows how firms acquire capital to the point where the price of capital services (the interest rate) equals the marginal efficiency of investment.

In Figure 35-2, the demand for investment loans (MEI) is reproduced from Figure 35-1, together with the supply of funds by lenders. This supply indicates how much businesses and households are willing to provide at various interest rates.[1] For example, the 4% interest rate that would just barely induce individual f to save and lend reflects how highly he or she values this money in its alternative use—current consumption. Individuals who value current consumption more highly won't be induced to save and lend until the interest rate rises above 4%. Therefore, they appear further to the right in this supply schedule. They are often described as having a stronger *time preference*; that is, they have a stronger preference for consuming now rather than in the future.

---

[1] Here, we ignore a number of macroeconomic complications, including the effects of the banking system on the supply of loans. These complications were studied in chapters 12 to 14.

In a perfectly competitive capital market, equilibrium is at E, where demand and supply intersect. In this example, the equilibrium rate of interest is 6%.

It is important to emphasize that this 6% interest rate reflects the height of the demand curve at E. In other words, *the marginal efficiency of investment is 6%.* We can take $1 worth of goods today and invest it to produce $1.06 of goods next year. In short, by investing in capital, we can convert present goods into a larger amount of future goods.

Through investment, present goods can be *exchanged for* a larger amount of future goods. Thus, present goods are *worth more* than future goods, with the interest rate telling us how much more.

Roundabout Production, with Interest as the Reward for Waiting

Investment is often described as **roundabout** or **indirect production**. Rather than using resources today to produce consumer goods directly, society produces an even greater amount of consumer goods *indirectly* by a roundabout method: First, resources are used to produce capital goods, and then this capital is used—together with labour and land—to produce consumer goods.

The greater quantity of consumer goods that is eventually produced in this way is the incentive for undertaking roundabout production. However, roundabout production is not possible unless some people are prepared to defer their consumption today; that is, people must be willing to save. This is necessary in order to release the resources that would otherwise go into producing consumer goods, and allow these resources to produce capital goods instead. For their decision to defer consumption—to wait before enjoying their income—savers receive an interest return. Thus, the interest rate can be viewed as a *reward to savers for waiting,* just as the wage rate is a reward to labour for its time and effort.

Risk and Other Influences on the Interest Rate

Although there is only one interest rate shown in Figure 35-2, in fact there are many rates of interest. A very large and financially sound corporation will be able to borrow funds at a low interest rate, since lenders view this loan as relatively risk-free. But a company in shaky financial condition will have to pay a higher interest rate to compensate lenders for the greater

risk that the loan will not be repaid. Thus, the interest rate shown in Figure 35-2 may be viewed as the "base rate of interest" that applies to a risk-free loan; as such, it is the best simple measure of the marginal efficiency of investment. Even though we continue to concentrate on this base rate, we should keep in mind that there is a whole array of interest rates on loans of varying risk.

Interest rates also reflect the *expectation of inflation.* (This macroeconomic issue was dealt with in Chapter 18. For simplicity, in this microeconomic analysis we describe a non-inflationary world.) In addition, interest rates today depend on the *length of term of the loans* and the *expectation of future changes in interest rates.* For example, suppose interest rates today are expected to rise next year because of an increase in the demand for loans by business. In this case, lenders will now be reluctant to lend money for a long period of, say, 5 or 10 years. They will prefer instead to lend their money for a short period of, say, a year, at which time they can then lend it out again at the expected higher interest rate. Thus, lenders now increase their supply of short-term loans, and this lowers the price (the interest rate) on these loans. At the same time, lenders now decrease their supply of long-term loans, raising the interest rate on these loans. Therefore, the expectation of a *future* change in interest rates will change the relationship between short-term and long-term interest rates *today.*

As we have seen in earlier chapters, an important question in product or labour markets is: What happens if the government intervenes to impose some restriction? This is also an important question in the capital market—that is, in the market for loans.

Effects of an Interest-Rate Ceiling

Figure 35-3 shows what happens in a perfectly competitive capital market when the government imposes a ceiling on the interest rate that can be charged by banks. Original equilibrium before the imposition of a ceiling is shown at E, with the interest rate at i_1. When the government sets a ceiling below this rate, say at i_2, the market no longer clears. There is a shortage of funds of GF. Unsatisfied borrowers cannot find loans.

One of the arguments in favour of an interest-rate ceiling is that it will reduce the burden of interest payments that must be paid by relatively poor individ-

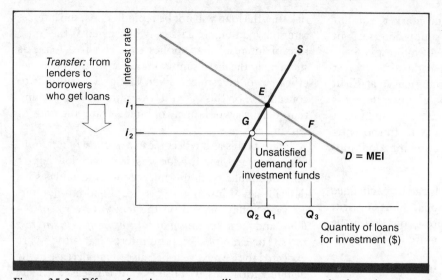

Figure 35-3 Effects of an interest-rate ceiling.
Before the interest rate ceiling, equilibrium in this competitive capital market is at E, with Q_1 of investment funds loaned out at interest rate i_1. When a ceiling of i_2 is imposed, borrowers are attracted by the lower rate and seek Q_3 loans; that is, borrowers try to move down their demand curve from E to F. However, only Q_2 of loans are available because lenders, discouraged by the reduced interest return, move down their supply curve from E to G. Thus, equilibrium shifts from E to G, loans are reduced from Q_1 to Q_2, and there is Q_2Q_3 unsatisfied demand for loans. Moreover, by lowering the interest rate that lenders receive and borrowers pay, the interest-rate ceiling results in the wide-arrow transfer from lenders to those borrowers who get funds.

uals and small firms. The lower interest rate does result in a transfer from lenders to borrowers—*but only to those borrowers lucky enough to get loans.* (This transfer is shown by the wide arrow on the left.) However, there is no guarantee that this redistribution will "help the poor." Some of the largest borrowers who get the bargain loans may be the rich who borrow to finance their big homes and business ventures. At the same time, some of the borrowers who are left unsatisfied may be the poor, who suffer as a consequence. Indeed, when funds are in short supply, poor borrowers are less likely to get them than are wealthy borrowers. If you had $100,000 to lend out and there were many groups who wanted to borrow it from you, would you lend it to the wealthy or to the poor?

Moreover, the interest-rate ceiling has two unfavourable effects on efficiency. First, it reduces the quantity of loanable funds available for investment from Q_1 to Q_2. This shift in the market away from its initial, perfectly competitive equilibrium results in the efficiency loss shown by the familar red triangle in Box 35-1. However, this problem—that there are now too few investment funds available—is not the only reason for an efficiency loss. A second reason is that the wrong borrowers may get the limited funds.

While this second source of inefficiency is also described in detail in Box 35-1, the basic problem can be understood in a fairly simple way. Because the interest-rate ceiling makes the demand for loans Q_3 greater than the supply Q_2, the limited supply of funds must be rationed in some way. Bankers may do this by a first come, first served procedure or some more complex method. But whatever the method, there will be a second efficiency loss unless the funds are rationed out to exactly the right set of borrowers—that is, those borrowers to the left of Q_2 in Figure 35-3, who have the investment projects with the highest productivity (MEI). It is unlikely that this will happen. Because the interest rate is so low, borrowers in the range Q_2Q_3, with lower-productivity investments, will also be trying to obtain funds, and some may succeed. If such a "rationing error" does occur, the second efficiency loss results: In the market for investment funds, high-productivity investments lose out to low-productivity ones.

This second source of inefficiency—above and beyond the red triangle in Figure 35-4—may be summarized as follows. In an unrestricted, perfectly competitive capital market, the interest rate is a price that allocates funds to the most productive investment projects. When the government intervenes to set an interest rate ceiling, some other allocating device must be used, and there is then a risk that the wrong set of projects will get the funds.

We emphasize that this is just another illustration

BOX 35-1

THE INEFFICIENCY OF AN INTEREST-RATE CEILING

Figure 35-4 reproduces the market for loanable funds from Figure 35-3, along with the ceiling that reduces the interest rate from i_1 to i_2. The first efficiency loss from this policy is shown by the red triangle. This loss occurs because suppliers of funds (savers) are discouraged by the lower interest rate and provide fewer funds, as shown by arrow a at the bottom of the diagram. Consequently, economically justified investment projects like g are "knocked out"—they cannot be undertaken. This results in a loss because the cost of this project would have been only the white bar under the supply curve (the cost to the lender of having to reduce consumption), while its benefit would have been the white bar plus the red bar under the demand curve (the return on this investment). Thus, the net loss because this particular project is cancelled is the red bar. The efficiency loss from all such cancellations in the relevant range shown by arrow a is the red triangle. Thus, the principle previously established in the market for goods and for labour— that a shift away from a perfectly competitive equilibrium such as E will result in an efficiency loss— is now shown to hold in a perfectly competitive market for investment funds as well.

The efficiency loss will be limited to this red triangle *only if* the investment projects knocked out by a lack of funds are those (like g) in the range a. If this is not the case, there will be a second efficiency loss. To illustrate, suppose, for example, that project j on the left is the one that is knocked out, not g. (The promoter of g may have been able to borrow by being more persuasive to a banker who is rationing loans.) An even greater efficiency loss is now

involved because an even more productive investment (j rather than g) is knocked out.

Moreover, this inefficiency may be even more serious. It is quite possible for j to lose out, not to g,

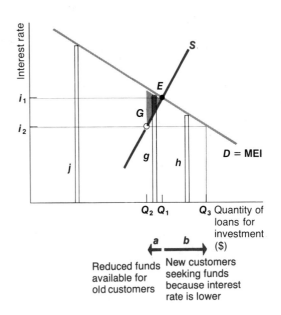

Figure 35-4 The inefficiencies created by an interest-rate ceiling.

but instead to an even lower-productivity project like h. In fact, h's productivity is so low that it would not even be considered at the original interest rate i_1; nobody would try to borrow to undertake it. The only reason someone is now applying for funds for h is the attraction of the artificially low interest rate. If the funds go to h rather than j, the efficiency loss from this rationing error—the reduction in the nation's output— will be even more severe. In this case, the loss will be the difference in j's high productivity and h's low productivity.

of the general problem that applies to *any* form of price fixing, such as our earlier example of rent control. Not only does rent control result in fewer apartments for rent. In addition, the "wrong" people may get the apartments. For example, a retired couple may continue to hang on to a choice Toronto apartment even though they now spend 9 months a year in Florida and would give up the apartment if they had to pay the higher free-market rent.

Returning to the interest-rate ceiling, we once again conclude: If we wish to transfer income from the rich to the poor, changing a market price like the interest rate may be an unwise way to do it. In the first place, an interest-rate ceiling may be an ineffective form of transfer because it may not move income from the rich to the poor at all. The statement that "borrowers benefit, therefore the poor benefit" involves two possible errors. First, borrowers as a group may not benefit, since some no longer get funds. Second, the borrowers who get cut off from funds tend to be the poor. Therefore, they bear the cost of this policy, whereas the rich who are still able to borrow are the ones who benefit from the lower interest rate. Moreover, an interest-rate ceiling may have damaging effects on efficiency. Isn't it better for the government to do any transferring directly, by taxing the rich and subsidizing the poor? The answer is yes, *provided* that the government can do so without incurring large efficiency losses of a different sort—an issue to be discussed in Chapter 37.

NORMAL PROFIT: A RETURN TO EQUITY CAPITAL

Thus far, we have assumed that all investment projects are financed by borrowing. Now let's broaden our analysis to include "equity finance"—that is, funds a firm raises by selling its stock (or by retaining some of its earnings). When a firm sells its stock, those who buy it obtain a share of the ownership and future profits of the firm.

In Chapter 22, we drew a distinction between two kinds of profit. First, **normal profit** reflects opportunity cost—the return necessary to induce and hold funds in one activity rather than another. Second, **above-normal profit** is any additional return beyond

this. We defer discussion of above-normal profit to a later section and concentrate here on normal profit.

For those who provide equity funds, what is their normal profit; that is, what is the opportunity cost of these funds? The answer is the return the funds could earn in their best alternative use. An alternative to buying stock is to buy interest-bearing securities. Thus, normal profit can be viewed as the base rate of interest plus an appropriate premium for risk—a risk that may be substantial because the entire amount that is put into the ownership of a firm may be wiped out. (Profit is sometimes described as a reward for risk taking. However, it is more than this, since it must also include a base rate of return needed to attract funds away from interest-bearing alternatives.)

Figure 35-2 can now be recast in the more general form shown in Figure 35-5, which represents the total market for investment funds. Now D includes the total demand by business for investment funds, whether these funds are raised by borrowing or by the sale of stock; and S is the corresponding supply. The result-

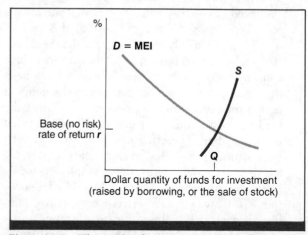

Figure 35-5   The market for investment funds (a generalization of Figure 35-2).
Whereas Figure 35-2 showed only borrowing, this diagram shows two ways that business may raise funds: by borrowing or by equity finance (the sale of stock). D is the demand for funds—in either debt or equity form—to finance new investment, while S is the corresponding supply of funds. In equilibrium, the base rate of return, in the absence of risk, would be r. However, in a risky world, the return any specific business must actually pay for the funds it raises will be r plus an appropriate amount to compensate the lender for risk.

ing equilibrium Q is the quantity of both debt and equity funds provided by savers to those who invest.

FOREIGN INVESTMENT AND THE RETURN TO FOREIGN CAPITAL

In the discussion so far, we have paid no attention to an important issue in Canada, namely the role of *foreign* savings in our economy. When we examine the quantity of savings (Q in Figure 35-5) that have financed Canada's capital requirements, we find that a substantial proportion has historically been supplied by foreign savers. (In recent years, most of the foreign capital coming in has come from the United States; during the late nineteenth and early twentieth century, most of it came from Britain.)

As we saw in the discussion of international capital flows in Chapter 15, foreign funds are invested in Canada in two ways. First, *direct investment* occurs when foreigners establish or expand firms that they

control, or when they buy control of an existing Canadian enterprise. Second, *portfolio investment* takes place when foreigners buy stocks, bonds, or other financial instruments issued by Canadian-controlled corporations, or by the Canadian federal or provincial governments.

The net flows of both types of foreign investment in Canada has fluctuated widely over the years. Relative to GNP, the largest total inflow occurred before World War I. During the Great Depression in the 1930s and during World War II, normal international capital movement essentially came to a halt. However, since World War II, Canada has again had large inflows of foreign capital: As Figure 35-6 shows, the net inflow was especially large (as a percentage of GNP) during most of the 1950s and early 1960s. During the 1970s and early 1980s, the capital inflow was smaller relative to GNP. In particular, the net flow of direct foreign investment has declined: While there was a substantial

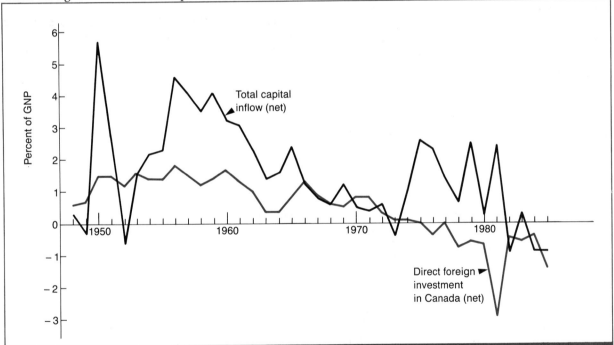

Figure 35-6   Net foreign capital inflows into Canada, 1946–1985 (percent of GNP).
During the 1950s and early 1960s, Canada received large net capital inflows, including substantial amounts of direct investment. Since the late 1960s, the inflows of capital have been smaller relative to GNP, and net direct foreign invest-

ment has at times been negative.

Sources: Compiled from K. Buckley and M. Urquhart, eds., *Historical Statistics of Canada*, 1st ed. (Toronto and Cambridge: Cambridge University Press and Macmillan of Canada, 1965) and *Bank of Canada Review*.

net inflow in this form during the fifties and sixties, in the late 1970s and early 1980s, net direct investment was negative—that is, Canadian direct investment in foreign countries (or takeovers of firms in Canada that were previously foreign-controlled) was larger than foreign direct investment in Canada. Statistics Canada estimates for 1979 put the total accumulated amount of foreign capital in Canada at a little less than $80 billion; the estimated return on this foreign-owned capital was roughly one-third of all income from capital in Canada.

Why is so much investment in Canada financed by foreign savers? Is it (1) because Canadians are unwilling to save as much as people in other countries? Or is it (2) because our economy has so many attractive investment opportunities?

There is little evidence to suggest that Canadians are less willing to save than other people. For example, during most of the 1970s, Canadians saved a larger fraction of their personal incomes than did U.S. citizens. Thus, we must look to the second explanation: Canada attracts foreign savings because its market and natural resources offer investment opportunities with a good return. Historically, domestic saving has not been sufficient to satisfy the large investment demand in Canada.

In Figure 35-7, S_d represents the supply of domestic saving in Canada, while S_t is the total supply of saving, including the foreign capital. (S_f is the supply of foreign capital to Canada; thus, S_t is found by horizontally adding S_f to S_d.) In the absence of foreign investment, equilibrium between supply and demand for investment funds would occur at E_d. But of course foreign capital does come into Canada, attracted by the relatively high rate of return here. With foreign funds coming in—and with the supply of savings accordingly being S_t, rather than just S_d—equilibrium occurs at E, rather than E_d. Thus, the inflow of foreign funds reduces the rate of return on investment in Canada from r_1 to r_2, and increases the amount of investment in Canada from Q_1 to Q_2. However, the quantity of investment in Canada that is financed *by Canadians* is reduced somewhat, from Q_1 to Q_3, with the balance Q_3Q_2 (which equals quantity $0Q_4$) now being supplied by foreigners.

The world as a whole benefits from the flow of foreign capital into Canada, since the rate of return is higher here than elsewhere; world saving is being used more efficiently than it would be if it were confined to

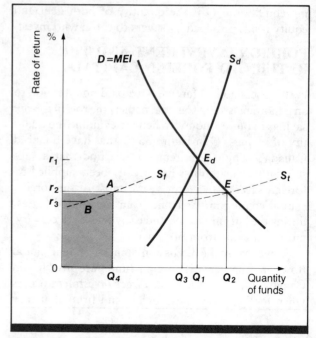

Figure 35-7   Adding foreign savings to the market for investment funds.

S_d is the supply curve showing the amounts that *domestic* Canadian savers would supply to the market for funds, at different rates of return. S_f shows the funds that *foreign* savers would be willing to invest in Canada. The *total* supply of funds is shown by curve S_t; it is found by adding the quantities of funds that domestic *and* foreign savers would supply at different rates of return.

Without foreign capital, equilibrium would be at E_d, the intersection of the demand curve for funds with the domestic supply curve. When foreign capital does come in, equilibrium occurs at E. At the equilibrium rate of return r_2, we can see from the S_f curve that foreign savers would supply the amount Q_4; this amount must be the same as Q_3Q_2.

lower-return investments outside Canada. But this does not *necessarily* mean that Canadians benefit. True, output is greater in Canada because investment is greater. But a lot of the benefit of this investment goes to foreigners. Specifically, foreigners earn a rate of return r_2 on their investment in Canada—that is, an income equal to the shaded rectangle.

To analyse whether or not Canadians on balance benefit, consider Figure 35-8. First, the inflow of foreign savings means that Canadians save Q_3Q_1 less; that is, their consumption increases by Q_3Q_1. But recall from Figure 35-2 that for any given amount of

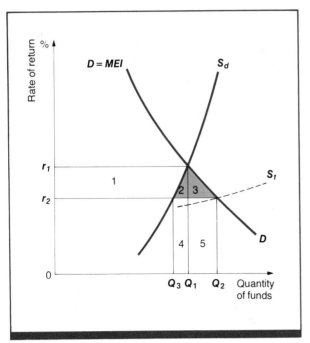

Figure 35-8 The effects of foreign investment in Canada.
The demand curve and the domestic and total supply curves for funds are reproduced from Figure 35-7. When Q_3Q_2 of foreign investment comes in, driving the equilibrium rate of return down from r_1 (the equilibrium rate without foreign capital) to r_2, there are two effects. First, total investment increases by Q_1Q_2; the return on this extra investment equals area 3 + 5. Second, Canadian savers increase current consumption, since their savings fall by Q_3Q_1; the value of this extra consumption is area 2 + 4. However, since area 4 + 5 (which is equal to the gray, shaded area in Figure 35-7) is paid as a return to the foreign investors, the net gain to Canada is only area 2 + 3. (Area 1 represents a transfer from Canadian savers to owners of other Canadian factors of production.)

saving, the height of the Canadian supply curve S_d reflects the value of an additional unit of current consumption. Therefore, the value that Canadians place on Q_3Q_1 additional units of consumption is area 2 + 4 under the curve S_d.

However, on this Q_3Q_1 of investment in Canada, income 4 must be paid to foreigners. (They are earning return r_2 on these funds.) Therefore, the net benefit to Canadians is area 2—the benefit Canadians receive because foreigners undertake some of the investing in Canada, thus allowing Canadians to use these funds for higher-valued consumption.

Second, the inflow of foreign savings into Canada

not only takes the place of Canadian savings. It also results in an increase (Q_2Q_1) in total investment in Canada, which results in additional output equal to area 3 + 5. (The return on the last unit of investment at Q_2 is r_2; the return on the preceding units are given by the height of the MEI curve.) Of this, area 5 is paid to foreign investors, leaving a net gain to Canada of area 3. This is the net benefit to Canada of using foreign funds whose productivity exceeds their cost.

Thus, economic analysis suggests that capital imports result in overall gains to Canada of areas 2 + 3—gains which are similar to the gains from the imports of goods, as may be seen by comparing Figure 35-8 to Figure 31-8. However, we saw earlier that while imports of goods provide an overall gain, they affect various groups differently, benefitting some, and hurting others. The same is true of capital imports. Specifically:

1. Canadian savers (owners of capital) lose, because the rate of return on investment in Canada is depressed from r_1 to r_2. (The return to Canadian capitalists is reduced by foreign competition.)
2. Canadian labour benefits because more capital in Canada means more demand for labour and a higher wage rate; for example, when the Ford Motor Co. builds a plant in St. Thomas, Ontario, employment and wages rise in the St. Thomas–London area. (With more capital in Canada, Canadians work with more and better equipment; consequently, labour productivity—and wages—rise.)

Thus, the inflow of foreign capital results in both an efficiency gain and a transfer of income from Canadian capital owners to Canadian labour.[2]

SOME COMPLICATIONS

While our simple approach suggests that there are gains from foreign investment, such investment is nevertheless very controversial—even more controversial

---

[2]In our discussion of the gains and losses from capital flows, we have ignored an important complication: A capital inflow this year affects not only the return on Canadian-owned capital, but also on foreign-owned capital invested in the past. This complication (which does not upset our conclusions) is taken into account in G.D.A. MacDougall, "The Benefits and Costs of Private Investment from Abroad: A Theoretic Approach," *Economic Record* (March 1960); reprinted in Richard E. Caves and Harry G. Johnson, eds., *Readings in International Economics* (Homewood, Ill.: Richard D. Irwin, 1968), pp. 172–94.

than international trade. The controversy focuses on a number of complications which have not been taken into account in our discussion of figures 35-7 and 35-8, most notably:

1. International investment can have political consequences. In particular, the question may be raised: Does a small country receiving a large volume of international investment suffer a reduction in its national independence because many decisions that are important for that country are not made there, but are instead made in the head offices of parent companies, in places like New York or London?

2. The fact that many firms operating in Canada are subsidiaries of American (or other foreign) firms may influence international trade. Are American subsidiaries more eager to import and slower to export than Canadian firms, thus reducing industrial production in Canada?

Because of the complexities which they introduce, these important elements of the controversy over capital imports are deferred to the appendix. Here we deal with two other complications.

1. The Taxation of the Returns to Capital

Foreign-owned firms are subject to the same basic rate of corporation income tax as domestic firms: 46% of profits. Moreover, most interest and dividends paid to foreigners are subject to a Canadian *withholding tax* of 15%. Thus, a fraction of the earnings of foreign capital do not go to foreigners at all; rather, they end up in the Canadian treasury. Therefore, areas 2 + 3 in Figure 35-8 may understate the Canadian gain from capital inflows. (It is interesting to note that this tax benefit to Canada is a loss to foreign countries. Specifically, when foreign firms invest in Canada rather than at home—in, say, the United States—there is a transfer of income from the Treasury in Washington to Ottawa. The profits of U.S.-owned firms operating in Canada are taxed by Ottawa; if the profits were earned in the United States instead, they would be taxed by Washington, to the benefit of American taxpayers.)

2. Can We Reduce the Cost of Foreign Capital?

In our discussion of international trade policy in Chapter 32, we noted that one logically valid argument in favour of a tariff was that by reducing imports, it may reduce the price we have to pay for them—that is, the price foreign firms get when they supply imports to us (point no. 7 in the section "Economic Arguments for Protection"). A similar argument applies to foreign capital: If we reduce our imports of capital, this may reduce the net returns we have to pay foreigners to induce them to supply capital to us. In short, we may acquire capital less expensively; and we will benefit from this, just as we would from less expensive imports from foreigners. (If, for example, capital imports were reduced from A to B in Figure 35-7, the net return we would have to offer to get this amount of foreign capital would be reduced from r_2 to r_3.)

However, the possibility of reducing the cost of foreign capital in this way is limited by two factors:

(a) The supply curve of foreign capital must be upward-sloping. That is, the country must be in a position where it has to pay a higher net return on foreign capital in order to attract more of it. (If the supply curve is horizontal, rather than upward-sloping, a reduction in the amount of foreign capital will not reduce its cost: The cost will remain at r_2 no matter how much capital we import.) Some Canadian economists believe that the supply curve of foreign capital facing Canada is virtually horizontal; others believe that it has a significant upward slope.

(b) The policies used to reduce the amount of foreign capital have to be carefully designed so that they don't change foreigners' perception of the attractiveness of Canada as a place to invest. If foreigners perceive government policy as hostile to foreign capital, the supply curve S_f may shift upward and to the left: Foreigners will demand a higher expected return to compensate for the risk of investing in a country whose policies are seen as hostile. Thus, the cost of foreign capital to Canada will rise. Moreover, if you redraw Figure 35-7 with a new, higher S_f curve, you will see that the amount of capital imports will be reduced to less than the original Q_3Q_2. In turn, this means that the taxes collected and other benefits to Canada of foreign investment (originally areas 2 + 3 in Figure 35-8) will also be reduced.

In the 1970s and early 1980s, some observers believed that the policies of Canada's *Foreign Investment Review Agency* (FIRA), the government agency charged with screening and restricting foreign investment, were having just this effect. American and other foreign investors complained that negotiations with FIRA were complicated and costly and that FIRA's decisions sometimes seemed arbitrary. By the mid-1980s, there was concern that resentment of FIRA by foreign investors might substantially raise the cost of foreign capital to Canada. After the Liberals were defeated in 1984, the Conservative government moved quickly to revamp FIRA, and reduce or eliminate the restrictions it had been imposing. (To emphasize its new image, FIRA was renamed "Investment Canada.")

Thus, we see that the issue of foreign investment is complicated. Moreover, the issues described here just begin to deal with the controversy over foreign investment. As noted earlier, other elements of the debate are considered in the appendix.

THE ROLE OF FACTOR PRICES

We have examined the pricing of two factors of production: labour and capital. We now pause to consider how factor prices influence both the individual firm's decisions on using these factors and the allocation of these factors across the economy as a whole.

How Factor Prices Influence Decisions by Individual Firms

In its decision making, a firm must address several issues. On the one hand, it must decide on how much labour and how much capital equipment it will use. At the same time, it must also decide which goods to produce and how much of each. To illustrate, suppose the wage rate rises. The firm responds by using less labour and more capital; that is, it substitutes capital for labour because labour has become more expensive. Moreover, because of the higher wage, the firm may also reduce the output of its final products, especially those requiring a great deal of labour.

As a further example of how factor and product decisions are interrelated, suppose there is an increase in the price of one of the firm's products. In response, the firm will increase its output of this good by hiring more factors of production and/or by shifting production away from one of its other outputs. In short, the firm's decisions on what to produce and the amount of factors to employ are not separate decisions. Instead, they are all *elements of one overall decision*.

How Factor Prices Influence the Allocation of Scarce Resources throughout the Economy

Just as price acts as the screening mechanism for deciding who will consume a good and who will not (Figure 24-5), so a factor price acts as a screening device to determine how a scarce resource will be used. For example, the wage rate acts as a screen to determine the particular activities in which society's scarce labour will be employed. In a competitive, fully employed economy, the wage rate rises as productivity increases. This conveys a clear message to those producers who can no longer afford the higher wage. The message is: Society can no longer afford to have its scarce labour employed in your activity. There are now too many other, more productive pursuits. This may seem harsh, but it is the sign of economic progress. Think back, for a moment, to all the things that labour used to do, but no longer does. At our current high wage rates, it doesn't pay to hire workers to hoe field corn anymore, as in the "good old days." Household servants have almost vanished.

Similarly, we have seen how the interest rate is a market price that acts as a screen to determine in which particular projects investment will take place. When that screening device is replaced by another—such as the rationing that occurs when an interest-rate ceiling is imposed—investment funds are unlikely to go to the most productive projects.

THE RETURN TO HUMAN CAPITAL

Income is earned not only by investment in machinery and other physical capital, but also by investment in *human capital*—the acquisition of skills, training, and education.[3] In many essential respects, an investment in human capital is similar to an investment in physical capital: Current consumption is reduced in the

---

[3]For a sample of early work in this field, see G.S. Becker, *Human Capital: A Theoretical and Empirical Analysis, with Special Reference to Education,* 2nd ed. (New York: National Bureau of Economic Research, 1975) and Jacob Mincer, *Schooling, Experience and Earning* (New York: National Bureau of Economic Research, 1974). For a survey of more recent research on the value of an education, see R.J. Willis, "Wage Determinants: A Survey and Reinterpretation of Human Capital Earnings Functions," in O.C. Ashenfelter and R. Layard, eds., *Handbook of Labor Economics* (Amsterdam: North Holland Press, 1985). An early Canadian work on human capital was Bruce Wilkinson, *Studies in the Economics of Education* (Ottawa: Department of Labour, 1965).

expectation of higher future income and consumption. For example, students give up the income they could make if they were not busy studying; they live frugally in the hope that the education will pay off in higher income after graduation. Similarly, apprentices may be willing to work for abnormally low wages if they are receiving training that is likely to lead to a better job.

By recognizing the importance of human capital, we recognize that everyone in the labour force is not equally productive; we are relaxing our earlier assumption that all workers are similar. In fact, the quality of labour depends on the amount of education, skill, and experience that various individuals have acquired. Some have a lot of human capital, others very little. Frequently, their incomes reflect this. This means that when we say that three-quarters of the national income is paid in the form of wages and salaries, we recognize that this includes not only a basic payment for the time and effort of unskilled labour, but also a return on the human capital that skilled workers have acquired.

Who pays for the investment in human capital? In the case of education, much of the investment is undertaken by the individuals who spend their time studying instead of earning an income. However, governments also invest: Federal, provincial, and municipal governments all help to finance education. One justification for these expenditures is that it is only fair to provide educational opportunity for all. Another is that education provides not only a benefit to those who acquire it, but also spillover benefits to others in society as well. For example, if a highly educated doctor discovers a new vaccine, it may not only increase the discoverer's own income, but will also benefit the public, which now has protection from a disease. In the face of such spillover benefits, the unaided free market may not provide enough investment in human capital, so the government also contributes.

On-the-job apprenticeship or training in industry also represents an investment in human capital. There are several ways the initial cost of this investment may be covered. For example, workers may accept a low wage during the apprenticeship period when their productivity is still low. However, as noted earlier, the possibility of using this arrangement is limited by the minimum-wage laws. Alternatively, employers may pay apprentices a standard wage and thereby bear the initial costs of this investment. But this option raises a serious problem for employers, since they are investing in an asset—in the form of skill or training—which they do not own. Workers are not slaves, and they can always quit and go to work elsewhere, taking the training with them. (Of course, the ease with which they can do so depends on how specific their expertise is to the company that trained them.) This is another reason why there may be underinvestment in human capital: Employers may not invest as heavily in training programs as they would if workers would guarantee to stay on the job and thus allow employers to "get their money back." More detail on this issue is provided in Box 35-2.

Human Capital and Discrimination

The problem of low income for a minority, such as blacks in the United States or Native people in Canada, may reflect more than present discrimination by employers. It may also be the result of the past inability of the minority to acquire human capital. The members of such a group may be caught in the following vicious circle. Past discrimination has meant that they have been receiving lower wages. Consequently, they have been unable to provide their children with an adequate education. As a result, their children are now paid lower wages—*even if employers today don't discriminate*. For example, American blacks remain at a disadvantage even if those now making important economic decisions are not prejudiced.

One way of breaking this vicious circle is to ensure equal educational opportunity for minorities. To make up for past discrimination, special efforts have been made under affirmative action programs to get blacks, other minorities, and women into training programs and positions where they can accumulate human capital. How far affirmative action should be extended to "reverse discrimination"—whereby women and minorities are given preferential treatment—is a controversial question. However, the concept of affirmative action is gaining ground: In its 1985 report, the MacDonald Commission endorsed it in principle, and recommended that it be introduced on an experimental basis in Crown corporations.

Measuring the Return on Human Capital: What Is a University Education Worth?

Acquiring a university education involves substantial costs. What is its future payoff?

In the 1950s and 1960s, the answer seemed clear: Those with post-secondary education were earning substantially higher incomes than those with only a high-school diploma. However, through the 1970s and early 1980s, there were a number of factors that combined to reduce the payoff on post-secondary schooling. In the United States, where the problem has been studied extensively, this decline has been brought out clearly by statistical evidence; the trends in Canada seem to have been broadly similar.[4] One of the factors tending to decrease the payoff was the increased supply of people with post-secondary degrees. Unprecedented numbers were being graduated, both because of the population bulge at the university age level and because an increasing proportion of that population was going to university or community colleges. At the same time, the demand for graduates was not increasing at the same pace—partly because of shrinking job opportunities in education, one of the areas of employment that requires a university degree. Elementary schools, high schools, and post-secondary institutions had already increased their staffs to handle the bulge in population.

Suppose we wish to calculate a percentage rate of return on a human investment like a university degree. This can be done in much the same way as we would calculate a percentage rate of return on a physical investment like machinery: The initial costs are compared with the eventual payoff, in the form of a higher income. Figure 35-9 shows a hypothetical income pattern for those with a university degree and those with only a high-school education.

What is the cost of a university education? First, there is the income foregone during the actual period of study. This cost can be visualized as a set of arrows like *a,* one for each year spent at university. But that's not the only sacrifice students make. Even after their education is complete, their average incomes at first are below the incomes of people without a degree who have four years of experience and seniority instead.

[4]For a survey of Canadian research in this field, see David Stager, "Economics of Higher Education: Research Publications in English in Canada, 1971–81," *The Canadian Journal of Higher Education,* vol. 12, no. 1 (1982): 17–28. Rate-of-return calculations up to the early 1970s are presented in Ozay Mehmet, "Economic Returns on Undergraduate Fields of Study in Canadian Universities: 1961 to 1972," *Relations Industrielles/Industrial Relations,* vol.32, no.3 (1977): 321–39.

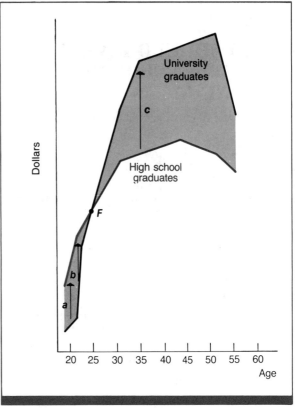

Figure 35-9   Typical lifetime profiles of income, with and without a university education.
Hypothetical earnings over the life cycle for high-school graduates and university graduates.

This cost to university students is the set of arrows like *b.* However, this income disadvantage of university graduates disappears fairly quickly. By point *F,* in their late twenties, they have caught up. Arrow *c* shows that by their late thirties they have gone well ahead— and they stay ahead.

Thus, the costs and benefits of a university education can be summed up as follows:

1. The *costs* include both (a) the income foregone during university and the later "catch-up period," shown as the red area in this diagram, and (b) a set of costs not shown in this diagram, including tuition and any higher costs of living in university residence than elsewhere.

2. The *benefits* come in the form of a higher income later, as shown by the gray area.

By comparing these initial costs and eventual bene-

BOX 35-2

WHO SHOULD INVEST IN APPRENTICESHIP TRAINING?

As one form of investment in human capital, on-the-job training of apprentices involves an initial cost that is expected to pay off with increased productivity in the future. In this box we consider the question: Who should pay this initial cost, the employees who receive the training or the employers?

THE EMPLOYEES

In Figure 35-10, the employees' wage (the red line) is always kept the same as their productivity (the black line). Therefore, the investment in the initial apprenticeship period (area 1) is paid by the employees who accept a wage during this period that is lower than the wage W_o they could earn in alternative jobs. They also get all the later payoff from the investment (area 2), since the wage W_n that they earn then is higher than the W_o they could earn without the training.

THE EMPLOYERS

In Figure 35-11, the employees bear none of the cost of the investment, nor do they capture any of the payoff from it. Throughout, their wage remains the same W_o that they could have earned in other jobs. It is now the employers who pay the total cost of the investment (area 1). The reason is that dur-

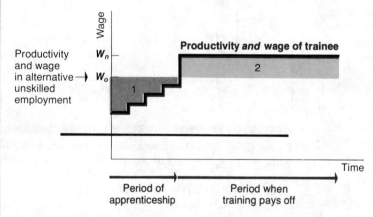

Figure 35-10 The employees invest in apprenticeship.

fits, we can calculate a percentage return on a university education (an investment in human capital) in much the same way as we earlier estimated the percentage return on physical capital such as machinery.

However, such calculations raise problems. For example, is it reasonable to claim that the higher income of graduates—shown by the gray area in Figure 35-9—is all due to their university education? The answer is no. One reason for their higher earnings is that they are, on average, more talented and hardworking; they aren't dropouts. Thus, even without a university education, they would still earn more, on average. Accord-

ingly, one task is to sort out how much of their higher income should be attributed to their education, and how much to their greater talent and perseverance. A second difficulty is that the *private* rate of return to the individual acquiring an education is not the same as the *social* rate of return to the nation as a whole. (For adjustments in the private rate necessary to derive the social rate, see Box 35-3.)

American studies that have attempted to take some of these complications into account found private returns on an undergraduate degree of 10% to 12% in the 1960s, with social returns probably being some-

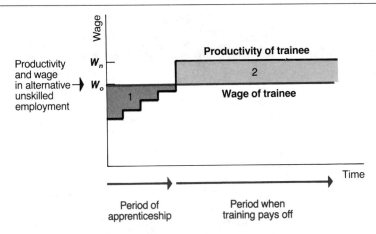

Figure 35-11 **The employers invest in apprenticeship.**

ing the apprenticeship period they get less productivity from the employees (black line) than the wage they pay them (red line). In theory, employers also get the later payoff from this investment (area 2) when the productivity of the employees exceeds their wage W_o.

However, the problem for employers is that they may not get this later payoff, since workers may leave once their training is completed. Specifically, workers may be attracted away by another employer offering higher wage W_n; there is now a very good chance of such an offer, since this is now what the workers' services are worth. This risk that employ-

ees will leave once their training is complete reduces the incentive for employers to undertake investment in human capital, even though it might yield high returns to society in terms of greater labour productivity.

These two panels represent the two sharpest alternatives. In practice, other more complicated arrangements are often introduced. For example, even employers in Figure 35-11 who pay the whole training cost almost always give the trainees some of the eventual payoff 2, in order to keep them from leaving.

what lower. Private return studies for Canada yield even higher figures: over 20% in 1969 and only somewhat less in 1972. Because the costs of post-secondary education are more heavily subsidized in Canada, the gap between the social and private returns are probably wider in Canada than in the United States.

Through the 1970s and early 1980s, the private rates of return fell—to as low as 5% to 9%, according to some estimates for the United States. These changes were caused in part by shifts in the age profile of earnings in Figure 35-9. As the population bulge reduced the advantage of university graduates during the 1970s,

the two curves came closer together; that is, gap c became smaller. In the process, catch-up point F moved to the right, with university graduates being older before they caught up to high-school graduates. (In the United States, there is some evidence that the relative earnings of college graduates may be rising again, so that the gap between the curves is once more widening, and the catch-up point F moving back toward the left. It is not yet clear whether such a trend is also emerging in Canada.)

Thus, we see that education is indeed an investment; costs incurred in acquiring an education today

BOX 35-3

WHY PRIVATE AND SOCIAL RETURNS ON EDUCATION DIFFER

To estimate the social return on investment in higher education, the estimated private rate of return should ideally be adjusted as follows:

1. Adjust it upward to take into account any external benefits, such as the spillover benefit from the education of the doctor who discovers a new vaccine.

2. Adjust it downward to take into account government subsidies to higher education. These are costs of the investment to society but not to the private individuals being educated. Because private individuals do not take these costs into account, they are not included in the calculation of private rates of return.

There are other reasons why private and social rates of return may differ. Employers pay university graduates more, not only because education has made them more productive, but also because it has given them a "credential." In other words, education acts as a screening device that tells employers which individuals have the capacity and diligence to learn. Because it gives graduates the best jobs, it provides them with a private return in the form of a higher income. But what benefit to society overall is provided by such a mechanism that gives the best jobs to one group rather than another? The traditional answer has been: Very little. How-

Courtesy Miller Services Limited

ever, it may be argued that there is some social benefit to screening because it tends to match up the more talented people with the best jobs. If there were no educational screening mechanism, it would take longer for these jobs and people to "find" each other, with some national output and income being lost during this period.

---

do yield a return in terms of higher income in the future. This is particularly true of a high-school education, which has traditionally had a higher return than a university education. Moreover, a high-school education is a relatively good investment in another sense: it yields returns that are favourable relative to returns on physical capital. Thus, if you wish, you could view your high-school education purely and simply as an investment; it needs no further justification.

While a university education may also be viewed as an investment, part of its justification may also lie in its other benefits in the form of "consumption" gains.

For example, a university education provides many individuals with a greater appreciation of history and literature. One might also consider the psychological benefits that well-educated people receive because they have more interesting and challenging jobs. To illustrate: Even if the income were the same, it would be more interesting and pleasant to design a bridge than to pour the cement. Then, too, jobs may come with what the British call "perks" (perquisites). For example, expense-paid business trips are often fun. On the other hand, those at the top often work hard, under great pressure.

The Complex Nature of Wages and Salaries

In the preceding section, we have seen some of the reasons why an individual's wage or salary may reflect far more than just a basic wage rate. For example, an individual's income may be higher because of education. Or it may be higher because of some specific talent or ability: Martina Navratilova was born with a great natural ability to hit a tennis ball; others are born with a special talent for solving mathematical problems.

Figure 35-12 illustrates this idea. An initial point of reference is provided on the left by the base income of $15,000 earned by an unskilled labourer with no special talent or training. The remaining three individuals work for a large firm. Individual A is educated up to an MBA and has five years' experience. He earns $33,000 income; this is also what he could earn in an alternative occupation. (This includes the $15,000 base

wage plus an $18,000 return on his education and experience.) In other words, $33,000 is his income and also his opportunity cost. Individual B has exactly the same education and experience as A, and the same $33,000 opportunity cost. However, her income is another $14,000 higher because she has a special flair for solving the problems encountered by this firm. Finally, individual C has exactly the same education, experience, and opportunity cost as A and B. But he has an even more incisive mind in dealing with this firm's problems. His income consequently is a hefty $75,000.

Three components of income can be distinguished:
1. The $15,000 base income for unskilled work.
2. The additional $18,000 of income that these consultants could earn in other jobs because of their education and experience.

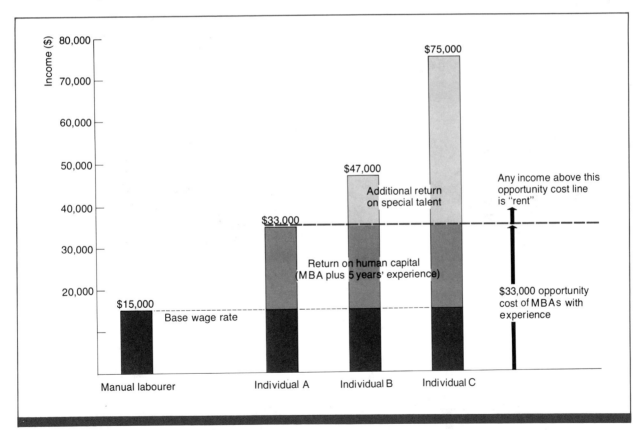

Figure 35-12 Dividing income into its components.
Individuals A, B, and C have the same qualifications—an MBA plus five years experience—and the same $33,000 opportunity cost, shown by the red dashed line. Any surplus income above this is rent. Thus A earns no rent, B earns $14,000 rent, and C—with the greatest natural talent for the job—earns $42,000 rent.

The first two components represent opportunity cost. The last one does not:

3. Additional returns to those with special talents. This third item falls under the economists' broad definition of *rent*.

Economists use the term *rent* in a broad sense, to identify the return to any factor of production in excess of its opportunity cost.

Thus, rent is the gap between what a factor *is* earning and what it *could* earn elsewhere. Expressed this way, we see that there are two reasons why an individual's income might include a very large rent component: (1) The income he or she *is* earning may be very high, and (2) what he or she *could* earn elsewhere is low. We continue to focus on the first reason here, while the second is considered in Box 35-4.

BOX 35-4

RENT AND OPPORTUNITY COST

Recall that rent is defined as the difference between what a factor is earning and what it could earn elsewhere (its opportunity cost). The three business executives in Figure 35-12 had the same $33,000 opportunity cost but different incomes, so they had different rents. Here, we consider individuals who have the same income but different opportunity

costs. Differences in rent occur in this case as well, as we shall now show.

In Figure 35-13 we show a labour market in which all individuals have the same salary Y. But their opportunity costs vary. Thus, individuals *a* and *b* have the two different opportunity costs shown by the two white bars. Therefore their rents will vary.

To show this in detail, first consider individual *a*. She has barely been attracted into this industry by income Y, since this is what she can earn elsewhere (her opportunity cost). Because there is no

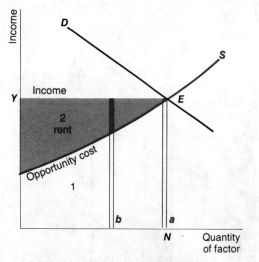
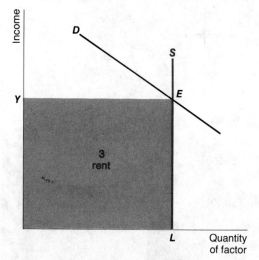

(a) All individuals in this panel earn the same income **Y**, but they have different opportunity costs, as given by the height of the curve **S**. The difference between their income and opportunity cost is rent. For individual **b**, this is the dark bar, while for individual **a**, it is zero. For all individuals, it is the shaded area.

(b) None of the plots of land in this panel has any other use. All plots have zero opportunity cost, and their supply is completely inelastic. Therefore, their entire income 3 is rent.

Figure 35-13 Rent of a factor of production that (a) has an alternative use (such as labour) and (b) one that does not (such as some types of land).

RENT

What do Wayne Gretzky, Placido Domingo, and an acre of southern Ontario farmland have in common? The answer to this question is: They all are like business executive C in Figure 35-12; they all earn an economic *rent* because of their superior quality. Domingo has an exceptional voice. Gretzky plays outstanding hockey. An acre of good Ontario land yields unusually large quantities of corn.

Rent on Agricultural Land, Based on Differences in Quality

All economic analyses begin with the cultivation of the earth. . . . To the economist, . . . the green plain is a sort of burial place of hidden treasure, where all the forethought and industry of man are set at naught by the caprice of the power which hid the treasure. . . . Thus is Man mocked by earth his stepmother, and never knows as he tugs at her closed hand whether it

---

difference between her income and her opportunity cost, she earns no rent.

The situation for individual *b* is different. His opportunity cost (potential income elsewhere) is shown by the lower white bar. The difference between this and his actual income *Y* is the red bar; this is his rent. Visualizing similar red bars repre-

senting the rents of other workers, we conclude that the rent earned by all *N* workers in this industry is the shaded triangle 2.

To sum up this example: The *N* workers, all earning salary *Y*, have a total salary income of areas 1 + 2. Of this, area 1 is their opportunity cost, while area 2 is their rent.

The income of any other factor of production can similarly be divided into opportunity cost and rent components. In particular, we are interested in the land shown in panel (*b*), which has a completely inelastic supply because it can't be used for anything but agriculture. In other words, quantity *L* will be supplied no matter what its price may be. Because this land can't earn anything in any other use (its opportunity cost is zero) all its income 3 is rent.

Finally, we can recap our discussion of rent with the simple example shown in Figure 35-14, which illustrates how an individual can earn rent because (1) he's very good at what he's doing (the issue addressed in the main text) or (2) he's very bad at anything else (the issue addressed in this box). Washington is a better basketball player than teammate McTavish, and his higher income reflects this. If they had the same opportunity costs—that is, the same ability to earn income elsewhere—Washington would have a higher rent. But they don't have the same opportunity costs. Whereas Washington could play pro football instead for $100,000 a year, McTavish has no other talent than basketball. His opportunity cost is the bare $15,000 that he could earn in unskilled manual labour. Because his opportunity cost is so low, almost all his income is rent; indeed, for this reason there's a higher rent component in his income than in Washington's.

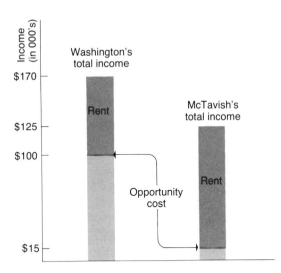

Figure 35-14 **Why rent depends both on (1) how productive a factor is in its present use and (2) how unproductive it is in any other use.**
Washington has more basketball talent and earns a higher salary. If the opportunity costs of the players were the same, Washington would earn the higher rent. But their opportunity costs are not the same. In fact, McTavish's is so much lower that rent makes up a larger part of his income than Washington's.

contains diamonds or flints, good red wheat or a few clayey and blighted cabbages.

George Bernard Shaw

Figure 35-15 shows three plots of land with no alternative use but to grow a crop. In other words, their opportunity cost is zero. It therefore follows from the preceding definition that any income they earn is rent. In this special case, economists' and the public's definition of rent coincide: It is the income earned by land.

Relatively poor land C has such low productivity that with a $3 price of wheat, it has just been brought into cultivation. The value of the wheat it produces is barely sufficient to cover the costs of fertilizer, machinery, the farmer's time, and other inputs. Therefore, it earns no rent. Land B is more fertile soil that grows enough wheat per acre to pay for other inputs and leave $60 per acre; that is, its rent is $60 per acre. Land A is even more productive and earns a rent of $150.

Of course, the rent on these plots of land depends on the price of wheat. Suppose that, because of crop failures elsewhere in the world, the price of wheat rises from the initial $3 a bushel (in Figure 35-15) to $4. The result is shown in Figure 35-16. Land C,

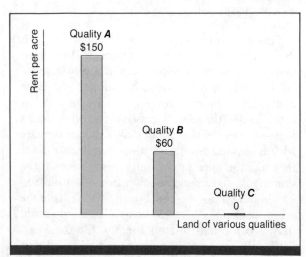

Figure 35-15   Rent based on differences in quality of land (based on wheat price of $3 per bushel).
Marginal land C, which is just barely fertile enough to cultivate, earns no rent. High-productivity land A earns the highest rent.

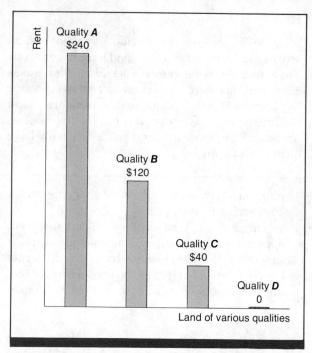

Figure 35-16   How rents increase when the price of wheat increases.
This figure is the same as Figure 35-15 except that the price of wheat has risen from $3 to $4 per bushel. Because of this increased price, all existing plots of land earn greater income—that is, greater rent. Moreover, less productive plot D is brought into cultivation for the first time.

which previously earned no rent, now does. And the rents earned by plots A and B increase. Land D is now the marginal land, just brought into cultivation and earning zero rent.

Another Example of Rent: The Income from Mineral Deposits

A mineral deposit may also earn an economic rent. To confirm this statement, reinterpret figures 35-15 and 35-16 as follows. Mineral deposit A is a rich vein of ore, easy to reach. Mineral deposit B is also a rich vein of ore, but difficult to reach and extract. Deposit C is of poorer quality and so difficult to reach that initially in Figure 35-15 it is barely being mined. In Figure 35-16 we see how an increase in the price of ore increases the rent earned on each of these deposits and induces the mining of low-yield deposit D for the first time.

Rent on Land Because of Its Location

Land may yield economic rent not only because of its fertility but also because of its location. To illustrate, land A in Figure 35-17 is in the prime business district of a city and can be used in a highly productive way. A business might wish to locate there for a variety of reasons: It might want to be close to suppliers and competitors so that it can easily keep up with new developments and innovations in the industry. Or it might wish to have access to the large labour pool that exists in this area of high-density population. Or it might wish to be close to the population centre in order to reduce the cost of transporting its product to market.

For all these reasons, location A earns a rent. Land B is less attractive, since it is not in this prime district, and it earns a smaller rent. Finally, land C earns no rent because it is even farther away and therefore involves even higher costs of inconvenience and transportation.

These blocks in Figure 35-17, just like the bars in the previous diagram, give us a picture of how rents compare. Because the selling price of land depends on the rent it can earn—as we shall soon see in more detail—these blocks also give us a picture of how land prices over an urban area will compare.

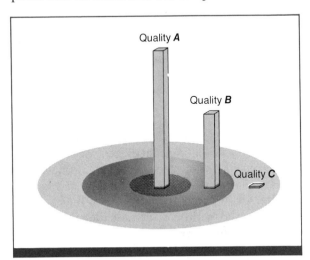

Figure 35-17 Rent based on differences in the location of land.
Compare with Figure 35-15. Because of its greater convenience and lower transport costs, land A earns a higher rent than land B. Land C, in a relatively poor location, earns no rent.

Finally, note that although the heights of the blocks have been drawn to reflect rents and land values, they may also provide some rough indication of where the tallest buildings will be constructed. Office space becomes more and more expensive to construct as a building gets higher and higher. Consequently, if land is cheap, you buy more land and build sideways. But if land is expensive enough, you conserve it by building up. Thus, buildings tend to be tallest in the prime, most expensive locations.

Above-Normal Profit as a Rent

Since above-normal profit is defined as a return above opportunity cost, it is, by definition, a rent. The most obvious illustration occurs in the case of monopoly. Specifically, the shaded area of above-normal profit in Figure 25-4 is a *monopoly rent*. It exists because entry by new firms into the industry is restricted. Therefore, it is a rent on whatever restricts entry. For example, it may be rent on a government licence that is granted to one firm (or a few) that blocks out other potential competitors. Or it may be rent on a patented product that other firms cannot copy. Or if there are economies of scale, the existing firm may earn a rent, since no other firm can afford to enter.

HOW RENTS ARE CAPITALIZED

If land plots A and B in Figure 35-17 are put up for sale, we would expect A to sell for a higher price; it will be more valuable because of the higher rent it can earn. This is generally true: Higher rents result in higher land values. But can't we be more precise about how the value of land is determined?

If you had the money and you were interested in buying land B in Figure 35-15, how much would you be willing to pay for it? Bear in mind that, as an alternative, you can always purchase bonds (or stocks) instead and earn a rate of return of, say, 6%. Because the rent of land B is $60 per year, you should be willing to pay about $1,000 for it. This gives you the same 6% rate of return on your land (a $60 return on $1,000) as on the alternative of buying bonds. Moreover, the competition of other potential buyers who feel the same way will ensure that the price of land B will settle at about $1,000—so long as the rent on B is expected to remain at $60 per year.

However, when the rent on land *B* doubles in Figure 35-16 to $120, potential buyers will be attracted by this higher income it can earn, and will begin to bid up the price of this land. This process will continue until the price of this land roughly doubles to $2,000, where its rate of return will again be the same 6% as before—that is, a $120 return on $2,000. To describe this process, we say that an increase in rent is *capitalized* in the value of the land.

In practice, there are many complications. In particular, the price of land will be affected not only by present rents but by expected *future* rents, too. If a single year's rent increases by 20%, the price of land may increase by more than 20% if people expect rents to continue rising.[5]

The fact that land prices reflect rents leads us to be skeptical of government programs to raise farm income by raising the price of commodities. One major effect of such programs may be to cause higher rents (a shift from Figure 35-15 to 35-16) and consequently a higher value for farmland. Thus the benefit tends to go to the owners of farmland when the programs are introduced. By and large, it does not go to those who want to farm by renting land. And, if new farmers purchase the land, they will be passing their eventual income increase from farming over to those who sell the land at a high price. Paradoxically, the higher price of farm products may make farming *less* attractive for newcomers: They now have a greater problem of raising the money necessary to purchase the higher-priced farm land. Thus government price supports designed to "help out the small farmer" may, in fact, keep those of limited means out of farming altogether.

As we saw in Chapter 25, some farm programs involve marketing boards that drive up prices of farm products by using a system of production quotas that limit the supply of the products. (Such programs exist in milk and egg production, for example.) The price increases brought about by these programs will also give rise to rent—but in this case, it is a rent earned by the quota owners. If these quotas can be bought and sold, the rent becomes capitalized into the value of a production quota. Thus, the benefit goes to those who are originally given production quotas by the government; new farmers will have to buy production quotas from the original quota owners if they want to enter the business.[6]

Moreover, serious problems arise even for those who do raise the necessary funds to buy land or production quotas by borrowing heavily on a big mortgage. They will be able to earn a living—and make those big mortgage payments—only if the government marketing boards continue to keep up the price. So these farmers *of necessity* become strong supporters of the marketing board programs: Without these programs, farm prices would fall, and the farmers would no longer be able to make their mortgage payments. In short, when government price-support programs are introduced, they benefit those who initially own the land, or who get the original production quotas. But if these initial owners sell the land or the quotas, they are "out-of-reach": For example, if they have retired to Florida on the proceeds of their sales, they cannot be damaged if the farm support program is then reversed. Instead, the damage all falls on the *new* owners.

Other economic rents—besides those on land or production quotas—may also be capitalized. Like other cities, Vancouver limits the number of taxis: A driver must have a licence to operate a cab. Because this requirement makes taxis scarce in Vancouver, the fares collected by each taxi are greater. But this higher income (rent) becomes capitalized in the value of the taxi licence. By 1980 the price of a Vancouver taxi licence had risen to $55,000, that is, to more than *seven times* the cost of a cab. Thus, someone who wants to own and operate a cab in Vancouver faces the same problem as someone who wants to start producing a crop that is regulated by a marketing board. He may be able to do reasonably well once he gets into the business, but how in the world does he raise the money to get started in the first place?

Finally, taxi licences raise this issue: Rather than let the licence owners benefit from the policy of restrict-

---

[5]Further detail on how an income flow (such as rent or interest) is capitalized in the value of an asset (such as land or a bond) was given in Box 13-1. The "capitalization of an income flow" is just another way of saying "the calculation of the present value of an income flow."

[6]Why does the rent get capitalized into the value of farmland in one case, and into the value of quota in the other? The answer is simple: In the first case, you can get access to the rent by buying land (since the government allows anybody to produce as much as they like). But with supply management in a marketing board system, land without quota does not give you access to the rent; only quota does.

ing the number of cabs, would it not have been better for Vancouver to have auctioned off the rights to operate cabs only for one or two years at a time? Then the city would have been able to collect the rents. Moreover, individual drivers could now enter the industry far more easily. They would have to buy only the right to operate a cab for one or two years, rather than the far more expensive right to operate it permanently (the cost they now incur when they buy the licences).

Taxing Rent

Rent has always been a natural target for taxation. About a century ago, Henry George built a powerful single-tax movement on the idea that nothing should be taxed but land rents. (His book *Progress and Poverty* sold millions of copies, and he almost won an election as mayor of New York.) Why, asked George, shouldn't we tax land rents, since they represent a pure windfall? Owners obviously don't produce the land, nor do they work for their rental incomes. Instead, they just hold the land and become wealthy from "unearned increments" as the population increases and rents rise. George argued that the land rents belong to the public as a whole, and should be taxed away from the owners and used for public purposes.

George's case was based not only on equity, but also on efficiency. A levy on land rents is one of the few taxes that need not distort resource allocation. Even if half the rent on land is taxed away, it will still remain in cultivation. What else can the owner do with it? And because the quantity of land in use is not affected, there is no reason to expect an efficiency loss. (Compare this with a tax on any other factor of production. For example, a tax on wages can affect the incentive to work and might thus affect the amount of work done.)

However, George's proposal to tax land rent raises two serious difficulties—in addition to the obvious problem that, as a single tax, it would not raise nearly enough money to cover today's large government expenditures. First, if present owners paid the current high price when they bought their land, rents are not a windfall to them at all but just a reasonable return on their large initial expenditure. (Why tax those who bought land and not those who bought stocks or bonds instead?) The only windfall is to the previous owners who sold the land for a high price. But they may now be living in Bermuda, beyond the reach of the taxing authority. Second, in practice it may be impossible to separate the rent on land from the return on buildings. If you tax a landlord's income, you will be taxing *both*. But the return on buildings—or on any other improvements on the land—is not a return on the land itself. Instead, it is a return to *capital*, and it cannot be taxed without causing distortion and inefficiency. For example, a tax on the returns from apartments will discourage the construction and maintenance of buildings.

KEY POINTS

1. Those who provide the nation's capital stock receive income in several forms. For example, those who own businesses receive profits. Those who lend money to businesses to purchase plant or equipment receive interest.

2. In a perfectly competitive capital market, the interest rate is determined by the demand and supply of loanable funds. Demand reflects how productive these funds will be when they are invested (the marginal efficiency of investment). Supply reflects how highly savers value money in its alternative use—consumption.

3. Because capital is productive, present goods can be exchanged for even more future goods. Therefore, present goods are worth more than future goods. The interest rate indicates how much more.

4. The interest rate also acts as a screening device that allocates funds to investment projects with the highest productivity. A government ceiling that lowers the interest rate below its perfectly competitive level results in two kinds of efficiency loss: (1) It reduces the total funds available for investment, and (2) it may result in funds being allocated to the wrong set of projects. It also results in a transfer from lenders to those borrowers who are able to get loans. This doesn't necessarily benefit poor individuals or small businesses, because they may be the potential borrowers who do *not* get loans;

banks prefer to lend to wealthy individuals and large businesses.

5. A large share of the total supply of investment in the Canadian economy is provided by foreign savers. Basic economic analysis indicates that there is a triangular efficiency gain (areas 2 + 3 in Figure 35-8) from such investment, similar to the efficiency gains from international trade.

6. Income is earned not only on machinery and other forms of physical capital, but also on human capital—that is, on skills, training, and education. The individuals who own the human capital are not the only ones who bear the initial cost of the investment. Governments also invest by subsidizing education, and businesses invest by subsidizing training programs. An inadequate past opportunity to accumulate human capital is one significant reason why the income of minority groups is depressed.

7. The return to an individual on an investment in a university degree was estimated to be as high as 20% in the late 1960s. However, several factors have tended to reduce the return in the 1970s and early 1980s, including the large increase in the number of people with degrees from universities and community colleges.

8. Economists define rent as the return to any factor of production above its opportunity cost. Those with superior talents in any occupation, whether it be business or hockey, earn a rent.

9. Land also earns a rent—except for plots that are not cultivated or have just barely been brought into cultivation. The most fertile plots earn the largest rent. If the price of farm products increases, rents on all cultivated plots of land rise and new plots are brought into cultivation.

10. Rent is also earned on land because of its location. Mineral deposits similarly earn rent, with the richest, most accessible deposits earning the highest rents. Above-normal profits earned by a firm are also a form of rent. In the case of monopoly, these rents are typically due to something—such as a patent or a government licence—that blocks entry by potential competitors.

11. The higher the rent earned by an asset such as a plot of land, the higher its value; thus, rents are "capitalized." This in turn has important implications for any agricultural supply-management policy that creates rent on production quotas. Although such a policy obviously benefits those who get the quotas, it won't necessarily increase the income of those who subsequently have to buy quotas to get into farming. Quite the contrary: It tends to discourage new entrants by increasing the initial cost of buying a quota.

KEY CONCEPTS

debt and equity capital
physical and human capital
marginal efficiency of investment
  (MEI)
direct foreign investment
foreign portfolio investment
efficiency gain from foreign
  investment
roundabout production
time preference
why present goods are worth
  more than future goods

base (risk-free) rate of interest
transfer and efficiency effects
  of an interest-rate ceiling
misallocation due to rationing
  of funds
normal and above-normal profit
*withholding tax
*increasing cost of foreign
  borrowing
substitution between factors
  of production

interest rate as an allocator
  of investment funds
human capital and
  discrimination
affirmative action programs
private and social returns to
  education
economists' broad definition
  of rent
rent on land due to fertility
rent on land due to location
monopoly rent
capitalization of rent

PROBLEMS

35-1 (This is a review of chapters 33, 34, and 35.) Why are wages and salaries higher in Canada and the United States than in most other countries? Why are our other forms of income also higher? The highest per capita incomes are not in North America or Western Europe, but in some of the smaller states along the Persian Gulf. Why?

35-2 Why is it that the rate of return on capital in Canada would probably be higher than it is now if there were no foreign capital in Canada? Explain how foreign investment in Canada is likely to reduce the income of some Canadian factors of production, but increase the income of other factors. Is it true that Canada as a whole will gain from foreign investment? (Explain your answer).

35-3 Using a three-panel diagram like Figure 24-5, show how the interest rate acts as a monitoring device to determine which investments will be undertaken and which will not.

35-4 If expectations change, with borrowers and lenders expecting that interest rates will fall in the future, what is likely to happen to the interest rate that a firm has to pay in order to sell long-term bonds today?

35-5 When economists speak of labour, capital, and land as factors of production, resources such as oil are included in the broad "land" category. Explain how the rapidly rising price of oil in the 1970s affected (1) decisions by individual firms as to the combination of factors they would use, and (2) the mix of final goods that was produced. (Use the examples of plastics and fertilizer—which both require large quantities of oil to produce—in your answer.)

35-6 "In a world in which labour is free to switch jobs, there will be inadequate investment in human capital in the form of job training." Do you agree? Explain why or why not. How might our minimum wage laws be changed to reduce this problem? Would such changes lead to other problems? (Read Box 35-2 before answering this question.)

35-7 Explain why the armed services have subsidized the university education of students who sign up to serve for several years after graduation. Explain why your answer is similar to one of the cases in Box 35-2.

35-8 Why might a firm pay a very high salary to attract an executive from a competing firm?

35-9 In Figure 35-12, does individual A receive more income than a manual labourer because of rent? Does B receive more than A because of rent? Explain your answer.

35-10 The public's idea of rent does not coincide with the economist's definition. How are the two concepts different? Give an example of (a) a return that an economist considers rent, but the public does not; (b) a return that the public considers rent, but the economist does not; and (c) a return that both consider rent.

35-11 Do you think that rent is an important or an insignificant part of the income of: (a) Gordon Lightfoot, (b) an elevator operator, (c) a textile worker?

35-12 Are these statements true or false? "An increase in the price of oil not only stimulates the search for oil. It also brings previously uneconomic sources of oil into production. But it does not affect rent on existing oil fields." If any of these statements is false, correct it.

35-13 Suppose that all the agricultural land within 100 miles of Toronto is equally fertile. Suppose, also, that all corn must be sold in Toronto and that the cost of transporting it there depends only on distance. What pattern of land rent would you expect over this area?

35-14 Suppose Vancouver imposed its taxi restriction by allowing only a restricted set of *individuals* to drive cabs. Would rents be generated in this case? If so, who would earn these rents?

35-15 The number of doctors is limited because anyone practising medicine must have a licence. Are rents generated in this case? To whom do they go? Is the objective of licensing to affect doctors' income, or is there some other reason?

35-16 When Dave Winfield decided to play baseball he turned down offers to play pro football (where, let's suppose, he might now be working for $100,000 a year) and basketball (for $500,000 a year). Divide his current income of about $2 million a year into rent and opportunity cost.

APPENDIX

THE ISSUE OF FOREIGN OWNERSHIP AND CONTROL

As we noted in the main text, the conclusion that capital imports yield net benefits is far from universally accepted. Many of the objections are based on complications left out of Figure 35-8; most notably, the potential political consequences of international investment. This appendix will look at some of the important complications. But before we address the controversial issues, we set the stage by considering several preliminary matters. First, we return to the distinction between direct and portfolio investment. Then we will look at the volume of foreign investment in Canada, and the objectives of those engaged in direct investment.

DIRECT AND PORTFOLIO INVESTMENT

Not all international investment is considered equally objectionable by those who are uneasy about its implications for our political independence.

Most critics express greatest concern over direct investment. After all, when foreigners (mostly Americans) own and control businesses in Canada, it is they who make the principal business decisions, not Canadians. On the other hand, no such overt control exists with portfolio investment, and as a result, this type of investment is generally considered less objectionable.

But before we turn to the debate over direct investment, it is worth noting that the difference between direct and portfolio investment can be exaggerated. Some loss of independence results from all sorts of international contacts—including merchandise trade or tourism. For example, if a country builds up its tourist industry to attract foreign visitors, then the country becomes economically vulnerable to events in other countries (for example, regulations by other countries on their citizens' spending abroad). And when a country sells many of its goods in foreign markets, trade sanctions (refusals to trade) may be used to put political pressure on that country. For example, the European Economic Community supported Britain in its 1982 war with Argentina over the Falkland Islands, by suspending purchases of Argentine goods.

Foreign portfolio investment may also limit a country's freedom of action. A country which has borrowed large amounts abroad is subject to constraints on its economic policy: It has to make sure it can repay interest and principal. Thus, for example, one element in Poland's political-economic crisis of 1981–82 was the obligation to make payments on its huge international debts, totalling over $25 billion. (This is not to suggest that Poland's foreign creditors were trying to destabilize the regime. On the contrary, they showed great concern for the political stability in Poland, because stability would increase their chances of being repaid.)

Indeed, one can argue that, in one important respect, borrowing from foreigners can cause greater problems than foreign direct investment. Borrowed funds may be squandered on immediate consumption or on half-baked investment projects. As a result, the country may receive little or no payoff from the borrowings. Yet the interest and principal payments must still be met. In contrast, in the case of direct investment, foreign investors are likely to pay close attention to the potential payoff of the projects they are undertaking. And if a mistake is made, with the wrong investments being undertaken, the foreign investors bear much of the damage: If there are no profits, they get nothing back from their investments. In other words, direct investment has one significant advantage over debt: With debt, payments are required regardless of the payoff from the investment. But with direct investment, foreigners receive returns only if the investment is profitable.

The same advantage, of course, applies to the purchase of minority equity (corporation stock) by foreigners: If no profits are made, the foreigners get no return. Furthermore, minority equity gives foreigners little or no control over the operation of the Canadian corporations. Thus, portfolio investment in stocks may be seen as the best possible type of foreign investment. But to want large amounts of this type of investment is to want the moon. Equity (stock) represents ownership; and large shareholders want a say in the management of the corporation. Therefore the large volumes of foreign capital are likely to be available mostly in two forms: direct investment and debt.

FOREIGN CONTROL IN THE CANADIAN ECONOMY

What is the extent of foreign control in the Canadian economy? As Table 35-1 shows, it is substantial, although it varies greatly among economic sectors. Mining and manufacturing have the highest degree of foreign ownership, with about 40% of the assets in those sectors owned by foreign-controlled firms. Manufacturing industries such as tobacco products and rubber products are entirely or almost entirely foreign-controlled, and foreign firms account for more than 70 percent of the assets in the large chemical (C3) and transportation equipment industries (C4, which includes the Canadian subsidiaries of the giant U.S. car manufacturers). Foreign ownership is also substantial in the energy sector: Oil and gas extraction and petroleum refining are included in categories B1 ("mineral fuels") and C5 ("petroleum and coal products"), both of which have large shares of foreign control. But foreign ownership in the energy sector has been falling: In the late 1970s, for example, foreigners controlled 60% to 70% of the assets in energy firms.

Other manufacturing industries (such as iron and steel, included in C8, and furniture making (C)) have relatively small shares of foreign ownership; and in

Table 35-1

Foreign-Controlled Firms' Share in Total Corporate Assets: Selected Industries, 1983 (Percent)

Industry	Percentage held by foreign-controlled firms
	Sector Averages
A. Agriculture, forestry, and fishing	4
B. Mining	35
1. Mineral fuels	39
2. Metal mining	23
C. Manufacturing	44
1. Tobacco products	100
2. Rubber products	92
3. Chemicals and chemical products	71
4. Transport equipment	73
5. Petroleum and coal products	61
6. Paper and allied industries	26
7. Food products	30
8. Primary metal manufacturing	15
9. Furniture industries	19
D. Construction	10
E. Public utilities	4
F. Wholesale trade	21
G. Retail trade	13
H. Services	15
Average for all sectors (non-financial industries)	24

SOURCE: *Annual Report of the Minister of Supply and Services Canada under the Corporations and Labour Unions Returns Act* 1983 (Ottawa: Statistics Canada and Minister of Supply and Services Canada, 1986), Part 1, *Corporations.*

Reproduced by permission of the Minister of Supply and Services Canada.

sectors other than mining and manufacturing, foreign control is relatively limited.

WHY DO THEY COME?

In some cases, foreign direct investment occurs when a group of foreign capitalists get together and start a new firm (or take over an existing one) in Canada. The International Nickel Corporation (INCO) in Sudbury is an example of this form of foreign investment. But a much more common form of direct investment occurs when a *multinational corporation* builds a plant in Canada or takes over ownership of a Canadian firm. Firms in Canada owned by American or other foreign multinationals are referred to as *subsidiaries* and Canadian plants owned by the multinationals or their subsidiaries are often called *branch plants*.

Why do firms find it worthwhile to establish subsidiaries and branch plants in foreign countries? In large part, they do so to gain the advantages of large organizations:

1. A firm with many plants and large output may have lower costs because research and development expenses can be spread over a larger volume of output. The advantages of size may be achieved by a foreign firm both by increasing its domestic production, and by acquiring foreign subsidiaries which can use the technology the firm has developed at home.

2. Similarly, there may be economies in advertising and marketing. This is particularly important in the U.S.-Canadian case: Most Canadians live close to the border, speak the same language as Americans, and are exposed to U.S. advertising. Because Canadians hear of Kodak film, for example, Kodak has a valuable advantage in selling in the Canadian market.

   (There may be other ways than foreign investment to exploit technological knowledge or marketing advantages. For example, a U.S. firm may license a Canadian firm to use the U.S. firm's technology or its brand name. But it may be expensive to transfer the technology. And there is a potential problem when a brand name is licensed: The licensee has less incentive to maintain quality. The licensing firm may take steps to protect the good name of its product by requiring specific quality controls. But it is clearly easier to control quality when you own the firm; that is, there are fewer problems with a subsidiary than with an independent licensee. Furthermore, it may be more difficult for a new Canadian firm to raise the necessary amount of capital than it is for the multinational. Hence,

the multinational may find it simpler and less risky to start its own subsidiary.)

3. There may also be economies in using management resources. For example, the present U.S. management may also be able to manage a Canadian subsidiary with relatively little additional effort. For a new firm trying to compete with the multinational, however, the cost of acquiring specialized management skills may be much higher.

In an important study of foreign investment in Canada, Richard Caves of Harvard University found that these three factors have been important explanations for foreign ownership of Canadian industry. In particular, the evidence suggested that industries with large research and development and marketing expenditures tend to have a large degree of foreign control. He also found that in industries marked by multi-plant firms (such as automobiles), foreign multinationals tend to dominate the Canadian market.[7]

4. Firms may reduce their risks by owning their own sources of supply, rather than buying these supplies on the open market. Thus, producers of metal products may own mines, and newspapers may own the forests used to produce pulp and paper. For this reason, U.S. firms may acquire Canadian mines or other resources.

5. Finally, foreign firms set up subsidiaries in Canada not only to gain the normal business advantages of size (listed in points 1 to 4), but also because of the Canadian tariff. In the automobile industry, for example, one of the reasons that U.S. firms originally came to Canada was to produce inside the Canadian tariff wall. (It was less expensive to produce in Canada than to produce in the United States and export to Canada, paying the required tariff.)

This last point helps to explain not only U.S. direct investment in Canada, but, more broadly, the overall increase in international investment. For example, Honda has decided to begin automobile production in the United States in order to be inside the U.S. market in the event of increased U.S. protection. And other Japanese automobile firms are being threatened with

[7]Richard E. Caves, "Causes of Direct Investment: Foreign Firms' Shares in Canadian and United Kingdom Manufacturing Industries," *Review of Economics and Statistics* (August 1974): 279–93.

greater U.S. and European protection unless they set up manufacturing subsidiaries, or agree to buy more auto parts from the countries that import their cars.

CONSEQUENCES OF FOREIGN OWNERSHIP AND CONTROL

Even though the growth of multinational corporations and of foreign ownership may represent an economically efficient pattern of production, many economists and politicians in Canada are concerned about foreign investment, and particularly direct investment, for other reasons. In many cases, the concern is based on considerations of political sovereignty, and on a fear that an excessive foreign influence will retard the growth of a distinctly Canadian culture.

With respect to the question of political sovereignty, the problem of *extraterritoriality* has long been a sore point in U.S.-Canadian relations. Extraterritoriality refers to an application of U.S. laws and regulations to foreign subsidiaries of U.S. firms, even though these subsidiaries are operating outside the United States. An example is the U.S. Trading with the Enemies Act. Under this Act, firms require approval by the U.S. government to export goods to certain communist countries, notably North Korea, North Vietnam, and Cuba. Because the Act has also applied to foreign subsidiaries of U.S. firms, several deals involving exports from subsidiaries in Canada to these countries have been blocked by lack of approval from the U.S. government. Another example of the extraterritoriality principle is the application of U.S. anti-trust laws to Canadian subsidiaries of U.S. firms. (Since U.S. anti-trust laws have been more restrictive than our anti-combines legislation, U.S. law has sometimes prevented Canadian subsidiaries from actions that would have been legal in Canada.) The economic consequences to Canada of extraterritoriality have probably not been very great. But from the viewpoint of asserting Canadian political independence, extraterritoriality is a major aggravation. (In 1982, extraterritoriality became a sore point in U.S.–West European relations as well, because of the U.S. government's directive to European subsidiaries of U.S. firms that prevented these subsidiaries from providing American technology or supplies in the construction of the USSR–Western European natural gas pipeline. In the face of strong objec-

tions by European governments this ruling was later lifted.)

Because of the desire to encourage a distinctly Canadian culture, special rules have been introduced to limit the extent of foreign involvement in our communications industry, such as radio, television, and the publishing of magazines and periodicals. These rules cover not only foreign ownership of firms in these industries, but also the content being communicated. Thus, an extensive set of rules specifies the amount of Canadian programming that radio and television stations must offer. And, in a well-known case a few years ago, a tightening of the regulations concerning Canadian content in weekly magazines caused *Time* magazine to stop publication of its Canadian edition.

ECONOMIC ISSUES

There are also economic issues that have led some Canadians to advocate restricting the amount of foreign control in Canada. It has been claimed that Canadian subsidiaries of foreign firms often behave in ways that are detrimental to the Canadian economy.

Specifically, it has been claimed that (1) they are less interested than Canadian firms in exporting their products; (2) they are reluctant to spend money on research and development in Canada or to buy advertising services from Canadian agencies; and (3) they tend to discriminate against Canadian firms or individuals in their purchases of goods and services. (They may find it easier to buy imported components rather than Canadian ones, and to rely on U.S. personnel rather than Canadians for senior executive positions.)

There is surprisingly little empirical evidence to indicate that the performance of foreign-owned companies is very different from comparable Canadian-owned firms. In an important study, *The Performance of Foreign-Owned Firms in Canada* (Toronto: Private Planning Association, 1969), A.E. Safarian of the University of Toronto found that foreign subsidiaries in Canada were as likely to export as were Canadian-owned firms, and their spending on research and development was not significantly less than the spending by Canadian-owned firms. And while he did find that foreign-owned firms were more likely to import many of their inputs, the difference between Canadian and foreign-owned firms was not very great in this area either.[8]

While it may seem surprising that there is so little evidence of differences in the behaviour of Canadian and foreign-owned firms, there is one good reason why one might in fact expect these differences to be small. The managers of both kinds of firms have a common objective: to make the largest possible profit. A manager of a foreign subsidiary is most likely to import components from the United States in cases where that country is the cheapest source of supply. But if the United States is the cheapest source of supply, managers of Canadian firms should also find it advantageous to import rather than buy from a Canadian source. Similarly, if it is profitable for a Canadian-owned firm to export, it is likely to be profitable for a foreign-owned subsidiary to do the same. Although there have been cases of foreign parent companies preventing their Canadian subsidiaries from exporting to third-country markets in competition with the parents, there appear to be offsetting pressures that make it easier for a subsidiary to export—especially in selected products in which the parent has given the subsidiary a "world product mandate" (that is, the exclusive right to develop, produce, and sell these products worldwide). In such cases, the subsidiary may be able to take advantage of the advertising and goodwill built up by the parent in these third-country markets in the past.

[8]There is, however, a substantial difference in the performance of U.S. *parent* firms compared to Canadian-owned firms (or compared to subsidiaries of these U.S. firms). One reason is the higher-volume U.S. market in which American parents operate. For example, they spend more on research and development, because they have a greater volume over which to spread costly research and development overhead. For more detail on recent research into the relevant issue here—the comparison of foreign subsidiaries in Canada with Canadian-owned firms—see Paul and R.J. Wonnacott, "Problems That Trade Barriers and Foreign Ownership Raise for Canada as We Enter the 80s" in *Developments Abroad and the Domestic Economy* (Toronto: Ontario Economic Council, 1980). But this observation about U.S. parents doesn't prove anything about foreign ownership in Canada; it simply confirms that firms in Canada, *regardless of their ownership*, face problems of small market size.

GOVERNMENT POLICY TOWARD FOREIGN INVESTMENT

Because of public criticisms, there have been many proposals to enact legislation to restrict foreign ownership. Not all of these have been passed by Parliament. For example, in the early 1960s, Parliament rejected Finance Minister Walter Gordon's proposals to discourage foreign direct investment; the legislation proposed by Gordon would have provided for a 30% tax on foreigners acquiring certain Canadian firms.

Another idea promoted by Walter Gordon was to strengthen Canadian ownership of our business sector by establishing a government-owned holding corporation that would take over ownership of profitable firms operating in Canada. This resulted in the creation of the *Canada Development Corporation* in 1971; the CDC now owns shares in a large number of firms. One of its most important moves was to buy a controlling interest in the Texasgulf Corporation, a firm with extensive mining interests in Canada.

In 1975, the government again moved to establish a government-owned Canadian holding company, this time in the oil and gas sector. This company, Petro-Canada, has taken over very substantial petroleum and refining resources, notably by buying the Canadian facilities of the European-owned firm, Petrofina. Under the National Energy Program of 1980, Petro-Canada was given major responsibility for expanding the role of the Canadian government in the energy field.

In addition to pursuing these strategies, the Canadian government has from time to time taken a number of other measures designed to limit and control foreign ownership. As we have already noted, special rules restrict foreign investors in certain key sectors such as broadcasting and magazine publishing, and during the 1970s and early 1980s, foreign investment proposals were screened by the Foreign Investment Review Agency (FIRA). The 1980 National Energy Program also contained a number of provisions to encourage a shift in ownership of Canada's oil and gas industry from foreign to Canadian hands. However, by the mid-1980s, policy was shifting in a less restrictive direction, with the revamping of FIRA and the elimination of many of the provisions of the National Energy Program.

Chapter 36

INCOME INEQUALITY

> There are many in this old world of ours who
> hold that things break about even for all of us.
> I have observed for example that we all get the
> same amount of ice. The rich get it in the
> summertime and the poor get it in the winter.
>
> Bat Masterson

In 1985, the average wage in Canadian manufacturing was about $11.50 an hour. Based on a 40-hour work week for 50 weeks, this wage would produce an annual income of $23,000. In that same year, the annual compensation paid Wayne Gretzky under his contract with the Edmonton Oilers hockey team was close to $1 *million* a year, guaranteed until the end of this century. His salary from the Oilers was only part of Gretzky's total income. In addition, he was earning a similar amount for endorsing a range of products, from breakfast cereal to the services of the Continental Bank. Gretzky was not alone. By the mid-1980s, top salaries in several sports had reached about $1 million a year, with the only question being, "For how many years?" (A contract signed in 1985 by Steve Young, a quarterback just out of college football, provided for about $1 million a year until his retirement at age 65, forty-three years into the future.)

All this raises a question: Should a hockey player earn that much more than the prime minister of Canada? Should a successful pop musician earn many times more than a highly talented violinist in a symphony orchestra?

Looking at the distribution of income in Canada, we can find many cases of large differentials between the incomes of people who all appear to work equally hard, and to be good at their jobs. In this chapter we will look at Canadian income distribution to see whether such examples are the exception or the rule. How unequal are Canadian incomes? Is inequality increasing or decreasing?

Our second task will be to address the question: What is a *fair* distribution of income? Is it the income distribution that results from the free play of market forces? Or is it an equal income for all? Or is it some compromise between the two?

To begin, we review why income differences arise in the first place. Why do some people earn so much more than others?

REVIEW: WHY DO INCOMES DIFFER?

In earlier chapters, we have seen how market forces result in quite different incomes for different people. For example, the high income of a surgeon is in part a return to *human capital*; it provides compensation for the years of foregone income and hard study in medical school. It may also be partly a *rent* on greater-than-average *innate talent*. Of course, other individuals have gifts of quite a different sort; star athletes and entertainers also earn very large rents.

Income differences also arise because of wealth.

Those who own assets such as stocks, bonds, and other forms of property receive income from them. There are even greater differences in asset holdings than in income. A study based on data from the late 1970s shows that the poorest ten percent of Canadian families had average assets of less than $1,000. At the other extreme, 1.7% of the families had assets over $300,000, with almost one-fourth of the total income from assets going to this small group of families.

Family background explains some income differences. Canada may be a land of opportunity where someone from a poor, low-status family can achieve prominence and success. However, coming from the "right family" does help, especially if parents provide not only a silver spoon but also practical advice and inspiration. And working women or members of minority groups may have a lower income because of *discrimination*.

In addition, income differences may arise because of the exercise of *market power*. People who find themselves in a monopoly position may be able to profit handsomely in terms of increased income.

There are also income differences because some people work at more dangerous or unpleasant jobs. Thus, the construction worker in a dangerous job may receive a *compensating wage differential*, that is, a higher wage to compensate for the risks faced. At the other extreme, artists may accept a lower income in order to pursue a career that they find particularly pleasant.

Income differences may also arise because some people *work harder* than others. For example, a specific doctor's income may be lower because of a personal decision to sacrifice income for leisure; an example is the doctor with a clinic at a ski resort who goes skiing in the morning and sets broken bones in the afternoon. On the other hand, many doctors work very long hours, and this helps to explain their high incomes.

Some income differences may be the result of differences in *health,* or just plain *luck*. An example is the talented hockey player who is injured in the eye by a high stick and must give up hockey and the large income that may go with it. Just as bad luck can lower income, good luck can raise it.

Being "the right person at the right time" is a way of earning a windfall income. When there is an oil well blowout, it must be capped as soon as possible, and a specialist like Red Adair commands a very large income because he is known as one of the "world's best."

Of all the causes of income differences, which is most important? It is difficult to give an unambiguous answer, but human capital appears to be a strong candidate. Statistics Canada data show that in comparison with low-income groups, families and individuals in high-income groups derive a much higher proportion of their income from wages and salaries. In a U.S. study, Jacob Mincer found that differences in human capital explained roughly 60% of differences in American incomes.[1]

HOW MUCH INCOME INEQUALITY IS THERE?

It's the rich whot gets the gryvy,
It's the poor whot gets the blime.

English ballad, World War II.

Are wide differences in individual incomes the exception or the rule? When we look at the income of all Canadians, how much inequality is there?

Table 36-1 shows the distribution of Canadian incomes. However, these figures were calculated before taking into account government policies that tend to raise the relative income of the poor, such as Unemployment Insurance, Old Age Security, and taxes. Excluding transfers, the poor are very poor indeed: The lowest-income fifth of the population receive less than 2% of the nation's income. At the other extreme, the highest-income fifth of the population receive about 45% of the nation's before-tax income.

This unequal distribution is illustrated with a *Lorenz curve*. The first step in drawing such a curve is to rearrange the data in panel (*a*) of Table 36-1 into *cumulative* form in panel (*b*). For example, in the second row, the poorest 40% of the population earn 11% of the nation's income. (To get this figure, we add the first two numbers in panel (*a*).) This point, labelled *J*, is then plotted in Figure 36-1, along with other points that are similarly calculated. The result is the Lorenz curve of Canadian income.

To get some feel for how much inequality this curve represents, we ask: What would this Lorenz curve look like if all families received exactly the same

[1] Jacob Mincer, "Education, Experience, Earnings and Employment," in F. Thomas Juster, ed., *Education, Income and Human Behavior* (New York: McGraw-Hill, 1975), p. 73.

Table 36-1
Before-Tax Income Distribution of Canadian Families in 1981 (before Taxes and Transfers)*

(a) INCOME DISTRIBUTION		(b) CUMULATIVE INCOME DISTRIBUTION			
Population	Share of Total Income	Population	Share of Total Income		Point in Figure 36-1
Low 20%	gets 1.4%	First 20%	gets	1.4%	H
Second 20%	gets 9.6	First 40%	gets 1.4 + 9.6	11.0	J
Third 20%	gets 17.8	First 60%	gets 11.0 + 17.8	28.8	K
Fourth 20%	gets 26.4	First 80%	gets 28.8 + 26.4	55.2	L
High 20%	gets 44.9	Total	gets 55.2 + 44.9	100	M

*Numbers may not add exactly because of rounding.
SOURCE: Based on F. Vaillancourt, "Income Distribution and Economic Security in Canada: an Overview," in *Income Distribution and Economic Security in Canada*, vol. 1 (Toronto: University of Toronto Press in co-operation with the Royal Commission on the Economic Union and Development Prospects for Canada, and the Canadian Government Publishing Centre, Supply and Services Canada, 1985), Table 1-5.

income? In that case, we would observe point *F* instead of point *J*: The "lowest" 40% of the population would receive 40% of the income. And instead of point *K*, we would observe point *G* (60% of the population would receive 60% of the income). When we join all points like *F* and *G*, the result is the "complete equality" line 0*FGM*; that is, the 45° straight line from the origin. Thus, income inequality is shown by the amount of bow in the Lorenz curve; that is, by the size of the red slice between the curve and the 45° line.

In fact, *inequality is not as serious a problem as this diagram suggests*. One reason: Even if each family were earning exactly the same *lifetime* income, the Lorenz curve would still not coincide with that 45° line. We would still observe some "inequality slice." The reason is that, during any single year, we would observe some young families starting out with a low income and some middle-aged families in their earning prime with a high income. Inequality exists in that year for these families, even though they have exactly the same lifetime income pattern.

Nonetheless, even when such influences are fully taken into account, a substantial degree of inequality exists. Society's response is to reduce this inequality by government taxation that concentrates more heavily on the rich, and government expenditure programs such as Old Age Security, Unemployment Insurance, and Family Allowances that raise the relative income of the poor.

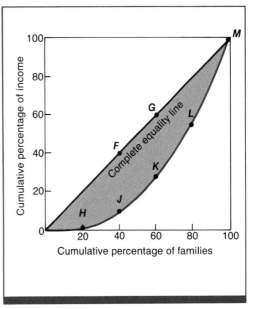

Figure 36-1 Lorenz curve showing before-tax-and-transfer income distribution in Canada.
If every family had exactly the same income, the Canadian income distribution would follow the 45° "complete equality" line. The actual income distribution is shown by the curve that lies below this—with the red slice between the two showing the amount of income inequality.

Source: Based on F. Vaillancourt, "Income Distribution and Economic Security in Canada: An Overview," in *Income Distribution and Economic Security in Canada*, vol. 1 (Toronto: University of Toronto Press in co-operation with the Royal Commission on the Economic Union and Development Prospects for Canada, and the Canadian Government Publishing Centre, Supply and Services Canada, 1985), Table 1-5.

HOW MUCH INEQUALITY DOES THE GOVERNMENT NOW ELIMINATE?

The degree to which government taxes and transfer payments reduce inequality in the nation's income distribution is shown in Figure 36-2. The coloured area is exactly the same as in Figure 36-1. However, here it is broken down into a light area that shows how much the government reduces inequality, and a darker area that shows how much still remains.

Whereas curve *a* is a reproduction of the before-taxes-and-transfers curve graphed in Figure 36-1, curve *b* shows the major shift toward equality that occurs as a result of government transfer programs, including social assistance, Old Age Security, and Unemployment Insurance. (Government programs that shift this curve are discussed in more detail in the next chapter.) Curve *c* shows the further shift that results from the effect of taxation. Together, transfers and taxes eliminate about one-fifth of total inequality.[2] In addition, however, the remaining inequality is reduced by transfers in kind: Because government programs provide the same standards of health care and education to rich and poor alike, and subsidizes the housing costs of low-income Canadians, total real income is more equal than after-tax money income. When all programs are considered, the overall picture is one of a government that is making substantial transfers of income to the poor, in the process eliminating more than a quarter of the nation's income inequality. Claims that the government is not very effective in changing the nation's income distribution have frequently been based on calculations that do not take into account all of these programs, in particular, in-kind transfers.

One surprise in this diagram is that taxation, often supposed to be a great income redistributor, is relatively ineffective in reducing income inequality. Certainly taxes are a large enough item in our income to make a big difference. But they do not change the nation's income distribution as much as one might expect because, on balance, they are not highly progressive. While it is true, as noted in Chapter 5, that *income* taxes are progressive—that is, the rates rise as incomes rise—other taxes are regressive. Moreover,

loopholes ease the burden of income taxes on the wealthy.

On the other hand, the more explicit transfer programs such as Unemployment Insurance, Old Age Security, and other forms of cash transfer seem, when taken together, to be more effective. However, we must be cautious about this conclusion. It is quite true that the payments they provide to the poor *directly* reduce inequality—that is, shift the Lorenz curve up from *a* to *b*. But *indirectly* they *increase* inequality (make the Lorenz curve *a* lower than it would otherwise be) because of their side effects. For example, the income guarantee provided by programs such as Unemployment Insurance makes unemployed people less desperate to get a job quickly, because they can at least survive without one. Moreover, for some couples the incentive to stay together may be reduced by an income guarantee that ensures that they can get welfare if they separate. When a couple breaks up, one medium-income family may become two poor families.

These effects reduce the per-family earned income at the low end of the scale and give Lorenz curve *a* a bigger bow than it would otherwise have. In short, income-support programs have two conflicting effects on income inequality. Indirectly they make it worse by giving the "before transfers" curve *a* a bigger bow. But directly they make it better, by shifting the Lorenz curve up from *a* to the "after transfers" curve *b*.

How has income inequality changed over time? If we look at the inequality of income after government transfers (curve *b* in Figure 36-2), we find a somewhat surprising result: Income inequality in Canada in 1981 was not much different than it was in 1951. In the two decades between 1951 and 1971, inequality appeared to actually *increase*. However, during the 1970s inequality was reduced, reflecting in part the rapid growth in transfer programs such as Old Age Security and increases in Unemployment Insurance benefit levels. Nevertheless, the share of the poorest 20% of the population in pre-tax income only rose from 4.4% in 1951 to 4.6% in 1981.

The relatively constant *share* of the poorest 20% in the distribution of income does not mean that the *level* of real income in this group has stayed constant. Instead, it means that the real income of the poorest 20% has been rising at about the same rate as the average income in the population as a whole. Thus, during the 1960s and 1970s, large numbers of people

---

[2] Perhaps more than this. Remember that if we were to achieve complete equality of *lifetime* incomes, the Lorenz curve would still have a bow below the 45° line, because in any specific year the middle-aged would have a higher income than the young.

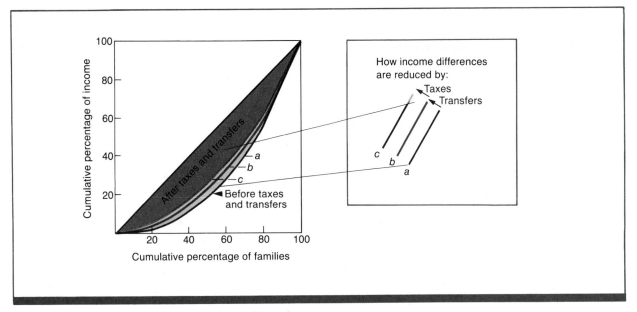

Figure 36-2 How government taxes and transfers reduce income inequality.

Taxes and transfers by all levels of government in 1981 reduced income inequality by about one-fifth. Taxes, which shifted the curve from *b* to *c*, were a relatively unimportant form of equalization compared to government transfer programs, which reduced inequality from curve *a* to curve *b*.

Source: Based on F. Vaillancourt, "Income Distribution and Economic Security in Canada: An Overview," in *Income Distribution and Economic Security in Canada*, vol. 1 (Toronto: University of Toronto Press in co-operation with the Royal Commission on the Economic Union and Development Prospects for Canada, and the Canadian Government Publishing Centre, Supply and Services Canada, 1985), Table 1-5.

were moving out of poverty, even though inequality did not change by much. In the next chapter, however, we will note a disturbing trend that has emerged in recent years: Following a decline in the 1960s and 1970s, the proportion of Canadians with incomes below the poverty line has been *rising* since the early 1980s.

This increase in the percentage of the population living in poverty also occurred in the United States during Ronald Reagan's first term as president. Some analysts have attributed this trend—and an apparent trend toward more inequality in the U.S. income distribution generally—to some of the Reagan administration policies, such as changes that make it more difficult for poor people to qualify for welfare. However, there were also other influences at work, such as the recessions of 1980 and 1982 that resulted in more severe job losses and income reductions for the poor.

Now let's turn from the question "What *is* the income distribution?" to "What *should* the income distribution *be*?"

In deriving policies that affect the distribution of income, what should we set as a target? Is there such a thing as a "fair" or "equitable" distribution?

WHAT IS AN EQUITABLE INCOME DISTRIBUTION?

See how the fates their gifts allot,
For A is happy—B is not.
Yet B is worthy, I dare say,
Of more prosperity than A.

If I were fortune—which I'm not—
B should enjoy A's happy lot,
And A should die in miserie—
That is, assuming I am B.

Gilbert and Sullivan,
The Mikado

A search for an equitable or just distribution of income for society will lead us into treacherous intellectual terrain, from which some of the world's noted philosophers have been unable to escape with reputations intact. Although we cannot expect to arrive at any definitive answer in this elementary treatment, we can at least identify some of the important issues.

To begin, we re-emphasize two important points made in Chapter 1. First, *equity and equality are two different concepts*. In our Lorenz curve description of income distribution, we have addressed only the question of equality: How equal *are* incomes? This is an empirical question. We can answer it by looking at the facts—by examining how much each Canadian family earns. On the other hand, the question of equity is not what incomes are, but rather what they *should be*. What income distribution is fair and just? This is an ethical issue on which people are not unanimous. Some believe that equity is equality—that it is fair for everyone to receive the same income. On the other hand, many believe that equity is not equality—for example, the individual who works harder or more effectively should be paid more.

> *Equal* means "of the same size." *Equitable* means "fair." The two are not necessarily the same.

Second, we re-emphasize that government policy cannot be designed just to achieve equity—that is, a fair division of the nation's income pie. Instead it must also take into account other, often conflicting goals such as efficiency—increasing the size of that pie. However, to sharpen our idea of equity, suppose for now that this is our only concern. *On grounds of equity alone*, what is the best distribution of income? Of the many possible answers, consider three: first, the distribution that results from the free play of the economic marketplace; second, a completely equal distribution of income; and third, some compromise between the two.

Is the Free Market's Distribution of Income Equitable?
Whatever is, is right.

Alexander Pope, Essay on Man

In economics, few would agree that whatever is, is necessarily right. *The free market does not do an entirely satisfactory job of distributing income.* Consider a monopolist who makes a fortune by successfully cornering the world's supply of a good, selling some at a very high price, and letting the unsold balance rot. In such cases it is very difficult to argue that the free market distributes income in a fair, equitable way.

However, our reservations about the free-market distribution are far more fundamental than this, and apply even when markets are perfectly competitive. Such markets will, under certain conditions (no externalities, etc.) allocate factors of production in an *efficient* way that will maximize the nation's total income. In the process, they determine a set of prices of both goods and factors of production—the wages of labour, rents on land, etc. Thus, they both maximize the nation's income pie and determine how it will be divided. But we can make no claim that they necessarily divide the pie up in a fair, equitable way. Remember: The size of the pie is maximized *for those who have the income to pay for it*. Output in a competitive market economy may include luxuries for the rich and too few necessities for the poor. Moreover, in many cases the poor—in particular, the disabled—may be destitute through no fault of their own.

Even the strongest supporters of the free market, while championing its efficiencies, will still vote for aid for those who are destitute. This point is important enough to repeat: The demonstrable virtues of a free, perfectly competitive market have to do with its efficiency, not its equity.

Perhaps the best illustration is this. In a perfectly competitive economy, rents on land efficiently direct the nation's scarce land into its most productive uses; if rents are forced below the competitive level, land may be used in wasteful ways. However, the payment of these rents to those who own the land does not necessarily give us a fair distribution of income. We can see this point by considering an extreme example of land that has been inherited by the idle rich. Why should they earn an income many times that of the able and hard-working people whom they hire to manage and work this land?

Equality as a Target
The idea that we should aim for complete equality has an immediate appeal (see Box 36-1). Since everyone has certain other rights such as the right to vote and equality before the law, why should each of us not have equality in our access to the marketplace—the right of equal economic reward? In other words, since

everyone has an equal vote to cast in elections, why shouldn't everyone have equal dollar "votes" to spend in the marketplace? In practice, it would be prohibitively costly to give everyone this right: An equal division of the pie would greatly shrink its size.

However, even if this cost did not exist, there would still be fundamental philosophical problems. For example, the right to an equal economic reward would come into conflict with the right of equality before the law—in particular, the principle that those who break the law should be punished for their crimes. Those who have to pay fines should *not* be left with an equal number of economic votes.

Moreover, there are practical problems. For example, how is equality to be defined? One way is to define it, most simply, as "equal money incomes." But this answer is not satisfactory, because not everyone works the same number of hours. Those who decide on shorter working hours are taking some of their potential income in the form of leisure, rather than cash. Therefore, income should be defined more broadly to include both income taken in the form of cash and "income" taken in the form of leisure. Fairness requires that an individual who takes a lot of income in one form— leisure—should get less in the other form—cash. Similarly, those whose work is dangerous should be paid higher money wages to compensate them for the risk. According to this approach, the *overall* economic position (rather than just money income) should be equalized.

Unfortunately, this broader approach raises as many problems as it solves. If the overall position of individuals is to be equalized, those who have unpleasant jobs should be paid high enough wages to compensate them, and those whose jobs are fun should accordingly be paid less. But how do we handle the following problem. Some people find a particular job—like teaching—extremely rewarding, while others find it a bore. Should the first group be paid less than the second, in order to make them equal? Quite apart from the practical problem of determining how much each teacher likes the job—in a situation in which they would all have an incentive to lie—this broad approach would lead to an unsatisfactory result: People would be paid for hating their jobs. Since those who love teaching generally make the best teachers, this would mean that the best teachers would be paid the least. Surely, this would not be fair.

Worse yet, bored, dissatisfied teachers often don't work so hard; they take "leisure on the job." Would it be fair to pay them a premium salary, when those taking a lot of leisure at home would receive low pay?

Therefore, we conclude that considerations of *equity alone* have not led us to complete equality as a meaningful objective. We are skeptical of this objective, just as we were skeptical earlier of the free-market determination of income. How about some compromise between the two?

A Compromise between the Free Market and Complete Equality

It is easy to conclude that both the free market and the complete equality approaches involve serious problems. What is far more difficult is to say where in the broad range in between we should aim. We will not be able to answer that question. But here are some suggestions for you to consider as you grapple with it (and you must, as a voter).

Make It a Fair Race, . . .

Suppose we think of participating in the economy as being in a race in which each runner's income is determined by his or her finish. The egalitarian view that "justice is income equality" implies that the government should equalize all rewards at the end of the race: Give everyone a bronze medal—no golds, and no booby prizes. As the Dodo in *Alice in Wonderland* put it, "Everybody has won, and all must have prizes."

An alternative view is that the responsibility of the government is only to ensure that the race is fair. Disadvantages should be eliminated: No one should start with a 50-yard handicap because of being a woman, or a Native Canadian, or the child of parents who are not influential. In this race, everyone has a right, but it is the right of equality of *opportunity*, not equality of *reward*. In brief, everyone should have the right to an equal *start*—but not to an equal *finish*.

While the idea of equal opportunity is appealing, it, too, is difficult to define. Buried in any definition of a fair race is a judgement as to *which advantages are unfair and should be removed, and which advantages should not*. Advantages of race, sex, and ethnic background clearly should be removed. But what should we do about advantages arising from differences in natural ability? Should an individual in the economic race be penalized for natural business talent so that all

BOX 36-1

RAWLS ON EQUALITY

Harvard philosophy professor John Rawls has argued that income equality is a desirable goal—except in special circumstances. His analysis starts in a promising way. A consensus on the fair distribution of income is difficult to achieve because everyone has a special axe to grind. Those with high incomes favour a system in which inequality is allowed, because it lets them keep their higher income. Those with low incomes are likely to advocate equality because it will improve their position. Rawls therefore suggests that, to get an objective view, people must be *removed from their present situation* and placed in an **original position** where they decide what the distribution of income should be, without knowing the specific place they themselves will eventually take in this distribution. What income distribution will they choose?

Here are the essentials of Rawls' argument. The typical person in the original position will think something like this: "Whatever income distribution is chosen, with my luck, chances are that I'll end up at the bottom. So I'll vote for the income distribution that will leave me, the lowest one on the totem pole, as well off as possible." Since everyone is similarly situated in the original position, Rawls argues that all will reason in the same way. He concludes that a consensus will develop in favour of an equal distribution of income—unless there is an unequal distribution that leaves *everyone* better off. This is what Rawls calls the **difference principle**.*

While Rawls' approach will generally lead to equality, there are circumstances in which it will not. To illustrate, we use two extreme examples, but the argument applies in less extreme cases as

*In his *Theory of Justice* (Cambridge: Harvard University Press, 1971), p. 63, Rawls was concerned with more than income: "All social values—liberty and opportunity, income and wealth, and the bases of self-respect—are to be distributed equally unless an unequal distribution of any, or all, of these values is to everyone's advantage."

While we consider the lowest-income individual in our examples, Rawls' focus is on a typical individual in the lowest-income group. But this does not seriously affect his conclusion or our evaluation of it.

Table 36-2
When Rawls' Theory Leads to Inequality:
An Example

	Income of all individuals (but one)	Income of last individual
Option A (equality)	$ 5,000	$5,000
Option B (inequality)	$10,000	$5,100*

*Option B chosen because everyone is better off

well. For the first example, suppose people in the original position choose between the two income distributions shown in Table 36-2. Option A represents complete equality, with everyone's annual income at $5,000. Now suppose it is possible to move to Option B, where everyone's income is $10,000 except for the last individual, whose income is $5,100. (Suppose that this move is possible because there was previously a very high tax aimed at equalizing income. When the tax is removed, people respond by working more.) Because everyone benefits, Rawlsian logic leads to a move from A to B—a move *away from equality*.† Most people would agree with such a move. So far, Rawls' theory is not controversial. In the circumstances shown in Table 36-2, Rawls, like almost everyone else, would allow inequality.

Table 36-3 illustrates the second, more likely situation, with options A and C. As before, the move away from equality (in this case, from A to C) benefits almost everyone by $5,000. But now we recognize that any such substantial change is likely to leave at least one person worse off. (Note in the last column how the income of the last individual is reduced by $100.) In this case, Rawls argues that people in an original position would choose option A. With their concern about ending up at the bottom of the totem pole, they would focus on the figures in the last column and prefer A with its

†Envy is not taken into account: It is assumed that nobody's happiness is reduced by the knowledge that someone else has become richer.

Table 36-3
When Rawls' Theory Leads to Equality:
An Example

	Income of all individuals (but one)	Income of last individual
Option A (equality)	$ 5,000	$5,000*
Option C (inequality)	$10,000	$4,900

*Option A chosen because a move to C would damage the last individual

$5,000 income to C with its $4,900 income. Thus, according to Rawls, people would choose equality.

It is here, when he puts forward a strong argument in favour of equality, that Rawls' theory is open to criticism. Ask yourself: If you were in Rawls' original position, without knowledge of where you would eventually end up, which option would you choose? Would you join the consensus Rawls expects in favour of option A? Most people would find C difficult to resist. The miniscule risk of being $100 worse off seems trivial in comparison with the near certainty of being $5,000 better off. This seems to be a risk well worth taking. Indeed, those who would select Rawls' option A are those who would *avoid risk at almost any cost*. How in the world would you find anyone so risk-averse? (Observe that the risk you would be taking in choosing income distribution C rather than A would be the same as your risk at the race track or the stock exchange if you were to bet $100 for a chance to win $5,000, with odds *in your favour* of 25 million to one. Why those odds? There are 25 million people in Canada. In moving from option A to C, they would all "win" $5,000—except for the one who would lose $100. With such odds, who in the world would turn down such a bet?)

(Try an experiment to see the difficulty with Rawls' argument. Change the number in the southwest corner of Table 36-3 to $100,000. Rawls' argument still leads to the choice of equality (option A). Would this be your choice? If so, would you

choose option A or C if the number were even higher, say $1 million? or $1 billion? Won't you eventually come around to option C and give up voting in a Rawlsian way?)

Because people in an original position would not necessarily vote for equality option A over C, Rawls does not make a convincing case for equality. The difficulty is that his argument is based on the assumption that people's only concern is with what is happening in the last column in those two tables—that is, with that last, poorest individual. Specifically, the choice is based on *maximizing* the *minimum* income; hence, this is often referred to as the *maximin* criterion. But why should we completely ignore the vast majority and be totally preoccupied with that last individual?

In a later reconsideration of the maximin criterion,‡ Rawls concluded that although he still viewed it as attractive, "a deeper investigation . . . may show that some other conception of justice is more reasonable. In any case, the idea that economists may find most useful . . . is that of the original position. This perspective . . . may prove illuminating for economic theory."

‡See John Rawls, "Some Reasons for the Maximin Criterion," *American Economic Review* (May 1974): 141–46.

Advocates of income equality were immediately attracted to Rawls' theory because it seemed to provide a firmer foundation for equality than the traditional argument. According to the earlier argument, equality is a desirable goal because it would maximize the total utility of all individuals in society. However, this conclusion follows only if it can be assumed that all individuals have the same capacity to enjoy income. (If this assumption does not hold, we can improve the outcome by moving away from complete equality, by transferring some income away from those who are less able to enjoy it to those who are more able to enjoy it.) Unfortunately, there is no way we can confirm or deny the assumption that people enjoy income equally. Remember, there is no way to meter people's heads to compare the satisfaction they get from $1 of income.

Therefore, this traditional argument does not provide convincing support for income equality. Nor, as we have seen in this box, does Rawls' theory. Like the older theory, it has a weak link, in this case the assumption that the only concern is for the lowest person on the totem pole. Moreover, many of those who believe in equality became less enthusiastic about Rawls' theory when they discovered that it allows for a very substantial degree of inequality—as we have seen in Table 36-2 and as Rawls himself has re-emphasized. (Rawls, "Some Reasons for the Maximin Criterion," p. 145.)

may start equal? Does it make any more sense to do this than to penalize a marathon runner for strong legs? If we were to embark on such a penalty or handicap system, we would end up in the world of Box 36-2, where Kurt Vonnegut's Handicapper General weighs down naturally talented ballerinas with bags of birdshot. In such a world, nobody would come close to breaking the 4-minute mile; the economy would fall far short of its potential.

. . . but Modify the Rewards

It is quite possible to have a fair race, yet still have a bad system of rewards. For example, suppose the winner were to be given a million dollars, and the loser were to be thrown, Roman style, to the lions? Believing in a fair economic race does not prevent us from modifying its rewards—in other words, using taxes and transfer payments to reduce the income differences that result.

To the authors, this idea of a fair race and a modified system of rewards that reduces but does not eliminate income inequality seems to be an appealing principle. But again, the idea is not as simple as it sounds. Is not an individual's economic life less like a standard race than like a relay race? Moreover, a relay race with no beginning or end? The race you run depends on the start you get, in terms of your whole background, including your family wealth. A first reaction is that it should not be like this. To keep the race fair, everyone should be started off equally, without any advantage of inherited wealth. Should we therefore tax away all inheritances and, for the same reason, gifts?

This is a difficult proposal to defend, even on equity grounds. Consider two men with equal incomes. One spends it all. The other wishes to save in order to pass wealth on to his children. Is it fair to impose a tax that

prohibits him from doing so? Is not charity a virtue? What can one say of a society that prevents gifts to family or friends?

Conclusions: Can We Pin Down the Idea of Equity?

Unfortunately, the answer is no. The only conclusions we have been able to reach are both negative. Equity is not complete equality of income, nor is it the income distribution that the free market generates. We are left somewhere between. We conclude that, in terms of equity considerations alone, we should move from a free-market distribution some distance, but not the whole way, toward equalizing incomes.

To further complicate matters, any such move tends to involve an efficiency cost in terms of a shrinking national pie. The reason—to be examined in detail in the next chapter—is that guaranteeing people an income tends to reduce their incentive to work, and they produce less. Because of this efficiency cost, it is desirable to stop short of the degree of equality that would be chosen if equity were the sole objective.

In practice, we have already introduced tax and expenditure policies that have moved us some distance toward equalizing incomes, as Figure 36-2 has illustrated. It is possible that we have not yet moved far enough; it is also possible that we have moved too far. The question of how the nation's income should be distributed is likely to remain an issue of continuing debate. However, it is important that the dispute about how the national income pie should be divided does not become so heated and exhausting that the total size of that pie is substantially reduced. To return to our earlier analogy: If all participants had spent their energies in a squabble about how the race should be run and how the rewards should be divided, no one would have broken the 4-minute mile.

BOX 36-2

KURT VONNEGUT ON WHY ONLY HORSES AND GOLFERS SHOULD BE HANDICAPPED*

The year was 2081, and everybody was finally equal. They weren't only equal before God and the law. They were equal every which way. Nobody was smarter than anybody else. Nobody was better looking than anybody else. Nobody was stronger or quicker than anybody else. All this equality was due to the 211th, 212th, and 213th Amendments to the Constitution, and to the unceasing vigilance of agents of the United States Handicapper General . . .

George [Bergeron, whose] intelligence was way above normal, had a little mental handicap radio in his ear. He was required by law to wear it at all times. It was tuned to a government transmitter. Every twenty seconds or so, the transmitter would send out some sharp noise to keep people like George from taking unfair advantage of their brains. . . .

On the television screen were ballerinas. . . . They weren't really very good—no better than anybody else would have been anyway. They were burdened with sashweights and bags of birdshot and their faces were masked, so that no one, seeing a free and graceful gesture or a pretty face, would feel like something the cat drug in. George was toying with the vague notion that maybe dancers shouldn't be handicapped. But he didn't get very far with it before another noise in his ear radio scattered his thoughts . . .

*Abridgment of "Harrison Bergeron" from *Welcome to the Monkey House* by Kurt Vonnegut, Jr. Copyright © 1961 by Kurt Vonnegut, Jr. Originally published in *Fantasy and Science Fiction*. Reprinted by permission of *Delacorte Press/Seymour Lawrence*.

George began to think glimmeringly about his abnormal son who was now in jail, about Harrison, but a twenty-one-gun salute in his head stopped that. "Boy," said Hazel, "that was a doozy, wasn't it?" It was such a doozy that George was white and trembling, and tears stood on the rims of his red eyes. Two of the eight ballerinas had collapsed to the studio floor, were holding their temples. . . .

The television program was suddenly interrupted for a news bulletin. It wasn't clear at first as to what the bulletin was about, since the announcer, like all announcers, had a serious speech impediment. For about half a minute, and in a state of high excitement, the announcer tried to say, "Ladies and gentlemen—"

He finally gave up, handed the bulletin to a ballerina to read. . . . "That's all right—" Hazel said of the announcer, "he tried. That's the big thing. He tried to the best he could with what God gave him. He should get a nice raise for trying so hard."

"Ladies and gentlemen—" said the ballerina, . . . "Harrison Bergeron, age fourteen . . . has just escaped from jail, where he was held on suspicion of plotting to overthrow the government. He is a genius and an athlete, is under-handicapped, and should be regarded as extremely dangerous."

A police photograph of Harrison Bergeron was flashed on the screen. . . . Harrison's appearance was Halloween and hardware. Nobody had ever borne heavier handicaps. . . . Instead of a little ear radio for a mental handicap, he wore a tremendous pair of earphones, and spectacles with thick wavy lenses. The spectacles were intended to make him not only half blind, but to give him whanging headaches besides.

Scrap metal was hung all over him. Ordinarily, there was a certain symmetry, a military neatness to the handicaps issued to strong people, but Harrison looked like a walking junkyard.

KEY POINTS

1. Large differences exist in the incomes of Canadians. Some have high incomes because of their human capital, wealth, native talent, family background, market power, or just plain luck. Others have low incomes because they enjoy none of these advantages or for some other reason. For example, they may suffer from discrimination.

2. If we examine the Canadian income distribution *before government taxes and transfers* are taken into account, we observe a great deal of inequality. The poorest 20% receive only 1.4% of the nation's income, while the highest 20% get 45%.

3. About a quarter of this inequality is eliminated by government transfer expenditures that are concentrated heavily on the poor, and by progressive taxes that draw heavily from the rich. However, our tax system overall is not as progressive as the income tax alone, and taxes do much less equalizing than government transfer payments.

4. The most effective government expenditure in equalizing income is transfers such as Old Age Security, social assistance, and Unemployment Insurance. But other government expenditures, both in cash and in kind, also play a role.

5. Equality is a question of fact: How equal *are* incomes? On the other hand, equity is a matter of judgement: What pattern of incomes is fair? A strong case can be made that neither a completely equal distribution of incomes nor the unequal free-market distribution is equitable. A desirable target seems to lie somewhere between.

6. While it is very difficult to be more precise than this, some rough guidelines have been suggested. For example, the "economic race" should be kept as fair as possible. In other words, everyone should have an equal opportunity. The government should ensure that no one starts at a disadvantage because of race or sex. However, the appealing principle of equality of opportunity conflicts with the equally appealing principle that parents should be able to help their children.

7. Equal opportunity need not result in equal reward. Even if everyone could be given an equal start, there is no reason to expect that all will finish in a tie. Some will get greater rewards than others. The second responsibility of the government is to modify rewards—that is, to reduce income inequality by taxes and transfer payments.

8. Finally, even if we could determine an equitable income distribution, it does not follow that the government should continue to redistribute income up to this point. The reason is that the act of redistributing income—changing the division of the national pie—affects the incentive to work and hence the level of efficiency (the size of that pie). Therefore, a compromise should be selected between the conflicting objectives of equity and efficiency.

KEY CONCEPTS

cumulative income distribution
  (Lorenz curve)
cash transfers
transfers in kind

difference between equity and
  equality
limitations of the free market
  as a distributor of income

*Rawls' difference principle
*maximin
  difference between equalizing
  opportunity and equalizing
  reward

*For those who have studied Box 36-1.

PROBLEMS

36-1 Explain to your very bright roommate (who is not studying economics) why some Canadians have much higher incomes than others.

36-2 Mark McCormack is, in his own words, an "engineer of careers." In one year, his company is reported to have grossed $35 million by charging a 15% to 40% agent's fee for managing 250 tennis stars and golfers. Do you think McCormack's large income is the result of (a) only luck; (b) luck and other reasons; or (c) just other reasons? If you answer (b) or (c), explain what the other reasons might be.

36-3 Explain how the marketplace generates a rental income for those with high reputation, just as for those with great skill.

36-4 Explain why you agree or disagree with the following statement: "Free-market prices of factors of production help to maximize the total national income pie and also divide it in an equitable way."

*36-5 (This question is based on Box 36-1.) Is the following statement true or false? If true, explain it. If false, correct it:
"Rawls' maximin principle is to *maximize* the *minimum* possible income. However, this is the preference only of people who are unwilling to risk any of their income in the hope of acquiring more. Many people are not like this, including all those individuals who bet a small part of their income at the races or Monte Carlo in the hope of winning more."

*36-6 In 1899, John Bates Clark wrote in the *Distribution of Wealth* that "free competition tends to give to labor what labor creates (that is, the value of the marginal product of labor), to capitalists what capital creates (that is, the marginal product of capital), and to entrepreneurs what the coordinating function creates." This sounds as though everyone gets what he or she deserves; that is, free competition distributes income in an equitable way. Do you agree? In your view, what does a free competitive market do well, and what does it do not so well?

Chapter 37

GOVERNMENT POLICIES TO REDUCE INEQUALITY: CAN WE SOLVE THE POVERTY PROBLEM?

Welfare has been indicted for encouraging family dissolution, promoting illegitimacy, degrading and alienating recipients, papering over the sins of a society that generates poverty, shielding the dissolute and lazy from their just deserts, failing to support life by providing too little assistance, and fostering sloth by providing too much. Conservatives, liberals, and radicals unite in attacking the welfare system but divide over its specific faults.

Henry J. Aaron

Although Canadians may differ on the question of how far we should go in reducing income inequality in general, an overwhelming majority agree that society has a responsibility to protect those at the bottom end of the income scale. Nobody should starve. No child should have to grow up in grinding poverty; nor should the elderly have to suffer deprivation in their declining years. Yet in 1984, poverty was still a fact of life for about one in seven Canadian families, and almost four out of ten individuals living alone. (In the official statistics, people living alone are referred to as "unattached individuals.")

The extent and effects of poverty are not as visible in Canada as they are in the United States, where they are depressingly illustrated in the run-down areas in the core of almost every large city. But while our poverty problem is less apparent, it is very real for the people affected by it. And poverty in North America is difficult to bear not only because it makes it hard for people to get even decent standards of food, housing, and clothing, but also because the poverty of the few contrasts so starkly with the comfort of the many.

This chapter is a study of the poor—the individuals who appeared in the bottom left-hand corner of the

Lorenz income curve in Figure 36-1. Who are the poor? Why are they poor? What programs has the government introduced to fight the war on poverty? Should these programs be viewed as a way of cleaning up an economic mess created by the system, or do they create the mess? And finally, can the faults in these programs be cured—and, if so, how?

POVERTY

The economic definition of poverty is "inadequate income." But this does not mean that poverty is strictly an economic condition. It is often also a state of mind, a condition in which the individual feels helpless and unable to cope. Therefore, poverty is a subject for sociologists and political scientists as well as economists. One of the difficulties encountered in studying poverty is the chicken-or-egg problem: Are people unable to cope because they are poor? Or are they poor because they are unable to cope? Undoubtedly the answer is, "Both."

> Poverty exists when people have inadequate income to buy the necessities of life. In 1984 it was defined, for a family of four in a medium-sized city, as an income of $19,000.

How the Poverty Line Is Defined

The problem in defining the poverty line—in the statistics, it is called the "low-income cut-off"—is to define what is meant by the necessities of life. For one thing, different families may have different "necessary" expenditures. For some it may be dental care or prescription drugs; for those who must drive to work, it may be the cost of a car. But some necessities must be paid for by every family: decent food and clothing, and a place to live. The importance of spending on food, clothing, and shelter can be seen in studies of family expenditure patterns. They show that the poorer the family, the larger the proportion of the family budget that is spent on these items: As the family becomes poorer, spending on luxury items will decline until all that remains is the cost of food, clothing, shelter, and a small amount of expenditures on other things.

The government defines the poverty line by estimating the income level at which an average family has to spend as much as three-fifths (more precisely, 58.5%) of its budget on food, clothing, and shelter. Because the cost of food and shelter differs between urban and rural areas, the poverty-line for a rural family of four is lower than it is for an urban family: about $14,700 for a rural family versus $19,000 for an urban family in a medium-sized city, in 1984. The poverty line is also adjusted for the size of the family unit: For an unattached individual living in a medium-sized urban area it was about $9,300 in 1984, but for an urban family of six it was $24,000.

Of course, the poverty line has to be adjusted upward periodically to take inflation into account. And historically, over the long term, it tends to rise for another reason as well: Our concept of poverty keeps shifting up. The poverty income of about $19,000 in 1984 would have been regarded before confederation as a very handsome income indeed (even after full adjustment is made for inflation). In fact, it would still have been considered a good income as late as the 1930s. So upward adjustments in the definition of poverty do occur. But beware: If the definition of poverty is made too flexible, the concept becomes meaningless. If, for example, poverty is defined as the income of the bottom one-tenth of the population, there is no hope of curing it: By this definition, one in ten Canadians will always be poor, no matter how much we may raise everyone's income. And the statement that one Canadian family in ten is living in poverty will tell us absolutely nothing about how serious the problem is, or how successful we have been in curing it.

Who Are the Poor?

As Table 37-1 shows, poverty in the mid-1980s was a more serious problem in some Canadian regions than

Table 37-1

Incidence of Low Income Families by Region (Percentage of population in 1984)

Atlantic provinces	18.0%
Quebec	16.8%
Ontario	11.4%
Prairie provinces	15.0%
British Columbia	15.2%

SOURCE: Statistics Canada, *Income Distribution by Size in Canada*, 1984. Reproduced by permission of the Minister of Supply and Services Canada.

in others. For example, the Atlantic provinces and Quebec had a relatively high percentage of families living in poverty—partly because of their high unemployment rates. On the other hand, the rate for Ontario was substantially below the national average.

From Table 37-2 one can also see that some specific kinds of families or individuals have much higher percentages below the poverty line. Often, poverty goes with other problems that make life difficult. Families in which the head of the household is a woman are three times as likely to be poor as the average family. And families with three or more children are more than twice as likely to be poor as a couple with no children. Poverty also goes with old age: Half the people over the age of 65 who live alone are below the poverty line. For many poor people, the explanation for poverty is simply a lack of jobs. In 1984, almost 70% of those who lived alone and had been employed

Table 37-2
Incidence of Low Income by Selected Characteristics, 1984

	Estimated Percentage below Poverty Line	
	Families	Unattached Individuals
All families and unattached individuals	14.5%	38%
By age of household head		
—24 and younger	30	47
—55–64 years	13	44
—65 and over	11	50
By sex of household head		
—Female	43	43
By marital status of household head		
neither married nor single†	37	42
By weeks worked		
—none	32	62
—10–19 weeks	32	67
—40–48 weeks	11	21
—49–52 weeks	6	12
By education of household head		
—0–8 years of school	20	58
—some secondary	16	36
By origin of household head		
—Canadian born	15	37
—non-Canadian born	14	40
By number of children younger than 16 years		
—none	10	38
—1	19	—
—2	18	—
—3 or more	26	—

SOURCE: Statistics Canada, *Income Distribution by Size in Canada*, 1984. †Divorced, separated, widowed.
Reproduced by permission of the Minister of Supply and Services Canada.

for less than 20 weeks, had incomes below the poverty level.

GOVERNMENT ANTI-POVERTY POLICIES

Programs to combat the problem of poverty have existed in Canada for a long time. Many of the early programs were organized by private charities; small-scale welfare schemes were also set up by municipal and provincial governments. (In the original British North America Act of 1867, social welfare came exclusively under provincial jurisdiction.) But the scope of the government programs has been growing steadily over time. Especially since the mid-1960s, government spending on programs designed to reduce poverty has been increasing very quickly: Between the mid-sixties and the early 1980s, transfer payments to individuals by federal and provincial governments grew by about ten times in dollar terms, and about four times when adjusted for inflation.

When the public thinks of anti-poverty programs, it is these government programs—such as Old Age Security, Unemployment Insurance and social assistance plans—that usually come to mind. But these outlays relieve only the *symptoms* of poverty: They make it more bearable without providing much hope that the problem will be cured (that is, that the poor will be able to increase their earnings). A more promising long-run approach to poverty is to attack its *causes*. For example, expenditures on education or training are designed to cure one of the causes of poverty: inadequate human capital. The objective is to allow people to accumulate this capital in order to provide for their own support in the future. (Although it is usually more promising to attack the causes of a problem than its symptoms, this is not always the case. In extreme cases of "clinical" poverty, where individuals have such a low innate capacity or skill that no amount of training will allow them to earn a living, straight support programs may be the more effective form of assistance.)

Policies to Reduce the Causes of Poverty

Before turning to the "symptom-relieving" policies, which are aimed at supporting people who are already poor, we consider policies that are intended to reduce the incidence of poverty by attacking its causes.

1. Subsidizing investment in human capital. Local governments (with financial contributions from the provinces) pay for the full cost of schooling until the end of high school. Because it is paid for, more individuals will finish high school; and high-school graduates are less likely to be poor than those with less education. University and community college education is also heavily subsidized by provincial governments. While most students pay part of the cost, the provinces generally have programs to assist community college and university students from low-income families.

For those no longer attending school, the government also supports on-the-job training: For example, under the *Adult Occupational Training Act*, the federal government pays part of the cost of retraining people who have lost their old jobs, and who might otherwise end up below the poverty line. Provincial governments also have different forms of human rights legislation that outlaw discrimination on the basis of race and sex. This is a useful way to attack poverty, since, as we have already seen, discrimination against minorities or women, in rates of pay or in hiring and firing practices, contributes to poverty.

2. Dealing with unemployment and disability. The most promising government policies to cure unemployment are those designed to keep the economy operating at a high level of output. But this provides no cure for those who cannot work, for example, because they are disabled. To reduce the incidence of disability due to work-related injuries or illness, we have federal and provincial legislation to govern safety and other conditions in the workplace (discussed in Chapter 27). The incomes of those workers who *do* become disabled are partially protected by provincial worker's compensation programs. In addition, provincial health insurance programs also provide health care at little or no cost to the user. By making high-quality health care available to everyone, these programs help prevent workers from losing their earning power due to illness.

3. Other policies. Some governments in Canada have organized special programs to assist welfare recipients in finding work. Another important policy of this type is the provision of free or subsidized daycare facilities for children. This is particularly important in reducing the incidence of poverty in the increasingly important group of families with only one parent in the home.

POLICIES TO REDUCE THE SYMPTOMS OF POVERTY: GOVERNMENT PROGRAMS TO MAINTAIN INCOMES

Even if it is not possible to cure a disease, it is very important to provide the patient with relief from the symptoms. While we are in the process of developing long-run cures for poverty (such as upgrading human capital and preventing disability) we also provide public assistance programs that keep many families from falling below the poverty line (Table 37-3).

Social Insurance Programs

Several of the government's transfer programs are not specifically designed to cure poverty, because the transfers are made to rich and poor alike. The most important of these general *social insurance programs* are Old Age Security, the Canada and Quebec Pension Plans, family allowances, Unemployment Insurance, and the provincial health insurance plans. Even though the transfers under these programs are not restricted to poor people, they play a key role in keeping many of the population from falling below the poverty line.

Old Age Security (OAS). All Canadian residents over the age of 65 are eligible for the Old Age Security program, though only those who have been Canadian residents for a long time get the full benefit. The OAS comes in the form of a monthly cheque, which is the same for all recipients. The amount is indexed to the consumer price index, and therefore increases from year to year. In 1986 it was $288 per month per recipient.

The Canada Pension Plan (CPP) and Quebec Pension Plan (QPP). The CPP, which covers most people in the labour force, provides for retirement benefits to people over 65, with the amount depending on the person's previous earnings. (The CPP may also pay certain other types of benefits, such as health benefits and pensions to surviving spouses and children when a beneficiary dies.) The CPP does not apply to people in Quebec, because Quebec has set up its own government pension plan, the QPP.

The CPP is a contributory plan, which means that it is financed by previous (before-retirement) contributions from workers and their employers. (In 1986, the workers' contribution was fixed at 1.8% of earnings up to a maximum of $419.40 per year. Employers had to contribute the same amount.) The maximum retirement pension (for those who have contributed the maximum amount during their earning years) was

Table 37-3
Major Government Programs to Maintain Income, 1982–83

Program	Total Cost ($ billion)	Government Responsible for Program
Old Age Security (OAS)	7.0	federal
Guaranteed Income Supplement (GIS)	2.4	federal
Canada/Quebec Pension Plan (CPP/QPP)	4.1	federal/provincial
Family allowances	2.2	federal
Refundable Child Tax Credit	1.5	federal
Workers' Compensation	2.0	provincial
Veterans' pensions	1.0	federal
Unemployment Insurance (UI)	8.6	federal
Hospital and medical Insurance	22.3	federal/provincial
Social welfare assistance and social welfare services	6.6	federal/provincial
Total Health Care and Social Services	57.7	

SOURCE: Åke Blomqvist, "Political Economy of the Canadian Welfare State" in David Laidler, ed., *Approaches to Economic Wellbeing*, Study No. 26 (Toronto: University of Toronto Press in co-operation with the Royal Commission on the Economic Union and Development Prospects for Canada, and the Canadian Government Publishing Centre, Supply and Services Canada, 1985), Table 5. Reproduced by permission of the Minister of Supply and Services Canada.

roughly $490 per month in 1986. Like the OAS payments, the retirement pensions under CPP are indexed to the consumer price index.

Family allowances. Canada's family allowance program was introduced in 1945. It was promptly given the name "baby bonus" by an unknown wit, and has kept that name. In most provinces, the baby bonus is a flat monthly amount for every child in the family under 18 years of age. (Quebec and Alberta have slightly different programs, with the second child drawing a larger monthly payment than the first, and so on.) The Family Allowances Act specifies that the monthly amount will be raised when the consumer price index increases, but not necessarily at the same rate. In 1976, indexing of family allowance benefits was temporarily suspended as part of a program of fiscal restraint, and in the May 1985 budget, Finance Minister Michael Wilson announced that from 1986 on, the government intended to modify the indexing so that benefits would increase at a rate three percentage points less than the inflation rate. (The original intention was to reduce the indexing of OAS payments the same way, but after a public outcry the government backed down and promised to continue regular indexing of OAS benefits.) By 1986, the monthly Family Allowance benefit had reached $31.58 per child in most provinces.

Unemployment Insurance. Canada's system of government unemployment insurance was started on a fairly modest scale in 1940. However, its scope was greatly expanded in 1971, and it now covers about nine-tenths of the labour force. The program is designed as an insurance scheme, with employers and workers paying a percentage of the workers' incomes into the system, so long as they remain employed. But as soon as they become unemployed, they receive benefits. Essentially, the weekly benefits are equal to 60% of previous earnings, but cannot be higher than a specified ceiling.

The number of people drawing unemployment insurance benefits has grown rapidly during the late 1970s and first half of the 1980s, for several reasons:

1. The economy has been operating well below capacity, thereby creating higher rates of unemployment among existing workers, especially following the 1982 recession.
2. There have been many new entrants to the labour force who have been able to find jobs for only short periods of time and have then become unemployed.
3. It has become easier to qualify, so more people are now receiving benefits. For example, the scheme now includes women who are unable to work because of pregnancy and some seasonal workers such as fishermen, who are eligible for insurance benefits in the off season.

Health insurance. As we have already noted, each province has a health insurance program that provides almost all health care services at little or no cost to almost all of its citizens. (Though some people are allowed to opt out of the program in some provinces, few choose to do so.) While they are still called "insurance" programs, most provinces finance the cost of health care out of their own tax receipts and transfers from the federal government. Only a few provinces (including Ontario) require their citizens to pay a health insurance premium, and even in those provinces, the premium revenue covers only a fraction of the total cost of health care.

Whereas programs such as Old Age Security and Unemployment Insurance provide cash transfers, health care insurance and programs such as free elementary and secondary education provide benefits ***in kind***, that is, specific goods or services instead of cash.

> ***Benefits in kind*** are transfers, not of cash, but of some good (like drugs) or service (medical care).

Targeted Transfer Programs

The government transfer programs we have been describing above are programs that are extended to all eligible beneficiaries regardless of income. Thus, while they help many people to escape poverty, they are not specifically designed for this purpose only, because they are not targeted to the poor. The programs we describe below, by contrast, are directly designed to combat poverty: They are available exclusively to people with low incomes.

Guaranteed Income Supplement (GIS). The GIS is a federal program which is designed to supplement the resources of people over 65 who have little income beyond Old Age Security. The maximum payment to a single person with no income other than OAS was $343 per month in 1986. For those over 65 with other income in addition to OAS, the GIS payments are reduced by 50% of the amount of other income. As we saw earlier, many elderly people in Canada are poor, and more than half of the people over 65 in fact receive money under the GIS program.

Child Tax Credit. Since 1978, the federal government provides a substantial tax credit for each child in low- and middle-income families. During the 1986 taxation year, the credit was $384 per child. Families with income of less than about $26,000 receive the full amount of the tax credit. For families with higher income, the credit is reduced by $5 per $100 of income in excess of this threshold.

Social assistance. This program encompasses what most people mean when they speak of somebody "being on welfare." Social assistance programs are the responsibility of the provinces, although municipal authorities may administer the programs at the local level. But the federal government shares in the cost under the *Canada Assistance Plan*: Of the roughly $6.6 billion spent on social assistance in 1982/83, the federal government paid about half. The amount of assistance a family receives is determined by its *cash deficit*—that is, the amount its income falls short of its necessary expenditure on basic food, clothing, shelter, and other essentials. Subject to various administrative limitations, social workers have fairly wide discretion in deciding what expenditures are necessary for the family, and may arrange payment for specific things that the family would not otherwise be able to afford, such as dental work or the services of a homemaker.

Other programs. In addition to the major welfare programs, local and provincial governments have been trying a variety of other ways to give assistance to people with low incomes. For example, several provinces have programs supplementing the federal OAS/GIS payments to needy persons over 65. Many governments provide subsidized public housing to welfare recipients and other poor people, or subsidize the cost of old-age homes, and programs exist to ensure that prescription drugs are available at no cost to those who would have difficulty paying for them.

ASSESSING THE PRESENT WELFARE PACKAGE

The cost of our social welfare programs is very high. In trying to assess whether the money is being well spent, one can consider two different but related questions:

1. How far have the welfare programs taken us toward the fundamental objective of eliminating poverty?
2. Is the current package of social welfare programs efficient? In other words, are we reducing poverty at minimum cost, or could we get the same reduction at a lower cost?

How Much Progress Have We Made?
Taking a long-run view, the message in Figure 37-1 is encouraging. From the early 1960s to the mid-1980s,

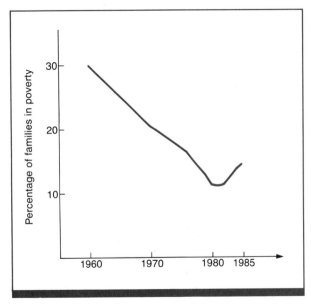

Figure 37-1 **How the percentage of the population below the poverty line is shrinking over time.**
By the low-income standard of the mid-1970s, the proportion of the population in poverty has declined substantially since the early 1960s. However, there was an upward trend in the population below the low-income cutoff in the early 1980s.
Sources: 1969–84 data from Statistics Canada, *Income Distribution by Size in Canada*, various years; 1961 figure from F. Vaillancourt, *Income Distribution and Economic Security in Canada*, vol. 1 (Toronto: University of Toronto Press in co-operation with the Royal Commission on the Economic Union and Development Prospects for Canada, and the Canadian Government Publishing Centre, Supply and Services Canada, 1985), Table 12. We have added 2.7 percentage points to all figures before 1979 to account for a change in Statistics Canada's definition of the poverty line. Statistics Canada data reproduced by permission of the Minister of Supply and Services Canada.

BOX 37-1

THE RISING COST OF HEALTH CARE

It is widely recognized that the quality of health care in Canada is as good as anywhere in the world. However, it has become *very* costly. In 1984, we spent some 8.5% of GNP on health care.

In Canada, most of the cost of health care is covered by provincial government health insurance plans. In the United States, government plans cover only those over age 65 (Medicare) and the poor (Medicaid); the rest of the population is either covered by private plans or not covered at all. Nevertheless, the U.S. health care system is even more costly than the Canadian one: In 1984–85, Americans spent as much as 10.5% of their GNP on health care.

One reason why health care has become so costly in Canada and the United States is that medical research has now made it possible to save lives in a variety of new ways. But many methods, such as heart transplants, are very expensive. All available life-saving opportunities cannot be seized unless a larger and larger percentage of the nation's GNP is directed into this effort. One can argue that, with the opening up of new life-saving opportunities, more of our GNP *should* be spent in this way. However, if we try to capture all of these opportunities, the cost would become extremely high. Therefore, society must have some way of deciding at what point its lifesaving efforts will be limited— that is, at what point funds that could save lives will be cut off. Which patients will be the lucky ones who will live because they get access to the limited number of lifesaving machines and treatments that society can afford?

No one likes to make this life-and-death decision about "who will get a seat in the lifeboat" and who will not. For this reason, there are a number of alternative ways of making this decision.

(a) *Delay*. In 1984, the British National Health Service provided about 110 free heart transplants. However, there was a waiting list of up to a year, during which most of those in line simply died.

(b) *Set an age limit*. Unofficially, heart trans-

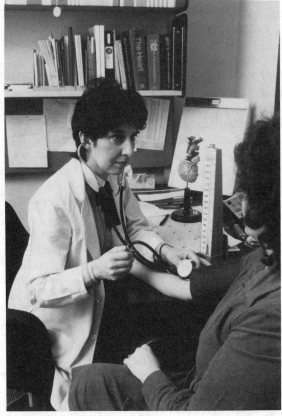

Courtesy Miller Services Limited

plants in the United States are given only to those less than 50 years of age. This was one reason why Barney Clark and William Schroeder, both over 50, were given artificial hearts instead.

(c) *Use chance*. Decide on who will live and die in some sort of a doomsday lottery. However, this makes no sense at all, because an Einstein may lose out in such a lottery to a suicidal derelict who places no value on his own life. (For more on this life-or-death choice, see Victor R. Fuchs, *Who Shall Live?* (New York: Basic Books, 1983).)

Because these methods are unsatisfactory or inadequate, the life-or-death decision frequently has to be made by doctors on the spot—or administrators or committees allocating funds. It's often an agonizing decision. We've seen earlier how difficult it is to put a value on a life. But the task of saying that one *particular* life is worth more than another— and therefore is the one that should be saved—is even more difficult. Therefore, whenever possible, those making such decisions understandably argue: Instead of choosing between two lives, let's save them both—if there is any conceivable way we can get the cost covered. This, then, is one reason there is persistent upward pressure on costs.

Another reason is that when most of the bills for a patient's health care is paid for by a government insurance plan (or by private insurance, for that matter), there is little pressure to cut costs. Patients have little or no incentive to seek out low-cost treatment; when your health is at stake you don't go bargain hunting, especially if the government or an insurance company is paying the tab.

Canadian governments have tried a variety of measures to counteract the upward pressure on the costs of health care. In most provinces, doctors are no longer allowed to set their own fees, but have to charge according to a fee schedule that has been negotiated with the provincial government. (In the mid-1980s, doctors in Alberta and Ontario were allowed to charge their patients in excess of the negotiated schedules ("extra billing"). However, following the passage of the Canada Health Act which provided for financial penalties by the federal government for provinces that allowed extra billing, it seemed only a matter of time before it would be banned across Canada; in Ontario, the government of Premier David Peterson introduced a bill to do so in 1986.) While hospitals in Canada are not technically "owned" by provincial governments, they get almost all their operating funds and most of their capital funds directly from the governments. Thus, one way in which provincial governments can cut back is simply by giving hospitals smaller budgets. Widespread complaints of government "underfunding" of the health care system in recent years is evidence that such cutbacks have been taking place.

A number of proposals have been made to increase the efficiency of the health care system by using various forms of financial incentives. For example, it has sometimes been argued that patients should be given at least *some* financial responsibility for the cost of their health care. While no one wants to allow life-and-death decisions to depend on the patient's ability to pay for treatment, the argument is that by making the patient pay at least some fraction of the cost of care (such as 10% of the cost or $200, whichever is less, for example), patients would at least become more conscious of the cost of care. With patients becoming more cost-conscious, so would doctors and hospitals.

Another promising alternative that is appearing in the United States is the so-called *Health Maintenance Organization* (HMO). HMOs are corporations that own their own hospitals and employ their own doctors. Instead of billing patients directly for the services produced, they provide hospital and physician services, at no direct charge, to people who have enrolled in the HMO plan and pay a fixed fee each year or month. (Such a plan is sometimes referred to as a "prepayment" plan.) Since the income per enrolled patient in an HMO is fixed, it makes more money the *fewer* the services it provides to its patients. In contrast, doctors and hospitals who bill their patients (or their patients' insurance companies) for services rendered, make more money if they provide *more* services. Even though the American Medical Association has long been opposed to HMOs, they have been growing in the United States, and in the long run they may help to keep costs from rising.

Finally, there is evidence from the United States that another explanation for the present high cost of health care may be that some doctors and hospitals have been defrauding the government health insurance plans. A U.S. Senate committee investigating the cost of Medicaid found that some doctors would carry out complete physical examinations—with the whole battery of laboratory tests—on essentially healthy people who came to their offices with a minor complaint. Through referrals, a group of specialist doctors may "ping-pong" patients back and forth among themselves. Moreover, Medicaid patients getting a doctor's appointment have sometimes been told to bring their children, too. The doctor can then take a brief look at the children and charge Medicaid the fee for an office visit for each. Attempts to fight this problem of "medifraud" have entailed the creation of costly administrative machinery to supervise the payments made under the plans.

the percentage of families classified as poor has fallen by half; in 1961 about one in three families was classified as poor, while in 1984 only about one in seven families was below Statistics Canada's "low-income cutoff" level. (If we look at individuals living alone, the progress appears less impressive, but the percentage classified as poor fell substantially in this category as well.)

In interpreting this evidence, we should keep in mind that some reduction in poverty would have occurred even if we had not expanded the system of welfare programs, because factors such as technological change and capital accumulation have been raising real incomes during this period.[1] Thus, it is difficult to say precisely what proportion of the reduction in poverty is due to the social welfare programs. Nevertheless, it is clear that our social welfare system has helped many Canadians escape poverty.

While the statistics are encouraging when we consider the whole period shown in Figure 37-1, it appears that most of the progress was made during the 1960s and 1970s; in the early 1980s, the extent of poverty seems to have *increased* . This is particularly disturbing when we take into account the fact that during this period, spending on our social welfare programs rose at an unprecedented rate.

The principal explanation for this recent trend is undoubtedly the poor performance of the overall economy during the early 1980s; the 1982 recesssion was the worst since World War II, and unemployment (one of the main factors contributing to poverty) reached record levels. Nevertheless, one of the purposes of the social welfare system is to protect Canadians from poverty during economic downturns, and it is discouraging that the system has not done a better job of

that in recent years. This brings us to the second question raised above: How efficient is the current system of welfare programs?

Problems with the Welfare System

Questions about the efficiency of our system of social welfare programs have been raised for a long time, and major proposals for reform date back to the late 1960s. While some critics simply would like to see less spending on social welfare, there are many others who are principally concerned with the possibility of changing the *pattern* (rather than the level) of expenditures so as to make more efficient use of the money already being spent. They have two main types of criticism of the present system:

1. The system is *too complex*. The complexity adds to the cost of the programs. (A simpler system would be less costly to administer.) Worse, the complexity has contributed to introducing many *inequities* in the system. For example, poor families may receive very different levels of income depending on where they live. Some families whose members earn some income from working end up with an income that is no higher (and may even be lower) than families in which no one is working. Furthermore, if we look at the overall impact of the complicated set of transfer programs, we cannot even be sure that we always provide the most help to those who are in the greatest need. For example, according to a calculation in the report of the MacDonald Commission (which contained an extensive discussion of social welfare programs), a family of four in 1985 with one income earner and an income of $100,000 received a combined benefit of $5,035 from the Family Allowance, the Child Tax Credit, and various tax deductions, whereas a similar family with two working adults earning a total income of only $25,000 received benefits of only $2,240. Thus, the critics charge, one of the shortcomings of our welfare package is that its benefits are not well enough *targeted* toward those low-income people who should receive the most help.

2. The second major criticism of the present system is that it creates *undesirable incentives*. Consider, for example, a hypothetical low-

---

[1]If we examined the recent income of Canadian families *before taxes and transfers*, we would find as many as one-fourth of them below the poverty line. Taxes and transfers reduce this to less than 15%. This sounds like clear evidence that taxes and transfers drastically reduce poverty. But this conclusion does not follow quite so simply. As noted earlier, if transfer payments did not exist, there would be a greater incentive to work. (Without welfare to fall back on, people would feel under more pressure to get a job. With more people working, there would be less than 25% initially below the poverty line.) In other words, because taxes and transfers have the indirect effect of reducing incentives to work, they are less effective in reducing poverty than they initially appear.

income family in which the wife normally works but is currently unemployed, and suppose she has been told of an opportunity for a temporary job which would allow her to contribute an extra $5,000 to the family's income this year. In deciding whether or not to take the job, she has several things to consider. (1) She will not be able to collect Unemployment Insurance benefits during the period she will be working. (2) If the family is currently living in subsidized low-income housing, the wife's extra earnings may make the family ineligible for this type of housing; thus, their housing costs would rise. (3) The increase in family income may also reduce the amount of the Child Tax Credit the family will collect, and make it ineligible for provincial subsidies such as sales tax or property tax rebates, or exemption from government health insurance premiums in a province like Ontario. Suppose the loss in Unemployment Insurance benefits and the other subsidies would amount to $3,500. The family may then ask: If the *net* increase in family earnings would be no more than $1,500—that is, the $5,000 gross earnings less $3,500 in lost subsidies—is it really worthwhile for her to take this job? Would $1,500 be enough to pay for things like daycare for the children and help with the housework?

Of the $5,000 that the wife in this example would earn by going out to work, only 30% ($1,500) represents a benefit; the other 70% (that is, $3,500) is offset by lost subsidies. It's just as if the family faced a 70% marginal tax rate on the extra earnings. In fact, this effect is referred to as an *implicit tax* built into the social welfare system.

> The *implicit tax* built into a welfare system is calculated by examining the loss of benefits or subsidies when a family earns another $1 of income. (If the loss is 70 cents, the implicit tax is 70%.)

As we shall see later, the implicit tax problem is especially severe for people on social assistance; for them, the implicit tax may be as high as 100% or even more.

According to critics of the present system, its com-

plexity and undesirable incentive effects make it very inefficient. It is no surprise, therefore, that most of the proposals for reform of the system have focused on *simplifying it* and *reducing its disincentives*.

A GUARANTEED MINIMUM INCOME: A CURE FOR THE POVERTY PROBLEM?

One proposal that clearly meets the objective of creating a simpler system is to eliminate poverty in one stroke by having the government guarantee everybody a minimum income equal to the poverty level. If any family's income were to fall below that level, the government would just cover the shortfall with a direct cash grant. What would this cost? If we add up the shortfall in income for every family currently below the poverty line, we would end up with something less than 2% of GNP. Given what we are already spending, why couldn't we commit ourselves to this sort of relatively modest spending increase, and eliminate poverty once and for all?

Unfortunately, it is not that easy.

Inefficiencies in a Subsidy Program

One problem is this: A program that raises the income of the poor by $1 billion costs the government (and therefore the Canadian taxpayer) far more than $1 billion. Waste occurs because such a program has adverse effects on incentives.

Disincentives for those paying for the subsidy. The first adverse incentive applies to those who pay the higher taxes necessary to finance this scheme. The heavier the tax rate, the more likely it is that an individual will ask, "Why am I working so hard when the government gets such a large slice of what I earn?" However, studies fail to show as substantial an effect as one might expect. One reason is that although a higher tax makes working less attractive (by reducing the reward), it also makes working more necessary (for anyone trying to maintain previous levels of spending); and these two effects tend to offset each other to some degree. But even though high taxes may not have a large effect on the incentive to work, they do encourage the search for tax loopholes. And as higher-income individuals engage in (or hire lawyers to engage in) socially unproductive efforts to minimize their tax payments, there is a consequent waste

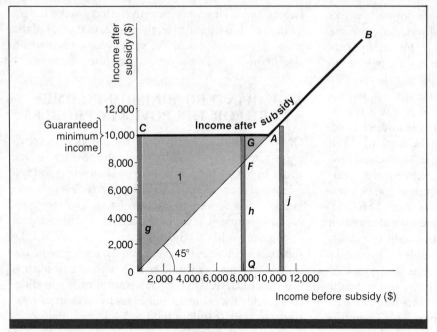

Figure 37-2 Possible disincentive effects of a guaranteed $10,000 minimum income.
The 45° line 0*AB* is the no-subsidy line. For example, at point *F* on this line, family *h* that earns $8,000 (measured left to right) would end up with $8,000 (measured up). On the other hand, heavy line *CAB* shows income with the subsidy. Family *h* is paid the $2,000 (dark gray bar) subsidy necessary to raise it to the guaranteed $10,000 level, while family *g* (which earns no income) must be paid a full $10,000 subsidy. This program erodes the incentive to work: Because *h*'s income will remain at the same $10,000 level, members of family *h* may stop working and thus join *g*.

imposed on society. As U.S. economist Arthur Okun has described it: "High tax rates are followed by attempts of ingenious men to beat them, as surely as snow is followed by little boys on sleds."[2]

Disincentives for those receiving the subsidy. Now let's turn to those at the bottom of the income scale who will receive this subsidy. Here one would expect more substantial incentive effects, for the reasons shown in Figure 37-2. In this diagram we concentrate on what happens to people at the bottom of the income scale. For simplicity, we disregard any taxes paid now by these people. To simplify further, we use a "round figure" minimum-income target of $10,000. Families are plotted along the horizontal axis according to how much income they originally earn. Thus, family *h* with an $8,000 earned income is plotted at point *Q* along the horizontal axis. Income after the implemen-

tation of this policy is measured up the vertical axis. If no subsidy were to be paid to family *h*, its "income after" would also be $8,000, as shown by the dark red bar. In other words, family *h* would be shown by point *F* on the 45° line, where its before and after incomes are equal. Hence this 45° line may be called the "same-before-and-after" line, or just the "no-subsidy" line.

But, of course, our minimum-income program does pay family *h* a subsidy—specifically, the $2,000 solid bar *FG* that is necessary to raise its income to the target $10,000 level. Since the income of any other family below the target income is similarly subsidized up to this $10,000 level, the "income after subsidy" line is the heavy line *CAB*. Shaded triangle 1 represents the shortfall income gap that the government must fill at an additional cost that we have already noted is likely to run to less than a few percent of our GNP—*provided people continue to work and earn as much after the subsidy as before.*

[2]Arthur M. Okun, *Equality and Efficiency: The Big Tradeoff* (Washington: The Brookings Institution, 1975), p. 97.

The problem is that, because they are being subsidized, some people will not work as hard as before. For example, the father of family h may realize: "If I don't work at all, the government will still guarantee us the same $10,000; so why should I work?" And if he stops working, that $8,000 of income he earned disappears. The position of that family on the horizontal axis therefore shifts all the way to the left, from situation h to situation g. At this point, nothing is being earned, that family has become totally unproductive, and it must be subsidized by the full $10,000 dark gray bar. Therefore, in order to raise this family's income by the original $2,000 shortfall, the government ends up paying out $10,000 (which, of course, it had to raise from the public in taxes). This example illustrates what Arthur Okun referred to as "transferring income with a leaky bucket": Although $10,000 has been spent to increase the income of a poor family, it has increased that income by only $2,000. The other $8,000 has "leaked away" because the family has stopped working. This leakage of the light red bar at h also represents the efficiency loss from this policy: The original income this family produced was the $8,000 light red bar at h, but this is now lost to society because no one in the family works any longer.

Disincentives that apply to the non-poor. Disincentive effects may apply not only to families like h with initial incomes below the $10,000 support level; they may also apply to families like j with incomes above $10,000. Suppose the breadwinner in family j has been earning the $10,800 shown, in a boring and unpleasant job. The subsidy program will now offer a tempting option: Go fishing, and receive a $10,000 income from the government. If this happens, family j also shifts to the left into position g, where it, too, qualifies for the full $10,000 subsidy. So the government has to subsidize not only those with initial incomes below the $10,000 target level, but also some with higher incomes, for whom this program was never intended.

In short, when the government attempts to fill an income gap by such a simple subsidy, its cost may far exceed the initial income shortfall that it set about to cure. The reason is that the subsidy disturbs incentives, and some people stop working. From the viewpoint of the government paying the subsidy, the problem appears in two forms: On the one hand, some poor families like h may absorb more subsidy than expected;

on the other hand, a whole new and unexpected group of families like j may appear on the scene, claiming the subsidy. Moreover, when a family like j goes onto the subsidy program, the overall efficiency loss to society is particularly severe. It is the light red bar at j—the $10,800 of income that is no longer produced because someone who used to work is now off fishing.

The reason that this policy is so inefficient is that the portion CA of the "income after subsidy" line is completely horizontal, leaving the poor no incentive to work. That is, they face an implicit tax of 100%; they have nothing to show for any additional $1 they earn, because their subsidy is reduced by the same $1.

Critics have charged that, in terms of its anti-work incentives, provincial social assistance programs are similar to this simple subsidy scheme. Recall that under the cash deficit method, a family's welfare payment is set equal to its shortfall in income. If actual income increases by $1,000, the shortfall and therefore the welfare payment will be reduced by the same $1,000. Since lost welfare benefits are equal to the entire increase in income, this system involves a 100% implicit tax. But in practice, because social workers have some discretion over the welfare allowances of recipients, the implicit tax may be a bit less. On the other hand, in some cases it may be more than 100%: For example, when a family's income goes up it may lose not only its social assistance, but also some in-kind subsidies such as free dental care or the right to subsidized public housing. Because of these complications a precise implicit tax rate is not easy to calculate. But in a rough and ready way, the guaranteed annual income scheme in Figure 37-2—with its 100% implicit tax—can be used to illustrate some of the problems of the current Canadian system.

CONFLICTING VIEWS ON WELFARE

Figure 37-2 illustrates why some observers view welfare as the *cure* for society's failure, while others view it as the *cause* of this failure. How can two views be so clearly in conflict?

Economic Failure: Is It Cured or Caused by Welfare?

Proponents of welfare programs point to individuals who are disabled or who simply cannot cope. Because they are unable to succeed economically, they are *ini-*

tially left at g. The (dark gray bar) welfare benefits raise them above the minimum-income level. In such cases, welfare *solves* a serious social problem.

On the other hand, welfare critics point to individuals who start out at *h* or *j*, and respond to welfare by shifting to *g*. According to this view, welfare payments provide potentially productive people with an incentive to stop producing—to stop earning the light red bar of income at *h* or *j* and instead go on the dole at *g*. In such cases, welfare *creates* a social problem.

In practice, a welfare system has both effects: It solves the poverty problem for people who start at *g*, and it creates a problem by inducing some of the people who start at *h* or *j* to move to *g*. In the Canadian system, what is the relative importance of these two effects? In particular, how much does welfare erode the incentive to work?

So far, no studies are available that give us the answer to this question. But studies in the United States seem to show that the negative incentive is not as powerful as the discussion of Figure 37-2 so far might suggest. Many families at *h* or *j* don't stop working (don't move to the left). Their (light red bar) productivity is not lost. Moreover, many people start at *g*. In their case, there is no "leak in the bucket" at all: Welfare can't reduce their productivity because they don't produce anything in the first place.

Even if the disincentive effects on the recipients are not all that severe, we must also take into account the losses from collecting the taxes necessary to finance the welfare expenditure, because taxation encourages the search for loopholes, and reduces the incentive to work of those who are taxed. Estimates of this "excess cost of taxation" vary widely, but suggest that 25% to 35% is the best range for estimating this additional leak, with 30% being perhaps the best single round number. When we add this to the leak that results because the recipients have an incentive to work less, we get a bucket with a leak of roughly 50%. When the other costs are taken into account—such as the administrative costs of running a welfare program— the picture is one of a bucket with somewhat more than a 50% leak.[3]

To recap this discussion, it is worth considering what we mean by a leak in the transfer bucket of about 50%. It does not mean that the government raises $100 in taxes but only delivers $50 to the poor. Instead, the hypothetical example in Figure 37-3 shows what happens. We begin at line 2 with the $100 the government collects in taxes. Most, but not all of this is delivered to the poor. In our example, we suppose that the government has $10 of administrative costs, so that only $90 can be delivered to the poor. The problem is that about 25% of this—let's say $25—leaks away. It does not raise the income of the poor at all; it just replaces the income they lose because they work less. (An extreme example was family *h* in Figure 37-2.) Thus the income of the poor is increased by only $90 − $25 = $65. Finally, we return to the top of this diagram and see that when the government raises the original $100 in taxes, this imposes a $30 excess cost on the economy because, for example, those who are taxed work less. When this $30 of excess cost is added to the $100 of taxes, it is costing the Canadian public $130 to provide a net benefit of $65 to the poor. It is in this sense that there is a 50% leak.

Such a large leak does not mean that welfare expenditures should necessarily be cut back because of the waste in the transfer process. However, it does illustrate that solving the poverty problem is a more expensive task than was once assumed.

Non-economic Benefits and Costs

Not surprisingly, economists focus on the economic consequences of programs such as welfare; for example, how much does the "bucket" leak? But we should recognize that many government programs—such as welfare—also have broader effects on our society.

---

[3]Estimating this number is difficult, because it depends on how the government is raising taxes and how it is spending the funds. Nonetheless, a fairly clear, though not precise, picture still emerges. In simulations 1 and 6 in Table 2 of "Welfare Costs per Dollar of Additional Tax Revenue in the United States," *American Economic Review* (June 1984) Charles Stuart estimates that the excess cost of taxation ranges from 7% to 53%. In his judgement, 30% to 40% is the most likely range. In Table 3 of "General Equilibrium Computations of the Marginal Welfare Costs of Taxes in the United States," *American Economic Review* (March 1985) C.L. Ballard, J.B. Shoven, and J. Whalley provide estimates of the marginal excess burden of taxation that range between 17% and 56%, with their best estimate being roughly 33%. With respect to the leak when the funds are spent, because welfare recipients work less, an estimate of 25% is given in S. Danziger et al., "How Income Transfer Programs Affect Work, Savings and the Income Distribution: A Critical Review," *Journal of Economic Literature* (September 1981): 975–1028.

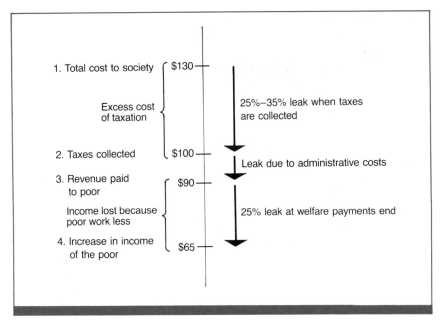

1. Total cost to society — $130

Excess cost of taxation

25%–35% leak when taxes are collected

2. Taxes collected — $100

Leak due to administrative costs

3. Revenue paid to poor — $90

Income lost because poor work less

25% leak at welfare payments end

4. Increase in income of the poor — $65

Figure 37-3   Leaks in the transfer bucket.

On the positive side, welfare programs are society's way of stating its commitment to the less fortunate. We would not want to live in a callous nation, which paid no heed to the sick and helpless. By contributing to a humane society, a welfare program can have social gains that go beyond the benefits to the welfare recipients themselves.

Because of the way in which welfare programs are a symbol of society's values, any inequities in the system can be demoralizing. Critics question whether our welfare system has unintended social consequences:

1. One of the reasons some fathers in unstable marriages remain in the home and support their families is the fear of what might happen if they were to leave. If a government welfare program guarantees child support and removes this fear, won't some fathers feel more free to leave? So welfare programs may be important in shaping our social structure, and in particular, the family unit.

2. Does welfare encourage a problem it is designed to cure: the "culture of poverty"? Does it encourage dependence and destroy pride and self-respect? Being the breadwinner may be one of the few sources of pride and self-respect for those with low-paying, no-promise jobs. If welfare provides as adequately for their families as they can, does it make them feel like so much excess baggage and destroy their self-respect?

THE KEY TRADE-OFF: EQUITY VERSUS EFFICIENCY

It all seemed so simple. As we look back over parts 5 and 6, the following message seemed to be emerging: Where product or factor markets are inefficient, the government should intervene to increase efficiency. (For example, it should intervene to tax polluters or to regulate monopoly price.) If this intervention also has favourable equity effects, so much the better; then there are no conflicts, and the appropriate policy choice is a simple one. (For example, it is easy to endorse ending discrimination in the labour market because this increases efficiency and also transfers income equitably to those who have faced disadvantages in the past because of their race or sex.) However, such cases are the exception, rather than the rule; conflicts often do arise. The search for efficiency in product and factor markets does not necessarily lead us to an equitable income distribution. Therefore, the argument goes, to achieve equity we should rely on direct government transfers, rather than inefficient interventions into factor or product markets (like the imposition of an interest-rate ceiling).

Unfortunately, it's not so easy after all, because of one weak link in this argument: Direct government transfers may not be very efficient either. In particular, government spending on the poor erodes the incentive to work and reduces national output. So we are still left with the trade-off between the objectives of equity and efficiency: The size of the national pie is reduced if we try to carve it up in a more equitable way.

This is not a recommendation that we go back to transferring income by the inefficient market interventions we have criticized in earlier chapters. Not only are they inefficient. Worse yet, as a means of raising the income of the poor, they are often ineffective. (An interest-rate ceiling benefits rich borrowers as well as poor, and in fact, may leave many relatively poor borrowers out in the cold completely. As another example, farm price guarantees benefit the rich farmer without lifting many poor farmers out of poverty.) The message remains: The way to reduce poverty is by direct government policies to aid the poor. But we should be searching for a better way of making these transfers than the simple subsidy programs we have been discussing so far. In particular, we should be seeking a way that is not only equitable (and that—unlike our present welfare system—treats all the poor alike). We should also be seeking a way that is efficient—in other words, that does not destroy the incentive to work.

THE NEGATIVE INCOME TAX: CAN WE COMBINE EQUITY AND EFFICIENCY?

How can we guarantee families a minimum income (for example, $10,000) without destroying their incentive to work? This is an essential question, and it is not an easy one to answer. One proposal is the *negative income tax*, which has been advocated by many of those on both the "left" and the "right" of the political spectrum who are critical of the present welfare system. To explain this proposal, let's put Figure 37-2 back on the drawing board in Figure 37-4. This new diagram has the same frame of reference as Figure 37-2, except that it is extended to the right to allow us to take into account not only families that receive a subsidy, but also higher-income families that pay the government a tax. The 45° "same-before-and-after" line 0QB now represents the "no-subsidy, no-tax" line

where families would be if the government neither subsidized nor taxed them.

Design of a Negative Income Tax

To see how a negative income tax would work, begin by assuming, as before, that the minimum income level is set at $10,000. Now, rather than subsidizing incomes just up to the line CA by filling gap 1 as we did in Figure 37-2, the government instead pays subsidies—that is, "negative taxes"—equal to areas 1 + 2 + 3, thereby bringing incomes up to the heavy line CQ. (Beyond an income of $20,000, a family pays "positive" taxes to the government, as shown by the red area 4.) Because the "income-after-tax" line CQH slopes upward, people have an incentive to work. The more income they earn (the more they move to the right in this diagram) the more income they get to keep (the higher they rise on line CQ). By providing this incentive to earn income, we attempt to reduce the leak in the bucket that occurs because people prefer going on welfare to working. Proponents of the negative income tax have usually suggested that it should replace all existing welfare programs, including programs such as subsidized housing. If some of these subsidies remain, the poor may get a higher income from these subsidies and the negative income tax than from working. They may therefore quit work to draw government benefits.

The negative income tax should not only improve efficiency. It should also move us toward a greater degree of equity in several ways: (1) It would guarantee a minimum income for all; (2) it would replace the wide variety of existing welfare programs with one consistent policy that would treat all families at the same income level in the same way; and (3) it would also satisfy another equity objective of most Canadians —it would leave those who work with a higher income than those who do not.

However, this would apparently be a very expensive program, since the subsidy is now area 1 plus areas 2 and 3. Specifically, the government now provides an even greater subsidy (area 1 + 2) to poor families earning less than $10,000, plus a subsidy 3 to families with incomes all the way up to $20,000. Of course, families earning even higher incomes pay a tax. For example, a family earning $24,000 pays the $2,000 tax shown as the red bar *t*. Thus, heavy line CQH shows how the government pays gray subsidies

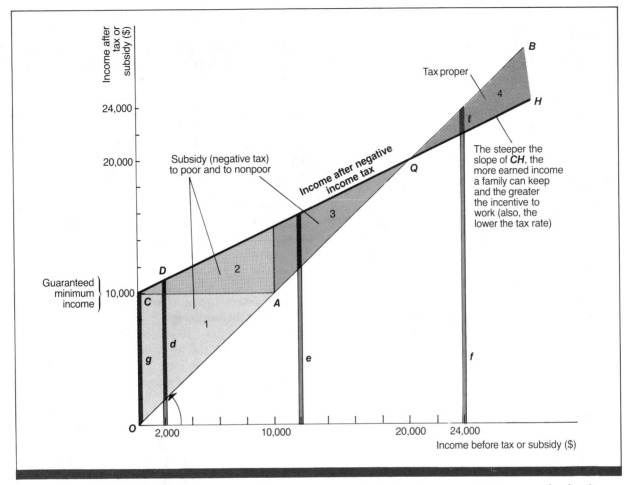

Figure 37-4 How a negative income tax should work. (**Compare with Figure 37-2.**)

Family *g* with a zero earned income is paid the dark gray bar grant of $10,000. But what do we do with family *d* with $2,000 of earned income? If we make the same mistake we made in Figure 37-2 and raise this income up only to that same $10,000 (by an $8,000 grant), this will leave that family with no incentive to keep working to earn that $2,000. So to provide an incentive to work, we grant this family $9,000 instead (as shown by the dark gray bar), thus bringing its total up to $11,000 at point *D*. If we continue in this way, always providing a $1,000 incentive for families to earn an additional $2,000 of income, we move up heavy line *CDQ* to cutoff point *Q*, where no subsidy is paid. Moreover, if we continue to allow families to keep half of any additional income they earn, we will tax incomes above this level down from *QB* to *QH*. Thus, red area 4 shows us how any income above $10,000 is subject to a tax. (For example, family *f* with a $24,000 income pays the $2,000 tax *t*.) At the same time, gray area 1 + 2 + 3 shows us how any income below $20,000 is subsidized ("taxed in reverse"). Hence, the name: negative income tax.

all the way up to point *Q*, and levies the red tax on incomes above this. (Although this line need not have a constant slope, it does in this simple example. Any family keeps half of any additional income it earns. For example, those with earned incomes of less than $20,000 get to keep half of any additional income they earn; in other words, they lose half of it, which means they face a 50% implicit tax. At the same time, those at the higher end of the income scale face a 50% regular tax on all their income over $20,000.)

Another problem with the negative income tax is that its apparent high cost is not limited to filling new gaps 2 + 3. In addition, the government loses the taxes previously collected from many non-poor families with incomes between $10,000 and $20,000. Under this program they would pay no tax; instead they would receive a subsidy. Moreover, this program would also reduce the taxes paid by some families with incomes above $20,000.[4] This was not the objective when we set out to ensure that poor families would have an income of at least $10,000.

When one takes into account all these considerations, doesn't the negative income tax come out badly in comparison with the simple subsidy scheme in Figure 37-2? Why would anyone recommend it? The answer is that it should have a favourable effect on incentives. The negative income tax should be a far less leaky bucket than a simple subsidy scheme, or our present welfare system. This point is worth considering in detail.

Why the Negative Income Tax Should Reduce the Leaks in the "Welfare Bucket"

By allowing families to keep half of any additional income they earn, the negative income tax should induce them to get out and earn more, and thus "move to the right" in Figure 37-4. Since this would reduce—and in some cases, perhaps even eliminate—the subsidy some families receive, the cost of this scheme should be less than the gray subsidy area in Figure 37-4 suggests.

Moreover, the cost of this scheme may be reduced even further by modifications. For example, the "after-tax" line CQH might be lowered by, say, $2,000. This would maintain the same incentive to work (the same slope of CQH), but would substantially reduce the cost (the subsidy areas 1 + 2 + 3). Moreover, by shifting critical point Q to the left, it would mean that families with an income in the $16,000 to $20,000 range would no longer receive a subsidy; instead they would pay a tax. Thus, this program would no longer allow so many families to escape taxes. However, one problem would remain. Those at C doing no work would now receive less than the $10,000 minimum target.

This problem might be reduced by providing a guaranteed $10,000 income to those who are aged, infirm, or disabled and *cannot* work. If these people can be clearly identified, guaranteeing them a minimum income would result in no inefficiency; it would not affect the amount they work, because they can't work. Such a program would also score high in terms of equity, by providing an adequate safety net for those who cannot do without it. Such a policy—of identifying specific groups with special needs—is called *categorization* or *tagging*.[5] The big problem is that, in practice, it is difficult to identify exactly who should be tagged as unable to work; it is often difficult to determine who is disabled. While people don't blind themselves to get welfare, some may falsely argue that they have been disabled, say, because of minor backaches that they exaggerate.

The Negative Income Tax Does Not Resolve All Conflicts

We can now extend this theoretical discussion of the negative income tax by noting how it gives rise to tension among the following three objectives:

1. Set the minimum-income level (C) high enough so no one will be left destitute.
2. Give CQH enough slope to provide people with a strong incentive to work. (Many would view the slope of CQH in Figure 37-4 as being too low and therefore providing inadequate incentive to work. Since people can keep only half of any additional income they earn, they all "spend half their time working for the government.")
3. Keep the subsidy areas 1 + 2 + 3 small, in order to keep the cost of the program down and avoid heavily subsidizing the non-poor.

It is impossible to achieve all these objectives at once, because they are in conflict. For example, the way to achieve the second objective is to make line CQH steeper. But a greater slope means that either C must be lower or subsidy areas 1 + 2 + 3 must be larger. Thus, objective 2 conflicts with objectives 1 and 3.

---

[4]To confirm this statement, consider a family with income just barely over $20,000. In Figure 37-4, it pays a miniscule tax that is less than the tax it used to pay.

[5]The advantages of tagging are discussed by George Akerlof in "The Economics of Tagging," *American Economic Review* (March 1978): 8–17. Its major disadvantage is that it provides a perverse incentive for people to get "tagged" and thus qualify for special treatment.

The Negative Income Tax in Practice: Results of Recent Experiments

Because it seemed such an appealing idea, negative income tax schemes have been tried out in practice in actual experiments in both the United States (in New Jersey, and in the cities of Denver and Seattle) and Canada (in Manitoba). In these experiments, a large number of families were subsidized and taxed according to a negative income tax, and the effects on their labour supply and other decisions have been studied.

At the time of writing, the results from the Manitoba experiments had not yet become available. The evidence from the U.S. experiments was somewhat mixed. Studies of the Seattle-Denver case were disappointing. A negative income tax designed to encourage people to work more seemed, in practice, to make them work less. The explanation for this surprising result appeared to be that the expected positive work incentive was more than offset by several influences that encouraged recipients to work less.

For one thing, when people participated in these experimental studies, their rights under the negative income tax were clearly explained to them—in particular, their right to stop working and still continue to receive an income. In contrast, people in the traditional U.S. welfare system often complain about the hassle they have to go through in order to find out what their rights are when they try to apply for welfare benefits. Thus, analysts speculate, many poor people continue working because they don't want to go through the hassle in the traditional system. Another important and related factor was that people in the experiments did not seem to feel that there was much of a stigma attached to quitting work and getting the negative income tax benefits. By comparison, many poor people are extremely reluctant to apply for traditional welfare in our present system and will not do so even if they would receive substantial welfare benefits.

WHERE DO WE GO FROM HERE?

While the evidence from the Seattle-Denver experiment is disappointing, results from other experiments have been somewhat more encouraging, and some analysts argue that the Seattle-Denver case may exaggerate the unfavourable effects of a negative income tax. Moreover, many people think it's unfair to have a

system where some poor people do not seek assistance because they fear that they will be hassled or because they fear a social stigma: Such a system favours those who don't mind the hassle rather than those most in need.

Thus, although there is less enthusiasm now than in the 1970s for a massive negative income tax as "the" solution to the welfare problem, there is still considerable support in Canada for the idea that a modified and more limited version of a negative income tax could have a useful role to play in our system of social welfare programs. Indeed, in Saskatchewan, Quebec, and Manitoba, limited versions of a negative income tax covering the "working poor" (those who are able to earn *some* income from work, but not enough to get above the poverty line) have already been introduced. And in 1985, the wide-ranging report of the MacDonald Commission included a long analysis of Canada's social welfare system: One of its major recommendations was that a range of federal welfare programs should be abolished and replaced by a version of a negative income tax.

Other approaches to designing a welfare system that provides a reasonable protection for poor people without seriously reducing work incentives have recently been considered as well. One suggestion is a **wage subsidy** that would increase the take-home pay of low-income workers. (The subsidy would be higher for workers with more dependents.) Because the government subsidy would come to the family via the worker's paycheque, it might increase the worker's pride in having a job and supporting a family. Moreover, by increasing the take-home wage, it would increase the incentive to work. (In contrast, the present welfare system reduces the amount kept by the worker because of the implicit taxes. And a negative income tax likewise reduces the amount the worker keeps.) Finally, by encouraging employment by private firms, a wage subsidy might be used to partially replace present government make-work programs. This, in turn, should increase productivity, since private employers don't hire people unless there is a productive job to fill; but there is no similar guarantee when the government is hiring as an "employer of last resort."

But this suggestion is also far from being problem-free. A wage subsidy would have to be accompanied by welfare payments to those "tagged" as unable to work because of disability or age. And this, in turn, means facing one of the most difficult issues in welfare. How do you decide who's in the "tagged" group that doesn't have to work, and how do you keep out others who want to get in?

KEY POINTS

1. Poverty is defined as inadequate income to buy the necessities of life. A specific poverty-line figure is determined by finding the income level at which an average family would have to spend as much as 58.5% of its income on food, clothing, and shelter alone. In 1984 the poverty line for a family of four in a medium-sized city was about $19,000. In 1984, one in seven Canadian families was still living in poverty. But this was still a big improvement on the figure of about one in three in the early 1960s when the government started many of the present income-maintenance programs.

2. As a result of our struggle against poverty, government income transfers have increased by almost ten times when measured in dollars; that is, by about four times when adjusted for inflation.

3. People in the Atlantic provinces are more likely to be poor than those living elsewhere in Canada, and older people are more likely to be poor than others. The less an individual is educated, the greater the risk of poverty. Poverty is a particularly serious problem in fatherless families.

4. In the long run, the most promising government anti-poverty policies are those that deal with the causes rather than the symptoms of poverty. These policies include subsidizing investment in human capital (both education and on-the-job training), and eliminating employment discrimination against minorities and women.

5. Government income-maintenance programs include Old Age Security and Unemployment Insurance, which are paid to poor and non-poor alike. But there are also many programs, like the Guaranteed Income Supplement to those over 65, and the provincial social assistance plans, that are designed specifically for the poor. The problem with these programs is that when the poor earn more income, there is a reduction in the subsidies they receive (an implicit tax). This reduces their incentive to work, thus lowering the nation's output and level of efficiency.

6. The package of present programs is also inequitable. Some of the poor are not lifted up to the poverty line, while others who qualify under several of the programs may be lifted above it—indeed, in some cases, even above the income earned by some of the people who pay taxes to support the anti-poverty program.

7. Why not, then, replace this present system with a single policy that would lift all the poor up to the same minimum income level? The answer is that the poor, with their incomes thus guaranteed, would have little or no economic incentive left to work. With lost potential output, the economy would operate at a low level of efficiency. Thus, the conflict between greater equality and efficiency persists: As we try to carve up the national pie more equally (by raising the income of the poor), the total size of that pie is reduced.

8. In theory, a negative income tax is a good method of reducing, but not entirely eliminating, this conflict. Under this policy, families would be allowed to keep part of any additional income they earn. This would leave them with an incentive to work. The program would also guarantee every family a minimum income.

KEY CONCEPTS

poverty line
causes of poverty
symptoms of poverty
policies to increase human capital
policies to eliminate discrimination
Old Age Security
Unemployment Insurance

Child Tax Credit
Canada Assistance Plan
Guaranteed Income Supplement
provincial health insurance plans
implicit tax
leak in the transfer bucket
guaranteed minimum income

non-economic benefits and
   costs of welfare
tagging
negative income tax
hassle and stigma effects
wage subsidy

PROBLEMS

37-1 What is meant by an implicit tax rate of 90%? Of 105%? What is the effect of such a tax rate?

37-2 Let's review the efficiency losses from our income redistribution policy in Figure 37-2. What is the efficiency loss if this subsidy induces the breadwinner of family h to go fishing? the breadwinner of family j? What is the efficiency loss if the breadwinner of family j takes one day off each week to go fishing? What is the efficiency loss from subsidizing a family like g that originally earned no income?

   How do you think the efficiency loss would change if the minimum income level were set at $12,000, rather than $10,000?

37-3 Explain to your bright roommate (who is taking economics but hasn't yet reached this chapter) exactly what you mean by a "leaky bucket."

37-4 Let's see if we can't reduce the costs to the government of the negative income tax in Figure 37-4. The incentive to work in that diagram is the $500 a family can keep out of each additional $1,000 it earns. Now suppose that the amount it can keep is reduced from $500 to $300.

(a) Redraw Figure 37-4 to take this into account.

(b) What has happened to the incentive to work?

(c) What has happened to the implicit tax in this welfare proposal?

(d) Are your answers to (b) and (c) related in any way? If so, how?

(e) What has happened to the total amount of subsidy the government must pay? (Be careful.)

(f) Has this transfer bucket become more or less leaky?

(g) Now regraph this policy making one further change: Set the poverty level at $4,000, rather than $5,000. Again answer questions (b), (c), and (e). What are the pros and cons of the two policies you have graphed?

37-5 Suppose you are designing a negative income tax. Graph your answers to each of the following questions:

(a) What do you consider a reasonable minimum family income (0C in Figure 37-4)?

(b) What do you consider to be the maximum reasonable implicit tax rate? How does the slope of CQ in your diagram therefore compare to CQ in Figure 37-4?

(c) From your answers to (a) and (b), calculate the break-even level of income (like the $10,000 at Q in Figure 37-4).

(d) Do you think the tax proper (on families to the right of the break-even point Q) should be greater or smaller than the implicit tax on families to the left of Q?

(e) Explain the possible "public finance problem" in your scheme. In other words, do you think your scheme would make it difficult for the government to collect enough taxes from those to the right of Q to cover the cost of subsidizing those to the left of Q—and cover other government expenditures as well? As real incomes rise, would this public finance problem become more serious, or less? Would you agree with the view that we should institute a negative income tax someday, with the only question being how soon we can afford it?

37-6 In economics, it is only in exceptional cases (such as with the negative income tax) that experiments are possible. Do you think that being unable to conduct experiments in other cases is a disadvantage for economists? Isn't it possible to establish the effects of a policy using theoretical arguments, rather than experimental evidence? (Use the negative income tax to illustrate your answer.)

Chapter 38

MARXISM AND MARXIST ECONOMIES

The capitalist gets rich . . . at the same rate as he
squeezes out the labour power of others, and then
forces on the labourer abstinence from all life's
enjoyments.

Karl Marx, *Das Kapital*

Historically, one of the major criticisms of the free
enterprise system has been that it does not distribute
income in an equitable way—largely because of the
income payments that go to private owners of factories and other forms of physical capital ("capitalists").
Moreover, many critics believe that the economic and
political power held by capitalists limits the government in its attempts to achieve a more equal and just
society. The solution, according to some of these critics,
is to replace our system with one that is fundamentally
different—specifically, a system in which capital is
owned by the state, and used on behalf of all the
people.

This chapter begins with a discussion of the ideas
of Karl Marx, whose writings over a century ago have
proved to be the most influential and durable criticisms ever levelled against the free enterprise system.
This is followed by an examination of the socialist
systems of the Soviet Union and Yugoslavia, two illustrations of the many alternative ways in which the
philosophy of Karl Marx can be put into practice.
Finally, we have a few brief observations about the
People's Republic of China.

KARL MARX

In proportion as capital accumulates, the lot of
the labourer, be his payment high or low, must
grow worse.

Karl Marx, *Das Kapital*

Today about one-third of the world lives under some
form of Marxist-communist economic system. In
addition, there are many followers of Marx who do
not support any of the existing communist states, but
who believe his ideas should be implemented in a different way. Clearly, this means that whether or not
Marx was right, he was certainly one of the most
influential writers in history.

Marx's criticism of the free market was based on
two theories. While both were controversial even in
Marx's day, they were nonetheless accepted by many
orthodox economists. These two theories were: (1)
the labour theory of value, and (2) the theory that
wages tended toward a socially defined subsistence
level. According to the labour theory of value, the
value of any good is determined buy the amount of

labour that goes into producing it. (But be careful: As Marx recognized, this value must include both the labour time directly required to produce the good and the labour time spent on, or "congealed in," the machinery used to produce the good.) Marx then asked: With labour being the source of all value, does it receive the total value of the nation's output in return for its effort? His answer was no: All that labour receives is a low wage representing only a fraction of what is produced. The rest is *surplus value* that goes to the employer or capitalist (the owner of the capital equipment which labour uses). Marx's conclusion: This surplus value should go to labour. Because it does not, the working class is exploited.

Surplus Value and the Class Struggle

According to Marx, the exploitation of the proletariat (workers) by the bourgeoisie (capitalists) results in a *class struggle.* He urged workers to organize themselves to fight in this struggle. In his words, "Let the ruling classes tremble at a Communist revolution. The proletarians have nothing to lose but their chains. They have a world to win. Working men of all countries, unite!"[1] In his view, the capitalist class would continue to accumulate more and more capital and use it to exploit labour more and more. Thus there would be ". . . an accumulation of misery, corresponding to the accumulation of capital." Marx's cure was a revolution—which he viewed as inevitable[2]—in which the workers would seize power and abolish the ownership of capital by individuals: "By despotic inroads on the rights of property [workers would] centralize all instruments of production in the hands of the State." Finally, after this new *socialist* system has been firmly established, the state would wither away, leaving Marx's ideal *communist* society.

[1] The source of quotes in this paragraph is Karl Marx and Friedrich Engels, *Manifesto of the Communist Party* (Peking: Foreign Languages Press, 1975), pp. 59 and 77. Note that Marx went far beyond an analysis of economic forces to suggest what should be done to change them. In taking such a normative approach, Marx and the Marxists strongly dispute the view of some economists that a positive, "value-free" economic analysis is possible.

[2] If this revolution is the inevitable result of an historical process governed by unchangeable economic laws—as Marx believed—what's the point of exhorting workers to struggle hard to achieve it? One possible answer: Even an inevitable event may be speeded up.

Socialism is an economic system in which the "means of production" (capital equipment, buildings, and land) are owned by the state.[3]

In Marxist countries like the Soviet Union, *communism* means an ideal system in which all means of production and other forms of property are no longer owned by the state, but instead are owned by the community as a whole, with all members of the community sharing in its work and income. The Soviet Union makes no claim to having achieved communism. Rather, it claims to be working "through socialism towards communism."

In the West, communism has a quite different meaning. It refers to the present economic and political system of countries like the Soviet Union.

How the Critic Has Been Criticized

Marx's critics have pointed out that a number of his predictions have proven false. For example, there is little evidence that any existing governments, such as that of the Soviet Union, are withering away, even though the Soviet state has existed for about 70 years. The idea that the state would "wither away" ranks as one of the most curious in the history of economic and political thought. One need not be as cynical as Lord Acton ("Power corrupts; absolute power corrupts absolutely") to doubt that those who have struggled for power will be prepared to give it up voluntarily.

Indeed, the most significant single weakness of Marxism, in the view of a number of its sympathetic critics, is that it provides enormous political power to individuals without providing adequate ways to con-

[3] "Socialism" has become an emotion-laden word that is now used loosely in a wide variety of meanings. To the campus radical, it is a tool for attacking the shortcomings of Canadian and American societies. To the American millionaire, it is a plot to deprive the wealthy of their hard-earned fortunes. To the Swedish politician, it means a mixed economic system, combining substantially free markets and a large degree of private ownership with a highly developed social welfare system. To Nobel prize winner Friedrich Hayek, it represents a loss of freedom by the individual to the state, and thus is a step along "the road to serfdom." To the British Fabian Socialist, it means the gradual evolution of a more humane economy, with a more equal distribution of income. With such diversity in the interpretation of the meaning of socialism, it is little wonder people have difficulty in debating its virtues and vices.

trol them—such as free elections in which the public can throw them out.[4] (Voting yes or no to a single slate of candidates is obviously not enough.) Thus, Marxism provides inadequate restraints against the ruthless exercise of power by a ruler like Joseph Stalin. The majority of Marxists now view Stalin as an aberration that no better reflects true Marxism than the Holy Wars reflected Christianity. While there may be some truth in this defence, we should be careful with it. Specifically, it is inappropriate to argue, as Marxists sometimes do, that every Marxist failure like Joseph Stalin is not true Marxism, while every capitalist failure proves that this system is corrupt and headed for collapse.

The principal point remains: There were in fact no controls in the Soviet system to prevent Stalin from rising to the top and, worse yet, from staying there. Nor are there safeguards against the accumulation of power by more recent Soviet leaders. Thus, Marxism is paradoxical. While it promises greater political freedom, it has delivered less wherever it has been tried. Although a Marxist society is initially revolutionary, it may become very conservative, with aging leaders clinging to power and maintaining the status quo.

Another criticism of Marxism is that, as capital has accumulated, there has not been the accumulation of misery that Marx predicted. Quite the contrary: Misery has been reduced. And for good reason. Over the long run, the accumulation of capital has raised the demand for labour, and thus has raised, rather than lowered, the wage rate. To cite an earlier example: Workers driving bulldozers are paid more than workers with shovels. While many Marxists concede that workers' income has indeed risen in *absolute* terms, they reinterpret Marx's prediction to mean that workers would become poorer, not in any absolute sense, but *relative* to other classes in society. Even this weaker claim is difficult to support with historical data.

Another way in which Marxists have reinterpreted Marx is to argue that although capitalists may have been unable to exploit labour in Europe and North America to the degree that Marx predicted, they have succeeded in exploiting labour in the less developed

countries (LDCs), which have become today's economically subjugated proletariat. Sometimes this argument is put very simply: "We are rich. They are poor. Therefore, we must have become rich by making them poor." This conclusion does not follow, because it is based on the "zero-sum" assumption—that the LDCs lose what we gain and vice versa. Our foreign investment in the LDCs can provide both a profit to investors and benefit to the LDCs, when foreign investors bid up wages and pay out part of their profits in taxes to LDC governments. Our trade with the LDCs isn't a zero-sum game either. As we saw in our earlier discussion of comparative advantage, both parties typically gain from trade.

We conclude that, short of a major reinterpretation of what Marx said, his prediction that workers would become poorer has proven false. Nonetheless, it is true that workers are paid less than what the nation produces. We have referred to the gap between the two as payments to other factors of production. Marx called it surplus value. In particular, he focused his attack on the payments going to owners of capital. Was he justified in dismissing these payments as simply the exploitation of labour?

How Are Capital Costs to Be Covered?

Here we must be careful. Part of the cost of capital is the payment for the labour time spent on producing machinery. As Marx recognized, this is an appropriate payment to labour. Therefore, it is not surplus value. However, Marx did regard as surplus value the interest and profit paid to those who provide the funds to finance investment. Remember: Investment requires that someone, somewhere, defers consumption. In our system, interest is a reward to those who voluntarily defer consumption.

The Marxist contention is that it is precisely the interest and profit payments that make our system inequitable. Moreover, Marxists maintain, it is possible to set up a system in which investment occurs even though there is no interest rate to act as an incentive to get the public to provide the necessary funds. The way to ensure that investment takes place is for the state to impose taxes high enough not only to cover current government expenditures, but also to provide the funds for investment. Under such a system, the ownership

---

[4]See Robert Heilbroner, *Marxism For and Against* (New York: Norton, 1980).

of capital is held by the state on behalf of the people, rather than by capitalists.

While communism may achieve Marx's objective of ending income payments to capitalists, it raises several new problems. First, raising investment funds by such a system of involuntary saving—that is, by taxes—may "hurt" more than our system of voluntary saving. Under our system, people can save when it is most convenient, and need not save when it is difficult to do so. Under a Marxist system, they are forced to save throughout their taxpaying lives. Taxes must be paid, no matter how much they hurt.

Second, can investment decisions made by government officials in a communist state be as flexible and innovative as decisions made by the owners of capital in a free enterprise system?

Investment Decisions

To invest wisely, two questions must be answered: (1) Should existing types of plant and equipment be expanded? (2) What new products and processes should be developed? There is less incentive for the second question to be asked in the Soviet Union than in a free enterprise economy. Whenever you compare the two systems in the future, ask yourself: Which innovations from free enterprise economies are the Soviets using? Which of their innovations are we using?

Consider the practical problems communist countries encounter in allocating investment funds across the economy, as they do when drawing up a five-year plan. To illustrate, first consider what happens in our economy if there is a major new discovery of, say, copper ore in northern Quebec. To finance its development, the mining companies increase their borrowing (or issue new stock), and the interest rate rises slightly. In response to this, marginal investments elsewhere in the nation are cut back. Thus, funds for this development are raised from all over the country (or all over North America, if foreign capital gets involved) as a result of a large number of individuals and firms reacting to a slight rise in the market interest rate. In comparison, what occurs in a communist country that, six months ago, set its five-year investment targets for each sector? Do the planners sit down and go through the planning process all over again? For a big enough discovery, they might. However, for less significant events they can't be continuously rewriting the plan.

The plan tends to get "locked in." New opportunities are not incorporated into the plan until the next time it is recalculated. Thus, adjustment to unexpected changes is much more difficult in a planned economy than in a free enterprise economy where markets are responding continuously to changes that occur.

Any society must have some mechanism to determine which investments are undertaken and which are not. In our economy, the interest rate and expected profits are the mechanism. They are used to direct funds toward the high-return investments, not to the low-return ones. While this system is far from perfect, it does provide a framework within which to make choices. Recognizing this, central planners now quietly make their interest-like calculations after all. (Nevertheless, major blunders are still made. A contributing factor in Poland's economic difficulties was the construction of a $5 million steel mill in a location that was poor from an economic point of view, but was the home town of the Communist party secretary. True, politicians anywhere may thus "feather their own nest"; however, this problem is potentially more serious in a Marxist economy where most capital is owned by the state and controlled by government officials.)

The Role of Profit

Recall that normal profit is a return to equity capital equal to the interest rate that could be earned elsewhere. Above-normal profit is any additional return beyond this; in a free enterprise economy, it goes to entrepreneurs. Is this justified? To throw light on this issue, consider two kinds of above-normal profit—monopoly profit, and profit from a successful innovation.

Above-normal monopoly profit. Many non-Marxist economists would agree that monopoly profit should be reduced or eliminated by "trustbusting" or regulation. However, Marxists charge that we are naïve if we believe that we can effectively deal with monopoly in our present economic and political system. The reason, Marxists argue, is that in our system, foreign or domestic monopolists can translate their economic power (money) into political power (votes) via campaign contributions. This power then allows them to thwart anti-monopoly action. In short, our elected officials are too often committed to the interests of the rich and powerful, rather than to the interests of the public. Thus, Marxists contend, the only effective way to deal with this problem is to change the system and to prevent the accumulation of wealth that makes such political corruption possible.

There is, of course, an element of truth in this criticism—more, perhaps, than we like to admit.[5] But the question is one of alternatives. If a system is to be set up based on the "public interest," how is that elusive concept to be defined? What better way is there to determine it than by elections? If there are no elections, and one party has the monopoly of power, what protection is there against the abuse of that power? It is scarcely satisfactory to say that elections between two or more contending parties are unnecessary in the Soviet Union because the Communist Party represents the interests of the workers. (This belief is one reason why Communist governments strongly resist the development of independent sources of power, such as the Solidarity union in Poland. An independent union implies that the Communist Party does not invariably represent the interests of the working people.) In Western countries, the prevailing practice is to let voters decide between two or more competing political parties. We have chosen to reform our existing political system rather than to replace it.

Above-normal profit from innovation. In our system, there are various kinds of innovation that may allow a firm to earn an above-normal profit. For example, a firm may develop a new product that better satisfies consumers. True, in the long run, such above-normal profit may disappear as competing firms follow suit. Nonetheless, this profit still provides the incentive for businesses to innovate and respond to changing consumer tastes. In short, the opportunity for profit is what makes our system go; it determines what will be produced and how. We tax away part of the profits, but not all; some incentive to innovate must be left. However, many Marxists take the view that although this profit system may have worked well enough in our early stages of development,[6] it is no longer satisfactory. The whole incentive system should

be changed and the economy directed in some other way. Precisely how, of course, is the big question.

This question is not answered by Marx's recommendation: "From each according to his ability; to each according to his need." This sounds fine in theory, but in practice it is a totally impractical guideline. If individuals define their own needs, the sum will always outrun a nation's ability to produce. Alternatively, if needs are defined by someone else, two questions remain. Who is to decide? and How does that person decide who needs what? (For a socialist country in the transition stage to communism, this guideline has been modified to: "From each according to his ability; to each according to his *work*." This is the policy in the Soviet Union.)

THE COMMAND ECONOMY OF THE SOVIET UNION

The Soviet Union is a riddle wrapped up in a mystery inside an enigma.

Sir Winston Churchill

The first country to attempt to put Marx's philosophy into practice was the Soviet Union, and for almost 30 years it was the only communist nation of any significance.

In 1917, the repressive and decaying czarist regime in Russia was overthrown by a moderate group led by Kerensky. In turn, Kerensky was overthrown by a small, militant group led by Lenin, a Marxist revolutionary. (The Germans, intent on destroying Russia as an enemy in the First World War, had transported Lenin from his exile in Switzerland, across Germany to the Russian border.) Lenin's control was consolidated when the Red Army defeated the White Russians in a bitter civil war, and turned back an invasion by Western countries trying to purge Russia of its new communist regime. It was only then that Lenin and the other communist leaders could turn their attention fully to the design of a new kind of economy.

As it has developed, that economy has differed from ours in two major respects: (1) Productive assets are predominantly owned by the state rather than by individuals; and (2) many production decisions are made on the command of a central authority. Our

---

[5]For a thoughtful, non-Marxist view of this problem, see the brief book by Elizabeth Drew, *Politics and Money: The New Road to Corruption* (New York: Macmillan, 1983).

[6]In the Communist Manifesto, Marx and Engels expressed great admiration for the growth generated by capitalism, which in the preceding 100 years "created more massive and colossal productive forces than have all preceding generations together."

Table 38-1
How the Soviet System of Public Ownership and Central Planning Differs from Our System

Basic issues	Soviet system	Modified free enterprise
1. Is ownership of productive assets held by the state or by private individuals?	State ownership—with some exceptions; for example, in parts of agriculture and retail trade	Private ownership—with exceptions like the post office, some utilities, and some transport systems
2. How are prices and outputs determined?	Largely by central planning agency	Largely in individual markets, in response to profit motive
3. How much freedom of choice do consumers have?	In theory, free choice in spending income; but in practice, items of desired style, size, etc., may be difficult to obtain	Essentially free choice in spending income, with producers more responsive to a wide variety of tastes

discussion of each of these is summarized for easy reference in Table 38-1.

Public versus Private Ownership

In Canada and the United States, the basic pattern is private ownership—with some exceptions, such as schools, Crown corporations, and public utilities. In the Soviet Union, in contrast, the basic pattern is public ownership, with some exceptions. For example, some retail and wholesale businesses are privately owned. In addition, over one-third of the houses in cities and virtually all houses on farms are privately owned. Moreover, private ownership in agriculture extends beyond housing. For example, each family working on a collective farm can use a small plot of land and the livestock and equipment to go with it. Finally, of course, personal assets like clothing and household tools are privately owned.

Otherwise, assets in the Soviet Union are predominantly owned by the state. These assets include the "means of production" that, in Marx's view, were used to exploit labour, such as factories, industrial machinery, transport and banking facilities, and natural resources.

Central Planning in the Soviet Economy

The second big difference between the two systems is that the important decisions on what will be produced in the Soviet Union are made "by command," by a central state planning agency—GOSPLAN. ("Gos" is

the abbreviation for the Russian word for "state.") In comparison, in our economy, most such decisions are made by individual producers responding to a profit incentive. (But not all: A number of our production decisions, such as the number of new schools or military transport vehicles to be produced, are made by federal, provincial, or local governments.)

In a complex planning process, the Soviet government decides on a five-year plan which establishes the desired rate of growth, including the necessary investment for that growth. Within this broad framework, a more detailed plan is drawn up for each year, specifying output targets throughout the economy. The targets are not chosen in a completely arbitrary way by government planners. Instead, they are the result of an elaborate set of consultations, in which each firm and industry suggests amendments to its targets. Nonetheless, the targets are eventually set by the planners, and each plant manager is given a specific quota to fulfill. The manager faces an array of incentives (bonuses, promotions, etc.) to reach or exceed the quota. Profits do exist in the Soviet Union, and can be calculated just as in our economy. However, profits do not provide the same sort of incentive as in our system, because most go to the state. Moreover, profits are calculated from output and input prices that are set by planners and are not very closely related to demand and supply conditions. *Since profits do not provide the same information, nor the same incentive to produce as in our system, they do not play the same key role in allocating resources.* To illustrate: The central planners may decide to contract an activity that is profitable in order to expand one that is unprofitable—a pattern exactly the opposite of what normally happens in our system. Thus, the plant manager tends to be a hired official carrying out a directive of what to produce, rather than an entrepreneur making decisions about what output will be.

The surprising thing about such a highly complicated planning system is not that it sometimes works badly, but that it works at all. Consider the problem that arises if the planners increase the target for steel, to be used in building bridges. Because steel production requires machinery, the machinery target must also be increased. But machinery production requires steel, so the steel target must be increased again. In turn, this results in a second-round increase in the machinery target, and so on, and on. Because steel is an input for machinery production and machinery is an input for steel production, one target cannot be set without regard to the other. Moreover, this interdependency illustrates only the simplest possible "loop" in the economic system. In reality, a complex economy like that of the Soviet Union is characterized by a myriad of much more complicated loops, with the output of one industry being used directly or indirectly as an input of almost all the others. Thus, a target cannot be set in isolation.

It is sometimes assumed that if there are economic problems, they can be solved by planning. Some may be solved, but others cannot. In particular, central planning tends to be inflexible, slowing the response of the economy to changing conditions (the weather, changes in the availability of raw materials, etc.). Moreover, the act of planning introduces a number of problems of its own. In theory, it should be possible to "get the plan right"—that is, to come up with a consistent set of outputs. However, there are millions of items produced in the Soviet Union. Such an economy is too complex and unpredictable to be adequately managed by any plan, and bottlenecks frequently occur. What happens if the production of steel is inadequate to meet the needs of the machinery industry and other steel-using industries? What can be done by a plant manager, desperate to acquire steel? The answer often is: Dispatch a *tolkache* (fixer), cognac and rubles in

hand, to acquire steel with the appropriate bribe. While bribery occurs in any economy, the difference is that this, and other similar forms of "fixing," are often quietly condoned in the Soviet Union because of the role they play in making the Soviet economy operate. Without such emergency measures, quotas would be even more difficult to achieve. Thus in the Soviet Union, a market economy has been replaced by a central-command quota system *and* a "second economy" that fills the inevitable cracks in the quota system. Black markets also exist in goods stolen from the state. In such a system, there is no clear line between what is silently tolerated and what is punished. The head of GUM (a large department store in Moscow) was unable to make this distinction and was executed for "excessive" operations in the second economy.

A second way in which bottleneck problems are reduced—but not eliminated—is for Soviet planners, faced with a shortage, to simply let consumers do without. If steel is in short supply, use it to produce industrial machinery rather than home refrigerators. With this set of priorities, it is no surprise that Soviet performance in heavy industry is better than in consumer goods and housing.

Growth in the Soviet Economy

The example just given is but one reflection of the Soviet emphasis on industrial growth at the expense of the consumer. In addition, planners aim for a high growth rate by diverting a large proportion of production away from consumption and into investment. Since investment has typically accounted for about 30% of GNP in the Soviet Union—as compared to below 25% in Canada, and even less in the United States—it is no surprise that, until recently, the Soviet growth rate often exceeded North American rates. If the Soviets had been able to continue their 6%–10% real growth rates of the 1960s, they would have eventually overtaken Canada or the United States. However, the higher Soviet growth rate in the past must be interpreted with care. It did not necessarily mean that the communist system was a relatively efficient way of generating growth. Instead, it reflected the fact that a very large share of Soviet GNP was being directed toward investment. The Soviet experience might be compared to that of Japan, a non-communist, market economy that has also been investing about 30% of its GNP. Japanese growth has far exceeded that of the Soviet Union.

Despite the continued heavy diversion of Soviet income from consumption into investment, the growth rate in the Soviet Union has recently become very disappointing.[7] In spite of its substantial insulation from the world economy, the Soviet Union has followed a pattern similar to that of most other countries, growing much more slowly since 1973 than before; indeed, by the end of the seventies, Soviet growth had fallen close to zero.

Soviet planners have two principal ways to divert production away from consumption. First is the planning process, which gives priority to investment rather than consumption, and often results in shortages of consumer goods. Second is a tax on consumer goods that accounts, on average, for about one-third of their price. This tax helps to finance investment, and takes income out of the hands of consumers, thus reducing their purchasing power. Consequently, shortages of consumer goods are reduced, although not avoided.

The Position of the Soviet Consumer

Consumers tend to be the forgotten people in the Soviet system—although their lot has gradually been improving. We have already seen how they are forced—via heavy taxation—to sacrifice current consumption to finance the investment the government undertakes; and how they are also forced to shoulder a special burden when bottlenecks develop. In addition, there is another cost in the Soviet command economy that consumers have to bear. To understand it, consider again the Soviet plant manager whose major concern is to produce a given quota of, say, nails. If planners have set the quota in terms of tons, the manager can most easily satisfy it by producing a relatively small number of large nails. (Visitors often wonder why so many things seem "heavy" in the Soviet Union. The reason is that many quotas are expressed in pounds or tons. Thus, an easy way to achieve a quota is to build weight into the product. It is no surprise that the Soviet Union is the world's largest producer of steel.)

[7]For detail on this and some of the other issues discussed in this chapter, see E. A. Hewett " Economic Reform in the Soviet Union," *The Brookings Review* (Spring 1984): 9.

On the other hand, suppose that the quota of nails is defined as a certain *number*. In this case, the manager will produce mostly small ones. Again, the resulting nail production will not satisfy the consumer, who wants a selection of various kinds. Of course, the consumer may be able to make a wrong-sized nail do in a pinch. But what does a person with big feet do if shoe producers meet their quota by concentrating on small sizes? The poor quality of goods and other problems facing the consumer (Box 38-1) remain one of the major weaknesses of the Soviet system. The problem can be stated very simply. The consumer is not king; the "customer" that producers are most concerned about is the central authority to which they must report.

Recently, Soviet leaders have, with mixed success, been trying to pay more attention to consumers. For example, auto production has been increased substantially, in cooperation with the Italian auto maker, Fiat. The result is the rugged but technologically backward Lada, which is sold on world markets at bargain prices, but is very expensive for Soviet purchasers.

How Much Can the Soviet Consumer Buy?

One way to compare standards of consumption across countries is to look at the number of hours an average worker has to work in order to buy specific items. By this standard, Russian workers are relatively poor. For example, feeding a family takes something like twice as many hours of work in Russia as in Canada, and for items like a small car or a colour television, perhaps ten times as many.

However, the lot of Soviet citizens is not as bad as this sounds because government subsidies provide Soviet citizens with bargain housing and free medical care. While this reduces the gap in living standards, it would be even more significant if Soviet citizens were able to acquire more of these services. Unfortunately, because of a housing scarcity, the average Soviet urban dweller doesn't get much housing—less than half the average for a Canadian family.

The Interplay of Economic and Political Systems

The Soviet system of rule by a single party is quite consistent with Marx's prediction that the overthrow of the capitalist system would be followed by a "dic-

BOX 38-1

A SHOPPER'S GUIDE TO THE SOVIET UNION*

Shopping in the Soviet Union is often a lottery. The stores seem well stocked, but typically with inferior or out-of-fashion items that nobody wants. When attractive goods arrive they are quickly snapped up. Long lines immediately form as passersby queue up, sometimes without even asking what's on sale. (They find that out later; sometimes nobody in the last 20 or 30 yards of a lineup will yet know.) When you get to the head of the line chances are you may have to deal with rude sales clerks, who know that you will buy anyway and who may be getting even for the frustrations they face in doing their own shopping. But all this you disregard in order to buy for yourself, your friends, your parents, and your cousins.

Buying this way involves a lot of luck and a lot of good management. Shoppers know by heart the sizes and colour preferences of relatives and friends;

they carry a lot of cash, because credit cards and cheques aren't used, and one never knows where lightning will strike next. To be ready, women carry a bag called an *avoska*, which is derived from the Russian word for "maybe." Soviet citizens have lined up through a freezing December night just to get on an 18-month long waiting list to buy a car, and viewed themselves as lucky when they succeeded. Thus, the efficiency loss in this centrally planned system includes not only the loss because consumers often get inferior products; it also includes the loss because consumers waste time in queues. The Soviet press estimates that the public spends 30 billion hours in line per year—a waste equal to having 15 million unemployed.

When this wasted time is taken into account, it means that there has been "disguised inflation"—goods cost more than the price the public pays for them.

*This box draws heavily on Hedrick Smith, *The Russians*, chap. II (New York: Quadrangle–New York Times Book Co., 1976). The situation for shoppers remains much the same a decade later.

---

tatorship of the proletariat." One of the interesting questions is whether a centrally planned economy like the Soviet system would work at all with the degree of political freedom that we enjoy. The more economic commands are issued by a central authority, the more dictatorial a system generally becomes.

This is an important issue, because a major Soviet criticism of our system—one that contains an element of truth—is that economic power corrupts political institutions. But if the Soviets' alternative economic system leads to an even worse form of government, what sort of cure is that?

Better Macroeconomic Balance?

The Soviets seem to be able to do a better job of curing unemployment than we do, since they can set their target outputs at a level to closely approximate full employment. However, while they face less overt unemployment, they have a greater problem with "disguised" unemployment, that is, workers on the

job who seem to be producing something, but who are in fact contributing little or nothing to the national product. An example is the labour used to produce undersize shoes that never get worn. While this may appear to be productive employment, it is, in fact, wasted effort. An oft-cited failure of the U.S. economy was Ford's decision in the 1950s to introduce the Edsel, an automobile that sold very poorly. Its failure represented a loss not only to Ford, but to the nation as a whole in terms of the resources wasted in the development of this car. In the Soviet Union, such a failure would not have occurred. Instead, the public would have bought the Edsel. It might not have been quite what people wanted, but they would not have had much choice. In North America, an incorrect decision results in a loss to producers and short-run unemployment in an industry; both of these can be identified and evaluated. On the other hand, a similarly erroneous decision in the Soviet Union results in a loss to consumers that may not be so obvious and so easy to measure, but may be just as real.[8] This suggests another question to keep in mind when comparing the Soviet and North American systems: Do Edsel-type goods that the public does not like still exist in the Soviet Union, or are they disappearing?

Which is the worse problem—the Soviets' disguised unemployment, or our overt unemployment? Our problem may be less damaging in the long run, because it is obvious to all. Therefore, a government is brought under pressure to reduce it. (There may be no similarly strong pressure in the Soviet Union to reduce disguised unemployment, precisely because it is disguised and therefore may go unrecognized.) A second consideration is that a system with overt unemployment allows rapid growth following a recession as the unemployed are put back to work. When growth slows in the Soviet Union—as it has in recent years—there is no pool of unemployed labour to fuel a rapid recovery; everyone already has a job.

However, in some respects, the Soviet problem of disguised unemployment may be less damaging than ours: The individuals involved are at least working, and hence feel productive even though they are not. Therefore, its psychological and social effects are less serious. One might also argue that disguised unemployment is more equitable than overt unemployment, because the winners are those who get a job who are

able to earn an income to support their families; in other words, the winners are those who would otherwise be jobless and at the low end of the economic ladder. The losers are those at all levels on the ladder—the poor and rich alike who get inferior products.

In the Soviet Union, the balance between aggregate demand and aggregate supply has been substantially different from that in Canada and other market economies. In Canada, demand has at times fallen, resulting in recessions, high unemployment, and a low rate of capital utilization. At other times, aggregate demand has risen rapidly, putting pressure on productive capacity and causing inflation. In the Soviet Union, demand has consistently been high compared to productive capacity. This is one reason for the low Soviet rate of unemployment. Inflation has been suppressed—though not completely—with price controls, and the resulting shortages mean that many consumer goods are hard to find. Even though capital-goods industries have been favoured in the planning process, shortages have also occurred there. The result has been a stretch-out of investment projects—projects planned for three or four years often take ten years or longer. The resulting inefficiencies provide one reason for the disappointing payoff from the large volume of capital formation. In the smaller, more open economies of Eastern Europe, the macroeconomic imbalances have also been reflected in stretch-outs of investment projects and shortages of consumer goods. Since such shortages create pressures to buy abroad, these countries have often had rising imports that have led to balance-of-payments crises in which they have been unable to pay for their imports from their earnings abroad.

[8]Or is it? After, all what difference does it make whether the public is driving an Edsel or a Mercury? In terms of basic transportation, they were quite similar cars; the main difference was in styling. This brings into focus again a fundamental criticism of our free enterprise system: What is the point of satisfying existing consumer desires when they are the result of advertising and the other methods producers use to manipulate consumers?

As pointed out earlier, this is an argument that sounds good, but in practice raises serious problems. First, who is to say which desires are basic, and which are contrived? In the last analysis, many things, from good music to dill pickles, represent an acquired rather than a "basic" taste. Second, although we may wish to reform advertising and the other means that are used to influence tastes, what is wrong, at any point in time, in satisfying existing consumer desires? This approach may not be ideal, but isn't it better than having someone or some group decide on what our desires should be?

Our democratic political system provides an interesting parallel. It is set up to respect the public's existing political preferences, even though they may have been formed by advertising and other forms of "manipulation." This may not, in theory, be an ideal system, but in practice we judge it better than a system in which "basic" or "ideal" political preferences are determined for the public by some individual or political party.

Is There Equality of Income in the Soviet Union?

The answer is no. The Soviets have allowed large differences in income to creep back into their system, as they have tried to increase production by providing incentives. Thus, scientists receive a much higher income than clerks, and skilled workers earn much more than unskilled workers. As a result, human capital is becoming a significant source of income difference in the Soviet Union. Because of this growing importance of *human capital*, a socialist policy that deals only with *physical capital* (by putting it in the hands of the state) can, at best, provide no more than a partial solution to the problem of serious income inequality.

This raises the question: Will the appeal of socialism to those who believe in equalizing incomes become less strong than in Marx's day?

Concluding Observations on the Soviet System

The ability of Soviet leaders to impose high taxes has provided substantial resources for investment, and for many years there was rapid growth in Soviet heavy industry. However, this growth has become particularly disappointing in the last decade. Moreover, the Soviet system has performed poorly in the many areas where decentralized decision making is the key to success. Nowhere is this more true than in agriculture, into which the Soviets pour more than 25% of their investment—several times more than in Canada. Yet despite this, Soviet agricultural productivity remains low. The principal problem is the organization of labour into collective farms where individuals have little incentive to work or innovate. (As much as a quarter to a third of the nation's total agricultural output is produced on the miniscule 2% of the Soviet farm land that is privately owned, where individuals are rewarded for hard work and initiative.) Soviet leaders have often attributed poor harvests to the weather, but grain was exported from these same lands before the First World War, and the weather doesn't present problems on adjacent privately owned plots of land. Some critics quip that, since 1917, the Soviet Union has announced a poor harvest due to bad weather 69 times.

The same sort of problems have dogged Soviet efforts over the last 50 years to close the technology gap. True, they have performed impressively in some ways. As early as 1957 they were graduating 80,000 engineers, several times the number trained in North America. Now they are world leaders in a number of fields, from theoretical mathematics to applied areas such as oceanography and polar research. Moreover, Soviet scientists developed the most promising line of research for the harnessing of power from nuclear fusion. However, they have not been successful in getting innovation across the board in a society that rewards caution and conformity, rather than risk taking. An important area in which Soviet technology has lagged is computers. Despite the Soviets' theoretical contributions to computer development and their ability to produce the large-scale computers necessary to put astronauts into space, they are concerned that they may have missed out on some of the early stages of the small computer revolution. One of the first reforms by Soviet leader Mikhail Gorbachev in 1985 was to introduce a crash program to get high school students familiar with computers.

It is not only the political leaders, concerned with maintaining power, who become devoted to the status quo. Plant managers do also, and resist experimenting with promising but risky new techniques because this may make it difficult for them to meet their quotas. Indeed, they may even resist *proven* risk-free innovations or style changes because introducing them will temporarily reduce their production and make their quotas more difficult to achieve. Moreover, Soviet managers lack an incentive to reduce costs by economizing in the use of inputs. Consequently, for example, the Soviet Union uses much more energy per unit of output than most Western countries. This profligate use is a cause—along with central planning—of the serious shortages of such inputs.

One of the most critical problems in the Soviet economy is the limited incentive to work. The scarcity of consumer goods means that additional pay may not provide a strong incentive—as illustrated by the Soviet joke: "They pretend to pay us, and we pretend to work." Alcoholism and absenteeism are serious problems. A cartoon shows two workers embracing in a factory, with the caption "Old friends meet. They haven't seen each other for two months; one or the other has been absent every day." This lack of incentives seems strange, since the authorities have introduced a number of incentives for individual workers that appear to be similar to—and sometimes even seem to exceed—those available to North American workers. Not only are Russian workers paid higher wages in some occupations than in others; in addition, high piecework rates (that is, payments according to the number of units produced) are more common as an incentive in the Soviet Union than in North America. Often the most productive workers are granted tangible rewards, such as free, government-financed holidays. Finally, there are other incentives which may seem odd to us but appear to have a certain appeal in the Soviet Union. For example, highly productive workers are decorated and cited as "Heroes of Socialist Labour."

Why, then, have Soviet workers not responded? Why has their productivity been disappointing? One possible reason is that wages are paid whether or not a factory meets its quota, and in the Soviet system there is no risk that a factory will go bankrupt. Another is that, after so many years of being told to reduce consumption today in order to enjoy a higher standard of living in the future, Soviet citizens have become cynical. While their paycheques are guaranteed, the goods they can buy continue to be disappointing.

In the Soviet system, problems of quality, preoccupation with quotas, and the heavy diversion of resources by the state from consumption into investment all mean that the consumer has been short-changed. This is one of the reasons why the Soviets have not, after all, achieved their objective of income equality. The elite not only receive a higher income; they also get to spend it on Black Sea resorts and in special stores which stock highly desirable items such as the French perfume and Yugoslavian toothpaste that are not available to the general public. The Soviets, like us, do not have complete equality. Their reply is that they are far closer to it than we are, because huge accumulations of wealth cannot be passed on from generation to generation. But there is an increasingly important kind of wealth that *can* be passed on: human capital. By arranging the best education and careers for their children, the Soviet elite pass on their privileged status.

However, as already noted, many Marxists in the West would argue that the Soviet Union is an example of communism gone wrong, not of any fundamental weaknesses in communism itself. The degree to which you accept this claim is a matter of judgement, on which you will have to decide for yourself. But before doing so, it is enlightening to consider the case of Yugoslavia, a communist country in which there is less accumulation of power by the central authority.

THE SOCIALIST MARKET ECONOMY OF YUGOSLAVIA

By the end of the Second World War, Soviet armies had swept the Germans out of the countries of Eastern Europe, imposing communist political and economic systems in their wake. Since that time, the history of these countries has been marked by a long and sometimes unrewarding struggle for political and economic reform. The story of Yugoslavia is somewhat different. That country was liberated from the Germans, not by the Soviet army, but instead by a Yugoslavian guerrilla movement. The civil war that followed was won by Marshall Tito, a communist who nonetheless was sufficiently independent to break politically with Moscow in 1948. He was then able to introduce his own kind of communism, which can best be described as *market socialism*. As in the Soviet Union or any other Marxist country, most capital is owned by the government. But Yugoslavia has a less centralized economy than the Soviet Union. The decision as to what will be produced depends more heavily on market signals from consumers than on decisions by central planners.

> *Market socialism* is an economic system which is based on the socialist idea of government ownership of the "means of production" (capital equipment, buildings, and land). At the same time, most of the decisions as to what will be produced are made by the market, that is, by the interaction of consumers and producers rather than by central planners.

Before we consider how the Yugoslavs have introduced a greater reliance on the market, it is important to keep their economy in perspective by noting the respects in which their government still does exercise a high degree of control. First, although many prices vary as a result of market pressures, they typically do so only within specified limits. Moreover, in some sectors, prices are controlled by the government. Second, the government follows a high-growth policy. As in the Soviet Union, about one-third of GNP is directed into investment. Third, the government determines which sectors will grow more rapidly than others by allocating investment funds to each. However, within each sector there is, typically, considerable competition among enterprises for available funds. Finally, the Yugoslavs, like the Soviets, draw up a five-year plan. However, the Yugoslav plan is less in the Soviet style of setting target outputs in each sector than in the French style of simply indicating what output levels are likely to be. Thus, a steel firm can see the expected level of output in industries that use steel, such as machinery and home appliances. It can then use this information in making its own decision as to how much steel to produce.

The Greater Degree of Market Freedom in Yugoslavia

In Yugoslavia, a firm may be owned by the state, but it is operated by its workers, who elect a manager to make day-to-day decisions. The manager acquires labour and other factors of production and sells the firm's output in more-or-less free markets, with the objective being to earn profits, which in turn are shared with the workers. The enterprise may succeed or it may not, depending on its ability to earn profits by responding to changes in consumer tastes and other market pressures. Moreover, within limits, the firm can change its prices.

Because production decisions are influenced by the profit motive and are sensitive to consumer wants, the Yugoslav system achieves some of the efficiencies of a free enterprise system. But (no surprise) it consequently also encounters some of its problems. First, managers who are in a monopoly position soon discover that they can exploit this position. They can increase their workers' profits by restricting supply and raising price.[9] Thus, the efficiency losses of monopoly may arise in such an economy, just as they do in ours.

Second, workers' income depends on earnings from the enterprise, rather than on just a formal wage. Since some enterprises are more successful financially than others, some workers have higher incomes. Thus, workers' ownership introduces incentives for labour to work harder (thereby increasing efficiency) but it also results in an uneven distribution of income that many socialists view as inequitable. Even in this socialist state, *there is still a conflict between the objectives of efficiency and equity.*

[9]At first, socialist theoreticians were optimistic that the monopoly problem could be solved by setting up a system in which planners would announce prices. This would force producers into the role of price takers. As a consequence, they would produce to the point where their marginal cost would be equal to price. At the same time, consumers would also take market price as given, and would consume to the point where their marginal benefit would be equal to price.

How would a planner decide on the price to announce? If the price that had been announced previously did not equate producers' supply and consumers' demand, the planner would change it until it did. With producers and consumers all acting as price takers, wouldn't such a socialist system provide the efficiency of perfect competition—even better than our imperfectly competitive free enterprise system? The answer is: Not necessarily. The profit-seeking manager with monopoly power would still be able to exercise it. As the only producer, the manager could just reduce the quantity supplied. The planner would then observe that supply was falling short of demand, and would raise price to the monopoly level the producer was seeking. In other words, a monopolist who figures out how the system works may not take price as given, even if it is announced by a central planner.

Third, compared with the Soviets, the Yugoslavs face a greater problem of overt unemployment[10]—though a smaller problem of disguised unemployment. The reason is that, in Yugoslavia, profits determine whether an enterprise will prosper or not, and if it does, it may expand. Hence, regions that have profitable enterprises may have no problem in absorbing a growing labour force and thus maintaining full employment. However, regions with unprofitable firms that do not grow may face an unemployment problem. There is no Soviet-type command for production to expand in these areas.

Special Problems

In Yugoslavia, there is still a relatively healthy, small-scale, privately owned sector where new firms are set up by individuals, just as in our system. However, if we concentrate on the rest of the economy where capital is publicly owned, an important question for this or any other socialist economy, is: Who sets up new enterprises? In Yugoslavia, existing firms develop new product lines and open up new branches. But how are *new* firms established?

This is a major issue because the entry—or even just the threat of entry—of new firms into an industry may reduce or prevent monopoly abuse, thus increasing the efficiency of the economy. Moreover, new firms may mean an even greater variety of new products will become available to satisfy consumer demand more effectively, as well as new jobs in regions of severe unemployment. New firms in our system are formed by entrepreneurs who know they will own them and expect to earn profits from them. But where private ownership is not allowed, what then? In Yugoslavia, new firms may be set up by a local community using government-supplied funds. But the problem is that the initiator loses control of the enterprise as soon as it is established and passes into the hands of its workers—so the incentive to exercise such an initiative is reduced.

CHINA: ANOTHER SOCIALIST EXPERIMENT

While the Soviet Union is the oldest of the communist governments, the communist party of China rules by

[10]See A. Sapir, "Economic Growth and Factor Substitution: What Happened to the Yugoslav Miracle?" *Economic Journal* (June 1980): 305.

far the largest population. For the first three decades after the 1949 victory of the Communist Party in the Civil War, China's economy was dominated by central planning, somewhat similar to that in the Soviet Union. Under Mao, China embarked on several nationwide campaigns—the "Great Leap Forward" of the late 1950s, aimed at spreading small-scale industrial production, and the "Cultural Revolution" aimed at ensuring ideological purity. Since Mao's death, there has been less emphasis on rigid ideological conformity. By 1984, in repudiation of the founding philosophy of the Communist Party, the official *People's Daily* newspaper stated that orthodox Marxism was out of date, and could not be relied upon to solve all of China's problems.

A major reason for this change in view was the favourable experience in agriculture, which was reformed in 1979. An incentive system was established that allowed peasants, once they had turned over a relatively modest quota of their crops to the government, to sell the rest on the open market. As a result, according to some estimates, Chinese grain output almost doubled between 1979 and 1985, and the Chinese were encouraged to reform other sectors of the economy. Private entrepreneurs are no longer considered enemies of the people. Private enterprise has been encouraged in some areas, and foreign investment welcomed, as China has taken major steps toward a market-oriented economy.

Moreover, the Chinese have also been moving away from the earlier Soviet-style emphasis on reduced consumption to finance investment and growth. By 1984, investment had fallen from a high of over one-third of national product to just over one-quarter.

The incentive systems that have been so successful in agriculture have been introduced in industry as well. State-owned enterprises have been encouraged to aim their efforts at increasing efficiency and better satisfying consumer wants. These enterprises have been made responsible for their profits or losses. Many of the enterprises incurring losses have been informed that their government subsidies will eventually be ended. Nowhere has reform gone further than in the area that borders Hong Kong. Indeed, in some respects its economy is now closer to the free enterprise economy of Hong Kong than to the rest of China.

By 1985, there was some indication that the Chinese authorities were becoming concerned that the free market reforms were moving too fast and that they might lose control. There was a report that there had been a crackdown; for example, the president of the Bank of China was reported to have been fired because he had violated discipline by giving himself and other bank officials excessive pay increases. The question was: Would the apparently successful move by the Chinese toward a free enterprise economy be allowed to continue? And if so, what sort of pressure for reform would this put on the Soviet Union, with its highly centralized system that lacks innovation and initiative? Would a Soviet reform be possible without stripping the central bureaucracy of its control over many dimensions of Soviet life?

CONCLUSIONS

In previous chapters we have seen how, in our system, redistributing income via government transfer payments reduces incentives—in particular, the incentive to work of those receiving the payments. In this chapter we have seen how incentives are also reduced in a socialist system where income is redistributed by the more drastic measure of giving the ownership of capital to the state. Most notably, a socialist system such as the Soviet Union reduces the incentives to initiate and innovate. Thus, there is no system that works ideally, solving all problems at once.

Judgement as to which economic system is better depends not on what it promises, but on what it delivers. *In practice*, which system does a better job of solving the basic economic problem of transforming resources into the satisfaction of human wants? As you evaluate this issue for yourself in the future, remember that the standard criticism of socialism is that it does not do a particularly good job of satisfying these wants. Also remember the basic criticism of free enterprise: It does a far better job of satisfying the wants of the rich than those of the poor.

Another criticism of free enterprise is that large corporations often exercise too much economic and political power—power that should be exercised by the government on behalf of the people. However, if communism cures this problem by transferring a great deal of the economic power (including the ownership of capital) to the government, does too much power then fall into the hands of the state? Lane Kirkland, an American union leader, has expressed labour's reservations about dealing with a powerful state:

> "We on the whole prefer to negotiate with private companies that have roughly equivalent bargaining power than with [government] corporations that control the courts, the police, the army, the navy, and the hydrogen bomb."

The problem of dealing with a powerful communist state has been faced recently by Polish workers when they formed a union. They discovered that a state that had always paid lip-service to the interests of the workers, could still strongly resist any attempt by workers to set up their own organization.

Finally, we must distinguish between the physical capital that a socialist state brings under government ownership and control, and the human capital that cannot be dealt with in this way: the skills, experience, and expertise we carry around in our heads. Labour is no longer as unskilled as when Marx wrote over a hundred years ago; workers now have widely differing skills. Consequently, our nation's capital today is in the hands not only of those who own physical plant and machinery, but also of those who own human capital. These people range all the way from semiskilled workers to managers and professionals. As a result, it is now much more difficult to argue that our society is simply divided into two groups: those who exploit (the capitalists) and those who are exploited (the workers). Most workers are also "capitalists"— some because they own physical capital, but most because they own significant quantities of human capital.

KEY POINTS

1. Most of the physical capital in our free enterprise system is owned by individuals; under socialism it is owned by the state on behalf of all the people. The theoretical appeal of socialism is that it eliminates one of the major causes of inequality in our system: the power and income enjoyed by those who own capital.

2. The two major economic characteristics of the system that exists in the Soviet Union today are: (a) physical capital is owned publicly rather than privately; and (b) investment and output levels are determined by a central planning authority.

3. One of the advantages of Soviet economy-wide central planning is that industry output targets can be set at a level that keeps unemployment low. But there are disadvantages. Central planning results in a great accumulation of power in the hands of the central political authorities. The more such power is centralized, the greater the risk that this power will be abused. A key question is: Could a Soviet-style command economy be run without political dictatorship?

4. A further problem with economy-wide planning is that it is extremely difficult to administer and therefore often results in bottlenecks and other inefficiencies. Accordingly, central planning tends to result in higher levels of disguised unemployment, with workers engaged in unproductive activities such as producing goods that poorly satisfy consumer tastes.

5. In recognition of this problem, the Soviets have recently been attempting to make their system more sensitive to "messages from the marketplace." This approach has brought them closer to Yugoslavia's economic system.

6. Yugoslavia is, like the Soviet Union, a socialist country in which productive capital is owned by the state. But it differs from the Soviet Union because much less economic decision making is done by a central authority and much more is handled by individual enterprises responding to profits and subject to market pressures.

7. For this reason, the Yugoslavian economy is closer to our system; as a consequence, the government encounters some of the same problems that we face, such as unemployment. Moreover, the fact that the Yugoslavs' capital is publicly owned means that they face a problem common to the Soviet Union or any other socialist country: how to attain the high levels of innovation and initiative that exist in a free enterprise system, where the people who own capital take great risks in order to earn future profits.

8. The Chinese have recently been moving away from the central planning of the Soviet Union toward a market-oriented economy.

KEY CONCEPTS

capitalist	bourgeoisie	output target
labour theory of value	class struggle	overt vs. disguised
subsistence level of wages	socialism	unemployment
surplus value	communism	market socialism
proletariat	Gosplan	worker management of firms
	five-year plan	

PROBLEMS

38-1 What did Marx mean by "surplus value"? Does it include some, all, or none of the costs of capital that must be paid by firms undertaking investment?

38-2 What are the two forms of unemployment? Which is worse in the Soviet system? Which is worse in our system? Explain.

38-3 In your view, what is the most important difference between the Soviet and the Yugoslav systems?

38-4 "Because many workers are hostile to capital, they oppose a rapid accumulation of it—either by a firm or by the nation as a whole. Thus they fail to understand their own interest, which is to be working with more, rather than less, capital." Do you agree that it is in the workers' interest to be working with more capital? or with less? Explain your answer.

38-5 Give your own concrete example to explain how a bottleneck may occur in a centrally planned economy. To what degree do you think socialism requires central planning?

38-6 Discuss why you think the free enterprise and socialist systems will, or will not, eventually converge into an "ideal" system.

38-7 Do we acquire more new technology from the Japanese, British, and Germans, or from the Russians and Czechs? Are there several reasons for your answer?

38-8 "Under unrestricted free enterprise, a stupid, shiftless individual who has inherited a great deal of valuable land can charge a high rent, and through the diligent pursuit of idleness, become very wealthy—indeed, far wealthier than the intelligent, hard-working person who rents the land. Something is wrong." Explain why you agree or disagree.

Now consider three alternative solutions to this problem, carefully criticizing each:

(a) Put a ceiling on rent. This would transfer income from landlords to tenants.

(b) Charge the maximum rent, but have the land owned by the state, with all income going to the state.

(c) Let the shiftless owner continue to own the land and charge a maximum rent. But place a heavy percentage tax on his income.

Which solution is closest to the socialist blueprint? Which is closest to our modified free enterprise system?

38-9 "Although socialism and communism promise less, they deliver more." Explain why you agree or disagree.

GLOSSARY

Not all these terms appear in the text; some are included here because they occur frequently in readings or lectures. Page numbers provide the primary references for the terms. For additional references, see the index.

(Some of the page numbers shown do not appear in *Microeconomics*, but refer to pages in *Macroeconomics*, the companion to this volume.)

ability-to-pay principle. The view that taxes should be levied according to the means of the various taxpayers, as measured by their incomes and/or wealth. Compare with *benefit principle*. (p. 98)

absolute advantage. A country (or region or individual) has an absolute advantage in the production of a good or service if it can produce that good or service with fewer resources than other countries (or regions or individuals). See also *comparative advantage*. (pp. 47, 665)

accelerationist. One who believes that an attempt to keep the unemployment rate low by expansive demand policies will cause more and more rapid inflation. (p. 365)

accelerator. The theory that investment depends on the change in sales. (p. 351)

accounts payable. Debts to suppliers of goods or services. (p. 113)

accounts receivable. Amounts due from customers. (p. 113)

action lag. The time interval between the recognition that adjustments in aggregate demand policies are desirable and the time when policies are actually changed. (p. 336)

actual investment. Investment as it appears in the GNP accounts; investment including undesired inventory accumulation. (p. 193)

adjustable peg system. A system whereby countries peg (fix) exchange rates but retain the right to change them in the event of fundamental disequilibrium. (In the adjustable peg system of 1945–73, most countries fixed the prices of their currencies in terms of the U.S. dollar; however, during the period 1950–62, Canada was an exception to the rule by allowing its currency to float.) (p. 315)

ad valorem tax. A tax collected as a percentage of the price or value of a good.

aggregate demand. (1) Total quantity of goods and services that would be bought at various possible average price levels. (pp. 169–70) (2) Total expenditures on consumer goods and services, government goods and services, (desired) investment, and net exports. (p. 214)

aggregate supply. (1) Total quantity of goods and services that would be offered for sale at various possible average price levels. (pp. 169–70) (2) Potential GNP.

allocative efficiency. Production of the best combination of goods with the lowest-cost combination of inputs. (p. 13)

annually balanced budget principle. The view that government expenditures should be limited each year to no more than government receipts during that year. (p. 227)

anti-combines legislation. The laws designed to limit monopoly power and business practices that reduce competition; the laws are contained in the Combines Investigation Act. (p. 576) See also *Competition Act*.

Anti-Inflation Board. Government body charged with overseeing the 1975–78 price and incomes policy.

appreciation (depreciation) of a currency. In a flexible exchange-rate system, a rise (fall) in the price of a currency in terms of another currency or currencies. (p. 319)

arbitrage. A set of transactions aimed at making a profit from inconsistent prices.

arbitration. See *compulsory arbitration* and *voluntary arbitration*.

arc elasticity of demand. The elasticity of demand between two points on a demand curve, calculated by the equation

$$\frac{\Delta Q}{Q_1 + Q_2} \div \frac{\Delta P}{P_1 + P_2}$$

asset. Something that is owned. (p. 112)

automatic stabilizer. A feature built into the economy that tends to reduce the amplitude of fluctuations. For example, tax collections tend to fall during a recession and rise during a boom, slowing the change in disposable incomes and aggregate demand. (Thus, they are an automatic fiscal stabilizer.) Another example is the tendency for imports to rise and fall as national income rises and falls; the leakage into imports also tends to reduce the fluctuations in the aggregate demand for Canadian goods and services. (p. 223)

average cost pricing. Setting the price where the average cost curve (including normal profit) intersects the demand curve. (p. 536)

average fixed cost. Fixed cost divided by the number of units of output. (p. 476)

average product. Total product divided by the number of units of the variable input used. (p. 472)

average propensity to consume. Consumption divided by disposable income.

average propensity to save. Saving divided by disposable income.

average revenue. Total revenue divided by the number of units sold. Where there is a single price, this price equals average revenue. (p. 528)

average total cost. Total cost divided by the number of units of output. (p. 476)

average variable cost. Variable cost divided by the number of units produced. (p. 476)

balanced budget. (1) A budget with revenues equal to expenditures. (2) More loosely (but more commonly), a budget with revenues equal to or greater than expenditures. (p. 89)

balanced budget multiplier. The change in equilibrium national product divided by the change in government spending when this spending is financed by an equivalent change in taxes.

balance of payments. The summary figure calculated from balance-of-payments credits less balance-of-payments debits, with certain monetary transactions excluded from the calculation. (There are various ways of defining monetary transactions; thus, there are various balance-of-payments definitions. The most common excludes official reserve transactions.) (p. 312)

balance-of-payments accounts. A statement of a country's transactions with other countries. (p. 309)

balance-of-payments surplus (deficit). A positive (negative) balance of payments. (p. 312)

balance of trade (or balance on merchandise account). The value of exports of goods minus the value of imports of goods. (p. 312)

balance sheet. The statement of a firm's financial position at a particular time, showing its assets, liabilities, and net worth. (p. 112)

band. The range within which an exchange rate could move without the government's being committed to intervene in exchange markets to prevent further movement. Under the adjustable peg system, governments were obliged to keep exchange rates from moving outside a band (of 1% either side of parity). (p. 315)

Bank Rate. The interest rate charged by the Bank of Canada on its loans to the chartered banks. (p. 265)

bank reserve. See *required reserves*.

bank run. A situation in which many owners of bank deposits attempt to make withdrawals because of their fear that the bank will be unable to meet its obligations. (p. 243)

bankruptcy. (1) A situation in which a firm (or individual) has legally been declared unable to pay its debts. (2) More

loosely, a situation in which a firm (or individual) is unable to pay its debts.

barrier to entry. An impediment that makes it difficult or impossible for a new firm to enter an industry. Examples: patents, economies of scale, accepted brand names. (p. 566)

barter. The exchange of one good or service for another without the use of money. (p. 42)

base year. The reference year, given the value of 100 when constructing a price index or other time series. (p. 137)

beggar-thy-neighbour policy (or beggar-my-neighbour policy). A policy aimed at shifting an unemployment problem to another country. Example: an increase in tariffs. (p. 682)

benefit-cost analysis. The calculation and comparison of the benefits and costs of a program or project. (p. 589)

benefit principle. The view that taxes should be levied in proportion to the benefits that the various taxpayers receive from government expenditures. Compare with *ability-to-pay principle*. (p. 98)

benefits in kind. Payments, not of cash, but of some good (like food) or service (like medical care). (p. 802)

bilateral monopoly. A market structure involving a single seller (monopolist) and a single buyer (monopsonist). (p. 742)

bill. See *Treasury bill*.

blacklist. A list of workers who are not to be given jobs because of union activity or other behaviour considered objectionable by employers. (p. 731)

black market. A market in which sales take place at a price above the legal maximum. (p. 69)

block grant. Grant that may be used in a broad area (such as education), and need not be spent on specific programs (such as reading programs for the handicapped). (p. 90)

bond. A written commitment to pay a scheduled series of interest payments plus the face value (principal) at a specified maturity date. (p. 110)

book value. The book value of a stock is its net worth per share. (It is calculated by dividing the total net worth of the company by the number of its shares outstanding.) (p. 113)

bourgeoisie. (1) In Marxist doctrine, capitalists as a social class. (2) The middle class. (3) More narrowly, shopkeepers. (p. 820)

boycott. A concerted refusal to buy (buyer's boycott) or sell (seller's boycott). A campaign to discourage people from doing business with a particular firm.

break-even point. (1) The output at which costs just equal revenues and therefore profits are zero. (p. 476) (2) The level of disposable income at which consumption just equals disposable income and therefore saving is zero. (p. 187)

broker. One who acts on behalf of a buyer or seller. (p. 118)

budget deficit. The amount by which budgetary outlays exceed revenues. (p. 89)

budget line (or income line or price line). The line on a diagram that shows the various combinations of commodities that can be bought with a given income at a given set of prices. (p. 463)

budget surplus. The amount by which budgetary revenues exceed outlays. (p. 89)

built-in stabilizer. See *automatic stabilizer.*

burden of tax. The amount of the tax ultimately paid by different individuals or groups. (For example, how much does a cigarette tax raise the price paid by buyers, and how much does it lower the net price received by sellers?) The incidence of the tax. (p. 98)

business cycle. The more or less regular upward and downward movement of economic activity over a period of years. A cycle has four phases: recession, trough, expansion, and peak. (pp. 147–48)

Canada Assistance Plan. A plan under which the federal government contributes to provincial and local spending on social welfare assistance to poor individuals and families. (p. 803)

Canadian Labour Congress (CLC). An organization of labour unions to which most of Canada's labour unions are affiliated. (p. 733)

Canadian Wheat Board. A government agency that has a monopoly on the marketing of all wheat, oats, and barley grown in the Prairie provinces. (p. 514)

cap. A limit on the upward adjustment of an indexed wage in response to a rise in the price index. (p. 400)

capital. (1) Real capital: buildings, equipment, and materials used in the productive process that have themselves been produced in the past. (p. 28) (2) Financial capital: either funds available for acquiring real capital *or* financial assets such as bonds or common stock. (p. 28) (3) Human capital: the education, training, and experience that make human beings more productive. (p. 763)

capital account. The account in a country's balance-of-payments accounts that records international transactions in existing assets. (p. 310)

capital consumption allowance. Depreciation, with adjustments for the effects of inflation on the measurement of capital. Loosely, depreciation. (p. 134)

capital flows. Purchases by foreign residents of Canadian assets (inflow), or by Canadian residents of foreign assets (outflow). Sometimes referred to as capital imports or exports. (p. 311) See also *direct foreign investment, portfolio investment.*

capital gain. The increase in the value of an asset over time.

capitalism. A system in which individuals are permitted to own large amounts of capital, and decisions are made primarily in private markets, with relatively little government interference. (p. 56)

capitalized value. The present value of the income stream that an asset is expected to produce. (p. 774)

capital market. A market in which financial instruments such as stocks and bonds are bought and sold.

capital-output ratio. The value of capital divided by the value of the annual output produced with this capital. (p. 354)

capital stock. The total quantity of capital.

cartel. A formal agreement among firms to set price and market shares. (p. 554)

cash reserves. See *required reserves.*

central bank. A banker's bank, whose major responsibility is the control of the money supply. A central bank also generally performs other functions, such as cheque clearing and the inspection of commercial or chartered banks. (p. 243)

central planning. Centralized direction of the resources of the economy, with the objective of fulfilling national goals. (p. 56)

certificate of deposit (CD). A marketable time deposit.

ceteris paribus. "Other things unchanged." In demand-and-supply analysis, it is common to make the *ceteris paribus* assumption; that is, to assume that none of the determinants of the quantity demanded or supplied is allowed to change, with the sole exception of price. (p. 61)

chartered bank. A privately owned, profit-seeking institution that accepts chequing and savings deposits, makes loans, and acquires other earning assets (particularly bonds and shorter-term debt instruments). There are only about a dozen domestic chartered banks in Canada; the five largest ones have as much as 90 percent of total chartered bank assets. (p. 244)

checkoff. The deduction of union dues from workers' pay by an employer, who then remits the dues to the union. (p. 733)

cheque clearing. The transfer of cheques from the bank in which they were deposited to the bank on which they were written, with the net amounts due to or from each bank being calculated. (p. 248)

chequing deposit. A deposit against which an order to pay (that is, a cheque) may be written.

circular flow of payments. The flow of payments from businesses to households in exchange for labour and other productive services and the return flow of payments from households to businesses in exchange for goods and services. (p. 44)

classical economics. (1) In Keynesian economics, the accepted body of macroeconomic doctrine prior to the publication of Keynes' *General Theory.* According to classical economics, a market economy tends toward an equilibrium with full employment; a market economy tends to be stable if monetary conditions are stable; and changes in the quantity of money are the major cause of changes in aggregate demand. (p. 170) (2) The accepted view, prior to about 1870, that value depends on the cost of production. In the late nineteenth century, this was replaced with the "neoclassical" view that value depends on both costs of production (supply) and utility (demand).

class struggle. In Marxist economics, the struggle for control between the proletariat and the bourgeoisie. (p. 820)

clean float. A situation where exchange rates are determined by market forces, without intervention by central banks or governments. (p. 325)

closed economy. An economy where exports and imports are very small relative to national product. (p. 220)

closed shop. A business that hires only workers who are already union members. (p. 734)

cobweb cycle. A switching back and forth between a situation of high production and low price and one of low production and high price. A cobweb cycle can occur if there are long lags in production and if producers erroneously assume that price this year is a good indicator of price next year.

coincidence of wants. Situation in which each of the parties involved in a barter has a product that the other wants. (p. 42)

collective bargaining. Negotiations between a union and management over wages and working conditions. (p. 730)

collective goods. Goods that, by their very nature, provide benefits to a large group of people.

collusion. An agreement among sellers regarding prices and/or market shares. The agreement may be explicit or tacit. (p. 554)

commercial bank. A term used in other countries to describe banks similar to Canada's chartered banks.

common property resource. A resource in which nobody has established property rights and which can be used by anyone. (p. 623)

commons. Land that is open for use by all or by a large group of people; for example, commonly owned pasture land. (p. 624)

common stock. Each share of common stock represents part ownership in a corporation. (p. 110)

communism. (1) In Marxist theory, the ultimate stage of historical development in which (a) all are expected to work and no one lives by owning capital, (b) exploitation has been eliminated and there is a classless society, and (c) the state has withered away. (2) A common alternative usage: the economic and political systems of China, the Soviet Union, and other countries in which a communist party is in power. (p. 820)

company union. A union dominated by the employer.

comparable worth. See *equal value, work of.*

comparative advantage. If two nations (or cities or individuals) have different opportunity costs of producing a good or service, then the nation (or city or individual) with the lower opportunity cost has a comparative advantage in that good or service. (pp. 49, 666) See also *absolute advantage.*

compensating wage differentials. Wage differences that may result if labour views some jobs as less attractive than others. (Employers have to pay a higher wage to fill the unattractive jobs.) (p. 749)

competition. See *perfect competition.*

Competition Act. Legislation introduced in Parliament in 1986 to reform Canada's competition policy and replace the Combines Investigation Act. (p. 581)

competition policy. Anti-combines laws and other policies to reduce monopoly power and strengthen competition in the economy. (p. 576)

competitive devaluations. A round of exchange-rate devaluations in which each of a number of countries tries to gain a competitive advantage by devaluing its currency. (Not all can be successful; each must fail to the extent that other countries also devalue.)

complementary goals. Goals such that the achievement of one helps in the achievement of the other. (Contrast with *conflicting goals.*) (p. 15)

complementary goods. Goods that are used together. A rise in the price of one causes a leftward shift in the demand curve for the other. (Contrast with *substitute.*) (p. 62)

complements in production. Goods produced together, as a package. A rise in the price of one causes a rightward shift in the supply curve of the other. Joint products. (p. 64)

compulsory arbitration. In a labour dispute, occurs when the government forces both parties to submit their dispute to an arbitrator, who then decides on a binding settlement. (p. 748)

concentration ratio. Usually, the fraction of an industry's total output made by the four largest firms. (Sometimes a different number of firms — such as eight — is chosen in calculating concentration ratios, and sometimes a different measure of size — such as assets — is chosen.) (p. 549)

conditional transfers. Contributions by the federal government to provincial budgets (or by provincial governments to local governments) which are conditional on the amounts spent by the receiving governments. (p. 89)

conflicting goals. Goals such that working toward one makes it more difficult to achieve the other. (p. 15)

conglomerate merger. See *merger.*

conspicuous consumption. Consumption whose purpose is to impress others. A term originated by Thorstein Veblen (1857–1929).

constant dollars (or real dollars). A series is measured in constant dollars if it is measured at the prices existing in a specified base year. Such a series has been adjusted to remove the effects of inflation or deflation. (p. 23) Contrast with *current dollars.*

constant returns (to scale). This occurs if an increase of x

percent in all inputs causes output to increase by the same *x* percent.

consumer price index (CPI). A weighted average of the prices of goods and services commonly purchased by an average household, as calculated by Statistics Canada. (p. 138)

consumer surplus. The net benefit that consumers get from being able to purchase a good at the prevailing price; the difference between the maximum amounts that consumers would be willing to pay and what they actually do pay. It is approximately the triangular area under the demand curve and above the market price. (pp. 454–55)

consumption. (1) The purchase of consumer goods and services. (p. 130) (2) The act of using goods and services to satisfy wants. (3) The using up of goods (as in capital consumption allowances).

consumption function. (1) The relationship between consumer expenditures and disposable income. (p. 186) (2) More broadly, the relationship between consumer expenditures and the factors that determine these expenditures.

contestable market. A market with only one or a few producers, whose market power is nevertheless severely limited by the ease with which additional producers may enter. (p. 569)

continental union. A Canadian labour union which is affiliated with a union in the United States (sometimes also called an *international union*).

convergence hypothesis. The proposition that the differences between communistic and capitalistic societies is decreasing.

convertible bond. A bond that can be exchanged for common stock under specified terms and prior to a specified date, at the option of the bondholder. (pp. 111–12)

cornering a market. Buying and accumulating enough of the commodity to become the single (or at least dominant) seller, and thus acquire the power to resell at a higher price. (p. 513)

corporation. An association of shareholders with a government charter that grants certain legal powers, privileges, and liabilities separate from those of the individual shareholder-owners. The major advantages of the corporate form of business organization are limited liability for the owners, continuity, and relative ease of raising capital for expansion. (p. 108)

correlation. The tendency of two variables (such as income and consumption) to move together.

cost-benefit analysis. See *benefit-cost analysis.*

cost-push inflation. Inflation caused principally by increasing costs — in the form of higher prices for labour, materials, and other inputs — rather than by rising demand. (p. 363) Contrast with *demand-pull inflation.*

countercyclical policy. (1) Policy that reduces fluctuations in economic activity. (2) Policy whose objective is to reduce fluctuations in economic activity.

countervailing power. Power in one group, which has grown as a reaction to power in another group. For example, a big labour union may develop to balance the bargaining power of a big corporation. A term originated by John Kenneth Galbraith. (p. 741)

craft union. A labour union whose members have a particular craft (skill or occupation). Examples: an electricians' union, or a plumbers' union. Contrast with *industrial union.* (p. 732)

crawling peg system. An international financial system in which par values would be changed frequently, by small amounts, in order to avoid large changes at a later date.

credit crunch. A situation of severe credit rationing. (p. 291)

credit instrument. A written promise to pay at some future date.

credit rationing. Allocation of available funds among borrowers when the demand for loans exceeds the supply at the prevailing interest rate. (p. 291)

creeping inflation. A slow but persistent upward movement of the average level of prices (not more than 2% or 3% per annum).

cross elasticity of demand. The percentage change in the quantity demanded of a good in response to a 1 percent change in the price of a related good. (p. 441)

cross-section data. Observations taken at the same time. For example, the consumption of different income classes in Canada in 1986.

cross-subsidization. A firm's or agency's use of revenues generated in profitable lines of activity to offset losses in other, less profitable lines of activity. (p. 583)

crowding out. A reduction in private investment demand caused when an expansive fiscal policy results in higher interest rates. (p. 295)

Crown corporation. A government-owned corporation, usually one that derives most of its revenue from the sale of goods and services to the public — for example, Air Canada, Ontario Hydro. (p. 92)

currency. (1) Coins and paper money (dollar bills, for instance). (2) In international economics, a national money, such as the British pound or the Japanese yen.

current account. The account in a country's balance-of-payments accounts that records that country's exports and imports of goods and services, as well as unilateral transfers. (p. 310)

current dollars. A series (like GNP) is measured in current dollars if each observation is measured at the prices that prevailed at the time. Such a series reflects both real changes in GNP *and* inflation (or deflation). Contrast with *constant dollars.* (p. 137)

current liabilities. Debts that are due for payment within a year.

customs union. An agreement among nations to eliminate trade barriers (tariffs, quotas, etc.) among themselves and to adopt common tariffs on imports from nonmember countries. Example: the European Economic Community.

cut-throat competition. Selling at a price below cost, with the objective of driving competitors out of the market (at which time prices may be raised and monopoly profits reaped). (p. 578)

cyclically adjusted budget. See *full-employment budget*.

cyclically balanced budget. A budget whose receipts over a whole business cycle are at least equal to its expenditures over the same cycle. Unlike an annually balanced budget, a cyclically balanced budget permits the use of countercyclical fiscal policies. Surpluses during prosperity may be used to cover deficits during recessions. (p. 228)

debasement of currency. (1) Reduction of the quantity of precious metal in coins. (p. 45) (2) More broadly, a substantial decrease in the purchasing power of money.

debt instrument. A written commitment to repay borrowed funds.

declining industry. An industry whose firms make less than normal profits. (Firms will therefore leave the industry.)

decreasing returns (to scale). Occurs if an *x* percent increase in all inputs results in an increase of output of less than *x* percent.

deficit. The amount by which expenditures exceed revenues. (p. 89) Contrast with *surplus*.

deflation. (1) A fall in the average level of prices; the opposite of inflation. (p. 11) (2) The removal of the effects of inflation from a series of observations by dividing each observation with a price index. The derivation of a constant-dollar series from a current-dollar series. (p. 138)

deflationary bias. Such a bias exists in a system if, on average, monetary and fiscal authorities are constrained from allowing aggregate demand to increase as rapidly as productive capacity. (The classical gold standard was criticized on the ground that it created a deflationary bias.)

deflationary gap. See *recessionary gap*.

demand. A schedule or curve showing how much of a good or service would be demanded at various possible prices, *ceteris paribus*. (p. 59)

demand deposit. A bank deposit withdrawable on demand and transferable by cheque.

demand management policy. A change in monetary and/or fiscal policy aimed at affecting aggregate demand. (pp.213–14)

demand-pull inflation. Inflation caused by excess aggregate demand. (p. 362) Contrast with *cost-push inflation*.

demand schedule. A table showing the quantities of a good or service that buyers would be willing and able to purchase at various market prices, *ceteris paribus*. (p. 59)

demand shift. A movement of the demand curve to the right or left as a result of a change in income or any other determinant of the quantity demanded (with the sole exception of the price of the good). (pp. 60–61)

demand shifter. Anything except its own price that affects the quantity of a good demanded. (pp. 61–62)

depletion allowance. A deduction, equal to a percentage of net taxable income, that certain extractive industries are permitted in calculating taxable profits. (p. 102)

deposit multiplier. See *money multiplier*.

depreciation. (1) The loss in the value of physical capital due to wear and obsolescence. (2) The estimate of such loss in business or economic accounts. (3) The amount that tax laws allow businesses to count as a cost of using plant or equipment. (p. 115)

depreciation of a currency. A decline in the value of a floating currency measured in terms of another currency or currencies. (p. 319)

depression. An extended period of very high unemployment and much excess capacity. (There is no generally accepted, precise, numerical definition of a depression. However, none of the economic slumps since World War II has been generally considered a depression.) (pp. 9, 150)

derived demand. The demand for an input that depends on the demand for the product or products it is used to make. For example, the demand for flour is derived from the demand for bread. (p. 713)

devaluation. In international economics, a reduction of the par value of a currency. (p. 316)

dictatorship of the proletariat. In Marxist economics, the dictatorship that occurs when a revolution has eliminated the capitalist class and power has fallen into the hands of the proletariat. (p. 826)

differentiated products. Similar products that retain some distinctive difference(s); close but not perfect substitutes. Examples: Ford and Chevrolet automobiles, different brands of toothpaste. (p. 553)

diminishing returns, law of eventually. If technology is unchanged, then the use of more and more units of a variable input, together with one or more fixed inputs, must eventually lead to a declining marginal product for the variable input. (p. 470)

direct foreign investment. Occurs when foreign residents establish or invest in firms in which foreign owners have a controlling interest. (p. 759)

dirty float. See *floating exchange rates*.

discounting. (1) The process by which the present value of one or more future payments is calculated, using an interest rate. See *present value*. (2) In central banking, lending by the central bank to a chartered bank or authorized investment dealer.

discount rate. (1) A term used to denote the rate of interest used to calculate discounted present value. (2) In the United States, the interest charged by the Federal Reserve when lending to commercial banks. See also *Bank Rate*.

discouraged worker. Someone who wants a job but is no

longer looking because work is believed to be unavailable. A discouraged worker is not included in either the labour force or the number of unemployed. (p. 155)

discretionary policy. Policy that is periodically changed in the light of changing conditions. The term is usually applied to monetary or fiscal policies that are adjusted to meet the objectives of high employment and stable prices. Contrast with *monetary rule.* (p. 333)

disposable (personal) income. Income that households have left after the payment of taxes. It is divided among consumption expenditures, the payment of interest on consumer debt, and saving. (p. 136)

dissaving. Negative saving.

dividend. The part of a corporation's profits paid out to its shareholders. (p. 109)

division of labour. The breaking up of a productive process into different tasks, each done by a different worker (for example, on an automobile assembly line). (p. 50)

dollar standard. An international system in which many international transactions take place in U.S. dollars and many countries hold sizeable fractions of their reserves in dollars. Also, other currencies may be pegged to the U.S. dollar.

double-entry bookkeeping. An accounting system in which each transaction results in equal entries on both sides. When double-entry bookkeeping is used, the two sides of the accounts must balance.

double taxation. The taxation of corporate profits first when they are earned and second when they are paid out in dividends. While double taxation of dividends has been effectively eliminated from Canada's tax system, it still exists in the United States. (p. 109)

dual labour market. A double labour market, where workers in one market are excluded from taking jobs in the other market. (p. 722)

dumping. The sale of a good at a lower price in a foreign market than in the home market — a form of price discrimination.

duopoly. A market in which there are only two sellers.

dynamic efficiency. Efficient change in an economy, particularly the most efficient use of resources, the best rate of technological change, and the most efficient rate of growth. (p. 507)

dynamic wage differential. A wage difference that arises because of changing demand or supply conditions in the labour market. It tends to disappear over time as labour moves out of relatively low-wage jobs and into those that pay a relatively high wage. (p. 749)

econometrics. The application of statistical methods to economic problems.

economic efficiency. See *allocative efficiency, dynamic efficiency,* and *technological efficiency.*

economic freedom. A situation in which people have the right to choose their own occupations, to enter contracts, and to spend their incomes as they please. (p. 9)

economic independence. A situation in which a nation's economy is controlled by its citizens, with relatively little influence by foreign decision makers. (p. 9)

economic integration. The elimination of tariffs and other barriers between nations. The partial or complete unification of the economies of different countries.

economic profit. Above-normal profit; profit after the opportunity costs of capital have been taken into account. (p. 480)

economic rent. The return to a factor of production in excess of its opportunity cost. (p. 772)

economics. (1) The study of how people acquire material necessities and comforts, the problems they encounter in doing so, and how these problems can be reduced. (p. 3) (2) Frequently, a narrower definition is used — the study of the allocation of scarce resources to satisfy human wants. (p. 40)

economies (diseconomies) of scale. Occur if an increase of x % in the quantity of every input causes the quantity of output to increase by more (less) than x %. (p. 50)

economize. To make the most of limited resources; to be careful in spending.

efficiency. The goal of getting the most out of our productive efforts. (p. 12) See also: *allocative efficiency, dynamic efficiency,* and *technological efficiency.*

effluent fee. A tax or other levy on a polluting activity, based on the quantity of pollution discharged. (p. 608)

elastic demand. Demand with an elasticity of more than one. A fall in price causes an increase in total expenditure on the product in question, because the percentage change in quantity demanded is greater than the percentage change in price. (p. 430)

elasticity of demand. The price elasticity of demand is

$$\frac{\text{Percentage change in quantity demanded}}{\text{Percentage change in price}}$$

Similarly, the income elasticity of demand is

$$\frac{\text{Percentage change in quantity demanded}}{\text{Percentage change in income}}$$

The unmodified term "elasticity" usually applies to price elasticity. (p. 430)

elasticity of supply. The (price) elasticity of supply is

$$\frac{\text{Percentage change in quantity supplied}}{\text{Percentage change in price}}$$

(p. 432)

elastic supply. Supply with an elasticity of more than one. A supply curve which, if extended in a straight line, would meet the vertical axis. (p. 432)

emission fee. See *effluent charge.*

employer of last resort. The government acts as the employer of last resort if it provides jobs for all those who are willing and able to work but cannot find jobs in the private sector. (p. 378)

employment rate. The percentage of the labour force employed.

endogenous variable. A variable explained within a theory.

Engel's laws. Regularities between income and consumer expenditures observed by nineteenth-century statistician Ernst Engel. Most important is the decrease in the percentage of income spent on food as income rises.

entrepreneur. One who organizes and manages production, makes business decisions, and innovates and bears risks. (p. 29)

envelope curve. A curve that encloses, by just touching, a series of other curves. For example, the long-run average-cost curve is the envelope of all the short-run average-cost curves (each of which shows costs, given a particular stock of fixed capital). (p. 486)

equal value, work of. "Equal pay for work of equal value" is a strengthening of the principle "equal pay for equal work" in legislation to eliminate pay discrimination between men and women. (p. 723)

equalization payments. Transfers by the federal government to "have-not" provinces, whose low tax base would make it difficult for them to finance adequate levels of public services without federal assistance. (p. 89)

equation of exchange. MV = PQ. (p. 292)

equilibrium. A situation in which there is no tendency for change. (p. 16)

equity. (1) Ownership, or amount owned. (p. 112) (2) Fairness. (p. 16)

escalated tariff. A tariff that is very low (or zero) on resources, but rises as goods become more and more highly processed. (p. 691)

escalator clause. A provision in a contract or law whereby a price, wage, or other monetary quantity is increased at the same rate as a specified price index (usually the consumer price index). (p. 400)

Established Programs Financing Act. The laws that state the amounts to be contributed by the federal government to provincial spending in the areas of health care, post-secondary education, and social assistance. (p. 89)

estate tax. A tax on property owned at the time of death.

Eurodollars. Deposits denominated in U.S. dollars but held in banks in countries outside of the United States (such as Canada or the European countries).

excess burden of a tax. The decrease in efficiency that results when people change their behaviour to reduce their tax payments. (p. 231)

excess demand. The amount by which the quantity demanded exceeds the quantity supplied at the existing price. A shortage. (p. 60)

excess reserves. Reserves held by a chartered bank in excess of the legally required amount. (p. 246)

excess supply. The amount by which the quantity supplied exceeds the quantity demanded at the existing price. A surplus. (p. 60)

Exchange Fund Account (EFA). A government account in which Canada's foreign exchange reserves are held. (p. 263)

exchange rate. The price of one national currency in terms of another. (p. 261)

exchange-rate appreciation (depreciation). See *appreciation (depreciation) of a currency.*

excise tax. A tax on the sale of a particular good. An *ad valorem tax* is collected as a percentage of the price of the good. A *specific tax* is a fixed number of cents or dollars collected on each unit of the good.

exclusion principle. The basis for distinguishing between public and nonpublic goods. If those who do not pay for a good can be excluded from enjoying it, then it is not a public good. (p. 648)

exogenous variable. A variable not explained within a theory; its value is considered to be given. Example: investment in the simple Keynesian theory.

expansion. The phase of the business cycle when output and employment are increasing. (p. 148)

export (X). Good or service sold to foreign nationals. (p. 132)

export of capital. Acquisition of foreign assets.

external cost. Cost borne by others. Pollution is an example of an external cost (sometimes called a *cost spillover* or a *neighbourhood cost*). (p. 603)

externality. An adverse or beneficial side effect of production or consumption. Also known as a *spillover* or *third-party effect.* (p. 95)

externally held public debt. Government securities held by foreigners. (p. 231)

extra-territoriality. Attempts by a country to apply its own laws to firms owned by its citizens but operating in another country; for example, the attempts by the U.S. government to enforce its anti-trust laws on U.S.-owned firms operating in Canada. (p. 781)

Fabian socialism. Form of socialism founded in Britain in the late nineteenth century, advocating gradual and evolutionary movement toward socialism within a democratic political system.

face value. The stated amount of a loan or bond. The amount that must be paid, in addition to interest, when the bond comes due. The principal. (p. 110)

factor mobility. Ease with which factors can be moved from one use to another.

factor of production. Resource used to produce a good or service. Land, labour, and capital are the three basic categories of factors of production. (p. 28)

fallacy of composition. The unwarranted conclusion that a proposition which is true of a single sector or market is necessarily true for the economy as a whole. (p. 210)

fair return. Return to which a regulated public utility should be entitled.

featherbedding. Make-work rules designed to increase the number of workers or the number of hours on a particular job. (p. 736)

federal-provincial transfers. Transfers of federal government revenue to provincial governments, as equalization payments or as payments under the Established Programs Financing Act. (p. 89)

fiat money. Paper money that is neither backed by nor convertible into precious metals but is nevertheless legal tender. Money that is money solely because the government says that it is. (p. 274)

final product. Product that has been acquired for final use and not for resale or for further processing. (p. 128)

financial capital. Financial assets such as common stocks, bonds, or bank deposits. (p. 28)

financial instrument. A legal document representing claims or ownership. Examples: bonds, Treasury bills.

financial intermediary. An institution that issues financial obligations (such as demand deposits) in order to acquire funds from the public. The institution then pools these funds and provides them in larger amounts to businesses, governments, or individuals. Examples: chartered banks, trust companies, insurance companies. (p. 115)

financial market. A market in which financial instruments (stocks, bonds, etc.) are bought and sold. (p. 115)

fine-tuning. An attempt to smooth out mild fluctuations in the economy by frequent adjustments in monetary and/or fiscal policies. (p. 334)

firm. A business organization that produces goods and/or services. A firm may own one or more plants. (p. 58)

fiscal dividend. A budget surplus, measured at the full-employment national product, that is generated by the growth of the productive capacity of the economy. (This term was most commonly used during the 1960s.)

fiscal drag. The tendency for rising tax collections to impede the healthy growth of the aggregate demand that is needed for the achievement and maintenance of full employment. (This term was most commonly used during the 1960s.)

fiscal policy. The adjustment of tax rates or government spending in order to affect aggregate demand. (p. 178) *Pure fiscal policy* involves a change in government spending or tax rates, unaccompanied by any change in the rate of growth of the money stock. (p. 295)

fiscal year. A 12-month period selected as the year for accounting purposes.

Fisher equation. The equation of exchange: $MV = PQ$. (p. 292)

fixed asset. A durable good, expected to last at least a year.

fixed cost. A cost that does not vary with output. (p. 468)

fixed exchange rate. An exchange rate that is held within a narrow band by the monetary authorities. (p. 314)

fixed factor. A factor whose quantity cannot be changed in the short run. (p. 468)

flat tax. A tax with only one rate applying to all income. A proportional tax. (p. 98)

floating (or flexible) exchange rate. An exchange rate that is not pegged by monetary authorities but is allowed to change in response to changing demand or supply conditions. If governments and central banks withdraw completely from the exchange markets, the float is *clean*. (That is, the exchange rate is *freely flexible*.) A float is *dirty* when governments or central banks intervene in exchange markets by buying or selling foreign currencies in order to influence exchange rates. (p. 325)

focal-point pricing. This occurs when independent firms quote the same price even though they do not explicitly collude. They are led by convention, rules of thumb, or similar thinking to the same price. (For example, $59.95 for a pair of shoes.) (p. 565)

forced saving. A situation where households lose control of their income, which is directed into saving even though they would have preferred to consume it. This can occur if the monetary authorities provide financial resources for investment, creating inflation which reduces the purchasing power of households' incomes (and therefore reduces their consumption). Alternatively, forced saving occurs if taxes are used for investment projects (such as dams).

foreign exchange. The currency of another country. (p. 306)

foreign exchange market. A market in which one national currency is bought in exchange for another national currency. (p. 306)

foreign exchange reserves. Foreign currencies held by the government or central bank. (p. 312)

Foreign Investment Review Agency (FIRA). An agency set up in the 1970s by the federal government to regulate and restrict direct foreign investment in Canada. Where policy toward foreign investment became less restrictive in the mid-1980s, FIRA was renamed *Investment Canada*. (p. 762)

forward price. A price established in a contract to be executed at a specified time in the future (such as three months from now). See also *futures market*.

fractional-reserve banking. A banking system in which banks keep reserves (generally in the form of currency or deposits in the central bank) equal to only a fraction of their deposit liabilities. (p. 243)

freedom of entry. The absence of barriers that make it difficult or impossible for a new firm to enter an industry. (p. 489)

free enterprise economy. One in which individuals are permitted to own large amounts of capital, and decisions are made primarily in markets, with relatively little government interference. (p. 57)

free good. A good or service whose price is zero, because at that price the quantity supplied is at least as great as the quantity demanded.

free-market economy. An economy in which the major questions "What?" "How?" and "For whom?" are answered by the actions of individuals and firms in the marketplace rather than by the government. (p. 55)

free rider. Someone who cannot be excluded from enjoying the benefits of a project, but who pays nothing (or pays a disproportionately small share) to cover its costs. (p. 650)

free trade. A situation in which no tariffs or other barriers exist on trade between countries.

free-trade area (or free-trade association). A group of countries that agrees to eliminate trade barriers (tariffs, quotas, etc.) within itself, while each country in the group retains the right to set its own tariffs on imports from nonmember countries. Compare with *customs union*.

frictional unemployment. Temporary unemployment associated with adjustments in a changing, dynamic economy. It arises for a number of reasons. For example, some new entrants into the labour force take time to find jobs, some with jobs quit to look for better ones, and others are temporarily unemployed by such disturbances as bad weather. (p. 160)

fringe benefits. Benefits other than wages (such as health insurance premiums, subsidized lunches, and employer contributions to employee pension plans) paid as part of the remuneration to employees.

front-loaded debt. A debt on which the payments, measured in constant dollars, are greater at the beginning than at the end of the repayment period. (p. 393)

full employment. (1) A situation in which there is no unemployment attributable to insufficient aggregate demand; that is, where all unemployment is due to frictional causes. (2) A situation where all who want to work can find jobs reasonably quickly. (p. 161)

full-employment budget (or high-employment budget). Full-employment government receipts (that is, the receipts that would be obtained with present tax rates if the economy were at full employment) minus full-employment government expenditures (that is, actual expenditures less expenditures directly associated with unemployment in excess of the full-employment level). (p. 224) Similar to *cyclically adjusted budget*.

full-employment GNP. The GNP that would exist if full employment were consistently maintained. Potential GNP. (p. 162)

full-employment rate of unemployment. See *natural rate of unemployment*.

full-line forcing. See *tied selling*.

fundamental disequilibrium (in international economics). A term used but not defined in the articles of agreement of the International Monetary Fund. The general idea is that a fundamental disequilibrium exists when an international payments imbalance cannot be eliminated without increasing trade restrictions or imposing unduly restrictive aggregate demand policies. (p. 330)

futures market. A market in which contracts are undertaken today at prices specified today for fulfillment at some specified future time. For example, a futures sale of wheat involves the commitment to deliver wheat (say) three months from today at a price set now.

gain from trade. Increase in real income that results from specialization and trade. (p. 667)

game theory. Theory dealing with conflict, in which alternative strategies are formally analysed. Sometimes used in the analysis of oligopoly.

general equilibrium. Situation where all markets are in equilibrium simultaneously.

general equilibrium analysis. Analysis taking into account interactions among markets.

general glut. This occurs when excess supply is a general phenomenon. The quantity of goods and services that producers are willing to supply greatly exceeds the quantity buyers are willing and able to purchase.

general inflation. An increase in all prices (including wages) by the same percent, leaving relative prices unchanged. (p. 171)

general price level. Price level as measured by a broad average, such as the consumer price index or the GNP deflator.

Giffen good. A good whose demand curve slopes upward to the right. (p. 466)

Gini coefficient. A measure of inequality derived from the Lorenz curve. It is the "bow" area (in Figure 36-1 on p. 785) between the curve and the diagonal line, divided by the entire area beneath the diagonal line. It can range from zero (if there is no inequality and the Lorenz curve corresponds to the diagonal line) to one (if there is complete inequality and the Lorenz curve runs along the horizontal axis).

GNP (price) deflator. Current dollar GNP divided by constant dollar GNP, times 100. Measure of the change in prices of the goods and services in GNP. (p. 138)

GNP gap. Amount by which actual GNP falls short of potential GNP. (p. 162)

gold point. Under the old gold standard, an exchange rate at which an arbitrager can barely cover the costs of shipping, handling, and insuring gold.

gold standard. System in which the monetary unit is defined in terms of gold, the monetary authorities buy and sell gold freely at that price, and gold may be freely exported or imported. If central banks follow the "rule of the gold standard game," they allow changes in gold to be reflected in changes in the money stock. (pp. 274, 314)

gold sterilization. A gold flow is sterilized when the central bank takes steps to cancel out the automatic effects of the gold flow on the country's money supply (that is, when the "rule of the gold standard game" is broken).

good. Tangible commodity, such as wheat, a shirt, or an automobile. (p. 27)

graduated-payment mortgage. A mortgage on which the money payments rise as time passes, in order to reduce front loading. If the money payments rise rapidly enough to keep real payments constant, then the mortgage is *fully* graduated. (p. 394)

Gresham's law. Essentially, "Bad money drives out good." More precisely: If there are two types of money whose values in exchange are equal while their values in another use (such as consumption) are different, the more valuable item will be retained for its other use while the less valuable item will continue to circulate as money. (p. 45)

gross domestic investment (I_g). Expenditures for new plant, equipment, and new residential buildings, plus the change in inventories. (p. 134)

gross national expenditure (GNE). Same as *gross national product*.

gross national product (GNP). Personal consumption expenditures plus government purchases of goods and services plus gross domestic investment plus net exports of goods and services. The total product of the nation, excluding double counting. (p. 134)

growth. An increase in the productive capacity of the economy. (p. 34)

Herfindahl index. A measure of concentration. Specifically, the sum of the squared market shares of all the firms. (p. 552)

high-employment GNP. The GNP that would exist if a high rate of employment were consistently maintained. Potential GNP. (p. 162)

holding company. A company that holds a controlling interest in the stock of one or more other companies.

horizontal merger. See *merger*.

human capital. Education and training that make human beings more productive. (p. 763)

hyperinflation. Very rapid inflation. (p. 12)

identification problem. The difficulty of determining the effect of variable *a* alone on variable *b* when *b* can also be affected by variables *c, d*, etc. (p. 446)

impact lag. The time interval between policy changes and the time when the major effects of the policy changes occur. (p. 336)

imperfect competition. A market in which some buyer(s) or seller(s) are large enough to have a noticeable effect on price. (p. 58)

implicit (or imputed) cost. The opportunity cost of using an input that is already owned by the producer. (p. 477)

implicit tax built into a welfare program. The benefits a family loses when it earns another \$1 of income. For example, if its benefits are reduced by 46¢, the implicit tax is 46%. (p. 807)

import (M). Good or service acquired from foreign nationals. (p. 132)

import of capital. Sale of financial assets to foreign nationals, or establishment by foreign nationals of firms in the domestic country.

import quota. A restriction on the quantity of a good that may be imported. (p. 677)

incidence of tax. The amount of the tax ultimately paid by different individuals or groups. (For example, how much does a cigarette tax raise the price paid by buyers, and how much does it lower the net price received by sellers?) (p. 99)

income-consumption line. The line or curve traced out by the points of tangency between an indifference map and a series of parallel budget (income) lines. It shows how a consumer responds to a changing income when relative prices remain constant.

income effect. Change in the quantity of a good demanded as a result of a change in real income with no change in relative prices. (p. 465)

income elasticity of demand. See *elasticity of demand*.

income line. See *budget line*.

incomes policy. A government policy (such as wage-price guidelines or wage and price controls) aimed at restraining the rate of increase in money wages and other money incomes. The purpose is to reduce the rate of inflation. (p. 379)

income statement. An accounting statement that summarizes a firm's revenues, costs, and income taxes over a given period of time (usually a year). A profit-and-loss statement. (p. 113)

increasing returns to scale. This occurs if an increase of *x* percent in all inputs results in an increase in output of more than *x* percent. (p. 487)

incremental cost. The term that business executives frequently use instead of "marginal cost."

incremental revenue. The term that business executives frequently use instead of "marginal revenue."

index. A series of numbers, showing how an average (of prices, or wages, or some other economic measure) changes over time. Each of these numbers is called an index number.

By convention, the index number for the base year is set at 100. (p. 138)

indexation. The inclusion in a contract or law of an automatic adjustment for inflation. A wage contract is *indexed* (p. 400) if it contains an *escalator clause* providing for an automatic increase in the wage in the event of a rise in the average level of prices (as measured, usually, by the consumer price index). The income tax is *indexed* (p. 395) when tax brackets, exemptions, and other provisions of the tax code automatically increase by the same proportion as the increase in the average level of prices.

indifference curve. A curve joining all points among which the consumer is indifferent. (p. 461)

indifference map. A series of indifference curves, each representing a different level of satisfaction or utility. (p. 462)

indirect tax. A tax that is thought to be passed on to others, and not borne by the one who originally pays it. Examples: sales taxes, excise taxes, import duties. (p. 134n)

induced investment. Additional investment demand that results from an increase in national product. (p. 209)

industrial union. A union open to all workers in an industry, regardless of their specific craft or skill. (p. 732) Contrast with *craft union*.

industry. The producers of a single good or service (or closely related goods or services). (p. 58)

inelastic demand. Demand with an elasticity of less than one. See *elasticity of demand*. (p. 430)

infant-industry argument for protection. The proposition that new domestic industries with economies of scale or large requirements of human capital need protection from foreign producers until they can become established. (p. 683)

inferior good. A good for which the quantity demanded decreases as income rises, *ceteris paribus*. (p. 62)

inflation. An increase in the average level of prices. (p. 11)

inflationary gap. The vertical distance by which the aggregate demand line is above the 45° line at the full-employment quantity of national product. (p. 216)

information cost. See *search cost*.

inheritance tax. Tax imposed on property received from a person who has died.

injection. Demand for a GNP component other than consumption. (p. 195)

innovation. A change in products or in the techniques of production.

inputs. Materials and services used in the process of production.

interest. Payment for the use of money.

interest rate. Interest as a percentage per annum of the amount borrowed.

interlocking directorate. Situation where one or more directors of a company sit on the boards of directors of one or more other companies that are competitors, suppliers, or customers of the first company.

intermediate product. A product intended for resale or further processing. (p. 128)

internal cost. Costs incurred by those who actually produce (or consume) a good. (p. 603) Contrast with *external cost*.

internalization. A process that results in a firm or individual taking into account an external cost (or benefit) of its actions. (p. 605)

international adjustment mechanism. Any set of forces that tends to reduce surpluses or deficits in the balance of payments. (p. 329)

international liquidity. The total amount of international reserves (foreign exchange, SDRs, etc.) held by the various nations. (p. 331)

inventories. Stocks of raw materials, intermediate products, and finished goods held by producers or marketing organizations. (p. 131)

investment. Accumulation of capital. (p. 28)

Investment Canada. See *FIRA*

investment dealer. A firm that markets common stock, bonds, and other securities. (p. 116)

investment demand. (Also known as *desired investment* or *planned investment*). This is the amount of new plant, equipment, and housing acquired during the year, plus additions to inventories that businesses wanted to acquire. Undesired inventory accumulation is excluded. (If undesired inventory accumulation is included, the result is *actual investment*.) (p. 193)

investment, domestic (I). See *gross domestic investment* and *net domestic investment*.

investment good. A capital good. Buildings, equipment, or inventory.

investment tax credit. A provision in the tax code providing a reduction in taxes to those who acquire capital equipment. (p. 102)

invisible. An intangible; a service (as contrasted with a good).

"invisible hand." Adam Smith's phrase expressing the idea that the pursuit of self-interest by individuals will lead to a desirable outcome for society as a whole. (p. 7)

iron law of wages. The view (commonly held in the nineteenth century) that the high birth rate creates a tendency for the supply of labour to outrun the productive capacity of the economy and the demand for labour. As a consequence, it was an iron law of nature that wages would be driven down to the subsistence level. (Any excess population at that wage would die from starvation, pestilence, or war.) (p. 78)

joint products. Goods such that the rise in the price of one causes a rightward shift in the supply curve of the other.

Complements in production. Products produced together. Example: meat and hides. (p. 64)

joint profit maximization. Formal or informal cooperation by oligopolists to pick the price that yields the most profit for the group. (p. 554)

key currency. A national currency commonly used by foreigners in international transactions and by foreign monetary authorities when intervening in exchange markets. Examples: the U.S. dollar, and, historically, the British pound. (p. 331)

Keynesian economics. The major macroeconomic propositions put forward by John Maynard Keynes in *The General Theory of Employment, Interest and Money* (1936): A market economy may reach an equilibrium with large-scale unemployment; steps to stimulate aggregate demand can cure a depression; and fiscal policies are the best way to control aggregate demand. (p. 174) Contrast with *classical economics.*

kinked demand curve. A demand curve that an oligopoly firm faces if its competitors follow any price cut it makes but do not follow any of its price increases. The kink in such a demand curve occurs at the existing price. (p. 561)

labour. The physical and mental talents of human beings, applied to the production of goods and services. (p. 28)

labour force. The number of people employed plus those actively seeking work. (p. 155)

labour-intensive product. A good whose production uses a relatively large quantity of labour and relatively small quantity of other resources. (p. 468)

labour participation rate. See *participation rate.*

labour productivity. See *productivity of labour.*

labour theory of value. Strictly, the proposition that the sole source of value is labour (including labour "congealed" in capital). Loosely, the proposition that labour is the principal source of value. (pp. 819–20)

labour union. See *union.*

Laffer curve. A curve showing how tax revenues change as the tax rate changes. (p. 420)

laissez-faire. Strictly translated, "let do." More loosely, "leave it alone." An expression used by the French physiocrats and later by Adam Smith, to describe the absence of government intervention in markets. (p. 7)

land. This term is used broadly by economists to include not only arable land but also the other gifts of nature (such as minerals) that come with the land. (p. 28)

law of diminishing marginal benefit (utility). As a consumer gets more and more of a good, the marginal benefit (utility) of that good will (eventually) decrease. (p. 452)

law of diminishing returns. See *diminishing returns, law of eventually.*

leading indicator. An economic variable that reaches a turning point (peak or trough) before the economy as a whole changes direction. (p. 347)

leakage. (1) A withdrawal of potential spending from the circular flow of income and expenditures (p. 195) (2) A withdrawal of currency from the banking system that reduces the potential expansion of the money stock.

leakages-injections approach. The determination of equilibrium national product by finding the size of the product at which leakages are equal to injections. (p. 221)

legal tender. An item that creditors must, by law, accept in payment of a debt. (p. 273)

leverage. The ratio of debt to net worth. (p. 117)

liability. (1) What is owed. (p. 112) (2) The amount that can be lost by the owners of a business if that business goes bankrupt. (p. 108)

life-cycle hypothesis. The proposition that consumption depends on expected lifetime income (as contrasted with the early Keynesian view that consumption depends on current income).

limited liability. The amount an owner-shareholder of a corporation can lose in the event of bankruptcy. This is limited to the amount paid to purchase shares of the corporation. (p. 108)

line of credit. Commitment by a bank or other lender to stand ready to lend up to a specified amount to a customer on request. (p. 117)

liquid asset. An asset that can be sold on short notice, at a predictable price, with little cost or bother. (p. 241)

liquidity. Ease with which an asset can be sold on short notice, at a predictable price, with little cost. (p. 116)

liquidity preference. The demand for money — that is, the willingness to hold money as a function of the interest rate.

liquidity preference theory of the interest rate. The theory put forward by J. M. Keynes that the interest rate is determined by the willingness to hold money (liquidity preference) and the supply of money (that is, the stock of money in existence). Contrast with *loanable funds theory of interest.*

liquidity trap. In Keynesian theory, the situation in which individuals and businesses are willing to hold all their additional financial assets in the form of money — rather than bonds or other debt instruments — at the existing interest rate. In such circumstances, the creation of additional money by the central bank cannot depress the interest rate further, and monetary policy cannot be used effectively to stimulate aggregate demand. (All additional money created is caught in the liquidity trap and is held as idle balances.) In geometric terms, the liquidity trap exists where the liquidity preference curve (the demand for money) is horizontal.

loanable funds theory of interest. The theory that the interest rate is determined by the demand for and the supply of funds in the market for bonds and other forms of debt. Contrast with *the liquidity preference theory of the interest rate.*

lockout. Temporary closing of a factory or other place of business in order to deprive workers of their jobs. A bargaining tool sometimes used in labour disputes; the employer's equivalent of a strike.

logarithmic (or log or ratio) scale. A scale in which equal percentage changes are shown as equal distances. For example, the distance from 100 to 200 is equal to the distance from 200 to 400. (Each involves a doubling.) (p. 22)

long run. (1) A period long enough for equilibrium to be reached. (2) A period of time long enough for the quantity of capital to be adjusted to the desired level. (p. 468) (3) Any extended period.

long-run Phillips curve. The curve (or line) traced out by the possible points of long-run equilibrium; that is, the points where people have adjusted completely to the prevailing rate of inflation. (p. 367)

long-run production function. A table showing various combinations of inputs and the maximum output that can be produced with each combination. For a simple firm with only two inputs (labour and capital), the production function can be shown by a two-dimensional table. (p. 495)

Lorenz curve. A curve showing cumulative percentages of income or wealth. For example, a point on a Lorenz curve might show the percentage of income received by the poorest half of the families. (The cumulative percentage of income is shown on the vertical axis. The family with the lowest income is counted first, and then other families are added successively in the order o their incomes. The cumulative percentage of families is on the horizontal axis.) Such a curve can be used to measure inequality; if all families have the same income, the Lorenz curve traces out a diagonal line. See also *Gini coefficient.* (p. 785)

lump-sum tax. A tax of a constant amount. The revenues from such a tax do not change when income changes. (p. 217)

M1. The narrowly defined money stock; consisting of the non-bank public's holdings of currency (coins and paper money) plus demand deposits in the chartered banks. Currency held by banks is excluded, as are deposits owned by banks or by the federal government. This was the definition of money used by the Bank of Canada as an indicator of monetary policy from the mid-1970s to the early 1980s. (p. 239)

M1A. Holding by the non-bank public of currency and all demand deposits in chartered banks. In recent years, this has become a more common basic definition of money. (p. 240)

M2. Defined as M1 *plus* all notice (savings) and personal term deposits in chartered banks. Excludes large term deposits held by corporations; these are included in M3. (p. 241)

M3. Defined as M2 plus non-personal term deposits, *plus* deposits owned by Canadian residents but denoted in foreign currency, in chartered banks. (p. 241)

macroeconomics. The study of the overall aggregates of the economy, such as total employment, the unemployment rate, national product, and the rate of inflation. (p. 125)

Malthusian problem. The tendency for population to outstrip productive capacity, particularly the capacity to produce food. This is the supposed consequence of a tendency for population to grow geometrically (1, 2, 4, 8, etc.) while the means of subsistence grows arithmetically (1, 2, 3, 4, etc.). The pressure of population will tend to depress the wage rate to the subsistence level and keep it there, with the excess population being eliminated by war, pestilence, or starvation. A problem described by Thomas Malthus in his *Essay on the Principle of Population* (1798) (p. 75)

managed float. A dirty float. See *floating exchange rate.*

marginal. The term commonly used by economists to mean "additional." For example: *marginal cost* is the additional cost when one more unit is produced; *marginal revenue* is the addition to revenue when one more unit is sold; *marginal utility* is the utility or satisfaction received from consuming one more unit of a good or service.

marginal benefit. The value (in money terms) that an individual would ascribe to having an additional unit of a good or service; that is, the amount of money the individual would be willing to pay for having an additional unit of the good or service. (An individual's marginal benefit schedule for a good or service is equivalent to the individual's demand curve for that good or service.) (p. 451)

marginal cost pricing. Setting price at the level where MC intersects the demand curve. (p. 535)

marginal efficiency of investment. The schedule or curve relating desired investment to the rate of interest. The investment demand curve. (p. 287)

marginal physical product. The additional output when one more unit of an input is used (with all other inputs being held constant). For example, the *marginal physical product of labour* (often abbreviated to the *marginal product of labour*) is the additional output when one more unit of labour is used. (p. 473)

marginal product. (1) Strictly, the marginal physical product. (2) Sometimes, the value of the marginal physical product.

marginal product of labour. See *marginal physical product.*

marginal propensity to consume (MPC). The change in consumption expenditures divided by the change in disposable income. (p. 188) *marginal propensity to import (MPM).* The change in imports of goods and services divided by the change in GNP.

marginal propensity to save (MPS). The change in saving divided by the change in disposable income. 1 – MPC. (p. 190)

marginal rate of substitution. The slope of the indifference curve. The ratio of the marginal utility of one good to the marginal utility of another. (p. 462)

marginal revenue. The increase in total revenue from the sale of one more unit. (p. 471)

marginal revenue product. The additional revenue when the firm uses one additional unit of an input (with all other inputs being held constant). (p. 710)

marginal tax rate. The fraction of additional income paid in taxes. (p. 88)

marginal utility. The satisfaction an individual receives from consuming one additional unit of good or service. (p. 452)

margin call. The requirement by a lender who holds stocks (or bonds) as security that more money be put up or the stocks (or bonds) will be sold. A margin call may be issued when the price of the stocks (or bonds) declines, making the stocks (or bonds) less adequate as security for the loan.

margin requirement. The minimum percentage that purchasers of stocks or bonds must put up in their own money. For example, if the margin requirement on stock is 60%, the buyer must put up at least 60% of the price in his or her own money and can borrow no more than 40% from a bank or stockbroker.

market. An institution in which items are bought and sold. (p. 55)

market economy. See *free-market economy.*

market failure. The failure of market forces to bring about the best allocation of resources. For example, when production of a good generates pollution, too many resources tend to go into the production of that good and not enough into the production of alternative goods and services.

market mechanism. The system whereby prices and the interaction of demand and supply help to answer the major economic questions "What will be produced?" "How?" and "For whom?" (p. 57)

market power. The ability of a single firm or individual to influence the market price of a good or service. (p. 526)

market-power inflation. See *cost-push inflation.*

market share. Percentage of an industry's sales accounted for by a single firm.

market structure. Characteristics that affect the behaviour of firms in a market, such as the number of firms, the possibility of collusion, the degree of product differentiation, and the ease of entry.

marketing board. A legally sanctioned producer organization in agriculture; some boards have the right to fix prices and control production of their product. (p. 545)

Marxist economy. One in which most of the capital is owned by the government. (Individuals may of course own small capital goods, such as hoes or hammers, but the major forms of capital — factories and heavy machinery — are owned by the state.) Political power is in the hands of a party pledging allegiance to the doctrines of Karl Marx. (p. 56)

measure of economic welfare (MEW). A comprehensive measure of economic well-being. Per capita real national product is adjusted to take into account leisure, pollution, and other such influences on welfare. (p. 141)

median. The item in the middle (that is, half of all items are above the median and half are below).

mediation (or conciliation). In labour disputes, occurs when major negotiations are deadlocked and an impartial outsider is brought in to suggest a settlement. (p. 747)

medium of exchange. Money; any item that is generally acceptable in exchange for goods or services; any item that is commonly used in buying goods or services (p. 44)

mercantilism. The theory that national prosperity can be promoted by a positive balance of trade and the accumulation of precious metals.

merchandise trade surplus. The excess of merchandise exports over merchandise imports. (p. 311)

merger. The bringing together of two or more firms under common control through purchase, exchange of common stock, or other means. A *horizontal merger* brings together competing firms. A *vertical merger* brings together firms that are each others' suppliers or customers. A *conglomerate merger* brings together firms that are not related in either of these ways. (p. 579)

merit good. A good or service that the government considers particularly desirable and that it therefore encourages by subsidy or regulation — such as the regulation that children must go to school to get the merit good of education. (p. 95)

microeconomics. The study of individual units within the economy — such as households, firms, and industries — and their interrelationships. The study of the allocation of resources and the distribution of income. (p. 125)

military-industrial complex. A loose term referring to the combined political power exerted by military officers and defence industries; those with a vested interest in military spending. (In his farewell address, President Eisenhower of the United States warned against the military-industrial complex.)

minimum wage. The lowest wage that an employer may legally pay for an hour's work. (p. 717)

mint parity. The exchange rate calculated from the official prices of gold in two countries under the gold standard.

mixed economy. An economy in which the private market and the government share the decisions as to what shall be produced, how, and for whom. (p. 56)

model. The essential features of an economy or economic problem, explained in terms of diagrams, equations, or words — or some combination of these.

monetarism. A body of thought that has its roots in classical economics and that rejects much of the teaching of Keynes' *General Theory*. According to monetarists, the most important determinant of aggregate demand is the quantity of money; the economy is basically stable if monetary growth is stable; and the authorities should follow a monetary rule, aiming for a steady growth of the money stock. Many monetarists also believe that the effects of fiscal policy on aggregate demand are weak (unless accompanied by changes in the quantity of money), that the government plays too active a role in the economy, and that the long-run Phillips curve is vertical. (The most famous contemporary monetarist is Milton Friedman).

monetary base. Currency held by the general public and by chartered banks plus the deposits of chartered banks in the Bank of Canada.

monetary policy. Central bank policies aimed at changing the rate of growth of the money stock; for example, open market operations or changes in required reserve ratios. (p. 178)

monetary rule. The rule, proposed by monetarists, that the central bank should aim for a steady rate of growth of the money stock. (p. 334)

money. Any item commonly used in buying goods or services.

money illusion. Strictly defined, people have money illusion if their behaviour changes in the event of a proportional change in prices, money incomes, and assets and liabilities measured in money terms. More loosely, people have money illusion if their behaviour changes when there is a proportional change in prices and money incomes.

money income. Income measured in dollars (or, in another country, income measured in the currency of that country).

money market. The market for short-term debt instruments (such as Treasury bills).

money multiplier (deposit multiplier). The number of dollars by which the money stock can increase as a result of a $1 increase in the reserves of chartered banks. (p. 251)

money stock (or supply). Narrowly, M1 or M1A. More broadly and less commonly, M2 or M3. (pp. 239–41)

monopolistic competition. A market structure with many firms selling a differentiated product, with low barriers to entry. (p. 568)

monopoly. (1) A market in which there is only a single seller. (2) The single seller in such a market. A *natural monopoly* occurs when the average total cost of a single firm falls over such an extended range that one firm can produce the total quantity sold at a lower average cost than could two or more firms. (p. 523)

monopoly rent. Above-normal profit of a monopoly. (p. 773)

monopsony. A market in which there is only one buyer. (p. 78)

moral suasion. Appeals or pressure by Bank of Canada intended to influence the behaviour of chartered banks. (p. 268)

most-favoured-nation clause. A clause in a trade agreement that commits a country to impose no greater barriers (tariffs, etc.) on imports from a second country than it imposes on imports from any other country.

multinational corporation. A corporation that carries on business (either directly or through subsidiaries) in more than one country. (p. 779)

multiplier. The change in equilibrium real national product divided by the change in investment demand (or in government expenditures, tax collections, or exports). In the simplest economy (with a marginal tax rate of zero and no imports), the multiplier is 1 ÷ (the marginal propensity to save). (p. 198) See also *money multiplier*.

Nash equilibrium. Equilibrium that exists when each firm assumes that none of its competitors will react to any changes it makes. (p. 564)

national debt. See *public debt*.

National Energy Program (NEP). A 1980 program outlining the federal government's policy on pricing and taxation of oil and gas, energy exports, and Canadianization of the energy sector. The NEP was largely abolished by the Conservative government in 1984–85. (p. 636)

national income. The return to all factors of production owned by the residents of a nation. (p. 128)

national product. See *gross national product* and *net national product*.

natural monopoly. See *monopoly*.

natural oligopoly. See *oligopoly*.

natural rate of unemployment. The equilibrium rate of unemployment that exists when people have adjusted completely to the existing rate of inflation. The rate of unemployment to which the economy tends when those making labour and other contracts correctly anticipate the rate of inflation. The rate of unemployment consistent with a stable rate of inflation. (p. 367)

national union. A Canadian labour union that is not affiliated with foreign labour unions. (p. 733)

near money. A highly liquid asset that can be quickly and easily converted into money. Examples: a savings deposit or a Treasury bill. (p. 241)

negative income tax. A reverse income tax, whereby the government makes payments to individuals and families with low incomes. (The lower the income, the greater the payment from the government.) (p. 812)

neocolonialism. The domination of the economy of a nation by the business firms or government of another nation or nations.

net domestic investment I_n. Gross domestic investment less depreciation. (p. 134)

net exports. Exports minus imports. (p. 220)

net national product (NNP). Personal consumption expenditures plus government purchases of goods and services plus net private domestic investment plus net exports of goods and services. GNP minus capital consumption allowances. (p. 134)

net official monetary movements. Changes in Canada's official foreign exchange reserves. An increase in reserves appears as a positive entry on the debit side of the balance-of-payments accounts, a decrease as a negative debit.

net worth. Total assets less total liabilities. The value of ownership. (p. 113)

neutrality of money. Money is neutral if a change in the quantity of money affects the price level without affecting relative prices or the distribution of income.

neutrality of taxes. (1) A situation where taxes do not affect relative prices. (2) The absence of an excess burden of taxes. (p. 96)

New Left. Radical economists; Marxists of the 1960s and 1970s.

nominal. Measured in money terms. Current dollar as contrasted to constant-dollar, or real. (p. 23) See also *current dollar.*

noncompeting groups. Groups of workers that do not compete with each other for jobs because their training or skills are different.

non-price competition. Competition by means other than price; for example, advertising or product differentiation. (p. 563)

non-renewable resource. Resource of which a finite quantity exists. (p. 631)

non-tariff barrier. Impediment to trade other than tariffs. Example: an import quota. (p. 687)

normal good. A good for which the quantity demanded rises as income rises, *ceteris paribus.* Contrast with an *inferior good.* (p. 62)

normal profit. The opportunity cost of capital and/or entrepreneurship. (Normal profit is considered a cost by economists but not by business accountants.) (p. 480)

normative statement. A statement about what should be. (p. 38). Contrast with *positive statement.*

notice deposit. A deposit in a chartered bank or other financial institution for which the institution has the legal right to insist on several days' or weeks' notice before being obliged to allow the depositor to withdraw his or her funds. (Though ordinary savings accounts are legally notice deposits, banks and trust companies routinely waive the notice requirement for small depositors.) (p. 239)

official settlements surplus. See *net official monetary movements.*

Okun's law. The observation that a change of 2% to 3% in real GNP (compared with its long-run trend) has been associated with a 1% change in the opposite direction in the unemployment rate. (Named after Arthur M. Okun.) (p. 156)

Old Age Security. A monthly transfer payment by the government to every Canadian or landed immigrant over the age of 65 (provided they meet certain residency requirements). (p. 84)

oligopoly. A market in which there are only a few sellers, who sell either a standarized or differentiated product. (p. 57) A *natural oligopoly* occurs when the average total costs of individual firms fall over a large enough range that a few firms can produce the total quantity sold at the lowest average cost. (p. 551) (Compare with *natural monopoly.*)

oligopsony. A market in which there are only a few buyers. (p. 78)

OPEC (the Organization of Petroleum Exporting Countries). A cartel of oil exporters that brought about the large increase in the world price of oil in the 1970s. (p. 556)

open economy. An economy where exports and imports are large relative to domestic national product. (p. 220)

open market operation. The purchase (or sale) of government (or other) securities by the Bank of Canada on the open market (that is, not directly from the issuer of the security). (p. 257)

open shop. A business that may hire workers who are not (and need not become) union members. (p. 734) Contrast with *closed shop* and *union shop.*

opportunity cost. (1) The alternative that must be foregone when something is produced. (p. 30) (2) The amount that an input could earn in its best alternative use. (p. 477)

output gap. The amount by which output falls short of the potential or full-employment level. The GNP gap. (p. 215)

panic. A rush for safety, historically marked by a switch out of bank deposits into currency and out of paper currency into gold. A run on banks. (p. 243) A *stock-market panic* occurs when there is a rush to sell and stock prices collapse.

paradox of thrift. The paradoxical situation, pointed out by Keynes, in which an increase in the desire to save can result in a decrease in the equilibrium quantity of saving. (p. 209)

paradox of value. The apparent contradiction, pointed out by Adam Smith, when an essential (such as water) has a low price while a nonessential (such as a diamond) has a high price. (p. 452)

Pareto improvement. Making one person better off without making anyone else worse off. (Named after Vilfredo Pareto, 1848–1923.) (p. 506)

Pareto optimum. A situation in which it is impossible to make any Pareto improvement. That is, it is impossible to make any individual better off without making someone else worse off. (p. 506)

partial equilibrium analysis. Analysis of a particular market or set of markets, ignoring feedbacks from other markets.

participation rate. Number of people in the labour force as a percentage of the population of working age.

partnership. An unincorporated business owned by two or more people. (p. 107)

par value. (1) Under the IMF adjustable peg system, the officially specified value of the currency in terms of gold or U.S. dollars. (2) A situation in which the Canadian dollar trades for precisely one U.S. dollar in the exchange market. (p. 315)

patent. Exclusive right, granted by the government to an inventor, to use an invention for a specified time period. (Such a right can be licensed or sold by the patent holder.)

payroll tax. A tax levied on wages and salaries, or on wages and salaries up to a specified limit. Example: social security tax.

peak. The month of greatest economic activity prior to the onset of a recession; one of the four phases of the business cycle. (p. 148)

peak-load pricing. Setting the price for a good or service higher during periods of heavy demand than at other times. The purpose is to encourage buyers to choose nonpeak periods and/or to raise more revenue. Examples: electricity, weekend ski tow.

penalty rate. A discount rate kept consistently above a short-term market rate of interest. (p. 266)

perfect competition. A market with many buyers and many sellers, with no single buyer or seller having any (noticeable) influence over price. That is, every buyer and every seller is a *price taker.* (p. 58)

permanent income. Normal income; income that is thought to be normal.

permanent-income hypothesis. The proposition that the principal determinant of consumption is permanent income (rather than current income).

personal consumption expenditures. See *consumption.*

personal income. Income received by households in return for productive services, and from transfers prior to the payment of personal taxes. (p. 136)

personal saving. (1) Loosely but commonly, disposable personal income less consumption expenditures. (p. 187) (2) More strictly, disposable personal income less consumption expenditures less payment of interest on consumer debt.

petrodollars. Liquid U.S. dollar assets held by oil-exporting nations, representing revenues received from the export of oil.

Phillips curve. The curve tracing out the relationship between the unemployment rate (on the horizontal axis) and the inflation rate or the rate of change of money wages (on the vertical axis). (p. 360) The *long-run Phillips curve* is the curve (or line) tracing out the relationship between the unemployment rate and the inflation rate when the inflation rate is stable and correctly anticipated. (p. 367)

planned investment. Desired investment; investment demand; *ex ante* investment. (p. 193)

plant. A physical establishment where production takes place. (p. 58)

policy dilemma. This occurs when a policy that helps to solve one problem makes another worse. (p. 361)

portfolio investment. Purchase by a foreign investor of bonds, stocks, or other Canadian financial assets in corporations or other firms which remain controlled by Canadian owners. (May also refer to purchases by foreigners of Canadian government securities.) (p. 759)

positive (or descriptive) statement. A statement about what is (or was) or about how something works. (p. 38) Contrast with *normative statement.*

potential output (or potential GNP). The GNP that would exist if a high rate of employment were consistently maintained. (p. 162)

poverty. Exists when people have inadequate income to buy the necessities of life. (p. 13)

poverty line (or poverty standard). An estimate of the income needed to avoid poverty. In 1983 it was $19,200 for a large-city family of four. (p. 798)

precautionary demand for money. The amount of money that households and businesses want to hold to protect themselves against unforeseen events.

preferred stock. A stock that is given preference over common stock when dividends are paid. That is, specified dividends must be paid on preferred stock before any dividend is paid on common stock. (p. 112)

premature inflation. Inflation that occurs before the economy reaches full employment.

present value. The value now of a future receipt or receipts, calculated using the interest rate, i. The present value (PV) of $\$X$ to be received n years hence is $\$X \div (1 + i)^n$. (p. 262)

price ceiling. The legally established maximum price.

price discrimination. The sale of the same good or service at different prices to different customers or in different markets, provided the price differences are not justified by cost differences such as differences in transportation costs. (p. 580)

price-earnings ratio. The ratio of the price of a stock to the annual (after-tax) earnings per share of the stock.

price elasticity of demand (supply). See *elasticity of demand (supply).*

price index. A weighted average of prices, as a percentage of prices existing in a base year. (pp. 137–38) *price leadership.* A method by which oligopolistic firms establish similar prices without overt collusion. One firm (the price leader) announces a new price, confident that the other firms will quickly follow. (p. 562)

price line. See *budget line.*

price maker. A monopolist (or monopsonist) who is able to set price because there are no competitors. (p. 526)

price mechanism. See *market mechanism.*

price searcher. A seller (or buyer) who is able to influence price, and who has competitors whose responses can affect the profit-maximizing price. An oligopolist (or oligopsonist). (p. 553)

price support. A commitment by the government to buy surpluses at a given price (the support price) in order to prevent the price from falling below that figure. (p. 519)

price system. See *market mechanism.*

price taker. A seller or buyer who is unable to affect the price and whose market decision is limited to the quantity to be sold or bought at the existing market price. A seller or buyer in a perfectly competitive market. (p. 526)

price-wage flexibility. The ease with which prices and wages rise or fall (especially fall) in the event of changing demand and supply. Contrast with *price-wage stickiness.*

price-wage stickiness. The resistance of prices and wages to a movement, particularly in a downward direction. (p. 173)

primary burden of a tax. The amount of tax collected. Compare with *excess burden of a tax.*

prime rate of interest. (1) A bank's publicly announced interest rate on short-term loans. (2) Historically, the interest rate charged by banks on loans to their most credit-worthy customers. (p. 261)

procyclical policy. A policy that increases the amplitude of business fluctuations. ("Procyclical" refers to results, not intentions.)

producer surplus. Net benefit that producers get from being able to sell a good at the existing price. Returns to capital and entrepreneurship in excess of their opportunity costs. Rents on capital and entrepreneurship. Measured by the area left of the supply curve between the break-even price and the existing price.

product differentiation. See *differentiated products.*

production function. The relationship showing the maximum output that can be produced with various combinations of inputs.

production possibilities curve. A curve showing the alternative combinations of outputs that can be produced if all productive resources are used. The boundary of attainable combinations of outputs. (p. 29)

productivity. Output per unit of input.

productivity of labour. The *average* productivity of labour is total output divided by the units of labour input. (pp. 156, 407) The *marginal* productivity of labour is the additional output when one more unit of labour is added, while all other factors are held constant. (p. 472)

profit. In economics, return to capital and/or entrepreneurship over and above normal profit. (p. 773) In business accounting, revenues minus costs. (pp. 113–14). Also sometimes used to mean profit after the payment of corporate income taxes. (pp. 113–14).

profit-and-loss statement. An accounting statement summarizing a firm's revenues, costs, and income taxes over a given period (usually a year). An income statement. (pp. 113–14).

progressive tax. A tax that takes a larger percentage of income as income rises. (p. 88)

proletariat. Karl Marx's term for the working class, especially the industrial working class.

proportional tax. A tax that takes the same percentage of income regardless of the level of income. (p. 88)

proprietors' income. The income of unincorporated firms.

prospectus. A statement of the financial condition and prospects of a corporation, presented when new securities are about to be issued. (p. 120)

protectionism. The advocacy or use of high or higher tariffs to protect domestic producers from foreign competition.

protective tariff. A tariff that is intended to protect domestic producers from foreign competition (as contrasted with a revenue tariff, intended to be a source of revenue for the government).

proxy. A temporary written transfer of voting rights at a shareholders' meeting. (p. 111)

proxy fight. A struggle between competing groups in a corporation to obtain a majority vote (and therefore control of the corporation) by collecting proxies of shareholders. (p. 111)

public debt. The debt owed by governments as a result of previous borrowing to finance budget deficits. Most of Canada's public debt is owed to Canadian holders of government debt instruments such as ordinary government bonds, Canada Savings Bonds, or Treasury bills. However, part of it is held by foreign capitalists. (p. 85)

public good. See *pure public good.*

public utility. A firm that is the sole supplier of an essential good or service in an area and that is regulated by the government. (p. 547)

pump priming. Short-term increases in government expenditures aimed at generating an upward momentum of the economy toward full employment.

purchase and resale agreement. An arrangement by which the Bank of Canada makes short-term loans to investment dealers; by purchasing Treasury bills from the dealers at an agreed price and specifying the price and date at which the dealer has to buy them back, the Bank is in effect making a short-term loan to the dealer.

purchasing power of money. The value of money in buying goods and services. The change in the purchasing power of money is measured by the change in the fraction 1 ÷ the price index. (p. 171) **general purchasing power.** Describes something that can be used to buy any of the goods and services offered for sale: e.g., money. (p. 43)

purchasing power parity theory. The theory that changes in exchange rates reflect and compensate for differences in the rate of inflation in different countries.

pure public good. A good (or service) with benefits that people cannot be excluded from enjoying, regardless of who pays for the good. (p. 648)

quantity theory (of money). The proposition that velocity is reasonably stable and that a change in the quantity of money will therefore cause nominal national product to change by approximately the same percentage. (p. 293)

quota. A numerical limit. For example, a limit on the amount of a good that may be imported. (p. 306)

Rand Formula. A famous arbitration ruling which settled a 1945 strike by Ford workers; it included compulsory contribution of union dues by workers and has had a great deal of influence on Canadian labour relations and labour law since that time. (p. 733)

random sample. A sample chosen from a larger group in such a way that every member of the group has an equal chance of being chosen.

rate base. Allowable capital of a public utility, to which the regulatory agency applies the allowable rate of return.

rate of exchange. The price of one national currency in terms of another. (p. 261)

rate of interest. Interest as a percentage per annum of the amount borrowed.

rate of return. (1) Annual profit as a percentage of net worth. (2) Additional annual revenue from the sale of goods or services produced by plant or equipment, less depreciation and operating costs such as labour and materials, expressed as a percentage of the value of the plant or equipment. (p. 286)

rational expectations. Expectations based on available information, including information about the policies being pursued by the authorities. If expectations are rational, people do not consistently make the same mistake. (p. 374)

rationing. (1) A method for allocating a good (or service) when the quantity demanded exceeds the quantity supplied at the existing price. (2) More loosely, any method for allocating a scarce resource or good. In this sense, we may speak of the market *rationing by price*.

ratio (or logarithmic) scale. A scale in which equal percentage changes are shown as equal distances. For example, the distance from 100 to 200 is equal to the distance from 200 to 400. (Each involves a doubling.) (p. 22)

Reaganomics. The economic program of U.S. President Reagan, including: (1) tax cuts, (2) restraint in domestic spending, (3) increases in defence spending, and (4) less regulation. (p. 100)

real. Measured in terms of quantity; adjusted to remove the effects of inflation. (p. 137)

real capital. Buildings, equipment, and other materials, including inventories, used in production, which have themselves been produced in the past. (p. 28)

real deficit. The *increase* in the real debt of the government. (p. 402)

real investment. The accumulation of machines and other real capital. (p. 28)

real rate of interest. The nominal rate of interest less the expected rate of inflation. (p. 390)

real wage. The quantity of goods and services that a money wage will buy; the nominal (or dollar) wage adjusted for inflation. (p. 710)

recession. A decline in output, income, employment, and trade, usually lasting six months to a year, and marked by widespread contractions in many sectors of the economy. (pp. 10, 148)

recessionary gap. The vertical distance by which the aggregate demand line is below the 45° line at the full-employment quantity of national product. (p. 214)

recognition lag. The time interval between the beginning of a problem and the time when the problem is recognized. (p. 336)

regression analysis. A statistical calculation of the relationship between two or more variables.

regressive tax. A tax that takes a smaller percentage of income as income rises. (p. 88)

rent. (1) In economics, any payment to a factor of production in excess of its opportunity cost. (p. 770) (2) A payment by the user of land to the owner. (3) Payments by users to the owners of land, buildings, or equipment.

replacement-cost depreciation. Depreciation based on the current replacement cost of buildings and equipment rather than their original acquisition cost. (p. 397)

required reserve ratio. The fraction of deposit liabilities that a chartered bank must keep in reserves. (p. 246)

required reserves. The reserves that, by law, a chartered bank must keep. Reserves are held in the form of currency or deposits in the Bank of Canada. (p. 245)

resale price maintenance. Practice whereby a manufacturer sets the minimum retail price of a product, thereby eliminating price competition among retailers of that product. The practice has long been illegal under Canadian anti-combines legislation, and has recently been made illegal in the United States as well. (p. 581)

rescheduling of debt. The renegotiation of the terms of the debt, to give the debtor more time to repay, and sometimes including a reduction in the interest rate.

reservation price of a resource. The cost of harvesting the resource today plus the amount necessary to compensate for the reduction in the quantity of the resource available in the future. (p. 628)

resource. Basic inputs used in the production of goods and services, namely, labour, land, and capital. (p. 28) See also *factor of production.*

restrictive agreement. Agreement among companies to restrain competition through practices such as price fixing or market sharing.

Restrictive Trade Practices Commission. The government bureau in charge of investigating violations of the Combines Investigation Act. (p. 581)

return to capital. See *rate of return.*

revaluation of a currency. In international economics, an increase in the par value of a currency. (p. 316)

revenue sharing. See *federal-provincial transfers.*

revenue tariff. See *protective tariff.*

right-to-work law. Law making it illegal to require union membership as a condition of employment. Equivalent to prohibition of closed shops and union shops. Such laws exist in some states in the United States, but do not exist in Canada. (p. 734)

risk premium. The difference between the yields on two grades of bonds (or other securities) because of differences in their risk. The additional interest or yield needed to compensate the holder of bonds (or other securities) for risk. (p. 117)

roundabout production. The production of capital goods and the use of these capital goods in the production of consumer goods. The production of goods in more than one stage. (p. 755)

rule of the gold standard game. The understanding that each country would permit its money stock to change in the same direction as the change in its gold stock. That is, if a country's gold stock were to rise, it should allow its money supply to increase, and vice versa.

rule of 70. A rule that tells approximately how many years it will take for something to double in size if it is growing at a compound rate. For example, a deposit earning 2% interest approximately doubles in $70 \div 2 = 35$ years. In general a deposit earning x percent interest will double in about $70 \div x$ years. (p. 394)

run. A rush to switch into safer assets; for example, a *run on banks.* (p. 243)

satisficing theory. The theory that firms do not try to maximize profits but rather aim for reasonable target levels of profits, sales, and other measures of performance.

saving. See *personal saving.*

saving function. (1) The relationship between personal saving and disposable income. (p. 188) (2) More broadly, the relationship between personal saving and the factors (like disposable income) that determine saving.

Say's law. The discredited view that supply in the aggregate creates its own demand (regardless of the general price level). (p. 208)

scarcity. (1) The inability to satisfy all wants because they exceed what we can produce with our available resources. (p. 27) (2) A shortage.

SDRs. See *special drawing rights.*

search cost. The time and money spent in collecting the information necessary to make a decision to buy or sell stocks or any other item. (p. 459)

seasonal adjustment. The removal of regular seasonal movements from a time series. (p. 149)

secondary boycott. Boycott against a firm to discourage it from doing business with a second firm, in order to exert pressure on the second firm (which may be in a strong position to withstand other forms of pressure).

secondary reserves. Chartered bank holdings of liquid assets (Treasury bills, etc.) that can readily be converted into primary reserves (currency or reserve deposits). The Bank Act gives the Bank of Canada the right to legally require the chartered banks to hold specific amounts of secondary reserves. (p. 245)

second best, theory of the. The theory of how to get the best results in remaining markets when one or more markets have defects about which nothing can be done. (p. 533)

secular stagnation. A situation of inadequate aggregate demand extending over many years. Consequently, large-scale unemployment persists, and it may even become increasingly severe.

secular trend. The trend in economic activity over an extended number of years.

sell short. See *short sale.*

seniority rules. Rules giving preference to those who have been longest on the job. Individuals with seniority are typically the last to be discharged or laid off, and the first to be rehired. (p. 730)

shortage. (1) The amount by which quantity supplied is less than quantity demanded at the existing price; the opposite of a surplus. (p. 60) (2) Any deficiency.

short run. (1) The period before the price level has adjusted to its equilibrium. (2) The period in which the quantity of plant and equipment cannot change. (p. 468) (3) The time period before equilibrium can be re-established. (4) Any brief time period.

short-run production function. The table showing the relationship between the amount of variable factors used and the amount of output that can be produced, in a situation where the quantity of capital is constant. For the simple case of a firm with just two inputs—capital and one variable factor—the short-run production function is one row in the long-run production function. (p. 472)

short sale. A contract to sell something at a later date for a price specified now.

shutdown point. The point where the MC curve cuts the AVC curve. If the price is below this point, the firm produces nothing. (p. 477)

single proprietorship. A business owned by an individual person. (p. 107) Contrast with *partnership* and *corporation*.

single-tax proposal. The proposal of Henry George (1839–1897) that all taxes be eliminated except one on land. (George argued that all returns to land represent an unearned surplus.) (p. 775)

slope. The vertical rise in a function divided by the horizontal run. (p. 25)

small, open economy. An economy that has substantial international transactions but is too small to have a substantial influence on the prices of the goods and services that are involved in the transactions.

snake. An agreement among some Western European countries to keep their currencies within a narrow band of fluctuation (the snake). Prior to 1973, they allowed their currencies to move jointly in a wider band with respect to the dollar. (This was called the *snake in the tunnel*.) (Since 1973, the snake has not been tied to the dollar.)

socialism. An economic system in which the means of production (capital equipment, buildings, and land) are owned by the state. (p. 820)

social security. Government programs such as Old Age Security, Unemployment Insurance, provincial health insurance plans, etc., which provide payments to people in specified circumstances such as old age, unemployment, or ill health. Social assistance, social insurance. (p. 86)

special drawing rights (SDRs). Bookkeeping accounts created by the International Monetary Fund to increase the quantity of international reserves held by national governments. SDRs can be used to cover balance-of-payments deficits. (p. 332)

specific tax. A fixed number of cents or dollars of tax on each unit of the good. Contrast with *ad valorem tax*.

speculation. The purchase (or sale) of an asset in the hope of making a quick profit from a rise (fall) in its price. (p. 317)

speculative demand for money. The schedule or curve showing how the rate of interest affects the amount of assets that firms and households are willing to hold in the form of money, rather than in bonds or other interest-bearing securities.

speculator. Anyone who buys or sells a foreign currency (or any other asset) in the hope of profiting from a change in its price. (p. 317)

spillover. See *externality*.

stagflation. The coexistence of a high rate of unemployment (stagnation) and inflation. (p. 360)

standard of value. The item (money) in which the prices of goods and services are measured. (p. 239)

sterilization of balance-of-payments surplus (deficit). Operations by the central bank to prevent a balance-of-payments surplus or deficit from causing changes in chartered bank reserves and, hence, in the money supply. (p. 318)

store of value. An asset that may be used to store wealth through time; an asset that may be used to finance future purchases. (p. 239)

structural unemployment. Unemployment due to a mismatch between the skills or location of the labour force and the skills or location required by employers. Unemployment due to a changing location or composition of jobs. (p. 160)

subsidy. A negative tax.

subsistence wage. Minimum living wage. A wage below which population will decline because of starvation or disease. (p. 77)

substitute. A good or service that satisfies similar needs. Two commodities are substitutes if a rise in the price of one causes a rightward shift in the demand curve for the other. (p. 62) (Contrast with *complementary goods*.)

substitution effect. The change in the quantity of a good demanded because of a change in its price when the real income effect of the change in price has been eliminated. That is, a change in the quantity demanded as a result of a movement along a single indifference curve. See also *income effect*. (p. 465)

sunspot theory. The theory put forward in the late nineteenth century that cycles in sunspot activity cause cycles in agricultural production and, hence, cycles in business activity.

superior good. A good for which the quantity demanded rises as income rises, *ceteris paribus*. A *normal good*. Contrast with an *inferior good*. (p. 62)

supply. The schedule or curve showing how the price of a good or service influences the quantity supplied, *ceteris paribus*. (p. 59)

supply of money. See *money stock*.

supply schedule. A table showing the quantities of a good or service that sellers would offer at various market prices, *ceteris paribus*. (p. 59)

supply shift. A movement of the supply curve of a good (or service) to the right or left as a result of a change in the price of inputs or any other determinant of the quantity supplied (except the price of the good or service itself). (p. 63)

supply shifter. Anything that affects the quantity of a good or service supplied except its own price. (p. 63)

supply side. The view that it is supply factors—such as the quantity of capital and the willingness to work—that are the principal constraints to growth. According to this view, a lack of aggregate demand is not the main constraint.

support price. Agricultural price guaranteed to farmers by the government. (If the market price falls short of the target price, the government pays farmers the difference.)

surplus. (1) The amount by which quantity supplied exceeds quantity demanded at the existing price. (p. 60) Contrast with *shortage*. (2) The amount by which revenues exceed expenditures. (p. 89) Contrast with *deficit*. Any excess or amount left over.

surplus value. In Marxist economics, the amount by which the value of a worker's output exceeds the wage; the share of output appropriated by capitalists. (p. 820)

sustainable yield. The amount of a renewable resource (like fish) that can be harvested while still leaving the population constant. (p. 626)

sympathy strike. A strike by a union that does not have a dispute with its own employer, but is trying to stengthen the bargaining position of another striking union.

syndicate. An association of investment bankers to market a large block of securities. (p. 116)

tacit collusion. The adoption of a common policy by sellers without explicit agreement. (p. 562)

takeoff. The achievement of sustained growth, in which capital can be accumulated without depressing the standard of living below its existing level. (p. 36)

tariff. A tax on an imported good. (p. 306)

tax base. The total amount of income or sales revenue subject to a specific tax (such as the personal income tax or a provincial sales tax). (p. 97)

tax-based incomes policy (TIP). An incomes policy backed up with tax penalties on violators or tax incentives for those who co-operate. (p. 381)

tax credit. A subtraction from the tax payable. (For example, if a $1000 machine is bought, a 10% investment tax credit means that $100 can be subtracted from the taxes that must be paid to the government.) (p. 102)

tax deduction. A subtraction from taxable income. Suppose an individual pays $1,000 in allowable charitable donations. This $1,000 can be deducted from taxable income. For someone in the 36% tax bracket, this results in a $360 reduction in taxes. (Note that the tax saving depends on the tax bracket. Thus, a $1,000 deduction reduces taxes more for someone in the 36% tax bracket than for a person in a lower bracket. Note also that the $1,000 deduction is worth only $360 to this individual, while a $1,000 tax credit is worth the full $1,000 in tax savings.) (p. 102)

tax incidence. See *incidence of tax*.

tax neutrality. (1) A situation in which taxes do not affect relative prices. (2) A situation in which the excess burden of taxes is zero.

tax shifting. This occurs when the initial taxpayer transfers all or part of a tax to others. (For example, a firm that is taxed may charge a higher price.) (pp. 435–36)

technological (or technical) efficiency. Providing the maximum output with the available resources and technology, while working at a reasonable pace. The avoidance of wasted effort and sloppy management. (p. 13)

term deposit. A deposit in a bank or other financial institution which has a specific term to maturity; a penalty is charged if the depositor wants to cash it in before maturity. (p. 241)

terms of trade. The average price of goods sold divided by the average price of goods bought. Often used to refer to the prices of a country's export and import goods. (p. 684)

theory of games. See *game theory*.

theory of public choice. Theory of how government spending decisions are made and how they should be made.

third world. Countries that are neither in the "first" world (the high-income countries of Western Europe and North America, plus a few others such as Japan) nor in the "second" world (the countries of Eastern Europe). Low- and middle-income countries other than those run by communist parties.

tied selling. Transaction in which purchaser is forced to buy another item or items in the seller's line of products in order to get the one that is really wanted. (p. 581)

time preference. The desire to have goods now rather than in the future. The amount by which goods now are preferred over goods in the future. (p. 754)

time series. A set of observations taken in successive time periods. For example, GNP in 1974, in 1975, in 1976, etc. (p. 20)

TIP. See *tax-based incomes policy*.

total cost. The sum of fixed costs and variable costs. (p. 469)

total revenue. Total receipts from the sale of a product. Where there is a single price, total revenue is the price times the quantity sold. (p. 429)

transactions demand for money. The amount of money that firms and individuals want to cover the time between the receipt of income and the making of expenditures.

transfer of government deposits. A technique of monetary control by which the Bank of Canada influences chartered bank reserves by depositing or withdrawing government funds held in the chartered banks. (p. 264)

transfer payment. A payment, usually made by the government to private individuals, that does not result from current productive activity. (p. 83) See also *federal-provincial transfers*.

Treasury bill. A short-term (less than a year, often three months) debt of the Bank of Canada. It carries no explicit interest payment; a purchaser gains by buying a bill for less than its face value. (p. 261)

trough. The month of lowest economic activity prior to

the beginning of a recovery; one of the four phases of the business cycle. (p. 148)

turning point. The trough or peak of a business cycle. (p. 149)

turnover tax. A tax on goods or services (whether they are intermediate or final products) whenever they are sold.

underemployed. (1) Workers who can find only part-time work when they want full-time work. (2) Workers who are being paid full time but are not kept busy because of low demand for output. (p. 156)

underground economy. Economic activity unobserved by tax collectors and government statisticians. (p. 142)

underwrite. Guarantee by an investment dealer that the whole new issue of stock will be sold. (An investment dealer unable to sell all the underwritten stock must buy the remainder.) (p. 116)

undesired inventory accumulation. Actual inventory accumulation less desired inventory accumulation. (p. 191)

undistributed corporate profits. After-tax corporate profits less dividends paid.

unemployment. The condition of people who are willing to work but cannot find jobs. More generally, the condition of any underutilized resource. (p. 9)

unemployment rate. The percentage of the labour force unemployed. (p. 155)

union. An association of workers, formed to negotiate over wages, fringe benefits, and working conditions. (p. 729)

union shop. A business where all nonunion workers must join the union within a brief period of their employment. (p. 734) Compare with *closed shop* and *right-to-work law*.

unit elasticity. Elasticity of one. If a demand curve has unit elasticity, total revenue remains unchanged as price changes. (The demand curve is a rectangular hyperbola.) If a supply curve has unit elasticity, it is a straight line that would, if extended, go through the origin. (p. 432)

unlimited liability. Responsibility for debts without limit. (p. 108)

utility. The ability to satisfy wants. (p. 452)

value added. Value of the product sold less the cost of intermediate products bought from other firms. (p. 129)

value of marginal product (VMP). Marginal physical product times product price. (p. 711)

variable costs. Any costs that increase as output increases. (p. 468)

variable-rate mortgage. A mortgage which has an interest rate that is periodically adjusted in response to changes in the market interest rate. (p. 399)

velocity of money. The average number of times per year that the average dollar in the money stock is spent. There are two principal ways of calculating velocity. (1) *Income velocity* is the number of times the average dollar is spent on final products (that is, GNP ÷ M). (p. 292) (2) *Transaction velocity* is the number of times the average dollar is spent on *any* transaction (including those for intermediate goods and financial assets). That is, total spending ÷ M.

vertical merger. See *merger*.

voluntary arbitration. In labour disputes, occurs when labour and management submit their conflict to an impartial third party and commit themselves in advance to accepting that third party's decision. (p. 748)

wage-price controls. See *incomes policy*.

withholding tax. A tax (generally of about 15 percent) charged (withheld) by the Canadian government on payments of interest and dividends from Canadian sources to foreign investors. (p. 762)

windfall. An unexpected increase in profit that accrues to existing producers in an industry as a result of an unforeseen price increase; an example is the increase in the profits of Canadian oil companies as a result of the rapid rise in the producer price of oil during the 1970s.

workable competition. A compromise that limits monopoly power while allowing firms to become big enough to reap economies of scale. A practical alternative to the often unattainable goal of perfect competition. (p. 582)

yellow-dog contract. Contract in which an employee agrees not to become a member of a union. (p. 731)

yield. The annual rate of discount that would make the present value of a stream of future payments equal to the price or present value of an asset. (p. 286n) The *rate of return*.

zero-base budgeting. A budgeting technique that requires items to be justified anew "from the ground up," without regard to how much has been spent on them in the past.

INDEX

NOTE: Key Concepts and Key Points at the end of appendices and chapters should also be consulted.

- - - CUT HERE - - -

STUDENT REPLY CARD

In order to improve the quality of future editions, we are seeking your comments on **Economics, Second Canadian Edition, by Blomqvist, Wonnacott, and Wonnacott.**

Thanks in advance for your feedback!

1. Name of school you attend: _____
   _____

2. If you are enrolled in a degree program, please indicate your field of study: ____
   _____

3. Approximately how much of this text did you use for your course? _____
   _____

4. What did you like best about this book? _____
   _____

- - - FOLD HERE - - -

5. What did you like *least*? _____
   _____
   _____

Other comments:

- - CUT HERE - -